How to use your Connected Casebook

Step 1: Go to **www.CasebookConnect.com** and redeem your access code to get started.

Access Code:

Step 2: Go to your **BOOKSHELF** and select your Connected Casebook to start reading, highlighting, and taking notes in the margins of your e-book.

Step 3: Select the **STUDY** tab in your toolbar to access a variety of practice materials designed to help you master the course material. These materials may include explanations, videos, multiple-choice questions, flashcards, short answer, essays, and issue spotting.

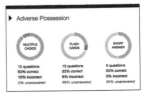

Step 4: Select the **OUTLINE** tab in your toolbar to access chapter outlines that automatically incorporate your highlights and annotations from the e-book. Use the My Notes area for copying, pasting, and editing your book notes or creating new notes.

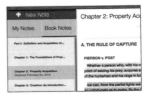

Step 5: If your professor has enrolled your class, you can select the **CLASS INSIGHTS** tab and compare your own study center results against the average of your classmates.

Is this a used casebook? Access code already scratched off?

You can purchase the Digital Version and still access all of the powerful tools listed above.
Please visit CasebookConnect.com and select Catalog to learn more.

PIN: 10050856-0002 BCnts6   10615

CONTRACTS

ASPEN CASEBOOK SERIES

CONTRACTS

Cases and Doctrine

Sixth Edition

Randy E. Barnett

Carmack Waterhouse Professor of Legal Theory
Georgetown University Law Center

Nathan B. Oman

Professor of Law
William & Mary Law School

Wolters Kluwer

Wolters Kluwer Legal & Regulatory U.S. serves customers worldwide with CCH,
Aspen Publishers, and Kluwer Law International products.
(www.WKLegaledu.com)

To contact Customer Service, e-mail customer.service@wolterskluwer.com,
call 1-800-234-1660, fax 1-800-901-9075, or mail correspondence to:

Wolters Kluwer
Attn: Order Department
PO Box 990
Frederick, MD 21705

Printed in the United States of America.

3 4 5 6 7 8 9 0

ISBN 978-1-4548-7103-3

Library of Congress Cataloging-in-Publication Data

Names: Barnett, Randy E., author. | Oman, Nathan, author.
Title: Contracts: cases and doctrine / Randy E. Barnett Carmack,
    Waterhouse Professor of Legal Theory, Georgetown University Law Center;
    Nathan B. Oman, Professor of Law, William & Mary Law School.
Description: Sixth edition. | New York: Wolters Kluwer, [2017] | Series:
    Aspen casebook series
Identifiers: LCCN 2016043983 | ISBN 9781454871033
Subjects: LCSH: Contracts—United States. | LCGFT: Casebooks.
Classification: LCC KF801.A7 B35 2017 | DDC 346.7302/2—dc23
LC record available at https://lccn.loc.gov/2016043983

About Wolters Kluwer Legal & Regulatory U.S.

Wolters Kluwer Legal & Regulatory U.S. delivers expert content and solutions in the areas of law, corporate compliance, health compliance, reimbursement, and legal education. Its practical solutions help customers successfully navigate the demands of a changing environment to drive their daily activities, enhance decision quality and inspire confident outcomes.

Serving customers worldwide, its legal and regulatory portfolio includes products under the Aspen Publishers, CCH Incorporated, Kluwer Law International, ftwilliam.com and MediRegs names. They are regarded as exceptional and trusted resources for general legal and practice-specific knowledge, compliance and risk management, dynamic workflow solutions, and expert commentary.

To my wife, Beth, and my kids, Laura and Gary, for all their love and support.
— Randy E. Barnett

For Jacob and Beth, third party beneficiaries.
— Nathan B. Oman

SUMMARY OF CONTENTS

CONTENTS

| 3 |

OTHER REMEDIES AND CAUSES OF ACTION

II

MUTUAL ASSENT

4

REACHING AN AGREEMENT

6

WRITTEN MANIFESTATIONS OF ASSENT   451

7

MULTIPARTY TRANSACTIONS   501

| | 11 | |

THE DOCTRINE OF PROMISSORY ESTOPPEL

685

14

BREACH   859

V

DEFENSES TO CONTRACTUAL OBLIGATION

15

LACK OF CONTRACTUAL CAPACITY

PREFACE

In the beginning there was the textbook. It consisted of explanatory text. Students studied contracts largely on their own using treatises such as those by Blackstone and Kent or summaries of these treatises written by learned practitioners. Next came the casebook. It consisted of cases. Casebooks were developed for teaching contracts in the university classroom setting using the "case method." Then came the multivolume modern specialized treatises, the Restatements, the Realist Revolution, the Uniform Commercial Code, and, most recently, an explosion of legal scholarship with an increasing emphasis on legal theory.

As contracts casebook authors struggled to cope with each of these developments, contracts casebooks were transformed into an amalgam of highly edited cases and "squibs," fragments of law review articles, excerpts from the Uniform Commercial Code and the Restatement — and, of course, the ubiquitous "note material." The idea was to integrate the diverse sources of contract law in a single tightly edited volume. However, this evolution from casebook to integrated snippets of material has resulted in several undesirable consequences.

First, contracts teaching materials are now predigested. Practicing lawyers and legal scholars must scan whole cases, whole articles, and whole statutes to glean the information relevant to their problem. Unfortunately, to get everything into a single volume, cases, articles, and other materials are so heavily edited that students are not required to sift through the materials themselves. The scanning has already been done for them by the casebook author. Rather than gleaning the message of a case or an article, the challenge posed to students and professors by today's casebooks is to decipher the casebook *author's* message hidden in the structure of the materials.

Further, because highly edited casebooks inevitably take on a heavy dose of their authors' views of contracts, novice professors are forced either to learn and accept the author's viewpoint or to swim heroically against the tide. Experienced professors with independent minds are less likely to engage in fighting the casebook and are more likely to supplement it with their own materials, perhaps eventually abandoning the casebook altogether. While it is inevitable that the author's views will be reflected in any casebook, the more heavily edited and integrated a casebook is, the more difficult it becomes for teachers to project to students their own views of contract.

Finally, to make room for more cases about complex commercial transactions, contracts casebooks have increasingly abandoned the classic cases that contracts professors still debate to this day. Complicated commercial fact patterns make contracts seem remote from the life experience of average first-year law students, who are required to take the course but may or may not be interested in pursuing careers practicing commercial law. As a result, contracts professors are at a competitive disadvantage with their colleagues who teach seemingly more engaging first-year subjects such as criminal law or torts.

This book charts a different course. It contains far fewer cases that are more lightly edited than has become the norm. In addition to commercial transactions, we have favored a mix of classic and very recent cases involving provocative controversies,[1] memorable fact patterns,[2] and public figures.[3] These are cases that lend themselves to discussing both basic contract doctrine and the broad philosophical, economic, and political implications of adhering to these legal rules and principles.

In place of vexatious note material, students will find "Study Guides" before most cases and, after each topic, "Reference" citations to the most popular and respected contract treatises.[4] In this way, students receive useful questions and suggestions *before* they read a case and ready access to more comprehensive and authoritative explanations of the material than is possible in a casebook. Each section also includes relevant provisions of the Uniform Commercial Code and the Restatement (Second) of Contracts.

We believe it is safe to say that this casebook contains a larger portion of the scholarship providing context on the famous contracts cases than any other. These "relational background" materials will enrich the students' understanding of the cases and will stimulate a deeper classroom discussion than will cases or statutes alone. Students actually *enjoy* them! They also illustrate that opinions of appellate courts are often surprisingly incomplete and that one's sympathies for the parties may shift upon learning more about the facts. In addition, historical, comparative, ethical, economic, statutory, procedural, empirical, commercial, and theoretical "background materials" were selected and edited to engage students with the subject of contracts and spark debate, but also to be accessible. They can be assigned as required or optional reading, or they may be skipped altogether without detracting from doctrinal coverage, thereby greatly shortening the book.

This sixth edition makes a few changes. Chief among these has been an effort to improve the "modularity" of the book, making it easier to teach sections independent of one another and allowing professors to pick and choose which doctrinal areas to cover, particularly those teaching shorter, one-semester courses. We have created a free-standing section on public policy defenses, which were covered only in the introduction of earlier

---

1. For example, surrogacy agreements, failed vasectomies, involuntary servitude, palimony claims, sexual harassment, reporters' promises of confidentiality, and children's rights.

2. For example, Chevy Corvettes, Carbolic Smokeballs, custom stereos, oil embargoes, cancelled coronations, football players, opera singers, college catalogues, employment manuals, computer software, and pregnant cows.

3. For example, Shirley Maclaine, Robert Reed, Brooke Shields, Jack Dempsey, Lee Marvin, Lillian Russell, and Elvis.

4. References are provided to Randy E. Barnett, The Oxford Introduction to U.S. Law: Contracts (2010), E. Allan Farnsworth, Contracts (4th ed. 2004), John D. Calamari & Joseph M. Perillo, Contracts (6th ed. 2009), and John E. Murray, Murray on Contracts (5th ed. 2011).

editions. We have also added a few new cases, included some classics over-looked by previous editions, and added newly published background materials.

- In Chapter 1, In re Baby M and the associated material has been replaced by Jordan v. Knafel along and background materials by Lawrence Cunningham.
- In Chapter 2, Tonglish v. Thomas has been replaced by KGM Harvesting Co. v. Fresh Network and Mistletoe Express Service v. Locke has been replaced by the classic case of Security Stove & Mfg. Co. v. American Ry. Express Co.
- Chapter 4 includes new background materials on Lucy v. Zehmer by Barak Richman, and has added Arnold Palmer Golf Company v. Fuqua Industries Inc., Copeland v. Baskin Robbins USA, the classic case of Lefkowitz v. Great Minneapolis Surplus Store, Inc., and Nguyen v. Barnes & Noble Inc., which replaces Specht v. Netscape. We have also added a drafting problem based on Arnold Palmer Golf Company, and a summary of empirical research by Florencia Marotta-Wurgler on online contracting replaces the ABA Working Materials on that topic.
- In Chapter 6, we replaced Brown v. Oliver with Masterson v. Sine and omitted In re RealNetworks.
- In Chapter 7, we added Lawrence v. Fox, along with historical background materials on this seminal case. We have omitted the section on Agency.
- In Chapter 9, we added Boothe v. Fitzpatrick and Harris v. Watson.
- In Chapter 11, we added Pitts v. McGraw-Edison Co.
- In Chapter 12, we replaced Step-Saver Data Sys. Inc. v. Wyse Technology with Vlases v. Montgomery Ward & Company.
- Finally, in Chapter 16 we added Samaniego v. Empire Today LLC to the section on arbitration agreements and added a new section on public policy defenses consisting of A.Z. v. B.Z. and Meyer v. Hawkinson.

For those professors who wish to teach contract theory by means of excerpts from legal scholarship, the anthology *Perspectives on Contract Law*[5] continues to mesh harmoniously with the organization of this casebook. In contrast to the complex and sometimes idiosyncratic organization of some other casebooks, a great effort was made to adhere to a comprehensible organization reflecting the cause of action for breach of contract: Enforcement, Mutual Assent, Enforceability, Performance and Breach, and Defenses. While starting with enforcement or remedies is sometimes controversial (and we explain this choice in the introduction to Chapter 2), the modular construction of the casebook permits professors easily to reorder these topics as they see fit.

Randy E. Barnett & Nathan B. Oman

November 2016

5. Randy E. Barnett, *Perspectives on Contract Law* (4th ed. 2009).

ACKNOWLEDGMENTS

This book would not have been possible without the assistance of a great many persons. First are the wonderful people at Little, Brown and now Aspen Publishers of Wolters Kluwer. Their commitment to excellence by means of repeated peer reviews of the original proposal and successive drafts immeasurably improved the final product. Special thanks are due to Carol McGeehan, who originally conceived of this project, Betsy Kenny, who ably assisted her in shepherding it from conception to completion, and Tony Perriello, who deftly edited the manuscript for the first edition. I owe a great debt as well to the professors who gave selflessly of themselves as anonymous reviewers of the manuscript: Miriam A. Cherry, Kevin Davis, David A. Hoffman, Kristin Madison, Katherine E. White, and Noah D. Zatz. Although I do not know who of them suggested which improvements to the text, I do know that, as a group, they functioned for me as a coauthor — looking over my shoulder to ensure that the book responded to the diverse needs and preferences of other contracts teachers. In addition, I received helpful suggestions from Ian Ayres, Sheldon Halpern, Alexander Mieklejohn, and Anthony Jon Waters. Several professors who used earlier editions of this casebook made a great many excellent suggestions for its improvement: Mark Chinen, Marcus Cole, Adrienne Davis, Mark Drumbl, Harold Dubroff, Mark Gergen, Grace Giesel, Henry Greely, Matthew Harrington, Michael Kelly, Kristin Madison, Carol Rose, Peter Siegleman, Robert Shepherd, Jim Smith, Eric Talley, Kellye Testy, William Vukowich, Kathy White, Christopher Wonnell, and David Snyder. My eagle-eyed BU colleague Mark Pettit (and contracts teacher *extraordinaire*) performed an enormous service by noting numerous typos and mistakes in the second edition.

Many improvements to previous drafts of this book were stimulated by class discussion with my contracts students at Northwestern University, Harvard Law School, Boston University School of Law, and Georgetown University Law Center. Finally, I wish also to thank my extraordinary research assistants: Dan Brown at Chicago-Kent College of Law (Class of 1994), at Boston University, Saba Khairi (Class of 1995), Kristin Taylor, Andrew White, Kathleen Eagan (Class of 1996), Leslie Ravestein (Class of 2000), Lourdes German (Class of 2004) and, at Harvard Law School, Jaime Byrnes (Class of 2004). In addition to their other contributions, these students are solely responsible for researching and writing the wonderful judicial biographies that set this casebook apart by giving readers a sense of the men and women who struggled both to decide the cases before them and to justify their decisions. The idea to include judicial biographies in a casebook was innovated by Professor Curtis R. Reitz and a few of his biographies are included here as well. The cases and materials on legal ethics in Chapters 6, 7, and 16 were suggested by the W M. Keck Foundation's project on legal ethics, which is administered by Geoffrey Hazard, Jr. and Susan Koniak.

Finally, with this edition, I welcome aboard Nate Oman as a coauthor. I have long held Nate in high regard and was most grateful when he accepted my invitation to join the book. I encouraged him to bring a fresh eye to everything in the last edition, while being mindful that we did not want to change things too much for existing users. I believe he has added enormous value with the revisions we've made to the Sixth Edition, which were all done at his behest.

Speaking for Nate and myself, we also wish to thank the following authors and publishers for permitting us to include excerpts from these works:

American Bar Association, excerpts from Model Rules of Professional Conduct. Copyright © 2002 by the American Bar Association. Reprinted with permission. Copies of ABA Model Rules of Professional Conduct 2002 are available from Service Center, American Bar Association, 750 North Lake Shore Drive, Chicago, IL 60611-4497, 1-800-285-2222.

American Law Institute, Restatement (Second) of Contracts. Copyright © by the American Law Institute. Reprinted with permission.

American Law Institute, Uniform Commercial Code. Copyright © by the American Law Institute. Reprinted with permission.

Barnett, Randy E., A Consent Theory of Contract, 86 Colum. L. Rev. 269 (1986). Copyright © 1986 by Columbia Law Review. Reprinted with permission.

Barnett, Randy E., and Becker, Mary E., Beyond Reliance: Promissory Estoppel, Contract Formalities, and Misrepresentations, 15 Hofstra L. Rev. 443 (1987). Copyright © 1987 by Hofstra Law Review. Reprinted with permission.

Bennett, James, G.M. Settles Suit Over Plant Closing, New York Times, April 15, 1994. Copyright © 1994 by The New York Times Company. Reprinted with permission.

Bernstein, Lisa, Opting Out of the Legal System: Extralegal Contractual Relations in the Diamond Industry, 21 J. Legal Stud. 115 (1992). Reprinted with permission.

Blinkoff, Samuel, Note, Contracts: Acceptance of an Offer for a Unilateral Contract: Effect of Tender, 14 Cornell L.Q. 81 (1928). Copyright © 1928 by Cornell University. All rights reserved.

Cox, Stephen, Mysteries of the Titanic, Liberty, May 1997. Copyright © 1997 Liberty. Reprinted with permission.

Cunningham, Lawrence A., Contracts in the Real World: Stories of Popular Contracts and Why They Matter. Copyright © 2012 Cambridge University Press. Reprinted with permission.

Danzig, Richard, *Hadley v. Baxendale:* A Study in the Industrialization of the Law, 4 J. Legal Studies 249 (1975). Copyright © 1975 by Journal of Legal Studies, University of Chicago Law School. Reprinted with permission.

Conference of Commissioners on Uniform State Laws, 676 North St. Clair Street, Suite 1700, Chicago, Illinois 60611, (312) 915-0195.

Petzinger, Thomas, The Texaco-Pennzoil Wars. Copyright © 1987 by Thomas Petzinger. Reprinted with permission of The Putnam Publishing Group.

Pomeroy, A Treatise on Equity Jurisprudence (2d ed. 1892). Copyright © 1892 by Bancroft-Whitney Company. Reprinted with permission of Bancroft-Whitney, a division of Thomson Legal Publishing, Inc.

Richman, Barak, Weinstock, Jordi, and Mehta, Jason, A Bridge, A Tax Revolt, and the Struggle to Industrialize: The Story and Legacy of Rockingham County v. Luten Bridge Co., 84 N.C. L.Rev. 1841, 1851-1879, 1906-1908 (2006). Copyright © 2006. Reprinted with permission.

Roberts, Jorie, Hawkins Case: A Hair-Raising Experience, Harvard Law Record, vol. 66, no. 6, March 11, 1978, p. 1. Copyright © 1978 by Harvard Law Record. Reprinted with permission.

Simpson, A. W. B., Contracts for Cotton to Arrive: The Case of the Two Ships Peerless, 11 Cardozo L. Rev. 287 (1990). Copyright © 1990 by Cardozo Law Review. Reprinted with permission.

Simpson, A. W. B., Quackery and Contract Law: The Case of the Carbolic Smokeball, 14 J. Legal. Stud. 345 (1985). Copyright © 1985. Reprinted with permission.

Simpson, A. W. B., The Doctrine of Consideration — Introduction. Reprinted from A History of the Common Law of Contract: The Rise of the Action of Assumpsit (1975 ed.). Out of Print. Reprinted with permission.

Threedy, Deborah L., A Fish Story: Alaska Packers Association v. Domenico, 2000 Utah L. Rev. 185. Copyright © Deborah L. Threedy. Reprinted with permission.

Von Mises, Ludwig, Human Action (revised ed. 1963). Copyright © 1963 by Contemporary Books. Reprinted with permission.

Waddams, Stephen, Dimensions of Private Law: Categories and Concepts in Anglo-American Legal Reasoning 23-27 (2003). Copyright © 2003 by Cambridge University Press. Reprinted with permission of Cambridge University Press.

Weintraub, Russell J., A Survey of Contract Practice and Policy, 1992 Wis. L. Rev. 1. Copyright © 1992 by the Board of Regents of the University of Wisconsin System. Reprinted with permission of the Wisconsin Law Review.

Whitford, William C. and Macaulay, Stewart, Hoffman v. Red Owl Stores: The Rest of the Story, 61 Hastings L.J. 801 (2009). Reprinted with permission of William C. Whitford, Stewart Macaulay, and University of California, Hastings College of the Law.

Williams, Sandra Boyd, The Indiana Supreme Court and the Struggle Against Slavery, 30 Indiana Law Review 305, 307-309 (1997). Copyright © 1997 Indiana University Law Review. Reprinted with permission.

Randy E. Barnett

November 2016

CONTRACTS

CONTRACTS

ENFORCING PRIVATE AGREEMENTS

I

INTRODUCTION TO CONTRACT LAW

A. STUDYING CONTRACT LAW

This book is organized around the cause of action for breach of contract. When one party to a lawsuit alleges that another person has breached a contract, certain legal consequences follow. What are these consequences? What must a party to a lawsuit establish to justify the use of legal coercion against another person? What responses are available to the other person to avoid the imposition of legal sanctions? The law of contract provides answers to these questions, and we shall examine each of these questions in turn. While this is by no means the only way to approach the study of contracts, it does provide a framework or structure within which to organize, in a coherent fashion, a great diversity of doctrines and theories.

1. The Structure of This Book

In Part I, we examine the *remedies* for breach of contract. Although a contract is created before remedies for its breach become an issue, the initial study of remedies will prove useful to understanding the elements of contract and breach. As explained in the introduction to Chapter 2, the different remedies being sought in the cases we shall read in Parts II, III, and IV reveal subtle differences in the underlying theories of obligation. Were the study of remedies left to the end, we would be unable to appreciate these differences. This should really come as no surprise. Judges are well aware that their decisions will be *enforced* and that enforcement will have serious consequences for both parties to the lawsuit. They are mindful of these consequences when deciding what must be shown to establish a breach of contract. In other words, were it not for the coercive remedies that result from a finding of breach of contract, the elements of contract formation and performance might well be very different than they are. For this reason, we begin our study of contract law by examining some public policy limitations that have been placed on the use of legal coercion to enforce contracts (Chapter 1) and then turn to the different types of remedies that may be imposed on the party in breach (Chapters 2 and 3).

In Parts II, III, and IV, we will study the three principal elements of an action for breach of contract: mutual assent, enforceability, and breach. Part II covers the element of *mutual assent*. How mutual assent is normally reached is discussed in Chapter 4. Assessing the meaning of the parties' assent is the subject of Chapter 5. Chapter 6 concerns the special problems that surround written manifestations of assent. Finally, in Chapter 7, we examine complications for "mutual" assent that arise when more than two parties are involved in the making or are affected by the enforcement of a contract.

Part III covers the element of *enforceability*. Not all manifestations of mutual assent will be enforced. In Chapter 8, we examine various theories that have been offered to distinguish those commitments that will be enforced from those that will not and we attempt to apply these theories to a controversial case. We then turn our attention to the three categories of doctrine that have been used by courts to answer the question of enforceability. In Chapter 9, we examine the doctrine of consideration. In Chapter 10, we consider the even older body of law that would enforce those manifestations of assent that are accompanied by some evidence of intention to be legally bound. In Chapter 11, we discuss the doctrine of promissory estoppel that has arisen as an alternative to the doctrine of consideration.

Parts II and III concern the elements of a valid contract. A cause of action for breach of contract requires that the party seeking relief establish an additional element: that the other party has failed to meet its obligation of performance and is therefore in breach. In Part IV, we approach the issue of *performance and breach* from two directions. Chapter 12 concerns the requirement of "good faith" performance and the ways that the requirement of performance can be expanded, limited, or modified by the parties' consent. In Chapter 13, we examine how lawyers use conditions to define when non-performance is justified and, therefore, not a breach. Then, in Chapter 14, we study the types of breaches that justify not merely money damages, but the unilateral cancellation of the contract by the victim of the breach, as well as another variation on the expectation interest.

The prima facie case of breach of contract comprises the elements of mutual assent, enforceability, and breach, discussed in Parts II, III, and IV. If a court knew nothing more about a particular transaction than that a breach of contract had occurred, it would be justified in awarding a remedy against the party in breach. But the party in breach may bring further facts and circumstances to the attention of the court that are deemed to be sufficient to rebut the normal legal consequences of the prima facie case of breach of contract. Alternatively, prior to any breach a party to a contract that satisfies the elements of mutual assent and enforceability may affirmatively assert a *defense* to avoid its enforcement. Defenses to contractual obligation are the subject of Part V.

In Chapter 15, we study the defenses of incompetence and infancy, which are based on the capacity of the party, against whom enforcement is sought, to assent to a contract. These defenses are often used affirmatively to bar enforcement of a contract before any breach has occurred. Chapter 16 concerns situations in which a party's assent is obtained by improper means, such as by fraud, duress, or undue influence. Finally, in Chapter 17, we conclude our study of contract law by considering the defenses of mistake, impracticability, and frustration, which are based on the failure of an assumption that was basic to the contract, as well as attempts by parties to allocate the risks of changed circumstances.

2. The Three Dimensions of Law

The first year of law school can be at once exhilarating and frustrating. Some days everything makes perfect sense. On others, the process seems to threaten one's very soul. One of the sources of this feeling of dislocation is that legal analysis takes place on three distinct levels. Students are therefore forced to think in fundamentally different ways, sometimes simultaneously. One of the antidotes to frustration is to make explicit these "three dimensions of law."

All law is three-dimensional. The three levels on which the law of *any* subject simultaneously exists are doctrine, facts, and theory. The dimension of *doctrine* consists of the rules and principles of law by which judges justify their decisions. This is what the general public thinks of as "the law" and is probably the only dimension of law many of you expected to study in law school. In this casebook, we shall learn the rules and principles primarily by reading the "classic" cases that have become famous for establishing them, the Restatement (Second) of the Law of Contract (published by the American Law Institute), and the Uniform Commercial Code.[1] In addition, we shall study some recent and controversial cases in which these traditional principles have either been reaffirmed or modified. For students desiring additional information about the rules and principles covered in the text, page references to the three most popular treatises or hornbooks are provided, along with references to an overview of contract law that I have authored. Be sure to check with your professor to see which of these books, if any, he or she prefers you to use as references.

The dimension of *facts* is the actual application of doctrine by courts and its effects on contracting parties and the public at large. While it is difficult to study legal practice in the classroom, we will gain important insight into practice by studying the many different fact situations contained in the appellate cases in this casebook. In addition, the factual backgrounds of many of the classic cases have been examined in rich detail by legal historians. To provide a broader context as well as to highlight the inherent limitations of appellate court opinions, liberal excerpts from these writings are included. Such excerpts designated as "Relational Background" provide additional information about the relationship between the parties, their particular transaction, and the subsequent litigation. You will learn that the reported cases often omit tantalizing facts that may affect your sympathies for the parties. "Historical Background" material places the case it follows in a wider historical context. In some of these cases, we shall also critically examine the lawyer's conduct in light of the rules of professional conduct that govern the ethics of legal practice. In the final analysis, however, practice cannot be taught. It must be experienced. This is an important function of "clinical" legal education.

The dimension of *theory* consists of the rationales or reasons for legal doctrine. The principal source of theory is the "common sense" of lawyers and judges, but often these intuitions are implicitly or explicitly informed by other disciplines such as history, economics, or philosophy. The number of possible rules we might apply to cases is virtually infinite. Legal theory tells

---

1. See E. Allan Farnsworth, Contract §§1.8-1.9 (4th ed. 2004).

us why we have chosen the ones we have. In cases where there are no existing rules, legal theory tells us what the new rule should be. In cases where the rules conflict, legal theory tells us which rule should prevail. In sum, an intuitive grasp of the theories that underlie legal doctrine helps practicing lawyers to predict how courts will behave in the absence of doctrine or in the face of conflicting doctrines. For this reason, in addition to inquiring about the rules and principles to be found in the cases, statutes, and Restatement sections in this book, your professor may ask about the underlying rationale or theory that accounts for these doctrines. And many professors who stress legal theory will supplement this casebook by assigning readings from books and law review articles — both classic and recent.

3. The Restatement and the Uniform Commercial Code

Some cases like Hadley v. Baxendale (Chapter 2) are famous for the rules they originated, and lawyers consult appellate court decisions to determine the law in their jurisdictions. But cases are more often studied in law school because of their facts — the more colorful and memorable the better. It is next to impossible to understand rules of law without knowing the sorts of factual problems the rules are designed to address. This is why we do not simply study a list of "black letter" rules. At some point, however, facts are not enough. As noted above, this casebook stresses two sources of law in addition to judicial decisions: the Restatement (Second) of Contracts and the Uniform Commercial Code.

The Restatement is the product of the American Law Institute (ALI), a private nonprofit select group of practicing lawyers, judges, and law professors. One of the institute's principal projects is the production of "restatements of the law" of numerous subjects. Their stated purpose is to "address uncertainty in the law through a restatement of basic legal subjects that would tell judges and lawyers what the law was." Although these Restatements are supposed to be summaries of existing law, by systematizing their subjects, they inevitably reshape the law being summarized. Sometimes the Restatement also tries its hand at consciously reforming the law in response to complaints by legal scholars or practitioners or both. Supreme Court Justice Benjamin Cardozo explained the importance of the Restatements as follows:

> When, finally, it goes out under the name and with the sanction of the Institute, after all this testing and retesting, it will be something less than a code and something more than a treatise. It will be invested with unique authority, not to command, but to persuade. It will embody a composite thought and speak a composite voice. Universities and bench and bar will have had a part in its creation. I have great faith in the power of such a restatement to unify our law.[2]

2. Benjamin N. Cardozo, The Growth of the Law 9 (1924).

Each Restatement has a reporter or reporters who are the focal point for organizing the massive task of drafting proposals, eliciting feedback, and trying to accommodate criticisms. The reporters also draft the comments, illustrations, and reporters' notes that follow each black letter rule. Here is how the ALI describes the drafting process:

> The project's Reporter initially prepares a *Preliminary Draft* of one or more substantial segments of the project for review by the Advisers. Preliminary Drafts are normally also reviewed by the Members Consultative Group for the project.
>
> When the Director determines that the subject matter of a Preliminary Draft is ready for consideration by the Council, the Reporter prepares a *Council Draft*, which incorporates revisions made in light of the previous review by the Advisers and Members Consultative Group. Upon completion of its review, the Council may decide that all or part of the draft should be revised and resubmitted. Most often it will conclude that all or part, subject to revisions agreed to, should be submitted to the ALI membership at an Annual Meeting.
>
> A *Tentative Draft*, incorporating any revisions directed or agreed to by the Council, is submitted to the Annual Meeting for action by the membership. It is distributed in advance to the membership as a whole, which is invited to submit written comments and suggestions, and it is also made available to the entire legal community. At the close of the discussion, the Tentative Draft, subject to any changes resulting from the Annual Meeting, may be approved in whole or part or remanded in whole or part to the Reporter for further revision and eventual resubmission to the membership.
>
> The Council may conclude that a draft is not yet ready for action by the membership but would nevertheless benefit from discussion at the Annual Meeting. It may therefore direct that the draft, as revised following the Council Meeting, be submitted to the membership for discussion only. Such a draft is denominated a *Discussion Draft*.
>
> The drafting cycle continues until each segment of the project has been accorded final approval by both the Council and the membership. When extensive changes are required, the Reporter may be asked to prepare a *Proposed Final Draft* of the entire work, or appropriate portions thereof, for review by the Council and membership. Review of such a draft is not de novo, and it will ordinarily be limited to consideration of whether the changes previously decided upon have been accurately and adequately carried out. Upon final approval of the project, the Reporter, subject to oversight by the Director, prepares the Institute's *official text* for publication.

The first Restatement of Contracts was published in 1932. Its reporter was the famous Harvard contracts professor Samuel Williston. The Restatement (Second) of Contracts was commenced in 1962 and completed in 1979; it carries a 1981 publication date. Its original reporter was Harvard law professor Robert Braucher (1916-1982). When Professor Braucher was appointed to a seat on the Supreme Judicial Court of Massachusetts in 1971, Columbia law professor E. Allan Farnsworth (1928-2005) became the reporter. In this casebook, we will sometimes compare sections from the first and second Restatements to determine the significance of revisions. For example, in Chapter 11, we contrast the two versions of §90 that define the doctrine of promissory estoppel to see how the theory of that doctrine evolved between the first and second Restatements.

The other principal source of legal doctrine we will study is the Uniform Commercial Code (UCC). A product of the nineteenth-century movement to harmonize and make uniform the laws of the 50 states, the UCC is a joint product of the ALI and the National Conference of Commissioners on Uniform State Laws (NCCUSL). The conference describes itself as providing

> states with non-partisan, well-conceived and well-drafted legislation that brings clarity and stability to critical areas of the law. NCCUSL's work supports the federal system and facilitates the movement of individuals and the business of organizations with rules that are consistent from state to state.
>
> Uniform Law Commissioners must be lawyers, qualified to practice law. They are lawyer-legislators, attorneys in private practice, state and federal judges, law professors, and legislative staff attorneys, who have been appointed by state governments as well as the District of Columbia, Puerto Rico and the U.S. Virgin Islands to research, draft and promote enactment of uniform state laws in areas where uniformity is desirable and practical.

The conference has drafted more than 200 uniform laws on numerous subjects and in various fields of law, setting patterns for uniformity across the nation. Uniform acts include the Uniform Probate Code, the Uniform Child Custody Jurisdiction Act, the Uniform Partnership Act, the Uniform Anatomical Gift Act, the Uniform Limited Partnership Act, and the Uniform Interstate Family Support Act. NCCUSL describes its drafting process as follows:

> Each uniform act is years in the making. The process starts with the Scope and Program Committee, which initiates the agenda of the Conference. It investigates each proposed act, and then reports to the Executive Committee whether a subject is one in which it is desirable and feasible to draft a uniform law. If the Executive Committee approves a recommendation, a drafting committee of commissioners is appointed. Drafting committees meet throughout the year. Tentative drafts are not submitted to the entire Conference until they have received extensive committee consideration.
>
> Draft acts are then submitted for initial debate of the entire Conference at an annual meeting. Each act must be considered section by section, at no less than two annual meetings by all commissioners sitting as a Committee of the Whole. With hundreds of trained eyes probing every concept and word, it is a rare draft that leaves an annual meeting in the same form it was initially presented.
>
> Once the Committee of the Whole approves an act, its final test is a vote by states — one vote per state. A majority of the states present, and no less than 20 states, must approve an act before it can be officially adopted as a Uniform or Model Act.
>
> At that point, a Uniform or Model Act is officially promulgated for consideration by the states. Legislatures are urged to adopt Uniform Acts exactly as written, to "promote uniformity in the law among the states." Model Acts are designed to serve as guideline legislation, which states can borrow from or adapt to suit their individual needs and conditions.
>
> When drafting is completed on an act, a commissioner's work has only begun. They advocate the adoption of uniform and model acts in their home jurisdictions. Normal resistance to anything "new" makes this the hardest part of a commissioner's job. But the result can be workable modern state law that helps keep the federal system alive.

In 1940, the conference decided to address the issue of commercial relations. In 1942, Karl Llewellyn (1893-1962) of Columbia was named the principal drafter of the UCC. His assistant on the project was Soia Mentschikoff (1915-1984), who joined the faculty of the Harvard Law School in 1947 as its first female professor. In 1949, she was named associate chief reporter. The two were married in 1947 and, in 1951, both joined the faculty of the University of Chicago School of Law.

It took 10 years to draft the UCC and another 14 years to see it adopted by the legislatures of every state except Louisiana, which still uses a version of the Napoleonic Code. Article 2 of the UCC concerns the *sale* of *goods*. Students must know that if a contractual transaction is *not a sale* or *does not involve goods*, it is not covered by Article 2 of the UCC. So a sale of land or an employment services contract is still regulated by the common law of each state, not by the UCC. The case of J.O. Hooker & Sons v. Roberts Cabinet Co. (Chapter 2) discusses how to categorize contracts dealing with both goods and services. One reason for the revision of the Restatement was to incorporate the various reforms adopted in the UCC to harmonize both documents. Still, the Restatement (Second) is of greatest importance with the many contracts that do not involve the sale of goods and are not governed by the UCC.

In 2003, the ALI and NCCUSL completed work on proposed revisions of Article 2. After a highly contentious meeting of the Committee of the Whole in Denver, Colorado, the proposal was withdrawn due to strong opposition. And speaking of unsuccessful proposals by NCCUSL, in Chapter 10 we will study the Uniform Written Obligations Act that was drafted in 1925 with the assistance of Samuel Williston but was adopted by the legislatures of just two states. It remains, however, the law in Pennsylvania.

Students are always curious about the authoritative weight of these sources of law. A judicial decision is binding only within its relevant jurisdiction, though it may be persuasive in the courts of other jurisdictions, especially when considering a matter for the first time. The Uniform Commercial Code is a statute adopted by the legislatures of 49 states and is binding on courts; it supersedes any common law rules that are inconsistent with its provisions. By contrast, the Restatement is good "authority" in the literal sense: It is widely respected because of how it was drafted and the learned "authorities" who drafted it. For this reason, courts often adopt its provisions as the law. When a state appellate court is deciding what doctrine to adopt, following the Restatement is likely to be considered a safe option. Note, however, that courts have sometimes adopted provisions of the first Restatement as the law in their jurisdictions, and then have not since revisited the issue after the second Restatement was published.

4. How to Brief Cases for This Class

Because your ability to appreciate the classroom discussion of cases depends so heavily on your knowledge of the facts and the legal analysis of the court, many students find it useful to "brief" the cases on a separate sheet of paper. Some professors — myself included — even require their students to do so, especially during the first semester of law school. Cases appearing in this material are either principal cases or are provided as background. *Background cases* are short excerpts and may not provide all the procedural and historical facts. They usually elaborate on or deviate from the principal cases they follow. They should be carefully studied (not skimmed), but your notes, or brief, of the case may be limited to the holding (if one is provided) and your analysis of how this material compares with the preceding principal cases. *Principal cases* are listed in italics in the table of contents and table of cases. Either all or a substantial portion of the case is reproduced in this casebook and is set apart from the rest of the text. They should be thoroughly briefed. This will greatly assist you in understanding the case, appreciating class discussion, and participating in class. Throughout this book, *Study Guide* questions are provided to guide and stimulate you while reading and briefing the cases. They are not intended to be comprehensive, and your professor may well choose to stress other issues.

There is no one right way to brief cases and eventually you will develop your own style, but you could do worse than to begin with this format:

a. Identify the PARTIES.
   - Who is suing whom? Determine who is the plaintiff/defendant, appellant/appellee, petitioner/respondent, etc.
b. Figure out the PROCEDURAL FACTS of the case.
   - What is the history of the *lawsuit itself*? For example, is this an appeal from the trial court to an appellate court? Was there a "finding of fact" in the lower court? By a judge or jury? The procedural context may govern which issues are to be argued.
c. Summarize the HISTORICAL FACTS that led to a lawsuit.
   - What happened between the parties that led someone to file a lawsuit?
d. What FORM OF RELIEF is being sought by the plaintiff/appellant?
   - For example, damages? Specific performance? Injunction?
e. Identify the ARGUMENTS of the parties.
   - What legal reason is the plaintiff/appellant/petitioner offering to justify the granting of relief? What arguments are made by the defendant/appellee/respondent against the granting of relief?
f. The OUTCOME of the case.
   - Who won? What, if any, relief was ordered by the court?
g. The REASONING of the court.
   - What reasons did the court offer for granting or denying relief? Did it summarize these reasons as a basic principle, or holding?
h. YOUR ANALYSIS.
   - Do you agree with the outcome of the case (who won)? How would you have decided the case?
   - Do you agree with the reasoning of the court? Can you give any other rationales for the outcome?
   - How does this case relate to other cases and materials you have read?
   - Both before and during the lawsuit, why have the parties behaved in the ways that they have?

Following many of the cases are various types of *background* materials that expand on the doctrinal material. These include relational, historical, comparative, ethical, economics, statutory, procedural, empirical, commercial, and theoretical background sections selected for their inherent interest to students and to enrich classroom discussion. Different professors will choose to emphasize different background materials, and few will discuss them all in class. Still, even if not assigned by your professor, you may find these additional readings to be interesting background to the assigned material. That is why they were included.

B. THE NATURE AND HISTORY OF CONTRACT

The cases and materials in Sections B and C are intended to give you a "first look" at the basic issues of contract law. They raise fundamental questions about the enforcement of private agreements. These questions will not all be answered here, but will remain with us for the entire course.

STUDY GUIDE: When reading the following case be sure to identify the court's response to each of the defendant's objections to the complaint. Although the elements or requirements of a contract will be covered in detail in Parts II and III, this case requires you to consider some preliminary questions about the nature and history of contract. For example, what does assumpsit *mean? What is the difference between this cause of action and one in* negligence? *Why do you suppose that Pennsylvania (and many other states) refuses to imply a "warranty of cure" from the words and conduct of a physician? Notice also how the court here used precedent to justify its decision. In refusing to award damages here, did it adhere to the standards provided by Mamlin v. Genoe? After reading this case, consider why Pennsylvania might have passed a statute in 1975 that reads: "In the absence of a special contract in writing, a health care provider is neither a warrantor nor a gurantor of a cure."*

SHAHEEN v. KNIGHT

Court of Common Pleas of Lycoming County, Pennsylvania,
11 Pa. D. & C.2d 41 (1957)

WILLIAMS, P.J.*
Plaintiff, Robert M. Shaheen, is suing defendant physician because of an operation. He alleges defendant contracted to make him sterile. According to the complaint, the operation occurred on September 16, 1954, and a "blessed event" occurred on February 11, 1956, when plaintiff's wife, Doris,

---

* *Charles Scott Williams* (1904-1966) was educated at Dickinson College (A.B., LL.B.) and served as President Judge on the Court of Common Pleas of Pennsylvania for two terms (1944-1954, 1954-1963). Prior to joining the bench, Williams served as U.S. Commissioner (1932-1936) and District Attorney (1936-1944) of Williamsport, Pennsylvania. — [This judicial biography was written by Kristin Taylor, hereinafter "K.T."]

was delivered of a fifth child as a result of marital relations continued after the operation.

Plaintiff in his complaint does not allege any negligence by defendant. The suit is based on contract.

Plaintiff does not claim that the operation was necessary because of his wife's health. He claims that in order to support his family in comfort and educate it, it is necessary to limit the size of his family, and that he would be emotionally unable to limit his family's size by reason or will power alone, or by abstention.

Plaintiff claims damages as follows: "That the Plaintiff, as a result, despite his love and affection for his fifth (5th) child, as he would have for any other child, now has the additional expenses of supporting, educating and maintaining said child, and that such expense will continue until the maturity of said child, none of which expense would have been incurred, had the Defendant, Dr. John E. Knight, fulfilled the contract and undertaking entered into by him, or fulfilled the representations made by him."

Defendant has filed preliminary objections to the complaint, alleging:

1. An alleged contract to sterilize a man whose wife may have a child without any hazard to her life is void as against public policy and public morals.

2. Under Pennsylvania law there is no [implied] "warranty of cure" by a physician.

3. That the complaint charges no lack of skill, malpractice, or negligence in any respect in the performance of the operation, a vasectomy, but merely seeks to recover upon the ground that the operation did not achieve the purpose sought and the results allegedly promised.

4. That while the complaint is said to be in assumpsit, it appears to be grounded on deceit, that is that the defendant made a statement, misrepresenting material facts, known to be false or made in ignorance or reckless disregard of its truth, with an intent to induce the plaintiff to act in reliance thereon, and the plaintiff, believing it to be true, did act thereon to his damage. If this be true the plaintiff has made no allegation of fraudulent intent on defendant's part, or any of the elements of deceit.

5. The duty of a physician or surgeon to bring skill and care to the amelioration of the condition of his patient does not arise from contract but has its foundation in public considerations which are inseparable from the nature and exercise of his calling; it is predicated by the law on the relation which exists between physician and patient, which is the result of a consensual transaction.

6. That the plaintiff has suffered no damage but "has been blessed with the fatherhood of another child."

We are of the opinion that a contract to sterilize a man is not void as against public policy and public morals. It was so held in Christensen v. Thornby, 192 Minn. 123, 255 N.W. 620. Also see 93 A.L.R. 570. It is argued, however, that in the *Christensen* case the operation was for a man whose wife could not have a child without hazard to her life, whereas in the instant case claimant has contracted for sterilization because he cannot afford children.

It is only when a given policy is so obviously for or against the public health, safety, morals or welfare that there is a virtual unanimity of opinion in regard to it, that a court may constitute itself the voice of the community in declaring such policy void: Mamlin v. Genoe, 340 Pa. 320. It has been said: "There must be a positive, well-defined, universal public sentiment, deeply integrated in the customs and beliefs of the people and in their conviction of what is just and right and in the interest of the public weal."

It is the faith of some that sterilization is morally wrong whether to keep [the] wife from having children or for any other reason. Many people have no moral compunctions against sterilization. Others are against sterilization, except when a man's life is in danger, when a person is low mentally, when a person is an habitual criminal. There is no virtual unanimity of opinion regarding sterilization. The Superior Court, in Wilson v. Wilson, 126 Pa. Superior Ct. 423, ruled that the incapacity to procreate is not an independent ground for divorce where it appears that the party complained against is capable of natural and complete copulation. This case so held whether or not there was natural or artificial creation of sterility, and recognized that in some cases there was artificial creation of sterility. It would appear that an exception would have been made had there been recognized any public policy against sterilization.

Defendant argues that there is no [implied] "warranty of cure" by physician[s] in Pennsylvania. He also argues that the duty of a physician or surgeon does not arise from contract and suggests that it is against public policy for such a contract to be upheld. . . .

A doctor and his patient, however, are at liberty to contract for a particular result. If that result be not attained, the patient has a cause of action for breach of contract. The cause of action is entirely separate from malpractice, even though both may arise out of the same transaction. The two causes of action are dissimilar as to theory, proof and damages recoverable. Negligence is the basis of malpractice, while the action in contract is based upon a failure to perform a special agreement. . . . Damages in a contract action between doctor and patient are restricted in some jurisdictions.

In the instant case plaintiff is suing, according to his claim, under a special contract in which defendant agreed to make him "immediately and permanently sterile and guaranteed the results thereof." Defendant's "warranty of cure" argument therefore does not apply to this case.

We see little merit in defendant's argument that the action seems to be grounded on deceit and that therefore we should dismiss the complaint.

Defendant argues, however, and pleads, that plaintiff has suffered no damage. We agree with defendant. The only damages asked are the expenses of rearing and educating the unwanted child. We are of the opinion that to allow damages for the normal birth of a normal child is foreign to the universal public sentiment of the people.

Many consider the sole purpose of marriage a union for having children.

As Chief Justice Gibson said in Matchin v. Matchin, 6 Pa. 332 [1847]:

> The great end of matrimony is not the comfort and convenience of the immediate parties, though these are necessarily embarked in it; but the procreation of a progeny having a legal title to maintenance by the father; and the reciprocal taking for better, for worse, for richer, for poorer, in sickness and in health, to love and cherish till death, are important, but only modal conditions of the contract, and no more than ancillary to the principal purpose of it. The civil rights created by them may be forfeited by the misconduct of either party; but though the forfeiture can be incurred, so far as the parties themselves are concerned, only by a responsible agent, it follows not that those rights must not give way without it to public policy, and the paramount purposes of the marriage — the procreation and protection of legitimate children, the institution of families, and the creation of natural relations among mankind; from which proceed all the civilization, virtue, and happiness to be found in the world.

To allow damages in a suit such as this would mean that the physician would have to pay for the fun, joy and affection which plaintiff Shaheen will have in the rearing and educating of this, defendant's [sic] fifth child. Many people would be willing to support this child were they given the right of custody and adoption, but according to plaintiff's statement, plaintiff does not want such. He wants to have the child and wants the doctor to support it. In our opinion to allow such damages would be against public policy.

RESTATEMENT (SECOND) OF CONTRACTS

Study Guide: Many of the cases in this book will be followed by sections taken from the Restatement (Second) of Contracts. The Restatement is an extremely influential source of law for courts dealing with contracts problems. (See page 6.) When you see these sections, try to apply them to the case or cases that immediately precede them. For example, apply the following definitions of contract, promise, and agreement to the facts of Shaheen v. Knight. Was there a promise according to the Restatement §2(1)? If so, how was the promise made (§4)? These sections are included here only for introductory purposes. They shall be of greater importance when studying manifesting assent in Part II. We shall consider the concept of bargain mentioned in §3 at length in Chapter 9.

§1.   CONTRACT DEFINED

A contract is a promise or a set of promises for the breach of which the law gives a remedy, or the performance of which the law in some way recognizes as a duty.

§2.   PROMISE; PROMISOR; PROMISEE; BENEFICIARY

(1) A promise is a manifestation of intention to act or refrain from acting in a specified way, so made as to justify a promisee in understanding that a commitment has been made.

(2) The person manifesting the intention is the promisor.

(3) The person to whom the manifestation is addressed is the promisee.

(4) Where performance will benefit a person other than the promisee, that person is a beneficiary.

§3.   AGREEMENT DEFINED; BARGAIN DEFINED

An agreement is a manifestation of mutual assent on the part of two or more persons. A bargain is an agreement to exchange promises or to exchange a promise for a performance or to exchange performances.

§4.   HOW A PROMISE MAY BE MADE

A promise may be stated in words either oral or written, or may be inferred wholly or partly from conduct.

REFERENCE: Barnett, xiii-xxvi
                 Farnsworth, §§1.1-1.11
                 Calamari & Perillo, §§1.1-1.3, 1.5-1.8
                 Murray, §§1-6, 32(c)*

Historical Background: From Status to Contract

STUDY GUIDE: *How does the following famous passage by the legal historian Sir Henry Maine bear on the Shaheen case?*

SIR HENRY MAINE, ANCIENT LAW 163-165 (3D AMERICAN FROM 6TH LONDON ED., 1864):   The movement of the progressive societies has been uniform in one respect. Through all its course it has been distinguished by the gradual dissolution of family dependency and the growth of individual obligation in its place. The individual is steadily substituted for the Family, as the unit of which civil laws take account. The advance has been accomplished at varying rates of celerity, and there are societies not absolutely stationary in which the collapse of the ancient organisation can only be perceived by careful study of the phenomena they present. But, whatever its pace, the change has not been subject to reaction or recoil,

---

*References are to Randy E. Barnett, The Oxford Introduction to U.S. Law: Contracts (2010), E. Allan Farnsworth, Contracts (4th ed. 2004), John D. Calamari & Joseph M. Perillo, Contracts (6th ed. 2009), John E. Murray, Murray on Contracts (5th ed. 2011).

and apparent retardations will be found to have been occasioned through the absorptions of archaic ideas and customs from some entirely foreign source. Nor is it difficult to see what is the tie between man and man which replaces by degrees those forms of reciprocity in rights and duties which have their origin in the Family. It is Contract. Starting, as from one terminus of history, from a condition of society in which all the relations of Persons are summed up in the relations of Family, we seem to have steadily moved towards a phase of social order in which all these relations arise from the free agreement of individuals. In Western Europe the progress achieved in this direction has been considerable. . . .

The word Status may be usefully employed to construct a formula expressing the law of progress thus indicated, which, whatever be its value, seems to me to be sufficiently ascertained. All the forms of Status taken notice of in the Law of Persons were derived from, and to some extent are still coloured by, the powers and privileges anciently residing in the Family. If then we employ Status, agreeably with the usage of the best writers, to signify these personal conditions only, and avoid applying the term to such conditions as are the immediate or remote result of agreement, we may say that the movement of the progressive societies has hitherto been a movement *from Status to Contract.*

Historical Background: The Rise of Assumpsit

STUDY GUIDE: *The court in* Shaheen *discusses the action of "assumpsit." Understanding the meaning and significance of this strange word will contribute to a better understanding of a host of contract doctrines that we shall study throughout the course. Notice also how competition among legal systems within the same legal order stimulated doctrinal change.*

E. ALLAN FARNSWORTH, CONTRACTS 11-18 (4TH ED. 2004):   No legal system has ever been reckless enough to make all promises enforceable. As a distinguished legal philosopher expressed it, some freedom to change one's mind is essential "for free intercourse between those who lack omniscience." Most of us "would shudder at the idea of being bound by every promise, no matter how foolish, without any chance of letting increased wisdom undo past foolishness."[3] In framing a basis for enforcing promises, however, one can approach the goal from two opposite extremes. One can begin with the assumption that promises are generally enforceable, and then create exceptions for promises considered undesirable to enforce. Or one can begin with the assumption that promises are generally unenforceable, and then create exceptions for promises thought desirable to enforce.

The common law courts chose this latter assumption, the same as that of Roman law: a mere promise does not give rise to an action. Their choice was scarcely surprising. It accorded well with the procedural niceties of common law courts, where recovery was not to be had unless the claim could be fitted within one of the established forms of action, and it suited

3. Cohen, The Basis of Contract, 46 Harv. L. Rev. 553, 573 (1932).

the status-oriented society of the Middle Ages, which was anything but conducive to the flowering of promise. Furthermore, no great pressure existed for enforceability of promises, because contracts were not yet a significant part of the business of the common law courts. At the end of the twelfth century, a writer apologized for the scant treatment of the subject in his treatise on English common law with the remark that "it is not the custom of the court of the lord king to protect private agreements, nor does it even concern itself with such contracts as can be considered to be like private agreements."[4]

Competing jurisdictions, however, were more hospitable to actions for breach of promise. Under the law merchant (the body of rules then applied in the commercial courts), the courts in the medieval fairs and markets entertained actions, as commerce required, on promises made by merchants. Under canon law, the Church courts regarded a sworn promise (by which one pledged one's "faith," i.e., one's hope of salvation) as enforceable and its breach as a sin subject to ecclesiastical censures, including excommunication, and there was support for the position that even an unsworn promise was sacred and therefore enforceable. And in equity, the Chancellor held that because a man was "damaged by the non-performance of the promise, he shall have a remedy."[5]

The general theory for enforcing promises that was ultimately fashioned by the common law courts succeeded less on its intrinsic merits than as an incident of the victories of those courts in their struggles to expand their own jurisdiction at the expense of their rivals. These victories were complete by the close of the sixteenth century. By that time the common law courts had so far succeeded in wresting jurisdiction from the commercial courts as to stifle the law merchant's practice of enforcing promises made by merchants in commerce. Although the Church courts had continued to enforce promises in the face of the prohibition of the Constitution of Clarendon of 1164, this business also dried up in the sixteenth century when the common law courts provided a forum for such causes.[6] And since, in equity, the Chancellor often intervened if he found the common law to be wanting, it is a tribute to the ingenuity and flexibility of the common law judges that they succeeded in moving fast enough to stay the Chancellor's hand. Credit for the development of the general basis for enforcing promises that we know today is therefore theirs and theirs alone.

The challenge faced and met by the common law courts in the fifteenth and sixteenth centuries was to develop a general basis for enforcing

---

4. R. de Glanville, Treatise on the Laws and Customs of the Realm of England, bk. 10, ch. 18 (G. Hall ed. 1965); see also bk. 10, ch. 8. Records are lacking to show the extent to which promises were enforced in local courts, and it was the king's courts that dictated the development of contract law.

5. Anon., Y.B. Pasch. 8 Edw. 4, fo. 4, pl. 11 (1468) (1640 ed.); C. Fifoot, History and Sources of the Common Law: Tort and Contract 304 (1949) (suit on promise to pay for services brought after performance); cf. F. Robinson (ed.), The Complete Works of Geoffrey Chaucer 537 (2d ed. 1957) ("Sometyme the world was so stedfast and stable that mannes word was obligacioun.").

6. See Helmholz, Assumpsit and *Fidei Laesio*, 91 L.Q. Rev. 406 (1975).

promises within the framework of the forms of action.[7] This they did, first by developing exceptions as the Romans had done, and then by fashioning those exceptions into something that the Romans had never achieved: a general basis for enforcing promises, including purely executory exchanges of promises. How was this brought about?

One possible vehicle for the development of a general basis for enforcing promises might have been a formal acknowledgment of liability, such as that on which the Roman stipulation was based. The common law action known as *covenant* that grew up in England near the end of the twelfth century became associated with such a formal acknowledgment in the form of a wax seal. Had the trend then been toward the relaxation of formalities, the action of covenant might have developed into a general contractual remedy. This possibility was foreclosed, however, by the middle of the fourteenth century, when it became settled that the seal was not merely evidentiary, so that an action of covenant could not be maintained unless the plaintiff produced a writing under seal. With this turn of events, any hope that covenant might serve as a general ground for contractual liability vanished, since a sealed writing was little better suited to an informal exchange of promises than the Roman stipulation had been.

Another possible avenue of evolution was through the concept of loan, which we have seen was familiar to most primitive societies. By the end of the twelfth century, this concept had given rise to the common law action known as *debt*, which would lie to recover a sum certain in money. But the defendant's liability in debt was not seen as based on a mere promise. It depended instead on the debtor's receipt of what the debtor had asked for — called a *quid pro quo* in imitation of the Romans — in the form of the loan. It was therefore thought to be unjust to allow the debtor to retain it without paying for it. The debtor's wrong was more in the nature of misfeasance than of nonfeasance.[8] Following this rationale, courts finally broadened the action of debt to allow recovery by anyone who had conferred a substantial benefit on the defendant, including one who had furnished personal services.

Suppose that an owner paid a builder $10,000 in return for the builder's promise to do specified work on the owner's house. If the builder failed to do the work, the action of debt was adequate to allow the owner to recover from the builder. Since the promisor, the builder, had received a

---

7. Under the formulary system, a plaintiff who sought relief in the common law courts had to state a case in accordance with one of a limited number of standard forms. According to Maitland's memorable description, "English law knows a certain number of forms of action, each with its own uncouth name. . . . The choice is not merely a choice between a number of queer technical terms, it is a choice between methods of procedure adapted to cases of different kinds. . . . The forms of action we have buried, but they still rule us from their graves." F. Maitland, The Forms of Action at Common Law 2 (1962).

8. Scholars disagree over whether the action of debt was conceived of as proprietary in nature (i.e., as founded on what the creditor owned, rather than on what the debtor owed). See [F. Maitland, The Forms of Action at Common Law 38 (1936): "vast gulf . . . to our minds divides the 'Give me what I own' and 'Give me what I am owed'"] and the critical discussion in A. Simpson, History of the Common Law of Contract 75-80 (paperback ed. 1987). It seems clear, however, that it was based on notions of unjust enrichment, rather than of obligation arising out of mere promise.

benefit in the amount of $10,000, recovery prevented the unjust enrich-
ment of the promisor.[9]

But it was clear that, for there to be a *quid pro quo*, the benefit must
have been actually conferred — a mere promise to confer it would not
suffice. Therefore the action of debt was no better suited than were the
innominate contracts of Roman law to the enforcement of a mere exchange
of promises, such as a promise to deliver apples in the future in return for a
promise to pay the price in the future. Moreover, the action of debt was
subject to the further inconvenience — difficult for the modern mind to
comprehend — that the defendant might avoid liability by a procedure
known as "wager of law," in which the defendant denied the debt under
oath accompanied by a number (usually 11) of oath-helpers, who swore that
the defendant was telling the truth.

How was the common law to break out of this mold? . . .

. . . The common law courts found the answer to this question in the
law of torts. They had already recognized that liability in tort arose when a
person undertook to perform a duty and then performed it in such a way as
to cause harm to the obligee. The obligee could sue on the variety of the
common law action of "trespass on the case" that came to be known as
assumpsit (from the Latin, meaning that the defendant undertook). At the
beginning of the fifteenth century it was available only if there had been
misfeasance in the performance of the undertaking.

This example was given in 1436: "If a carpenter makes a [promise to]
me to make me a house good and strong and of a certain form, and he
makes me a house which is weak and bad and of another form, I shall have
an action of trespass on my case."[10] Such a case of misfeasance cried out for
recovery. The promisee, who was left with a worthless house, had been
harmed by relying on the promise. Justice could be done by requiring
the promisor to pay compensation in an amount sufficient to put the promisee in as good a position as the promisee would have been in had the
promise never been made. The promisee's claim to recovery based on
the reliance interest was less compelling than that based on the restitution
interest, since the reliance interest did not depend on any benefit received
by the promisor (i.e., it was not founded on the concept of unjust enrichment). Nevertheless, the promisee's right to recovery seemed clear on principles developed in tort cases.

But might not a remedy lie when there had merely been nonfeasance, a
failure by the promisor to perform the undertaking? At first the answer was
no. In 1409 it was said: "Certainly it would lie [if the carpenter had built the
house badly], because he would then answer for the wrong which he had
done, but when a man makes a [promise] and does nothing under that
[promise], how can you have an action against him without a [writing
under seal]?"[11] Nevertheless, by the second half of the fifteenth century

---

9. The amount of recovery in debt at common law was not, however, limited to the value
of the benefit conferred, but could be any definite amount of money or goods that the debtor
had promised to pay. Ames, Parol Contracts Prior to Assumpsit, 8 Harv. L. Rev. 252, 260 (1894).

10. Y.B. 14 Hy. 6 [1679 ed.], p. 18, pl. 58 (1436), 3 W. Holdsworth, History of English
Law 430 (4th ed. 1935).

11. Y.B. Mich. 11 Hy. 4 [1605 ed.], p. 33, pl. 60 (1409), 3 W. Holdsworth, supra note
[10], at 433-434.

there was a growing inclination among common law judges, conscious of their rival jurisdictions, to make a major extension in the action of assumpsit by enforcing such promises, even where there had been only nonfeasance. But some limits had to be placed on which promises would be enforced, for the judges were not about to allow "that one shall have trespass for any breach of covenant in the world."[12] The courts were therefore forced to find a test to distinguish instances in which nonfeasance was actionable from those in which it was not.

Since the misfeasance cases that had originally given rise to the action in assumpsit were characterized by a detriment incurred by the promisee in reliance on the promise, it was natural to formulate an analogous test and to allow enforcement if the promisee had changed position on the faith of the promise and had been consequently damaged by its nonperformance. Doing nothing can make things worse.[13] Suppose, for instance, that a builder promised to do specified work on an owner's house in return for the owner's promise to pay the builder $10,000 on its completion, and, in reliance on the builder's promise, the owner rented and moved to another house to permit the builder to do the work. If the builder failed to do the work, the law could justify protecting the owner because of the detriment sustained. To the extent that the promisee incurred expenses in preparing to perform or suffered loss by forgoing other opportunities, a broken promise resulted in waste. Because the loss was purely economic, as contrasted with cases of misfeasance that had resulted in loss to person or property, the claim to recovery may have seemed less compelling. But in a society that depended on promises for cooperation, there was reason to protect those who relied on promises by placing the cost of that waste on those who broke them.

This first major extension of the action of assumpsit fell short, however, of recognizing claims based on purely executory exchanges of promises, in which there had been no reliance at all by the claimant. As the sixteenth century drew to a close, the common law courts made a second and dramatic extension of the action of assumpsit by allowing such claims. It was held that even if one had given only a promise in exchange for the other's promise, one had nonetheless suffered a detriment by having one's freedom of action fettered: one was in turn bound by one's own promise. Suppose again that the builder promised to do specified work on the owner's house and, in return, the owner promised to pay the builder $10,000. On this reasoning, if the builder repudiated the bargain before the owner had done anything in reliance on the builder's promise, the owner had a claim for breach of contract. The reasoning is, of course, circular, since the conclusion that there was a detriment to the promisee, in this case the owner, assumed that the promisee was in turn bound by a promise, even though nothing but a promise had been given for it. Nevertheless, by the end of the sixteenth century

12. Y.B. Hil. 3 Hy. 6 [1679 ed.], p. 36, pl. 33 (1425), 3W. Holdsworth, supra note [10], at 435.

13. In 1499, Fyneux C.J. said that "if a man covenants to build me a house by such a day, and he does nothing towards it, I shall have an action on my case upon this nonfeasance as well as if he had done it badly." But it has been suggested that if "Fyneux C.J. really did not think prepayment essential, his views differed from those of his contemporaries." 2 J. Baker (ed.), The Reports of Sir John Spelman 269-270 (Selden Soc. 1978). For an example in addition to that given in the text, suppose that a builder promised to repair an owner's barn by December 1 and, when this was not done, the owner's livestock died from cold weather.

the common law courts were enforcing exchanges of promises where no performance had been rendered on either side.[14] . . .

The action of assumpsit was still subject to one important restriction. It had been held that where the action of debt was available, the action of assumpsit was not. This proved a disadvantage to creditors, since in assumpsit the plaintiff was entitled to a jury trial, while in debt the defendant could resort to wager of law. The next important step in the common law's development of a law of contract was therefore to permit assumpsit to supplant debt. By the middle of the sixteenth century, it had been recognized that an action in assumpsit could be brought against a defendant who, being already indebted (*indebitatus*), expressly undertook (*assumpsit*) to pay a particular sum. This action in *indebitatus assumpsit* was also described as "general assumpsit," to distinguish it from the older action of "assumpsit," which was known as "special assumpsit" because of the specifics that had to be pleaded.[15] (Only special and not general assumpsit could be used for the enforcement of a purely executory contract, in which there had been an exchange of promises but no performance on either side.) Toward the end of the century, it began to be held that a debt alone, without a subsequent express promise, would support such an action of general assumpsit. The final triumph of this view came at the beginning of the seventeenth century in *Slade's Case*, in which the plaintiff sued for the price of a crop sold and delivered to the defendant. On a jury finding that "there was no other promise or assumption, but only the said bargain," it was decided by all of the common law judges assembled to pass upon this important matter that every such bargain "imports in itself an assumpsit."[16] The creditor could sue in assumpsit as an alternative to debt, even though there was no subsequent promise. The creditor was at last assured of the benefits of jury trial in place of wager of law.

Over the course of the fifteenth and sixteenth centuries, the common law courts thus had succeeded in developing the action of

---

14. Strangborough v. Warner, 4 Leo. 3, 74 Eng. Rep. 686 (K.B. 1588). Perhaps the pressure to take this step in England was lessened by the availability of the action of debt for a purely executory contract of sale, on the theory that the promise to pay was a sufficient quid pro quo for the promise to deliver. See Holdsworth, Debt, Assumpsit, and Consideration, 11 Mich. L. Rev. 347 (1913). . . .

15. In *indebitatus assumpsit*, the plaintiff could state the origin of the debt in general terms, followed by a statement that, being indebted, the defendant promised to pay. This general statement of the source of the debt was the beginning of what later came to be known as the common counts of general assumpsit. . . . [In another section of his book, Professor Farnsworth explains that "[t]he action of general assumpsit, which after *Slade's Case* was the standard remedy for recovery of debts, was divided into what were known as the 'common counts.' By means of one of these, the plaintiff might allege that the defendant was indebted to the plaintiff for money lent; by means of another (*quantum meruit*) for work done; by another (*quantum valebant*), for goods sold and delivered; and so on. Quantum meruit gradually became a flexible basis for recovery where a benefit had been received by the defendant and it would be inequitable for the defendant to retain it." E. Allan Farnsworth, Contracts §2.20 n.6 (4th ed. 2004). — EDS.]

16. *Slade's Case*, 4 Co. Rep. 92b, 94a, 76 Eng. Rep. 1074, 1077 (1602). This landmark decision was handed down by all the judges of the central courts assembled in a special chamber, after argument by Sir Edward Coke, then Attorney General, for the plaintiff, and Sir Francis Bacon, Coke's bitter rival, for the defendant. For a detailed discussion, including the jurisdictional dispute between the courts of King's Bench and Common Pleas, see Baker, New Light on Slade's Case, 29 Camb. L.J. 51, 213 (1971).

assumpsit into a general basis for enforcing promises, including purely executory exchanges of promises.

REFERENCE: Barnett, §§1.1-1.5

C.   THE BOUNDARIES OF CONTRACT

Regret is a ubiquitous feature of contracting. Parties frequently enter contracts that after the fact they wish they had not made. Sometimes they undertake contracts in situations or on terms that they would prefer to avoid. For obvious reasons, the mere fact that someone regrets having entered into a contract is not a defense to contractual liability. Such a rule would effectively gut the idea of a legally enforceable commitment. We want our agreements with others to be legally enforceable in large part because we want the law to hold others to their promises later, when they wish to escape from their obligations. Yet this doesn't mean that all regretted agreements will be enforced.

In Jordan v. Knafel, basketball superstar Michael Jordan allegedly made a contract that he later wished to escape. Amid the tangle of sex, adultery, and their consequences, the Appellate Court of Illinois had to grapple with the distinction between a regretted agreement in unfortunate circumstances and a promise that the law should refuse to enforce. Later in this book, we will examine various defenses to contractual liability in detail. For now, try to get a feel for why the law might refuse to enforce some promises and how parties compete to characterize their transactions in order to bring them within the ambit of contractual enforceability or, alternatively, beyond the pale of the law.

STUDY GUIDE: Jordan claims to be the victim of an "extortionate" agreement. What is the difference between an "extortionate" agreement and one in which one party gets money in exchange for doing or not doing some action? Don't all commercial agreements involve extracting money by making a threat, if only the threat to withhold goods and services if the seller's price isn't met? How does Knafel characterize the agreement with Jordan?

JORDAN v. KNAFEL
Appellate Court of Illinois, First District, Fourth Division,
355 Ill. App. 3d 534, 823 N.E.2d 1113 (2005)

Justice THEIS* delivered the opinion of the court:
Plaintiff Michael Jordan sought a declaratory judgment that a contract asserted by defendant Karla Knafel was extortionate and void against public

*Mary Jane Theis (1949-†) was born in Chicago and attended Loyola University of Chicago for her undergraduate studies. She studied law at the University of San Francisco, graduating in 1974, and began her legal career as a public defender in Cook County, Illinois. In 1983, she was selected to be a judge on the Circuit Court of Cook County. She proceeded to move up the judicial ranks, and is now an Illinois Supreme Court Justice. — S.Q. [Judicial biographies by S.Q. were authored by Sebastian Quitmeyer and † will denote "date unknown" throughout the text. — EDS.]

policy. Knafel filed a counterclaim, alleging that Jordan owed her $5 million for breach of a confidential settlement agreement. The trial court dismissed the complaint and counterclaim, finding that Jordan failed to allege an actual controversy and that Knafel's alleged contract was unenforceable. . . .

On appeal, Knafel contends that the trial court erred in holding that the contract was unenforceable as extortionate and that it violated public policy. . . . For the following reasons, we . . . reverse . . . and remand for further proceedings.

BACKGROUND

On October 23, 2002, Jordan filed a complaint for a declaratory judgment and injunctive relief against Knafel, a woman with whom he had an intimate relationship. Therein, he alleged that Knafel, through her attorneys, was attempting to extort money from Jordan by threatening to publicly expose their relationship unless Jordan paid Knafel $5 million. He further alleged that Knafel had previously extorted $250,000 from him under threat of publicly exposing their relationship. Jordan denied that he agreed to pay Knafel $5 million pursuant to a purported second agreement and sought a declaratory judgment that her demand for payment was unenforceable because (i) extortionate agreements violate public policy; (ii) there would be no consideration to support any such agreement due to Knafel's existing obligation not to publicly expose their relationship; (iii) any such agreement would violate the statute of frauds because there is no agreement in writing; and (iv) any such agreement would be barred by the statute of limitations. Additionally, Jordan sought an order enjoining Knafel, and any other persons acting on her behalf, from engaging in further efforts to extort money from him.

Knafel responded to the complaint by filing a verified answer and affirmative defenses denying the material allegations of the complaint. Therein, she admitted that Jordan paid her $250,000, but stated that it was for her mental pain and anguish arising from their romantic relationship. In addition, Knafel filed a verified counterclaim asserting theories of breach of contract and anticipatory breach of contract based on Jordan's alleged breach of his promise to pay Knafel $5 million "when he retired from professional basketball in exchange for her agreement not to file a paternity suit against him and for her agreement to keep their romantic involvement publicly confidential." The following relevant facts were alleged in the verified counterclaim.

In the spring of 1989, Knafel was performing in a band at a hotel in Indianapolis, Indiana. The Chicago Bulls were in town to play the Indiana Pacers. After her performance, Knafel was introduced to Jordan over the telephone by Eddie Rush, a National Basketball Association referee, who had approached Knafel at the hotel. Knafel declined an invitation from Jordan to meet him at the Indianapolis airport and continued to decline his invitations to meet during the spring and summer of 1989. Nevertheless, Jordan and Knafel continued long-distance telephone conversations during that time.

On September 2, 1989, Jordan married his wife, Juanita. In December 1989, Knafel traveled to Chicago to meet Jordan, where they had unprotected sex. Thereafter, in November 1990, Knafel stayed with Jordan in Phoenix, Arizona, where they again had unprotected sex. In early 1991, Knafel learned that she was pregnant. She believed the baby was Jordan's, but kept silent about the pregnancy for some time. The Bulls were on their way to their first NBA championship. Jordan's product endorsements were earning him large sums of money. Knafel alleged that as a result, Jordan was "troubled" when she told him she was pregnant with his child in the spring of 1991. He was worried about destroying his public image, which he and his agent had carefully cultivated, and was concerned about the loss of future endorsements. Knafel further alleged that Jordan demanded that she abort the baby, but because of her personal beliefs, she refused.

According to Knafel, in the spring of 1991, Jordan offered, and urged Knafel to accept, his proposed settlement agreement to resolve their problems. Jordan offered to pay her "$5 million when he retired from professional basketball in return for her agreement not to file a paternity suit against him in a court of law and for her agreement to keep their romantic involvement publicly confidential." Knafel accepted Jordan's offer. In consideration for his promise to pay her, she agreed to forbear filing a public paternity action against him and agreed to keep their romantic relationship confidential.

In July 1991, Knafel's child was born. Jordan paid certain hospital bills and medical costs and paid Knafel $250,000 for "her mental pain and anguish arising from her relationship with him." Knafel did not file a paternity suit against Jordan and she kept their relationship confidential. In October 1993, Jordan announced his retirement from the Bulls. However, in March of 1995, he returned to the NBA again to play for the Bulls. Knafel had not contacted Jordan to demand her payment of the $5 million amount which he had allegedly promised her in 1991. In September 1998, Knafel approached Jordan while he was vacationing in Las Vegas. During their conversation, Knafel reminded Jordan of his obligation to pay her the money under their agreement. Knafel alleged that Jordan reaffirmed his agreement to pay her the $5 million. A few months later, Jordan retired from professional basketball again.

Two years later, Knafel's counsel contacted Jordan's counsel to resolve their contract dispute. Jordan denied that he had promised to pay Knafel $5 million. Knafel's counterclaim sought $5 million for breach of contract. Additionally, at the time Knafel filed her counterclaim, it was alleged that Jordan was playing basketball for the Washington Wizards. Accordingly, she also alleged an anticipatory breach of their 1991 contract and 1998 reaffirmation.

Thereafter, Jordan filed a hybrid motion for judgment on the pleadings, which was directed to his complaint, and a motion to dismiss Knafel's counterclaim pursuant to section 2-615 of the Illinois Code of Civil Procedure (the Code) (735 ILCS 5/2-615 (West 2002)). Therein, Jordan argued that the alleged agreement was unenforceable because it violated public policy or, in the alternative, that it was induced by fraud or mutual mistake of fact regarding the paternity of her child. The trial court initially struck the allegations raised in the motion for judgment on the pleadings that went beyond those pled in the declaratory judgment complaint, and struck the exhibits attached to Knafel's response brief. The court further declined to proceed with a hearing on the combined motions, and by agreement of the parties, proceeded to hear the motion for judgment on the pleadings. Jordan was then granted leave to file a separate motion to dismiss the counterclaim. Thereafter, Jordan filed his motion to dismiss the counterclaim pursuant to section 2-615 of the Code. He argued that the alleged agreement was unenforceable because (1) it was contrary to public policy; (2) it was fraudulently induced; and (3) if not fraudulently induced, it was based on a mutual mistake of fact as to paternity.

After a separate hearing on both motions, the trial court dismissed Jordan's complaint for declaratory judgment and denied his motion for judgment on the pleadings. The court found that Jordan failed to allege an actual controversy and that issuing a declaratory judgment on a hypothetical contract would constitute the rendering of an advisory opinion. The trial court further dismissed the counterclaim, finding the agreement to be extortionate and against public policy. Knafel subsequently filed a motion for leave to amend her verified counterclaims. Therein, she added a count for promissory and equitable estoppel and common law fraud. Her motion for leave to amend her verified counterclaims was denied.

ANALYSIS

Knafel initially contends that the trial court erred in dismissing her counterclaim and finding the alleged $5 million contract unenforceable as extortionate and against public policy. This issue comes before this court on a motion to dismiss the counterclaim pursuant to section 2-615 of the Code (735 ILCS 5/2-615 (West 2002)). A section 2-615 motion attacks the sufficiency of the counterclaim and raises the question of whether the allegations, when viewed in the light most favorable to the plaintiff, are sufficient to state a cause of action upon which relief can be granted. 735 ILCS 5/2-615 (West 2002); Wallace v. Smyth, 203 Ill. 2d 441, 447, 272 Ill. Dec. 146, 786 N.E.2d 980, 984 (2002). Further, the trial court should dismiss the cause of action only if it is clearly apparent that no set of facts can be proven which will entitle the plaintiff to recovery. Canel v. Topinka, 212 Ill. 2d 311, 317, 288 Ill. Dec. 623, 818 N.E.2d 311, 317 (2004). All well-pleaded facts are taken as true and all reasonable inferences that can be drawn from those facts are drawn in favor of the plaintiff. Bryson v. News America Publications, Inc., 174 Ill. 2d 77, 86, 220 Ill. Dec. 195, 672 N.E.2d 1207, 1213 (1996).

In the present case, Jordan does not assert that Knafel failed to properly plead the elements of the claims asserted in her counterclaims. Rather, Jordan asserts that the contract is unenforceable because it is against public policy. That argument appears on the face of the pleadings and is therefore "peculiarly within the area of confluence between section 2-615 and 2-619(a)(9)." Illinois Graphics Co. v. Nickum, 159 Ill. 2d 469, 486, 203 Ill. Dec. 463, 639 N.E.2d 1282, 1290 (1994). Accordingly, we may review Jordan's motion pursuant to section 2-615(a), and our review is *de novo*. *Wallace*, 203 Ill. 2d at 447, 272 Ill. Dec. 146, 786 N.E.2d at 984.

We must begin our analysis with the premise that Illinois public policy strongly favors freedom to contract, and courts will not declare a contract illegal unless it expressly contravenes the law or a known public policy of this state. H & M Commercial Driver Leasing, Inc. v. Fox Valley Containers, Inc., 209 Ill. 2d 52, 57, 282 Ill. Dec. 160, 805 N.E.2d 1177, 1180 (2004). Public policy is the legal principle that no one may lawfully do that which has the tendency to injure the welfare of the public. O'Hara v. Ahlgren, Blumenfeld & Kempster, 127 Ill. 2d 333, 341, 130 Ill. Dec. 401, 537 N.E.2d 730 (1989). Thus, agreements are not void as against public policy unless they are

> " 'clearly contrary to what the constitution, the statutes or the decisions of the courts have declared to be the public policy or unless they [are] manifestly injurious to the public welfare.' " H & M Commercial Driver Leasing, Inc., 209 Ill. 2d at 57, 282 Ill. Dec. 160, 805 N.E.2d at 1180, quoting Schumann-Heink v. Folsom, 328 Ill. 321, 330, 159 N.E. 250, 254 (1927).

The question of whether a contract is injurious to the public welfare is ultimately a conclusion of law (Rome v. Upton, 271 Ill. App. 3d 517, 520, 208 Ill. Dec. 163, 648 N.E.2d 1085, 1087-88 (1995)), and turns on the particular facts and circumstances of each case (O'Hara, 127 Ill. 2d at 341-42, 130 Ill. Dec. 401, 537 N.E.2d at 734).

In arguing that the alleged contract is unenforceable, Jordan asks this court to adopt a public policy in Illinois that all contracts involving the payment of money in exchange for silence are inherently extortionate. In contrast, Knafel argues that the trial court's ruling that the contract is extortionate would render all valid settlement agreements that incorporate a term of confidentiality to be against public policy. We make neither ruling today, but, rather, consider the law as it applies to the facts and circumstances presented by this case under the procedural posture before us.

Not all contracts for silence violate public policy. Rather, there is a presumption of validity and enforceability attaching to settlement agreements which include confidentiality provisions. Fidelity Financial Services, Inc. v. Hicks, 267 Ill. App. 3d 887, 892, 204 Ill. Dec. 858, 642 N.E.2d 759, 762 (1994) (confidentiality clauses are common attributes of settlement agreements). Confidentiality agreements have often been utilized in various settings to protect the disclosure of valuable information. See, e.g., Coady v. Harpo, Inc., 308 Ill. App. 3d 153, 241 Ill. Dec. 383, 719 N.E.2d 244 (1999) (confidentiality agreement restricting ability of former senior associate producer for well-known television talk show to disseminate confidential information she obtained while in the employ of the show's maker was reasonable and enforceable). However, we also recognize that there are contracts for silence that are unenforceable. For example, they may suppress information about harmful products or information about public safety, they may conceal criminal conduct, or they may constitute extortion or blackmail. See generally, Garfield, Promises of Silence: Contract Law and Freedom of Speech, 83 Cornell L. Rev. 261 (1998).

In Illinois, "extortion" and "blackmail" are synonymous terms. Becker v. Zellner, 292 Ill. App. 3d 116, 129, 226 Ill. Dec. 175, 684 N.E.2d 1378, 1388 (1997), citing People v. Mahumed, 381 Ill. 81, 84, 44 N.E.2d 911 (1942).

Blackmail has been defined as "[a] threatening demand made without jus-tification." Black's Law Dictionary 163 (7th ed. 1999). The gravamen of these offenses is the exercise of coercion or an improper influence. People v. Hubble, 81 Ill. App. 3d 560, 564, 37 Ill. Dec. 189, 401 N.E.2d 1282, 1285 (1980). While Jordan does not argue that the alleged agreement is extor-tionate in the criminal sense, he argues that it is extortionate because the agreement involves the exchange of money for silence, which is inherently coercive and exploitive. He relies on the case of In re Yao, 661 N.Y.S.2d 199, 231 A.D.2d 346 (1997), for support.

In *Yao*, an attorney brought a breach of contract action against Mr. Bult, a wealthy financial executive with whom he had a brief, intimate rela-tionship. In his complaint, the attorney alleged that he and Bult had entered into an enforceable oral contract pursuant to which Bult agreed to pay him $10,000 per month for life in exchange for his promise not to publicize certain embarrassing information about Bult's personal life. Bult refused to abide by such an agreement and the attorney filed the complaint. Bult moved to dismiss the complaint for failure to state a cause of action upon which relief could be granted. *Yao*, 661 N.Y.S.2d at 200-201, 231 A.D.2d at 347-48. The trial court found the alleged oral agreement to be illegal, finding it "nothing more than an attempt to extort money from an apparently wealthy but vulnerable individual." *Yao*, 661 N.Y.S.2d at 201, 231 A.D.2d at 348.

Yao is distinguishable from the present case. Here, Knafel's promise is twofold. Unlike *Yao*, we are not examining an exchange of money for silence in a vacuum but rather must look at the contract as a whole. Owens v. McDermott, Will & Emery, 316 Ill. App. 3d 340, 344, 249 Ill. Dec. 303, 736 N.E.2d 145, 150 (2000) (contracts must be interpreted as a whole rather than focusing on isolated portions). Knafel allegedly approached Jordan with the fact that she was pregnant with his child. According to the com-plaint, she alleged that based upon that statement, Jordan subsequently approached her with a proposed settlement agreement, and "[t]hey dis-cussed possible resolutions of their dilemma." If she agreed to forbear filing a paternity action and to remain silent about the details of their affair, he would pay her $5 million when he retired from professional basketball. Accordingly, here, there is an alleged nexus to a good-faith claim of right, a right to file a paternity action, which distinguishes this case from *Yao* and makes the alleged exchange one that is not necessarily a demand without legal justification or motivated by an improper influence.

The case of Kaplan v. Kaplan, 25 Ill. 2d 181, 182 N.E.2d 706 (1962), is instructive. There, a husband and wife in the midst of a divorce entered into a property settlement agreement. Three years later, the husband filed a complaint, alleging that the agreement had been entered into as the result of duress. He alleged that during the pendency of their separate mainte-nance action, his wife threatened to publicize embarrassing photographs depicting immoral behavior between the husband and another woman by suing the other woman for alienation of affections. Under duress, he agreed to sign the property settlement agreement. *Kaplan*, 25 Ill.2d at 183-84, 182 N.E.2d at 708.

The court in *Kaplan* held that such a threat is not duress where the threatened action is made in the honest belief that a good cause of action exists and does not involve some actual or threatened abuse of process. Based on the allegations of the complaint, the wife had a cause of action for alienation of affections. The court found that any use of the photographs in such a proceeding, or personal embarrassment suffered by plaintiff or his friend, as a result, would be no more than incidents of the suit. *Kaplan*, 25 Ill. 2d at 188, 182 N.E.2d at 710. The court also held that duress is not shown by subjecting someone to annoyance and vexation and that a threat of personal embarrassment does not rise above annoyance and vexation. *Kaplan*, 25 Ill. 2d at 188, 182 N.E.2d at 710.

Therein, the court also cited the case of Schumm v. Berg, 37 Cal. 2d 174, 231 P.2d 39 (1951). In *Schumm*, the supreme court of California held that the expressed intention of the mother of an illegitimate child to institute a paternity proceeding against the putative father if he did not enter into a contract for the support of the child did not make the contract unenforceable as having been obtained by a threat to expose the affair and injure the father's reputation. The father, like Jordan, was a wealthy celebrity who would suffer unfavorable publicity if the paternity suit was brought and the facts of the affair were made public. The *Schumm* court found that the complaint did not allege that the mother would injure his character if he did not enter into the contract. Rather, it alleged that she would commence a suit, a right she clearly had. "A sufference by him of unfavorable publicity would only be an incident of the suit." *Schumm*, 37 Cal. 2d at 185-86, 231 P.2d at 45.

Thus, as alleged, Knafel's agreement to refrain from suing for paternity coupled with her agreement to remain quiet about the affair is not inherently coercive or exploitive or motivated by an improper influence. Rather, taking the facts alleged in the light most favorable to Knafel, as we must do when reviewing a section 2-615 motion to dismiss, the agreement could be construed as a good-faith settlement of her paternity claim with a confidentiality provision which is not violative of public policy. This court reiterated in *Becker* that declaring that " 'one intends to use the courts to insist upon what he believes to be his legal rights' [is] not actionable" as intimidation, extortion or blackmail. *Becker*, 292 Ill. App. 3d at 129, 226 Ill. Dec. 175, 684 N.E.2d at 1388, quoting Enslen v. Village of Lombard, 128 Ill. App. 3d 531, 533, 83 Ill. Dec. 768, 470 N.E.2d 1188, 1190-91 (1984).

Furthermore, we adhere to the view that the trial court should dismiss a cause of action on the pleadings only if it is clearly apparent that no set of facts can be proven which will entitle a plaintiff to recover. *Nickum*, 159 Ill. 2d at 488, 203 Ill. Dec. 463, 639 N.E.2d at 1291. We find that whether this particular oral agreement was exploitive or coercive is a matter best left to the trier of fact. Knafel alleged that she told Jordan she was pregnant with his child, that he did not want the publicity, and that he made her an offer to deal with their problem. While we agree with Jordan that there need not be an explicit threat for a contract to be coercive or exploitive, this court has stated that an inquiry regarding the coercive nature of the language used is a fact intensive inquiry:

> "[W]hile the issue of whether particular words have a reasonable tendency to coerce or cause apprehension is essentially an objective determination, the subjective reactions of the recipients is a proper factor to consider. 'It is not

the abstract meaning of words that constitutes an expression [of] a threat, but their reasonable tendency under the circumstances to place another in fear that the threat-maker will perform the threatened act. An innocent expression may be threatening because of the ominous circumstances in which it is made. Similarly, a statement that is literally a declaration of intent to do harm to another is not a threat if the context negatives any reasonable apprehension that the speaker intends what he says he intends.'" People v. Peterson, 306 Ill. App. 3d 1091, 1103-04, 240 Ill. Dec. 164, 715 N.E.2d 1221, 1227-28 (1999), quoting Landry v. Daley, 280 F. Supp. 938, 962 (N.D. Ill. 1968).

Accordingly, where these are factual determinations and credibility determinations that have yet to be resolved, we cannot make a determination on the pleadings alone that this contract is extortionate. . . . [W]e reverse the dismissal of Jordan's complaint for declaratory judgment and reverse the dismissal of Knafel's counterclaim. Additionally, we affirm the dismissal of Jordan's motion for judgment on the pleadings and remand this cause to the circuit court for further proceedings.

Affirmed in part and reversed in part; cause remanded.

REID, P.J., and QUINN, J., concur.

Relational Background

STUDY GUIDE: *The material below provides a summary of the final resolution of Jordan v. Knafel. Notice the way that Knafel's lawyers ultimately argued themselves into a corner.*

LAWRENCE A. CUNNINGHAM, CONTRACTS IN THE REAL WORLD: STORIES OF POPULAR CONTRACTS AND WHY THEY MATTER 41-44 (2012). Michael Jordan, the legendary basketball star for the Chicago Bulls, met Karla Knafel, a lounge singer, in the spring of 1989. After several months of long-distance phone conversations, Jordan and Knafel got together in December 1989. Jordan was married, but Jordan and Knafel engaged in unprotected sex at that time and once again in November 1990. Throughout that year, Knafel dated other men and had unprotected sex with at least one. She became pregnant and, inferring the date of conception back to November, claimed Jordan was the father.

During the spring of 1991, the Bulls were heading for another NBA championship and Jordan was earning millions from the team and from product endorsements. It was in Jordan's interest to keep the extramarital affair and his possible paternity from the public. Knafel later claimed that Jordan suggested she get an abortion, which she refused to do. Jordan ultimately offered to pay her $5 million, upon his retirement from basketball, if she would keep the matter confidential and not file a paternity suit. Knafel accepted. After she gave birth in July 1991, Jordan paid the bills and gave Knafel $250,000. In exchange, she kept quiet and never filed a paternity suit. A month later, Jordan determined through blood testing that he was not the baby's father.

When Jordan retired from playing professional basketball, Knafel asked him to pay up. Jordan refused and instead sued to have the alleged contract declared illegal and unenforceable. Jordan argued that, as a matter of public policy, all contracts involving paying money in exchange for silence are extortionate. Knafel contended that to hold the contract extortionate would unwisely render all settlement agreements containing confidentiality clauses invalid as against public policy. The court rejected both extreme positions. Confidentiality agreements may have some special features, but are presumed valid and are common in settlement agreements. On the other hand, some are suspect, such as those commanding silence about harmful products, threats to public safety, criminal enterprises, or those constituting blackmail — often targeted to the rich and famous.

An example of such suspect deals confronted David Letterman, host of the popular CBS television show, "Late Night."[17] A once-respected CBS news executive, Robert Halderman, knew that Letterman was having extramarital affairs with staff members. Using an assortment of evidence — pictures, letters, and one woman's diary — Halderman wrote a screenplay depicting Letterman facing public humiliation from the disclosure. Halderman gave that evidence and the screenplay to Letterman's limousine driver on September 9, 2009. One week later, Halderman told Letterman's lawyer, Jim Jackoway, he would go public with it unless Letterman paid him $2 million. Letterman promptly called the police, who assisted him in preparing a bogus check for $2 million. After Halderman deposited that check, police arrested him for attempted grand larceny. He spent six months in jail, followed by four years of probation.[18]

In contrast to Jordan and Knafel's case, no valid contract could possibly have been formed between Halderman and Letterman in the circumstances because there was no other relationship between them.[19] The deal was based solely on a spontaneous threat from a stranger to extract cash for silence. Such cases involve money for silence, and nothing else. To recognize these as valid contracts would encourage people to engage in behavior that criminal law seeks to deter.[20]

Knafel contended that her contract with Jordan was more like the valid bargain found in an old-fashioned case involving Hilda Boehm and one Louis Fiege, who had a romantic relationship in the 1950s.[21] Hilda got pregnant, named Louis as the father, and claimed he agreed to pay child support if she refrained from filing a paternity suit. Louis denied all of this, pointing to later blood tests proving he was not the father, contradicting Hilda's confident assertions of paternity.

---

17. Bill Carter & Brian Stelter, Letterman Extortion Raises Questions for CBS, *N.Y. Times* (Oct. 2, 2009).

18. Federal statutes declare it illegal to threaten to harm a person's reputation unless money is paid. 18 U.S.C. §875(d). The law does not stop people from trying, as Bill Cosby can also tell you. In January 1997, a twenty-two-year-old woman named Autumn Jackson claimed Cosby was her father and eventually demanded that he pay her $40 million in exchange for not making this claim public. She was arrested, prosecuted, convicted, and landed in jail on federal criminal charges of threatening reputation harm unless money is paid. *See* United States v. Jackson, 180 F.3d 55 (2d Cir. 1999).

19. Another comparable case is In re Yao, 661 N.Y.S.2d 199 (1997).

20. See Juliet P. Kostrinsky, Illegal Contracts and Efficient Deterrence: A Study in Modern Contract Theory, Iowa Law Review 74 (1988): 115.

21. Friege v. Boehm, 123 A.2d 316 (Md. App. 1956).

Ancient common law declared that fathers of children born out of wedlock had no legal duty to care for them. Courts often found a father's promise to provide financial support unenforceable for lack of consideration. After many states enacted paternal support statutes, however, such promises could be supported by consideration if the mother gave up valid rights to pursue statutory paternity proceedings. A statute applicable in the case of Hilda and Louis authorized mothers to sue putative fathers for support, persuading the court that there is no public policy objection to bargains such as theirs.

Even though such precedents were helpful to Knafel, she was not home-free in her dispute with Jordan because any such bargain must still meet standard contract law tests for enforceability. With money-for-silence deals suspect, the place to look for consideration is foreswearing legal action. Cases dating to early English law recognized as consideration a promise not to sue, so long as the claimant held an honest and reasonable belief in the validity of the claim being sworn off.[22] Courts refused to recognize giving up "entirely baseless" claims as consideration but validated claims so long as they were "colorable" or "tenable" or "possible." To paraphrase one court's poetic summary of the cases: Consideration includes giving up a claim that makes a mountain out of a mole hill, but there must be some mole hill to begin with.[23]

Knafel and Jordan thus disputed whether they had settled a mole-hill's worth of quarreling. Knafel stressed that in paternity cases, consideration is provided by a mother giving up valid statutory rights, putting her claim squarely in the line of cases running back to that of Hilda and Louis. Taken at face value, that could have spelled the end of the Jordan-Knafel case in her favor, but the famous Jordan made a novel argument that lured Knafel into a damning concession.

Jordan contended that their contract was unenforceable because it was induced by Knafel's fraud. Fraud in the inducement of a contract occurs when someone knowingly misleads another into a bargain they would not likely make otherwise. Knafel resisted the assertion of fraud by stressing that she believed in good faith that Jordan was the baby's father. She claimed that the authenticity of paternity was not so important to Jordan that, without her statements, he would have acted differently. Jordan countered that the paternity issue was an inducement to his promise: Had he known he was not the baby's father, he likely would not have agreed to pay to avoid a suit or obtain confidentiality. True, Jordan feared damaging his public image, which induced him to agree, but that was not the sole motivating factor.

---

22. Hart v. Stahl, 27 Md. 157 (Md. App. 1867).

23. Duncan v. Black, 324 S.W.2d 483 (Mo. App. 1959). This case involved a farm sale when federal law regulated cotton by authorizing production on specific acreage and banning production elsewhere. In a sale of several hundred acres, the seller promised the buyer a "65 acre cotton allotment." When authorities allotted that farm only 50 acres for the following year, the seller let the buyer use another 15 he kept. The buyer asked the seller to make up the shortfall in the next year's allotment too, but the seller refused. After the buyer threatened suit, the seller settled by promising payment of money. The buyer later sued to enforce that promise, but the court found that it lacked consideration. Giving up a right to sue when federal law barred the basis for the claim did not "make a mountain out of a molehill" — the ban covering the acreage meant that there was no "molehill" of a dispute to settle.

The court agreed with Jordan. To accept Knafel's claim that Jordan's agreement was not induced by the paternity issue would suggest that the two had haggled over and settled nothing by their agreement. But that would make the case equivalent to that of the blackmail of David Letterman — silence for money. Concerning the paternity issue, Michael Jordan's fame and fortune, and the fling he and Karla Knafel had, did suggest reasons to be more skeptical of Knafel's story than that of the claim Hilda Boehm made against her obscure partner, Louis Fiege.[24]

24. For more on this topic and the Knafel-Jordan case, see Michelle Oberman, Sex, Lies, and the Duty to Disclose, Arizona Law Review 47 (2005): 871.

2

DAMAGES FOR BREACH
OF CONTRACT

A. WHY STUDY REMEDIES FIRST?

Some students may find it odd that we begin our study with contract remedies instead of the elements of contract formation (Parts II and III) and
defenses (Part V). The reason is quite straightforward. Although contract
formation and defenses are in some respects issues that logically precede
the determination of a remedy, the cases we shall discuss under those topics
can be much better understood if one is already familiar with the different
forms of available remedies (damages, specific performance, injunctions,
etc.) and the different damage "interests" (expectation, reliance, and restitution). This is especially true when trying to understand the doctrine of
promissory estoppel in Chapter 11. Notice, for example, that while the
section on remedies in Professor Farnsworth's treatise, Contracts, is at
the end of the book, his summary of the three damage interests (excerpted
in Section B) appears near the beginning of his book and *before* his discussion of contract formation.[1]

We shall see throughout these materials that the precise remedy
sought by the parties and awarded by the court will reveal important information about the formation of contract. Therefore, if the study of remedies
is left to the end of the course, it would be impossible to fully appreciate the
subtleties of the cases in Parts II and III. The converse is not true, however.
One can fully grasp the distinctions among contract remedies (while simply
assuming a contract exists) without being familiar with the nuances of contract formation. Accordingly we begin at the end.

B. THE THREE DAMAGE INTERESTS

Many professors assign their students to read what is undoubtedly the most
famous law review article about contracts ever written: Lon L. Fuller &
William R. Perdue, Jr., The Reliance Interest in Contract Damages (pt. 1),
46 Yale L.J. 52 (1936). In this path-breaking work Fuller & Perdue identify
what they called the three damage interests: expectation, reliance, and restitution. They spend a good deal of time defining these concepts, explaining

---

1. See E. Allan Farnsworth, Contracts 45-47 (4th ed. 2004).

their different rationales, and relating them to each other. What follows is a brief summary of these concepts by Professor E. Allan Farnsworth.

Legal Background: Introduction to Damage Interests

E. ALLAN FARNSWORTH, EXPECTATION, RELIANCE, AND RESTITUTION INTERESTS, from CONTRACTS 46 (4TH ED. 2004):   Occasionally a court grants a promisee specific relief by ordering the promisor to perform the promise. But in our legal system such specific relief is the exception rather than the rule. Usually a court grants the promisee substitutional relief by awarding a sum of money intended to compensate for the harm to the promisee's interests caused by the promisor's failure to perform the promise. It is common to discuss the measure of this liability of the promisor in terms of the promisee's expectation, reliance, and restitution interests.

In general, the amount of the award is measured by the promisee's *expectation interest* or, as it is sometimes said, "the benefit of the bargain." The court attempts to put the *promisee in the position in which the promisee would have been had the promise been performed* (i.e., had there been no breach). This is the measure generally used today in actions founded on promises that are enforceable because supported by consideration. But it is not the only possible measure of recovery.

If the promisee changed its position to its detriment in reliance on the promise — as by incurring expenses in performing or preparing to perform — the court might award a sum of money intended to compensate for this loss. Recovery would then be measured by the promisee's *reliance interest*, in an attempt to put the *promisee back in the position in which the promisee would have been in had the promise not been made.* Because such recovery does not take account of the promisee's lost profit, it is ordinarily less generous than recovery measured by the promisee's expectation interest.[2]

If the promisee conferred a benefit on the promisor in the course of the transaction — as by delivering something to the promisor or improving the promisor's property — the court might award the promisee a sum of money intended to deprive the promisor of this benefit. Recovery would then be measured by the promisee's *restitution interest*, in an attempt to put the *promisor back in the position in which the promisor would have been had the promise not been made.* Because such recovery does not take account of either the promisee's lost profit or reliance by the promisee that produces no benefit to the promisor, it is ordinarily less generous than recovery measured by the promisee's expectation or reliance interest.

---

2. Courts generally have not taken account of lost opportunities in figuring the reliance interest. . . .

REFERENCE: Barnett, §§2.1-2.3.1
                Farnsworth, §§12.1-12.3
                Calamari & Perillo, §§14.1-14.3
                Murray, §§118(A), 120

STUDY GUIDE: *Identify the damage interest awarded by the court in* Hawkins. *Does the court consider any alternative measures? Notice that, unlike* Shaheen, *the court in this case is enforcing an express warranty of cure. Why is it reasonable to conclude that such a warranty was made by Dr. McGee?*

HAWKINS v. McGEE
Supreme Court of New Hampshire,
84 N.H. 114, 146 A. 641 (1929)

Assumpsit, against a surgeon for breach of an alleged warranty of the success of an operation. Trial by jury, and verdict for the plaintiff. The writ also contained a count in negligence upon which a nonsuit was ordered, without exception.

. . . The defendant seasonably moved to set aside the verdict . . . because the damages awarded by the jury were excessive. The court . . . found that the damages were excessive, and made an order that the verdict be set aside unless the plaintiff elected to remit all in excess of $500. The plaintiff having refused to remit, the verdict was set aside "as excessive and against the weight of the evidence," and the plaintiff excepted. . . .

BRANCH, J.* 1. The operation in question consisted in the removal of a considerable quantity of scar tissue from the palm of the plaintiff's right hand and the grafting of skin taken from plaintiff's chest in place thereof. The scar tissue was the result of a severe burn caused by contact with an electric wire, which the plaintiff received about nine years before the time of the transactions here involved. There was evidence to the effect that before the operation was performed the plaintiff and his father went to the defendant's office and that the defendant in answer to the question, "How long will the boy be in the hospital?", replied, "Three or four days, . . . not over four; then the boy can go home, and it will be just a few days when he will be able to go back to work with a perfect hand." Clearly this and other testimony to the same effect would not justify a finding that the doctor contracted to complete the hospital treatment in three or four days or that the plaintiff would be able to go back to work within a few days thereafter. The above statements could only

Oliver Winslow Branch (1879-1956) was a graduate of Phillips Andover Academy (1897), Harvard College (A.B., 1901, A.M., 1902), and Harvard Law School (LL.B., 1904). He engaged in private practice with his father until he was appointed associate justice of the Superior Court of New Hampshire in 1913, where he served as Chief Justice from 1924 until 1926, when he became a justice of the Supreme Court of New Hampshire. In 1946, Branch was appointed Chief Justice, which he remained until his retirement in 1949. The 1945 legislature established the Judicial Council, to which Branch was elected as a representative of the Supreme Court. He continued to represent the court until his retirement, at which time he was appointed directly to the council by the governor and council and served until October 1955. — K.T.

be construed as expressions of opinion or predictions as to the probable duration of the treatment and plaintiff's resulting disability, and the fact that these estimates were exceeded would impose no contractual liability upon the defendant. The only substantial basis for the plaintiff's claim is the testimony that the defendant also said before the operation was decided upon, "I will guarantee to make the hand a hundred per cent perfect hand" or "a hundred per cent good hand." The plaintiff was present when these words were alleged to have been spoken, and if they are to be taken at their face value, it seems obvious that proof of their utterance would establish the giving of a warranty in accordance with his contention.

The defendant argues, however, that even if these words were uttered by him, no reasonable man would understand that they were used with the intention of entering into any "contractual relation whatever," and that they could reasonably be understood only "as his expression in strong language that he believed and expected that as a result of the operation he would give the plaintiff a very good hand." It may be conceded, as the defendant contends, that before the question of the making of a contract should be submitted to a jury, there is a preliminary question of law for the trial court to pass upon, i.e. "whether the words could possibly have the meaning imputed to them by the party who founds his case upon a certain interpretation," but it cannot be held that the trial court decided this question erroneously in the present case. It is unnecessary to determine at this time whether the argument of the defendant based upon "common knowledge of the uncertainty which attends all surgical operations" and the improbability that a surgeon would ever contract to make a damaged part of the human body "one hundred per cent perfect" would, in the absence of countervailing considerations, be regarded as conclusive, for there were other factors in the present case which tended to support the contention of the plaintiff. There was evidence that the defendant repeatedly solicited from the plaintiff's father the opportunity to perform this operation, and the theory was advanced by plaintiff's counsel in cross-examination of defendant, that he sought an opportunity to "experiment on skin grafting" in which he had had little previous experience. If the jury accepted this part of the plaintiff's contention, there would be a reasonable basis for the further conclusion that if defendant spoke the words attributed to him, he did so with the intention that they should be accepted at their face value, as an inducement for the granting of consent to the operation by the plaintiff and his father, and there was ample evidence that they were so accepted by them. The question of the making of the alleged contract was properly submitted to the jury.

2. The substance of the charge to the jury on the question of damages appears in the following quotation: "If you find the plaintiff entitled to anything, he is entitled to recover for what pain and suffering he has been made to endure and what injury he has sustained over and above the injury he had before." To this instruction the defendant seasonably excepted. By it, the jury was permitted to consider two elements of damage, (1) pain and suffering due to the operation, and (2) positive ill effects of the operation upon the plaintiff's hand. Authority for any specific rule of damages in cases of this kind seems to be lacking, but when tested by general principle and by analogy, it appears that the foregoing instruction was erroneous.

"By 'damages' as that term is used in the law of contracts, is intended compensation for a breach, measured in the terms of the contract." . . . The purpose of the law is to "put the plaintiff in as good a position as he would have been in had the defendant kept his contract." 3 Williston, Cont., §1338. . . . The measure of recovery "is based upon what the defendant should have given the plaintiff, not what the plaintiff has given the defendant or otherwise expended." 3 Williston, Cont., §1341. "The only losses that can be said fairly to come within the terms of a contract are such as the parties must have had in mind when the contract was made, or such they either knew or ought to have known would probably result from a failure to comply with its terms." Davis v. [New England Cotton Yarn Co.], 77 N.H. 403, 404. . . .

The present case is closely analogous to one in which a machine is built for a certain purpose and warranted to do certain work. In such cases, the usual rule of damages for breach of warranty in the sale of chattels is applied and it is held that the measure of damages is the difference between the value of the machine if it had corresponded with the warranty and its actual value, together with such incidental losses as the parties knew or ought to have known would probably result from a failure to comply with its terms. . . . The rule thus applied is well settled in this state. "As a general rule, the measure of the vendee's damages is the difference between the value of the goods as they would have been if the warranty as to the quality had been true, and the actual value at the time of the sale, including gains prevented and losses sustained, and such other damages as could be reasonably anticipated by the parties as likely to be caused by the vendor's failure to keep his agreement, and could not by reasonable care on the part of the vendee have been avoided." . . . We, therefore, conclude that the true measure of the plaintiff's damage in the present case is the difference between the value to him of a perfect hand or a good hand, such as the jury found the defendant promised him, and the value of his hand in its present condition, including any incidental consequences fairly within the contemplation of the parties when they made their contract. . . . Damages not thus limited, although naturally resulting, are not to be given.

The extent of the plaintiff's suffering does not measure this difference in value. The pain necessarily incident to a serious surgical operation was a part of the contribution which the plaintiff was willing to make to his joint undertaking with the defendant to produce a good hand. It was a legal detriment suffered by him which constituted a part of the consideration given by him for the contract. It represented a part of the price which he was willing to pay for a good hand, but it furnished no test of the value of a good hand or the difference between the value of the hand which the defendant promised and the one which resulted from the operation.

It was also erroneous and misleading to submit to the jury as a separate element of damage any change for the worse in the condition of the plaintiff's hand resulting from the operation, although this error was probably more prejudicial to the plaintiff than to the defendant. Any such ill effect of the operation would be included under the true rule of damages set forth above, but damages might properly be assessed for the defendant's failure to improve the condition of the hand even if there were no evidence that its condition was made worse as a result of the operation.

It must be assumed that the trial court, in setting aside the verdict, undertook to apply the same rule of damages which he had previously given to the jury, and since this rule was erroneous, it is unnecessary for us to consider whether there was any evidence to justify his finding that all damages awarded by the jury above $500 were excessive.

3. Defendant's requests for instructions were loosely drawn and were properly denied. A considerable number of issues of fact were raised by the evidence, and it would have been extremely misleading to instruct the jury in accordance with defendant's request number 2, that "The only issue on which you have to pass is whether or not there was a special contract between the plaintiff and the defendant to produce a perfect hand." Equally inaccurate was defendant's request number 5, which reads as follows: "You would have to find, in order to hold the defendant liable in this case, that Dr. McGee and the plaintiff both understood that the doctor was guaranteeing a perfect result from this operation." If the defendant said that he would guarantee a perfect result and the plaintiff relied upon that promise, any mental reservations which he may have had are immaterial. The standard by which his conduct is to be judged is not internal but external. . . .

New trial.

STUDY GUIDE: *Although the* Hawkins *case has come to be associated with the "hairy hand," there is no such reference in the opinion. This fact appears in a subsequent case in which Dr. McGee sues his malpractice insurer who had refused to reimburse him for the damages awarded in the lawsuit. Before reading the opinion, can you predict the outcome of that lawsuit? We also learn that the trial described in the above opinion was, in fact, the second one held.*

McGEE v. UNITED STATES FIDELITY & GUARANTY CO., U.S. COURT OF APPEALS, FIRST CIRCUIT, 53 F.2D 953 (1931): ANDERSON, Circuit Judge.* In October, 1925, George Hawkins brought a suit against the appellant in the superior court of Coos County, N.H. The declaration in his writ contains two counts, as follows: . . .

[T]he defendant . . . so unskillfully and negligently operated and treated the same that by his unskillfulness and negligence, the new tissue grafted upon said hand became matted, unsightly, and so healed and attached to said hand as to practically fill the hand with an unsightly growth, restricting the motion of the plaintiff's hand so that said hand has become useless to the plaintiff wherein, previous to said operation by the said defendant, it was a practical, useful hand, all through the negligence and unskillful treatment of said defendant and to the damage of the plaintiff as he claims in the sum of $10,000.

* *George Weston Anderson* (1861-1938) was educated at the Cushing Academy, Williams College (A.B., LL.D.), and Boston University School of Law (LL.B., summa cum laude). He began practice in Boston in 1890 and was an unsuccessful Democratic candidate for attorney general of Massachusetts in 1911 and 1912. In 1913, Anderson was appointed to the Public Service Commission for a term of four years, which he resigned in 1914 to assume the post of United States District Attorney for Massachusetts. He served as a member of the Interstate Commerce Commission from October 1917 to November 1918 when he became judge of the United States Circuit Court of Appeals in Boston. — K.T.

And in a further plea of assumpsit, for that the defendant, in Berlin, on the 21st day of January, 1922, promised the plaintiff that he was possessed of the skill necessary to properly operate upon his right hand aforesaid, and that the defendant would not be obliged to remain in the hospital for a longer period than six days, and that the scar to be left upon that part of the body wherein said defendant stated he would graft said new skin, would be a small scar, and would hardly be noticeable after healing, and that the plaintiff further avers that relying upon said promises as aforesaid, he consented to be treated by the said defendant as aforesaid, and the plaintiff says further that the defendant did not possess the skill that he held himself out to possess, but that he experimented upon said plaintiff, and that by reason of said operation, the plaintiff was laid up in said hospital for a long time, to wit, three months, that the scar left upon the chest of the plaintiff is a long, large, unsightly scar, and that the hand of said plaintiff has been made useless, and that the results are not as promised him by the said defendant, and that if the plaintiff had not relied on the several promises of the defendant, he would not have submitted to said operation. All to the damage of the plaintiff, as he says, in the sum of $10,000.

The defense of this suit was undertaken and conducted by the appellee, until December, 1926. At the first trial, the jury disagreed. In December, 1926, the case came on for another trial, before Judge Scammon and a jury. At the close of the plaintiff's evidence, on defendant's motion, the court directed a verdict for defendant on the first count, but denied the motion as to the second count. Pending the court's order on this motion, the Guaranty Company served, on December 17, 1926, a notice on Dr. McGee, as follows:

This is to notify you that in the event that a nonsuit is ordered on the count in negligence in the suit of George Hawkins v. Dr. E. R. B. McGee, the United States Fidelity & Guaranty Company, the insurer of Dr. McGee, disclaims any liability to reimburse the said Dr. McGee for any damages or costs awarded to the said George Hawkins based on a finding of the jury that Dr. McGee guaranteed the result of the operation on said George Hawkins, claiming that its policy does not cover cases where the Doctor makes a contract to perfect a cure or guarantees the result of his treatment, and you are notified that the Company is not waiving any of its rights under said policy or any of its rights in law or equity by reason of the fact that Irving A. Hinkley counsel for the said Insurance Company continues to participate in the trial after the issue of negligence has been taken from the jury.

The trial proceeded on the second count, counsel for the Guaranty Company continuing to assist counsel for Dr. McGee, so that the jury would not be prejudiced by his withdrawal. The result of the trial on the second count was a verdict for Hawkins for $3,000. Dr. McGee saved numerous exceptions.

On motion before Judge Scammon, the *Hawkins* verdict was set aside, on the ground that the damage was excessive. But this ruling was, on Hawkins' exceptions, reversed by the New Hampshire court, Hawkins v. McGee, 84 N.H. 114, 146 A. 641.

On December 22, 1926, appellant's attorney addressed to the Guaranty Company's agent a letter of protest against the attitude of the Guaranty Company, sufficiently asserting the appellant's present contention of the Guaranty Company's full liability under the policy.

Just prior to a third trial, McGee notified the Guaranty Company's agent that the claim against him could be adjusted for $1,400; that the company might proceed at its own risk with the trial and defense of the suit; that, if it refused so to do, McGee proposed to purchase his peace by paying this $1,400, and would look to the Guaranty Company for payment of said sum and his expenses.

The company refused; McGee settled the Hawkins suit for $1,400; and brought this suit to recover the $1,400 and his expenses, mostly attorney's fees. The court found that, if entitled to recover, he is entitled to judgment for $4,248.48.

The finding of controlling importance is as follows:

> In the *Hawkins* Case Dr. McGee's liability resulted not from the implied contract applicable to every physician in the treatment of his patient but because of the special contract to give his patient "a perfect hand one hundred percent good." (Plff's Ex. 36, p. 27.)
>
> In the submission of the *Hawkins* Case to the jury the only question submitted by Judge Scammon was whether or not Dr. McGee made a special contract and if so did he fail in its performance and what were the damages. This is made clear from a perusal of Judge Scammon's charge.
>
> The jury found that such a special contract was made and that the Doctor failed to perform. These findings have not been controverted in this action. It follows that the expenses herein sought to be recovered resulted from the findings of a jury that there was a special contract between Dr. McGee and his patient and not because of "malpractice, error or mistake" in treatment.

The court ruled that the policy in question did not extend to such special contract, and therefore entered judgment for the defendant. . . .

The court below was plainly right in ruling that defendant's policy did not cover Dr. McGee's liability under a special contract so to cure Hawkins "that he should have a perfect hand, one hundred per cent good."

The judgment of the District Court is affirmed, with costs.

Relational Background: Before and After the Lawsuit

JORIE ROBERTS, *HAWKINS* CASE: A HAIR-RAISING EXPERIENCE, HARVARD LAW RECORD, VOL. 66, NO. 6, MARCH 11, 1978, P. 1:
. . . The case originated in 1922 in Berlin, New Hampshire, a small mill town near the Canadian border, when Dr. Edward McGee, a general practitioner, promised to restore George Hawkins' slightly scarred hand to "perfect condition" through surgery. Instead, Hawkins' hand was permanently disfigured and crippled. . . .

George Hawkins was born in January, 1904 — the second of Rose Wilkinson and Charles Augustus Hawkins' six children. . . .

One morning in 1915, 11-year-old George burned his right hand while preparing breakfast for his father on the family's woodburning stove. At the time, George was trying to turn on the kitchen light to illuminate the stove, but an electrical storm the night before had damaged the wiring so that George received a severe shock.

One of George's younger brothers, Howard Hawkins, now an insurance agent in Berlin, described George's initial scar as a "small pencil-size scar" which was between his thumb and index finger and did not substantially affect his use of the hand. Nevertheless, Charles Hawkins took his son George to skin specialists in Montreal after the accident; but there the doctors advised the Hawkinses against doing anything to restore the hand.

During this period, the family physician, Edward McGee, while treating one of George's younger brothers for pneumonia, also became aware of George's scarred hand. Later, in 1919, after returning from several years of medical service in Europe during World War I, McGee requested George and his parents to let him operate on the hand in order to restore it to "perfect" condition.

According to Dorothy St. Hilaire, George's younger sister, McGee claimed to have done a number of similar skin grafts on soldiers in Germany during the war, although he later admitted that he had really only observed such operations.

St. Hilaire recollects that McGee, in persuading George to undergo the surgery, emphasized the social problems which his scarred hand might create. McGee encouraged the Hawkinses to allow him to operate on the hand for three years, until finally George agreed shortly after his 18th birthday. St. Hilaire remembers that, while her parents had strong doubts about the operation, they trusted McGee's judgment and were hesitant to oppose George's decision and the physician's advice.

McGee operated on George's hand in the St. Louis Hospital in Berlin in March of 1922. The skin graft operation was supposed to be quick, simple, and effective, and to require only a few days of hospitalization. Instead, St. Hilaire recalls that her brother bled very badly for several days; the sight of the saturated surgical dressings caused her mother to faint when they first visited George at the hospital after what they thought to be minor surgery.

Moreover, while McGee had earlier stated that the skin for the graft was to come from George's thigh, Mrs. Hawkins and Dorothy, then age 13, saw that George's hand was bandaged to his chest. George was, in the words of his brother Howard, "in the throes of death" for quite a while after the operation because of his extensive bleeding and the ensuing infection. Moreover, the post-operation scar covered his thumb and two fingers and was densely covered with hair.

Howard Hawkins remembered that George's hand was partially curled up and continued to bleed periodically throughout his life. St. Hilaire, in describing the skin on George's chest from where McGee had taken the graft, compared it to thin onion skin.

After the operation failed so completely to give George the "100 percent perfect hand" which McGee had promised, Ovide Coulombe, a lawyer friend of the Hawkins and mayor of Berlin, encouraged the Hawkinses to take the case to court. He represented the Hawkinses, while McGee engaged three lawyers from Concord.

The jury only awarded the Hawkins $3,000 for damages, and the final settlement was for $1,400 and lawyers fees. St. Hilaire believes the jurors, while at heart solidly behind the Hawkinses' cause, were afraid to return heavier damages against McGee because he was one of the more prominent physicians in the area. Charles Hawkins took the $1,400 and his injured son to Montreal to see if any subsequent operations would alleviate George's deformity, but the doctors there said that the grafted skin was so tough that nothing more could be done. . . .

Apparently, the unsuccessful operation did not significantly reduce McGee's business. According to Arthur Bergeron, a Berlin lawyer, McGee's medical practice grew and he and two other doctors formed a clinic in Berlin. Bergeron recalls that McGee was popular in Berlin and even served as mayor of the town. He was also very musically inclined and directed McGee's Symphony Orchestra, which performed around northern New Hampshire, as a hobby.

Hawkins' crippled hand affected his employment and outlook throughout his lifetime. After the operation, George Hawkins never returned to high school, even though, in Howard's opinion, "George was very bright, learned quickly, and had a pleasing personality." He was encouraged by his parents to finish school, but would not because, in his siblings' view, he was embarrassed by his hand.

George also gave up tennis and riflery after the operation, although previously he had won several medals as a marksman for the State Home Guard. Because of his hand, George was unable to perform any heavy manual labor or learn to type. He worked for many years in the printing division of the Brown Company, a pulp and paper manufacturer in Berlin, and later in a tire store. He then entered the military service for a short time in 1943, where he was stationed at Fort Devens in eastern Massachusetts.

George married late in life and never had any children. He and his wife worked as a chauffeur-maid team for a wealthy couple in Massachusetts for several years, then returned to Berlin in 1952. After George died of a heart attack in 1958, his widow went to work in North Conway, New Hampshire. . . .

The Hawkins family was unaware of the widespread study of Hawkins v. McGee in law schools until, in 1964, Howard and Edith Hawkins' daughter Gail encountered the case early in her contracts course at Boston University Law School. Moreover, the Hawkins family did not know about the case's use in "The Paper Chase" contracts class scene until Edith Hawkins happened to see the 1972 movie during its first run.

Howard Hawkins, however, believes that George was somewhat aware of the case's importance before his 1958 death. Howard states: "I think he became aware of the importance of his case through a lawyer friend, an O. (Ovide) J. Coulombe. I think it gave him a sense of importance, in that this was bringing the facts out in public eye, but this was only temporary, as he really lived with this incapacity all his life, and he did suffer mentally as well as physically."

RESTATEMENT (SECOND) OF CONTRACTS

§347.   MEASURE OF DAMAGES IN GENERAL

Subject to the limitations stated in §§350-353, the injured party has a right to damages based on his expectation interest as measured by

(a) the loss in the value to him of the other party's performance caused by its failure or deficiency, plus

(b) any other loss, including incidental or consequential loss, caused by the breach, less

(c) any cost or other loss that he has avoided by not having to perform.

REFERENCE: Barnett, §§2.3.2-2.3.4
               Farnsworth, §12.9
               Calamari & Perillo, §14.4
               Murray, §120

STUDY GUIDE: What follows is the unabridged text of the shortest opinion in the casebook; yet it is considered a noteworthy case on the issue of damages. Which measure of damages does it represent? How does the Restatement formula in §347 apply to this case? Can you think of more contemporary examples of this type of damages?

NURSE v. BARNS
King's Bench,
Sir T. Raym 77 (1664)

DAMAGES

The plaintiff declares, that the defendant in consideration of 10*l.* promised to let him enjoy certain iron mills for six months; and it appeared that the iron mills were worth but 20*l.* per annum, and yet damages were given to 500*l.* by reason of the loss of stock laid in; and per Curiam the jury may well find such damages, for they are not bound to give only the 10*l.* but also all the special damages.

DIFFERENTIATING DAMAGE INTERESTS: A PROBLEM

To better test your ability to distinguish the three damage interests, consider the following problem. In addition to identifying the three interests, consider how the Restatement formula found in §347 would apply.

FACTS

I agree to sell to you a copy of the Restatement (to be delivered tomorrow), in return for your agreement to pay me $10.00 and to give me a photocopy of your class notes. Assume that the Restatement has a market value of $15.00; that your notes have a market value of $1.00; and that it costs you $3.00 to photocopy your notes. You pay me the $10.00 and give me a photocopy of your notes. I refuse to deliver or return your money or the notes. You sue for damages.

CALCULATING DAMAGES

1. How much would you be entitled to:
    a. If limited to the *restitution interest?*
    b. If limited to the *reliance interest?*
    c. Applying the holding of Hawkins v. McGee?

VARIATIONS ON THE FACTS

2. If you photocopied your notes and gave them to me, but had not paid me anything in advance, what amount would you be entitled to?
3. If you had not paid me anything in advance and had not photocopied your notes, what amount would you be entitled to?
4. If the market value of the Restatement was $9.00 (and you prepaid the $10.00 and gave me the notes (that cost you $3.00 to photocopy and had a market value of $1.00)) what amount would you recover if damages were measured by the:
    a. *Expectation interest?*
    b. *Reliance interest?*
    c. *Restitution interest?*
5. Assuming, once again, that the market value of the Restatement was $15.00, if you had photocopied your notes, but had not given them to me and had not paid me anything in advance, what amount would you be entitled to? Why?

Try varying the facts of the hypothetical and see how each interest is affected by the change (for example, you only prepay $5.00).

STUDY GUIDE: *To what extent does the court deviate from the approach of* Hawkins? *Which measure of damages does it adopt and why? Does the plaintiff's waiver deprive this decision of any of its potential significance?*

SULLIVAN v. O'CONNOR
Supreme Judicial Court of Massachusetts,
363 Mass. 579, 296 N.E.2d 183 (1973)

KAPLAN, Justice.*
The plaintiff patient secured a jury verdict of $13,500 against the defendant surgeon for breach of contract in respect to an operation upon the

Benjamin Kaplan (1911-2010) was the Royall Professor of Law at Harvard Law School, where he joined the faculty in 1948, before he became a Justice on the Supreme Judicial Court of Massachusetts, where he sat from 1972 to 1981. The James S. Carpentier Lectures he delivered in 1966 at Columbia were published as An Unhurried View of Copyright (1967). He also served as a reporter for the Restatement (Second) of Judgments (1982). He was a colonel on Justice William Douglas's staff at the Nuremberg trials and was a prosecutor in the trials. He graduated from the City College of New York in 1929 and received his law degree from Columbia University in 1933 where he was a student of Karl Llewellyn. His former students include Justices Ruth Bader Ginsburg and Stephen Breyer. [This judicial biography was written by Jennifer Locke Davitt, hereinafter "J.L.D."]

plaintiff's nose. The substituted consolidated bill of exceptions presents questions about the correctness of the judge's instructions on the issue of damages.

The declaration was in two counts. In the first count, the plaintiff alleged that she, as patient, entered into a contract with the defendant, a surgeon, wherein the defendant promised to perform plastic surgery on her nose and thereby to enhance her beauty and improve her appearance; that he performed the surgery but failed to achieve the promised result; rather the result of the surgery was to disfigure and deform her nose, to cause her pain in body and mind, and to subject her to other damage and expense. The second count, based on the same transaction, was in the conventional form for malpractice, charging that the defendant had been guilty of negligence in performing the surgery. Answering, the defendant entered a general denial.

On the plaintiff's demand, the case was tried by jury. At the close of the evidence, the judge put to the jury, as special questions, the issues of liability under the two counts, and instructed them accordingly. The jury returned a verdict for the plaintiff on the contract count, and for the defendant on the negligence count. The judge then instructed the jury on the issue of damages.

As background to the instructions and the parties' exceptions, we mention certain facts as the jury could find them. The plaintiff was a professional entertainer, and this was known to the defendant. The agreement was as alleged in the declaration. More particularly, judging from exhibits, the plaintiff's nose had been straight, but long and prominent; the defendant undertook by two operations to reduce its prominence and somewhat to shorten it, thus making it more pleasing in relation to the plaintiff's other features. Actually the plaintiff was obliged to undergo three operations, and her appearance was worsened. Her nose now had a concave line to about the midpoint, at which it became bulbous; viewed frontally, the nose from bridge to midpoint was flattened and broadened, and the two sides of the tip had lost symmetry. This configuration evidently could not be improved by further surgery. The plaintiff did not demonstrate, however, that her change of appearance had resulted in loss of employment. Payments by the plaintiff covering the defendant's fee and hospital expenses were stipulated at $622.65.

The judge instructed the jury, first, that the plaintiff was entitled to recover her out-of-pocket expenses incident to the operations. Second, she could recover the damages flowing directly, naturally, proximately, and foreseeably from the defendant's breach of promise. These would comprehend damages for any disfigurement of the plaintiff's nose — that is, any change of appearance for the worse — including the effects of the consciousness of such disfigurement on the plaintiff's mind, and in this connection the jury should consider the nature of the plaintiff's profession. Also consequent upon the defendant's breach, and compensable, were the pain and suffering involved in the third operation, but not in the first two. As there was no proof that any loss of earnings by the plaintiff resulted from the breach, that element should not enter into the calculation of damages.

By his exceptions the defendant contends that the judge erred in allowing the jury to take into account anything but the plaintiff's out-of-pocket expenses (presumably at the stipulated amount). The defendant excepted to the judge's refusal of his request for a general charge to that effect, and, more specifically, to the judge's refusal of a charge that the plaintiff could not recover for pain and suffering connected with the third operation or for impairment of the plaintiff's appearance and associated mental distress.

The plaintiff on her part excepted to the judge's refusal of a request to charge that the plaintiff could recover the difference in value between the nose as promised and the nose as it appeared after the operations. However, the plaintiff in her brief expressly waives this exception and others made by her in case this court overrules the defendant's exceptions; thus she would be content to hold the jury's verdict in her favor.

We conclude that the defendant's exceptions should be overruled.

It has been suggested on occasion that agreements between patients and physicians by which the physician undertakes to effect a cure or to bring about a given result should be declared unenforceable on grounds of public policy. But there are many decisions recognizing and enforcing such contracts, and the law of Massachusetts has treated them as valid, although we have had no decision meeting head on the contention that they should be denied legal sanction. These causes of action are, however, considered a little suspect, and thus we find courts straining sometimes to read the pleadings as sounding only in tort for negligence, and not in contract for breach of promise, despite sedulous efforts by the pleaders to pursue the latter theory.

It is not hard to see why the courts should be unenthusiastic or skeptical about the contract theory. Considering the uncertainties of medical science and the variations in the physical and psychological conditions of individual patients, doctors can seldom in good faith promise specific results. Therefore it is unlikely that physicians of even average integrity will in fact make such promises. Statements of opinion by the physician with some optimistic coloring are a different thing, and may indeed have therapeutic value. But patients may transform such statements into firm promises in their own minds, especially when they have been disappointed in the event, and testify in that sense to sympathetic juries. If actions for breach of promise can be readily maintained, doctors, so it is said, will be frightened into practising [sic] "defensive medicine." On the other hand, if these actions were outlawed, leaving only the possibility of suits for malpractice, there is fear that the public might be exposed to the enticements of charlatans, and confidence in the profession might ultimately be shaken. The law has taken the middle of the road position of allowing actions based on alleged contract, but insisting on clear proof. Instructions to the jury may well stress this requirement and point to tests of truth, such as the complexity or difficulty of an operation as bearing on the probability that a given result was promised.

If an action on the basis of contract is allowed, we have next the question of the measure of damages to be applied where liability is found. Some cases have taken the simple view that the promise by the physician is to be treated like an ordinary commercial promise, and accordingly that the successful plaintiff is entitled to a standard measure of recovery for breach of contract — "compensatory" ("expectancy") damages, an amount intended to put the plaintiff in the position he would be in if the contract had been performed, or, presumably, at the plaintiff's election, "restitution" damages, an amount corresponding to any benefit conferred by the plaintiff upon the defendant in the performance of the contract disrupted by the defendant's breach. See Restatement: Contracts §329 and comment a, §§347, 384(1). Thus in Hawkins v. McGee, the defendant doctor was taken to have promised the plaintiff to convert his damaged hand by means of an operation into a good or perfect hand, but the doctor so operated as to damage the hand still further. The court, following the usual expectancy formula, would have asked the jury to estimate and award to the plaintiff the difference between the value of a good or perfect hand, as promised, and the value of the hand after the operation. (The same formula would apply, although the dollar result would be less, if the operation had neither worsened nor improved the condition of the hand.) If the plaintiff had not yet paid the doctor his fee, that amount would be deducted from the recovery. There could be no recovery for the pain and suffering of the operation, since that detriment would have been incurred even if the operation had been successful; one can say that this detriment was not "caused" by the breach. But where the plaintiff by reason of the operation was put to more pain that he would have had to endure, had the doctor performed as promised, he should be compensated for that difference as a proper part of his expectancy recovery. It may be noted that on an alternative count for malpractice the plaintiff in the *Hawkins* case had been nonsuited; but on ordinary principles this could not affect the contract claim, for it is hardly a defence to a breach of contract that the promisor acted innocently and without negligence. . . .

Other cases, including a number in New York, without distinctly repudiating the *Hawkins* type of analysis, have indicated that a different and generally more lenient measure of damages is to be applied in patient-physician actions based on breach of alleged special agreements to effect a cure, attain a stated result, or employ a given medical method. This measure is expressed in somewhat variant ways, but the substance is that the plaintiff is to recover any expenditures made by him and for other detriment (usually not specifically described in the opinions) following proximately and foreseeably upon the defendant's failure to carry out his promise. This, be it noted, is not a "restitution" measure, for it is not limited to restoration of the benefit conferred on the defendant (the fee paid) but includes other expenditures, for example, amounts paid for medicine and nurses; so also it would seem according to its logic to take in damages for any worsening of the plaintiff's condition due to the breach. Nor is it an "expectancy" measure, for it does not appear to contemplate recovery of the whole difference in value between the condition as promised and the condition actually resulting from the treatment. Rather the tendency of the formulation is to put the plaintiff back in the position he occupied just before the parties entered upon the agreement, to compensate him for the detriments he suffered in reliance upon the agreement. This kind of intermediate pattern of recovery for breach of contract is discussed in the suggestive article by Fuller and Perdue, The Reliance Interest in Contract Damages, 46 Yale L.J. 52, 373, where the authors show that, although not attaining the currency of the standard measures, a "reliance" measure has for special reasons been applied by the courts in a variety of settings, including noncommercial settings.[3]

For breach of the patient-physician agreements under consideration, a recovery limited to restitution seems plainly too meager, if the agreements are to be enforced at all. On the other hand, an expectancy recovery may well be excessive. The factors, already mentioned, which have made the cause of action somewhat suspect, also suggest moderation as to the breadth of the recovery that should be permitted. Where, as in the case at bar and in a number of the reported cases, the doctor has been absolved of negligence by the trier, an expectancy measure may be thought harsh. We should recall here that the fee paid by the patient to the doctor for the alleged promise would usually be quite disproportionate to the putative expectancy recovery. To attempt, moreover, to put a value on the condition that would or might have resulted, had the treatment succeeded as promised, may sometimes put an exceptional strain on the imagination of the fact finder. As a general consideration, Fuller and Perdue argue that the reasons for granting damages for broken promises to the extent of the expectancy are at their strongest when the promises are made in a business context, when they have to do with the production or distribution of goods or the allocation of functions in the market place; they become weaker as the context shifts from a commercial to a noncommercial field.

There is much to be said, then, for applying a reliance measure to the present facts, and we have only to add that our cases are not unreceptive to the use of that formula in special situations. We have, however, had no previous occasion to apply it to patient-physician cases.

The question of recovery on a reliance basis for pain and suffering or mental distress requires further attention. We find expressions in the decisions that pain and suffering (or the like) are simply not compensable in actions for breach of contract. The defendant seemingly espouses this proposition in the present case. True, if the buyer under a contract for the purchase of a lot of merchandise, in suing for the seller's breach, should claim damages for mental anguish caused by his disappointment in the transaction, he would not succeed; he would be told, perhaps, that the asserted psychological injury was not fairly foreseeable by the defendant as a probable consequence of the breach of such a business contract. See Restatement: Contracts, §341, and comment a. But there is no general rule barring such items of damage in actions for breach of contract.

It is all a question of the subject matter and background of the contract, and when the contract calls for an operation on the person of the plaintiff, psychological as well as physical injury may be expected to figure somewhere in the recovery, depending on the particular circumstances. . . . Suffering or distress resulting from the breach going beyond that which was envisaged by the treatment as agreed, should be compensable on the same ground as the worsening of the patient's condition because of the

3. Some of the exceptional situations mentioned where reliance may be preferred to expectancy are those in which the latter measure would be hard to apply or would impose too great a burden; performance was interfered with by external circumstances; the contract was indefinite.

breach. Indeed it can be argued that the very suffering or distress "contracted for" — that which would have been incurred if the treatment achieved the promised result — should also be compensable on the theory underlying the New York cases. For that suffering is "wasted" if the treatment fails. Otherwise stated, compensation for this waste is arguably required in order to complete the restoration of the status quo ante.[4]

In the light of the foregoing discussion, all the defendant's exceptions fail: the plaintiff was not confined to the recovery of her out-of-pocket expenditures; she was entitled to recover also for the worsening of her condition, and for the pain and suffering and mental distress involved in the third operation. These items were compensable on either an expectancy or a reliance view. We might have been required to elect between the two views if the pain and suffering connected with the first two operations contemplated by the agreement, or the whole difference in value between the present and the promised conditions, were being claimed as elements of damage. But the plaintiff waives her possible claim to the former element, and to so much of the latter as represents the difference in value between the promised condition and the condition before the operations.

REFERENCE: Barnett, §2.3.2

STUDY GUIDE: The next case concerns the measurement of the expectation interest. Why was the jury in error to award damages for the rental expense of storing the cabinets but not for the salary of its general manager, given that it had to pay for both expenses whether or not there was a breach by the buyer? Why was the shutdown of the factory not directly relevant to the computation of lost profits? (Keep your answer in mind when we read the case of Hadley v. Baxendale in Section C.) This case also introduces Article 2 of the Uniform Commercial Code, which has been adopted by every state except Louisiana to govern contracts for the sale of goods. Note well: This means that if a contract is not a sale, or not for goods, the common law of contract and not the U.C.C. still applies. In light of this, notice how the court here deals with a contract that is a mixture of goods and services. Notice also the use of procedure of remittitur and additur.

---

4. Recovery on a reliance basis for breach of the physician's promise tends to equate with the usual recovery for malpractice, since the latter also looks in general to restoration of the condition before the injury. But this is not paradoxical, especially when it is noted that the origins of contract lie in tort. See Farnsworth, The Past of Promise: An Historical Introduction to Contract, 69 Col. L. Rev. 576, 594-596. . . . A few cases have considered possible recovery for breach by a physician of a promise to sterilize a patient, resulting in birth of a child to the patient and spouse. If such an action is held maintainable, the reliance and expectancy measures would, we think, tend to equate, because the promised condition was preservation of the family status quo. But cf. . . . Shaheen v. Knight, 11 Pa. D. & C. 2d 41. It would, however, be a mistake to think in terms of strict "formulas." For example, a jurisdiction which would apply a reliance measure to the present facts might impose a more severe damage sanction for the wilful use by the physician of a method of operation that he undertook not to employ.

J. O. HOOKER & SONS v. ROBERTS CABINET CO.
Supreme Court of Mississippi,
683 So. 2d 396 (1996)

PRATHER, P.J.,* for the Court:

INTRODUCTION

This case calls upon this Court to review the granting of a motion for summary judgment in favor of a subcontractor against a general contractor who breached a subcontract agreement. This Court considers the granting of the summary judgment motion to have been well taken, but we order a remittitur of $1,260 to the amount of $41,610.

STATEMENT OF THE FACTS

In 1991, J. O. Hooker & Sons, Inc. ("Hooker") served as the general contractor for the renovation of residences owned by the Bessemer Public Housing Authority ("BPHA") in Bessemer, Alabama. The renovation involved tearing out fixtures, such as cabinets, and Hooker's contract with the BPHA provided that the BPHA, as the owner of the property, had the option to either keep or salvage fixtures which needed to be torn out during the renovation process. The contract further provided that, in the event that the BPHA elected to keep the cabinets, Hooker would be required to remove the cabinets and move them to a location of the BPHA's choosing. Under said general contract, the cabinets were to become the property of Hooker and to be removed by him in the event that the BPHA elected not to keep said cabinets.

Hooker entered into a subcontract agreement with Roberts Cabinet Co., Inc. ("Roberts"), pursuant to which Roberts was required to "furnish cabinets, tops, plastic laminates on walls and furr down materials and fronts for hot water heaters as per plans and specs for the price listed below." The agreement also provided that "the price includes the cost of tear-out [sic] old cabinets and installation of new cabinets."

As the date when the cabinets would be needed approached, Roberts informed Hooker that he had underestimated the costs of the job and demanded an additional $23,000, which, Hooker asserts, he had no choice but to pay given the time constraints which were present. Later, a dispute arose between Hooker and Roberts as to which party had the duty to dispose of the cabinets as the BPHA required in the general contract. Roberts

---

* *Lenore Loving Prather* (1931-†) was educated at Mississippi State College for Women (B.S.) and the University of Mississippi (J.D.). After admission to practice in Mississippi in 1955, she began her legal practice in West Point, and continued working there until 1965 when she became a West Point City Judge (1965-1971). Judge Prather later became the first female Chancellor on the Chancery Court Bench of the Fourteenth Judicial District (1971-1982) and in 1982, the first woman member of the Mississippi Supreme Court, where she served as Chief Justice. Her term on the Court ended in 2000. [This judicial biography was written by Leslie Ravestein, hereinafter "L.R."]

asserted that the subcontract did not obligate him to dispose of the cabinets, but Hooker contends that the "as per specs and plans" language in the subcontract agreement served to incorporate by reference the general contract and that Roberts thus assumed Hooker's duties to dispose of the cabinets.

The parties were unable to resolve their dispute, and on December 13, 1991, Hooker sent Roberts a fax in which he stated that he had consulted with his lawyer and was considering the contract null and void. Hooker offered to buy from Roberts the cabinets that Roberts had already constructed, but the parties were unable to come to an agreement.

STATEMENT OF THE CASE

On December 18, 1991, Roberts Cabinet Co., Inc., filed suit against J. O. Hooker & Sons, Inc., alleging that Hooker had wrongfully breached a subcontract agreement with Roberts after Roberts had already begun performance. On September 16, 1992, the trial court granted summary judgment in favor of Roberts, finding that Hooker had no legal right to unilaterally terminate the contract in the present case.

On December 10, 1992, a trial was held for the sole purpose of determining the amount of damages suffered by Roberts as a result of Hooker's actions, and a jury determined Robert's damages to be in the amount of $42,870. On January 8, 1993, the trial court denied Hooker's motions for a new trial or in the alternative a remittitur of the jury's verdict, and Hooker filed a timely appeal. . . .

Hooker asserts that the contract in question should be interpreted in the context of Article 2 of the Uniform Commercial Code, Miss. Code Ann. §75-2-101 et seq., given that the transaction involved was for the sale of goods, namely cabinets. Hooker cites no authority for this proposition, and Roberts does not address this issue at all, but it is of importance to determine what law should apply to the contract. There appear to be no Mississippi cases directly on point, but this Court finds that, although the transaction in this case did involve a sale of goods, the dispute in this case actually concerns the performance of services and the delegation of duties under a contract.

A number of states which have considered this issue have concluded, based on an interpretation of UCC §2-102, that Article 2 does not apply to construction or service contracts. See Perlmutter v. Don's Ford, Inc., 96 Misc. 2d 719, 409 N.Y.S.2d 628 (1978); Christiansen Bros., Inc. v. State, 90 Wash. 2d 872, 586 P.2d 840 (1978). The present contract, however, is properly viewed as a mixed transaction of goods and services, and courts have reached differing conclusions as to whether the UCC should apply to such mixed transactions.

In Snyder v. Herbert Greenbaum & Associates, Inc., 38 Md. App. 144, 380 A.2d 618 (1977), the Maryland Court of Appeals held that a contract for the installation of carpeting in a large apartment complex was primarily a contract for sale, rather than installation, of such carpeting and thus was subject to UCC Article 2. In Freeman v. Shannon Const., Inc., 560 S.W.2d 732 (Tex. Civ. App. 7th Dist. 1977), by contrast, a Texas appellate court held that a contract between a general contractor and subcontractor, pursuant to which the subcontractor was to complete cement construction work on an apartment project, was in essence a service contract, even though it did involve the transfer of goods, and thus the UCC should not apply.

It is very often the case that a construction contract will involve the furnishing of goods by a subcontractor, and this Court holds that, in such a mixed transaction, whether or not the contract should be interpreted under the UCC or our general contract law should depend upon the nature of the contract and also upon whether the dispute in question primarily concerns the goods furnished or the services rendered under the contract. The present case clearly does not concern the cabinets manufactured, but rather the refusal of Roberts to assume duties which Hooker contractually obligated itself to perform. This Court would not hesitate to apply Article 2 if the present case involved, for example, a dispute over the quality of the cabinets, but the present case is in actuality a fairly standard contract dispute involving delegation of duties under a contract and the right to unilaterally rescind said contract. The fact that goods were furnished in the present contract has no bearing on the legal analysis involved, given that the dispute in this case clearly concerns the service aspect of this mixed transaction. . . .

WERE THE DAMAGES AWARDED BY THE JURY THE RESULT OF BIAS, PASSION AND PREJUDICE, AND/OR AGAINST THE WEIGHT OF THE OVERWHELMING EVIDENCE?

Hooker . . . argues that this Court should grant a substantial remittitur based on the damages in the jury's verdict being against the overwhelming weight of the evidence. Miss. Code Ann. §11-1-55, "Authority to impose condition of additur or remittitur," provides:

> The supreme court or any other court of record in a case in which money damages were awarded may overrule a motion for new trial or affirm on direct or cross appeal, upon condition of an additur or remittitur, if the court finds that the damages are excessive or inadequate for the reason that the jury or trier of the facts was influenced by bias, prejudice, or passion, or that the damages awarded were contrary to the overwhelming weight of the credible evidence. If such additur or remittitur be not accepted then the court may direct a new trial on damages only. If the additur or remittitur is accepted and the other party perfects a direct appeal, then the party accepting the additur or remittitur shall have the right to cross appeal for the purpose of reversing the action of the court in regard to the additur or remittitur.

Plaintiff's Exhibit 6 listed the following damages:

Reliance	$ 5,117.28	Net Loss on Manufactured Cabinets
	$ 3,775.04	Countertops
	$ 886.25	Laminate
	$ 72.38	Travel Expenses]→ Incidental
	$ 1,760.00	Administrative Time]→ Incidental
	$ 1,440.00	Storage of Cabinets]→ Incidental
Expectation	$30,000.00	Lost profit on job (lowered)
	$43,050.95	Total Damages

Although Roberts originally requested $51,309.29 in total damages, he was shown on cross-examination to have overestimated his lost profits, and Roberts accordingly lowered his total damages requested during closing arguments to $43,050.95. The excessive amount claimed was due to an accounting error and is not a subject of dispute in this appeal. Hooker does not contest on appeal the jury's awards with regard to the first four items listed above, namely the net loss on the manufactured cabinets, as well as the countertops, laminate, and travel expenses. Hooker does, however, contest the jury's awards relating to the storage and administrative costs, and, especially, the lost profits. These damages will be considered separately.

A.   STORAGE AND ADMINISTRATIVE COSTS

With regard to the storage costs for the cabinets, it is clear that Roberts would have incurred said costs regardless of any breach on the part of Hooker, given that the cabinets were stored in space which Roberts had already leased. Roberts argues that:

> As to the cost of storage, Hooker suggests that Roberts cannot allocate any costs for storage, because it was storing them in a building that it was paying rent on anyway. However, it was paying rent for a 30,000 square foot building. As a result of Hooker's breach, it was paying the same rent but on a reduced square foot building. Roberts only applied the percentage of the lease which was specifically attributable to the area being used to store Hooker's cabinets. Therefore, these costs are directly attributable to Hooker's breach.

Roberts' argument is without merit. Roberts is only entitled to recover damages for expenses in storing the cabinets that it would not otherwise have incurred absent Hooker's breach. As noted by Hooker, Roberts was not forced to rent additional space to store the cabinets, but merely utilized storage facilities that it had already leased. Roberts' rental fees were not raised a single penny by the storage of the cabinets in question, and it was not forced to rent additional space to store other materials as a result of a lack of space arising from the storage of the cabinets. Roberts' claim for recovery in this regard is based solely on the abstract economic value of previously empty storage space which it filled with the cabinets in question. Allowing Roberts to recover for the cost of storing the cabinets would place it in a better position than if the contract had been fully performed. Under these facts, Roberts' claimed damages of $1,440 for storage costs are disallowed in their entirety.

A somewhat similar analysis may appear to apply with regard to the "administrative time" damages of $1,760 which were cited by Roberts as having been incurred in paying Kevin Roberts for his time as general manager. With regard to these damages, Roberts argues that:

> Finally, as to the percentage of the general manager's salary allocated as damages, Hooker suggests that this percentage of the salary which was applicable to time spent on Hooker's project was not recoverable, because the

general manager was paid this salary anyway. However, Hooker misses the point. The general manager is not the Plaintiff in this action. Rather, Roberts is the Plaintiff in this action. Paying the general manager a salary to work on a contract which cannot be performed is the equivalent of paying the general manager a salary for reading the newspaper. It is wasted money and time that could have been spent on a contract that it was allowed to perform. Consequently, although the general manager may not have lost his salary, Roberts lost the benefit from paying its general manager this salary.

As with the expenses relating to storage space, Roberts' expenses in paying Kevin Roberts were exactly the same as they would have been if Hooker had not breached the contract. Kevin Roberts' salary, however, is not comparable to the storage costs in an important respect.

It is clear that the time which Kevin spent working on the Hooker project could, and presumably would, have been spent productively in other projects. As such, Roberts suffered an economic loss by having to pay an important employee his salary for working on a contract which would eventually be canceled. Kevin testified that he spent approximately forty percent of his working hours over a two-month period on the Hooker project. It is true that Roberts would have paid Kevin regardless of whether he had spent that time working on the Hooker project. However, the distinction is that, unless reimbursed for these expenses, the salary paid by Roberts for this time spent will have been paid for no resulting economic value. Given that Kevin Roberts was a salaried employee of Roberts who was directly engaged in working on the Hooker project, it can not be disputed that Roberts suffered expenses related to the contract in question by paying Kevin for his work.

The issue arises as to whether compensating Roberts for both its lost profits and for the salary of Kevin Roberts would amount to a double recovery. The answer to this question depends upon whether Kevin Roberts' salary was included in the $120,000 in expenses which Roberts estimated it would have incurred in completing the project. If said salary was included in the expenses, then the recovery would not amount to a double recovery, given that the amount of the salary would have already served to reduce the amount of profits in the calculation of damages.

The record does not reveal whether Roberts included an estimate of Kevin Roberts' salary allocable to the Hooker contract in his determination of his expenses. It is reasonable to assume, however, that a subcontractor includes in his bid estimate the salaries which he will be required to pay to all employees who will be directly involved in the project in question. It naturally adds to the expense of a project if a company is required to utilize the services of managerial personnel who may be unable to perform other tasks as a result of said project. Roberts suffered expenses by paying Kevin Roberts his salary without being able to utilize his expertise on other jobs for which they would be receiving the full amount of contract value. On these facts, it cannot be said that the jury's awarding of these administrative costs was against the overwhelming weight of the evidence.

B. Lost Profits

The main issue with regard to damages in this appeal concerns the extent of Roberts' lost profits as a result of the breach by Hooker. In awarding damages for breach of contract, this Court's purpose is to put the injured party in as good a position as he would have been in but for the breach. . . . 22 Am. Jur. 2d "Damages" §45 notes that:

> Contract damages are ordinarily based on the injured party's expectation interest and are intended to give him the benefit of the bargain by awarding him a sum of money that will, to the extent possible, put him in as good a position as he would have been in had the contract been performed.

It is clear that damages awarded by the jury were in the nature of expectation damages, and said damages included Roberts' lost profit from the deal, along with expenses that Roberts incurred in manufacturing the cabinets that it was unable to mitigate. The jury's awarding of Roberts' direct expenses in partially performing the contract in addition to lost profits was entirely proper, given that failing to do so would under-compensate Roberts by forcing him to pay for said expenses out of his net profits.

Of considerable dispute at trial was Roberts' claimed profit percentage on the deal with Hooker of twenty-six percent. Hooker testified that such a percentage was not a "usual and ordinary profit to be expected in the con-struction business" and that one would be unable to "win any jobs on public works with bids including a 26% profit margin." Hooker testified that his usual profit margin was approximately 4%, although Roberts argued that a manufacturer such as Roberts should expect a greater profit margin than a general contractor such as Hooker.

Also in dispute at trial was the evidence regarding the daily manufac-turing output of Roberts' factory and the number of days that the produc-tion was curtailed at said factory as a result of the breach by Hooker. Kevin testified at trial that Roberts' average daily manufacturing output was between $6,000 and $8,000 in 1991, although he estimated during discov-ery that such output amounted to only $6,000. Hooker asserts that, even assuming that the twenty-six percent profit margin is correct, the $6,000/day output constitutes a gross sales figure, and that Roberts would thus only expect a profit of approximately $1,500/day from the contract.

Hooker thus argues that Roberts' lost profits should be measured by the four-day period during which production at Roberts' factory was shut down. However, the shut-down period at the factory would be much more relevant with regard to determining the amount of consequential damages resulting from the breach rather than measuring Roberts' amount of lost profits. The relevant inquiry is not the amount of profit that Roberts would have been able to make in the four days that the factory was shut down, but rather the amount of profit it would have been able to make on the deal as a whole had the contract not been breached by Hooker.

Roberts' daily manufacturing output would only be relevant in deter-mining the amount of lost profits on the deal as a whole if it could be shown exactly how many days it would have taken for Roberts to manufacture the cabinets, and there was no exact proof in this regard at trial. Given the bid price of over $150,000, however, it is clear that it would have taken Roberts many more than four days to complete the contract, considering the daily manufacturing output of the factory of only $6,000/day. Kevin testified that the factory was capable of generating a daily production output considerably in excess of $6,000/day, but the completion of the contract would have taken weeks even at an increased rate of production.

Kevin testified that, in making his bid, he estimated the costs that his company would have incurred in manufacturing the cabinets to be approximately $120,000, and then factored in his desired profit margin of twenty-six percent, for a total of an approximately $151,000 total bid. Thus, Kevin testified that, had the contract been completed, Roberts expected to receive a profit of around thirty thousand dollars. Bids in construction situations are rarely susceptible of exact proof as to what the manufacturing costs and profits would have been, and, while the profit margin of twenty-six percent may appear high, Hooker's sole proof regarding the excessive nature of Roberts' claimed profit margin was his testimony regarding his own experiences as a general contractor, rather than a manufacturer/subcontractor.

This Court thus has only the conflicting testimony of Hooker and Roberts with which to determine the true profit margin, and, on these facts, it cannot be said that the jury's verdict was against the overwhelming weight of the evidence. . . . The only damages granted by the jury which this Court considers to be against the overwhelming weight of the evidence are the damages for the storage of the cabinets. While the storage costs constitute a rather insignificant portion of the damages, the fact remains that the awarding of the $1,440 in storage costs was clearly erroneous and an abuse of discretion, given that Hooker suffered no real economic loss as a result of being forced to store the cabinets at his factory. Having established that a rather minor remittitur is in order, this Court's role is to reduce the damages to such an amount that the verdict is not in conflict with the overwhelming weight of the evidence.

Accordingly, this Court grants a remittitur of $1,260.00, which constitutes the difference between the $42,870.00 sum awarded by the jury and the sum of $41,610.00, which, this Court concludes, is not against the overwhelming weight of the evidence. . . .

Affirmed on condition of remittitur; if remittitur refused, reversed and remanded for a new trial on damages only.

SALES CONTRACTS: THE UNIFORM COMMERCIAL CODE

§1-103.   SUPPLEMENTARY GENERAL PRINCIPLES OF CONTRACT LAW APPLICABLE

Unless displaced by the particular provisions of this Act, the principles of law and equity, including the law merchant and the law relative to capacity to contract, principal and agent, estoppel, fraud, misrepresentation, duress, coercion, mistake, bankruptcy, or other validating or invalidating cause shall supplement its provisions.

§2-102. SCOPE; CERTAIN SECURITY AND OTHER TRANSACTIONS EXCLUDED FROM THIS ARTICLE

Unless the context otherwise requires, the Article applies to transactions in goods; it does not apply to any transaction which although in the form of an unconditional contract to sell or present sale is intended to operate only as a security transaction nor does this Article impair or repeal any statute regulating sales to consumers, farmers or other specified classes of buyers.

§2-105. DEFINITIONS: TRANSFERABILITY; "GOODS" . . .

(1) "Goods" means all things (including specially manufactured goods) which are movable at the time of identification to the contract for sale other than the money in which the price is to be paid, investment securities (Article 9) and things in action. "Goods" also includes the unborn young of animals and growing crops and other identified things attached to realty as described in goods to be severed from realty (Section 2-107). . . .

§2-106. DEFINITIONS: "CONTRACT"; "AGREEMENT"; "CONTRACT FOR SALE"; "SALE"; "PRESENT SALE" . . .

(1) In this Article unless the context otherwise requires "contract" and "agreement" are limited to those relating to the present or future sale of goods. "Contract for sale" includes both a present sale of goods and a contract to sell goods at a future time. A "sale" consists in the passing of title from the seller to the buyer for a price (Section 2-401). A "present sale" means a sale which is accomplished by the making of a contract. . . .

REFERENCE: Barnett, §2.3.5
Farnsworth, §§1.9-1.10
Calamari & Perillo, §1.7
Murray, §§9-12

STUDY GUIDE: In the next opinion, does the court award the plaintiff expectation damages, reliance damages, restitution damages, or something else? Does the plaintiff receive a windfall? What incentive does the rule applied by the court create for parties in similar situations in the future who might be contemplating breach? Who ultimately bore the costs of the defendant's breach? Were they compensated for their losses? Should we care?

KGM HARVESTING CO. v. FRESH NETWORK
Court of Appeal, Sixth District, California,
42 Cal. Rptr. 2d 286 (1995),
36 Cal. App. 4th 376 (1995)

COTTLE,* Presiding Justice.

California lettuce grower and distributor KGM Harvesting Company (hereafter seller) had a contract to deliver 14 loads of lettuce each week to Ohio lettuce broker Fresh Network (hereafter buyer). When the price of lettuce rose dramatically in May and June 1991, seller refused to deliver the required quantity of lettuce to buyer. Buyer then purchased lettuce on the open market in order to fulfill its contractual obligations to third parties. After a trial, the jury awarded buyer damages in an amount equal to the difference between the contract price and the price buyer was forced to pay for substitute lettuce on the open market. On appeal, seller argues that the damage award is excessive. We disagree and shall affirm the judgment. In a cross-appeal, buyer argues it was entitled to prejudgment interest from August 1, 1991, as its damages were readily ascertainable from that date. We agree and reverse the trial court's order awarding prejudgment interest from 30 days prior to trial.

FACTS

In July 1989 buyer and seller entered into an agreement for the sale and purchase of lettuce. Over the years, the terms of the agreement were modified. By May 1991 the terms were that seller would sell to buyer 14 loads of lettuce each week and that buyer would pay seller 9 cents a pound for the lettuce. (A load of lettuce consists of 40 bins, each of which weighs 1,000 to 1,200 pounds. Assuming an average bin weight of 1,100 pounds, one load would equal 44,000 pounds, and the 14 loads called for in the contract would weigh 616,000 pounds. At 9 cents per pound, the cost would approximate $55,440 per week.)

Buyer sold all of the lettuce it received from seller to a lettuce broker named Castellini Company who in turn sold it to Club Chef, a company that chops and shreds lettuce for the fast food industry (specifically, Burger King, Taco Bell, and Pizza Hut). Castellini Company bought lettuce from buyer on a "cost plus" basis, meaning it would pay buyer its actual cost plus a small commission. Club Chef, in turn, bought lettuce from Castellini Company on a cost plus basis.

Seller had numerous lettuce customers other than buyer, including seller's subsidiaries Coronet East and West. Coronet East supplied all the lettuce for the McDonald's fast food chain.

---

* Christopher Cottle (1940-†) attended law school at Stanford University, and received his J.D. in 1966. He served as the Santa Cruz County District Attorney from 1975-1977. He was appointed to the 6th District Court of Appeal in California in 1988, and served as the Presiding Justice until his retirement in 2001. He played football while attending Stanford. — S.Q.

In May and June 1991, when the price of lettuce went up dramatically, seller refused to supply buyer with lettuce at the contract price of nine cents per pound. Instead, it sold the lettuce to others at a profit of between $800,000 and $1,100,000. Buyer, angry at seller's breach, refused to pay seller for lettuce it had already received. Buyer then went out on the open market and purchased lettuce to satisfy its obligations to Castellini Company. Castellini covered all of buyer's extra expense except for $70,000. Castellini in turn passed on its extra costs to Club Chef which passed on at least part of its additional costs to its fast food customers.

In July 1991 buyer and seller each filed complaints under the Perishable Agricultural Commodities Act (PACA). Seller sought the balance due on its outstanding invoices ($233,000), while buyer sought damages for the difference between what it was forced to spend to buy replacement lettuce and the contract price of nine cents a pound (approximately $700,000).

Subsequently, seller filed suit for the balance due on its invoices, and buyer cross-complained for the additional cost it incurred to obtain substitute lettuce after seller's breach. At trial, the parties stipulated that seller was entitled to a directed verdict on its complaint for $233,000, the amount owing on the invoices. Accordingly, only the cross-complaint went to the jury, whose task was to determine whether buyer was entitled to damages from seller for the cost of obtaining substitute lettuce and, if so, in what amount. The jury determined that seller breached the contract, that its performance was not excused, and that buyer was entitled to $655,960.22, which represented the difference between the contract price of nine cents a pound and what it cost buyer to cover by purchasing lettuce in substitution in May and June 1991. It also determined that such an award would not result in a windfall to buyer and that buyer was obligated to the Castellini Company for the additional costs. The court subtracted from buyer's award of $655,960.22 the $233,000 buyer owed to seller on its invoices, leaving a net award in favor of buyer in the amount of $422,960.22. The court also awarded buyer prejudgment interest commencing 30 days before trial.

DISCUSSION

A.   SELLER'S APPEAL

Section 2711 of the California Uniform Commercial Code provides a buyer with several alternative remedies for a seller's breach of contract. The buyer can " 'cover' by making in good faith and without unreasonable delay any reasonable purchase of . . . goods in substitution for those due from the seller." (§2712, subd. (1).) In that case, the buyer "may recover from the seller as damages the difference between the cost of cover and the contract price. . . ." (§2712, subd. (2).) If the buyer is unable to cover or chooses not to cover, the measure of damages is the difference between the market price and the contract price. (§2713.) Under either alternative, the buyer may also recover incidental and consequential damages. (§§2711, 2715.) In addition, in certain cases the buyer may secure specific performance or replevin "where the goods are unique" (§2716) or may recover goods identified to a contract (§2502).

In the instant case, buyer "covered" as defined in section 2712 in order to fulfill its own contractual obligations to the Castellini Company. Accordingly, it was awarded the damages called for in cover cases — the difference between the contract price and the cover price. (§2712.)

In appeals from judgments rendered pursuant to section 2712, the dispute typically centers on whether the buyer acted in "good faith," whether the "goods in substitution" differed substantially from the contracted for goods, whether the buyer unreasonably delayed in purchasing substitute goods in the mistaken belief that the price would go down, or whether the buyer paid too much for the substitute goods. (See generally White & Summers, Uniform Commercial Code (3d ed. 1988) Buyer's Remedies, Cover, §6-3, pp. 284-292 [hereinafter White & Summers], and cases cited therein.)

In this case, however, none of these typical issues is in dispute. Seller does *not* contend that buyer paid too much for the substitute lettuce or that buyer was guilty of "unreasonable delay" or a lack of "good faith" in its attempt to obtain substitute lettuce. Nor does seller contend that the lettuce purchased was of a higher quality or grade and therefore not a reasonable substitute.

Instead, seller takes issue with section 2712 itself, contending that despite the unequivocal language of section 2712, a buyer who covers should not *necessarily* recover the difference between the cover price and the contract price. Seller points out that because of buyer's "cost plus" contract with Castellini Company, buyer was eventually able to pass on the extra expenses (except for $70,000) occasioned by seller's breach and buyer's consequent purchase of substitute lettuce on the open market. It urges this court under these circumstances not to allow buyer to obtain a "windfall."[5]

The basic premise of contract law is to effectuate the expectations of the parties to the agreement, to give them the "benefit of the bargain" they struck when they entered into the agreement. In its basic premise, contract law therefore differs significantly from tort law. As the California Supreme Court explained in Foley v. Interactive Data Corp. (1988) 47 Cal. 3d 654, 254 Cal. Rptr. 211, 765 P.2d 373, "contract actions are created to enforce the intentions of the parties to the agreement [while] tort law is primarily designed to vindicate 'social policy.' " (*Id.* at p. 683, 254 Cal. Rptr. 211, 765 P.2d 373, citing Prosser, Law of Torts (4th ed. 1971) p. 613.)

" 'The basic object of damages is *compensation*, and in the law of contracts the theory is that the party injured by breach should receive as nearly as possible the equivalent of the benefits of performance.

---

5. In answering special interrogatories, the jury found (1) that if buyer were awarded the difference between the contract price and the cost of cover, it would not result in a windfall to buyer, and (2) that buyer had an obligation to pay Castellini Company for the amount Castellini Company paid buyer to acquire the substitute lettuce. On appeal, seller contends that these findings were not supported by substantial evidence. As we shall explain, however, these findings were not necessary to justify the section 2712 award. Accordingly, we need not reach the issue whether the evidence supports the jury's findings on these two special interrogatories.

[Citations.]' " (Lisec v. United Airlines, Inc. (1992) 10 Cal. App. 4th 1500, 1503, 11 Cal. Rptr. 2d 689.) A compensation system that gives the aggrieved party the benefit of the bargain, and no more, furthers the goal of "predictability about the cost of contractual relationships . . . in our commercial system." (Foley v. Interactive Data Corp., supra, 47 Cal. 3d at p. 683, 254 Cal. Rptr. 211, 765 P.2d 373; Putz & Klippen, *Commercial Bad Faith: Attorney Fees — Not Tort Liability — Is the Remedy for "Stonewalling"* (1987) 21 U.S.F. L. Rev. 419, 432.)

With these rules in mind, we examine the contract at issue in this case to ascertain the reasonable expectations of the parties. The contract recited that its purpose was "to supply [buyer] with a consistent quality raw product at a fair price to [seller], which also allows [buyer] profitability for his finished product." Seller promised to supply the designated quantity even if the price of lettuce went up ("We agree to supply said product and amount at stated price regardless of the market price or conditions") and buyer promised to purchase the designated quantity even if the price went down "[Buyer] agrees to purchase said product and amounts at stated price regardless of the market price or conditions, provided quality requirements are met"). The possibility that the price of lettuce would fluctuate was consequently foreseeable to both parties.

Although the contract does not recite this fact, seller was aware of buyer's contract with the Castellini Company and with the Castellini Company's contract with Club Chef. This knowledge was admitted at trial and can be inferred from the fact that seller shipped the contracted for 14 loads of lettuce directly to Club Chef each week. Thus, seller was well aware that if it failed to provide buyer with the required 14 loads of lettuce, buyer would have to obtain replacement lettuce elsewhere or would itself be in breach of contract. This was within the contemplation of the parties when they entered into their agreement.

As noted earlier, the object of contract damages is to give the aggrieved party " 'as nearly as possible the equivalent of the benefits of performance.' " (Lisec v. United Airlines, Inc., supra, 10 Cal. App. 4th at p. 1503, 11 Cal. Rptr. 2d 689; see also §1106 ["The remedies provided by this code shall be liberally administered to the end that the aggrieved party may be put in as good a position as if the other party had fully performed. . . ."].) In the instant case, buyer contracted for 14 loads of lettuce each week at 9 cents per pound. When seller breached its contract to provide that lettuce, buyer went out on the open market and purchased substitute lettuce to fulfill its contractual obligations to third parties. However, purchasing replacement lettuce to continue its business did not place buyer "in as good a position as if the other party had fully performed." This was because buyer paid more than nine cents per pound for the replacement lettuce. Only by reimbursing buyer for the additional costs above nine cents a pound could buyer truly receive the benefit of the bargain. This is the measure of damages set forth in section 2712.

As White and Summers point out, "Since 2-712 measures buyer's damages by the difference between his actual cover purchase and the contract price, the formula will often put buyer in the identical economic position that performance would have." (White & Summers, supra, §6-3, p. 285.) Therefore, "[i]n the typical case a timely 'cover' purchase by an aggrieved buyer will preclude any 2-715 [incidental and consequential] damages." (*Ibid.*) "Not only does the damage formula in 2-712 come close to putting the aggrieved buyer in the same economic position as actual performance would have," White and Summers conclude, "but it also enables him to achieve his prime objective, namely that of acquiring his needed goods." (*Id.* at p. 292.)

In this case, the damage formula of section 2712 put buyer in the identical position performance would have: it gave buyer the contracted for 14 loads of lettuce with which to carry on its business at the contracted for price of 9 cents per pound.

Despite the obvious applicability and appropriateness of section 2712, seller argues in this appeal that the contract-cover differential of section 2712 is inappropriate in cases, as here, where the aggrieved buyer is ultimately able to pass on its additional costs to other parties. Seller contends that section 1106's remedial injunction to put the aggrieved party "in as good a position as if the other party had fully performed" demands that all subsequent events impacting on *buyer*'s ultimate profit or loss be taken into consideration (specifically, that buyer passed on all but $70,000 of its loss to Castellini Company, which passed on all of its loss to Club Chef, which passed on most of its loss to its fast food customers).[6] For this proposition, seller relies on two cases limiting a buyer's damages under a different provision of the Commercial Code, section 2713 (Allied Canners & Packers, Inc. v. Victor Packing Co. (1984) 162 Cal. App. 3d 905, 209 Cal. Rptr. 60; H-W-H Cattle Co., Inc. v. Schroeder (8th Cir. 1985) 767 F.2d 437), and on one section 2712 cover case in which damages were apparently limited (Sun Maid Raisin Growers v. Victor Packing Co. (1983) 146 Cal. App. 3d 787, 194 Cal. Rptr. 612).

We begin with the cover case. In Sun-Maid Raisin Growers v. Victor Packing Co., supra, 146 Cal. App. 3d 787, 194 Cal. Rptr. 612, the seller (Victor) repudiated a contract to sell 610 tons of raisins to Sun-Maid after "disastrous" rains damaged the raisin crop and the price of raisins nearly doubled. Sun-Maid attempted to cover but was only partially successful. It was able to obtain only 200 tons of comparable raisins. For the remaining 410 tons, it had to purchase inferior raisins that had to be reconditioned at a substantial cost. Apparently the total cost of purchasing the 200 tons of high quality raisins and of purchasing and reconditioning the remaining 410 tons was $377,720 over the contract price.

The trial court awarded Sun-Maid, as consequential damages under section 2715, $295,339.40 for its lost profits. Victor appealed, arguing that the amount of lost profits was unforeseeable by either party when the contracts were formed. The Court of Appeal affirmed, noting that the evidence established that Victor knew Sun-Maid was purchasing the raisins for resale.

In its discussion, the court recounted the various measures of damages available to an aggrieved buyer under the Uniform Commercial Code for a seller's nondelivery of goods or repudiation of contract, citing sections

---

6. Seller, not surprisingly, does not focus on post-breach events impacting on *seller*'s ultimate profit or loss. As noted earlier, seller made a profit of between $800,000 and $1,100,000 for selling the lettuce at the higher market price rather than the lower nine cent per pound contract price.

2712, 2713, 2715 and 2723. The court seemed to wonder why the trial court had chosen lost profits rather than the cost of cover as damages, noting that the court did not specify why it had determined damages in that manner and that neither party had requested findings. However, as neither Sun-Maid nor Victor was contesting that measure of damages on appeal (the only issue was whether lost profits were foreseeable consequential damages), the court observed that the trial court "probably found that damages should be limited to the amount that would have put Sun-Maid in 'as good a position as if the other party had fully performed.' (§1106.)" (*Id.* at p. 792, 194 Cal. Rptr. 612.)

From this simple observation, seller claims that "[i]n cases, like the instant case, involving forward contracts, *California courts hold that section 1106 limits the damages to be awarded under section 2712* (*i.e.,* the cover damages statute) and section 2713 (*i.e.,* the market damages statute) for the very reason that the non-breaching party is entitled to nothing more than to be placed in the position which would result from the breaching party's full performance of the agreement. See Sun-Maid Raisin Growers v. Victor Packing Co. (1983) 146 Cal. App. 3d 787, 792, [194 Cal. Rptr. 612] (cover case); Allied Canners & Packers, Inc. v. Victor Packing Co. (1984) 162 Cal. App. 3d 905, 915 [209 Cal. Rptr. 60] (non-cover case)." (Emphasis added.)

In fact, the *Sun-Maid* court held no such thing. It simply offered one possible explanation for the trial court's award, which no one was contesting. Under the facts of that case, the cost of cover might have been unduly difficult to calculate. Sun-Maid was able to purchase only 200 tons of comparable raisins in a timely manner. There were no other Thompson seedless free tonnage raisins available within a reasonable time after seller's breach (August 1976). It was considerably later before buyer could find another 410 tons to purchase, and those raisins were damaged in part because of rains occurring *after* the breach, in September 1976.[7] Under these circumstances, the trial court and the parties may simply have chosen to focus on the easily calculable consequential damages (which buyer claimed were foreseeable and seller denied were foreseeable) and to ignore the difficult to calculate cover damages.

We now look to the "non-cover" case relied upon by seller, Allied Canners & Packers, Inc. v. Victor Packing Co., supra, 162 Cal. App. 3d at 915, 209 Cal. Rptr. 60, which in fact does hold that section 1106 acts as a limitation on the amount of damages otherwise recoverable under *section 2713.* Before discussing the *Allied Canners* case, however, a few observations on the differences between the contract-cover differential of section 2712 and the contract-market differential of section 2713 are called for.

---

7. Section 2712's requirement that buyer purchase goods "in substitution for those due from seller" does not "envisage[ ] . . . goods . . . identical with those involved but commercially usable as reasonable substitutes under the circumstances of the particular case. . . ." (U.C.C. comment 2 to §2712.) Where, as here, the goods purchased to cover differ significantly from the contracted for goods, is the section 2712 damage formula even appropriate? Should the breaching seller be responsible for the post-breach rains in September 1976? If not, should the damage formula of section 2712 be adjusted to take these matters into consideration?

As noted earlier, section 2712 "will often put buyer in the identical economic position that performance would have." (White & Summers, supra, §6-3, p. 285.) In contrast, the contract-market differential of section 2713 "bears no necessary relation to the change in the buyer's economic status that the breach causes. It is possible that this differential might yield the buyer a handsome sum even though the breach actually saved him money in the long run (as for example when a middleman buyer's resale markets dry up after the breach). It is also quite possible that the buyer's lost profit from resale or consumption would be greater than the contract-market difference." (*Id.*, §6-4, at p. 294.)

White and Summers argue that the drafters of section 2713 could *not* have intended to put the buyer in the same position as performance since "[p]erformance would have given the buyer certain goods for consumption or resale" (White & Summers, supra, at p. 294) which would have resulted in "either a net economic gain for the buyer or a net economic loss." (*Ibid.*) The best explanation of section 2713, they suggest, is that it is a "statutory liquidated damage clause, a breach inhibitor the payout of which need bear no close relation to the plaintiff's actual loss." (*Id.* at p. 295; accord Peters, *Remedies for Breach of Contracts Relating to the Sale of Goods Under the Uniform Commercial Code: A Roadmap for Article Two* (1963) 73 Yale L.J. 199, 259.) In discussing the "problem of a buyer who has covered but who seeks to ignore 2-712 and sue for a larger contract-market differential under 2-713," the authors suggest: "If the Code's goal is to put the buyer in the same position as though there had been no breach, and if 2-712 will accomplish that goal but 2-713 will do so only by coincidence, why not force the covering buyer to use 2-712?" (*Id.* at p. 304.) Professor Robert Childres has actually called for the repeal of section 2713 and the requirement of compulsory cover. (Childres, *Buyer's Remedies: The Danger of Section 2-713* (1978) 72 Nw. U. L. Rev. 837.)

With these prefatory comments in mind, we look to the *Allied Canners* case. In *Allied Canners,* the same raisin supplier (Victor Packing Company) involved in the *Sun Maid* case breached another contract to sell raisins in 1976. The buyer, Allied Canners, had contracts to resell the raisins it bought from Victor to two Japanese companies for its cost plus 4 percent. Such a resale would have resulted in a profit of $4,462.50 to Allied. When Victor breached the contract, Allied sued for the difference between the market price and the contract price as authorized by section 2713. As the market price of raisins had soared due to the disastrous 1976 rains, the market-contract price formula would have yielded damages of approximately $150,000. Allied did not purchase substitute raisins and did not make any deliveries under its resale contracts to the Japanese buyers. One of the Japanese buyers simply released Allied from its contract because of the general unavailability of raisins. The other buyer did not release Allied, but it did not sue Allied either. By the time Allied's case against Victor went to trial, the statute of limitations on the Japanese buyer's claim had run.

Under these circumstances, the court held that the policy of section 1106 (that the aggrieved party be put in as good a position as if the other party had performed) required that the award of damages to Allied be limited to its actual loss. It noted that for this limitation to apply, three conditions must be met: (1) "the seller knew that the buyer had a resale contract";

(2) "the buyer has not been able to show that it will be liable in damages to the buyer on its forward contract";[8] and (3) "there has been no finding of bad faith on the part of the seller. . . ." (Allied Canners & Packers, Inc. v. Victor Packing Co., supra 162 Cal. App. 3d at p. 915, 209 Cal. Rptr. 60.)[9]

[handwritten margin note: Incorrect! under 2713 Market price subtracted from contract price]

[handwritten margin note: No role in Contract "all about money"]

The result in Allied Canners seems to have derived in large part from the court's finding that Victor had not acted in bad faith in breaching the contract. The court noted, "It does appear clear, however, that, as the trial court found, the rains caused a severe problem, and Victor made substantial efforts [to procure the raisins for Allied]. We do not deem this record one to support an inference that windfall damages must be awarded the buyer to prevent unjust enrichment to a deliberately breaching seller. (Compare Sun-Maid Raisin Growers v. Victor Packing Co., supra, 146 Cal. App. 3d 787, 194 Cal. Rptr. 612 [where, in a case coincidentally involving Victor, Victor was expressly found by the trial court to have engaged in bad faith by gambling on the market price of raisins in deciding whether to perform its contracts to sell raisins to Sun-Maid].)" (162 Cal. App. 3d at p. 916, 209 Cal. Rptr. 60.)[10]

We believe that this focus on the good or bad faith of the breaching party is inappropriate in a commercial sales case. As our California Supreme Court recently explained, courts should not differentiate between good and bad motives for breaching a contract in assessing the measure of the non-breaching party's damages. (Applied Equipment Corp. v. Litton Saudi Arabia Ltd. (1994) 7 Cal. 4th 503, 513-515, 28 Cal. Rptr. 2d 475, 869 P.2d 454.) Such a focus is inconsistent with the policy "to encourage contractual relations and commercial activity by enabling parties to estimate in advance the financial risks of their enterprise." (Id. at p. 515, 28 Cal. Rptr. 2d 475, 869 P.2d 454.) " 'Courts traditionally have awarded damages for breach of contract to compensate the aggrieved party rather than to punish the breaching party.' [Citations.]" (Foley v. Interactive Data Corp., supra, 47 Cal. 3d at p. 683, 254 Cal. Rptr. 211, 765 P.2d 373.)

8. The court apparently never considered anything other than whether the Japanese buyers would sue Allied Canners. For example, it did not consider whether the breach adversely affected Allied Canners' goodwill with its Japanese customers. Should the court not have also considered Allied Canners' potential loss of future contracts?

9. The other section 2713 case on which seller relies, an Eighth Circuit case, H-W-H Cattle Co. v. Schroeder, supra, 767 F.2d 437, also limited a buyer's damages to its anticipated commissions on the resale of the cattle rather than the full contract-market differential.

10. In view of Allied Canners' three part test, we assume the results would have been different here if the court had found Victor was "a deliberately breaching seller." Perhaps in that case, the court would not have focused on what the aggrieved buyer ultimately would have received on resale but might have focused on what benefits the seller reaped from breaching. In Allied Canners, the price of raisins went up from 30 cents a pound to 87 cents a pound. If seller had not breached, it would have had to go out on the market and buy raisins for Allied at considerably more than it was contracted to sell them for to Allied. By breaching, it avoided a loss that might have been more in the $150,000 range (market-contract differential) than the $4,000 range (Allied's lost profits). Thus, the court prevented a windfall to Allied at the cost of providing a windfall to Victor. Such a result is curious if the intent of contract damages is to effectuate the expectations of the parties to the contract. Here, the parties clearly contemplated when they entered into their fixed price agreement that the price of raisins would fluctuate and that sometimes buyer would receive a price better than the market price and that other times it would have to pay more than the market price.

The *Allied Canners* opinion has been sharply criticized in numerous law review articles and in at least one sister-state opinion. In Tongish v. Thomas (1992) 251 Kan. 728, 840 P.2d 471, the Kansas Supreme Court rejected the *Allied Canners* approach and instead applied the "majority view [which] would award market damages even though in excess of plaintiff's loss." (*Id.*, 840 P.2d at p. 475.) Relying on an article by Professors Simon and Novack, *Limiting the Buyer's Market Damages to Lost Profits: A Challenge to the Enforceability of Market Contracts* (1979) 92 Harv. L. Rev. 1395, the *Tongish* court explained that use of the market price/contract price damage scheme of section 2713 " 'encourages a more efficient market and discourages the breach of contracts.' " (Tongish v. Thomas, *supra*, 840 P.2d at p. 476.)

Similarly, in Schneider, *UCC Section 2-713: A Defense of Buyers' Expectancy Damages* (1986) 22 Cal. W. L. Rev. 233, 264, the author states the "[b]y limiting buyer to lost resale profits, the [*Allied Canners*] court ignored the clear language of section 2-713's compensation scheme to award expectation damages in accordance with the parties' allocation of risk as measured by the difference between contract price and market price on the date set for performance. If the court wanted to avoid giving greater damages, it would have been better for it to view what occurred to the availability and price of raisins as being beyond the risks contemplated by the parties and thus to have ruled under the doctrine of commercial impracticability as provided in section 2-615(a)."

In addition numerous New York courts have chosen not to limit a buyer's damages to actual losses. (See e.g., Fertico Belgium v. Phosphate Chem. Export (1987) 70 N.Y.2d 76, 517 N.Y.S.2d 465, 510 N.E.2d 334; Apex Oil Co. v. Vanguard Oil & Service Co. Inc. (2d Cir. 1985) 760 F.2d 417; G.A. Thompson & Co. v. Wendell J. Miller, Etc. (S.D.N.Y. 1978) 457 F. Supp. 996.)

As the foregoing discussion makes clear, we have serious reservations about whether the result in *Allied Canners*, with its emphasis on the good faith of the breaching party, is appropriate in an action seeking damages under section 2713. We have no reservations, however, in not extending the *Allied Canners* rationale to a section 2712 case. As noted earlier, no section 2712 case, including Sun Maid Growers v. Victor Packing Co., *supra*, 146 Cal. App. 3d 787, 194 Cal. Rptr. 612, has ever held that cover damages must be limited by section 1106. The obvious reason is that the cover-contract differential puts a buyer who covers in the exact same position as performance would have done. This is the precisely what is called for in section 1106. In this respect, the cover/contract differential of section 2712 is very different than the market/contract differential of section 2713, which "need bear no close relation to the plaintiff's actual loss." (White & Summers, *supra*, at p. 295.

In summary, we hold that where a buyer " 'cover[s]' by making in good faith and without unreasonable delay any reasonable purchase of . . . goods in substitution for those due from the seller, . . . [that buyer] may recover from the seller as damages the difference between the cost of cover and the contract price. . . ." (§2712.) This gives the buyer the benefit of its bargain. What the buyer chooses to do with that bargain is not relevant to the determination of damages under section 2712.

. . .

DISPOSITION

The order of the trial court awarding prejudgment interest from 30 days before trial is reversed and the cause is remanded. The trial court is directed to enter a new order awarding buyer prejudgment interest from August 1, 1991. In all other respects, the judgment is affirmed. Costs on appeal to buyer.

PREMOL and ELIA, JJ., concur.

SALES CONTRACTS: THE UNIFORM COMMERCIAL CODE

§1-106. REMEDIES TO BE LIBERALLY ADMINISTERED

(1) The remedies provided by this Act shall be liberally administered to the end that the aggrieved party may be put in as good a position as if the other party had fully performed but neither consequential or special nor penal damages may be had except as specifically provided in this Act or by other rule of law. . . .

§2-712. "COVER"; BUYER's PROCUREMENT OF SUBSTITUTE GOODS

(1) After a breach within the preceding section the buyer may "cover" by making in good faith and without unreasonable delay any reasonable purchase of or contract to purchase goods in substitution for those due from the seller.

(2) The buyer may recover from the seller as damages the difference between the cost of cover and the contract price together with any incidental or consequential damages as hereinafter defined (Section 2-715), but less expenses saved in consequence of the seller's breach.

(3) Failure of the buyer to effect cover within this Section does not bar him from any other remedy.

§2-713. BUYER's DAMAGES FOR NON-DELIVERY — Hypothetical in a way OR REPUDIATION

(1) Subject to the provisions of this Article with respect to proof of market price (Section 2-723), the measure of damages for non-delivery or repudiation by the seller is the difference between the market price at the time when the buyer learned of the breach and the contract price together with any incidental and consequential damages provided in this Article (Section 2-715), but less expenses saved in consequence of the seller's breach.

(2) Market price is to be determined as of the place for tender or, in cases of rejection after arrival or revocation of acceptance, as of the place of arrival.

§2-715.   BUYER's INCIDENTAL AND CONSEQUENTIAL DAMAGES

(1) Incidental damages resulting from the seller's breach include expenses reasonably incurred in inspection, receipt, transportation and care and custody of goods rightfully rejected, any commercially reasonable charges, expenses or commissions in connection with effecting cover and any other reasonable expense incident to the delay or other breach.

(2) Consequential damages resulting from the seller's breach include

(a) any loss resulting from general or particular requirements and needs of which the seller at the time of contracting had reason to know and which could not reasonably be prevented by cover or otherwise; and

(b) injury to person or property proximately resulting from any breach of warranty.

§2-717.   DEDUCTION OF DAMAGES FROM THE PRICE

The buyer on notifying the seller of his intention to do so may deduct all or any part of the damages resulting from any breach of the contract from any part of the price still due under the same contract.

C.   THREE LIMITATIONS ON DAMAGES

While the expectancy interest provides the normal upper limit of contract damages, your analysis is not over when you have calculated this interest. You must then take into account several limitations in awarding the expectancy interest. We shall consider the three most common limitations: remoteness or foreseeability of harm, certainty of harm, and avoidability of harm. When these limitations on the expectancy apply, you may find that courts award damages measured by the reliance or restitution interests instead. When you read these materials, ask yourself why courts might have adopted these limitations on damage recoveries.

REFERENCE: Barnett, §2.4
               Farnsworth, §12.8

1.   Remoteness or Foreseeability of Harm

STUDY GUIDE: In Chapter 7 we shall study some of the legal rules governing problems that arise when persons manifest their assent through an agent. In addition to reading the next case to discern its famous rule(s) limiting contract damages, consider how the agency problem bears on the circumstances that arose here and may have influenced the legal rule decided upon.

HADLEY v. BAXENDALE
In the Court of Exchequer,
9 Ex. 341, 156 Eng. Rep. 145 (1854)

[handwritten margin note: ? Traveling Courts]

. . . At the trial before CROMPTON, J., at the last Gloucester Assizes, it appeared that the plaintiffs carried on an extensive business as millers at Gloucester; and that, on the 11th of May, their mill was stopped by a breakage of the crank shaft by which the mill was worked. The steam-engine was manufactured by Messrs. Joyce & Co., the engineers, at Greenwich, and it became necessary to send the shaft as a pattern for a new one to Greenwich. The fracture was discovered on the 12th, and on the 13th the plaintiffs sent one of their servants to the office of the defendants, who are the well-known carriers trading under the name of Pickford & Co., for the purpose of having the shaft carried to Greenwich. The plaintiffs' servant told the clerk that the mill was stopped, and that the shaft must be sent immediately and in answer to the inquiry when the shaft would be taken, the answer was, that if it was sent up by twelve o'clock any day, it would be delivered at Greenwich on the following day. On the following day the shaft was taken by the defendants, before noon, for the purpose of being conveyed to Greenwich, and the sum of £2. 4s. was paid for its carriage for the whole distance; at the same time the defendants' clerk was told that a special entry, if required, should be made to hasten its delivery. The delivery of the shaft at Greenwich was delayed by some neglect; and the consequence was, that the plaintiffs did not receive the new shaft for several days after they would otherwise have done, and the working of their mill was thereby delayed, and they thereby lost the profits they would otherwise have received.

[In their pleadings, plaintiffs had claimed (a) that defendants promised to deliver the shaft by the next day and failed to do so and (b) that defendants assumed a duty of care to deliver the shaft promptly and breached that duty. They claimed damages in the amount of £300 for lost business and for wages paid to their idle employees. Defendants denied making the promise and tendered £25 to the court in satisfaction of any liability for their negligence. In response, the plaintiffs entered a *nolle prosequi* as to the first count; and as to the second, replied that the sum paid into the court was insufficient to satisfy their claim.]

[handwritten margin note: ? Breach resulted ~ loss of profit which it did]

On the part of the defendants, it was objected that these damages were too remote, and that the defendants were not liable with respect to them. The learned Judge left the case generally to the jury, who found a verdict with £25 damages beyond the amount paid into Court.

Whateley [Barrister for the Defendant] . . . obtained a rule nisi for a new trial, on the ground of misdirection.

Keating and Dowdeswell [Barrister for the Plaintiffs] . . . shewed cause. The plaintiffs are entitled to the amount awarded by the jury as damages. These damages are not too remote, for they are not only the natural and necessary consequence of the defendants' default, but they are the only loss which the plaintiffs have actually sustained. The principle upon which damages are assessed is found upon that of rendering compensation to the injured party. This important subject is ably treated in Sedgwick on the Measure of Damages. And this particular branch of it is discussed in the third chapter, where . . . he says, "It is sometimes said, in regard to contracts that the defendant shall be held liable for those damages only which both parties may fairly be supposed to have at the time contemplated as likely to result from the nature of the agreement, and this appears to be the rule adopted by the writers upon the civil law." In a subsequent passage he says, "In cases of fraud the civil law made a broad distinction"; and he adds, that "in such cases the debtor was liable for all the consequences." It is difficult, however, to see what the ground of such principle is, and how the ingredient of fraud can affect the question. For instance, if the defendants had maliciously and fraudulently kept the shaft, it is not easy to see why they should have been liable for these damages, if they are not to be held so where the delay is occasioned by their negligence only. . . .

[PARKE, B.[11] The sensible rule appears to be that which has been laid down in France, and which is declared in their code . . . and which is thus translated in *Sedgwick*: "The damages due the creditor consist in general of the loss that he has sustained, and the profit which he has been prevented from acquiring, subject to the modifications hereinafter contained. The debtor is only liable for the damages foreseen, or which might have been foreseen, at the time of the execution of the contract, when it is not owing to his fraud that the agreement has been violated. . . ."] If that rule is to be adopted, there was ample evidence in the present case of the defendant's knowledge of such a state of things as would necessarily result in the damage the plaintiffs suffered through the defendant's default. The authorities are in the plaintiffs' favour upon the general ground. In Nurse v. Barns (1 Sir T. Raym. 77), which was an action for the breach of an agreement for the letting of certain iron mills, the plaintiff was entitled to a sum of 500*l.*, awarded by reason of loss of stock laid in, although he had only paid 10*l.* by way of consideration. . . . The recent decision of this Court, in Waters v. Towers (8 Ex. 401), seems to be strongly in the plaintiffs' favour. The defendants there had agreed to fit up the plaintiffs' mill within a reasonable time, but had not completed their contract within such time; and it was held that the plaintiffs were entitled to recover, by way of damages, the loss of profit upon a contract they had entered into with third parties, and which they were unable to fulfil by reason of the defendants' breach of contract. [Parke, B. The defendants there must of necessity have known that the consequence of their not completing their contract would be to stop the working of the mill. But how could the defendants here know that any such result would follow?] There was ample evidence that the defendants knew the purpose for which this shaft was sent, and that the result of its non-delivery in due time would be the stoppage of the mill; for the defendants' agent, at their place of business, was told that the mill was then stopped, that the shaft must be delivered immediately, and that if a special entry was necessary to hasten its delivery, such an entry should be made. The defendants must, therefore, be held to have contemplated at the time what in fact did follow, as the necessary and natural result of their wrongful act. . . .

11. [Baron Parke was one of the judges, interposing a question to counsel. Such questions appear in brackets in old English law reports. — EDS.]

Whateley, Willes, and Phipson, in support of the rule . . . It has been contended, on the part of the plaintiffs, that the damages found by the jury are a matter fit for their consideration; but still the question remains, in what way ought the jury to have been directed? It has been also urged, that, in awarding damages, the law give compensation to the injured individual. But it is clear that complete compensation is not to be awarded. . . . Take the case of the breach of a contract to supply a rick-cloth, whereby and in consequence of bad weather the hay, being unprotected, is spoiled, that damage could not be recoverable. . . . Sedgwick says, "In regard to the quantum of damages, instead of adhering to the term compensation, it would be far more accurate to say . . . 'that the object is to discriminate between that portion of the loss which must be borne by the offending party and that which must be borne by the sufferer.' The law in fact aims not at the satisfaction but at a division of the loss." . . . Several of the cases which were principally relied upon by the plaintiffs are distinguishable. In Waters v. Towers ([8] Exch. 401) there was a special contract to do the work in a particular time, and the damage occasioned by the non-completion of the contract was that to which the plaintiffs were held to be entitled. . . .

ALDERSON, B.* We think that there ought to be a new trial in this case; but, in so doing, we deem it to be expedient and necessary to state explicitly the rule which the Judge, at the next trial, ought, in our opinion, to direct the jury to be governed by when they estimate the damages.

It is, indeed, of the last importance that we should do this; for, if the jury are left without any definite rule to guide them, it will, in such cases as these, manifestly lead to the greatest injustice. . . .

Now we think the proper rule in such a case as the present is this: — Where two parties have made a contract which one of them has broken, the damages which the other party ought to receive in respect of such breach of contract should be such as may fairly and reasonably be considered either arising naturally, i.e., according to the usual course of things, from such breach of contract itself, or such as may reasonably be supposed to have been in the contemplation of both parties, at the time they made the contract, as the probable result of the breach of it. Now, if the special circumstances under which the contract was actually made were communicated by the plaintiffs to the defendants, and thus known to both parties, the damages resulting from the breach of such a contract, which they would reasonably contemplate, would be the amount of injury which would ordinarily follow from a breach of contract under these special circumstances so known and communicated. But, on the other hand, if these special circumstances were wholly unknown to the party breaking the contract, he, at the most, could only be supposed to have had in his contemplation the amount of injury which would arise generally, and in the great multitude of cases

* *Sir Edward Hall Alderson* (1787-1857) was educated at the Charterhouse and Caius College (Cambridge). He was admitted to the bar in 1811, and entered a legal practice that lasted until 1830; during part of that period, he was also reporter to the King's Bench (1817-1822). In 1830, Alderson was made judge in the Court of Common Pleas; four years later, he was transferred to the Court of Exchequer, where he remained until his death. — [This biography was written by Professor Curtis Reitz, "C.R." hereinafter, who innovated the idea of judicial biographies in his casebook. — EDS.]

not affected by any special circumstances, from such a breach of contract. For, had the special circumstances been known, the parties might have specially provided for the breach of contract by special terms as to the damages in that case; and of this advantage it would be very unjust to deprive them. . . . Now, in the present case, if we are to apply the principles above laid down, we find that the only circumstances here communicated by the plaintiffs to the defendants at the time the contract was made, were, that the article to be carried was the broken shaft of a mill, and that the plaintiffs were the millers of that mill. But how do these circumstances shew reasonably that the profits of the mill must be stopped by an unreasonable delay in the delivery of the broken shaft by the carrier to the third person? Suppose the plaintiffs had another shaft in their possession put up or putting up at the time, and that they only wished to send back the broken shaft to the engineer who made it; it is clear that this would be quite consistent with the above circumstances, and yet the unreasonable delay in the delivery would have no effect upon the intermediate profits of the mill. Or, again, suppose that, at the time of the delivery to the carrier, the machinery of the mill had been in other respects defective, then, also, the same results would follow. Here it is true that the shaft was actually sent back to serve as a model for a new one, and that the want of a new one was the only cause of the stoppage of the mill, and that the loss of profits really arose from not sending down the new shaft in proper time, and that this arose from the delay in delivering the broken one to serve as a model. But it is obvious that, in the great multitude of cases of millers sending off broken shafts to third persons by a carrier under ordinary circumstances, such consequences would not, in all probability, have occurred; and these special circumstances were here never communicated by the plaintiffs to the defendants. It follows, therefore, that the loss of profits here cannot reasonably be considered such a consequence of the breach of contract as could have been fairly and reasonably contemplated by both the parties when they made this contract. For such loss would neither have flowed naturally from the breach of this contract in the great multitude of such cases occurring under ordinary circumstances, nor were the special circumstances, which, perhaps, would have made it a reasonable and natural consequence of such breach of contract, communicated to or known by the defendants. The Judge ought, therefore, to have told the jury, that, upon the facts then before them, they ought not to take the loss of profits into consideration at all in estimating the damages. There must therefore be a new trial in this case.

Rule absolute.

REFERENCE: Barnett, xxi-xxii, §2.4.1
                  Farnsworth, §12.14
                  Calamari & Perillo, §14.5
                  Murray, §121(A)

Historical Background: Putting Hadley in Context

STUDY GUIDE: *In the following historical analysis, note how the growth of the law of contract damages was influenced by institutional considerations — particularly the efforts of judges to control juries and the small number of appellate judges in England at the time.*

RICHARD DANZIG, HADLEY v. BAXENDALE: A STUDY IN THE INDUSTRIALIZATION OF THE LAW, 4 J. LEG. STUD. 249 (1975):   Of the many thousands of students who graduate from American law schools every year, probably all save a few hundred are required to read the 1854 English Exchequer case of Hadley v. Baxendale. It is, indeed, one of a startlingly small number of opinions to which graduates from law school will almost assuredly have been exposed even if they attended different institutions, used a variety of textbooks, and opted for disparate electives. The exceptional pedagogical centrality of the case is further underscored by the similarly widespread attention the case receives in the curricula of all Commonwealth law schools.

But if the case is unusually widely read, it is typically narrowly studied. In the first-year law curriculum, where the opinion usually appears, cases are normally treated like doctrinal fruits on a conceptual tree: some bulk large, some are almost insignificant; some display a wondrous perfection of development, others are shown to be rotten at the core; some are further out along conceptual branches than others; but all are quite erroneously treated as though they blossomed at the same time, and for the same harvest.

This ahistorical view may have some didactic advantages, but it overlooks much that is important. Cases are of different vintages; they arise in different settings. It matters that Hadley v. Baxendale was decided in 1854 in England, and not in 1974 in California. Without reflecting on the ramifications of these facts of timing and setting, perhaps teachers and students can understand black letter law as it now is, but neither can comprehend the processes of doctrinal innovation, growth, and decay. . . .

To understand the origins and the limitations of the rule in Hadley v. Baxendale we must appreciate the industrial and legal world out of which it came and for which it was designed. In 1854 Great Britain was in a state of extraordinary flux. Between 1801 and 1851 its population rose from 10.6 to 20.9 million people and its gross national product increased from £10.7 to £523.3 million. By 1861 its population was 23.2 million and its GNP £668.0 million. Contemporaries saw the magnitude of this change and were aware of its impact on the law. As one writer, surveying the scene in 1863, put it:

> What our Law was then [in 1828], it is not now; and what it is now, can best be understood by seeing what it was, then. It is like the comparison between England under former, and present, systems of transit, for persons, property, and intelligence: between the days of lumbering wagons, stage coaches, and a creeping post — and of swift, luxurious railroads and lightening telegraphs. All is altered: material, inducing corresponding moral and social changes.[12]

---

12. S. Warren, A Popular and Practical Introduction to Law Studies 12 (3d ed. 1863).

Arising squarely in the middle of the "industrial revolution" and directly in the midst of the "Great Boom" of 1842-1874, Hadley v. Baxendale was a product of these times. The case was shaped by the increasing sophistication of the economy and the law — and equally significantly by the gaps, the naiveté, and the crudeness of the contemporary system. . . .

[W]hat of the legal system which had to deal with that transition? This system was also modernizing, but, at the time of Hadley v. Baxendale, it was still strikingly underdeveloped. The case itself indicates the rudimentary and uneven development of the commercial law of the period. Hadley v. Baxendale is frequently described as a case involving a claim for damages consequent on a breach of a negotiated contract for especially quick delivery of a consigned package; but in fact, although this was the first of two counts on which the Hadleys initially pressed their suit, both the official and the contemporary press reports make it clear that before going to trial against Baxendale they abandoned all claim to damages based on a specific contract. Instead their pleadings claimed damages arising as a consequence of Pickford's failure to effect delivery "within a reasonable time" as it was obliged to do because of its status as a common carrier. If, as Maine posited ten years after Hadley v. Baxendale, the process of modernization involves a movement from status to contract, this most famed of modern contract cases is peculiarly antiquarian!

The pleadings' emphasis on status rather than contract appears to have been related to the underdeveloped nature of the law of agency in England at the time. The Gloucester Journal report of the Assize trial comments:

> The declaration had originally contained two counts; the first charging the defendants with having contracted to deliver the crank within the space of two days, which they did in truth do, but there was a doubt how far Mr. Perrett, the agent of the defendants, had authority to bind them by any special contract which would vary their ordinary liability. It was therefore thought not prudent to proceed upon that count, but upon the count of not delivering within a reasonable time.[13]

The Hadleys' counsel apparently reasoned that a jury verdict against Baxendale predicated on what was said to or by the Pickfords' clerk might be upset by an appellate court on a theory that personal liability could not be imputed to Baxendale through comment to or by an agent. The situation was summarized by Baxendale's counsel in the argument on appeal:

> Here the declaration is founded upon the defendants' duty as common carriers, and indeed there is no pretense for saying that they entered into a special contract to bear all the consequences of the non-delivery of the article in question. They were merely bound to carry it safely, and to deliver it within a reasonable time. The duty of the clerk, who was in attendance at the defendants' office, was to enter the article, and to take the amount of the carriage; but a mere notice to him, such as was here given, could not make the defendants, as carriers, liable as upon a special contract. Such matters, therefore, must be rejected from the consideration of the question.[14]

13. Gloucester Journal, Supplement August 13, 1853, at 1, col. 3.
14. 9 Ex. 341, 352, 156 Eng. Rep. 145, 150 (1854).

Baxendale's counsel here overstates the case, but at the least it appears that there was an uncertainty in the rudimentary law of agency as it existed at the time.

This uncertainty may explain Baron Alderson's surprising assertion that the Hadleys failed to serve notice that the mill operations were dependent on the quick return of the shaft. It may be that as a factual matter the Hadleys never served notice on the Pickfords' clerk of their extreme dependence on the shaft, and that the Court reporter simply erred in asserting that notice had been served to this effect.[15]

But it is also possible that Baron Alderson saw the case as the Pickfords' counsel urged: ". . . a mere notice . . . was here given . . . [but it] could not make the defendants liable . . . [and therefore it was to] be rejected from the consideration of the question."

This agency problem underscores the fact that the case is Hadley v. Baxendale, not Hadley v. Pickford's Moving Co.; in other words, that the opinion was handed down at a time and in a situation in which principals were personally liable for the misfeasance of their companies. Although the principle of limited liability was already recognized in England for exceptional "chartered" companies, it was not until 1855 that Parliament extended the right to ordinary entrepreneurs, and it was not until 1901 that Pickfords (and many other companies) incorporated. In 1854 the desirability of limiting personal liability for corporate debts was a major item of parliamentary debate and the legal world's most hotly disputed subject.

15. Lord Asquith took this position ("the headnote is definitely misleading") in Victoria Laundry v. Newman Indus. Ltd., 2 K.B. 528, 537 (1949). The best available account of the Assize trial supports this view. It reports the Hadleys' counsel as saying only:

> On the morning of the 12th of May, it was discovered that the shaft of the steam-mill was broken, rendering it necessary to forward it to Messrs. Joyce. . . . A clerk of the plaintiffs was therefore dispatched on Friday, the 13th of May, to the office of Messrs. Pickford and Co., where he saw their agent, Mr. Perrett, to whom he stated what had occurred and that the plaintiffs were anxious that the crank should be delivered to Messrs. Joyce and Co. as soon as possible. . . . The shaft was not [promptly] received by Messrs. Joyce. Meanwhile the mills of the plaintiff were stopped.

Gloucester Journal, supra note [13], at 1, col. 3. A contemporary newspaper report of the Exchequer proceedings, moreover, paraphrases Baxendale's counsel as saying, "there was no special contract, and the defendants had no knowledge of the inconvenience to which the plaintiff was subject by the delay." 7 Cty. Cts. Chron. 133 (June 1854). On the other hand, two remarks in the course of argument strongly suggest that notice of the stoppage was in fact given to Pickfords' clerk. Baron Parke attempted to distinguish Waters v. Towers, [8 Ex. 401, 155 Eng. Rep. 1404 (1853)], by saying that "[t]he defendants there must of necessity have known that the consequence of their not completing their contract would be to stop the working of the mill. But how could the defendants here know that any such result would follow?" 9 Ex. 341, 349, 156 Eng. Rep. 145, 149 (1854). To this the Hadleys' counsel is reported as having answered flatly: "There was ample evidence that the defendants knew the purpose for which this shaft was sent, and that the result of its non-delivery in due time would be the stoppage of the mill; for the defendants' agent, at their place of business, was told that the mill was then stopped, that the shaft must be delivered immediately, and that if a special entry was necessary to hasten its delivery, such an entry should be made." Ibid. The comment of Baxendale's counsel (which I have quoted in the text accompanying note [14] supra) is even more striking. The argument is that "a mere notice [to the clerk], *such as was here given*, could not make the defendants, as carriers, liable as upon a special contract. Such matters, therefore, must be rejected from the consideration of the question." 9 Ex. 341, 352, 156 Eng. Rep. 145, 150 (1854) (emphasis added).

This contemporary ferment was fed by, and in turn reinforced, related areas of concern about the run of liability: A Royal Commission was meeting in 1854 to consider expanding the right to petition for bankruptcy; the right to limit liability for torts by means of a prior contract was being pondered in the courts; and the alleged right of common carriers to limit liability for property loss by mere prior notification was being keenly debated.

Under these conditions the concept of a severe restriction on the scope of damages in contract actions must have seemed both less alien than it would have appeared to a judge a decade earlier, and more important than it would have seemed to a judge a decade later. For in 1854 judges were, at one and the same time, confronted with a growing acceptance of the idea of limited liability and yet with a situation of unlimited personal liability for commercial misfeasance. This was a time, moreover, when commercial interactions involved increasing agglomerations of capital and a pyramiding and interlocking of transactions, so that any error might lead to damages that could significantly diminish annual profits[16] or even destroy the personal fortunes of those sharing in thinly financed ventures. . . .

Other more comprehensive studies of Victorian judges and legislators will have to explore this tension between Parliamentary and judicial dispositions toward the entrepreneur,[17] and particularly the common carrier, but insofar as a case study can shed any light on the matter, it is worth noting that the predisposition of this panel seems clear. Two of the three Exchequer judges were tied to Pickfords in contexts likely to make them sympathetic to the company. Baron Martin had represented Pickfords before ascending to the bench, and Baron Parke's brother had been the managing director of the company before Baxendale.[18]

The opinion in Hadley v. Baxendale is written in general terms and has had a broad impact on the law of contracts for 120 years. But at the time of its conception it was probably seen and shaped by its authors in the context of uncertainties about the law of agency and conflicts about the shape of the

16. Pickfords' profits during the period 1853-1857 have been estimated at £21,954 per year. . . . By this calculus, the Hadley damage claim of £300 would alone absorb 1.5% of those profits. . . .

17. The interaction of Parliamentary and judicial lawmaking becomes of particular interest in this period, as the propensity for legislation rose dramatically. See generally Alan Harding, [A Social History of English Law (1966)], especially at 355, quoting Pollock: "Our modern law of real property is simply founded on judicial evasions of Acts of Parliament." I do not mean to imply by this discussion that one can simplistically say that the courts were sympathetic to the nationwide entrepreneur and Parliament antithetic to him. This dichotomy is blurred, for example, by evidence that in 1847, 178 M.P.s were directors of railway companies, P. Mathias, [The First Industrial Nation (1969)], at 282, and by Laski's observation (cited in Cornish, [untitled, unpublished manuscript]), that between 1832 and 1906 57% of the judges appointed had been M.P.s.

18. See Evidence of Joseph Baxendale, Select Committee on Railroads, Gt. Brit., Parl. Papers, H.C. 1844, Vol. XI, at 249, Q. 3402, remarking that his predecessor as manager was "the brother of Mr. Baron Parke, Major Parke." That this web of relationships seems to have been not uncommon or thought improper at the time provides yet another indication of the distance between this period and our own age. The idea of impersonalization of business relationships, which the "rule" of this case both reflected and encouraged, had not yet been applied, it appears, to relations between those on the bench and those before them. These personal involvements may go some way, it should be noted, to explaining Baron Alderson's activism in asserting what he took to be common practice when mill shafts were shipped.

law of liability — particularly common carriers' liability — which are now generally forgotten.

An understanding of the relationship of the rule in Hadley v. Baxendale to the contemporary law affecting common carriers may be a predicate to comprehending the impulse behind the rule and its form, but standing alone it tells only a part of the story. I think the rule in Hadley v. Baxendale may have had its most significant contemporary effects not for the entrepreneurs powering a modernizing economy, but rather for the judges caught up in their own problems of modernization.

By the middle of the nineteenth century Parliament had acted to modernize the judicial system in a number of important ways. Successive law revision commissions and ensuing enactments had effected changes in the substantive laws of tort, debt, criminal law and, as we have seen, contractual liability. Antiquated aspects of pleading and procedure were similarly remodeled. But the size and case disposition capacity of the common law courts remained remarkably stagnant. . . .

In 1854 it must have been apparent to the fifteen judges who composed the national judicial system that they had no hope of reviewing half a million cases or even that fraction of them which dealt with genuinely contested issues. Moreover the relatively small stakes involved in County Court cases left all but a miniscule proportion of litigants disinclined to incur the costs of appeal.[19] Under these conditions it is not surprising that *ad hoc* review gave way to attempts at a crystallized delineation of instructions for dispute resolution which more closely resembled legislation than they did prior common law adjudication.

In its centralization of control, the judicial invention here examined paralleled the industrial developments of the age. The importance of the centralization of control is particularly evident when the rule is put back into the context in which it was promulgated: in terms of judges' control over juries. . . . The tension inherent in the conflict of perspectives between the two decision-making centers — local juries and appellate judges — is underscored when one focuses on the particular decision-makers in this case. . . . If life in the mid-nineteenth century was anything like life in our times, the jury members, themselves local merchants who must have suffered frustration or injury from the then frequent occurrence of carrier error, probably sympathized much more readily with the Hadleys than with Baxendale. . . . Under these conditions the invention of the case must have seemed particularly appealing to its promulgators. It led not simply to a resolution of this case for Baxendale, but also, more generally, to a rule of procedure and review which shifted power from more parochial to more cosmopolitan decision-makers. As Baron Alderson put the matter, "we deem it to be expedient and necessary to state explicitly the rule which . . . the jury [ought] to be governed by . . . for if the jury are left

---

19. Extant County Court Returns show a total of only 142 appeals for the years 1850-1855, and 55 of these were dropped before they were decided. Returns, County Courts 4 (1856, L). [S.]. Warren, [A Popular and Practical Introduction to Law Studies (3d ed. 1863)] at 46, reports that there were only 20 appeals generated from 744,652 county court complaints filed in 1857.

without any definite rule to guide them, it will, in such cases as these, manifestly lead to the greatest injustice."[20]

From a less personal perspective the invention also effected a modernization by enhancing efficiency as a result of taking matters out of the hands of the jurors. Whatever its other characteristics, jury justice is hand-crafted justice. Each case is mulled on an *ad hoc* basis with reference to little more than, as Chitty put it, "the circumstances of the case."[21] In an age of rapidly increasing numbers of transactions and amounts of litigation, a hand-crafted system of justice had as little durability as the hand-crafted system of tool production on which the Hadleys relied for their mill parts. By moving matters from a special jury — which cost £24, untold time to assemble, and a half hour to decide — to a judge, the rule in Hadley v. Baxendale facilitated the production of the judicial product.[22] And by standardizing the rule which a judge employed, the decision compounded the gain — a point of particular importance in relation to the County Courts where juries were rarely called.

Thus, the judicial advantages of Hadley v. Baxendale can be summarized: after the opinion the outcome of a claim for damages for breach of contract could be more readily predicted (and would therefore be less often litigated) than before; when litigated the more appropriate court could more often be chosen; the costs and biases of a jury could more often be avoided; and County Court judges and juries alike could be more readily confined in the exercise of their discretion. Clearly the rule invented in the case offered substantial rewards to the judges who promulgated it and in later years reaffirmed it. . . .

How does an opinion whose primary functions seem to correlate with a quarrel over an 1830 transport act and with the needs of a judicial system in the 1850s come to be viewed as "a fixed star in the jurisprudential firmament" 120 years later?[23]

The fame and widespread acceptance of the innovation effected by this case seems particularly remarkable when we remember that this was a decision of one of three equal intermediate courts. Other Exchequer opinions were vulnerable to rejection or recasting by Queens Bench and Common Pleas judges sitting either in their appellate capacity as the Exchequer Chamber, or within their own systems as Assize and nisi prius judges. Why did this case escape overruling and anonymity? The theme of invention suggests an answer. For an invention to be widely employed it must not only fill a need and be well fabricated; it must also be marketed. In mid-nineteenth century England it was perhaps easier than ever before for a judge-created rule to take hold and influence other judges and lay conduct. Prompt press reporting of opinions and an expanding bar served to transmit at least the gist of commercial opinions to those likely to be affected by them. More important, an increasing professionalization of the system of

20. 9 Ex. 341, 353-54, 156 Eng. Rep. 145, 150 (1854).

21. J. Chitty, [A Practical Treatise on the Law of Contracts (4th ed. 1850)].

22. It is doubtful that the parties to the decision in Hadley v. Baxendale were insensitive to this phenomenon. In the early 1850s Sir James Shaw Willes and Baron Martin were principal members of the Common Law Commission, whose second report decried the inefficiencies associated with jury trial.

23. Grant Gilmore, The Death of Contract 49 (1974).

court reporting made the then common tactic of "doubting" the accuracy of an adverse reported opinion[24] more difficult, and thus enhanced the power of precedent.

There was another factor at play which has been lost sight of by modern observers. Sir James Shaw Willes . . . to whom I have ascribed much of the responsibility for the invention in the case, appears to have been remarkably situated to effect the marketing of the invention by virtue of his position as co-editor of the foremost legal textbook of the time: Smith's Leading Cases. Yet more remarkably — and this underscores the already mentioned intimacy of the mid-century British legal world — Willes' opposing counsel on appeal (and the counsel for the Hadleys at trial), Sir Henry Singer Keating, was the other editor of Smith's.

The two "editors" wasted no time in converting their litigation arguments into an academic analysis, so that a primary difference between the 1852 edition of Smith's Leading Cases and the 1856 edition was a lengthy description of and commentary on Hadley v. Baxendale. The impact of such notoriety cannot, of course, be precisely ascertained, but it seems fair to surmise that it was substantial. The breadth of Smith's readership and the respect with which it was regarded can be inferred in part from the frequency with which it is noted as referred to by judges in the official reports. Our rudimentary sources, moreover, show Smith's note on *Hadley* quoted by litigants in cases where the *Hadley* rule might apply and in public discussion of the rule.

Nor did Sir Henry and Sir James end their association with Hadley v. Baxendale upon enshrining the opinion in Smith's. Both culminated illustrious careers by elevation to the Superior Courts; and Sir James, in particular, in his capacity as an appellate judge had frequent occasion to endorse and expound on the opinion in Hadley v. Baxendale. Within a year of arguing for Baxendale he was one of three judges offering an opinion in the case in which the Court of Common Pleas accepted the Exchequer rule. Over the next decade Willes established himself as the outstanding commercial law judge of the latter half of the century. He then crafted the most significant nineteenth century opinion interpreting and endorsing Hadley v. Baxendale,[25] and followed it, four years later, with the next most often cited elaboration of the rule[26] — in this instance in an opinion reviewed and sustained by the Exchequer Chamber.[27]

In sum, Sir James was a central actor in the importation, spread and interpretation of the rule of Hadley v. Baxendale; and he contributed toward these ends as an academic, as a litigator and as an esteemed

---

24. The argument in Hadley v. Baxendale itself provides an example of this practice. When counsel for the Hadleys cited Borradaile v. Brunton, 8 Taunt. 535, 2 B. Moo. 582 (1818), the official reports record Baron Parke as remarking that "Sedgwick doubts the correctness of that report," and the report adds the footnoted observation that "the learned Judge has frequently observed of late that the 8th Taunton is of but doubtful authority, as the cases were not reported by Mr. Taunton himself." 9 Ex. 341 at 347, 156 Eng. Rep. 145, 148 (1854). (22 Law Times Reports 69 (1854) attributes the remark to Baron Alderson in the form: "I should very much doubt that case, both in law and in fact.")

25. British Columbia Saw-Mill v. Nettleship, 3 C.P. 449 (1868).

26. Horn v. Midland Rail Co., 7 C.P. 583 (1872).

27. Horn v. Midland Rail Co., 8 C.P. 131 (1873).

appellate judge. If the common law is thought to be some "brooding omni-presence" working itself pure, it obviously acquired some substantial human assistance in this instance.

STUDY GUIDE: *The next case concerns the meaning of "foreseeable" and when notice of "special" damages is required. How does the court distinguish the dragline that was delayed in shipment in this case from the crankshaft in* Hadley? *Why was notice of the consequences of delay in delivery required in* Hadley, *but not in this case? What does the court mean when it distinguishes between "one common law method for computing damages" and "the underlying common law rule of awarding reasonable compensation for foreseeable injury from a contract's breach"?*

HECTOR MARTINEZ AND CO. v. SOUTHERN PACIFIC TRANSPORTATION CO.
United States Court of Appeals, Fifth Circuit,
606 F.2d 106 (1979)

VANCE, C.J.:* Martinez appeals the trial court's dismissal of his claim . . . for losses resulting from delay and damage in transportation by carrier Southern Pacific. The district court granted Southern Pacific's motion under Rule 12(b)(6) to dismiss the claim, for delay damages. It held that such damages are special and Martinez failed to allege that the carrier had any notice of the possibility that such damages would accrue upon a breach of the contract between the parties. We reverse and remand for trial on the claim for some but not all of the damages sought.

Martinez's agent delivered a 2400 Lima Dragline,[28] Model 66, to the Penn Central Railroad, the origin carrier, on February 11, 1974, for

Robert S. Vance (1931-1989) was educated at the University of Alabama (B.S., J.D.) before serving two years in the Army with the Judge Advocate Corps (1952-1954) and eventually completing his education at George Washington University (LL.M.). During his years in practice in Birmingham, Alabama (1956-1977), Vance enlisted in the effort by a small group of Democrats to wrest control of the state Democratic Party from Gov. George C. Wallace and the segregationist forces that controlled it. He later served as chairman of the Alabama Democratic Party. In 1978, Vance was appointed by President Carter to the U.S. Court of Appeals, 5th Circuit (1978-1981). Judge Vance thereafter served on the U.S. Court of Appeals, 11th Circuit (newly formed from the 5th Circuit) until 1989, when he was killed and his wife seriously injured by a mail bomb delivered to his home. In 1991, Walter Leroy Moody, Jr. — a law school dropout who had appeared in Vance's courtroom several years before and had waged an obsessive battle over nearly two decades against the federal courts — was convicted on 71 counts, including threats to kill 17 judges and sending two other mail bombs that were intercepted at the 11th Circuit courthouse and the NAACP office in Jacksonville, Florida. — L.R.

28. [This is a large excavation machine used in surface mining to remove overburden (layers of rock and soil) covering a coal seam. The dragline casts a wire rope-hung bucket a considerable distance, collects the dug material by pulling the bucket toward itself on the ground with a second wire rope (or chain), elevates the bucket, and dumps the material on a spoil bank, in a hopper, or on a pile. The capacity of a dragline bucket can range from 50 to 100 cubic yards. Draglines are electrically powered and can run 24 hours a day. — EDS.]

shipment from New Philadelphia, Ohio to Eagle Pass, Texas. The dragline was loaded onto five separate railroad cars. A single uniform bill of lading, which described the dragline as "used strip mining machinery and parts," was issued by Penn Central, listing Martinez's agent in Eagle Pass as the consignee.

The last of the five cars, which were shipped separately, arrived in Eagle Pass on April 2, 1974. Martinez had to make reasonable repairs in the amount of $14,467.00 because the dragline was damaged in transit. These repairs were not completed until June 20, 1974. Martinez also alleges delay damages in the amount of $117,600.00 because the dragline could not be used from March 1, when he contends that the last of the cars should have arrived, until June 20. The claimed sum represents the dragline's fair rental value during this period.

After filing a claim as prescribed by the bill of lading, Martinez sued Southern Pacific, which as delivering carrier is liable for all recoverable damages. Martinez framed his original complaint to allege three separate claims. . . . First, Martinez sought recovery of the cost of repairing the damage to the dragline. Second, he sought the refund of certain demurrage or storage charges assessed by Southern Pacific and paid at the time of delivery. Third, Martinez sought compensation for wrongful deprivation of the dragline's use during the periods of delay in transit and of repair.

Martinez and Southern Pacific had already settled the first two of these claims, when Southern Pacific filed its Rule 12(b)(6) motion to dismiss the third claim for loss of use. Southern Pacific argues that, because such damages are special, they are not recoverable . . . absent notice of the possibility of such damages. The trial court denied this motion upon condition that Martinez amend his complaint to allege such notice. When Martinez refused, the district court granted Southern Pacific's motion under Rule 12(b)(6). This ruling, which had the effect of dismissing all that remained of Martinez's suit, is the basis of this appeal.

Martinez's delay claim involves two very different items. Lost use during the period of March 1 until April 2 resulted from a delay in transit. Lost use from April 2 until June 20 resulted from repair of the damaged goods. Neither the parties nor the district court have focused on the full import of this distinction. Martinez's claimed loss during repair is not severable from the physical damage to the dragline but is a part of the same legal claim. Thus Martinez necessarily settled his claim regarding damages for the repair period when he settled his first claim for damages to the dragline. The surviving issue is the appropriate measure of damages for the claimed loss resulting from Southern Pacific's unreasonable delay in transportation.

[W]e first examine the extent to which the innocent party actually has been injured by the alleged breach. This inquiry assists in determining how the innocent party can be restored to the position in which he would have been had the contract been fully performed. . . .

Normally, the remedy is an award of money damages to the aggrieved party as compensation for his economic injury.[29] This rule in effect protects the innocent party's expectation interest, giving him the "benefit of the

---

29. In some situations in which money damages cannot adequately compensate the innocent party, the court may order specific performance of the contract.

bargain."[30] Martinez's alleged injury in this case was deprivation of the dragline's use between March 1, when it should have been delivered, and April 2. Besides compensating the injured plaintiff, the common law also seeks to protect the defendant from unforeseeable large losses to the plaintiff.[31] This limitation makes good sense. An award of full compensation for all of the plaintiff's losses due to the breach, no matter how unforeseeable or bizarre these losses are, would simply be unfair to the defendant as well as possibly paralyzing to commerce.

We next assess the reasonable foreseeability of the plaintiff's actual injury at the time of entry into the contract here the bill of lading. Globe Refining Co. v. Landa Cotton Oil Co., 190 U.S. 540, 544, 23 S. Ct. 754, 47 L.Ed. 1171 (1903). . . . Our analysis on this point begins with Hadley v. Baxendale, 9 Ex. 341, 156 Eng. Rep. 145 (1854). There, mill operators were forced to close operations to ship a broken shaft for repairs, and the carrier negligently delayed shipment. The carrier, however, had not been informed of the situation at the mill. The court refused to award profits lost during the period of delay because such damages were not in the contemplation of the parties. The court articulated the rules, still almost universally followed,[32] Damage is foreseeable by the carrier if it is the proximate and usual consequence of the carrier's action. 11 Williston on Contracts, supra §1344, at 226. that general damages are awarded only if injury were foreseeable to a reasonable man and that special damages are awarded only if actual notice were given the carrier of the possibility of injury.[33]

Martinez asserts that his loss resulting from the delay in shipment was reasonably foreseeable when he entered the contract to transport his dragline. Hadley held that the damages arising from an inoperative mill were not foreseeable results of delayed shipment of a shaft, without specific notice. It was not obvious that the shaft in Hadley was an indispensable element of a mill. In the instant case, however, it was obvious that the dragline is a machine which of itself has a use value. Some cases after Hadley have suggested that the injury resulting from loss of a machine's use are not foreseeable results of delayed transport, because it is not a usual

30. Damages may be awarded for the expectation interest, the reliance interest, or the restitution interest of the aggrieved party. Fuller Perdue, The Reliance Interest in Contract Damages (pts. 1-2), 46 Yale L.J. 52, 373 (1936-1937); J. Calamari & J. Perillo, Contracts §205, at 328-29 (1970). If it is impossible to calculate a plaintiff's expectation interest, courts award damages to protect his reliance interest, to restore him to his position before the contract was entered. If reliance damages do not represent a fair measure of recovery, courts calculate damages on the basis of the restitution interest, to restore the benefit received from the plaintiff's performance.

31. In addition to the foreseeability limitation, damages may also be limited because of uncertainty . . . , or because of failure to mitigate damages. . . .

32. J. Calamari & J. Perillo, supra note 30, at 329. As Professor Gilmore admonished, Hadley "has meant all things to all men." G. Gilmore, The Death of Contract 50 (1974).

33. There are two tests for determining special damages. The more restrictive test requires proof both that notice was given of special circumstances and that the defendant impliedly or expressly assented to bearing the risk of these damages. Globe Refining Co. v. Landa Cotton Oil Co., 190 U.S. 540, 23 S. Ct. 754, 47 L. Ed. 1171 (1903). The more common test rejects the added showing of a tacit agreement for special damages. E.g., . . . U.C.C. §2-715, Comment 2.

consequence although it is a proximate consequence. See 11 Williston on Contracts, supra §1344, at 226-27. These decisions are unwarranted extensions of *Hadley* and employ arbitrary and inflexible definitions of foreseeability. Capital goods such as machinery have a use value, which may equal the rental value of the equipment or may be an interest value. The latter is ordinarily interest at the market rate on the value of the machine. It might be quite foreseeable that deprivation of the machine's use because of a carriage delay will cause a loss of rental value or interest value during the delay period.[34] See generally F. Kessler & G. Gilmore, Contracts 1042 (2d ed. 1970). We must not lose sight of the basic, common law rule, enunciated in *Hadley,* of damages for foreseeable loss. The amount of damages that was reasonably foreseeable involves a fact question that Martinez is entitled to present to a jury.

Southern Pacific replies that it was as foreseeable that the goods were to be sold as that they were to be used. This contention proves too much because *Hadley* allows recovery for harms that should have been foreseen. The general rule does not require the plaintiff to show that the actual harm suffered was the *most* foreseeable of possible harms. He need only demonstrate that his harm was not so remote as to make it unforeseeable to a reasonable man at the time of contracting. Even if the dragline were being shipped for sale it does not follow that delay in shipment would cause no recoverable loss.

Southern Pacific argues that, because only market value damages are foreseeable under common law, damages for lost rental value must be special and therefore require notice by Martinez. This argument confuses one common law method for computing damages with the underlying common law rule of awarding reasonable compensation for foreseeable injury from a contract's breach.

The common law employs a number of methods for computing damages recoverable for unreasonable delay in shipment. One of these is the market value test that measures damages by the diminution in the goods' value between the time of dispatch and the time of actual delivery. . . . That test, however, "is merely a method," and it "is not applied in cases where . . . another rule will better compute actual damages." Great Atlantic & Pacific Tea Co. v. Atchison, T. & Ste. F. Ry., 333 F.2d 705, 708 (7th Cir. 1964), *cert. denied,* 379 U.S. 967, 85 S. Ct. 661, 13 L. Ed. 2d 560 (1965). . . . Lost rental value is frequently an appropriate measure of damages from a delay in shipment of machinery.[35] . . . In deciding which

34. Unlike loss of use, Martinez would have had to plead notice had he sought to recover for a variety of damages that could not have been foreseeable here such as lost profits, the cost of idle labor hired to operate the dragline, the cost of idle equipment that had been rented to be used with the dragline, or the daily royalties Martinez was paying for the land on which he planned to run his dragline. . . . Thus Martinez may recover for lost use of the machine but not for the costs of the mining operations in which the machine was to be involved. Similarly, *Hadley* held that one cannot equate a shaft with the operation of an entire mill unless notice of the shaft's use had been given to the carrier. The result in *Hadley* might have been different had the plaintiff sought to recover solely for the loss of use of the shaft.

35. Diminution in market value is a proper measure of damages from a delay in carriage of food and other non-rentable goods. . . . However, this test is generally not as accurate a measure of injury from a delay in transport of capital goods, with an ascertainable

measure of damage to apply, courts look to the actual loss suffered by the plaintiff and the common law rule of compensating that loss.

> There is only one rule, of universal application, . . . and that is to give compensation for the loss suffered. Frequently, this ideal is found impossible of complete attainment; perhaps generally the market value rule is found to be the nearest approach to reaching the actual loss. But the market value rule is inapplicable when, on the facts, it is not the nearest practicable approach to an ascertainment of the actual loss. Each case must be governed by its own facts.

United States v. Palmer & Parker Co., 61 F.2d 455, 459 (1st Cir. 1932). . . .

Martinez has stated a claim for damages resulting from the delay in shipment. We reverse the district court's order of dismissal on this point, and remand for trial. We affirm, however, the district court's decision to dismiss Martinez's claim for damages resulting from the delay during repair.

RESTATEMENT (SECOND) OF CONTRACTS

§351. UNFORESEEABILITY AND RELATED LIMITATIONS ON DAMAGES

(1) Damages are not recoverable for loss that the party in breach did not have reason to foresee as a probable result of the breach when the contract was made.

(2) Loss may be foreseeable as a probable result of a breach because it follows from the breach

   (a) in the ordinary course of events, or
   (b) as a result of special circumstances, beyond the ordinary course of events, that the party in breach had reason to know.

(3) A court may limit damages for foreseeable loss by excluding recovery for loss of profits, by allowing recovery only for loss incurred in reliance, or otherwise if it concludes that in the circumstances justice so requires in order to avoid disproportionate compensation.

STUDY GUIDE: In a footnote [33] in the previous case, the court refers to a "more restrictive test" that "requires proof both that notice was given of special circumstances and that the defendant impliedly or expressly assented to bearing the risk of these damages." It also notes that this test has been rejected by most jurisdictions and by the U.C.C. The Official Comment to U.C.C. §2-715 (p. 68) — which governs the sale of goods in 49 states — says: "The 'tacit agreement' test for the recovery of consequential damages is rejected." Arkansas is one jurisdiction that employs the "more restrictive" tacit agreement test. Although the following

---

rental value for the machinery or interest value of the invested sum. Otherwise, a carrier could breach its contractual duties with impunity as long as the market value of the equipment did not drop, even though the shipper might lose a substantial use value or pay high installment purchase costs.

case does not involve the sale of goods, consider how it would have been decided if §2-715 had been applied. Why might the authors of the U.C.C. have rejected this approach? Does the concept of "default rules" illuminate this theoretical disagreement?

MORROW v. FIRST NATIONAL BANK
OF HOT SPRINGS
Supreme Court of Arkansas,
261 Ark. 568, 550 S.W. 429 (1977)

GEORGE ROSE SMITH, J.* For a number of years before 1971 the two plaintiffs, Morrow and Goslee, collected coins, individually and as partners. In 1971 a substantial part of the collection was kept at Morrow's home in Hot Springs. On September 4 of that year someone broke into the house and stole coins valued at $32,155.17. Almost three years later the plaintiffs brought this action against the defendant bank to recover the value of the stolen coins. The complaint alleges a breach of contract, in that the bank failed to notify the plaintiffs of the availability, on August 30, 1971, of safety-deposit boxes in a new bank building. This appeal is from a summary judgment in favor of the bank.

We state the facts most favorably to the plaintiffs. Morrow collected coins for many years. In about 1964 he had metal cabinets built in a closet in his house, so arranged that a burglar would have to go through eleven sets of locks to reach the coins. In about 1969, as insurance rates were becoming prohibitive, the two plaintiffs began to look for large safety-deposit boxes in which to keep their coins. No boxes were available in Hot Springs. From time to time Morrow discussed the problem with one or more employees of the defendant bank, where he was a regular customer.

In the summer of 1971 the bank was planning to move into its new building. Safety-deposit boxes were advertised. On June 25 the plaintiffs reserved three large boxes in the new building, paying $25 for each box. It was expected that the boxes would be available in from 30 to 60 days. Morrow explained his need for the boxes, adding that he particularly wanted them by September 1, when his husky teenage son would leave for college. The bank was perhaps on notice, through a loan application to a different department, that the coins were worth at least $12,000.

One or two employees of the bank promised to notify Morrow as soon as the boxes were available. The burglary occurred on the evening of Saturday, September 4, while Morrow and his wife were out to dinner. When Morrow inquired about the safety-deposit boxes on the following Tuesday, after Labor Day, he learned that the boxes had become available on August 30. An employee of the bank explained that "we just didn't have time" to

---

* *George Rose Smith* (1911-1992) was educated at Washington and Lee University and the University of Arkansas (LL.B.) and was admitted to the Arkansas bar in 1933. He practiced law privately at Little Rock and was an instructor at the University of Arkansas Law School (1935-1942, 1949-1955). In 1949, he became a member of the Arkansas Supreme Court. Smith was also a member of the U.S. Army Air Corps during World War II. — K.T.

notify Morrow that the boxes were ready. The plaintiffs immediately moved the rest of their coins into the safety-deposit boxes. We do not reach the bank's argument that the plaintiffs' acceptance of the rental contract was a waiver of their right to claim a breach.

We consider this case to be controlled by our holding in Hooks Smelting Co. v. Planters' Compress Co., 72 Ark. 275, 79 S.W. 1052 (1904). There we adopted what is now known as the "tacit agreement test" for the recovery of consequential damages for a breach of contract. By that test the plaintiff must prove more than the defendant's mere knowledge that a breach of contract will entail special damages to the plaintiff. It must also appear that the defendant at least tacitly agreed to assume responsibility. Justice Riddick's entire opinion in *Hooks* is enlightening, but we emphasize this particular language:

> It seems then that mere notice is not always sufficient to impose on the party who breaks a contract damages arising by reason of special circumstances, and the reason why this is so was referred to in a recent decision by the Supreme Court of the United States. In that case Mr. Justice Holmes, who delivered the opinion of the court, after remarking that one who makes a contract usually contemplates performance, not a breach, of his contract, said: "The extent of liability in such cases is likely to be within his contemplation, and whether it is or not, should be worked out on terms which it fairly may be presumed he would have assented to if they had been presented to his mind." Globe Refining Co. v. Landa Oil Co., 190 U.S. 540 [23 S. Ct. 754, 47 L. Ed. 1171].
>
> Now, where the damages arise from special circumstances, and are so large as to be out of proportion to the consideration agreed to be paid for the services to be rendered under the contract, it raises a doubt at once as to whether the party would have assented to such a liability had it been called to his attention at the making of the contract unless the consideration to be paid was also raised so as to correspond in some respect to the liability assumed. To make him liable for the special damages in such a case, there must not only be knowledge of the special circumstances, but such knowledge "must be brought home to the party sought to be charged under such circumstances that he must know that the person he contracts with reasonably believes that he accepts the contract with the special condition attached to it." In other words, where there is no express contract to pay such special damages, the facts and circumstances in proof must be such as to make it reasonable for the judge or jury trying the case to believe that the party at the time of the contract tacitly consented to be bound to more than ordinary damages in case of default on his part. . . .

In the case at bar there is no proof to support a finding that the bank, in return for box rentals of $75, agreed in effect to issue a burglary insurance policy to the plaintiffs in the amount of at least $32,155.17 and probably much more, as the actual loss was only partial. The bank's bare promise to notify the plaintiffs as soon as the boxes were available did not amount to a tacit agreement that the bank, for no consideration in addition to its regular rental for the boxes, would be liable for as much as $32,000 if the promised notice was not given.

The tacit agreement rule is a minority rule, but we think it to be sound. We did not lightly adopt it. To the contrary, we relied upon three textbooks and a number of decisions, including one written by Justice Holmes. This language from the *Hooks* opinion expresses what Holmes described as "common sense":

> Suppose, for instance, that a large manufacturing establishment is driven by power from a single engine, and that, by reason of an accident to some small but important part of the engine or machinery, it becomes necessary to stop the operation of the whole plant until a new part can be made or the old one repaired. If thereupon a blacksmith or machinist is called in, and, for the price of a few dollars, undertakes to make the repairs, but through some mistake or unskillfulness the part supplied by him should fail to fit, requiring it to be remade and entailing still further delay, would any court hold that the blacksmith or machinist could be held liable for all the damages entailed by the delay when they were large, in the absence of a contract on his part to be thus liable, unless the notice and the circumstances under which he made the contract were such that he ought reasonably to have known that in the event of his failure to perform his contract the other party would look to him to make good the loss?

The tacit agreement test, to be sure, has been questioned and was rejected by the draftsmen of the Uniform Commercial Code. . . . We do not attach great importance to the Commercial Code provision, simply because the legislature, in adopting a uniform act containing hundreds of sections, certainly did not specifically and consciously decide that the rule of the *Hooks* case should be changed in all situations. We adhere to that decision.

Alternatively, the plaintiffs argue that the bank's breach of its contract should be treated as a tort, for which liability may be imposed without regard to the tacit agreement test. As Prosser points out, a breach of contract is not treated as a tort if it consists merely of a failure to act (nonfeasance) as distinguished from an affirmatively wrongful act (misfeasance). . . .

Affirmed.

We agree. HARRIS, C.J., and HOLT and ROY, JJ.

REFERENCE: Barnett, §2.4.1
              Farnsworth, §12.14
              Calamari & Perillo, §14.5

2. Certainty of Harm

STUDY GUIDE: What measure of recovery was awarded in the following case? Consider what reasons might exist for denying the damages sought by the plaintiff. ["Jack" Dempsey, nicknamed the Manassa Mauler, was the undisputed heavyweight champion of the world from 1919 until he was beaten by Gene Tunney in Philadelphia on September 23, 1926, before a record crowd of 130,000. On September 22, 1927, in front of more than 102,000 spectators, he lost a rematch held in Chicago at Soldier Field, during which the famous "Long Count" in the seventh round saved Tunney from an apparent knockout. Tunney won in a ten-round decision.

Information about Harry Wills and the controversy surrounding the ill-fated match-up between him and Dempsey follows the case.]

CHICAGO COLISEUM CLUB v. DEMPSEY
Illinois Court of Appeals, First District,
265 Ill. App. 542 (1932)

MR. JUSTICE WILSON* delivered the opinion of the court.

Chicago Coliseum Club, a corporation, as plaintiff, brought its action against William Harrison Dempsey, known as Jack Dempsey, to recover damages for breach of a written contract executed March 13, 1926, but bearing date of March 6 of that year.

Plaintiff was incorporated as an Illinois corporation for the promotion of general pleasure and athletic purposes and to conduct boxing, sparring and wrestling matches and exhibitions for prizes or purses. The defendant William Harrison Dempsey was well known in the pugilistic world and, at the time of the making and execution of the contract in question, held the title of world's Champion Heavy Weight Boxer.

Under the terms of the written agreement, the plaintiff was to promote a public boxing exhibition in Chicago, or some suitable place to be selected by the promoter, and had engaged the services of one Harry Wills, another well known boxer and pugilist, to engage in [a] boxing match with the defendant Dempsey for the championship of the world. By the terms of the agreement Dempsey was to receive $10, receipt of which was acknowledged, and the plaintiff further agreed to pay to Dempsey the sum of $300,000 on the 5th day of August 1926, — $500,000 in cash at least 10 days before the date fixed for the contest, and a sum equal to 50 per cent of the net profits over and above the sum $2,000,000 in the event the gate receipts should exceed that amount. In addition the defendant was to receive 50 per cent of the net revenue derived from moving picture concessions or royalties received by the plaintiff, and defendant agreed to have his life and health insured in favor of the plaintiff in a manner and at a place to be designated by the plaintiff. Defendant further agreed not to engage in any boxing match after the date of the agreement and prior to the date on which the contest was to be held. Certain agreements previously entered into by the defendant with one Floyd Fitzsimmons for a Dempsey-Wills boxing match were declared to be void and of no force and effect. Certain

---

* Francis Servis Wilson (1872-1951), educated at Western Reserve Academy in Hudson, Ohio, and Western Reserve University (LL.B.), was admitted to the Ohio bar in 1896. He was nominated for judge of Probate Court, Mahoning County, in 1896, but removed to Chicago in 1897. For a number of years, he was a member of the firms Darrow, Masters & Wilson, and Felsenthal & Wilson, during which time he was nominated for judge of the Municipal Court of Chicago on an independent ticket (1906), and served as county attorney for Cook County (1911-1912). In 1920, Wilson began his judicial career as Circuit Court judge of Cook County. He was elevated to justice of the Appellate Court of Illinois in 1927, and served as that court's Presiding Justice from 1930 until 1935, when he was appointed justice of the Supreme Court of Illinois. He became Chief Justice in 1939, which he remained until his death. — K.T.

other mutual agreements were contained in the written contract which are not necessary in a consideration of this case.

March 6, 1926, the plaintiff entered into an agreement with Harry Wills, in which Wills agreed to engage in a boxing match with the Jack Dempsey named in the agreement hereinbefore referred to. Under this agreement the plaintiff, Chicago Coliseum Club, was to deposit $50,000 in escrow in the National City Bank of New York City, New York, to be paid over to Wills on the 10th day prior to the date fixed for the holding of the boxing contest. Further conditions were provided in said contract with Wills, which, however, are not necessary to set out in detail. There is no evidence in the record showing that the $50,000 was deposited nor that it has ever been paid, nor is there any evidence in the record showing the financial standing of the Chicago Coliseum Club, a corporation, plaintiff in this suit. This contract between the plaintiff and Wills appears to have been entered into several days before the contract with Dempsey.

March 8, 1926, the plaintiff entered into a contract with one Andrew C. Wcisberg, under which it appears that it was necessary for the plaintiff to have the services of an experienced person skilled in promoting boxing exhibitions and the said Weisberg was possessed of such qualifications and that it was necessary for the plaintiff to procure his help in the promoting of the exhibition. It appears further from the agreement that it was necessary to incur expenditures in the way of traveling expenses, legal services and other costs in and about the promotion of the boxing match, and Weisberg agreed to investigate, canvass and organize the various hotel associations and other business organizations for the purpose of securing accommodations for spectators and to procure subscriptions and contributions from such hotels and associations and others for the erection of an arena and other necessary expense in order to carry out the enterprise and to promote the boxing match in question. Under these agreements Weisberg was to furnish the funds for such purposes and was to be reimbursed out of the receipts from the sale of tickets for the expenses incurred by him, together with a certain amount for his services.

Both the Wills contract and the Weisberg contract are referred to at some length, inasmuch as claims for damages by plaintiff are predicated upon these two agreements. Under the terms of the contract between the plaintiff and Dempsey and the plaintiff and Wills, the contest was to be held during the month of September, 1926.

July 10, 1926, plaintiff wired Dempsey at Colorado Springs, Colorado, stating that representatives of life and accident insurance companies would call on him for the purpose of examining him for insurance in favor of the Chicago Coliseum Club, in accordance with the terms of his contract, and also requesting the defendant to begin training for the contest not later than August 1, 1926. In answer to this communication plaintiff received a telegram from Dempsey, as follows:

BM Colorado Springs Colo.   July 10th 1926
B.E. Clements

President Chicago Coliseum Club Chgo Entirely too busy training for my coming Tunney match to waste time on insurance representatives stop as you have <u>no contract</u> suggest you stop kidding yourself and me also Jack Dempsey.

Breach
and Repudiation

We are unable to conceive upon what theory the defendant could contend that there was no contract, as it appears to be admitted in the proceeding here and bears his signature and the amounts involved are sufficiently large to have created a rather lasting impression on the mind of anyone signing such an agreement. It amounts, however, to a repudiation of the agreement and from that time on Dempsey refused to take any steps to carry out his undertaking. It appears that Dempsey at this time was engaged in preparing himself for a contest with Tunney to be held at Philadelphia, Pennsylvania, sometime in September, and on August 3, 1926, plaintiff, as complainant, filed a bill in the superior court of Marion county, Indiana, asking to have Dempsey restrained and enjoined from engaging in the contest with Tunney, which complainant was informed and believed was to be held on the 16th day of September, and which contest would be in violation of the terms of the agreement entered into between the plaintiff and defendant at Los Angeles, March 13, 1926.

Why Indiana first

Personal service was had upon the defendant Dempsey in the proceeding in the Indiana court and on August 27, 1926, he entered his general appearance, by his attorneys, and filed his answer in said cause. September 13, 1926, a decree was entered in the superior court of <u>Marion county</u>, finding that the contract was a valid and subsisting contract between the parties, and that the complainant had expended large sums of money in carrying out the terms of the agreement, and entering a decree that Dempsey be perpetually restrained and enjoined from in any way, wise, or manner, training or preparing for or participating in any contracts or engagements in furtherance of any boxing match, prize fight or any exhibition of like nature, and particularly from engaging or entering into any boxing match with one Gene Tunney, or with any person other than the one designated by plaintiff.

It is insisted among other things that the costs incurred by the plaintiff in procuring the injunctional order in Marion county, Indiana, were properly chargeable against Dempsey for his breach of contract and recoverable in this proceeding. Under the evidence in the record in this proceeding there appears to have been a valid subsisting agreement between the plaintiff and Dempsey, in which Dempsey was to perform according to the terms of the agreement and which he refused to do, and the plaintiff, as a matter of law, was entitled at least to nominal damages. For this reason, if for no other, judgment should have been for the plaintiff.

During the proceeding in the circuit court of this county it was sought to introduce evidence for the purpose of showing damages, other than nominal damages, and in view of the fact that the case has to be retried, this court is asked to consider the various items of expense claimed to have been incurred and various offers of proof made to establish damages for breach of the agreement. Under the proof offered, the question of damages naturally divides itself into the four following propositions:

1st. Loss of profits which would have been derived by the plaintiff in the event of the holding of the contest in question;

2nd. Expenses incurred by the plaintiff prior to the signing of the agreement between the plaintiff and Dempsey;

3rd. Expenses incurred in attempting to restrain the defendant from engaging in other contests and to force him into a compliance with the terms of his agreement with the plaintiff; and

4th. Expenses incurred after the signing of the agreement and before the breach of July 10, 1926.

Proposition 1: Plaintiff offered to prove by one Mullins that a boxing exhibition between Dempsey and Wills held in the City of Chicago on September 22, 1926, would bring a gross receipt of $3,000,000, and that the expense incurred would be $1,400,000, leaving a net profit to the promoter of $1,600,000. The court properly sustained an objection to this testimony. The character of the undertaking was such that it would be impossible to produce evidence of a probative character sufficient to establish any amount which could be reasonably ascertainable by reason of the character of the undertaking. The profits from a boxing contest of this character, open to the public, is dependent upon so many different circumstances that they are not susceptible of definite legal determination. The success or failure of such an undertaking depends largely upon the ability of the promoters, the reputation of the contestants and the conditions of the weather at and prior to the holding of the contest, the accessibility of the place, the extent of the publicity, the possibility of other and counter attractions and many other questions which would enter into consideration. Such an entertainment lacks utterly the element of stability which exists in regular organized business. This fact was practically admitted by the plaintiff by the allegation of its bill filed in the Marion county court of Indiana asking for an injunction against Dempsey. Plaintiff in its bill in that proceeding charged, as follows:

> That by virtue of the premises aforesaid, the plaintiff will, unless it secures the injunctive relief herein prayed for, suffer great and irreparable injury and damages, not compensable by any action at law in damages, the damages being incapable of commensuration, and plaintiff, therefore, has no adequate remedy at law.

Compensation for damages for breach of contract must be established by evidence from which a court or jury are able to ascertain the extent of such damages by the usual rules of evidence and to a reasonable degree of certainty. We are of the opinion that the performance in question is not susceptible of proof sufficient to satisfy the requirements and the damages, if any, are purely speculative. . . .

Can't award damages you can't prove!

Proposition 2: Expenses incurred by the plaintiff prior to the signing of the agreement between the plaintiff and Dempsey.

The general rule is that in an action for a breach of contract a party can recover only on damages which naturally flow from and are the result of the act complained of. O'Conner v. Nolan, 64 III. App. 357.[36] The Wills contract was entered into prior to the contract with the defendant and was not made contingent upon the plaintiff's obtaining a similar agreement with the defendant Dempsey. Under the circumstances the plaintiff speculated as to the result of his efforts to procure the Dempsey contract. It may be argued that there had been negotiations pending between plaintiff and Dempsey which clearly indicated an agreement between them, but the agreement in fact was never consummated until sometime later. The action is based upon the written agreement which was entered into in Los Angeles. Any obliga-, tions assumed by the plaintiff prior to that time are not chargeable to the defendant. Moreover, an examination of the record discloses that the $50,000 named in the contract with Wills, which was to be payable upon a signing of the agreement, was not and never has been paid. There is no evidence in the record showing that the plaintiff is responsible financially, and, even though there were, we consider that it is not an element of damage which can be recovered for breach of the contract in question.

Proposition 3: Expenses incurred in attempting to restrain the defendant from engaging in other contests and to force him into a compliance with the terms of his agreement with the plaintiff.

After the repudiation of the agreement by the defendant, plaintiff was advised of defendant's match with Tunney which, from the evidence, it appears, was to take place in Philadelphia in the month of September and was in direct conflict with the terms of the agreement entered into between plaintiff and defendant. plaintiff's bill, filed in the superior court of Marion county, Indiana, was an effort on the part of the plaintiff to compel defendant to live up to the terms of his agreement. The chancellor in the Indiana court entered his decree, which apparently is in full force and effect, and the defendant in violating the terms of that decree, after personal service, is answerable to that court for a violation of the injunctional order entered in said proceeding. The expenses incurred, however, by the plaintiff in procuring that decree are not collectible in an action for damages in this proceeding; neither are such similar expenses as were incurred in the trips to Colorado and Philadelphia, nor the attorney's fees and other expenses thereby incurred. Cuyler Realty Co. v. Teneo Co., Inc., 188 N.Y.S. 340. The plaintiff having been informed that the defendant intended to proceed no further under his agreement, took such steps at its own financial risk. There was nothing in the agreement regarding attorney's fees and there was nothing in the contract in regard to the services of the defendant from which it would appear that the action for specific performance would lie. After the clear breach of contract by the defendant, the plaintiff proceeded with this character of litigation at its own risk. We are of the opinion that the trial court properly held that this was an element of damages which was not recoverable.

Proposition 4: Expenses incurred after the signing of the agreement and before the breach of July 10, 1926.

36. [*O'Conner* includes an extensive discussion of Hadley v. Baxendale, and the principle for which the *Chicago Coliseum* court cites *O'Conner* is adopted explicitly from *Hadley*. — EDS.]

After the signing of the agreement plaintiff attempted to show expenses incurred by one Weisberg in and about the furtherance of the project. Weisberg testified that he had taken an active part in promoting sports for a number of years and was in the employ of the Chicago Coliseum Club under a written contract during all of the time that his services were rendered in furtherance of this proposition. This contract was introduced in evidence and bore the date of March 8, 1926. Under its terms Weisberg was to be reimbursed out of the gate receipts and profits derived from the performance. His compensation depended entirely upon the success of the exhibition. Under his agreement with the plaintiff there was nothing to charge the plaintiff unconditionally with the costs and expenses of Weisberg's services. The court properly ruled against the admissibility of the evidence.

We find in the record, however, certain evidence which should have been submitted to the jury on the question of damages sustained by the plaintiff. The contract on which the breach of the action is predicated shows a payment of $10 by the plaintiff to the defendant and the receipt acknowledged. It appears that the stadium located in the South Park District, known as the Soldier's Field, was considered as a site for the holding of the contest and plaintiff testified that it paid $300 to an architect for plans in the event the stadium was to be used for the performance. This item of damage might have been made more specific and may not have been the best evidence in the case but, standing alone, it was sufficient to go to the jury. There were certain elements in regard to wages paid assistant secretaries which may be substantiated by evidence showing that they were necessary in furtherance of the undertaking. If these expenses were incurred they are recoverable if in furtherance of the general scheme. The defendant should not be required to answer in damages for salaries paid regular officials of the corporation who were presumed to be receiving such salaries by reason of their position, but special expenses incurred are recoverable. The expenses of Hoffman in going to Colorado for the purpose of having Dempsey take his physical examination for insurance, if before the breach and reasonable, are recoverable. The railroad fares for those who went to Los Angeles for the purpose of procuring the signing of the agreement are not recoverable as they were incurred in a furtherance of the procuring of the contract and not after the agreement was entered into. The services of Shank in looking after railroad facilities and making arrangements with the railroad for publicity and special trains and accommodations were items which should be considered and if it develops that they were incurred in a furtherance of the general plan and properly proven, are items for which the plaintiff should be reimbursed.

The items recoverable are such items of expense as were incurred between the date of the signing of the agreement and the breach of July 10, 1926, by the defendant and such as were incurred as a necessary expense in furtherance of the performance. Proof of such items should be made subject to the usual rules of evidence.

For the reasons stated in this opinion the judgment of the circuit court is reversed and the cause remanded for a new trial.

Judgment reversed and cause remanded.

Relational and Historical Background: Why Didn't Dempsey Fight Wills? The Role of Race

Great controversy surrounds the failure of Jack Dempsey — the "Manassa Mauler" and then heavyweight champion of the world — to fight Harry Wills. Wills was one of the leading contenders for the crown, who was known as the "New Orleans Brown Panther" — a fighter whose "size was as impressive as his record; at six feet, four inches, and 220 pounds, he was a well-proportioned athlete who could box as well as punch."[37] Most of the speculation concerns the fact that Dempsey was white and Wills was black. Dempsey vehemently denied that race deterred him from fighting Wills or that he ducked him at all. In his later years, when asked by a reporter whether he and his manager, Jack Kearns, had deliberately avoided Wills, he replied:

> You know that is false. You were with Kearns, Bob Edgren, Vincent Treanor, Jimmy Dawson of the *New York Times*, and me in the office of [fight promoter Tex] Rickard at the time he had arranged to stage the fight [with Wills] in Jersey City, when Tex, after a dispute with Mullins, Wills' manager, turned to Kearns and said, "The fight cannot be held in Jersey City. I just spoke with Frank Hague, the Democratic boss of Jersey City, and he told me the governor won't stand for it. I'm now going to get another opponent for an outdoor show. We'll forget Wills."
>
> That's the true reason why I never fought Wills. To stop Mullins from complaining and to stop unwarranted attacks against me by the press. I had accepted the proposition of Floyd Fitzsimmons to fight Wills in Michigan but when the time came for Floyd to put up the money, he said he gave Mullins $50,000 for Wills' share and couldn't raise any more. That's why the fight never took place.[38]

The fight at issue in *Chicago Coliseum* was promoted by Floyd Fitzsimmons, and Wills was to receive $50,000, so it is possible that years later Dempsey was simply mistaken in his recollection about the proposed location of the match. But there appears to have been multiple contracts between Dempsey and promoters of a Dempsey-Wills match. In a statement released to the press in August 1926, Dempsey stated:

> In September of last year I signed papers in Niles, Mich., for a Wills bout, but it fell through because the promoters could not put up the initial $125,000 that was to be paid me on signing the contract. Incidentally I got for Wills $55,000 cash at that time which he has never turned back to the promoters. I did not get a red cent myself.
>
> In October at Huntington, W. Va., we again met only to see the match fall through because the would-be promoters could not put up the necessary $125,000.
>
> In March of this year at Los Angeles we went through the motions again and the initial and necessary payment, this time $100,000, was not forthcoming.[39]

---

37. Randy Roberts, Jack Dempsey: The Manassa Mauler (Baton Rouge, LA: Louisiana State University Press, 1979), p. 141.

38. Nat Fleischer, Jack Dempsey (New Rochelle, NY: Arlington House, 1972), p. 134.

39. Dempsey Publicly Challenges Wills, *New York Times*, August 19, 1926, p. 17.

March 1926 is when the contract in *Chicago Coliseum* was signed. A month after issuing this statement, the Indiana courts issued an injunction against him fighting Tunney in Pennsylvania, and Dempsey was quoted as saying: "The only contract I signed is the one I have in my possession, and this I regard as voided in view of the fact that I never received a penny from the promoters and they failed to live up to the money payments as provided in the contract."[40] Tex Rickard said: "There is no ground for holding Dempsey to a match with Wills. Dempsey some time since tried to collect on the deal and, failing to do so, tore up his contract."[41] In the *Chicago Coliseum* opinion, the court suggests that Wills too might not have been paid: "There is no evidence in the record showing that the $50,000 [for Wills] was deposited nor that it has ever been paid, nor is there any evidence in the record showing the financial standing of the Chicago Coliseum Club."

As to the issue of race, Dempsey years later said:

> I've been accused of discrimination against Wills because he was black. Any promoter who could or would have put up the money for my end of the purse could have had the fight. But no one came forth.
> If you recall, William Muldoon, a member of the boxing commission, called a meeting of the press and told reporters that while he definitely wanted a Wills-Dempsey match, so long as he was a member of the commission, there would be no heavyweight championship mixed match in New York. Yet he insisted that I sign for such a fight. How ridiculous![42]

Dempsey's last remark suggests that, even if he did not deliberately avoid a match with Wills — whether for racial or other reasons — race appeared to play a substantial role in preventing the fight.

> . . . Wills's fate was hampered by two shadows. First, he was black, and although in the 1920s blacks were permitted to fight for the title in lower divisions, they were not allowed to compete for the heavyweight crown. This situation was an heirloom of Wills second shadow: Jack Johnson. Every time a Wills-Dempsey bout was proposed, the image of the gold-toothed, smiling former champion surfaced in the minds of race-conscious promoters. All black heavyweights between 1908 and the mid-1930s were handicapped by the stigma of Jack Johnson. It became so difficult for a black to get a match with a good white fighter that the leading black boxers were forced to fight each other numerous times.[43]

The memory was not only of a black fighter considered by some whites to be swaggering and arrogant. It was also of the racial violence sparked by Johnson's successful defense, on July 4, 1910, of his championship against the retired and undefeated former champion, James J. Jeffries — a fight that had been both promoted and officiated by Tex Rickard.

---

40. Injunction Amuses Backers of Dempsey, *New York Times*, September 15, 1926, at 20.
41. Id.
42. Fleischer, supra note 38, at pp. 134-135.
43. Roberts, supra note 37, at 141.

Almost as soon as the gloves were cut off, a wave of interracial rioting and violence swept the country. In Little Rock two blacks were killed by whites; in Houston a white cut a black to death; in Roanoke six blacks attacked a white, and whites retaliated with a "lynching bee"; in Atlanta a black ran "amuck" with a knife; in Washington, D.C., two whites were fatally stabbed by blacks; in New York, one black was beaten to death and scores were injured; in Pueblo, Colorado, thirty people were killed by white assailants. Every section of the country experienced the racial violence and the Johnson-Jeffries fight was named as the catalyst. . . . Never before had a single event caused such widespread rioting. Not until the assassination of Martin Luther King would another event elicit a similar reaction.[44]

These events very nearly led to the legal prohibition of boxing.[45] Indeed the film of the fight was banned in many states and in most major cities.[46]

According to author Randy Roberts, "Dempsey was perfectly willing to fight Wills."[47] He had fought black fighters before.[48] "[B]ut there can be no doubt that after the fiasco of the Johnson-Jeffries bout, a match that Rickard promoted, the Madison Square Garden czar opposed interracial heavyweight title fights on principle. Rickard believed that to promote an interracial title bout was to tamper with the delicate balance of race relations in the United States."[49] In this he was greatly aided by William Muldoon, chairman of the New York State Athletic Commission, who, at least initially, imposed impossible conditions on any fight with the purpose of preventing any Dempsey-Wills bout.[50] Another author, Bruce Evansen, however, refers to "Dempsey's determination to draw the color line and his refusal to fight black champion Harry Wills."[51]

Even before he fought Tunney, Dempsey publicly denied this charge, though his lengthy and candid statement published in August 1926 also confirms the racial impediment to any Dempsey-Wills match:

> Since I won the championship in 1919 I wanted a bout with Wills. The powers that be in New York and the responsible promoters throughout the country do not want a heavyweight championship bout with a negro and they have carefully prevented it from taking place. The Jack Johnson mess killed fight pictures and nearly killed the game and the men who control the sport are scared to death of a repetition. Meanwhile I have had to be the goat and remain silent while I have been accused of running away from Wills.

44. Id. at 23-24.

45. Id. at 24-25.

46. See id. at 25.

47. Id. at 143.

48. In 1916, Dempsey fought black boxer John Lester Johnson at the Harlem Sporting Club. Although the ten-round bout ended in no decision, Johnson broke three of Dempsey's ribs. See id. at 30-31. See also Fleischer, supra note 38, at 133 ("Thereafter, there were many more Negroes on the list of his opponents.").

49. Id. at 143.

50. See id. at 144-148.

51. Bruce J. Evensen, When Jack Dempsey Fought Tunney: Heroes, Hokum, and Storytelling in the Jazz Age (Knoxville, TN: Univ. of Tennessee Press, 1996), p. 61. Evensen notes that, prior to this, the black community liked Dempsey because "he had beaten the man who had beaten Jack Johnson." Id.

Three years ago when I fought Firpo and Wills tried to tie up the boxing commission with an injunction the commission openly stated that no responsible promoter had come forward to stage a Wills bout. That was true then and has been true since.

The Boxing Commission in that case took the position that no one had come forward to promote a Wills bout. Yet they did not have the courage to say that it was because Wills was a Negro. . . . The commission did not want to antagonize the Negro race. Since then, however, in some unknown way, their hands have been called and they have tried to cover up and force me into a Wills bout with some such promoter as Tom O'Rourke. . . .

If any bull-dosing of the boxing authorities has induced Tex Richard to undertake the job of promoting a Wills bout, Tex knows he could have had my signature to any contract he wanted to write.

For the past year I have traveled thousands of miles and spent much time trying to book Wills for a fight. I have never drawn the color line. Wills was the only man I wanted. . . . Those who have tried to promote the Wills match have realized that every possible wire in opposition to it is being pulled to every reformer and publicity seeker in the country.

But that bout will take place if I am still the champion after the Tunney match. I refuse longer [sic] to remain silent and be the goat. I will fight Wills or I will know the reason why. I want every one that is interested to know that I am open for bids for a Wills bout to take place not later than Jan. 1, 1927, to take place anywhere in the United States or Mexico, except in the State of New York. If we cannot stage this fight in the United States then we will take it to Tia Juana.

For the benefit of Mr. Mullins and Mr. Wills, who have been such favorites with the boxing authorities of New York, my friend and manager Gene Normile, on my behalf has today deposited with Mr. Thomas J. Shaw, one of the best-known sportsmen in the country and who is now at the Saratoga track, $150,000 against which Mr. Wills and Mr. Mullins must deposit an equal amount, the winner to take all. If I lose my title to Tunney all money will be returned. If Mr. Wills and Mr. Mullins really want to fight they will cover that amount. If they cannot do so then maybe Mr. Farley, Mr. Phelan or Mr. Wear may help them out. These men want to see the fight and I want to accommodate them.[52]

Why did the plaintiffs in *Chicago Coliseum* seek equitable relief in Indiana? According to the *Indianapolis Star Tribune*, "Dempsey was on his way eastward to train for the proposed bout with Tunney and stopped over in Indianapolis. Attorneys for the Chicago Coliseum Club had been following Dempsey's movements since he left his home in Los Angeles, Cal., hoping to get service on him notifying him of the pending suit. Indianapolis was his first stopover."[53] However, the Indiana injunction against Dempsey

52. Dempsey Publicly Challenges Wills, *New York Times*, August 19, 1926, p. 17.

53. Court Enjoins Big Bout, Holds Dempsey Encounter with Tunney Illegal, *Indianapolis Star Tribune*, September 14, 1926, p. 1. My thanks to Professor Douglas Boshkoff for this information and for providing me with a copy of the article, which contains two other pertinent pieces of information: During argument, Dempsey's attorney told the Indiana court that "the first contract which was entered into by South Bend promoters and which was later sold to the Chicago Coliseum Club was signed in Niles Mich." Id. at p. 3. And fight promoter Fitzsimmons "testified that the contract which Dempsey signed with the Chicago club was never delivered to the club officials. . . . Dempsey signed the contract in Los Angeles, Cal., and gave it to Fitzsimmons. Later the contracts were placed in escrow in a Chicago bank, he said." Id.

"operated only for the month of September 1926,"[54] the month that Dempsey fought Tunney. The entire case was dismissed in 1928 on mootness grounds, without a determination of the propriety of the initial injunction. 88 Ind. App. 251, 162 N.E. 237. "Apparently no contempt proceedings were ever started against Dempsey in Indiana."[55] Moreover, at the time of the lawsuit, heavyweight prizefights were illegal in Indiana.[56]

On June 22, 1937, Joe Louis became heavyweight boxing champion of the world by dethroning James Braddock in front of 41,675 paying customers in Comiskey Park. In the first heavyweight title fight in Chicago since the "Long Count" Dempsey-Tunney rematch in 1927, Louis at age 23 became the youngest heavyweight champion to date and the first black man to hold the crown since Jack Johnson. The color line was broken. Among the many luminaries in attendance were both Gene Tunney and Jack Dempsey.[57]

STUDY GUIDE: *The court in the next case offers a defense of the doctrine of uncertainty. Especially noteworthy is its discussion of the advantages and disadvantages of following rules of law. This is a topic typically discussed in Jurisprudence. Consider how the court's attitude about the need for rules to guide juries reflects the historical developments discussed by Richard Danzig in his treatment of Hadley v. Baxendale.*

WINSTON CIGARETTE MACHINE CO. v. WELLS-WHITEHEAD TOBACCO CO., SUPREME COURT OF NORTH CAROLINA, 141 N.C. 284, 53 S.E. 885 (1906): WALKER, J.* It is clear that whenever profits are rejected as an item in the calculation of damages, it is because they are subject to too many contingencies and are too dependent upon the fluctuations of markets and the chances of business to constitute a safe criterion for an estimate of damages.

> The law may, and often does, fail of doing complete justice, from the imperfection of its means for ascertaining truth, and tracing and apportioning effects to their various causes; but it is not liable to the reproach of doing positive injustice by design. Such a doctrine would tend not only to make the

54. John P. Dawson, William B. Harvey, & Stanley D. Henderson, Contracts: Cases and Comment (7th ed. 1998), p. 91.

55. Id.

56. Indiana Court Enjoins Dempsey-Tunney Bout; Lawyers Differ on Effect in Pennsylvania, *New York Times*, September 14, 1926, at 1. According to this press account, "Judge Given held that the ownership of the contract by the Chicago club represented a property right. He said that although a prizefight was not sanctioned by Indiana law, and an Indiana court could not properly take juridical cognizance of a contract for a 'prizefight' contrary to Indiana law, the State did recognize property rights, and that this was what he construed the contract to be."

57. See Mike Conklin, June 22, 1937: Joe Louis Ushers In a New Boxing Era, *Chicago Tribune*, June 22, 1987, §3, at 3.

Platt D. Walker (1849-1923) was educated at the University of North Carolina (A.B.) and the University of Virginia (LL.B.). After his admission to the bar in 1870, he entered private practice. In 1903, following the impeachment of a number of Republican justices of the North Carolina Supreme Court, Walker was elected to fill one of the vacancies and was re-elected in 1910 and 1918. — [This judicial biography was written by Jaime Byrnes, hereinafter "J.B."]

law itself odious, but to corrupt its administration, by fostering a disregard of the just rights of parties. In actions upon contract, especially, and in those nominally in tort, but substantially upon contract, courts have thought it generally safer, upon the whole, to adopt certain definite rules for the government of the jury by which the damages could be estimated, at the risk of falling somewhat short of the actual damages, by rejecting such as could not be estimated by a fixed rule than to leave the whole matter entirely at large with the jury, without any rule to govern their discretion, or to detect or correct errors or corruption in the verdict. In such cases, therefore, there has been a strong inclination to seize upon such elements of certainty as the case might happen to present, and as might approximate compensation, and to frame thereon rules of law for the measurement of damages, though it might be evident that further damages must have been suffered, which, however, could only be estimated as matter of opinion, and must, therefore, be excluded under the rules thus adopted.

Allison v. Chandler, 11 Mich., 542. . . .

The distinction between such profits as can be thus definitely ascertained by some standard furnished by the contract itself or by the law, and those for the calculation of which there is no standard, but which are shadowy, uncertain, and speculative and therefore incapable of legal computation, is clearly recognized. . . .

. . . Judge Story said that, independent of all authorities, he was satisfied upon principle that an allowance of damages, upon the basis of a calculation of profits, is inadmissible where there is no certain standard to guide the jury. The rule would be in the highest degree unfavorable to the interest of the community and the subject would be involved in utter uncertainty. The computation would proceed upon contingencies, and would require a knowledge of markets to an exactness in point of time and value which would sometimes present embarrassing obstacles. Much would depend upon the vigilance and activity of the party who it is supposed would have made the profits and much upon the momentary demand and other considerations purely speculative. After all, it would be a mere calculation upon conjectures and not upon facts. . . . Any such estimate would be based upon imaginary and uncertain profits depending upon a variety of circumstances, the failure of any one of which would subvert the whole calculation and, for this reason they would be too remote and indeterminate to enter into the measure of damages. . . . Should the rule contended for prevail, the breach of a very simple contract, or failure in some part, might bring ruin upon the party in default, by leaving the damages to the unbridled discretion of the jury, when in fact no such loss was contemplated. The adoption of such a rule would, therefore, be extremely dangerous. If such consequences are to follow, it is much better that the parties, when contracting, expressly provide for such enlarged responsibility. This they may do by liquidating the amount when the damages cannot be otherwise ascertained and are such as the law will not allow because of their uncertainty. . . .

A party who has broken his contract cannot, we admit, escape liability because of the difficulty there may be in finding a perfect measure of damages. In this case it appears that the jury, by their verdict, have said that the defendant violated the contract without any just cause or legal excuse. . . . While the bad faith of the defendant would ordinarily entitle it to little consideration from the court, it cannot have the effect to reverse a well settled rule of law, which must be general in its application. We should administer the law as we find it. Its proper administration will sometimes apparently work individual hardship, but this is true of all general rules. It is a much less evil than to construe it to meet the supposed injustice of the particular case or merely to redress a wrong, because we may think it is of so grievous a nature that it should be, in this way, specially rebuked, without regard to the strict principles of the law which have been adopted for all cases. "It is then an established rule to abide by former precedents, stare decisis, where the same points come again in litigation, as well to keep the scales of justice even and steady, and not liable to waver with every new judge's opinion, and also because, the law in that case being solemnly declared and determined, what before was uncertain and perhaps indifferent, is now become a permanent rule, which it is not in the breast of any subsequent judge to alter or swerve from according to his private sentiments; he being sworn to determine, not according to his own private judgment, but according to the known laws and customs of the land, — not delegated to pronounce a new law, but to maintain and expound the old one. . . ." The defendant, it is true, has willfully broken the contract at a time too late for the plaintiff to repair the wrong or retrieve the resulting loss, but this should not change the rule of law, although it may justly provoke our condemnation of the act. "Our duty," said Baron Alderson, "is plain. It is to expound and not to make the law, to decide on it as we find it, not as we may wish it to be." . . . It is not our province to invent new rules for avoiding hardship, however unjustly we may think a party has been dealt with, but to discover and be governed by those rules which were adopted by our predecessors for their guidance. . . .

RESTATEMENT (SECOND) OF CONTRACTS

§346. AVAILABILITY OF DAMAGES

(1) The injured party has a right to damages for any breach by a party against whom the contract is enforceable unless the claim for damages has been suspended or discharged.

(2) If the breach caused no loss or if the amount of the loss is not proved under the rules stated in this Chapter, a small sum fixed without regard to the amount of loss will be awarded as nominal damages.

§349. DAMAGES BASED ON RELIANCE INTEREST

As an alternative to the measure of damages stated in §347, the injured party has a right to damages based on his reliance interest, including expenditures made in preparation for performance or in performance, less any loss that the party in breach can prove with reasonable certainty the injured party would have suffered had the contract been performed.

§352.   UNCERTAINTY AS A LIMITATION ON DAMAGES

Damages are not recoverable for loss beyond an amount that the evidence permits to be established with reasonable certainty.

Study Guide: How does the court's assessment of damages differ from that employed in Chicago Coliseum Club v. Dempsey? Does the measure of recovery in the next case suggest that the "reliance interest" identified by Lon Fuller may be a misnomer? Can you think of another way of characterizing this damage interest? Once again, notice how this contractual difficulty for Mr. Reed stemmed from the power of his agent to make contracts on his behalf. [Robert Reed, a Shakespearean actor by training, is best known for his role as Mike Brady, the father in TV's "The Brady Bunch," which made its debut in 1969. Some also remember him for having co-starred in the early sixties with E.G. Marshall in the gritty television series "The Defenders," in which he played Kenneth Preston, the junior half of a father-son New York criminal defense firm. (It was this show that first motivated the author of this casebook to become a lawyer.) Mr. Reed died in 1992 at the age of 59.]

ANGLIA TELEVISION LTD. v. REED
Court of Appeal, Civil Division,
[1971] 3 All E.R. 690

Lord Denning Mr.* Anglia Television Ltd were minded in 1968 to make a film of a play for television entitled "The Man in the Wood." It portrayed an American married to an English woman. The American has an adventure in an English wood. The film was to last for 90 minutes. Anglia Television made many arrangements in advance. They arranged for a place where the play was to be filmed. They employed a director, a designer and a stage manager, and so forth. They involved themselves in much expense. All this was done before they got the leading man. They required a strong actor capable of holding the play together. He was to be on the scene the whole time. Anglia Television eventually found the man. He was Mr. Robert Reed, an American who has a very high reputation as an actor. He was very suitable for this part. By telephone conversation on 30th August 1968 it was agreed by Mr. Reed through his agent that he would come to England and be available between 9th September and 11th October 1968 to rehearse and play in this film. He was to get a performance fee of £1,050, living expenses of £100 a week, his first class fares to and from the United States, and so forth. It was all subject to the permit of the Ministry of Labour for him to come here. That was duly given on 2nd September 1968. So the contract was concluded. But

---

*Alfred Thompson Denning (Baron Denning of Whitchurch) (1899-1999) was educated at Magdalen College, Oxford, and was called to the bar in 1923. He became King's Counsel in 1938 and became High Court Judge in 1944. He has also served as Lord Justice of Appeal (1946-1947), Lord of Appeal in Ordinary (1957-1962), and Master of the Rolls (1962-1982). In 1963, he conducted the inquiry into the Profumo scandal. — K.T.

unfortunately there was some muddle with the bookings. It appears that Mr. Reed's agent had already booked him in America for some other play. So on 3rd September 1968 the agent said that Mr. Reed would not come to England to perform in this play. He repudiated his contract. Anglia Television tried hard to find a substitute but could not do so. So on 11th September they accepted his repudiation. They abandoned the proposed film. They gave notice to the people whom they had engaged and so forth.

Anglia Television then sued Mr. Reed for damages. He did not dispute his liability, but a question arose as to the damages. Anglia Television do not claim their profit. They cannot say what their profit would have been on this contract if Mr. Reed had come here and performed it. So, instead of claim for loss of profits, they claim for the wasted expenditure. They had incurred the director's fees, the designer's fees, the stage manager's and assistant manager's fees, and so on. It comes in all to £2,750. Anglia Television say that all that money was wasted because Mr. Reed did not perform his contract.

Mr. Reed's advisers take a point of law. They submit that Anglia Television cannot recover for expenditure incurred *before* the contract was concluded with Mr. Reed. They can only recover the expenditure *after* the contract was concluded. They say that the expenditure *after* the contract was only £854.65, and that is all that Anglia Television can recover. The master rejected that contention; he held that Anglia Television could recover the whole £2,750; and now Mr. Reed appeals to this court.

Counsel for Mr. Reed has referred us to the recent unreported case of Perestrello & Compania Limitada v. United Paint Co. Ltd. (No. 2),[58] in which Thesiger, J., quoted the words of Lord Tindal, CJ., in 1835 in Hodges v. Earl of Litchfield:[59]

> The expenses preliminary to the contract ought not to be allowed. The party enters into them for his own benefit at a time when it is uncertain whether there will be any contract or not.

THESIGER, J., applied those words, saying: "In my judgment pre-contract expenditure, though thrown away, is not recoverable. . . ."

I cannot accept the proposition as stated. It seems to me that a plaintiff in such a case as this had an election: he can either claim for his loss of profits; or for his wasted expenditure. But he must elect between them. He cannot claim both. If he has not suffered any loss of profits — or if he cannot prove what his profits would have been — he can claim in the alternative the expenditure which has been thrown away, that is, wasted, by reason of the breach. That is shown by Cullinane v. British "Rema" Manufacturing Co. Ltd.[60]

If the plaintiff claims the wasted expenditure, he is not limited to the expenditure incurred *after* the contract was concluded. He can claim also the expenditure incurred *before* the contract, provided that it was such as would reasonably be in the contemplation of the parties as likely to be wasted if the contract was broken. Applying that principle here, it is plain

58. (1969) 113 Sol. J. 324.
59. (1835) 1 Bing N.C. 492 at 498, [1835-42] All E.R. Rep. 551 at 552, 553.
60. [1953] 2 All E.R. 1257 at 1261, 1264, 1265, [1954] 1 Q.B. 292 at 303, 308.

that, <u>when Mr. Reed entered into this contract, he must have known per-fectly well that much expenditure had already been incurred on director's fees and the like</u>. He must have contemplated — or, at any rate, it is reason-ably to be imputed to him — that if he broke his contract, all that expen-diture would be wasted, whether or not it was incurred before or after the contract. He must pay damages for all the expenditure so wasted and thrown away. This view is supported by the recent decision of Brightman, J., in Lloyd v. Stanbury.[61] There was a contract for the sale of land. In anticipation of the contract — and before it was concluded — the pur-chaser went to much expense in moving a caravan to the site and in getting his furniture there. The seller afterwards entered into a contract to sell, the land to the purchaser, but afterwards broke his contract. The land had not increased in value, so the purchaser could not claim for any loss of profit. But Brightman, J., held that he could recover the cost of moving the caravan and furniture, because it was "within the contemplation of the parties when the contract was signed."[62] That decision is in accord with correct principle, namely, that wasted expenditure can be recovered when it is wasted by reason of the defendant's breach of contract. It is true that, if the defendant had never entered into the contract, he would not be liable, and the expen-diture would have been incurred by the plaintiff without redress; but, the defendant having made his contract and broken it, it does not lie in his mouth to say he is not liable, when it was because of his breach that the expenditure has been wasted.

I think the master was quite right and this appeal should be dismissed. Appeal dismissed.

STUDY GUIDE: In the next case, what would the plaintiff's expectation damages have been? What reason does the court give for awarding reli-ance damages instead? Is the court trying to compensate the plaintiff for harm inflicted by the defendant's misconduct in this case, or is the court trying to give the plaintiff the value of what was promised?

SECURITY STOVE & MANUFACTURING CO. v. AMERICAN RAILWAY EXPRESS CO.

Kansas City Court of Appeals, Missouri, 227 Mo. App. 175, 51 S.W.2d 572 (1932)

BLAND, J.*

This is an action for damages for the failure of defendant to transport, from Kansas City to Atlantic City, New Jersey, within a reasonable time, a furnace equipped with a combination oil and gas burner. The cause was

---

61. [1971] 2 All E.R. 267, [1971] 1 W.L.R. 535.

62. [1971] 2 All E.R. at 276, [1971] 1 W.L.R. at 547.

* Ewing C. Bland (1882-1949) served on the Kansas City Court of Appeals. He was the son of Richard P. Bland, who was a Missouri congressman for over 20 years, a Freemason and a supporter of the free silver movement. In 1913, he was nominated by Woodrow Wilson to be the U.S. Marshal for the Eastern District of Missouri, but the Senate rejected this nomina-tion. — S.Q.

tried before the court without the aid of a jury, resulting in a judgment in favor of plaintiff in the sum of $801.50 and interest, or in a total sum of $1,000.00. Defendant has appealed.

The facts show that plaintiff manufactured a furnace equipped with a special combination oil and gas burner it desired to exhibit at the American Gas Association Convention held in Atlantic City in October, 1926. The president of plaintiff testified that plaintiff engaged space for the exhibit for the reason "that the Henry L. Dougherty Company was very much interested in putting out a combination oil and gas burner; we had just developed one, after we got through, better than anything on the market and we thought this show would be the psychological time to get in contact with the Dougherty Company"; that "the thing wasn't sent there for sale but primarily to show"; that at the time the space was engaged it was too late to ship the furnace by freight so plaintiff decided to ship it by express, and, on September 18th, 1926, wrote the office of the defendant in Kansas City, stating that it had engaged a booth for exhibition purposes at Atlantic City, New Jersey, from the American Gas Association, for the week beginning October 11th; that its exhibit consisted of an oil burning furnace, together with two oil burners which weighed at least 1,500 pounds; that, "In order to get this exhibit in place on time it should be in Atlantic City not later than October the 8th. What we want you to do is to tell us how much time you will require to assure the delivery of the exhibit on time."

. . .

[P]laintiff's president made arrangements to go to Atlantic City to attend the convention and install the exhibit, arriving there about October 11th. When he reached Atlantic City he found the shipment had been placed in the booth that had been assigned to plaintiff. The exhibit was set up, but it was found that one of the packages shipped was not there. This missing package contained the gas manifold, or that part of the oil and gas burner that controlled the flow of gas in the burner. This was the most important part of the exhibit and a like burner could not be obtained in Atlantic City.

Wires were sent and it was found that the stray package was at the "over and short bureau" of defendant in St. Louis. Defendant reported that the package would be forwarded to Atlantic City and would be there by Wednesday, the 13th. plaintiff's president waited until Thursday, the day the convention closed, but the package had not arrived at the time, so he closed up the exhibit and left. About a week after he arrived in Kansas City, the package was returned by the defendant.

. . .

The petition upon which the case was tried alleges that plaintiff ". . . relying upon defendant's promise and the promises of its agents and servants, that said parcels would be delivered at Atlantic City by October 8th, 1926, if delivered to defendant by October 4th, 1926, plaintiff herein hired space for an exhibit at the American Gas Association Convention at Atlantic City, and planned for an exhibit at said Convention and sent men in the employ of this plaintiff to Atlantic City to install, show and operate said exhibit, and that these men were in Atlantic City ready to set up this plaintiff's exhibit at the American Gas Association Convention on October 8th, 1926."

That defendant, in violation of its agreement, failed and neglected to deliver one of the packages to its destination on October 8th, 1926.

"That the package not delivered by defendant contained the essential part of plaintiff's exhibit which plaintiff was to make at said convention on October 8th, was later discovered in St. Louis, Missouri, by the defendant herein, and that plaintiff, for this reason, could not show his exhibit."

Plaintiff asked damages, which the court in its judgment allowed as follows: $147.00 express charges (on the exhibit); $45.12 freight on the exhibit from Atlantic City to Kansas City; $101.39 railroad and pullman fares to and from Atlantic City, expended by plaintiff's president and a workman taken by him to Atlantic City; $48.00 hotel room for the two; $150.00 for the time of the president; $40.00 for wages of plaintiff's other employee and $270.00 for rental of the booth, making a total of $801.51.

Defendant contends that . . . the court erred in allowing plaintiff's expenses as damages; that the only damages, if any, that can be recovered in cases of this kind, are for loss of profits and that plaintiff's evidence is not sufficient to base any recovery on this ground.

. . .

We think, under the circumstances in this case, that it was proper to allow plaintiff's expenses as its damages. Ordinarily the measure of damages where the carrier fails to deliver a shipment at destination within a reasonable time is the difference between the market value of the goods at the time of the delivery and the time when they should have been delivered. But where the carrier has notice of peculiar circumstances under which the shipment is made, which will result in an unusual loss by the shipper in case of delay in delivery, the carrier is responsible for the real damage sustained from such delay if the notice given is of such character, and goes to such extent, in informing the carrier of the shipper's situation, that the carrier will be presumed to have contracted with reference thereto. Central Trust Co. of New York v. Savannah & W. R. Co. (C. C.) 69 F. 683, 685.

In the case at bar defendant was advised of the necessity of prompt delivery of the shipment. Plaintiff explained to Johnson the "importance of getting the exhibit there on time." Defendant knew the purpose of the exhibit and ought to respond for its negligence in failing to get it there. As we view the record this negligence is practically conceded. The undisputed testimony shows that the shipment was sent to the over and short department of the defendant in St. Louis. As the packages were plainly numbered this, prima facie, shows mistake or negligence on the part of the defendant. No effort was made by it to show that it was not negligent in sending it there, or not negligent in not forwarding it within a reasonable time after it was found.

There is no evidence of claim in this case that plaintiff suffered any loss of profits by reason of the delay in the shipment. In fact defendant states in its brief:

"The plaintiff introduced not one whit of evidence showing or tending to show that he would have made any sales as a result of his exhibit but for the negligence of the defendant. On the contrary Blakesley testified that the main purpose of the exhibit was to try to interest the Henry L. Dougherty Company in plaintiff's combination oil and gas burner, yet that was all the evidence that there was as to the benefit plaintiff expected to get from the exhibit.

As a matter of evidence, it is clear that the plaintiff would not have derived a great deal of benefit from the exhibit by any stretch of the imagination.

No where does plaintiff introduce evidence showing that the Henry L. Dougherty Company in all probability would have become interested in the combination oil and gas burner and made a profitable contract with the plaintiff."

There is evidence that the exhibit was not sent to make a sale.

In support of its contention that plaintiff can sue only for loss of profit, if anything, in a case of this kind, defendant, among other cases cites that of Adams Exp. Co. v. Egbert, 36 Pa. 360, 78 Am. Dec. 382. That case involved the shipment of a box containing architectural drawings or plans for a building to a building committee of the Touro Almshouse, in New Orleans. This committee had offered a premium of $500.00 to the successful competitor. These plans arrived after the various plans had been passed upon and the award made to another person. It was sought in that case to recover the value of the plans. The evidence, howover, showed that the plans would not have won the prize had they arrived on time. The court held that the plans, under the circumstances, had no appreciable value and recovery could not be had for them and there was no basis for recovery for loss of the opportunity to compete for the prize. The opinion states that in denying recovery for the plans it is contrary to the English rule in such cases. Other cases cited by defendant involve loss of profits or the loss of opportunity to compete in such events as horse racing and the like. In one case, Delta Table & Chair Co. v. R.R., 105 Miss. 861, 63 So. 272, it was held that the plaintiff could recover for loss of profits that might have been made in the sale of its commodity, as a result of exhibiting a sample at an exhibition, where the shipment was delayed too late for the exhibit. Some of the cases cited by defendant hold that such profits in those classes of cases are not recoverable, and others to the contrary.

Defendant contends that plaintiff "is endeavoring to achieve a return of the status quo in a suit based on a breach of contract. Instead of seeking to recover what he would have had, had the contract not been broken, plaintiff is trying to recover what he would have had, had there never been any contract of shipment"; that the expenses sued for would have been incurred in any event. It is no doubt, the general rule that where there is a breach of contract the party suffering the loss can recover only that which he would have had, had the contract not been broken, and this is all the cases decided upon which defendant relies, including C., M. & St. P. Ry. v. McCaull-Dinsmore Co., 253 U.S. 97, 100, 40 S. Ct. 504, 64 L. Ed. 801. But this is merely a general statement of the rule and is not inconsistent with the holdings that, in some instances, the injured party may recover expenses incurred in relying upon the contract, although such expenses would have been incurred had the contract not been breached. See Morrow v. Railroad, 140 Mo. App. 200, 212, 213, 123 S.W. 1034; Bryant v. Barton, 32 Neb. 613, 616, 49 N.W. 331; Woodbury v. Jones, 44 N.H. 206; Driggs v. Dwight, 17 Wend. (N.Y.) 71, 31 Am. Dec. 283.

In Sperry et al. v. O'Neill-Adams Co. (C. C. A.) 185 F. 231, the court held that the advantages resulting from the use of trading stamps as a means of increasing trade are so contingent that they cannot form a basis on which to rest a recovery for a breach of contract to supply them. In lieu of compensation based thereon the court directed a recovery in the sum expended in preparation for carrying on business in connection with the use of the stamps. The court said, loc. cit. 239:

"Plaintiff in its complaint had made a claim for lost profits, but, finding it impossible to marshal any evidence which would support a finding of exact figures, abandoned that claim. Any attempt to reach a precise sum would be mere blind guesswork. Nevertheless a contract, which both sides conceded would prove a valuable one, had been broken and the party who broke it was responsible for resultant damage. In order to carry out this contract, the plaintiff made expenditures which otherwise it would not have made. The trial judge held, as we think rightly, that plaintiff was entitled at least to recover these expenses to which it had been put in order to secure the benefits of a contract of which defendant's conduct deprived it."

In the case of Gilbert v. Kennedy, 22 Mich. 117, involved the question of the measure of plaintiff's damages, caused by the conduct of defendant in wrongfully feeding his cattle with plaintiff's in the latter's pasture, resulting in plaintiff's cattle suffering by the overfeeding of the pasture. The court said loc. cit. 135, 136:

"There being practically no market value for pasturage when there was none in the market, that element of certainty is wanting, even as to those cattle which were removed from the Pitcher farm to the home farm of the plaintiff for pasturage; and, as it could not apply to the others at all, and there being no other element of certainty by which the damages can be *accurately* measured, resort must be had to such principle or basis of calculation applicable to the circumstances of the case (if any be discoverable) as will be most likely to *approximate* certainty, and which may serve as a guide in making the most probable estimate of which the nature of the case will admit; and, though it may be less certain as a scale of measurement, yet if the principle be just in itself, and more likely to approximate the *actual damages*, it is better than any rule, however certain, which must certainly produce injustice, by excluding a large portion of the damages actually sustained."

In Hobbs v. Davis, 30 Ga. 423, a negro slave was hired to make a crop, but she was taken away by her owner in the middle of the year, the result of which the crop was entirely lost. The court said, loc. cit. 425:

"As it was, the true criterion of damages was, perhaps, the hire of the negro, the rent of the land and all the expense incurred, and actual loss sustained by the misconduct of the defendant, rather than the conjecture of the witness, as to what the crop would have been worth."

"Compensation is a fundamental principle of damages whether the action is in contract or in tort. Wicker v. Hoppock, 6 Wall. 94, 99, 18 L. Ed. 752. One who fails to perform his contract is justly bound to make good all damages that accrue naturally from the breach: and the other party is entitled to be put in as good a position pecuniarily as he would have been by performance of the contract." Miller v. Robertson, 266 U.S. 243, 257, 258, 45 S. Ct. 73, 78, 69 L. Ed. 265.

The case at bar was to recover damages for loss of profits by reason of the failure of the defendant to transport the shipment within a reasonable time, so that it would arrive in Atlantic City for the exhibit. There were no profits contemplated. The furnace was to be shown and shipped back to Kansas City. There was no money loss, except the expenses, that was of such a nature as any court would allow as being sufficiently definite or lacking in pure speculation. Therefore, unless plaintiff is permitted to recover the expenses that it went to, which were a total loss to it by reason of its inability to exhibit the furnace and equipment, it will be deprived of any substantial compensation for its loss. The law does not contemplate any such injustice. It ought to allow plaintiff, as damages, the loss in the way of expenses that it sustained, and which it would not have been put to if it had not been for its reliance upon the defendant to perform its contract. There is no contention that the exhibit would have been entirely valueless and whatever it might have accomplished defendant knew of the circumstances and ought to respond for whatever damages plaintiff suffered. In cases of this kind the method of estimating the damages should be adopted which is the most definite and certain and which best achieves the fundamental purpose of compensation. 17 C. J. p. 846; Miller v. Robertson, 266 U.S. 243, 257, 45 S. Ct. 73, 78, 69 L. Ed. 265. Had the exhibit been shipped in order to realize a profit on sales and such profits could have been realized, or to be entered in competition for a prize, and plaintiff failed to show loss of profits with sufficient definiteness, or that he would have won the prize, defendant's cases might be in point. But as before stated, no such situation exists here.

While, it is true that plaintiff already had incurred some of these expenses, in that it had rented space at the exhibit before entering into the contract with defendant for the shipment of the exhibit and this part of plaintiff's damages, in a sense, arose out of a circumstance which transpired before the contract was even entered into, yet, plaintiff arranged for the exhibit knowing that it could call upon defendant to perform its common law duty to accept and transport the shipment with reasonable dispatch. The whole damage, therefore, was suffered in contemplation of defendant performing its contract, which it failed to do, and would not have been sustained except for the reliance by plaintiff upon defendant to perform it. It can, therefore, be fairly said that the damages or loss suffered by plaintiff grew out of the breach of the contract, for had the shipment arrived on time, plaintiff would have had the benefit of the contract, which was contemplated by all parties, defendant being advised of the purpose of the shipment.

The judgment is affirmed.

All concur.

REFERENCE: Barnett, §2.4.2
                Farnsworth, §§12.15-12.16
                Calamari & Perillo, §§14.8-14.10
                Murray, §122

Economics Background: The Subjectivity of Valuation

STUDY GUIDE: The subject of damages — indeed of legal obligation — cannot be understood without taking into account the subjectivity of value. What follows is a brief description of this concept. Can you see how the subjectivity of value renders all computations of contract damages to some degree "uncertain"? We shall return to this issue time and again throughout these materials. While reading this passage consider whether this view of the subjectivity of valuation is inconsistent with the idea that valuations of right and wrong, good and bad could — in some sense — be objective or true.

LUDWIG VON MISES, HUMAN ACTION 97, 204-205 (REV. ED. 1963):   The difference between the value of the price paid (the costs incurred) and that of the goal attained is called gain or profit or net yield. Profit in this primary sense is purely subjective, it is an increase in the acting man's happiness, it is a psychical phenomenon that can be neither measured nor weighed. There is a more and a less in the removal of uneasiness felt; but how much one satisfaction surpasses another one can only be felt; it cannot be established and determined in an objective way. A judgment of value does not measure, it arranges in a scale of degrees, it grades. It is expressive of an order of preference and sequence, but not expressive of measure and weight. Only the ordinal numbers can be applied to it, but not the cardinal numbers. . . .

Now, we must realize that valuing means to prefer *a* to *b*. There is — logically, epistemologically, psychologically, and praxeologically — only one pattern of preferring. It does not matter whether . . . a man [prefers] one friend to other people, an amateur one painting to other paintings, or a consumer one loaf of bread to a piece of candy. Preferring always means to love or to desire *a* more than *b*. Just as there is no standard and no measurement of sexual love, of friendship and sympathy, and of aesthetic enjoyment, so there is no measurement of the value of commodities. If a man exchanges two pounds of butter for a shirt, all that we can assert with regard to this transaction is that he — at the instant of the transaction and under the conditions which this instant offers to him — prefers one shirt to two pounds of butter. It is certain that every act of preferring is characterized by a definite psychic intensity of the feelings it implies. These are grades in the intensity of the desire to attain a definite goal and this intensity determines the psychic profit which the successful action brings to the acting individual. But psychic quantities can only be felt. They are entirely personal, and there is no semantic means to express their intensity and to convey information about them to other people.

There is no method available to construct a unit of value. Let us remember that two units of a homogeneous supply are necessarily valued differently. The value attached to the nth unit is lower than that attached to the $(n–1)$th unit.

REFERENCE: Barnett, §2.3.6
                  Calamari & Perillo, §§14.12-14.14

3.   Avoidability of Harm

STUDY GUIDE: *Can you think of a principle of justice that accounts for the rules discussed in the following cases? What policy reasons might exist for these rules?*

ROCKINGHAM COUNTY v. LUTEN BRIDGE CO.
Circuit Court of Appeals, Fourth Circuit,
35 F.2d 301 (1929)

Appeal from the District Court of the United States for the Middle District of North Carolina, at Greensboro. . . .

PARKER, C.J.* This was an action at law instituted in the court below by the Luten Bridge Company, as plaintiff, to recover of Rockingham county, North Carolina, an amount alleged to be due under a contract for the construction of a bridge. The county admits the execution and breach of the contract, but contends that notice of cancellation was given the bridge company before the erection of the bridge was commenced, and that it is liable only for the damages which the company would have sustained, if it had abandoned construction at that time. The judge below . . . excluded evidence offered by the county in support of its contentions as to notice of cancellation and damages, and instructed a verdict for plaintiff for the full amount of its claim. From judgment on this verdict the county has appealed.

The facts out of which the case arises . . . are as follows: On January 7, 1924, the board of commissioners of Rockingham county voted to award to plaintiff a contract for the construction of the bridge in controversy. Three of the five commissioners favored the awarding of the contract and two opposed it. Much feeling was engendered over the matter, with the result that on February 11, 1924, W. K. Pruitt, one of the commissioners who had voted in the affirmative, sent his resignation to the clerk of the superior court of the county. The clerk received this resignation on the same day, and immediately accepted same and noted his acceptance thereon. Later in the day, Pruitt called him over the telephone and stated that he wished to withdraw the resignation, and later sent him written notice to the same effect. The clerk, however, paid no attention to the attempted withdrawal, and proceeded on the next day to appoint one W. W. Hampton as a member of the board to succeed him.

After his resignation, Pruitt attended no further meetings of the board, and did nothing further as a commissioner of the county. Likewise Pratt and McCollum, the other two members of the board who had voted with him in favor of the contract, attended no further meetings. Hampton, on the other

John Johnston Parker (1885-1958) completed his studies at the University of North Carolina (A.B., LL.B., LL.D.). After being admitted to the North Carolina bar in 1908, Parker entered private practice and eventually became a senior partner at Parker, Stewart, McRae & Bobbit in Charlotte, North Carolina. Judge Parker entered federal service as Special Assistant to the Attorney General of the United States in 1924, and in 1925 assumed office at the United States Court of Appeals, Fourth Circuit. — L.R.

hand, took the oath of office immediately upon his appointment and entered upon the discharge of the duties of a commissioner. He met regularly with the two remaining members of the board, Martin and Barber, in the courthouse at the county seat, and with them attended to all of the business of the county. Between the 12th of February and the first Monday in December following, these three attended, in all, 25 meetings of the board.

At one of these meetings, a regularly advertised called meeting held on February 21st, a resolution was unanimously adopted declaring that the contract for the building of the bridge was not legal and valid, and directing the clerk of the board to notify plaintiff that it refused to recognize same as a valid contract, and that plaintiff should proceed no further thereunder. This resolution also rescinded action of the board theretofore taken looking to the construction of a hard-surfaced road, in which the bridge was to be a mere connecting link. The clerk duly sent a certified copy of this resolution to plaintiff.

At the regular monthly meeting of the board on March 3d, a resolution was passed directing that plaintiff be notified that any work done on the bridge would be done by it at its own risk and hazard, that the board was of the opinion that the contract for the construction of the bridge was not valid and legal, and that, even if the board were mistaken as to this, it did not desire to construct the bridge, and would contest payment for same if constructed. A copy of this resolution was also sent to plaintiff. At the regular monthly meeting on April 7th, a resolution was passed, reciting that the board had been informed that one of its members was privately insisting that the bridge be constructed. It repudiated this action on the part of the member and gave notice that it would not be recognized. At the September meeting, a resolution was passed to the effect that the board would pay no bills presented by plaintiff or any one connected with the bridge. At the time of the passage of the first resolution, very little work toward the construction of the bridge had been done, it being estimated that the total cost of labor done and material on the ground was around $1,900; but, notwithstanding the repudiation of the contract by the county, the bridge company continued with the work of construction.

On November 24, 1924, plaintiff instituted this action against Rockingham county, and against Pruitt, Pratt, McCollum, Martin, and Barber, as constituting its board of commissioners. Complaint was filed, setting forth the execution of the contract and the doing of work by plaintiff thereunder, and alleging that for work done up until November 3, 1924, the county was indebted in the sum of $18,301.07. . . .

At the trial . . . [t]he county elicited . . . proof as to the state of the work at the time of the passage of the resolutions to which we have referred. It then offered these resolutions in evidence . . . ; but . . . this evidence was excluded, and the jury was instructed to return a verdict for plaintiff for the full amount of its claim. The county preserved exceptions to the rulings which were adverse to it, and contends that there was error on the part of the judge below . . . in excluding the evidence offered . . . of the resolutions attempting to cancel the contract and the notices sent plaintiff pursuant thereto; and in directing a verdict for plaintiffs in accordance with its claim.

As the county now admits the execution and validity of the contract, and the breach on its part, the ultimate question in the case is one as to the measure of plaintiff's recovery, and the exceptions must be considered with this in mind. . . . [W]e do not think that, after the county had given notice, while the contract was still executory, that it did not desire the bridge built and would not pay for it, plaintiff could proceed to build it and recover the contract price. It is true that the county had no right to rescind the contract, and the notice given plaintiff amounted to a breach on its part; but, after plaintiff had received notice of the breach, it was its duty to do nothing to increase the damages flowing therefrom. If A enters into a binding contract to build a house for B, B, of course, has no right to rescind the contract without A's consent. But if, before the house is built, he decides that he does not want it, and notifies A to that effect, A has no right to proceed with the building and thus pile up damages. His remedy is to treat the contract as broken when he receives the notice, and sue for the recovery of such damages, as he may have sustained from the breach, including any profit which he would have realized upon performance, as well as any other losses which may have resulted to him. In the case at bar, the county decided not to build the road of which the bridge was to be a part, and did not build it. The bridge, built in the midst of the forest, is of no value to the county because of this change of circumstances. When, therefore, the county gave notice to the plaintiff that it would not proceed with the project, plaintiff should have desisted from further work. It had no right thus to pile up damages by proceeding with the erection of a useless bridge.

The contrary view was expressed by Lord Cockburn in Frost v. Knight, L.R. 7 Ex. 111, but, as pointed out by Prof. Williston (Williston on Contracts, vol. 3, p. 2347), it is not in harmony with the decisions in this country. The American rule and the reasons supporting it are well stated by Prof. Williston as follows:

> There is a line of cases running back to 1845 which holds that, after an absolute repudiation or refusal to perform by one party to a contract, the other party cannot continue to perform and recover damages based on full performance. This rule is only a particular application of the general rule of damages that a plaintiff cannot hold a defendant liable for damages which need not have been incurred; or, as it is often stated, the plaintiff must, so far as he can without loss to himself, mitigate the damages caused by the defendant's wrongful act. The application of this rule to the matter in question is obvious. If a man engages to have work done, and afterwards repudiates his contract before the work has been begun or when it has been only partially done, it is inflicting damage on the defendant without benefit to the plaintiff to allow the latter to insist on proceeding with the contract. The work may be useless to the defendant, and yet he would be forced to pay the full contract price. On the other hand, the plaintiff is interested only in the profit he will make out of the contract. If he receives this it is equally advantageous for him to use his time otherwise.

The leading case on the subject in this country is the New York case of Clark v. Marsiglia, 1 Denio (N.Y.) 317, 43 Am. Dec. 670. In that case defendant had employed plaintiff to paint certain pictures for him, but countermanded the order before the work was finished. Plaintiff, however, went on and completed the work and sued for the contract price. In reversing a judgment for plaintiff, the court said:

> The plaintiff was allowed to recover as though there had been no countermand of the order; and in this the court erred. The defendant, by requiring the plaintiff to stop work upon the paintings, violated his contract, and thereby incurred a liability to pay such damages as the plaintiff should sustain. Such damages would include a recompense for the labor done and materials used, and such further sum in damages as might, upon legal principles, be assessed for the breach of the contract; but the plaintiff had no right, by obstinately persisting in the work, to make the penalty upon the defendant greater than it would otherwise have been.

And the rule as established by the great weight of authority in America is summed up in the following statement in 6 R.C.L. 1029 . . . :

> While a contract is executory a party has the power to stop performance on the other side by an explicit direction to that effect, subjecting himself to such damages as will compensate the other party for being stopped in the performance on his part at that stage in the execution of the contract. The party thus forbidden cannot afterwards go on and thereby increase the damages, and then recover such damages from the other party. The legal right of either party to violate, abandon, or renounce his contract, on the usual terms of compensation to the other for the damages which the law recognizes and allows, subject to the jurisdiction of equity to decree specific performance in proper cases, is universally recognized and acted upon.

> . . . It follows that there was error in directing a verdict for plaintiff for the full amount of its claim. The measure of plaintiff's damage, upon its appearing that notice was duly given not to build the bridge, is an amount sufficient to compensate plaintiff for labor and materials expended and expense incurred in the part performance of the contract, prior to its repudiation, plus the profit which would have been realized if it had been carried out in accordance with its terms. . . . The judgment below will accordingly be reversed, and the case remanded for a new trial.
> Reversed.

[handwritten margin notes: "Reliance Damages" and "Expectation Interests"]

Relational Background: Why Did the County Change Its Mind? Why Did the Company Keep Building?

STUDY GUIDE: *Do the following background facts shed any additional light on contract law issues considered in Judge Parker's opinion? Do you think the Luten Bridge Company could have been completely confident in the command it received to desist construction?*

BARAK RICHMAN, JORDI WEINSTOCK & JASON MEHTA, A BRIDGE, A TAX REVOLT, AND THE STRUGGLE TO INDUSTRIALIZE: THE STORY AND LEGACY OF ROCKINGHAM COUNTY v. LUTEN BRIDGE CO., 84 N.C. L. REV. 1841, 1851-1879, 1906-1908 (2006):   The central figure in Rockingham County's decision to build a new bridge at Fishing Creek was Colonel Benjamin Franklin

Mebane, Jr. Throughout the first quarter of the twentieth century, Mebane, a flamboyant industrialist living in a changing South, was the undisputed king of Rockingham County. In his time, Mebane's power and notoriety seemed limitless. Contemporaries noted that he was "the ideal of a cavalier, young, successful, brave and handsome — and he knows how to sit on a horse."

Mebane exploited this power and his oversized personality to reign supreme over a wide variety of local industries. The Rockingham industrialist's vast enterprises included raising cattle, running a variety of publishing companies, managing the Imperial Bank and Trust Company, and establishing the Spray Institute of Technology. . . . But Mebane's primary enterprise — and the one in which he left an indelible imprint on the county — was textile manufacturing. During his reign, Mebane saw northern Rockingham Country transform from a sleepy rural community into a thriving industrial center, featuring new factories, roads, and bridges. Indeed, much of Rockingham County's growth was a by-product of Mebane's own industry. . . .

Mebane's economic empire came to dominate Rockingham County, and by 1905, nearly all of Spray's 5,000 residents worked for him in some capacity. . . . The price of expansion, however, caught up with Mebane. Despite his vast holdings, Mebane was forced to borrow heavily to finance his development, and by 1910 he had overextended his credit. Mebane's primary creditor, Marshall Field & Company, promptly took control of all of Mebane's mills except Morehead Mills and Leaksville Mill. . . . Nonetheless, Mebane's aspirations did not wane after these massive setbacks. To the contrary, he had a plan — as ambitious and as audacious as any previous scheme — that would reassert his economic dominance in the region.

Mebane's plan, developed in the early 1920s, was reportedly to build a massive chemical factory in "the Meadows," a large series of fields that the Spray Water Power & Land Company owned between Spray and Draper. . . . However, Mebane's oversized dream, which might also have included attracting new residents near the chemical factory and laying the foundations of a new town, was hindered by the lack of infrastructure in the immediate area. . . . Seeking to facilitate passageway onto his property, Mebane decided an additional bridge should be built, this one near the confluence of the Dan River and the Fishing Creek. As a result, much of the debate about whether to build what would be called the Fishing Creek Bridge (and much of the controversy that accompanied its construction) was in fact a debate over B. Frank Mebane.

Even though Mebane would be the obvious primary beneficiary of the construction of a new bridge, the project was consistent with his larger plan to develop Rockingham County, so he wanted the county to pay for it. Thus, his plan began with the Rockingham County Board of Commissioners. In 1922, Mebane, himself an avid Republican in heavily Democratic Rockingham County, channeled his substantial charisma, powers of persuasion, and financial resources to recruit three Democrats to support his industrial agenda and run for the county's board of commissioners: Josiah Ferre McCollum, Thomas Ruffin Pratt, and William Franklin Pruitt. Both Pruitt and McCollum were farmers, Pratt was a modest merchant, and all three were late in years. . . .

Mebane quietly helped Pratt, Pruitt, and McCollum get elected to the five-member board of commissioners in the 1922 election along with two other Democrats — R. B. Chance and J. R. Martin. Pratt, Pruitt, and McCollum promptly initiated Mebane's bridge plan, issuing a proposal to build a new bridge near Mebane's Meadows property. Chance and Martin, however, were quite reluctant to fund the project, especially since another bridge would soon be completed only a mile and a half upstream. Initially, the three Mebane loyalists were undeterred. In a March 19, 1923, resolution introduced by Commissioner W. F. Pruitt, the board of county commissioners deemed it "a public necessity" to build a bridge across the Dan River near its juncture with the Fishing Creek. The proposal, receiving the support of Commissioners Pratt and McCollum while confronting strong opposition from Commissioners Martin and Chance, authorized the board to spend $50,000 on the bridge and to employ an engineer to lead the construction effort. At the same meeting, the board (led by Mebane's commissioners) voted three to two to build a hard-surface road from the town of Madison to Settle's bridge at an additional cost of $250,000. Neither of those figures, though, included the additional $100,000 that would be needed to build a road to and from the Fishing Creek site — the bridge plan was initiated without a plan to provide road access.

These very substantial public expenditures were unprecedented for Rockingham County and forced dramatic changes in the county's finances. The county commissioners raised county property taxes to bankroll much of these new public works projects. . . . The commissioners also issued new bonds at significant interest rates, increasing the county's debt by nearly one-third and leaving Rockingham County in 1925 with the third-highest indebtedness among North Carolina's ninety-eight counties. . . . The rising taxes, and the apparent cronyism behind them and the project they financed, quickly led to a backlash against Mebane's proposal.

The board's construction plans immediately drew the ire of many of Rockingham County's citizens. The heavily Democratic county was like many Democratic bastions of the time in the South, comprised primarily of rural voters opposed to substantial government spending of any kind, particularly spending on public works designed to foster industrialization. The county's rural taxpayers were especially hostile to public spending fueled by property taxes since they would bear most of the burden while most of the benefits would accrue to their industrializing neighbors. Moreover, the board of commissioners had been elected in 1922 on a platform of fiscal restraint, so the additional spending was seen as both extravagant and a breach of the voters' trust by many of the commissioners' traditional supporters. . . .

As political opposition gained momentum, Mebane's opponents mounted a legal attack on the project. A group of local lawyers . . . filed for an injunction in local state court to prevent the county board from entering into a contract to build the proposed bridge. . . . The complaint successfully convinced Judge H. P. Lane of North Carolina's Eleventh District (and a native of Leaksville) to impose a temporary injunction to prevent the county board from entering into a contract to build the Fishing Creek Bridge. However, Superior Court Judge Thomas J. Shaw later dissolved the injunction on appeal, concluding that as long as nothing illegal was being done, the county's elected officials could decide matters of public expenditures as they saw fit. Since the schedule of the appellate courts made it unlikely that any further appeal would be heard before construction of the bridge was completed, opponents of the bridge opted instead to arouse political pressure and called for a series of "mass meetings" to organize and defeat the Mebane plan. . . .

At [one] mass meeting, which . . . coincided with a meeting of the board and at which a Luten Bridge Company representative was in attendance, Citizens' Committee Chairman Montgomery vigorously attacked the proposal, promised that the Citizens' Committee would not back down, and then invoked the image of the Ku Klux Klan, which reputedly counted among its ranks members of the Citizens' Committee leadership. He declared, "I don't know much about this organization, . . . but when we have to go after anything we are not going to mask but we will go if it is necessary." The *Gazette* also noted an association between the Klan and the anti-bridge movement, referring to their mass meetings as "masked meetings." . . .

By January of 1924, many people in Rockingham County assumed that Mebane's bridge would not be built. Then, on January 7, 1924, like a "bolt from the clear sky," the board of county commissioners voted three to two, with Commissioners Pratt, Pruitt, and McCollum voting in favor, and Commissioners Barber and Martin voting in opposition, to approve the construction of the Fishing Creek Bridge. A contract in the amount of $39,675 was awarded to the Luten Bridge Company of Knoxville, Tennessee. . . . To the Luten Bridge Company, this was yet another routine contract with a community.

Many in the county, however, met the news with public outcry and immediately charged Pratt, Pruitt, and McCollum with being improperly swayed by Mebane's deep pockets. Political pressure swelled to a fever pitch as the parties entered February 1924, which would prove to be the pivotal month in which the composition of the board of commissioners, and the contours of the bridge debate, drastically changed.

On February 11, 1924, W. Franklin Pruitt sent a letter of resignation from the board of county commissioners to Hunter K. Penn, the Rockingham County clerk:

> As my health has so failed me that I fear that I cannot attend the meetings of the Board of Co. Commissioners as I should and feeling that it would be to the best interest of my health I hereby tender my resignation as a member of said Board, my resignation effective at once. I have desired to do my duty as one of the Board, and do hope that a good man will be chosen as my successor.

Pruitt, however, promptly reconsidered his resignation, and later that same afternoon he contacted the clerk's office requesting to rescind his resignation. Pruitt then sent another letter the same day, addressed to the board and sent to Clerk Penn, saying that "after due consideration I request the Board not to take any action on the [resignation], and I still consider myself a member of said Board." He later explained, in a remark that suggests Mebane's forceful hand, that "friends" had "urged upon [him] that it was his duty to remain faithful to the County interests to which he had been elected."

Penn disregarded both Pruitt's call and letter and instead accepted Pruitt's resignation. The next day, Penn wrote to W. W. Hampton, a Leaksville businessman, appointing him "as a County Commissioner for Rockingham County to fill the unexpired term of W. F. Pruitt, resigned." Hampton was described by the *Reidsville Review* as "a dyed-in-the-wool democrat" and "a booster at all times for this great county." His loyalties to the county's Democrats ensured that Hampton would oppose construction of the bridge, thus changing the balance of power on the five-member board.

For the following eleven months, both Pruitt and Hampton claimed to be on the county board of commissioners, leaving the actual membership of that body in dispute. But even as Pruitt continued to claim a place on the board, he, Chairman Pratt, and Commissioner McCollum stopped attending board meetings. . . . Pratt and McCollum explained their own continued absences from their rightful place at the board meetings with claims of poor health.

Meanwhile, the anti-bridge commissioners — Martin, Barber, and Hampton — immediately asserted control over Rockingham County matters and started implementing a traditional Democratic agenda. In its first meeting, on February 21, 1924, the board agreed to cut spending projects throughout the county. It first resolved "that any new public road, or new construction on same decided on by Board . . . be stopped at once" and then ordered "to rescind any and all orders in regard to new public road, leading from Spray-Draper hard surface road to proposed site of Fishing Creek Bridge." Next on the chopping block was the bridge itself. The board proclaimed that the Fishing Creek Bridge was "not in the public interest, but on the contrary against the public interest." As such, they ordered the clerk to notify the Luten Bridge Company that the county "refuses to recognize the said paper writing as a valid contract and to advise said Bridge Company to proceed no further thereunder." At the time of this proclamation, the Luten Bridge Company had incurred only $1,900 in costs. . . .

The two parallel boards, and the confusion over who spoke for the county, wreaked significant uncertainty over county policy. When the anti-bridge board met on March 3, 1924, the three commissioners noted that they had "been informed that a member of this Board was privately insisting on the Luten Bridge Company building the Fishing Creek Bridge in opposition to the action of this Board." Notwithstanding this claim, the board reiterated its refusal to pay for the bridge, resolving that the Luten Bridge Company should be notified that:

> [A]ny and all work or expense incurred by it in regard to said bridge will be done by it at its own hazard and risk. The Board is of the opinion that the paper writing signed by T. R. Pratt purporting to be a contract with the Luten Bridge Company for the construction of this bridge is not a valid and legal contract as heretofore expressed by resolution of this Board, but if this Board should be mistaken about the legality of said paper writing, this Board does not desire to construct this bridge and will contest the payment for same if constructed.

Nonetheless, the Luten Bridge Company continued to build. The *Tri-City Daily Gazette* reported, "It is thought that attorneys for the bridge company were looking into the legal status of the matter and found that the only safe thing to do, was to fulfill their contract signed by themselves and the commissioners." Some believed that the reason the bridge company continued to build was that B. Frank Mebane promised to pay for the bridge if the company was unable to secure payment from the county. Indeed, years after the incident, one newspaper reported that Mebane personally gave the Luten Bridge Company $25,000 in Liberty Bonds to continue building the bridge. . . .

Whatever its reason, the Luten Bridge Company appeared steadfast in its plans to build the bridge. Even after Rockingham County indicated that it would not pay for the bridge, W. H. Long, vice president of the Luten Bridge Company, traveled to Rockingham County and defiantly proclaimed in an interview with the *Reidsville Review* that not only would the bridge be completed, but also that it would be "the finest bridge in [the] county." The company also issued a more direct response to the county's rescission by sending a letter to the board of county commissioners, stating:

> We are unable to agree with you that this contract is for any reason invalid or illegal, and we cannot consent to its recision [sic] or cancellation or to any other conduct upon your part which will excuse you from the full and complete execution and compliance therewith upon the part of the Board of Commissioners of Rockingham County. We have already assembled a lot of material, organized our forces and performed a portion of the contract. It shall be our purpose to live up to and carry out the contract upon our part, and this is to advise you that we shall expect you to do the same upon your part and that we will be paid by the county in accordance with the contract for the material and work done by us in the completion of the construction of the said bridge. We shall proceed at once and vigorously the construction of this bridge [sic] in fulfillment of our contract with full confidence that the county will fulfill its part and pay for the same.

The Luten Bridge Company and the three opposing commissioners continued to play a slow-paced cat-and-mouse game throughout the summer. After each board of commissioners meeting, the board passed a resolution, and gave notice to the company, decreeing that the county refused to meet its end of the contract. Meanwhile, county engineer J. S. Trogdon came to the courthouse each month with a new estimate of what the county owed the Luten Bridge Company, and every month the county rejected the bill on its face. . . . [T]he county's residents grew increasingly divided about the issue, torn between supporting the commissioners' decisions or supporting the initial bridge plan. . . .

The battle over the bridge became even more contentious in late 1924 when the county commissioners were up for reelection. When Pratt, Pruitt, and McCollum all declined to seek reelection, Mebane (who, after all, was a Republican himself) pledged his support behind the 1924 Republican campaign and the Republican challengers for the county commission. As the November election approached, it clearly became a referendum on not only the bridge project but also on B. Frank Mebane himself. . . .

The election clearly reflected the county's anger. With a record voter turnout and in a categorical rebuke of Mebane's plan, the previous anti-bridge commissioners, Barber, Martin, and Hampton, were all reelected . . . and the Republican candidates were handily beaten. . . . With the board now firmly and indisputably in the hands of the Fishing Creek Bridge's opponents, the stage was set for a legal battle with the Luten Bridge Company. . . .

B. Frank Mebane never saw any of the trials related to his bridge. He died suddenly on June 15, 1926, after three days of illness in New York City, while traveling en route to London to meet his wife. Dying without children, Mebane left his entire estate, then valued at $2,000,000, to Lily. News of his death received national attention and was the major news story of the week in the *North Carolina Piedmont*, with headlines such as "His Name is Written Large in Economic History of Rockingham County." . . . Judge Parker lived into his thirty-third year as a circuit judge, dying in 1958 while still on the bench. Few judges had careers as accomplished as Parker's, but it is likely that he never knew of the fame and legacy he would enjoy from his *Luten Bridge* opinion. Though the case appeared in Williston's casebook two years before Parker's death, it was not until the early 1960s that it became a staple in first-year contracts texts. And perhaps the penultimate testament to the lasting significance of the case did not arrive until 1979, fifty years after Judge Parker wrote the famous opinion, when *Luten Bridge* was included in the Restatement (Second) of the Law of Contracts to demonstrate the duty to mitigate principle.

After the tumult of the 1920s, the Fishing Creek Bridge sat quietly over the Dan River during the 1930s, unencumbered by traffic and alone in the woods. Occasionally the remote bridge played host to picnics and parties attended by young people from the area, including some elegant dinners and dances. Through the following decades, the absurdity of the Fishing Creek Bridge's existence became part of Rockingham County folklore and soon "Mebane's Bridge" also became known as "Mebane's Folly." . . .

In 1968, the State Department of Transportation finally paved a road on both sides of the bridge. Dismissing the span's actual name, the Fishing Creek Bridge, the new street signs read "Mebane Bridge Road." And what might be the bridge's final chapter arrived in the fall of 2003, when the famous bridge was permanently closed to traffic. The single-lane bridge still crosses high above the Dan River and remains available for pedestrians, and it now ingloriously supports a sewage pipe leading to Eden's water treatment facility. There have been threats that North Carolina's Department of Transportation might decide to demolish the bridge, but that sewage pipe might just save the bridge from destruction. However long it remains above the Dan River, Mebane's Bridge will serve as a monument to industrial ambition, cronyism, a countryside in transition, Judge Parker's most famous opinion, and one of the most bizarre and heated moments in Rockingham County's history.

STUDY GUIDE: How does the situation in the following case differ from that in Rockingham County v. Luten Bridge Co.? What countervailing difficulties of principle and policy arise when we try to extend the approach taken there to this setting? [Beginning in the 1950s, Shirley MacLaine has made over 40 feature films including Irma la Douce, Sweet Charity, Two

Mules for Sister Sarah *(a western with Clint Eastwood released in 1970),* The Turning Point, Terms of Endearment *(for which she won an Academy award for best actress),* Postcards from the Edge, *and* Guarding Tess.*]*

SHIRLEY MacLAINE PARKER v. TWENTIETH CENTURY-FOX FILM CORP.

Supreme Court of California, 3 Cal. 3d 176, 89 Cal. Rptr. 737, 474 P.2d 689 (1970)

BURKE, J.*

Defendant Twentieth Century-Fox Film Corporation appeals from a summary judgment granting to plaintiff the recovery of agreed compensation under a written contract for her services as an actress in a motion picture. As will appear, we have concluded that the trial court correctly ruled in plaintiff's favor and that the judgment should be affirmed.

Plaintiff is well known as an actress, and in the contract between plaintiff and defendant is sometimes referred to as the "Artist." Under the contract, dated August 6, 1965, plaintiff was to play the female lead in defendant's contemplated production of a motion picture entitled "Bloomer Girl." The contract provided that defendant would pay plaintiff a minimum "guaranteed compensation" of "[$]53,571.42 per week for 14 weeks commencing May 23, 1966," for a total of $750,000. Prior to May 1966 defendant decided not to produce the picture and by a letter dated April 4, 1966, it notified plaintiff of that decision and that it would not "comply with our obligations to you under" the written contract.

By the same letter and with the professed purpose "to avoid any damage to you," defendant instead offered to employ plaintiff as the leading actress in another film tentatively entitled "Big Country, Big Man" (hereinafter, "Big Country"). The compensation offered was identical, as were 31 of the 34 numbered provisions or articles of the original contract.[63] Unlike "Bloomer Girl," however, which was to have been a musical production, "Big Country" was a dramatic "western type" movie. "Bloomer Girl" was to have been filmed in California; "Big Country" was to be produced in Australia. Also, certain terms in the proffered contract varied from those of the original.[64]

Lloyd Hudson Burke (1916-1988) was educated at St. Mary's College (A.B.) and Boalt Hall, University of California at Berkeley (LL.B.). He began his career as a Deputy District Attorney for Alameda County, California (1940-1953), before serving as the U.S. Attorney for the Northern District of California (1953-1958). In 1958, he was appointed to the U.S. District Court for the Northern District of California, where he served until 1979 (senior status, 1979-1988). Judge Burke also served in the U.S. Army. — J.B.

63. Among the identical provisions was the following found in the last paragraph of Article 2 of the original contract: "We [defendant] shall not be obligated to utilize your [plaintiff's] services in or in connection with the Photoplay hereunder, our sole obligation, subject to the terms and conditions of this Agreement, being to pay you the guaranteed compensation herein provided for."

64. Article 29 of the original contract specified that plaintiff approved the director already chosen for "Bloomer Girl" and that in case he failed to act as director plaintiff was to have approval rights of any substitute director. Article 31 provided that plaintiff

Plaintiff was given one week within which to accept; she did not and the offer lapsed. Plaintiff then commenced this action seeking recovery of the agreed guaranteed compensation.

The complaint sets forth two causes of action. The first is for money due under the contract; the second, based upon the same allegations as the first, is for damages resulting from defendant's breach of contract. Defendant in its answer admits the existence and validity of the contract, that plaintiff complied with all the conditions, covenants and promises and stood ready to complete the performance, and that defendant breached and "anticipatorily repudiated" the contract. It denies, however, that any money is due to plaintiff either under the contract or as a result of its breach, and pleads as an affirmative defense to both causes of action plaintiff's allegedly deliberate failure to mitigate damages, asserting that she unreasonably refused to accept its offer of the leading role in "Big Country."

Plaintiff moved for summary judgment under Code of Civil Procedure section 437c, the motion was granted, and summary judgment for $750,000 plus interest was entered in plaintiff's favor. This appeal by defendant followed. . . .

As stated, defendant's sole defense to this action which resulted from its deliberate breach of contract is that in rejecting defendant's substitute offer of employment plaintiff unreasonably refused to mitigate damages.

The general rule is that the measure of recovery by a wrongfully discharged employee is the amount of salary agreed upon for the period of service, less the amount which the employer affirmatively proves the employee has earned or with reasonable effort might have earned from

---

was to have the right of approval of the "Bloomer Girl" dance director, and Article 32 gave her the right of approval of the screenplay.

Defendant's letter of April 4 to plaintiff, which contained both defendant's notice of breach of the "Bloomer Girl" contract and offer of the lead in "Big Country," eliminated or impaired each of those rights. It read in part as follows:

> The terms and conditions of our offer of employment are identical to those set forth in the "BLOOMER GIRL" Agreement, Articles 1 through 34 and Exhibit A to the Agreement, except as follows:

(1)   Article 31 of said Agreement will not be included in any contract of employment regarding "BIG COUNTRY, BIG MAN" as it is not a musical and it thus will not need a dance director.

(2)   In the "BLOOMER GIRL" agreement, in Articles 29 and 32, you were given certain director and screenplay approvals and you had preapproved certain matters. Since there simply is insufficient time to negotiate with you regarding your choice of director and regarding the screenplay and since you already expressed an interest in performing the role in "BIG COUNTRY, BIG MAN," we must exclude from our offer of employment in "BIG COUNTRY, BIG MAN" any approval rights as are contained in said Articles 29 and 32; however, we shall consult with you respecting the director to be selected to direct the photoplay and will further consult with you with respect to the screenplay and any revisions or changes therein, provided, however, that if we fail to agree . . . the decision of . . . [defendant] with respect to the selection of a director and to revisions and changes in the said screenplay shall be binding upon the parties to said agreement.

other employment. . . .[65] However, before projected earnings from other employment opportunities not sought or accepted by the discharged employee can be applied in mitigation, the employer must show that the other employment was comparable, or substantially similar, to that of which the employee has been deprived; the employee's rejection of or failure to seek other available employment of a different or inferior kind may not be resorted to in order to mitigate damages. . . .

In the present case defendant has raised no issue of *reasonableness of efforts* by plaintiff to obtain other employment; the sole issue is whether plaintiff's refusal of defendant's substitute offer of "Big Country" may be used in mitigation. Nor, if the "Big Country" offer was of employment different or inferior when compared with the original "Bloomer Girl" employment, is there an issue as to whether or not plaintiff acted reasonably in refusing the substitute offer. Despite defendant's arguments to the contrary, no case cited or which our research has discovered holds or suggests that reasonableness is an element of a wrongfully discharged employee's option to reject, or fail to seek, different or inferior employment lest the possible earnings therefrom be charged against him in mitigation of damages.[66]

65. Although it would appear that plaintiff was not *discharged* by defendant in the customary sense of the term, as she was not permitted by defendant to enter upon performance of the "Bloomer Girl" contract, nevertheless the motion for summary judgment was submitted for decision upon a stipulation by the parties that "plaintiff Parker was discharged."

66. Instead, in each case the reasonableness referred to was that of the *efforts* of the employee to obtain other employment that was not different or inferior; his right to reject the latter was declared as an unqualified rule of law. Thus, Gonzales v. Internat. Assn. of Machinists, supra, 213 Cal. App. 2d 817, 823-824, 29 Cal. Rptr. 190, 194, holds that the trial court correctly instructed the jury that plaintiff union member, a machinist, was required to make "such *efforts* as the average (member of his union) desiring employment would make at that particular time and place" (italics added); but, further, that the court *properly rejected* defendant's *offer of proof of the availability of other kinds of employment* at the same or higher pay than plaintiff usually received and all outside the jurisdiction of his union, as plaintiff could not be required to accept different employment or a nonunion job. In Harris v. Nat. Union, etc., Cooks and Stewards, supra, 116 Cal. App. 2d 759, 761, 254 P.2d 673, 676, the issues were stated to be, inter alia, whether comparable employment was open to each plaintiff employee; and if so whether each plaintiff made a *reasonable effort* to secure such employment. It was held that the trial court *properly sustained an objection to an offer to prove a custom of accepting a job in a lower rank when work in the higher rank* was not available, as "The duty of mitigation of damages . . . does not require the plaintiff 'to seek or to accept other employment of a different or inferior kind.' " (p. 764[5], 254 P.2d p. 676.) See also: Lewis v. Protective Security Life Ins. Co. (1962) 208 Cal. App. 2d 582, 583, 584, 25 Cal. Rptr. 213, 214: "*honest effort* to find similar employment. . . ." (Italics added.) De La Falaise v. Gaumont-British P. Corp., supra, 39 Cal. App. 2d 461, 469, 103 P.2d 447: "reasonable effort." Erler v. Five Points Motors, Inc. (1967) 249 Cal. App. 2d 560, 562, 57 Cal. Rptr. 516, 518. Damages may be mitigated "by a showing that the employee, by the exercise of *reasonable diligence and effort,* could have procured comparable employment. . . ." (Italics added.) Savitz v. Gallaccio (Pa. 1955) 179 Pa. Super. 589, 118 A.2d 282, 286; Atholwood Development Co. v. Houston (1941) 179 Md. 441, 19 A.2d 706, 708; Harcourt Co. v. Heller (1933) 250 Ky. 321, 62 S.W.2d 1056; Alaska Airlines v. Stephenson (9th Cir. 1954) 217 F.2d 295, 299, 15 Alaska 272; United Protective Workers of America, Local No. 2 v. Ford Motor Co. (7th Cir. 1955) 223 F.2d 49, 52; Chisholm v. Preferred Bankers' Life Assur. Co. (1897) 112 Mich. 50, 70 N.W. 415; each of which held that the *reasonableness of the employee's efforts,* or his excuses for failure, to find other similar employment was properly submitted to the

Applying the foregoing rules to the record in the present case, with all intendments in favor of the party opposing the summary judgment motion — here, defendant — it is clear that the trial court correctly ruled that plaintiff's failure to accept defendant's tendered substitute employment could not be applied in mitigation of damages because the offer of the "Big Country" lead was of employment both different and inferior, and that no factual dispute was presented on that issue. The mere circumstance that "Bloomer Girl" was to be a musical review calling upon plaintiff's talents as a dancer as well as an actress, and was to be produced in the City of Los Angeles, whereas "Big Country" was a straight dramatic role in a "Western Type" story taking place in an opal mine in Australia, demonstrates the difference in kind between the two employments; the female lead as a dramatic actress in a western style motion picture can by no stretch of imagination be considered the equivalent of or substantially similar to the lead in a song-and-dance production.

Additionally, the substitute "Big Country" offer proposed to eliminate or impair the director and screenplay approvals accorded to plaintiff under the original "Bloomer Girl" contract (see fn. [64], ante), and thus constituted an offer of inferior employment. No expertise or judicial notice is required in order to hold that the deprivation or infringement of an employee's rights held under an original employment contract converts the available "other employment" relied upon by the employer to mitigate damages, into inferior employment which the employee need not seek or accept. . . .

Statements found in affidavits submitted by defendant in opposition to plaintiff's summary judgment motion, to the effect that the "Big Country" offer was not of employment different from or inferior to that under the "Bloomer Girl" contract, merely repeat the allegations of defendant's answer to the complaint in this action, constitute only conclusionary assertions with respect to undisputed facts, and do not give rise to a triable factual issue so as to defeat the motion for summary judgment. . . .

In view of the determination that defendant failed to present any facts showing the existence of a factual issue with respect to its sole defense — plaintiff's rejection of its substitute employment offer in mitigation of damages — we need not consider plaintiff's further contention that for various reasons, including the provisions of the original contract set forth in footnote [64], ante, plaintiff was excused from attempting to mitigate damages.

The judgment is affirmed.

McComb, Peters, and Tobriner, JJ., and Kaus, J. pro tem., and Roth, J. pro tem., concur.

---

jury as a question of fact. NB: *Chisholm* additionally *approved* a jury *instruction* that a *substitute offer* of the employer to work for a lesser compensation was *not to be considered in mitigation,* as the employee was not required to accept it. Williams v. National Organization, Masters, etc. (1956) 384 Pa. 413, 120 A.2d 896, 901(13): "Even assuming that plaintiff . . . could have obtained employment in ports other than . . . where he resided, *legally* he was not compelled to do so in order to mitigate his damages." (Italics added.)

SULLIVAN, Acting C.J.* (dissenting).

The basic question in this case is whether or not plaintiff acted reasonably in rejecting defendant's offer of alternate employment. The answer depends upon whether that offer (starring in "Big Country, Big Man") was an offer of work that was substantially similar to her former employment (starring in "Bloomer Girl") or of work that was of a different or inferior kind. To my mind this is a factual issue which the trial court should not have determined on a motion for summary judgment. The majority have not only repeated this error but have compounded it by applying the rules governing mitigation of damages in the employer-employee context in a misleading fashion. Accordingly, I respectfully dissent.

The familiar rule requiring a plaintiff in a tort or contract action to mitigate damages embodies notions of fairness and socially responsible behavior which are fundamental to our jurisprudence. Most broadly stated, it precludes the recovery of damages which, through the exercise of due diligence, could have been avoided. Thus, in essence, it is a rule requiring reasonable conduct in commercial affairs. This general principle governs the obligations of an employee after his employer has wrongfully repudiated or terminated the employment contract. Rather than permitting the employee simply to remain idle during the balance of the contract period, the law requires him to make a reasonable effort to secure other employment. He is not obliged, however, to seek or accept any and all types of work which may be available. Only work which is in the same field and which is of the same quality need be accepted.[67]

Over the years the courts have employed various phrases to define the type of employment which the employee, upon his wrongful discharge, is under an obligation to accept. Thus in California alone it has been held that he must accept employment which is "substantially similar" . . . ; "comparable employment" . . . ; employment "in the same general line of the first employment" . . . ; "equivalent to his prior position" . . . ; employment which is "not . . . of a different or inferior kind. . . ."

For reasons which are unexplained, the majority cite several of these cases yet select from among the various judicial formulations which contain they [sic] one particular phrase, "Not of a different or inferior kind," with which to analyze this case. I have discovered no historical or theoretical reason to adopt this phrase, which is simply a negative restatement of the affirmative standards set out in the above cases, as the exclusive standard.

Raymond L. Sullivan (1907-1999) was appointed to the California Court of Appeals (1961-1966) before serving on the California Supreme Court (1966-1975). Known for his eloquence and scholarship, Sullivan received many honors, including the state bar's Witkin Medal (1994) for particularly distinguished service to the law that has "changed the landscape of California jurisprudence." Stating that Sullivan "brought true justice to the state high court with his commitment to the principles of fairness and equality," whether addressing education finance or prohibiting contributory negligence, the Lieutenant Governor of California ordered that flags be flown at half-staff when he received news of Sullivan's death.

67. This qualification of the rule seems to reflect the simple and humane attitude that it is too severe to demand of a person that he attempt to find and perform work for which he has no training or experience. Many of the older cases hold that one need not accept work in an inferior rank or position nor work which is more menial or arduous. This suggests that the rule may have had its origin in the bourgeois fear of resubmergence in lower economic classes.

Indeed, its emergence is an example of the dubious phenomenon of the law responding not to rational judicial choice or changing social conditions, but to unrecognized changes in the language of opinions or legal treatises. However, the phrase is a serviceable one and my concern is not with its use as the standard but rather with what I consider its distortion.

The relevant language excuses acceptance only of employment which is of a *different* kind. . . . It has never been the law that the mere existence of *differences between two jobs in the same field* is sufficient, as a matter of law, to excuse an employee wrongfully discharged from one from accepting the other in order to mitigate damages. Such an approach would effectively eliminate any obligation of an employee to attempt to minimize damage arising from a wrongful discharge. The only alternative job offer an employee would be required to accept would be an offer of his former job by his former employer.

Although the majority appear to hold that there was a difference "in kind" between the employment offered plaintiff in "Bloomer Girl" and that offered in "Big Country" . . . , an examination of the opinion makes crystal clear that the majority merely point out differences between the two *films* (an obvious circumstance) and then apodictically assert that these constitute a difference in the *kind of employment.* The entire rationale of the majority boils down to this: that the *"mere circumstances "* that "Bloomer Girl" was to be a musical review while "Big Country" was a straight drama "demonstrates the difference in kind" since a female lead in a western is not "the equivalent of or substantially similar to" a lead in a musical. This is merely attempting to prove the proposition by repeating it. It shows that the vehicles for the display of the star's talents are different but it does not prove that her employment as a star in such vehicles is of necessity different *in kind* and either inferior or superior.

I believe that the approach taken by the majority (a superficial listing of differences with no attempt to assess their significance) may subvert a valuable legal doctrine.[68] The inquiry in cases such as this should not be whether differences between the two jobs exist (there will always be differences) but whether the differences which are present are substantial enough to constitute differences in the *kind* of employment or, alternatively, whether they render the substitute work employment of an *inferior kind.*

It seems to me that *this* inquiry involves, in the instant case at least, factual determinations which are improper on a motion for summary judgment. Resolving whether or not one job is substantially similar to another or whether, on the other hand, it is of a different or inferior kind, will often (as here) require a critical appraisal of the similarities and differences between them in light of the importance of these differences to the employee. This necessitates a weighing of the evidence, and it is precisely this undertaking which is forbidden on summary judgment. . . .

---

68. The values of the doctrine of mitigation of damages in this context are that it minimizes the unnecessary personal and social (e.g., nonproductive use of labor, litigation) costs of contractual failure. If a wrongfully discharged employee can, through his own action and without suffering financial or psychological loss in the process, reduce the damages accruing from the breach of contract, the most sensible policy is to require him to do so. I fear the majority opinion will encourage precisely opposite conduct.

This is not to say that summary judgment would never be available in an action by an employee in which the employer raises the defense of failure to mitigate damages. No case has come to my attention, however, in which summary judgment has been granted on the issue of whether an employee was obliged to accept available alternate employment. Nevertheless, there may well be cases in which the substitute employment is so manifestly of a dissimilar or inferior sort, the declarations of the plaintiff so complete and those of the defendant so conclusionary and inadequate that no factual issues exist for which a trial is required. This, however, is not such a case.

It is not intuitively obvious, to me at least, that the leading female role in a dramatic motion picture is a radically different endeavor from the leading female role in a musical comedy film. Nor is it plain to me that the rather qualified rights of director and screenplay approval contained in the first contract are highly significant matters either in the entertainment industry in general or to this plaintiff in particular. Certainly, none of the declarations introduced by plaintiff in support of her motion shed any light on these issues. Nor do they attempt to explain why she declined the offer of starring in "Big Country, Big Man." Nevertheless, the trial court granted the motion, declaring that these approval rights were "critical" and that their elimination altered "the essential nature of the employment." . . .

I cannot accept the proposition that an offer which eliminates *any* contract right, regardless of its significance, is, as a matter of law, an offer of employment of an inferior kind. Such an absolute rule seems no more sensible than the majority's earlier suggestion that the mere existence of differences between two jobs is sufficient to render them employment of different kinds. Application of such per se rules will severely undermine the principle of mitigation of damages in the employer-employee context.

I remain convinced that the relevant question in such cases is whether or not a particular contract provision is so significant that its omission creates employment of an inferior kind. This question is, of course, intimately bound up in what I consider the ultimate issue: whether or not the employee acted reasonably. This will generally involve a factual inquiry to ascertain the importance of the particular contract term and a process of weighing the absence of that term against the countervailing advantages of the alternate employment. In the typical case, this will mean that summary judgment must be withheld.

In the instant case, there was nothing properly before the trial court by which the importance of the approval rights could be ascertained, much less evaluated. Thus, in order to grant the motion for summary judgment, the trial court misused judicial notice. In upholding the summary judgment, the majority here rely upon per se rules which distort the process of determining whether or not an employee is obliged to accept particular employment in mitigation of damages.

I believe that the judgment should be reversed so that the issue of whether or not the offer of the lead role in "Big Country, Big Man" was of employment comparable to that of the lead role in "Bloomer Girl" may be determined at trial.

Rehearing denied; SULLIVAN, J., dissenting.

MOSK, J., did not participate.

Relational Background: A Feminist Interpretation of Parker

STUDY GUIDE: When reading the following, consider how the subjectivism of economics intersects with Professor Frug's use of feminist analysis.

MARY JOE FRUG, SHIRLEY MACLAINE AND THE MITIGATION OF DAMAGES RULE: RE-UNITING LANGUAGE AND EXPERIENCE IN LEGAL DOCTRINE, from RE-READING CONTRACTS: A FEMINIST ANALYSIS OF A CONTRACTS CASEBOOK, 34 AM. U. L. REV. 1065, 1115-1119 (1985):   By calling attention to the majority opinion's conclusory application of the "different or inferior" qualification, the dissenting opinion encourages the . . . reader to feel uncertain about how to use the mitigation rule in the employment context. It will seem unjust, to some readers, that Shirley MacLaine is apparently going to get $750,000, after this decision, for doing nothing. The mitigation rule seems to lose all of its muscle as a result of this "different or inferior" qualification. Would MacLaine have been entitled to damages if she had refused the lead in "Annie Hall," because that extremely successful film, is not a musical? Would she have been denied damages if she had turned down "Springtime for Hitler"?[69] How can you tell?

I believe The Feminist Reader and the Reader with a Chip on her Shoulder (as well as other readers who are familiar with feminist social history) might find the majority's application of the "different or inferior" standard much less mysterious than other readers. Their views would be based on their acquaintance either with Amelia Bloomer, a mid-nineteenth century feminist, suffragist, and abolitionist, or with "bloomers," the loose trousers that some women wore under a short skirt, without hoops, multiple petticoats, or restricting underwear, in the early 1850s. (Bloomer, whose magazine, The Lily, was the first American magazine published by and for women, publicized and stirred enthusiasm among some women for the trousers, or pantelettes, as they were sometimes known, and they came to be called after her.) These readers might have the intuition, as I did in reading the *Parker* case, that a film entitled "Bloomer Girl" was related in some way to the radical effort feminists in the last century made to achieve more freedom of movement and control over what they wore by reforming their dress. Moreover, simply because Shirley MacLaine is a woman, these readers might assume that the role in "Bloomer Girl" had personal significance for the actress;[70] even if the film treated women's issues in the light-hearted fashion typical of musical comedy, it would still link the actress with events that are historically significant to other women.[71] "Bloomer Girl"

---

69. "Springtime for Hitler" was the musical comedy created within the film "The Producers" solely for the purpose of obtaining a financial loss for its originators. The producers designed the musical hoping it would be a commercial disaster. See *N.Y. Times*, Mar. 19, 1968, at 38, col. 1 (reviewing "The Producers").

70. Although the actress's decision to reject "Big Country, Big Man" may not have been politically motivated, feminists who read the case now may identify MacLaine as a feminist and they are likely to assume that her decision more than twenty years ago was politically motivated. . . .

71. Indeed, while the spirited campaign for bloomers was ultimately unsuccessful in reforming women's dress of the period, it contained themes familiar to modern feminists —

would seem different, from this perspective, not only from a western but from other musical comedies, because of its political overtones.

In contrast with their favorable attitudes toward "Bloomer Girl," The Feminist Reader as well as the Reader with a Chip on her Shoulder would probably assume that a movie entitled "Big Country, Big Man" would offer a leading actress the inferior kind of leading role westerns have typically offered women. Like Miss Kitty in "Gunsmoke," a woman in a western is usually very much subordinated to the main focus of such films — the cowboy-hero. Because feminist readers oppose the subordination of women, they are likely to believe that, assuming "Big Man" portrayed women as men's sidekicks, it would be "inferior" to "Bloomer Girl," where women were probably shown leading their sisters to fight for control over their own bodies. Thus, the readers' gender-related presumptions regarding the political overtones of "Big Country, Big Man" would affect their opinion of why the film would seem "different or inferior" to "Bloomer Girl."

Although these readers might not know whether "Bloomer Girl" had feminist themes[72] or whether "Big Country, Big Man" portrayed women according to the usual demeaning western stereotype,[73] because of their skepticism about women's roles in westerns and their intuitions regarding "Bloomer Girl's" feminist themes, they might understand MacLaine's rejection of the "Big Country, Big Man" role in terms of their own efforts to reconcile their politics with their careers. These readers would be able to ground the language of the "different or inferior" qualification in their own lives.[74] They might assume that MacLaine not only sought to refuse a role that would be

---

bloomer advocates sought to free themselves from the confines of fashion constraints which they blamed men for imposing on them. Cf. S. Brownmiller, Femininity 77-102 (1984); K. Chernin, The Obsession: Reflections on the Tyranny of Slenderness (1981); Note, Gender-Specific Clothing Regulation: A Study in Patriarchy, 5 Harv. Women's L.J. 73 (1982).

72. It turns out that "Bloomer Girl" did have feminist themes, as Charles Knapp has pointed out in his contracts casebook. . . . My own intuitions about "Bloomer Girl" were confirmed by reading John Gregory Dunne's review of a book by "Danny Santiago" in the New York Review of Books last year. Dunne, The Secret of Danny Santiago (Book Review), 31 N.Y. Rev. of Books 17 (Aug. 16, 1984) (reviewing D. Santiago, Famous All Over Town (1984)). "Danny Santiago" was revealed in that review to be the *nom de plume* of Dan James, a Hollywood writer who was blacklisted during the fifties because of his past membership in the Communist Party. Dunne mentioned that the Broadway musical "Bloomer Girl" was based on a play that James and his wife Lilith co-authored. The inspiration for the James' play stemmed from "a Party-endorsed workshop on women's rights." Id. at 20. . . .

73. The court in *Parker* states that "Big Country" was a " 'western type' story taking place in an opal mine in Australia." . . . Marlene Lasky, library assistant with the Academy of Motion Picture Arts and Sciences, stated in a telephone interview that although Sean Connery and Diane Cilento were signed to play the lead roles, the movie was probably never made. Telephone interview with Marlene Lasky, Library Assistant, Academy of Motion Picture Arts and Sciences (July 22, 1985). Ms. Lasky thinks the film was about the settlement of Australia.

74. These readers might also be able to find support for their views in other language of the majority opinion. By describing the "Big Man" role as a "*female* lead as a dramatic actress in a *western* style motion picture," the majority may be indicating their awareness that women are traditionally given subordinate roles in western films. . . . In contrast, the dissent describes the "Big Country, Big Man" role as "the leading female role in a dramatic motion picture." . . . By not referring to the "dramatic motion picture" as a "western," the dissent seems insensitive to the issue of female subordination in westerns, thus suggesting that attitudes toward the importance of sex roles may explain the silent rationale of the majority opinion, as well as the distinctions between the two opinions in the case. . . .

demeaning to her as a woman, but that she also wanted to avoid contributing to the oppressed images of women in popular culture. Rather than thinking that Shirley MacLaine is being paid to do nothing in *Parker*, and that the "different or inferior" qualification to the mitigation rule was unfairly applied, their attitude toward the two films could enable them to infer an ascertainable but complicated standard for determining when the "different or inferior" qualification should be applied in employment cases. That is, they would assume that *Parker* demonstrates that an employee's serious and recognized personal goals should be respected and protected when they are connected to a concern that is respected and acknowledged by others. Under this interpretation, some degree of mitigation can be required (mitigation does not lose all of its muscle in *Parker*), and yet a wrongly discharged employee would not have to take just any substitute employment. Money would not be the only test for determining whether jobs are comparable, and yet other employment objectives would require social as well as personal significance in order to be protected under the "different or inferior" qualification.

The interpretation of *Parker* generated by feminist attitudes and information about the social history related to the case offers readers useful guidance in applying the "different or inferior" qualification to other situations. This interpretation also allows readers who identify with Shirley MacLaine (because she is a woman) to attribute dignity to her conduct.

Relational Background: The Rise and Fall of the Bloomer Girl *Project*

STUDY GUIDE: *In a brilliant chapter analyzing the legal theories of the* Parker *case, explaining the rationales for entertainment contracts with similar clauses, and criticizing the California Supreme Court's opinion in the case, Professor Goldberg also provides more details about the relationship of the parties.*

VICTOR GOLDBERG, FRAMING CONTRACT LAW: AN ECONOMIC PERSPECTIVE 281-284 (2006): *Bloomer Girl* was an adaptation of a stage musical, written by Harold Arlen and Yip Harburg, that ran for 654 performances on Broadway in the mid-1940s. Harburg's son summarized the play's plot and political themes:

> *Bloomer Girl* concerns the political activities of Amelia (renamed Dolly) Bloomer and the effect they have on the pre–Civil War family of her brother-in-law, hoopskirt king Horace Applegate, and his feminist daughter, Evalina. Evalina is the youngest and only remaining unmarried Applegate daughter; her older sisters are all married to company salesmen, and as *Bloomer Girl* begins, Horace is trying to unify business and family by encouraging his chief Southern salesman, Jefferson Calhoun, to court Evalina. On the eve of the Civil War, *Bloomer Girl* centers around Evalina's tutelage of Jeff in matters of gender and racial equality. Evalina, Dolly, and the other feminists of Cicero Falls not only campaign against Applegate's hoopskirts and sexism but also stage their own version of Uncle Tom's Cabin and conceal a runaway slave — Jeff's own manservant, Pompey. It was, said Yip, a show about the "the indivisibility of human freedom."

Bloomer Girl interweaves the issues of black and female equality and war and peace with the vicissitudes of courtship and pre–Civil War politics. . . . [I]t was at no point an escapist entertainment. "There were so many new issues coming up with Roosevelt in those years," Yip once said, "and we were trying to deal with the inherent fear of change — to show that whenever a new idea or a new change in society arises, there'll always be a majority that will fight you, that will call you a dirty radical or a red."

. . .

When she entered into her contract to make *Bloomer Girl* in August 1965, Shirley MacLaine was one of the biggest female stars in Hollywood, having received three Academy Award nominations for Best Actress in a five-year span. (The nominations were for *Irma La Douce* (United Artists, 1963) in 1964, *The Apartment* (United Artists, 1960) in 1961, and *Some Came Running* (Metro-Goldwyn-Mayer, 1959) in 1960.) The contract negotiation had taken about seven months. Shooting was to begin the following May and was expected to take fourteen weeks. MacLaine would receive 10% of the gross profits of the film to be offset against her guaranteed compensation ($750,000) and expenses of $50,000. She had the right to approve the screenplay and the director. In fact, the director, George Cukor, had already been approved. His previous film, *My Fair Lady*, had been both an artistic and a commercial success, both the film and Cukor winning Academy Awards in 1964. If the movie had been produced, and if it had been as successful at the box office as *My Fair Lady*, MacLaine would have earned over $3 million from the domestic box office alone. . . .

While waiting for shooting to begin on *Bloomer Girl*, MacLaine turned down a role in *Casino Royale*, for which she would have received guaranteed compensation of $1 million plus an unspecified percentage. It is not clear whether she was to receive a percentage of the gross receipts, as in *Bloomer Girl*, or of some other amount. The large number of stars associated with *Casino Royale* (and her counsel's silence) suggests that the contingent compensation was less favorable for *Casino Royale*. She did, nonetheless, manage to fit one film in; according to her agent, she "consented to perform in the motion picture called 'Gambit' for Universal Pictures only because she knew at the time that the motion picture 'Bloomer Girl' would follow."

In March 1966, Fox decided to terminate the *Bloomer Girl* project for reasons unspecified. Fox's letter to MacLaine said, in part:

Because of circumstances which have arisen since the date of the Agreement, we have determined not to proceed with the production of the photoplay as originally contemplated. Therefore, we cannot and will not utilize your services as contemplated by the Agreement nor otherwise comply with our obligations to you under that Agreement. In order to avoid any damage to you, the Corporation hereby offers to employ you to portray the leading feminine role in a photoplay tentatively entitled "Big Country, Big Man," which role you previously expressed interest in performing.

Big Country, Big Man (BCBM) was a western-style drama, set, and to be filmed in, Australia. She had read the screenplay in June 1965 and had expressed interest in doing the film if there were a different director.

The record is silent on the identity of the director and whether that director was still associated with the project when it was proposed in 1966. In the March discussions, her agent informed Fox that she was no longer interested in the alternative project. A few weeks later, Fox sent a letter (characterized by her counsel as artfully drafted) to MacLaine informing her that her services would not be utilized in *Bloomer Girl* and offering her the female lead in *BCBM* as a substitute, giving her one week to accept the offer. The terms of the second contract would be the same, with a few exceptions. In fact, of the thirty-four clauses in the *Bloomer Girl* contract, thirty-one were identical. The second contract eliminated the clause giving her approval rights regarding the dance director (since there would be none) and modified her approval rights of the director and the screenplay.

There are hints in the record that the *BCBM* offer was not entirely sincere. Her agent stated in his declaration that Fox had informed him in December 1965 that *BCBM* was off schedule and if it were to be done at all, it would probably be in 1967. In the March discussion of the termination of the *Bloomer Girl* project, Richard Zanuck (Fox's executive vice president in charge of production) purportedly told her agent that the script was much better now and could be produced in July or August 1966. . . . In his declaration, Zanuck claimed the offer was "a bona fide good faith offer and the defendant would have complied with the terms of that offer, had plaintiff accepted them." Fox's sincerity would have been a fact question and probably would have survived the summary judgment motion.

MacLaine refused the substitute offer and, according to her agent, was unable to find alternative employment in the *Bloomer Girl* shooting period. She brought suit against Fox to recover the $750,000 guarantee, stating two causes of action: money due under a written contract, and damages for breach of a written contract. She rejected a settlement offer of $400,000. Fox conceded that it had breached the original agreement and offered as its only defense her failure to mitigate damages by her refusal to accept the *BCBM* offer. Her failure to mitigate, claimed Fox, meant that MacLaine should receive only nominal damages. On a very thin record consisting of the *Bloomer Girl* contract, Fox's letter proposing the *BCBM* contract, short declarations by her agent and lawyer, Fox's in-house counsel, and Richard Zanuck, an affidavit by MacLaine that she did not work or receive compensation during the fourteen-week shooting period, and a few stipulations, MacLaine asked for and received summary judgment. That result was upheld on appeal.

RESTATEMENT (SECOND) OF CONTRACTS

§350.   AVOIDABILITY AS A LIMITATION ON DAMAGES

(1) Except as stated in Subsection (2), damages are not recoverable for loss that the injured party could have avoided without undue risk, burden or humiliation.

(2) The injured party is not precluded from recovery by the rule stated in Subsection (1) to the extent that he has made reasonable but unsuccessful efforts to avoid loss.

Employment contract - Employee makes reasonable effort to find comparable employment ✗

REFERENCE: Barnett, §2.4.3
               Farnsworth, §§12.10, 12.12
               Calamari & Perillo, §§14.15-14.17
               Murray, §123

STUDY GUIDE: *What is the rationale for the "lost volume" doctrine described in the next case? Why should a retailer recover profits on both sales, when Twentieth Century-Fox would get to deduct from what it owed Shirley MacLaine any money she earned while acting in another movie she might choose to make during the period covered by the contract? Is this an example of courts favoring capital over labor? Was the court in* Neri *correct in refusing to award attorney's fees to the defendant? As a matter of statutory construction, why didn't U.C.C. §2-718 apply as the plaintiff claimed? (We shall return to §2-718 in Section C when we study the enforceability of "liquidated damages" clauses.)*

NERI v. RETAIL MARINE CORP.
Court of Appeals of New York,
334 N.Y.S.2d 165, 30 N.Y.2d 393, 285 N.E.2d 311 (1972)

GIBSON, J.*

The appeal concerns the right of a retail dealer to recover loss of profits and incidental damages upon the buyer's repudiation of a contract governed by the Uniform Commercial Code. This is, indeed, the correct measure of damage in an appropriate case and to this extent the code (§2-708, subsection (2)) effected a substantial change from prior law, whereby damages were ordinarily limited to "the difference between the contract price and the market or current price."[75] Upon the record before us, the courts below erred in declining to give effect to the new statute and so the order appealed from must be reversed.

The plaintiffs contracted to purchase from defendant a new boat of a specified model for the price of $12,587.40, against which they made a deposit of $40. They shortly increased the deposit to $4,250 in consideration of the defendant dealer's agreement to arrange with the manufacturer for immediate delivery on the basis of "a firm sale," instead of the delivery within approximately four to six weeks originally specified. Some six days

---

James Gibson (1902-1992), son and great-grandson of judges, was educated at Princeton and Albany Law School. After graduating from law school in 1926, he began a general law practice. During World War II, he served as a captain in the army. In 1952, Gibson was elected to the New York Supreme Court, and in 1955 he was promoted to the Appellate Division. In 1964, as an Associate Justice on the Appellate Division, he ruled that the phrase "under God" in the Pledge of Allegiance did not violate the constitutional separation of church and state. The Court of Appeals upheld his decision and the U.S. Supreme Court denied review. Gibson served on the Court of Appeals from 1969 to 1978, continuing on special assignment until he retired in 1984. — Kathleen A. Eagan.

75. Personal Property Law, Consol. Laws, c.41, §145, repealed by Uniform Commercial Code, §10-102 (L.1962, ch. 553, eff. Sept. 27, 1964). . . .

after the date of the contract plaintiff's lawyer sent to defendant a letter rescinding the sales contract for the reason that plaintiff Neri was about to undergo hospitalization and surgery, in consequence of which, according to the letter, it would be "impossible for Mr. Neri to make any payments." The boat had already been ordered from the manufacturer and was delivered to defendant at or before the time the attorney's letter was received. Defendant declined to refund plaintiff's deposit and this action to recover it was commenced. Defendant counterclaimed, alleging plaintiff's breach of the contract and defendant's resultant damage in the amount of $4,250, for which sum defendant demanded judgment. Upon motion, defendant had summary judgment on the issue of liability tendered by its counterclaim; and Special Term directed an assessment of damages, upon which it would be determined whether plaintiffs were entitled to the return of any portion of their down payment.

Upon the trial so directed, it was shown that the boat ordered and received by defendant in accordance with plaintiffs' contract of purchase was sold some four months later to another buyer for the same price as that negotiated with plaintiffs. From this proof the plaintiffs argue that defendant's loss on its contract was recouped, while defendant argues that but for plaintiff's default, it would have sold two boats and have earned two profits instead of one. Defendant proved, without contradiction, that its profits on the sale under the contract in suit would have been $2,579 and that during the period the boat remained unsold incidental expenses aggregating $674 for storage, upkeep, finance charges and insurance were incurred. Additionally, defendant proved and sought to recover attorneys' fees of $1,250.

The trial court found "untenable" defendant's claim for loss of profit, inasmuch as the boat was later sold for the same price that plaintiffs had contracted to pay; found, too, that defendant had failed to prove any incidental damages; further found "that the terms of [§718(2)(b)] of the Uniform Commercial Code were applicable and same make adequate and fair provision to place the sellers in as good a position as performance would have done" and, in accordance with paragraph (b) of subsection (2) thus relied upon, awarded defendant $500 upon its counterclaim and directed that plaintiffs recover the balance of their deposit, amounting to $3,750. The ensuing judgment was affirmed, without opinion, at the Appellate Division . . . and defendant's appeal to this court was taken by our leave.

The issue is governed in the first instance by section 2-718 of the Uniform Commercial Code which provides, among other things, that the buyer, despite his breach, may have restitution of the amount of which his payment exceeds: (a) reasonable liquidated damages stipulated by the contract or (b) absent such stipulation, 20% of the value of the buyer's total performance or $500, whichever is smaller (§2-718, subsection (2), pars. (a), (b)). As above noted, the trial court awarded defendant an offset in the amount of $500 under paragraph (b) and directed restitution to plaintiffs of the balance. Section 2-718, however, establishes, in paragraph (a) of subsection (3), an alternative right of offset in favor of the seller, as follows: "(3) The buyer's right to restitution under subsection (2) is subject to offset to the extent that the seller establishes (a) a right to recover damages under the provisions of this Article other than subsection (1)."

Among "the provisions of this Article other than subsection (1)" are those to be found in §2-708, which the courts below did not apply. Subsection (1) of that section provides that "the measure of damages for non-acceptance or repudiation by the buyer is the difference between the market price at the time and place for tender and the unpaid contract price together with any incidental damages provided in this Article (Section 2-710), but less expenses saved in consequence of the buyer's breach." However, this provision is made expressly subject to subsection (2), providing: "(2) If the measure of damages provided in subsection (1) is inadequate to put the seller in as good a position as performance would have done then the measure of damages is the profit (including reasonable overhead) which the seller would have made from full performance by the buyer, together with any incidental damages provided in this Article (Section 2-710), due allowance for costs reasonably incurred and due credit for payments or proceeds of resale." . . .

. . . The buyer's right to restitution was established at Special Term upon the motion for summary judgment, as was the seller's right to proper offsets, in each case pursuant to §2-718; and, as the parties concede, the only question before us, following the assessment of damages at Special Term, is that as to the proper measure of damage to be applied. The conclusion is clear from the record — indeed with mathematical certainty — that "the measure of damages provided in subsection (1) is inadequate to put the seller in as good a position as performance would have done" (Uniform Commercial Code, §2-708, subsection (2)) and hence — again under subsection (2) — that the seller is entitled to its "profit (including reasonable overhead) . . . together with any incidental damages . . . , due allowance for costs reasonably incurred and due credit for payments or proceeds of resale."

It is evident, first, that this retail seller is entitled to its profit and, second, that the last sentence of subsection (2), as hereinbefore quoted, referring to "due credit for payments or proceeds of resale" is inapplicable to this retail sales contract.[76] Closely parallel to the factual situation now before us is that hypothesized by Dean Hawkland as illustrative of the operation of rules: "Thus, if a private party agrees to sell his automobile to a buyer for $2,000, a breach by the buyer would cause the seller no loss (except incidental damages, i.e., expense of a new sale) if the seller was able to sell the automobile to another buyer for $2,000. But the situation is different with dealers having an unlimited supply of standard-priced goods. Thus, if an automobile dealer agrees to sell a car to a buyer at the standard price of $2,000, a breach by the buyer injures the dealer, even though he is able to

---

76. The concluding clause, "due credit for payments or proceeds of resale," is intended to refer to "the privilege of the seller to realize junk value when it is manifestly useless to complete the operation of manufacture." . . . The commentators who have considered the language have uniformly concluded that "the reference is to a resale as scrap under . . . Section 2-704" (1956 Report of N.Y. Law Rev. Comm., p.397 . . .). Another writer, reaching the same conclusion, after detailing the history of the clause, says that " 'proceeds of resale' previously meant the resale value of the goods in finished form; now it means the resale value of the components on hand at the time plaintiff learns of breach" (Harris, Seller's Damages, 18 Stan. L. Rev. 66, 104).

sell the automobile to another for $2,000. If the dealer has an inexhaustible supply of cars, the resale to replace the breaching buyer costs the dealer a sale, because, had the breaching buyer performed, the dealer would have made two sales instead of one. The buyer's breach, in such a case, depletes the dealer's sales to the extent of one, and the measure of damages should be the dealer's profit on one sale. Section 2-708 recognizes this, and it rejects the rule developed under the Uniform Sales Act by many courts that the profit cannot be recovered in this case." (Hawkland, Sales and Bulk Sales (1958 ed.), pp. 153-154; and see Comment, 31 Fordham L. Rev. 749, 755-756.)

The record which in this case establishes defendant's entitlement to damages in the amount of its prospective profit, at the same time confirms defendant's cognate right to "any incidental damages provided in this Article (Section 2-710)"[77] (Uniform Commercial Code, §2-708, subsection (2)). From the language employed it is too clear to require discussion that the seller's right to recover loss of profits is not exclusive and that he may recoup his "incidental" expenses as well. . . . Although the trial court's denial of incidental damages in the uncontroverted amount of $674 was made in the context of its erroneous conclusion that paragraph (b) of subsection (2) of §2-718 was applicable and was "adequate . . . to place the sellers in as good a position as performance would have done," the denial seems not to have rested entirely on the court's mistaken application of the law, as there was an explicit finding "that defendant completely failed to show that it suffered any incidental damages." We find no basis for the court's conclusion with respect to a deficiency of proof inasmuch as the proper items of the $674 expenses (being for storage, upkeep, finance charges and insurance for the period between the date performance was due and the time of the resale) were proven without objection and were in no way controverted, impeached or otherwise challenged, at the trial or on appeal. Thus the court's finding of a failure of proof cannot be supported upon the record and, therefore, and contrary to plaintiffs' contention, the affirmance at the Appellate Division was ineffective to save it.

The trial court correctly denied defendant's claim for recovery of attorney's fees incurred by it in this action. Attorney's fees incurred in an action such as this are not in the nature of the protective expenses contemplated by the statute (Uniform Commercial Code, §1-106, subd. (1); §2-710; §2-708, subsection (2)). . . .

It follows that plaintiffs are entitled to restitution of the sum of $4,250 paid by them on account of the contract price less an offset to defendant in the amount of $3,253 on account of its lost profit of $2,579 and its incidental damages of $674.

The order of the Appellate Division should be modified, with costs in all courts, in accordance with this opinion, and, as so modified, affirmed.

---

77. "Incidental damages to an aggrieved seller include any commercially reasonable charges, expenses or commissions incurred in stopping delivery, in the transportation, care and custody of goods after the buyer's breach, in connection with return or resale of the goods or otherwise resulting from the breach" (Uniform Commercial Code, §2-710).

SALES CONTRACTS: THE UNIFORM COMMERCIAL CODE

§2-706.   SELLER's RESALE INCLUDING CONTRACT FOR RESALE

(1) Under the conditions stated in Section 2-703 on seller's remedies, the seller may resell the goods concerned or the undelivered balance thereof. Where the resale is made in good faith and in a commercially reasonable manner the seller may recover the difference between the resale price and the contract price together with any incidental damages allowed under the provisions of this Article (Section 2-710), but less expenses saved in consequence of the buyer's breach.

(2) Except as otherwise provided in subsection (3) or unless otherwise agreed resale may be at public or private sale including sale by way of one or more contracts to sell or of identification to an existing contract of the seller. Sale may be as a unit or in parcels and at any time and place and on any terms but every aspect of the sale including the method, manner, time, place and terms must be commercially reasonable. The resale must be reasonably identified as referring to the broken contract, but it is not necessary that the goods be in existence or that any or all of them have been identified to the contract before the breach.

(3) Where the resale is at private sale the seller must give the buyer reasonable notification of his intention to resell.

(4) Where the resale is at public sale

(a) only identified goods can be sold except where there is a recognized market for a public sale of futures in goods of the kind; and

(b) it must be made at a usual place or market for public sale if one is reasonably available and except in the case of goods which are perishable or threaten to decline in value speedily the seller must give the buyer reasonable notice of the time and place of the resale; and

(c) if the goods are not to be within the view of those attending the sale the notification of sale must state the place where the goods are located and provide for their reasonable inspection by prospective bidders; and

(d) the seller may buy.

(5) A purchaser who buys in good faith at a resale takes the goods free of any rights of the original buyer even though the seller fails to comply with one or more of the requirements of this section.

(6) The seller is not accountable to the buyer for any profit made on any resale. A person in the position of a seller (Section 2-707) or a buyer who has rightfully rejected or justifiably revoked acceptance must account for any excess over the amount of his security interest, as hereinafter defined (subsection (3) of Section 2-711).

§2-708.   SELLER's DAMAGES FOR NON-ACCEPTANCE OR REPUDIATION

(1) Subject to subsection (2) and to the provisions of this Article with respect to proof of market price (Section 2-723), the measure of damages

for non-acceptance or repudiation by the buyer is the difference between the market price at the time and place for tender and the unpaid contract price together with any incidental damages provided in this Article (Section 2-710), but less expenses saved in consequence of the buyer's breach.

(2) If the measure of damages provided in subsection (1) is inadequate to put the seller in as good a position as performance would have done then the measure of damages is the profit (including reasonable overhead) which the seller would have made from full performance by the buyer, together with any incidental damages provided in this Article (Section 2-710), due allowance for costs reasonably incurred and due credit for payments or proceeds of resale.

§2-710.   SELLER's INCIDENTAL DAMAGES

Incidental damages to an aggrieved seller include any commercially reasonable charges, expenses or commissions incurred in stopping delivery, in the transportation, care and custody of goods after the buyer's breach, in connection with return or resale of the goods or otherwise resulting from the breach.

§2-718.   LIQUIDATION OR LIMITATION OF DAMAGES; DEPOSITS

(1) Damages for breach by either party may be liquidated in the agreement but only at an amount which is reasonable in the light of the anticipated or actual harm caused by the breach, the difficulties of proof of loss, and the inconvenience or nonfeasibility of otherwise obtaining an adequate remedy. A term fixing unreasonably large liquidated damages is void as a penalty.

(2) Where the seller justifiably withholds delivery of goods because of the buyer's breach, the buyer is entitled to restitution of any amount by which the sum of his payments exceeds

(a) the amount to which the seller is entitled by virtue of terms liquidating the seller's damages in accordance with subsection (1), or

(b) in the absence of such terms, 20% of the value of the total performance for which the buyer is obligated under the contract or $500, whichever is smaller.

(3) The buyer's right to restitution under subsection (2) is subject to offset to the extent that the seller establishes

(a) a right to recover damages under the provisions of this Article other than subsection (1), and

(b) the amount or value of any benefits received by the buyer directly or indirectly by reason of the contract.

(4) Where a seller has received payment in goods their reasonable value or the proceeds of their resale shall be treated as payments for the purposes of subsection (2); but if the seller has notice of the buyer's breach

before reselling goods received in part performance, his resale is subject to the conditions laid down in this Article on resale by an aggrieved seller (Section 2-706).

D.   CONTRACTING AROUND THE DEFAULT RULES OF DAMAGES

Most contract rules are *default rules*, meaning that they can be contracted around by inserting an expressed clause to the contrary. The liability for breach specified by the default rules governing contract damages can either be expanded or contracted. Express clauses may disclaim liability for consequential damages, even though such damages may be foreseeable. Damages may be either limited or expanded by the use of liquidated damage clauses. In this section, we shall examine both of these important and quite common types of clauses.

REFERENCE: Barnett, xxi-xxii

1.   Express Limitations on Consequential and Incidental Damages

Parties may seek to limit their liability under the default rules of contract damages by including a warranty clause that is expressly intended to be the *exclusive* remedy for breach of contract, thereby excluding damages for other foreseeable losses. An example of an attempt to limit liability established by the default rules of contract damages can be found on the back of Federal Express Airbill (Rev. Date 10/06). Can you spot the passage that tries to contract around the rule of Hadley v. Baxendale?

LIMITATIONS ON OUR LIABILITY AND LIABILITIES NOT ASSUMED

- Our liability in connection with this shipment is limited to the lesser of the actual damages or $100, unless you declare a higher value, pay an additional charge, and document your actual loss in a timely manner. You may pay an additional charge for each $100 of declared value. The declared value does not constitute, nor do we provide, cargo insurance.
- In any event, we will not be liable for any damage, whether direct, incidental, special, or consequential, in excess of the declared value of a shipment, whether or not FedEx has knowledge that such damages might be incurred, including but not limited to loss of income and profits. . . .

Keeps prices down
Policy considerations

MONEY-BACK GUARANTEE   In the event of untimely delivery, FedEx will, at your request and with some limitations, refund or credit all transportation charges. See the current FedEx Service Guide for more information.

SALES CONTRACTS: THE UNIFORM COMMERCIAL CODE

§2-719. CONTRACTUAL MODIFICATION OR LIMITATION OF REMEDY

(1) Subject to the provisions of subsections (2) and (3) of this Section and of the preceding section on liquidation and limitation of damages,

(a) the agreement may provide for remedies in addition to or in substitution for those provided in this Article and may limit or alter the measure of damages recoverable under this Article, as by limiting the buyer's remedies to return of the goods and repayment of the price or to repair and replacement of non-conforming goods or parts; and

(b) resort to a remedy as provided is optional unless the remedy is expressly agreed to be exclusive, in which case it is the sole remedy.

(2) Where circumstances cause an exclusive or limited remedy to fail of its essential purpose, remedy may be had as provided in this Act.

(3) Consequential damages may be limited or excluded unless the limitation or exclusion is unconscionable. Limitation of consequential damages for injury to the person in the case of consumer goods is prima facie unconscionable but limitation of damages where the loss is commercial is not.

2. Liquidated Damages vs. Penalty Clauses

Prior to the rise of assumpsit, most important promises were enforced by an action in debt. This was accomplished by the use of a formal sealed document called a "bond." As Professor A. W. B. Simpson has noted,

> it was by the use of conditioned bonds that important agreements were made actionable in the days when the bond was the basic contractual institution. . . . Suppose Hugo proposes to lend Robert £100. Robert will execute a bond in favour of Hugo for a larger sum, normally twice the sum lent, thus binding himself to pay Hugo £200 on a fixed day; the bond will be made subject to a condition of defeasance, which provides that if he pays the £100 before the day the bond is to be void. This condition will normally be endorsed on (i.e. written on the back of) the bond. What is essentially the same technique could be employed in the case of a contract for the sale of land, or indeed any agreement where what was desired was the performance of some act, or the granting of some forbearance.[78]

Thus, by the use of a conditional "penal" bond could any promise be reduced to debt. For when the condition was not met, the promisor was indebted to the promisee for the amount of money specified in the bond. In this period penalty clauses were the rule, not the exception, in important agreements.

---

78. A. W. B. Simpson, A History of the Common Law of Contract 90 (1975).

Professor Simpson also traces the decline in this practice:

The primary factor which led to the decline of the conditioned penal bond was the evolution, originally in the Court of Chancery, of the practice of relieving defaulting obligors from forfeiture of the penalty due under bonds; this led eventually to the acceptance both in equity and at common law of the modern principle of contract law, according to which a distinction is drawn between a "penalty" and "liquidated damages."[79]

The reason for this change was the acceptance of the theory that "a contracting party should only be permitted to recover compensation for loss actually suffered through default, such compensation being assessed, broadly speaking, with a view to putting the innocent party into the position he would have achieved if the contract had been performed."[80] Simpson notes that this principle reflects one of two ideas concerning contractual enforcement that have long been in tension:

On the one hand we have the idea that the real function of contractual institutions is to make sure, so far as possible, that agreements are performed; the institution of the penal bond and the practice of the courts in upholding such bonds exemplified this idea. On the other hand we have the idea that it suffices for the law to provide compensation for loss suffered by failure to perform agreements. This second idea is not, of course, necessarily incompatible with the pursuit of the aim of encouraging contractual performance, but it is bound to impose a limitation upon the enthusiasm with which that aim is pursued, and there can well be contexts (for example, contracts for personal service) in which a positive value is attached to the right to break the contract so long as the defaulting party is made to pay compensation. Now if securing performance is the aim to be pursued, the use of penalties *in terrorem* of the party from whom performance is due is the natural and obvious technique. Thus today the decree of specific performance is given teeth by the threat of imprisonment for contempt, and in the criminal courts we are familiar with such institutions as the granting of bail and the entry into recognizances to keep the peace, which institutions, to those who are not over-impressed by labels, are nothing more than modern versions of the conditioned bond used to bind persons to the performance of contracts. What has happened is not that contracts *in terrorem* have been outlawed, or that the use of penal mechanisms no longer plays any part in contract law, but only that the courts have come to acquire a monopolistic control over the use of terror. It is today the courts which may do things which in former ages private citizens might do.[81]

The next three cases examine the modern distinction between those clauses that operate as "penalties" and are therefore unenforceable and those "liquidated damage" clauses that are enforceable.

STUDY GUIDE: *Why does the court in the next case think that "liquidated damage" clauses ought to be enforceable? Why did it conclude that the clause in question was an unenforceable penalty clause? Was this the only*

79. Id. at 118.
80. Id. at 123.
81. Id. at 123-24.

conclusion that the court might have reached? Might we evaluate a clause to see if it operates as a penalty from any other perspective?

<u>KEMBLE v. FARREN</u>
Court of Common Pleas,
6 Bing. 141, 130 Eng. Rep. 1234 [1829]

Assumpsit by the manager of Covent Garden Theatre against an actor, to recover liquidated damages for the violation of an engagement to perform at Covent Garden for four seasons. . . .

TINDAL, C.J.* This is a rule which calls upon the Defendant to show cause why the verdict, which has been entered for the Plaintiff for £750., should not be increased to £1000.

The action was brought upon an agreement made between the Plaintiff and the Defendant, whereby the Defendant agreed to act as a principal comedian at the Theatre Royal, Covent Garden, during the four then next seasons, commencing October 1828, and also to conform in all things to the usual regulations of the said Theatre Royal, Covent Garden; and the Plaintiff agreed to pay the Defendant £3. 6s. 8d. every night on which the theatre should be open for theatrical performances, during the next four seasons, and that the Defendant should be allowed one benefit night during each season, on certain terms therein specified. And the agreement contained a clause, that if either of the parties should neglect or refuse to fulfil the said agreement, or any part thereof, or any stipulation therein contained, such party should pay to the other the sum of £1000., to which sum it was thereby agreed that the damages sustained by any such omission, neglect, or refusal, should amount; and which sum was thereby declared by the said parties to be liquidated and ascertained damages, and not a penalty or penal sum, or in the nature thereof.

The breach alleged in the declaration was, that the Defendant refused to act during the second season, for which breach, the jury, upon the trial, assessed the damages at £750.; which damages the Plaintiff contends ought by the terms of the agreement to have been assessed at £1000.

It is, undoubtedly, difficult to suppose any words more precise or explicit than those used in the agreement; the same declaring not only affirmatively that the sum of £1000. should be taken as liquidated damages, but negatively also that it should not be considered as a penalty, or in the nature thereof. And if the clause had been limited to breaches which were of an uncertain nature and amount, we should have thought it would have had the effect of ascertaining the damages upon any such breach at £1000.

---

* Sir Nicholas Conyngham Tindal (1776-1846) was educated at Oxford University (B.A., M.A.), then studied law with Sir John Richardson and practiced as a special pleader. In 1824, he entered Parliament as a Tory member, and became solicitor-general in 1826. At that time he received the honor of knighthood. In 1827 Tindal was elected to representative of the University of Cambridge and during his tenure, twice declined to assume the role of attorney-general. In 1829 he was appointed Chief Justice of the Common Pleas and occupied that position until his death. He continued to serve on the bench to within ten days of his death, when he succumbed to paralysis. — K.T.

For we see nothing illegal or unreasonable in the parties, by their mutual agreement, settling the amount of damages, uncertain in their nature, at any sum upon which they may agree. In many cases, such an agreement fixes that which is almost impossible to be accurately ascertained; and in all cases, it saves the expense and difficulty of bringing witnesses to that point. But in the present case, the clause is not so confined; it extends to the breach of any stipulation by either party. If, therefore, on the one hand, the Plaintiff had neglected to make a single payment of £3.6s. 8d. per day, or on the other hand, the Defendant had refused to conform to any usual regulation of the theatre, however minute or unimportant, it must have been contended that the clause in question, in either case, would have given the stipulated damages of £1000. But that a very large sum should become immediately payable, in consequence of the nonpayment of a very small sum, and that the former should not be considered as a penalty, appears to be a contradiction in terms; the case being precisely that in which courts of equity have always relieved, and against which courts of law have, in modern times, endeavoured to relieve, by directing juries to assess the real damages sustained by the breach of the agreement. It has been argued at the bar, that the liquidated damages apply to those breaches of the agreement only which are in their nature uncertain, leaving those which are certain to a distinct remedy, by the verdict of a jury. But we can only say, if such is the intention of the parties, they have not expressed it; but have made the clause relate, by express and positive terms, to all breaches of every kind. We cannot, therefore, distinguish this case, in principle, from that of Astley v. Weldon, in which it was stipulated, that either of the parties neglecting to perform the agreement should pay to the other of them the full sum of £200., to be recovered in his Majesty's courts at Westminster. Here there was a distinct agreement, that the sum stipulated should be liquidated and ascertained damages: there were clauses in the agreement, some sounding in uncertain damages, others relating to certain pecuniary payments; the action was brought for the breach of a clause of an uncertain nature; and yet it was held by the Court, that for this very reason it would be absurd to construe the sum inserted in the agreement as liquidated damages, and it was held to be a penal sum only. As this case appears to us to be decided on a clear and intelligible principle, and to apply to that under consideration, we think it right to adhere to it, and this makes it unnecessary to consider the subsequent cases, which do not in any way break in upon it. The consequence is, we think the present verdict should stand, and the rule for increasing the damages be discharged.

Rule discharged.

STUDY GUIDE: In the next case, what standard does the court use to evaluate the enforceability of liquidated damage clauses? Do you think that this court would have reached the same outcome in Kemble v. Farren? What does the court say about the effect of a liquidated damage clause on an employee's "duty to mitigate" damages? Was there a clause in Shirley MacLaine's contract with the studio to which this analysis would apply? Notice the effect on appeal of the employer's failure to make an "offer of proof" at trial as to the employee's earnings from his new job. Does the court's approach differ in any way from that of U.C.C. §2-718 (p. 137)?

WASSENAAR v. TOWNE HOTEL
Supreme Court of Wisconsin,
331 N.W.2d 357 (1983)

ABRAHAMSON, J.* This is a review of an unpublished decision of the court of appeals filed May 6, 1982, reversing a judgment of the circuit court for Milwaukee county, Louis J. Ceci, Circuit Judge. The circuit court entered a judgment in favor of an employee, Donald Wassenaar, against his former employer, Theanne Panos, d/b/a The Towne Hotel, enforcing the stipulated damages clause in the employment contract and confirming a $24,640 jury award. The circuit court interpreted the stipulated damage clause in the contract as providing that in the event of wrongful discharge the employee was to be paid a sum equal to his salary for the unexpired term of the contract. The court of appeals reversed, holding the stipulated damages clause unenforceable as a penalty and remanding the cause to the circuit court for a new trial on the issue of damages only.

This court granted the employee's petition for review limiting the issue on review to whether the clause in the employment contract stipulating damages is a valid and enforceable liquidated damages provision or is, as a matter of public policy, an unenforceable penalty. We use the term "stipulated damages" herein to refer to the contract and the term "liquidated damages" to refer to stipulated damages which a court holds to be reasonable and will enforce. This court also asked the parties to address the sub-issue of whether a liquidated damages clause in an employment contract may serve to eliminate the employee's duty to mitigate damages, a question the court of appeals did not address. We conclude that where the stipulated damages clause is a valid provision for liquidated damages, the doctrine of mitigation of damages is not applicable to determine the damages awarded the nonbreaching party. In this case we hold that the stipulated damages clause is a valid provision for liquidated damages, not a penalty, and that the employee's earnings after the breach do not reduce the damages award. Accordingly, we reverse the decision . . . of the court of appeals and affirm the judgment of the circuit court.

The dispute centers on the stipulated damages clause of a written employment contract by which the employee-plaintiff, Donald Wassenaar, was hired as general manager of the employer-defendant, Towne Hotel. The employment contract is brief. It sets forth the employee's duties, his beginning salary, and his periodic pay increases. The contract further provides for a three-year term of employment beginning on January 1, 1977, renewable at the employee's option, and stipulates damages in case the employer terminates the employee's employment before the

---

* *Shirley Schlanger Abrahamson* (1933-†) was born in New York, New York, in 1933 and completed her studies at New York University (A.B.), Indiana University School of Law (J.D.), and University of Wisconsin School of Law (S.J.D.). She began legal practice in Madison, Wisconsin, in 1962 and continued her work there until being appointed in 1976 to the Wisconsin Supreme Court by Governor Patrick J. Lucey, a position to which she has repeatedly been reelected. Since 1996, she has served as the Chief Justice. Justice Abrahamson has also served as a law professor at the University of Wisconsin School of Law since 1966. — L.R.

expiration of the contract. The stipulated damages clause in issue here reads as follows:

> IT IS FURTHER UNDERSTOOD, that should this contract be terminated by the Towne Hotel prior to its expiration date, the Towne Hotel will be responsible for fulfilling the entire financial obligation as set forth within this agreement for the full period of three (3) years.[82]

The employer terminated Wassenaar's employment as of March 31, 1978, 21 months prior to the contract's expiration date. Wassenaar was unemployed from April 1, 1978, until June 14, 1978, when he obtained employment in a Milwaukee area hotel where he remained employed at least until the time of trial in May, 1981.

The employee sued for damages. The employer answered the complaint and as an affirmative defense asserted that the employee had failed to mitigate damages. In a pretrial motion to strike the employer's affirmative defense that the employee had failed to mitigate damages, the employee argued that mitigation was irrelevant because the contract contained a valid stipulated damages clause. The circuit court struck the employer's affirmative defense, ruling that the employee had no duty to mitigate damages, apparently inferentially ruling that the stipulated damages clause was valid.

After a trial on the remaining issues and in response to special verdict questions, the jury found that the person negotiating the contract on behalf of the employer was authorized as the employer's agent to enter into the employment contract and that the employer terminated the employment without just cause. The circuit court, over the employee's objection, submitted to the jury the question of what sum of money would compensate the employee for his losses resulting from the breach of the employment agreement. The jury answered $24,640, which is the sum the employee had calculated as his damages on the basis of the stipulated damages clause of the contract, that is, his salary for 21 months, the unexpired term of the contract.

On review, the court of appeals . . . scrutinized the stipulated damages clause and decided that the clause was void as a penalty. The court of appeals reached that conclusion reasoning that the amount of damages for breach of an employment contract could easily be measured and proved at trial and that the contractual formula fixing damages at full salary without considering how long the employee would need to find a new job or the probable earnings from substitute employment was unreasonable on its face. In its analysis, the court of appeals did not consider any facts other than the actual contract language and the black-letter law relating to the measure of damages for breach of employment contracts. . . .

Because the employer sought to set aside the bargained-for contractual provision stipulating damages, it had the burden of proving facts which would justify the trial court's concluding that the clause should not be enforced. . . . Placing the burden of proof on the challenger is consistent

---

82. The clause can be interpreted to provide that the employee will receive the entire salary for three years regardless of when the employment was terminated. We reject this interpretation of the clause, as did the employee and the circuit court.

with giving the nonbreaching party the advantage inherent in stipulated damages clauses of eliminating the need to prove damages, and with the general principle that the law assumes that bargains are enforceable and that the party asking the court to intervene to invalidate a bargain should demonstrate the justice of his or her position. As we discuss below, we conclude that the employer failed to carry its burden, and we affirm the circuit court's conclusion that the stipulated damages clause is valid.

We turn now to the test that the trial court (and the appellate court) should apply in deciding whether a stipulated damages clause is valid. The overall single test of validity is whether the clause is reasonable under the totality of circumstances. See sec. 356(1), Restatement (Second) of Contracts (1979), and sec. 402.718(1), Stats. 1979-80 [U.C.C. §2-718].

The reasonableness test is a compromise the courts have struck between two competing viewpoints toward stipulated damages clauses, one favoring enforcement of stipulated damages clauses and the other disfavoring such clauses.

Enforcement of stipulated damages clauses is urged because the clauses serve several purposes. The clauses allow the parties to control their exposure to risk by setting the payment for breach in advance. They avoid the uncertainty, delay, and expense of using the judicial process to determine actual damages. They allow the parties to fashion a remedy consistent with economic efficiency in a competitive market, and they enable the parties to correct what the parties perceive to be inadequate judicial remedies by agreeing upon a formula which may include damage elements too uncertain or remote to be recovered under rules of damages applied by the courts. In addition to these policies specifically relating to stipulated damages clauses, considerations of judicial economy and freedom of contract favor enforcement of stipulated damages clauses.

[handwritten margin note: Good for business]

A competing set of policies disfavors stipulated damages clauses, and thus courts have not been willing to enforce stipulated damages clauses blindly without carefully scrutinizing them. Public law, not private law, ordinarily defines the remedies of the parties. Stipulated damages are an exception to this rule. Stipulated damages allow private parties to perform the judicial function of providing the remedy in breach of contract cases, namely, compensation of the nonbreaching party, and courts must ensure that the private remedy does not stray too far from the legal principle of allowing compensatory damages. Stipulated damages substantially in excess of injury may justify an inference of unfairness in bargaining or an objectionable *in terrorem* agreement to deter a party from breaching the contract, to secure performance, and to punish the breaching party if the deterrent is ineffective.

The reasonableness test strikes a balance between the two competing sets of policies by ensuring that the court respects the parties' bargain but prevents abuse. See Macneil, Power of Contract and Agreed Remedies, 47 Cornell L.Q. 495 (1962).

Over time, the cases and commentators have established several factors to help determine whether a particular clause is reasonable: (1) Did the parties intend to provide for damages or for a penalty? (2) Is the injury caused by the breach one that is difficult or incapable of accurate estimation at the time of contract? and (3) Are the stipulated damages a reasonable forecast of the harm caused by the breach?

Recent discussions of the test of reasonableness have generally discarded the first factor, subjective intent of the parties, because subjective intent has little bearing on whether the clause is objectively reasonable.[83] The label the parties apply to the clause, which might indicate their intent, has some evidentiary value, but it is not conclusive. . . .

The second factor, sometimes referred to as the "difficulty of ascertainment" test, is generally viewed as helpful in assessing the reasonableness of the clause. The greater the difficulty of estimating or proving damages, the more likely the stipulated damages will appear reasonable. . . . If damages are readily ascertainable, a significant deviation between the stipulated amount and the ascertainable amount will appear unreasonable. . . . The "difficulty of ascertainment" test has several facets, depending on whether the stipulated damages clause is viewed from the perspective of the time of contracting or the time of breach (or trial). These facets include the difficulty of producing proof of damages at trial; the difficulty of determining what damages the breach caused; the difficulty of ascertaining what damages the parties contemplated when they contracted; the absence of a standardized measure of damages for the breach; and the difficulty of forecasting, when the contract is made, all the possible damages which may be caused or occasioned by the various possible breaches.

The third factor concerns whether the stipulated damages provision is a reasonable forecast of compensatory damages. Courts test the reasonableness of the parties' forecast, as they test the "difficulty of ascertainment" by looking at the stipulated damages clause from the perspective of both the time of contracting and the time of the breach (or trial).

The second and third factors are intertwined, and both use a combined prospective-retrospective approach. Although courts have frequently said that the reasonableness of the stipulated damages clause must be judged as of the time of contract formation (the prospective approach) and that the amount or existence of actual loss at the time of breach or trial is irrelevant, except as evidence helpful in determining what was reasonable at the time of contracting (the retrospective approach), the cases demonstrate that the facts available at trial significantly affect the courts' determination of the reasonableness of the stipulated damages clause. If the damages provided for in the contract are grossly disproportionate to the actual harm sustained, the courts usually conclude that the parties' original expectations were unreasonable. Our prior decisions indicate that this court has employed the prospective-retrospective approach in determining the reasonableness of the stipulated damages clauses and has looked at the harm anticipated at the time of contract formation and the actual harm at the time of breach (or trial). See, e.g., Fields Foundation, Ltd. v. Christensen, 103 Wis.2d 465, 475-76, 309 N.W.2d 125 (Ct. App. 1981). . . .

As the above discussion demonstrates, the various factors and approaches to determine reasonableness are not separate tests, each of which must be satisfied for the stipulated damages clause to stand. Reasonableness of the stipulated damages clause cannot be determined by a

83. 5 Williston, Contracts, sec. 778, pp. 687, 693 (Jaeger 3d ed. 1961); 5 Corbin, Contracts, sec. 1058, p. 337 (1964); Calamari and Perillo, Law of Contracts, sec. 14.31, p. 565 (2d ed. 1977); Restatement (Second) of Contracts, sec. 356(1), comment c (1979).

mechanical application of the three factors cited above. . . . Courts may give different interpretations to or importance to the various factors in particular cases. . . .

In ruling on the reasonableness of a stipulated damages clause, the trial judge should take into account not only these factors but also the policies that gave rise to the adoption of the reasonableness test as the test for distinguishing between enforceable liquidated damages provisions and unenforceable penalty provisions.[84]

With the reasonableness test and the policies underlying the test in mind, we now consider the circuit court's conclusion that the stipulated damages clause is reasonable. The employer argues that the stipulated damages clause is void as a penalty because the harm to the employee was capable of estimation at the formation of the contract and was relatively easy to prove at trial. The employer further contends that calculating damages based on the entire wage for the unexpired term of the employment contract does not reasonably forecast the loss caused by the breach because such a calculation gives the employee a windfall recovery. The employer's arguments are not without merit. Under the rules of appellate review we will review the record for facts which support the circuit court's conclusion that the stipulated damages clause is reasonable.

When the parties to an employment contract estimate the harm which might result from the employer's breach, they do not know when a breach might occur, whether the employee will find a comparable job, and if he or she does, where the job will be or what hardship the employee will suffer. Nevertheless, the standard measure of damages provides, as the court of appeals noted in its opinion, a simple formula which is generally fairly easy to apply. According to black-letter law, when an employee is wrongfully discharged, damages are the salary the employee would have received during the unexpired term of the contract plus the expenses of securing other employment reduced by the income which he or she has earned, will earn, or could with reasonable diligence earn, during the unexpired term. These damages are usually easily ascertainable at the time of trial.

The standard calculation of damages after breach, however, may not reflect the actual harm suffered because of the breach. In addition to the damages reflected in the black-letter formulation, an employee may suffer consequential damages, including permanent injury to professional reputation, loss of career development opportunities, and emotional stress. When calculating damages for wrongful discharge courts strictly apply the rules of foreseeability, mitigation, and certainty and rarely award consequential damages. Damages for injury to the employee's reputation, for example, are generally considered too remote and not in the parties'

84. For a discussion of policies favoring judicial acceptance of stipulated damages and those justifying the courts' scrutiny of such clauses, see generally: Restatement (Second) of Contracts, sec. 356, comment a (1979); Dobbs, Law of Remedies, sec. 12.5, p. 823 (1973); Clarkson, Miller, and Muris, Liquidated Damages v. Penalties: Sense or Nonsense?, 1978 Wis. L. Rev. 351; Goetz and Scott, Liquidated Damages, Penalties and the Just Compensation Principle: Some Notes on an Enforcement Model and a Theory of Efficient Breach, 77 Colum. L. Rev. 554 (1977); Sweet, Liquidated Damages in California, 60 Calif. L. Rev. 84 (1972); Macneil, Power of Contract and Agreed Remedies, 47 Cornell L.Q. 495 (1962); Note, Liquidated Damages as Prima Facie Evidence, 51 Ind. L.J. 189 (1975).

contemplation. Thus, actual harm suffered and damages that would be awarded in a legal action for breach of contract may not be the same. Nevertheless, in providing for stipulated damages, the parties to the contract could anticipate the types of damages not usually awarded by law. The usual arguments against allowing recovery for consequential damages — that they are not foreseeable and that no dollar value can be set by a court — fail when the parties foresee the possibility of such harm and agree on an estimated amount.

We do not know in the case at bar how the parties calculated the stipulated amount, but we do know that both the employee and employer were concerned about job security. The employee desired a steady, long-term job and the employer wanted the employee, who was experienced in managing the Towne Hotel, to remain on the job. The parties did not suggest that the stipulated damages clause resulted from unequal bargaining power. The contract drafted by the employer provided for a fixed term of employment with a provision for stipulated damages in the amount of unpaid wages if the employer breached. Under these circumstances it is not unreasonable to assume that the parties might have anticipated elements of consequential damages and drafted the stipulated damages clause to include salary lost while out of work, expenses of finding a new job, lower salary on the new job, and consequential damages.

In examining the instant stipulated damages clause and the record, we conclude that the parties' estimate at the time of contract formation of anticipated damages was reasonable when consequential damages are taken into account. Consequential damages may be difficult to ascertain at the time of contracting or breach and are difficult to prove at trial. The contract formula of full salary for the period after breach seems to be a simple and fair way of calculating all damages.

The employer argues that even if the stipulated amount is a reasonable forecast at the time of contract formation of anticipated loss, the amount is unreasonable from the perspective of the time of trial because the employee suffered no loss whatsoever, or if he suffered any loss it is disproportionate to (that is, significantly less than) the stipulated damages.

This court appears to have adopted the position that if the nonbreaching party suffers no damage the stipulated damages clause is a penalty. See Hathaway v. Lynn, 75 Wis. 186, 43 N.W. 956 (1889). Apparently the court reasons, first, that if there is no damage, awarding stipulated damages violates the compensation principle of contract damages, and, second, that since one way to test reasonableness of stipulated damages is by comparing the estimated damages with actual harm suffered, if there is no harm the stipulated damages is automatically disproportionate to the harm. . . .

In this case we find it difficult to uphold the employer's position that the employee suffered no harm, because there is evidence in the record that the employee did suffer harm in being unemployed for approximately two and a half months after his discharge. At the end of this time, the employee obtained employment at another hotel, but there is no evidence that the jobs he held were comparable in terms of salary, opportunity for advancement, etc., to the job he held as manager of the Towne Hotel. There is no evidence that the employee's total compensation from the new job was equal to or exceeded the salary under the breached contract, and the record does not reveal whether the employee suffered consequential damages. All we know is that the employee appears to have suffered some harm. . . .

Since the record in this case can be read to show that the employee suffered some harm, the question remains whether the stipulated damages are so much greater than the loss suffered by the employee that the stipulated damages constitute a penalty.

The employer has repeatedly asserted that this clause is a penalty because it does not take into account the amount the employee earned during the unexpired term of the contract. The employer argues that allowing the employee to recover the stipulated damages in this case gives the employee a windfall because he receives both the agreed upon salary and the ability to sell his services to another employer during the unexpired term of the contract: the employee will receive 21 months salary from the defendant employer and 18 months salary from the new employer. Ordinarily the circuit court would, in this type of stipulated damages case, use evidence of the employee's actual or potential earnings in assessing the overall reasonableness of the clause, since subsequent earnings would be relevant to the issue of the employee's actual loss resulting from the breach. In this case, . . . there is no evidence in the record showing the employee's subsequent earnings, so there is no evidence supporting the employer's position that the employee would get a windfall from enforcement of the stipulated damages clause.

. . . When the employee challenged the employer's affirmative defense of failure to mitigate damages in a pretrial motion to strike the defense, he pointed out the effect of the stipulated damages clause and clearly set forth the applicable law concerning the test to be applied to determine the validity of the clause. . . . The circuit court granted the employee's motion to strike the defense on the basis of pretrial briefs, ruling that the employee had no duty to mitigate damages because the parties had stipulated their damages as part of their bargain. The circuit court thus inferentially upheld the validity of the clause.

At trial the employer attempted to put in evidence regarding the employee's salary at his new job. The circuit court refused to admit this evidence indicating that it had already ruled on the mitigation issue. . . . Although the employer attempted to elicit testimony from the employee regarding how much he earned on the new job, in order to prove the unreasonableness of the damages clause, the employer made no offer of proof as to what the testimony would be. An offer of proof is needed to preserve the facts underlying the objection for the record, sec. 901.03(1)(b), Stats. 1979-80.

The employer failed to get facts into the record showing that the employee suffered no damages or that his damages were significantly less than the stipulated amount. In short, the employer did not meet his burden of proof on the unreasonableness of the stipulated damages clause. Since we conclude that the record shows that the employee suffered some actual injury and that the record does not show that actual damages are disproportionate to the stipulated damages, we affirm the circuit court's ruling that the stipulated damages provision is reasonable and enforceable.

This court asked the parties to brief what it characterized as a sub-issue, namely, the employee's duty to mitigate damages. In breach of contract cases not involving liquidated damages clauses, this court has consistently held that a discharged employee has a duty to use ordinary care and reasonable efforts to seek other comparable employment and that in calculating damages the employer should be credited to the extent that the employee obtains work and earns wages or might have done so. Klug v. Flambeau Plastics Corp., 62 Wis.2d 141, 155, 214 N.W.2d 281 (1974). . . .

While evidence of the employee's earnings after the employer's breach may be relevant in meeting the employer's burden of proving that the stipulated damages clause is unreasonable, once the court determines that the clause is reasonable, proof of the employee's actual loss (including what he earned or might have earned on another job) is no longer relevant. . . . We hold that once a stipulated damages clause is found reasonable, the liquidated damages should not be reduced at trial by an amount the employee did earn or could have earned. . . . Recalculating liquidated damages to credit the breaching party with the amount the employee earned or could have earned is antithetical to the policies favoring liquidated damages clauses. Our holding comports with the rule in other jurisdictions where courts have not required employees to reduce the amount recovered under a liquidated damages provision by other earnings. . . .

For the reasons set forth, we conclude that the judgment of the circuit court should be affirmed.

RESTATEMENT (SECOND) OF CONTRACTS

§355.   PUNITIVE DAMAGES

Punitive damages are not recoverable for a breach of contract unless the conduct constituting the breach is also a tort for which punitive damages are recoverable.

§356.   LIQUIDATED DAMAGES AND PENALTIES

(1) Damages for breach by either party may be liquidated in the agreement but only at an amount that is reasonable in the light of the anticipated or actual loss caused by the breach and the difficulties of proof of loss. A term fixing unreasonably large liquidated damages is unenforceable on grounds of public policy as a penalty.

(2) A term in a bond providing for an amount of money as a penalty for non-occurrence of the condition of the bond is unenforceable on grounds of public policy to the extent that the amount exceeds the loss caused by such non-occurrence.

Reread: U.C.C. §2-718 (p. 137)

STUDY GUIDE: Why should not parties be able to contract for a penalty clause if they wish? In the next opinion, Judge Posner expresses his skepticism about the merits of the prohibition on the enforceability of penalty clauses. Why is he skeptical? Nevertheless, he argues that penalty clauses may inhibit "efficient breaches" of contract. What is an efficient breach? Why does Judge Posner think that such breaches are desirable? Do you agree? Notice how Judge Posner's ultimate determination harkens back to the reasoning of Kemble v. Farren.

LAKE RIVER CORP. v. CARBORUNDUM CO.
United States Court of Appeals, Seventh Circuit,
769 F.2d 1284 (1985)

POSNER, C.J.*

This diversity suit between Lake River Corporation and Carborundum Company requires us to consider questions of Illinois commercial law, and in particular to explore the fuzzy line between penalty clauses and liquidated-damages clauses. . . .

. . . Deep as the hostility to penalty clauses runs in the common law, . . . we still might be inclined to question, if we thought ourselves free to do so, whether a modern court should refuse to enforce a penalty clause where the signator is a substantial corporation, well able to avoid improvident commitments. Penalty clauses provide an earnest of performance. . . . On the other side it can be pointed out that by raising the cost of a breach of contract to the contract breaker, a penalty clause increases the risk to his other creditors; increases (what is the same thing and more, because bankruptcy imposes "deadweight" social costs) the risk of bankruptcy; and could amplify the business cycle by increasing the number of bankruptcies in bad times, which is when contracts are most likely to

*Richard Allen Posner (1939-†) was educated at Yale University (A.B.) and Harvard University (LL.B.), where he graduated first in his class. Upon graduation, he clerked for Justice William Brennan, Jr., and then worked for the Federal Trade Commission (1963-1965); for Thurgood Marshall, then Solicitor General of the United States (1965-1967); and as general counsel for President Johnson's Task Force on Communications Policy (1967-1968). He began teaching in 1968 at Stanford Law School before becoming a professor at the University of Chicago Law School in 1969, where he continues to serve as senior lecturer. In 1981, he was appointed to the U.S. Court of Appeals for the Seventh Circuit and was Chief Judge from 1993 to 2000. He is now a senior judge. By far the most prolific legal scholar of his generation, he has written around 40 books and more than 300 articles on an astonishing array of topics. His recent books include Overcoming Law (1995), Aging and Old Age (1995), The Federal Courts (2d ed. 1996), Law and Legal Theory in England and America (1996), The Economic Analysis of Law (5th ed. 1998), Law and Literature (rev. ed. 1998), The Problematics of Moral and Legal Theory (1999), An Affair of State: The Investigation, Impeachment, and Trial of President Clinton (1999), Antitrust Law (2d ed. 2001), Breaking the Deadlock: The 2000 Election, the Constitution, and the Courts (2001), Frontiers of Legal Theory (2001), Public Intellectuals: A Study of Decline (2002), The Economic Structure of Intellectual Property Law (with William M. Landes) (2003), Preventing Surprise Attacks: Intelligence Reform in the Wake of 9/11 (2005), Catastrophe: Risk and Response (2005), Uncertain Shield: The U.S. Intelligence System in the Throes of Reform (2006), Not a Suicide Pact: The Constitution in a Time of National Emergency (2006), The Problems of Jurisprudence (2007), The Little Book of Plagiarism (2007), Countering Terrorism: Blurred Focus, Halting Steps (2008), How Judges Think (2008), A Failure of Capitalism: The Crisis of '08 and the Descent into Depression (2009), and The Crisis of Capitalist Democracy (2010). — [This judicial biography was written by Randy Barnett, hereinafter "R.B."]

be broken. But since little effort is made to prevent businessmen from assuming risks, these reasons are no better than makeweights.

A better argument is that a penalty clause may discourage efficient as well as inefficient breaches of contract. Suppose a breach would cost the promisee $12,000 in actual damages but would yield the promisor $20,000 in additional profits. Then there would be a net social gain from breach. After being fully compensated for his loss the promisee would be no worse off than if the contract had been performed, while the promisor would be better off by $8,000. But now suppose the contract contains a penalty clause under which the promisor if he breaks his promise must pay the promisee $25,000. The promisor will be discouraged from breaking the contract, since $25,000, the penalty, is greater than $20,000, the profits of the breach; and a transaction that would have increased value will be forgone.

On this view, since compensatory damages should be sufficient to deter inefficient breaches (that is, breaches that cost the victim more than the gain to the contract breaker), penal damages could have no effect other than to deter some efficient breaches. But this overlooks the earlier point that the willingness to agree to a penalty clause is a way of making the promisor and his promise credible and may therefore be essential to inducing some value-maximizing contracts to be made. It also overlooks the more important point that the parties (always assuming they are fully competent) will, in deciding whether to include a penalty clause in their contract, weigh the gains against the costs — costs that include the possibility of discouraging an efficient breach somewhere down the road — and will include the clause only if the benefits exceed those costs as well as all other costs.

On this view the refusal to enforce penalty clauses is (at best) paternalistic — and it seems odd that courts should display parental solicitude for large corporations. But however this may be, we must be on guard to avoid importing our own ideas of sound public policy into an area where our proper judicial role is more than usually deferential. The responsibility for making innovations in the common law of Illinois rests with the courts of Illinois, and not with the federal courts in Illinois. And like every other state, Illinois, untroubled by academic skepticism of the wisdom of refusing to enforce penalty clauses against sophisticated promisors, see, e.g., Goetz & Scott, Liquidated Damages, Penalties and the Just Compensation Principle, 77 Colum. L. Rev. 554 (1977), continues steadfastly to insist on the distinction between penalties and liquidated damages. . . . To be valid under Illinois law a liquidation of damages must be a reasonable estimate at the time of contracting of the likely damages from breach, and the need for estimation at that time must be shown by reference to the likely difficulty of measuring the actual damages from a breach of contract after the breach occurs. If damages would be easy to determine then, or if the estimate greatly exceeds a reasonable upper estimate of what the damages are likely to be, it is a penalty. . . .

REFERENCE: Barnett, §§2.3.4, 2.3.6
                Farnsworth, §12.18
                Calamari & Perillo, §§14.31-14.35
                Murray, §126

3

OTHER REMEDIES AND CAUSES OF ACTION

In this chapter we shall examine legal remedies and causes of action that are outside the garden variety suits for breach of contract, but which are still encountered frequently enough to merit study. By identifying the edges of normal breach of contract actions, these other remedies and alternative causes of action also help us to better understand the nature and limits of contract. In the next section, we consider the exceptional or equitable remedies of specific performance and injunctions. We then turn our attention in Section B to causes of action other than breach of contract that may arise in contractual situations. The two we shall study are actions for restitution and for tortious interference with contract. In Chapter 16, we shall briefly discuss the cause of action for fraud when we distinguish this tort from the contract defense of misrepresentation.

A. SPECIFIC PERFORMANCE AND INJUNCTIONS

Money damages is the normal or presumptive remedy for breach of contract. Other remedies — sometimes deemed "extraordinary" — are also available. Traditionally, damages were available in courts of *law* (also known as common law courts) while extraordinary relief was available in chancery courts or courts of *equity*. Consequently, money damages came to be known as *legal* relief, while these other remedies were called *equitable* relief.

Legal Background: Introduction to Equitable Remedies

DAN B. DOBBS, INTRODUCTION TO EQUITY AND EQUITABLE REMEDIES, from HANDBOOK ON THE LAW OF REMEDIES 24-28 (1973):

Equity Substance and Procedure. In one sense, the word *equity* implies right, justice, or moral quality. Relatedly, it may mean flexibility rather than rigidity. In a judicial sense, the word refers to what was once an entirely separate body of judicial rules, procedures, remedies, and to the separate courts that administered this juridical mass.

The Court of Chancery was the court that administered equity in England. It was a court committed, in theory, to doing equity in the sense of higher justice, and also committed to doing equity in the sense of providing flexible approaches where the law had become too rigid.

The Chancellors of England were powerful and often innovative men. They developed an enormous body of equity doctrine, much of which survives today in some form. Sometimes this is difficult to identify as equitable, because it has often been codified in statutes, or adopted and used regularly by law courts as well as equity courts. Both the modern trust and the modern mortgage were developed mainly by actions of the equity courts. For various reasons, equity has a hand in the management of insolvent's estates, and in some aspects of decedent's estates. Statutory law of divorce, bankruptcy, and estate administration is partly the product of, partly the subject matter of, equity courts. In each case, the substantive rules of equity were made in response either to unduly rigid legal rules, or to their entire inadequacy, and in each case the substantive rules were purportedly based on higher moral principle.

Equitable procedure, too, was different. Equity cases were begun by bill, not by a writ keyed to the forms of action. In the equity court it did not matter whether the facts fitted some established form; relief would be given on the chancellor's sense of need and justice. Nor did the chancellor use a jury (or any of the other means of trials at law). He decided the case himself, and he compelled what the law courts would not even permit — the testimony of the actual parties. On the other hand, the chancellor did not see the parties, and could not judge their demeanor, since he took testimony by means of written interrogatories. Much of the chancellor's procedure as well as his substantive rules, remain with us today. . . .

Equitable Remedies.   Roughly speaking, the Chancellor's remedies were either coercive, restitutionary, declaratory, or in some cases, all of these. The coercive remedies turned on the Chancellor's unique power to enter an authoritarian personal order against the defendant commanding conduct of some specified sort, and subjecting the defendant to a punishment if he did not obey. This power to issue personal orders was not at all like the power of the law courts. The law courts' power was the power to declare law. The judgment at law adjudicated that A owed B money in a certain sum, or that O had title to Blackacre and that C did not. Such a judgment might be enforced: The sheriff might put O in possession of Blackacre, or sell A's chattels to pay the debt declared in the law courts. But the judgment at law did not command obedience because it was not a command at all, only an adjudication. The defendant at law was thus subjected to *enforcement* of the judgment, not *punishment* for disobedience. The decree in equity, with its personal order to the defendant, coupled with the power of punishment, was a considerable departure from the relatively limited remedies available at law.

The coercive remedies of the chancellors could be applied to a variety of situations, since the chancellors were not restricted to the limited number of cases that fell within defined forms of actions at common law.

The injunction was the main form of the personal order directed to the defendant. He might be enjoined to act, or not to act. For example, he might be enjoined not to commit nuisance, or he might be enjoined to remove boulders wrongly deposited on the plaintiff's land. The specific performance order is a form of injunction that compels the defendant to act to perform his contract with the plaintiff. . . .

. . . Declaratory relief in equity was often obscured because it was, in form, associated with some other remedy, such as the injunction. However, there were many instances in which the plaintiff's ultimate purpose in seeking equitable relief was to obtain a declaration of his rights, even though at some early stage in the proceeding he might be obliged to seek an injunction or claim some established remedy in order to do this. Nevertheless, many claims in equity for rescission of a transaction or cancellation of an instrument, claims for reformation, bills of peace and interpleader, had as their real purpose a declaration of rights, so that the plaintiff might proceed with an intelligent understanding of what he could and could not legally do. Such claims still exist in equity, as where the plaintiff seeks to enjoin the enforcement of a statute alleged to be unconstitutional. In many instances, though he does indeed wish an injunction, his main purpose is to test the constitutionality, and he knows that if he establishes the invalidity of the law, the injunction is usually not needed. In this and other cases, the availability today of a declaratory judgment under the declaratory judgment statutes has slowly eroded the need for coercive relief, though such relief may still be granted where needed.

. . . Restitutionary remedies given by equity courts were a little different. These remedies operated essentially to restore to the plaintiff something that, in good conscience, belonged to him. This restoration might be enforced, if need be, by personal order, and thus the coercive element, always strong in equity, would be present. However, the restitutionary remedies for the most part could just as well be enforced by the procedures known to the law courts. The coercive means of enforcing the restitutionary remedies, then, is accidental, a result of the fact that restitution happened to be sought and granted in an equity court.

Restitution has always been given at law as well as in equity. However, restitution at law was for centuries based solely on legal title. Thus the plaintiff could be restored to his chattels by way of a replevin or detinue action at law, or to his real property by way of ejectment action at law. But if legal title had passed to the defendant, the law courts refused to aid the plaintiff, even though that legal title might have been gained by fraud or undue influence or breach of fiduciary duty. In these cases, then, equity took jurisdiction to force restitution. Equity was also quicker to act on the shift from a landed to a money economy, and to force restitution of money, as distinct from tangible goods or property.

Restitution means "restoration," but in equity cases the term was given expanded interpretation. If a trustee took money that belonged to this beneficiary and invested it in Blackacre, equity would say that Blackacre was held on constructive trust and force the trustee to convey it to his beneficiary. If the trustee invested in a stock, or a business, equity would declare him a constructive trustee of the stock, or make him account for the profits of the business. In these cases the plaintiff-beneficiary got not only a literal restoration of what had been taken from him, but the profits or gains as well. This is restitution or restoration only in the sense that the profits can be identified as the product of, and hence "belonging" to, the values appropriated from the plaintiff. This whole idea has been expanded in the modern American cases to furnish this kind of expanded restitution even where there is no fiduciary relationship.[1]

Remedial Limits.   It is usually assumed that if the defendant has violated the plaintiff's substantive rights, the plaintiff is entitled to the appropriate legal remedy as a matter of course, and no one debates whether that remedy is more, or less, appropriate than an equitable remedy. This may not be a sound approach, especially since the courts of law and equity have been merged in most states. Sound or not, however, it is not the approach taken in equity cases.

When the plaintiff seeks an equitable remedy, particularly a coercive one, the rule is that he may have the remedy only if the remedy at law is inadequate. Furthermore, the chancellor must take into account practical questions, whether he can enforce any remedy he grants, since he does not wish to issue a personal command and have it flouted, and whether enforcement would be too burdensome to the court. In addition to these considerations, the chancellor may also take into account the plaintiff's moral standing. Because the chancellor has always claimed a particular concern for high moral standards he may refuse relief to a plaintiff who has in some way misbehaved, or whose activities have prejudiced the defendant, or even to the plaintiff who has delayed unduly. It is important to understand that, though equity enforced substantive rules of moral behavior, the ones just mentioned are not substantive but remedial. The plaintiff of poor moral standing does not lose his claim; he loses his remedy in equity. Much of traditional equity is based on analysis of concepts like adequacy, practicality, clean hands, estoppel, laches, and hardship, in an effort to determine whether the equity remedy will be granted.

The Merger of Law and Equity.   The profession almost always speaks of law and equity as though they remained separate even today, and this introduction has spoken in the same way. But this is shorthand for much more complex ideas. Equity courts were indeed separate courts for hundreds of years, but, with the exception of a handful of states, probably four or five, the courts of law and the courts of equity have ceased to have separate existences. The superior courts of most states, and the Federal District Courts now enjoy all of the powers formerly vested in the separate courts. The judge of the Superior Court of North Carolina or the Supreme Court of New York or the Federal District Court anywhere can hear a criminal case in the morning, a negligence suit in the afternoon, and issue a temporary restraining order at night.

Thus the reference to "equity" is partly a reference to a history that has been changed. Yet, jury trial was given in actions at common law and not in suits in equity, and a jury trial may still be granted or not, according to

---

1. Thus it may be an appropriate device to remedy mistake, duress, fraud, undue influence, or violation of statutory duty. . . .

whether the case is classified as one in equity or at law. For reasons of this sort the distinction remains, for some purposes, a viable one.

What Makes a Case an Equitable One? What do lawyers and judges mean when they say the case is an equitable one, or that it is not? They may mean the case is one that equity would have taken before the merger, because of some substantive defect in the legal rule. An example of this is the relief equity gave to debtors who had mortgaged their lands. The case was "equitable" because equity courts took the case, and equity courts took the case because the substantive rule at law was oppressive and out of accord with the developing money economy.

More often today a case is called an equitable one because some equitable remedy, usually of a coercive nature, is sought. Thus if an injunction is sought or specific performance of a contract, the case is equitable in the eyes of most professionals, even though the substantive law rules in the case are all rules of the law courts, and equity's only function is to add a remedy not available at law.

Finally, a case is sometimes referred to as equitable in the rather loose sense that it involves questions of discretion, or judgment, or calls for principles of justice and conscience rather than rigid "legal" rules. . . .

REFERENCE: Barnett, §2.5
               Farnsworth, §12.4
               Calamari & Perillo, §16.1
               Murray, §128(A)

1. Contracts for Land

Traditionally, money damages were the presumptive form of legal relief. This is reflected in Justice Oliver Wendell Holmes, Jr.'s famous observation that: "The only universal consequence of a legally binding promise is, that the law makes the promisor pay damages if the promised event does not come to pass."[2] Holmes was not denying that one could, in exceptional circumstances, obtain specific relief. Instead, he was asserting that the only remedy available in principle in *every* case is money damages.

As was discussed in the excerpt from Dobbs, an injunction for specific performance is equitable relief that is available when legal relief is, for some reason, inadequate. One uniformly accepted reason for inadequacy is that the property in question is unique. Traditionally, land has been presumed to be unique, so in land sales contracts the presumption actually shifts in favor of specific performance. In sales of personal property, however, there is no such presumption and uniqueness or some other reason why damages are inadequate must be established by the victim of the breach.

STUDY GUIDE: Why are damages presumptively inadequate when a contract for the sale of land is breached? Each of the opinions in the following case illustrates a different method of interpreting this traditional presumption.

2. Oliver W. Holmes, Jr., The Common Law 301 (1881).

LOVELESS v. DIEHL
Supreme Court of Arkansas, 235 Ark. 805,
236 Ark. 129, 364 S.W.2d 317 (1963)

ED. F. McFADDIN, A.J.* Appellees, W. A. Diehl and wife, filed suit against Appellants, J. E. Loveless and wife, for specific performance of an option contract, and in the alternative prayed for damages. Appellants, Loveless and wife, denied the claim for specific performance; and, by counterclaim, sought judgment on a note. Trial in the Chancery Court resulted in a decree awarding Diehl and wife specific performance and damages; and also awarding Loveless judgment on the note. Both sides have appealed.

Mr. and Mrs. Loveless owned a farm of 79 acres in Faulkner County; and they leased the farm to Mr. and Mrs. Diehl for a 3-year term beginning December 15, 1956, at a rental of $100.00 per month, payable in advance. The lease instrument also contained this option:

> It is mutually agreed and understood between the parties hereto that Lessees shall have an option to purchase said property at any time during the life of this lease, it being specifically understood that at any time between December 15, 1956, and December 15, 1959, that said option can be exercised by the Lessees wherein they will be permitted to purchase said lands for a total purchase price of $21,000.00.

[handwritten margin note: Option Contract — present promises with choice]

The Diehls took possession of the land and spent several thousand dollars in improvements. Also, Mr. Diehl purchased from Mr. Loveless a "pipeline milking system complete with two walk through stalls," and executed therefor his promissory note for $1440.95; and no part of this note has been paid. The Diehls evidently intended to seasonably exercise the option to purchase the land; but as time went on they found it impossible to do so. In order to salvage what they could from the expenditures they had made for improvements, the Diehls listed the property with real estate brokers, hoping to find a purchaser who would pay in excess of the $21,000.00, the amount required to be paid to exercise the option with Loveless.

Shortly before the option expired, the Diehls agreed with Dr. J. W. Hart to sell him the place for $22,000.00; which, after paying the Loveless option of $21,000.00, would have left the Diehls $1,000.00. It is clear that Dr. Hart could have paid the $22,000.00 for the property. The evidence is in conflict as to the conversations and dealings between the Diehls and Dr. Hart on the one side, and the Lovelesses on the other; but it is reasonably clear that before December 15, 1959, Dr. Hart would have paid the $22,000.00 if Mr. Loveless had not interfered with the Diehl-Hart trade, by disclaiming any intention to sell the property to Diehl. Such interference and disavowal by Loveless made unnecessary any further tender of the $21,000.00 to him. . . .

---

* *Edward Fitzgerald McFaddin* (1894-1982) was educated at Hendrix College, Hardin-Simmons University (A.B.), the University of Texas (LL.B.), and Columbia University (LL.M.). Admitted to the Arkansas bar in 1916, he practiced law in Arkansas prior to being elected to the Supreme Court of Arkansas in 1943. McFaddin retired from the bench in 1966. — K.T.

After December 15, 1959 the Diehls moved a portion of their property from the premises; and the Lovelesses took forcible possession, and rented the property to Mr. Waggoner for $100.00 per month; and there are claims and counterclaims because of such forcible possession, and also claims for rent, and damages. No useful purpose would be served by detailing the testimony of the various witnesses and differentiating our conclusions from those of the learned Chancellor. After a careful study of all the evidence, we have decided that the best way to conclude this litigation is as follows:

Traditional Contract Damages

1. The Diehls are entitled to judgment against the Lovelesses for $1,000.00, being the amount the Diehls would have realized if they had purchased the property from the Lovelesses for $21,000.00 and sold it to Dr. Hart for $22,000.00. Under the situation as it existed in December 1959, the judgment of $1,000.00 gives the Diehls all the relief that a deed from the Lovelesses would have given them. The Diehls admitted that they could not have purchased the property except by obtaining the money through resale to Dr. Hart. He was ready, able, and willing to purchase in December 1959, but was not bound to do so thereafter. Furthermore, the Diehls prayed for damages in the alternative to specific performance, and we conclude that the amount of $1,000.00 is the amount of damages they established in connection with the option to purchase; and this conclusion eliminates any rental claims of the Diehls after December 15, 1959. In thus awarding the clearly established damages in lieu of specific performance, we are exercising the sound discretion which a court of equity has in cases involving specific performance. . . .

2. Mr. Loveless is entitled to judgment against Mr. Diehl on the milking equipment note for $1,440.95, with interest at six per cent per annum from January 15, 1957 until paid. The $1,000.00 damages as awarded the Diehls in the paragraph just above is to be credited on the Loveless judgment as of December 15, 1959; and Mr. Loveless will have judgment against Mr. Diehl for the balance. The appellees' claim to strike this note item was correctly denied by the Chancery Court.

3. The claim of the Lovelesses for balance of rents, and the claims of the Diehls for loss of property were considered by the learned Chancellor as offsetting. At least, each claim was so disputed by evidence as to be unproved; and in this we agree.

It follows that the Chancery decree is reversed and the cause remanded, with directions to enter a decree in keeping with this opinion; and each party will bear the cost of the entire case that such party has incurred.

JOHNSON, J., not participating. . . .

GEORGE ROSE SMITH, J., on rehearing. This is an appeal by the sellers from a decree directing specific performance of a contract for the sale of land. In our original opinion, in the belief that we were achieving substantial justice, we set aside the chancellor's award of specific performance and instead limited the purchasers to their monetary damages, which we fixed as the difference between the contract price and the slightly greater sum for which the purchasers had agreed to sell the property to a third person. . . .

This possibility of substituting damages for specific performance was not mentioned in the original briefs. In their petition for rehearing the appellees earnestly insist that our decision did not in fact reach a completely just result. Briefing the legal point for the first time, counsel contend that the court's denial of specific performance is not warranted in the circumstances of this case.

After reconsidering the question we have concluded that the petition for rehearing is well-founded.

Our prior decisions recognize the possibility that in a few unusual situations a court of equity may in its discretion deny the plaintiff the right of specific performance. But the remedy of specific performance, in giving the complaining party exactly what he bargained for, ordinarily affords complete and perfect relief and therefore is usually to be awarded *as a matter of course.*

The point was discussed in Sims v. Best, 140 Ark. 384, 215 S.W. 519, where we said:

> Finally, it is insisted that the right to specific performance is not absolute, but is a matter of discretion with the chancellor. While this is true, the discretion is a sound judicial discretion controlled by established principles of equity, and where the contract is in writing, is certain in its terms, is for a valuable consideration, is fair and just in all its provisions, and is capable of being enforced without hardship to either party, *it is as much a matter of course for a court of equity to decree its specific performance* as for a court of law to award a judgment of damages for its breach.

(Italics added.) It will be noted that every one of the conditions just mentioned (a written contract, certainty, etc.) is present in the case at bar.

Much to the same effect is this holding in Dollar v. Knight, 145 Ark. 522, 224 S.W. 983:

> Where land or any estate or interest in land is the subject-matter of the agreement, the jurisdiction to enforce specific performance is undisputed, and does not depend upon the inadequacy of the legal remedy in the particular case. It is as much *a matter of course* for courts of equity to decree a specific performance of a contract for the conveyance of real estate, which is in its nature un-objectionable, as it is for courts of law to give damages for its breach.

(Italics added.)

In the present case we find no valid reason for a denial of specific performance. To the contrary, the equities in the case strongly demand that this remedy be afforded. The purchasers, according to the great weight of the evidence, expended some $5,000 or more, in money or in labor, in improving the property. Apparently the land in its improved state is worth more than the contract price, for otherwise the sellers would hardly be so strenuously resisting this suit for enforcement of the agreement. To deny specific performance, and to award instead an amount of damages far below the buyers' expenditures in improving the property, would result in the sellers' being unjustly enriched for their culpable refusal to carry out their promise.

The only reason that occurs to us for a denial of specific performance is the fact that the buyers entered into an agreement to sell the land to

Dr. Hart. It is plain enough, however, that they had a perfect right to resell the land if they wanted to. Whether they kept it, sold it, or gave it away was of no concern to the sellers. To refuse specific relief on account of the proposed resale would establish an unsound precedent, diminishing the transferability of property, since in similar situations prospective buyers would be reluctant to bind themselves to a purchase contract, for fear that it might prove to be unenforceable. . . .

The decree is modified as indicated, and the cause is remanded so that the account may be stated in accordance with this opinion and a final decree be entered.

JOHNSON, J., not participating.

HARRIS, C.J., and MCFADDIN, J., dissent.

CARLETON HARRIS, C.J.* (dissenting). . . .
The majority state,

> The purchasers, according to the great weight of the evidence, expended some $5,000 or more, in money or in labor, in improving the property. Apparently the land in its improved state is worth more than the contract price, for otherwise the sellers would hardly be so strenuously resisting this suit for enforcement of the agreement. To deny specific performance, and to award instead an amount of damages far below the buyers' expenditures in improving the property, would result in the sellers' being unjustly enriched for their culpable refusal to carry out their promise.

I should like to point out that Diehl, entirely voluntarily, wanted to sell this property to Dr. Hart for $22,000.00, which means, according to the majority statement just quoted, that he would lose $4,000.00 by making the sale. In other words, since he was willing to lose $4,000.00 (if he expended $5,000.00 on the place) there certainly was no reason for this court to go beyond the figure that he was willing to accept himself. Diehl was willing to accept $1,000 more than his purchase price, which was the amount of damages we awarded him. Nor can I see that specific performance is called for either legally or equitably, when the sole beneficiary of this holding by the court will be Dr. Hart, a rank outsider — who never had a contract — who was not a party to the litigation — who suffered no loss — and who, according to my view, never did tender to Loveless the $21,000.00 in cash.

I, therefore, respectfully dissent to the granting of the rehearing.

ED. F. MCFADDIN, A.J. (dissenting). I dissent from the opinion of this Court granting a rehearing; and stoutly maintain that the opinion of December 3, 1962, was correct and should stand. . . .

Carleton Harris (1909-1980) attended Union University (Jackson, Tennessee) and Cumberland University (LL.B.). He practiced privately in Pine Bluff (1932-1948), was a member of the Arkansas House of Representatives (1933-1938), and was prosecuting attorney of the Eleventh Judicial District (1947-1948) before being appointed judge of the Fourth Chancery District of Arkansas in 1949. He was justice of the Arkansas Supreme Court from 1957 to 1980. Judge Harris also served as Disaster Relief chairman for the Jefferson County American Red Cross for nearly forty years until his death. — K.T.

The present opinion granting the rehearing uses this language:

> Our prior decisions recognize the possibility that in a few unusual situations a court of equity may in its discretion deny the plaintiff the right of specific performance. But the remedy of specific performance, in giving the complaining party exactly what he bargained for, ordinarily affords complete and perfect relief and therefore is usually to be awarded *as a matter of course.*

The opinion quotes from Sims v. Best, 140 Ark. 384, 215 S.W 519, and Dollar v. Knight, 145 Ark. 522, 224 S.W 983, following the above quoted language. But the opinion on rehearing fails to quote this language from Dollar v. Knight:

> It is allowable in the exercise of a sound discretion to deny specific performance "where the case is not clear, or where the complainant is in the wrong, or there are considerable countervailing equities." Watkins v. Turner, supra.

The case at bar comes within the last quotation from Dollar v. Knight, because (a) the case is not clear; and (b) there are considerable countervailing equities. The dissenting opinion of the Chief Justice in this case shows that it is not entirely clear that the Diehls made a sufficient tender of any kind; and there are certainly countervailing equities because the sum of $1,000.00 is all that the Diehls would have gained if they had received the deed under the contract; and to grant them judgment for that amount is to end the litigation. In Watkins v. Turner, 34 Ark. 663, Judge Eakin denied specific performance because the case was not clear. . . .

The plaintiffs' prayer to the complaint in the case at bar was in this language:

> WHEREFORE, Plaintiffs pray that defendants be required to specifically perform said lease agreement and the option therein contained, and that plaintiffs be adjudged to be entitled to conveyance of said lands from defendants; that, in the alternative, defendants be required to reimburse plaintiffs for expenditures made by plaintiffs in making permanent improvements to and upon said lands in the sum of $7,000.00, and for judgment against defendants for breach of contract in the sum of $2,000.00; for the costs herein, and for all other relief to which they may be entitled.

When the plaintiffs prayed for damages as an alternative to specific performance, the court of equity has the right to decide whether to award specific performance or damages; certainly when the case is not clear and when there are countervailing equities, as in the case at bar. Without prolonging this dissent, it is sufficient to say that I stoutly maintain that the opinion of December 3, 1962 reached a practical result in giving the Diehls $1,000.00 as damages, which is all they would have received if the deed had been delivered to them; and the opinion of December 3, 1962, therefore, would have ended the litigation. Now the majority is continuing the litigation by remanding it for further consideration by the Chancery Court.

REFERENCE: Barnett, §2.5.1
                    Farnsworth, §12.6
                    Calamari & Perillo, §16.2
                    Murray, §128(B)(2)(b) & (c)

2. Contracts for Goods

Each case in this section concerns personal property or *goods*, and the last two apply the Uniform Commercial Code's provision on specific performance (§2-716).

STUDY GUIDE: When reading the following cases consider what function the uniqueness test is serving. Why exactly is the burden placed on the victim to establish that the subject of a contract is unique? Should this be the rule? How does the U.C.C. liberalize the traditional approach to specific performance of contracts for the sale of goods?

CUMBEST v. HARRIS
Supreme Court of Mississippi,
363 So. 2d 294 (1978)

Before PATTERSON, C.J., ROBERTSON and WALKER, JJ.

WALKER, J.,* for the Court:

This is an appeal from an order of the Chancery Court of Jackson County, Mississippi, dismissing appellant Cumbest's bill of complaint.

The sole question presented is whether the personal property, which was the subject of the controversy, is of such peculiar, sentimental or unique value as to come within the exception to the general rule that a chancery court will not ordinarily decree specific performance of a contract involving personal property.

Cumbest's bill of complaint and exhibits attached thereto aver, among other things, that on May 19, 1976, Donald Ronnie Cumbest and Bedford Harris, respectively, contracted for the sale and purchase of certain hi-fi equipment via a bill of sale. An option agreement was also signed on the same date allowing Cumbest to repurchase the audio equipment on or before 5:00 P.M., Monday, June 7, 1976. The language of these two instruments is clear and unambiguous and both were signed and notarized.

The complainant averred that the transaction was intended to be a loan, in substance, and that the audio equipment was to serve as collateral. It also states that from early morning on Monday, June 7, 1976, until late that evening every effort humanly possible was made to pay the required amount of money to the defendant. The defendant purposely avoided meeting with him at various places during the day, thereby fraudulently and deliberately evading the receipt of the money as contracted for in The Option to Repurchase Agreement. In desperation the complainant

---

* *Harry Grey Walker* (1924-†) was educated at the University of Mississippi (LL.B.). He has served as Mississippi State Reporter (1964), judge on the County Court of Harrison County (1964-1968), judge on the Circuit Court of Mississippi (1968-1973), and justice on the Mississippi Supreme Court (1973-1987). Walker served as Presiding Justice of that body from 1982-1986 and as Chief Justice from 1986-1987. Prior to his judicial career, he held a private practice at Gulfport, Mississippi (1952-1964). — K.T.

deposited the required amount of money with the defendant's landlord on the evening of June 7, 1976, and approximately a week later initiated this lawsuit seeking equitable relief. Subsequently, the landlord, Mrs. Neuhaus, turned the money over to her attorney, Mr. Schroeder. Both of these parties have been joined as defendants in this lawsuit and the money paid into the registry of the court.

The amended complaint further averred that the complete assemblage of the audio equipment took several years for the appellant to acquire and because of the unique nature and irreplaceability of much of the equipment the court should assert jurisdiction of the case and grant such equitable relief as it deems appropriate. Finally, the complainant prays for the defendant to be enjoined against the disposition, sale or removal of the property and for the court to mandate specific performance of the contract to reconvey.

The chancellor allowed a hearing solely on the question of whether the property was of such sentimental value or so unique as to come within the exception to the general rule that the chancery court will not ordinarily decree specific performance of a contract involving personal property.

Cumbest was the only witness to testify at the proceeding. The property involved was a stereo system allegedly valued at $10,000. The system consisted of twenty separate parts accumulated over a period of fifteen years. There was testimony that Cumbest had acquired experience in stereophonic and recording equipment over the years by working in hi-fi stores in Oxford and Gulfport. He also did some recording of a professional nature. According to him, the items involved were a part of a recording studio which consisted of carefully matched parts, rather than a mere stereo set as contended by the defendant. The parts involved could not function alone, and could not be matched to just any standard stereo system. Cumbest testified that many of the integral parts of the system could no longer be replaced, e.g., the main reel to reel recorder; a stereo quadraphonic four channel logic decoder which, according to Cumbest, was originally on order for two years; a stereo three channel crossover preamplifier with bass boost and turn over frequency control; some speaker components, and the particular diamond needle in the turntable system. Other equipment was personally designed and built by Cumbest himself. He testified that he purchased the parts and assembled the speakers to accommodate his particular system, and that the cabinets were designed and handmade by him after extensive study and research to meet the needs of his particular system.

> I designed and built each one of the [7] speakers myself. I ordered each part and component and especially ordered the cross-over preamplifier and there isn't another one like it, and the speakers I built.

In explaining construction of certain speaker systems, Cumbest testified:

> I designed and read over 15 articles on midfrequency sound and quadrosonic sound and what would produce the best and I ordered the speakers and built the cabinets to match the speakers. I cut each piece of wood. They are covered

with rosewood type material and made specially to place in each corner for quadraphonic sound.

In other testimony he pointed out that even those items which are still available are of the type which require special order purchases and that in obtaining them originally there were six months to two years waiting periods. As to sentimental value, Cumbest testified:

> As far as the snetimental [sic] value of the equipment, it is very great, blood sweat and tears have gone into it, I spent 15 years acquiring it piece by piece and I would never seel [sic] it at any price.

Defendant put on no witnesses to contradict Cumbest's testimony. As the chancellor recited in his order, the general rule is that, ordinarily, specific performance will not be decreed if the subject matter of the contract sought to be enforced is personalty. However, this general principle is subject to several well recognized exceptions, such as: (1) Where there is no adequate remedy at law; (2) Where the specific articles or property are of peculiar, sentimental or unique value; and (3) Where due to scarcity the chattel is not readily obtainable. 81 C.J.S. Specific Performance §§81-83 (1977). These exceptions are partly founded on the principle of the inadequacy of a remedy at law and the remedy may, in a proper case, be allowed where damages are not readily ascertainable.

> The tests to determine whether or not specific performance of a contract should be granted are the same in case of contracts for the sale of personalty as in the case of contracts for the sale of realty, namely, whether the damages for the breach are the equivalent of the promised performance, and whether the remedy at law is inadequate.

81 C.J.S. Specific Performance §80 (1977). Such equitable relief is justified by the fact that the legal remedy of replevin is subject to defects of procedure which prevent the successful plaintiff from invariably recovering possession of the chattel. There is also considerable authority, old and new, showing liberality in the granting of an equitable remedy. 11 Williston Contracts §1419 (3d ed. 1968); Miss. Code Ann. §75-2-716 (1972).

In the present case, there was uncontradicted testimony that some components of the system were irreplaceable. Other components were replaceable but only with difficulty and long waiting periods. Additionally, Cumbest testified that the system was acquired over a fifteen-year span and that he personally designed and built parts of it specifically to match that particular system. Based on that testimony, we must conclude the property had both a unique value and falls into the category of property which is not readily obtainable due to scarcity.

For the above reasons, we hold that the chancellor erred in not finding that the property was sufficiently unique to justify the equitable jurisdiction of a chancery court. The cause will be remanded for a hearing on the merits.

Reversed and remanded for a hearing on the merits.

SCHOLL v. HARTZELL
Court of Common Pleas of Pennsylvania, Northampton County, 20 Pa. D. & C.3d 304 (1981)

GRIFO, J.,* . . .

On April 3, 1981, defendant placed a newspaper advertisement in the Allentown Morning Call Newspaper for the sale of a 1962 Chevrolet Corvette automobile and miscellaneous parts for the sale price of $4,000. Plaintiff, in response to the aforementioned advertisement, met with defendant on April 3 to inspect the automobile and component parts which formed the basis of defendant's offer to sell. Subsequent to the inspection of said automobile and parts, defendant and plaintiff entered into an agreement of sale for the total sale price of $4,000, at which time plaintiff gave defendant a deposit of $100. A receipt was given to plaintiff noting said deposit, and indicating that a balance of $3,900 would be due and payable upon pick up of the vehicle. Thereafter, on the same date, plaintiff advised defendant that he had obtained a bank money order, payable to defendant, for the balance of the said price, which he would hand deliver to defendant when the vehicle and parts were tendered. On April 5, 1981, pursuant to a phone conversation, defendant advised plaintiff that he would not accept plaintiff's tender of the balance of the sale price. Thereafter, defendant returned plaintiff's initial payment of $100, and has continued to ignore plaintiff's demand that defendant accept plaintiff's tender of the full amount of the sale price.

Based on the foregoing, plaintiff has filed an action in replevin, wherein he demands that possession of said automobile and automotive parts be delivered to plaintiff following payment of the sale price. In the alternative, plaintiff demands a judgment against defendant in the amount of $4,655, which he alleges represents the difference between the sale price and the value of the property to be replevied.

Generally speaking, replevin lies wherever one person claims personal property in the possession of another, provided the claimant has the exclusive and immediate right to possession of the goods in question: Robinson v. Tool-O-Matic, Inc., 216 Pa. Superior Ct. 258, 263 A.2d 914 (1970). . . . Defendant has alleged that plaintiff has failed to establish his exclusive right to the automotive parts in question. Indeed, defendant avers that the complaint, at best, raises a question of contract. He further contends that in order to permit an action in replevin to lie in this action, it would also have to lie in any situation where a prospective buyer places a deposit on a piece of merchandise. We agree.

In Morgan v. East, 25 N.E. 867 (1890), the Indiana Supreme Court held that an action in replevin would not lie to enforce an unexecuted contract, and concluded that the parties are left to an action for the breach of the agreement. In the instant matter, it would appear that if a contract were

---

Richard D. Grifo (1919-2009) was educated at Lafayette College (B.A.) and the University of Pennsylvania (LL.B.), and was admitted to the Pennsylvania bar in 1943. He held a legal practice in Easton from 1943 to 1968, except while serving as County Solicitor for Northampton County (1951-1955). Judge Grifo was appointed to the Court of Common Pleas in 1968, where he sat until his retirement at the age of seventy, as required by the Pennsylvania Constitution. — K.T.

indeed created through the tender of the deposit and the signed receipt, it was still executory since further performance was required by both parties; namely, the tendering of the balance due and the transfer of title to the automobile and miscellaneous parts. We do not believe that plaintiff, through said tendering of the deposit, acquired a right to immediate and exclusive possession of the goods in question within the meaning of Robinson v. Tool-O-Matic, supra.

Reasoning

We believe that to allow plaintiff to maintain his present action in replevin would allow plaintiff to accomplish indirectly what he cannot do directly. That is to say, plaintiff by his replevin action is attempting to force defendant to specifically perform the contract in issue. Specific performance is an equitable remedy and only available when plaintiff has no adequate remedy at law. Our Commonwealth Court had held that specific performance should only be granted where facts clearly establish plaintiff's rights thereto, where no adequate remedy at law exists, and where justice requires it: Hilton v. State Employees' Retirement Board, 23 Pa. Commonwealth Ct. 639, 353 A.2d 883 (1976), revised on other grounds, 470 Pa. 301, 368 A.2d 640 (1977).

In support of his contentions, plaintiff has argued that the Pennsylvania Uniform Commercial Code specifies that a replevin action is one of the buyer's remedies in a breach of contract situation, and has cited [U.C.C. §2-716] as his authority. . . .

Plaintiff further submits that Official Comment 3 explains that [§2-716] permits a buyer to avail himself of the legal remedy of replevin in cases in which cover is reasonably unavailable and goods have been identified to the contract. We find plaintiff's argument unpersuasive. Official Comment No. 2 to [§2-716] provides:

> In view of this article's emphasis on the commercial feasibility of replacement, a new concept of what are "unique" goods is introduced under this section. Specific performance is no longer limited to goods which are already specific or ascertained at the time of contracting. The test of uniqueness under this section must be made in terms of the total situation which characterizes the contract. Output and requirements contracts involving a particular or peculiarly available source or market presents today a typical commercial performance situation, as contrasted with contracts for the sale of heirlooms or priceless works of art which were usually involved in the older cases. However, uniqueness is not the sole basis of the remedy under this section for the relief may also be granted "in other proper circumstances" and inability to cover is strong evidence of "other proper circumstances."

Although a 1962 Chevrolet Corvette automobile may be considered by many to be a collector's item, the court fails to find that it is of the "unique" goods contemplated by [§2-716]. Moreover, plaintiff has not alleged in his complaint that he has been unable to cover as provided in [§2-716]. We conclude that plaintiff's action does not lie in replevin, but should more appropriately be in assumpsit. . . .

Holding

Plaintiff is given leave to file an amended complaint.

STUDY GUIDE: *Is the car in question in the following case found to be unique? What principle underlies the court's approach to specific performance?*

SEDMAK v. CHARLIE'S CHEVROLET, INC.
Missouri Court of Appeals, Eastern District, Division
Four, 622 S.W.2d 694 (Mo. App. 1981)

Satz, J.*

Holdings ← This is an appeal from a decree of specific performance. We affirm.

Contract ← In their petition, plaintiffs, Dr. and Mrs. Sedmak (Sedmaks), alleged they entered into a contract with defendant, Charlie's Chevrolet, Inc. (Charlie's), to purchase a Corvette automobile for approximately $15,000.00. The Corvette was one of a limited number manufactured to commemorate the selection of the Corvette as the Pace Car for the Indianapolis 500. Charlie's breached the contract, the Sedmaks alleged, when, after the automobile was delivered, an agent for Charlie's told the Sedmaks they could not purchase the automobile for $15,000.00 but would have to bid on it. . . .

Breach ←

. . . [T]he record reflects the Sedmaks to be automobile enthusiasts, who, at the time of trial, owned six Corvettes. In July, 1977, "Vette Vues," a Corvette fancier's magazine to which Dr. Sedmak subscribed, published an article announcing Chevrolet's tentative plans to manufacture a limited edition of the Corvette. The limited edition of approximately 6,000 automobiles was to commemorate the selection of the Corvette as the Indianapolis 500 Pace Car. The Sedmaks were interested in acquiring one of these Pace Cars to add to their Corvette collection. In November, 1977, the Sedmaks asked Tom Kells, sales manager at Charlie's Chevrolet, about the availability of the Pace Car. Mr. Kells said he did not have any information on the car but would find out about it. Kells also said if Charlie's were to

?? ← receive a Pace Car, the Sedmaks could purchase it.

On January 9, 1978, Dr. Sedmak telephoned Kells to ask him if a Pace Car could be ordered. Kells indicated that he would require a deposit on the car, so Mrs. Sedmak went to Charlie's and gave Kells a check for $500.00. She was given a receipt for that amount bearing the names of Kells and Charlie's Chevrolet, Inc. At that time, Kells had a pre-order form listing both standard equipment and options available on the Pace Car. Prior to tendering the deposit, Mrs. Sedmak asked Kells if she and Dr. Sedmak

Verbal ← were "definitely going to be the owners." Kells replied, "yes." After the
Contract deposit had been paid, Mrs. Sedmak stated if the car was going to be theirs, her husband wanted some changes made to the stock model. She asked Kells to order the car equipped with an L82 engine, four speed standard transmission and AM/FM radio with tape deck. Kells said that he would try to arrange with the manufacturer for these changes. Kells was able to make the changes, and, when the car arrived, it was equipped as the Sedmaks had requested.

Kells informed Mrs. Sedmak that the price of the Pace Car would be the manufacturer's retail price, approximately $15,000.00. The dollar figure could not be quoted more precisely because Kells was not sure what the

Harold L. Satz (1927-2007) was educated at Washington University at St. Louis (A.B., LL.B.) and worked as a patent examiner for the U.S. Patent Office before entering private practice in St. Louis. In 1970, he was appointed to the Circuit Court and, in 1979, moved to the Missouri Court of Appeals, where he became its Chief Judge (1987-1989). Since his retirement from the bench in 1992, he has presided as a mediator or arbitrator in over 400 cases for the American Arbitration Association and the federal district court. Satz also served in the Merchant Marine (1950-1952). — J.B.

ordered changes would cost, nor was he sure what the "appearance package" — decals, a special paint job — would cost. Kells also told Mrs. Sedmak that, after the changes had been made, a "contract" — a retail dealer's order form — would be mailed to them. However, no form or written contract was mailed to the Sedmaks by Charlie's.

On January 25, 1978, the Sedmaks visited Charlie's to take delivery on another Corvette. At that time, the Sedmaks asked Kells whether he knew anything further about the arrival date of the Pace Car. Kells replied he had no further information but he would let the Sedmaks know when the car arrived. Kells also requested that Charlie's be allowed to keep the car in their showroom for promotional purposes until after the Indianapolis 500 Race. The Sedmaks agreed to this arrangement.

On April 3, 1978, the Sedmaks were notified by Kells that the Pace Car had arrived. Kells told the Sedmaks they could not purchase the car for the manufacturer's retail price because demand for the car had inflated its value beyond the suggested price. Kells also told the Sedmaks they could bid on the car. The Sedmaks did not submit a bid. They filed this suit for specific performance.

Mr. Kells' testimony about his conversations with the Sedmaks regarding the Pace Car differed markedly from the Sedmaks' testimony. Kells stated that he had no definite price information on the Pace Car until a day or two prior to its arrival at Charlie's. He denied ever discussing the purchase price of the car with the Sedmaks. He admitted, however, that after talking with the Sedmaks on January 9, 1978,[3] he telephoned the zone manager and requested changes be made to the Pace Car. He denied the changes were made pursuant to Dr. Sedmak's order. He claimed the changes were made because they were "more favorable to the automobile" and were changes Dr. Sedmak "preferred." In ordering the changes, Kells said he was merely taking Dr. Sedmak's advice because he was a "very knowledgeable man on the Corvette." There is no dispute, however, that when the Pace Car arrived, it was equipped with the options requested by Dr. Sedmak.

Mr. Kells also denied the receipt for $500.00 given him by Mrs. Sedmak on January 9, 1978, was a receipt for a deposit on the Pace Car. On direct examination, he said he "accepted a five hundred dollar ($500) deposit from the Sedmaks to assure them the first opportunity of purchasing the car." On cross-examination, he said: "We were accepting bids and with the five hundred dollar ($500) deposit it was to give them the first opportunity to bid on the car." Then after acknowledging that other bidders had not paid for the opportunity to bid, he explained the deposit gave the Sedmaks the "last opportunity" to make the final bid. Based on this evidence, the trial court found the parties entered into an oral contract for the purchase and sale of the Pace Car at the manufacturer's suggested retail price. . . .

. . . Charlie's contends the Sedmaks failed to show they were entitled to specific performance of the contract. We disagree. Although it has been stated that the determination whether to order specific performance lies within the discretion of the trial court, Landau v. St. Louis Public Service Co.,

3. According to Kells' testimony, both Dr. and Mrs. Sedmak visited Charlie's on January 9, 1978. Mrs. Sedmak testified only she visited Charlie's on that date.

273 S.W2d 255, 259 (Mo. 1954), this discretion is, in fact, quite narrow. When the relevant equitable principles have been met and the contract is fair and plain, "'specific performance goes as a matter of right.'" Miller v. Coffeen, 280 S.W2d 100, 102 (Mo. 1955). Here, the trial court ordered specific performance because it concluded the Sedmaks "have no adequate remedy at law for the reason that they cannot go upon the open market and purchase an automobile of this kind with the same mileage, condition, ownership and appearance as the automobile involved in this case, except, if at all, with considerable expense, trouble, loss, great delay and inconvenience." Contrary to defendant's complaint, this is a correct expression of the relevant law and it is supported by the evidence.

Under the Code, the court may decree specific performance as a buyer's remedy for breach of contract to sell goods "where the goods are unique or in other proper circumstances." §400.2-716(1) [U.C.C. §2-716] (R.S. Mo. 1978). The general term "in other proper circumstances" expresses the drafters' intent to "further a more liberal attitude than some courts have shown in connection with the specific performance of contracts of sale." §400.2-716 [U.C.C. §2-716], U.C.C., Comment 1. This Comment was not directed to the courts of this state, for long before the Code, we, in Missouri, took a practical approach in determining whether specific performance would lie for the breach of contract for the sale of goods and did not limit this relief only to the sale of "unique" goods. Boeving v. Vandover, 240 Mo. App. 117, 218 S.W.2d 175 (1945). In *Boeving*, plaintiff contracted to buy a car from defendant. When the car arrived, defendant refused to sell. The car was not unique in the traditional legal sense but, at that time, all cars were difficult to obtain because of war-time shortages. The court held specific performance was the proper remedy for plaintiff because a new car "could not be obtained elsewhere except at considerable expense, trouble or loss, which cannot be estimated in advance and under such circumstances [plaintiff] did not have an adequate remedy at law." Thus, *Boeving* presaged the broad and liberalized language of [U.C.C. §2-716] and exemplifies one of the "other proper circumstances" contemplated by this subsection for ordering specific performance. [U.C.C. §2-716], Missouri Code Comment 1. The present facts track those in *Boeving*.

The Pace Car, like the car in *Boeving*, was not unique in the traditional legal sense. It was not an heirloom or, arguably, not one of a kind. However, its "mileage, condition, ownership and appearance" did make it difficult, if not impossible, to obtain its replication without considerable expense, delay and inconvenience. Admittedly, 6,000 Pace Cars were produced by Chevrolet. However, as the record reflects, this is limited production. In addition, only one of these cars was available to each dealer, and only a limited number of these were equipped with the specific options ordered by plaintiffs. Charlie's had not received a car like the Pace Car in the previous two years. The sticker price for the car was $14,284.21. Yet Charlie's received offers from individuals in Hawaii and Florida to buy the Pace Car for $24,000.00 and $28,000.00 respectively. As sensibly inferred by the trial court, the location and size of these offers demonstrated this limited edition was in short supply and great demand. We agree with the trial court. This case was a "proper circumstance" for ordering specific performance.

Judgment affirmed.

Photograph by Mike Millian of a 1978 Indy Pace Car Chevrolet Corvette that was left in a barn for 33 years. The car is shown sitting in the showroom of Corvette Mike New England in Plymouth, Massachusetts. When it was recovered from a barn in Detroit, Michigan, it had not been driven in 33 years and had logged only 13 miles. The interior still had a "new car" smell and the plastic from the factory still covered the bucket seats and steering wheel. Everything was original, including the dealer's key ring. The original owner bought the car in 1978 as an investment and never drove it. In 1995 he sold his house and moved into a high-rise apartment and had no place to put the car, so he put it in a barn. He then locked the door and walked away from it for 16 years. When the owner decided to sell the car to a dealer, it was buried under boxes. Although covered in dust, the Corvette was undamaged and it started right up even with half a tank of 33-year-old gas. The engine was not frozen up and the seals never got a chance to rust and go bad. The only thing that had to be changed was a dead battery. According to the dealer, Mike Millian, a limited number of 6,502 of the 1978 Indy Pace Car Corvette replicas were made, one for every dealer in the country. The limited edition black and silver T-top with 350 V-8 engine was part of the 25th anniversary year of the Corvette. In 1978, the original list price of the Corvette in 1978 was approximately $15,000. In 2011, Mike sold it to a collector for $50,000.

SALES CONTRACTS: THE UNIFORM
COMMERCIAL CODE

§2-716. BUYER'S RIGHT TO SPECIFIC PERFORMANCE
OR REPLEVIN

(1) Specific performance may be ordered where the goods are unique or in other proper circumstances.

(2) The judgment (decree) for specific performance may include such terms and conditions as to payment of the price, damages, or other relief as the court may deem just.

(3) The buyer has a right of replevin for goods identified to the contract if after reasonable effort he is unable to effect cover for such goods or the circumstances reasonably indicate that such effort will be unavailing or if the goods have been shipped under reservation and satisfaction of the security interest in them has been made or tendered.

REFERENCE: Barnett, §2.5.2
              Farnsworth, §12.6
              Calamari & Perillo, §16.3
              Murray, §128(B)(2)(a)

3.   Contracts for Personal Services

We now examine whether the principles that govern specific performance remedies for breach of contracts for the sale of goods and land do and should govern contracts for personal services. This subject merits careful consideration because of the serious problems it raises. When reading the next group of cases consider the following quote from an 1833 American case involving a New York opera singer:

> Upon the merits of the case, I suppose it must be concluded that the complainant is entitled to a specific performance of this contract; as the law appears to have been long since settled that a bird that can sing and will not sing must be made to sing. (Old adage.)[4]

In *Corsetti*, the court offered the following rather flippant analysis of the practical problems raised by the case:

> Although the authority before cited shows the law to be in favor of the complainant, so far at least as to entitle him to a decree for the singing, I am not aware that any officer of this court has that perfect knowledge of the Italian language, or possesses that exquisite sensibility in the auricular nerve which is necessary to understand, and to enjoy with a proper zest, the peculiar beauties of the Italian opera, so fascinating to the fashionable world. There

---

4. De Rivafinoli v. Corsetti, 4 Paige Ch. (N.Y.) 264, 270 (1833). Despite the dicta favoring specific performance, the chancellor in *Corsetti* found that the lower court's order jailing the defendant until he agreed to perform was prematurely granted because he had not yet breached the contract.

might be some difficulty, therefore, even if the defendant was compelled to sing under the direction and in the presence of a master in chancery, in ascertaining whether he performed his engagement according to its spirit and intent. It would also be very difficult for the master to determine what effect coercion might produce upon the defendant's singing, especially in the livelier airs; although the fear of imprisonment would unquestionably deepen his seriousness in the graver parts of the drama. But one thing at least is certain; his songs will be neither comic, or even semi-serious, while he remains confined in that dismal cage, the debtor's prison of New York.[5]

STUDY GUIDE: What moral problems are raised by applying the "old adage" from the Corsetti *case to breaches of contracts for personal services? Do all contracts for services involve personal services? We shall consider these questions at some length because of what they reveal about our underlying theories of contractual obligation.*

THE CASE OF MARY CLARK, A WOMAN
OF COLOUR
Supreme Court of Judicature of the State of Indiana,
1 Blackf. 122 (Ind. 1821)

Appeal from the *Knox* Circuit Court.

HOLMAN, J.* In obedience to a writ of habeas corpus, issued by the *Knox* Circuit Court, G. W. Johnston brought before that Court the body of Mary Clark, (a woman of colour,) said to be illegally detained by him; and assigned as the cause of her detention, that she was his servant by indenture, executed at Vincennes in this state, on the 24th of October, 1816: which indenture is set out in the return, regularly executed and acknowledged, by which the said Mary (being a free woman) voluntarily bound herself to serve him as an indentured servant and house maid for 20 years. This cause of detention was deemed sufficient by the Circuit Court, and the said Mary remanded to the custody of the said Johnston. She has appealed to this Court.

This application of Mary Clark to be discharged from her state of servitude, clearly evinces that the service she renders to the obligee is involuntary; and the constitution, having determined that there shall be no involuntary servitude in this state, seems at the first view to settle this case in favour of the appellant. But a question still remains, whether her service, although involuntary in fact, shall not be considered voluntary by operation of law, being performed under an indenture voluntarily

---

5. Id.

Jesse Lynch Holman (1784-1842) wrote and published Errors of Education (under auspices of Henry Clay) in 1804. He became prosecuting attorney for Dearborn County (Indiana) in 1811 and was elected to the Indiana Territorial Legislature in 1814, where he became speaker. Holman was circuit judge of the Indiana Territory (1814-1816) and United States District Judge for Indiana (1834-1842). He was also a founder of both Indiana University and Franklin College. — K.T.

Constitutional Basis

Rule

executed. This indenture is a writing obligatory. The clause in the 7th section of the 11th article of the constitution that provides, that no indenture hereafter executed by any negro or mulatto without the bounds of this state, shall be of any validity within this state, has no bearing on it. An indenture executed by a negro or mulatto out of this state, is, by virtue of this provision, absolutely void; and can be set up neither as a demand for the services therein specified, nor as a remuneration in damages for a non-performance. But the constitution, having confirmed the liberty of all our citizens, has considered them as possessing equal right and ability to contract, and, without any reference to the colour of the contracting parties, has given equal validity to all their contracts when executed within the state. We shall, therefore, discard all distinctions that might be drawn from the colour of the appellant; and consider this indenture as a writing obligatory; and test it, in all its bearings, by the principles that are applicable to all cases of a similar nature. It is a covenant for personal service; and the obligee requires a specific performance. It may be laid down as a general rule, that neither the common law nor the statutes in force in this state, recognize the coercion of a specific performance of contracts. The principal if not the only exceptions to this general rule are statutory provisions; few if any of which are applicable to this state; and none of them has any bearing on this case. Apprentices are compellable to a specific performance of the articles of apprenticeship; but their case rests on principles of a different nature. They are not considered as performing a contract of their own; but acting in conformity to the will of those whose right and duty it was to exact obedience from them. That right and duty existed by nature in the parent, and are, by legal regulations, transferable to the master during the minority of the child: and when transferred, either by the parent, or those who stand *in loco parentis*, the duty of obedience arises, and is enforced, on the ground of parental authority, and not on the principle of a specific performance of contracts; and cannot be urged as an exception to the general rule, that the coercion of a specific performance of contracts is not contemplated in law. The case of soldiers and sailors depends on national policy, and cannot be used in the elucidation of matters of private right.

There are some covenants that may be specifically enforced in equity; but they are of a very different nature from the contract before us. They are mostly covenants for the conveyance of real estate, and in no case have any relation to the person. But if the law were silent, the policy of enforcing a specific performance of a covenant of this nature, would settle this question. Whenever contracting parties disagree about the performance of their contract, and a Court of justice of necessity interposes to settle their different rights, their feelings become irritated against each other; and the losing party feels mortified and degraded in being compelled to perform for the other what he had previously refused, and the more especially if that performance will place him frequently in the presence or under the direction of his adversary. But this state of degradation, this irritation of feeling, could be in no other case so manifestly experienced, as in the case of a common servant, where the master would have a continual right of command, and the servant be compelled to a continual obedience. Many covenants, the breaches of which are only remunerated in damages, might be specifically performed, either by a third person at a distance from the adversary, or in a short space of time. But a covenant for service, if performed at all, must be personally performed under the eye of the master; and might, as in the case before us, require a number of years. Such a performance, if enforced by law, would produce a state of servitude as degrading and demoralizing in its consequences, as a state of absolute slavery; and if enforced under a government like ours, which acknowledges a personal equality, it would be productive of a state of feeling more discordant and irritating than slavery itself. Consequently, if all other contracts were specifically enforced by law, it would be impolitic to extend the principle to contracts for personal service. Very dissimilar is the case of apprentices. They are minors, and for the want of discretion, are necessarily under the control of parents, guardians, or masters; and obedience is exacted from them, whether considered as children, wards, or apprentices. They are incapable of regulating their own conduct, and are subjected by nature and by law to the government of others; and that government, instead of humbling and debasing the mind, has a tendency to give it a regular direction, and a suitable energy for future usefulness. . . . The appellant in this case is of legal age to regulate her own conduct; she has a right to the exercise of volition; and, having declared her will in respect to the present service, the law has no intendment that can contradict that declaration. We must take the fact as it appears, and declare the law accordingly. The fact then is, that the appellant is in a state of involuntary servitude; and we are bound by the constitution, the supreme law of the land, to discharge her therefrom.

> *[handwritten margin note: Reasoning ?]*
> *[handwritten margin note: → Holding]*

Per Curiam. The judgment is reversed, with costs; and the woman discharged.

Relational Background: The Nature of Mary Clark's "Voluntary" Indenture

SANDRA BOYD WILLIAMS, THE INDIANA SUPREME COURT AND THE STRUGGLE AGAINST SLAVERY, 30 IND. L. REV. 305, 307-309 (1997):   On November 6, 1821, the supreme court decided the case of "a woman of colour called Mary Clark." Court records reveal that in 1814 Mary had been purchased as a "slave for life" by Benjamin L. Harrison in Kentucky.[6] Harrison brought Mary to Vincennes, Indiana in 1815, and freed her. Contemporaneously with her release from slavery, Mary contracted with Harrison to be his indentured servant for thirty years. On October 24, 1816, Harrison "cancelled, annulled and destroyed" the contract for indenture, thereby liberating Mary.[7] On the same day, however, Mary, "a free woman of colour," bound herself to General W. Johnston, his heirs, executor, administrator and assigns as an indentured servant and house maid for twenty years. On his part, General Johnston agreed to:

---

6. Record at 4, Mary Clark v. General W. Johnston (Knox Cir. Ct. 1821) (handwritten) (contained in Indiana Supreme Court case file, Mary Clark v. G.W. Johnston, Nov. term, 1821, on file with Indiana State Archives, commission on Public Records, Indianapolis).
    7. Id. at 4-5.

find, provide and allow unto her, during all her aforesaid term of servitude, good and wholesome meat, drink, lodging, washing and apparel both linen and woollen, fit and convenient for such a servant. And upon the expiration of her term of servitude, she serving out her present indenture faithfully, give unto her one suit of new clothes (not to exceed however in value twenty dollars) and also one flax wheel.[8]

Mary's signature was indicated on the contracts with an "X."

Mary filed for a writ of habeas corpus, claiming that General Johnston "without any just or legal claim" held her as a slave. General Johnston argued that he had purchased Mary from Harrison for $350 that Harrison had emancipated Mary and that Mary had indentured herself to Johnston for twenty years. The circuit court determined that Mary should be returned to General Johnston, her putative master, to serve out the remainder of her indenture. The circuit court also ordered that General Johnston "recover . . . his costs and charges" from Mary.

The Indiana Supreme Court reversed. As it had in *Lasselle*, the court relied on the Indiana Constitution's unequivocal prohibition of slavery and involuntary servitude. After noting that all Indiana citizens (including Mary, a woman of colour) could properly enter into contracts, the supreme court held that contracts for personal service could not be enforced through specific performance. . . . Mary was awarded costs of eighteen dollars and seventy-four and one half cents.[9] Apparently, however, Mary never received her costs from Johnston. The return of the writ of execution states that Johnston had no property or real estate to satisfy the judgment.[10]

. . . Mary was represented by Charles Dewey, who, fifteen years later, was appointed to the Indiana Supreme Court. . . . Judge Holman, the author of the supreme court opinion, was considered a moderate abolitionist. When Holman came to Indiana from Kentucky around 1810, he brought his wife's slaves with him and freed them.

STUDY GUIDE: On page 744 of his treatise, Professor Farnsworth appears to suggest that Lumley v. Wagner stands for the following proposition: "Often, however, an injunction is used as an indirect means of enforcing a duty to act. Instead of ordering that the act be done, as a court would in granting specific performance, the court orders forbearance from inconsistent action. This is done most often in cases in which specific performance is objectionable on some ground that can be avoided by the use of an injunction." Does this description fit the Lord Chancellor's opinion? [Johanna Wagner was the niece of the famous German composer Richard Wagner and cantatrice of the court of the King of Prussia.]

---

8. Id. at 6.

9. Letter from Henry P. Coburn, Indiana Supreme Court Clerk, to Harrison County Sheriff (Dec. 1, 1821) (contained in Indiana Supreme Court case file, Mary Clark v. G.W. Johnston, Nov. term, 1821, on file with Indiana State Archives, Commission on Public Records, Indianapolis).

10. Note dated Apr. 2, 1822, on reverse side of letter from Henry P. Coburn, Indiana Supreme Court Clerk, to Harrison County Sheriff (Feb. 26, 1822) (contained in Indiana Supreme Court Case file, Mary Clark v. G.W. Johnston, Nov. term, 1821, on file with Indiana State Archives, Commission of Public Records, Indianapolis).

LUMLEY v. WAGNER

Chancery Division,
1 De G., M. & G. 604, 42 Eng. Rep. 687 [1852]

The bill in this suit was filed on the 22d April 1852, by Benjamin Lumley, the lessee of Her Majesty's Theatre, against Johanna Wagner, Albert Wagner, her father, and Frederick Gye, the lessee of Covent Garden Theatre: it stated that in November 1851 Joseph Bacher, as the agent of the Defendants Albert Wagner and Johanna Wagner, came to and concluded at Berlin an agreement in writing in the French language, bearing date the 9th November 1851, and which agreement, being translated into English, was as follows:

> The undersigned Mr. Benjamin Lumley, possessor of Her Majesty's Theatre at London, and of the Italian Opera at Paris, of the one part, and Mademoiselle Johanna Wagner, cantatrice of the Court of His Majesty the King of Prussia, with the consent of her father, Mr. A. Wagner, residing at Berlin, of the other part, have concerted and concluded the following contract: — First, Mademoiselle Johanna Wagner binds herself to sing three months at the theatre of Mr. Lumley, Her Majesty's, at London, to date from the 1st of April 1852 (the time necessary for the journey comprised therein), and to give the parts following: 1st, Romeo, Montecchi; 2d, Fides, Prophète; 3d, Valentine, Huguenots; 4th, Anna, Don Juan; 5th, Alice, Robert le Diable; 6th, an opera chosen by common accord. — Second, The three first parts must necessarily be, 1st, Romeo, 2d, Fides, 3d, Valentine; these parts once sung, and then only she will appear, if Mr. Lumley desires it, in the three other operas mentioned aforesaid. — Third, These six parts belong exclusively to Mademoiselle Wagner, and any other cantatrice shall not presume to sing them during the three months of her engagement. If Mr. Lumley happens to be prevented by any cause soever from giving these operas, he is, nevertheless, held to pay Mademoiselle Johanna Wagner the salary stipulated lower down for the number of her parts as if she had sung them. — Fourth, In the case where Mademoiselle Wagner should be prevented by reason of illness from singing in the course of a month as often as it has been stipulated, Mr. Lumley is bound to pay the salary only for the parts sung. — Fifth, Mademoiselle Johanna Wagner binds herself to sing twice a week during the run of the three months; however, if she herself was hindered from singing twice in any week whatever, she will have the right to give at a later period the omitted representation. — Sixth, If Mademoiselle Wagner, fulfilling the wishes of the direction, consent to sing more than twice a week in the course of three months, this last will give to Mademoiselle Wagner £50 sterling for each representation extra. — Seventh, Mr. Lumley engages to pay Mademoiselle Wagner a salary of £400 sterling per month, and payment will take place in such manner that she will receive £100 sterling each week. — Eighth, Mr. Lumley will pay, by letters of exchange, to Mademoiselle Wagner at Berlin, the 15th of March 1852, the sum of £300 sterling, a sum which will be deducted from her engagement in his retaining £100 each month. — Ninth, In all cases except that where a verified illness would place upon her a hindrance, if Mademoiselle Wagner shall not arrive in London eight days after that from whence dates her engagement, Mr. Lumley will have the right to regard the non-appearance as a rupture of the contract, and will be able to demand an indemnification. — Tenth, In the case where Mr. Lumley should cede his enterprise to another, he has the right to transfer this contract to his

successor, and in that case Mademoiselle Wagner has the same obligations and the same rights towards the last as towards Mr. Lumley.

Johanna Wagner.
Albert Wagner.

Berlin, the 9th November 1851.

The bill then stated in November 1851 Joseph Bacher met the Plaintiff in Paris, when the Plaintiff objected to the agreement as not containing an [sic] usual and necessary clause, preventing the Defendant Johanna Wagner from exercising her professional abilities in England without the consent of the Plaintiff, whereupon Joseph Bacher, as the agent of the Defendants Johanna Wagner and Albert Wagner, and being fully authorized by them for the purpose, added an article in writing in the French language to the agreement, and which, translated into English, was as follows: —

Mademoiselle Wagner engages herself not to use her talents at any other theatre, nor in any concert or reunion, public or private, without the written authorization of Mr. Lumley.

Dr. Joseph Bacher,
For Mademoiselle Johanna Wagner, and authorized by her.

The bill then stated that J. and A. Wagner subsequently made another engagement with the Defendant F. Gye, by which it was agreed that the Defendant J. Wagner should, for a larger sum than that stipulated by the agreement with the Plaintiff, sing at the Royal Italian Opera, Covent Garden, and abandon the agreement with the Plaintiff. . . .

The bill prayed that the Defendants Johanna Wagner and Albert Wagner might be restrained from violating or committing any breach of the last article of the agreement; that the Defendant Johanna Wagner might be restrained from singing and performing or singing at the Royal Italian Opera, Covent Garden, or at any other theatre or place without the sanction or permission in writing of the Plaintiff. . . .

Mr. Bethell, Mr. Malins and Mr. Martindale, in support of the appeal motion. We submit that the agreement in the present case being one of which the Court cannot decree specific performance, the jurisdiction by injunction does not attach. . . . We contend that the agreement is a purely personal contract, for the infraction of which damages are a complete and ample remedy: the agreement is, in fact, nothing more than a contract of hiring and service, and whatever the relation between the employer and employed may be, whether master and servant, or principal and agent, or manager and actor, this Court will, in all such cases, abstain from interfering, either directly or indirectly; Kemble v. Kean (6 Sim. 333), Kimberly v. Jennings (6 Sim. 340), Stocker v. Brockelbank (3 Mac. & G. 250).

[The Lord Chancellor. In the case of Stocker v. Brockelbank there was no negative covenant.] . . .

Mr. Bacon and Mr. H. Clarke, contra, in support of the injunction. The prayer of the bill in the present case is not for specific performance and for an injunction as ancillary to that relief, but for an injunction simply, to prevent the violation of the negative stipulation in the Defendants' agreement. . . .

THE LORD CHANCELLOR [Lord St. Leonards*]. The question which I have to decide in the present case arises out of a very simple contract, the effect of which is, that the Defendant Johanna Wagner should sing at Her Majesty's Theatre for a certain number of nights, and that she should not sing elsewhere (for that is the true construction) during that period. As I understand the points taken by the Defendants' counsel in support of this appeal they in effect come to this, namely, that a Court of Equity ought not to grant an injunction except in cases connected with specific performance, or where the injunction being to compel a party to forbear from committing an act (and not to perform an act), that injunction will complete the whole of the agreement remaining unexecuted. . . .

The present is a mixed case, consisting not of two correlative acts to be done — one by the Plaintiff, and the other by the Defendants, which state of facts may have and in some cases has introduced a very important difference — but of an act to be done by J. Wagner alone, to which is super-added a negative stipulation on her part to abstain from the commission of any act which will break in upon her affirmative covenant; the one being ancillary to, concurrent and operating together with the others. The agreement to sing for the Plaintiff during three months at his theatre, and during that time not to sing for anybody else, is not a correlative contract, it is in effect one contract; and though beyond all doubt this Court could not interfere to enforce the specific performance of the whole of this contract, yet in all sound construction, and according to the true spirit of the agreement, the engagement to perform for three months at one theatre must necessarily exclude the right to perform at the same time at another theatre. It was clearly intended that J. Wagner was to exert her vocal abilities to the utmost to aid the theatre to which she agreed to attach herself. I am of opinion that if she had attempted, even in the absence of any negative stipulation, to perform at another theatre, she would have broken the spirit and true meaning of the contract as much as she would now do with reference to the contract into which she has actually entered.

Wherever this Court has not proper jurisdiction to enforce specific performance, it operates to bind men's consciences, as far as they can be bound, to a true and literal performance of their agreements; and it will

---

Edward Burtenshaw Sugden, Baron St. Leonards (1781-1875), educated at Cambridge (LL.D.) and Oxford (D.C.L.), was admitted in 1802 as a student at Lincoln's Inn. He was elected a bencher in 1822, and treasurer in 1836. In 1805, he published his Practical Treatise of the Law of Vendors and Purchasers of Estates, which became the standard textbook on its subject. He was soon called to handle all important cases turning on the construction of wills or deeds. He entered Parliament in 1828, after several prior unsuccessful attempts, and retained his seat after being knighted in 1829. In 1832, Sugden was offered a place on the exchequer bench, which he declined. In 1834, Sugden held the great seal of Ireland, and during his second tenure in Ireland, he developed a systematic code of procedure. In 1852, he was appointed Lord Chancellor and became Baron St. Leonards of Slaugham, Sussex. He held this post for less than a year due to the fall of the government. After this, he continued to take an active part in the judicial deliberations of the House of Lords and privy council to the time of his death. — K.T.

not suffer them to depart from their contracts at their pleasure, leaving the party with whom they have contracted to the mere chance of any damages which a jury may give. The exercise of this jurisdiction has, I believe, had a wholesome tendency towards the maintenance of that good faith which exists in this country to a much greater degree perhaps than in any other; and although the jurisdiction is not to be extended, yet a Judge would desert his duty who did not act up to what his predecessors have handed down as the rule for his guidance in the administration of such an equity.

It was objected that the operation of the injunction in the present case was mischievous, excluding the Defendant J. Wagner from performing at any other theatre while this Court had no power to compel her to perform at Her Majesty's Theatre. It is true, that I have not the means of compelling her to sing, but she has no cause of complaint, if I compel her to abstain from the commission of an act which she has bound herself not to do, and thus possibly cause her to fulfil her engagement. The jurisdiction which I now exercise is wholly within the power of the Court, and being of opinion that it is a proper case for interfering, I shall leave nothing unsatisfied by the judgment I pronounce. The effect, too, of the injunction in restraining J. Wagner from singing elsewhere may, in the event of an action being brought against her by the Plaintiff, prevent any such amount of vindictive damages being given against her as a jury might probably be inclined to give if she had carried her talents and exercised them at the rival theatre: the injunction may also, as I have said, tend to the fulfilment of her engagement; though, in continuing the injunction, I disclaim doing indirectly what I cannot do directly. . . .

The authority of Clarke v. Price (2 Wils. 157) was much pressed upon me by the learned counsel for the Defendants; but that is a case which does not properly belong to their argument, because there was no negative stipulation, and I quite admit that this Court cannot enforce the performance of such an affirmative stipulation as is to be found in that case; there the Defendant having agreed to take notes of cases in the Court of Exchequer, and compose reports for the Plaintiff, and having failed to do so, the Plaintiff, Mr. Clarke, filed a bill for an injunction, and Lord Eldon, when refusing the injunction, in effect, said, I cannot compel Mr. Price to sit in the Court of Exchequer and take notes and compose reports; and the whole of his judgments shews that he proceeded (and so it has been considered in later cases) on the ground that there was no covenant, on the part of the Defendant, that he would not compose reports for any other person. The expressions in the judgment are: — "I cannot . . . say that I will induce him to write for the Plaintiff by preventing him from writing for any other person;" and then come these important words "for that is not the nature of the agreement." Lord Eldon, therefore, was of opinion, upon the construction of that agreement, that it would be against its meaning to affix to it a negative quality and import a covenant into it by implication, and he, therefore, very properly, as I conceive, refused that injunction; that case, therefore, in no respect touches the question now before me, and I may at once declare that if I had only to deal with the affirmative covenant of the Defendant J. Wagner that she would perform at Her Majesty's Theatre, I should not have granted any injunction. . . .

Relational Background: In the End Everyone Except the Lawyers Were Losers

STUDY GUIDE: *The facts provided in the following excerpt explain why both Johanna Wagner and Frederick Gye might have thought that she was free to accept his rival offer. The case of Lumley v. Gye appears later in this chapter in the section on tortious interference with contract. The concept of "condition precedent" is covered in Chapter 13.*

STEPHEN WADDAMS, DIMENSIONS OF PRIVATE LAW 23-27 (2003):   The twin cases of Lumley v. Wagner (1852) and Lumley v. Gye (1853), decisions respectively of the courts of Chancery and Queen's Bench, were perceived in their time, and indeed have been perceived ever since, to have determined crucial issues of fundamental importance in English private law. . . .

The background of these cases was a fierce rivalry between two London theatres, Her Majesty's Theatre, Haymarket, managed by Benjamin Lumley, and the then fairly new Royal Italian Opera, Covent Garden, managed by Frederick Gye. . . . The rivalry had been the cause of earlier litigation. There had been a dispute (with the interests of the parties effectively reversed) in 1847, involving Jenny Lind, who, having signed first with another theatre, broke her contract and later sang at Her Majesty's, and was held liable for damages (£2,500, later settled for £2,000) for breach of contract. Lumley, who was alleged to have taken advantage of Lind's breach of contract in order to meet the competition from the new opera house at Covent Garden, had made a very handsome profit out of the transaction, even after indemnifying Lind and paying her fee. This earlier case, suggesting both that the ordinary remedy of damages for breach of contract was ineffective in these circumstances and that the real dispute was between the rival employers, must have been in the minds of the judges when they came to deal with Lumley's cases against Wagner and Gye four years later. It is significant that Lind's case appeared to raise no legal point of interest, and was not reported in any law reports, whereas the Wagner dispute, on very similar facts, interested all the law reporters and produced two leading cases.

Johanna Wagner was, like Jenny Lind, a star performer. Lumley, who had profited so handsomely from Lind's London appearance, confidently anticipated equal success with Wagner, and witnesses at the trial said that "the Wagner fever" was "quite as violent" as the "Lind fever." The history of the negotiations was complex, and shows the extraordinary efforts of the two rival houses to secure Johanna Wagner's services. She was first in contact with Gye, but in November 1851 she entered into an agreement with Lumley, for £1,200 for a three-month engagement.

By the terms of the agreement, Wagner was to commence her engagement on 1 April 1852, and Lumley was to make an advance payment of £300 on 15 March. On 6 February, Wagner requested a postponement of the starting date to 15 April, and Lumley assented, no mention being made by either party of changing the date for payment of the advance. By February, Johanna Wagner and her father, Albert, were regretting their bargain, having formed the view that they could have obtained a much better price for Johanna's services. Moreover, they were changing their opinion of the comparative merits of the two theatres. Lumley's financial position was now unstable, and on 13 March he was arrested for debt. The date of 15 March came and went without payment of the £300. Gye now wrote twice to Wagner (9 and 30 March), ostensibly to enquire whether her engagement with Lumley was firm, and, deducing from the absence of a reply that there might be doubt about this, he travelled to Germany and made her a very attractive offer: £2,000 for a two-month engagement, with £1,000 payable in advance. Wagner told him that Lumley was in default of payment of the sum due on 15 March and that she therefore considered herself free, and she accepted Gye's terms, repudiating her contract with Lumley.

Johanna Wagner arrived in London with Gye, and her debut was announced for 24 April at Covent Garden. But Gye's victory was short-lived. On 23 April Lumley obtained a temporary injunction from a Vice-Chancellor (Sir James Parker) to restrain her from appearing. The injunction was continued by the Vice-Chancellor on 10 May, and an appeal was dismissed by the Lord Chancellor (Lord St. Leonards) on 26 May. Just as Gye's victory was short-lived, so also was Lumley's, for in the end Wagner did not sing at either theatre, and the 1852 season was a disaster for Lumley, and for Her Majesty's theatre, which closed from 1853 to 1855, Lumley attributing the closure largely to Johanna Wagner's defection. Lumley eventually lost his legal action against Gye for damages, so in the end Lumley, Gye, Wagner, and the opera-going public — everyone in fact except the lawyers — were all losers.

Few modern lawyers, asked to recall the facts of the cases, would mention Lumley's omission to make the advance payment originally promised for 15 March. Yet it was this omission that caused Wagner to accept Gye's proposal, and, though held by three courts for different reasons to be legally inconclusive, it eventually proved to be crucial. The Vice-Chancellor, revealing a surprising ignorance of the common law, and of the obvious purpose of an advance payment, said that non-payment would not, as a matter of law, entitle Wagner to terminate the contract, that is that it was not a condition precedent. In the higher Chancery court this last question was determined as a matter of law in Wagner's favour, but Lord St. Leonards found another reason for reaching the same conclusion as the Vice-Chancellor: this was that Lumley had in fact paid the money to his agent (Joseph Bacher) for transmission to Wagner in good time, and she had been informed of this. He thought that Wagner had deliberately evaded receipt of the money in order to escape from the contract: "I think it is entirely her own fault, and that she intended, as far as she could, to prevent the money being paid in order to escape the liability of performing the contract."

Lord St. Leonards, seeking to derive the facts from the affidavits, relied very heavily on Bacher's statement that he had written to Albert Wagner on 10 March offering to pay the £300, deducing that the statement must be true because Bacher would not take the risk of swearing falsely to the contents of a letter that might be produced to contradict him. But when it came to the trial, Bacher's evidence on this point was shaken and Lumley's counsel pressed an alternative argument that, even if Bacher had not tendered the money on 10 March, the time for payment had been impliedly extended to and beyond 5 April by a letter written, in French, by Albert Wagner to

Lumley in March saying "if you send the bill of exchange, be good enough to address it either at this time to Berlin, or from (dès) the 2nd of April, to Hamburgh, to Engel & Co, Ferdinand Street, where we shall remain some time." Lord Campbell directed the jury that they could find that the time for payment had been impliedly extended, and it seems likely that this was the basis for the jury finding that the contract remained in force on 5 April. Thus, the fact that the advance money had not been paid on 15 March — apparently an important breach of Lumley's obligation — was held by three judges not to be legally conclusive, and for three quite different and inconsistent reasons: in the Vice-Chancellor's court because it was found not to be a condition precedent, in the Lord Chancellor's court because it was found as a fact that Bacher had offered to pay by his letter of 10 March, and (when Bacher's evidence on this point was later shaken) in the common law court because the time for payment might have been impliedly extended to and beyond 5 April, and it was for the jury to say whether this had occurred. This successive variety of reasons shows how a fact, apparently relevant, may be made irrelevant by framing of the legal issues, or by findings of other facts. But ultimately Lumley's omission did turn out to be crucial, because at the trial Gye said that he honestly believed that Wagner was free to terminate her engagement with Lumley on this ground, and his defence succeeded.

STUDY GUIDE: The next case represents one of the earliest American considerations of the English case of Lumley v. Wagner. Notice that this court cites the Corsetti *case as authority for refusing to grant specific performance.*

FORD v. JERMON
District Court of Philadelphia,
6 Phila. 6 (Dist. Ct. 1865)

Demurrer to bill in equity. Opinion by HARE, J.*

The prayer of the bill filed in this case was originally for the specific performance of a written agreement by which the respondent bound herself to act, during a stipulated period, for the complainant, and that the respondent should be enjoined from playing or appearing at any theatre not under the management of the complainant, until the season for which she had agreed to serve him should have expired. But the former part of the prayer

---

John Innes Clark Hare (1816-1905) graduated with honors from the University of Pennsylvania, after which he studied chemistry for nearly four years, two of them in Europe, before studying law. In 1841, he was admitted to the bar, and in 1851, he was elected to the district court of Philadelphia, where he served first as an associate and after 1867 as Presiding Judge. In 1875, he was appointed judge of the City Court of Common Pleas, from which he resigned in 1896. He also served as professor of law at the University of Pennsylvania (1868-1888), where his lectures included the subject of contracts. Hare's published works include The Law of Contracts (1887) and American Constitutional Law (2 vols., 1889). He contributed greatly to the establishment of the newly introduced equity system in Pennsylvania and is considered one of the six greatest judges that Pennsylvania has produced. — K.T.

has since been abandoned as untenable, and the complainant now only asks that the respondent shall be prevented from playing for others, not that she should be compelled to perform for him. This change of ground will be found on examination to contain an admission that the whole fabric of the bill is unsound. For if the case is not one in which the respondent ought to be compelled to perform her agreement directly, it cannot be right to substitute an indirect method of compulsion, more injurious to her and less beneficial to the complainant than a positive command that she should appear on his stage and act the parts assigned to her.

One reason why the courts will not attempt to force an unwilling performer before the public, is the harshness of compelling obedience by imprisonment, and the difficulty or rather impossibility of knowing whether his obedience is real or illusory, when he finally consents to appear. In order to render such a decree effectual, it would be necessary to appoint a master, whose duty should be to frequent the theatre and decide whether the mistakes or incongruities by which the part might be disfigured, were in contempt of the order of the court, or unintentional. I am unable to see that these difficulties are likely to be less, because the mode of compulsion is the indirect one of obliging the actor to remain idle until necessity forces him to comply. We are asked to say that Mrs. Jermon shall not play at all, unless she will consent to play for the complainant; are we also to declare that she shall not sing? shall not earn her bread by writing or by her needle? To debar her from one pursuit would be vain and futile, unless she were also excluded from others, that might, so far as we can tell, be more profitable. Are such decrees to be made solely with reference to actors, or shall lawyers be held to their clients, mechanics to their employers, and servants to their masters, by the same process? Is it not obvious that a contract for personal services thus enforced would be but a mitigated form of slavery, in which the party would have lost the right to dispose of himself as a free agent, and be, for a greater or less length of time, subject to the control of another? And as this objection is to the substance of the relief desired, and not to the form, it must prevail, even when the agreement to render the service, is coupled with a stipulation that the contracting party will not enter into the employment of another master, or engage in work of any other kind. Otherwise the court might be compelled to transcend the limits within which its jurisdiction ought to be confined, and engage in a contest where the sympathies of mankind would be all with the weaker party, by the simple expedient of coupling the affirmative words with a negative stipulation, that the covenantor will not do for others what he agrees to do for the covenantee. I deem it unnecessary to carry the argument further on a point which must be intuitively apprehended by every man of sound judgment. The case of Lumley v. Wagner, 6 Jurist, 871, has been cited as an authority for the relief desired, but the fact that amidst the multitude of quarrels that have distracted the green room or disturbed the stage, there has been but one instance of such interference, may be thought to indicate that it should be regarded as a warning rather than followed as a precedent. I prefer to rely on the cases of Kemble v. Kean, 6 Simons, 333; Corsetti v. Rivafinoli, 4 Paige, 464; Sanquirico v. Benedetti, 1 Barbour, 316; and Hamblin v. Durneford, 2 Edwards, 529 which show conclusively, that the objections to enforcing contracts for personal services specifically, apply with peculiar force in the case of those whose business is to amuse as well as instruct, and whose labors are worth nothing if given grudgingly, without the spirit that should pervade and give life to art. We therefore dismiss this bill as without our province, and belonging to a sphere more likely to be marred than improved, by the most formal decree that counsel could devise or the court award.

STUDY GUIDE: In the next case pay close attention to the issue of the negative covenant that played so crucial a role in both Lumley *and* Ford. *Does the rationale of this case represent a departure from* Lumley v. Wagner?

DUFF v. RUSSELL
*Superior Court of New York City,
60 Super. 80, 14 N.Y.S. 134 (1891)*

PER CURIAM. This action is brought by the plaintiff, a theatrical and operatic manager, to restrain the defendant from appearing as a singer or actress upon the stage of the Casino, in the city of New York, during the period of her contract with the plaintiff.

A preliminary injunction having been granted, and it appearing, upon the hearing of the motion for the continuance of the injunction during the pendency of the action, that the defendant had made a contract in writing with the manager of the Casino, and had been extensively advertised to appear at that theatre within a few days thereafter, it was arranged between the parties, but without prejudice to the rights of either, that the defendant upon giving an undertaking in the sum of $2,000, conditioned to pay that sum as liquidated damages in case it should be finally determined that the plaintiff is entitled to an injunction herein, might go on and fulfill her contract at the Casino.

The undertaking having been given as agreed, and the rights of both parties having been expressly preserved, the fact that plaintiff's contract with defendant has since that time expired, is not to be considered, and the case still calls upon the court to determine plaintiff's original right to injunctive relief.

The material facts, as they appear from the pleadings and the evidence, are that by written contract the defendant agreed with the plaintiff to appear in the soprano roles of such operas as the plaintiff might produce during the seasons of 1887-[188]8 and 1888-[188]9, and in such cities in the United States as he might select; that in the production of each opera the plaintiff was to supply the costumes; that in New York seven performances were to be given each week, exclusive of Sundays; that each season was to commence in the month of October or November of each year and to last until May or June of the following year; that the plaintiff was to have the right to terminate each season by giving two weeks' notice; and that the defendant, for the faithful performance of her part of the said contract, was to receive the sum of $300 per week; that the defendant was and is an actress and singer distinguished in her profession and a great artistic acquisition both in name and dramatic and operatic service, to any theatre where comic operas are produced; that the plaintiff, relying upon his contract, announced the defendant at large expense in the daily newspapers of this city and widely throughout the United States as a member of his company to the end of the season of 1889; that the defendant refused to perform in plaintiff's opera, which was produced at the Standard Theatre, in the city of New York, on Monday evening, January 7, 1889, and which was to be continued for some weeks; that at that time the defendant had agreed to perform as an actress and singer at the Casino, a rival of and competitor with the theatre, so far as the production of operas are concerned, which the plaintiff had engaged for his company, and had been announced with her consent to appear at the said Casino on Monday, January 14, 1889, and to continue to the end of the operatic season; that the plaintiff unsuccessfully protested against it; that it was not possible for the plaintiff to replace the defendant for the remainder of the season by any other actress and singer of equal repute; and that in consequence thereof the plaintiff was likely to, and in fact did, sustain irreparable damage. The proof on the part of the plaintiff, that in this and other cities he did sustain large damages in consequence of defendant's act, and that the extent of such damages cannot be accurately measured, is unusually clear and convincing.

The facts, so far referred to contain all the elements necessary to sustain, within the rule laid down in Daly v. Smith, 38 N.Y. Super. Ct. Rep. 158, and followed in several cases since that time, an injunction against defendant's appearance at the Casino.

It therefore remains to be seen whether there is anything else in the case which calls for a different conclusion.

The defendant's counsel insists that, inasmuch as there is no negative stipulation in the contract by which the defendant agreed not to appear elsewhere, the court cannot interfere. But, as was shown in Daly v. Smith, supra, the court is bound to look to the substance and not to the form of the contract. As the defendant had agreed to appear in seven performances in each week (exclusive of Sundays) which the plaintiff's company might give in New York, it was not possible for her to perform elsewhere in New York without a violation of her contract with the plaintiff, and a negative clause was unnecessary to secure to the plaintiff exclusively the services of the defendant.

It is also insisted . . . that the defendant was justified in breaking her contract with the plaintiff because the plaintiff refused to substitute a more healthful costume for the tights in which the defendant had appeared in a certain opera, and the wearing of which she had objected to on the ground of danger to her health. It appears that the opera in question was called The Queen's Mate. In this opera the defendant was to appear in a part which required her to wear tights. Before the production of the opera she was consulted by the plaintiff with regard to it, and informed that it would be necessary for her to wear tights, and she agreed that she would so appear. This had been admitted by her, but at the same time she claimed that she agreed to do so only during the summer. But in point of fact the plaintiff [sic] did appear in tights during cold weather and never claimed exemption by agreement during such weather, and inasmuch as the plaintiff had not only the right to prescribe the costumes but also the duty to furnish them, and no evidence has been adduced that the costumes of an opera change with the seasons of the year, or that the defendant ever claimed any right to such a change, I cannot find that the claim now advanced by the defendant in this respect has any foundation in fact. In point of fact the defendant did appear in this part and in tights for at least 150 nights, and from twenty to thirty chorus girls appeared in the same costume during each performance. Any change which might have been made in the costume of the defendant would have necessitated a corresponding change in the costumes of from twenty to thirty other persons. . . .

A further circumstance of great significance is that on December 5, 1888, the defendant wrote to the plaintiff that she was ready and willing to assume her part in the said opera in Boston for two weeks, and to appear in tights for that period, provided the plaintiff would pay her the additional sum of $150 per week. Other incidents might be referred to, but it is not necessary to go any further. The conclusion is unavoidable that the excuse now advanced by the defendant for the breach of her contract with the plaintiff should not be sustained.

Upon the whole case, the plaintiff is entitled to judgment, with costs.

Historical and Relational Background: Sex and Specific Performance

LEA S. VANDERVELDE, THE GENDERED ORIGINS OF THE *LUMLEY* DOCTRINE: BINDING MEN'S CONSCIENCES AND WOMEN'S FIDELITY, 101 YALE L.J. 775, 800-804, 812-815, 818, 821-822, 825 (1992):[11]   . . . In the early part of the [nineteenth] century, acting was considered a suspect profession; actors were characterized as drunkards and actresses as harlots by the religious establishment. Actresses were particularly susceptible to being mistaken for prostitutes because the theater was one of the few public places that prostitutes could enter to ply their trade. Many theaters reserved their third tiers for prostitutes. The presence of prostitutes in the theater perpetuated the negative image of the acting profession. But, by mid-century, prostitutes were swept out of the elite theaters to make the theater acceptable for the bourgeoisie to attend in mixed company. Between 1870 and 1880, the status of the acting profession began to improve markedly.

During the second period, women were coming into their own in the theater. Broadway was expanding and flourishing, and the American theater was becoming big business. As never before, women were performing more openly in public, forming theater companies, designing careers, commanding top billings and top dollars, and heading up touring companies. There were opportunities for income, travel, independence, and autonomy.

Outside the theater, however, the Victorian ideology was prescribing a stricter code of propriety and conduct for middle class women than that of earlier decades. The notion that a woman's life should be limited to hearth and home became more and more generally accepted. According to

11. Reprinted by permission of The Yale Law Journal Company and Fred B. Rothman & Company from The Yale Law Journal, vol. 101, pp. 775-852.

historian Barbara Welter, "The attributes of True Womanhood, by which a woman judged herself and was judged by her husband, her neighbors and society, could be divided into four cardinal virtues — piety, purity, submissiveness and domesticity. Put them all together and they spelled mother, daughter, sister, wife — woman."[12] Historian Mary Ryan adds, "[W]omen were conscripted into a code of public conduct which prescribed that they present themselves as 'ladies' outside the home."[13] When women did not comport themselves according to the strictures of propriety, the standard reproach was to label them prostitutes.

It is important to emphasize that although this ideology had a pervasive influence in shaping attitudes about women generally, it was a white, middle class ideology. As an ideology, it was a simplification of life with terms that were regularly contradicted by the everyday experiences of working class women. "These ideas had not developed out of the situation of working class women, nor were they consistent with it, yet they informed the ideology of the period so thoroughly that they dominated prevailing attitudes toward working women, and shaped the terms in which those women interpreted their own experience."[14] To the extent that Victorian ideology recognized women as working outside the home at all, it was expected that their working station would be temporary and transitional. Women were denied access to most professions and many trades, and they customarily earned less than men, even in factories. Women who sought to work for wages outside the home met with numerous obstacles ranging from social disapproval to legal and economic sanctions.

These two contrary trends placed the actress in a precarious position. In the words of historian Claudia Johnson, the late nineteenth-century actress "was able to anticipate professional rewards which few other women in the age enjoyed, but only at considerable sacrifice of intangibles precious to nineteenth-century women — personal esteem and social acceptability."[15]

By the very act of performing in public, actresses defied the social norm that the place for women was in the home, and that the proper roles of women were as faithful mothers, wives, and daughters, obligated to serve. Moreover, actresses appeared in a mode of dress that violated the expectations of the piety of "true womanhood." In an era when women were sensitive, if not oversensitive, to the norms of modesty and some even put skirts on the legs of their pianos, Lillian Russell appeared in public in tights.

> [T]he actress, it was thought, had little claim on modesty. Her work required her to be in close association with men: She had to change costumes frequently in the same general backstage area with men; she often had to travel with men when shows went on tour; and on stage she would play love scenes with men. Untenably immodest behavior was demanded of the actress

12. [Barbara Welter, Dimity Convictions: The American Woman in the Nineteenth Century 21 (1976).]

13. [Mary P. Ryan, Woman in Public — Between Banners and Ballots, 1825-1880 (1990), at 3.]

14. [Sarah Eisenstein, Give Us Bread but Give Us Roses 55 (1983).]

15. [Claudia D. Johnson, American Actress — Perspective on the Nineteenth Century 3-78 (1984), at 4.]

on stage. She was seen dispensing "lascivious smiles, wanton glances, and dubious compliments."[16]

As a result, despite the banishment of prostitutes from the theaters, actresses as a group were still apt to be characterized as fallen women.

Their precarious social position was reflected in their legal position. Female performers were being sued for specific performance and injunction in greater numbers than were men during the period. They were also less able to make clean breaks from their employment contracts with only liability for damages. After 1860, cases involving women performers dominated the litigation: Annetta Galetti, Auguste Sohlke, Fanny Morant, Loie Fuller, and most importantly, Lillian Russell, who appears in three of the major reported cases of the period, but whose memoirs disclose that she was involved in many similar disputes.

The canon of negative injunction was based on Daly v. Smith and two cases involving Lillian Russell, but the broader litigation base included a number of other cases, most of which involved women performers. During this critical period when American courts were deliberating whether they would exercise any equitable jurisdiction over quitting performers, there were roughly twice as many cases involving actresses as cases involving actors.[17] In the cases involving actors, no permanent injunction for the term of the contract was ever issued; the only equitable orders ever granted against actors were preliminary injunctions, and none survived appeal.[18]

Significantly, the *only* cases during the entire century that permanently enjoined performers from appearing elsewhere for the duration of the

16. [Id.] at 30.

17. From 1860 to 1900, 17 cases were recorded where theatrical performers were sued by male theater managers. Of these 17, 12 involved female performers and five involved male performers. . . .

There was a single case in which a female head of an acting company sued a male actor. . . . In addition, there were several parallel suits involving men in professions other than the theater. Wollensak v. Briggs, 20 Ill. App. 50 (1886) (male machine inventor); Strobridge Lithographing Co. v. Crane, 12 N.Y.S. 898 (Sup. Ct. 1890) (male lithographic sketch artist); Sternberg v. O'Brien, 48 N.J. Eq. 370 (1891) (male debt collector in installment clothing business); W. J. Johnston Co. v. Hunt, 21 N.Y.S. 314 (Sup. Ct. 1892) (advertising man), *aff'd*, 37 N.E. 564 (N.Y. 1894); Burney v. Ryle, 17 S.E. 986 (Ga. 1893) (male insurance company manager). These suits are without female parallel in the nineteenth century. For the most part, women were not present in any of these occupations during the nineteenth century in anything but trace numbers. . . .

Other suits that parallel this line of cases were brought against baseball players — again, all male populations. . . .

18. . . . I acknowledge the methodological difficulty in classifying the results in some of these cases. I have counted a case as resulting in an injunction only if the final recorded opinion in the case actually ordered the defendant enjoined *for the term of the contract* or sustained the exercise of the lower court's injunction. Several of the men's cases and most of the women's cases make reference to injunctive orders equivalent to temporary restraining orders. These orders were not counted as injunctions *for the term of the contract* unless they were sustained in the last written opinion in the case. In certain cases it is difficult from the record to distinguish between temporary restraining orders, preliminary injunctions of some duration, and permanent injunctions for the term of the contract.

contract term were five cases involving women performers.[19] The contracts
at issue in these cases often ran for several years, so the effect of an injunction could have been a serious impairment of the defendant's career
and her ability to work. Although three of the cases involved women of
considerable stature in the theater, two enjoined far less powerful and
financially independent women performers. Moreover, in three of the
five cases, the courts enjoined actresses even when the contracts did not
contain any negative covenants or clauses pertaining to an exclusive right to
their services. These opinions indicate the courts' willingness to surpass
even the language of the contracts in fashioning for the actresses a status
subservient to their male employers' control. The essence of the courts'
rulings was: if the lady's employer could not have her services, no one
could. . . .

One actress' litigation fate seemed to shape and reinforce judicial and
public attitudes regarding the breach of employment contracts by women.
Lillian Russell's losses in two major cases during the next decade reinforced
the rule adopted in Daly v. Smith. By 1897, on the authority of Fanny Morant
Smith's case and one of Lillian Russell's suits, Pomeroy's Specific Performance could state that the English rule of Lumley v. Wagner was followed in
the United States.[20] More importantly, the opinion in one of Lillian Russell's
cases indicated that something beyond the abstract application of a capital-
protective legal rule was at work. The opinion in the second case carried
Lumley's rationale to the point of legal absurdity.

Lillian Russell, both as a popular symbol and as an individual, was the
ideal foil for reinforcing this more restrictive legal rule concerning the freedom of women performers.[21] She was a larger-than-life symbol of American
femininity in the American consciousness. Her face adorned cigar boxes,
and her voice was chosen for the first publicized long distance telephone
conversation to demonstrate Alexander Graham Bell's new invention; the
cable was laid from her dressing room on Broadway to the White House.
She was the woman who made all men swoon, America's sweetheart, the
major attraction of the Columbian Exposition of 1893. Her public presence
was feminine *non plus ultra*, sweet, gracious, youthful, and, above all,
submissive. She never played serious roles. At a critical juncture in her
career she deliberately elected to confine her singing talents to light oper-
ettas rather than attempt serious opera. In the realm of light comic operas,

19. Daly v. Smith, 49 How. Pr. (n.s.) 150 (N.Y. Super. Ct. 1874); McCaull v. Braham,
16 F. 37 (C.C.S.D.N.Y. 1883); Hoyt v. Fuller, 19 N.Y.S. 962 (Super. Ct. 1892); Duff v. Russell,
14 N.Y.S. 134 (Super. Ct. 1891), *aff'd*, 31 N.E. 622 (N.Y. Ct. App. 1892); Edwards v. Fitzgerald
(N.Y. Sup. Ct. 1895), *cited in* Hammerstein v. Sylvia, 124 N.Y.S. 535, 539-40 n.1 (Sup. Ct.
1910); see also Canary v. Russell, 30 N.Y.S. 122 (Sup. Ct. 1894) (defendant could perform
elsewhere during summer season not covered by contract, but was enjoined from
performing elsewhere during period covered by plaintiffs' contract).
20. [John N. Pomeroy, Specific Performance of Contracts 31 & n.2 (New York, Banks &
Bros. 2d ed. 1897).] . . .
21. The biographical details in this section are drawn from John Burke, Duet in Diamonds: The Flamboyant Saga of Lillian Russell and Diamond Jim Brady in America's Gilded
Age (1972); [Parker Morrell, Lillian Russell: The Era of Plush 58-66 (1940)]; and the
somewhat rosy, autobiographical account in Lillian Russell, Lillian Russell's Reminiscences
(pts. 1-8), Cosmopolitan, Feb. 1922, at 13, Mar. 1922, at 25, Apr. 1922, at 23, May 1922, at 69,
June 1922, at 81, July 1922, at 93, Aug. 1922, at 80, Sept. 1922, at 73.

she was immensely popular at the box office and could command salaries unheard of previously.

Despite her popularity as an actress, she belonged to a suspect profession, and both her private and professional life were major topics of the gossip newspapers. Although billed as America's sweetheart, the public still considered her scandalous and risqué. Russell appeared on the stage wearing tights and décolleté costumes. She fully enjoyed the independence that her fame and power gave her. She smoked cigars and played poker in her home with the shades drawn. For exercise, she rode her famous diamond-studded bicycle in Central Park. She was the daughter of a well-known feminist suffragette and editorial writer, who was also the first woman to run for Mayor of New York City. As a result of her very unconventional lifestyle, she was snubbed by high society.[22] But most importantly, Lillian Russell broke off her four unhappy marriages and her unhappy contracts with equally innocent abandon.

Russell's habit of breaking off contracts led to McCaull v. Braham[23] and Duff v. Russell,[24] litigation that spanned a decade. The press covered these cases closely, reporting on each of her depositions, occasionally on her testimony, but much more often on what she wore, and her gracious, light, and submissive demeanor.

Russell's first experience in court occurred early in her career. The theater production covered by the contract was her first hit, and, as a young actress, she had not yet developed widespread popularity or a strong box office draw. Over the course of the play's run, her contract was revised several times to raise her salary. Lillian Russell was sued not because she would not perform for the plaintiff theater, but because she proposed to sing at other engagements on off-nights. Since Lillian Russell was not seeking to repudiate the contract, but merely to retain her ability to perform outside of scheduled performances under the contract, the issue of her right to quit was not squarely presented in McCaull v. Braham. Nonetheless, this case was used as precedent in later cases where employees did seek to quit.

The theater manager, Colonel McCaull, sought to enjoin her from performing *anywhere* without his consent. McCaull, who had begun his career as an attorney for Ford's Theater, had drafted an iron-clad contract with three different clauses spelling out the theater's desire to maintain exclusive control over Russell's singing engagements. One of the clauses stipulated that she would forfeit either a week's salary or the entire contract, at McCaull's option, if she sang at a competing theater during the season. Another stated that McCaull would have additional rights to pursue remedies notwithstanding the forfeiture clause. The only serious legal issue the court saw was whether the forfeiture clause constituted a liquidated

---

22. On one highly publicized occasion, she was publicly refused entry to the V.I.P. gallery at the Chicago Race Track, only to have the press and public create such a stir as she was seated in the regular galleries that the race had to be delayed. She was also the most famous person not invited to the Duke of Windsor's dinner to celebrate the Chicago Exposition. . . .

23. 16 F. 37 (C.C.S.D.N.Y. 1883). Lillian Russell was sued under her then married name, Mrs. Helen Braham.

24. 14 N.Y.S. 134 (Super. Ct. 1891), *aff'd*, 31 N.E. 622 (N.Y. Ct. App. 1892).

damages provision or an additional penalty. The court took the latter position.

In contrast with the *Jermon* court, the *McCaull* court never considered whether it should look beyond the language of the well-drafted contract to the substantive effect on the young actress. In interpreting the language of the agreement, the *McCaull* court did not evaluate who had the upper hand in drafting the contract's terms. Not only did the court enforce the exclusivity clause by ordering an injunction, even when the defendant's performance for the plaintiff theater would continue undisturbed, it enforced the forfeiture as a special penalty in addition to the injunction, rather than as a provision for liquidated damages. The court used the difficulty in evaluating damages for breach to justify invoking its equitable powers.

When the second case arose eight years later, Lillian Russell's position as the preeminent female performer had been established. By that time, she had broken off dozens of contracts. In one instance, she fled to England while her managers issued legal summons and press statements about her dishonorable conduct, only to return several months later to these same managers' welcoming arms greeting her as a "prodigal daughter." Her lawyers had also learned not to let her sign exclusivity clauses. Her ability to set her own terms was described in the published words of one of her attorneys: "When you want to engage Miss Russell, she'll tell you." Managers knew that they had to assume risks if they wanted to cast Lillian Russell. One manager stated, "She has broken various other engagements in London. I shan't be surprised if she breaks mine. I hope she won't, though." In this instance, the performer clearly had the upper hand and reflected that power in favorable contract language, and the capital interests quite willingly took the risks of her nonperformance.

One would not have expected the same actress represented by the same attorneys to fall under an equitable injunction again. After all, in 1887, Lillian Russell had been quoted in the press as saying that she never signed contracts with conditions in them. One certainly would not have anticipated that the second time a manager sued to enjoin her, it would be assigned to Judge Freedman, the same judge who had decided Daly v. Smith. . . .

What prompted James Duff to sue Lillian Russell? As absorbed as Judge Freedman was with Lillian Russell's refusal to wear tights, he never probed Duff's reasons for bringing suit. A limerick published in a contemporary New York newspaper provides some insight.

> There was a young lady named Russell
> Who wouldn't wear tights 'neath her bustle
> 'Cause it gave her a cold
> Where it cannot be told
> And she and Jim Duff had a tussle.
> Then, Jimmy, the young man, he sued her
> Rather tough for a person who'd wooed her
> But you can't quite explain
> The regrets in the brain
> Of a man who finds out he don't suit her.

The celebrated case ended in a monetary settlement. . . .

The men's cases were far fewer in number than the women's were. Most of the male performers won on appeal, if not in the first instance. In the men's cases, actor Moritz Hahn, baritone Giuseppe Del Puente, acrobats Lassard and Lucifer, actor William Ferguson, tenor Agostino Montegriffo, and even performer Henry Willio, who was initially enjoined and then released, all successfully defended themselves against their theater managers' attempts to enjoin them. In fact, the first permanent injunction of a male performer of any kind was that of a baseball player, Napolean Lajoie,[25] which did not occur until 1902, almost thirty years after the decision in Daly v. Smith and fifty years after *Lumley*.

The men's cases generally were not resolved by repudiating the *Lumley* rule, but instead were decided by excusing the male performer from the operation of the rule through one of a number of exceptions. . . .

A close reading of the case histories suggests that the gender ratios reflected in the case results were not purely coincidental. Simply put, without the women's cases, there would have been no *Lumley* rule in the United States in the nineteenth century. Moreover, not only did women performers lose more cases than men did, women performers were sued more often than men were. One may argue that in time the *Lumley* rule would have been accepted in America in any case. The free labor sentiment certainly was in decline at the end of the nineteenth century, even in cases involving men;[26] the women's cases may only have hastened its arrival. But even in this scenario, gender played a role in facilitating the acceptance of a rule that had, at its core, the use of equitable compulsion to hold people to their employer's consent. Actresses, due to their precarious social position in a highly gendered society, served as a lightning rod for these forces to touch down.

STUDY GUIDE: Does the legal principle followed in the next case differ from that of Lumley v. Wagner? Does it support Professor Farnsworth's generalization quoted in the Study Guide before that case?

DALLAS COWBOYS FOOTBALL CLUB v. HARRIS
Court of Civil Appeals of Texas, Dallas,
348 S.W.2d 37 (1961), Rehearing Denied June 23, 1961

DIXON, C.J.*

PRELIMINARY STATEMENT

Appellant Dallas Cowboys Football Club, Inc., hereinafter called the Club, a member of the National Football League, brought this action against

---

25. Philadelphia Ball Club v. Lajoie, 54 Cent. L.J. 446 (Pa. Sup. Ct. 1902).

26. See, e.g., Payne v. Western Atl. R.R., 81 Tenn. 507 (1884) The Slaughter-House Cases, 83 U.S. (16 Wall.) 36 (1873).

Dick Dixon (1897-†) was educated at Blackburn College (A.A.), Eureka College (A.B.), and Chicago-Kent College of Law (J.D.). Admitted to the Texas bar in 1923, he practiced law in Dallas from 1923 to 1935 and served as City Attorney of University Park (1930-1936). In 1936, Dixon was appointed judge of the District Court of Texas, and became Chief Justice of the Texas Court of Civil Appeals in 1953, and served there until his retirement in 1970. — K.T.

James B. Harris for injunction to restrain Harris from playing professional football, or engaging in any activities related to professional football for anyone except the Club. Appellant alleged that Harris was bound by the terms of a written contract to play football for the Club and no one else, but that in violation of his contract he was playing football for the Dallas Texans Football Club, a member of the American Football League. The suit was for injunction only. No money judgment was sought.

After hearing and upon execution of $15,000 injunction bond a temporary injunction was granted to the Club on July 29, 1960. Harris took an appeal from this temporary order.

Meantime the trial court had reached the main suit for trial on the merits, and on September 21, 1960, following return of a jury verdict favorable to Harris, had rendered judgment that the Club take nothing by its suit against Harris. The Club took an appeal from the judgment on the merits. . . .

CLUB'S APPEAL FROM JUDGMENT ON MERITS

In June 1958 James B. Harris for a consideration of $8,000 signed a contract to play football and to engage in activities related to football only for the Los Angeles Rams Football Club, a member of the National Football League. This contract covered a period of time beginning with the execution of the contract and extending to the first day of May following the 1958 football season, which latter date was May 1, 1959. The contract also included a clause providing that the Club at its option might renew the contract for an additional year.

Both Harris and the Los Angeles Rams Football Club performed the primary contract which by its terms expired May 1, 1959. A controversy arose between the parties with reference, among other things, to the exercise by the Los Angeles Rams Club of its option on Harris' services for another year. As a result Harris chose not to play professional football during the 1959 season. Instead he reentered the University of Oklahoma as a student and also accepted a position as assistant football coach at the University.

In April 1960 Harris signed a contract to play football during the 1960 season for the Dallas Texans Football Club of the newly organized American Football League.

Harris' contract with the Los Angeles Rams was by its terms assignable. On July 22, 1960 the contract was assigned to the Dallas Cowboys Football Club, Inc., a new member of the National Football League. On the same date this suit was instituted against Harris by the latter Club to restrain Harris from playing football for anyone except the Club.

Since the Club contends that Harris, as a matter of law, is bound by the terms of the 1958 contract and its option to play football only for the Club for an additional year, we deem it advisable to reproduce material parts of the contract:

> 2. The player agrees during the term of this contract he will play football and will engage in activities related to football only for the Club and as directed by the Club. . . .

3. For the Player's services . . . , and for his agreement not to play football or engage in activities related to football for any other person, firm, corporation or institution during the term of this contract, and for the option hereinafter set forth . . . the Club promises to pay the Player . . . the sum of $8,000.00. . . .

5. The Player promises and agrees that during the term of this contract he will not play football or engage in activities related to football for any other person, firm, corporation or institution except with the prior written consent of the Club and the Commissioner. . . .

8. The Player hereby represents that he has special, exceptional and unique knowledge, skill and ability as a football player, the loss of which cannot be estimated with any certainty and cannot be fairly or adequately compensated by damages and therefore agrees that the Club shall have the right, in addition to any other rights which the Club may possess, to enjoin him by appropriate injunction proceedings against playing football or engaging in activities related to football for any person, firm, corporation or institution and against any other breach of this contract. . . .

10. On or before the date of expiration of this contract, the Club may, upon notice in writing to the Player, renew this contract for a further term until the first day of May following said expiration on the same terms as are provided by this contract, except that (1) the Club may fix the rate of compensation to be paid by the Club to the Player during said period of renewal, which compensation shall not be less than ninety percent (90%) of the amount paid by the Club to the Player during the preceding season, and (2) after such renewal this contract shall not include a further option to the Club to renew the contract. . . .

Should Player . . . retire from football prior to the expiration of this contract or any option contained herein, and subsequently . . . return to professional football, then . . . the time elapsed between . . . his retiring from professional football and his return thereto, shall be considered as tolled, and the term of his contract shall be considered as extended for a period beginning with the player's . . . return to professional football . . . and ending after a period of time equal to the portion of the term of this contract which was unexpired at the time the Player . . . retired from professional football; and the option contained herein shall be considered as continuously in effect from the date of this contract until the end of such extended term. . . .

It is well established in this State and other jurisdictions that injunctive relief will be granted to restrain violation by an employee of negative covenants in a personal service contract if the employee is a person of exceptional and unique knowledge, skill and ability in performing the service called for in the contract. Mission Independent School Dist. v. Diserens, 144 Tex. 107, 188 S.W.2d 568, 161 A.L.R. 877; Winnipeg Rugby Football Club v. Freeman, D.C., 140 F. Supp. 365; Philadelphia Ball Club v. Lajoie, 202 Pa. 210, 51 A. 973, 58 L.R.A. 227. . . .

But in this case there is a fact finding by a jury in answer to Special Issue No. 1 to the effect that at the time of the trial Harris did *not* have exceptional and unique knowledge, skill and ability as a football player. If the record reveals any evidence of probative force in support of this finding it was not error for the court to submit Special Issue No. 1 to the jury, nor was it error to overrule the Club's motions for summary judgment, directed verdict and judgment non obstante veredicto. . . . If an issue of fact is raised by the evidence, it must go to the jury, though a verdict based on such evidence would have to be set aside as not supported by sufficient evidence. . . .

In one of its points the Club takes the position that Harris by the express representations contained in his contract is estopped, as a matter of law, from disputing the fact that he possesses exceptional and unique knowledge, skill and ability as a football player.

We see no merit in the Club's claim of estoppel. We think the rule applicable here is stated correctly in 31 C.J.S. Estoppel §79, p. 288: "To create an estoppel the representation relied on must be a statement of a material fact, and not a mere expression of opinion." . . .

The part of the contract above referred to and relied on by the Club is properly to be interpreted as an expression of opinion by Harris of his own capabilities. In this connection the testimony of Tom Landry, Head Coach of the Club, is of interest. We quote from his testimony:

Q.   . . . Paragraph 8 of the Plaintiff's contract says: "Player hereby represents he has special, exceptional and unique knowledge and skill and ability as a football player. . . ."?
A.   Well, I think the boy probably represents himself as being unique in that respect. Now, maybe he is not the best judge of his ability.
Q.   Well, whether or not a man is unique is a matter of opinion, isn't it?
A.   I think that is probably true as far as forming a conclusion yes.

The record discloses that appellee Harris himself on cross-examination testified that he *thought* he had a certain amount of unique skill and ability.

But later a definition of the word "unique" was introduced without objection from appellant and in that connection Harris then testified as follows:

Q.   Now, have you looked up the definition of "unique" in the dictionary?
A.   No, sir I haven't.
Q.   Well, I am reading from the New Century Dictionary here, and it says: "Of which there is but one, or sole, or only" Do you think you are the only defensive halfback?
A.   Not by any means of the imagination.
Q.   It says, "Unparalleled, or unequal" — you think you are unparalleled or unequal?
A.   I wish I were, now.
Q.   Do you think you are?
A.   No, sir I am not. I know my own ability.
Q.   It says, "something of which there is only one" are you the only defensive halfback?
A.   No. I am not.
Q.   "Something without parallel or equal of its kind" are you that kind of defensive halfback?
A.   No. I wish I was.

In view of the above testimony we are unable to agree with appellant Club that there is no evidence in the record of probative force to support the fact finding of the jury to the effect that Harris did not have exceptional and unique knowledge, skill and ability as a football player. Certainly we may not ignore the testimony, especially in view of the fact that it was admitted without objection. . . . We overrule the Club's eight points on appeal in so far as they assert that the Club, under the record before us, was entitled to injunctive relief as a matter of law and that it was error for the court to submit Special Issue No. 1 and to overrule the motions for summary judgment, directed verdict and judgment non obstante veredicto. . . .

Among the several grounds of error urged by the Club in its sixth point on appeal was this: the court erred in refusing to grant a new trial because the great weight and preponderance of the evidence showed that Harris did possess special, exceptional and unique knowledge, skill and ability as a football player, contrary to the answer of the jury. . . .

[T]hough there may be some evidence in the record which raises a fact issue necessitating the submission of the case to the jury, nevertheless it may be the duty of the court afterwards to grant a new trial if the record evidence is "insufficient" to support the jury verdict, that is, if the evidence is so against the overwhelming weight and preponderance of the evidence as to be manifestly wrong.

We think that is true in this case. The definition of the word "unique" introduced in evidence was too narrow and limited.[27] We agree with the statement in Philadelphia Ball Club v. Lajoie, 202 Pa. 210, 51 A. 973, 58 L.R.A. 227, as follows:

> We think, however, that in refusing relief unless the defendant's services were shown to be of such a character as to render it impossible to replace him he has taken extreme ground. It seems to us that a more just and equitable rule is laid down in Pom. Spec. Perf. p. 31, where the principle is thus declared: "Where one person agrees to render personal services to another, which requires [sic] and presuppose a special knowledge[,] skill, and ability in the employee, so that in case of a default *the same service could not easily* be obtained from others, . . . its performance will be negatively enforced by enjoining its breach. . . ." We have not found any case going to the [same] length of requiring, as a condition of relief, proof of the impossibility of obtaining equivalent service.

(Emphasis ours).

After a careful study of all the record evidence in this case we are of the opinion that the evidence is "insufficient" to support the jury finding.

All of those witnesses, whose testimony has any bearing on the question testified very positively that Harris was possessed of unique skill and ability. Prior to the introduction of the narrow and limited definition of "unique" Harris himself testified as follows:

Q. Jimmy, you signed contracts with both of them in which you represented that you did have unique skill and ability, didn't you?
A. I thought I did.
Q. Well, you know that is in both of the contracts, don't you?
A. That's right.
Q. . . . Then you know you do have unique skill and ability, don't you?
A. I think I have a certain amount yes.

---

27. Appellant's counsel quoted only part of the definition of the word "unique" as the definition appears in the "New Century Dictionary." The complete definition includes this also: ". . . loosely, rare or unusual. . . ."

Q.   . . . You yourself told both clubs in your written contracts that you
       did have skill and ability, didn't you?
A.   That's right.
Q.   . . . You now tell this jury that you have got that skill and ability,
       don't you?
A.   Right.

      We also quote from the testimony of Don Rossi, General Manager of
the Dallas Texans Football Club, who was a witness for Harris:

Q.   . . . In your opinion, Mr. Rossi, he does have exceptional skill and
       ability, doesn't he?
A.   Yes, sir. . . .
Q.   Well, haven't you already testified that he was above the average?
A.   Well, yes, sir average or above average.
Q.   That's right.
A.   Well, we will go along with that.
Q.   Well, he is above average, isn't he?
A.   We will buy that.
Q.   . . . not buy it you are just swearing to it?
A.   Yes sir.

      The testimony of Schramm and Landry was even more positive. It is
true that the witnesses named other professional football players who are
"equal or better" than Harris as players, but the testimony was that players
of Harris' ability were not available to the Club.
      We sustain that part of the Club's sixth point on appeal wherein
the Club asserts error in the court's refusing to grant a new trial
because the great weight and preponderance of the evidence clearly
showed that Harris did possess special, exceptional and unique knowledge, skill and ability as a football player, contrary to the answers of
the jury. . . .
      We cannot support Harris' contention that the contract is so unrea-
sonable and harsh as to be unenforceable in equity. Holdings to the
contrary have been made in regard to similar contracts. Philadelphia Ball
Club v. Lajoie, 202 Pa. 210, 51 A. 973, 58 L.R.A. 227; Shubert Theatrical Co. v.
Rath, 2 Cir., 271 F. 827, 837, 20 A.L.R. 846; Winnipeg Rugby Football Club v.
Freeman, D.C., 140 F. Supp. 365, 367. . . .
      The judgment on the merits to the effect that the Club take nothing by
its suit is reversed and the cause remanded for another trial.
      The order granting a temporary injunction in favor of the Club is
affirmed.

Reread: Uniform Commercial Code §2-716 (p. 172)

REFERENCE: Barnett, §2.5.3
              Farnsworth, §§12.5, 12.7
              Calamari & Perillo, §16.5
              Murray, §127 (E)(2)

Constitutional Background: The Thirteenth Amendment and Contractual Freedom

STUDY GUIDE: Although the following case is not an action for specific performance of a contract, it does concern a statutory scheme that raises similar moral and constitutional issues.

BAILEY v. STATE OF ALABAMA, 219 U.S. 219 (1911):   Mr. JUSTICE HUGHES* delivered the opinion of the court.

This is a writ of error to review a judgment of the Supreme Court of the State of Alabama, affirming a judgment of conviction in the Montgomery City Court. The statute, upon which the conviction was based, is assailed as in violation of the Fourteenth Amendment of the Constitution of the United States upon the ground that it deprived the plaintiff in error of his liberty without due process of law and denied him the equal protection of the laws, and also of the Thirteenth Amendment, and of the act of Congress providing for the enforcement of that Amendment, in that the effect of the statute is to enforce involuntary servitude by compelling personal service in liquidation of a debt. . . .

. . . Upon the trial the following facts appeared: On December 26, 1907, Bailey entered into a written contract with the Riverside Company, which provided:

> That I, Lonzo Bailey for and in consideration of the sum of Fifteen Dollars in money, this day in hand paid to me by said The Riverside Co., the receipt whereof, I do hereby acknowledge, I, the said Lonzo Bailey do hereby consent, contract and agree to work and labor for the said Riverside Co. as a farm hand on their Scotts Bend Place in Montgomery County, Alabama, from the 30 day of Dec. 1907, to the 30 day of Dec. 1908, at and for the sum of 12.00 per month.
>
> And the said Lonzo Bailey agrees to render respectful and faithful service to the said The Riverside Co. and to perform diligently and actively all work pertaining to such employment, in accordance with the instructions of the said The Riverside Co., or *ag't*.
>
> And the said The Riverside Co. in consideration of the agreement above mentioned of the said Lonzo Bailey hereby employs the said Lonzo Bailey as such farm hand for the time above set out, and agrees to pay the said Lonzo Bailey the sum of $10.75 per month.

* *Charles Evans Hughes* (1862-1948) studied at Colgate University, Brown University (A.B., A.M.), and Columbia University (LL.B.). He practiced law privately in New York (1884-1906), and was counsel for the New York Legislature (1905-1906) and a special assistant to the U.S. Attorney-General (1906). He served as governor of New York for two terms (1907-1910), resigning to accept an appointment to the United States Supreme Court. He resigned as Justice in 1916 when he was nominated for President of the United States by the Republican Party. He received 254 electoral votes for the presidency, against 277 for Woodrow Wilson. He returned to private practice again, except to serve as Secretary of State in the cabinets of Presidents Harding and Coolidge (1921-1925). He was appointed by President Coolidge to the Permanent Court of Arbitration, The Hague, in 1926, and by the Council and Assembly of League of Nations as judge of the Permanent Court of International Justice in 1928, both of which he resigned in 1930 to accept appointment by President Hoover as Chief Justice of the United States Supreme Court, from which he retired in 1941. During his professional career, he also served as professor of law and special lecturer at Cornell Law School. — K.T.

The manager of the employing company testified that at the time of entering into this contract there were present only the witness and Bailey and that the latter then obtained from the company the sum of fifteen dollars; that Bailey worked under the contract throughout the month of January and for three or four days in February, 1908, and then, "without just cause and without refunding the money, ceased to work for said Riverside Company, and has not since that time performed any service for said Company in accordance with or under said contract, and has refused and failed to perform any further service thereunder, and has, without just cause, refused and failed to refund said fifteen dollars." He also testified, in response to a question from the attorney for the defendant and against the objection of the state, that Bailey was a negro. No other evidence was introduced.

The court, after defining the crime in the language of the statute, charged the jury, in accordance with its terms, as follows:

> And the refusal of any person who enters into such contract to perform such act or service, or refund such money, or pay for such property, without just cause, shall be prima facie evidence of the intent to injure his employer, or to defraud him.

Bailey excepted to these instructions, and requested the court to instruct the jury that the statute, and the provision creating the presumption, were invalid, and further that

> the refusal or failure of the defendant to perform the service alleged in the indictment, or to refund the money obtained from the Riverside Co. under the contract between it and the defendant, without cause, does not of itself make out a prima facie case of the defendant's intent to injure or defraud said Riverside Company.

The court refused these instructions and Bailey took exception.

The jury found the accused guilty, fixed the damages sustained by the injured party at fifteen dollars, and assessed a fine of thirty dollars. Thereupon Bailey was sentenced by the court to pay the fine of thirty dollars and the costs, and in default thereof to hard labor "for twenty days in lieu of said fine, and one hundred and sixteen days on account of said costs."

On appeal to the Supreme Court of the State the constitutionality of the statute was again upheld and the judgment affirmed. . . .

We at once dismiss from consideration the fact that the plaintiff in error is a black man. While the action of a State, through its officers charged with the administration of a law, fair in appearance, may be of such a character as to constitute a denial of the equal protection of the laws . . . , such a conclusion is here neither required nor justified. The statute, on its face, makes no racial discrimination, and the record fails to show its existence in fact. No question of a sectional character is presented, and we may view the legislation in the same manner as if it had been enacted in New York or in Idaho. Opportunities for coercion and oppression, in varying circumstances, exist in all parts of the Union, and the citizens of all the States are interested in the maintenance of the constitutional guaranties, the consideration of which is here involved. . . .

We cannot escape the conclusion that, although the statute in terms is to punish fraud, still its natural and inevitable effect is to expose to conviction for crime those who simply fail or refuse to perform contracts for personal service in liquidation of a debt, and judging its purpose by its effect that it seeks in this way to provide the means of compulsion through which performance of such service may be secured. The question is whether such a statute is constitutional. . . .

In the present case it is urged that the statute as amended, through the operation of the presumption for which it provides, violates the Thirteenth Amendment of the Constitution of the United States and the act of Congress passed for its enforcement.

The Thirteenth Amendment [1865] provides:

> Section 1. Neither slavery nor involuntary servitude, except as a punishment for crime whereof the party shall have been duly convicted, shall exist within the United States, or any place subject to their jurisdiction.
> Section 2. Congress shall have power to enforce this article by appropriate legislation. . . .

The language of the Thirteenth Amendment was not new. It reproduced the historic words of the ordinance of 1787 for the government of the Northwest Territory and gave them unrestricted application within the United States and all places subject to their jurisdiction. While the immediate concern was with African slavery, the Amendment was not limited to that. It was a charter of universal civil freedom for all persons, of whatever race, color or estate, under the flag.

The words involuntary servitude have a "larger meaning than slavery."

> It was very well understood that in the form of apprenticeship for long terms, as it had been practiced in the West India Islands, on the abolition of slavery by the English government, or by reducing the slaves to the condition of serfs attached to the plantation, the purpose of the article might have been evaded, if only the word 'slavery' had been used.

Slaughter-House Cases, 16 Wall. p. 69 [21 L. Ed. 406]. The plain intention was to abolish slavery of whatever name and form and all its badges and incidents; to render impossible any state of bondage; to make labour free, by prohibiting that control by which the personal service of one man is disposed of or coerced for another's benefit which is the essence of involuntary servitude.

While the Amendment was self-executing, so far as its terms were applicable to any existing condition, Congress was authorized to secure its complete enforcement by appropriate legislation. As was said in the *Civil Rights* cases:

> By its own unaided force and effect it abolished slavery, and established universal freedom. Still, legislation may be necessary and proper to meet all the various cases and circumstances to be affected by it, and to prescribe proper modes of redress for its violation in letter or spirit. And such legislation may be primary and direct in its character; for the Amendment is not a mere prohibition of state laws establishing or upholding slavery, but an

absolute declaration that slavery or involuntary servitude shall not exist in any part of the United States.

109 U.S. 20 [3 S. Ct. 18, 27 L. Ed. 842].

The act of March 2, 1867 (Rev. Stat., §§1990, 5526, supra), was a valid exercise of this express authority. . . . It declared that all laws of any State, by virtue of which any attempt should be made "to establish, maintain, or enforce, directly or indirectly, the voluntary or involuntary service or labor of any persons as peons, in liquidation of any debt or obligation, or otherwise," should be null and void.

Peonage is a term descriptive of a condition which has existed in Spanish America, and especially in Mexico. The essence of the thing is compulsory service in payment of a debt. A peon is one who is compelled to work for his creditor until his debt is paid. And in this explicit and comprehensive enactment, Congress was not concerned with mere names or manner of description, or with a particular place or section of the country. It was concerned with a fact, wherever it might exist; with a condition, however named and wherever it might be established, maintained or enforced.

The fact that the debtor contracted to perform the labor which is sought to be compelled does not withdraw the attempted enforcement from the condemnation of the statute. The full intent of the constitutional provision could be defeated with obvious facility if, through the guise of contracts under which advances had been made, debtors could be held to compulsory service. It is the compulsion of the service that the statute inhibits, for when that occurs the condition of servitude is created, which would be not less involuntary because of the original agreement to work out the indebtedness. The contract exposes the debtor to liability for the loss due to the breach, but not to enforced labor. . . .

The act of Congress, nullifying all state laws by which it should be attempted to enforce the "service or labor of any persons as peons, in liquidation of any debt or obligation, or otherwise," necessarily embraces all legislation which seeks to compel the service or labor by making it a crime to refuse or fail to perform it. Such laws would furnish the readiest means of compulsion. The Thirteenth Amendment prohibits involuntary servitude except as punishment for crime. But the exception, allowing full latitude for the enforcement of penal laws, does not destroy the prohibition. It does not permit slavery or involuntary servitude to be established or maintained through the operation of the criminal law by making it a crime to refuse to submit to the one or to render the service which would constitute the other. The State may impose involuntary servitude as a punishment for crime, but it may not compel one man to labor for another in payment of a debt, by punishing him as a criminal if he does not perform the service or pay the debt.

If the statute in this case had authorized the employing company to seize the debtor and hold him to the service until he paid the fifteen dollars, or had furnished the equivalent in labor, its invalidity would not be questioned. It would be equally clear that the State could not authorize its constabulary to prevent the servant from escaping and to force him to work out his debt. But the State could not avail itself of the sanction of the criminal law to supply the compulsion any more than it could use or authorize the use of physical force.

> In contemplation of the law the compulsion to such service by the fear of punishment under a criminal statute is more powerful than any guard which the employer could station.

Ex parte Hollman (S. Car.), 60 S.E. Rep. 24 [79 S.C. 22, 21 L.R.A. (N.S.) 249, 14 A.E. Ann. Cas. 1109].

What the State may not do directly it may not do indirectly. If it cannot punish the servant as a criminal for the mere failure or refusal to serve without paying his debt, it is not permitted to accomplish the same result by creating a statutory presumption which upon proof of no other fact exposes him to conviction and punishment. Without imputing any actual motive to oppress, we must consider the natural operation of the statute here in question . . . , and it is apparent that it furnishes a convenient instrument for the coercion which the Constitution and the act of Congress forbid; an instrument of compulsion peculiarly effective as against the poor and the ignorant, its most likely victims. There is no more important concern than to safeguard the freedom of labor upon which alone can enduring prosperity be based. The provision designed to secure it would soon become a barren form if it were possible to establish a statutory presumption of this sort and to hold over the heads of laborers the threat of punishment for crime, under the name of fraud but merely upon evidence of failure to work out their debts. The act of Congress deprives of effect all legislative measures of any State through which directly or indirectly the prohibited thing, to wit, compulsory service to secure the payment of a debt may be established or maintained; and we conclude that §4730, as amended, of the Code of Alabama, in so far as it makes the refusal or failure to perform the act or service, without refunding the money or paying for the property received, prima facie evidence of the commission received of the crime which the section defines, is in conflict with the Thirteenth Amendment and the legislation authorized by that Amendment, and is therefore invalid.

In this view it is unnecessary to consider the contentions which have been made under the Fourteenth Amendment. As the case was given to the jury under instructions which authorized a verdict in accordance with the statutory presumption, and the opposing instructions requested by the accused were refused, the judgment must be reversed.

Reversed and cause remanded for further proceedings not inconsistent with this opinion.

MR. JUSTICE HOLMES,* with whom concurred MR. JUSTICE LURTON, dissenting.

*Oliver Wendell Holmes, Jr. (1841-1935) was educated at Harvard College (A.B., LL.B.) and admitted to the Massachusetts bar in 1867. He practiced in Boston and served as an instructor and professor of law at Harvard College (1870-1871, 1882) before being appointed to the Supreme Judicial Court of Massachusetts in 1882. He spent the last three years of his tenure on that bench as Chief Justice and in 1902 he was appointed to the

We all agree that this case is to be considered and decided in the same way as if it arose in Idaho or New York. Neither public document nor evidence discloses a law which by its administration is made something different from what it appears on its face, and therefore the fact that in Alabama it mainly concerns the blacks does not matter. . . . I shall begin then by assuming for the moment what I think is not true and shall try to show not to be true, that this statute punishes the mere refusal to labor according to contract as a crime, and shall inquire whether there would be anything contrary to the Thirteenth Amendment or the statute if it did, supposing it to have been enacted in the State of New York. I cannot believe it. The Thirteenth Amendment does not outlaw contracts for labor. That would be at least as great a misfortune for the laborer as for the man that employed him. For it certainly would affect the terms of the bargain unfavorably for the laboring man if it were understood that the employer could do nothing in case the laborer saw fit to break his word. But any legal liability for breach of a contract is a disagreeable consequence which tends to make the contractor do as he said he would. Liability to an action for damages has that tendency as well a fine. If the mere imposition of such consequences as tend to make a man keep to his promise is the creation of peonage when the contract happens to be for labor, I do not see why the allowance of a civil action is not, as well as an indictment ending in fine. Peonage is service to a private master at which a man is kept by bodily compulsion against his will. But the creation of the ordinary legal motives for right conduct does not produce it. Breach of a legal contract without excuse is wrong conduct, even if the contract is for labor, and if a State adds to civil liability a criminal liability to fine, it simply intensifies the legal motive for doing right, it does not make the laborer a slave.

But if a fine may be imposed, imprisonment may be imposed in case of a failure to pay it. Nor does it matter if labor is added to the imprisonment. Imprisonment with hard labor is not stricken from the statute books. On the contrary, involuntary servitude as a punishment for crime is excepted from the prohibition of the Thirteenth Amendment in so many words. Also the power of the States to make breach of contract a crime is not done away with by the abolition of slavery. But if breach of contract may be made a crime at all, it may be made a crime with all the consequences usually attached to crime. There is produced a sort of illusion if a contract to labor ends in compulsory labor in a prison. But compulsory work for no private master in a jail is not peonage. If work in a jail is not condemned in itself, without regard to what the conduct is it punishes, it may be made a consequence of any conduct that the State has power to punish at all. I do not blink the fact that the liability to imprisonment may work as a motive when a fine without it would not, and that it may induce the laborer to keep on when he would like to leave. But it does not strike me as an objection to a law that it is effective. If the contract is one that ought not to be made, prohibit it. But if it is a perfectly fair and proper contract, I can see no reason why the State

---

Supreme Court of the United States. He retired from that bench in 1932. A much-published author, his most famous work, The Common Law, was published in 1881; he also served as editor of the 12th edition of Kent's Commentaries. Holmes was wounded three times during his service in the Civil War. — K.T.

should not throw its weight on the side of performance. There is no relation between its doing so in the manner supposed and allowing a private master to use private force upon a laborer who wishes to leave. . . .

To sum up, I think that obtaining money by fraud may be made a crime as well as murder or theft; that a false representation, expressed or implied, at the time of making a contract of labor that one intends to perform it and thereby obtaining an advance, may be declared a case of fraudulently obtaining money as well as any other; that if made a crime it may be punished like any other crime, and that an unjustified departure from the promised service without repayment may be declared a sufficient case to go to the jury for their judgment; all without in any way infringing the Thirteenth Amendment or the statutes of the United States.

MR. JUSTICE LURTON concurs in this dissent.

B. RESTITUTION — DAMAGE INTEREST AND CAUSE OF ACTION

You are already familiar with the restitution interest of contract damages. The legal concept of restitution generally pertains to situations where one person has — without intending to make a gift — conferred a benefit on another.[29] Restitution notions arise in a variety of legal contexts. Sometimes restitution arises as part of contract law, for example, as a remedy for breach of contract. Sometimes a restitution-based remedy is given to the party who has committed a breach of contract. Restitution can also provide an independent cause of action when there is no contract at all. (There is, for example, a Restatement of Restitution published by the American Law Institute.) Occasionally this cause of action is called *quantum meruit* or *quasi-contract*. The subject of noncontractual restitution is typically dealt with more extensively in a remedies course. We will read three cases encompassing three different uses of restitution so that you have some familiarity with the concept.

1. Restitution for Breach of Contract

STUDY GUIDE: This case illustrates the difference between damages as measured by the expectation interest and as measured by the restitution interest. Why would an exception to the ordinary rule favoring the expectancy be made here? Notice that in this unusual report, after an opinion from a dissenting judge appears, an opinion from a judge in the majority follows that answers the dissenter's argument.

29. An entirely distinct use of the term *restitution* appears in criminal justice theory — as in "restitution to victims of crime." See, e.g., Randy E. Barnett, Restitution: A New Paradigm of Criminal Justice, 87 Ethics 279 (1977); Randy E. Barnett, The Justice of Restitution, 25 Am. J. Juris. 117 (1980).

BUSH v. CANFIELD
Supreme Court of Errors,
2 Conn. 485 (1818)

This was an action on the case, brought by the plaintiffs as the only surviving partners of the late firm of Norton & Bush. The declaration stated, that Norton & Bush, on the 20th of February 1812, entered into a contract in writing with the defendant, in these words:

It is agreed by and between the parties here subscribing, that Judson Canfield agrees to deliver to the order of Norton & Bush, at New-Orleans, 2000 barrels *superfine* wheat flour, to be delivered in good shipping order, on or before the first day of May next: the flour to be regularly inspected at New-Orleans, at the time of delivery the price of the superfine to be 7 dollars *per* barrel; and in case the whole quantity to be delivered should not pass as *superfine*, but should pass as good merchantable *fine* flour, the said Canfield will have a right to deliver of the above named 2000, say 1000, barrels, that should be inspected and branded *fine*, at 50 cents less than the price of *superfine*, as above. And Norton & Bush do agree to receive the flour as here described, at the port of New-Orleans, and to pay therefor 5000 dollars in advance, as is agreed by us, calculating to be in 15 or 20 days from this date 3000 dollars more to be advanced at four months from the date of the first advance for the said flour; and the balance then remaining due to be paid in six months from the date of the delivery of the said flour. It is agreed, that Norton & Bush shall be allowed four months interest on 1000 dollars.

[Signed.]   *Judson Canfield,*

                                                    Norton & Bush.

That in pursuance of this contract, Norton & Bush paid over to the defendant, on the 12th of March 1812, the sum of 5,000 dollars; and were ready, at New-Orleans, on the 1st of May 1812, to receive the flour; and have kept and performed all the covenants on their part; concluding with a general assignment of breach, on the part of the defendant, and a demand of damages.

The defendant pleaded Not guilty, and several special pleas, on which issues were taken.

The cause was tried at Litchfield, February term, 1818, before Edmond and Smith, Js.

On the trial, it was proved, that the price of superfine flour at New-Orleans, on the 1st of May, 1812, was 5 dollars, 50 cents, per barrel, and no more. The court, in their charge to the jury, directed them, that if they should find the issues in favour of the plaintiffs, the rule of damages would be, the amount of the sum advanced by the plaintiffs to the defendant, and the interest thereof, from the time it was so advanced. The jury found a verdict for the plaintiffs, with 6,771 dollars damages; and the defendant moved for a new trial, on the ground of a mis-direction. . . .

SWIFT, Ch. J.* Where a man contracts to deliver any article besides money, and fails to do it, the rule of damages is the value of the article at

---

Zephaniah Swift (1759-1823) received degrees from Yale (B.A., M.A.). His public service career included posts as member of the Connecticut General Assembly (1787-

the time and place of delivery, and the interest for the delay. Though the promisee may have suffered a great disappointment and loss, by the failure to fulfil the contract; yet these remote consequences cannot, in such cases, be taken into consideration by courts, in estimating the damages. It is always supposed, that the party could have supplied himself with the article at that price; and if he intends to provide against the inconvenience arising from such a disappointment, he must make a contract adapted to such objects. In the present case, if the plaintiffs had paid to the defendants the full sum for the two thousand barrels of flour contracted for, then they would have been entitled to recover the value of it at New-Orleans, where it was to have been delivered. If the price had risen between the time of purchase and delivery, they would have made a profitable speculation; otherwise, if it had fallen. If they had paid nothing, if the flour had advanced in price, they would have been entitled to recover the amount of such advance. If the price had fallen, they would have been entitled to recover nominal damages for the breach of the contract; though they might have been subjected to a great loss, if the contract had been fulfilled. This proves, that the actual damages suffered by a party cannot always be the rule of estimating damages for a breach of contract.

Reasons for why general rule cannot always apply

In this case, the plaintiffs advanced a part of the purchase money; that is, the sum of five thousand dollars; and no parallel case has been adduced to shew what ought to be the rule of damages for not delivering the flour. I think the one adopted by the court at the circuit, to be just and reasonable. *→ Holding* The defendant has violated his contract; and it is not for him to say, that if he had fulfilled it, the plaintiffs would have sustained a great loss, and that this ought to be deducted from the money advanced. It is not for him to say, that the plaintiffs shall only recover the reduced value of a part of the flour which was to have been delivered, in proportion to the advanced payment. The contract was for the delivery of an entire quantity of flour; and no rule can be found for an apportionment in such a manner. The plaintiffs have been disappointed in their arrangements; the defendant has neglected his duty; and retains in his hands five thousand dollars of the money of the plaintiffs, without consideration. Nothing can be more just than that he should refund it; and I am satisfied, that a better rule cannot be adopted in similar cases.

→ Reasoning

TRUMBULL, J.* concurred, substantially, in this opinion. He remarked, that the plaintiffs, by paying the 5,000 dollars, have performed all that the contract required them to do, before the receiving of the flour. As the flour was not delivered, they were not bound, by the contract, to pay any more. The defendant, on the other hand, has wholly failed of performance, at the time stipulated. He is liable for the breach; and it will be conceded

---

1793), where he was clerk of the lower house for four sessions and speaker in 1792, and as a member of the U.S. House of Representatives from Connecticut (Third and Fourth Congresses, 1793-1797). Swift served as secretary to Oliver Ellsworth on a mission to France (1800). He was appointed judge of the Connecticut Supreme Court (1801-1810), and served as Chief Justice (1806-1819). Swift served as a member of the Connecticut House of Representatives (1820-1822) shortly before his death. — K.T.

*John Trumbull (1750-1831) was educated at Yale University (M.A.) and studied law under John Adams. Admitted to the Connecticut bar in 1773, he was state's attorney for Hartford County in 1789 and a member of the Connecticut Legislature (1792-1800). In 1801, Trumbull was elevated to the Supreme Court of Connecticut and took a seat on the Supreme Court of Errors in 1808, where he served until 1819. Trumbull was also an active writer, with a volume of his poems being published in 1820. — K.T.

that if the plaintiffs had done nothing, they would be entitled to judgment, with nominal damages. Shall they not now recover what they have advanced upon the contract, previous to the breach? This sum is the actual loss, which they have sustained, by the breach. Complete justice has been done; and no new trial ought to be granted.

EDMOND, SMITH, BRAINARD and PETERS, Js. were of the same opinion.

HOSMER, J.* This is an action on an express contract, to recover damages for its non-performance. On the 20th day of February 1812, the defendant agreed to deliver to Norton & Bush, at New-Orleans, two thousand barrels of superfine flour, on or before the 1st day of May the next. On their part, they contracted to pay 7 dollars per barrel. Of this sum 5,000 dollars were advanced, and the residue was payable at different periods, posterior to the time prefixed for the delivery of the flour. It was not delivered, and the jury have given their verdict for damages in the sum of 6,771 dollars. At the time when the flour should have been delivered, the price of that article, at New-Orleans, was 5 dollars, 50 cents, per barrel, and no more. The court directed the jury, that "if they found the issues joined in favour of the plaintiffs, they should find for them to recover of the defendant 5,000 dollars, being the amount of the sum advanced by the plaintiffs to the defendant, and the interest thereof from the time the same was so advanced." For a supposed misdirection, the defendant now applies for a new trial.

Had the contract been rescinded, in an action for money had and received to recover the sum advanced, the charge to the jury would have been precisely correct. The agreement, however, was open; the action is founded upon it, and damages are demanded for the breach of it. So long as the agreement is open, it must be stated specifically . . . and the consideration paid cannot be recovered. . . .

The jury should have been directed to give the plaintiffs the damages sustained by the breach of the agreement, on the day when it should have been performed. In other words, the plaintiffs were entitled to the price of the flour estimated at 5 dollars, 50 cents, per barrel; and on this basis, connected with the other circumstances relative to the point of damages, the verdict should have been founded. The rule laid down, is indispensable, to give efficacy to the implied condition attendant on every express covenant. "If I fail in my part of the agreement, I shall pay the other party such damages as he has sustained by such my neglect or refusal." 2 Black. Comm. 443. In conformity with this, it is said by Spencer, J. in Pitcher v. Livingston, 4 Johns. Rep. 15. that "in actions for a breach of covenant, the damages are to be estimated according to the value of the thing when the covenant was broken." There have been many determinations for not transferring stock pursuant to contract; and the established rule of damages is, the price of it at the time of trial, or on the day when it should have been transferred. . . . In the case of Gray v. Portland Bank, 3 Mass. Rep. 390, it is said by the court, "that the price of stock at the time it should be transferred or delivered,

*Stephen T. Hosmer (1763-1834) was the son of the Connecticut Court of Appeals Judge Titus Hosmer. He was educated at Yale (LL.B.). Hosmer served as a member of the Council for ten years, a judge of the Superior Court for four years, and Chief Judge of that court for fourteen years. — K.T.

(and the same rule applies to other personal property,) shall be that by which the damages shall be assessed."

He who controverts the principle advanced in the cases cited, must supply a better. If he would sustain the charge to the jury in this case, he must contend, that for a breach of contract the sum to be recovered is, not the damages sustained by the non-performance, but the consideration which the plaintiff may have advanced. A rule so unwarranted as this, so opposed to familiar practice, and numerous decisions, so arbitrary, bearing not at all on the contract of the parties, and mistaking the very ground of the complaint, cannot be supported.

It is contended, that the plaintiffs have not recovered a greater sum than is due to them; and that justice does not require a new trial. To this proposition I cannot accede. If the benefit derivable to the plaintiffs from a compliance with the agreement, can be ascertained, we shall possess an infallible criterion of the damages sustained. Now the facts stated, furnish unquestionable *data*, and reduce the enquiry to a mere question of calculation. The damages sustained, were, the price of the flour when the contract was first broken; that is, the sum of 11,000 dollars. If the contract is to be considered as mutual and independent, the plaintiffs are entitled to that sum, and are bound to pay the defendant 14,000 dollars, the sum stipulated for the purchase. But, if the agreement is dependent on the prior performance of the contract by the defendant, there must be deducted from the above mentioned sum, the balance which would be payable to him on delivery of the flour, that is, 9,000 dollars. The effect of this would be precisely the same, as if the flour had been delivered, and the plaintiffs had performed the agreement on their part. *Quacunque via data*, the verdict is not conformable to legal justice. This view of the subject makes it unnecessary to consider what was the precise character of the contract.

That the plaintiffs have sustained a considerable loss on the supposed legal result, is unquestionably manifest. A fallacy has existed in not ascribing it to the right cause. It did not arise from the non-performance of the defendant's agreement. Before the period had arisen when the flour was to have been delivered, the loss had accrued by the fall of it in the market. It is equally obvious, that the defendant had derived a correspondent benefit. The verdict of the jury, in opposition to the contract of the parties, reverses their condition. It rescues the plaintiffs from their loss, and deprives the defendant of his gain. In effect, it arbitrarily subjects the defendant to a warranty, that flour shall not sink in price, and renders him the victim of the plaintiffs' unfortunate speculation.

It has been contended, that in as much as the defendant did not fulfil his contract, he ought not to derive a profit from it. To this I reply, that the obligations of the parties depend exclusively upon their own voluntary agreement. There was a hazard accompanying the contract. If flour rose in the market, the defendant would become, proportionably, a loser; and if it fell, he would be a gainer. The event on which the result was suspended, was favourable to him; and of this he cannot be deprived, unless it is the duty of courts to *make* contracts, *not to enforce* them.

I am clear in my opinion, that a new trial ought to be granted.

PETERS, J.* The rule of damages prescribed by the court on the circuit, seems to have done substantial justice between the parties; as it is admitted, that in an action for money had and received, the charge would have been precisely correct. And we are now called upon to deprive the plaintiffs of a righteous verdict, and to turn them round to another form of action wherein the damages must be *the same*, or to another trial wherein the damages will be *greater*, on a mere technical objection. If, however, the rule relied on be fixed and inflexible, this must be done; and instead of *fiat justitia*, our maxim must be *fiat lex . . . ruat coelum*. But with due deference to the learned opinion, which we have just heard, the rule of damages, in cases of this sort is not so much like the laws of the *Medes* and *Persians* as it has been represented. Even in Gray v. The Portland Bank, 3 Mass. Rep. 390, though Sedgwick, J., said, that "the price of personal property, at the time when it should be delivered, shall be that by which damages shall be assessed"; yet Sewall, J., fortified this rule by the equitable circumstances of the case — "that the plaintiff made no payment, and after tendering it, was not obliged to deposit his money, or hold it unemployed." But this decision, though made by *two* able and learned judges, is not to be considered as authority in opposition to a recent and unanimous opinion of the court of King's Bench; whose decisions are the best evidence of the common law. I allude to the case of Shepherd v. Johnson, 2 East, 211, which was debt on bond, conditioned to replace stock on a given day; and the question was, whether damages should be calculated at the price when the stock was to be delivered, or on the day of trial? The learned judge who tried the cause, was of opinion, that as the agreement had been broken, and the stock never replaced, the plaintiff was entitled to recover the larger sum, (the value on the day of trial,) and the verdict was taken accordingly, with leave to the defendant to move the court to reduce the damages. But this opinion was sanctioned by the court. Grose, J., said, "the true measure of damages, in all these cases, is that which will completely indemnify the plaintiff for the breach of the engagement. If the defendant neglect to replace the stock at the day appointed, and the stock afterwards rise in value, the plaintiff can only be indemnified by giving him the price of it *at the time of trial*. And it is no answer to say, that the defendant may be prejudiced by the plaintiff's delaying to bring his action; for it is his own fault that he does not perform his engagement at the time." . . .

But it is said, the rule of damages in *assumpsit* is not applicable to this case, because here is an express contract. But in Weaver v. Bentley, 1 Caines, 47, money advanced under a sealed contract, was recovered in assumpsit; and the court said, "We are of the opinion he (the plaintiff) had his election, either to proceed on the covenant, and recover damages for the breach, or to disaffirm the contract, and resort to his assumpsit to recover back what he had paid." And Livingston, J., who dissented merely with respect to the form of action, said, that covenant will lie on the instrument to recover back *all that has been paid*.

But what can the defendant gain by a new trial? Does he wish to be subjected to the value of the flour, when it should have been delivered, or

---

*John Thompson Peters (1765-1834) was educated at Yale University (LL.B.) and practiced law at Hartford, Connecticut. In 1818, he became a judge of the Supreme Court of Connecticut, where he served for many years. — R.B.

at the time of the trial, at the hazard of recovering the sums stipulated, without any pretence of fulfilling the contract on his part? Or, does he expect the court will aid him in his iniquity, by giving him 3,000 dollars of the money advanced for his breach of faith? Though the flour might have been purchased at New-Orleans, at less than the stipulated price, *non constat* that it would have been an unprofitable cargo in some other market. And after the plaintiffs had advanced their money, and been at the hazard and expense of a voyage to New-Orleans to ship it home, or to some other market, is it to be endured that the defendant should pocket their money and bid them defiance? "Flour, gentlemen," says this honest defendant, "is plenty and cheap at New-Orleans. You may buy it, if you can find money and credit, *there*, and get your money back, in Connecticut, when you can." I take it to be well settled, that "a new trial ought to be granted to attain *real justice*, but not to gratify litigious passions upon every point of *summum jus*" — Farewell v. Chaffey & al. 1 Burr. 54.: That "an application for a new trial is to the discretion of the court, who ought to exercise that discretion in such a manner as will best answer the ends of justice"; and where "complete and substantial justice has been done," the court will not "send the cause down to be re-tried on a technical objection in point of law" — Edmonson v. Machell, 2 Term Rep. 4.: That "though the ground of the verdict should be wrong, yet if it clearly appeared to the court now, that, upon the whole, no injustice had been done to the defendant; or if it clearly appeared to the court now, that the plaintiffs, by another form of action, could recover all they have got by this verdict; the court ought not to grant a new trial," Foxcroft & al. v. Devonshire & al. 2 Burr. 396.

Gould and Chapman, Js., gave no opinion, having formerly been of counsel in the cause.

New trial not to be granted.

RESTATEMENT (SECOND) OF CONTRACTS

§371. MEASURE OF RESTITUTION INTEREST

If a sum of money is awarded to protect a party's restitution interest, it may as justice requires be measured by either

(a) the reasonable value to the other party of what he received in terms of what it would have cost him to obtain it from a person in the claimant's position, or

(b) the extent to which the other party's property has been increased in value or his other interests advanced.

§373. RESTITUTION WHEN OTHER PARTY IS
IN BREACH

(1) Subject to the rule stated in Subsection (2), on a breach by non-performance that gives rise to a claim for damages for total breach or on a repudiation, the injured party is entitled to restitution for any benefit that he has conferred on the other party by way of part performance or reliance.

(2) The injured party has no right to restitution if he has performed all of his duties under the contract and no performance by the other party

remains due other than payment of a definite sum of money for that performance.

REFERENCE: Farnsworth, §§12.19-12.20
              Calamari & Perillo, §§19.40-19.46
              Murray, §127

2.   Restitution to the Party in Breach

STUDY GUIDE: For most of the nineteenth century, the approach taken by the New Hampshire courts was considered the minority approach. It is now generally accepted. When reading the next case, consider whether the contract between the parties is irrelevant to the cause of action. Is there reason to doubt the court's claim that parties are free to contract around the rule it establishes?

BRITTON v. TURNER
Superior Court of Judicature of New Hampshire,
6 N.H. 481, 26 Am. Dec. 713 (1834)

Assumpsit for work and labour, performed by the plaintiff, in the service of the defendent [sic], from March 9th, 1831, to December 27, 1831. The declaration contained the common counts, and among them a count in *quantum meruit,* for the labor, averring it to be worth one hundred dollars.

At the trial in the C. C. Pleas, the plaintiff proved the performance of the labor as set forth in the declaration. The defence was that it was performed under a special contract — that the plaintiff agreed to work one year, from some time in March, 1831, to March, 1832, and that the defendant was to pay him for said year's labor the sum of one hundred and twenty dollars; and the defendant offered evidence tending to show that such was the contract under which the work was done. Evidence was also offered to show that the plaintiff left that defendant's service without his consent, and it was contended by the defendant that the plaintiff had no good cause for not continuing in his employment. There was no evidence offered of any damage arising from the plaintiff's departure farther than was to be inferred from his nonfulfillment of the entire contract.

The court instructed the jury, that if they were satisfied from the evidence that the labor was performed, under a contract to labor a year, for the sum of one hundred and twenty dollars, and if they were satisfied that the plaintiff labored only the time specified in the declaration, and then left the defendant's service, against his consent, and without any good cause, yet the plaintiff was entitled to recover, under his *quantum meruit* count, as much as the labor he performed was reasonably worth, and under this direction the jury gave a verdict for the plaintiff for the sum of $95. The defendant excepted to the instructions thus given to the jury. . . .

PARKER, J.,* delivered the opinion of the court. It may be assumed, that the labor performed by the plaintiff, and for which he seeks to recover a compensation in this action, was commenced under a special contract to labor for the defendant the term of one year, for the sum of one hundred and twenty dollars, and that the plaintiff has labored but a portion of that time, and has voluntarily failed to complete the entire contract. It is clear, then, that he is not entitled to recover upon the contract itself, because the service, which was to entitle him to the sum agreed upon, has never been performed.

But the question arises, can the plaintiff, under these circumstances, recover a reasonable sum for the service he has actually performed, under the count in *quantum meruit*. Upon this, and questions of a similar nature, the decisions to be found in the books are not easily reconciled.

It has been held, upon contracts of this kind for labor to be performed at a specified price, that the party who voluntarily fails to fulfil the contract by performing the whole labor contracted for, is not entitled to recover anything for the labor actually performed, however much he may have done toward the performance, and this has been considered the settled rule of law upon this subject. . . . That such rule in its operation may be very unequal, not to say unjust, is apparent.

A party who contracts to perform certain specified labor, and who breaks his contract in the first instance, without any attempt to perform it, can only be made liable to pay the damages which the other party has sustained by reason of such nonperformance, which in many instances may be trifling — whereas a party who in good faith has entered upon the performance of his contract, and nearly completed it, and then abandoned the further performance — although the other party has had the full benefit of all that has been done, and has perhaps sustained no actual damage — is in fact subjected to a loss of all which has been performed, in the nature of damages for the nonfulfillment of the remainder, upon the technical rule, that the contract must be fully performed, in order to a recovery of any part of the compensation.

By the operation of this rule, then, the party who attempts performance may be placed in a much worse situation than he who wholly disregards his contract, and the other party may receive much more, by the breach of the contract, than the injury which he has sustained by such breach, and more than he could be entitled to were he seeking to recover damages by an action.

The case before us presents an illustration. Had the plaintiff in this case never entered upon the performance of his contract, the damage could not probably have been greater than some small expense and trouble incurred in procuring another to do the labor which he had contracted to perform.

Joel Parker (1795-1875) graduated from Dartmouth (A.B.) and was a member of the New Hampshire Legislature (1824-1826). Appointed to the New Hampshire Superior Court in 1833, he served as Chief Justice from 1838 until 1848. Parker was also a professor of law at Harvard University (1847-1868), and delegate from Cambridge to the Massachusetts Constitutional Convention (1853). He was commissioner to revise the statutes of Massachusetts, and authored many works including A Charge to the Grand Jury on the Uncertainty of Law (1854); The Non-Extension of Slavery (1856); Personal Liberty Laws and Slavery in the Territories (1861); The Right of Secession (1861); The War Powers of Congress and the President (1863); and The Three Powers of Government (1869). — K.T.

But having entered upon the performance, and labored nine and a half months, the value of which labor to the defendant as found by the jury is $95, if the defendant can succeed in this defence, he in fact receives nearly five sixths of the value of a whole year's labor, by reason of the breach of contract by the plaintiff a sum not only utterly disproportionate to any probable, not to say possible damage which could have resulted from the neglect of the plaintiff to continue the remaining two and a half months, but altogether beyond any damage which could have been recovered by the defendant, had the plaintiff done nothing towards the fulfillment of his contract. . . .

It is said, that where a party contracts to perform certain work, and to furnish material, as, for instance, to build a house, and the work is done, but with some variations from the mode prescribed by the contract, yet if the other party has the benefit of the labor and materials he should be bound to pay so much as they are reasonably worth. . . .

A different doctrine seems to have been holden in Ellis v. Hamlen, 3 Taunt. 52, and it is apparent, in such cases, that if the house has not been built in the manner specified in the contract, the work has not been done. The party has no more performed what he contracted to perform, than he who has contracted to labor for a certain period, and failed to complete the time. It is in truth virtually conceded in such cases that the work has not been done, for if it had been, the party performing it would be entitled to recover the contract itself, which, it is held he cannot do.

Those cases are not to be distinguished, in principle, from the present, unless it be in the circumstance, that where the party has contracted to furnish materials, and do certain labor, as to build a house in a specified manner, if it is not done according to the contract, the party for whom it is built may refuse to receive it — elect to take no benefit from what has been performed — and therefore if he does receive, he shall be bound to pay the value — whereas, in a contract for labor, merely, from day to day, the party is continually receiving the benefit of the contract under an expectation that it will be fulfilled, and cannot, upon the breach of it, have an election to refuse to receive what has been done, and thus discharge himself from payment. But we think this difference in the nature of the contracts does not justify the application of a different rule in relation to them.

The party who contracts for labor merely, for a certain period, does so with full knowledge that he must, from the nature of the case, be accepting part performance, and with knowledge also that the other may eventually fail of completing the entire term. If, under such circumstance he actually receives a benefit from the labor performed, over and above the damage occasioned by the failure to complete, there is as much reason why he should pay the reasonable worth of what has thus been done for his benefit, as there is when he enters and occupies the house which has been built for him, but not according to the stipulation of the contract, and which he perhaps enters, not because he is satisfied with what has been done, but because circumstance compel him to accept it such as it is, that he should pay for the value of the house. . . .

So where a person contracts for the purchase of a quantity of merchandize, at a certain price, and receives a delivery of part only, and he keeps that part, without any offer of a return, it has been held that he must pay the value of it. . . .

It is said, that in those cases where the plaintiff has been permitted to recover there was an acceptance of what had been done. The answer is, that where the contract is to labor from day to day, for certain period, the party for whom the labor is done in truth stipulates to receive it from day to day, as it is performed, and although the other may not eventually do all he has contracted to do, there has been, necessarily, an acceptance of what has been done in pursuance of the contract, and the party must have understood when he made the contract that there was to be such acceptance.

If then the party stipulates in the outset to receive part performance from time to time, with a knowledge that the whole may not be completed, we see no reason why he should not equally be holden to pay for the amount of value received, as where he afterwards takes the benefit of what has been done, with a knowledge that the whole which was contracted for has not been performed. . . .

If on such failure to perform the whole, the nature of the contract be such that the employer can reject what has been done, and refuse to receive any benefit from the part performance, he is entitled so to do, and in such case is not liable to be charged, unless he has before assented to and accepted of what has been done, however much the other party may have done towards the performance. He has in such case received nothing, and having contracted to receive nothing but the entire matter contracted for, he is not bound to pay, because his express promise was only to pay on receiving the whole, and having actually received nothing the law cannot and ought not raise an implied promise to pay. But where the party receives value — takes and uses the materials, or has advantage from the labor, he is liable to pay the reasonable worth of what he has received. . . . And the rule is the same whether it was received and accepted by the assent of the party prior to the breach, under a contract by which, from its nature, he was to receive labor, from time to time until the completion of the whole contract; or whether it was received and accepted by an assent subsequent to the performance of all which was in fact done. If he received it under such circumstances as precluded him from rejecting it afterwards, that does not alter the case — it has still been received by his assent. . . .

It is easy, if parties so choose, to provide by an express agreement that nothing shall be earned, if the laborer leaves his employer without having performed the whole service contemplated, and then there can be no pretense for a recovery if he voluntarily desert the service before the expiration of the time.

The amount, however, for which the employer ought to be charged, where the laborer abandons his contract, is only the reasonable worth, or the amount of advantage he receives upon the whole transaction, . . . and, in estimating the value of the labor, the contract price for the service cannot be exceeded. . . . If a person makes a contract fairly he is entitled to have it fully performed, and if this is not done he is entitled to damages. He may maintain a suit to recover the amount of damage sustained by the non-performance.

The benefit and advantage which the party takes by the labor, therefore, is the amount of value which he receives, if any, after deducting the amount of damage; and if he elects to put this in defence he is entitled so to do, and the implied promise which the law will raise, in such case, is to pay such amount of the stipulated price for the whole labor, as remains after deducting what it would cost to procure a completion of the residue of the service, and also any damage which has been sustained by reason of the nonfulfillment of the contract.

If in such case it be found that the damages are equal to, or greater than the amount of the labor performed, so that the employer, having a right to the full performance of the contract, has not upon the whole case received a beneficial service, the plaintiff cannot recover.

This rule, by binding the employer to pay the value of the service he actually receives, and the laborer to answer in damages where he does not complete the entire contract, will leave no temptation to the former to drive the laborer from his service, near the close of his term, by ill treatment, in order to escape from payment; nor to the latter to desert his service before the stipulated time, without a sufficient reason; and it will in most instances settle the whole controversy in one action, and prevent a multiplicity of suits and cross actions. . . .

Judgment on the verdict.

VINES v. ORCHARD HILLS, INC.
Supreme Court of Connecticut,
181 Conn. 501, 435 A.2d 1022 (1980)

PETERS, A.J.* This case concerns the right of purchasers of real property, after their own default, to recover moneys paid at the time of execution of a valid contract of sale. The plaintiffs, Euel D. Vines and his wife Etta Vines, contracted, on July 11, 1973, to buy Unit No. 10, Orchard Hills Condominium, New Canaan, Connecticut, from the defendant Orchard Hills, Inc. for $78,800. On or before that date, they had paid the defendant $7880 as a down payment toward the purchase. Alleging that the sale of the property was never consummated, the plaintiffs sought to recover their down payment. The trial court . . . overruled the defendant's demurrer to the plaintiffs' amended complaint; subsequently, after a hearing, the trial court . . . rendered judgment for the plaintiffs for $7880 plus interest. The defendant's appeal maintains that its demurrer should have been sustained, that its liquidated damages clause should have been enforced, and that evidence of the value of the property at the time of the trial should have been excluded.

The facts underlying this litigation are straightforward and undisputed. When the purchasers contracted to buy their condominium in July, 1973,

---

*Ellen Ash Peters (1930-†) studied at Swarthmore College (B.A.) and Yale University (LL.B.). In 1957, after clerking for Judge Charles E. Clark, U.S. Court of Appeals, Second Circuit (1954-1955), Justice Peters was admitted to practice in Connecticut, where she became a law professor at Yale Law School (1955-1978). While a professor, she served as an advisor for the Restatement of Contracts (1963-1980) and, after being appointed to the Connecticut Supreme Court in 1978, continued as an advisor for the Restatement of Restitution (1978-1980). After serving as Justice and Chief Justice of the Connecticut Supreme Court, Justice Peters retired. Since then, she has been a regular visiting professor at the University of Connecticut School of Law — teaching contracts among other subjects — and is also a judge trial referee who sits on occasion with the appellate court. — L.R.

they paid $7880, a sum which the contract of sale designated as liquidated damages.[30] The purchasers decided not to take title to the condominium because Euel D. Vines was transferred by his employer to New Jersey; the Vines so informed the seller by a letter dated January 4, 1974. There has never been any claim that the seller has failed, in any respect, to conform to his obligations under the contract, nor does the complaint allege that the purchasers are legally excused from their performance under the contract. In short, it is the purchasers and not the seller whose breach precipitated the present cause of action.

In the proceedings below, the purchasers established that the value of the condominium that they had agreed to buy for $78,800 in 1973 had, by the time of the trial in 1979, a fair market value of $160,000. The trial court relied on this figure to conclude that, because the seller had gained what it characterized as a windfall of approximately $80,000, the purchasers were entitled to recover their down payment of $7880. Neither the purchasers nor the seller proffered any evidence at the trial to show the market value of the condominium at the time of the purchasers' breach of their contract or the damages sustained by the seller as a result of that breach. . . .

The ultimate issue on this appeal is the enforceability of a liquidated damages clause as a defense to a claim of restitution by purchasers in default on a land sale contract. Although the parties, both in the trial court and here, have focused on the liquidated damages clause per se, we must first consider when, if ever, purchasers who are themselves in breach of a valid contract of sale may affirmatively invoke the assistance of judicial process to recover back moneys paid to, and withheld by, their seller.

The right of a contracting party, despite his default, to seek restitution for benefits conferred and allegedly unjustly retained has been much disputed in the legal literature and in the case law. See 5A Corbin, Contracts §§1122-1135 (1964); Dobbs, Remedies §12.14 (1973); 1 Palmer, Restitution, c. 5 (1978). . . . Although earlier cases often refused to permit a party to bring an action that could be said to be based on his own breach; see, e. g., Hansbrough v. Peck, 72 U.S. (5 Wall.) 497, 506, 18 L. Ed. 520 (1867); . . . many of the more recent cases support restitution in order to prevent unjust enrichment and to avoid forfeiture. See, e. g., Hook v. Bomar, 320 F.2d 536, 541 (5th Cir. 1963) . . . ; and see Restatement (Second), Contracts §[374].

A variety of considerations, some practical and some theoretical, underlie this shift in attitude toward the plaintiff in breach. As Professor Corbin pointed out in his seminal article, "The Right of a Defaulting Vendee to the Restitution of Instalments Paid," 40 Yale L.J. 1013 (1931), the anomalous result of denying any remedy to the plaintiff in breach is to punish more severely the person who has partially performed, often in good faith, than the person who has entirely disregarded his contractual obligations from the outset. Only partial performance triggers a claim for restitution,

30. Paragraph 9 of the contract of sale provided: "DEFAULT: In the event Purchaser fails to perform any of the obligations herein imposed on the Purchaser, the Seller performing all obligations herein imposed on the Seller, the Seller shall retain all sums of money paid under this Contract, as liquidated damages, and all rights and liabilities of the parties hereto shall be at an end."

and partial performance will not, in the ordinary course of events, have been more injurious to the innocent party than total nonperformance. Recognition of a claim in restitution is, furthermore, consistent with the economic functions that the law of contracts is designed to serve. . . . The principal purpose of remedies for the breach of contract is to provide compensation for loss[,] . . . and therefore a party injured by breach of contract is entitled to retain nothing in excess of that sum which compensates him for the loss of his bargain. Indeed, there are those who argue that repudiation of contractual obligations is socially desirable, and should be encouraged, whenever gain to the party in breach exceeds loss to the party injured by breach. Birmingham, "Breach of Contract, Damage Measures, and Economic Efficiency," 24 Rut. L. Rev. 273, 284 (1970); Posner, Economic Analysis of Law §4.9, pp. 89-90 (2d Ed. 1977). To assign such primacy to inferences drawn from economic models requires great confidence that the person injured by breach will encounter no substantial difficulties in establishing the losses for which he is entitled to be compensated. It is not necessary to push the principle of compensatory damages that far, or to disregard entirely the desirability of maintaining some incentives for the performance of promises. A claim in restitution, although legal in form, is equitable in nature, and permits a trial court to balance the equities, to take into account a variety of competing principles to determine whether the defendant has been unjustly enriched. "Even though we adhere to the rule that only compensatory damages are to be awarded, there are other important questions of policy to be considered. One is whether aid is to be given to one who breaches his contract, particularly when the breach is deliberate and without moral justification. Another is whether restitution can be administered without leaving the innocent party with uncompensated damages." 1 Palmer, Restitution §5.1, p. 574 (1978). . . .

In this state, at the turn of the century, in Pierce v. Staub, 78 Conn. 459, 466, 62 A. 760 (1906), this court acknowledged the equitable claim of a purchaser in breach to recover moneys paid under a contract to purchase real property. . . . Apart from Pierce v. Staub, we have never directly decided whether a purchaser of real estate may, despite his breach, recover payments made to his seller. But Pierce v. Staub is an impressive, and an impressively early, guidepost toward permitting such a cause of action. . . . We therefore conclude that a purchaser whose breach is not willful has a restitutionary claim to recover moneys paid that unjustly enrich his seller. In this case, no one has alleged that the purchasers' breach, arising out of a transfer to a more distant place of employment, should be deemed to have been willful. The trial court was therefore not in error in initially overruling the seller's demurrer and entertaining the purchasers' cause of action.

The purchaser's right to recover in restitution requires the purchaser to establish that the seller has been unjustly enriched. The purchaser must show more than that the contract has come to an end and that the seller retains moneys paid pursuant to the contract. To prove unjust enrichment, in the ordinary case, the purchaser, because he is the party in breach, must prove that the damages suffered by his seller are less than the moneys received from the purchaser. . . . It may not be easy for the purchaser to prove the extent of the seller's damages, it may even be strategically advantageous for the seller to come forward with relevant evidence of the losses he has incurred and may expect to incur on account of the buyer's breach. Nonetheless, only if the breaching party satisfies his burden of proof that the innocent party has sustained a net gain may a claim for unjust enrichment be sustained. . . .

In the case before us, the parties themselves stipulated in the contract of sale that the purchasers' down payment of 10 percent of the purchase price represents the damages that would be likely to flow from the purchasers' breach. The question then becomes whether the purchasers have demonstrated the seller's unjust enrichment in the face of the liquidated damages clause to which they agreed.

This is not a suitable occasion for detailed review of the checkered history of liquidated damages clauses. Despite the judicial resistance that such clauses have encountered in the past[,] . . . this court has recognized the principle that there are circumstances that justify private agreements to supplant judicially determined remedies for breach of contract. *Berger v. Shanahan*, 142 Conn. 726, 731-32, 188 A.2d 311 (1955). . . . This court has however refused to enforce an otherwise valid liquidated damages clause upon a finding that no damages whatsoever ensued from the particular breach of contract that actually occurred. *Norwalk Door Closer Co. v. Eagle Lock & Screw Co.*, 153 Conn. 681, 689, 220 A.2d 263 (1966).

Most of the litigation concerning liquidated damages clauses arises in the context of an affirmative action by the party injured by breach to enforce the clause in order to recover the amount therein stipulated. In such cases, the burden of persuasion about the enforceability of the clause naturally rests with its proponent. . . . In the case before us, by contrast, where the plaintiffs are themselves in default, the plaintiffs bear the burden of showing that the clause is invalid and unenforceable. . . . It is not unreasonable in these circumstances to presume that a liquidated damages clause that is appropriately limited in amount bears a reasonable relationship to the damages that the seller has actually suffered. See Restatement (Second), Contracts §[374], esp. subsection (2). The seller's damages . . . include not only his expectation damages suffered through loss of his bargain, and his incidental damages such as broker's commissions, but also less quantifiable costs arising out of retention of real property beyond the time of the originally contemplated sale. . . . A liquidated damages clause allowing the seller to retain 10 percent of the contract price as earnest money is presumptively a reasonable allocation of the risks associated with default. . . .

The presumption of validity that attaches to a clause liquidating the seller's damages at 10 percent of the contract price in the event of the purchaser's unexcused nonperformance is, like most other presumptions, rebuttable. The purchaser, despite his default, is free to prove that the contract, or any part thereof, was the product of fraud or mistake or unconscionability. . . . In the alternative, the purchaser is free to offer evidence that his breach in fact caused the seller no damages or damages substantially less than the amount stipulated as liquidated damages. See [*Norwalk Door Closer*], supra.

The trial court concluded that the plaintiff purchasers had successfully invoked the principle of [*Norwalk Door Closer*] by presenting evidence of increase in the value of the real property between the date of the contract of sale and the date of the trial. That conclusion was in error. The relevant time at which to measure the seller's damages is the time of breach. . . . Benefits to the seller that are attributable to a rising market subsequent to breach rightfully accrue to the seller. . . . There was no evidence before the court to demonstrate that the seller was not injured at the time of the purchasers' breach by their failure then to consummate the contract. Neither the seller's status as a developer of a condominium project nor the absence of willfulness on the part of the purchasers furnishes a justification for disregarding the liquidated damages clause, although these factors may play some role in the ultimate determination of whether the seller was in fact unjustly enriched by the down payment he retained.

Because the availability of, and the limits on, restitutionary claims by a plaintiff in default have not previously been clearly spelled out in our cases, it is appropriate to afford the purchasers herein another opportunity to proffer evidence to substantiate their claim. What showing the purchasers must make cannot be spelled out with specificity in view of the sparsity of the present record. The purchasers may be able to demonstrate that the condominium could, at the time of their breach, have been resold at a price sufficiently higher than their contract price to obviate any loss of profits and to compensate the seller for any incidental and consequential damages. Alternatively, the purchasers may be able to present evidence of unconscionability or of excuse, to avoid the applicability of the liquidated damages clause altogether. The plaintiffs' burden of proof is not an easy one to sustain, but they are entitled to their day in court.

There is error, the judgment is set aside, and the case is remanded for further proceedings in conformity with this opinion.

RESTATEMENT (SECOND) OF CONTRACTS

§374.   RESTITUTION IN FAVOR OF PARTY IN BREACH

(1) Subject to the rule stated in Subsection (2), if a party justifiably refuses to perform on the ground that his remaining duties of performance have been discharged by the other party's breach, the party in breach is entitled to restitution for any benefit that he has conferred by way of part performance or reliance in excess of the loss that he has caused by his own breach.

(2) To the extent that, under the manifested assent of the parties a party's performance is to be retained in the case of breach, that party is not entitled to restitution if the value of the performance as liquidated damages is reasonable in the light of the anticipated or actual loss caused by the breach and the difficulties of proof of loss.

REFERENCE: Farnsworth, §8.14
            Murray, §127(B) & (C)

3.   Restitution and "Quasi-Contract"

STUDY GUIDE: Is Cotnam v. Wisdom a genuine contracts case? Why or why not? Your serious consideration of this question will prove very useful shortly when we reach the materials that discuss contract formation.

COTNAM v. WISDOM
Supreme Court of Arkansas,
83 Ark. 601, 104 S.W. 164 (1907)

Action by F. L. Wisdom and another against T. T. Cotnam, administrator of A. M. Harrison, deceased, for services rendered by the plaintiffs as surgeons to defendant's intestate. Judgment for plaintiffs. Defendant appeals. Reversed and remanded. ——> SCOA Holding! L—> Trial Court Holding

Instructions 1 and 2, given at the instance of plaintiffs, are as follows:

(1) If you find from the evidence that plaintiffs rendered professional services as physicians and surgeons to the deceased, A. M. Harrison, in a sudden emergency following the deceased's injury in a street car wreck, in an endeavor to save his life, then you are instructed that plaintiffs are entitled to recover from the estate of the said A. M. Harrison such sum as you may find from the evidence reasonable compensation for the services rendered.

(2) The character and importance of the operation, the responsibility resting upon the surgeon performing the operation, his experience and professional training, and the ability to pay of the person operated upon, are elements to be considered by you in determining what is a reasonable charge for the services performed by plaintiffs in the particular case.

HILL, C.J.* (after stating the facts). The Reporter will state the issues and substance of the testimony, and set out instructions one and two at instance of appellees, and it will be seen therefrom that instruction one amounted to a preemptory instruction to find for the plaintiff in some amount.

The first question is as to the corrections of this instruction. As indicated therein, the facts are that Mr. Harrison, appellant's intestate, was thrown from a street car, receiving serious injuries which rendered him unconscious, and while in that condition the appellees were notified of the accident and summoned to his assistance by some spectator, and performed a difficult operation in an effort to save his life, but they were

Joseph Morrison Hill (1864-1951) attended the University of Arkansas (LL.D.). After being admitted to the bar, he practiced at Eureka Springs and Ft. Smith, Arkansas (1883-1904), then served as Chief Justice of the Supreme Court of Arkansas (1904-1909). Upon resignation from the court, he served as chief counsel for the State of Arkansas, winning the litigation over railroad rate cases in 1913 and over taxation of railroads in bankruptcy in 1941 for the State in the U.S. Supreme Court. Hill was also a compiler of Sandels and Hill's Digest of the Statutes of Arkansas (1894). — K.T.

unsuccessful, and he died without regaining consciousness. The appellant says: "Harrison was never conscious after his head struck the pavement. . . . However merciful or benevolent may have been the intention of the appellees, a new rule of law, of contract by implication of law, will have to be established by this court in order to sustain the recovery." Appellant is right in saying that the recovery must be sustained by a contract by implication of law, but is not right in saying that it is a new rule of law, for such contracts are almost as old as the English system of jurisprudence. They are usually called "implied contracts." More properly they should be called "*quasi*-contracts" or "constructive contracts." . . .

Contract by Implication

The following excerpts from Sceva v. True, 53 N.H. 627, are peculiarly applicable here:

> We regard it as well settled by the cases referred to in the briefs of counsel . . . that an insane person, an idiot, or a person utterly bereft of all sense and reason by the sudden stroke of an accident or disease, may be held liable, in assumpsit, for necessaries furnished to him in good faith while in that unfortunate and helpless condition. And the reasons upon which this rests are too broad, as well as too sensible and humane, to be overborne by any deductions which a refined logic may make from the circumstances that in such cases there can be no contract or promise, in fact — no meeting of the minds of the parties. The cases put it on the ground of an implied contract; and by this is not meant, as the defendant's counsel seems to suppose, an actual contract — that is, an actual meeting of the minds of the parties, an actual, mutual understanding, to be inferred from language, acts, and circumstances by the jury — but a contract and promise, said to be implied by the law, where, in point of fact, there was no contract, no mutual understanding, and so no promise. The defendant's counsel says it is usurpation for the court to hold, as a matter of law, that there is a contract and a promise, when all the evidence in the case shows that there was not a contract, nor the semblance of one. It is doubtless a legal fiction, invented and used for the sake of the remedy. If it was originally usurpation, certainly it has now become very inveterate, and firmly fixed in the body of the law.
>
> Illustrations might be multiplied, but enough has been said to show that, when a contract or promise implied by law is spoken of, a very different thing is meant from a contract in fact, whether express or tacit. The evidence of an actual contract is generally to be found, either in some writing made by the parties, or in verbal communications which passed between them, or in their acts and conduct considered in the light of the circumstances of each particular case. A contract implied by law, on the contrary, rests upon no evidence. It has no actual existence. It is simply a mythical creation of the law. The law says it shall be taken that there was a promise when, in point of fact, there was none. Of course, this is not good logic, for the obvious and sufficient reason that it is not true. It is a legal fiction, resting wholly for its support on a plain legal obligation, and a plain legal right. If it were true, it would not be a fiction. There is a class of legal rights, with their correlative legal duties, analogous to the *obligationes quasi ex contractu* of the civil law, which seem to lie in the region between contracts on the one hand and torts on the other, and to call for the application of a remedy not strictly furnished either by actions *ex contractu* or actions *ex delicto*. The common law supplies no action of *duty*, as it does of assumpsit and trespass; and hence the somewhat awkward contrivance of this fiction to apply the remedy of assumpsit where there is no true contract and no promise to support it. . . .

2. The defendant sought to require the plaintiff to prove, in addition to the value of the services, the benefit, if any, derived by the deceased from the operation, and alleges error in the court refusing to so instruct the jury. The court was right in refusing to place this burden upon the physicians. The same question was considered in <u>Ladd v. Witte,</u> 116 Wis. 35, [92 N.W. 365], where the court said:

> <u>That is not at all the test.</u> So that <u>a surgical operation be conceived and performed with due skill and care, the price to be paid therefor does not depend upon the result.</u> The event so generally lies with the forces of nature that all intelligent men know and understand that the surgeon is not responsible therefor. In absence of express agreement, the surgeon, who brings to such a service due skill and care earns the reasonable and customary price therefor, whether the outcome be beneficial to the patient or the reverse.

3. The court permitted to go to the jury the fact that Mr. Harrison was a bachelor, and that his estate would go to his collateral relatives, and also permitted proof to be made of the <u>value of the estate, which amounted to about $18,500, including $10,000</u> from accident and life insurance <u>policies.</u>

There is a conflict in the authorities as to whether it is proper to prove the value of the estate of a person for whom medical services were rendered, or the financial condition of the person receiving such services. In Robinson v. Campbell, 47 Iowa, 625, it was said: "There is no more reason why this charge should be enhanced on account of the ability of the defendant to pay than that the merchant should charge them more for a yard of cloth, or the druggist for filling a prescription, or a laborer for a day's work." . . .

Whatever may be the true principle governing this matter in contracts, the court is of the opinion that the financial condition of a patient cannot be considered where there is no contract and recovery is sustained on a legal fiction which raises a contract in order to afford a remedy which the justice of the case requires. . . .

It was improper to let it go to the jury that <u>Mr. Harrison was a bachelor</u> and <u>that his estate was left to nieces and nephews. This was relevant to no issue in the case, and its effect might well have been prejudicial.</u> While this verdict is no higher than some of the evidence would justify, yet it is much higher than some of the other evidence would justify, and hence it is impossible to say that this was harmless error.

Judgment is reversed, and cause remanded.

STUDY GUIDE: The next case explains further the distinction between "implied-in-fact" contracts and quasi-contracts that are "implied in law." Be sure you understand the difference. In denying recovery to a "volunteer," is the court contradicting Cotnam? *Was not the doctor in* Cotnam *a volunteer? Also be aware that some courts, but not all, add an additional element of recovery under quasi-contract: that services be performed under circumstances that put the recipient of the benefit on notice that the party performing the services expected to be paid.*

MARTIN v. LITTLE, BROWN AND CO.
Superior Court of Pennsylvania,
304 Pa. Super. 424, 450 A.2d 984 (1981)

WIEAND, J.* This appeal was taken from an order sustaining preliminary objections in the nature of a demurrer to appellant's pro se complaint in assumpsit. The trial court held that a contract had not been made and that there could be no recovery on quantum meruit where appellant had volunteered information which enabled appellee, a publisher of books, to effect a recovery against a third person for copyright infringement. We agree and, accordingly, affirm.

The averments of the complaint disclose that on September 28, 1976, the appellant, James L. Martin [identified by the court as a law student], directed a letter to Bantam Books, Inc. in which he advised the addressee that portions of a paperback publication entitled "How to Buy Stocks" had been plagiarized by the authors of a later book entitled "Planning Your Financial Future." Appellant's letter offered to provide a copy of the book, in which appellant had highlighted the plagiarized passages, with marginal references to the pages and paragraphs of the book from which the passages had been copied. By letter dated October 21, 1976 and signed by Robin Paris, Editorial Assistant, the appellee, Little, Brown and Company, Inc., invited appellant to send his copy of "Planning Your Financial Future." This was done, and appellee acknowledged receipt thereof in writing. Thereafter, appellant made inquiries about appellee's investigation but received no response. Appellant was persistent, however, and upon learning that appellee had agreed with his assertions and was pursuing a claim of copyright infringement, he demanded compensation for his services. Appellee denied that it had contracted with appellant or was otherwise obligated to compensate appellant for his work or for his calling the infringement to the publisher's attention. Nevertheless, appellee offered an honorarium in the form of a check for two hundred dollars, which appellant retained but did not cash. Instead, he filed suit to recover one-third of the recovery effected by appellee.

These facts and all reasonable inferences therefrom have been admitted by appellee's demurrer. . . . In determining whether they are sufficient to state a cause of action we are guided by the rule that a demurrer may be sustained only in clear cases, and all doubts must be resolved in favor of the sufficiency of the complaint. . . .

The facts alleged in the complaint are insufficient to establish a contractual relationship between appellant and appellee. Appellant's initial letter did not expressly or by implication suggest a desire to negotiate.

Donald E. Wieand (1926-1996) was educated at Muhlenberg College, Villanova University (A.B. cum laude), and Dickinson School of Law (LL.B.). After being called to the Pennsylvania bar in 1951, Judge Wieand engaged in private practice in Allentown, Pennsylvania, and served as an Instructor in Law at Muhlenberg College (1955-1957) and the American Institute of Banking (1954-1957) until becoming a Judge for the Pennsylvania Court of Common Pleas Thirty-first Judicial District (1963-1978). Judge Wieand was appointed to the Superior Court of Pennsylvania in 1978 and reappointed in 1980, before being elected to the same position in 1981. After his re-election in 1991, he remained on the court until his death. — L.R.

Neither did appellee's letter of October 21, 1976, which invited appellant to send his copy of the offending publication, constitute an offer to enter a unilateral contract. It was no more than a response to an initial letter by appellant in which he notified appellee of a copyright infringement and expressed a willingness to forward a copy of the infringing work in which he had highlighted copied portions and cited pages of appellee's work which had been copied. Appellant's letter did not suggest that he intended to be paid, and appellee's response did not contain an offer to pay appellant if he forwarded his copy of the infringing work. In brief, payment to appellant was not discussed in any of the correspondence which preceded the forwarding of appellant's work to appellee.

"A contract, implied in fact, is an actual contract which arises where the parties agree upon the obligations to be incurred, but their intention, instead of being expressed in words, is inferred from their acts in the light of the surrounding circumstances. . . ." Home Protection Building & Loan Association Case, 143 Pa. Super. 96, 98, 17 A.2d 755, 756 (1941). An implied contract is an agreement which legitimately can be inferred from the intention of the parties as evidenced by the circumstances and "the ordinary course of dealing and the common understanding of men." Hertzog v. Hertzog, 29 Pa. 465, 468 (1857).

> Generally, there is an implication of a promise to pay for valuable services rendered with the knowledge and approval of the recipient, in the absence of a showing to the contrary. A promise to pay the reasonable value of the service is implied where one performs for another, with the other's knowledge, a useful service of a character that is usually charged for, and the latter expresses no dissent or avails himself of the service. A promise to pay for services can, however, only be implied when they are rendered in such circumstances as authorized the party performing to entertain a reasonable expectation of their payment by the party benefitted. The service or other benefit must not be given as a gratuity or without expectation of payment, and the person benefitted must do something from which his promise to pay may be fairly inferred.

Home Protection Building & Loan Association Case, supra, . . . When a person requests another to perform services, it is ordinarily inferred that he intends to pay for them, unless the circumstances indicate otherwise. Restatement Restitution §107(2) (1937). However, where the circumstances evidence that one's work effort has been voluntarily given to another, an intention to pay therefor cannot be inferred. In the instant case, the facts alleged in the complaint disclose a submission of information from appellant to appellee without any discussion pertaining to appellee's payment therefor. Clearly, there was no basis upon which to infer the existence of a unilateral contract.

Similarly, there is no factual premise to support a finding that appellant is entitled to recover in quasi-contract for the information supplied by appellant. Where one person has been unjustly enriched at the expense of another he or she must make restitution to the other. . . . However, unjust enrichment is the key to an action for restitution. . . . The vehicle for achieving restitution is a quasi-contract, or contract implied in law. "Unlike true contracts, quasi-contracts are not based on the apparent intention of the parties to undertake the performances in question, nor are they

promises. They are obligations created by law for reasons of justice."
Schott v. Westinghouse Electric Corporation, 436 Pa. 279, 290, 259 A.2d
443, 449 (1969), quoting Restatement (Second) of Contracts, §5, comment
b. at 24. "Quasi-contracts may be found in the absence of any expression of
assent by the party to be charged and may indeed be found in spite of the
party's contrary intention." Schott v. Westinghouse Electric Corporation,
supra. . . . To sustain a claim of unjust enrichment, it must be shown by
the facts pleaded that a person wrongly secured or passively received a
benefit that it would be unconscionable to retain. . . .

As a general rule, volunteers have no right to restitution. Reiver v. Safeguard Precision Products, Inc., 240 Pa. Super. 572, 576, 361 A.2d 371, 373,
(1976); . . . Restatement, Restitution §1, comment (c). Appellant was a
volunteer. It was he who made the unsolicited suggestion that he would
be willing to submit to appellee his copy of "Planning Your Financial Future"
with notations to show which portions had been purloined from "How to
Buy Stocks." His offer to do so was not conditioned upon payment of any
kind. He did not suggest, either expressly or by implication, that he expected
to be paid for this information or for time spent in reducing the same to
writing. Thus, the facts averred in the complaint establish that he was purely a
volunteer and cannot properly be reimbursed for unjust enrichment.[31] . . .

Order affirmed.

REFERENCE: Farnsworth, §2.20
            Murray, §127(B)(1)

C. Tortious Interference with Contract

*STUDY GUIDE: The lawsuit that culminated in the next opinion grew out
of the case of Lumley v. Wagner. [On remand, the defendant ultimately
prevailed at trial by successfully claiming that he believed Johanna
Wagner was legally free of her obligation to Lumley.]*

<hr />

LUMLEY v. GYE
Queen's Bench,
2 El. & Bl. 215, 118 Eng. Rep. 749 (1853)

ERLE, J.* The question raised upon this demurrer is, whether an action
will lie by the proprietor of a theatre against a person who maliciously
procures an entire abandonment of a contract to perform exclusively at

<hr />

31. The parties have not briefed and our decision makes it unnecessary that we consider the damages which appellant would otherwise be entitled to recover. It is clear,
however, that such damages are measured by the reasonable value of services rendered
and not by a percentage of the recovery achieved by appellee as a result of the copyright
infringement first observed by appellant. See: Pulli v. Warren National Bank, 488 Pa. 194, 412
A.2d 464 (1970); Lach v. Fleth, 361 Pa. 340, 64 A.2d 821 (1949).

Sir William Erle (1793-1880) was educated at Winchester and New College, Oxford
(B.C.L.O.) He was called to the bar in 1819 and became a bencher of the Inner Society in

that theatre for a certain time; whereby damage [including special damages on the contract] was sustained? And it seems to me that it will. . . . He who maliciously procures a damage to another by violation of his right ought to be made to indemnify; and that, whether he procures an actionable wrong of a breach of contract. He who procures the non-delivery of goods according to contract may inflict an injury, the same as he who procures the abstraction of goods after delivery; and both ought on the same ground to be made responsible. The remedy on the contract may be inadequate, as where the measure of damages is restricted; or in the case of non-payment of a debt where the damage may be bankruptcy to the creditor who is disappointed, but the measure of damages against the debtor is interest only; or, in the case of the non-delivery of the goods, the disappointment may lead to a heavy forfeiture under a contract to complete a work within a time, but the measure of damages against the vendor of the goods for non-delivery may be only the difference between the contract price and the market value of the goods in question at the time of the breach. In such cases, he who procures the damage maliciously might justly be made responsible beyond the liability of the contractor. . . .

COLERIDGE, J.* . . . [T]he remedy for breach of contract is by the general rule of our law confined to the contracting parties. I need not argue that, if there be any remedy by action against a stranger, it must be by action [in tort for trespass] on the case. Now, to found this, there must be both injury in the strict sense of the word (that is a wrong done), and loss resulting from that injury: the injury or wrong done must be the act of the defendant; and the loss must be a direct and natural, not a remote and indirect, consequence of the defendant's act. Unless there be a loss thus directly and proximately connected with the act, the mere intention, or even the endeavor, to produce it will not found the action. The existence of the intention, that is the malice, will in some cases be an essential ingredient in order to constitute the wrongfulness or injurious nature of the act; but it will neither supply the want of the act itself, or its hurtful consequence: however complete the injuria, and whether with malice or without, if the act be after all sine damno, no action on the case will lie. . . . If a contract has been made between A and B that the latter should go supercargo for the former on a voyage to China, and C, however maliciously, persuades B to break his contract, but in vain, no one, I suppose, would contend that any action would lie against

---

1834. He served in Parliament from 1837 to 1841 and as counsel to the Bank of England prior to his appointment to the Court of Common Pleas in 1844. In the following year, he was transferred to the Queen's Bench, remaining with that body until he was raised to Lord Chief Justice of the Common Pleas in 1859. He retired in 1866. — K.T.

   Sir John Taylor Coleridge (1790-1876) was educated first by his uncle, the Rev. George Coleridge, at Ottery St. Mary, then at Eton and at Corpus Christi College, Oxford. He was called to the bar in 1819, but, under the influence of his uncle, Samuel Taylor Coleridge, he directed his attention for some time to literature. In 1832, he became serjeant-at-law and recorder of Exeter, and in 1835, he took a seat on the King's Bench, where he sat for twenty-three years. Upon retirement, he was sworn as privy council, where his knowledge of ecclesiastical law proved of great service. — K.T.

C. On the other hand, suppose a contract of the same kind made between the same parties to go to Sierra Leone, and *C* urgently and bonafide advises *B* to abandon this contract, which on consideration *B* does, whereby loss results to *A;* I think no one will be found bold enough to maintain that an action would lie against *C.* In the first case no loss has resulted; . . . in the second, though a loss has resulted from the act, that act was not *C*'s, but entirely and exclusively *B*'s own. If so, let malice be added, and let *C* have persuaded, not bonafide but mala-fide and maliciously, still, all other circumstances remaining the same, the same reason applies; for it is malitia sine damno, if the hurtful act is entirely and exclusively *B*'s, which last circumstance cannot be affected by the presence or absence of malice in *C.* . . . To draw a line between advice, persuasion, enticement and procurement is practically impossi-ble in a court of justice; who shall say how much of a free agents' [sic] resolution flows from the interference of other minds, or the independent resolution of his own? This is a matter for the casuist rather than the jurist; still less is it for the juryman. . . . Again, if, instead of limiting our recourse to the agent, actual or constructive, we will go back to the person who immediately persuades or procures him one step, why are we to stop there? The first mover, and the malicious mover too, may be removed several steps backward from the party actually induced to break the contract: why are we not to trace him out? Morally he may be the most guilty. . . . [I]f we go the first step, we can shew no good reason for not going fifty. And, again, I ask how is it that, if the law really be as the plaintiff contends, we have no discussions upon such questions as those in our books, no decisions in our reports? Surely such cases would not have been of rare occurrence: they are not of slight importance, and could hardly have been decided without reference to the Courts in Banc. . . .

[Judgment was for the plaintiff.]

Historical and Relational Background: The Impact of Lumley v. Gye on Johanna Wagner

STUDY GUIDE: Elsewhere in her article, Professor VanderVelde notes that, while finding for Lumley, the jury refused to award more than nominal damages.

LEA S. VANDERVELDE, THE GENDERED ORIGINS OF THE *LUMLEY* DOCTRINE: BINDING MEN'S CONSCIENCES AND WOMEN'S FIDELITY, 101 YALE L.J. 775, 792-793 (1992): Lumley v. Wagner was actually one of two cases, based on the same incident, that played an important role in imposing conditions on an employee's right to quit. In the related case, Lumley v. Gye, Benjamin Lumley sued the rival theater that enticed Madame Wagner away. He sued under the partially statutory, partially common law, cause of action for enticement, which allowed an individual who had an interest in the services of another to sue anyone who interfered with the employee's services by enticing the employee away from his or her contract. Naturally, a rival employer, who hired the departing employee, fell within the scope of potential defendants to these actions.

The lineage of enticement actions is significant in that the cause of action originated in conditions of compulsory labor. One historical antecedent of enticement actions was the English medieval statute of Laborers and Artificers, which required compulsory service of menial laborers and which was brought to the American colonies in various forms. The other significant antecedent was the multitude of cases seeking recovery of runaway slaves and indentured servants.

When the English courts ruled against Johanna Wagner in both cases, they legitimated the employer's use of enticement actions and injunctions to control a class of workers: the professional class under general employment contracts, who had never before been subject to either type of employer control. Historically, only menial laborers had been subject to these actions. Taken together, the effect of these two causes of action was to impose legal and equitable constraints on a performer's election to quit employment. The injunction prevented the performer from using her talents and skills else-where. The enticement action discouraged demand for currently employed performers. In essence, these sanctions increased the employer's leverage over employees contemplating quitting. In Johanna Wagner's case, even though the original contract term was only for three months, the combined effect of these suits kept her off the London stage for four years.

RESTATEMENT (SECOND) OF TORTS

§766. INTENTIONAL INTERFERENCE WITH PERFORMANCE OF CONTRACT BY THIRD PERSON

One who intentionally and improperly interferes with the performance of a contract (except a contract to marry) between another and a third person by inducing or otherwise causing the third person not to perform the contract, is subject to liability to the other for the pecuniary loss resulting to the other from the failure of the third person to perform the contract.

STUDY GUIDE: *The next case is included here to serve two distinct functions: First, it permits a contemporary reconsideration of the action of tortious interference with contract we have just discussed. Is the Texaco v. Pennzoil case really the same as Lumley v. Gye? Second, it provides a transition between the discussion of contract remedies in Part I and the requirements of a contract in Parts II and III. Was there really a contract here for Texaco to interfere with? For now, however, we shall consider only the first of these two issues.*

TEXACO v. PENNZOIL
Court of Appeals of Texas, Houston, First District,
729 S.W.2d 768 (1987)

WARREN, J.*

This is an appeal from a judgment awarding Pennzoil damages for Texaco's tortious interference with a contract between Pennzoil and the "Getty entities" (Getty Oil Company, the Sarah C. Getty Trust, and the J. Paul Getty Museum).

The jury found, among other things, that:

(1) At the end of a board meeting on January 3, 1984, the Getty entities intended to bind themselves to an agreement providing for the purchase of Getty Oil stock, whereby the Sarah C. Getty Trust would own 4/7th of the stock and Pennzoil the remaining 3/7th; and providing for a division of Getty Oil's assets, according to their respective ownership if the Trust and Pennzoil were unable to agree on a restructuring of Getty Oil by December 31, 1984;

(2) Texaco knowingly interfered with the agreement between Pennzoil and the Getty entities;

(3) As a result of Texaco's interference, Pennzoil suffered damages of $7.53 billion;

(4) Texaco's actions were intentional, willful, and in wanton disregard of Pennzoil's rights; and,

(5) Pennzoil was entitled to punitive damages of $3 billion.

The main questions for our determination are: (1) whether the evidence supports the jury's finding that there was a binding contract between the Getty entities and Pennzoil, and that Texaco knowingly induced a breach of such contract; (2) whether the trial court properly instructed the jury on the law pertinent to the case; (3) whether the evidence supported the jury's damage awards; (4) whether the trial court committed reversible error in its admission and exclusion of certain evidence; (5) whether the conduct and posture of the trial judge denied Texaco a fair trial; and (6) whether the judgment violates certain articles of the United States Constitution.

Though many facts are disputed, the parties' main conflicts are over the inferences to be drawn from, and the legal significance of, these facts. There is evidence that for several months in late 1983, Pennzoil had followed with interest the well-publicized dissension between the board of directors of Getty Oil Company and Gordon Getty, who was a director of Getty Oil and also the owner, as trustee, of approximately 40.2% of the outstanding shares of Getty Oil. On December 28, 1983, Pennzoil announced an unsolicited, public tender offer for 16 million shares of Getty Oil at $100 each.

Soon afterwards, Pennzoil contacted both Gordon Getty and a representative of the J. Paul Getty Museum, which held approximately 11.8% of the shares of Getty Oil, to discuss the tender offer and the possible

---

James F. Warren (1932-1990) was educated at the University of Houston Law School (LL.B.) and practiced law privately (1960-1967). He was formerly a judge on the Texas District Court for the 12th Judicial District (1972-1978). Warren was appointed to the Texas Court of Appeals in 1978 and was elected to the same in 1980 and 1986. He served on the bench until his death. — K.T.

purchase of Getty Oil. In the first two days of January 1984, a "Memorandum of Agreement" was drafted to reflect the terms that had been reached in conversations between representatives of Pennzoil, Gordon Getty, and the Museum.

Under the plan set out in the Memorandum of Agreement, Pennzoil and the Trust (with Gordon Getty as trustee) were to become partners on a 3/7ths to 4/7ths basis respectively, in owning and operating Getty Oil. Gordon Getty was to become chairman of the board, and Hugh Liedtke, the chief executive officer of Pennzoil, was to become chief executive officer of the new company.

The Memorandum of Agreement further provided that the Museum was to receive $110 per share for its 11.8% ownership, and that all other outstanding public shares were to be cashed in by the company at $110 per share. Pennzoil was given an option to buy an additional 8 million shares to achieve the desired ownership ratio. The plan also provided that Pennzoil and the Trust were to try in good faith to agree upon a plan to restructure Getty Oil within a year, but if they could not reach an agreement, the assets of Getty Oil were to be divided between them, 3/7ths to Pennzoil and 4/7ths to the Trust.

The Memorandum of Agreement stated that it was subject to approval of the board of Getty Oil, and it was to expire by its own terms if not approved at the board meeting that was to begin on January 2. Pennzoil's CEO, Liedtke, and Gordon Getty, for the Trust, signed the Memorandum of Agreement before the Getty Oil board meeting on January 2, and Harold Williams, the president of the Museum, signed it shortly after the board meeting began. Thus, before it was submitted to the Getty Oil board, the Memorandum of Agreement had been executed by parties who together controlled a majority of the outstanding shares of Getty Oil.

The Memorandum of Agreement was then presented to the Getty Oil board, which had previously held discussions on how the company should respond to Pennzoil's public tender offer. A self-tender by the company to shareholders at $110 per share had been proposed to defeat Pennzoil's tender offer at $100 per share, but no consensus was reached.

The board voted to reject recommending Pennzoil's tender offer to Getty's shareholders, then later also rejected the Memorandum of Agreement price of $110 per share as too low. Before recessing at 3 A.M., the board decided to make a counter-proposal to Pennzoil of $110 per share plus a $10 debenture. Pennzoil's investment banker reacted to this price negatively. In the morning of January 3, Getty Oil's investment banker, Geoffrey Boisi, began calling other companies, seeking a higher bid than Pennzoil's for the Getty Oil shares.

When the board reconvened at 3 P.M. on January 3, a revised Pennzoil proposal was presented, offering $110 per share plus a $3 "stub" that was to be paid after the sale of a Getty Oil subsidiary ("ERC"), from the excess proceeds over $1 billion. Each shareholder was to receive a pro rata share of these excess proceeds, but in any case, a minimum of $3 per share at the end of five years. During the meeting, Boisi briefly informed the board of the status of his inquiries of other companies that might be interested in bidding for the company. He reported some preliminary indications of interest, but no definite bid yet.

The Museum's lawyer told the board that, based on his discussions with Pennzoil, he believed that if the board went back "firm" with an offer of $110 plus a $5 stub, Pennzoil would accept it. After a recess, the Museum's president (also a director of Getty Oil) moved that the Getty board should accept Pennzoil's proposal provided that the stub be raised to $5, and the board voted 15 to 1 to approve this counter-proposal to Pennzoil. The board then voted themselves and Getty's officers indemnity for any liability arising from the events of the past few months. Additionally, the board authorized its executive compensation committee to give "golden parachutes" (generous termination benefits) to the top executives whose positions "were likely to be affected" by the change in management. There was evidence that during another brief recess of the board meeting, the counter-offer of $110 plus a $5 stub was presented to and accepted by Pennzoil. After Pennzoil's acceptance was conveyed to the Getty board, the meeting was adjourned, and most board members left town for their respective homes.

That evening, the lawyers and public relations staff of Getty Oil and the Museum drafted a press release describing the transaction between Pennzoil and the Getty entities. The press release, announcing an agreement in principle on the terms of the Memorandum of Agreement but with a price of $110 plus a $5 stub, was issued on Getty Oil letterhead the next morning, January 4, and later that day, Pennzoil issued an identical press release.

On January 4, Boisi continued to contact other companies, looking for a higher price than Pennzoil had offered. After talking briefly with Boisi, Texaco management called several meetings with its in-house financial planning group, which over the course of the day studied and reported to management on the value of Getty Oil, the Pennzoil offer terms, and a feasible price range at which Getty might be acquired. Later in the day, Texaco hired an investment banker, First Boston, to represent it with respect to a possible acquisition of Getty Oil. Meanwhile, also on January 4, Pennzoil's lawyers were working on a draft of a formal "transaction agreement" that described the transaction in more detail than the outline of terms contained in the Memorandum of Agreement and press release.

On January 5, the Wall Street Journal reported on an agreement reached between Pennzoil and the Getty entities, describing essentially the terms contained in the Memorandum of Agreement. The Pennzoil board met to ratify the actions of its officers in negotiating an agreement with the Getty entities, and Pennzoil's attorneys periodically attempted to contact the other parties' advisors and attorneys to continue work on the transaction agreement.

The board of Texaco also met on January 5, authorizing its officers to make an offer for 100% of Getty Oil and to take any necessary action in connection therewith. Texaco first contacted the Museum's lawyer, Lipton, and arranged a meeting to discuss the sale of the Museum's shares of Getty Oil to Texaco. Lipton instructed his associate, on her way to the meeting in progress of the lawyers drafting merger documents for the Pennzoil/Getty transaction, to not attend that meeting, because he needed her at his meeting with Texaco. At the meeting with Texaco, the Museum outlined various issues it wanted resolved in any transaction with Texaco, and then agreed to sell its 11.8% ownership in Getty Oil.

That evening, Texaco met with Gordon Getty to discuss the sale of the Trust's shares. He was informed that the Museum had agreed to sell its shares to Texaco. Gordon Getty's advisors had previously warned him that the Trust shares might be "locked out" in a minority position if Texaco bought, in addition to the Museum's shares, enough of the public shares to achieve over 50% ownership of the company. Gordon Getty accepted Texaco's offer of $125 per share and signed a letter of his intent to sell his stock to Texaco, as soon as a California temporary restraining order against his actions as trustee was lifted.

At noon on January 6, Getty Oil held a telephone board meeting to discuss the Texaco offer. The board voted to withdraw its previous counterproposal to Pennzoil and unanimously voted to accept Texaco's offer. Texaco immediately issued a press release announcing that Getty Oil and Texaco would merge.

Soon after the Texaco press release appeared, Pennzoil telexed the Getty entities, demanding that they honor their agreement with Pennzoil. Later that day, prompted by the telex, Getty Oil filed a suit in Delaware for declaratory judgment that it was not bound to any contract with Pennzoil. The merger agreement between Texaco and Getty Oil was signed on January 6; the stock purchase agreement with the Museum was signed on January 6; and the stock exchange agreement with the Trust was signed on January 8, 1984. . . .

SPECIAL ISSUE NO. 2

Texaco's next points of error concern the jury's finding in Special Issue No. 2 that Texaco knowingly interfered with the agreement, if so found, between Pennzoil and the Getty entities. . . .

First, Texaco asserts that Pennzoil failed to prove that Texaco had actual knowledge that a contract existed.

New York law requires knowledge by a defendant of the existence of contractual rights as an element of the tort of inducing a breach of that contract. . . . However, the defendant need not have full knowledge of all the detailed terms of the contract. . . .

There is even some indication that a defendant need not have an accurate understanding of the exact legal significance of the facts giving rise to a contractual duty, but rather may be liable if he knows those facts, but is mistaken about whether they constitute a contract. Restatement (Second) of Torts §766, comment i (1977). . . . For example, the commentary to the Restatement (Second) of Torts describes the knowledge requirement as follows:

> *Actor's knowledge of other's contract.* To be subject to liability . . . the actor must have knowledge of the contract with which he is interfering. . . . [I]t is not necessary that the actor appreciate the legal significance of the facts giving rise to the contractual duty. . . . If he knows those facts, he is subject to liability even though he is mistaken as to their legal significance and believes that the agreement is not legally binding. . . .

Sec. 766, comment i. New York's highest court has followed the principles and precepts embodied in the Restatement in this developing area of tort law. . . .

The element of knowledge by the defendant is a question of fact, and proof may be predicated on circumstantial evidence. . . . Since there was no direct evidence of Texaco's knowledge of a contract in this case, the question is whether there was legally and factually sufficient circumstantial evidence from which the trier of fact reasonably could have inferred knowledge. . . .

The jury was not required to accept Texaco's version of events in this case, and this Court may not substitute its own interpretation of the evidence for the decision of the trier of fact. There was legally and factually sufficient evidence to support an inference by the jury that Texaco had the required knowledge of an agreement. Point of Error 49 is overruled.

The second major issue Texaco raises under Special Issue No. 2 is that the evidence was legally and factually insufficient to show that Texaco actively induced breach of the alleged Pennzoil/Getty contract.

A necessary element of the plaintiff's cause of action is a showing that the defendant took an active part in persuading a party to a contract to breach it. . . . Merely entering into a contract with a party with the knowledge of that party's contractual obligations to someone else is not the same as inducing a breach. . . . It is necessary that there be some act of interference or of persuading a party to breach, for example by offering better terms or other incentives, for tort liability to arise. . . . The issue of whether a defendant affirmatively took steps to induce the breach of an existing contract is a question of fact for the jury. . . .

Texaco contends that it did not actively procure the alleged breach and that the required inducement did not occur. Texaco argues that it merely responded to a campaign of active solicitation by Getty Oil and the Museum, who were dissatisfied by the terms of Pennzoil's offer.

There was testimony that on January 2, Getty's investment advisor, Boisi, was instructed to seek a higher price for Getty's shares than Pennzoil had offered. Early on the morning of January 3, Boisi contacted Texaco's president, DeCrane, among others, to tell him that the Getty Oil board was meeting that day and to get a specific expression of interest in Getty's sale. DeCrane told Boisi that Texaco was interested in more information and to keep him informed.

That afternoon, Boisi told the Getty board of directors that he had been calling other potential bidders and that some of those contacts had expressed interest in Getty's sale. After the board recessed, Boisi talked with some of the board members in more detail about his conversations and told them he thought that Getty could get more than Pennzoil's $110 per share.

Later in the evening on January 3, despite Boisi's report of other interest in Getty, the board of Getty Oil voted 15 to 1 to accept "the Pennzoil proposal," provided that the price per share be increased to $110 plus a minimum $5 stub. Pennzoil accepted the higher price, and the board was told that Pennzoil had accepted its counter-proposal. Yet, one of Getty's directors testified, for the defendant, that the board's consensus at that time was to encourage the overall bidding process. Petersen, the chairman of Getty, told Boisi to continue to search for a better price.

On January 4 Texaco called Boisi early in the morning. Getty Oil issued its press release that morning, and it appeared on the Dow Jones broad tape under the headline "Getty Oil Announces Merger." Boisi was not in his office yet, but returned the call later that morning to explain the press release. Boisi testified that he told DeCrane that the Getty board had voted on a price with Pennzoil; that no definitive merger contract had been signed yet, so there was no binding agreement; and that open issues remained for negotiation. Boisi testified that Texaco expressed a heightened degree of interest in Getty, and Texaco's witnesses testified that Texaco's interest in Getty increased as Texaco got more information.

As discussed above, Texaco assembled its in-house financial planning group, which worked all day on January 4 to study Getty and the Pennzoil situation and then reported to management. The evidence of Texaco's strong motivation to acquire Getty's reserves, given Texaco's own declining reserves and high finding costs, is also relevant here. There was testimony that in the afternoon of January 4, Texaco decided to pursue its interest in Getty, and it hired First Boston investment bankers to advise it on the most effective strategy to purchase Getty. Meetings with Texaco executives and First Boston advisors continued through the evening.

There was testimony for Texaco that on January 4, other representatives of the Getty entities told Texaco that Getty Oil wanted to receive bids and would be pleased to hear a proposal from Texaco. These representatives included one of Getty's directors, another Getty advisor from its investment bankers Goldman Sachs, and Getty's chairman. There was testimony that Texaco and its advisors were told that there were other potential competitors for Getty and that Texaco should put its "best shot" forward.

The evidence discussed above on Texaco's calculated formulation and implementation of its ideal strategy to acquire Getty is also inconsistent with its contention that it was merely the passive target of Getty's aggressive solicitation campaign and did nothing more than to accept terms that Getty Oil and the Museum had proposed. The evidence showed that Texaco knew it had to act quickly, and that it had "24 hours" to "stop the train." Texaco's strategy was to approach the Museum first, through its "key person" Lipton, to obtain the Museum's shares, and then to "talk to Gordon." It knew that the Trust instrument permitted Gordon Getty to sell the Trust shares only to avoid a loss, and it knew of the trustee's fear of being left in a powerless minority ownership position at Getty Oil. Texaco notes indicated a deliberate strategy to "create concern that he will take a loss"; "if there's a tender offer and Gordon doesn't tender, then he could wind up with paper"; and "pressure." This evidence contradicts the contention that Texaco passively accepted a deal proposed by the other parties.

Texaco then implemented its plan by contacting the Museum's lawyer, Lipton, arranging for a meeting on the evening of January 5 to discuss an offer by Texaco for Getty Oil. Lipton ordered his associate, on her way to join the meeting of attorneys drafting Pennzoil's transaction agreement, to not attend that meeting, because he needed her assistance in the meeting with Texaco. At the Texaco meeting, Lipton reviewed an outline of points that the Museum wanted covered in any sale of its Getty shares to Texaco; for example, it wanted price protection and an indemnity against any claim brought by Pennzoil. Texaco agreed to the Museum's demands, and the Museum agreed to sell. Lipton testified that though he asked repeatedly about price, the Texaco officers at that time would say only that Texaco's chairman, McKinley, wanted to do the talking about price.

Texaco then contacted the Trust to arrange for a meeting between Texaco's chairman, McKinley, and Gordon Getty, the trustee. There was evidence that the initial meeting did not go well, and Lipton was asked to go over to Gordon Getty's hotel suite to speak with the trustee. Lipton testified that he went over because all the parties wanted to act together, and it was his understanding from Texaco that it wanted the Museum, the Trust, and the company to each "desire" a proposal from Texaco and express that desire. After talking to Gordon Getty, Lipton joined the Texaco people in the lobby and told them that the trustee did want to receive a proposal. When McKinley went back to Gordon Getty's suite, the trustee accepted Texaco's offer before McKinley could even name the price. Texaco initially offered the Getty entities $125 per share, compared to Pennzoil's price of $110 plus a $5 stub (present value $112.50), and eventually paid $128 per share.

Texaco argues that its testimony shows that Getty Oil and the Museum were the real moving forces that eventually led to the Texaco contract. However, we find that there is legally and factually sufficient evidence in the record to support the jury's finding that Texaco actively induced the breach of the Getty entities' agreement with Pennzoil.

. . . We overrule Points of Error 48 and 50, contending that there was no evidence or factually insufficient evidence to support the jury's finding that Texaco knowingly induced the breach of Pennzoil's agreement. . . .

REMITTITUR

In its 65th through 68th points of error, Texaco claims that the jury's award of both compensatory and punitive damages are grossly excessive and prays that we remand on that basis or grant a remittitur. Though the size of the award was indeed large, so were the stakes.

Although the verdict is large and the trial court, in the exercise of its sound discretion, could have set it aside, an appellate court will not disturb the verdict in the absence of circumstances tending to show that it was the result of passion, prejudice, or other improper motive; or that the amount fixed was not the result of a deliberate and conscientious conviction in the minds of the jury and the court; or that the amount was so excessive as to shock a sense of justice of the appellate court. . . .

Though the compensatory damages are large, they are supported by the evidence, and were not the result of mere passion, prejudice, or improper motive. We have received many amicus curae briefs suggesting that the verdict should be greatly reduced or overturned because of the adverse economic impact it would have, if allowed to stand, on certain states and industries, and on Texaco's many shareholders. Though we are mindful of the economic effect the judgment might have on some individuals and institutions, and we are sympathetic with those who might be affected by the verdict through no fault of their own, we are not authorized by law to substitute our judgment for that of the jury, and to make redress as we deem appropriate. Because we are of the opinion that the evidence supports the jury's award of compensatory damages, we do not consider a remittitur of those damages appropriate.

In New York, punitive damages have been allowed in cases where the wrong complained of is morally culpable, or is actuated by evil and reprehensible motives, not only to punish the defendant but to deter him as well as others from indulging in similar conduct in the future. . . . It is not the form of the action that gives the right to punitive damages, but the moral culpability of the defendant. . . . Punitive damages are recoverable in tort actions where there exist ingredients of malice, fraud, oppression, insult, wanton or reckless disregard of plaintiff's rights, or other circumstances of aggravation. Such damages are also recoverable for intentional torts committed wantonly or maliciously. . . .

The jury in our case found that Texaco's actions were intentional, willful, and in wanton disregard of the rights of Pennzoil. We consider this a sufficient finding under New York law to support an award of punitive damages in a tortious inducement of a breach of contract cause of action.

The amount of exemplary or punitive damages to be awarded depends on the facts of the case and rests largely within the sound discretion of the jury. . . . Under Texas law, exemplary damages must be reasonably proportioned to actual damages. . . . Factors to be considered in determining whether an award of exemplary damages is reasonable include: (1) the nature of the wrong, (2) the character of the conduct involved, (3) the degree of culpability of the wrongdoer, (4) the situation and sensibilities of the parties concerned, and (5) the extent to which such conduct offends a public sense of justice and propriety. Id. at 910.

The proportion of punitive damages to actual damages presents no problem. The punitive damages awarded only amount to approximately 40% of actual damages, which in itself is not excessive. Under New York law, punitive damages need bear no ratio to compensatory damages. Hartford Accident & Indemnity Co. v. Village of Hempstead, 48 N.Y.2d 218, 422 N.Y.S.2d 47, 397 N.E.2d 737 (1979).

But when considering the other factors listed above, our task is more difficult. From the evidence, the jury could have concluded that Texaco deliberately seized upon an opportunity to wrest an immensely valuable contract from a less affluent competitor, by using its vast wealth to induce the Museum, Gordon Getty, and Getty Oil to breach an existing contract. The evidence shows that the wrongful conduct came not from servants or mid-level employees but from top level management. Apparently the jury believed that the conduct of Texaco's top level management was less than the public was entitled to expect from persons of such stature. There is no evidence that Texaco interfered with the contract to injure Pennzoil, but the jury could reasonably conclude from the evidence at trial that Texaco cared little if such injury resulted from its interference. Points of Error 61 through 66 and Point 68 are overruled.

Considering the type of action, the conduct involved, and the need for deterrence, we are of the opinion that the punitive damages are excessive and that the trial court abused its discretion in not suggesting a remittitur. Though our Texas guidelines are similar to those of New York, New York courts have adopted a more conservative stance on punitive damages. There is a point where punitive damages may overstate their purpose and serve to confiscate rather than to deter or punish. In this case, punitive damages of one billion dollars are sufficient to satisfy any reason for their being awarded, whether it be punishment, deterrence, or encouragement of the victim to bring legal action. We conclude that the award of punitive damages is excessive by two billion dollars. . . .

Texaco's Points of Error 1 through 66, and 68 through 90 are over-ruled. Point of Error 67 is sustained.

If within thirty days from the date of this judgment, Pennzoil files in this Court a remittitur of two billion dollars, as suggested above, the judgment will be reformed and affirmed as to the award of $7.53 billion in compensatory damages and $1 billion in exemplary damages; otherwise the judgment will be reversed and remanded.

Procedural Background: The Most Expensive Legal Mistake in the History of the World

STUDY GUIDE: Some seasoned lawyers become slovenly about deadlines and other formalities. A common attitude is that "we can always get an extension" or "we can always amend." This excerpt from a fascinating journalistic study of the Texaco-Pennzoil lawsuit describes how such an attitude on the part of some unknown (to us) attorney led to the largest jury verdict in history. When reading it keep in mind the following (under)statement by Judge Solomon Casseb, Jr., the Texas state trial judge who handled the case: "Home territory does help." Finally, note Judge Brown's opinion that "the existence or nonexistence of a contract is a question of the intentions of the parties." We shall return to this issue in Part III when we consider the element of enforceability.

THOMAS PETZINGER, JR., OIL AND HONOR: THE TEXACO-PENNZOIL WARS 251-262 (1987): Pennzoil's hearing before Judge Grover Brown of the Delaware Chancery Court on January 25, 1984, made a few things very plain. Hard feelings abounded, especially on the Pennzoil side; [Pennzoil's President J. Hugh] Liedtke's Houston law firm of Baker Botts — the same firm that had failed to get the definitive agreement signed — would also handle the courtroom work, and they were willing to play rough. In addition, it was clear that the battle had been transformed into a full-employment case for lawyers some thirty were in attendance, with the total legal bill already approaching $1 million. . . .

After a full day of arguments, Judge Brown dismissed the lawyers, promising to render a decision . . . as soon as possible. "This is a massive task," he said. . . .

A week later, on February 6, 1984, Delaware Judge Brown handed down a forty-nine page opinion with the last paragraph reading: "The application of Pennzoil for preliminary injunction is denied. It is so ordered." For Hugh Liedtke, Getty Oil was gone for good.

But what the judge wrote on the preceding forty-eight pages would send a shock wave through the law. . . .

. . . Under the law of New York, the existence or nonexistence of a contract is a question of the intention of the parties . . . to be determined objectively, based on their expressed words and deeds as manifested at the time. . . .

I can only conclude that on the present record Pennzoil has made a sufficient preliminary showing that in all probability a contract did come into being between the four parties.

The judge then turned his attention to whether Texaco was legally responsible. "The point is a close one," he said.

I have no doubt that Texaco deliberately set out to use what are said to be its superior financial resources in an effort to wrest the acquisition of an interest in Getty from Pennzoil, and to acquire all of Getty for itself. But on the present record, I cannot conclude that Texaco did so with full knowledge that a contract had already been entered into. . . .

But despite everything else the judge had to say, he ultimately refused to thwart the Texaco merger and award three-sevenths of Getty Oil to Pennzoil. Pennzoil could obtain an injunction only by proving that it had no other way to make itself whole. And Pennzoil did have a recourse, the judge said. It could present the case all over again at a full-blown trial, right in Delaware, and try to convince a judge to award it money instead of oil-in-the-ground.

Seldom do judicial opinions circulate as quickly as did Judge Brown's. . . . Judge Brown did not know that while he was writing his opinion in Pennzoil v. Getty, a federal appeals court had quietly reversed the very lower-court decision [involving SCM Corporation] on which Brown had relied in his finding that Pennzoil probably did have a contract. SCM, the appeals court found, had reserved the right "not to be bound" before a definitive agreement had been signed.

"There are still situations," the appeals court said, four days before Brown published his opinion, "where the absence of a signed, formal agreement is fatal."

. . . But Judge Brown's denial of Pennzoil's demand for an injunction did not free Pennzoil to go running into the Texas courts; Pennzoil had started the lawsuit in Delaware, and by all legal protocol was bound to see the case through to completion there. Pennzoil *could* ask the Delaware judge for permission to dismiss the case there and file it in a state court elsewhere. But Texaco and the Getty group were certain to put up a fierce fight to remain in the familiar jurisdiction of Delaware. Moreover, there was no clear jurisdiction for suing the entire Getty group in Texas: Gordon [Getty] lived in San Francisco, and the museum and the [Getty] company were headquartered in Los Angeles.

But while studying the unfamiliar (to him) terrain of the Delaware courts, [Baker & Botts' Irv] Terrell had come upon a seldom-used rule: If someone fails to file a formal answer to a lawsuit, the lawsuit may be dismissed at any stage of the case — without even asking the judge for permission. Getty Oil had filed a response. So had the trust and the museum. *Texaco hadn't.* As near as Terrell could tell, Pennzoil was now free to drop Texaco from the Delaware lawsuit without even having to ask the judge for permission, then refile the case anywhere in the country where both companies had operations. That, of course, meant Hugh Liedtke's Houston.

While awaiting the decision on the injunction motion, Terrell discussed the move to nonsuit Texaco with the Pennzoil local law firm in Delaware, which agreed that the move just might succeed. However, special security measures were required. The Chancery Court of Delaware is a genteel court, where local custom requires the lawyers on one side of a case to notify their adversaries in advance of any filings. Doing so in this case would obviously permit Texaco to hustle up a piece of paper formally answering Pennzoil's suit.

"Maintain silence," Terrell told his cohorts in Delaware. "We're not gonna follow this gentlemanly rule."

At midnight the day that Judge Brown finally dashed Pennzoil's hope of restoring its deal, Terrell conferred with his partner [John] Jeffers and with Liedtke, who were in Washington appearing before the Federal Trade Commission in yet another effort to thwart the Texaco deal. (It too would fail.) Liedtke gave the go-ahead. Early the following morning, Pennzoil gave the Delaware court clerk a $25,000 check to cover its costs in the case and filed a one-sentence document: "Please take notice that plaintiff, Pennzoil Company, hereby dismisses this action without prejudice as to defendant Texaco Inc. pursuant to Chancery Court Rule 41(a)(1)(i)."

Fifteen minutes later, Terrell filed the case of Pennzoil Company v. Texaco Incorporated, Cause #84-05905, in the District Court of Harris County, Texas. In the last paragraph of the twenty-page document, Pennzoil made the greatest damages demand ever seen in Harris County, and probably anywhere in the world: "Pennzoil respectfully prays that upon trial by jury, this Court enter judgment against Texaco in such amount as is proper, but in no event less than $7,000,000,000 actual damages and $7,000,000,000 punitive damages."

The amounts would later be increased to $7.53 billion each, after Pennzoil had more fully refined its case.

MUTUAL ASSENT

4

REACHING AN AGREEMENT

Formation of a contract requires two basic elements: (1) the mutual *assent* of the parties and (2) some showing that this assent is the *kind* that the law will enforce. Each of the chapters in Part II discusses some aspect of mutual assent. The chapters in Part III discuss the element of enforceability. In this chapter, we begin our study of mutual assent by distinguishing, in Section A, between the "subjective" and "objective" conceptions of assent. Is it necessary that a person consciously make a commitment to another person, or is it enough that she *appeared* to be committing herself? We shall see that, while it is commonly said that contract law adopts the objective approach, what is called the "objective" approach contains a "subjective" element as well. We then examine various doctrines that courts use to ascertain the existence of mutual assent — particularly those that concern the making of offers (Section B) and acceptances (Section C) — before considering, in Section D, how these doctrines may or may not apply in the context of electronic commerce.

A.   THE OBJECTIVE THEORY OF ASSENT

In Dickinson v. Dodds, which we shall read in the next section, James, L.J., stated: "It must, to constitute a contract, appear that the two minds were at one at the same moment of time . . ."; and that "the existence of the same mind between the two parties . . . is essential in point of law to the making of an agreement." This idea is often referred to as the requirement that there be a "meeting of the minds." In this section we shall begin to examine whether this is an accurate description of contract formation. We will return to this issue in Chapter 5 when discussing methods of interpreting assent. When we do, we will consider what difference, if any, may exist between the objective theory of assent in the contract *formation* stage and an objective approach to contract *interpretation*.

STUDY GUIDE: What does the next case suggest for a claim that contracts require a "meeting of the minds"? According to the court, are the subjective mental states of the parties entirely irrelevant?

243

EMBRY v. HARGADINE, McKITTRICK DRY GOODS CO.
St. Louis Court of Appeals,
127 Mo. App. 383, 105 S.W. 777 (1907)

GOODE, J.* . . . The appellant was an employee of the respondent company under a written contract to expire December 15, 1903, at a salary of $2,000 per annum. His duties were to attend to the sample department of respondent, of which he was given complete charge. It was his business to select samples for the traveling salesmen of the company, which is a wholesale dry goods concern, to use in selling goods to retail merchants. Appellant contends that on December 23, 1903, he was re-engaged by respondent, through its president, Thos. H. McKittrick, for another year at the same compensation and for the same duties stipulated in his previous written contract. On March 1, 1904, he was discharged, having been notified in February, that on account of the necessity of retrenching expenses, his services and that of some other employees, would no longer be required. The respondent company contends that its president never re-employed appellant after the termination of his written contract and hence that it had a right to discharge him when it chose. The point with which we are concerned requires an epitome of the testimony of appellant and the counter-testimony of McKittrick, the president of the company, in reference to the alleged re-employment. Appellant testified that several times prior to the termination of his written contract on December 15, 1903, he had endeavored to get an understanding with McKittrick for another year, but had been put off from time to time; that on December 23d, eight days after the expiration of said contract, he called on McKittrick, in the latter's office, and said to him that as appellant's written employment had lapsed eight days before, and as there were only a few days between then and the 1st of January in which to seek employment with other firms, if respondent wished to retain his services longer he must have a contract for another year or he would quit respondent's service then and there; that he had been put off twice before and wanted an understanding or contract at once so that he could go ahead without worry; that McKittrick asked him how he was getting along in his department, and appellant said he was very busy as they were in the height of the season getting men out — had about 110 salesmen on the line and others in preparation; that McKittrick then said:

— Go ahead, you're all right; get your men out and don't let that worry you;

that appellant took McKittrick at his word and worked until February 15th without any question in his mind. It was on February 15th that he was notified his services would be discontinued on March 1st. McKittrick denied

---

Richard Livingson Goode (1855-1927) graduated from Drury College, Springfield, Missouri (M.A.), and thereafter studied law with a practitioner in Springfield. After 20 years of practice, he became a judge on the St. Louis Court of Appeals, sitting from 1901 to 1910; during the last five years of that period, he was also a professor of law at Washington University. Judge Goode became dean of that law school in 1915 and, with the exception of service on the Supreme Court of Missouri from 1919 to 1921, remained in that position until his death. — C.R.

this conversation as related by appellant and said that when accosted by the latter on December 23rd, he (McKittrick) was working on his books in order to get out a report for stockholders' meeting and when appellant said if he did not get a contract he would leave, that he (McKittrick) said:

> Mr. Embry, I am just getting ready for the stockholders' meeting tomorrow, I have no time to take it up now; I have told you before I would not take it up until I had these matters out of the way; you will have to see me at a later time. I said: "Go back upstairs and get your men out on the road." I may have asked him one or two other questions relative to the department, I don't remember. The whole conversation did not take more than a minute.

Embry also swore that when he was notified he would be discharged, he complained to McKittrick about it, as being a violation of their contract, and McKittrick said it was due to the action of the board of directors, and not to any personal action of his and that others would suffer by what the board had done as well as Embry. Appellant request[ed] an instruction to the jury setting out in substance the conversation between him and McKittrick according to his version and declaring that those facts, if found to be true, constituted a contract between the parties that defendant would pay the plaintiff the sum of $2,000 for another year, provided the jury believed from the evidence that plaintiff commenced said work believing he was to have $2,000 for the year's work. This instruction was refused but the court gave another embodying in substance appellant's version of the conversation, and declaring it made a contract

> if you (the jury) find both parties thereby intended and did contract with each other for plaintiff's employment for one year from and including December 23, 1903, at a salary of $2,000 per annum.

. . . It is assigned for error that the court required the jury, in order to return a verdict for appellant, not only to find the conversation occurred as appellant swore, but that both parties intended by such conversation to contract with each other for plaintiff's employment for the year from December, 1903, at a salary of $2,000. If it appeared from the record that there was dispute between the parties as to the terms on which appellant wanted re-employment, there might have been sound reason for inserting this clause in the instruction; but no issue was made that they split on terms; the testimony of McKittrick tending to prove only that he refused to enter into a contract with appellant regarding another year's employment until the annual meeting of stockholders was out of the way. Indeed, as to the proposed terms McKittrick agrees with Embry; for the former swore as follows:

> Mr. Embry said he wanted to know *about the renewal of his contract*; said if he did not have the contract made he would leave.

As the two witnesses coincided as to the terms of the proposed re-employment, there was no reason for inserting the abovementioned clause in the instruction in order that it might be settled by the jury whether or not plaintiff, if employed for one year from December 23, 1903, was to be paid

$2,000 a year. Therefore it remains to determine whether or not this part of the instruction was a correct statement of the law in regard to what was necessary to constitute a contract between the parties; that is to say, whether the formation of a contract by what, according to Embry was said, depended on the intention of both Embry and McKittrick. Or, to put the question more precisely, did what was said constitute a contract of re-employment on the previous terms irrespective of the intention or purpose of McKittrick? Judicial opinion and elementary treatises abound in statement of the rule that to constitute a contract there must be a meeting of the minds of the parties and both must agree to the same thing in the same sense. Generally speaking this may be true; but it is not literally or universally true. That is to say, the inner intention of parties to a conversation subsequently alleged to create a contract, cannot either make a contract of what transpired or prevent one from arising, if the words used were sufficient to constitute a contract. In so far as their intention is an influential element, it is only such intention as the words or acts of the parties indicate; not one secretly cherished which is inconsistent with those words or acts. The rule is thus stated by a text-writer and many decisions are cited in support of his test:

> The primary object of construction in contract law is to discover the intention of the parties. This intention in express contracts is, in the first instance embodied in the words which the parties have used and is to be deduced therefrom. This rule applies to oral contracts, as well as to contracts in writing, and is the rule recognized by courts of equity. . . .

So it is said in another work:

> Now this measure of the contents of the promise will be found to coincide, in the usual dealings of men of good faith and ordinary competence, both with the actual intention of the promisor and with the actual expectation of the promisee. But this is not a constant or a necessary coincidence. In exceptional cases a promisor may be bound to perform something which he did not intend to promise, or a promisee may not be entitled to require that performance which he understood to be promised to him. . . .

In Brewington v. Mesker, 51 Mo. App. 348, 356, it is said that the meetings of minds which is essential to the formation of a contract, is not determined by the secret intention of the parties, but by their expressed intention, which may be wholly at a variance with the former. In Machine Co. v. Criswell, 58 Mo. App. 471, an instruction was given on the issue of whether the sale of a machine occurred, which told the jury that an intention on the part of the seller to pass the title and of the purchaser to receive and accept the machine for the purpose of making it his own, was essential to a sale, and if the jury believed such intention did not exist in the minds of both parties at the time and was not made known to each other, then there was no sale notwithstanding the delivery. In commenting on this instruction the court said:

> The latter clause of the instruction is erroneous and misleading. It is true that in every case of purchase the question of sale or no sale is a matter of intention; but such intention must always be determined by the conduct, acts, and

express declarations, of the parties and not by the secret intention existing in the mind or minds of the contracting parties. If the validity of such a contract depended on the secret intentions of the parties, then no oral contract of sale could be relied on with safety. . . .

In Smith v. Hughes, L.R. 6 Q.B. 597, 607, it was said:

If, whatever a man's real intention may be, he so conducts himself that a reasonable man would believe that he was assenting to the terms proposed by the other party, and that other party upon that belief enters into the contract with him, the man thus conducting himself would be equally bound as if he had intended to agree to the other party's terms.

And that doctrine was adopted in Phillip v. Gallant, 62 N.Y. 256. In 9 Cyc. 245, we find the following text:

The law imputes to a person an intention corresponding to the reasonable meaning of his words and acts. It judges his intention by his outward expressions and excludes all questions in regard to his unexpressed intention. If his words or acts, judged by a reasonable standard, manifest an intention to agree in regard to the matter in question, that agreement is established, and it is immaterial what may be the real but unexpressed state of his mind on the subject.

Even more pointed was the language of Baron Bramwell in Brown v. Hare, 3 Hurlst. & N. *484, *495:

Intention is immaterial till it manifests itself in an act. If a man intends to buy, and says so to the intended seller, and he intends to sell and says so to the intended buyer, there is a contract of sale; and so there would be if nether [sic] had the intention.

In view of those authorities we hold that though McKittrick may not have intended to employ Embry by what transpired between them according to the latter's testimony, yet if what McKittrick said would have been taken by a reasonable man to be an employment, and Embry so understood it, it constituted a valid contract of employment for the ensuing year. The next question is whether or not the language used was of that character; namely, was such that Embry, as a reasonable man, might consider he was re-employed for the ensuing year on the previous terms, and act accordingly. We do not say that in every instance it would be for the court to pronounce on this question, because, peradventure, instances might arise in which there would be such an ambiguity in the language relied on to show an assent by the obligor to the proposal of the obligee, that it would be for the jury to say whether a reasonable mind would take it to signify acceptance of the proposal. . . . In Lancaster v. Elliott, 28 Mo. App. 86, 92, the opinion, as to the immediate point, reads:

The interpretation of a contract in writing is always a matter of law for determination by the court, and equally so, upon like principles, is the question what acts and words, in nearly every case, will suffice to constitute an acceptance by one party, of a proposal submitted by the other, so that contract or agreement thereby becomes matured.

The general rule is that it is for the court to construe the effect of writings relied on to make a contract and also the effect of unambiguous oral words. . . . However, if the words are in dispute, the question of whether they were used or not is for the jury. . . . With the rules of law in mind, let us recur to the conversation of December 23d between Embry and McKittrick as related by the former. Embry was demanding a renewal of his contract, saying he had been put off from time to time and that he had only a few days before the end of the year in which to seek employment from other houses, and that he would quit then and there unless he was re-employed. McKittrick inquired how he was getting along with the department and Embry said they (i.e., the employees of the department) were very busy getting out salesmen; whereupon McKittrick said:

Go ahead, you are all right; get your men out and do not let that worry you.

We think no reasonable man would construe that answer to Embry's demand that he be employed for another year, otherwise than as an assent to the demand, and that Embry had the right to rely on it as an assent. The natural inference is, though we do not find it testified to, that Embry was at work getting samples ready for the salesmen to use during the ensuing season. Now when he was complaining of the worry and mental distress he was under because of his uncertainty about the future, and his urgent need, either of an immediate contract with respondent, or a refusal by it to make one, leaving him free to seek employment elsewhere, McKittrick must have answered as he did for the purpose of assuring appellant that any apprehension was needless, as appellant's services would be retained by the respondent. The answer was unambiguous, and we rule that if the conversation was according to appellant's version and he understood he was employed, it constituted in law a valid contract of re-employment, and the court erred in making the formation of a contract depend on a finding that both parties intended to make one. It was only necessary that Embry, as a reasonable man, had a right to and did so understand. . . .

The judgment is reversed and the cause remanded. All concur.

THE OBJECTIVE THEORY OF ASSENT: A PROBLEM

Suppose that McKittrick wrote the following memorandum to his Board of Directors immediately after Embry left his office. Would it provide objective evidence of his intent? Would it be relevant evidence on the issue of McKittrick's objective assent?

MCKITTRICK DRY GOODS COMPANY
Interoffice Memorandum

TO: The Board of Directors
FROM: Tom McKittrick, Pres.
DATE: December 23, 1903
RE: Conversation with employee Embry

In case it is ever disputed, I wish to report an encounter I had today with one of our employees. Today, Embry, our sample manager, came to see me and demanded that I renew his contract for another year. He told me that if I refused, he would quit on the spot. As you know we are in the height of our busiest season and I was not about to agree to anything with a gun to my head. I agreed to nothing and simply told him to go back to work, which, to my great relief, he did.

I must advise you that since we no longer have a long-term employment contract with Embry, and since we cannot find a replacement in the middle of the season, the success of our sales operation is at the mercy of this one man. I am hopeful, however, that he will decide to stay on through our busy season. After that you may wish to replace him.

Study Guide: *According to the objective theory, was Ida Zehmer's testimony about her conversation with her husband relevant to the issue of assent? As in* Embry, *consider whether the objective approach entirely precludes consideration of subjective understanding. For example, would the court have reached the same conclusion had Lucy subjectively understood Zehmer to have been joking?*

LUCY v. ZEHMER

Supreme Court of Appeals of Virginia,
196 Va. 493, 84 S.E.2d 516 (1954)

BUCHANAN, J.* delivered the opinion of the court.

This suit was instituted by W. O. Lucy and J. C. Lucy, complainants, against A. H. Zehmer and Ida S. Zehmer, his wife, defendants, to have specific performance of a contract by which it was alleged the Zehmers had sold to W. O. Lucy a tract of land owned by A. H. Zehmer in Dinwiddie county containing 471.6 acres, more or less, known as the Ferguson farm, for $50,000. J. C. Lucy, the other complainant, is a brother of W. O. Lucy, to whom W. O. Lucy transferred a half interest in his alleged purchase.

The instrument sought to be enforced was written by A. H. Zehmer on December 20, 1952, in these words: "We hereby agree to sell to W. O. Lucy the Ferguson Farm complete for $50,000.00, title satisfactory to buyer," and signed by the defendants, A. H. Zehmer and Ida S. Zehmer.

The answer of A. H. Zehmer admitted that at the time mentioned W. O. Lucy offered him $50,000 cash for the farm, but that he, Zehmer, considered that the offer was made in jest; that so thinking, and both he and Lucy having had several drinks, he wrote out "the memorandum" quoted above and induced his wife to sign it; that he did not deliver the memorandum to Lucy, but that Lucy picked it up, read it, put it in his pocket, attempted to offer

---

*Archibald C. Buchanan (1890-1979) attended Hampden-Sydney College (A.B.) and Washington and Lee University (LL.B.). During his career, Buchanan had a general practice in the state and federal courts (1915-1927); was a member of the law partnership of Chapman, Peery and Buchanan, Tazewell, Virginia; and was mayor of Tazewell (1917-1921). After 20 years as judge of the twenty-second judicial circuit of Virginia, he served as justice of the Supreme Court of Appeals of Virginia from 1946 until his retirement in 1969. — K.T.

Zehmer $5 to bind the bargain, which Zehmer refused to accept, and realizing for the first time that Lucy was serious, Zehmer assured him that he had no intention of selling the farm and that the whole matter was a joke. Lucy left the premises insisting that he had purchased the farm.

Depositions were taken and the decree appealed from was entered holding that the complainants had failed to establish their right to specific performance, and dismissing their bill. The assignment of error is to this action of the court.

W. O. Lucy, a lumberman and farmer, thus testified in substance: He had known Zehmer for fifteen or twenty years and had been familiar with the Ferguson farm for ten years. Seven or eight years ago he had offered Zehmer $20,000 for the farm which Zehmer had accepted, but the agreement was verbal and Zehmer backed out. On the night of December 20, 1952, around eight o'clock, he took an employee to McKenney, where Zehmer lived and operated a restaurant, filling station and motor court. While there he decided to see Zehmer and again try to buy the Ferguson farm. He entered the restaurant and talked to Mrs. Zehmer until Zehmer came in. He asked Zehmer if he had sold the Ferguson farm. Zehmer replied that he had not. Lucy said, "I bet you wouldn't take $50,000.00 for that place." Zehmer replied, "Yes, I would too; you wouldn't give fifty." Lucy said he would and told Zehmer to write up an agreement to that effect. Zehmer took a restaurant check and wrote on the back of it, "I do hereby agree to sell to W. O. Lucy the Ferguson Farm for $50,000 complete." Lucy told him he had better change it to "We" because Mrs. Zehmer would have to sign it too. Zehmer then tore up what he had written, wrote the agreement quoted above and asked Mrs. Zehmer, who was at the other end of the counter ten or twelve feet away, to sign it. Mrs. Zehmer said she would for $50,000 and signed it. Zehmer brought it back and gave it to Lucy, who offered him $5 which Zehmer refused, saying, "You don't need to give me any money, you got the agreement there signed by both of us."

The discussion leading to the signing of the agreement, said Lucy, lasted thirty or forty minutes, during which Zehmer seemed to doubt that Lucy could raise $50,000. Lucy suggested the provision for having the title examined and Zehmer made the suggestion that he would sell it "complete, everything there," and stated that all he had on the farm was three heifers.

Lucy took a partly filled bottle of whiskey into the restaurant with him for the purpose of giving Zehmer a drink if he wanted it. Zehmer did, and he and Lucy had one or two drinks together. Lucy said that while he felt the drinks he took he was not intoxicated, and from the way Zehmer handled the transaction he did not think he was either.

December 20 was on Saturday. Next day Lucy telephoned to J. C. Lucy and arranged with the latter to take a half interest in the purchase and pay half of the consideration. On Monday he engaged an attorney to examine the title. The attorney reported favorably on December 31 and on January 2 Lucy wrote Zehmer stating that the title was satisfactory, that he was ready to pay the purchase price in cash and asking when Zehmer would be ready to close the deal. Zehmer replied by letter, mailed on January 13, asserting that he had never agreed or intended to sell.

Mr. and Mrs. Zehmer were called by the complainants as adverse witnesses. Zehmer testified in substance as follows:

He bought this farm more than ten years ago for $11,000. He had had twenty-five offers, more or less, to buy it, including several from Lucy, who had never offered any specific sum of money. He had given them all the same answer, that he was not interested in selling it. On this Saturday night before Christmas it looked like everybody and his brother came by there to have a drink. He took a good many drinks during the afternoon and had a pint of his own. When he entered the restaurant around eight-thirty Lucy was there and he could see that he was "pretty high." He said to Lucy, "Boy, you got some good liquor, drinking, ain't you?" Lucy then offered him a drink. "I was already high as a Georgia pine, and didn't have any more better sense than to pour another great big slug out and gulp it down, and he took one too."

After they had talked a while Lucy asked whether he still had the Ferguson farm. He replied that he had not sold it and Lucy said, "I bet you wouldn't take $50,000.00 for it." Zehmer asked him if he would give $50,000 and Lucy said yes. Zehmer replied, "You haven't got $50,000 in cash." Lucy said he did and Zehmer replied that he did not believe it. They argued "pro and con for a long time," mainly about "whether he had $50,000 in cash that he could put up right then and buy that farm."

Finally, said Zehmer, Lucy told him if he didn't believe he had $50,000, "you sign that piece of paper here and say you will take $50,000.00 for the farm." He, Zehmer, "just grabbed the back off of a guest check there" and wrote on the back of it. At that point in his testimony Zehmer asked to see what he had written to "see if I recognize my own handwriting." He examined the paper and exclaimed, "Great balls of fire, I got 'Firgerson' for Ferguson. I have got satisfactory spelled wrong. I don't recognize that writing if I would see it, wouldn't know it was mine."

After Zehmer had, as he described it, "scribbled this thing off," Lucy said, "Get your wife to sign it." Zehmer walked over to where she was and she at first refused to sign but did so after he told her that he "was just needling him [Lucy], and didn't mean a thing in the world, that I was not selling the farm." Zehmer then

> took it back over there . . . and I was still looking at the dern thing. I had the drink right there by my hand, and I reached over to get a drink, and he said, "Let me see it." He reached and picked it up, and when I looked back again he had it in his pocket and he dropped a five dollar bill over there, and he said, "Here is five dollars payment on it." . . . I said, "Hell no, that is beer and liquor talking. I am not going to sell you the farm. I have told you that too many times before."

Mrs. Zehmer testified that when Lucy came into the restaurant he looked as if he had had a drink. When Zehmer came in he took a drink out of a bottle that Lucy handed him. She went back to help the waitress who was getting things ready for next day. Lucy and Zehmer were talking but she did not pay too much attention to what they were saying. She heard Lucy ask Zehmer if he had sold the Ferguson farm, and Zehmer replied that he had not and did not want to sell it. Lucy said, "I bet you wouldn't take $50,000 cash for that farm," and Zehmer replied, "You haven't got $50,000 cash." Lucy said, "I can get it." Zehmer said he might form a company and get it, "but you haven't got $50,000.00 cash to pay me tonight." Lucy asked him if he would put it in writing that he would sell him this farm. Zehmer then wrote on the back of a pad, "I agree to sell the Ferguson Place to W. O. Lucy for $50,000.00 cash." Lucy said, "All right, get your wife to sign it." Zehmer came back to where she was standing and said, "You want to put your name to this?" She said "No," but he said in an undertone, "It is nothing but a joke," and she signed it.

She said that only one paper was written and it said: "I hereby agree to sell," but the "I" had been changed to "We." However, she said she read what she signed and was then asked, "When you read 'We hereby agree to sell to W. O. Lucy,' what did you interpret that to mean, that particular phrase?" She said she thought that was a cash sale that night; but she also said that when she read that part about "title satisfactory to buyer" she understood that if the title was good Lucy would pay $50,000 but if the title was bad he would have a right to reject it, and that that was her understanding at the time she signed her name.

On examination by her own counsel she said that her husband laid this piece of paper down after it was signed; that Lucy said to let him see it, took it, folded it and put it in his wallet, then said to Zehmer, "Let me give you $5.00," but Zehmer said, "No, this is liquor talking. I don't want to sell the farm, I have told you that I want my son to have it. This is all a joke." Lucy then said at least twice, "Zehmer, you have sold your farm," wheeled around and started for the door. He paused at the door and said, "I will bring you $50,000.00 tomorrow. . . . No, tomorrow is Sunday. I will bring it to you Monday." She said you could tell definitely that he was drinking and she said to her husband, "You should have taken him home," but he said, "Well, I am just about as bad off as he is."

The waitress referred to by Mrs. Zehmer testified that when Lucy first came in "he was mouthy." When Zehmer came in they were laughing and joking and she thought they took a drink or two. She was sweeping and cleaning up for next day. She said she heard Lucy tell Zehmer, "I will give you so much for the farm," and Zehmer said, "You haven't got that much." Lucy answered, "Oh, yes, I will give you that much." Then "they jotted down something on paper . . . and Mr. Lucy reached over and took it, said let me see it." He looked at it, put it in his pocket and in about a minute he left. She was asked whether she saw Lucy offer Zehmer any money and replied, "He had five dollars laying up there, they didn't take it." She said Zehmer told Lucy he didn't want his money "because he didn't have enough money to pay for his property, and wasn't going to sell his farm." Both of them appeared to be drinking right much, she said.

She repeated on cross-examination that she was busy and paying no attention to what was going on. She was some distance away and did not see either of them sign the paper. She was asked whether she saw Zehmer put the agreement down on the table in front of Lucy, and her answer was this: "Time he got through writing whatever it was on the paper, Mr. Lucy reached over and said, 'Let's see it.' He took it and put it in his pocket," before showing it to Mrs. Zehmer. Her version was that Lucy kept raising his offer until it got to $50,000.

The defendants insist that the evidence was ample to support their contention that the writing sought to be enforced was prepared as a bluff or dare to force Lucy to admit that he did not have $50,000; that the whole matter was a joke; that the writing was not delivered to Lucy and no binding contract was ever made between the parties.

It is an unusual, if not bizarre, defense. When made to the writing admittedly prepared by one of the defendants and signed by both, clear evidence is required to sustain it.

In his testimony Zehmer claimed that he "was high as a Georgia pine," and that the transaction "was just a bunch of two doggoned drunks bluffing to see who could talk the biggest and say the most." That claim is inconsistent with his attempt to testify in great detail as to what was said and what was done. It is contradicted by other evidence as to the condition of both parties, and rendered of no weight by the testimony of his wife that when Lucy left the restaurant she suggested that Zehmer drive him home. The record is convincing that Zehmer was not intoxicated to the extent of being unable to comprehend the nature and consequences of the instrument he executed, and hence that instrument is not to be invalidated on that ground. . . . It was in fact conceded by defendants' counsel in oral argument that under the evidence Zehmer was not too drunk to make a valid contract.

The evidence is convincing also that Zehmer wrote two agreements, the first one beginning "I hereby agree to sell." Zehmer first said he could not remember about that, then that "I don't think I wrote but one out." Mrs. Zehmer said that what he wrote was "I hereby agree," but that the "I" was changed to "We" after that night. The agreement that was written and signed is in the record and indicates no such change. Neither are the mistakes in spelling that Zehmer sought to point out readily apparent.

The appearance of the contract, the fact that it was under discussion for forty minutes or more before it was signed; Lucy's objection to the first draft because it was written in the singular, and he wanted Mrs. Zehmer to sign it also; the rewriting to meet that objection and the signing by Mrs. Zehmer; the discussion of what was to be included in the sale, the provision for the examination of the title, the completeness of the instrument that was executed, the taking possession of it by Lucy with no request or suggestion by either of the defendants that he give it back, are facts which furnish persuasive evidence that the execution of the contract was a serious business transaction rather than a casual, jesting matter as defendants now contend.

On Sunday, the day after the instrument was signed on Saturday night, there was a social gathering in a home in the town of McKenney at which there were general comments that the sale had been made. Mrs. Zehmer testified that on that occasion as she passed by a group of people, including Lucy, who were talking about the transaction, $50,000 was mentioned, whereupon she stepped up and said, "Well, with the high-price whiskey you were drinking last night you should have paid more. That was cheap." Lucy testified that at that time Zehmer told him that he did not want to "stick" him or hold him to the agreement because he, Lucy, was too tight and didn't know what he was doing, to which Lucy replied that he was not too tight; that he had been stuck before and was going through with it. Zehmer's version was that he said to Lucy: "I am not trying to claim it wasn't a deal on account of the fact the price was too low. If I had wanted to sell $50,000.00 would be a good price, in fact I think you would get stuck at $50,000.00." A disinterested witness testified that what Zehmer said to

Lucy was that "he was going to let him up off the deal, because he thought he was too tight, didn't know what he was doing. Lucy said something to the effect that 'I have been stuck before and I will go through with it.'"

If it be assumed, contrary to what we think the evidence shows, that Zehmer was jesting about selling his farm to Lucy and that the transaction was intended by him to be a joke, nevertheless the evidence shows that Lucy did not so understand it but considered it to be a serious business transaction and the contract to be binding on the Zehmers as well as on himself. The very next day he arranged with his brother to put up half the money and take a half interest in the land. The day after that he employed an attorney to examine the title. The next night, Tuesday, he was back at Zehmer's place and there Zehmer told him for the first time, Lucy said, that he wasn't going to sell and he told Zehmer, "You know you sold that place fair and square." After receiving the report from his attorney that the title was good he wrote to Zehmer that he was ready to close the deal.

Not only did Lucy actually believe, but the evidence shows he was warranted in believing, that the contract represented a serious business transaction and a good faith sale and purchase of the farm.

In the field of contracts, as generally elsewhere, "We must look to the outward expression of a person as manifesting his intention rather than to his secret and unexpressed intention. 'The law imputes to a person an intention corresponding to the reasonable meaning of his words and acts.'" First Nat. Bank v. Roanoke Oil Co., 169 Va. 99, 114, 192 S.E. 764, 770.

At no time prior to the execution of the contract had Zehmer indicated to Lucy by word or act that he was not in earnest about selling the farm. They had argued about it and discussed its terms, as Zehmer admitted, for a long time. Lucy testified that if there was any jesting it was about paying $50,000 that night. The contract and the evidence show that he was not expected to pay the money that night. Zehmer said that after the writing was signed he laid it down on the counter in front of Lucy. Lucy said Zehmer handed it to him. In any event there had been what appeared to be a good faith offer and a good faith acceptance, followed by the execution and apparent delivery of a written contract. Both said that Lucy put the writing in his pocket and then offered Zehmer $5 to seal the bargain. Not until then, even under the defendants' evidence, was anything said or done to indicate that the matter was a joke. Both of the Zehmers testified that when Zehmer asked his wife to sign he whispered that it was a joke so Lucy wouldn't hear and that it was not intended that he should hear.

The mental assent of the parties is not requisite for the formation of a contract. If the words or other acts of one of the parties have but one reasonable meaning, his undisclosed intention is immaterial except when an unreasonable meaning which he attaches to his manifestations is known to the other party. Restatement of the Law of Contracts, Vol. I, §71, p. 74.

". . . The law, therefore, judges of an agreement between two persons exclusively from those expressions of their intentions which are communicated between them. . . ." Clark on Contracts, 4 ed., §3, p. 4.

An agreement or mutual assent is of course essential to a valid contract but the law imputes to a person an intention corresponding to the reasonable meaning of his words and acts. If his words and acts, judged by a reasonable standard, manifest an intention to agree, it is immaterial what may be the real but unexpressed state of his mind. 17 C.J.S., Contracts, §32, p. 361; 12 Am. Jur., Contracts, §19, p. 515.

So a person cannot set up that he was merely jesting when his conduct and words would warrant a reasonable person in believing that he intended a real agreement, 17 C.J.S., Contracts, §47, p. 390; Clark on Contracts, 4 ed., §27, at p. 54.

Whether the writing signed by the defendants and now sought to be enforced by the complainants was the result of a serious offer by Lucy and a serious acceptance by the defendants, or was a serious offer by Lucy and an acceptance in secret jest by the defendants, in either event it constituted a binding contract of sale between the parties.

Defendants contend further, however, that even though a contract was made, equity should decline to enforce it under the circumstances. These circumstances have been set forth in detail above. They disclose some drinking by the two parties but not to an extent that they were unable to understand fully what they were doing. There was no fraud, no misrepresentation, no sharp practice and no dealing between unequal parties. The farm had been bought for $11,000 and was assessed for taxation at $6,300. The purchase price was $50,000. Zehmer admitted that it was a good price. There is in fact present in this case none of the grounds usually urged against specific performance.

Specific performance, it is true, is not a matter of absolute or arbitrary right, but is addressed to the reasonable and sound discretion of the court. First Nat. Bank v. Roanoke Oil Co., supra, 169 Va. At p. 116, 192 S.E. at p. 771. But it is likewise true that the discretion which may be exercised is not an arbitrary or capricious one, but one which is controlled by the established doctrines and settled principles of equity; and, generally, where a contract is in its nature and circumstances unobjectionable, it is as much a matter of course for courts of equity to decree a specific performance of it as it is for a court of law to give damages for a breach of it. Bond v. Crawford, 193 Va. 437, 444, 69 S.E. 2d 470, 475.

The complainants are entitled to have specific performance of the contracts sued on. The decree appealed from is therefore reversed and the cause is remanded for the entry of a proper decree requiring the defendants to perform the contract in accordance with the prayer of the bill.

Reversed and remanded.

Holding ←

Relational Background: The Politics and Economics of Lucy v. Zehmer

STUDY GUIDE: *After revealing the economics behind the deal in Lucy v. Zehmer, Barak Richman and Dennis Schmelzer argue that these facts show "the deep limitations of that method. Although 'objective' connotes a scientific approach, relying on different outward manifestations can lead to different conclusions." Do you agree? Why should the fact that each party subjectively valued the property differently than the other affect the communicative content of their words and deeds? Does not every buyer subjectively value the other's performance more than the purchase price? Does not every seller subjectively value the price more than what* *is being sold? At the time of formation, wasn't the land worth more to Lucy (given his knowledge) than it was to Zehmer (given his)? Did Lucy "owe" Zehmer the benefit of his expertise? Would Zehmer owe Lucy a refund if Lucy had miscalculated the lumber market? With these facts in mind, can you see how the ruling of the Court of Appeals secured the feasibility of profitable investments? We will return to these issues when considering the contract defenses that are based on a failure of basic assumptions.*

BARAK RICHMAN & DENNIS SCHMELZER, WHEN MONEY GREW ON TREES: LUCY v. ZEHMER AND CONTRACTING IN A BOOM MARKET, 61 DUKE L.J. 1511 (2012): The history of the Zehmer family is very much the history of McKenney, the small town in Dinwiddie County where the Zehmers lived. Named after William Robertson McKenney, a railroad attorney from Richmond, McKenney was founded around 1900 when the railroad was built to connect the isolated and rural south of Dinwiddie County to the Richmond market to the north. Many local institutions, such as the local bank, were established during this period to meet the sudden demand generated by this growing commercial link. Among these institutions were several businesses established by the Zehmer family, businesses that cemented the Zehmers' influence in the town.

. . .

This business had a natural limit, and the family looked to use its land holdings for alternative businesses once the local railroad line had been established. In the 1920s, the family began to farm tobacco, a profitable cash crop at the time. Less than 20 years later, they supplemented their income by raising cattle, a business that was naturally followed by dairy farming. As each business reached what seemed like its natural limit, other family businesses were established, including a local grocery store, a local hardware store, and, ultimately, Ye Olde Virginnie, the small "tourist court" operated by Hardy Zehmer.

Image 1. Hardy Zehmer's Tourist Court

. . .

The Lucy brothers came from a world far away from the Zehmers' privilege. Though also born into a farming family — their father ran a tobacco farm — the Lucy brothers lost everything when their father's farm went bankrupt in the early years of the Depression; and the five Lucy children were left to fend for themselves. John Cleveland Lucy, Welford's older brother and a coplaintiff, never finished the seventh grade and went to work in the lumber industry as a teenager. Eventually scraping together enough money to buy a small sawmill, John enjoyed the freedom that came from running his own business, even though he took on an occasional partner on larger projects.

. . .

Welford, unlike his brother, was not content remaining in his native Brunswick County. Instead, he looked further north to neighboring Dinwiddie County, at first driving a truck for a local businessman and then getting into lumber and cattle farming. In the 1940s, he purchased an estate along Highway 1, not too far from Zehmer's tourist court. This change marked the first time, but not the last time, that Welford would feel the need to move to a new community to pursue new business opportunities.

Welford arrived in McKenney as an outsider, and although he would become a close associate of several residents — including Harrison Zehmer, a cousin of Hardy Zehmer who would often spend his evenings at Hardy's restaurant — views vary as to whether Welford ever integrated himself into the area. Some residents recall that Lucy was known to be shady with his business and that — like many of the county's lumbermen at the time — he was eager to make quick profits off of the land of others.

. . .

When John C. Lucy began his career as a lumberman in the 1930s, economic trends that had begun in the 1920s and that had accelerated throughout the 1950s were rapidly changing the business of lumbermen across the American South. During much of this period, the lumber industry of southern Virginia — the region's traditional driver of prices for raw-timber resources — was waning in the face of declining demand for southern pine. Yet far from slowing down, business was heating up for lumbermen in the region, as industrial leaders addressed weak markets for lumber by investing heavily in plants to make wood pulp, a valuable raw material used to produce paper. The new capacity for paper manufacturing made harvesting timber for wood pulp quite lucrative, which in turn created a shock to local timber prices. Demand for timber spiked as companies sought to acquire more timberlands to guarantee their timber supplies, and speculation over timberlands spread. This economic boom provides the context essential to understanding the 1952 encounter in Zehmer's restaurant.

. . .

Figure 1. Rapid Increase in Market Price for Southern Pine

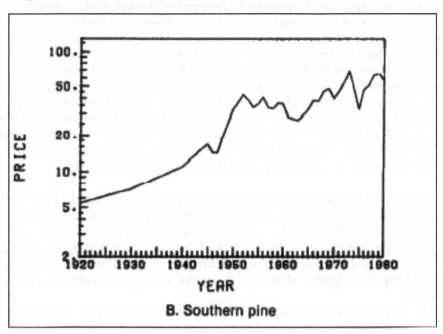

B. Southern pine

As these companies pursued standing timber across vast new tracts of land, they recognized the potential public outcry in communities encroached upon by the paper industry's expanding reach. For a variety of reasons, the industry ultimately followed a business model that relied on middlemen to obtain the timber resources necessary to sustain its tremendous growth — a strategy that would eventually bring Lucy and Zehmer face-to-face over drinks a few nights before Christmas in 1952.

. . .

In part, *Lucy v. Zehmer* is a tale of two brothers in southern Virginia who . . . made a fortune by buying undervalued forested properties in remote areas and selling the timber from those properties for more money than they had paid for the land as a whole. The Lucys' rise to prosperity, however, was a distinct reflection of the region's industrialization, as the brothers capitalized on the regional mills' need for timber brokers. The brothers thus contributed to the transformation of southern Virginia's economy from one that relied on farming to one that rested on harvesting natural resources for industrial use.

Property records reveal that the Lucy brothers signed dozens of land and timber deeds between the 1930s and the 1960s. Though generally involving properties smaller than the 471.6-acre Ferguson farm, these deeds reflect a pattern of business activity in Dinwiddie and Brunswick Counties: The Lucy brothers would purchase farmland and then harvest the timber for sale to the Camp Manufacturing Company or another large paper mill. Sometimes the Lucys would resell the land after removing the timber, but often the immediate returns from harvesting would enable the Lucys to keep much of the land.

Engaging in such activity required a keen eye for "cruising," the process of strolling through a property to determine the value of its timber, and the descendants of John and Welford Lucy described Welford as a true master of the trade. Cruising usually involved taking careful measurements of a land's timber and making calculations based on market prices, but Lucy family lore describes Welford as someone who could stroll around a property and intuitively make an accurate assessment of its value. In fact, Welford admitted in a deposition that he had driven around Zehmer's property several times in the years prior to making his offer of $50,000 in December 1952, including one trip three weeks before the disputed sale. Those trips suggest that Welford's eventual offer was based on a reasoned analysis of the value of the property's timber rather than on an impulsive wager.

. . .

The record suggests that the Zehmers, by contrast, thought little of the land's natural resources — or at least that they were much less attuned to the land's timber value than the nearby community of lumbermen. Ida and Hardy Zehmer, for example, both testified that the farm had no equipment or value except for the presence of a farmhouse and two head of cattle; they said nothing to suggest that the property contained valuable natural resources.[1]

Viewing the conversation between Zehmer and Lucy through this lens, one can understand why Zehmer might have thought that $50,000 was an attractive price at first but changed his mind after realizing that it was so agreeable to Lucy. Zehmer likely became aware of his land's potential value only after Lucy walked out of Zehmer's restaurant excitedly waving the restaurant receipt-cum-contract. Lucy's zeal in enforcing the contract and Zehmer's strong resistance to selling are in tension with Justice Buchanan's proclamation that $50,000 was, if not a windfall for Zehmer, a fair price for the land. A careful examination of Dinwiddie property records provides reason to question the accuracy of Justice Buchanan's valuation.

Subsequent events reveal the true value of the Ferguson farm. On December 17, 1954, Hardy and Ida Zehmer finally conveyed the Ferguson farm to the Lucys for the bargained-for price of $50,000. On January 5, 1955, less than a month after the final sale, the Lucy brothers executed a timber deed granting the right to all the merchantable timber on the property to

---

1. A review of Ida Zehmer's deposition testimony, for example, reveals a telling exchange in which Harrison pushed Ida to describe objects of value on the property:

Q. What else did the word, "complete," include other than the land and buildings thereon?
A. I know of nothing else except the cows.
Q. There was no farming equipment on the property at the time?
A. Not that I know of.
Q. The property consisted of farm and buildings thereon? And two heads of cattle?
A. That is right.

Harrison proceeded to ask Hardy Zehmer similar questions, and he received similar answers. [For example,] Harrison asked whether "there [was] anything else [on the property] except a couple cows" and Zehmer replied, "No, sir.").

the Lumber Distribution Company of Petersburg, Virginia. To execute this purchase, the Lumber Distribution Company borrowed $85,000, suggesting that at least that much — and perhaps more — was paid to the Lucy brothers.

By April 1956, the Lumber Distribution Company had removed all the merchantable timber from the formerly forested portions of the property and had filed a deed of release, freeing the Lucy brothers from their obligations under the contract and enabling them to otherwise dispose of the property. Immediately thereafter, Welford Lucy sold the formerly wooded portion of the property, which amounted to 367.7 of the original 471.6 acres, to the Continental Timber Lands Corporation, an affiliate of the Continental Can Company. Because the Continental Timber Lands Corporation evidently had no need to secure financing for the transaction, there is no public record of what Welford received in his truncated sale of the property.

Following this sale, Welford leased the remaining 103.9 acres of the Ferguson farm — the portion suitable for farming — to W. Franklin Townsend, enabling Townsend to reside on the property as a tenant farmer and granting him an option to buy the property for $12,000 as early as 1961. On May 14, 1962, after Townsend had informed Lucy that he intended to exercise this option and had arranged for the payment of the $12,000, Lucy — not one to shy away from a fight or an opportunity — refused to deliver title to the property. Townsend and his wife filed a complaint to compel performance, again in Judge Jefferson's court, and later settled with Lucy for a revised price of $15,000.

Based on this evidence, we can begin to piece together the profits the Lucy brothers made from their purchase and truncated sale of the Ferguson farm. Assuming that the Lucy brothers sold the farm's timber for $85,000 — the price that the Lumber Distribution Company borrowed from the Petersburg Savings and American Trust Bank — and that the 367.7 acres of land sold to Continental were sold at the same per-acre price as the price originally agreed to by Welford and Townsend — $12,000 for 103.9 acres — we estimate that by 1962 the Lucy brothers had earned at least $142,000 from their $50,000 investment less than a decade earlier.

This is not a scientific calculation. It assumes for convenience that the previously wooded 367.7 acres were sold at the same price as the 103.9 acres that were used for farming and that contained the dwellings and farm equipment. Our calculation also does not include the income from leasing the farm to Townsend before the sale in 1962. Nonetheless, it is our best approximation based on the available evidence. If anything, reports from the Lucy descendants suggest that our estimate might be too conservative. John C. Lucy III, for example, recalled being told that John and Welford had earned at least four times what they had paid for the farm in 1954. Taken together, the evidence convincingly suggests that Lucy, and not Zehmer, reaped windfall profits from the sale enforced by the Virginia Supreme Court in *Lucy v. Zehmer*.

. . .

This was the context in which Lucy met Zehmer for a drink before Christmas in 1952, and understanding this context changes the interpretation of the case. Justice Buchanan, looking at the outward manifestations of Zehmer's reported conduct and believing that $50,000 was more than a fair price, concluded that Lucy had been reasonable in thinking that Zehmer had intended to become contractually bound and thus enforced the written instrument. Our research suggests that the value of the farm's timber alone far exceeded $50,000. We also know that Dinwiddie County was swarming with aggressive timber brokers like the Lucy brothers, many of whom employed unseemly tactics, many of whom had their eyes on the Ferguson farm, and many of whom — the record indicates as many as twenty-five — had been previously rebuffed by Zehmer. In light of this context of rapidly rising land values and hastily created contracts, one can understand Judge Jefferson's refusal to intervene and enforce the contract.

We conclude that the outward manifestations observed by Justice Buchanan and the Virginia Supreme Court revealed only part of what was well known to the parties — and likely well known to the trial judge as well. Ironically, the historical analysis of the case that is most often used to teach the objective method of contracts in fact demonstrates the deep limitations of that method. Although "objective" connotes a scientific approach, relying on different outward manifestations can lead to different conclusions.

Cicero demanded that historians, above all, must tell the truth. The story of Lucy v. Zehmer reveals that the truth frequently offers sufficient material for talented historians and creative lawyers to construct alternative narratives. Although our reconstruction of Lucy v. Zehmer contrasts sharply with the traditional telling, the case remains a useful tool for studying the objective theory of contracts. Both Justice Buchanan's account and our own are supported by facts. Therein lies the art of the objective method.

RESTATEMENT (SECOND) OF CONTRACTS

§17.   REQUIREMENT OF A BARGAIN

(1) Except as stated in Subsection (2), the formation of a contract requires a bargain in which there is a manifestation of mutual assent to the exchange and a consideration.

(2) Whether or not there is a bargain a contract may be formed under special rules applicable to formal contracts or under the rules stated in §§82-94.

COMMENT . . .

c. "Meeting of the minds." The element of agreement is sometimes referred to as a "meeting of the minds." The parties to most contracts give actual as well as apparent assent, but it is clear that a mental reservation of a party to a bargain does not impair the obligation he purports to undertake.

The phrase used here, therefore, is "manifestation of mutual assent," as in the definition of "agreement" in §3.

§18.   MANIFESTATION OF MUTUAL ASSENT

Manifestation of mutual assent to an exchange requires that each party either make a promise or begin or render a performance.

§19.   CONDUCT AS MANIFESTATION OF ASSENT

(1) The manifestation of assent may be made wholly or partly by written or spoken words or by other acts or by failure to act.

(2) The conduct of a party is not effective as a manifestation of his assent unless he intends to engage in the conduct and knows or has reason to know that the other party may infer from his conduct that he assents.

(3) The conduct of a party may manifest assent even though he does not in fact assent. In such cases a resulting contract may be voidable because of fraud, duress, mistake, or other invalidating cause.

Reread: Restatement, §3 (p. 15)

REFERENCE: Barnett, §3.1
                       Farnsworth, §3.6
                       Calamari & Perillo, §§2.2, 2.3
                       Murray, §31

B.   WHAT IS AN OFFER?

Traditionally, courts and commentators conceived of mutual assent in terms of *offers* and *acceptances.* Most complex commercial transactions, however, involve multiple drafts of written documents, which are then submitted to both parties for their signatures. During this process, while mutual assent is clearly manifested, it becomes next to impossible to distinguish the offeror from the offeree. Nevertheless, the offer-acceptance mode of assent survives, and various doctrines governing mutual assent are still understood by courts in terms of "offers" and "acceptances."

In this section, we begin by examining some of the problems that can arise when determining the existence of an offer. Section 24 of the Restatement (Second) of Contracts defines an offer as "the manifestation of willingness to enter into a bargain, so made as to justify another person in understanding that his assent to that bargain is invited and will conclude it." In each of the cases that follow in Sections 1 and 2, the alleged offeror claims that the other party was not justified "in understanding that his assent to that bargain is invited and will conclude it." In Section 3, we consider the revocability of an offer.

1. Preliminary Negotiations

NEBRASKA SEED CO. v. HARSH
Supreme Court of Nebraska,
98 Neb. 89, 152 N.W. 310 (1915)

MORRISSEY, C.J.*

Plaintiff, a corporation, engaged in buying and selling seed in the city of Omaha, Nebraska, brought this action against the defendant, a farmer, residing at Lowell, Kearney county, Nebraska. The petitioner alleges:

That on the 26th day of April, 1912, the plaintiff purchased of and from the defendant 1,800 bushels of millet seed at the agreed price of $2.25 per hundred weight, f.o.b. Lowell, Nebraska, which said purchase and contract was evidenced by writing and correspondence passing between the respective parties, of which the following is a copy:

Lowell, Nebraska, 4-24-1912.
Neb. Seed Co.
Omaha, Neb.

Gentlemen:

I have about 1800 bu. or thereabouts of millet seed of which I am mailing you a sample. This millet is recleaned and was grown on sod and is good seed. I want $2.25 per cwt. for this seed f.o.b. Lowell.

(free on board)
(risk of loss shifts   Yours truly,
 when seller ships   H. F. Harsh.
 goods (sends))

Said letter was received by the plaintiff at its place of business in Omaha, Nebraska, on the 26th day of April, 1912, and immediately thereafter the plaintiff telegraphed to the defendant at Lowell, Nebraska, a copy of which is as follows:

4-26-12.

H. F. Harsh, Lowell, Nebr. Sample and letter received. Accept your offer. Millet like sample two twenty-five per hundred. Wire how soon can load. The Nebraska Seed Co.

On the same day, to wit, April 26, 1912, the plaintiff, in answer to the letter of the said defendant, wrote to him a letter and deposited the same in the United States mail, directed to the said defendant at Lowell, Nebraska, which said letter was duly stamped, and which the plaintiff charges that the

---

Andrew Marcus Morrissey (1871-1933) was admitted to the Nebraska bar in 1896, and practiced at Valentine and Lincoln, Nebraska, except while serving in the Spanish-American War in 1898. In 1915, he was appointed, and later that year elected, Chief Justice of the Supreme Court of Nebraska, and was reelected in 1920 to the term ending in 1927. Morrissey was a member of the faculty of Northwestern University Law College during the summer 1925 term. — K.T.

defendant in due course of mail received; that a copy of said letter is as follows:

4-26-12.

Mr. H. F. Harsh
Lowell, Neb.

Dear Sir:

We received your letter and sample of millet seed this morning and at once wired you as follows: 'Sample and letter received. Accept your offer. Millet like sample two twenty-five per hundred, wire how soon can load.' We confirm this message. Have booked purchase of you[r] 1,800 bushels of millet seed to be fully equal to sample you sent us at $2.25 per cwt., your track. Please be so kind as to load this seed at once and ship to us at Omaha. We thank you in advance for prompt attention. When anything further in the line of millet to offer, let us have samples.

Yours truly, Nebraska Seed Co.

It alleges that defendant refused to deliver the seed, after due demand and tender of the purchase price, and prays judgment in the sum of $900. Defendant filed a demurrer, which was overruled. He saved an exception to the ruling, and answered, denying that the petition stated a cause of action; that the correspondence set out constituted a contract, etc. There was a trial to a jury, with verdict and judgment for plaintiff, and defendant appeals.

In our opinion, the letter of defendant cannot be fairly construed into an offer to sell to the plaintiff. After describing the seed, the writer says: "I want $2.25 per cwt. For this seed f.o.b. Lowell." He does not say, "I offer to sell to you." The language used is general, and such as may be used in an advertisement, or circular addressed generally to those engaged in the seed business, and is not an offer by which he may be bound, if accepted, by any or all of the persons addressed.

> If a proposal is nothing more than an invitation to the person to whom it is made to make an offer to the proposer, it is not such an offer as can be turned into an agreement by acceptance. Proposals of this kind, although made to definite persons and not to the public generally, are merely invitations to trade; they go no further than what occurs when one asks another what he will give or take for certain goods. Such inquiries may lead to bargains, but do not make them. They ask for offers which the proposers [sic] has a right to accept or reject as he pleases.

9 Cyc. 278e.

The letter as a whole shows that it was not intended as a final proposition, but as a request for bids. It did not fix a time for delivery, and this seems to have been regarded as one of the essentials by plaintiff, for in his telegram he requests defendant to "wire how soon can load."

"The mere statement of the price at which property is held cannot be understood as an offer to sell." Knight v. Cooley, 34 Ia. 218.

The letter of acceptance is not in the terms of the offer. Defendant stated that he had 1,800 bushels or thereabouts. He did not fix a definite and certain amount. It might be 1,800 bushels; it might be more; it might be less; but plaintiff undertook to make an acceptance for 1,800 bushels — no more, no less. Defendant might not have this amount, and therefore be unable to deliver, or he might have a greater amount, and, after filling plaintiff's order, have a quantity of seed left for which he might find no market. We may assume that when he wrote the letter he did not contemplate the sale of more seed than he had, and that he fixed the price on the whole lot, whether it was more or less than 1,800 bushels.

We do not think the correspondence made a complete contract. To so hold where a party sends out letters to a number of dealers would subject him to a suit by each one receiving a letter, or invitations to bid, even though his supply of seed were exhausted. In Lyman v. Robinson, 14 Allen (Mass.) 242, 254, the supreme court of Massachusetts has sounded the warning: "Care should always be taken not to construe as an agreement letters which the parties intended only as a preliminary negotiation."

Holding, as we do, that there was no binding contract between the parties, it is unnecessary to discuss the other questions presented. The judgment of the district court is

Reversed. ———> Holding

STUDY GUIDE: In the next case, the court struggles with the question of when a communication becomes an offer. Ordinarily, advertisements are not construed to be offers, but rather merely "invitations to bargain." Why might the courts favor such a rule? Why does the court in Lefkowitz *reach a different conclusion? According to the court's reasoning, should all advertisements now be treated as offers?*

LEFKOWITZ v. GREAT MINNEAPOLIS SURPLUS STORE, INC.
Supreme Court of Minnesota,
251 Minn. 188, 86 N.W.2d 689 (1957)

MURPHY,* Justice.

This is an appeal from an order of the Municipal Court of Minneapolis denying the motion of the defendant for amended findings of fact, or, in the alternative, for a new trial. The order for judgment awarded the plaintiff the sum of $138.50 as damages for breach of contract.

This case grows out of the alleged refusal of the defendant to sell to the plaintiff a certain fur piece which it had offered for sale in a newspaper advertisement. It appears from the record that on April 6, 1956, the defendant published the following advertisement in a Minneapolis newspaper:

> "Saturday 9 A.M. Sharp 3 Brand New Fur Coats Worth to $100.00
>   First Come First Served $1 Each"

_____

* William P. Murphy (1898-1986) served on the Minnesota Supreme Court from 1955-1972. He was born in St. Cloud, Minnesota, and graduated from St. Paul College of Law in 1924. — S.Q.

On April 13, the defendant again published an advertisement in the same newspaper as follows:

"Saturday 9 A.M. 2 Brand New Pastel Mink 3-Skin Scarfs Selling for $89.50
  Out they go Saturday. Each . . . $1.00
  1 Black Lapin Stole Beautiful, worth $139.50 . . . $1.00
  First Come First Served"

The record supports the findings of the court that on each of the Saturdays following the publication of the above-described ads the plaintiff was the first to present himself at the appropriate counter in the defendant's store and on each occasion demanded the coat and the stole so advertised and indicated his readiness to pay the sale price of $1. On both occasions, the defendant refused to sell the merchandise to the plaintiff, stating on the first occasion that by a "house rule" the offer was intended for women only and sales would not be made to men, and on the second visit that plaintiff knew defendant's house rules.

The trial court properly disallowed plaintiff's claim for the value of the fur coats since the value of these articles was speculative and uncertain. The only evidence of value was the advertisement itself to the effect that the coats were "Worth to $100.00," how much less being speculative especially in view of the price for which they were offered for sale. With reference to the offer of the defendant on April 13, 1956, to sell the "1 Black Lapin Stole worth $139.50" the trial court held that the value of this article was established and granted judgment in favor of the plaintiff for that amount less the $1 quoted purchase price.

1. The defendant contends that a newspaper advertisement offering items of merchandise for sale at a named price is a "unilateral offer" which may be withdrawn without notice. He relies upon authorities which hold that, where an advertiser publishes in a newspaper that he has a certain quantity or quality of goods which he wants to dispose of at certain prices and on certain terms, such advertisements are not offers which become contracts as soon as any person to whose notice they may come signifies his acceptance by notifying the other that he will take a certain quantity of them. Such advertisements have been construed as an invitation for an offer of sale on the terms stated, which offer, when received, may be accepted or rejected and which therefore does not become a contract of sale until accepted by the seller; and until a contract has been so made, the seller may modify or revoke such prices or terms. Montgomery Ward & Co. v. Johnson, 209 Mass. 89, 95 N.E. 290; Nickel v. Theresa Farmers Co-op. Ass'n, 247 Wis. 412, 20 N.W.2d 117; Lovett v. Frederick Loeser & Co. Inc., 124 Misc. 81, 207 N.Y.S. 753; Schenectady Stove Co. v. Holbrook, 101 N.Y. 45, 4 N.E. 4; Georgian Co. v. Bloom, 27 Ga. App. 468, 108 S.E. 813; Craft v. Elder & Johnson Co., 38 N.E.2d 416, 34 Ohio L.A. 603; Annotation, 157 A.L.R. 746.

The defendant relies principally on Craft v. Elder & Johnston Co. supra. In that case, the court discussed the legal effect of an advertisement offering for sale, as a one-day special, an electric sewing machine at a named price. The view was expressed that the advertisement was (38 N.E.2d 417, 34 Ohio L.A. 605) "not an offer made to any specific person but was made to the public generally. Thereby it would be properly designated as a unilateral offer and not being supported by any consideration could be withdrawn at will and without notice." It is true that such an offer may be withdrawn before acceptance. Since all offers are by their nature unilateral because they are necessarily made by one party or on one side in the negotiation of a contract, the distinction made in that decision between a unilateral offer and a unilateral contract is not clear. On the facts before us we are concerned with whether the advertisement constituted an offer, and, if so, whether the plaintiff's conduct constituted an acceptance.

There are numerous authorities which hold that a particular advertisement in a newspaper or circular letter relating to a sale of articles may be construed by the court as constituting an offer, acceptance of which would complete a contract. J. E. Pinkham Lumber Co. v. C. W. Griffin & Co., 212 Ala. 341, 102 So. 689; Seymour v. Armstrong & Kassebaum, 62 Kan. 720, 64 P. 612; Payne v. Lautz Bros. & Co., City Ct., 166 N.Y.S. 844, affirmed, 168 N.Y.S. 369, affirmed, 185 App. Div. 904, 171 N.Y.S. 1094; Arnold v. Phillips, 1 Ohio Dec. Reprint 195, 3 West. Law J. 448; Oliver v. Henley, Tex. Civ. App., 21 S.W.2d 576; Annotation, 157 A.L.R. 744, 746.

The test of whether a binding obligation may originate in advertisements addressed to the general public is "whether the facts show that some performance was promised in positive terms in return for something requested." 1 Williston, Contracts (Rev. ed.) §27.

The authorities above cited emphasize that, where the offer is clear, definite, and explicit, and leaves nothing open for negotiation, it constitutes an offer, acceptance of which will complete the contract. The most recent case on the subject is Johnson v. Capital City Ford Co., La. App., 85 So. 2d 75, in which the court pointed out that a newspaper advertisement relating to the purchase and sale of automobiles may constitute an offer, acceptance of which will consummate a contract and create an obligation in the offeror to perform according to the terms of the published offer.

Whether in any individual instance a newspaper advertisement is an offer rather than an invitation to make an offer depends on the legal intention of the parties and the surrounding circumstances. Annotation, 157 A.L.R. 744, 751; 77 C.J.S., Sales, §25b; 17 C.J.S., Contracts, §389. We are of the view on the facts before us that the offer by the defendant of the sale of the Lapin fur was clear, definite, and explicit, and left nothing open for negotiation. The plaintiff having successful managed to be the first one to appear at the seller's place of business to be served, as requested by the advertisement, and having offered the stated purchase price of the article, he was entitled to performance on the part of the defendant. We think the trial court was correct in holding that there was in the conduct of the parties a sufficient mutuality of obligation to constitute a contract of sale.

2. The defendant contends that the offer was modified by a "house rule" to the effect that only women were qualified to receive the bargains advertised. The advertisement contained no such restriction. This objection may be disposed of briefly by stating that, while an advertiser has the right at any time before acceptance to modify his offer, he does not have the right, after acceptance, to impose new or arbitrary conditions not contained in the published offer. Payne v. Lautz Bros. & Co., City Ct., 166 N.Y.S. 844, 848; Mooney v. Daily News Co., 116 Minn. 212, 133 N.W. 573, 37 L.R.A., N.S., 183.

Affirmed.

STUDY GUIDE: *In the next case, PepsiCo claims that it made a joke in an advertisement where it offered a Harrier fighter jet as a reward for "Pepsi Points" earned by consuming Pepsi products. How can this case be distinguished from* Lucy v. Zehmer? *From* Lefkowitz?

LEONARD v. PEPSICO, UNITED STATES DISTRICT COURT, SOUTHERN DISTRICT OF NEW YORK, 88 F. SUPP. 2D 116 (1999): KIMBA M. WOOD,* District Judge. Plaintiff brought this action seeking, among other things, specific performance of an alleged offer of a Harrier Jet, featured in a television advertisement for defendant's "Pepsi Stuff" promotion. Defendant has moved for summary judgment. . . . For the reasons stated below, defendant's motion is granted.

. . .

Because whether the television commercial constituted an offer is the central question in this case, the Court will describe the commercial in detail. The commercial opens upon an idyllic, suburban morning, where the chirping of birds in sun-dappled trees welcomes a paperboy on his morning route. As the newspaper hits the stoop of a conventional two-story house, the tattoo of a military drum introduces the subtitle, "MONDAY 7:58 AM." The stirring strains of a martial air mark the appearance of a well-coiffed teenager preparing to leave for school, dressed in a shirt emblazoned with the Pepsi logo, a red-white-and-blue ball. While the teenager confidently preens, the military drumroll again sounds as the subtitle "T-SHIRT 75 PEPSI POINTS" scrolls across the screen. Bursting from his room, the teenager strides down the hallway wearing a leather jacket. The drumroll sounds again, as the subtitle "LEATHER JACKET 1450 PEPSI POINTS" appears. The teenager opens the door of his house and, unfazed by the glare of the early morning sunshine, puts on a pair of sunglasses. The drumroll then accompanies the subtitle "SHADES 175 PEPSI POINTS." A voiceover then intones, "Introducing the new Pepsi Stuff catalog," as the camera focuses on the cover of the catalog.[2]

The scene then shifts to three young boys sitting in front of a high school building. The boy in the middle is intent on his Pepsi Stuff Catalog, while the boys on either side are each drinking Pepsi. The three boys gaze in awe at an object rushing overhead, as the military march builds to a crescendo. The Harrier Jet is not yet visible, but the observer senses the presence of a mighty plane as the extreme winds generated by its flight create a

---

Kimba M. Wood (1944-†) attended the Sorbonne in Paris and received her B.A. from Connecticut College and her M.A. from the London School of Economics before graduating from Harvard Law School in 1969. After working in the legal services program for the poor at the federal Office of Economic Opportunity, she entered private practice, where she became a litigator and antitrust expert. Since assuming her position on the U.S. District Court, Southern District of New York in 1988 after being nominated by President Reagan, her most highly publicized case was the securities fraud sentencing hearing for junk-bond king Michael Milken. In 1993, after the failed nomination of Zoe Baird to be Attorney General, President Clinton was poised to nominate Judge Wood when it was disclosed that she had employed an illegal immigrant as a nanny. Janet Reno was then nominated in her place. Judge Wood's parents picked her name after leafing through an atlas and settling on Kimba, a small town on South Australia's Eyre Peninsula. In 2009, she assumed senior status. — R.B.

2. At this point, the following message appears at the bottom of the screen: "Offer not available in all areas. See details on specially marked packages."

paper maelstrom in a classroom devoted to an otherwise dull physics lesson. Finally, the Harrier Jet swings into view and lands by the side of the school building, next to a bicycle rack. Several students run for cover, and the velocity of the wind strips one hapless faculty member down to his underwear. While the faculty member is being deprived of his dignity, the voiceover announces: "Now the more Pepsi you drink, the more great stuff you're gonna get."

The teenager opens the cockpit of the fighter and can be seen, helmetless, holding a Pepsi. "[L]ooking very pleased with himself," the teenager exclaims, "Sure beats the bus," and chortles. The military drumroll sounds a final time, as the following words appear: "HARRIER FIGHTER 7,000,000 PEPSI POINTS." A few seconds later, the following appears in more stylized script: "Drink Pepsi — Get Stuff." With that message, the music and the commercial end with a triumphant flourish.

Inspired by this commercial, plaintiff set out to obtain a Harrier Jet. . . .

Although plaintiff initially set out to collect 7,000,000 Pepsi Points by consuming Pepsi products, it soon became clear to him that he "would not be able to buy (let alone drink) enough Pepsi to collect the necessary Pepsi Points fast enough." Reevaluating his strategy, plaintiff "focused for the first time on the packaging materials in the Pepsi Stuff promotion," and realized that buying Pepsi Points would be a more promising option. Through acquaintances, plaintiff ultimately raised about $700,000.

On or about March 27, 1996, plaintiff submitted an Order Form, fifteen original Pepsi Points, and a check for $700,008.50. Plaintiff appears to have been represented by counsel at the time he mailed his check; the check is drawn on an account of plaintiff's first set of attorneys. At the bottom of the Order Form, plaintiff wrote in "1 Harrier Jet" in the "Item" column and "7,000,000" in the "Total Points" column. In a letter accompanying his submission, plaintiff stated that the check was to purchase additional Pepsi Points "expressly for obtaining a new Harrier jet as advertised in your Pepsi Stuff commercial."

On or about May 7, 1996, defendant's fulfillment house rejected plaintiff's submission and returned the check. . . .

In evaluating the commercial, the Court must not consider defendant's subjective intent in making the commercial, or plaintiff's subjective view of what the commercial offered, but what an objective, reasonable person would have understood the commercial to convey. See Kay-R Elec. Corp. v. Stone & Webster Constr. Co., 23 F.3d 55, 57 (2d Cir. 1994) ("[W]e are not concerned with what was going through the heads of the parties at the time [of the alleged contract]. Rather, we are talking about the objective principles of contract law."); *Mesaros*, 845 F.2d at 1581 ("A basic rule of contracts holds that whether an offer has been made depends on the objective reasonableness of the alleged offeree's belief that the advertisement or solicitation was intended as an offer."). . . .

If it is clear that an offer was not serious, then no offer has been made:

> What kind of act creates a power of acceptance and is therefore an offer? It must be an expression of will or intention. It must be an act that leads the offeree reasonably to conclude that a power to create a contract is conferred. This applies to the content of the power as well as to the fact of its existence. *It*

is on this ground that we must exclude invitations to deal or acts of mere preliminary negotiation, and *acts evidently done in jest* or without intent to create legal relations.

Corbin on Contracts, §1.11 at 30 (emphasis added). An obvious joke, of course, would not give rise to a contract. See, e.g., Graves v. Northern N.Y. Pub. Co., 260 A.D. 900, 22 N.Y.S.2d 537 (1940) (dismissing claim to offer of $1000, which appeared in the "joke column" of the newspaper, to any person who could provide a commonly available phone number). On the other hand, if there is no indication that the offer is "evidently in jest," and that an objective, reasonable person would find that the offer was serious, then there may be a valid offer. See *Barnes*, 549 P.2d at 1155 ("[I]f the jest is not apparent and a reasonable hearer would believe that an offer was being made, then the speaker risks the formation of a contract which was not intended."); see also Lucy v. Zehmer, 196 Va. 493, 84 S.E.2d 516, 518, 520 (1954) (ordering specific performance of a contract to purchase a farm despite defendant's protestation that the transaction was done in jest as "'just a bunch of two doggoned drunks bluffing'"). . . .

plaintiff's insistence that the commercial appears to be a serious offer requires the Court to explain why the commercial is funny. Explaining why a joke is funny is a daunting task; as the essayist E. B. White has remarked, "Humor can be dissected, as a frog can, but the thing dies in the process. . . ." The commercial is the embodiment of what defendant appropriately characterizes as "zany humor.". . .

For the reasons stated above, the Court grants defendant's motion for summary judgment. . . .

RESTATEMENT (SECOND) OF CONTRACTS

§22. MODE OF ASSENT: OFFER AND ACCEPTANCE

(1) The manifestation of mutual assent to an exchange ordinarily takes the form of an offer or proposal by one party followed by an acceptance by the other party or parties.

(2) A manifestation of mutual assent may be made even though neither offer nor acceptance can be identified and even though the moment of formation cannot be determined.

§24. OFFER DEFINED

An offer is the manifestation of willingness to enter into a bargain, so made as to justify another person in understanding that his assent to that bargain is invited and will conclude it.

§26. PRELIMINARY NEGOTIATIONS

A manifestation of willingness to enter into a bargain is not an offer if the person to whom it is addressed knows or has reason to know that the person making it does not intend to conclude a bargain until he has made a further manifestation of assent.

§29.   TO WHOM AN OFFER IS ADDRESSED

(1) The manifested intention of the offeror determines the person or persons in whom is created a power of acceptance.

(2) An offer may create a power of acceptance in a specified person or in one or more of a specified group or class of persons, acting separately or together, or in anyone or everyone who makes a specified promise or renders a specified performance.

§33.   CERTAINTY

(1) Even though a manifestation of intention is intended to be understood as an offer, it cannot be accepted so as to form a contract unless the terms of the contract are reasonably certain.

(2) The terms of a contract are reasonably certain if they provide a basis for determining the existence of a breach and for giving an appropriate remedy.

(3) The fact that one or more terms of a proposed bargain are left open or uncertain may show that a manifestation of intention is not intended to be understood as an offer or as an acceptance.

SALES CONTRACTS: THE UNIFORM COMMERCIAL CODE

STUDY GUIDE: How does the Nebraska Seed *case square with the following provisions of the Uniform Commercial Code that govern formation and contracts with open terms? What are the arguments that the case would be decided differently under these provisions? What are the arguments that the outcome of the case would be unchanged? We will return to these sections in Chapter 5 when discussing methods of filling gaps in agreements, so be especially familiar with §2-204.*

§2-204.   FORMATION IN GENERAL

(1) A contract for sale of goods may be made in any manner sufficient to show agreement, including conduct by both parties which recognizes the existence of such a contract.

(2) An agreement sufficient to constitute a contract for sale may be found even though the moment of its making is undetermined.

(3) Even though one or more terms are left open a contract for sale does not fail for indefiniteness if the parties have intended to make a contract and there is a reasonably certain basis for giving an appropriate remedy.

§2-206. OFFER AND ACCEPTANCE IN FORMATION OF CONTRACT

(1) Unless otherwise unambiguously indicated by the language or circumstances

(a) an offer to make a contract shall be construed as inviting acceptance in any manner and by any medium reasonable in the circumstances;

(b) an order or other offer to buy goods for prompt or current shipment shall be construed as inviting acceptance either by a prompt promise to ship or by the prompt or current shipment of conforming or nonconforming goods, but such a shipment of non-conforming goods does not constitute an acceptance if the seller seasonably notifies the buyer that the shipment is offered only as an accommodation to the buyer.

(2) Where the beginning of a requested performance is a reasonable mode of acceptance an offeror who is not notified of acceptance within a reasonable time may treat the offer as having lapsed before acceptance.

§2-305. OPEN PRICE TERM

(1) The parties if they so intend can conclude a contract for sale even though the price is not settled. In such a case the price is a reasonable price at the time for delivery if

(a) nothing is said as to price; or

(b) the price is left to be agreed by the parties and they fail to agree; or

(c) the price is to be fixed in terms of some agreed market or other standard as set or recorded by a third person or agency and it is not so set or recorded.

(2) A price to be fixed by the seller or by the buyer means a price for him to fix in good faith.

(3) When a price left to be fixed otherwise than by agreement of the parties fails to be fixed through fault of one party the other may at his option treat the contract as cancelled or himself fix a reasonable price.

(4) Where, however, the parties intend not to be bound unless the price be fixed or agreed and it is not fixed or agreed there is no contract. In such a case the buyer must return any goods already received or if unable so to do must pay their reasonable value at the time of delivery and the seller must return any portion of the price paid on account.

§2-308. ABSENCE OF SPECIFIED PLACE FOR DELIVERY

Unless otherwise agreed

(a) the place for delivery of goods is the seller's place of business or if he has none his residence; but

(b) in a contract for sale of identified goods which to the knowledge of the parties at the time of contracting are in some other place, that place is the place for their delivery; and

(c) documents of title may be delivered through customary banking channels.

§2-309.   ABSENCE OF SPECIFIC TIME PROVISIONS; NOTICE OF TERMINATION

(1) The time of shipment or delivery or any other action under a contract if not provided in this Article or agreed upon shall be a reasonable time.

(2) Where the contract provides for successive performances but is indefinite in duration it is valid for a reasonable time but unless otherwise agreed may be terminated at any time by either party.

(3) Termination of a contract by one party except on the happening of an agreed event requires that reasonable notification be received by the other party and an agreement dispensing with notification is invalid if its operation would be unconscionable.

§2-310.   OPEN TIME FOR PAYMENT OR RUNNING OF CREDIT; AUTHORITY TO SHIP UNDER RESERVATION

Unless otherwise agreed

(a) payment is due at the time and place at which the buyer is to receive the goods even though the place of shipment is the place of delivery; and

(b) if the seller is authorized to send the goods he may ship them under reservation, and may tender the documents of title, but the buyer may inspect the goods after their arrival before payment is due unless such inspection is inconsistent with the terms of the contract (Section 2-513); and

(c) if delivery is authorized and made by way of documents of title otherwise than by subsection (b) then payment is due at the time and place at which the buyer is to receive the documents regardless of where the goods are to be received; and

(d) where the seller is required or authorized to ship the goods on credit the credit period runs from the time of shipment but post-dating the invoice or delaying its dispatch will correspondingly delay the starting of the credit period.

2.   Written Memorial Contemplated

Many complex business transactions are negotiated by many persons over an extended period of time. At some point after an agreement is reached, one or both parties may expect that it be reduced to a single writing. Suppose one party changes her mind before the writing is executed. Is she bound nonetheless?

STUDY GUIDE: When parties sign an "agreement in principle" or "letter of intent," what exactly are they agreeing to? If such agreements are not binding, then why bother with them? Under what circumstances does Judge Easterbrook think such agreements are binding? Is there any middle ground between finding such agreements to be completely binding or not binding at all? In this regard, consider Empro's fallback request for relief.

EMPRO MANUFACTURING CO. v. BALL-CO MANUFACTURING, INC.
United States Court of Appeals, Seventh Circuit,
870 F.2d 423 (1989)

EASTERBROOK, C.J.* We have a pattern common in commercial life. Two firms reach concord on the general terms of their transaction. They sign a document, captioned "agreement in principle" or "letter of intent," memorializing these terms but anticipating further negotiations and decisions — an appraisal of the assets, the clearing of a title, the list is endless. One of these terms proves divisive, and the deal collapses. The party that perceives itself the loser then claims that the preliminary document has legal force independent of the definitive contract. Ours is such a dispute.

Ball-Co Manufacturing, a maker of specialty valve components, floated its assets on the market. Empro Manufacturing showed interest. After some preliminary negotiations, Empro sent Ball-Co a three-page "letter of intent" to purchase the assets of Ball-Co and S.B. Leasing, a partnership holding title to the land under Ball-Co's plant. Empro proposed a price of $2.4 million, with $650,000 to be paid on closing and a 10-year promissory note for the remainder, the note to be secured by the "inventory and equipment of Ballco." The letter stated "[t]he general terms and conditions of such proposal (which will be subject to and incorporated in a formal, definitive Asset Purchase Agreement signed by both parties)." Just in case Ball-Co might suppose that Empro had committed itself to buy the assets, paragraph four of the letter stated that "Empro's purchase shall be subject to the satisfaction of certain conditions precedent to closing including, but not limited to" the definitive Asset Purchase Agreement and, among five other conditions, "[t]he approval of the shareholders and board of directors of Empro."

Although Empro left itself escape hatches, as things turned out Ball-Co was the one who balked. The parties signed the letter of intent in November 1987 and negotiated through March 1988 about many terms. Security for the note proved to be the sticking point. Ball-Co wanted a security interest in the land under the plant; Empro refused to yield.

When Empro learned that Ball-Co was negotiating with someone else, it filed this diversity suit. Contending that the letter of intent obliges Ball-Co to sell only to it, Empro asked for a temporary restraining order. The district judge set the case for a prompt hearing and, after getting a look at the letter of intent, dismissed the complaint under Fed. R. Civ. P. 12(b)(6) for failure

---

*Frank H. Easterbrook (1948-†) graduated from Swarthmore College (B.A) and the University of Chicago (J.D). Upon graduation, Easterbrook served as law clerk for Judge Levin H. Campbell, U.S. Court of Appeals, First Circuit (1973-1974). He then spent several years in the federal government as Assistant to the Solicitor General of the U.S. Department of Justice (1974-1977) and Deputy Solicitor General of the U.S. (1978-1979). Prior to being appointed in 1985 to the U.S. Court of Appeals, Seventh Circuit, by President Ronald Reagan, Judge Easterbrook served as the Lee and Brena Freeman Professor of Law at the University of Chicago and has continued as a Senior Lecturer since his appointment. Easterbrook has co-authored several books, including Antitrust (1981) with Richard A. Posner, and The Economic Structure of Corporate Law (1991) with Daniel R. Fischel. Since 2006, he has been the Chief Judge of the Circuit. — L.R.

to state a claim on which relief may be granted. Relying on Interway, Inc. v. Alagna, 85 Ill. App. 3d 1094, 41 III. Dec. 117, 407 N.E.2d 615 (1st Dist. 1980), the district judge concluded that the statement, appearing twice in the letter, that the agreement is "subject to" the execution of a definitive contract meant that the letter has no independent force.

Empro insists on appeal that the binding effect of a document depends on the parties' intent, which means that the case may not be dismissed — for Empro says that the parties intended to be bound, a factual issue. Empro treats "intent to be bound" as a matter of the parties' states of mind, but if intent were wholly subjective there would be no parol evidence rule, no contract case could be decided without a jury trial, and no one could know the effect of a commercial transaction until years after the documents were inked. That would be a devastating blow to business. Contract law gives effect to the parties' wishes, but they must express these openly. Put differently, "intent" in contract law is objective rather than subjective — a point Interway makes by holding that as a matter of law parties who make their pact "subject to" a later definitive agreement have manifested an (objective) intent not to be bound, which under the parol evidence rule becomes the definitive intent even if one party later says that the true intent was different. As the Supreme Court of Illinois said in Schek v. Chicago Transit Authority, 42 Ill. 2d 362, 364, 247 N.E.2d 886, 888 (1969), "intent must be determined solely from the language used when no ambiguity in its terms exists." See also Feldman v. Allegheny International, Inc., 850 F.2d 1217 (7th Cir. 1988) (Illinois law). . . . Parties may decide for themselves whether the results of preliminary negotiations bind them, . . . but they do this through their words.

Because letters of intent are written without the care that will be lavished on the definitive agreement, it may be a bit much to put dispositive weight on "subject to" in every case, and we do not read Interway as giving these the status of magic words. They might have been used carelessly, and if the full agreement showed that the formal contract was to be nothing but a memorial of an agreement already reached, the letter of intent would be enforceable. Borg-Warner Corp. v. Anchor Coupling Co., 16 Ill. 2d 234, 156 N.E.2d 513 (1958). Conversely, Empro cannot claim comfort from the fact that the letter of intent does not contain a flat disclaimer, such as the one in Feldman pronouncing that the letter creates no obligations at all. The text and structure of the letter — the objective manifestations of intent — might show that the parties agreed to bind themselves to some extent immediately. Borg-Warner is such a case. One party issued an option, which called itself "firm and binding"; the other party accepted; the court found this a binding contract even though some terms remained open. After all, an option to purchase is nothing if not binding in advance of the definitive contract. The parties to Borg-Warner conceded that the option and acceptance usually would bind; the only argument in the case concerned whether the open terms were so important that a contract could not arise even if the parties wished to be bound, a subject that divided the court. See 156 N.E.2d at 930-36 (Schaefer, J., dissenting).

A canvass of the terms of the letter Empro sent does not assist it, however. "Subject to" a definitive agreement appears twice. The letter also recites, twice, that it contains the "general terms and conditions," implying that each side retained the right to make (and stand on) additional demands. Empro insulated itself from binding effect by listing, among the conditions to which the deal was "subject," the "approval of the shareholders and board of directors of Empro." The board could veto a deal negotiated by the firm's agents for a reason such as the belief that Ball-Co had been offered too much (otherwise the officers, not the board, would be the firm's final decisionmakers, yet state law vests major decisions in the board). The shareholders could decline to give their assent for any reason (such as distrust of new business ventures) and could not even be required to look at the documents, let alone consider the merits of the deal. See Earl Sneed, The Shareholder May Vote As He Pleases: Theory and Fact, 22 U. Pittsburgh L. Rev. 23, 31-36, 40-42 (1960) (collecting cases). Empro even took care to require the return of its $5,000 in earnest money "without set off, in the event this transaction is not closed," although the seller usually gets to keep the earnest money if the buyer changes its mind. So Empro made clear that it was free to walk.

> Deposit

Neither the text nor the structure of the letter suggests that it was to be a one-sided commitment, an option in Empro's favor binding only Ball-Co. From the beginning Ball-Co assumed that it could negotiate terms in addition to, or different from, those in the letter of intent. The cover letter from Ball-Co's lawyer returning the signed letter of intent to Empro stated that the "terms and conditions are generally acceptable" but that "some clarifications are needed in Paragraph 3(c) (last sentence)," the provision concerning Ball-Co's security interest. "Some clarifications are needed" is an ominous noise in a negotiation, foreboding many a stalemate. Although we do not know what "clarifications" counsel had in mind, the specifics are not important. It is enough that even on signing the letter of intent Ball-Co proposed to change the bargain, conduct consistent with the purport of the letter's text and structure.

Highlights no intent to be bound

The shoals that wrecked this deal are common hazards in business negotiations. Letters of intent and agreements in principle often, and here, do no more than set the stage for negotiations on details. Sometimes the details can be ironed out; sometimes they can't. Illinois, as . . . *Interway* and *Feldman* show, allows parties to approach agreement in stages, without fear that by reaching a preliminary understanding they have bargained away their privilege to disagree on the specifics. Approaching agreement by stages is a valuable method of doing business. So long as Illinois preserves the availability of this device, a federal court in a diversity case must send the disappointed party home empty-handed. Empro claims that it is entitled at least to recover its "reliance expenditures," but the only expenditures it has identified are those normally associated with pre-contractual efforts: its complaint mentions the expenses "in negotiating with defendants, in investigating and reviewing defendants' business, and in preparing to acquire defendants' business." Outlays of this sort cannot bind the other side any more than paying an expert to tell you whether the painting at the auction is a genuine Rembrandt compels the auctioneer to accept your bid.

Reliance Damages not recoverable b/c there is no contract

Expenses pre-contract are not recoverable

Affirmed.

Reread: Restatement §26 (p. 271)

RESTATEMENT (SECOND) OF CONTRACTS

§27.   EXISTENCE OF CONTRACT WHERE WRITTEN MEMORIAL IS CONTEMPLATED

Manifestations of assent that are in themselves sufficient to conclude a contract will not be prevented from so operating by the fact that the parties also manifest an intention to prepare and adopt a written memorial thereof; but the circumstances may show that the agreements are preliminary negotiations. (Embro v. Ball Co.)

STUDY GUIDE: In the next case, the court finds that a preliminary memorandum can constitute a binding contract. Can the facts in this case be distinguished from those in Empro? *Given the court's reasoning, could the memorandum have been drafted so as to be either clearly enforceable or clearly unenforceable?*

ARNOLD PALMER GOLF CO. v. FUQUA INDUSTRIES, INC.
United States Court of Appeals, Sixth Circuit,
541 F.2d 584 (1976)

McCree,* Circuit Judge.

This is an appeal from the district court's grant of summary judgment in favor of defendant Fuqua Industries, Inc. (Fuqua) in an action for breach of contract. The district court determined that a document captioned "Memorandum of Intent" and signed by both parties was not a contract because it evidenced the intent of the parties not to be contractually bound. We reverse and remand for trial. —> Holding!

Arnold Palmer Golf Company (Palmer) was incorporated under Ohio law in 1961, and has been primarily engaged in designing and marketing various lines of golf clubs, balls, bags, gloves, and other golf accessories. Palmer did none of its own manufacturing, but engaged other companies to produce its products. In the late 1960's, Palmer's management concluded that it was essential for future growth and profitability to acquire manufacturing facilities.

To that end, in January, 1969, Mark McCormack, Palmer's Executive Vice-President, and E. D. Kenna, Fuqua's President, met in New York City to consider a possible business relationship between the two corporations. The parties' interest in establishing a business relationship continued and they held several more meetings and discussions where the general outline of the proposed relationship was defined. In November 1969, Fuqua, with Palmer's assistance and approval, acquired Fernquest and Johnson, a

---

*Wade H. McCree (1920-1987) earned his law degree from Harvard Law School in 1944. He was one of the most influential African-American judges of the twentieth century. He was appointed to serve on the Federal District Court in Detroit in 1961, and then served on the Court of Appeals for the 6th Circuit from 1966-1977. At the time of his death, he was working as a law professor at the University of Michigan. — S.Q.

California manufacturer of golf clubs. The minutes of the Fuqua Board of Directors meeting on November 3, 1969, reveal that Fuqua:

> Proposed that this Corporation participate in the golf equipment industry in association with Arnold Palmer Golf Co. and Arnold Palmer Enterprises, Inc. The business would be conducted in two parts. One part would be composed of a corporation engaged in the manufacture and sale of golf clubs and equipment directly related to the playing of the game of golf. This Corporation would be owned to the extent of 25% by Fuqua and 75% by the Arnold Palmer interests. Fuqua would transfer the Fernquest & Johnson business to the new corporation as Fuqua's contribution.

In November and December of 1969 further discussions and negotiations occurred and revised drafts of a memorandum of intent were distributed.

The culmination of the discussions was a six page document denominated as a Memorandum of Intent. It provided in the first paragraph that:

> This memorandum will serve to confirm the general understanding which has been reached regarding the acquisition of 25% of the stock of Arnold Palmer Golf Company ("Palmer") by Fuqua Industries, Inc. ("Fuqua") in exchange for all of the outstanding stock of Fernquest and Johnson Golf Company, Inc. ("F & J"), a wholly-owned California subsidiary of Fuqua, and money in the amount of $700,000; and for the rendition of management services by Fuqua.

The Memorandum of Intent contained detailed statements concerning, *inter alia*, the form of the combination, the manner in which the business would be conducted, the loans that Fuqua agreed to make to Palmer, and the warranties and covenants to be contained in the definitive agreement.

Paragraph 10 of the Memorandum of Intent stated:

> (10) *Preparation of Definitive Agreement.* Counsel for Palmer and counsel for Fuqua will proceed as promptly as possible to prepare an agreement acceptable to Palmer and Fuqua for the proposed combination of businesses. Such agreement will contain the representations, warranties, covenants and conditions, as generally outlined in the example submitted by Fuqua to Palmer. . . .

In the last paragraph of the Memorandum of Intent, the parties indicated that:

> (11) *Conditions.* The obligations of Palmer and Fuqua shall be subject to fulfillment of the following conditions:
> (i) preparation of the definitive agreement for the proposed combination in form and content satisfactory to both parties and their respective counsel;
> (ii) approval of such definitive agreement by the Board of Directors of Fuqua; . . .

The Memorandum of Intent was signed by Palmer and by the President of Fuqua. Fuqua had earlier released a statement to the press upon Palmer's signing that "Fuqua Industries, Inc., and The Arnold Palmer Golf Co. have agreed to cooperate in an enterprise that will serve the golfing industry, from the golfer to the greens keeper."

In February, 1970, the Chairman of Fuqua's Board of Directors, J. B. Fuqua, told Douglas Kenna, Fuqua's President, that he did not want to go through with the Palmer deal. Shortly thereafter Kenna informed one of Palmer's corporate officers that the transaction was terminated.

Palmer filed the complaint in this case on July 24, 1970. Nearly three and one-half years later, on January 14, 1974, the defendant filed a motion for summary judgment. More than one year after the briefs had been filed by the parties, on May 30, 1975, the district court granted defendant's motion.

The district court determined that:

> The parties were not to be subject to any obligations until a definitive agreement satisfactory to the parties and their counsel had been prepared. The fact that this agreement had to be "satisfactory" implies necessarily that such an agreement might be unsatisfactory. . . . The parties by the terms they used elected not to be bound by this memorandum and the Court finds that they were not bound.

The primary issue in this case is whether the parties intended to enter into a binding agreement when they signed the Memorandum of Intent, and the primary issue in this appeal is whether the district court erred in determining this question on a motion for summary judgment. The substantive law of Ohio applies.

We agree with the district court that both parties must have a clear understanding of the terms of an agreement and an intention to be bound by its terms before an enforceable contract is created.[3] As Professor Corbin has observed:

> The courts are quite agreed upon general principles. The parties have power to contract as they please. They can bind themselves orally or by informal letters or telegrams if they like. On the other hand, they can maintain

---

3. *See, e.g., McMillen v. Willys Sales Corp.*, 118 Ohio App. 20, 193 N.E.2d 160 (1962). Section 26 of the Restatement of Contracts states the general rule that Ohio follows:

> Mutual manifestations of assent that are in themselves sufficient to make a contract will not be prevented from so operating by the mere fact that the parties also manifest an intention to prepare and adopt a written memorial thereof; but other facts may show that the manifestations are merely preliminary expressions as stated in Section 25.

Comment a to Section 26 of the Restatement explains the considerations that enter into a determination whether a binding contract exists:

> Parties who plan to make a final written instrument as the expression of their contract, necessarily discuss the proposed terms of the contract before they enter into it and often, before the final writing is made, agree upon all the terms which they plan to incorporate therein. This they may do orally or by exchange of several writings. It is possible thus to make a contract to execute subsequently a final writing which shall contain certain provisions. If parties have definitely agreed that they will do so, and that the final writing shall contain these provisions and no others, they have then fulfilled all the requisites for the formation of a contract. On the other hand, if the preliminary agreement is incomplete, it being apparent that the determination of certain details is deferred until the writing is made out; or if an intention is manifested in any way that legal obligations between the parties shall be deferred until the writing is made, the preliminary negotiations and agreements do not constitute a contract.

complete immunity from all obligation, even though they have expressed agreement orally or informally upon every detail of a complex transaction. The matter is merely one of expressed intention. If their expressions convince the court that they intended to be bound without a formal document, their contract is consummated, and the expected formal document will be nothing more than a memorial of that contract. 1 Corbin on Contracts, §30 (1963). (Footnote omitted.)

The decision whether the parties intended to enter a contract must be based upon an evaluation of the circumstances surrounding the parties' discussions. The introduction of extrinsic evidence does not violate the parol evidence rule because that rule applies only after an integrated or a partially integrated agreement has been found. Itek Corp. v. Chicago Aerial, 248 A.2d 625 (Del. 1968), Smith v. Dotterweich, 200 N.Y. 299, 93 N.E. 985 (1911), 3 Corbin on Contracts, ss 576, 577. As Judge Kalbfleisch observed in New York Central Railroad Co. v. General Motors Corp., 182 F. Supp. 273, 285 (N.D. Ohio 1960):

> The greatest latitude should be given in developing the surrounding situations and conditions attending the negotiations for the consummation of a contract, and the language employed in a contract should be construed in the light of circumstances surrounding the contracting parties at the time. *Circumstantial evidence is as competent to prove a contract as it is to prove a crime.* (Emphasis added.)

At bottom, the question whether the parties intended a contract is a factual one, not a legal one, and, except in the clearest cases, the question is for the finder of fact to resolve. See Godfrey v. Heublein, 219 F.2d 654, 656 (2d Cir. 1955), 1 Corbin on Contracts, §30.

We held in S. J. Groves & Sons Co. v. Ohio Turnpike Comm'n, 315 F.2d 235 (6th Cir.), *cert. denied*, 375 U.S. 824, 84 S. Ct. 65, 11 L. Ed. 2d 57 (1963), also a case governed by the substantive law of Ohio, that summary judgment was inappropriate in a breach of contract case that involved "complex facts and issues." Judge Shackelford Miller, writing for the court, stated:

> It is often the case that although the basic facts are not in dispute, the parties in good faith may nevertheless disagree about the inferences to be drawn from these facts, what the intention of the parties was as shown by the facts, or whether an estoppel or a waiver of certain rights admitted to exist should be drawn from such facts. Under such circumstances the case is not one to be decided by the Trial Judge on a motion for summary judgment. 315 F.2d at 237-38.

The Delaware Supreme Court considered a case similar to this one in Itek Corp. v. Chicago Aerial, *supra*. Like the district court here, the trial court in *Itek* granted defendants' motion for summary judgment in a breach of contract action based upon a letter of intent. The letter of intent provided that the parties:

> [S]hall make every reasonable effort to agree upon and have prepared as quickly as possible a contract providing for the foregoing purchase by Itek

and sale by CAI, subject to the approval of CAI stockholders, embodying the above terms and such other terms and conditions as the parties shall agree upon. If the parties fail to agree upon and execute such a contract they shall be under no further obligations to one another. 248 A.2d at 627.

The trial judge decided in favor of the defendants because of the last sentence quoted above. The Delaware Supreme Court, considering the entire document and other evidence submitted by the plaintiff, reversed, determining that:

There is evidence which, if accepted by the trier of fact, would support the conclusion that . . . Itek and CAI intended to be bound. . . . There is also evidence which, if accepted by the trier of fact, would support the conclusion that subsequently, . . . CAI willfully failed to negotiate in good faith and to make "every reasonable effort" to agree upon a formal contract, as it was required to do. 248 A.2d at 629.

In a Third Circuit opinion, Melo-Sonics Corp. v. Cropp, 342 F.2d 856 (1965), the court reversed a district court's judgment in favor of defendants on a motion to dismiss a complaint. The plaintiffs contended that they had a contract with defendants which the latter had breached. Plaintiffs relied on a telegram they sent to defendants, and defendants' subsequent acceptance, as constituting a contractual agreement. The telegram provided in pertinent part:

My three clients are willing to sell their capital stock in said corporations for the total price of one million five hundred thousand ($1,500,000) dollars subject to formalizing a preliminary agreement along lines previously discussed. Will be in your office at 10:00 A.M. on February 15, 1960 with my clients for purpose of formalizing such an agreement. 342 F.2d at 858.

The defendants eventually notified plaintiffs that they would not sign the agreement, whereupon plaintiffs filed suit.

The reviewing court pointed out that it would be permissible for the district court to make a finding of fact that no contract existed after it had conducted a full hearing, but that where no trial had been conducted and no findings of fact had been made it was improper to grant the defendants' motion to dismiss because plaintiffs' claim, if proved, entitled them to recovery.

Considering this appeal in the light of these authorities, we determine that our proper course is to remand this case to the district court for trial because we believe that the issue of the parties' intention to be bound is a proper one for resolution by the trier of fact. Upon first blush it may appear that the Memorandum of Intent is no more than preliminary negotiation between the parties. A cursory reading of the conditions contained in paragraph 11, by themselves, may suggest that the parties did not intend to be bound by the Memorandum of Intent.

Nevertheless, the memorandum recited that a "general understanding (had) been reached." And, as the *Itek* court noted, the entire document and relevant circumstances surrounding its adoption must be considered in making a determination of the parties' intention.[4] In this case we find an extensive document that appears to reflect all essential terms concerning the transfer of Arnold Palmer stock to Fuqua in exchange for all outstanding stock in Fernquest and Johnson. The form of combination, the location of the principal office of Palmer, the license rights, employment contracts of Palmer personnel and the financial obligations of Fuqua are a few of the many areas covered in the Memorandum of Intent, and they are all described in unqualified terms. The Memorandum states, for instance, that "Fuqua *will* transfer all of the . . . stock," that the "principal office of Palmer *will* be moved to Atlanta," that "Palmer . . . *shall* possess an exclusive license," and that "Fuqua *agrees* to advance to Palmer up to an aggregate of $700,000. . . ." (Emphasis added.)

Paragraph 10 of the Memorandum states, also in unqualified language, that counsel for the parties "will proceed as promptly as possible to prepare an agreement acceptable to (the parties). . . ." We believe that this paragraph may be read merely to impose an obligation upon the parties to memorialize their agreement. We do not mean to suggest that this is the correct interpretation. The provision is also susceptible to an interpretation that the parties did not intend to be bound.

As we have indicated above, it is permissible to refer to extrinsic evidence to determine whether the parties intended to be bound by the Memorandum of Intent. In this regard, we observe that Fuqua circulated a press release in January 1970 that would tend to sustain Palmer's claim that the two parties intended to be bound by the Memorandum of Intent. Fuqua's statement said that the two companies "have agreed to cooperate in an enterprise that will serve the golfing industry."

Upon a review of the evidence submitted in connection with the motion for summary judgment, we believe that there is presented a factual issue whether the parties contractually obligated themselves to prepare a definitive agreement in accordance with the understanding of the parties contained in the Memorandum of Intent. Just as in *S. J. Groves, supra*, we believe that the parties may properly "disagree about the inferences to be drawn from (the basic facts that are not in dispute or) what the intention of the parties was as shown by the facts." 315 F.2d at 237. Because the facts and the inferences from the facts in this case indicate that the parties may have intended to be bound by the Memorandum of Intent, we hold that the district court erred in determining that no contract existed as a matter of law.

We reject appellee's argument that summary judgment was appropriate because the obligations of the parties were subject to an express condition that was not met. We believe a question of fact is presented whether the parties intended the conditions in paragraph 11 to operate only if the definitive agreement was not in conformity with the general understanding contained in the Memorandum of Intent. See Frank Horton & Co. v. Cook Electric Co., 356 F.2d 485, 490 (7th Cir.), *cert. denied*, 384 U.S. 952, 86 S. Ct.

---

4. Parties may orally or by informal memoranda, or by both, agree upon all essential terms of the contract and effectively bind themselves, if that is their intention, even though they contemplate the execution, at a later time, of a formal document to memorialize their undertaking. Comerata v. Chaumont, Inc., 52 N.J. Super. 299, 145 A.2d 471 (1958).

1572, 16 L. Ed. 2d 548 (1966). The parties may well have intended that there should be no binding obligation until the definitive agreement was signed, but we regard this question as one for the fact finder to determine after a consideration of the relevant evidence.

Appellee also argues that the district court's judgment should be affirmed because, as a matter of law, Palmer cannot recover lost profits in any amount. Appellant prayed for damages in its complaint in the amount of $18,750,000. Appellee contends that because Palmer had a history of losses and because Ohio law does not permit recovery of lost profits in a new business, the district court's grant of summary judgment in favor of defendant should be upheld.[5]

We believe that this issue must abide further proofs. As appellant points out (1) it seeks damages for more than lost profits, and (2) the damages sought for lost profits relate in large part to an established business that was to be acquired by Palmer.

Accordingly, the judgment of the district court is reversed and the case is remanded for proceedings not inconsistent with this opinion.

STUDY GUIDE: Below is the entire Memorandum in Arnold Palmer. *Reading the document, do you think that it should be read as creating a contract or not? If you were representing the defendant, how would you have drafted the language differently to secure your client's interests? What if you were representing the plaintiff?*

MEMORANDUM OF INTENT FOR THE ACQUISITION OF 25% OF THE STOCK OF ARNOLD PALMER GOLF COMPANY IN EXCHANGE FOR CERTAIN ASSETS OF FUQUA INDUSTRIES, INC.

This memorandum will serve to confirm the general understanding which has been reached regarding the acquisition of 25% of the stock of Arnold Palmer Golf Company ("Palmer") by Fuqua Industries, Inc. ("Fuqua") in exchange for all of the outstanding stock of Fernquest and Johnson Golf Company, Inc. ("F & J"), a wholly-owned California subsidiary of Fuqua, and money in the amount of $700,000; and for the rendition of management services by Fuqua.

(1) *Form of the Combination.* Fuqua will transfer to Palmer all of the issued and outstanding stock of Fernquest & Johnson Golf Company and cash in the amount of $700,000 in exchange for an amount of common stock, $.50 par value, of Palmer ("Palmer Common Stock") equal to 25% of the total number of shares of Palmer Common Stock which will be outstanding, subject to option, or issuable upon conversion, after such issuance.

---

5. We note that the district court did not consider either the loss of profits issue or the express condition issue.

(2) *Conduct of Business.* The principal office of Palmer will be moved to Atlanta, Georgia, and the transfer of operations will occur as quickly as possible after Palmer has been qualified to do business in the state of Georgia. Fuqua will provide Palmer with management services including financial, marketing, legal, industrial engineering, insurance procurement, corporate planning, data processing, purchasing and general management services at Fuqua's cost. The general operating manager of Palmer, with the title of President and Chief Operating Officer, will be nominated by Fuqua but shall be subject to the approval of the Board of Directors of Palmer and shall serve at the pleasure of such Board. Arnold Palmer, individually, shall be Chairman of the Board of Palmer, and Mark McCormack will be Vice Chairman of the Board of Palmer.

(3) *License Rights to the Use of the Name "Arnold Palmer."* Palmer and/or a wholly-owned subsidiary shall possess an exclusive license or licenses in the form attached hereto for the use of the name "Arnold Palmer" in connection with the manufacture and sale of golf clubs, golf balls, golf bags and golf gloves in the United States and Canada. The licenses are for a period expiring in the year 1991 and are exclusive licenses. Certified copies of the licenses shall be attached as exhibits to the definitive agreement for the acquisition provided for in paragraph 10 below. Palmer shall represent and warrant as to the validity, exclusiveness and duration of such licenses.

(4) *Employment Contracts.* Palmer and/or its wholly-owned subsidiary will have employment contracts with Arnold Palmer and Mark McCormack expiring in the year of 1991 in the form attached hereto. Palmer will have no other written employment contracts except an acceptable contract with Robert Robinson.

(5) *Loans and Investments by Fuqua.* Fuqua agrees to advance to Palmer up to an aggregate of $700,000, payable 150 days after demand with interest payable from time to time at the rate then charged, giving effect to compensating balances, to Fuqua by The Chase Manhattan Bank, N.A. and successor lenders, plus one quarter of one per cent as an administrative charge, and secured by a pledge of the F & J common stock. From such funds Palmer shall cause F & J to repay to Fuqua up to the sum of $200,000 which Fuqua acknowledges will be the maximum amount owed by F & J to Fuqua. Additional funds may be advanced by Fuqua to Palmer upon such terms and conditions as the Board of Directors of Palmer and Fuqua may determine.

(6) *Investment Intent and Registration Rights.* The stock of Palmer issued to Fuqua shall be issued and received for investment and not with a view to the sale or other distribution thereof; Fuqua will execute an agreement evidencing the foregoing intent; and the certificates evidencing such shares shall be appropriately legended to express such investment intent. Fuqua will have "piggy-back" registration rights.

(7) *Palmer Qualified Stock Options.* Palmer has adopted a "Qualified Stock Option Plan" pursuant to the Internal Revenue Code of 1954, as amended. No options have been granted thereunder and all proposals to grant shares thereunder shall be canceled (EDK) (AJL). No other options will be granted prior to the Closing.

(8) *Financial Statements.* On or before the Closing, Palmer shall submit to Fuqua financial statements as of December 31, 1969, certified by Arthur Anderson and Company, independent public accountants, including (i) a balance sheet as of that date which shall not reflect any material adverse change in the condition of Palmer since the balance sheet audited by Arthur Anderson and Company as of December 31, 1968, a copy of which has been submitted to Fuqua, except for changes incurred as a result of the operating loss incurred in the calendar year 1969, and (ii) an income statement for the year then ended which shall reveal an operating loss of not in excess of $200,000. Fuqua has already delivered to Palmer a copy of the acquisition agreement pursuant to which Fuqua acquired F & J, including financial statements attached thereto as exhibits, and shall represent and warrant that there has not been any material adverse change in the condition of F & J and its wholly-owned subsidiary as set forth in said acquisition agreement since the date thereof.

(9) *Representations, Warranties, Conditions and Covenants.* The definitive agreement provided for in paragraph 10 below for the combination of the businesses shall contain representations, warranties, conditions, and covenants in the general form used by Fuqua in connection with the acquisition of businesses by Fuqua. Fuqua has delivered to Palmer an example of such provisions.

In addition, such agreement will provide that the following shall be conditions to the obligations of Fuqua thereunder:

(a) Professional Golf Company ("Pro Golf") will advise Palmer in writing that its requirements contract with Palmer dated October 27, 1961, does not obligate Palmer to purchase future requirements from Pro Golf.

(b) There will be no obligation on the part of Palmer to continue under any lease from Pro Golf to Palmer.

(c) Termination of requirements contract with Windbreaker-Danville Company, dated January 20, 1962.

(d) The life insurance policies on the lives of Arnold Palmer and Mark McCormack will be assets of Palmer.

(e) There will be a warranty by Arnold Palmer that he has no present obligation to Wilson Sporting Goods Co.

(f) Palmer will have the written authority to disapprove any proposed future "premium sales" of golf clubs, golf balls, golf bags and golf gloves arranged by Arnold Palmer Enterprises, Inc. in the territories in which Palmer and/or its subsidiary are licensed to sell such products.

(g) Remlap Company shall be a wholly-owned subsidiary of Palmer.

(h) Palmer will warrant that there is no present obligation to pay royalties to Jack Harkins on the sale of golf balls and that there will not be in the future unless steel center golf balls are sold.

(10) *Preparation of Definitive Agreement.* Counsel for Palmer and counsel for Fuqua will proceed as promptly as possible to prepare an agreement acceptable to Palmer and Fuqua for the proposed combination of businesses. Such agreement will contain the representations, warranties, covenants and conditions, as generally outlined in the example submitted by Fuqua to Palmer and referred to in paragraph 9 hereof. In addition, the definitive agreement will provide for indemnification of

Fuqua by the principal stockholders of Palmer (Arnold Palmer, Robert Caldwell, Mark McCormack and Hardwick Caldwell) (EDK) (AJL) for a period of three years after the closing in the event that Palmer shall have undisclosed liabilities in excess of $100,000, pursuant to which said principal stockholders will be obligated to indemnify Fuqua in an amount equal to only 25% of so much, if any, of such undisclosed liabilities as are in excess of $100,000 and shall as a group in no event be obligated to make payments in excess of a total of $1,000,000 for all four stockholders combined (EDK) (AJL).

(11) *Conditions.* The obligations of Palmer and Fuqua shall be subject to fulfillment of the following conditions:

(i) preparation of the definitive agreement for the proposed combination in form and content satisfactory to both parties and their respective counsel;

(ii) approval of such definitive agreement by the Board of Directors of Fuqua;

(iii) approval of such definitive agreement by the Board of Directors of Palmer;

(iv) approval by the stockholders of Palmer of certain amendments to the Articles & Regulations of Palmer which are necessary in order to consummate said agreement;

(v) approval by the respective counsel of Palmer and Fuqua of all legal matters;

(vi) that between the date of the definitive agreement and the Closing, there shall have been no material adverse change in the business or financial condition of Palmer or F & J;

(vii) requisite approval by creditors of Palmer and Fuqua;

(viii) the Closing shall have occurred not later than March 31, 1970.

(12) *Publicity.* All announcements and publicity relating to the proposed combination shall be subject to the mutual approval of Palmer and Fuqua.

The foregoing correctly setting forth the general understanding and agreement of the respective parties, and parties hereby confirm their acceptance by signing and delivering copies of this memorandum, as of this day of December, 1969.

ARNOLD PALMER GOLF COMPANY
By/s/ Arthur J. Lafave, Jr.
President's Designee
FUQUA INDUSTRIES, INC.
By/s/ E. D. Kenna
President

STUDY GUIDE: In the following case, the court faced an issue similar to that presented in Empro *and* Arnold Palmer. *Does the court in this case enforce the memorandum as a contract? How did it alter the remedy? Does it respond adequately to the traditional objections against enforcing "agreements to agree"?*

COPELAND v. BASKIN ROBBINS U.S.A.
Court of Appeal, Second District, Division 7, California,
96 Cal. App. 4th 1251, 117 Cal. Rptr. 2d 875 (2002)

JOHNSON,* Acting P.J.

We address an unsettled question in California: may a party sue for breach of a contract to negotiate an agreement or is such a "contract" merely an unenforceable "agreement to agree"? We hold a contract to negotiate an agreement is distinguishable from a so-called "agreement to agree" and can be formed and breached just like any other contract. We further hold, however, even if the plaintiff in this case could establish the defendant's liability for breach of contract he is limited to reliance damages — a form of recovery he has disavowed and defendant has shown he cannot prove. For this reason we affirm the trial court's judgment for defendant.

FACTS AND PROCEEDINGS BELOW

The following facts are undisputed.

Baskin Robbins operated an ice cream manufacturing plant in the city of Vernon. When the company announced its intention to close the plant, Copeland expressed an interest in acquiring it. The parties commenced negotiations. Copeland made clear from the outset his agreement to purchase the plant was contingent on Baskin Robbins agreeing to purchase the ice cream he manufactured there. Copeland testified at his deposition the ice cream purchase arrangement, known as "co-packing," was "critical" and "a key to the deal." Without co-packing, Copeland testified, "this deal doesn't work." Baskin Robbins does not deny the co-packing arrangement was an indispensable part of the contract to purchase the plant.

After several months of negotiations an agreement took shape under which Copeland would purchase the plant's manufacturing assets and sublease the plant property. Baskin Robbins would purchase seven million gallons of ice cream from Copeland over a three-year period.

In May 1999 Baskin Robbins sent Copeland a letter, which stated in relevant part: "This letter details the terms which our Supply Chain executives have approved for subletting and sale of our Vernon manufacturing facility/equipment and a product supply agreement. . . . (1) Baskin Robbins will sell [Copeland] Vernon's ice cream manufacturing equipment . . . for $1,300,000 cash. . . . (2) Baskin Robbins would agree, subject to a separate co-packing agreement and negotiated pricing, to provide [Copeland] a three year co-packing agreement for 3,000,000 gallons in year 1, 2,000,000 gallons in year 2 and 2,000,000 in year 3. . . . If the above is acceptable please acknowledge by returning a copy of this letter with a non-refundable

---

*Earl Johnson, Jr. (1933-†) was born in Watertown, South Dakota. He received his Bachelor's degree from Northwestern University and attended law school at the University of Chicago. After serving in the United States Navy from 1955-1958, he worked in the U.S. Attorney's office and was a law professor at USC. He was appointed to the California Court of Appeal in 1982, and served there until his retirement in 2007. — S.Q.

check for three thousand dollars. . . . We should be able to coordinate a closing [within] thirty days thereafter." Copeland signed a statement at the bottom of the letter agreeing "[t]he above terms are acceptable" and returned the letter to Baskin Robbins along with the $3000 deposit.

After Copeland accepted the terms in the May 1999 letter, the parties continued negotiating over the terms of the co-packing agreement. Among the issues to be settled were the price Baskin Robbins would pay for the ice cream, the flavors Copeland would produce, quality standards and controls, who would bear the loss from spoilage, and trademark protection. Copeland testified he believed in June 1999 he reached an oral agreement with Baskin Robbins on a price for the ice cream of his cost plus 85 cents per tub. He conceded, however, the parties had not agreed on how the cost component was to be determined and so far as he knew there was no written memorandum of this pricing agreement. None of the other issues were settled before Baskin Robbins allegedly breached the contract.

In July 1999, Baskin Robbins wrote to Copeland breaking off negotiations over the co-packing arrangement and returning his $3000 deposit. The letter explained Baskin Robbins' parent company had "recently . . . made strategic decisions around the Baskin Robbins business" and "the proposed co-packing arrangement [is] out of alignment with our strategy." Therefore, Baskin Robbins informed Copeland, "we will not be engaging in any further negotiations of a co-packing arrangement." Although Baskin Robbins offered to proceed with the agreement for the sale and lease of the Vernon plant assets it did not insist on doing so, apparently accepting Copeland's view the lack of a co-packing agreement was a "deal-breaker."

In his suit for breach of contract, Copeland alleged he and Baskin Robbins entered into a contract which provided Baskin Robbins would enter into a co-packing agreement with Copeland under the terms set out in the May 1999 letter and additional terms to be negotiated. Baskin Robbins breached this contract by "unreasonably and wrongfully refusing to enter into any co-packing agreement with [Copeland]." As a result of this breach of contract Copeland suffered expectation damages "in the form of lost profits . . . as well as lost employment opportunities and injury to his reputation." In response to a discovery request, Copeland stated his damages consisted of "lost profits from [the] three year co-packing agreement with defendants" as well as lost profits from other sales he could have made had he acquired the plant and the profit he could have earned from selling the plant equipment. Copeland's discovery responses did not provide or allege he could provide evidence of damages he suffered as a result of his relying on Baskin Robbins' promise to negotiate a co-packing agreement.

The trial court granted Baskin Robbins' motion for summary judgment based on the undisputed facts described above. The court concluded the May 1999 letter was susceptible to several interpretations but no matter how it was interpreted it failed as a contract because the essential terms of the co-packing deal were never agreed to and there was no reasonable basis upon which to determine them. Copeland filed a timely appeal from the subsequent judgment.

For the reasons discussed below we affirm the judgment albeit on a ground different from those relied upon by the trial court.

DISCUSSION

I.   A Cause of Action Will Lie for the Breach of a Contract to Negotiate an Agreement

When Baskin Robbins refused to continue negotiating the terms of the co-packing agreement Copeland faced a dilemma. "Many millions of dollars" in anticipated profits had melted away like so much banana ripple ice cream on a hot summer day. True enough, he could proceed with the contract for the purchase and lease of the Vernon plant's assets and use those assets to produce ice cream for other retailers. But, as he explained in his deposition, without the Baskin Robbins co-packing agreement he could not afford to purchase the assets and pay the on-going costs of operating the plant while he searched for other business. Alternatively he could attempt to sue Baskin Robbins for breach of the co-packing agreement on the theory the terms of the agreement set out in the May 1999 letter plus additional terms supplied by the court constituted an enforceable contract. Such a suit, however, had a slim prospect of success. While courts have been increasingly liberal in supplying missing terms in order to find an enforceable contract they do so only where the "reasonable intentions of the parties" can be ascertained. It is still the general rule that where any of the essential elements of a promise are reserved for the future agreement of both parties, no legal obligation arises "until such future agreement is made." Here, the parties agreed in the May 1999 letter as to the amount of ice cream Baskin Robbins would purchase over a three year period but, as Copeland candidly admitted, "a variety of complex terms" remained for agreement before the co-packing contract could be completed. These included price, the flavors to be manufactured, quality control standards, and responsibility for waste.

Copeland chose a third course. Rather than insist the parties had formed a co-packing contract and Baskin Robbins had breached it, he claimed the May 1999 letter constituted a contract to negotiate the remaining terms of the co-packing agreement and Baskin Robbins breached this contract by refusing without excuse to continue negotiations or, alternatively, by failing to negotiate in good faith. This path too has its difficulties. No reported California case has held breach of a contract to negotiate an agreement gives rise to a cause of action for damages. On the other hand numerous California cases have expressed the view the law provides no remedy for breach of an "agreement to agree" in the future. We believe, however, these difficulties could be overcome in an appropriate case.

Initially, we see no reason why in principle the parties could not enter into a valid, enforceable contract to negotiate the terms of a co-packing agreement. A contract, after all, is "an agreement to do or not to do a certain thing." Persons are free to contract to do just about anything that is not illegal or immoral. Conducting negotiations to buy and sell ice cream is neither.

Furthermore, as we will demonstrate below, purported contracts which the courts have dismissed as mere "agreements to agree" are distinguishable from contracts to negotiate in at least two respects.

A contract to negotiate the terms of an agreement is not, in form or substance, an "agreement to agree." If, despite their good faith efforts, the parties fail to reach ultimate agreement on the terms in issue the contract to negotiate is deemed performed and the parties are discharged from their obligations. Failure to agree is not, itself, a breach of the contract to negotiate. A party will be liable only if a failure to reach ultimate agreement resulted from a breach of that party's obligation to negotiate or to negotiate in good faith. For these reasons, criticisms of an "agreement to agree" as "absurd" and a "contradiction in terms" do not apply to a contract to negotiate an agreement.

In addition, it is important to note courts which have found purported contracts to be unenforceable "agreements to agree" have focused on the enforceability of the underlying substantive contract, not on whether the agreement to negotiate the terms of that contract is enforceable in its own right. In Autry v. Republic Productions, for example, after stating the law "provides [no] remedy for breach of an agreement to agree" the court explained this was so because "[t]he court may not imply what the parties will agree upon."

Our decision in Beck v. American Health Group illustrates the distinction between an "agreement to agree" and a contract to negotiate the terms of an agreement.

In *Beck*, the plaintiff sued the defendant for breach of contract. The alleged contract was contained in a letter to plaintiff from defendant's executive director which began: " 'It is a pleasure to draft the outline of our future agreement. . . .' " After outlining the terms of the agreement, the letter concluded: " 'If this is a general understanding of the agreement, I ask that you sign a copy of this letter, so that I might forward it to Corporate Counsel for the drafting of a contract. When we have a draft, we will discuss it and hopefully shall have a completed contract and operating unit in the very near future.' " Noting that " 'preliminary negotiations or an agreement for future negotiations *are not the functional equivalent of a valid, subsisting agreement*' " we concluded the letter "did not constitute a binding contract, but was merely 'an agreement to agree' which cannot be made the basis of a cause of action." We based our conclusion on the words of the letter which "manifest an intention of the parties that no binding contract would come into being until the terms of the letter were embodied in a formal contract to be drafted by corporate counsel."

Assume, however, the defendant in *Beck* did not present plaintiff with a draft contract and an opportunity to negotiate its terms as promised in its letter. Instead, defendant presented plaintiff with a final contract on a take-it-or-leave-it basis, refusing to negotiate any of the contract terms the plaintiff found unacceptable. Under the law as we see it, plaintiff could have a cause of action for breach of contract on the theory the letter signed by the parties constituted a contract to negotiate the terms of an agreement and defendant breached that contract by refusing to negotiate.

Most jurisdictions which have considered the question have concluded a cause of action will lie for breach of a contract to negotiate the terms of an agreement.

The *Channel Home Centers* case is illustrative. There the parties executed a letter of intent to enter into the lease of a store in a shopping center.

The letter stated, inter alia, Grossman the lessor " 'will withdraw the store from the rental market, and only negotiate the above described leasing transaction to completion.' " After Channel Home Centers expended approximately $25,000 in activities associated with the negotiations, Grossman unilaterally terminated negotiations. The following day Grossman leased the store to one of Channel Home Centers' competitors, Mr. Good Buys. Channel Home Centers sued Grossman for breach of contract based on the letter of intent. After a court trial, the court awarded judgment to Grossman. The Third Circuit Court of Appeals reversed. Distinguishing this case from one alleging merely the breach of an agreement to agree the court pointed out: "[I]t is Channel's position that [the letter of intent] is enforceable as a mutually binding obligation *to negotiate in good faith.* By unilaterally terminating negotiations with Channel and precipitously entering into a lease agreement with Mr. Good Buys, Channel argues, Grossman acted in bad faith and breached his promise to 'withdraw the Store from the rental market and only negotiate the above-described leasing transaction to completion.' " The court concluded under Pennsylvania law an agreement to negotiate in good faith is an enforceable contract.

Baskin Robbins maintains there are sound public policy reasons for not enforcing a contract to negotiate an agreement. In doing so, we would be injecting a covenant of good faith and fair dealing into the negotiation process whether or not the parties specifically agreed to such a term. Citing Professor Farnsworth, Baskin Robbins argues that instead of having a salutary effect on contract negotiations, imposing a regime of good faith and fair dealing would actually discourage parties from entering into negotiations, especially where the chances of success were slight. Alternatively, such an obligation might increase the pressure on the parties to bring the negotiations to a hasty, even if unsatisfactory conclusion, rather than risk being charged with the ill-defined wrong of bad faith negotiation. Most parties, Baskin Robbins suggests, would prefer to risk losing their out-of-pocket costs if the negotiation fails rather than risk losing perhaps millions of dollars in expectation damages if their disappointed negotiating partner can prove bad faith. Finally, Baskin Robbins argues, any precontractual wrong-doing can be adequately remedied by existing causes of action for unjust enrichment, promissory fraud and promissory estoppel.

We find Baskin Robbins' policy arguments unpersuasive.

Allowing a party to sue for breach of a contract to negotiate an agreement would not inject a covenant of good faith and fair dealing into the negotiation process in violation of the parties' intent. When two parties, under no compulsion to do so, engage in negotiations to form or modify a contract neither party has any obligation to continue negotiating or to negotiate in good faith. Only when the parties are under a contractual compulsion to negotiate does the covenant of good faith and fair dealing attach, as it does in every contract. In the latter situation the implied covenant of good faith and fair dealing has the salutary effect of creating a disincentive for acting in bad faith in contract negotiations.

Professor Farnsworth's criticisms were not directed toward a cause of action for breach of a contract to negotiate the terms of an agreement. On the contrary, Farnsworth supports such a cause of action. Rather, his criticisms were directed at the theory propounded by some European courts and legal scholars that, even absent a contractual agreement to negotiate, a general obligation of fair dealing arises out of the negotiations themselves. We rejected this theory of liability in Los Angeles Equestrian Center, Inc. v. City of Los Angeles, as did the court in Racine & Laramie.

Arguing bad faith is an uncertain concept which could cost the defendant millions of dollars in expectation damages is also without merit. For the reasons we explain below, the appropriate remedy for breach of a contract to negotiate is not damages for the injured party's lost expectations under the prospective contract but damages caused by the injured party's reliance on the agreement to negotiate. Furthermore, we disagree with those who say the courts, unlike the National Labor Relations Board or labor arbitrators, are ill equipped to determine whether people are negotiating with each other in good faith. While few of us will ever negotiate a multi-million dollar contract, each of us participates in some form of negotiation nearly every day. In most cases the question whether the defendant negotiated in good faith will be a question of fact for the jury. In our view ordinary citizens applying their experience and common sense are very well equipped to determine whether the parties negotiated with each other in good faith.

Recovery for unjust enrichment in the context of contract negotiations is usually based on ideas disclosed or services rendered during the negotiations. Where, as here, the negotiations are over the sale of goods, the subject matter of the contract is not an idea nor does the potential seller typically confer a precontractual service on the potential buyer.

A cause of action for promissory fraud is based on "[a] promise made without any intention of performing it." In many cases the defendant may have intended to negotiate in good faith when it contracted to do so but changed its mind later when, for example, a more attractive contracting partner came along.

Thus, we conclude neither unjust enrichment nor promissory fraud provide a party an adequate vehicle for relief when its negotiating partner breaks off negotiations or negotiates in bad faith.

The doctrine of promissory estoppel is generally used to enforce the defendant's clear and unambiguous promise when the plaintiff has reasonably and foreseeably relied on it. We agree a cause of action for promissory estoppel might lie if the defendant made a clear, unambiguous promise to negotiate in good faith and the plaintiff reasonably and foreseeably relied on that promise in incurring expenditures connected with the negotiation. We may also assume for the sake of argument such a cause of action could be based on an implied promise to negotiate in good faith. If these propositions are correct, then promissory estoppel is just a different rubric for determining the enforceability of a contract to negotiate an agreement.

Finally, we believe there are sound public policy reasons for protecting parties to a business negotiation from bad faith practices by their negotiating partners. Gone are the days when our ancestors sat around a fire and bargained for the exchange of stone axes for bear hides. Today the stakes are much higher and negotiations are much more complex. Deals are rarely made in a single negotiating session. Rather, they are the product of a gradual process in which agreements are reached piecemeal on a variety of issues in a series of face-to-face meetings, telephone calls, e-mails and letters involving corporate officers, lawyers, bankers, accountants, architects, engineers and others. As Professor Farnsworth observes, contracts today are not formed by discrete offers, counter-offers and acceptances. Instead they result from a gradual flow of information between the parties followed by a series of compromises and tentative agreements on major points which are finally refined into contract terms. These slow contracts are not only time-consuming but costly. For these reasons, the parties should have some assurance "their investments in time and money and effort will not be wiped out by the other party's footdragging or change of heart or taking advantage of a vulnerable position created by the negotiation." This concept is not new to California law. In Drennan v. Star Paving Co. the court applied the doctrine of promissory estoppel to hold that where a general contractor used the bid of a subcontractor in formulating its own successful bid for a job the court would imply a promise by the subcontractor not to revoke its bid in order "to preclude the injustice that would result if the offer could be revoked after the offeree had acted in detrimental reliance thereon."

For obvious reasons, damages for breach of a contract to negotiate an agreement are measured by the injury the plaintiff suffered in relying on the defendant to negotiate in good faith. This measure encompasses the plaintiff's out-of-pocket costs in conducting the negotiations and may or may not include lost opportunity costs. The plaintiff cannot recover for lost expectations (profits) because there is no way of knowing what the ultimate terms of the agreement would have been or even if there would have been an ultimate agreement.

II.   Baskin Robbins Is Entitled to Summary Judgment Because It Has Shown Copeland Cannot Establish Reliance Damages

A defendant is entitled to summary judgment if it "show[s] that one or more elements of the cause of action . . . cannot be established" by the plaintiff. The defendant may not make this showing through argument alone but may do so through the plaintiff's discovery responses if those responses demonstrate "the plaintiff does not possess, and cannot reasonably obtain, needed evidence" to establish his cause of action.

As we explained in Part I, reliance damages are the only form of recovery available in an action on a contract to negotiate an agreement. Baskin Robbins has shown through Copeland's complaint and discovery responses he cannot establish reliance damages.

The only damages Copeland seeks in his complaint are derived from what he would have received if the underlying contract had been consummated, e.g., the profits he hoped to earn through the co-packing agreement and other ice cream sales. Satisfactory proof of such damages is impossible because there is no way to know what the eventual terms of the co-packing agreement would have been, or even if the parties would have reached an agreement. Copeland's complaint disavowed reliance damages, e.g., time spent, expenses incurred, opportunities missed while negotiating with Baskin Robbins.

More importantly, in response to interrogatories from Baskin Robbins, Copeland stated his damages were his lost profits from the ice cream deals and the profit he could have made from selling the plant equipment. We conclude the allegations in Copeland's complaint together with his discovery responses constitute a sufficient showing Copeland "does not possess, and cannot reasonably obtain, needed evidence" to establish reliance damages and, therefore, Baskin Robbins was entitled to summary judgment.

DISPOSITION

The judgment is affirmed.

REFERENCE: Barnett, §§3.2, 3.2.1, 3.2.2
Farnsworth, §§3.10-3.11
Calamari & Perillo, §§2.5-2.6
Murray, §§34, 35, 40

3. Revoking an Offer

Once there is an offer, the question arises of when or whether it may be revoked by the offeror. This issue is addressed by the next case and the materials that follow it.

STUDY GUIDE: Justice James says that it was the plaintiff who added the postscript to the memorandum of June 10. Would it have made a difference to the outcome if the defendant had then raised the price of the land?

DICKINSON v. DODDS
In the Court of Appeal,
2 Ch. D. 463 (1876)

On Wednesday, the 10th of June, 1874, the Defendant John Dodds signed and delivered to the Plaintiff, George Dickinson, a memorandum, of which the material part was as follows:

> I hereby agree to sell to Mr. George Dickinson the whole of the dwelling-houses, garden ground, stabling, and outbuildings thereto belonging, situate at Crest, belonging to me, for the sum of £800. As witness my hand this tenth day of June, 1874.
>
> > (Signed) *John Dodds.*
>
> P.S. — This offer to be left over until Friday, 9 o'clock, A.M. *J.D.* (the twelfth), 12th June, 1874.
>
> > (Signed) *J. Dodds.*

The bill alleged that Dodds understood and intended that the Plaintiff should have until Friday 9 A.M. within which to determine whether he would or would not purchase, and that he should absolutely have until that time the refusal of the property at the price of £800, and that the Plaintiff in fact determined to accept the offer on the morning of Thursday, the 11th of June, but did not at once signify his acceptance to Dodds, believing that he had the power to accept it until 9 A.M. on the Friday.

In the afternoon of the Thursday the Plaintiff was informed by a Mr. Berry that Dodds had been offering or agreeing to sell the property to Thomas Allan, the other Defendant. Thereupon the Plaintiff, at about half-past seven in the evening, went to the house of Mrs. Burgess, the mother-in-law of Dodds, where he was then staying, and left with her a formal acceptance in writing of the offer to sell the property. According to the evidence of Mrs. Burgess this document never in fact reached Dodds, she having forgotten to give it to him.

On the following (Friday) morning, at about seven o'clock, Berry, who was acting as agent for Dickinson, found Dodds at the Darlington railway station, and handed to him a duplicate of the acceptance by Dickinson, and explained to Dodds its purport. He replied that it was too late, as he had sold the property. A few minutes later Dickinson himself found Dodds entering a railway carriage, and handed him another duplicate of the notice of acceptance, but Dodds declined to receive it, saying, "You are too late. I have sold the property."

It appeared that on the day before, Thursday, the 11th of June, Dodds had signed a formal contract for the sale of the property to the Defendant Allan for £800, and had received from him a deposit of £40.

The bill in this suit prayed that the Defendant Dodds might be decreed specifically to perform the contract of the 10th of June, 1874; that he might be restrained from conveying the property to Allan; that Allan might be restrained from taking any such conveyance; that, if any such conveyance had been or should be made, Allan might be declared a trustee of the property for, and might be directed to convey the property to, the Plaintiff; and for damages.

The cause came on for hearing before Vice-Chancellor Bacon on the 25th of January, 1876. . . .

BACON, V.C.,* after remarking that the case involved no question of unfairness or inequality, and after stating the terms of the document of the 10th of June, 1874, and the statement of the Defendant's case as given in his answer, continued: . . .

. . . It is clear that a plain, explicit acceptance of the contract was, on Thursday, the 11th of June, delivered by the Plaintiff at the place of abode of the Defendant, and ought to have come to his hands. Whether it came to his hands or not, the fact remains that, within the time limited, the Plaintiff did

---

* *Sir James Bacon* (1798-1895) was called to the bar in 1827 and in 1846 was elected bencher of Lincoln's Inn. He served the Master of the Rolls from 1859 to 1868, when he became Commissioner in Bankruptcy for the London district. Bacon advanced to Chief Justice under the Bankruptcy Act of 1869, which he held concurrently with the office of Vice-Chancellor beginning in 1870. In 1871, Bacon was knighted and continued performing duties in both offices until the Chief Justiceship in Bankruptcy was abolished in 1883. He retired from the bench at the age of 88 and continued as a member of privy council until his death. — K.T.

accept and testify his acceptance. From that moment the Plaintiff was bound, and the Defendant could at any time, notwithstanding Allan, have filed a bill against the Plaintiff for the specific performance of the contract which he had entered into, and which the Defendant had accepted.

I am at a loss to guess upon what ground it can be said that it is not a contract which the Court will enforce. It cannot be on the ground that the Defendant had entered into a contract with Allan, because, giving to the Defendant all the latitude which can be desired, admitting that he had the same time to change his mind as he, by the agreement, gave to the Plaintiff— the law, I take it, is clear on the authorities, that if a contract, unilateral in its shape, is completed by the acceptance of the party on the other side, it becomes a perfectly valid and binding contract. It may be withdrawn from by one of the parties in the meantime, but, in order to be withdrawn from, information of that fact must be conveyed to the mind of the person who is to be affected by it. It will not do for the Defendant to say, "I made up my mind that I would withdraw, but I did not tell the Plaintiff; I did not say anything to the Plaintiff until after he had told me by a written notice and with a loud voice that he accepted the option which had been left to him by the agreement." In my opinion, after that hour on Friday, earlier than nine o'clock, when the Plaintiff and Defendant met, if not before, the contract was completed, and neither party could retire from it. . . .

There will be a decree for specific performance, with a declaration that Allan has no interest in the property; and the Plaintiff will be at liberty [to] deduct his costs of the suit out of his purchase-money.

From this decision both the Defendants appealed, and the appeals were heard on the 31st of March and the 1st of April, 1876. . . .

JAMES, L.J.,* after referring to the document of the 10th of June, 1874, continued:

The document, though beginning "I hereby agree to sell," was nothing but an offer, and was only intended to be an offer, for the Plaintiff himself tells us that he required time to consider whether he would enter into an agreement or not. Unless both parties had then agreed there was no concluded agreement then made; it was in effect and substance only an offer to sell. The Plaintiff, being minded not to complete the bargain at that time, added this memorandum — "This offer to be left over until Friday, 9 o'clock A.M., 12th June, 1874." That shows it was only an offer. There was no consideration given for the undertaking or promise, to whatever extent it may be considered binding, to keep the property unsold until 9 o'clock on Friday morning; but apparently Dickinson was of opinion, and probably Dodds was of the same opinion, that he (Dodds) was bound by that

* *Sir William Milbourne James* (1807-1881) was educated at the University of Glasgow (MA.). After a bout of ill health hampered his practice of law, he slowly developed a practice which included work with the treasury in equity, junior counsel to Woods and Forests department, the Inland Revenue, and the Board of Works. In 1853 he became a queen's counsel and Vice-Chancellor of the Duchy of Lancaster. James became Vice-Chancellor of the Court of Chancery and a knight, and he became Lord Justice of Appeal in 1870. During his tenure on the court, he served as a member of commissions on equity procedure and on the Indian code commission and the army purchase commission. During this time, James also recommended abolishment of pleadings. — K.T.

promise, and could not in any way withdraw from it, or retract it, until 9 *"naked promise"*
o'clock on Friday morning, and this probably explains a good deal of what
afterwards took place. But it is clear settled law, on one of the clearest
principles of law, that this promise, being a mere *nudum pactum* was
not binding, and that at any moment before a complete acceptance by
Dickinson of the offer, Dodds was as free as Dickinson himself. Well, that
being the state of things, it is said that the only mode in which Dodds could
assert that freedom was by actually and distinctly saying to Dickinson, "Now
I withdraw my offer." It appears to me that there is neither principle nor
authority for the proposition that there must be an express and actual withdrawal of the offer, or what is called a retractation. It must, to constitute a
contract, appear that the two minds were at one, at the same moment of
time, that is, that there was an offer continuing up to the time of the acceptance. If there was not such a continuing offer, then the acceptance comes
to nothing. Of course it may well be that the one man is bound in some way
or other to let the other man know that his mind with regard to the offer has
been changed; but in this case, beyond all question, the Plaintiff knew that
Dodds was no longer minded to sell the property to him as plainly and
clearly as if Dodds had told him in so many words, "I withdraw the
offer." This is evident from the plaintiff's own statements in the bill.

The Plaintiff says in effect that, having heard and knowing that Dodds
was no longer minded to sell to him, and that he was selling or had sold to
someone else, thinking that he could not in point of law withdraw his offer,
meaning to fix him to it, and endeavouring to bind him, "I went to the house
where he was lodging, and saw his mother-in-law, and left with her an
acceptance of the offer, knowing all the while that he had entirely changed
his mind. I got an agent to watch for him at 7 o'clock the next morning, and
I went to the train just before 9 o'clock, in order that I might catch him and
give him my notice of acceptance just before 9 o'clock, and when that
occurred he told my agent, and he told me, you are too late, and he then
threw back the paper." It is to my mind quite clear that before there was any
attempt at acceptance by the Plaintiff, he was perfectly well aware that
Dodds had changed his mind, and that he had in fact agreed to sell the
property to Allan. It is impossible, therefore, to say there was ever that
existence of the same mind between the two parties which is essential in
point of law to the making of an agreement. I am of opinion, therefore, that
the Plaintiff has failed to prove that there was any binding contract between
Dodds and himself.

MELLISH, L.J.* I am of the same opinion. . . .
. . . If an offer has been made for the sale of property, and before that
offer is accepted, the person who has made the offer enters into a binding
agreement to sell the property to somebody else, and the person to whom
the offer was first made receives notice in some way that the property has
been sold to another person, can he after that make a binding contract by

* *Sir George Mellish* (1814-1877) was educated at Eton and University College, Oxford
(B.A., M.A.), and studied law privately. He practiced law as a pleader until being called to the
bar in 1848. Several times, he refused lower court judgeships until in 1870 he was appointed
lord justice of appeal in chancery, which he held until his death. — K.T.

the acceptance of the offer? I am of opinion that he cannot. The law may be right or wrong in saying that a person who has given to another a certain time within which to accept an offer is not bound by his promise to give that time; but, if he is not bound by that promise, and may still sell the property to some one else, and if it be the law that, in order to make a contract, the two minds must be in agreement at some one time, that is, at the time of the acceptance, how is it possible that when the person to whom the offer has been made knows that the person who has made the offer has sold the property to someone else, and that, in fact, he has not remained in the same mind to sell it to him, he can be at liberty to accept the offer and thereby make a binding contract? It seems to me that would be simply absurd. If a man makes an offer to sell a particular horse in his stable, and says, "I will give you until the day after tomorrow to accept the offer," and the next day goes and sells the horse to somebody else, and receives the purchase-money from him, can the person to whom the offer was originally made then come and say, "I accept," so as to make a binding contract, and so as to be entitled to recover damages for the non-delivery of the horse? If the rule of law is that a mere offer to sell property, which can be withdrawn at any time, and which is made dependent on the acceptance of the person to whom it is made, is a mere *nudum pactum*, how is it possible that the person to whom the offer has been made can by acceptance make a binding contract after he knows that the person who has made the offer has sold the property to someone else? It is admitted law that, if a man who makes an offer dies, the offer cannot be accepted after he is dead, and parting with the property has very much the same effect as the death of the owner, for it makes the performance of the offer impossible. I am clearly of opinion that, just as when a man who has made an offer dies before it is accepted it is impossible that it can then be accepted, so when once the person to whom the offer was made knows that the property has been sold to someone else, it is too late for him to accept the offer, and on that ground I am clearly of opinion that there was no binding contract for the sale of this property by Dodds to Dickinson, and even if there had been, it seems to me that the sale of the property to Allan was first in point of time. However, it is not necessary to consider, if there had been two binding contracts, which of them would be entitled to priority in equity, because there is no binding contract between Dodds and Dickinson.

BAGGALLAY, J.A.: I entirely concur in the judgments which have been pronounced.

JAMES, L.J.: — The bill will be dismissed with costs.

Swanston, Q.C. [attorney for defendant Dodds]: — We shall have the costs of the appeal.

Kay, Q.C. [attorney for plaintiff]: — There should only be the costs of one appeal.

Sir H. Jackson, Q.C. [attorney for defendant Allan]: — The Defendant Allan was obliged to protect himself.

MELLISH, L.J.: — He had a separate case. There might, if two contracts had been proved, have been a question of priority.

JAMES, L.J.: — I think the Plaintiff must pay the costs of both appeals.

RESTATEMENT (SECOND) OF CONTRACTS

§17. REQUIREMENT OF A BARGAIN

(1) Except as stated in Subsection (2), the formation of a contract requires a bargain in which there is a manifestation of mutual assent to the exchange and a consideration.

(2) Whether or not there is a bargain a contract may be formed under special rules applicable to formal contracts or under the rules stated in §§82-94.

§18. MANIFESTATION OF MUTUAL ASSENT

Manifestation of mutual assent to an exchange requires that each party either make a promise or begin or render a performance.

§22. MODE OF ASSENT: OFFER AND ACCEPTANCE

(1) The manifestation of mutual assent to an exchange ordinarily takes the form of an offer or proposal by one party followed by an acceptance by the other party or parties.

(2) A manifestation of mutual assent may be made even though neither offer nor acceptance can be identified and even though the moment of formation cannot be determined. —→ Ask question —→ Answered (Leftkowitz)

§24. OFFER DEFINED

An offer is the manifestation of willingness to enter into a bargain, so made as to justify another person in understanding that his assent to that bargain is invited and will conclude it. (Carlill v. Carbolic Smoke)

§25. OPTION CONTRACTS

An option contract is a promise which meets the requirements for the formation of a contract and limits the promisor's power to revoke an offer.

§35. THE OFFEREE's POWER OF ACCEPTANCE

(1) An offer gives to the offeree a continuing power to complete the manifestation of mutual assent by acceptance of the offer.

(2) A contract cannot be created by acceptance of an offer after the power of acceptance has been terminated in one of the ways listed in §36.

§36. METHODS OF TERMINATION OF THE POWER OF ACCEPTANCE

(1) An offeree's power of acceptance may be terminated by
  (a) rejection or counter-offer by the offeree, or
  (b) lapse of time, or
  (c) revocation by the offeror, or
  (d) death or incapacity of the offeror or offeree.
(2) In addition, an offeree's power of acceptance is terminated by the non-occurrence of any condition of acceptance under the terms of the offer.

§37. TERMINATION OF POWER OF ACCEPTANCE UNDER OPTION CONTRACT

Notwithstanding §§38-49, the power of acceptance under an option contract is not terminated by rejection or counter-offer, by revocation, or by death or incapacity of the offeror, unless the requirements are met for the discharge of a contractual duty.

§42. REVOCATION BY COMMUNICATION FROM OFFEROR RECEIVED BY OFFEREE

An offeree's power of acceptance is terminated when the offeree receives from the offeror a manifestation of an intention not to enter into the proposed contract.

§43. INDIRECT COMMUNICATION OF REVOCATION

An offeree's power of acceptance is terminated when the offeror takes definite action inconsistent with an intention to enter into the proposed contract and the offeree acquires reliable information to that effect. (Dickinson v. Dodds)

Legal Background: The Emergence of "Firm Offers"

Had it involved a sale of goods rather than land, it is likely that the *Dickinson* case would be decided differently today, but for reasons that do not pertain to "offer and acceptance." Rather, they pertain generally to the developments in the doctrine of consideration and particularly the enforceability of an option. We shall return to this issue in Chapter 11 when we discuss the doctrine of promissory estoppel. U.C.C. §2-205 codifies situations where offers to buy or sell goods will be irrevocable.

SALES CONTRACTS: THE UNIFORM COMMERCIAL CODE

§2-205.   FIRM OFFERS

An offer by a merchant to buy or sell goods in a signed writing which by its terms gives assurance that it will be held open is not revocable, for lack of consideration, during the time stated or if no time is stated for a reasonable time, but in no event may such period of irrevocability exceed 3 months; but any such term of assurance on a form supplied by the offeree must be separately signed by the offeror.

C.   WHAT IS AN ACCEPTANCE?

Because an offer can be revoked until it is accepted (unless it is an option), the issue of mutual assent sometimes turns on whether or not an offeree has accepted. In this section, we consider a number of sometimes perplexing problems that arise when determining the existence of an acceptance.

1.   Acceptance That Varies Terms — The Mirror Image Rule

It is easy to see how a contract is formed when, as in Dickinson v. Dodds, an offeree unambiguously accepts all the terms stated in the offer. What happens when a purported "acceptance" differs from the offer in some way? Has a contract been formed nonetheless? The answer may vary depending on whether the contract has been partially performed. Before performance, it is easier to contest the existence of mutual assent to contract by finding that a purported "acceptance" was really a "counter-offer" and therefore a rejection of the original offer. There being no mutual assent, a contract was not formed. This doctrine, known as the Mirror Image Rule, was summarized by the Supreme Court of Minnesota in Langellier v. Shaefer, 36 Minn. 361, 363 (1887):

> An offer of a bargain by one person to another imposes no obligation upon the former, unless it is accepted by the latter according to the terms on which the offer was made. Any qualification of or departure from those terms invalidates the offer, unless the same is agreed to by the party who made it. Where the negotiations are by letters, they will constitute no agreement unless the answer to the offer is a simple acceptance, without the introduction of any new term.

After performance has begun, however, it is often clearer that there was mutual assent to enter into a contract — but because the terms of an "offer" differ from those of the "acceptance," it may be difficult to discern the terms to which both parties assented. Though we know the parties intended to contract, we then are faced with the problem of identifying the terms to which they agreed when their manifestations of assent conflict. We shall study how contract law deals with this problem in Chapter 5, where we shall see that the Mirror Image Rule is no longer used when performance indicates the existence of a contract. Now, however, consider a modern case that asserts the continued vitality of the Mirror Image Rule to determine whether a contract is formed in the first instance.

STUDY GUIDE: *In the following case, has performance by either party yet occurred? Do these circumstances raise any doubts as to whether both parties intended to contract? Pay attention to the court's inquiry as to whether the acceptance was "a qualified acceptance or . . . an absolute acceptance together with a mere inquiry concerning a collateral matter."*

ARDENTE v. HORAN
Supreme Court of Rhode Island,
366 A.2d 162 (1976)

DORIS,* Justice. Ernest P. Ardente, the plaintiff, brought this civil action in Superior Court to specifically enforce an agreement between himself and William A. and Katherine L. Horan, the defendants, to sell certain real property. The defendants filed an answer together with a motion for summary judgment. . . . [J]udgment was entered by a Superior Court justice for the defendants. The plaintiff now appeals.

In August 1975, certain residential property in the city of Newport was offered for sale by defendants. The plaintiff made a bid of $250,000 for the property which was communicated to defendants by their attorney. After defendants' attorney advised plaintiff that the bid was acceptable to defendants, he prepared a purchase and sale agreement at the direction of defendants and forwarded it to plaintiff's attorney for plaintiff's signature. After investigating certain title conditions, plaintiff executed the agreement. Thereafter plaintiff's attorney returned the document to defendants along with a check in the amount of $20,000 and a letter dated September 8, 1975, which read in relevant part as follows:

> My clients are concerned that the following items remain with the real estate: a) dining room set and tapestry wall covering in dining room; b) fireplace fixtures throughout; c) the sun parlor furniture. I would appreciate your confirming that these items are a part of the transaction, as they would be difficult to replace.

*John E. Doris (1917-†) was educated at Providence College (A.B. 1937) and Boston University School of Law (LL.B. 1947) and entered the Rhode Island bar in 1947 after serving in the U.S. Army during WWII, where he attained the rank of Captain, Quartermasters Corps. He was a representative to the general assembly from Woonsocket (1953-1961), where he became deputy majority leader. He was appointed Associate Justice of the Family Court in 1961, where he sat until his elevation in 1972 to the Supreme Court of Rhode Island, from which he has retired. — R.B.

The defendants refused to agree to sell the enumerated items and did not sign the purchase and sale agreement. They directed their attorney to return the agreement and the deposit check to plaintiff and subsequently refused to sell the property to plaintiff. This action for specific performance followed.

In Superior Court, defendants moved for summary judgment on the ground that the facts were not in dispute and no contract had been formed as a matter of law. The trial justice ruled that the letter quoted above constituted a conditional acceptance of defendants' offer to sell the property and consequently must be construed as a counteroffer. Since defendants never accepted the counteroffer, it followed that no contract was formed, and summary judgment was granted. . . .

The [plaintiff contends] that the trial justice incorrectly applied the principles of contract law in deciding that the facts did not disclose a valid acceptance of defendants' offer. . . . [W]e cannot agree.

The trial justice proceeded on the theory that the delivery of the purchase and sale agreement to plaintiff constituted an offer by defendants to sell the property. Because we must view the evidence in the light most favorable to the party against whom summary judgment was entered, in this case plaintiff, we assume as the trial justice did that the delivery of the agreement was in fact an offer.[6]

The question we must answer next is whether there was an acceptance of that offer. The general rule is that where, as here, there is an offer to form a bilateral contract, the offeree must communicate his acceptance to the offeror before any contractual obligation can come into being. A mere mental intent to accept the offer, no matter how carefully formed, is not sufficient. The acceptance must be transmitted to the offeror in some overt manner. . . . A review of the record shows that the only expression of acceptance which was communicated to defendants was the delivery of the executed purchase and sale agreement accompanied by the letter of September 8. Therefore it is solely on the basis of the language used in these two documents that we must determine whether there was a valid acceptance. Whatever plaintiff's unexpressed intention may have been in sending the documents is irrelevant. We must be concerned only with the language actually used, not the language plaintiff thought he was using or intended to use.

There is no doubt that the execution and delivery of the purchase and sale agreement by plaintiff, without more, would have operated as an acceptance. The terms of the accompanying letter, however, apparently conditioned the acceptance upon the inclusion of various items of personalty. In assessing the effect of the terms of that letter we must keep in mind certain generally accepted rules. To be effective, an acceptance must be definite and unequivocal. "An offeror is entitled to know in clear terms

6. The conclusion that the delivery of the agreement was an offer is not unassailable in view of the fact that defendants did not sign the agreement before sending it to plaintiff, and the fact that plaintiff told defendants' attorney after the agreement was received that he would have to investigate certain conditions of title before signing the agreement. If it was not an offer, plaintiff's execution of the agreement could itself be no more than an offer, which defendants never accepted.

whether the offeree accepts his proposal. It is not enough that the words of a reply justify a probable inference of assent." 1 Restatement Contracts §58, comment a (1932). The acceptance may not impose additional conditions on the offer, nor may it add limitations. "An acceptance which is equivocal or upon condition or with a limitation is a counteroffer and requires acceptance by the original offeror before a contractual relationship can exist." John Hancock Mut. Life Ins. Co. v. Dietlin, 199 A.2d 311, 313 (1964). . . .

Court makes a distinction between counter-offer and contract dealing with a collateral matter

However, an acceptance may be valid despite conditional language if the acceptance is clearly independent of the condition. Many cases have so held. Williston states the rule as follows:

> Frequently an offeree, while making a positive acceptance of the offer, also makes a request or suggestion that some addition or modification be made. So long as it is clear that the meaning of the acceptance is positively and unequivocally to accept the offer whether such request is granted or not, a contract is formed. 1 Williston, Contracts §79 at 261-62 (3d ed. 1957).

Corbin is in agreement with the above view. 1 Corbin, [Corbin on Contracts] §84 at 363-65. Thus our task is to decide whether plaintiff's letter is more reasonably interpreted as a qualified acceptance or as an absolute acceptance together with a mere inquiry concerning a collateral matter.

? Issue before the court

In making our decision we recognize that, as one text states, "The question whether a communication by an offeree is a conditional acceptance or counter-offer is not always easy to answer. It must be determined by the same common-sense process of interpretation that must be applied in so many other cases." 1 Corbin, supra §82 at 353. In our opinion the language used in plaintiff's letter of September 8 is not consistent with an absolute acceptance accompanied by a request for a gratuitous benefit. We interpret the letter to impose a condition on plaintiff's acceptance of defendants' offer. The letter does not unequivocally state that even without the enumerated items plaintiff is willing to complete the contract. In fact, the letter seeks "confirmation" that the listed items "are a part of the transaction." Thus, far from being an independent, collateral request, the sale of the items in question is explicitly referred to as a part of the real estate transaction. Moreover, the letter goes on to stress the difficulty of finding replacements for these items. This is a further indication that plaintiff did not view the inclusion of the listed items as merely collateral or incidental to the real estate transaction. . . .

? Reasoning

Accordingly, we hold that since the plaintiff's letter of acceptance dated September 8 was conditional, it operated as a rejection of the defendants' offer and no contractual obligation was created. The plaintiff's appeal is denied and dismissed, the judgment appealed from is affirmed and the case is remanded to the Superior Court. *→ Holding!*

RESTATEMENT (SECOND) OF CONTRACTS

§61.   ACCEPTANCE WHICH REQUESTS CHANGE OF TERMS

An acceptance which requests a change or addition to the terms of the offer is not thereby invalidated unless the acceptance is made to depend on an assent to the changed or added terms.

COMMENT

a. *Interpretation of Acceptance.* An acceptance must be unequivocal. But the mere inclusion of words requesting a modification of the proposed terms does not prevent a purported acceptance from closing the contract unless, if fairly interpreted, the offeree's assent depends on the offeror's further acquiescence in the modification. See Uniform Commercial Code §2-207(1).

2. Acceptance by Correspondence — The Mailbox Rule *"Acceptance at a distance"*

When an acceptance takes place at a distance, a problem can arise when it is sent by the offeree but not received by the offeror. When is acceptance effective? Upon being sent by the offeree? Upon being received by the offeror? While this problem has largely been overcome by modern forms of near instantaneous communication, even an e-mail can be sent and not received.

The traditional way of handling this situation is called the Mailbox Rule but could better be termed the deposited acceptance rule. According to this rule, an *acceptance is effective upon dispatch.* Its rationale was explained by Karl Llewellyn:

> As between hardship on the offeror which is really tough, and hardship on the offeree which would be even tougher, the vital reason for throwing the hardship of an odd delayed or lost letter upon the offeror remains this: the offeree is already relying, with the best reason in the world, on the deal being on; the offeror is only holding things open; and, in view of the efficiency of communication facilities, we can protect the offerees in *all* these deals at the price of hardship on offerors in very few of them.[7]

In evaluating the choice to protect the offeree rather than offeror, one must always remember that, as "master" of his offer, the offeror is free to insist upon acceptance being effective only upon receipt, as was observed in the case of Lewis v. Browning, 130 Mass. 173, 175-176 (1881): "[T]he person making the offer may always, if he chooses, make the formation of the contract which he proposes dependent upon the actual communication to himself of the acceptance."

The deposited acceptance rule or Mailbox Rule provides ready answers to a series of questions that may arise when an offer is accepted from a distance:

1. May an offeror attempt to revoke an offer after the mailing of the acceptance but before receipt?

    No. An offeror retains the power of revocation up to the time that the offer is accepted. An acceptance creates a *contract* out of an offer. An offeror cannot "revoke" a contract without the agreement of the

7. Karl N. Llewellyn, Our Case-Law of Contract, Offer and Acceptance (pt. 2), 48 Yale L.J. 779, 795 (1939).

other party. The Mailbox Rule specifies that the time of acceptance is *when acceptance is mailed* and not when it is received. So when an acceptance is mailed, there is a contract and a contract cannot be "revoked" by the offeror (without the consent of the offeree).

2. Is there a contract when the acceptance is lost or delayed in transit?

Yes. The Mailbox Rule says that a contract is formed upon dispatch, so what happens after that point does not affect the formation of the contract. However, the offeror's *duty to perform* her obligations under the contract may be affected by delay or loss. The language of the offer may be interpreted as making the offeror's performance conditional upon receipt of the acceptance. Note however that the analysis is that the contract is *discharged*. This is not the same thing as saying that there is or was not a contract. For one thing, after acceptance is dispatched, the offeror may no longer revoke the offer. The contract formed was a "conditioned" one. There *was* a contract, but when the condition was not fulfilled, the contractual obligation was subsequently discharged. Where the receipt of notice is essential to enable the offeror to perform, such a condition is normally implied.

3. What if the offeree attempts to revoke her acceptance?

The Mailbox Rule is that a contract is formed upon dispatch of the acceptance. So any attempt to revoke after acceptance is dispatched will not deprive the contract of legal effect. Otherwise, if the offeror could not revoke the offer after acceptance is mailed (for the reasons given above), but the offeree could revoke the acceptance until it is received, then the offeree can speculate — for example, on a rise or fall of the price — during that period at the expense of the offeror.

4. What if the offeree is able to recapture the acceptance before receipt?

This does not change the Mailbox Rule that acceptance is effective upon dispatch. But, of course, as a practical matter, an offeror cannot enforce an acceptance that he never knows about.

5. What if the offeree sends a revocation that is received by the offeror before the acceptance?

According to the Mailbox Rule, any such communication will not be an effective revocation. However, some rights of the parties may be affected, depending on the circumstances. Here are some examples: (a) The communication may be considered an *offer to revoke* (which may then be accepted by the other party); (b) it may bar or *estop* the offeree from suing to enforce the contract; (c) it may be considered a *repudiation* of the contract (as in "anticipatory repudiation"), which would give the original offeror the right to avoid the contract; or (d) similarly such a purported revocation might also justify the offeror in withholding performance and demanding adequate assurance that perfomance will be forthcoming. For example, U.C.C. §2-609 gives a party under some circumstances the right to stop performance until it receives adequate assurances from the other side that it is prepared and able to perform. We shall discuss both anticipatory repudiation and the right to demand adequate assurances of performance in Chapter 14.

6. What happens when an offer is in the form of an option?

The general rule is that, in such a case, acceptance is operative only *upon receipt* by the offeror — the opposite of the Mailbox Rule. The original rationale for the Mailbox Rule is that, in deciding whether or not to accept an offer, an offeree needs a reliable way of knowing that she has a deal. Unlike a normal offer, which can be revoked until it is accepted, the existence of the option limiting the offeror's right of revocation provides this assurance, so the Mailbox Rule is no longer needed. Speculation at the expense of the offeror is not objectionable when, by voluntarily limiting his right of revocation, the offeror has assumed that risk. Given the fact that the offeree's interests are protected by the existence of the option, we now pick the rule that protects the offeror's interest in learning that his option has been accepted and he is now bound. If there is a time limit attached to the offer, as is usually the case, the acceptance must be received within that time. And conversely from when the Mailbox Rule is in effect, the offeree remains free to revoke her acceptance after it is dispatched but before it is received.

RESTATEMENT (SECOND) OF CONTRACTS

§63. TIME WHEN ACCEPTANCE TAKES EFFECT

Unless the offer provides otherwise,
(a) an acceptance made in a manner and by a medium invited by an offer is operative and completes the manifestation of mutual assent as soon as put out of the offeree's possession, without regard to whether it ever reaches the offeror; but
(b) an acceptance under an option contract is not operative until received by the offeror.

§64. ACCEPTANCE BY TELEPHONE OR TELETYPE

Acceptance given by telephone or other medium of substantially instantaneous two-way communication is governed by the principles applicable to acceptances where the parties are in the presence of each other.

§65. REASONABLENESS OF MEDIUM OF ACCEPTANCE

Unless circumstances known to the offeree indicate otherwise, a medium of acceptance is reasonable if it is the one used by the offeror or one customary in similar transactions at the time and place the offer is received.

§66. ACCEPTANCE MUST BE PROPERLY DISPATCHED

An acceptance sent by mail or otherwise from a distance is not operative when dispatched, unless it is properly addressed and such other precautions taken as are ordinarily observed to insure safe transmission of similar messages.

REFERENCE: Farnsworth, §3.22
                 Calamari & Perillo, §2.23
                 Murray, §48

3. Acceptance by Performance or "Unilateral" Contracts?

While an offeror normally seeks an acceptance in the form of a promise to perform from the offeree, as in *Dickinson* and *Ardente*, Restatement (Second) of Contracts §30 permits offerors to specify that acceptance may take the form of "performing or refraining from performing a specified act." Therefore, on rare occasions an offeror will invite the offeree to accept by actually performing the acts that the offeror is bargaining for. When this occurs, special problems of notification, revocation, and reliance in the form of partial performance can arise. The cases that follow examine these problems.

In this area, courts have traditionally distinguished between "bilateral" and "unilateral" contracts. According to the Restatement, the only difference between these are the modes of acceptance. On this view, bilateral contracts are simply those agreements that result from acceptance by a promise, while unilateral contracts are those that result from acceptance by performance. Consequently, the Restatement has disregarded the terminology of bilateral and unilateral contracts. Nonetheless we shall consider these "unilateral" contracts as a distinct category, because, the Restatement notwithstanding, something other than the mode of acceptance may distinguish them from bilateral contracts. In particular, to what extent do such contracts involve *mutual* assent?[8]

REFERENCE: Farnsworth, §3.4
                 Calamari & Perillo, §2.10
                 Murray, §18, 46(B)

STUDY GUIDE: When reading the cases in this section, consider the definitions of offer *and* promise. *Could a distinction between these two concepts help to differentiate between bilateral and unilateral contracts?*

8. See Peter Meijes Tiersma, Reassessing Unilateral Contracts: The Role of Offer, Acceptance and Promise, 26 U.C. Davis L. Rev. 1 (1992).

CARLILL v. CARBOLIC SMOKE BALL CO.
In the Court of Appeal,
1 Q.B 256 (1893)

Appeal from a decision of HAWKINS, J.

The defendants, who were the proprietors and vendors of a medical preparation called "The Carbolic Smoke Ball," inserted in the Pall Mall Gazette of November 13, 1891, and in other newspapers, the following advertisement:

£100. reward will be paid by the Carbolic Smoke Ball Company to any person who contracts the increasing epidemic influenza, colds, or any disease caused by taking cold, after having used the ball three times daily for two weeks according to the printed directions supplied with each ball. £1000. is deposited with the Alliance Bank, Regent Street, shewing our sincerity in the matter.

During the last epidemic of influenza many thousand carbolic smoke balls were sold as preventives against this disease, and in no ascertained case was the disease contracted by those using the carbolic smoke ball.

One carbolic smoke ball will last a family several months, making it the cheapest remedy in the world at the price, 10s., post free. The ball can be refilled at a cost of 5s. Address, Carbolic Smoke Ball Company, 27, Princes Street, Hanover Square, London.

The plaintiff, a lady, on the faith of this advertisement, bought one of the balls at a chemist's, and used it as directed, three times a day, from November 20, 1891, to January 17, 1892, when she was attacked by influenza. Hawkins, J., held that she was entitled to recover the £100. The defendants appealed. . . .

LINDLEY, L.J.* [The Lord Justice stated the facts, and proceeded:] . . . We must first consider whether this was intended to be a promise at all, or whether it was a mere puff which meant nothing. Was it a mere puff? My answer to that question is No, and I base my answer upon this passage: "£1000. is deposited with the Alliance Bank, shewing our sincerity in the matter." Now, for what was that money deposited or that statement made except to negative the suggestion that this was a mere puff and meant nothing at all? The deposit is called in aid by the advertiser as proof of his sincerity in the matter — that is, the sincerity of his promise to pay this £100. in the event which he has specified. I say this for the purpose of giving point to the observation that we are not inferring a promise; there is the promise, as plain as words can make it.

Then it is contended that it is not binding. In the first place, it is said that it is not made with anybody in particular. Now that point is common to

Reflects seriousness of offer [handwritten margin note]

Hyperbol [handwritten margin note]

---

* *Nathaniel Lindley,* Baron Lindley (1828-1921), studied at University College School and University College. He began his study of the law in 1847 and was called to the bar in 1850. He practiced privately and, after publishing a treatise on the law of partnership, began to retain pupils, including one who later became Chief Justice. After serving for several years as revising barrister of Middlesex County, he was given the post of judgeship in the Common Pleas in 1875; Lindley later served as lord justice of appeal from 1881 to 1897, master of the Rolls from 1897 to 1900, and a lord of appeal in ordinary from 1900 until he resigned from the bench in 1905. — K.T.

the words of this advertisement and to the words of all other advertisements offering rewards. They are offers to anybody who performs the conditions named in the advertisement, and anybody who does perform the condition accepts the offer. In point of law this advertisement is an offer to pay £100. to anybody who will perform these conditions, and the performance of the conditions is the acceptance of the offer. That rests upon a string of authorities, the earliest of which is Williams v. Carwardine, which has been followed by many other decisions upon advertisement offering rewards.

But then it is said, "Supposing that the performance of the conditions is an acceptance of the offer, that acceptance ought to have been notified." Unquestionably, as a general proposition, when an offer is made, it is necessary in order to make a binding contract, not only that it should be accepted, but that the acceptance should be notified. But is that so in cases of this kind? I apprehend that they are an exception to that rule, or, if not an exception, they are open to the observation that the notification of the acceptance need not precede the performance. This offer is a continuing offer. It was never revoked, and if notice of acceptance is required . . . the person who makes the offer gets the notice of acceptance contemporaneously with his notice of the performance of the condition. If he gets notice of the acceptance before his offer is revoked, that in principle is all you want. I, however, think that the true view, in a case of this kind, is that the person who makes the offer shews by his language and from the nature of the transaction that he does not expect and does not require notice of the acceptance apart from notice of the performance. . . .

It appears to me, therefore, that the defendants must perform their promise, and, if they have been so unwary as to expose themselves to a great many actions, so much the worse for them.

BOWEN, L.J.* I am of the same opinion. . . .

Was it intended that the £100., should, if the conditions were fulfilled, be paid? The advertisement says that £1000. is lodged at the bank for that purpose. Therefore, it cannot be said that the statement that £100. would be paid was intended to be a mere puff. I think it was intended to be understood by the public as an offer which was to be acted upon.

But it was said there was no check on the part of the persons who issued the advertisement, and that it would be an insensate thing to promise £100. to a person who used the smoke ball unless you could check or superintend his manner of using it. The answer to that argument seems to me to be that if a person chooses to make extravagant promises of this kind he probably does so because it pays him to make them, and, if he has made them, the extravagance of the promises is no reason in law why he should not be bound by them.

Charles Synge Christopher Bowen (1835-1894) was born in Woolaston, Gloucestershire, and was the grandson of an Irish baronet. He entered Balliol College, Oxford, in 1853 and graduated with first-class honors. He studied law at Lincoln's Inn and was called to the bar in January 1861. After several years of private practice, he was designated junior counsel to the Treasury in 1872, representing the Crown. He was knighted in 1879 and appointed to serve as a judge of the Queen's Bench Division. In 1882, he was elevated to the Court of Appeal, where he served for nine years. He was appointed to the House of Lords as a Lord of Appeal in Ordinary in 1893 but died shortly thereafter at the age of 59. — R.B.

It was also said that the contract is made with all the world — that is, with everybody; and that you cannot contract with everybody. It is not a contract made with all the world. There is the fallacy of the argument. It is an offer made to all the world; and why should not an offer be made to all the world which is to ripen into a contract with anybody who comes forward and performs the condition? It is an offer to become liable to anyone who, before it is retracted, performs the condition, and, although the offer is made to the world, the contract is made with a limited portion of the public who come forward and perform the condition on the faith of the advertisement. It is not like cases in which you offer to negotiate, or you issue advertisements that you have got a stock of books to sell, or houses to let, in which case there is no offer to be bound by any contract. Such advertisements are offers to negotiate — offers to receive offers — offers to chaffer, as, I think, some learned judge in one of the cases has said. If this is an offer to be bound, then it is a contract the moment the person fulfils the condition. . . .

Then it was said that there was no notification of the acceptance of the contract. One cannot doubt that, as an ordinary rule of law, an acceptance of an offer made ought to be notified to the person who makes the offer, in order that the two minds may come together. Unless this is done the two minds may be apart, and there is not that consensus which is necessary according to the English law — I say nothing about the laws of other countries — to make a contract. But there is this clear gloss to be made upon that doctrine, that as notification of acceptance is required for the benefit of the person who makes the offer, the person who makes the offer may dispense with notice to himself if he thinks it desirable to do so, and I suppose there can be no doubt that where a person in an offer made by him to another person, expressly or impliedly intimates a particular mode of acceptance as sufficient to make the bargain binding, it is only necessary for the other person to whom such offer is made to follow the indicated method of acceptance; and if the person making the offer, expressly or impliedly intimates in his offer that it will be sufficient to act on the proposal without communicating acceptance of it to himself, performance of the condition is a sufficient acceptance without notification.

Now, if that is the law, how are we to find out whether the person who makes the offer does intimate that notification of acceptance will not be necessary in order to constitute a binding bargain? In many cases you look to the offer itself. In many cases you extract from the character of the transaction that notification is not required, and in the advertisement cases it seems to me to follow as an inference to be drawn from the transaction itself that a person is not to notify his acceptance of the offer before he performs the condition, but that if he performs the condition notification is dispensed with. It seems to me that from the point of view of common sense no other idea could be entertained. If I advertise to the world that my dog is lost, and that anybody who brings the dog to a particular place will be paid some money, are all the police or other persons whose business it is to find lost dogs to be expected to sit down and write me a note saying that they have accepted my proposal? Why, of course, they at once look after the dog, and as soon as they find the dog they have performed the condition. The essence of the transaction is that the dog should be found, and it is not necessary under such circumstances, as it seems to me, that in order to make the contract binding there should be any notification of acceptance. It follows from the nature of the thing that the performance of the condition is sufficient acceptance without the notification of it, and a person who makes an offer in an advertisement of that kind makes an offer which must be read by the light of that common sense reflection. He does, therefore, in his offer impliedly indicate that he does not require notification of the acceptance of the offer. . . .

Appeal dismissed.

Relational Background: The Smoke Ball and Nineteenth-Century Patent Medicine

A. W. B. SIMPSON, QUACKERY AND CONTRACT LAW: THE CASE OF THE CARBOLIC SMOKE BALL, 14 J. LEG. STUD. 345 (1985): All lawyers, and indeed many nonlawyers, are familiar with the case of Carlill v. Carbolic Smoke Ball Company.[9] Continuously studied though it has been by lawyers and law students for close to a century, it has never been investigated historically. Even the form taken by the celebrated smoke ball itself remains a mystery, as indeed it was in 1892 at least to one of the members of the Court of Appeal who decided the case. For Lord Justice Lindley is reported to have referred to it as "a thing they call the 'Carbolic Smoke Ball.' What that is I don't know."[10]

Happily, a considerable volume of material survives that makes it possible to recreate at least something of the historical background and significance of this landmark in the history of contract law and its relationship to the seedy world of the late nineteenth-century vendors of patent medical appliances. . . .

The Patenting of the Smoke Ball. On October 30, 1889, one Frederick Augustus Roe, "of 202 Regent St. in the County of Middlesex, Gentleman," submitted an application to patent what he described as "An Improved Device for Facilitating the Distribution, Inhalation and Application of Medicated and other Powder." . . . As described in the specification, the improved device "comprises a compressible hollow ball or receptacle of India Rubber or other suitable elastic material, having an orifice or nozzle provided with a porous or perforated disc or diaphragm consisting of muslin, silk, wire or gauze, perforated sheet metal or the like, through which, when the ball or receptacle is compressed, the powder will be forced *in a cloud of infinitesimally small particles resembling smoke.*"[11] Accompanying drawings . . . showed two variant forms of this elegant medical

---

9. [1892] 2 Q.B. 484, before Hawkins J., (1893) 1 Q.B. 256, before the Court of Appeal. . . . The report in 8 T.L.R. adds further information including Lindley's ignorance of what the object was; other reports do not add anything. . . . Much the fullest reporting of the case is in the professional journals: the Patent Medicines J. (1892) at 196; 40 Chemist and Druggist 875 (1892), and 41 id. 39, 48, 839 (1892).

10. 41 Chemist and Druggist 843 (1892).

11. Patent No. 17,220 of 1889 (emphasis added). . . .

appliance, the beauty of which, so its inventor claimed, lay in the fact that the inrush of air when the ball filled prevented the screen from clogging, thus enabling the user to discharge "a cloud or diffused stream of powder resulting from each compression of the said receptacle." When exhausted the receptacle could of course be refilled. Aesthetic claims were also made; the fact that the powder was both put in and puffed out through a single orifice, so Roe argued, greatly improved the appearance of the appliance. The invention also possessed considerable development potential. It could, for example, be modified so as to have two nozzles, or two oval outlets, "to enable the apparatus to be applied to both nostrils at once" in a swift and concerted assault on the seat of infection. By a fortunate chance the directions for use of the ball as marketed survive in the *Inventor*.[12]

> Hold the ball by the loose end below the silk floss, with the thumb and forefinger in front of the mouth. Snap or flip rapidly on the side of the ball, on the place marked "S" and a fine powder resembling smoke will arise. Inhale this smoke or powder as it arises, as shown in the above illustration. This will cause sneezing, and for a few moments you will feel as if you were taking cold. This feeling will soon pass away and the cure has commenced. If you do not feel the effects at the first inhalation by it making you sneeze, take a second in same manner.

The Marketing of the Ball.

The Marketing of the Ball.   Whether the ball was in fact marketed in America, perhaps as "the Pulverator," is unknown, but late in 1889 or early in 1890 Roe began to market his Carbolic Smoke Ball in England, moving his premises to 27 Princes Street, Hanover Square, at about this time. The influenza epidemic which had begun . . . in December of 1889, must have come as a godsend to his new enterprise, but the utility of the ball was by no means restricted to this single ailment. The earliest of his advertisements that I have located appeared in the Illustrated London News on January 11, 1890. He claimed that the ball, to be had from the Carbolic Smoke Ball Company at their new premises for a price of ten shillings, "Will positively cure Influenza, Catarrh, Asthma, Bronchitis, Hay Fever, Neuralgia, Throat Deafness, Hoarseness, Loss of Voice, Whooping Cough, Croup, Coughs, Colds, and all other ailments caused by Taking Cold." Behind this optimism lay a theory, more fully articulated in some of his later advertisements. It was that all these ailments arose from a single cause, taking cold, and were therefore all amenable to the same single remedy, the Carbolic Smoke Ball. His advertisements exhibited a note of caution in insisting that the ball was to be used for inhalation only. Carbolic acid, though not at the time a scheduled poison, could be fatal if taken internally in more than small amounts. Inhaling the powder through the nostrils must certainly have produced a numbing and astringent effect and been somewhat disagreeable and, as the directions for use indicate, caused sneezing. . . .

Frederick Roe was only one of many advertisers who made claims to cure or ward off influenza. It was the practice of the patent medicine vendors to adapt their claims, rather than their products, to the current needs

---

12. 6 Inventor (1890) at 189. . . .

of the market, and Roe was merely doing what was normal in the trade. The product remained the same; its function changed.

According to his later claims the ball was widely sold during this epidemic, and gave great satisfaction. There is no particular reason to doubt this. In the catalog of Barclay and Sons, Ltd., published for the trade in 1890, it appears in two obscurely different forms, "the Carbolic Smoke Ball" and "the Carbolic Smoke (India Rubber) Ball." The wholesale prices were eighty-eight shillings and ninety-four shillings a dozen, respectively, with a retail price of ten shillings. During 1890 the appliance does not seem to have been heavily advertised, though a more exhaustive search through the newspapers and journals of the period might reveal advertising that I have missed. During 1891, however, the ball was heavily and imaginatively advertised in the Illustrated London News at what must have been considerable expense; a full page at this time cost £100 for one issue. Thus on January 24 a series of very specific claims was made: the ball would cure cold in the head or chest in twelve hours, catarrh in three months, asthma "in every case" with relief in ten minutes, hoarseness in twelve hours, influenza in twenty-four hours, the bizarre ailment called throat deafness in three weeks, and so on. If used before retiring the ball would also prevent snoring. After running this advertising for three months new copy was inserted on April 4. The list of diseases remained the same, but the theory of the smoke ball was made explicit: "As all these diseases mentioned above proceed from the same cause — viz. taking cold, they may all be cured by one remedy — viz. the Carbolic Smoke Ball." An appeal was also made to the snobbery of the readers by providing a list of distinguished people who, it was claimed, used the ball; the use of such testimonials, which could be fraudulent, was standard practice in the quack medicine world. This list included the duchess of Sutherland; the earls of Wharncliffe, Westmoreland, Cadogan, and Leitrim; the countesses Dudley, Pembroke, and Aberdeen; the marchionesses of Bath and Conyngham; a continental count, Count Gleichen; and a brace of run-of-the-mill lords, Rossmore and Norton. Further lists of satisfied customers appeared on April 18, May 2, and May 16. In addition to aristocrats — nine dukes — doctors now began to appear, including the distinguished Sir Henry Acland, K.C.B., a particularly important client; he was at the time Regius Professor of Medicine at Oxford and physician to the Prince of Wales.

With the coming of spring Roe's advertising changed again; on May 30 the ball was offered as a cure for hay fever, indeed as the only cure for "a disease that has hitherto baffled the skill of the most eminent physicians." The approach of winter brought a new advertisement on November 14, with testimonials from, for example, the Reverend Dr. Reade of Banstead Downs, Surrey, and Dr. Colbourne M.D., of 60 Maddox Street in London. I have not traced Dr. Reade, but a W. W. Colbourne does feature in the Medical Directory for 1892, with no address given. Testimonials from clerics and doctors were much favored in quack medicine advertisements, both professions combining respectability and status with a close association with death, and Roe used the names of very eminent doctors indeed.[13]

13. See also November 28. Of the doctors mentioned during the year in Roe's advertisements, Henry Wentworth Dyke Acland (1815-1900) was one of the leading physicians of

Whether he had their permission it is quite impossible to tell. On December 5 he inserted a much larger advertisement, showing not merely an adult lady using the ball but a child as well; the undated advertising leaflet preserved in Oxford also directed attention to children, who could, it pointed out, be medicated when asleep, thus preserving them from illnesses which "usually led to fatal results." The new advertisement embodied further illustrious testimonials: "as prescribed by Sir Morell Mackenzie, M.D." The duke of Portland was also quoted as writing "I am much obliged for the Carbolic Smoke Ball which you sent me, and which I find most efficacious." And no less than His Grace the bishop of London confessed that "the Carbolic Smoke Ball has helped me greatly," though whether spiritually or physically was not made clear. The advertisement in the special Christmas supplement went even further by reproducing the Royal Arms — "By Royal Letters Patent" — with the obvious intention of suggesting that Her Majesty herself had in some way approved the ball. This form of deception was then common in the trade.

The Recurrence of Influenza, 1891-92.

Influenza again became established in London during 1891, first in June and July and again during the winter of 1891-92. According to Dr. Parson's meticulous report, the winter epidemic started in November and reached its peak in the week ending January 23, 1892, when 506 deaths were attributed to it, as a primary cause, in London alone and a further 86 as a secondary cause. . . . The epidemic died out in February of 1892. At this time Frederick Roe was, as we have seen, advertising heavily. . . .

The advertisement that gave rise to the litigation first appeared not in the Illustrated London News but in the Pall Mall Gazette on November 13, 1891, and again on November 24 and December 8; apparently it also appeared in substantially the same form in other newspapers, not all of which I have identified. One such was the Illustrated London News, which carried the advertisement in substantially the same form on January 30 with a facsimile reproduction of the Duke of Portland's handwritten testimonial, dated March 1, 1891, from 2 Grosvenor Square. The Pall Mall Gazette, despite its high moral tone, carried at this period many advertisements for dubious remedies. Thus readers on November 11 were exhorted to buy Clarke's World Famous Blood Mixture, "warranted to cleanse the blood of all impurities, from whatever cause arising. For Scrofula, Scurvy, Eczema, Skin and Blood Diseases, Pimples and Sores of all kinds, its effects are marvellous." On November 19 Beecham's Pills, "for regulating the system and for all Bilious and Nervous Disorders such as Headaches,

---

the time; he held the chair at Oxford from 1857 to 1894. . . . Sir James Paget, first baronet (1814-1899), was sergeant surgeon to Queen Victoria, surgeon to the Prince of Wales, and vice-chancellor of London University 1884-95. . . . Sir William Scovell Savory (1826-1895) was surgeon extraordinary to the Queen, 1887, and Hunterian Professor at St. Bartholomews. . . . Sir Edward Henry Sieveking (1816-1904) was physician to the Queen and the Prince of Wales. . . . [In an omitted portion of this article, Professor Simpson notes that "[s]o far as I have been able to check all the names quoted by Roe were of real people, and his testimonials may have been quite genuine." 14 J. Leg. Stud. at 368. He also observes that "[f]alse testimonials were widely used in the trade, but genuine ones were sent in by satisfied customers, some of whom may have been sent free smoke balls." Id. at 369 n.82. — EDS.]

Constipation, Weak Stomach, Impaired Digestion, Disordered Livers etc.,"
were advertised together with Towle's Penny-royal and Steel Pills for
Females, a thinly disguised and no doubt wholly ineffective abortifacient
("quickly corrects all Irregularities and Relieves the Distressing Symptoms
so Prevalent with the Sex"). Pepsolic, advertised on December 15, was even
claimed to prevent divorce, which the copywriter attributed to indigestion:
"Causes Bad Temper, Irritability, Peppery Disposition, Domestic Quarrels,
Separation and — The Divorce Court." Issues of January 8 and 9, 1892,
published advertisements for Holloway's celebrated ointment, Dr. Henry
Paterson's Electrolytic Pill, Sequah's Prairie Flower, Dr. Durbar's Alkaram
Inhalant, and Epp's Glycerine Jube-Jubes. Between them they cured more
or less everything.

But if Frederick Roe was typical in his extravagant claims, he was early
off the mark in directing his advertising specifically to influenza, and none of
his competitors seems to have gone so far as to offer a substantial sum of
money to purchasers of the ball if it failed to protect them. . . .

To the lasting benefit of the law of contract, Mrs. Carlill saw this advertisement on the evening of November 13, 1891.

The Carlill Family.   Her full name was Louisa Elizabeth Carlill. She
used the name Elizabeth. Her maiden name was Flamank, and she was born
at 10:15 A.M. on October 22, 1845. . . . On December 17, 1873, at All Saints
Church, Clapton Park, she married James Briggs Carlill. . . . [A]ccording to
family tradition he was an actuary. . . . I have not been able to confirm his
occupation. Whatever he eventually became, he was originally a solicitor.
He was admitted to the role in 1870, and practiced in Hull until 1882. . . . As
for Mrs. Carlill herself, she was described by counsel in the legal proceedings as "a literary lady." This was a slightly mocking expression at the time,
but it is clear that she had, as a writer, an income of her own. I have been
unable to trace any writings by her either under her own names, Carlill or
Flamank, or a pseudonym. The point is one to which I return.

Mrs. Carlill saw the advertisement, and on November 20 she purchased
a smoke ball from Messrs. Wilcox and Company, who operated a druggist's
shop at 239 Oxford Street.[14] She paid for the ball out of her literary earnings.
The vendors, as we have seen, were actively promoting the ball at the time.
According to her account of the matter, which was given in evidence at the
trial and not disputed, she assiduously used the ball three times daily for
two weeks, in accordance with the already quoted printed instructions
supplied with it: "In the morning before breakfast, at about 2 o'clock,
and again when I went to bed." Whether she continued to use the ball
thereafter does not appear. On January 17, that is, at the height of the
epidemic, she contracted influenza. She remained ill under the care of a
Dr. Robertson for some two weeks.

14. This account of the litigation and the facts of the case is based on the law reports
and newspapers cited in note [9] supra, and material in the Public Record Office. This
consists of J54/740 (pleadings), J54/748 (notice of change of solicitor), and KB25/10
(Court of Appeal Order Book). None of the letters mentioned in the case survives in the
public records, but texts can be recovered from the professional journals.

On January 20 her husband, James Briggs Carlill, wrote to the Carbolic Smoke Ball Company informing them of what had occurred; possibly her letter was only one of many received at this time:

> Dear Sir,
>   Seeing your offer of a reward, dated July 20, in the Pall Mall Gazette of November 13, my wife purchased one of your smoke balls, and has used it three times a day since the beginning of December. She was, however, attacked by influenza. Dr. Robertson, of West Dulwich, attended, and will no doubt be able to certify in the matter. I think it right to give you notice of this, and shall be prepared to answer any inquiry or furnish any evidence you require. I am, yours obediently,
>
>   J. B. Carlill.

This was ignored. He wrote again, threatening to place the matter in the hands of his solicitors, and received in reply a post card saying the matter would receive attention. He wrote a third time, and received in reply a printed circular, undated, endorsed "In answer to your letter of January 20." This remarkable document read:

> Re reward of £100 — The Carbolic Smoke Ball Company, seeing that claims for the above reward have been made by persons who have either not purchased the smoke ball at all, or else have failed to use it as directed, consider it necessary that they should state the conditions in which alone such reward would be paid. They have such confidence in the efficacy of the carbolic smoke ball, if used according to the printed directions supplied to each person, that they made the aforesaid offer in entire good faith, believing it impossible for the influenza to be taken during the daily inhalation of the smoke ball as prescribed. In order to protect themselves against all fraudulent claims, the Carbolic Smoke Ball Company require that the smoke ball be administered, free of charge, at their office, to those who have already purchased it. Intending claimants must attend three times daily for three weeks, and inhale the smoke ball under the directions of the Smoke Ball Company. These visits will be specially recorded by the secretary in a book. 27 Princes St., Hanover Square, London.

Why this gem was not quoted in the law reports must forever remain a mystery, for it goes a long way toward explaining the hostile judicial attitude to the company. It certainly irritated James Briggs Carlill, who replied, insisting his claim was perfectly honest. To this Roe replied that "the company considered his letter impertinent and gave him the names of his solicitors." And so it was that on February 15 an action was commenced to claim the £100 promised. . . .

    . . . Carlill v. Carbolic Smoke Ball Co. came on for trial . . . on June 16, 1892, in court number five at the Royal Courts of Justice in the Strand, built, ironically enough, on the site of the premises of a celebrated maker and advertiser of patent medicines, Thomas Holloway. The judge was Sir Henry Hawkins, assisted by his fox terrier Jack, which always sat on the bench with him,[15] with a special jury. . . . The defense was led by no less than Herbert

---

15. See Richard Harris, The Reminiscences of Sir Henry Hawkins, (1904), especially 2 id. 45-64. Two pictures of Jack appear in this work. There is an obituary for the animal in the Illustrated London News for December 15, 1894, at 736.

Henry Asquith, Q.C., future prime minister; his junior was H. W. Loehnis. . . . Notwithstanding the formal denials of Loehnis, the facts of the case were not in any real dispute, and a full trial before the special jury would have further inflated the costs. Mrs. Carlill did indeed go into the witness box, and the judge inspected the letters and the document setting out the instructions for use, and showing a lady using the ball — the picture appears in many of Roe's advertisements and in the Inventor. Asquith asked her when she used the ball, but did not cross examine as the facts were undisputed. Counsel agreed to leave the decision to the judge, giving him power to enter whatever verdict the jurymen, in his view, ought to have found; the jury was discharged. The case was then adjourned until Saturday June 18, when the judge heard counsels' argument on the points of law involved. He then reserved judgment to consider their arguments, eventually, on July 4, entering a verdict in favor of Mrs. Carlill, for the £100 claimed, together with costs, and refusing an application for a stay of execution of the judgment.[16] The form of procedure adopted, which bypassed the jury, was a significant factor in the conversion of the dispute into a leading case, for the judge gave reasons for his decision in a complex written opinion. Had the matter gone to a jury the case would have terminated in a laconic jury verdict, and although there could have been an appeal based on the judge's directions to the jury, it is unlikely that the legal elaboration of the case would have proceeded so far as it did. . . .

. . . No doubt there were at the time genuinely satisfied users of the Carbolic Smoke Ball; indeed, initially Mrs. Carlill was one, for in the witness box she explained how she had recommended the ball to her friends. Although the claims made for its efficacy were ludicrously optimistic, the puffing of carbolic powder up the nostrils as a mode of treatment was not in itself any odder than many of the procedures employed at the time by orthodox medicine.

For in the Victorian world the distinction between quackery and legitimate scientific medicine was by no means as clear as it now seems. It depended, at least in part, purely on who was prescribing the treatment. Much of what the doctors did was either useless or positively harmful, except insofar as it may have improved the morale of the patient. Quack medicine was not obviously any worse as a morale booster and could, especially if available on mail order, be considerably cheaper. Considered merely as an appliance the ball was not in itself in any way unorthodox. It was what was and indeed still is known in the business as an insufflator, close cousin to an inhaler. Frederick Roe indeed used "Inhalations London" as his telegraphic address. The medical press of the period regularly reported on new developments in the field of medical appliances, so long as a regular doctor had invented or approved of them, describing and depicting, for example, contraptions such as Dr. Blenkarne's Improved Insufflator with Adjustable Tongue Depressor, which it claimed, surpassed

16. [In an omitted portion of the article, Professor Simpson adds: "The reason for the attempt to stay execution was principally sexist. Being a married woman Mrs. Carlill might be unable to refund the money if she lost the appeal. The [appellate] judges rejected this; as a 'literary lady' she had her own earnings, and might indeed make as much as £1,000 a year, so Lord Justice Kay, no doubt slightly frivolously, suggested." 14 J. Leg. Stud. at 364. — EDS.]

the old established insufflator associated with the name of Dr. Osborne. Also advertised in this way in the British Medical Journal for 1890 was the more alarming New Vaginal Insufflator. For no human orifice was safe from the assaults of Victorian medical science, and vast ingenuity was expended in perfecting suitable instruments, or even mechanisms for storing them in serried ranks, ready for instant use, such as Reynolds Enema Rack, whose virtues were extolled in the Lancet in 1892. The availability of suitable materials encouraged this hideous trade. It was the age of rubber, gutta percha, and vulcanite. It was also the golden age of the enema, which reached the summit of its development in America with the invention of the J.B.L. Cascade, promoted by Dr. Charles A. Tyrrell, author of The Royal Road to Health, a horrendous and obscene work on the mythical condition of auto-intoxication, which reached, so its author claimed, its thirty-seventh edition in 1901. For those in pursuit merely of the more restrained practice of insufflation, Roe's device was one among many, and, for those desiring elegance there was an abundance of ivory, which Frederick Roe mentioned in his patent specification as a possible material for the orifice.

Nor of course were the external surfaces of the body in any way immune from the products of the mechanical ingenuity of the time; one might, if suffering from hysteria, be set upon with Dr. Andrew Smart's Dermic Punctator, which enabled the medical man to puncture one's skin simultaneously, and with little effort, with large numbers of needles to produce what was euphemistically called counterirritation. If need be, dilute acid could then be applied to the skin to enhance and sharpen the effect. But Frederick Roe never widened his activities to become involved either with the external surfaces or more intimate parts of the Victorian anatomy.

The smoke ball's active ingredient, carbolic acid, is a poison, and from 1882 onward the Pharmaceutical Society had waged a campaign to persuade the Privy Council to add it to the list of scheduled poisons, a campaign which was eventually partially successful in 1900. Earlier it had been freely available, and an article by Dr. Robert Lee in the Lancet for 1892 indicates that inhaling carbolic acid fumes was a recognized form of treatment for some conditions. We may be fairly confident that it did little more good to his patients than inhaling carbolic dust did for the purchasers of the Carbolic Smoke Ball, but we must not judge Frederick Roe too harshly for his optimism. And, so far as influenza is concerned the use of the ball compares favorably with the heroic measures adopted for the same condition by Dr. J. C. Voight, a product of the medical school at Edinburgh; rectal injections of eucalyptus oil, or the milder methods of Dr. John Crerar, who relied on large and repeated doses of potassium bicarbonate. These were inventive spirits; more typical perhaps was the scatter-gun system followed by Dr. E. C. Barnes, divisional surgeon to the Metropolitan Police: "I gave all cases carbonate of ammonia early, with citrate of potass. and Liq. ammon. Acetatis, followed quickly or even accompanied with quinine pills in one grain dose three times a day. For the bilious cases two grains calomel, one grain opium followed in two hours with haust. rhei and a mixture containing sodae bicarb, ammonia and chlorodyne. I also found liniment of chloroform and belladonna very valuable." This list excludes the extras for coughs or rheumatic symptoms. To be fair to the good doctor his patients did also receive gruel, beef tea, and brandy, which they surely deserved and needed. But it is perhaps not too surprising that some sufferers preferred the regular use of the Carbolic Smoke Ball.

Roe Goes Public. . . . On December 16, shortly after the decision had gone against him in the Court of Appeal, Frederick Roe, together with one Henry Edwin Teasdale Turner, agreed to form a limited company to market the ball and another product, a tonic known as "Sunilla." . . .

Now it might be supposed that December 1892, just after the loss of the action, was hardly the moment for forming the new company. A flood of claims ought surely to have arrived to drive Roe into the bankruptcy court, for his personal liability for the payment of the £100 rewards would in no way be affected by the later acquisition of limited liability. . . . But in fact no flood of claims seems to have occurred. On February 25 we find the managing director of the new company boldly publishing in the Illustrated London News a new advertisement, cunningly framed in order to turn the whole affair to his advantage. In it he pointed out that a reward of £100 pounds had recently been promised to anyone who contracted influenza, or eleven other diseases "caused by taking cold," after using the ball according to the instructions. The text continues: "Many thousand Carbolic Smoke Balls were sold on these advertisements, but only three persons claimed the reward of £100, thus proving conclusively that this invaluable remedy will prevent and cure the above mentioned disease. THE CARBOLIC SMOKE BALL COMPANY LTD. now offer £200 REWARD to the person who purchases a Carbolic Smoke Ball and afterwards contracts any of the following diseases. . . ." There followed a list of nineteen ailments: influenza, coughs, cold in the head, cold in the chest, catarrh, asthma, bronchitis, sore throat, hoarseness, throat deafness, loss of voice, laryngitis, snoring, sore eyes, diphtheria, croup, whooping cough, neuralgia, headache (see illustration). It will be noted that this offer appears to envisage only a single prize, and the small print went on to restrict the scope of the offer still further in a way which suggests legal advice: "This offer is made to those who have purchased a Carbolic Smoke Ball since Jan. 1, 1893, and is subject to conditions to be obtained on application, a duplicate of which must be signed and deposited with the Company in London by the applicant before commencing the treatment specified in the conditions. This offer will remain open only till March 31, 1893."

What these conditions were, or whether anyone succeeded in claiming the reward, does not appear. But no similar offer appears to have been made in later advertisements, so perhaps the experiment proved costly. . . .

Epilogue.   [Records in St. Catherine's House show that Roe . . . died of tuberculosis and valvular heart disease on June 3, 1899, at his premises, 3 Princes Street; he was fifty-seven, and his occupation of "Patent Medicine Proprietor" failed to protect him. He left a widow, but no will.[17]]

And as for Louisa Elizabeth Carlill herself, . . . she long survived her adventure with the law. After her husband died on October 6, 1930, she lived in a flat in Blackheath, but by 1939 she was established in a hotel on the south coast, probably in Hastings, where she was renowned for her

17. [From 14 J. Leg. Stud. at 375. — EDS.]

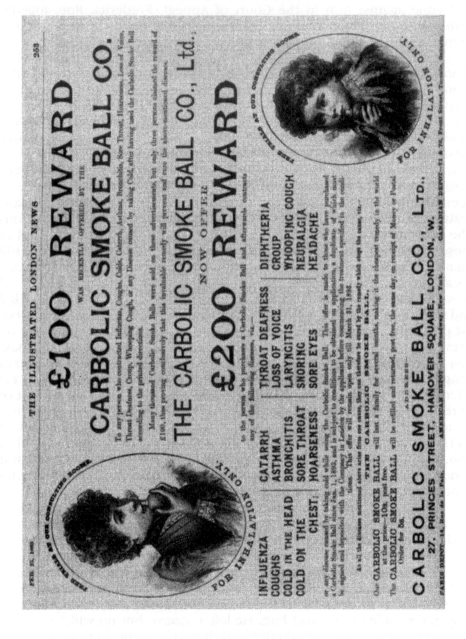

punctuality and her settled practice of drinking one glass of claret with her lunch. She then went to live with her daughter Dorothy Brousson at Swan House, in the village of Sellindge, near Folkestone, a lively spot to choose at the time of the Battle of Britain. There she died on March 10, 1942, at the age of ninety-six years, principally, as her death certificate records, of old age.

The other cause noted by her medical man, Dr. Joseph M. Yarman, was influenza.

Reread: Restatement §§2 (p. 15) & 24 (p. 300)
                 Uniform Commercial Code, §§2-204(1) & 2-206 (p. 272-273)

RESTATEMENT (SECOND) OF CONTRACTS

§54. ACCEPTANCE BY PERFORMANCE; NECESSITY OF NOTIFICATION TO OFFEROR

(1) Where an offer invites an offeree to accept by rendering a performance, no notification is necessary to make such an acceptance effective unless the offer requests such a notification.

(2) If an offeree who accepts by rendering a performance has reason to know that the offeror has no adequate means of learning of the performance with reasonable promptness and certainty, the contractual duty of the offeror is discharged unless

(a) the offeree exercises reasonable diligence to notify the offeror of acceptance, or

(b) the offeror learns of the performance within a reasonable time, or

(c) the offer indicates the notification of acceptance is not required.

REFERENCE: Barnett, §3.2.3
                Farnsworth, §3.15
                Calamari & Perillo, §2.15
                Murray, §47

STUDY GUIDE: How does the problem of acceptance by performance that arose in the next case differ from that which arose in Carlill? *In each case, what is it that the offeror wants from the offeree?*

WHITE v. CORLIES & TIFFT
Court of Appeals of New York,
46 N.Y. 467 (1871)

Appeal from judgment of the General Term of the first judicial district, affirming a judgment entered upon a verdict for plaintiff.

The action was for an alleged breach of contract.

The plaintiff was a builder, with his place of business in Fortieth street, New York city.

The defendants were merchants at 32 Dey street.

In September, 1865, the defendants furnished the plaintiff with specifications, for fitting up a suit [sic] of offices at 57 Broadway, and requested him to make an estimate of the cost of doing the work.

On September twenty-eighth the plaintiff left his estimate with the defendants, and they were to consider upon it, and inform the plaintiff of their conclusions.

On the same day the defendants made a change in their specifications and sent a copy of the same, so changed, to the plaintiff for his assent under his estimate, which he assented to by signing the same and returning it to the defendants.

On the day following the defendants' book-keeper wrote the plaintiff the following note:

NEW YORK, September 29th.

Upon an agreement to finish the fitting up of offices 57 Broadway in two weeks from date, you can begin at once.

The writer will call again, probably between five and six this P.M.

W. H. R.,
For J.W. Corlies & Co.,

32 Dey street.

No reply to this note was ever made by the plaintiff; and on the next day the same was countermanded by a second note from the defendants.

Immediately on receipt of the note of September twenty-ninth, and before the countermand was forwarded, the plaintiff commenced a performance by the purchase of lumber and beginning work thereon.

And after receiving the countermand, the plaintiff brought this action for damages for a breach of contract.[18]

The court charged the jury as follows: "From the contents of this note which the plaintiff received, was it his duty to go down to Dey street (meaning to give notice of assent), before commencing the work?"

"In my opinion it was not. He had a right to act upon this note and comence [sic] the job, *and that was a binding contract between the parties.*"

To this defendants excepted.

L. Henry, for appellants. The manifestion [sic] of assent must be such as tends to give notice to proposing party. . . .

18. ["Some additional facts, taken from the record on appeal of White's testimony may be helpful. Corlies' initial request was to have the office done in black walnut, a hard wood, within 21 days. White replied that he could not do the job in a hard wood in that time. Corlies then requested an estimate for white pine, a soft wood. White left the estimate on September 28, but did not indicate the time within which he would finish. Corlies made a change in the specifications to which White assented. There followed the letter of September 29 from Corlies. The countermand from Corlies said that it had decided to do the office in black walnut and requested an estimate for that in place of pine. Record, pp. 7-12." E. Allan Farnsworth & William F. Young, Cases and Materials on Contracts 166 (4th ed. 1988).]

Mr. Field, for respondent. Not necessary that the fact of concurrence by one party should be made known to the other. . . . An agent acting, apparent authority binds the principal. . . .

FOLGER, J.* We do not think that the jury found, or that the testimony shows, that there was any agreement between the parties, before the written communication of the defendants of September thirtieth was received by the plaintiff. This note did not make an agreement. It was a proposition, and must have been accepted by the plaintiff before either party was bound, in contract, to the other. The only overt action which is claimed by the plaintiff as indicating on his part an acceptance of the offer, was the purchase of the stuff necessary for the work, and commencing work, as we understand the testimony, upon that stuff.

We understand the rule to be, that where an offer is made by one party to another when they are not together, the acceptance of it by that other must be manifested by some appropriate act. It does not need that the acceptance shall come to the knowledge of the one making the offer before he shall be bound. But though the manifestation need not be brought to his knowledge before he becomes bound, he is not bound, if that manifestation is not put in a proper way to be in the usual course of events, in some reasonable time communicated to him. Thus a letter received by mail containing a proposal, may be answered by letter by mail, containing the acceptance. And in general, as soon as the answering letter is mailed, the contract is concluded. Though one party does not know of the acceptance, the manifestation thereof is put in the proper way of reaching him.

In the case in hand, the plaintiff determined to accept. But a mental determination not indicated by speech, or put in course of indication by act to the other party, is not an acceptance which will bind the other. Nor does an act, which, in itself, is no indication of an acceptance, become such, because accompanied by an unevinced mental determination. Where the act uninterpreted by concurrent evidence of the mental purpose accompanying it, is as well referable to one state of facts as another, it is no indication to the other party of an acceptance, and does not operate to hold him to his offer.

Conceding that the testimony shows that the plaintiff did resolve to accept this offer, he did no act which indicated an acceptance of it to the defendants. He, a carpenter and builder, purchased stuff for the work. But it was stuff as fit for any other like work. He began work upon the stuff, but as he would have done for any other like work. There was nothing in his thought formed but not uttered, or in his acts that indicated or set in motion an indication to the defendants of his acceptance of their offer, or which could necessarily result therein.

But the charge of the learned judge was fairly to be understood by the jury as laying down the rule to them, that the plaintiff need not indicate to

---

* *Charles James Folger* (1818-1884) graduated from Hobart College (M.A., LL.D.) and was admitted to the Albany (New York) bar in 1839. He was a county judge and member of the New York State Senate (1861-1869), where he was president pro tem for four years, before being appointed associate judge of the New York State Court of Appeals in 1870. After leaving that court in 1871, Folger was also assistant U.S. treasurer (1869-1871), Chief Justice of the New York Supreme Court in 1880, and Secretary of Treasury under President Arthur from 1881 until his death. — K.T.

the defendants his acceptance of their offer; and that the purchase of stuff and working on it after receiving the note, made a binding contract between the parties. In this we think the learned judge fell into error.

The judgment appealed from must be reversed, and a new trial ordered, with costs to abide the event of the action.

All concur, but ALLEN, J., not voting.

Judgment reversed, and new trial ordered.

↓ Holding

Poetic Background: Llewellyn's Verse

The following poem was found by Professor David Snyder among the papers of Karl Llewellyn (1893-1962), professor at the University of Chicago Law School and the intellectual force behind the Uniform Commercial Code.

white and corlies

I

White and Corlies had a spat; —
Whether White had promised that
He'd do the job in two weeks flat.

"Listen, Corlies" Whitey plead,
"Can't you get it through your head
No matter how your note is read
I've done all it could have said?

You need a promise? Well, you've got it!
Any imbecile could spot it!

Why then don't you face the fact
That I promised thru an act,*
And let me carry through our pact?"

But Corlies was a hard boiled guy —
So cold the stare that left his eye
'Twould seem that winter had drawn nigh.

And what he said is nothing new —
Ages past have heard it too —
"Sue, damn you, sue!"

That icy stare didn't work quite right —
It boiled the fighting-blood in White,
Who said, "All right, you louse, I'll fight!"

* performance does not rhyme — excuse it, please.

II

So a lawyer was sought
And a suit was brought
To the proper court —
(And alas poor White!)
'Twas all for nought.

The judge with high disdain decreed
That he could nohow seem to read
In any fact that White agreed.

RESTATEMENT (SECOND) OF CONTRACTS

STUDY GUIDE: To which of the previous two cases — Carlill or White — do you think the following Restatement sections were intended to apply? Would they affect the outcome?

Reread: Restatement (Second) of Contracts §19 (p. 263)

§30. FORM OF ACCEPTANCE INVITED

(1) An offer may invite or require acceptance to be made by an affirmative answer in words, or by performing or refraining from performing a specified act, or may empower the offeree to make a selection of terms in his acceptance.

(2) Unless otherwise indicated by the language or the circumstances, an offer invites acceptance in any manner and by any medium reasonable in the circumstances.

§32. INVITATION OF PROMISE OR PERFORMANCE

In case of doubt an offer is interpreted as inviting the offeree to accept either by promising to perform what the offer requests or by rendering the performance, as the offeree chooses.

STUDY GUIDE: No discussion of offer and acceptance would be complete without the famous case of Petterson v. Pattberg. When reading the opinions consider whether the majority and the dissent are actually disagreeing about the rules governing the formation of unilateral contracts. Does this case differ in any respect from Dickinson v. Dodds?

PETTERSON v. PATTBERG
Court of Appeals of New York,
248 N.Y. 86, 161 N.E. 428 (1928)

Appeal from a judgment of the Appellate Division of the Supreme Court in the second judicial department, entered November 18, 1927, affirming a judgment in favor of plaintiff entered upon a verdict directed by the court. . . .

KELLOGG, J.* The evidence given upon the trial sanctions the following statement of facts: John Petterson, of whose last will and testament the plaintiff is the executrix, was the owner of a parcel of real estate in Brooklyn, known as 5301 Sixth avenue. The defendant was the owner of a bond executed by Petterson, which was secured by a third mortgage upon the parcel. On April 4th, 1924, there remained unpaid upon the principal the sum of $5,450. This amount was payable in installments of $250 on April 25th, 1924, and upon a like monthly date every three months thereafter. Thus the bond and mortgage had more than five years to run before the entire sum became due. Under [the] date of the 4th of April, 1924, the defendant wrote Petterson as follows:

Female executor of a will

Offer

> I hereby agree to accept cash for the mortgage which I hold against premises 5301 6th Ave., Brooklyn, N.Y. It is understood and agreed as a consideration I will allow you $780 providing said mortgage is paid on or before May 31, 1924, and the regular quarterly payment due April 25, 1924, is paid when due.

On April 25, 1924, Petterson paid the defendant the installment of principal due on that date. Subsequently, on a day in the latter part of May, 1924, Petterson presented himself at the defendant's home, and knocked at the door. The defendant demanded the name of his caller. Petterson replied:

> It is Mr. Petterson. I have come to pay off the mortgage.

The defendant answered that he had sold the mortgage. Petterson stated that he would like to talk with the defendant, so the defendant partly opened the door. Thereupon Petterson exhibited the cash and said he was ready to pay off the mortgage according to the agreement. The defendant refused to take the money. Prior to this conversation Petterson had made a contract to sell the land to a third person free and clear of the mortgage to the defendant. Meanwhile, also, the defendant had sold the bond and mortgage to a third party. It, therefore, became necessary for Petterson to pay to such person the full amount of the bond and mortgage. It is claimed that he

---

* Henry Theodore Kellogg (1869-1942) was educated at Rock Point Military Academy, Burlington, Vermont, and Harvard University (A.B., LL.B.). Upon graduation in 1892, he entered the firm of his father, Supreme Court Justice S. Alonzo Kellogg, and practiced there until he became partner in the firms of Shedden & Kellogg, then Kellogg & Johnson. He became referee in bankruptcy (1898-1903), then served as a County Court judge until he was appointed by the governor to replace his father as supreme court judge. He served on this court until his appointment as judge of the appellate division in 1918. In 1926, he was elected associate judge of the New York Court of Appeals, which he resigned due to ill health in 1934. — K.T.

thereby sustained a loss of $780, the sum which the defendant agreed to allow upon the bond and mortgage if payment in full of principal, less that sum, was made on or before May 31st, 1924. The plaintiff has had a recovery for the sum thus claimed, with interest.

Clearly the defendant's letter proposed to Petterson the making of a unilateral contract, the gift of a promise in exchange for the performance of an act. The thing conditionally promised by the defendant was the reduction of the mortgage debt. The act requested to be done, in consideration of the offered promise, was payment in full of the reduced principal of the debt prior to the due date thereof.

> If an act is requested, that very act and no other must be given.

(Williston on Contracts, sec. 73.)

> In case of offers for a consideration, the performance of the consideration is always deemed a condition.

(Langdell's Summary of the Law of Contracts, sec. 4.)

It is elementary that any offer to enter into a unilateral contract may be withdrawn before the act requested to be done has been performed. . . . A bidder at a sheriff's sale may revoke his bid at any time before the property is struck down to him. . . . The offer of a reward in consideration of an act to be performed is revocable before the very act requested has been done. . . . So, also, an offer to pay a broker commissions, upon a sale of land for the offeror, is revocable at any time before the land is sold, although prior to revocation the broker performs services in an effort to effectuate a sale. . . . An interesting question arises when, as here, the offeree approaches the offeror with the intention of proffering performance and, before actual tender is made, the offer is withdrawn. Of such a case Williston says:

> The offeror may see the approach of the offeree and know that an acceptance is contemplated. If the offeror can say "I revoke" before the offeree accepts, however brief the interval of time between the two acts, there is no escape from the conclusion that the offer is terminated.

(Williston on Contracts, sec. 60-b.) In this instance Petterson, standing at the door of the defendant's house, stated to the defendant that he had come to pay off the mortgage. Before a tender of the necessary moneys had been made the defendant informed Petterson that he had sold the mortgage. That was a definite notice to Petterson that the defendant could not perform his offered promise and that a tender to the defendant, who was no longer the creditor, would be ineffective to satisfy the debt.

> An offer to sell property may be withdrawn before acceptance without any formal notice to the person to whom the offer is made. It is sufficient if that person has actual knowledge that the person who made the offer has done some act inconsistent with the continuance of the offer, such as selling the property to a third person.

(Dickinson v. Dodds, 2 Ch. Div. 463, headnote.) . . .

Thus, it clearly appears that the defendant's offer was withdrawn before its acceptance had been tendered. It is unnecessary to determine, therefore, what the legal situation might have been had tender been made before withdrawal. It is the individual view of the writer that the same result would follow. This would be so, for the act requested to be performed was the completed act of payment, a thing incapable of performance unless assented to by the person to be paid. . . . Clearly an offering party has the right to name the precise act performance of which would convert his offer into a binding promise. Whatever the act may be until it is performed the offer must be revocable. However, the supposed case is not before us for decision. We think that in this particular instance the offer of the defendant was withdrawn before it became a binding promise, and, therefore, that no contract was ever made for the breach of which the plaintiff may claim damages.

The judgment of the Appellate Division and that of the Trial Term should be reversed and the complaint dismissed, with costs in all courts.

LEHMAN, J.* (dissenting). The defendant's letter to Petterson constituted a promise on his part to accept payment at a discount of the mortgage he held, provided the mortgage is paid on or before May 31st, 1924. Doubtless by the terms of the promise itself, the defendant made payment of the mortgage by the plaintiff, before the stipulated time, a condition precedent to performance by the defendant of his promise to accept payment at a discount. If the condition precedent has not been performed, it is because the defendant made performance impossible by refusing to accept payment, when the plaintiff came with an offer of immediate performance.

It is a principle of fundamental justice that if a promisor is himself the cause of the failure of performance either of an obligation due him or of a condition upon which his own liability depends, he cannot take advantage of the failure.

(Williston on Contracts, section 677.) The question in this case is not whether payment of the mortgage is a condition precedent to the performance of a promise made by the defendant, but, rather, whether at the time the defendant refused the offer of payment, he had assumed any binding obligation, even though subject to condition.

The promise made by the defendant lacked consideration at the time it was made. Nevertheless the promise was not made as a gift or mere gratuity to the plaintiff. It was made for the purpose of obtaining from the [plaintiff] something which the [defendant] desired. It constituted an offer which was to become binding whenever the plaintiff should give, in return for the defendant's promise, exactly the consideration which the defendant requested.

Here the defendant requested no counter promise from the plaintiff. The consideration requested by the defendant for his promise to accept

---

Irving Lehman (1876-1945) graduated from Columbia University (A.M., LL.B.). Upon graduation in 1898, he held a private practice at New York until he was elected justice of the Supreme Court of New York. He was reelected in 1923, but left the court to accept election as judge of the Court of Appeals in 1924. He served as Chief Judge from 1940 until his death. — K.T.

payment was, I agree, some act to be performed by the plaintiff. Until the act requested was performed, the defendant might undoubtedly revoke his offer. Our problem is to determine from the words of the letter read in the light of surrounding circumstances what act the defendant requested as consideration for his promise.

The defendant undoubtedly made his offer as an inducement to the plaintiff to "pay" the mortgage before it was due. Therefore, it is said, that "the act requested to be performed was the completed act of payment, a thing incapable of performance unless assented to by the person to be paid." In unmistakable terms the defendant agreed to accept payment, yet we are told that the defendant intended, and the plaintiff should have understood, that the act requested by the defendant, as consideration for his promise to accept payment, included performance by the defendant himself of the very promise for which the act was to be consideration. The defendant's promise was to become binding only when fully performed; and part of the consideration to be furnished by the plaintiff for the defendant's promise was to be the performance of that promise by the defendant. So construed, the defendant's promise or offer, though intended to induce action by the plaintiff, is but a snare and delusion. The plaintiff could not reasonably suppose that the defendant was asking him to procure the performance by the defendant of the very act which the defendant promised to do, yet we are told that even after the plaintiff had done all else which the defendant requested, the defendant's promise was still not binding because the defendant chose not to perform.

I cannot believe that a result so extraordinary could have been intended when the defendant wrote the letter. "The thought behind the phrase proclaims itself misread when the outcome of the reading is injustice or absurdity." (See opinion of Cardozo, C. J., in Surace v. Danna, 248 N.Y. 18.) If the defendant intended to induce payment by the plaintiff and yet reserve the right to refuse payment when offered he should have used a phrase better calculated to express his meaning than the words: "I agree to accept." A promise to accept payment, by its very terms, must necessarily become binding, if at all, not later than when a present offer to pay is made.

I recognize that in this case only an offer of payment, and not a formal tender of payment, was made before the defendant withdrew his offer to accept payment. Even the plaintiff's part in the act of payment was then not technically complete. Even so, under a fair construction of the words of the letter I think the plaintiff had done the act which the defendant requested as consideration for his promise. The plaintiff offered to pay with present intention and ability to make that payment. A formal tender is seldom made in business transactions, except to lay the foundation for subsequent assertion in a court of justice of rights which spring from refusal of the tender. If the defendant acted in good faith in making his offer to accept payment, he could not well have intended to draw a distinction in the act requested of the plaintiff in return, between an offer which unless refused would ripen into completed payment, and a formal tender. Certainly the defendant could not have expected or intended that the plaintiff would make a formal tender of payment without first stating that he had come to make payment. We should not read into the language of the defendant's offer a meaning which would prevent enforcement of the defendant's promise after it had been accepted by the plaintiff in the very way which the defendant must have intended it should be accepted, if he acted in good faith.

The judgment should be affirmed.

Relational Background: Additional Information About Petterson v. Pattberg

STUDY GUIDE: Do the following facts affect either the legal or the equitable result in Petterson? *If so, exactly how?*

SAMUEL BLINKOFF, NOTE, 14 CORNELL L.Q. 81, 84 N.18 (1928):   Other facts in the case, not appearing in the opinion, may have influenced the court. The record of the trial (folios 95-97) reveals that the defendant was prevented from testifying as to a letter, sent to the plaintiff's testator, revoking the offer because such testimony was inadmissible under §347 of the Civil Practice Act, which excludes the testimony of one of the interested parties, to a transaction, where the other is dead and so unable to contradict the evidence.[19] The record (folio 59) also seems to suggest that the mortgagor knew of the previous sale of the mortgage, since he brought $4,000 in cash with him, and was accompanied by his wife and a notary public as witnesses: anticipation of the defendant's refusal by seeking to get evidence on which to base this action seems to be a plausible explanation. There was no actual proof of knowledge of the defendant's inability to carry out his offer but the situation was suspicious.

Reread: Restatement §§42 & 43 (p. 301)

STUDY GUIDE: Would §45 change the outcome in Petterson v. Pattberg? *If so, can you think of situations in which §45 would impose a hardship on offerors? If not, does this mean that the approach adopted by the court in* Petterson *made more sense than it may seem at first? Why does §62 define the tender or beginning of performance as an acceptance, while §45 defines the tender or beginning of performance as creating only an option to accept?*

RESTATEMENT (SECOND) OF CONTRACTS

§45.   OPTION CONTRACT CREATED BY PART PERFORMANCE OR TENDER

(1) Where an offer invites an offeree to accept by rendering a performance and does not invite a promissory acceptance, an option contract is created when the offeree tenders or begins the invited performance or tenders a beginning of it.   (Petterson v. Pattberg)

19. [Such enactments are known as "Deadman Statutes." — EDS.]

(2) The offeror's duty of performance under any option contract so created is conditional on completion or tender of the invited performance in accordance with the terms of the offer.

§62.   EFFECT OF PERFORMANCE BY OFFEREE WHERE OFFER INVITES EITHER PERFORMANCE OR PROMISE

(1) Where an offer invites an offeree to choose between acceptance by promise and acceptance by performance, the tender or beginning of the invited performance or a tender of a beginning of it is an acceptance by performance.

[handwritten margin note: Offeree accepts other thrust the beginning of performance]

(2) Such an acceptance operates as a promise to render complete performance.

4.   Acceptance by Silence

We have seen that an offer can be accepted by the promise or performance of an offeree. Can it also be accepted by doing nothing at all?

STUDY GUIDE: What issues of principle and policy are raised by the possibility of binding persons to contracts when they do not expressly refuse an offer that has been made to them? In the next opinion, does Holmes run afoul of these considerations? Consider a music or book club that sends you CDs or books that you must pay for if you do not return them within a specified time. Can you apply the holding of Hobbs to that type of situation? Despite its brevity, the doctrine of acceptance by silence will be of interest to us when considering how assent can be manifested in various e-commerce situations in the next section and again in Chapter 5.

HOBBS v. MASSASOIT WHIP CO.
Supreme Judicial Court of Massachusetts,
158 Mass. 194 (1893)

[This is] an action by Charles A. Hobbs against the Massasoit Whip Company to recover for skins shipped defendant, and retained by him several months without notifying plaintiff whether he had accepted them. . . . [P]laintiff had made several prior shipments to defendant, which it had accepted and paid for. . . .

Judgment for plaintiff, and defendant excepts. Exceptions overruled. . . .

HOLMES, J. This is an action for the price of eelskins sent by the plaintiff to the defendant, and kept by the defendant some months, until they were destroyed. It must be taken that the plaintiff received no notice that the defendants declined to accept the skins. The case comes before us on exceptions to an instruction to the jury, that, whether there was any prior contract or not, if skins are sent to the defendant, and it sees fit, whether it has agreed to take them or not, to lie back, and to say nothing, having reason to suppose that the man who has sent them believes that it is taking them, since it says nothing about it, then, if it fails to notify, the jury would be warranted in finding for the plaintiff.

Standing alone, and unexplained, this proposition might seem to imply that one stranger may impose a duty upon another, and make him a purchaser, in spite of himself, by sending goods to him, unless he will take the trouble, and be at the expense, of notifying the sender that he will not buy. The case was argued for the defendant on that interpretation. But, in view of the evidence, we do not understand that to have been the meaning of the judge, and we do not think that the jury can have understood that to have been his meaning. The plaintiff was not a stranger to the defendant, even if there was no contract between them. He had sent eelskins in the same way four or five times before, and they had been accepted and paid for. On the defendant's testimony, it was fair to assume that, if it had admitted the eelskins to be over twenty-two inches in length, and fit for its business, as the plaintiff testified, and the jury found that they were, it would have accepted them; that this was understood by the plaintiff; and, indeed, that there was a standing offer to him for such skins. In such a condition of things, the plaintiff was warranted in sending the defendant skins conforming to the requirements, and even if the offer was not such that the contract was made as soon as skins corresponding to its terms were sent, sending them did impose on the defendant a duty to act about them; and silence on its part, coupled with a retention of the skins for an unreasonable time, might be found by the jury to warrant the plaintiff in assuming that they were accepted, and thus to amount to an acceptance. . . . The proposition stands on the general principle that conduct which imports acceptance or assent is acceptance or assent in the view of the law, whatever may have been the actual state of mind of the party, — a principle sometimes lost sight of in the cases. . . .

Exceptions overruled.

RESTATEMENT (SECOND) OF CONTRACTS

§69.   ACCEPTANCE BY SILENCE OR EXERCISE OF DOMINION

(1) Where an offeree fails to reply to an offer, his silence and inaction operate as an acceptance in the following cases only:

(a) Where an offeree takes the benefit of offered services with reasonable opportunity to reject them and reason to know that they were offered with the expectation of compensation.

(b) Where the offeror has stated or given the offeree reason to understand that assent may be manifested by silence or inaction, and the offeree in remaining silent and inactive intends to accept the offer.

(c) Where because of previous dealings or otherwise, it is reasonable that the offeree should notify the offeror if he does not intend to accept.

(2) An offeree who does any act inconsistent with the offeror's ownership of offered property is bound in accordance with the offered terms unless they are manifestly unreasonable. But if the act is wrongful as against the offeror it is an acceptance only if ratified by him.

REFERENCE: Farnsworth, §3.14
              Calamari & Perillo, §§2.18-2.19
              Murray, §52

D. E-COMMERCE AND MUTUAL ASSENT

The materials in this section concern manifestations of assent in e-commerce: contracting on the World Wide Web. They weave together all of the doctrines governing mutual assent we have considered to this point, such as objective assent, acceptance by performance, and acceptance by silence. These cases also raise an important additional issue: Is the new electronic medium of contracting something wholly novel, requiring a new set of governing principles? Or can age-old principles of contract law be applied here, as they were applied to such formerly new technologies as the steamship, railroad, telegraph, telephone, and fax machine?

STUDY GUIDE: Are you persuaded by the court's reasoning that Verio had assented to the terms on Register.com's website? Do you think Register.com reasonably thought that Verio had assented? If Verio's subjective awareness of Register.com's conditions on use indicates Verio's assent, why does not Register.com's subjective awareness of Verio's refusal to assent to its terms not negate the existence of mutual assent? In other words, what role is the objective theory of assent playing in this case and how does the "subjective twist" work in this context? As a practical matter, is there any other way for Register.com to obtain a manifestation of consent by Verio? If so, must it employ it?

REGISTER.COM, INC. v. VERIO, INC.
United States Court of Appeals, Second Circuit,
356 F.3d 393 (2004)

LEVAL, Circuit Judge.*
Defendant, Verio, Inc. ("Verio") appeals from an order of the United States District Court for the Southern District of New York (Barbara S. Jones, J.) granting the motion of plaintiff Register.com, Inc. ("Register") for a

---

*Pierre Nelson Leval (1936-†) received his B.A. degree from Harvard College and his J.D. from Harvard Law School. Between his degrees, Judge Leval served in the U.S. Army. He clerked for Judge Henry J. Friendly of the U.S. Court of Appeals for the Second Circuit before serving as an Assistant United States Attorney in the Southern District of New York, eventually becoming Chief Appellate Attorney. After practicing with Cleary, Gottlieb, Steen & Hamilton in New York, he joined the New York County District Attorney's Office as First Assistant District Attorney and later as Chief Assistant District Attorney. In 1977, he was appointed to the United States District Court for the Southern District of New York, and in 1993, President Bill Clinton appointed him to the Court of Appeals. Judge Leval assumed senior status in 2002. — R.B.

preliminary injunction. The court's order enjoined Verio from (1) using Register's trademarks; (2) representing or otherwise suggesting to third parties that Verio's services have the sponsorship, endorsement, or approval of Register; (3) accessing Register's computers by use of auto-mated software programs performing multiple successive queries; and (4) using data obtained from Register's database of contact information of registrants of Internet domain names to solicit the registrants for the sale of web site development services by electronic mail, telephone calls, or direct mail. We affirm.[20]

BACKGROUND

This plaintiff Register is one of over 50 companies serving as registrars for the issuance of domain names on the world wide web. As a registrar, Register issues domain names to persons and entities preparing to establish web sites on the Internet. Web sites are identified and accessed by reference to their domain names.

Register was appointed a registrar of domain names by the Internet Corporation for Assigned Names and Numbers, known by the acronym "ICANN." ICANN is a private, nonprofit public benefit corporation which was established by agencies of the U.S. government to administer the Inter-net domain name system. To become a registrar of domain names, Register was required to enter into a standard form agreement with ICANN, desig-nated as the ICANN Registrar Accreditation Agreement, November 1999 version (referred to herein as the "ICANN Agreement").

Applicants to register a domain name submit to the registrar contact information, including at a minimum, the applicant's name, postal address, telephone number, and electronic mail address. The ICANN Agreement, referring to this registrant contact information under the rubric "WHOIS information," requires the registrar, under terms discussed in greater detail below, to preserve it, update it daily, and provide for free public access to it through the Internet as well as through an independent access port, called port 43. . . .

Section II.F.5 of the ICANN Agreement (which furnishes a major basis for the appellant Verio's contentions on this appeal) requires that the regis-trar "not impose terms and conditions" on the use made by others of its WHOIS data "except as permitted by ICANN-adopted policy." In specifying what restrictions may be imposed, the ICANN Agreement requires the regis-trar to permit use of its WHOIS data "for any lawful purposes except

---

20. Judge Parker was not in agreement with this disposition. Deliberations have fol-lowed an unusual course. Judge Parker initially was assigned to prepare a draft opinion affirming the district court. In the course of preparing the draft, Judge Parker changed his mind and proposed to rule in favor of the defendant, overturning the injunction in most respects. Judge Parker's draft opinion, however, failed to convince the other members of the panel, who adhered to the view that the injunction should be affirmed. Judge Parker died shortly thereafter, prior to the circulation of a draft opinion affirming the injunction, from which Judge Parker presumably would have dissented. We attach Judge Parker's draft opi-nion as an Appendix . . . to expose Judge Parker's views, which would have been set forth in a dissenting opinion, but for his death. . . .

to: . . . support the transmission of mass unsolicited, commercial advertising or solicitations *via email* (*spam*); [and other listed purposes not relevant to this appeal]." (emphasis added). . . .

In compliance with §II.F.1 of the ICANN Agreement, Register updated the WHOIS information on a daily basis and established Internet and port 43 service, which allowed free public query of its WHOIS information. An entity making a WHOIS query through Register's Internet site or port 43 would receive a reply furnishing the requested WHOIS information, captioned by a legend devised by Register, which stated,

> By submitting a WHOIS query, you agree that you will use this data only for lawful purposes and that under no circumstances will you use this data to . . . support the transmission of mass unsolicited, commercial advertising or solicitation via email.

The terms of that legend tracked §II.F.5 of the ICANN Agreement in specifying the restrictions Register imposed on the use of its WHOIS data. Subsequently, as explained below, Register amended the terms of this legend to impose more stringent restrictions on the use of the information gathered through such queries.

In addition to performing the function of a registrar of domain names, Register also engages in the business of selling web-related services to entities that maintain web sites. These services cover various aspects of web site development. In order to solicit business for the services it offers, Register sends out marketing communications. Among the entities it solicits for the sale of such services are entities whose domain names it registered. However, during the registration process, Register offers registrants the opportunity to elect whether or not they will receive marketing communications from it.

The defendant Verio, against whom the preliminary injunction was issued, is engaged in the business of selling a variety of web site design, development and operation services. In the sale of such services, Verio competes with Register's web site development business. To facilitate its pursuit of customers, Verio undertook to obtain daily updates of the WHOIS information relating to newly registered domain names. To achieve this, Verio devised an automated software program, or robot, which each day would submit multiple successive WHOIS queries through the port 43 accesses of various registrars. Upon acquiring the WHOIS information of new registrants, Verio would send them marketing solicitations by e-mail, telemarketing and direct mail. To the extent that Verio's solicitations were sent by e-mail, the practice was inconsistent with the terms of the restrictive legend Register attached to its responses to Verio's queries. . . .

Register changed the restrictive legend it attached to its responses to WHOIS queries. While previously the legend conformed to the terms of §II. F.5, which authorized Register to prohibit use of the WHOIS information for mass solicitations "via e-mail," its new legend undertook to bar mass solicitation "via direct mail, electronic mail, or by telephone."[21] Section II.F.5

---

21. By submitting a WHOIS query, you agree that . . . under no circumstances will you use this data to . . . support the transmission of mass unsolicited . . . advertising or solicitations via direct mail, electronic mail, or by telephone.

of Register's ICANN Agreement . . . required Register to permit use of the WHOIS data "for any lawful purpose except to . . . support the transmission of mass unsolicited solicitations via e-mail (spam)." Thus, by undertaking to prohibit Verio from using the WHOIS information for solicitations "via direct mail . . . or by telephone," Register was acting in apparent violation of this term of its ICANN Agreement.

Register wrote to Verio demanding that it cease using WHOIS information derived from Register not only for e-mail marketing, but also for marketing by direct mail and telephone. Verio ceased using the information in e-mail marketing, but refused to stop marketing by direct mail and telephone.

Register brought this suit on August 3, 2000, and moved for a temporary restraining order and a preliminary injunction. . . . On December 8, 2000, the district court entered a preliminary injunction. . . . The injunction barred Verio from . . . [a]ccessing Register.com's computers and computer networks in any manner, including, but not limited to, by software programs performing multiple, automated, successive queries, provided that nothing in this Order shall prohibit Verio from accessing Register.com's WHOIS database in accordance with the terms and conditions thereof. . . . Verio appeals from that order.

DISCUSSION

. . .

Verio contends that it . . . never became contractually bound to the conditions imposed by Register's restrictive legend because, in the case of each query Verio made, the legend did not appear until after Verio had submitted the query and received the WHOIS data. Accordingly, Verio contends that in no instance did it receive legally enforceable notice of the conditions Register intended to impose. Verio therefore argues it should not be deemed to have taken WHOIS data from Register's systems subject to Register's conditions.

Verio's argument might well be persuasive if its queries addressed to Register's computers had been sporadic and infrequent. If Verio had submitted only one query, or even if it had submitted only a few sporadic queries, that would give considerable force to its contention that it obtained the WHOIS data without being conscious that Register intended to impose conditions, and without being deemed to have accepted Register's conditions. But Verio was daily submitting numerous queries, each of which resulted in its receiving notice of the terms Register exacted. Furthermore, Verio admits that it knew perfectly well what terms Register demanded. Verio's argument fails.

The situation might be compared to one in which plaintiff P maintains a roadside fruit stand displaying bins of apples. A visitor, defendant D, takes an apple and bites into it. As D turns to leave, D sees a sign, visible only as one turns to exit, which says "Apples-50 cents apiece." D does not pay for the apple. D believes he has no obligation to pay because he had no notice when he bit into the apple that 50 cents was expected in return. D's view is that he never agreed to pay for the apple. Thereafter, each day, several times a day, D revisits the stand, takes an apple, and eats it. D never leaves money.

P sues *D* in contract for the price of the apples taken. *D* defends on the ground that on no occasion did he see *P*'s price notice until after he had bitten into the apples. *D* may well prevail as to the first apple taken. *D* had no reason to understand upon taking it that *P* was demanding the payment. In our view, however, *D* cannot continue on a daily basis to take apples for free, knowing full well that *P* is offering them only in exchange for 50 cents in compensation, merely because the sign demanding payment is so placed that on each occasion *D* does not see it until he has bitten into the apple.

Verio's circumstance is effectively the same. Each day Verio repeatedly enters Register's computers and takes that day's new WHOIS data. Each day upon receiving the requested data, Verio receives Register's notice of the terms on which it makes the data available — that the data not be used for mass solicitation via direct mail, e-mail, or telephone. Verio acknowledges that it continued drawing the data from Register's computers with full knowledge that Register offered access subject to these restrictions. Verio is no more free to take Register's data without being bound by the terms on which Register offers it, than *D* was free, in the example, once he became aware of the terms of *P*'s offer, to take *P*'s apples without obligation to pay the 50-cent price at which *P* offered them.

Verio seeks support for its position from cases that have dealt with the formation of contracts on the Internet. An excellent example, although decided subsequent to the submission of this case, is Specht v. Netscape Communications Corp., 306 F.3d 17 (2d Cir. 2002). The dispute was whether users of Netscape's software, who downloaded it from Netscape's web site, were bound by an agreement to arbitrate disputes with Netscape, where Netscape had posted the terms of its offer of the software (including the obligation to arbitrate disputes) on the web site from which they downloaded the software. We ruled against Netscape and in favor of the users of its software because the users would not have seen the terms Netscape exacted without scrolling down their computer screens, and there was no reason for them to do so. The evidence did not demonstrate that one who had downloaded Netscape's software had necessarily seen the terms of its offer.

Verio, however, cannot avail itself of the reasoning of *Specht*. In *Specht*, the users in whose favor we decided visited Netscape's web site one time to download its software. Netscape's posting of its terms did not compel the conclusion that its downloaders took the software subject to those terms because there was no way to determine that any downloader had seen the terms of the offer. There was no basis for imputing to the downloaders of Netscape's software knowledge of the terms on which the software was offered. This case is crucially different. Verio visited Register's computers daily to access WHOIS data and each day saw the terms of Register's offer; Verio admitted that, in entering Register's computers to get the data, it was fully aware of the terms on which Register offered the access.

Verio's next argument is that it was not bound by Register's terms because it rejected them. Even . . . acknowledging that Verio was fully aware of Register's terms, Verio contends that it still is not bound by Register's terms because it did not agree to be bound. In support of its claim, Verio cites a district court case from the Central District of California, Ticketmaster Corp. v. Tickets.com, Inc. (C.D. Cal. Aug. 10, 2000), in which the court rejected Ticketmaster's application for a preliminary injunction to enforce posted terms of use of data available on its web site against a regular user. Noting that the user of Ticketmaster's web site is not required to check an "I agree" box before proceeding, the court concluded that there was insufficient proof of agreement to support a preliminary injunction.

We acknowledge that the *Ticketmaster* decision gives Verio some support, but . . . we are not inclined to agree with the *Ticketmaster* court's analysis. There is a crucial difference between the circumstances of *Specht*, where we declined to enforce Netscape's specified terms against a user of its software because of inadequate evidence that the user had seen the terms when downloading the software, and those of *Ticketmaster*, where the taker of information from Ticketmaster's site knew full well the terms on which the information was offered but was not offered an icon marked, "I agree," on which to click. Under the circumstances of *Ticketmaster*, we see no reason why the enforceability of the offeror's terms should depend on whether the taker states (or clicks), "I agree."

We recognize that contract offers on the Internet often require the offeree to click on an "I agree" icon. And no doubt, in many circumstances, such a statement of agreement by the offeree is essential to the formation of a contract. But not in all circumstances. While new commerce on the Internet has exposed courts to many new situations, it has not fundamentally changed the principles of contract. It is standard contract doctrine that when a benefit is offered subject to stated conditions, and the offeree makes a decision to take the benefit with knowledge of the terms of the offer, the taking constitutes an acceptance of the terms, which accordingly become binding on the offeree. See, e.g., Restatement (Second) of Contracts §69(1)(a) (1981) ("[S]ilence and inaction operate as an acceptance . . . [w]here an offeree takes the benefit of offered services with reasonable opportunity to reject them and reason to know that they were offered with the expectation of compensation."); 2 Richard A. Lord, Williston on Contracts §6:9 (4th ed. 1991) ("[T]he acceptance of the benefit of services may well be held to imply a promise to pay for them if at the time of acceptance the offeree has a reasonable opportunity to reject the service and knows or has reason to know that compensation is expected."); Arthur Linton Corbin, Corbin on Contracts §71 (West 1 vol. ed. 1952) ("The acceptance of the benefit of the services is a promise to pay for them, if at the time of accepting the benefit the offeree has a reasonable opportunity to reject it and knows that compensation is expected."). . . .

Returning to the apple stand, the visitor, who sees apples offered for 50 cents apiece and takes an apple, owes 50 cents, regardless whether he did or did not say, "I agree." The choice offered in such circumstances is to take the apple on the known terms of the offer or not to take the apple. As we see it, the defendant in *Ticketmaster* and Verio in this case had a similar choice. Each was offered access to information subject to terms of which they were well aware. Their choice was either to accept the offer of contract, taking the information subject to the terms of the offer, or, if the terms were not acceptable, to decline to take the benefits.

We find that the district court was within its discretion in concluding that Register showed likelihood of success on the merits of its contract claim.

APPENDIX

Draft Opinion of Judge Fred I. Parker

F. I. PARKER,* Circuit Judge. . . .

Verio admits that it knew of Register.com's terms when it submitted queries. Register.com argues that Verio's course of conduct — repeatedly submitting queries while being aware of the proposed terms — objectively demonstrates its assent to be bound by Register.com's terms and that Verio's conduct would reasonably lead Register.com to infer Verio's assent. On the other hand, Verio argues that even though it knew of the terms, it rejected them and never manifested assent. Based on the circumstances of this case, . . . we find Verio's argument convincing.

We do not believe that one can reasonably infer that Verio assented to Register.com's proposed terms simply because Verio submitted multiple queries with knowledge of those terms. Verio (and every other end-user) may repeatedly submit WHOIS queries to Register.com based on an (accurate) understanding that Register.com does not own WHOIS information and that such information must be made freely and publicly available (with two specified restrictions) pursuant to the ICANN Agreement. Viewed in this manner, Register.com's repeated proposals that terms not authorized by the ICANN Agreement be adopted could reasonably have been repeatedly rejected by Verio. There is no basis to infer that Verio in fact assented to Register.com's mass marketing restriction. Cf. Step-Saver Data Sys., Inc. v. Wyse Tech., 939 F.2d 91, 103-04 (3d Cir. 1991); accord Expeditors Int'l of Washington, Inc. v. The Official Creditors Comm. (In re CFLC. Inc.), 166 F.3d 1012, 1017 (9th Cir. 1999) ("Course of dealing analysis is not proper in an instance where the only action taken has been the repeated delivery of a particular form by one of the parties.").[22]

Finally, we note that Register.com's position is undercut by the fact that WHOIS information is public information owned by no one. Register .com does not "own" the information. . . . By the time an end-user receives

---

Fred I. Parker (1938-2003) attended the University of Massachusetts and Georgetown University Law Center. After practicing briefly in Boston, he practiced in Vermont from 1966 to 1990 except for a term as Deputy Attorney General of Vermont. In 1990, President George H. W. Bush nominated Parker to serve as a judge of the U.S. District Court for the District of Vermont. In 1994, President Clinton promoted Parker to the U.S. Court of Appeals for the Second Circuit, where he served until his death. — R.B.

22. As the Ninth Circuit noted in adopting the *Step-Saver* approach:

The *Step-Saver* court gave two reasons for refusing to extend course of dealing analysis to a situation where the parties had not previously taken any action with respect to the matters addressed by the disputed terms. First, the repeated exchange of forms merely indicated the seller's desire to have these terms included. The failure to obtain the purchaser's express assent to those terms indicates the seller's agreement to do business on other terms — those expressly agreed upon by the parties. Second, a seller in multiple transactions will typically have the opportunity to negotiate the precise terms of the parties' agreement. The seller's unwillingness or inability to obtain a negotiated agreement reflecting its desired terms strongly suggests that those terms are not a part of the parties' commercial bargain.

the WHOIS information and Register.com's proposed terms, Register.com's WHOIS database has already been accessed and the information has already been delivered to the end-user. Absent an ownership right in the information itself, which might allow some use restrictions despite disclosure, there is nothing to prevent an end-user from simply rejecting Register.com's proposed terms and then proceeding to use the information in any desired manner.

In conclusion, because (1) Register.com did not condition access to its database on acceptance of its terms but instead granted access, thereby giving Verio possession of the WHOIS information; and (2) Register.com's terms were an attempt to unilaterally impose use restrictions not authorized by the ICANN Agreement on information that Register.com does not own, Register.com has failed to establish a sufficient likelihood of success on the merits of its contract claim.

STUDY GUIDE: In the next case, notice how the judge distinguishes between the existence of a contract (which he says is a matter of state law) and the enforceability of the arbitration clause (which he says is governed by federal law). Ironically, then, both state and federal law are needed to decide if an arbitrator rather than either a state or a federal judge is to consider the merits of the case. Are consumers less likely to read "browsewrap" terms than "clickwrap"? Should the likelihood that consumers will read the terms matter?

NGUYEN v. BARNES & NOBLE INC.
United States Court of Appeals, Ninth Circuit,
763 F.3d 1171 (2014)

NOONAN,* Circuit Judge:

Barnes & Noble, Inc. ("Barnes & Noble") appeals the district court's denial of its motion to compel arbitration against Kevin Khoa Nguyen ("Nguyen") pursuant to the arbitration agreement contained in its website's Terms of Use. In order to resolve the issue of arbitrability, we must address whether Nguyen, by merely using Barnes & Noble's website, agreed to be bound by the Terms of Use, even though Nguyen was never prompted to assent to the Terms of Use and never in fact read them. We agree with the district court that Barnes & Noble did not provide reasonable notice of its Terms of Use, and that Nguyen therefore did not unambiguously manifest assent to the arbitration provision contained therein.

. . .

*John T. Noonan, Jr. (1926-†) received his law degree from Harvard in 1954. He worked as a law professor at Notre Dame from 1961-1966. He was appointed to the U.S. Court of Appeals for the Ninth Circuit in 1985 and was named Senior Judge of that court in 1996. He has been a noted legal scholar concerning issues of law and religion. — S.Q.

I. BACKGROUND

A.

The underlying facts are not in dispute. Barnes & Noble is a national bookseller that owns and operates hundreds of bookstores as well as the website <www.barnesandnoble.com>. In August 2011, Barnes & Noble, along with other retailers across the country, liquidated its inventory of discontinued Hewlett-Packard Touchpads ("Touchpads"), an unsuccessful competitor to Apple's iPad, by advertising a "fire sale" of Touchpads at a heavily discounted price. Acting quickly on the nationwide liquidation of Touchpads, Nguyen purchased two units on Barnes & Noble's website on August 21, 2011, and received an email confirming the transaction. The following day, Nguyen received another email informing him that his order had been cancelled due to unexpectedly high demand. Nguyen alleges that, as a result of "Barnes & Noble's representations, as well as the delay in informing him it would not honor the sale," he was "unable to obtain an HP Tablet during the liquidation period for the discounted price," and was "forced to rely on substitute tablet technology, which he subsequently purchased . . . [at] considerable expense."

B.

In April 2012, Nguyen filed this lawsuit in California Superior Court on behalf of himself and a putative class of consumers whose Touchpad orders had been cancelled, alleging that Barnes & Noble had engaged in deceptive business practices and false advertising in violation of both California and New York law. Barnes & Noble removed the action to federal court and moved to compel arbitration under the Federal Arbitration Act ("FAA"), arguing that Nguyen was bound by the arbitration agreement in the website's Terms of Use.

The website's Terms of Use are available via a "Terms of Use" hyperlink located in the bottom left-hand corner of every page on the Barnes & Noble website, which appears alongside other hyperlinks labeled "NOOK Store Terms," "Copyright," and "Privacy Policy." These hyperlinks also appear underlined and set in green typeface in the lower lefthand corner of every page in the online checkout process.

Nguyen neither clicked on the "Terms of Use" hyperlink nor actually read the Terms of Use. Had he clicked on the hyperlink, he would have been taken to a page containing the full text of Barnes & Noble's Terms of Use, which state, in relevant part: "By visiting any area in the Barnes & Noble .com Site, creating an account, [or] making a purchase via the Barnes & Noble.com Site . . . a User is deemed to have accepted the Terms of Use." Nguyen also would have come across an arbitration provision, which states:

XVIII. DISPUTE RESOLUTION

Any claim or controversy at law or equity that arises out of the Terms of Use, the Barnes & Noble.com Site or any Barnes & Noble.com Service (each a

"Claim"), shall be resolved through binding arbitration conducted by tele-phone, online or based solely upon written submissions where no in-person appearance is required. In such cases, arbitration shall be administered by the American Arbitration Association under its Commercial Arbitration Rules (including without limitation the Supplementary Procedures for Consumer-Related Disputes, if applicable), and judgment on the award ren-dered by the arbitrator(s) may be entered in any court having jurisdiction thereof.

. . .

Any claim shall be arbitrated or litigated, as the case may be, on an individual basis and shall not be consolidated with any Claim of any other party whether through class action proceedings, class arbitration proceedings or otherwise.

. . .

Each of the parties hereby knowingly, voluntarily and intentionally waives any right it may have to a trial by jury in respect of any litigation (including but not limited to any claims, counterclaims, cross-claims, or third party claims) arising out of, under or in connection with these Terms of Use. Further, each party hereto certifies that no representative or agent of either party has represented, expressly or otherwise, that such a party would not in the event of such litigation, seek to enforce this waiver of right to jury trial provision. Each of the parties acknowledges that this section is a material inducement for the other party entering into these Terms of Use.

Nguyen contends that he cannot be bound to the arbitration provision because he neither had notice of nor assented to the website's Terms of Use. Barnes & Noble, for its part, asserts that the placement of the "Terms of Use" hyperlink on its website put Nguyen on constructive notice of the arbitra-tion agreement. Barnes & Noble contends that this notice, combined with Nguyen's subsequent use of the website, was enough to bind him to the Terms of Use. The district court disagreed, and Barnes & Noble now appeals.

II. STANDARD OF REVIEW

"We review the denial of a motion to compel arbitration de novo." Cox v. Ocean View Hotel Corp., 533 F.3d 1114, 1119 (9th Cir. 2008). Underlying factual findings are reviewed for clear error, Balen v. Holland Am. Line Inc., 583 F.3d 647, 652 (9th Cir. 2009), while "[t]he interpretation and meaning of contract provisions" are reviewed de novo, Milenbach v. Comm'r, 318 F.3d 924, 930 (9th Cir. 2003).

III. DISCUSSION

A.

The FAA, 9 U.S.C. §1 *et seq.*, requires federal district courts to stay judicial proceedings and compel arbitration of claims covered by a written and enforceable arbitration agreement. *Id.* §3. The FAA limits the district court's role to determining whether a valid arbitration agreement exists, and whether the agreement encompasses the disputes at issue. *See* Chiron Corp. v. Ortho Diagnostic Sys., Inc., 207 F.3d 1126, 1130 (9th Cir. 2000). The parties do not quarrel that Barnes & Noble's arbitration agreement, should it be found enforceable, encompasses Nguyen's claims. The only issue is whether a valid arbitration agreement exists.

In determining whether a valid arbitration agreement exists, federal courts "apply ordinary state-law principles that govern the formation of contracts." First Options of Chicago, Inc. v. Kaplan, 514 U.S. 938, 944, 115 S. Ct. 1920, 131 L. Ed. 2d 985 (1995), Federal courts sitting in diversity look to the law of the forum state — here, California — when making choice of law determinations. Hoffman v. Citibank (S.D.), N.A., 546 F.3d 1078, 1082 (9th Cir. 2008) (per curiam). Under California law, the parties' choice of law will govern unless section 187(2) of the Restatement (Second) of Conflict of Laws dictates a different result. *Id.*

Here, the parties agree that the validity of the arbitration agreement is governed by New York law, as specified by the Terms of Use's choice of law provision. But whether the choice of law provision applies depends on whether the parties agreed to be bound by Barnes & Noble's Terms of Use in the first place. As the district court acknowledged in its order, we need not engage in this circular inquiry because both California and New York law dictate the same outcome. Thus, in evaluating the validity of Barnes & Noble's arbitration agreement, we apply New York law, to the extent possible.

For the reasons that follow, we hold that Nguyen did not enter into Barnes & Noble's agreement to arbitrate.

B.

"While new commerce on the Internet has exposed courts to many new situations, it has not fundamentally changed the principles of contract." Register.com, Inc. v. Verio, Inc., 356 F.3d 393, 403 (2d Cir. 2004). One such principle is the requirement that "[m]utual manifestation of assent, whether by written or spoken word or by conduct, is the touchstone of contract." Specht v. Netscape Commc'ns Corp., 306 F.3d 17, 29 (2d Cir. 2002) (applying California law).

Contracts formed on the Internet come primarily in two flavors: "clickwrap" (or "click-through") agreements, in which website users are required to click on an "I agree" box after being presented with a list of terms and conditions of use; and "browsewrap" agreements, where a website's terms and conditions of use are generally posted on the website via a hyperlink at the bottom of the screen. *See Register.com*, 356 F.3d at 428-30. Barnes & Noble's Terms of Use fall in the latter category.

"Unlike a clickwrap agreement, a browsewrap agreement does not require the user to manifest assent to the terms and conditions expressly . . . [a] party instead gives his assent simply by using the website." Hines v. Overstock.com, Inc., 668 F. Supp. 2d 362, 366-67 (E.D.N.Y. 2009) (citation and quotation marks omitted) (alteration in original). Indeed, "in a pure-form browsewrap agreement, 'the website will contain a notice that — by merely using the services of, obtaining information from, or initiating applications within the website — the user is agreeing to and is bound by the site's terms of service.' " Fteja v. Facebook, Inc., 841 F. Supp. 2d 829, 837 (S.D.N.Y. 2012) (quoting United States v. Drew, 259 F.R.D. 449, 462 n. 22 (C.D. Cal. 2009)). Thus, "by visiting the website — something that the user has already done — the user agrees to the Terms of Use not listed on the site itself but available only by clicking a hyperlink." *Id.* "The defining feature of browsewrap agreements is that the user can continue to use the website or its services without visiting the page hosting the browsewrap agreement or even knowing that such a webpage exists." Be In, Inc. v. Google Inc., No. 12-CV-03373-LHK, 2013 WL 5568706, at *6 (N.D. Cal. Oct. 9, 2013). "Because no affirmative action is required by the website user to agree to the terms of a contract other than his or her use of the website, the determination of the validity of the browsewrap contract depends on whether the user has actual or constructive knowledge of a website's terms and conditions." Van Tassell v. United Mktg. Grp., LLC, 795 F. Supp. 2d 770, 790 (N.D. Ill. 2011) (citing Sw. Airlines Co. v. Board-First, LLC, No. 06-CV-0891-B, 2007 WL 4823761, at *4 (N.D. Tex. Sept. 12, 2007)); see also Mark A. Lemley, Terms of Use, 91 Minn. L. Rev. 459, 477 (2006) ("Courts may be willing to overlook the utter absence of assent only when there are reasons to believe that the [website user] is aware of the [website owner's] terms.").

Were there any evidence in the record that Nguyen had actual notice of the Terms of Use or was required to affirmatively acknowledge the Terms of Use before completing his online purchase, the outcome of this case might be different. Indeed, courts have consistently enforced browsewrap agreements where the user had actual notice of the agreement. See, e.g., *Register.com*, 356 F.3d at 401-04 (finding likelihood of success on the merits in a breach of browsewrap claim where the defendant "admitted that . . . it was fully aware of the terms" of the offer); *Sw. Airlines Co.*, 2007 WL 4823761, at *4-6 (finding proper contract formation where defendant continued its breach after being notified of the terms in a cease and desist letter); Ticketmaster Corp. v. Tickets.Com, Inc., No. CV-997654, 2003 WL 21406289, at *2C (C.D. Cal. Mar. 7, 2003) (denying defendants' summary judgment motion on browsewrap contract claim where defendants continued breaching contract after receiving letter quoting the browsewrap contract terms). Courts have also been more willing to find the requisite notice for constructive assent where the browsewrap agreement resembles a clickwrap agreement — that is, where the user is required to affirmatively acknowledge the agreement before proceeding with use of the website. See, e.g., Zaltz v. JDATE, 952 F. Supp. 2d 439, 451-52 (E.D.N.Y. 2013) (enforcing forum selection clause where prospective members had to check box confirming that they both read and agreed to the website's Terms and Conditions of Service to obtain account); *Fteja*, 841 F. Supp. 2d at 838-40 (enforcing forum selection clause in website's terms of service where a notice below the "Sign Up" button stated, "By clicking Sign Up, you are indicating that you have read and agree to the Terms of Service," and user had clicked "Sign Up").

But where, as here, there is no evidence that the website user had actual knowledge of the agreement, the validity of the browsewrap agreement turns on whether the website puts a reasonably prudent user on inquiry notice of the terms of the contract. *Specht*, 306 F.3d at 30-31; see also In re Zappos.com, Inc. Customer Data Sec. Breach Litig., 893 F. Supp. 2d 1058, 1064 (D. Nev. 2012). Whether a user has inquiry notice of a browsewrap agreement, in turn, depends on the design and content of the website and the agreement's webpage. *Google*, 2013 WL 5568706, at *6. Where the link to a website's terms of use is buried at the bottom of the page or tucked away in obscure corners of the website where users are unlikely to see it, courts have refused to enforce the browsewrap agreement. *See, e.g., Specht*, 306 F.3d at 23 (refusing to enforce terms of use that "would have become visible to plaintiffs only if they had scrolled down to the next screen"); *In re Zappos.com*, 893 F. Supp. 2d at 1064 ("The Terms of Use is inconspicuous, buried in the middle to bottom of every Zappos.com webpage among many other links, and the website never directs a user to the Terms of Use."); *Van Tassell*, 795 F. Supp. 2d at 792-93 (refusing to enforce arbitration clause in browsewrap agreement that was only noticeable after a "multi-step process" of clicking through non-obvious links); *Hines*, 668 F. Supp. 2d at 367 (plaintiff "could not even see the link to [the terms and conditions] without scrolling down to the bottom of the screen — an action that was not required to effectuate her purchase"). On the other hand, where the website contains an explicit textual notice that continued use will act as a manifestation of the user's intent to be bound, courts have been more amenable to enforcing browsewrap agreements. See, e.g., Cairo, Inc. v. Crossmedia Servs., Inc., No. 04-04825, 2005 WL 756610, at *2, *4-5 (N.D. Cal. Apr. 1, 2005) (enforcing forum selection clause in website's terms of use where every page on the website had a textual notice that read: "By continuing past this page and/or using this site, you agree to abide by the Terms of Use for this site, which prohibit commercial use of any information on this site"). *But see* Pollstar v. Gigmania, Ltd., 170 F. Supp. 2d 974, 981 (E.D. Cal. 2000) (refusing to enforce browsewrap agreement where textual notice appeared in small gray print against a gray background). In short, the conspicuousness and placement of the "Terms of Use" hyperlink, other notices given to users of the terms of use, and the website's general design all contribute to whether a reasonably prudent user would have inquiry notice of a browsewrap agreement.

Barnes & Noble argues that the placement of the "Terms of Use" hyperlink in the bottom left-hand corner of every page on the Barnes & Noble website, and its close proximity to the buttons a user must click on to complete an online purchase, is enough to place a reasonably prudent user on constructive notice. It is true that the location of the hyperlink on Barnes & Noble's website distinguishes this case from *Specht*, the leading authority on the enforceability of browsewrap terms under New York law. There, the Second Circuit refused to enforce an arbitration provision in a website's licensing terms where the hyperlink to the terms was located at the bottom of the page, hidden below the "Download" button that users had to click to initiate the software download. See *Specht*, 306 F.3d at 30. Then–Second Circuit Judge Sotomayor, writing for the panel, held that "a reference to the existence of license terms on a submerged screen is not sufficient to place consumers on inquiry or constructive notice of those terms." *Id.* at 32. By contrast, here the "Terms of Use" link appears either directly below the relevant button a user must click on to proceed in the checkout process or just a few inches away. On some pages, the content of the webpage is compact enough that a user can view the link without scrolling. On the remaining pages, the hyperlink is close enough to the "Proceed with Checkout" button that a user would have to bring the link within his field of vision in order to complete his order.

But the proximity or conspicuousness of the hyperlink alone is not enough to give rise to constructive notice, and Barnes & Noble directs us to no case law that supports this proposition.[23] The most analogous case the court was able to locate is PDC Labs., Inc. v. Hach Co., an unpublished district court order cited by neither party. No. 09-1110, 2009 WL 2605270 (C.D. Ill. Aug. 25, 2009). There, the "Terms [and Conditions of Sale] were hyperlinked on three separate pages of the online . . . order process in underlined, blue, contrasting text." *Id.* at *3. The court held that "[t]his contrasting text is sufficient to be considered conspicuous," thereby placing a reasonable user on notice that the terms applied. *Id.* It also observed, however, that the terms' conspicuousness was reinforced by the language of the final checkout screen, which read, " 'STEP 4 of 4: *Review terms*, add any comments, and submit order,' " and was followed by a hyperlink to the Terms. *Id.* (emphasis added).

As in *PDC*, the checkout screens here contained "Terms of Use" hyperlinks in underlined, color-contrasting text. But *PDC* is dissimilar in that the final screen on that website contained the phrase "Review terms." *PDC Labs.*, 2009 WL 2605270, at *3. This admonition makes *PDC* distinguishable, despite the court's explanation that the blue contrasting hyperlinks were sufficiently conspicuous on their own. That the *PDC* decision couched its holding in terms of procedural unconscionability rather than contract formation further distinguishes it from our case. See *id.*

In light of the lack of controlling authority on point, and in keeping with courts' traditional reluctance to enforce browsewrap agreements against individual consumers,[24] we therefore hold that where a website makes its terms of use available via a conspicuous hyperlink on every

23. Indeed, in cases where courts have relied on the proximity of the hyperlink to enforce a browsewrap agreement, the websites at issue have also included something more to capture the user's attention and secure her assent. See, e.g., 5381 Partners LLC v. Sharesale.com, Inc., No. 12-CV-4263 JFB AKT, 2013 WL 5328324, at *7 (E.D.N.Y. Sept. 23, 2013) (in addition to hyperlink that appeared adjacent to the activation button users had to click on, website also contained a text warning near the button that stated "By clicking and making a request to Activate, you agree to the terms and conditions in the [agreement]"); *Zaltz*, 952 F. Supp. 2d at 451-52 (users required to check box confirming that they had reviewed and agreed to website's Terms and Conditions, even though hyperlink to Terms and Conditions was located on the same screen as the button users had to click on to complete registration).

24. See Woodrow Hartzog, Website Design as Contract, 60 Am. U. L. Rev. 1635, 1644 (2011) (observing that courts "tend to shy away from enforcing browsewrap agreements that require no outward manifestation of assent"); Lemley, 91 Minn. L. Rev. at 472-77 ("An examination of the cases that have considered browsewraps in the last five years demonstrates that the courts have been willing to enforce terms of use against corporations, but have not been willing to do so against individuals.").

page of the website but otherwise provides no notice to users nor prompts them to take any affirmative action to demonstrate assent, even close proximity of the hyperlink to relevant buttons users must click on — without more — is insufficient to give rise to constructive notice. While failure to read a contract before agreeing to its terms does not relieve a party of its obligations under the contract, Gillman v. Chase Manhattan Bank, N.A., 73 N.Y.2d 1, 11, 537 N.Y.S.2d 787, 534 N.E.2d 824 (1988), the onus must be on website owners to put users on notice of the terms to which they wish to bind consumers. Given the breadth of the range of technological savvy of online purchasers, consumers cannot be expected to ferret out hyperlinks to terms and conditions to which they have no reason to suspect they will be bound.

Barnes & Noble's argument that Nguyen's familiarity with other websites governed by similar browsewrap terms, including his personal website <www. kevinkhoa.com>, gives rise to an inference of constructive notice is also of no moment. Whether Nguyen has experience with the browsewrap agreements found on other websites such as Facebook, LinkedIn, MySpace, or Twitter, has no bearing on whether he had constructive notice of Barnes & Noble's Terms of Use. There is nothing in the record to suggest that those browsewrap terms are enforceable by or against Nguyen, much less why they should give rise to constructive notice of Barnes & Noble's browsewrap terms.

. . .

We hold that Nguyen had insufficient notice of Barnes & Noble's Terms of Use, and thus did not enter into an agreement with Barnes & Noble to arbitrate his claims.

AFFIRMED.

Statutory Background:
Uniform Computer Information Transactions Act

The Prefatory Note dubs the Uniform Computer Information Transactions Act (UCITA) "a commercial contract code for the computer information transactions." It describes UCITA as "the first uniform contract law designed to deal specifically with the new information economy. Transactions in computer information involve different expectations, different industry practices, and different policies from transactions in goods. For example, in a sale of goods, the buyer owns what it buys and has exclusive rights in that subject matter (e.g., the toaster that has been purchased). In contrast, someone that acquires a copy of computer information may or may not own that copy, but in any case rarely obtains all rights associated with the information. . . . What rights are acquired or withheld depends on what the contract says. This point only is implicit in Article 2 for goods such as books; UCITA makes it explicit for the information economy where, unlike in the case of a book, the contract (license) is the product." As with all uniform acts, UCITA must be adopted by state legislatures to be effective. As of the publication date of this casebook, two states had adopted the Act; it is pending in seven others and the District of Columbia.

SECTION 112.   MANIFESTING ASSENT; OPPORTUNITY TO REVIEW

(a) A person manifests assent to a record or term if the person, acting with knowledge of, or after having an opportunity to review the record or term or a copy of it:

(1) authenticates the record or term with intent to adopt or accept it; or

(2) intentionally engages in conduct or makes statements with reason to know that the other party or its electronic agent may infer from the conduct or statement that the person assents to the record or term.

(b) An electronic agent manifests assent to a record or term if, after having an opportunity to review it, the electronic agent:

(1) authenticates the record or term; or

(2) engages in operations that in the circumstances indicate acceptance of the record or term.

(c) If this [Act] or other law requires assent to a specific term, a manifestation of assent must relate specifically to the term.

(d) Conduct or operations manifesting assent may be proved in any manner, including a showing that a person or an electronic agent obtained or used the information or informational rights and that a procedure existed by which a person or an electronic agent must have engaged in the conduct or operations in order to do so. Proof of compliance with subsection (a)(2) is sufficient if there is conduct that assents and subsequent conduct that reaffirms assent by electronic means.

(e) With respect to an opportunity to review, the following rules apply:

(1) A person has an opportunity to review a record or term only if it is made available in a manner that ought to call it to the attention of a reasonable person and permit review.

(2) An electronic agent has an opportunity to review a record or term only if it is made available in a manner that would enable a reasonably configured electronic agent to react to the record or term.

(3) If a record or term is available for review only after a person becomes obligated to pay or begins its performance, the person has an opportunity to review only if it has a right to a return if it rejects the record. However, a right to a return is not required if:

(A) the record proposes a modification of contract or provides particulars of performance under Section 305; or

(B) the primary performance is other than delivery or acceptance of a copy, the agreement is not a mass-market transaction, and the parties at the time of contracting had reason to know that a record or term would be presented after performance, use, or access to the information began.

(4) The right to a return under paragraph (3) may arise by law or by agreement.

(f) The effect of provisions of this section may be modified by an agreement setting out standards applicable to future transactions between the parties.

(g) Providers of online services, network access, and telecommunications services, or the operators of facilities thereof, do not manifest assent to a contractual relationship simply by their provision of those services to other parties, including, without limitation, transmission, routing, or providing connections, linking, caching, hosting, information location tools, or storage of materials, at the request or initiation of a person other than the service provider.

OFFICIAL COMMENT

1. Scope of Section. This section provides standards for "manifestation of assent" and "opportunity to review." In this Act, having an opportunity to review a record is a precondition to manifesting assent.

2. General Theme. The term "manifesting assent" comes from Restatement (Second) of Contracts §19. This section corresponds to Restatement §19, but more fully explicates the concept. Codification establishes uniformity that is lacking in common law.

Restatement (Second) of Contracts §19(1) provides: "The manifestation of assent may be made wholly or partly by written or spoken words or by other acts or by failure to act." This section adopts that view. Conduct can convey assent as clearly as words. This rule is important in electronic commerce, where most interactions involve conduct rather than words. Subsection (b) adapts that principle to electronic agent contracting

Statutory Background: Uniform Electronic Transactions Act (1999)

From the Prefatory Note: "With the advent of electronic means of communication and information transfer, business models and methods for doing business have evolved to take advantage of the speed, efficiencies, and cost benefits of electronic technologies. These developments have occurred in the face of existing legal barriers to the legal efficacy of records and documents which exist solely in electronic media. Whether the legal requirement that information or an agreement or contract must be contained or set forth in a pen and paper writing derives from a statute of frauds affecting the enforceability of an agreement, or from a record retention statute that calls for keeping the paper record of a transaction, such legal requirements raise real barriers to the effective use of electronic media. . . .

It is important to understand that the purpose of the UETA is to remove barriers to electronic commerce by validating and effectuating electronic records and signatures. It is NOT a general contracting statute — the substantive rules of contracts remain unaffected by UETA. Nor is it a digital signature statute. To the extent that a State has a Digital Signature Law, the UETA is designed to support and complement that statute."

Study Guide: In what sense is there "mutual assent" between two parties "if no individual was aware of or reviewed the electronic agents' actions or the resulting terms and agreements"?

SECTION 14.   AUTOMATED TRANSACTION

In an automated transaction, the following rules apply:

(1) A contract may be formed by the interaction of electronic agents of the parties, even if no individual was aware of or reviewed the electronic agents' actions or the resulting terms and agreements.

(2) A contract may be formed by the interaction of an electronic agent and an individual, acting on the individual's own behalf or for another person, including by an interaction in which the individual performs actions that the individual is free to refuse to perform and which the individual knows or has reason to know will cause the electronic agent to complete the transaction or performance.

(3) The terms of the contract are determined by the substantive law applicable to it.

COMMENT

1. This section confirms that contracts can be formed by machines functioning as electronic agents for parties to a transaction. It negates any claim that lack of human intent, at the time of contract formation, prevents contract formation. When machines are involved, the requisite intention flows from the programming and use of the machine. As in other cases, these are salutary provisions consistent with the fundamental purpose of the Act to remove barriers to electronic transactions while leaving the substantive law, e.g., law of mistake, law of contract formation, unaffected to the greatest extent possible.

2. The process in paragraph (2) validates an anonymous click-through transaction. It is possible that an anonymous click-through process may simply result in no recognizable legal relationship, e.g., A goes to a person's website and acquires access without in any way identifying herself, or otherwise indicating agreement or assent to any limitation or obligation, and the owner's site grants A access. In such a case no legal relationship has been created.

On the other hand it may be possible that A's actions indicate agreement to a particular term. For example, A goes to a website and is confronted by an initial screen which advises her that the information at this site is proprietary, that A may use the information for her own personal purposes, but that, by clicking below, A agrees that any other use without the site owner's permission is prohibited. If A clicks "agree" and downloads the information and then uses the information for other, prohibited purposes, should not A be bound by the click? It seems the answer properly should be, and would be, yes.

If the owner can show that the only way A could have obtained the information was from his website, and that the process to access the subject information required that A must have clicked the "I agree" button after having the ability to see the conditions on use, A has performed actions which A was free to refuse, which A knew would cause the site to grant her access, i.e., "complete the transaction." The terms of the resulting contract will be determined under general contract principles, but will include the limitation on *A*'s use of the information, as a condition precedent to granting her access to the information. . . .

Empirical Evidence on the Use of Online Contracting

STUDY GUIDE: Numerous scholars, policy makers, and judges have expressed concerns about online contracting, based mainly on individual cases, anecdotes, and speculation. One exception to this approach is the work of Professor Florencia Marotta-Wurgler, who has conducted one of the only broad-based empirical studies of electronic contracting. In the excerpts from the article below, she summarizes some of her key findings. To what extent do they support those concerned about online contracting? To what extent do they undermine the assumptions of those who defend or attack "clickwrap" or "browsewrap" agreements?

FLORENCIA MAROTTA-WURGLER, SOME REALITIES OF ONLINE CONTRACTING, 19 SUP. CT. ECON. REV. 11 (2011):   Online mass transactions challenge traditional contract paradigms. One fear is that these new ways of doing business and of contracting will undermine the notion of assent, making consumers vulnerable to seller exploitation. Like their brick-and-mortar counterparts, online sellers typically offer take-it-or-leave-it standard form contracts. An additional wrinkle in the online world is the widespread use of browsewraps and "pay now, terms later" (PNTL) contracts. In the former, sellers present their contracts as hyperlinks at the end of a webpage or somewhere in their site with relatively little notice to consumers; in the latter, sellers do not make their contracts available to consumers until *after* they purchase the product. Obviously, lack of notice or delayed disclosure makes it costlier for consumers to become informed about the relevant terms and decreases their ability to comparison shop on this dimension. Along the same lines, online (and traditional) sellers with market power could take advantage of consumers' lack of choice and impose abusive, one-sided terms.

Ultimately, the concern about online standard form contracts is that reduced choice and lack of disclosure results in terms being biased towards sellers. In particular, sellers could offer the minimum legally enforceable rights and protections against product failure. Commentators and consumer advocates have been particularly concerned about sellers' use of draconian dispute resolution clauses, such as forum selection clauses and class action waivers that virtually eliminate consumers' ability to seek redress expost. Other academics and policy makers have proposed eliminating PNTL contracts and increasing the disclosure of such contracts as software end user license agreements (EULAs).
. . .

The only way to understand the software industry's contracting practices is to go beyond anecdote and examine the actual content of their contracts in detail. In *What's in a Standard Form Contract! A Study of End User Software License Agreements*, I study a sample of 647 EULAs of pre-packaged software and report the incidence of 23 common terms that allocate rights and risks between buyers and sellers.[25] The EULAs correspond to software published by 598 companies from 114 different markets (as classified by Amazon.com), ranging from anti-virus to word processing, and sold online through the company website. The companies in the sample range from small sellers to giants like Microsoft and Adobe. There is also wide variation in the product prices that correspond to the sample EULAs. The average product price is $763 and the median is $200.

The 23 terms that I track can be grouped into seven different categories that are regarded as important by industry participants and courts. . . .

Next, I construct an index that captures each EULA's net "buyer friendliness" in a way that allows for systematic analysis. I compare each of the 23 terms to the relevant default rules, Article 2 of the Uniform Commercial Code (UCC). Should the buyer offer the software without a EULA or should the EULA be silent on a particular term, a court would rely on these rules to resolve most disputes. For each term that is more pro-buyer than the default rules, I give it a plus one-point score. If a term matches the default rules or is missing, I give it a score of 0. If a term is more pro-seller relative to the rules of Article 2, I give it a minus one-point score. I then add up all the scores into an overall score, a "bias index," that reflects the buyer friendliness relative to Article 2 of that EULA.

. . .

The results present some interesting conclusions about the content of EULAs. On net, EULAs tend to be biased towards sellers relative to the default rules of Article 2. The average EULA has five terms that are more pro-seller than the default rules (i.e., the average net "buyer-friendliness" for the sample is 4.85). Certain terms are more likely to be restrictive than others. Over 90% of the sample EULAs include terms restricting buyers' ability to transfer the software, disclaimers of implied warranties, and disclaimers of consequential damages. The remaining terms, however, present significant variation. Perhaps surprisingly, this result contradicts the perception that standard form contracts in any given market tend to be all the same.

The differences across EULAs are related to interesting company characteristics. Larger and, controlling for size, younger companies, tend to offer EULAs that are more tilted towards sellers. This might be because larger companies might benefit from the drafting skill of in-house counsel, who might be better able to decrease sellers' liability. Another surprising finding is that EULAs of products directed towards members of the general public are not significantly more biased than EULAs directed to business users. That is, members of the general public are not more exposed to being taken advantage than more sophisticated buyers.

. . .

Of the many terms in standard form contracts, consumer advocates and policy makers have expressed particular concern over sellers' widespread use of dispute resolution clauses (DRCs). DRCs direct how eventual contractual disputes are to be resolved. Choice of law clauses specify the law that will govern the dispute and choice of forum clauses dictate which court

---

25. Florencia Marotta-Wurgler, What's in a Standard Form Contract? An Empirical Analysis of Software License Agreements, J. Emp. L. Stud. 4 (2007).

or in which jurisdiction the dispute will be heard. Mandatory arbitration clauses deprive consumers of the option to seek redress in court altogether.

While sellers might use DRCs to reduce litigation costs by restricting the number of laws or geographic locations where disputes will be brought, some are concerned that they might also use these clauses to take advantage of consumers. For example, sellers might exploit their superior bargaining power or consumers' inattention to fine print by requiring disputes to be heard in a convenient forum where sellers have political clout. The growth of online commerce has only exacerbated this problem, as transactions between buyers and sellers are more likely to be distant, thus increasing the likelihood that sellers will make choice of law and forum selections that are not convenient for buyers. Numerous commentators have also claimed that sellers select laws that are more favorable to seller interests, or include mandatory arbitration to preclude class actions. Fear about sellers' strategic use of DRCs has resulted in strong opposition against the adoption of the Uniform Computer Information Transactions Act (UCITA), a proposed statute governing transactions of computer information. One of UCITA's goals is to increase choice of law flexibility in said transactions where the parties' physical location is likely to be of little importance.

In *"Unfair" Dispute Resolution Clauses: Much Ado About Nothing?*[26] I analyze a sub-sample of 597 EULAs to see the extent to which sellers use DRCs and whether they are used in ways that exploit consumers. For each EULA, I note whether the seller includes choice of law, choice of forum, and/or arbitration clauses. Given that some states have more seller-friendly laws than others, I also note the state whose laws or fora were selected to govern the dispute. I also collect information about each seller's size (in terms of revenue), location of headquarters, state of incorporation, and age to ascertain whether sellers use DRCs strategically.

The main descriptive findings are surprising: sellers don't generally include draconian dispute resolution in their EULAs. Choice of law clauses appear in 75% of the sample EULAs. Forum selection clauses, which often present severe limitations on buyers' ability to seek redress ex post, appear in 28% of the contracts in the sample. But only 6% of sellers offer arbitration clauses, and not one includes a class action waiver. The low incidence of forum selection and arbitration clauses casts doubt that these clauses should be a major concern, at least in the online software market.

Similarly, I find little to suggest that sellers are using DRCs strategically. Among sellers that include choice of law clauses, 86% select the law of the state where it is headquartered. As a result, sellers in the sample select the laws of California and Massachusetts 40% of the time, and these are two states known for their consumer-friendly laws. Moreover, sellers located in more seller-friendly states, such as Maryland and Virginia (two states that adopted the controversial UCITA), are in fact less likely to include choice of law clauses than sellers in more consumer-friendly states, such as California and Massachusetts. Choice of forum clauses always stipulate the same state chosen for law, which in turn is typically the headquarters state. Although it

---

26. Florencia Marotta-Wurgler, "Unfair" Dispute Resolution Clauses: Much Ado About Nothing? In Omri Ben-Shahar, ed., Boilerplate: Foundations of Market Contracts (Cambridge University Press 2007).

is possible that sellers could be selecting a local forum to obtain beneficial treatment from courts, it doesn't seem likely. The median firm with a choice of forum clause has only thirty-five employees, which seems far too small to have any meaningful political clout. The more likely explanation is that firms simply select the most convenient forum, which is the local forum.

. . .

As mentioned earlier, a common concern is that sellers in non-competitive markets or with market power lack sufficient competitive pressure to offer desirable standard terms to buyers. Most courts believe that a lack of competition increases buyers' vulnerability. They invalidate oppressive terms using the doctrine of unconscionability, a consideration of which is whether the seller has significant market share or is a monopolist.

In *Competition and the Quality of Standard Form Contracts: An Empirical Analysis of Software License Agreements*, I test whether this claim manifests itself in online software markets. I ask whether sellers in more competitive markets within the software industry or those with less market share offer more buyer-friendly terms than other sellers.[27] I use the aforementioned sample of 647 EULAs then collect data on competitive conditions for the associated companies. As mentioned earlier, the sample spans 114 different software markets. Common market-level measures of competitive conditions are concentration ratios, which represent the sum of the total market share of the largest n firms in a market, and the Herfindahl-Hirschman index (HHI), which is the sum of the squares of the market shares of the firms in a market. The latter measure is generally preferred. At the company level, I use market share measures, which indicate how powerful a company is in a given market.

. . .

With these competition measures in hand we can ask whether sellers in less competitive markets offer less buyer-friendly terms . . . in any meaningful way. The results may be surprising: there is no meaningful relationship. Firms in markets with higher HHIs . . . do not offer more one-sided terms than firms in markets with lower HHIs. The results are similar with concentration ratios. Within a given market, firms with higher market share generally do not impose more pro-seller terms than terms with little or no market share. An exception is terms related to dispute resolution. I find that firms with larger market share are more likely to offer more restrictive terms in this category; however, the same firms are also more likely to give notice regarding acceptance of the license. These patterns hold across as well as within markets, and upon controlling for various firm and product characteristics.

Although the analysis cannot address whether standard form contract terms are pro-seller or pro-buyer in an absolute sense, it directly speaks to the debate whether competitive conditions affect terms bias. The main conclusion is that term bias appears to be unrelated to competitive conditions, at least in the case of software sold online. The most immediate implication is that courts might want to de-emphasize competitive conditions in their determination of procedural unconscionability.

. . .

27. Florencia Marotta-Wurgler, Competition and the Quality of Standard Form Contracts: A Test Using Software License Agreements, 5 J. Emp. L. Stud. 447 (2008).

The fourth study described here considers whether sellers that use PNTL contracts, in which buyers cannot read the contract until after they purchase the product, take advantage of delayed disclosure to include particularly onerous terms. In a typical transaction involving this type of standard form contract, a buyer orders a good over the phone or the Internet and is only able to review the terms until after receiving the product, as the contract is bundled together with the good. Shrinkwrap software licenses are familiar examples. Buyers can only access the contract after they open the box. Although PNTL contracts generally allow buyers to reject their terms by returning the product to the seller for a period of time after purchase (usually 30 days), they pose an obstacle to any buyer who might wish to comparison shop for those products with the most favorable terms.

Several scholars have argued that PNTLs should not be enforceable because sellers will take advantage of delayed disclosure and increased comparison shopping costs to sneak in one-sided or abusive terms.[28] These concerns led to a concerted effort to block the adoption of UCITA, which allows the use of PNTLs. Also, the American Law Institute has recently approved the "Principles of the Law of Software Contracts," a set of recommendations for courts that advocates increased contract disclosure as way of strengthening competition and protecting consumers. The principles recommend refusing enforcement of PNTLs as they require sellers to post their terms on their websites for buyers to review prior to purchase.

The view that PNTLs are detrimental to buyers has been challenged by those who think that "terms later" contracting might just be the most efficient way of contracting between distant buyers and sellers.[29] They note that since the majority of buyers rarely reads fine print it doesn't really matter whether terms are disclosed before or after purchase, and also the buyer can return the product if she finds the terms disagreeable. Even widespread failure to read shouldn't be a concern, some argue, as the presence of an informed minority of consumers who are sensitive to terms might suffice to discipline sellers in sufficiently competitive markets. Thus, absent systematic evidence of seller abuse, this side recommends not interfering with contractual innovations.

In *Are "Pay Now, Terms Later" Contracts Worse for Buyers? Evidence from Software License Agreements*, I analyze empirically whether delayed disclosure is associated with more onerous terms for buyers.[30] The online software market is a particularly nice environment to address this question because there is a wide variation in how forthcoming sellers are in presenting their terms to buyers. Some sellers use PNTLs while others post their EULAs in their websites as hyperlinks that buyers must click to access the contract. Finally, a small group of sellers requires buyers to agree to the

28. See, for example, Roger C. Bern, "Terms Later" Contracting: Bad Economics, Bad Morals, and a Bad Idea, Judge Easterbrook Notwithstanding, 12 J. L. & Pol. 641 (2004); Jean Braucher, Delayed Disclosure in Consumer E-Commerce as an Unfair and Deceptive Practice, 46 Wayne. L. Rev. 1806 (2000).

29. See Douglas Baird, Letter to Lawrence J. Bugge, Chair, UCC Article 2 Drafting Committee (March 9, 1999).

30. Florencia Marotta-Wurgler, Are "Pay Now, Terms Later" Contracts Worse for Buyers? Evidence from Software License Agreements, 38 J. L. Stud. 309 (2009).

EULA prior to purchase by displaying it in a textbox or in a hyperlink next to a box to which buyers must click "I agree" (these are known as clickwraps).

I study a sample of 515 EULAs for which I could gather contract disclosure information. Of this group, 269 are PNTL contracts. For the remaining EULAs (that are available on the seller's website), I develop a methodology to measure the relative accessibility of a contract, defined as the number of clicks it takes to access the EULA from the homepage or the main path to purchase. For example, a EULA that is available on a hyperlink at the bottom of a company's homepage would obtain a score of 1 since it only takes one click to access the EULA from the main purchase path. Similarly, a score of 2 would correspond to a EULA that is 2 clicks away from the main path of purchase, and so on. I give those EULAs that are presented to buyers in the form of clickwraps a score of 0 (for those who present the text box with the terms) and 0.5 (for those that post the terms on a hyperlink next to a box that must be clicked on).

Are PNTL contracts worse for buyers? No. Sellers that use PNTLs do not offer more pro-seller terms than sellers that disclose their contract on their website. This is true for both business and consumer-oriented products and for each of the seven categories of terms included in the bias index. Indeed, non-PNTL contracts are less seller-friendly than PNTL contracts by an average of 0.67 terms, a statistically significant (yet economically meaningless) difference. I also find that clickwraps, have the most pro-seller terms of all, with an average of 1.18 more pro-seller terms than non-clickwraps.

The conclusion is that disclosure is unrelated to the content of standard form terms, at least in the context of software sold online. The implication is that would be highly optimistic to believe that increased disclosure or efforts to curtail the use of PNTL contracts will create pro-buyer changes. In general, the results indicate that regulators shouldn't be particularly concerned about rolling contracts. The focus should be on the quality of the terms offered, not how they are offered.

5

DISCERNING THE AGREEMENT

Once it is concluded that there has been mutual assent to a contract, there remains the task of ascertaining the terms that will bind the parties. This job can be divided into three parts, each of which addresses a different problem that can arise in practice. In Section A, we consider the task of *interpreting* the meaning of the words the parties used. In Section B, we address the issue of *gap-filling* when a situation arises that is not explicitly handled by the terms of the parties' agreement. Finally, in Section C, we study the problem of *identifying which term* is adopted by the parties when, though it is clear the parties intended to enter into contractual relations, the terms of the offer differ from the terms of the acceptance.

A. INTERPRETING THE MEANING OF THE TERMS

Contractual interpretation is the activity of finding the meaning of words. Some problems of interpretation involve "ambiguous" terms that have more than one meaning and the challenge is to find which meaning, if any, was intended by the parties. For example, in the sentence, "This feather is light," the term "light" could refer to the feather's weight, or it could refer instead to its shade. Another type of interpretive problem involves "vagueness," when the question is whether a term was meant to apply beyond its clear core meaning. For example, while the core meaning of a "light feather" undoubtedly includes a white feather and excludes a black one, it is unclear how dark a gray feather must be before we cease considering it as being light.[1]

As we learned in Chapter 4, American contract law has adopted what is known as the "objective" theory of assent. This approach was most starkly described by Judge Learned Hand in the case of Hotchkiss v. National City Bank, 200 F. 287, 293 (S.D.N.Y. 1911):

A contract has, strictly speaking, nothing to do with the personal, or individual, intent of the parties. A contract is an obligation attached by the mere force of law to certain acts of the parties, usually words, which ordinarily accompany and represent a known intent. If, however, it were proved by twenty bishops that either party when he used the words intended something else than the usual meaning which the law imposes on them, he would still be held, unless there were mutual mistake or something else of the sort. Of

1. For an explanation of the difference between ambiguity and vagueness, see E. Allan Farnsworth, "Meaning" in the Law of Contract, 76 Yale L.J. 939 (1967).

course, if it appear by other words, or acts, of the parties, that they attribute a peculiar meaning to such words as they use in the contract, that meaning will prevail, but only by virtue of the other words, and not because of their unexpressed intent.

Like the issue of mutual assent, however, when it comes to interpreting the meaning of terms, courts have adopted an objective approach with a significant subjective twist. In what sense is the "objective theory" really objective? Also, do the outcomes in these cases reveal any practical difference between a term that is ambiguous and one that is vague?

REFERENCE: Barnett, §3.3

1. Ambiguous Terms

In this section, we consider the problem of "misunderstanding," which can occur when words have more than one meaning and a question arises as to which, if any, was the meaning agreed to by both parties.

STUDY GUIDE: *Is the following case consistent with the objective theory of contract — as Justice Oliver Wendell Holmes, Jr., contended — or does it represent the application of a subjective approach — as contended by Grant Gilmore in the excerpt that follows the case?*

RAFFLES v. WICHELHAUS
Court of Exchequer, 1864,
2 H. & C. 906, 159 Eng. Rep. 375

Declaration. For that it was agreed between the plaintiff and the defendants, to wit, at Liverpool, that the plaintiff should sell to the defendants, and the defendants buy of the plaintiff, certain goods, to wit, 125 bales of Surat cotton, guaranteed middling fair merchant's Dhollorah, to arrive ex "Peerless" from Bombay; and that the cotton should be taken from the quay, and that the defendants would pay the plaintiff for the same at a certain rate, to wit, at the rate of 17 1/4 *d.* per pound, within a certain time then agreed upon after the arrival of the said goods in England. Averments: that the said goods did arrive by the said ship from Bombay in England, to wit, at Liverpool, and the plaintiff was then and there ready and willing and offered to deliver the said goods to the defendants, etc. Breach: that the defendants refused to accept the said goods or pay the plaintiff for them.

Plea. That the said ship mentioned in the said agreement was meant and intended by the defendants to be the ship called the "Peerless," which sailed from Bombay, to wit, in October; and that the plaintiff was not ready and willing, and did not offer, to deliver to the defendants any bales of cotton which arrived by the last-mentioned ship, but instead thereof was only ready and willing, and offered to deliver to the defendants 125 bales of Surat cotton which arrived by another and different ship, which was also called the "Peerless," and which sailed from Bombay, to wit, in December. Demurrer, and joinder therein.

MILWARD in support of the demurrer. The contract was for the sale of a number of bales of cotton of a particular description, which the plaintiff was ready to deliver. It is immaterial by what ship the cotton was to arrive, so that it was a ship called the "Peerless." The words "to arrive ex 'Peerless,'" only meant that if the vessel is lost on the voyage, the contract is to be at an end. [Pollock, C.B. It would be a question for the jury whether both parties meant the same ship called the "Peerless."] That would be so if the contract was for the sale of a ship called the "Peerless"; but it is for the sale of cotton on board a ship of that name. [Pollock, C.B. The defendant only bought that cotton which was to arrive by a particular ship. It may as well be said, that if there is a contract for the purchase of certain goods in warehouse A that is satisfied by the delivery of goods of the same description in warehouse B.] In that case there would be goods in both warehouses; here it does not appear that the plaintiff had any goods on board the other "Peerless." [Martin, B. It is imposing on the defendant a contract different from that which he entered into. Pollock, C.B. It is like a contract for the purchase of wine coming from a particular estate in France or Spain, where there are two estates of that name.] The defendant has no right to contradict by parol evidence a written contract good upon the face of it. He does not impute misrepresentation or fraud, but only says that he fancied the ship was a different one. Intention is of no avail, unless stated at the time of the contract. [Pollock, C.B. One vessel sailed in October and the other in December.] The time of sailing is no part of the contract.

MELLISH (Cohen with him) in support of the plea. There is nothing on the face of the contract to show that any particular ship called the "Peerless" was meant; but the moment it appears that two ships called the "Peerless" were about to sail from Bombay there is a latent ambiguity, and parol evidence may be given for the purpose of showing that the defendant meant one "Peerless" and the plaintiff another. That being so, there was no consensus ad idem, and therefore no binding contract. He was then stopped by the court.

Per Curiam. There must be judgment for the defendants.

Relational Background: What "to arrive ex Peerless" Really Meant

STUDY GUIDE: In the following excerpts Grant Gilmore and A. W. Brian Simpson offer conflicting accounts of the meaning of the crucial term "to arrive ex Peerless." Also included is Gilmore's criticism of Oliver Wendell Holmes, Jr.'s interpretation of the case. When reading it, consider whether Holmes's "objective" interpretation of the case is as ridiculous as Gilmore implies.

GRANT GILMORE, THE DEATH OF CONTRACT 35-
41 (1974): In the course of the preceding lecture the point was made
that Holmes and his successors substituted an "objectivist" approach to the
theory of contract for the "subjectivist" approach which the courts had —
almost instinctively, it would seem, and without giving any thought to the
matter — been following. At this point we must inquire what the switch
from "subjective" to "objective" involved, what difference (if any) it made in
the results which the courts were supposed to arrive at and what relationship the newly minted theory of "objectivism" had to the main lines of the
general theory of contract.

We may begin our inquiry with the celebrated case of Raffles v. Wichelhaus which, it may be, is to the ordinary run of case law as the recently
popular theatre of the absurd is to the ordinary run of theatre. Appropriately
enough, even the report of the case is weird. It starts with a fairly detailed
résumé of the pleadings, continues with a colloquy between losing counsel
and two of the three judges who made up the court, gives the argument of
the winning counsel who, after two sentences was "stopped by the Court"
which, giving no reasons, abruptly announced: "There must be judgment
for the defendants."

According to the declaration (or complaint) there was a contract for
the sale of 125 bales of cotton to be shipped from Bombay and delivered at
the dock in Liverpool. The contract term was that the cotton was "to arrive
ex Peerless from Bombay" — "Peerless" being the name of the carrying
ship. The plaintiff (seller) alleged that the cotton had arrived in Liverpool
on the Peerless which had sailed from Bombay, that he had offered to
deliver the cotton and that the defendant had breached the contract by
refusing to accept or pay for it. The defendant's plea did not deny any of
the allegations but stated that the Peerless which the defendant "meant and
intended" was a ship which had sailed from Bombay in October (on which
the plaintiff had shipped no cotton) and that the ship on which the plaintiff's cotton arrived "was another and different ship, which was also called
the Peerless, and which sailed from Bombay, to wit, in December."

At that point there was a joinder in demurrer. As a piece of trial strategy, the decision of plaintiff's counsel to demur to the plea — thus conceding that the defendant meant to contract for goods to be carried on the
October Peerless and not for the goods actually carried on the December
Peerless — seems as mystifying as it proved to be mistaken. No doubt his
thought was that, even with that concession, his client's case was
overwhelming — and, from the point of view of a commercial lawyer,
there was (and is) much to be said in favor of that position. Counsel had
the bad luck, however, to come up with a trio of judges who were apparently incapable of understanding the fairly simple point which he tried,
unavailingly, to make.[2]

Presumably, the buyer's real reason for rejecting the cotton was that, at
the time of tender, the Liverpool market price had fallen below the contract

2. The three judges were Pollock, Martin, and Pigott — none of them known to fame as
an expounder of commercial law.

price of 17 1/2d. per pound.[3] The fact that the buyer's Peerless had sailed from Bombay two months before the seller's Peerless suggests the possibility that the ship which sailed first also arrived first and that the market price had broken between the two arrival dates. In that case, it could be argued, the buyer had indeed suffered loss because of the seller's choice of the later ship. If that had been the case, however, the buyer would presumably have pleaded those facts, which would obviously have strengthened his case. In any event it does not necessarily follow that a ship sailing from Bombay in October would have made port in Liverpool before a ship sailing in December. Either Peerless may have been a sailing vessel, subject to the vagaries of wind and weather — or both of them may have been — and either one (or both) may have called at intermediate ports. Since the buyer did not in his plea raise any issue about the time of the seller's tender in Liverpool, we may, I think, safely assume that there was no such issue to be raised. Furthermore, as Milward (plaintiff's counsel) correctly pointed out, there was no provision in the contract relating to the time of sailing from Bombay.

The "fairly simple" point which Milward tried to make was that, under the contract term "to arrive ex Peerless," "it was immaterial by what ship the cotton was to arrive, so that it was a ship called the Peerless" and that the term meant only that "if the vessel is lost on the voyage, the contract is to be at an end" (that is, the seller would bear the loss but the buyer would have no claim for damages for non-delivery). In commercial understanding, that is exactly what the terms mean today and there is no reason to believe that they meant anything else a hundred years ago.[4] In technical language, Milward's argument was that the identity of the carrying ship was not a true condition of the contract. Thus, even on the assumption that the buyer had meant the October Peerless (and that his meaning was entitled to prevail), he would not have been justified in rejecting the tender of the cotton which arrived on the December Peerless. For mistake to justify rescission of a contract the mistake must relate to some fundamental aspect of the contractual performance; it was, as Milward said, given the commercial meaning of the contract term and the fact that no issue relating to the time of tender was raised, "immaterial" on which Peerless the cotton arrived.

---

3. The date of the case (1864) suggests a plausible explanation of why there should have been a break in the price of cotton in English markets at this time. During the early years of our Civil War, the effective Northern naval blockade prevented cotton from being shipped out of Southern ports. After the capture of New Orleans and other ports by Northern forces, the Lincoln administration confiscated large stocks of cotton, which were sold for export. I assume that American cotton could be sold in England more cheaply than Indian cotton of comparable quality because of reduced transportation costs.

4. On "to arrive" see U.C.C. §2-324 ("No Arrival, No Sale" Term). According to the Official Comment: "The 'no arrival, no sale' term [equivalent to "to arrive"] in a 'destination' overseas contract leaves risk of loss on the seller but gives him an exemption from liability for non-delivery." On "ex Peerless" see U.C.C. §2-322 (Delivery "Ex-Ship"). According to the Official Comment: "Delivery need not be made from any particular vessel under a clause calling for delivery 'ex ship' even though a vessel on which shipment is to be made originally is named in the contract, unless the agreement by appropriate language, restricts the clause to delivery from a named vessel." Thus, under the Code formulation, Milward need not even have made the concession that the cotton had to arrive on a ship called Peerless.

Milward got absolutely nowhere in explaining this point to the court. Two of the judges, Pollock and Martin, kept interrupting him with questions which suggest that they had no idea what he was talking about. Their evident assumption was that if the contract said Peerless, then Peerless was a fundamental term (or condition) of the contract and Milward could go on talking until he was blue in the face without shaking them. There seems to be an air of increasing desperation in Milward's attempts to deal with the wooly-headed questions from the bench. Toward the end of his argument, perhaps distracted, he suddenly switched to an obviously unsound line: that parol evidence was not admissible to show which Peerless was meant — a diversionary tactic which the Court treated with the silent contempt it deserved.

Mellish, as counsel for the buyer, answered Milward. His first sentence effectively demolished Milward's unfortunate attempt to drag in the parol evidence rule. His second sentence was:

> That being so [i.e. the parol evidence being admissible], there was no consensus ad idem, and therefore no binding contract.

At that point he was stopped by the Court which forthwith announced judgment for Mellish's client.

There are really only two things we can make out of this curious case. One is that the judges, no doubt mistakenly, believed that the identity of the carrying ship was important — a true condition of the contract. The other is that they seem to have been immediately convinced by Mellish's consensus ad idem argument — that if buyer "meant" the October Peerless while seller "meant" the December Peerless (which was admitted by the demurrer), then there could be no contract since their minds had never met. None of the judges thought of asking Mellish what would seem to be obvious questions. Would a reasonably well-informed cotton merchant in Liverpool have known that there were two ships called Peerless? Ought this buyer to have known? If in fact the October Peerless had arrived in Liverpool first, had the buyer protested the seller's failure to tender the cotton? The failure of the judges, who had given Milward such a hard time, to put any questions to Mellish suggests that they were entirely content to let the case go off on the purely subjective failure of the minds to meet at the time the contract was entered into. . . .

My principal reason for focusing our discussion on Raffles v. Wichelhaus is that [Oliver Wendell] Holmes [Jr.] has left us an altogether astonishing explanation of the true meaning of the case. In the lecture on Void and Voidable Contracts in The Common Law he stated the facts of the case and continued:

> It is commonly said that such a contract is void, because of mutual mistake as to the subject matter, and because therefore the parties did not consent to the same thing. But this way of putting it seems to me misleading. The law has nothing to do with the actual state of the parties' minds. In contract, as elsewhere, it must go by externals, and judge parties by their conduct. If there had been but one "Peerless," and the defendant had said "Peerless" by mistake,

meaning "Peri," he would have been bound.[5] The true ground of the decision was not that each party meant a different thing from the other, as is implied by the explanation which has been mentioned, but that each said a different thing. The plaintiff offered one thing, the defendant expressed his assent to another.[6]

[handwritten margin note: → 2 ships / 1 ship in / Oct. defendant / wanted did not / have cotton]

Even for Holmes this was an extraordinary tour de force. In the preceding lecture we observed at considerable length the process of "reinterpretation" to which the "leading cases" were subjected before being admitted to the pantheon. The magician who could "objectify" Raffles v. Wichelhaus . . . could, the need arising, objectify anything. . . .

A. W. B. SIMPSON, CONTRACTS FOR COTTON TO ARRIVE: THE CASE OF THE TWO SHIPS *PEERLESS*, 11 CARDOZO L. REV. 287 (1989): Some leading cases only achieve their special status posthumously, and Raffles v. Wichelhaus[7] is a striking example. . . .

Since 1868 the case has been under continuous discussion, and it has come to be one of the best known old chestnuts of the common law. Perhaps the best known modern discussion is that of Grant Gilmore in The Death of Contract. No student of the law of contract could regard his education as complete without either reading the case in the reports themselves, or, more commonly, acquiring some acquaintance with the case from one of the abbreviated, and sometimes garbled, accounts which appear in the legal casebooks or hornbooks. Yet in spite of the incredible number of hours which, since 1864, must have been devoted to discussing the case, virtually nothing is known about it. . . .

***II. The Maritime Background.* . . .**   There were reports of at least eleven ships called Peerless sailing the seven seas at the time, for the name was a popular one. The Mercantile Navy List for 1863 lists nine British registered sailing vessels of that name, their ports of registration being London, Aberystwyth, Dartmouth, Greenock, Halifax, Windsor (Nova Scotia), Hull, and Liverpool, which boasted two such ships. There were also two American ships named Peerless from Boston and Baltimore. The existence of so many vessels of the same or a similar name could obviously cause confusion in shipping movement reports. There was nothing unusual however in this state of affairs. Ships commonly shared the same name, particularly popular names such as Annie. But the two vessels with which we are concerned can readily be identified as the two which were registered at Liverpool. At the time it was the practice in the shipping press to differentiate vessels bearing the same name by the names of their captains, not, as one might expect, by using their unique registered number. Contrary to assumptions often made, for example by those impressed by the economic analysis of law, commercial practices in this period at least seem to have

---

5. Why?

6. Holmes, The Common Law 242 ([1881] Howe ed. 1963). . . .

7. The case of Raffles v. Wichelhaus is reported in 2 H. & C. 906, 159 Eng. Rep. 375 (Ex. 1864), and in 33 L.J.N.S. 160 (Ex. 1864). The second report is clearer and gives marginally more information.

been governed as much by tradition and conservatism as by cold rationality.[8] . . .

III. The Commercial Background: Speculation in Cotton.

The immediate commercial background to the transaction litigated in Raffles v. Wichelhaus was the Lancashire cotton famine,[9] created by the blockade of the southern American states during the Civil War. Spinners were forced to turn to other sources of supply, particularly to India, and the price of cotton from all sources rose sharply and became extremely volatile. The year 1862 saw the sharpest rise. In consequence there was much speculative dealing in the cotton market. . . .

. . . In the early nineteenth century factors which militated against any considerable trade in cotton which was not on the spot were the great variations in quality and type of the material, as well as the weights of bales. Such variations made inspection before purchase essential. The problems which discouraged trade in cotton which was not on the spot were eventually solved by the evolution of sophisticated grading, and by the use of samples, and by cheap arbitration together with arbitrated price adjustments both to solve disputes and to cope with variations from the contract description. In the early half of the century these devices had not been much developed.

Nevertheless, in spite of the difficulties, there existed a trade in cotton *in transitu*, purchased for forward delivery. The contracts involved were called "contracts to arrive" or "arrival" contracts. They do not appear to have been common until the 1850s. There are references in The Economist as early as 1851, and later in the decade they are more common. By the 1860s reference to them became standard form in market reports. Such contracts were attractive to speculators, since they avoided warehousing costs if the cotton was promptly sold on arrival or if the rights of the purchaser were assigned. In the absence of prepayment they also avoided locking up capital.

The explanation for their development, claimed J. Todd in 1934, was technological rather than legal.[10] The invention of the steamship and its use in the Atlantic trade by the Cunard Line, formed in 1840, made it possible for news of the American crop size, and samples of cotton, to be conveyed across the Atlantic ahead of the slower sailing vessels which carried bulk cotton from the principal source of supply, the southern states: "Merchants were advised of cotton coming by certain ships, and transactions took place in cotton 'to arrive,' which accounts for the fact that in certain offices in Liverpool to-day the futures department is still called the Arrivals Department."[11] Quite apart from the steamship, telegraphs and railways also enabled news of a vessel's progress, cargo, and bills of lading to travel faster

8. However a vessel's number was neither displayed upon it nor was it a matter of general quayside knowledge. Instead its name and captain would be known, so that an agent reporting a ship to Lloyd's would naturally use this information. So perhaps there is an economic explanation after all!

9. Lancashire was then home to the largest cotton processing industry in the world, and no larger factory organized processing industry then existed in any other commodity.

10. J. Todd, The Marketing of Cotton (1934).

11. Id. at 66. . . .

than the vessel. Thus, as we have seen, there were "ports of call" such as Falmouth in England or Cork in Ireland where sailing vessels, including our Peerless (Flavin), called or reported for orders, and were placed in touch with the markets by telegraph; since 1852 Cork had been in direct touch with Liverpool.

The extension of international telegraph services enhanced the possibilities. The telegraph between England and India, which passed down the Persian Gulf, was not effectively connected until February 1865, but parts of the distance were serviced before this. Lines at the European end reached Corfu and Malta by 1857, and Aden by 1859. The Red Sea cable from Suez to Karachi was connected in 1860, but frequently failed.

In addition, the practice of mutual speaking and reporting of ships on passage often enabled news of the progress of a particular vessel to be available in Britain before the vessel arrived. Thus in a variety of ways information travelled more rapidly than bulk cargoes. . . .

IV. The Form of Arrival Contracts.   A contract for cotton "to arrive" was a contract for forward delivery, or as they are sometimes called, a "time contract." One might expect that such a contract would normally specify a time for delivery. For it is the moment when the goods become available in the market which is of paramount importance to the purchaser, particularly if the purchaser wants the goods for use. But the world in which such contracts originated was one in which this was not really possible. Although one could discover, after an interval, when a sailing ship had left, or, more approximately, proposed to leave its port of departure, it was very uncertain when, if ever, it would arrive at its destination. Even when it did arrive, there were uncertain delays in finding a berth to unload its cargo. Hence such contracts did not originally specify the time of arrival, much less delivery, even within some fixed period. All they did was to identify which shipment of cotton was being sold; presumably the rationale of this was that the buyer, so long as he knew which shipment was being sold, would be able to form his own estimate of the probable time of arrival. This would not of course be a point in time but a period. It is said that originally such contracts were only made when an arrival was imminent, the ship typically having been reported off Point Lynas, which is on the north coast of Anglesey, some fifty miles from Liverpool. Presumably there was a signal station there. No doubt also cotton was sometimes sold as the ship lay in the river, waiting to berth. In such cases the date of delivery could be guessed with some precision, though a square rigged vessel, if it did not employ a steam tug, could take a long and unpredictable time to cover even fifty miles.[12]

There were no doubt various contractual forms used in the early days, and various possible ways of identifying the shipment which would directly or indirectly indicate the date of departure and make possible an estimate of the approximate date of arrival. One technique was to name the ship. These were "ship named" contracts. From this, and knowledge of the port of departure, and through the system of reporting ships' movements, the probable date of arrival could be estimated. In addition, the port of origin

---

12. Nineteenth-century sailing vessels did not carry auxiliary engines, whereas steam vessels did carry auxiliary sails.

could be named in the contract — ex Peerless Bombay. A contract could also specify the time of departure, not a precise day but a period — ex Peerless Bombay guaranteed October shipment — and what a tragedy that would have been! . . .

In July of 1862, in response to the imminent cotton famine, the cotton market became very excited. By August 30 it was reported that it "bordered on wildness."[13] On September 6 it was reported of the London market that "[t]he speculation has been enormous, and very wild."[14] In these conditions dealings in cotton "to arrive" became more common; no doubt some were purely speculative, but others represented attempts by or on behalf of spinners to safeguard future supplies. Market reports for the first time quote dates in addition to type, quality, and price. The dates of shipment show sailing by month, and they indicate some dealings in cotton which were not due to arrive for some considerable time. In July there is even a report of a sale of cotton, August shipment: This would not arrive until December 1862 or January 1863. By late August the market reports settle into a more or less standard form, quoting shipment dates from April up to August in single months, and in one instance in coupled months (July and August). . . .

V. The Peerless Contract and the Litigation. . . .   Peerless (Major) duly arrived on February 18, 1863, and on February 26, 1863, Gore's General Advertiser reported her docked and unloading in the Albert Dock. She did not lack for cotton. Her cargo included, in addition to 414 bales for designated Liverpool merchants, 3,439 1/2 bales of the material; indeed it principally consisted of cotton. The cotton market at this period was reported to be quiet. The Times of February 19, 1863 reported that "[t]he cotton market continues peculiarly dull and inanimate, and this day's sales do not exceed 1,500 bales — 500 on speculation."[15] The Economist quotes the London spot prices for Dhollerah "Middling" on February 21, 1863, as 15 1/4d[16] and on February 28 as 15d.[17] So the Liverpool market price would be well below the contract price at the time the vessel was discharging, for prices continued to fall. Given the state of the market and level of prices, it is very difficult to understand why Raffles, if he had cotton of appropriate type and quality on the vessel, would fail to tender delivery, since it would clearly have been in his economic interest to do so. We must conclude that he genuinely believed the contract did not relate to a shipment on this vessel. In all probability he would not have had cotton on this ship, as was indicated in argument by his counsel, Clement Milward, "[h]ere it does not appear that the plaintiff had any goods on board the other 'Peerless.'"[18]

Plainly Wichelhaus and Busch could at this point have complained over Raffles's failure to tender delivery, or indeed they might even have sued. But

---

13. The Economist, Aug. 30, 1862, at 971. The reference is to the Liverpool market.

14. The Economist, Sept. 6, 1862, at 981.

15. The Times (London), Feb. 19, 1863, at 7, col. 5.

16. The Economist, Feb. 21, 1863, at 217.

17. The Economist, Feb. 28, 1863, at 242.

18. Raffles v. Wichelhaus, 2 H. & C. 906, 159 Eng. Rep. 375 (Ex. 1864). The Law Journal text is: "It does not appear that the plaintiff had any goods on board the other 'Peerless.'" *Raffles*, 33 L.J.N.S. 160 (Ex. 1864).

it is easy to see why they had no economic motive for doing so. As matters stood they had made a bad bargain.

The second vessel, Peerless (Flavin), arrived off Liverpool on Sunday April 19, 1863, and Gore's General Advertiser reports her unloading in Queen's dock on April 23, 1863. Her cargo was more exotic, including eleven tons of buffalo horns, but again it principally consisted of cotton — 1,079 bales for specified merchants (one of whom must have been Raffles) and 3,723 bales and two half bales not bespoke. By now the Liverpool price of Dhollerah cotton was slightly better than it had been; "Dhollerah Fair" stood at 17 1/2d. on April 24 and then fell to 17 1/4d. in the following week, according to some sources. The Economist has Dhollerah in the London market at 16d. for "Middling" and 17 3/4d. for "Fair," noting a sale of 200 bales of "Middling Fair" "to arrive" at 16 5/8d.; "Middling Oomrawattee" at Liverpool stood at 15d., and "Fair" at 17 3/4d.[19] This level of prices would still not have enabled the purchasers to break even, for "Middling Fair" would fetch around 16 3/4d.; they would have suffered a substantial loss, though not so great a loss as in late February and early April. Prices over the next four weeks rose slightly, but not enough to give the buyers a profit. There was in consequence no economic advantage to them in accepting delivery from Raffles off the second ship, Peerless (Flavin); obviously if there had been they would have done so. Nor was there by now any chance of Raffles being able to sue them for failing to accept delivery from the first ship, Peerless (Major). Delivery had never been tendered, and it was now too late to remedy this. In any event, Raffles had in all probability no cotton from the ship to deliver. . . .

Now suppose the matter had been arbitrated by professionals. What solution would have been reached? There are of course a number of possibilities, but one would have been particularly attractive and is, I think, hinted at in the reports of the case. Assuming there to have been a genuine misunderstanding, neither side initially realizing that there were two vessels of the same name loading cotton in Bombay, what harm had this done to Wichelhaus and Busch? If cotton had been delivered to them from Peerless (Major), the vessel they claimed to have intended, they would have suffered a *larger* loss than they would incur by now taking delivery from Peerless (Flavin). The misunderstanding had in a sense worked in their favor (*en passant* I cannot but wonder whether some contracts teacher has ever thought of this "hypo" when teaching from the case). They had nothing to complain about. This is the point behind counsel's remark, reported only in the Law Journal Report: "If the defendants had said their speculation had fallen through in consequence, it might have been different."[20] The defendants' speculation had indeed failed, in the sense of failing to be profitable, because the price had not risen as they expected, and Milward would know that and so would the judges. Milward could not have been trying to suggest the contrary. But the consequence of the misunderstanding which led to tender of cotton from the second ship had reduced their loss, not increased it, and so their

19. The Economist, Apr. 25, 1863, at 464, 467.
20. Raffles v. Wichelhaus, 33 L.J.N.S. 160 (Ex. 1864).

speculation had not failed because of the misunderstanding at all. This surely is the point Milward is making.

Had the matter been settled in the normal way arbitrators might well have decided that the sensible and decent way to handle the problem, the equitable solution, would be to require them to take delivery from Raffles,[21] or even, though this would be less favorable to them, to do something which courts are always reluctant to do — split the difference. Furthermore, if Wichelhaus and Busch deliberately kept quiet when no cotton was tendered by Raffles from Peerless (Major), hoping that when the second ship arrived, the price would have moved in their favor, it would hardly seem fair to allow them both to have their cake and eat it by now refusing to accept the cotton when they discovered that their hopes had been in vain. Raffles may well have decided to litigate because he was irritated by the failure of Wichelhaus and Busch to do the decent thing — either accept the cotton or go to arbitration.

What of Grant Gilmore's discussion of the case in The Death of Contract? His speculations as to the background are inevitably misconceived, being unrelated to evidence.[22] But his principal point was that the judges in the case foolishly failed to grasp, in spite of Clement Milward's attempts to put the point to them, that in terms of commercial understanding the identity of the carrying ship was immaterial. Its only relevance was to the risk of loss. He backs this claim up with a classic statement of the ahistorical attitude to legal sources: "In commercial understanding, that is exactly what the terms mean today and there is no reason to believe that they meant anything else a hundred years ago."[23] And to be sure, Gilmore is correct in saying that there is no reason if we pay no attention whatever to the historical context in which the dispute arose. But from what I have said, it is perfectly plain that in arrival contracts where ship and port were named, the identity of the carrying vessel was of central importance. It was the identity of the carrying vessel that fixed the time of arrival and delivery. In the volatile cotton market, that time was critical to the success or failure of the speculation. The reason why time was not specified directly was technological, and as the technology changed, "shipments" were to be superseded by a new form of contract, "deliveries," which did directly specify time. Out of transactions involving this newer form of arrival contract was to develop the practice of futures trading, but that is another story.

Study Guide: *The next case illustrates a modern application of the approach to misunderstandings taken by the court in* Raffles.

---

21. In terms of a money award, compensate Raffles by paying the difference between the contract price and market price.

22. For example, "[e]ither Peerless may have been a sailing vessel, subject to the vagaries of wind and weather — or both of them may have been — and either one (or both) may have called at intermediate ports." [G. Gilmore, The Death of Contract 37 (1974).]

23. Id. at 37.

OSWALD v. ALLEN
United States Court of Appeals, Second Circuit,
417 F.2d 43 (1969)

MOORE, C.J.:*

Dr. Oswald, a coin collector from Switzerland, was interested in Mrs. Allen's collection of Swiss coins. In April of 1964 Dr. Oswald was in the United States and arranged to see Mrs. Allen's coins. The parties drove to the Newburgh Savings Bank of Newburgh, New York, where two of her collections referred to as the Swiss Coin Collection and the Rarity Coin Collection were located in separate vault boxes. After examining and taking notes on the coins in the Swiss Coin Collection, Dr. Oswald was shown several valuable Swiss coins from the Rarity Coin Collection. He also took notes on these coins and later testified that he did not know that they were in a separate "collection." The evidence showed that each collection had a different key number and was housed in labeled cigar boxes.

On the return to New York City, Dr. Oswald sat in the front seat of the car while Mrs. Allen sat in the back with Dr. Oswald's brother, Mr. Victor Oswald, and Mr. Cantarella of the Chase Manhattan Bank's Money Museum, who had helped arrange the meeting and served as Dr. Oswald's agent. Dr. Oswald could speak practically no English and so depended on his brother to conduct the transaction. After some negotiation a price of $50,000 was agreed upon. Apparently the parties never realized that the references to "Swiss coins" and the "Swiss Coin Collection" were ambiguous. The trial judge found that Dr. Oswald thought the offer he had authorized his brother to make was for all of the Swiss coins, while Mrs. Allen thought she was selling only the Swiss Coin Collection and not the Swiss coins in the Rarity Coin Collection.

On April 8, 1964, Dr. Oswald wrote to Mrs. Allen to "confirm my purchase of all your Swiss coins (gold, silver and copper) at the price of $50,000.00." The letter mentioned delivery arrangements through Mr. Cantarella. In response Mrs. Allen wrote on April 15, 1964, that "Mr. Cantarella and I have arranged to go to Newburgh Friday April 24." This letter does not otherwise mention the alleged contract of sale or the quantity of coins sold. On April 20, realizing that her original estimation of the number of coins in the Swiss Coin Collection was erroneous, Mrs. Allen offered to permit a re-examination and to undertake not to sell to anyone else. Dr. Oswald cabled from Switzerland to Mr. Alfred Barth of the Chase Manhattan Bank, giving instruction to proceed with the transaction. Upon receiving the cable, Barth wrote a letter to Mrs. Allen stating Dr. Oswald's understanding of the agreement and requesting her signature on a copy of the letter as a "mere formality." Mrs. Allen did not sign and return this letter. On April 24, Mrs. Allen's husband told Barth that his wife did not wish to proceed with the sale because her children did not wish her to do so.

Leonard Page Moore (1898-1982) received degrees from Amherst College (A.B.) and Columbia University (LL.B.). He practiced privately in New York City (1929-1953) until his appointment as U.S. Attorney for the Eastern District of New York (1953-1957). Moore was appointed to the Second Circuit Court of Appeals in 1957 and became Senior Circuit Judge in 1971, remaining on the court until his death. — K.T.

Appellant attacks the conclusion of the Court below that a contract did not exist since the minds of the parties had not met. The opinion below states:

> . . . plaintiff believed that he had offered to buy all Swiss coins owned by the defendant while defendant reasonably understood the offer which she accepted to relate to those of her Swiss coins as had been segregated in the particular collection denominated by her as the "Swiss Coin Collection." . . .

285 F. Supp. 488, 492 (S.D.N.Y. 1968). The trial judge based his decision upon his evaluation of the credibility of the witnesses, the records of the defendant, the values of the coins involved, the circumstances of the transaction and the reasonable probabilities. Such findings of fact are not to be set aside unless "clearly erroneous." Fed. R. Civ. P. 52(a). There was ample evidence upon which the trial judge could rely in reaching this decision.

In such a factual situation the law is settled that no contract exists. The Restatement of Contracts in section 71(a) adopts the rule of Raffles v. Wichelhaus, 2 Hurl. & C. 906, 159 Eng. Rep. 375 (Ex. 1864). Professor Young states that rule as follows:

> when any of the terms used to express an agreement is ambivalent, and the parties understand it in different ways, there cannot be a contract unless one of them should have been aware of the other's understanding.

Young, Equivocation in Agreements, 64 Colum. L. Rev. 619, 621 (1964). Even though the mental assent of the parties is not requisite for the formation of a contract (see Comment to Restatement of Contracts §71 (1932)), the facts found by the trial judge clearly place this case within the small group of exceptional cases in which there is "no sensible basis for choosing between conflicting understandings." Young, at 647. The rule of Raffles v. Wichelhaus is applicable here. . . .

Affirmed. . . .

REFERENCE: Barnett, §3.3.1

RESTATEMENT (SECOND) OF CONTRACTS

STUDY GUIDE: The following Restatement sections provide a useful roadmap to contractual interpretation. How would they apply to Raffles? *How would they apply to the next two cases? Do they represent an objective or subjective approach to interpretation? Do they support Learned Hand's view that "[a] contract has, strictly speaking, nothing to do with the personal, or individual, intent of the parties" or Holmes's view that "[t]he law has nothing to do with the actual state of the parties' minds"?*

§200.   INTERPRETATION OF PROMISE OR AGREEMENT

Interpretation of a promise or agreement or a term thereof is the ascertainment of its meaning.

§201. WHOSE MEANING PREVAILS

(1) Where the parties have attached the same meaning to a promise or agreement or a term thereof, it is interpreted in accordance with that meaning.

(2) Where the parties have attached different meanings to a promise or agreement or a term thereof, it is interpreted in accordance with the meaning attached by one of them if at the time the agreement was made

(a) that party did not know of any different meaning attached by the other, and the other knew the meaning attached by the first party; or

(b) that party had no reason to know of any different meaning attached by the other, and the other had reason to know the meaning attached by the first party.

(3) Except as stated in this Section, neither party is bound by the meaning attached by the other, even though the result may be a failure of mutual assent. (Oswald v. Allen)

No contract b/c "no meeting of the minds"

§202. RULES IN AID OF INTERPRETATION

(1) Words and other conduct are interpreted in the light of all the circumstances, and if the principal purpose of the parties is ascertainable it is given great weight.

(2) A writing is interpreted as a whole, and all writings that are part of the same transaction are interpreted together.

(3) Unless a different intention is manifested,

(a) where language has a generally prevailing meaning, it is interpreted in accordance with that meaning;

(b) technical terms and words of art are given their technical meaning when used in a transaction within their technical field.

(4) Where an agreement involves repeated occasions for performance by either party with knowledge of the nature of the performance and opportunity for objection to it by the other, any course of performance accepted or acquiesced in without objection is given great weight in the interpretation of the agreement.

(5) Wherever reasonable, the manifestations of intention of the parties to a promise or agreement are interpreted as consistent with each other and with any relevant course of performance, course of dealing, or usage of trade.

SALES CONTRACTS: THE UNIFORM
COMMERCIAL CODE

STUDY GUIDE: Notice how §2-208 establishes a hierarchy of evidence relevant to establishing the meaning of the agreement.

§1-205.   COURSE OF DEALING AND USAGE OF TRADE

(1) A course of dealing is a sequence of previous conduct between the parties to a particular transaction which is fairly to be regarded as establishing a common basis of understanding for interpreting their expressions and other conduct.

(2) A usage of trade is any practice or method of dealing having such regularity of observance in a place, vocation or trade as to justify an expectation that it will be observed with respect to the transaction in question. The existence and scope of such a usage are to be proved as facts. If it is established that such a usage is embodied in a written trade code or similar writing the interpretation of the writing is for the court.

(3) A course of dealing between parties and any usage of trade in the vocation or trade in which they are engaged or of which they are or should be aware give particular meaning to and supplement or qualify terms of an agreement.

(4) The express terms of an agreement and an applicable course of dealing or usage of trade shall be construed wherever reasonable as consistent with each other; but when such construction is unreasonable express terms control both course of dealing and usage of trade and course of dealing controls usage of trade.

(5) An applicable usage of trade in the place where any part of performance is to occur shall be used in interpreting as to that part of the performance.

(6) Evidence of a relevant usage of trade offered by one party is not admissible unless and until he has given the other party such notice as the court finds sufficient to prevent unfair surprise to the latter.

§2-208.   COURSE OF PERFORMANCE OR
PRACTICAL CONSTRUCTION

(1) Where the contract for sale involves repeated occasions for performance by either party with knowledge of the nature of the performance and opportunity for objection to it by the other, any course of performance accepted or acquiesced in without objection shall be relevant to determine the meaning of the agreement.

(2) The express terms of the agreement and any such course of performance, as well as any course of dealing and usage of trade, shall be construed whenever possible as consistent with each other; but when such construction is unreasonable, express terms shall control course of performance and course of performance shall control both course of dealing and usage of trade.

(3) Subject to the provisions of the next section on modification and waiver, such course of performance shall be relevant to show a waiver or modification of any term inconsistent with such course of performance.

OFFICIAL COMMENT

Purposes

1. The parties themselves know best what they have meant by their words of agreement and their action under that agreement is the best indication of what that meaning was. This section thus rounds out the set of factors which determines the meaning of the "agreement" and therefore also of the "unless otherwise agreed" qualification to various provisions of this Article.

2.   Vague Terms

The words that give rise to disputes in the next two cases are not ambiguous in the sense that they have entirely different meanings that either or both parties intended to employ. Instead, the disputes arose over whether and to what extent the words used were meant to apply beyond their agreed core meaning. Once again, you should consider in what respect (or to what extent) the approach taken here by the courts is "objective."

WEINBERG v. EDELSTEIN
Supreme Court, Special Term, New York County, Part VI,
201 Misc. 343, 110 N.Y. Supp. 2d 806 (1952)

MATTHEW M. LEVY, J.* The plaintiff and the defendant operate retail stores in the same building. The plaintiff's lease, entered into in June 1949, for a five-year term, entitles him to sell "ladies dresses, coats and suits and ladies sports clothes." The landlord in that lease covenanted with the plaintiff "not to rent any other store in the same building for the retail sale of ladies dresses, coats and suits." The defendant's lease was assigned to him in June 1950, for somewhat more than a five-year term, and authorized the defendant to sell at retail "ladies hosiery, gloves, lingerie, brassieres, girdles, bathing suits, sweaters, bags and accessories, blouses, skirts and beachwear." This assignment was made to and accepted by defendant after discussion and agreement among plaintiff, defendant and defendant's predecessor, as to the wording of the use-clause, with knowledge on defendant's part of the restrictive covenant in plaintiff's

---

*Matthew Malltz Levy (1899-1971) was born in Brest Litovsk, Russia, and was brought to the United States in 1904. He served in the U.S. Army in 1918, then continued his education at the University of Georgia (B.S.) and Harvard University (LL.B.). He practiced privately in New York before working in the New York Attorney General's office (1927-1938). Levy served as judge in the New York City Municipal Court (1938) and became justice of the Supreme Court of New York (1951-1971). Between these appointments, Levy directed two jewelry corporations and served as attorney to various nonprofit organizations, working on behalf of tenants and labor. In 1932, he was an unsuccessful Socialist Party candidate to the New York Supreme Court, and in 1943 he was an unsuccessful American Labor Party candidate to the same court. — K.T.

lease, and with knowledge on plaintiff's part that the defendant's assignor had, for some time, sold skirt-blouse combinations.

Defendant is displaying, offering for sale and selling, among other items, matched skirts and blouses. Claiming that these are in reality two-piece dresses — the sale of which is forbidden the defendant — the plaintiff has brought this suit for an injunction to restrain the defendant from thus violating the restrictive covenant. The applicable legal principles are not in dispute. Restrictive covenants are enforced by injunction against takers with notice . . . , and one who subsequently rents premises with knowledge of a prior restrictive covenant agreed to by his lessor in favor of another tenant will also be enjoined. . . . The issue is the applicability of the covenant, and I must endeavor to ascertain, from the evidence before me, the meaning of the terms used in the leases so as to fulfill the intent of the parties. . . .

Plaintiff asserted during the trial, in modification of the demand in the complaint, that he is entitled to an injunction restraining the defendant from selling one-piece or two-piece dresses of any kind, and also from selling to the same customer at the same time skirts and blouses made from the same material or otherwise co-ordinated, matched or related by ornamentation, decoration, embroidery, trim or design — because, as claimed by the plaintiff, the combination thereby became a "dress." The defendant claims no right to sell conventional one-piece dresses, that is, garments which are manufactured in a variety of styles, fabrics and designs, and which have the common characteristic of being used as a single outerwear article, and of covering the woman's form from above the bust to the hemline. Nor does the defendant assert the right to sell the conventional two-piece dress, consisting of a bottom or lower garment plus an upper vest, jacket or bolero.

The problem presented here is whether, when a restrictive covenant interdicts the sale of "dresses," it also necessarily precludes the sale of a "blouse-skirt combination," sometimes also called a "dress." I cannot rely upon naked dictionary definitions. However incongruous it may seem to purists in the spheres of lexicography and logic, the legal conclusion may well be that, under certain conditions, a matched-skirt-and-blouse garment, although identical with a two-piece dress of the same material, does not come within the restriction — and so, theoretically, a "dress" is not a "dress." Whether such two-piece ensemble should be considered a dress depends in large measure on the practices and customs of the trade. To resolve the issue requires some consideration of the background of the vast and changing ladies' garment industry, and proof was presented to me in that regard.

In that industry there has been a long-established division between houses which manufacture dresses, and sportswear houses which manufacture skirts and blouses. (There are separate blouse and skirt houses also.) Organization of the manufacturing industry, whether from the angle of the trade association or of the employees' unions, has corresponded to this same division; there are a skirt union, a blouse union and a dress union — each with separate collective bargaining machinery and contracts entered into with its own respective employers' group. Two-piece dresses have long been and now are manufactured by dress houses, and usually consist of a skirt with a bodice or other upper raiment having almost complete unification of style, ornamentation, color and material. These two-piece dresses are sold at a single-unit price, and it is the custom of women to wear the two-piece costume as a unit. The sportswear houses, on the other hand, had been accustomed to manufacture unrelated skirts and blouses and to charge a separate price for each item — skirt or blouse — and it has been the habit of women to wear each without relation to the other.

A recent style trend, emanating from the sportswear houses, and begun some time before the execution of the present leases, has resulted in the manufacture of "separates," "mix-matches," "co-ordinates," "pair-offs," or "match-mates," as they are variously termed. These are matched skirts and blouses which can be worn together or in combination with other blouses and skirts. Such garments are generally made by other than dress manufacturers, usually sportswear houses, and comprise, as wholly separate units, skirts, blouses, sweaters and other similar articles, no one of which is adapted for use as a sole article of outerwear, but must be worn together — a skirt plus an upper garment. They are not necessarily worn in any specific combination; they may be worn either in matched pairs, in contrasting pairs, or in any combination of units, to suit the whim of the wearer. Sizes, too, may vary — for example, a size twelve blouse may be matched with a size fourteen skirt of the same pattern, which, I am told, is a great advantage to many women; while, on the other hand, the entire costume must be of the same size when a two-piece dress is purchased. That matched skirts and blouses are considered sportswear can be noted in large metropolitan retail department stores, where blouses and skirts (although matched) are sold in the sportswear section, and not in the dress division — and where there are separate and even competing buyers, stylists, advertisers and salesmen. As "separates" are actually blouses and skirts, manufactured and sold by sportswear and not generally by dress, houses, the two parts of the garment are priced individually and both the retailer and the consumer can buy blouse and skirt separately or in combination.

The purpose of this style change was to permit the purchase at individual prices of various skirts and blouses, which, when worn together, look like dresses, and yet at the same time can be worn separately with other garments — thus increasing the number, utility and variety of the garments which the ingenious and stylish American woman, ever desirous of being variedly well-dressed, has at her disposal — and this, notwithstanding a limited pocketbook. The main characteristic, therefore, of "separates" is that, although approximating the outward appearance of dresses, they are really skirts and blouses that can be worn with other blouses and skirts. Because of the inability of the consumer to distinguish, at times, between the two-piece dress and the two-piece ensemble, it may be that the plaintiff will be competitively injured. But I cannot hold, under the language used and the facts proved, that the defendant must ignore an almost universal trend in the sportswear industry, even though the garments he sells tend to resemble the apparel sold by the plaintiff. At the time when the leases were made, the style change had already become established — and the language of the restriction in plaintiff's favor and the use-clause granted defendant (both of which the plaintiff in a measure formulated) should and could have been more precise.

If the restrictive covenant did not merely employ the generic and currently ambiguous term of "dress," but clearly forbade the sale of "blouse and skirt combinations," the conclusion might be different. But the covenant is not so worded. Just as certain as it is that plaintiff has the exclusive right to sell ladies' dresses, coats and suits, equally certain is it that the defendant has the undoubted right to sell, among other things, ladies' sweaters, blouses and skirts. Reading the two leases together, as I think we should, I must endeavor to make out some construction which will not do violence to the language of either contract, and yet give appropriate effect to the words used in each. It is to be noted too that the use-clause in the plaintiff's lease is broader than the restrictive covenant invoked against the defendant. While the plaintiff may sell "ladies dresses, coats and suits *and ladies sports clothes*" (italics supplied), the defendant is prohibited from selling "ladies dresses, coats and suits" only. The omission of "ladies sports clothes," it seems to me, is significant in the light of the use-clause in the defendant's lease — including, among other things, "sweaters," "blouses, skirts and beachwear" — which provision was arranged for after discussion with the plaintiff.

Due to the policy of our law against unduly restricting the free use of land . . . , the covenant is construed strictly against the person seeking its enforcement, particularly when the intent of the restriction is not clear. . . . I am of the view that the garments defendant has been selling are not "dresses." In any event, I am certain that they are "skirts" and "blouses." As such, I hold that they are not affected by the restrictive covenant. In my view, the two-piece ensembles may truly be considered "dresses," within the meaning of the contract, only when made by a dress manufacturer, designed and styled as to be normally worn together as a single costume and not normally intended to be worn in combination with other outerwear garments, passing through the channels of trade in the dress industry as distinguished from the sportswear industry, and sold both to the dealer and to the consumer as a single unit at a single price. At the very least, the commodities overlap. The line of commercial and physical demarcation between a traditional two-piece dress on the one hand and an ensemble of matched skirt-and-blouse on the other seems to have become somewhat vague and uncertain. To the extent of such overlapping, the plaintiff is subject to permissible competition. Restrictive covenants have not been enforced by the courts when articles protected by the covenant and articles sold by the defendant do overlap. . . .

The application for the injunction as prayed for is denied. However, the defendant may not compel the purchase of a skirt and blouse combination as a unit, and is to permit the purchase by his customers of skirts and blouses separately or together, as the customer wishes — and in any case, each at an individual price.

During the trial, some issue was raised as to the right of the defendant to sell "sun-backs." These garments expose a large part of the female back, and frequently of the upper front, and are sometimes of one piece and sometimes in the form of a skirt and separate halter. They are not normally worn at business or social functions; they are sometimes worn informally at home, and generally are used at beach or camp. They have some of the physical characteristics of dresses. But they were called "sun-togs" by the defendant and are claimed by him to have been developed from beachwear garments. It is not necessary, however, to arrive at a judicial conclusion as to the status of this type of apparel, as the defendant on final submission has agreed to forego the claimed and disputed right to sell such articles.

This opinion constitutes the decision of the court. Submit judgment on notice accordingly.

STUDY GUIDE: In Weinberg, *both parties were assumed to be in the same community of discourse and therefore either knew or had reason to know of the special meaning attached to the word "dress" in their trade. In the next case, this assumption is questioned. Does this change affect the method of interpretation?*

FRIGALIMENT IMPORTING CO. v. B.N.S. INTERNATIONAL SALES CORP.

United States District Court, Southern District of New York,
190 F. Supp. 116 (1960)

FRIENDLY, C.J.*

The issue is, what is chicken? Plaintiff says "chicken" means a young chicken, suitable for broiling and frying. Defendant says "chicken" means any bird of that genus that meets contract specifications on weight and quality, including what it calls "stewing chicken" and plaintiff pejoratively terms "fowl." Dictionaries give both meanings, as well as some others not relevant here. To support its [definition], plaintiff sends a number of volleys over the net; defendant essays to return them and adds a few serves of its own. Assuming that both parties were acting in good faith, the case nicely illustrates Holmes' remark "that the making of a contract depends not on the agreement of two minds in one intention, but on the agreement of two sets of external signs — not on the parties' having meant the same thing but on their having said the same thing." The Path of the Law, in Collected Legal Papers, p. 178. I have concluded that plaintiff has not sustained its burden of persuasion that the contract used "chicken" in the narrower sense. *[handwritten: → Holding]*

The action is for breach of the warranty that goods sold shall correspond to the description, New York Personal Property Law, McKinney's Consol. Laws, c. 41, §95. Two contracts are in suit. In the first, dated May 2, 1957, defendant, a New York sales corporation, confirmed the sale to plaintiff, a Swiss corporation, of

[handwritten margin note: Principles to follow]

---

* *Henry J. Friendly* (1903-1986) graduated summa cum laude from Harvard College in 1923 and earned a degree from Harvard Law School in 1927. After clerking for Justice Louis D. Brandeis of the U.S. Supreme Court, Friendly worked in private practice, rising to the position of general counsel to Pan American World Airways. In 1959, President Dwight Eisenhower appointed Friendly to the Court of Appeals for the Second Circuit. Friendly served as Chief Justice from 1971 to 1973 and was mentioned as a candidate for nomination to the Supreme Court during the Nixon administration. In 1974, Friendly took on the additional role of presiding judge on a special court that dealt with the reorganization of many of the nation's railroads. In the 1970s, he changed his status to senior judge, but even in his semi-retired state, he worked on 125 cases per year. Judge Friendly died, apparently by suicide, a year after the death of Sophine, his wife of 55 years. — Andrew J. White.

US Fresh Frozen Chicken, Grade A, Government Inspected, Eviscerated
   2½-3 lbs. and 1½-2 lbs. each
   all chicken individually wrapped in cryovac, packed in secured fiber
cartons or wooden boxes, suitable for export

   75,000 lbs. 2-3 lbs. . . . . . @$33.00
   25,000 lbs. 1-2 lbs. . . . . . @$36.50
   per 100 lbs. FAS New York

scheduled May 10, 1957 pursuant to instructions from Penson & Co.,
New York.[24]

   The second contract, also dated May 2, 1957, was identical save that
only 50,000 lbs. of the heavier "chicken" were called for, the price of the
smaller birds was $37 per 100 lbs., and shipment was scheduled for May 30.
The initial shipment under the first contract was short but the balance was
shipped on May 17. When the initial shipment arrived in Switzerland, plaintiff found, on May 28, that the 2½-3 lbs. birds were not young chicken
suitable for broiling and frying but stewing chicken or "fowl"; indeed,
many of the cartons and bags plainly so indicated. Protests ensued. Nevertheless, shipment under the second contract was made on May 29, the 2½-3
lbs. birds again being stewing chicken. Defendant stopped the transportation of these at Rotterdam.
   This action followed. Plaintiff says that, notwithstanding that its acceptance was in Switzerland, New York law controls under the principle of
Rubin v. Irving Trust Co., 1953, 305 N.Y. 288, 305, 113 N.E.2d 424, 431;
defendant does not dispute this, and relies on New York decisions. I shall
follow the apparent agreement of the parties as to the applicable law.
   Since the word "chicken" standing alone is ambiguous, I turn first to
see whether the contract itself offers any aid to its interpretation. Plaintiff
says the 1½-2 lbs. birds necessarily had to be young chicken since the older
birds do not come in that size, hence the 2½-3 lbs. birds must likewise be
young. This is unpersuasive — a contract for "apples" of two different sizes
could be filled with different kinds of apples even though only one species
came in both sizes. Defendant notes that the contract called not simply for
chicken but for "US Fresh Frozen Chicken, Grade A, Government
Inspected." It says the contract thereby incorporated by reference the
Department of Agriculture's regulations, which favor its interpretation;
I shall return to this after reviewing plaintiff's other contentions.
   The first hinges on an exchange of cablegrams which preceded execution of the formal contracts. The negotiations leading up to the contracts
were conducted in New York between defendant's secretary, Ernest R.
Bauer, and a Mr. Stovicek, who was in New York for the Czechoslovak
government at the World Trade Fair. A few days after meeting Bauer at
the fair, Stovicek telephoned and inquired whether defendant would be
interested in exporting poultry to Switzerland. Bauer then met with

---

   24. The Court notes the contract provision whereby any disputes are to be settled by
arbitration by the New York Produce Exchange; it treats the parties' failure to avail themselves of this remedy as an agreement eliminating that clause of the contract.

Stovicek, who showed him a cable from plaintiff dated April 26, 1957, announcing that they "are buyer" of 25,000 lbs. of chicken 2½-3 lbs. weight, Cryovac packed, grade A Government inspected, at a price up to 33¢ per pound, for shipment on May 10, to be confirmed by the following morning, and were interested in further offerings. After testing the market for price, Bauer accepted, and Stovicek sent a confirmation that evening. Plaintiff stresses that, although these and subsequent cables between plaintiff and defendant, which laid the basis for the additional quantities under the first and for all of the second contract, were predominantly in German, they used the English word "chicken"; it claims this was done because it understood "chicken" meant young chicken whereas the German word, "Huhn," included both "Brathuhn" (broilers) and "Suppenhuhn" (stewing chicken), and that defendant, whose officers were thoroughly conversant with German, should have realized this. Whatever force this argument might otherwise have is largely drained away by Bauer's testimony that he asked Stovicek what kind of chickens were wanted, received the answer "any kind of chickens," and then, in German, asked whether the cable meant "Huhn" and received an affirmative response. Plaintiff attacks this as contrary to what Bauer testified on his deposition in March, 1959, and also on the ground that Stovicek had no authority to interpret the meaning of the cable. The first contention would be persuasive if sustained by the record, since Bauer was free at the trial from the threat of contradiction by Stovicek as he was not at the time of the deposition; however, review of the deposition does not convince me of the claimed inconsistency. As to the second contention, it may well be that Stovicek lacked authority to commit plaintiff for prices or delivery dates other than those specified in the cable; but plaintiff cannot at the same time rely on its cable to Stovicek as its dictionary to the meaning of the contract and repudiate the interpretation given the dictionary by the man in whose hands it was put. . . .

[P]laintiff's next contention is that there was a definite trade usage that "chicken" meant "young chicken." Defendant showed that it was only beginning in the poultry trade in 1957, thereby bringing itself within the principle that "when one of the parties is not a member of the trade or other circle, his acceptance of the standard must be made to appear" by proving either that he had actual knowledge of the usage or that the usage is "so generally known in the community that his actual individual knowledge of it may be inferred." 9 Wigmore, Evidence (3d ed. 1940) §2464. Here there was no proof of actual knowledge of the alleged usage; indeed, it is quite plain that defendant's belief was to the contrary. In order to meet the alternative requirement, the law of New York demands a showing that "the usage is of so long continuance, so well established, so notorious, so universal and so reasonable in itself, as that the presumption is violent that the parties contracted with reference to it, and made it a part of their agreement." Walls v. Bailey, 1872, 49 N.Y. 464, 472-473.

Plaintiff endeavored to establish such a usage by the testimony of three witnesses and certain other evidence. Strasser, resident buyer in New York for a large chain of Swiss cooperatives, testified that "on chicken I would definitely understand a broiler." However, the force of this testimony was considerably weakened by the fact that in his own transactions the witness, a careful businessman, protected himself by using "broiler" when that was what he wanted and "fowl" when he wished older birds. Indeed, there are some indications, dating back to a remark of Lord Mansfield, Edie v. East India Co., 2 Burr. 1216, 1222 (1761), that no credit should be given "witnesses to usage, who could not adduce instances in verification." 7 Wigmore, Evidence (3d ed. 1940), §1954. . . . While Wigmore thinks this goes too far, a witness' consistent failure to rely on the alleged usage deprives his opinion testimony of much of its effect. Niesielowski, an officer of one of the companies that had furnished the stewing chicken to defendant, testified that "chicken" meant "the male species of the poultry industry. That could be a broiler, a fryer or a roaster," but not a stewing chicken; however, he also testified that upon receiving defendant's inquiry for "chickens," he asked whether the desire was for "fowl or frying chickens" and, in fact, supplied fowl, although taking the precaution of asking defendant, a day or two after plaintiff's acceptance of the contracts in suit, to change its confirmation of its order from "chickens," as defendant had originally prepared it, to "stewing chickens." Dates, an employee of Urner-Barry Company, which publishes a daily market report on the poultry trade, gave it as his view that the trade meaning of "chicken" was "broilers and fryers." In addition to this opinion testimony, plaintiff relied on the fact that the Urner-Barry service, the Journal of Commerce, and Weinberg Bros. & Co. of Chicago, a large supplier of poultry, published quotations in a manner which, in one way or another, distinguish between "chicken," comprising broilers, fryers and certain other categories, and "fowl," which, Bauer acknowledged, included stewing chickens. This material would be impressive if there were nothing to the contrary. However, there was, as will now be seen.

Defendant's witness Weininger, who operates a chicken eviscerating plant in New Jersey, testified "Chicken is everything except a goose, a duck, and a turkey. Everything is a chicken, but then you have to say, you have to specify which category you want or that you are talking about." Its witness Fox said that in the trade "chicken" would encompass all the various classifications. Sadina, who conducts a food inspection service, testified that he would consider any bird coming within the classes of "chicken" in the Department of Agriculture's regulations to be a chicken. The specifications approved by the General Services Administration include fowl as well as broilers and fryers under the classification "chickens." Statistics of the Institute of American Poultry Industries use the phrases "Young chickens" and "Mature chickens," under the general heading "Total chickens." [A]nd the Department of Agriculture's daily and weekly price reports avoid use of the word "chicken" without specification.

Defendant advances several other points which it claims affirmatively support its construction. Primary among these is the regulation of the Department of Agriculture, 7 C.F.R. 70.300-70.370, entitled, "Grading and Inspection of Poultry and Edible Products Thereof" and in particular 70.301 which recited:

Chickens. The following are the various classes of chickens:
  (a) Broiler or fryer. . . .
  (b) Roaster. . . .
  (c) Capon. . . .

(d) Stag. . . .
(e) Hen or stewing chicken or fowl. . . .
(f) Cock or old rooster. . . .

Defendant argues, as previously noted, that the contract incorporated these regulations by reference. Plaintiff answers that the contract provision related simply to grade and Government inspection and did not incorporate the Government definition of "chicken," and also that the definition in the Regulations is ignored in the trade. However, the latter contention was contradicted by Weininger and Sadina; and there is force in defendant's argument that the contract made the regulations a dictionary, particularly since the reference to Government grading was already in plaintiff's initial cable to Stovicek.

Defendant makes a further argument based on the impossibility of its obtaining broilers and fryers at the 33¢ price offered by plaintiff for the 2½-3 lbs. birds. There is no substantial dispute that, in late April, 1957, the price for 2½-3 lbs. broilers was between 35 and 37¢ per pound, and that when defendant entered into the contracts, it was well aware of this and intended to fill them by supplying fowl in these weights. It claims that plaintiff must likewise have known the market since plaintiff had reserved shipping space on April 23, three days before plaintiff's cable to Stovicek, or, at least, that Stovicek was chargeable with such knowledge. It is scarcely an answer to say, as plaintiff does in its brief, that the 33¢ price offered by the 2½-3 lbs. "chickens" was closer to the prevailing 35¢ price for broilers than to the 30¢ at which defendant procured fowl. Plaintiff must have expected defendant to make some profit — certainly it could not have expected defendant deliberately to incur a loss.

Finally, defendant relies on conduct by the plaintiff after the first shipment had been received. On May 28 plaintiff sent two cables complaining that the larger birds in the first shipment constituted "fowl." Defendant answered with a cable refusing to recognize plaintiff's objection and announcing "We have today ready for shipment 50,000 lbs. chicken 2-3 lbs. 25,000 lbs. broilers 1-2 lbs.," these being the goods procured for shipment under the second contract, and asked immediate answer "whether we are to ship this merchandise to you and whether you will accept the merchandise." After several other cable exchanges, plaintiff replied on May 29 "Confirm again that merchandise is to be shipped since resold by us if not enough pursuant to contract chickens are shipped the missing quantity is to be shipped within ten days stop we resold to our customers pursuant to your contract chickens grade A you have to deliver us said merchandise we again state that we shall make you fully responsible for all resulting costs."[25] Defendant argues that if plaintiff was sincere in thinking it was entitled to young chickens, plaintiff would not have allowed the shipment under the second contract to go forward, since the distinction between broilers and chickens drawn in defendant's cablegram must have made it clear that the larger birds would not be broilers. However, plaintiff answers that the cables show plaintiff was

25. These cables were in German; "chicken," "broilers" and, on some occasions, "fowl," were in English.

insisting on delivery of young chickens and that defendant shipped old ones at its peril. Defendant's point would be highly relevant on another disputed issue — whether if liability were established, the measure of damages should be the difference in market value of broilers and stewing chicken in New York or the larger difference in Europe, but I cannot give it weight on the issue of interpretation. Defendant points out also that plaintiff proceeded to deliver some of the larger birds in Europe, describing them as "poulets"; defendant argues that it was only when plaintiff's customers complained about this that plaintiff developed the idea that "chicken" meant "young chicken." There is little force in this in view of plaintiff's immediate and consistent protests.

When all the evidence is reviewed, it is clear that defendant believed it could comply with the contracts by delivering stewing chicken in the 2½-3 lbs. size. Defendant's subjective intent would not be significant if this did not coincide with an objective meaning of "chicken." Here it did coincide with one of the dictionary meanings, with the definition in the Department of Agriculture Regulations to which the contract made at least oblique reference, with at least some usage in the trade, with the realities of the market, and with what plaintiff's spokesman had said. Plaintiff asserts it to be equally plain that plaintiff's own subjective intent was to obtain broilers and fryers; the only evidence against this is the material as to market prices and this may not have been sufficiently brought home. In any event it is unnecessary to determine that issue. For plaintiff has the burden of showing that "chicken" was used in the narrower rather than in the broader sense, and this it has not sustained.

This opinion constitutes the Court's findings of fact and conclusions of law. Judgment shall be entered dismissing the complaint with costs.

REFERENCE: Barnett, §§3.3.2, 3.3.3
                        Farnsworth, §§7.7-7.11
                        Calamari & Perillo, §§3.9-3.14, 3.17
                        Murray, §§87-91

B.   FILLING GAPS IN THE TERMS

Courts and commentators often distinguish between *interpreting* terms that were expressly manifested between the parties and *supplying* terms when contracts are silent on a particular issue. The latter of these activities is sometimes called "gap-filling." When courts fill gaps in contracts, commentators traditionally have distinguished between those terms that are implied-in-fact and those that are implied-in-law. According to this distinction, *implied-in-fact* terms are those that the parties actually, albeit implicitly, have agreed to; so-called *implied-in-law* terms are thought to be imposed on parties without their consent. The Restatement (Second) of Contracts speaks instead of courts *supplying* terms.[26] Modern contract

---

26. See, e.g., Restatement (Second) of Contracts §204, infra, p. 392.

theorists have identified two types of judicially supplied gap-fillers: default rules and immutable rules. *Default rules* refer to those legal rules that the parties can avoid or vary by means of an express clause that differs from the term a court will otherwise supply by default. *Immutable rules*, by contrast, may not be varied by consent and will override any express clause to the contrary. According to this distinction, only some of the implied-in-law terms supplied by a court — those coming from immutable rules — are imposed on the parties without their consent. Like acceptance by silence, which we studied in Chapter 4, parties may have consented to those terms supplied by default rules by remaining silent and deferring to the law of contract.[27]

In each of the cases in this section, there has been a manifestation of mutual assent but some important terms are missing. Because courts traditionally were — and to some extent remain — reluctant to fill gaps in parties' agreements, the question that then arises is whether this incomplete manifestation is sufficient to warrant legal enforcement. For this reason, the issues discussed in these cases concern both (a) *when* a manifestation of assent is sufficient to justify concluding that a legally enforceable contract exists and (b) *how* to interpret the assent that *has* been manifested.

1.   Agreements to Agree

STUDY GUIDE: Can you distinguish this situation from that of Nebraska Seed v. Harsh or Leonard v. PepsiCo? Does Judge Easterbrook's reasoning in Empro v. Ball-Co (p. 275) suggest that this case is rightly or wrongly decided? How could you argue that the dissenting opinion by Judge Crane actually supports Judge Cardozo's holding? Which judge was favoring freedom of contract? Or does this dispute reveal a potential conflict between two aspects of contractual freedom. Would this case be decided the same way under the Uniform Commercial Code §§2-204, 2-305, and 2-309? Does the approach of §2-204 represent a rejection or affirmation of freedom of contract?

---

27. This inference from the parties' silence assumes that they or their lawyers are knowledgeable about the default rules of contract — or that a reasonable person would have such knowledge. While such an assumption may be warranted in the case of commercial *repeat players* who engage repeatedly in similar transactions, it is less likely to be accurate in the case of *one-shot players* such as typical consumers. Therefore, for run-of-the-mill transactions, if we are to infer from the silence of consumers (and other one-shot players) their consent to the terms supplied by the default rules of contract law, then the term supplied must conform to the reasonable expectations of most consumers (as opposed to the expectations of the repeat players with whom they are contracting). On the other hand, when transactions are sufficiently extraordinary or large — for example, the sale or purchase of a home or business — to warrant consultation of an attorney for even one-shot players, then we may infer from their silence a consent to whatever terms are supplied by the default rules in effect in that jurisdiction.

SUN PRINTING & PUBLISHING ASS'N v.
REMINGTON PAPER & POWER CO.
Court of Appeals of New York,
235 N.Y. 338, 139 N.E. 470 (1923)

Action by Sun Printing & Publishing Association against the Remington Paper & Power Company, Inc. From an order of the Appellate Division . . . which reversed an order of the Special Term denying plaintiff's motion for judgment on the pleadings, and granted said motion, defendant, by permission, appeals. The following question was certified: "Does the complaint state facts sufficient to constitute a cause of action?" Order of Appellate Division reversed, and that of Special Term affirmed, with costs in the Appellate Division, and question answered.

CARDOZO, J.* Plaintiff agreed to buy and defendant to sell 1,000 tons of paper per month during the months of September, 1919, to December, 1920, inclusive, 16,000 tons in all. Sizes and quality were adequately described. Payment was to be made on the 20th of each month for all paper shipped the previous month. The price for shipments in September, 1919, was to be $3.73 3/4 per 100 pounds, and for shipments in October, November and December, 1919, $4 per 100 pounds.

For the balance of the period of this agreement the price of the paper and length of terms for which such price shall apply shall be agreed upon by and between the parties hereto fifteen days prior to the expiration of each period for which the price and length of term thereof have been previously agreed upon, said price in no event to be higher than the contract price for newsprint charged by the Canadian Export Paper Company to the large consumers, the seller to receive the benefit of any differentials in freight rates.

Between September, 1919, and December of that year, inclusive, shipments were made and paid for as required by the contract. The time then arrived when there was to be an agreement upon a new price and upon the term of its duration. The defendant in advance of that time gave notice that the contract was imperfect, and disclaimed for the future an obligation to deliver. Upon this, the plaintiff took the ground that the price was to be ascertained by resort to an established standard. It made demand that during each month of 1920 the defendant deliver 1,000 tons of paper at the contract price for newsprint charged by the Canadian Export Paper Company to the large consumers, the defendant to receive the benefit of any differentials in freight rates. The demand was renewed month by month till the expiration of the year. This action has been brought to recover the ensuing damage.

---

* *Benjamin Nathan Cardozo* (1870-1938) is among the best-known judges who ever sat on an American court. He was educated at Columbia University (A.B., A.M.). He practiced law from 1891 to 1914, when he was designated to serve as a judge on the New York Court of Appeals. In 1927, he was elected Chief Judge of the Court of Appeals. Judge Cardozo was subsequently appointed to the Supreme Court of the United States, where he served from 1932 until his death. Justice Cardozo was also an author; his most noted work, The Nature of the Judicial Process, was published in 1921. — C.R.

Seller and buyer left two subjects to be settled in the middle of December and at unstated intervals thereafter. One was the price to be paid. The other was the length of time during which such price was to govern. Agreement as to the one was insufficient without agreement as to the other. If price and nothing more had been left open for adjustment, there might be force in the contention that the buyer would be viewed, in the light of later provisions, as the holder of an option. . . . This would mean that in default of an agreement for a lower price, the plaintiff would have the privilege of calling for delivery in accordance with a price established as a maximum. The price to be agreed upon might be less, but could not be more than "the contract price for newsprint charged by the Canadian Export Paper Company to the large consumers." The difficulty is, however, that ascertainment of this price does not dispense with the necessity for agreement in respect of the term during which the price is to apply. Agreement upon a maximum payable this month or today is not the same as an agreement that it shall continue to be payable next month or tomorrow. Seller and buyer understood that the price to be fixed in December for a term to be agreed upon, would not be more than the price then charged by the Canadian Export Paper Company to the large consumers. They did not understand that if during the term so established the price charged by the Canadian Export Paper Company was changed, the price payable to the seller would fluctuate accordingly. This was conceded by plaintiff's counsel on the argument before us. The seller was to receive no more during the running of the prescribed term, though the Canadian maximum was raised. The buyer was to pay no less during that term, though the maximum was lowered. In brief, the standard was to be applied at the beginning of the successive terms, but once applied was to be maintained until the term should have expired. While the term was unknown, the contract was inchoate.

The argument is made that there was no need of an agreement as to time unless the price to be paid was lower than the maximum. We find no evidence of this intention in the language of the contract. The result would then be that the defendant would never know where it stood. The plaintiff was under no duty to accept the Canadian standard. It does not assert that it was. What it asserts is that the contract amounted to the concession of an option. Without an agreement as to time, however, there would be not one option, but a dozen. The Canadian price today might be less than the Canadian price tomorrow. Election by the buyer to proceed with performance at the price prevailing in one month would not bind it to proceed at the price prevailing in another. Successive options to be exercised every month would thus be read into the contract. Nothing in the wording discloses the intention of the seller to place itself to that extent at the mercy of the buyer. Even if, however, we were to interpolate the restriction that the option, if exercised at all, must be exercised only once, and for the entire quantity permitted, the difficulty would not be ended. Market prices in 1920 happened to rise. The importance of the time element becomes apparent when we ask ourselves what the seller's position would be if they had happened to fall. Without an agreement as to time, the maximum would be lowered from one shipment to another with every reduction of the standard. With such an agreement, on the other hand, there would be stability and certainty. The parties attempted to guard against the contingency of failing to come together as to price. They did not guard against the contingency of failing to come together as to time. Very likely they thought the latter contingency so remote that it could safely be disregarded. In any event, whether through design or through inadvertence, they left the gap unfilled. The result was nothing more than "an agreement to agree." . . . Defendant "exercised its legal right" when it insisted that there was need of something more. . . . The right is not affected by our appraisal of the motive. . . .

We are told that the defendant was under a duty, in default of an agreement, to accept a term that would be reasonable in view of the nature of the transaction and the practice of the business. To hold it to such a standard is to make the contract over. The defendant reserved the privilege of doing its business in its own way, and did not undertake to conform to the practice and beliefs of others. . . . We are told again that there was a duty, in default of other agreement, to act as if the successive terms were to expire every month. The contract says they are to expire at such intervals as the agreement may prescribe. There is need, it is true, of no high degree of ingenuity to show how the parties, with little change of language, could have framed a form of contract to which obligation would attach. The difficulty is that they framed another. We are not at liberty to revise while professing to construe.

We do not ignore the allegation of the complaint that the contract price charged by the Canadian Export Paper Company to the large consumers "constituted a definite and well defined standard of price that was readily ascertainable." The suggestion is made by members of the court that the price so charged may have been known to be one established for the year, so that fluctuation would be impossible. If that was its character, the complaint should so allege. The writing signed by the parties calls for an agreement as to time. The complaint concedes that no such agreement has been made. The result, prima facie, is the failure of the contract. In that situation, the pleader has the burden of setting forth the extrinsic circumstances, if there are any, that make agreement unimportant. There is significance, moreover, in the attitude of counsel. No point is made in brief or in argument that the Canadian price, when once established, is constant through the year. On the contrary, there is at least a tacit assumption that it varies with the market. The buyer acted on the same assumption when it renewed the demand from month to month, making tender of performance at the prices then prevailing. If we misconceive the course of dealing, the plaintiff by amendment of its pleading can correct our misconception. The complaint as it comes before us leaves no escape from the conclusion that agreement in respect of time is as essential to a completed contract as agreement in respect of price. The agreement was not reached, and the defendant is not bound.

The question is not here whether the defendant would have failed in the fulfillment of its duty by an arbitrary refusal to reach any agreement as to time after notice from the plaintiff that it might make division of the terms in any way it pleased. No such notice was given so far as the complaint discloses. The action is not based upon a refusal to treat with the defendant and attempt to arrive at an agreement. Whether any such theory of liability would be tenable we need not now inquire. Even if the plaintiff might have stood upon the defendant's denial of obligation as amounting to such a refusal, it did not elect to do so. Instead, it gave its own construction to the contract, fixed for itself the length of the successive terms, and thereby coupled its demand with a condition which there was no duty to accept. . . . We find no allegation of readiness and offer to proceed on any other basis. The condition being untenable, the failure to comply with it cannot give a cause of action.

The order of the Appellate Division should be reversed and that of the Special Term affirmed, with costs in the Appellate Division and in this court, and the question certified answered in the negative.

CRANE, J.* (dissenting). I cannot take the view of this contract that has been adopted by the majority. The parties to this transaction beyond question thought they were making a contract for the purchase and sale of 16,000 tons rolls news print. The contract was upon a form used by the defendant in its business, and we must suppose that it was intended to be what it states to be, and not a trick or device to defraud merchants. It begins by saying that in consideration of the mutual covenants and agreements herein set forth the Remington Paper and Power Company, Incorporated, of Watertown, state of New York, hereinafter called the seller, agrees to sell and hereby does sell and the Sun Printing and Publishing Association of New York city, state of New York, hereinafter called the purchaser, agrees to buy and pay for and hereby does buy the following paper, 16,000 tons rolls news print. The sizes are then given. Shipment is to be at the rate of 1,000 tons per month to December, 1920, inclusive. There are details under the headings consignee, specifications, price and delivery, terms, miscellaneous, cores, claims, contingencies, cancellations.

Under the head of miscellaneous comes the following:

The price agreed upon between the parties hereto, for all papers shipped during the month of September, 1919, shall be $3.73 3/4 per hundred pounds gross weight of rolls on board cars at mills.

The price agreed upon between the parties hereto for all shipments made during the months of October, November and December, 1919, shall be $4.00 per hundred pounds gross weight of rolls on board cars at mills.

For the balance of the period of this agreement the price of the paper and length of terms for which such price shall apply shall be agreed upon by and between the parties hereto fifteen days prior to the expiration of each period for which the price and length of term thereof has been previously agreed upon, said price in no event to be higher than the contract price for newsprint charged by the Canadian Export Paper Company to the large consumers, the seller to receive the benefit of any differentials in freight rates.

It is understood and agreed by the parties hereto that the tonnage specified herein is for use in the printing and publication of the various editions of the Daily and Sunday New York Sun, and any variation from this will be considered a breach of contract.

* *Frederick Evan Crane* (1869-1947) was educated at Columbia University (LL.B.). He practiced law in Brooklyn, New York, from 1890 to 1901, before starting his judicial career as a county judge in Kings County. In 1906, Judge Crane was elected to the Supreme Court of New York; he was appointed to the Court of Appeals in 1917. He was elected to a full term on the Court of Appeals in 1920 and became Chief Judge of that body in 1934. Judge Crane retired at the end of 1939. — C.R.

After the deliveries for September, October, November and December, 1919, the defendant refused to fix any price for the deliveries during the subsequent months, and refused to deliver any more paper. It has taken the position that this document was no contract, that it meant nothing, that it was formally executed for the purpose of permitting the defendant to furnish paper or not, as it pleased.

Surely these parties must have had in mind that some binding agreement was made for the sale and delivery of 16,000 tons rolls of paper, and that the instrument contained all the elements necessary to make a binding contract. It is a strain upon reason to imagine the paper house, the Remington Paper and Power Company, Incorporated, and the Sun Printing and Publishing Association, formally executing a contract drawn up upon the defendant's prepared form which was useless and amounted to nothing. We must, at least, start the examination of this agreement by believing that these intelligent parties intended to make a binding contract. If this be so, the court should spell out a binding contract, if it be possible.

I not only think it possible, but think the paper itself clearly states a contract recognized under all the rules at law. It is said that the one essential element of price is lacking; that the provision above quoted is an agreement to agree to a price, and that the defendant had the privilege of agreeing or not, as it pleased; that if it failed to agree to a price there was no standard by which to measure the amount the plaintiff would have to pay. The contract does state, however, just this very thing. Fifteen days before the first of January, 1920, the parties were to agree upon the price of the paper to be delivered thereafter, and the length of the period for which such price should apply. However, the price to be fixed was not "to be higher than the contract price for newsprint charged by the Canadian Export Paper Company to large consumers." Here surely was something definite. The 15th day of December arrived. The defendant refused to deliver. At that time there was a price for newsprint charged by the Canadian Export Paper Company. If the plaintiff offered to pay this price, which was the highest price the defendant could demand, the defendant was bound to deliver. This seems to be very clear.

But while all agree that the price on the 15th day of December could be fixed, the further objection is made that the period during which that price should continue was not agreed upon. There are many answers to this.

We have reason to believe that the parties supposed they were making a binding contract; that they had fixed the terms by which one was required to take and the other to deliver; that the Canadian Export Paper Company price was to be the highest that could be charged in any event. These things being so, the court should be very reluctant to permit a defendant to avoid its contract. . . .

On the 15th of the fourth month, the time when the price was to be fixed for subsequent deliveries, there was a price charged by the Canadian Export Paper Company to large consumers. As the defendant failed to agree upon a price, made no attempt to agree upon a price and deliberately broke its contract, it could readily be held to deliver the rest of the paper, a thousand rolls a month, at this Canadian price. There is nothing in the complaint which indicates that this is a fluctuating price, or that the price of paper as it was on December 15th was not the same for the remaining twelve months.

Or we can deal with this contract, month by month. The deliveries were to be made 1,000 tons per month. On December 15th 1,000 tons could have been demanded. The price charged by the Canadian Export Paper Company on the 15th of each month on and after December 15th, 1919, would be the price for the thousand ton delivery for that month.

Or again, the word as used in the miscellaneous provision quoted is not "price," but "contract price" — "in no event to be higher than the contract price." Contract implies a term or period and if the evidence should show that the Canadian contract price was for a certain period of weeks or months, then this period could be applied to the contract in question.

Failing any other alternative, the law should do here what it has done in so many other cases, apply the rule of reason and compel parties to contract in the light of fair dealing. It could hold this defendant to deliver its paper as it agreed to do, and take for a price the Canadian Export Paper Company contract price for a period which is reasonable under all the circumstances and conditions as applied in the paper trade.

To let this defendant escape from its formal obligations when any one of these rulings as applied to this contract would give a practical and just result is to give the sanction of law to a deliberate breach. (Wood v. Duff-Gordon, 222 N.Y. 88. . . .)

For these reasons I am for the affirmance of the courts below.

Hiscock, C.J., Pound, McLaughlin, and Andrews, JJ., concur with Cardozo, J. Order reversed, etc.

Reread: Restatement (Second) of Contracts §33 (p. 272)
            Uniform Commercial Code, §§2-204 (p. 272), 2-305
            (p. 273) & 2-309 (p. 274)

Reference: Barnett, §3.4

RESTATEMENT (SECOND) OF CONTRACTS

Study Guide: Can you see any meaningful difference between the wording of U.C.C. §2-204 and that of Restatement (Second) §204?

§34. CERTAINTY AND CHOICE OF TERMS; EFFECT OF PERFORMANCE OR RELIANCE

(1) The terms of a contract may be reasonably certain even though it empowers one or both parties to make a selection of terms in the course of performance.

(2) Part performance under an agreement may remove uncertainty and establish that a contract enforceable as a bargain has been formed.

(3) Action in reliance on an agreement may make a contractual remedy appropriate even though uncertainty is not removed.

§204. SUPPLYING AN OMITTED ESSENTIAL TERM

When the parties to a bargain sufficiently defined to be a contract have not agreed with respect to a term which is essential to a determination of their rights and duties, a term which is reasonable in the circumstances is supplied by the court.

2. Illusory Promises

STUDY GUIDE: In the next three cases, the issue is whether the promise of one of the parties is "illusory" because it leaves complete discretion to perform or not in the hands of the purported promisor. In each of the cases, the court fills this gap in the manifestation of assent by supplying an obligation to exercise this discretion in "good faith." Here we are concerned only with how and why the court fills the gap, in contrast with Sun Printing, *where it refused to do so. In Chapter 12, we shall study what a duty of good faith performance requires and when it is breached.*

NEW YORK CENTRAL IRON WORKS CO. v. UNITED STATES RADIATOR CO.
Court of Appeals of New York,
174 N.Y. 331, 66 N.E. 967 (1903)

O'BRIEN, J.* This action was to recover damages for the breach of a written executory contract between the parties for the sale and delivery of goods. The contract was an open one as to the quantity of goods which the defendant was to deliver. The defendant became bound to furnish the plaintiff "with their entire radiator needs for the year 1899" on the terms and at the prices specified, as to which there is no dispute. The defense is that the defendant filled all orders from the plaintiff until forty-eight thousand feet of radiation had been delivered, which was as much as the plaintiff had ever required before, but that the plaintiff continued to send in orders that would bring the aggregate for the year up to one hundred thousand feet, and these orders in excess of the amount delivered the defendant refused to fill. The defendant construed the contract as calling for only the usual amount of goods and not materially exceeding the quantity delivered in any one year before under a similar contract. The defendant claimed in its answer that there was a mutual mistake in framing the contract, since the intention was to limit the quantity of goods to be delivered to an amount such as had been called for in previous years of similar dealing between the parties, and asked that the contract be reformed in this respect.

---

* *Denis O'Brien* (1837-1909) served as the Mayor of Watertown, New York, and as the Attorney General of the State of New York (1884-1887) before being elected in 1889 an associate judge of the New York Court of Appeals, where he sat until 1907. His son, John F. O'Brien, was also appointed as an associate judge. — R.B.

The proof given at the trial was directed to that issue, but the facts were found against the defendant and the defense failed. The contention of the learned counsel for the defendant now is that such a limitation was necessarily imported into the contract and it should be construed as containing it. We think that the contention cannot be sustained. The defendant bound the plaintiff to deal exclusively in goods to be ordered from it under the contract and to enlarge and develop the market for the defendant's wares so far as possible. Hence, the parties left the contract open and indefinite as to the quantity of goods that the plaintiff might order from time to time. It is quite probable that this controversy originated in a circumstance which the defendant, at least, had not anticipated or provided for. After the execution of the contract there was a large advance in the market price of iron and the manufactured products of iron, and, consequently, the value and selling price of the goods covered by this contract advanced in the same or possibly in a greater proportion. The *needs* of the plaintiff could be indefinitely enlarged when the market was in such a condition as to enable it to undersell its competitors in the same business in consequence of a favorable contract with the manufacturer of the goods. If a party contracts for goods upon a rising market he is ordinarily entitled to such profits as may accrue to him by reason of a prudent or favorable contract. We cannot perceive that there is any error of law in this judgment, although the plaintiff has recovered a considerable sum in damages for the breach. . . .

But we do not mean to assert that the plaintiff had the right under the contract to order goods to any amount. Both parties in such a contract are bound to carry it out in a reasonable way. The obligation of good faith and fair dealing towards each other is implied in every contract of this character. The plaintiff could not use the contract for the purpose of speculation in a rising market since that would be a plain abuse of the rights conferred and something like a fraud upon the seller. The plaintiff's claim for damages in this case might have been affected by the condition and customs of the trade, and any breach of good faith on its part could be taken into account. In such a case it would be competent for the defendant to plead and prove facts to show that the orders were in excess of the plaintiff's reasonable needs and were not justified by the conditions of the business or the customs of the trade. In other words, that the plaintiff was not acting reasonably or in good faith, but using the contract for a purpose not within the contemplation of the parties; that is to say, for speculative as distinguished from regular and ordinary business purposes. But no defense of this kind was either pleaded or proved in this case, and so the judgment must be affirmed, with costs.

PARKER, C.J., BARTLETT, HAIGHT, VANN, CULLEN and WERNER, JJ., concur.
Judgment affirmed.

STUDY GUIDE: *When reading the next case pay close attention to U.C.C. §2-306(1), which was relied upon by the court. Does Comment 2, quoted by the court, operate in the same manner as the section? Can these two passages be rendered consistent with each other?*

EASTERN AIR LINES, INC. v. GULF OIL CORP.
United States District Court, Southern District of Florida,
415 F. Supp. 429 (1975)

JAMES LAWRENCE KING, D.J.*

Eastern Air Lines, Inc., hereafter Eastern, and Gulf Oil Corporation, hereafter Gulf, have enjoyed a mutually advantageous business relationship involving the sale and purchase of aviation fuel for several decades.

This controversy involves the threatened disruption of that historic relationship and the attempt, by Eastern, to enforce the most recent contract between the parties. On March 8, 1974 the correspondence and telex communications between the corporate entities culminated in a demand by Gulf that Eastern must meet its demand for a price increase or Gulf would shut off Eastern's supply of jet fuel within fifteen days.

Eastern responded by filing its complaint with this court, alleging that Gulf had breached its contract . . . and requesting preliminary and permanent mandatory injunctions requiring Gulf to perform the contract in accordance with its terms. By agreement of the parties, a preliminary injunction preserving the status quo was entered on March 20, 1974, requiring Gulf to perform its contract and directing Eastern to pay in accordance with the contract terms, pending final disposition of the case.

Gulf answered Eastern's complaint, alleging that the contract was not a binding requirements contract, was void for want of mutuality, and, furthermore, was "commercially impracticable" within the meaning of Uniform Commercial Code §2-615; Fla. Stat. §§672.614 and 672.615. . . .

The extraordinarily able advocacy by the experienced lawyers for both parties produced testimony at the trial from internationally respected experts who described in depth economic events that have, in recent months, profoundly affected the lives of every American.

The Contract

On June 27, 1972, an agreement was signed by the parties which, as amended, was to provide the basis upon which Gulf was to furnish jet fuel to Eastern at certain specific cities in the Eastern system. Said agreement supplemented an existing contract between Gulf and Eastern which, on June 27, 1972, had approximately one year remaining prior to its expiration.

The contract is Gulf's standard form aviation fuel contract and is identical in all material particulars with the first contract for jet fuel, dated 1959, between Eastern and Gulf and, indeed, with aviation fuel contracts antedating the jet age. It is similar to contracts in general use in the aviation fuel

---

*James Lawrence King (1927-†) studied at the University of Florida (B.A., J.D.). After serving in the United States Air Force, he began practicing law in 1955. He served as judge of the 11th Judicial Circuit at Dade County (1964-1970), temporary associate justice on the Supreme Court of Florida (1965) and the U.S. Court of Appeals (second, third, and fourth circuits, 1965-1968), before being appointed judge of the U.S. District Court for the Southern District of Florida in 1970. King served as temporary judge of the U.S. Court of Appeals for the Fifth Circuit (1977, 1978) and then as Chief Judge of the U.S. District Court (1984-1991). He is now a senior district judge. — K.T.

trade. The contract was drafted by Gulf after substantial arm's length negotiation between the parties. Gulf approached Eastern more than a year before the expiration of the then-existing contracts between Gulf and Eastern, seeking to preserve its historic relationship with Eastern. Following several months of negotiation, the contract, consolidating and extending the terms of several existing contracts, was executed by the parties in June, 1972, to expire January 31, 1977.

Against this factual background we turn to a consideration of the legal issues.

I

THE "REQUIREMENTS" CONTRACT

Gulf has taken the position in this case that the contract between it and Eastern is not a valid document in that it lacks mutuality of obligation; it is vague and indefinite; and that it renders Gulf subject to Eastern's whims respecting the volume of jet fuel Gulf would be required to deliver to the purchaser Eastern.

The contract talks in terms of fuel "requirements."[28] The parties have interpreted this provision to mean that any aviation fuel purchased by Eastern at one of the cities covered by the contract, must be bought from Gulf. Conversely, Gulf must make the necessary arrangements to supply Eastern's reasonable good faith demands at those same locations. This is the construction the parties themselves have placed on the contract and it has governed their conduct over many years and several contracts.

In early cases, requirements contracts were found invalid for want of the requisite definiteness, or on the grounds of lack of mutuality. Many such cases are collected and annotated at 14 A.L.R. 1300.

As reflected in the foregoing annotation, there developed rather quickly in the law the view that a requirements contract could be binding where the purchaser had an operating business. The "lack of mutuality" and "indefiniteness" were resolved since the court could determine the volume of goods provided for under the contract by reference to objective evidence of the volume of goods required to operate the specified business. Therefore, well prior to the adoption of the Uniform Commercial Code, case law generally held requirements contracts binding. See 26 A.L.R.2d 1099, 1139.

The Uniform Commercial Code, adopted in Florida in 1965, specifically approves requirements contracts in F.S. 672.306 (U.C.C. §2-306(1)).

(1) A term which measures the quantity by the output of the seller or the requirements of the buyer means such actual output or requirements as may occur in good faith, except that no quantity unreasonably disproportionate to any stated estimate or in the absence of a stated estimate to any normal or otherwise comparable prior output or requirements may be tendered or demanded.

28. "Gulf agrees to sell and deliver to Eastern, and Eastern agrees to purchase, receive and pay for their requirements of Gulf Jet A and Gulf Jet A-1 at the locations listed. . . ."

The Uniform Commercial Code Official Comment interprets §2-306(1) as follows:

> 2. Under this Article, a contract for output or requirements is not too indefinite since it is held to mean the actual good faith output or requirements of the particular party. Nor does such a contract lack mutuality of obligation since, under this section, the party who will determine quantity is required to operate his plant or conduct his business in good faith and according to commercial standards of fair dealing in the trade so that his output or requirements will approximate a reasonably foreseeable figure. Reasonable elasticity in the requirements is expressly envisaged by this section and good faith variations from prior requirements are permitted even when the variation may be such as to result in discontinuance. A shut-down by a requirements buyer for lack of orders might be permissible when a shut-down merely to curtail losses would not. The essential test is whether the party is acting in good faith. Similarly, a sudden expansion of the plant by which requirements are to be measured would not be included within the scope of the contract as made but normal expansion undertaken in good faith would be within the scope of this section. One of the factors in an expansion situation would be whether the market price has risen greatly in a case in which the requirements contract contained a fixed price. Reasonable variation of an extreme sort is exemplified in Southwest Natural Gas Co. v. Oklahoma Portland Cement Co., 102 F.2d 630 (C.C.A. 10, 1939).

Some of the prior Gulf-Eastern contracts have included the estimated fuel requirements for some cities covered by the contract while others have none. The particular contract contains an estimate for Gainesville, Florida requirement.

The parties have consistently over the years relied upon each other to act in good faith in the purchase and sale of the required quantities of aviation fuel specified in the contract. During the course of the contract, various estimates have been exchanged from time to time, and, since the advent of the petroleum allocations programs, discussions of estimated requirements have been on a monthly (or more frequent) basis.[29]

The court concludes that the document is a binding and enforceable requirements contract.

STUDY GUIDE: We now turn from requirements *contracts to* exclusive dealings *contracts. Glance back at Judge Crane's opinion in* Sun Printing, *where he later relies on the next case. Was he correct to do so? In* Sun Printing, *did Cardozo change his mind about the approach he takes in the next case?*

---

29. A requirements contract under the U.C.C. may speak of "requirements" alone, or it may include estimates, or it may contain maximums and minimums. In any case, the consequences are the same, as Official Comments 2 and 3 indicate. Comment 2 is set out in the text above. Comment 3 provides:

> 3. If an estimate of output or requirements is included in the agreement, no quantity unreasonably disproportionate to it may be tendered or demanded. Any minimum or maximum set by the agreement shows a clear limit on the intended elasticity. In similar fashion, the agreed estimate is to be regarded as a center around which the parties intend the variation to occur.

WOOD v. LUCY, LADY DUFF-GORDON
Court of Appeals of New York,
222 N.Y. 88, 118 N.E. 214 (1917)

Appeal from a judgment entered April 24, 1917 upon an order of the Appellate Division of the Supreme Court in the first judicial department, which reversed an order of Special Term denying a motion by defendant for judgment in her favor upon the pleadings and granted said motion. . . .

CARDOZO, J. The defendant styles herself "a creator of fashions." Her favor helps a sale. Manufacturers of dresses, millinery and like articles are glad to pay for a certificate of her approval. The things which she designs, fabrics, parasols and what not, have a new value in the public mind when issued in her name. She employed the plaintiff to help her to turn this vogue into money. He was to have the exclusive right, subject always to her approval, to place her indorsements on the designs of others. He was also to have the exclusive right to place her own designs on sale, or to license others to market them. In return, she was to have one-half of "all profits and revenues" derived from any contracts he might make. The exclusive right was to last at least one year from April 1, 1915, and thereafter from year to year unless terminated by notice of ninety days. The plaintiff says that he kept the contract on his part, and that the defendant broke it. She placed her indorsement on fabrics, dresses and millinery without his knowledge, and withheld the profits. He sues her for the damages, and the case comes here on demurrer.

The agreement of employment is signed by both parties. It has a wealth of recitals. The defendant insists, however, that it lacks the elements of a contract. She says that the plaintiff does not bind himself to anything. It is true that he does not promise in so many words that he will use reasonable efforts to place the defendant's indorsements and market her designs. We think, however, that such a promise is fairly to be implied. The law has outgrown its primitive stage of formalism when the precise word was the sovereign talisman, and every slip was fatal. It takes a broader view today. A promise may be lacking, and yet the whole writing may be "instinct with an obligation," imperfectly expressed (Scott, J., in McCall Co. v. Wright, 133 App. Div. 62 . . .). If that is so, there is a contract.

The implication of a promise here finds support in many circumstances. The defendant gave an *exclusive* privilege. She was to have no right for at least a year to place her own indorsements or market her own designs except through the agency of the plaintiff. The acceptance of the exclusive agency was an assumption of its duties. . . . We are not to suppose that one party was to be placed at the mercy of the other. . . . Many other terms of the agreement point the same way. We are told at the outset by way of recital that

> the said Otis F. Wood possesses a business organization adapted to the placing of such indorsements as the said Lucy, Lady Duff-Gordon has approved.

The implication is that the plaintiff's business organization will be used for the purpose for which it is adapted. But the terms of the defendant's compensation are even more significant. Her sole compensation for the grant of an exclusive agency is to be one-half of all the profits resulting from the plaintiff's efforts. Unless he gave his efforts, she could never get anything. Without an implied promise, the transaction cannot have such business "efficacy as both parties must have intended that at all events it should have" (Bowen, L.J., in *The Moorcock*, 14 P.D. 64, 68). But the contract does not stop there. The plaintiff goes on to promise that he will account monthly for all moneys received by him, and that he will take out all such patents and copyrights and trademarks as may in his judgment be necessary to protect the rights and articles affected by the agreement. It is true, of course, as the Appellate Division has said, that if he was under no duty to try to market designs or to place certificates of indorsement, his promise to account for profits or take out copyrights would be valueless. But in determining the intention of the parties, the promise *has* a value. It helps to enforce the conclusion that the plaintiff *had* some duties. His promise to pay the defendant one-half of the profits and revenues resulting from the exclusive agency and to render accounts monthly, was a promise to use reasonable efforts to bring profits and revenues into existence. For this conclusion, the authorities are ample. . . .

The judgment of the Appellate Division should be reversed, and the order of the Special Term affirmed, with costs in the Appellate Division and in this court.

CUDDEBACK, MCLAUGHLIN and ANDREWS, JJ., concur; HISCOCK, C.J., CHASE and CRANE, JJ., dissent.

Biographical Background: Who Was Lucy, Lady Duff-Gordon?

STUDY GUIDE: *Although Judge Cardozo spoke rather condescendingly of the defendant's occupation (she "styles herself 'a creator of fashions' "), the excerpt that follows reveals Lady Duff-Gordon to be a woman of considerable accomplishment and fame. In addition to the authors' views of the significance of her life and accomplishments, I have included excerpts describing her activities during the period in which the lawsuit took place. (No mention of the case appears in this biography.) Following these is an excerpt from a different source that recounts the roles played by Lucy Lady Duff-Gordon and her husband Cosmo during the sinking of the* Titanic *in 1912. The character of Lady Duff-Gordon makes a brief appearance in the 1997 film* Titanic. *Coincidentally, in 1924, her colorful sister, author Elinor Glyn, was embroiled in another famous nautical incident aboard publisher William Randolph Hearst's yacht, which involved the mysterious death of one of the passengers, film pioneer Thomas Ince — an incident that was the subject of the film* The Cat's Meow, *released in 2002. Other guests included Hearst's longtime mistress, actress Marion Davies; actor Charlie Chaplin; and future Hollywood gossip columnist Louella Parsons.*

MEREDITH ETHERINGTON-SMITH & JEREMY PILCHER, THE "IT" GIRLS: LUCY, LADY DUFF-GORDON, THE COUTURIÈRE "LUCILE," AND ELINOR GLYN, ROMANTIC NOVELIST xiii-xiv, 174-178 (NEW YORK: HARCOURT BRACE JOVANOVICH, 1986):   The purpose of this biography is to reveal the truth behind Elinor Glyn's self-constructed legend and to contrast it — as she was contrasted in life — with the less durable reputation of her equally formidable sister Lucy Lady Duff Gordon, better known as the couturière Lucile. Legends endure, but reputations are more fragile and "Lucile" has been largely forgotten by fashion historians.

Both women were remarkable. Typical children of mid-Victorian middle class notions of "polite" up-bringing, they were repressed and lonely when young. But through circumstance and force of personality, they were unwittingly instrumental in announcing a more liberated age for women. Elinor wrote about female sensuality, illicit passion and a relationship between an older, dominant woman and a younger, dominated man. Her sister gave these attitudes outward form in the shape of feathery trailing chiffon tea-dresses, worn sans corset over rose-pink chiffon underwear.

They came into their own in the extravagant hey-day of Edwardian England, a period which prized maturity and savoir-faire in a woman, and they were typical of the age in their over-heated excessiveness and in their extravagance. They dealt in mystery; in love-letters; in emeralds worn with clouds of purple chiffon; in secret passion. Silk roses festooned their drawing rooms and boudoirs, which were among the first to be decorated in a manner inspired by the last years of the eighteenth century. They surrounded themselves with sensation: the smell of gardenias and tuberoses; the adoration of young men; the romance of escaping to foreign lands.

To their contemporaries they were fascinating because they embodied an entirely individual sense of heightened reality, whether in the way they dressed, in the way they decorated their surroundings, or in what they said, wrote or designed.

The success they achieved in their chosen metiers would have been outstanding in any age; considering the restrictive mood of the late Victorian age, when they both began their careers, it was little less than miraculous. So was the fact that — though each earned her own living (and supported her husband and children) — they were accepted by society in an era when to be in trade or to write risqué novels was virtually a sentence of social suicide for a "lady." That they were both "ladies" was never questioned by their contemporaries, although their antecedents were far less grand than they persuaded their peers to believe.

These antecedents, and the sisters' escape from them, played a vital part in shaping these very diverse women. So did a shadowy figure who is as much a subject of this biography as Elinor and Lucy — their mother. Had it not been for Mrs. Kennedy's determination and her support of her two daughters, they would never have succeeded as they did. Mrs. Kennedy was the centre of their lives: their prop and their critic, the one person they could never deceive. They were competitive, one with another, and never more so than in the tom-tiddler's game they played to come first in her affections. She never failed them and she inspired them to survive and to triumph over defeat.

Lucy and Elinor were temperamentally so different that they could never really get on with each other. Lucy was the Red Queen, Elinor the White. Lucy loved dramas and arguments. Elinor loved solitude, peace and good manners. Nonetheless their lives were inextricably entwined and have a curious interior relationship.

Lucy's frail cobweb creations are now in museums. Elinor's novels are primarily of interest to students of the early years of the century. But the sisters' sense of adventure and daring, their courage and their wonderful follies, cannot be gainsaid. They were the first of a new self-determined breed of woman who came into her own after the First World War. . . .

Early in 1915, encouraged by her continuing success, Lucy took much bigger premises in New York, moving Lucile ["The Maison Lucile," as she called her couturière business establishment] from its original location on 36th Street to a former private house on the corner of 57th Street and Fifth Avenue. In this, she was following the move her society clients had begun to make up town, a trend spear-headed by Bessie Marbury's and Elsie de Wolfe's move to Sutton Place. This new house served as both showroom and couture ateliers for Lucy's private clients. Lucy herself avoided visiting it, for she had lost interest in her couture clientèle and had begun to have very grandiose ideas, fired by her missionary ideal, about making wholesale fashions for the masses.[30]

In late 1915, she took in American partners to finance this new venture, out of which she confidently expected to make millions of dollars. She exhibited a hundred and fifty of her designs at a wholesale show in New York. It was not a success, but this did not deter Lucy, whose attitude toward failure was to ignore it.

She now did most of her work at her model studio, which occupied a loft just below the Flatiron building on Lower Fifth Avenue. Here, life was very different from the scented hush of the couture house. The space was taken up, not by eighteenth-century chairs, but by worktables, dressmaker's dummies and seamstresses. Partitions at the back of the studio gave the four assistant designers a bit of privacy as they sketched ideas. Next door was a room in which the mannequins relaxed in their grey crêpe kimonos while waiting to be called for fittings. Across the front of the loft, looking out across Fifth Avenue, was a suite of grey-panelled rooms littered with rainbows of colour where, in the words of Howard Greer, "the outstanding phenomenon of her day conceived, changed, worried and perfected the gowns that defined new trends."

No one entered this holy of holies unbidden. In the corridor outside, employees walked on tiptoe and greeted each other in whispers that genius might be left undisturbed. Lucy was so impressed with a sense of her own importance that no other tenant in the building was allowed to enter one of its public lifts when she was in it. Fortunately for the other tenants, she came down to the studio only three or four times a week, arriving around ten o'clock in the morning from the house in Mamaroneck. . . .

A Lucile opening was an important social event in New York and, although Lucy made no secret of her preference for Haute Bohemia, this did not deter her smart customers. On opening day, these clients were met by a social secretary, dressed in the inevitable grey taffetas, who checked the admittance cards. Once they were all seated, Lucy swept in a royal last and sat in a chair placed forward from the front row facing the chiffon-draped

30. [Later, Lady Duff Gordon would design fashions to be sold in the Sears Roebuck catalogue. The project was not a commercial success. — EDS.]

stage. This was the cue for the string orchestra to play a waltz and for another Lucile show to begin.

In the autumn of 1915, the society audience saw the beginnings of a change in the Lucile silhouette. For the past three years she had designed clothes with a strong oriental influence. But now she abandoned her draped, straight line with a high bust and hobbled skirts, and went back in history to 1828 to create elaborately frilled, bowed and furred dresses with a natural waist, invariably accentuated by a sash and a shorter bell-shaped skirt. Her choice of materials changed, too. Abandoning the lamé and brocades she had been using, Lucy returned to much lighter, transparent fabrics. She used lace as priceless as it was delicate and then re-embroidered it; chiffon; georgette; muslin. She based her designs on paintings of the era, and her trimmings became more and more lavish. These dresses were made in many diaphanous layers, one colour on top of another creating a shimmering diffused effect. She had been using black velvet edged with rhinestones to trim dresses; now she started to use bands of fur or jewelled embroidery. . . .

Lucy's list of clients read like a combination of the Social Register, a silent film set and Broadway. The Dolly sisters dressed identically in lace crinolines, Irene Castle in drifts of chiffon and pailettes, Isadora Duncan in Greek draperies, Norma Talmadge in ruffled net. Vanderbilts and Astors jostled Lily Langtry and Fanny Brice in the elegant fitting rooms.

Mary Pickford, just starting her long career in films, was employed by Lucy for the then enormous sum of one thousand dollars to advertise a Lucile dress — encouraged by her venal mother. But as she grew more successful Mary too became a paying client and, when she went on a bond-selling tour of America late in 1917, wore a specially-tailored khaki uniform designed for her by Lucy.

Not content with her continuing success as a couturière, Lucy launched herself into a secondary career as a fashion journalist — however, she wrote only of her own collections. Most of these articles appeared in *Harper's Bazaar*, owned by William Randolph Hearst. Here is what she had to say about fashion, late in 1915:

> The boudoir fantasies of a dainty woman are ever a delightful theme: I write of them with pleasure. This winter, the dressing gown is a dream of coziness and beauty. I'm using for its outer surface a soft, silky material called "Zenana" which I like with a blanket-like wool of matching colour. Broad bands of satin bind the neck, sleeves, front panels and hem. Pink in its lovely range of flesh to deepest rose, I use for these robes intimes, as well as the paler hues.
>
> For the belle who would seek her couch without delay, but would wait awhile before she sleeps, I have designed a dear little bed jacket of warm velvet. In deep rose bordered with ermine, it is inexpressibly adorable. . . . You ask me for a prophecy; I rejoice in the newest trend of fashion — the return of frills and bows and furbelows. . . .

. . . In spring, 1916, Lucy departed from the normal practice of showing her collection in her salon and mounted a series of *tableaux vivants* in a theatre. The tableaux were called *Fleurette's Dream at Péronne* and concerned the trials and tribulations of "Fleurette" in the war-torn town of Péronne in France. . . .

The tableaux starred the statuesque Dolores [one of her famous mannequins from London] and were presented at the Little Theatre. Billie Burke, then married to Florenz Ziegfeld, was a customer and brought her husband to one of the matinees. So impressed was Ziegfeld that he asked Lucy whether he could employ Dolores (dressed, naturally, by Lucile) and several other mannequins in his current *Follies*. "But they do not know how to sing or dance, let alone talk," Lucy is reputed to have said. Ziegfeld assured her that all they would have to do would be to walk around and carry her beautiful costumes, just as they had in *Péronne*.

Thus was born a great American tradition: the Showgirl. Dolores became the most beautiful star the *Follies* ever featured, taking the town by storm dressed as "Empress of Fashion, The Discourager of Hesitancy," in a scene entitled "Ladies of Fashion — An Episode in Chiffon." So successful was this innovation that Lucy designed the *Follies* costumes until 1920. She created siren gowns, Egyptian costumes (for a Cleopatra scene), Chu Chin Chow Chinese costumes; she dressed showgirls as bouquets of flowers, as nautch girls. She dressed the leading ladies: Irene Castle, Billie Burke, Marion Davies (Hearst's mistress), Peggy Hopkins Joyce (the blonde showgirl who was one of the prototypes for Lorelei Lee in *Gentlemen Prefer Blondes*). The *Follies* gave Lucy a new outlet for her fantasy designs.

STUDY GUIDE: In testimony not discussed below, Lady Duff-Gordon said she initially refused to board a lifeboat and had "quite made up my mind that I was going to be drowned." Later, the lifeboat crew discussed the danger of "suction" should the Titanic *sink. She heard "terrible cries" before the sinking, but afterward "I never heard a cry. . . . My impression was that there was absolute silence." Nor did anyone suggest they go back for survivors.*

STEPHEN COX, MYSTERIES OF THE TITANIC, LIBERTY, MAY 1997, P. 24:   The most arresting non-rescue story is the little epic of lifeboat No. 1. Among the boat's occupants were two persons aptly named for the ludicrous parts they were to play — Sir Cosmo Duff Gordon and his wife Lady Duff Gordon, best known as "Lucile," a fashionable dress designer. With them was her secretary, Miss Francatelli. The lifeboat was not exactly filled. It could accommodate 40 people, but through the haste of the supervising officer it had been lowered with only twelve. Seven of the twelve were crewmen.

On entering No. 1, Sir Cosmo somehow found his accommodations cramped. He did not realize, he told Lord Mersey,[31] that "there was plenty of room in the boat for more people." He admitted that it did occur to him "that people in the water could be saved by a boat," but it was evidently not his boat he was thinking of. The idea of personally trying to save anybody

_____

31. [Elsewhere in his article (on p. 17), Cox writes: "Lord Mersey, a canny old judge who looked like the little man in the Monopoly game, presided over the court [convened by the British Board of Trade] as Wreck Commissioner. He was assisted by Attorney-General Sir Rufus Isaacs and attorneys representing White Star, the third-class passengers, labor unions, and various other interests. The record of the 36-day British inquiry is a monument of intelligence and fairness. Mersey and the lawyers practicing before him showed distinguished analytical ability. . . ." — EDS.]

never crossed his mind. He was too busy worrying about his wife, who became violently seasick as soon as No. 1 touched the (absolutely calm) waters of the ocean: "We had a rather serious evening, you know." Sir Cosmo noticed that someone was rowing the lifeboat, but he didn't know where, and he didn't know why, and he didn't care. He speculated that the rowers wanted to make enough noise to "stop the sound" of the dying.

Crewman Charles Hendrickson testified that he suggested going back, but his suggestion was quashed by the Duff Gordons, or by Lady Duff Gordon and Miss Francatelli: "they were scared to go back for fear of being swamped." So Hendrickson stopped suggesting.

> *Mersey:* Then am I to understand that because two of the passengers said it would be dangerous you all kept your mouths shut and made no attempt to rescue anybody?
> *Hendrickson:* That is right, Sir.

The only rescue that the crewmen of No. 1 attempted was the rescue of the Duff Gordons from the British inquiry. The crew's attachment to the Duff Gordon family had been improved by charitable contributions of five pounds each, delivered by Sir Cosmo on the decks of the [rescue ship] *Carpathia*. Most of the crew showed up to testify that *nobody* in No. 1 had wanted to go back. But why not?

> *Mersey:* I want to know why? What was it that you were afraid of? —
> *George Symons (crewman in charge of No. 1):* I was not afraid of anything; I was only afraid of endangering the lives of the people I had on the boat.
> How? What was the danger? The ship had gone to the bottom. She was no longer a danger. What were you afraid of? — At that time the ship had only just disappeared.
> Never mind, it had disappeared, and had gone down to the bottom, two miles down, or something like that. What were you afraid of? — I was afraid of the swarming.
> Of what? — Of the swarming people — swamping the boat.
> That is it, that is what you were afraid of. You were afraid that there were too many people in the water? — Yes.
> And that your boat would be swamped? — Yes.
> I am not satisfied at all.

And no wonder. It would have been quite a job for anybody to crawl out of the freezing water into a lightly loaded boat standing high in the water, unless he had had help from the people inside. Boat No. 1 could hardly have been swamped by the human "swarm"; it would have had plenty of time to turn back before being engulfed.

Biographical and Relational Background: Who Was Otis Wood and Why Did He Omit a "Best Efforts" Clause?

STUDY GUIDE: *If the deal was the one suggested below by Professor Goldberg, can you think of any reason why an experienced business woman such as Lucy (who, as Professor Goldberg shows, also had experienced business advisors) would have put herself, in Cardozo's words, "at the mercy" of Otis Wood in so one-sided an arrangement? Is there any other way of construing the contract? Hint: Suppose it was a unilateral contract? Would that interpretation be consistent with all its terms?*

VICTOR GOLDBERG, FRAMING CONTRACT LAW: AN ECONOMIC PERSPECTIVE 45-46, 52-53, 55-58, 63 (2006): Otis's father was a three-time mayor of New York. He amassed a considerable fortune early in his career in shipping and later in New York real estate. He married Otis's mother (his third wife) when he was forty-eight and she was sixteen. . . . In 1867, Wood and Boss Tweed secured a nomination to the New York Supreme Court for Albert Cardozo. Shortly thereafter Cardozo ruled in Wood's favor in the so-called *Wood's Lease* case (New York v. Wood), a controversial decision in which Wood was accused of procuring a lucrative lease arrangement from the city by fraud or bribery; the judge rejected the city's evidence on technical grounds, giving a directed verdict for Wood. (Cardozo subsequently resigned from the bench when confronted with impeachment for misbehavior in other cases.) A half-century later Albert's son, Benjamin, found in favor of Fernando's son, Otis. Fernando spent the last two decades of his life in the House of Representatives, eventually becoming chairman of the Ways and Means Committee. He died while still in office in 1881. . . .

Born in the same year that Albert Cardozo decided the *Wood's Lease* case, Otis died a bachelor in 1939. His business career spanned almost fifty years, but from the few shards of historical material available, we can't say whether the promotion/agency activity promised to Lucy was a core part of his business or merely a sideline. . . . He began his career writing for the *Philadelphia Inquirer*. His first known employment in New York was as cofounder of a firm engaged in lithography in Manhattan in 1892. Within a few years, business directories have him listed as both a lithographer in Manhattan and a publisher in Staten Island (his home). In 1901, the Types Publishing Company, of which he was one of three directors, was dissolved. (The other two directors were his younger brother Benjamin and Benjamin's brother-in-law E. F. Hutton, who founded the eponymous brokerage house a few years later.) . . .

We have no idea how many other clients Wood had, but of one we are certain. Less than two years before entering into the contract with Lucy, Otis entered into an agreement with Rose O'Neill to promote her Kewpie dolls, and two months before the Lucy deal, he sued O'Neill for breach. O'Neill was a prominent illustrator with hundreds of illustrations in *Puck* and other major periodicals. She also did illustrations for advertisements, Kellogg's Corn Flakes and Jell-O being two of her more significant clients. She illustrated books, wrote books, and wrote poetry. In 1907, she divorced her second husband, the author and playwright Harry Leon Wilson. . . . Two years later, she published drawings of Kewpies along with some of her poetry in the *Ladies Home Journal*. They were a big hit, indeed a phenomenon. Rose had copyright and trademark rights in the Kewpies, and in March 1913 she obtained patent rights. Weeks later she entered into her contract with Otis, and shortly thereafter production of Kewpie dolls commenced. Kewpies were everywhere. As she wrote in her autobiography, there were "Kewpies holding candlesticks, ash-trays, ink-pots, umbrellas, puppies, kittens, rabbits, Easter-chicks. They were painted on dishes and cards, fans, and all sorts of objects. They appeared on buttons, jewelry, children's clothing, toy furniture." . . .

The initial contract with O'Neill was a three-year exclusive contract dated March 19, 1913. . . . Some of the terms were similar to those in the Lucy contract. Wood had the exclusive right to negotiate sale and disposition of Kewpies, to represent her in all publicity in connection with Kewpies, and to promote sales, licenses, and rights for "Kewpie forms and figures made up into all kinds and classes of merchandise." . . . While in the Lucy contract all revenues were to go first to Wood, who would then pay Lucy her share, in the Kewpie contract all revenues were to be paid to a named trustee, who would then disburse the funds to both Wood and O'Neill.

Two other differences were of much greater significance, putting a new spin on the Lucy contract. First, the Kewpie contract included a "best efforts" term: He "will use his best efforts and devote so much of his time as shall be necessary diligently to promote the sale or licenses and rights for said 'Kewpies' in all materials, and that in agreements for the manufacture and sale of said 'Kewpies' which he shall negotiate, he, as her agent, will use his best efforts to obtain, and will obtain, for [her] the highest possible royalty." The existence of an explicit "best efforts" promise in the Kewpie contract makes Cardozo's implication of such a promise in Lucy's contract (entered into only one year later) at least problematic.

Second, the compensation arrangement was different and somewhat more complicated. . . . [F]or all . . . business obtained by Wood, he would get 40%. For business obtained by her without his assistance, Wood would get 20%; the burden of proof as to who generated the business would be on her. The clear implication of this formula is that "exclusive" refers only to other agents. O'Neill had the right under the agreement to enter into deals directly, but if she did so, Wood would still get 20% of the revenue. The exclusivity appears to mean only that she was not free to work with another agent to generate business. The significant point is that even though the contract labeled Wood's right "exclusive," it clearly presumed that Rose O'Neill was free to develop business on her own. . . .

It appears that Wood's performance in the first term of the contract was satisfactory. . . . Wood succeeded in placing a number of commercial endorsements, including a new Manhattan retail outlet, Bedell Fashion Shop, Essanay Film Studios, Mallinson Silks, the Model Brassiere Co., Heatherbloom Petticoats, Hartmann Trunks, and O'Conner-Goldberg Shoes. Things began to unravel in year two when Lucy bypassed Wood and directly entered into a contract with Sears, Roebuck & Co. The Sears ad announcing the new arrangement appeared in the October 1916 *Ladies Home Journal*. The Sears deal was an attempt to reach an entirely new market. The advertisement, in the form of an interview, gives Lucy's rationale:

> Yes, of course, I have designed gowns for most women of note in the world, I suppose — Queen Mary of England, Queen Victoria of Spain, the Duchess of Roxborough, for coronation ceremonies and millionaires' weddings — and I shall continue to do this through the "Lucile" establishments in London,

Paris, New York, and Chicago. But what of that? It is nothing. This other it has been my one dream to make clothes for the women who have not hundreds of dollars to spend on one frock. They have not come to me naturally because they could not through the house of "Lucile." But now these men in Chicago who have grasped my idea are giving us our opportunity to reach each other. I am going to design clothes for the women who have twenty-five or fifty or ten dollars to spend. The garments will be made up under my personal supervision and this great Chicago house of yours will then pass them on to these women. Oh, I can help them so much with their clothes! Won't you tell them so for me?

There is some controversy as to how successful the Sears move was. The two extreme versions are embodied in the following quotation. . . . Sears sold about $90,000 worth of Lucy's dresses in six months at about $26,000 less than it paid for them. While the venture ultimately turned out poorly for Sears, it was, at least initially, pretty good for Lucy. . . . [I]n the first season her collection almost completely sold out, but that it did less well in the second (and last) season.

Wood's complaint cited Lucy's contracts with Sears and Chalmers Motors. The logic behind her deal with Sears is easy to understand. Less obvious is her deal with Chalmers Motors. What, one might reasonably ask, does a dress designer have to contribute to automobile sales? Her answer is in the opening lines of a full-page advertisement in the *Saturday Evening Post* signed by Lucy:

I have been engaged by the Chalmers Motor Company to select materials for furnishing the interiors of their new closed cars.

As for myself — I am not interested in the exterior of this Chalmers town car. If external things interest you, glance at the picture.

Neither am I concerned in the least with the motor. I know not and care not whether it be what mechanical men call a six, a 22, or a 3400. *Les détails m'ennuie*. I leave them to Monsieur Chauffeur.

My only interest is in the vitally important thing — the interior. All important because there is where I have to sit. It is my sun-parlor on wheels, and if colors clash or upholstery fabric grates on my nerves, how am I to love the car?

Nothing can recompense for poor taste.

The Sears dresses were marketed to the middle class; they were generally in the $20-45 price range. Given that per capita annual income at the time was $450 (Johnston and Williamson 2002), this was a considerable part of the farmer's wife's budget, which probably explains why Sears dropped the line. Nonetheless, it was at least within the reach of the mass market. Not so the Chalmers car with its list price of $2,480. Those able to buy such a car could, no doubt, leave the mechanical details to Monsieur Chauffeur. . . .

Before starting this project, I had assumed that in the Lucy era, parties did not write "best efforts" or similar language into agreements. I believe that among contracts scholars I was not alone. The fact that Wood had a "best efforts" clause in the earlier Kewpie contract puts matters in a different light. Why imply a particular level of effort when Wood chose to exclude an express promise? What can we infer from the absence of the "best efforts" clause in Lucy's contract? Had the two contracts been otherwise identical, we could be confident that the omission was deliberate. Wood, we could reasonably conclude, modified his way of doing business in response to problems that surfaced during the Kewpie litigation. The two contracts, however, are not the same. It is possible that the hand that drafted the Lucy contract knew of neither the Kewpie language nor the Kewpie dispute. I think it more likely than not that the Lucy contract was informed by the Kewpie experience, but we will never know for sure. Assuming this to be so, the absence of "best efforts" was most likely deliberate, an attempt to get the benefits of the arrangement while shielding Wood from the potential exposure. O'Neill used the "best efforts" clause as the basis for her counterclaim, although it is possible that Wood did not know of nor anticipate the counterclaim, since O'Neill's response was not filed until May 8, about six weeks after the Lucy contract. Nonetheless, it is at least plausible that by eliminating the clause, Wood would have hoped to shield himself from a counterclaim (and the bargaining leverage inherent in a plausible counterclaim). On the basis of the Kewpie contract, I would be willing to draw the negative inference that the absence of any mention of effort in the contract was deliberate and that Cardozo was wrong to find that any level of effort was implied.

SALES CONTRACTS: THE UNIFORM COMMERCIAL CODE

§2-306. OUTPUT, REQUIREMENTS AND EXCLUSIVE DEALINGS

(1) A term which measures the quantity by the output of the seller or the requirements of the buyer means such actual output or requirements as may occur in good faith, except that no quantity unreasonably disproportionate to any stated estimate or in the absence of a stated estimate to any normal or otherwise comparable prior output or requirements may be tendered or demanded.

(2) A lawful agreement by either the seller or the buyer for exclusive dealing in the kind of goods concerned imposes unless otherwise agreed an obligation by the seller to use best efforts to supply the goods and by the buyer to use best efforts to promote their sale.

OFFICIAL COMMENT

5. Subsection (2), on exclusive dealing, makes explicit the commercial rule embodied in the Act under which the parties to such contracts are held to have impliedly, even when not expressly, bound themselves to use reasonable diligence as well as good faith in their performance of the contract. Under such contracts the exclusive agent is required, although no express commitment has been made, to use reasonable effort and due diligence in the expansion of the market or the promotion of the product, as the case may be. The principal is expected under such a contract to refrain from supplying any other dealer or agent within the exclusive territory. An exclusive dealing agreement brings into play all of the good faith aspects of the output and requirement problems of subsection (1). It also raises questions of insecurity and right to adequate assurance under this Article.

REFERENCE: Barnett, §3.4.2
                    Farnsworth, §§7.15-7.17
                    Calamari & Perillo, §§3.14-3.17
                    Murray, §91

C.   IDENTIFYING THE TERMS OF THE AGREEMENT

1.   Form Contracts or "Contracts of Adhesion"

We now turn our attention to the issue of form contracts, which are sometimes referred to pejoratively as "contracts of adhesion." Form contracts are ubiquitous in modern commerce, yet have long been the subject of concern from contracts scholars. In light of the fact that they are so often written by one of the parties and are unread by the other, such contracts challenge our notions of assent. And as we shall see in the next section, when the form used by one party conflicts with the form used by the other, we are faced with the problem of identifying which terms govern. Many see adhesion contracts as closely related to the doctrine of unconscionability, which we shall study in Chapter 16. There is reason to keep these topics distinct, however, because the theoretical and practical problems of form contracts can exist even when the circumstances that are thought to make an agreement unconscionable do not. These problems are examined by the U.S. Supreme Court in the next, much-discussed case.

STUDY GUIDE: Does the Court enforce the terms in the form contract in the same manner as any other contract terms? Where does Justice Stevens in dissent think the majority goes wrong?

CARNIVAL CRUISE LINES v. SHUTE
United States Supreme Court,
499 U.S. 585 (1991)

Justice BLACKMUN* delivered the opinion of the Court.
In this admiralty case we primarily consider whether the United States Court of Appeals for the Ninth Circuit correctly refused to enforce a forum-

---

* Harry Andrew Blackmun (1908-1999) grew up in Minneapolis and St. Paul, Minnesota, and was a childhood friend of future U.S. Supreme Court Chief Justice Warren Burger. (Before their judicial opinions sharply diverged, they were once dubbed "the Minnesota twins.") He attended Harvard Law School and graduated in 1932. That year, he won admission to the Minnesota bar and clerked for Judge John B. Sanborn of the U.S. Court of Appeals for the Eighth Circuit. In 1934, he entered private practice, specializing in tax law and estate planning, and he later became resident counsel for the Mayo Clinic in Rochester, Minnesota. In 1959, President Dwight D. Eisenhower nominated Blackmun to fill a vacancy on the Eighth Circuit, where he served for over a decade. He was elevated to the Supreme Court by President Richard Nixon in 1970. During his tenure, he played an important role in several key decisions, most prominently by writing the majority opinion in Roe v. Wade in 1973. Justice Blackmun retired in 1994 and died five years later at his home in Virginia. — R.B.

selection clause contained in tickets issued by petitioner Carnival Cruise Lines, Inc., to respondents Eulala and Russel Shute.

The Shutes, through an Arlington, Wash., travel agent, purchased passage for a 7-day cruise on petitioner's ship, the *Tropicale*. Respondents paid the fare to the agent who forwarded the payment to petitioner's headquarters in Miami, Fla. Petitioner then prepared the tickets and sent them to respondents in the State of Washington. The face of each ticket, at its left-hand lower corner, contained this admonition:

SUBJECT TO CONDITIONS OF CONTRACT ON LAST PAGES **IMPORTANT!** PLEASE READ CONTRACT — ON LAST PAGES 1, 2, 3. App. 15

The following appeared on "contract page 1" of each ticket:

TERMS AND CONDITIONS OF PASSAGE CONTRACT TICKET

3. (a) The acceptance of this ticket by the person or persons named hereon as passengers shall be deemed to be an acceptance and agreement by each of them of all of the terms and conditions of this Passage Contract Ticket. . . .

8. It is agreed by and between the passenger and the Carrier that all disputes and matters whatsoever arising under, in connection with or incident to this Contract shall be litigated, if at all, in and before a Court located in the State of Florida, U.S.A., to the exclusion of the Courts of any other state or country. Id., at 16.

The last quoted paragraph is the forum-selection clause at issue.

Respondents boarded the *Tropicale* in Los Angeles, Cal. The ship sailed to Puerto Vallarta, Mexico, and then returned to Los Angeles. While the ship was in international waters off the Mexican coast, respondent Eulala Shute was injured when she slipped on a deck mat during a guided tour of the ship's galley. Respondents filed suit against petitioner in the United States District Court for the Western District of Washington, claiming that Mrs. Shute's injuries had been caused by the negligence of Carnival Cruise Lines and its employees. Id., at 4.

Petitioner moved for summary judgment, contending that the forum clause in respondents' tickets required the Shutes to bring their suit against petitioner in a court in the State of Florida. Petitioner contended, alternatively, that the District Court lacked personal jurisdiction over petitioner because petitioner's contacts with the State of Washington were insubstantial. The District Court granted the motion, holding that petitioner's contacts with Washington were constitutionally insufficient to support the exercise of personal jurisdiction. See App. to Pet. for Cert. 60a.

The Court of Appeals reversed. Reasoning that "but for" petitioner's solicitation of business in Washington, respondents would not have taken the cruise and Mrs. Shute would not have been injured, the court concluded that petitioner had sufficient contacts with Washington to justify the District Court's exercise of personal jurisdiction. 897 F.2d 377, 385-386 (CA9 1990).

Turning to the forum-selection clause, the Court of Appeals acknowledged that a court concerned with the enforceability of such a clause must begin its analysis with The Bremen v. Zapata Off Shore Co., 407 U.S. 1

(1972), where this Court held that forum selection clauses, although not "historically . . . favored," are "prima facie valid." Id., at 9-10. See 897 F.2d, at 388. The appellate court concluded that the forum clause should not be enforced because it "was not freely bargained for." Id., at 389. As an "independent justification" for refusing to enforce the clause, the Court of Appeals noted that there was evidence in the record to indicate that "the Shutes are physically and financially incapable of pursuing this litigation in Florida" and that the enforcement of the clause would operate to deprive them of their day in court and thereby contravene this Court's holding in *The Bremen.* 897 F.2d, at 389.

We granted certiorari to address the question whether the Court of Appeals was correct in holding that the District Court should hear respondents' tort claim against petitioner. 498 U.S. 807-808 (1990). Because we find the forum-selection clause to be dispositive of this question, we need not consider petitioner's constitutional argument as to personal jurisdiction. . . .

We begin by noting the boundaries of our inquiry. First, this is a case in admiralty, and federal law governs the enforceability of the forum-selection clause we scrutinize. . . . Second, we do not address the question whether respondents had sufficient notice of the forum clause before entering the contract for passage. Respondents essentially have conceded that they had notice of the forum-selection provision. Brief for Respondent 26 ("The respondents do not contest the incorporation of the provisions nor [sic] that the forum selection clause was reasonably communicated to the respondents, as much as three pages of fine print can be communicated."). Additionally, the Court of Appeals evaluated the enforceability of the forum clause under the assumption, although "doubtful," that respondents could be deemed to have had knowledge of the clause. See 897 F.2d, at 389 and n.11.

Within this context, respondents urge that the forum clause should not be enforced because, contrary to this Court's teachings in *The Bremen*, the clause was not the product of negotiation, and enforcement effectively would deprive respondents of their day in court. Additionally, respondents contend that the clause violates the Limitation of Vessel Owner's Liability Act, 46 U.S.C. App. §183c. We consider these arguments in turn. . . .

As an initial matter, we do not adopt the Court of Appeals' determination that a nonnegotiated forum-selection clause in a form ticket contract is never enforceable simply because it is not the subject of bargaining. Including a reasonable forum clause in a form contract of this kind well may be permissible for several reasons: First, a cruise line has a special interest in limiting the fora in which it potentially could be subject to suit. Because a cruise ship typically carries passengers from many locales, it is not unlikely that a mishap on a cruise could subject the cruise line to litigation in several different fora. . . . Additionally, a clause establishing *ex ante* the forum for dispute resolution has the salutary effect of dispelling any confusion about where suits arising from the contract must be brought and defended, sparing litigants the time and expense of pretrial motions to determine the correct forum, and conserving judicial resources that otherwise would be devoted to deciding those motions. . . . Finally, it stands to reason that passengers who purchase tickets containing a forum clause like that at issue in

[handwritten margin note: Yes, but [illegible] ... cases where they set injured]

this case benefit in the form of reduced fares reflecting the savings that the cruise line enjoys by limiting the fora in which it may be sued. . . .

It bears emphasis that forum-selection clauses contained in form passage contracts are subject to judicial scrutiny for fundamental fairness. In this case, there is no indication that petitioner set Florida as the forum in which disputes were to be resolved as a means of discouraging cruise passengers from pursuing legitimate claims. Any suggestion of such a bad-faith motive is belied by two facts: petitioner has its principal place of business in Florida, and many of its cruises depart from and return to Florida ports. Similarly, there is no evidence that petitioner obtained respondents' accession to the forum clause by fraud or overreaching. Finally, respondents have conceded that they were given notice of the forum provision and, therefore, presumably retained the option of rejecting the contract with impunity. In the case before us, therefore, we conclude that the Court of Appeals erred in refusing to enforce the forum-selection clause. . . .

[handwritten margin note: Reasoning]

The judgment of the Court of Appeals is reversed. *[handwritten: → Holding!]*

It is so ordered.

Justice STEVENS,* with whom Justice MARSHALL joins, dissenting.

The Court prefaces its legal analysis with a factual statement that implies that a purchaser of a Carnival Cruise Lines passenger ticket is fully and fairly notified about the existence of the choice of forum clause in the fine print on the back of the ticket. See ante, at 1524. Even if this implication were accurate, I would disagree with the Court's analysis. But, given the Court's preface, I begin my dissent by noting that only the most meticulous passenger is likely to become aware of the forum-selection provision. I have therefore appended to this opinion a facsimile of the relevant text, using the type size that actually appears in the ticket itself. A careful reader will find the forum-selection clause in the 8th of the 25 numbered paragraphs.

Of course, many passengers, like the respondents in this case, see ante, at 1524, will not have an opportunity to read paragraph 8 until they have actually purchased their tickets. By this point, the passengers will already have accepted the condition set forth in paragraph 16(a), which provides that "[t]he Carrier shall not be liable to make any refund to passengers in respect of . . . tickets wholly or partly not used by a passenger." Not

*John Paul Stevens (1920-†) received degrees from the University of Chicago (A.B.) and Northwestern University (J.D.). Admitted to the Illinois bar in 1947, he practiced law in Chicago (1948-1970) and was law clerk to U.S. Supreme Court Justice Wiley Rutledge (1947-1948). Appointed U.S. Circuit judge in 1970, Stevens was nominated by President Ford to be a Justice on the Supreme Court of the United States in 1975. He has also lectured on the law at Northwestern University School of Law (1953) and the University of Chicago Law School (1954-1955). He was decorated with a Bronze Star for his service with the U.S. Naval Reserve during World War II. After 34 years, 6 months, and 11 days of service on the Court, Stevens stepped down on June 29, 2010. He is now tied with Justice Stephen J. Field for second place on the all-time list for continuous service, superseded only by Justice William O. Douglas. — K.T.

knowing whether or not that provision is legally enforceable, I assume that
the average passenger would accept the risk of having to file suit in Florida
in the event of an injury, rather than canceling — without a refund — a
planned vacation at the last minute. The fact that the cruise line can reduce
its litigation costs, and therefore its liability insurance premiums, by forcing
this choice on its passengers does not, in my opinion, suffice to render the
provision reasonable. Cf. Steven v. Fidelity & Casualty Co. of New York, 58
Cal. 2d 862, 883, 27 Cal. Rptr. 172, 186, 377 P.2d 284, 298 (1962) (refusing
to enforce limitation on liability in insurance policy because insured "must
purchase the policy before he even knows its provisions"). . . .

   Clauses limiting a carrier's liability or weakening the passenger's right
to recover for the negligence of the carrier's employees come in a variety of
forms. Complete exemptions from liability for negligence or limitations on
the amount of the potential damage recovery, requirements that notice of
claims be filed within an unreasonably short period of time, provisions
mandating a choice of law that is favorable to the defendant in negligence
cases, and forum-selection clauses are all similarly designed to put a thumb
on the carrier's side of the scale of justice.[32]

   Forum selection clauses in passenger tickets involve the intersection of
two strands of traditional contract law that qualify the general rule that
courts will enforce the terms of a contract as written. Pursuant to the first
strand, courts traditionally have reviewed with heightened scrutiny the
terms of contracts of adhesion, form contracts offered on a take-or-leave
basis by a party with stronger bargaining power to a party with weaker
power. Some commentators have questioned whether contracts of adhesion can justifiably be enforced at all under traditional contract theory
because the adhering party generally enters into them without manifesting
knowing and voluntary consent to all their terms. See, e.g., Rakoff, Contracts of Adhesion: An Essay in Reconstruction, 96 Harv. L. Rev. 1173, 1179-
1180 (1983); Slawson, Mass Contracts: Lawful Fraud in California, 48 S. Cal.
L. Rev 1, 12-13 (1974); K. Llewellyn, The Common Law Tradition 370-371
(1960).

   The common law, recognizing that standardized form contracts
account for a significant portion of all commercial agreements, has taken
a less extreme position and instead subjects terms in contracts of adhesion
to scrutiny for reasonableness. Judge J. Skelly Wright set out the state of the
law succinctly in Williams v. Walker-Thomas Furniture Co., 121 U.S. App.
D.C. 315, 319-320, 350 F.2d 445, 449-450 (1965) (footnotes omitted):

> Ordinarily, one who signs an agreement without full knowledge of its terms
> might be held to assume the risk that he has entered a one-sided bargain. But

---

32. All these clauses will provide passengers who purchase tickets containing them
with a "benefit in the form of reduced fares reflecting the savings that the cruise line enjoys
by limiting [its exposure to liability]." See ante, at 594. Under the Court's reasoning, all these
clauses, including a complete waiver of liability, would be enforceable, a result at odds with
longstanding jurisprudence.

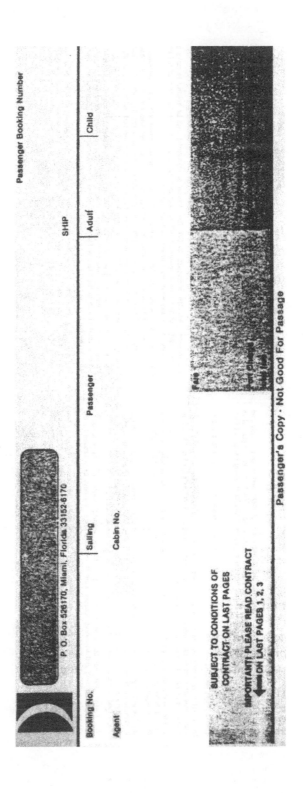

TERMS AND CONDITIONS OF PASSAGE CONTRACT TICKET

1 (a) Whenever the word "Carrier" is used in this Contract it shall mean and include, jointly and severally, the Vessel, its owners, operators, charterers and tenders. The term "Passenger" shall include the plural where appropriate, and all persons engaging to and/or traveling under this Contract. The masculine includes the feminine.

(b) The Master, Officers and Crew of the Vessel shall have the benefit of all of the terms and conditions of this contract.

2 This ticket is valid only for the person or persons named hereon as the passenger or passengers and cannot be transferred without the Carrier's consent written hereon. Passage money shall be deemed to be earned when paid and not refundable.

3 (a) The acceptance of this ticket by the person or persons named hereon as passengers shall be deemed to be an acceptance and agreement by each of them of all of the terms and conditions of this Passage Contract Ticket.

(b) The passenger admits a full understanding of the character of the Vessel and assumes all risk incident to travel and transportation and handling of passengers and cargo. The Vessel may or may not carry a ship's physician at the election of the Carrier. The fare includes full board, ordinary ship's food during the voyage, but no spirits, wine, beer or mineral waters.

4 The Carrier shall not be liable for any loss of life or personal injury or delay whatsoever wheresoever arising and howsoever caused even though the same may have been caused by the negligence or default of the Carrier or its servants or agents. No undertaking or warranty is given or shall be implied respecting the seaworthiness, fitness or condition of the Vessel. This exemption from liability shall extend to the employees, servants and agents of the Carrier and for this purpose this exemption shall be deemed to constitute a Contract entered into between the passenger and the Carrier on behalf of all persons who are or become from time to time its employees, servants or agents and all such persons shall to this extent be deemed to be parties to this Contract.

5 The Carrier shall not be liable for losses of valuables unless stored in the Vessel's safety depository and then not exceeding $500 in any event.

6 If the Vessel carries a surgeon, physician, masseuse, barber, hair dresser or manicurist, it is done solely for the convenience of the passenger and any such person in dealing with the passenger is not and shall not be considered in any respect whatsoever, as the employee, servant or agent of the Carrier and the Carrier shall not be liable for any act or omission of such person or those under his orders or assisting him with respect to treatment, advice or care of any kind given to any passenger.

The surgeon, physician, masseuse, barber, hair dresser or manicurist shall be entitled to make a proper charge for any service performed with respect to a passenger and the Carrier shall not be concerned in any way whatsoever in any such arrangement.

7 The Carrier shall not be liable for any claims whatsoever of the passenger unless full particulars thereof in writing be given to the Carrier or their agents within 185 days after the passenger shall be landed from the Vessel or in the case the voyage is abandoned within 185 days thereafter. Suit to recover any claim shall not be maintainable in any event unless commenced within one year after the date of the loss, injury or death.

8 It is agreed by and between the passenger and the Carrier that all disputes and matters whatsoever arising under, in connection with or incident to this Contract shall be litigated, if at all, in and before a Court located in the State of Florida, U.S.A., to the exclusion of the Courts of any other state or country.

9 The Carrier, in arranging for the service called for by all shore feature coupons or shore excursion tickets, acts only as agent for the holder thereof and assumes no responsibility and in no event shall be liable for any loss, damage, injury or delay to or of said person and/or baggage, property or effects in connection with said services, nor does Carrier guarantee the performance of any such service.

CONTRACT PAGE 1

when a party of little bargaining power, and hence little real choice, signs a commercially unreasonable contract with little or no knowledge of its terms, it is hardly likely that his consent, or even an objective manifestation of his consent, was ever given to all of the terms. In such a case the usual rule that the terms of the agreement are not to be questioned should be abandoned and the court should consider whether the terms of the contract are so unfair that enforcement should be withheld.

See also *Steven*, 58 Cal. 2d, at 879-883, 377 P.2d, at 295-297; Henningsen v. Bloomfield Motors, Inc., 32 N.J. 358, 161 A.2d 69 (1960).

The second doctrinal principle implicated by forum-selection clauses is the traditional rule that "contractual provisions, which seek to limit the place or court in which an action may . . . be brought, are invalid as contrary to public policy." See Dougherty, Validity of Contractual Provision Limiting Place or Court in Which Action May Be Brought, 31 A.L.R.4th 404, 409, §3 (1984). . . . Although adherence to this general rule has declined in recent years, . . . the prevailing rule is still that forum-selection clauses are not enforceable if they were not freely bargained for, create additional expense for one party, or deny one party a remedy. See 31 A.L.R.4th, at 409-438 (citing cases). A forum-selection clause in a standardized passenger ticket would clearly have been unenforceable under the common law . . . and, in my opinion, remains unenforceable under the prevailing rule today. . . .

I respectfully dissent.

COMPAGNO v. COMMODORE CRUISE LINE, LTD., UNITED STATES DISTRICT COURT, E.D. LOUISIANA, 1994 WL 462997 (1994): LIVAUDAIS, District Judge.* When *Shute* was decided in 1991, 46 U.S.C. §183c provided in pertinent part:

It shall be unlawful for the . . . owner of any vessel transporting passengers between ports of the United States . . . and a foreign port to insert in any . . . contract . . . any provision or limitation . . . (2) purporting [in the event of bodily injury] to lessen, weaken, or avoid the right of any claimant to a trial by court of competent jurisdiction on the question of liability for such loss or injury, or the measure of damages therefor. All such provisions or limitations contained in any such . . . contract . . . are declared to be against public policy and shall be null and void and of no effect.

In 1992, the House of Representatives added "any" immediately before the phrase "court of competent jurisdiction." Senator Breaux later remarked that the 1992 House addition

---

Marcel Livaudais, Jr. (1925-2009) served in the United States Navy (1943) before completing his education at Tulane University (B.A., J.D.). After being admitted to the Louisiana bar (1949), Livaudais began his practice in New Orleans, entering judicial service in 1977 as Magistrate Judge for the United States District Court for the Eastern District of Louisiana. Livaudais was appointed a District Court Judge in the same Court by President Ronald Reagan in 1984. He presided over several high-profile cases while on the bench, most notably the first two criminal trials of former Louisiana Governor Edwin Edwards. His favorite saying was "Love many, trust a few, and always paddle your own canoe." — L.R.

was intended by the House to overturn the Supreme Court decision in *Shute* by making it unlawful for cruise ship operators to use provisions in passenger contracts to limit a claimant's right to a trial in any court of competent jurisdiction.

140 CONG. REC. S1847-02, S1847 (daily ed. February 24, 1994). When "any" was deleted from 46 U.S.C. §183c in 1993, Congressman Studds of Massachusetts stated on the record: "Section 309 of H.R. 2150 should not be CONSTRUED to mean that a vessel owner may enforce a FORUM SELECTION CLAUSE in a passenger ticket." 139 CONG. REC. H10928-01, H10941 (daily ed. November 22, 1993). However, Congressman Studds' statement was later expressly disclaimed by the Senate.[33]

Accordingly, this Court is guided by the *Shute* decision. . . .

REFERENCE: Barnett, §§3.5.1-3.5.4
                  Farnsworth, §4.26
                  Calamari & Perillo, §§9.41-9.45
                  Murray, §98

---

33. Senator Stevens stated:

The House section-by-section analysis of the Coast Guard Authorization Act states that "SECTION 309 of H.R. 2150 should not be CONSTRUED to mean that a vessel owner may enforce a FORUM SELECTION CLAUSE in a passenger ticket." This statement contradicts what we intended. Our intent was that section 309 should be interpreted to allow vessels to enforce such clauses, as upheld by the Supreme Court in the *Shute* case.

140 Cong. Rec. S1847-02. S1847 (daily ed. February 24, 1994.)
    Senator Hollings remarked:

The other distinguished body made a mistake with regard to the statute. . . . The language in the Senate amendment restores the statute to exactly how it appeared prior to the Oceans Act of 1992.

    It is unfortunate that the House included an explanation of the Senate amendment, section 309, that differs so greatly from what we intended and from the clear meaning of the provision. We disagree with the November 22, 1993, statement made by the House regarding section 309 of the Coast Guard Authorization Act of 1993.

Id. Senator Breaux explained:

While it is perfectly legitimate for the Congress to overturn a Supreme Court decision within the bounds of the Constitution, we do not believe such changes should be made without notification to, and careful consideration by, the Members of Congress responsible for enactment of the legislation. As part of this consideration, we believe that the interested parties should have an opportunity to comment on any changes. At no time prior to the passage of the Oceans Act of 1992 was legislation introduced or did the House or Senate hold hearings on the cruise ship venue concern. . . . It is for this reason that the Senate supported a provision in the Coast Guard Authorization Act of 1993 to restore section 4283B to the wording as it read prior to the passage of the Oceans Act of 1992. Section 309 reinstates the Supreme Court decision in the *Shute* case as the applicable law for interpreting forum selection clauses.

Id.

CASPI v. MICROSOFT NETWORK
Superior Court of New Jersey, Appellate Division,
323 N.J. Super. 118, 732 A.2d 528 (1999)

KESTIN,* J.A.D. We are here called upon to determine the validity and enforceability of a forum selection clause contained in an on-line subscriber agreement of the Microsoft Network (MSN), an on-line computer service. The trial court granted defendants' motion to dismiss the complaint on the ground that the forum selection clause in the parties' contracts called for plaintiffs' claims to be litigated in the State of Washington. Plaintiffs appeal. We affirm. → Holding

The amended class action complaint in eighteen counts sought divers relief against two related corporate entities, The Microsoft Network, L.L.C. and Microsoft Corporation (collectively, Microsoft). Plaintiffs asserted various theories including breach of contract, common law fraud, and consumer fraud in the way Microsoft had "rolled over" MSN membership into more expensive plans. . . . Shortly thereafter, defendants moved to dismiss the amended complaint for lack of jurisdiction and improper venue by reason of the forum selection clause which, defendants contended, was in every MSN membership agreement and bound all the named plaintiffs and all members of the class they purported to represent. That clause, paragraph 15.1 of the MSN membership agreement, provided:

> This agreement is governed by the laws of the State of Washington, USA, and you consent to the exclusive jurisdiction and venue of courts in King County, Washington in all disputes arising out of or relating to your use of MSN or your MSN membership. . . .

Plaintiffs [contend that they] did not receive adequate notice of the forum selection clause, and therefore that the clause never became part of the membership contract which bound them. . . . Defendants respond by arguing that 1) in the absence of fraud, a contracting party is bound by the provisions of a form contract even if he or she never reads them; 2) this clause met all reasonable standards of conspicuousness; and 3) the sign-up process gave plaintiffs ample opportunity to review and reject the agreement. . . .

The holding in Carnival Cruise Lines v. Shute does not dispose of the notice question because the plaintiffs there had "essentially . . . conceded that they had notice of the forum-selection provision[,]" by stating that they "'[did] not contest . . . that the forum selection clause was reasonably

---

Howard H. Kestin (1937-†). A New Jersey native, he received his B.S. from St. Louis University (1959), his J.D. from Rutgers University School of Law (1962), and his LL.M. from the University of Virginia School of Law (1995). After entering the bar in 1962, clerking for the N.J. Supreme Court (1962-1963), and serving as a N.J. deputy attorney general (1963-1965), he worked in private practice, for the State Office of Legal Services to the Poor Program, and, as a member of the Rutgers faculty (1969-1978), he directed the New Jersey Institute for Continuing Legal Education. While at Rutgers, he also taught as an adjunct professor at Seton Hall University School of Law. In 1978, he became Chief Administrative Law Judge and director of the Office of Administrative Law (1978-1983). In 1983, he became judge on the Superior Court, first in the Chancery Division and, since 1992, in the Appellate Division where, in 2002, he was made Presiding Judge. In 2009, Judge Kestin retired from the bench. — R.B.

communicated to [them], as much as three pages of fine print can be communicated.'" The dissenting justices described the format in which the forum selection clause had been presented as "in the fine print on the back of the [cruise] ticket." (Stevens, J., dissenting).

The scenario presented here is different because of the medium used, electronic versus printed; but, in any sense that matters, there is no significant distinction. The plaintiffs in *Carnival* could have perused all the fine-print provisions of their travel contract if they wished before accepting the terms by purchasing their cruise ticket. The plaintiffs in this case were free to scroll through the various computer screens that presented the terms of their contracts before clicking their agreement.

Also, it seems clear that there was nothing extraordinary about the size or placement of the forum selection clause text. By every indication we have, the clause was presented in exactly the same format as most other provisions of the contract. It was the first item in the last paragraph of the electronic document. We note that a few paragraphs in the contract were presented in upper case typeface, presumably for emphasis, but most provisions, including the forum selection clause, were presented in lower case typeface. We discern nothing about the style or mode of presentation, or the placement of the provision, that can be taken as a basis for concluding that the forum selection clause was proffered unfairly, or with a design to conceal or de-emphasize its provisions. To conclude that plaintiffs are not bound by that clause would be equivalent to holding that they were bound by no other clause either, since all provisions were identically presented. Plaintiffs must be taken to have known that they were entering into a contract; and no good purpose, consonant with the dictates of reasonable reliability in commerce, would be served by permitting them to disavow particular provisions or the contracts as a whole. . . .

We agree with the trial court that, in the absence of a better showing than has been made, plaintiffs must be seen to have had adequate notice of the forum selection clause. . . .

Affirmed.

RESTATEMENT (SECOND) OF CONTRACTS

§211.   STANDARDIZED AGREEMENTS

(1) Except as stated in Subsection (3), where a party to an agreement signs or otherwise manifests assent to a writing and has reason to believe that like writings are regularly used to embody terms of agreements of the same type, he adopts the writing as an integrated agreement with respect to the terms included in the writing.

(2) Such a writing is interpreted wherever reasonable as treating alike all those similarly situated, without regard to their knowledge or understanding of the standard terms of the writing.

(3) Where the other party has reason to believe that the party manifesting such assent would not do so if he knew that the writing contained a particular term, the term is not part of the agreement.

COMMENT

a. *Utility of standardization.* Standardization of agreements serves many of the same functions as standardization of goods and services; both are essential to a system of mass production and distribution. Scarce and costly time and skill can be devoted to a class of transactions rather than to details of individual transactions. Legal rules which would apply in the absence of agreement can be shaped to fit the particular type of transaction, and extra copies of the form can be used for purposes such as record-keeping, coordination and supervision. Forms can be tailored to office routines, the training of personnel, and the requirements of mechanical equipment. Sales personnel and customers are freed from attention to numberless variations and can focus on meaningful choice among a limited number of significant features: transaction-type, style, quantity, price, or the like. Operations are simplified and costs reduced, to the advantage of all concerned.

b. *Assent to unknown terms.* A party who makes regular use of a standardized form of agreement does not ordinarily expect his customers to understand or even to read the standard terms. One of the purposes of standardization is to eliminate bargaining over details of individual transactions, and that purpose would not be served if a substantial number of customers retained counsel and reviewed the standard terms. Employees regularly using a form often have only a limited understanding of its terms and limited authority to vary them. Customers do not in fact ordinarily understand or even read the standard terms. They trust to the good faith of the party using the form and to the tacit representation that like terms are being accepted regularly by others similarly situated. But they understand that they are assenting to the terms not read or not understood, subject to such limitations as the law may impose.

c. *Review of unfair terms.* Standardized agreements are commonly prepared by one party. The customer assents to a few terms, typically inserted in blanks on the printed form, and gives blanket assent to the type of transaction embodied in the standard form. He is commonly not represented in the drafting, and the draftsman may be tempted to overdraw in the interest of his employer. The obvious danger of overreaching has resulted in government regulation of insurance policies, bills of lading, retail installment sales, small loans, and other particular types of contracts. Regulation sometimes includes administrative review of standard terms, or even prescription of terms. Apart from such regulation, standard terms imposed by one party are enforced. But standard terms may be superseded by separately negotiated or added terms (§203), they are construed against the draftsman (§206), and they are subject to the overriding obligation of good faith (§205) and to the power of the court to refuse to enforce an unconscionable contract or term (§208). Moreover, various contracts and terms are against public policy and unenforceable.

2. Which Terms Were Agreed to?

When the terms of an acceptance vary from those of an offer, it becomes necessary to determine which, if either, should constitute the terms of the agreement. As we saw in Chapter 4, before any performance has taken place, it is easier to contest the existence of mutual assent to contract by finding that a purported "acceptance" was really a counteroffer and therefore a rejection of the original offer. There being no mutual assent, a contract was not formed. After performance has begun, however, it is often clearer that there *was* mutual assent to enter into a contract — but because the terms of an offer differ from those of the acceptance, it is difficult to discern the terms to which both parties assented. Though we know the parties intended to contract, we then are faced with the problem of identifying the terms to which they agreed when their manifestations of assent conflict. Because this problem often arises as a result of conflicting writings, it is referred to as the "battle of the forms." As we shall see, the modern resolution of this problem has, to some extent, but not completely, undermined the traditional understanding of offer and acceptance, in which offerors were said to be "masters" of their offers.

STUDY GUIDE: Can you see how the problem raised by the next case differs from that which arose in Ardente v. Horan, discussed in Chapter 4? The U.C.C. has tried to address the problem of acceptances that vary from the terms of an offer once the parties have manifested an intent to form a contract. This approach is both described and illustrated by the next case. When reading this case, you should consult the complete text of §2-207 (and the Official Comments), which is reproduced after the case.

STEP-SAVER DATA SYSTEMS, INC. v. WYSE TECHNOLOGY

United States Court of Appeals, Third Circuit,
939 F.2d 91 (1991)

WISDOM, C.J.:*

The "Limited Use License Agreement" printed on a package containing a copy of a computer program raises the central issue in this appeal. The trial judge held that the terms of the Limited Use License Agreement governed the purchase of the package, and, therefore, granted the software producer, The Software Link, Inc. ("TSL"), a directed verdict on claims of breach of warranty brought by a disgruntled purchaser, Step-Saver Data Systems, Inc. We disagree with the district court's determination of the legal effect of the license, and reverse and remand the warranty claims for further consideration. . . .

John Minor Wisdom (1905-1999) was educated at Washington and Lee University (A.B.) and Tulane University (LL.B.) and admitted to the Louisiana bar in 1929. He practiced privately for nearly 30 years and was professor of law at Tulane University (1938-1957) before being appointed judge on the U.S. Court of Appeals for the Fifth Circuit in 1957. Wisdom played a critical role in the civil rights movement when he ordered the integration of the Louisiana public school system in the 1950s, and he received the Presidential Medal of Freedom in 1993. Judge Wisdom also served in the U.S. Army Air Corps (1942-1946). He participated in this Third Circuit case while sitting by designation. — K.T.

I. FACTUAL AND PROCEDURAL BACKGROUND

The growth in the variety of computer hardware and software has created a strong market for these products. It has also created a difficult choice for consumers, as they must somehow decide which of the many available products will best suit their needs. To assist consumers in this decision process, some companies will evaluate the needs of particular groups of potential computer users, compare those needs with the available technology, and develop a package of hardware and software to satisfy those needs. Beginning in 1981, Step-Saver performed this function as a value added retailer for International Business Machine (IBM) products. It would combine hardware and software to satisfy the word processing, data management, and communications needs for offices of physicians and lawyers. It originally marketed single computer systems, based primarily on the IBM personal computer.

As a result of advances in micro-computer technology, Step-Saver developed and marketed a multi-user system. With a multi-user system, only one computer is required. Terminals are attached, by cable, to the main computer. From these terminals, a user can access the programs available on the main computer.[34]

After evaluating the available technology, Step-Saver selected a program by TSL, entitled Multilink Advanced, as the operating system for the multi-user system. Step-Saver selected WY-60 terminals manufactured by Wyse, and used an IBM AT as the main computer. For applications software, Step-Saver included in the package several off-the-shelf programs, designed to run under Microsoft's Disk Operating System ("MS-DOS"),[35] as well as several programs written by Step-Saver. Step-Saver began marketing the system in November of 1986, and sold one hundred forty-two systems mostly to law and medical offices before terminating sales of the system in March of 1987. Almost immediately upon installation of the system, Step-Saver began to receive complaints from some of its customers.[36]

Step-Saver, in addition to conducting its own investigation of the problems, referred these complaints to Wyse and TSL, and requested technical assistance in resolving the problems. After several preliminary attempts to address the problems, the three companies were unable to reach a satisfactory solution, and disputes developed among the three concerning

---

34. In essence, the terminals are simply video screens with keyboards that serve as input output devices for the main computer. The main computer receives data from all of the terminals and processes it appropriately, sending a return signal to the terminal. To someone working on one of the terminals of a properly operating multi-user system, the terminal appears to function as if it were, in fact, a computer. Thus, an operator could work with a word processing program on a terminal, and it would appear to the operator the same as would working with the word processing program on a computer. The difference is that, with a set of computers, the commands of each user are processed within each user's computer, whereas with a multi-user system, the commands of all of the users are sent to the main computer for processing.

35. MS-DOS was the standard operating system for IBM and compatible personal computers.

36. According to the testimony of Jeffrey Worthington, an employee of Step-Saver, twenty to twenty-five of the purchasers of the multi-user system had serious problems with the system that were never resolved.

responsibility for the problems. As a result, the problems were never solved. At least twelve of Step-Saver's customers filed suit against Step-Saver because of the problems with the multi-user system.

[In this suit, Step-Saver alleged] breach of warranties by both TSL and Wyse and intentional misrepresentations by TSL. . . .

. . . [T]he trial judge . . . directed a verdict in favor of TSL on Step-Saver's remaining warranty claims, and dismissed TSL from the case.

The trial proceeded on Step-Saver's breach of warranties claims against Wyse. . . . Over Step-Saver's objection, the district court found insufficient evidence to support a finding that Wyse had breached its implied warranty of merchantability, and refused to instruct the jury on such warranty. The jury returned a verdict in favor of Wyse on the two warranty issues submitted.

Step-Saver appeals on [the grounds that] . . . Step-Saver and TSL did not intend the box-top license to be a complete and final expression of the terms of their agreement. . . .

II.   THE EFFECT OF THE BOX-TOP LICENSE . . .

. . . From August of 1986 through March of 1987, Step-Saver purchased and resold 142 copies of the Multilink Advanced program. Step-Saver would typically purchase copies of the program in the following manner. First, Step-Saver would telephone TSL and place an order. (Step-Saver would typically order twenty copies of the program at a time.) TSL would accept the order and promise, while on the telephone, to ship the goods promptly. After the telephone order, Step-Saver would send a purchase order, detailing the items to be purchased, their price, and shipping and payment terms. TSL would ship the order promptly, along with an invoice. The invoice would contain terms essentially identical with those on Step-Saver's purchase order: price, quantity, and shipping and payment terms. No reference was made during the telephone calls, or on either the purchase orders or the invoices with regard to a disclaimer of any warranties.

Printed on the package of each copy of the program, however, would be a copy of the box-top license. The box-top license contains five terms relevant to this action:

(1)   The box-top license provides that the customer has not purchased the software itself, but has merely obtained a personal, non-transferable license to use the program.

(2)   The box-top license, in detail and at some length, disclaims all express and implied warranties except for a warranty that the disks contained in the box are free from defects.

(3)   The box-top license provides that the sole remedy available to a purchaser of the program is to return a defective disk for replacement; the license excludes any liability for damages, direct or consequential, caused by the use of the program.

(4)   The box-top license contains an integration clause, which provides that the box-top license is the final and complete expression of the terms of the parties' agreement.

(5) The box-top license states: "Opening this package indicates your acceptance of these terms and conditions. If you do not agree with them, you should promptly return the package unopened to the person from whom you purchased it within fifteen days from date of purchase and your money will be refunded to you by that person."

The district court, without much discussion, held, as a matter of law, that the box-top license was the final and complete expression of the terms of the parties' agreement. Because the district court decided the questions of contract formation and interpretation as issues of law, we review the district court's resolution of these questions *de novo.* . . .

Step-Saver contends that the contract for each copy of the program was formed when TSL agreed, on the telephone, to ship the copy at the agreed price. The box-top license, argues Step-Saver, was a material alteration to the parties' contract which did not become a part of the contract under U.C.C. §2-207. . . . Alternatively, Step-Saver argues that the undisputed evidence establishes that the parties did not intend the box-top license as a final and complete expression of the terms of their agreement, and, therefore, the parol evidence rule of U.C.C. §2-202 would not apply.

TSL argues that the contract between TSL and Step-Saver did not come into existence until Step-Saver received the program, saw the terms of the license, and opened the program packaging. TSL contends that too many material terms were omitted from the telephone discussion for that discussion to establish a contract for the software. Second, TSL contends that its acceptance of Step-Saver's telephone offer was conditioned on Step-Saver's acceptance of the terms of the box-top license. Therefore, TSL argues, it did not accept Step-Saver's telephone offer, but made a counteroffer represented by the terms of the box-top license, which was accepted when Step-Saver opened each package. Third, TSL argues that, however the contract was formed, Step-Saver was aware of the warranty disclaimer, and that Step-Saver, by continuing to order and accept the product with knowledge of the disclaimer, assented to the disclaimer.

In analyzing these competing arguments, we first consider whether the license should be treated as an integrated writing under U.C.C. §2-202, as a proposed modification under U.C.C. §2-209, or as a written confirmation under U.C.C. §2-207. Finding that U.C.C. §2-207 best governs our resolution of the effect of the box-top license, we then consider whether, under U.C.C. §2-207, the terms of the box-top license were incorporated into the parties' agreement.

A. Does U.C.C. §2-207 Govern the Analysis?

As a basic principle, we agree with Step-Saver that U.C.C. §2-207 governs our analysis. We see no need to parse the parties' various actions to decide exactly when the parties formed a contract. TSL has shipped the product, and Step-Saver has accepted and paid for each copy of the program. The parties' performance demonstrates the existence of a contract. The dispute is, therefore, not over the existence of a contract, but the nature of its terms. . . . When the parties' conduct establishes a contract, but the parties have failed to adopt expressly a particular writing as the terms of their agreement, and the writings exchanged by the parties do not agree, U.C.C. §2-207 determines the terms of the contract.

As stated by the official comment to §2-207:

> 1. This section is intended to deal with two typical situations. The one is the written confirmation, where an agreement has been reached either orally or by informal correspondence between the parties and is followed by one or more of the parties sending formal memoranda embodying the terms so far as agreed upon and adding terms not discussed. . . .
>
>   2. Under this Article a proposed deal which in commercial understanding has in fact been closed is recognized as a contract. Therefore, any additional matter contained in the confirmation or in the acceptance falls within subsection (2) and must be regarded as a proposal for an added term unless the acceptance is made conditional on the acceptance of the additional or different terms.

Although U.C.C. §2-202 permits the parties to reduce an oral agreement to writing, and U.C.C. §2-209 permits the parties to modify an existing contract without additional consideration, a writing will be a final expression of, or a binding modification to, an earlier agreement only if the parties so intend. It is undisputed that Step-Saver never expressly agreed to the terms of the box-top license, either as a final expression of, or a modification to, the parties' agreement. In fact, Barry Greebel, the President of Step-Saver, testified without dispute that he objected to the terms of the box-top license as applied to Step-Saver. In the absence of evidence demonstrating an express intent to adopt a writing as a final expression of, or a modification to, an earlier agreement, we find U.C.C. §2-207 to provide the appropriate legal rules for determining whether such an intent can be inferred from continuing with the contract after receiving a writing containing additional or different terms. . . .

To understand why the terms of the license should be considered under §2-207 in this case, we review briefly the reasons behind §2-207. Under the common law of sales, and to some extent still for contracts outside the U.C.C., . . . an acceptance that varied any term of the offer operated as a rejection of the offer, and simultaneously made a counteroffer. . . . This common law formality was known as the mirror image rule, because the terms of the acceptance had to mirror the terms of the offer to be effective.[37] If the offeror proceeded with the contract despite the differing terms of the supposed acceptance, he would, by his performance, constructively accept the terms of the "counteroffer," and be bound by its terms. As a result of these rules, the terms of the party who sent the last form, typically the seller, would become the terms of the parties' contract. This result was known as the "last shot rule."

The U.C.C., in §2-207, rejected this approach. Instead, it recognized that, while a party may desire the terms detailed in its form if a dispute, in fact, arises, most parties do not expect a dispute to arise when they first

---

37. See, e.g., Daitom, Inc. v. Pennwalt Corp., 741 F.2d 1569, 1578 (10th Cir. 1984).

enter into a contract. As a result, most parties will proceed with the transaction even if they know that the terms of their form would not be enforced.[38]

The insight behind the rejection of the last shot rule is that it would be unfair to bind the buyer of goods to the standard terms of the seller, when neither party cared sufficiently to establish expressly the terms of their agreement, simply because the seller sent the last form. Thus, U.C.C. §2-207 establishes a legal rule that proceeding with a contract after receiving a writing that purports to define the terms of the parties' contract is not sufficient to establish the party's consent to the terms of the writing to the extent that the terms of the writing either add to, or differ from, the terms detailed in the parties' earlier writings or discussions. In the absence of a party's express assent to the additional or different terms of the writing, §2-207 provides a default rule that the parties intended, as the terms of their agreement, those terms to which both parties have agreed,[39] along with any terms implied by the provisions of the U.C.C.

The reasons that led to the rejection of the last shot rule, and the adoption of §2-207, apply fully in this case. TSL never mentioned during the parties' negotiations leading to the purchase of the programs, nor did it, at any time, obtain Step-Saver's express assent to, the terms of the box-top license. Instead, TSL contented itself with attaching the terms to the packaging of the software, even though those terms differed substantially from those previously discussed by the parties. Thus, the box-top license, in this case, is best seen as one more form in a battle of forms, and the question of whether Step-Saver has agreed to be bound by the terms of the box-top license is best resolved by applying the legal principles detailed in §2-207.

B.   APPLICATION OF §2-207

TSL advances several reasons why the terms of the box-top license should be incorporated into the parties' agreement under a §2-207 analysis. First, TSL argues that the parties' contract was not formed until Step-Saver received the package, saw the terms of the box-top license, and opened the package, thereby consenting to the terms of the license. TSL argues that a contract defined without reference to the specific terms provided by the box-top license would necessarily fail for indefiniteness. Second, TSL argues that the box-top license was a conditional acceptance and counter-offer under §2-207(1). Third, TSL argues that Step-Saver, by continuing to order and use the product with notice of the terms of the box-top license, consented to the terms of the box-top license.

---

38. As Judge Engel has written:

Usually, these standard terms mean little, for a contract looks to its fulfillment and rarely anticipates its breach. Hope springs eternal in the commercial world and expectations are usually, but not always, realized.

McJunkin Corp. v. Mechanicals, Inc., 888 F.2d [481 (6th Cir. 1989)] at 482.

39. The parties may demonstrate their acceptance of a particular term either "orally or by informal correspondence," U.C.C. §2-207, Comment 1, or by placing the term in their respective form.

1. Was the Contract Sufficiently Definite?

TSL argues that the parties intended to license the copies of the program, and that several critical terms could only be determined by referring to the box-top license. Pressing the point, TSL argues that it is impossible to tell, without referring to the box-top license, whether the parties intended a sale of a copy of the program or a license to use a copy. TSL cites Bethlehem Steel Corp. v. Litton Industries in support of its position that any contract defined without reference to the terms of the box-top license would fail for indefiniteness.[40]

From the evidence, it appears that the following terms, at the least, were discussed and agreed to, apart from the box-top license: (1) the specific goods involved; (2) the quantity; and (3) the price. TSL argues that the following terms were only defined in the box-top license: (1) the nature of the transaction, sale or license; and (2) the warranties, if any, available. TSL argues that these two terms are essential to creating a sufficiently definite contract. We disagree.

Section 2-204(3) of the U.C.C. provides:

> Even though one or more terms are left open a contract for sale does not fail for indefiniteness if the parties have intended to make a contract and there is a reasonably certain basis for giving an appropriate remedy.

Unlike the terms omitted by the parties in *Bethlehem Steel Corp.*, the two terms cited by TSL are not "gaping holes in a multi-million dollar contract that no one but the parties themselves could fill."[41] First, the rights of the respective parties under the federal copyright law if the transaction is characterized as a sale of a copy of the program are nearly identical to the parties' respective rights under the terms of the box-top license.[42] Second, the U.C.C. provides for express and implied warranties if the seller fails to disclaim expressly those warranties.[43] Thus, even though warranties are an important term left blank by the parties, the default rules of the U.C.C. fill in that blank.

We hold that contract was sufficiently definite without the terms provided by the box-top license. . . .

2. The Box-Top License as a Counter-Offer?

TSL advances two reasons why its box-top license should be considered a conditional acceptance under U.C.C. §2-207(1). First, TSL argues that

---

40. 507 Pa. 88, 488 A.2d 581 (1985).

41. 488 A.2d at 591.

42. The most significant difference would be that, under the terms of the license, Step-Saver could not transfer the copies without TSL's consent, while Step-Saver could do so under the federal copyright law if it had purchased the copy. Even if we assume that federal law would not preempt state law enforcement of this aspect of the license, this difference is not material to this case in that both parties agree that Step-Saver had the right to transfer the copies to purchasers of the Step-Saver multi-user system.

43. See U.C.C. §§2-312, 2-313, 2-314, & 2-315.

the express language of the box-top license, including the integration clause and the phrase "opening this product indicates your acceptance of these terms," made TSL's acceptance "expressly conditional on assent to the additional or different terms."[44] Second, TSL argues that the box-top license, by permitting return of the product within fifteen days if the purchaser does not agree to the terms stated in the license (the "refund offer"), establishes that TSL's acceptance was conditioned on Step-Saver's assent to the terms of the box-top license, citing Monsanto Agricultural Products Co. v. Edenfield.[45] While we are not certain that a conditional acceptance analysis applies when a contract is established by performance,[46] we assume that it does and consider TSL's arguments.

To determine whether a writing constitutes a conditional acceptance, courts have established three tests. Because neither Georgia nor Pennsylvania has expressly adopted a test to determine when a written confirmation constitutes a conditional acceptance, we consider these three tests to determine which test the state courts would most likely apply. . . .

Under the first test, an offeree's response is a conditional acceptance to the extent it states a term "materially altering the contractual obligations solely to the disadvantage of the offeror."[47] Pennsylvania, at least, has implicitly rejected this test. In Herzog Oil Field Service, Inc.,[48] a Pennsylvania Superior Court analyzed a term in a written confirmation under U.C.C. §2-207(2), rather than as a conditional acceptance even though the term materially altered the terms of the agreement to the sole disadvantage of the offeror.[49]

Furthermore, we note that adopting this test would conflict with the express provision of U.C.C. §2-207(2)(b). Under §2-207(2)(b), additional terms in a written confirmation that "materially alter [the contract]" are construed "as proposals for addition to the contract," not as conditional acceptances.

A second approach considers an acceptance conditional when certain key words or phrases are used, such as a written confirmation stating that the terms of the confirmation are "the only ones upon which we will accept

44. U.C.C. §2-207(1).
45. 426 So. 2d 574 (Fla. Dist. Ct. App. 1982).
46. Even though a writing is sent after performance establishes the existence of a contract, courts have analyzed the effect of such a writing under U.C.C. §2-207. . . . The official comment to U.C.C. §2-207 suggests that, even though a proposed deal has been closed, the conditional acceptance analysis still applies in determining which writing's terms will define the contract.

2. Under this Article a proposed deal which in commercial understanding has in fact been closed is recognized as a contract. Therefore, any additional matter contained in the confirmation or in the acceptance falls within subsection (2) and must be regarded as a proposal for an added term *unless the acceptance is made conditional on the acceptance of the additional or different terms.*

47. *Daitom, Inc.*, 741 F.2d at 1576. See, e.g., Roto-Lith Ltd. v. F. P. Bartlett & Co., 297 F.2d 497 (1st Cir. 1962).
48. 391 Pa. Super. 133, 570 A.2d 549 (Pa. Super. Ct. 1990).
49. The seller/offeree sent a written confirmation that contained a term that provided for attorney's fees of 25 percent of the balance due if the account was turned over for collection. 570 A.2d at 550.

orders."[50] The third approach requires the offeree to demonstrate an unwillingness to proceed with the transaction unless the additional or different terms are included in the contract. . . .

Although we are not certain that these last two approaches would generate differing answers,[51] we adopt the third approach for our analysis because it best reflects the understanding of commercial transactions developed in the U.C.C. Section 2-207 attempts to distinguish between: (1) those standard terms in a form confirmation, which the party would like a court to incorporate into the contract in the event of a dispute; and (2) the actual terms the parties understand to govern their agreement. The third test properly places the burden on the party asking a court to enforce its form to demonstrate that a particular term is a part of the parties' commercial bargain. . . .

Using this test, it is apparent that the integration clause and the "consent by opening" language is not sufficient to render TSL's acceptance conditional. As other courts have recognized, . . . this type of language provides no real indication that the party is willing to forego the transaction if the additional language is not included in the contract.

The second provision provides a more substantial indication that TSL was willing to forego the contract if the terms of the box-top license were not accepted by Step-Saver. On its face, the box-top license states that TSL will refund the purchase price if the purchaser does not agree to the terms of the license.[52] Even with such a refund term, however, the offeree/counterofferor may be relying on the purchaser's investment in time and energy in reaching this point in the transaction to prevent the purchaser from returning the item. Because a purchaser has made a decision to buy a particular product and has actually obtained the product, the purchaser may use it despite the refund offer, regardless of the additional terms specified

---

50. Ralph Shrader, Inc. v. Diamond Intl. Corp., 833 F.2d 1210, 1214 (6th Cir. 1987). . . . Note that even though an acceptance contains the key phrase, and is conditional, these courts typically avoid finding a contract on the terms of the counteroffer by requiring the offeree/counterofferor to establish that the offeror assented to the terms of the counteroffer. Generally, acceptance of the goods, alone, is not sufficient to establish assent by the offeror to the terms of the counteroffer. . . . If the sole evidence of assent to the terms of the counteroffer is from the conduct of the parties in proceeding with the transaction, then the courts generally define the terms of the parties' agreement under §2-207(3). . . .

51. Under the second approach, the box-top license might be considered a conditional acceptance, but Step-Saver, by accepting the product, would not be automatically bound to the terms of the box-top license. . . . Instead, courts have applied U.C.C. §2-207(3) to determine the terms of the parties' agreement. The terms of the agreement would be those "on which the writings of the parties agree, together with any supplementary terms incorporated under any other provisions of this Act." U.C.C. §2-207(3). Because the writings of the parties did not agree on the warranty disclaimer and limitation of remedies terms, the box-top license version of those terms would not be included in the parties' contract; rather, the default provisions of the U.C.C. would govern.

52. One Florida Court of Appeals has accepted such an offer as a strong indication of a conditional acceptance. *Monsanto Agricultural Prods. Co.*, 426 So. 2d at 575-576. Note that the Monsanto warranty label was conspicuous and available to the purchaser before the contract for the sale of the herbicide was formed. When an offeree proceeds with a contract with constructive knowledge of the terms of the offer, the offeree is typically bound by those terms, making the conditional acceptance finding unnecessary to the result reached in *Monsanto*.

after the contract formed. But we need not decide whether such a refund offer could ever amount to a conditional acceptance; the undisputed evidence in this case demonstrates that the terms of the license were not sufficiently important that TSL would forego its sales to Step-Saver if TSL could not obtain Step-Saver's consent to those terms.

As discussed, Mr. Greebel testified that TSL assured him that the box-top license did not apply to Step-Saver, as Step-Saver was not the end user of the Multilink Advanced program. Supporting this testimony, TSL on two occasions asked Step-Saver to sign agreements that would put in formal terms the relationship between Step-Saver and TSL. Both proposed agreements contained warranty disclaimer and limitation of remedy terms similar to those contained in the box-top license. Step-Saver refused to sign the agreements; nevertheless, TSL continued to sell copies of Multilink Advanced to Step-Saver.

Additionally, TSL asks us to infer, based on the refund offer, that it was willing to forego its sales to Step-Saver unless Step-Saver agreed to the terms of the box-top license. Such an inference is inconsistent with the fact that both parties agree that the terms of the box-top license *did not represent the parties' agreement* with respect to Step-Saver's right to transfer the copies of the Multilink Advanced program. Although the box-top license prohibits the transfer, by Step-Saver, of its copies of the program, both parties agree that Step-Saver was entitled to transfer its copies to the purchasers of the Step-Saver multi-user system. Thus, TSL was willing to proceed with the transaction despite the fact that one of the terms of the box-top license was not included in the contract between TSL and Step-Saver. We see no basis in the terms of the box-top license for inferring that a reasonable offeror would understand from the refund offer that certain terms of the box-top license, such as the warranty disclaimers, were essential to TSL, while others such as the non-transferability provision were not.

Based on these facts, we conclude that TSL did not clearly express its unwillingness to proceed with the transactions unless its additional terms were incorporated into the parties' agreement. The box-top license did not, therefore, constitute a conditional acceptance under U.C.C. §2-207(1). . .

4. *Public Policy Concerns*

TSL has raised a number of public policy arguments focusing on the effect on the software industry of an adverse holding concerning the enforceability of the box-top license. We are not persuaded that requiring software companies to stand behind representations concerning their products will inevitably destroy the software industry. We emphasize, however, that we are following the well established distinction between conspicuous disclaimers made available before the contract is formed and disclaimers made available only after the contract is formed.[53] When a disclaimer is not

53. Compare Hill v. BASF Wyandotte Corp., 696 F.2d 287, 290-291 (4th Cir. 1982). In that case, a farmer purchased seventy-three five-gallon cans of a herbicide from a retailer. Because the disclaimer was printed conspicuously on each can, the farmer had constructive knowledge of the terms of the disclaimer before the contract formed. As a result, when he

expressed until after the contract is formed, U.C.C. §2-207 governs the interpretation of the contract, and, between merchants, such disclaimers, to the extent they materially alter the parties' agreement, are not incorporated into the parties' agreement.

If TSL wants relief for its business operations from this well-established rule, their arguments are better addressed to a legislature than a court. Indeed, we note that at least two states have enacted statutes that modify the applicable contract rules in this area,[54] but both Georgia and Pennsylvania have retained the contract rules provided by the U.C.C. . . .

VI

We will reverse the holding of the district court that the parties intended to adopt the box-top license as the complete and final expression of the terms of their agreement. We will remand for further consideration of Step-Saver's express and implied warranty claims against TSL. Finding a sufficient basis for the other decisions of the district court, we will affirm in all other respects.

[Trial court's discussion of express and implied warranties appears in Chapter 12.]

REFERENCE: Barnett, §3.5.5
                Farnsworth, §3.21
                Calamari & Perillo, §2.21
                Murray, §50

Reread: U.C.C. §§2-204 (p. 272), 2-206 (p. 273)

SALES CONTRACTS: THE UNIFORM COMMERCIAL CODE

§2-207.   ADDITIONAL TERMS IN ACCEPTANCE OR CONFIRMATION

(1) A definite and seasonable expression of acceptance or a written confirmation which is sent within a reasonable time operates as an acceptance even though it states terms additional to or different from those offered or agreed upon, unless acceptance is expressly made conditional on assent to the additional or different terms.

selected each can of the herbicide from the shelf and purchased it, the law implies his assent to the terms of the disclaimer. See also Bowdoin v. Showell Growers, Inc., 817 F.2d 1543, 1545 (11th Cir. 1987) (disclaimers that were conspicuous before the contract for sale has formed are effective; post-sale disclaimers are ineffective). . . .

54. Louisiana Software License Enforcement Act, La. R.S. §§51:1961-1966 (1987); Illinois Software Enforcement Act, Ill. Ann. Stat. ch. 29, para. 801-808 (Smith-Hurd 1987).

(2) The additional terms are to be construed as proposals for addition to the contract. Between merchants such terms become part of the contract unless:

(a) the offer expressly limits acceptance to the terms of the offer;

(b) they materially alter it; or

(c) notification of objection to them has already been given or is given within a reasonable time after notice of them is received.

(3) Conduct by both parties which recognizes the existence of a contract is sufficient to establish a contract for sale although the writings of the parties do not otherwise establish a contract. In such case the terms of the particular contract consist of those terms on which the writings of the parties agree, together with any supplementary terms incorporated under any other provisions of this Act.

OFFICIAL COMMENT

Purposes of Changes

1. This section is intended to deal with two typical situations. The one is the written confirmation, where an agreement has been reached either orally or by informal correspondence between the parties and is followed by one or both of the parties sending formal memoranda embodying the terms so far as agreed upon and adding terms not discussed. The other situation is offer and acceptance, in which a wire or letter expressed and intended as an acceptance or the closing of an agreement adds further minor suggestions or proposals such as "ship by Tuesday," "rush," "ship draft against bill of lading inspection allowed," or the like. A frequent example of the second situation is the exchange of printed purchase order and acceptance (sometimes called "acknowledgment") forms. Because the forms are oriented to the thinking of the respective drafting parties, the terms contained in them often do not correspond. Often the seller's form contains terms different from or additional to those set forth in the buyer's form. Nevertheless, the parties proceed with the transaction. [Comment 1 was amended in 1966.]

2. Under this Article a proposed deal which in commercial understanding has in fact been closed is recognized as a contract. Therefore, any additional matter contained in the confirmation or in the acceptance falls within subsection (2) and must be regarded as a proposal for an added term unless the acceptance is made conditional on the acceptance of the additional or different terms. [Comment 2 was amended in 1966.]

3. Whether or not additional or different terms will become part of the agreement depends upon the provisions of subsection (2). If they are such as materially to alter the original bargain, they will not be included unless expressly agreed to by the other party. If, however, they are terms which would not so change the bargain they will be incorporated unless notice of objection to them has already been given or is given within a reasonable time.

4. Examples of typical clauses which would normally "materially alter" the contract and so result in surprise or hardship if incorporated without express awareness by the other party are: a clause negating such standard

warranties as that of merchantability or fitness for a particular purpose in circumstances in which either warranty normally attaches; a clause requiring a guaranty of 90% or 100% deliveries in a case such as a contract by cannery, where the usage of the trade allows greater quantity leeways; a clause reserving to the seller the power to cancel upon the buyer's failure to meet any invoice when due; a clause requiring that complaints be made in a time materially shorter than customary or reasonable.

5. Examples of clauses which involve no element of unreasonable surprise and which therefore are to be incorporated in the contract unless notice of objection is seasonably given are: a clause setting forth and perhaps enlarging slightly upon the seller's exemption due to supervening causes beyond his control, similar to those covered by the provision of this Article on merchant's excuse by failure of presupposed conditions or a clause fixing in advance any reasonable formula of proration under such circumstances; a clause fixing a reasonable time for complaints within customary limits, or in the case of a purchase for sub-sale, providing for inspection by the sub-purchaser; a clause providing for interest on overdue invoices or fixing the seller's standard credit terms where they are within the range of trade practice and do not limit any credit bargained for; a clause limiting the right of rejection for defects which fall within the customary trade tolerances for acceptance "with adjustment" or otherwise limiting remedy in a reasonable manner (see §§2-718 and 2-719).

6. If no answer is received within a reasonable time after additional terms are proposed, it is both fair and commercially sound to assume that their inclusion has been assented to. Where clauses on confirming forms sent by both parties conflict each party must be assumed to object to a clause of the other conflicting with one on the confirmation sent by himself. As a result the requirement that there be notice of objection which is found in subsection (2) is satisfied and the conflicting terms do not become a part of the contract. The contract then consists of the terms originally expressly agreed to, terms on which the confirmations agree, and terms supplied by this Act, including subsection (2). The written confirmation is also subject to §2-201. Under that section a failure to respond permits enforcement of a prior oral agreement; under this section a failure to respond permits additional terms to become part of the agreement. [Comment 6 was amended in 1966.]

7. In many cases, as where goods are shipped, accepted and paid for before any dispute arises, there is no question whether a contract has been made. In such cases, where the writings of the parties do not establish a contract, it is not necessary to determine which act or document constituted the offer and which the acceptance. See §2-204. The only question is what terms are included in the contract, and subsection (3) furnishes the governing rule. [Comment 7 was added in 1966.]

§2-316.   EXCLUSION OR MODIFICATION OF WARRANTIES

(1) Words or conduct relevant to the creation of an express warranty and words or conduct tending to negate or limit warranty shall be construed wherever reasonable as consistent with each other; but subject to the

provisions of this Article on parol or extrinsic evidence (§2-202) negation or limitation is inoperative to the extent that such construction is unreasonable.

(2) Subject to subsection (3), to exclude or modify the implied warranty of merchantability or any part of it the language must mention merchantability and in case of a writing must be conspicuous, and to exclude or modify any implied warranty of fitness the exclusion must be by writing and conspicuous. Language to exclude all implied warranties of fitness is sufficient if it states, for example, that "There are no warranties which extend beyond the description on the face hereof." . . .

STUDY GUIDE: How does Judge Posner discern the difference between (a) an "additional" term in a later form that becomes part of the agreement and (b) a "material alteration" that cannot become a part of the agreement without some further expression of assent?

UNION CARBIDE CORP. v. OSCAR MAYER FOODS CORP.
United States Court of Appeals, Seventh Circuit,
947 F.2d 1333 (1991)

POSNER, Circuit Judge.

This is a diversity suit for breach of contract, brought by Union Carbide against Oscar Mayer and resolved in the defendant's favor on summary judgment. Union Carbide sold Oscar Mayer plastic casings that Oscar Mayer uses in manufacturing sausages. The prices in Union Carbide's invoices to Oscar Mayer included two 1 percent sales taxes that are applicable to sales which originate in Chicago. Another supplier of plastic sausage casings to Oscar Mayer began charging a price that was 1 percent lower than Union Carbide's. This supplier had begun accepting orders at an office outside of Chicago and had decided that therefore it didn't have to pay one of the sales taxes (why one but not both is unclear). When Oscar Mayer informed Union Carbide of this, Union Carbide instructed its customers likewise to send their orders to an address outside Chicago, and it stopped paying both sales taxes and therefore deleted them from the invoices it sent Oscar Mayer. Thus Union Carbide had met and indeed beat the other supplier's discount by lowering its price 2 percent compared to the other supplier's reduction of 1 percent.

All this was in 1980. Eight years later the Illinois tax authorities decided that the two sales taxes were due notwithstanding the change of address and assessed Union Carbide $88,000 in back taxes on sales to Oscar Mayer and $55,000 in interest thereon. Union Carbide paid and then turned around and brought this suit to recover what it had paid from Oscar Mayer, claiming that Oscar Mayer had agreed to indemnify it for all sales tax liability. It relied on the following provision printed on the back of its invoices to Oscar Mayer and also in a "price book" that it sent its customers: "In addition to the purchase price, Buyer shall pay Seller the amount of all governmental taxes . . . that Seller *may be required* to pay with respect to the production, sale or transportation of any materials delivered hereunder." (Emphasis added.)

Union Carbide's claim nestles comfortably within this language, but that is only the beginning of analysis. The language is equally comfortably read to mean simply that the seller shall be permitted to add on to the agreed purchase price the amount of whatever sales tax is applicable to the purchase — which is a quite different reading from supposing that it imposes on the buyer an open-ended liability to pay back taxes, interest, and even fraud penalties (though an attempt to shift the last might be forbidden as contrary to public policy), perhaps many years after taking delivery, because the seller blundered in computing its tax liability. That may be a semantically permissible, but it is an economically implausible, reading. . . . We think that Union Carbide has misread the contract and that this is clear enough to be determined without a trial. . . .

We also agree with the district judge that if read as an indemnity clause the quoted provision is a material alteration in the parties' contract and is therefore unenforceable against Oscar Mayer because not agreed to. The common law rule was that if the purported acceptance of an offer was not identical to the offer, the acceptance was a fresh offer and had to be expressly accepted by the original offeror for the parties to have a contract. Step-Saver Data Systems, Inc. v. Wyse Technology, 939 F.2d 91, 99 (3d Cir. 1991). This "mirror image" rule was widely believed to take insufficient account of the incorrigible fallibility of human beings engaged in commercial as in other dealings, and is changed by the Uniform Commercial Code, which allows an acceptance to make a contract even if it adds terms to the offer. UCC §2-207(1). Moreover, if it is a contract between "merchants" (in the sense of "pros," UCC §2-104(1) and Official Comment thereto — as Union Carbide and Oscar Mayer are), the additional terms become part of the contract. UCC §2-207(2). But not any additional terms; only those to which the offeror would be unlikely to object, because they fill out the contract in an expectable fashion, and hence do not alter it materially. If a term added by the offeree in his acceptance works a material alteration of the offer, the acceptance is still effective, but the term is not: that is, the contract is enforceable minus the term the offeree tried to add. UCC §§2-207(1), (2); . . . see generally Caroline N. Brown, "Restoring Peace in the Battle of the Forms: A Framework for Making Uniform Commercial Code Section 2-207 Work," 69 N.C. L. Rev. 893 (1991).

An alteration is material if consent to it cannot be presumed. That is our gloss; the cases more commonly speak of "unreasonable surprise." But it comes to the same thing. What is expectable, hence unsurprising, is okay; what is unexpected, hence surprising, is not. Not infrequently the test is said to be "surprise or hardship," but this appears to be a misreading of Official Comment 4 to UCC §2-207. The comment offers examples of "typical clauses which would normally 'materially alter' the contract *and so result in surprise or hardship* if incorporated without express awareness by the other party" (emphasis added). Hardship is a consequence, not a criterion. (Surprise can be either.) You cannot walk away from a contract that you can fairly be deemed to have agreed to, merely because performance turns out to be a hardship for you, unless you can squeeze yourself into the impossibility defense or some related doctrine of excuse.

This is not the end of the analysis, however. Like most doctrines of contract law, the doctrine of material alteration is an aid to interpretation rather than an ironclad rule. Even if the alteration is material, the other party can, of course, decide to accept it, and then the doctrine of material alteration is out the window. Put differently, consent can be inferred from other things besides the unsurprising character of the new term: even from silence, in the face of a course of dealings that makes it reasonable for the other party to infer consent from a failure to object.

Cases such as Schulze & Burch Biscuit Co. v. Tree Top, Inc.[, 831 F.2d 709 (7th Cir. 1987)], merging the question of material alteration with that of silence as consent, hold that if the new term is contained in a succession of invoices or other forms, the recipient cannot claim unfair surprise and is therefore bound by it (the "therefore" implicitly deriving from the principle that a course of dealings can be the basis for treating silence as acceptance of an offer). But it assists clear analysis to separate the two issues. They are close but distinct. If the new term does not effect a material alteration, silence is consent, period. If it does effect a material alteration, the party who proposed it must present additional evidence, beyond the term itself, to show that he was reasonable to infer consent to the new term from the other party's failure to object (silence); ordinarily this will be evidence of prior dealings, unnecessary if the new term did not effect a material alteration. Finally, an offeror can protect himself against additional terms, material or not, by expressly limiting acceptance to the terms of the offer. UCC §2-207(2)(a).

To summarize, a term inserted by the offeree is ineffectual (1) if the offer expressly limits acceptance to the terms of the offer, or (2) if the new term (a) makes a material alteration, in the sense that consent to it cannot be presumed, and (b) there is no showing that the offeror in fact consented to the alteration — whether (i) expressly, or (ii) by silence against the background of a course of dealings.

Having got the law as straight as we can, let us return to the facts. The record does not reveal the origins of Union Carbide's dealings with Oscar Mayer. All we know is that in 1980 the parties' method of dealing was as follows. Oscar Mayer would from time to time send large purchase orders to Union Carbide which would not be filled immediately but instead would be filed for future reference. When Oscar Mayer actually needed casings it would phone Union Carbide and tell it how many it needed and Union Carbide would ship the casings the next day. After the casings arrived Oscar Mayer would send Union Carbide a purchase order for the shipment on the same form used for the standing orders. These "release orders," as the specific purchase orders were called, were like checks written against a bank account (the standing orders) — only this was a sausage-casings account. At about the same time that Oscar Mayer sent Union Carbide a release order, Union Carbide would send Oscar Mayer an invoice for the shipment — and the so-called indemnity clause was, as we noted at the outset, on the back of the invoice and also in a price book that Union Carbide sent its customers from time to time. So every actual purchase of sausage casings involved an exchange of four documents: the standing order, the price book, the release order, the invoice. Such a pattern of sequential exchange of documents governing a single sale is a prototypical situation for the application of UCC §2-207.

Union Carbide does not question that for purposes of our decision the purchase orders by Oscar Mayer are the offers and Union Carbide's invoices are the acceptances, and that the price book, if it be assumed to be an offer, was never accepted. So the indemnity clause (if, contrary to our view, that is what it was) was binding on Oscar Mayer only if the clause did not work a material alteration of the terms in the purchase orders.

Those orders don't exactly discuss taxes, but they contain a space for sales tax to be added into the purchase price, and Union Carbide points out that, consistent with this indication of willingness to pay sales tax, Oscar Mayer paid uncomplainingly all sales taxes that appeared on Union Carbide's invoices. Nor does Oscar Mayer deny that it was contractually obligated to do so, by virtue less of anything said in the documents than of a tacit understanding inferable from the parties' previous dealings. UCC §1-205(1). If the sales tax rates had risen, Oscar Mayer would have had to pay the higher rates. What difference does it make, asks Union Carbide, if the increase took the form of an assessment of back taxes? It makes a big difference, amounting to a material alteration to which Oscar Mayer did not consent either explicitly or implicitly. If a tax increase showed up on an invoice, Oscar Mayer would have to pay but might then decide to cease buying casings from Union Carbide, as it had every right to do; it did not have a requirements contract with Union Carbide but could switch at will to other suppliers, some of whom might not be subject to the tax. To assume responsibility for taxes shown on an individual invoice is quite different from assuming an open-ended, indeed incalculable, liability for back taxes. Construed (improperly in our view) as an indemnity clause, as Union Carbide urges, the tax clause altered the contract materially; and since the clause was at best ambiguous about indemnity, this is not a case where consent can realistically be inferred from Oscar Mayer's silence in the face of a succession of acceptances (Union Carbide's invoices) containing the new term.

There was no breach of contract. The judgment for the defendant is AFFIRMED.

3.   Terms That Follow Later

The next three cases do not concern conflicting forms, so one issue is whether or not §2-207 governs. But a more fundamental question is whether a party can be said to have assented to terms that he or she could not examine until sometime after a purchase was made. Can you manifest consent to be bound by terms to which you only later gain access? In this regard, these cases address a problem raised by the facts of *Carnival Cruise* but avoided by the Supreme Court: The terms of the agreement were on the back of the ticket that was delivered to the passengers after they paid for their tickets. In what sense did or could the purchasers consent to terms they had yet to see at the time of the sale?

STUDY GUIDE: In the next case, do you agree with Judge Easterbrook that §2-207 does not apply because there are no conflicting forms? What about the terms of the purchase at the time of the sale? Don't the software licensing terms inside the box provide terms that are either "additional" or that "materially alter" the terms of the sale? So shouldn't they be governed by §2-207? Is §2-207 limited to the battle of the forms?

ProCD v. ZEIDENBERG
United States Court of Appeals, Seventh Circuit,
86 F.3d 1447 (1996)

EASTERBROOK, Circuit Judge. Must buyers of computer software obey the terms of shrinkwrap licenses? The district court held not, for two reasons: first, they are not contracts because the licenses are inside the box rather than printed on the outside; second, federal law forbids enforcement even if the licenses are contracts. The parties and numerous *amici curiae* have briefed many other issues, but these are the only two that matter — and we disagree with the district judge's conclusion on each. Shrinkwrap licenses are enforceable unless their terms are objectionable on grounds applicable to contracts in general (for example, if they violate a rule of positive law, or if they are unconscionable). Because no one argues that the terms of the license at issue here are troublesome, we remand with instructions to enter judgment for the plaintiff.

I

ProCD, the plaintiff, has compiled information from more than 3,000 telephone directories into a computer database. We may assume that this database cannot be copyrighted, although it is more complex, contains more information (nine-digit zip codes and census industrial codes), is organized differently, and therefore is more original than the single alpha- betical directory at issue in Feist Publications, Inc. v Rural Telephone Ser- vice Co., 499 U.S. 340 (1991). See Paul J. Heald, The Vices of Originality, 1991 Sup. Ct. Rev. 143, 160-168. ProCD sells a version of the database, called SelectPhone (trademark), on CD-ROM discs. . . . The "shrinkwrap license" gets its name from the fact that retail software packages are covered in plastic or cellophane "shrinkwrap," and some vendors, though not ProCD, have written licenses that become effective as soon as the customer tears the wrapping from the package. (Vendors prefer "end user license," but we use the more common term.) A proprietary method of compressing the data serves as effective encryption too. Customers decrypt and use the data with the aid of an application program that ProCD has written. This program, which is copyrighted, searches the database in response to users' criteria (such as "find all people named Tatum in Tennessee, plus all firms with 'Door Systems' in the corporate name"). The resulting lists (or, as ProCD prefers, "listings") can be read and manipulated by other software, such as word processing programs.

The database in SelectPhone (trademark) cost more than $10 million to compile and is expensive to keep current. It is much more valuable to some users than to others. The combination of names, addresses, and SIC codes enables manufacturers to compile lists of potential customers. Man- ufacturers and retailers pay high prices to specialized information interme- diaries for such mailing lists; ProCD offers a potentially cheaper alternative. People with nothing to sell could use the database as a substitute for calling long distance information, or as a way to look up old friends who have moved to unknown towns, or just as an electronic substitute for the local phone book. ProCD decided to engage in price discrimination, selling its database to the general public for personal use at a low price (approximately $150 for the set of five discs) while selling information to the trade for a higher price. It has adopted some intermediate strategies too: access to the SelectPhone (trademark) database is available via the America Online service for the price America Online charges to its clients (approximately $3 per hour), but this service has been tailored to be useful only to the general public.

If ProCD had to recover all of its costs and make a profit by charging a single price — that is, if it could not charge more to commercial users than to the general public — it would have to raise the price substantially over $150. The ensuing reduction in sales would harm consumers who value the information at, say, $200. They get a consumer surplus of $50 under the current arrangement but would cease to buy if the price rose substantially. If because of high elasticity of demand in the consumer segment of the market the only way to make a profit turned out to be a price attractive to commercial users alone, then all consumers would lose out — and so would the commercial clients, who would have to pay more for the listings because ProCD could not obtain any contribution toward costs from the consumer market.

To make price discrimination work, however, the seller must be able to control arbitrage. An air carrier sells tickets for less to vacationers than to business travelers, using advance purchase and Saturday-night-stay requirements to distinguish the categories. A producer of movies segments the market by time, releasing first to theaters, then to pay-per-view services, next to the videotape and laserdisc market, and finally to cable and commercial tv. Vendors of computer software have a harder task. Anyone can walk into a retail store and buy a box. Customers do not wear tags saying "commercial user" or "consumer user." Anyway, even a commercial-user-detector at the door would not work, because a consumer could buy the software and resell to a commercial user. That arbitrage would break down the price discrimination and drive up the minimum price at which ProCD would sell to anyone.

Instead of tinkering with the product and letting users sort themselves — for example, furnishing current data at a high price, that would be attractive only to commercial customers, and two-year-old data at a low price — ProCD turned to the institution of contract. Every box containing its consumer product declares that the software comes with restrictions stated in an enclosed license. This license, which is encoded on the CD-ROM disks as well as printed in the manual, and which appears on a user's screen every time the software runs, limits use of the application program and listings to non-commercial purposes.

Matthew Zeidenberg bought a consumer package of SelectPhone (trademark) in 1994 from a retail outlet in Madison, Wisconsin, but decided to ignore the license. He formed Silken Mountain Web Services, Inc., to resell the information in the SelectPhone (trademark) database. The corporation makes the database available on the Internet to anyone willing to pay its price — which, needless to say, is less than ProCD charges its commercial customers. Zeidenberg has purchased two additional SelectPhone (trademark) packages, each with an updated version of the database, and made the latest information available over the World Wide Web, for a price, through his corporation. ProCD filed this suit seeking an injunction against further dissemination that exceeds the rights specified in the licenses (identical in each of the three packages Zeidenberg purchased). The district court held the licenses ineffectual because their terms do not appear on the outside of the packages. The court added that the second and third licenses stand no different from the first, even though they are identical, because they *might* have been different, and a purchaser does not agree to — and cannot be bound by — terms that were secret at the time of purchase.

II

Following the district court, we treat the licenses as ordinary contracts accompanying the sale of products, and therefore as governed by the common law of contracts and the Uniform Commercial Code. Whether there are legal differences between "contracts" and "licenses" (which may matter under the copyright doctrine of first sale) is a subject for another day. . . . Zeidenberg does not argue that Silken Mountain Web Services is free of any restrictions that apply to Zeidenberg himself, because any effort to treat the two parties as distinct would put Silken Mountain behind the eight ball on ProCD's argument that copying the application program onto its hard disk violates the copyright laws. Zeidenberg does argue, and the district court held, that placing the package of software on the shelf is an "offer," which the customer "accepts" by paying the asking price and leaving the store with the goods. In Wisconsin, as elsewhere, a contract includes only the terms on which the parties have agreed. One cannot agree to hidden terms, the judge concluded. So far, so good — but one of the terms to which Zeidenberg agreed by purchasing the software is that the transaction was subject to a license. Zeidenberg's position therefore must be that the printed terms on the outside of a box are the parties' contract — except for printed terms that refer to or incorporate other terms. But why would Wisconsin fetter the parties' choice in this way? Vendors can put the entire terms of a contract on the outside of a box only by using microscopic type, removing other information that buyers might find more useful (such as what the software does, and on which computers it works), or both. The "Read Me" file included with most software, describing system requirements and potential incompatibilities, may be equivalent to ten pages of type; warranties and license restrictions take still more space. Notice on the outside, terms on the inside, and a right to return the software for a refund if the terms are unacceptable (a right that the license expressly extends), may be a means of doing business valuable to buyers and sellers alike. See E. Allan Farnsworth, 1 Farnsworth on Contracts §4.26 (1990); Restatement (2d) of Contracts §211 comment a (1981) ("Standardization of agreements serves many of the same functions as standardization of goods and services; both are essential to a system of mass production and distribution. Scarce and costly time and skill can be devoted to a class of transactions rather than the details of individual transactions."). Doubtless a state could forbid the use of standard contracts in the software business, but we do not think that Wisconsin has done so.

Transactions in which the exchange of money precedes the communication of detailed terms are common. Consider the purchase of insurance. The buyer goes to an agent, who explains the essentials (amount of coverage, number of years) and remits the premium to the home office, which sends back a policy. On the district judge's understanding, the terms of the policy are irrelevant because the insured paid before receiving them. Yet the device of payment, often with a "binder" (so that the insurance takes effect immediately even though the home office reserves the right to withdraw coverage later), in advance of the policy, serves buyers' interests by accelerating effectiveness and reducing transactions costs. Or consider the purchase of an airline ticket. The traveler calls the carrier or an agent, is quoted a price, reserves a seat, pays, and gets a ticket, in that order. The ticket contains elaborate terms, which the traveler can reject by canceling the reservation. To use the ticket is to accept the terms, even terms that in retrospect are disadvantageous. See Carnival Cruise Lines, Inc. v. Shute, 499 U.S. 585 (1991). . . . Just so with a ticket to a concert. The back of the ticket states that the patron promises not to record the concert; to attend is to agree. A theater that detects a violation will confiscate the tape and escort the violator to the exit. One *could* arrange things so that every concertgoer signs this promise before forking over the money, but that cumbersome way of doing things not only would lengthen queues and raise prices but also would scotch the sale of tickets by phone or electronic data service.

Consumer goods work the same way. Someone who wants to buy a radio set visits a store, pays, and walks out with a box. Inside the box is a leaflet containing some terms, the most important of which usually is the warranty, read for the first time in the comfort of home. By Zeidenberg's lights, the warranty in the box is irrelevant; every consumer gets the standard warranty implied by the UCC in the event the contract is silent; yet so far as we are aware no state disregards warranties furnished with consumer products. Drugs come with a list of ingredients on the outside and an elaborate package insert on the inside. The package insert describes drug interactions, contraindications, and other vital information — but, if Zeidenberg is right, the purchaser need not read the package insert, because it is not part of the contract.

Next consider the software industry itself. Only a minority of sales take place over the counter, where there are boxes to peruse. A customer may place an order by phone in response to a line item in a catalog or a review in a magazine. Much software is ordered over the Internet by purchasers who have never seen a box.

Increasingly software arrives by wire. There is no box; there is only a stream of electrons, a collection of information that includes data, an application program, instructions, many limitations ("MegaPixel 3.14159 cannot be used with BytePusher 2.718"), and the terms of sale. The user purchases a serial number, which activates the software's features. On Zeidenberg's arguments, these unboxed sales are unfettered by terms — so the seller has made a broad warranty and must pay consequential damages for any shortfalls in performance, two "promises" that if taken seriously would drive prices through the ceiling or return transactions to the horse-and-buggy age.

According to the district court, the UCC does not countenance the sequence of money now, terms later. . . . One of the court's reasons — that by proposing as part of the draft Article 2B a new UCC

§2-203 that would explicitly validate standard-form user licenses the American Law Institute and the National Conference of Commissioners on Uniform Laws have conceded the invalidity of shrinkwrap licenses under current law — depends on a faulty inference. To propose a change in a law's *text* is not necessarily to propose a change in the law's *effect*. New words may be designed to fortify the current rule with a more precise text that curtails uncertainty. To judge by the flux of law review articles discussing shrinkwrap licenses, uncertainty is much in need of reduction — although businesses seem to feel less uncertainty than do scholars, for only three cases (other than ours) touch on the subject, and none directly addresses it. See Step-Saver Data Systems, Inc. v. Wyse Technology, 939 F.2d 91 (3d Cir. 1991); Vault Corp. v. Quaid Software Ltd., 847 F.2d 255, 268-270 (5th Cir. 1988); Arizona Retail Systems, Inc. v. Software Link, Inc., 831 F. Supp. 759 (D. Ariz. 1993). As their titles suggest, these are not consumer transactions. *Step-Saver* is a battle-of-the-forms case, in which the parties exchange incompatible forms and a court must decide which prevails. . . . Our case has only one form; UCC §2-207 is irrelevant. *Vault* holds that Louisiana's special shrinkwrap-license statute is preempted by federal law, a question to which we return. And *Arizona Retail Systems* did not reach the question, because the court found that the buyer knew the terms of the license before purchasing the software.

What then does the current version of the UCC have to say? We think that the place to start is §2-204(1): "A contract for sale of goods may be made in any manner sufficient to show agreement, including conduct by both parties which recognizes the existence of such a contract." A vendor, as master of the offer, may invite acceptance by conduct, and may propose limitations on the kind of conduct that constitutes acceptance. A buyer may accept by performing the acts the vendor proposes to treat as acceptance. And that is what happened. ProCD proposed a contract that a buyer would accept by *using* the software after having an opportunity to read the license at leisure. This Zeidenberg did. He had no choice, because the software splashed the license on the screen and would not let him proceed without indicating acceptance. So although the district judge was right to say that a contract can be, and often is, formed simply by paying the price and walking out of the store, the UCC permits contracts to be formed in other ways. ProCD proposed such a different way, and without protest Zeidenberg agreed. Ours is not a case in which a consumer opens a package to find an insert saying "you owe us an extra $10,000" and the seller files suit to collect. Any buyer finding such a demand can prevent formation of the contract by returning the package, as can any consumer who concludes that the terms of the license make the software worth less than the purchase price. Nothing in the UCC requires a seller to maximize the buyer's net gains.

Section 2-606, which defines "acceptance of goods," reinforces this understanding. A buyer accepts goods under §2-606(1)(b) when, after an opportunity to inspect, he fails to make an effective rejection under §2-602(1). ProCD extended an opportunity to reject if a buyer should find the license terms unsatisfactory; Zeidenberg inspected the package, tried out the software, learned of the license, and did not reject the goods. We refer to §2-606 only to show that the opportunity to return goods can be important; acceptance of an offer differs from acceptance of goods after delivery, . . . but the UCC consistently permits the parties to structure their relations so that the buyer has a chance to make a final decision after a detailed review.

Some portions of the UCC impose additional requirements on the way parties agree on terms. A disclaimer of the implied warranty of merchantability must be "conspicuous." UCC §2-316(2), incorporating UCC §1-201(10). Promises to make firm offers, or to negate oral modifications, must be "separately signed." UCC §§2-205, 2-209(2). These special provisos reinforce the impression that, so far as the UCC is concerned, other terms may be as inconspicuous as the forum-selection clause on the back of the cruise ship ticket in *Carnival Lines*. Zeidenberg has not located any Wisconsin case — for that matter, any case in any state — holding that under the UCC the ordinary terms found in shrinkwrap licenses require any special prominence, or otherwise are to be undercut rather than enforced. In the end, the terms of the license are conceptually identical to the contents of the package. Just as no court would dream of saying that SelectPhone (trademark) must contain 3,100 phone books rather than 3,000, or must have data no more than 30 days old, or must sell for $100 rather than $150 — although any of these changes would be welcomed by the customer, if all other things were held constant — so, we believe, Wisconsin would not let the buyer pick and choose among terms. Terms of use are no less a part of "the product" than are the size of the database and the speed with which the software compiles listings. Competition among vendors, not judicial revision of a package's contents, is how consumers are protected in a market economy. Digital Equipment Corp. v. Uniq Digital Technologies, Inc., 73 F.3d 756 (7th Cir. 1996). ProCD has rivals, which may elect to compete by offering superior software, monthly updates, improved terms of use, lower price, or a better compromise among these elements. As we stressed above, adjusting terms in buyers' favor might help Matthew Zeidenberg today (he already has the software) but would lead to a response, such as a higher price, that might make consumers as a whole worse off. . . . REVERSED AND REMANDED.

STUDY GUIDE: Given the academic controversy raised by the decision in the next case, you should ask yourself: What, if anything, did Gateway do wrong here? What, if anything, should it have done differently? What exactly is improper about the burden placed on the consumer by this transaction? Does the way Gateway structured the transaction here run afoul of the rules of offer and acceptance? Who is the offeror? Who is the offeree? Why do we care? How about U.C.C §2-204? Are the doctrines of acceptance by silence and acceptance by performance, which we studied in Chapter 4, at all relevant here?

HILL v. GATEWAY 2000
United States Court of Appeals, Seventh Circuit,
105 F.3d 1147 (1997)

EASTERBROOK, Circuit Judge. A customer picks up the phone, orders a computer, and gives a credit card number. Presently a box arrives,

containing the computer and a list of terms, said to govern unless the customer returns the computer within 30 days. Are these terms effective as the
parties' contract, or is the contract term-free because the order-taker did not
read any terms over the phone and elicit the customer's assent?

One of the terms in the box containing a Gateway 2000 system was an
arbitration clause. Rich and Enza Hill, the customers, kept the computer
more than 30 days before complaining about its components and performance. They filed suit in federal court arguing, among other things, that the
product's shortcomings make Gateway a racketeer (mail and wire fraud are
said to be the predicate offenses), leading to treble damages under RICO for
the Hills and a class of all other purchasers. Gateway asked the district court
to enforce the arbitration clause; the judge refused, writing that "[t]he
present record is insufficient to support a finding of a valid arbitration
agreement between the parties or that the plaintiffs were given adequate
notice of the arbitration clause." Gateway took an immediate appeal, as is its
right. 9 U.S.C. §16(a)(1)(A).

The Hills say that the arbitration clause did not stand out: they concede
noticing the statement of terms but deny reading it closely enough to discover the agreement to arbitrate, and they ask us to conclude that they
therefore may go to court. Yet an agreement to arbitrate must be enforced
"save upon such grounds as exist at law or in equity for the revocation of any
contract." 9 U.S.C. §2. Doctor's Associates, Inc. v. Casarotto, 517 U.S. 681
(1996), holds that this provision of the Federal Arbitration Act is inconsistent with any requirement that an arbitration clause be prominent.
A contract need not be read to be effective; people who accept take the
risk that the unread terms may in retrospect prove unwelcome. Carr v.
CIGNA Securities, Inc., 95 F.3d 544, 547 (7th Cir. 1996); Chicago Pacific
Corp. v. Canada Life Assurance Co., 850 F.2d 334 (7th Cir. 1988). Terms
inside Gateway's box stand or fall together. If they constitute the parties'
contract because the Hills had an opportunity to return the computer after
reading them, then all must be enforced.

ProCD, Inc. v. Zeidenberg, 86 F.3d 1447 (7th Cir. 1996), holds that
terms inside a box of software bind consumers who use the software after an
opportunity to read the terms and to reject them by returning the product.
Likewise, Carnival Cruise Lines, Inc. v. Shute, 499 U.S. 585 (1991), enforces
a forum-selection clause that was included among three pages of terms
attached to a cruise ship ticket. *ProCD* and *Carnival Cruise Lines* exemplify
the many commercial transactions in which people pay for products with
terms to follow; *ProCD* discusses others. The district court concluded in
ProCD that the contract is formed when the consumer pays for the software;
as a result, the court held, only terms known to the consumer at that
moment are part of the contract, and provisos inside the box do not
count. Although this is one way a contract could be formed, it is not the
only way: "A vendor, as master of the offer, may invite acceptance by conduct, and may propose limitations on the kind of conduct that constitutes
acceptance. A buyer may accept by performing the acts the vendor proposes
to treat as acceptance." Id. at 1452. Gateway shipped computers with the
same sort of accept-or-return offer ProCD made to users of its software.
ProCD relied on the Uniform Commercial Code rather than any peculiari-
ties of Wisconsin law; both Illinois and South Dakota, the two states whose

law might govern relations between Gateway and the Hills, have adopted the UCC; neither side has pointed us to any atypical doctrines in those states that might be pertinent; *ProCD* therefore applies to this dispute.

Plaintiffs ask us to limit *ProCD* to software, but where's the sense in that? *ProCD* is about the law of contract, not the law of software. Payment preceding the revelation of full terms is common for air transportation, insurance, and many other endeavors. Practical considerations support allowing vendors to enclose the full legal terms with their products. Cashiers cannot be expected to read legal documents to customers before ringing up sales. If the staff at the other end of the phone for direct-sales operations such as Gateway's had to read the four-page statement of terms before taking the buyer's credit card number, the droning voice would anesthetize rather than enlighten many potential buyers. Others would hang up in a rage over the waste of their time. And oral recitation would not avoid customers' assertions (whether true or feigned) that the clerk did not read term X to them, or that they did not remember or understand it. Writing provides benefits for both sides of commercial transactions. Customers as a group are better off when vendors skip costly and ineffectual steps such as telephonic recitation, and use instead a simple approve-or-return device. Competent adults are bound by such documents, read or unread. For what little it is worth, we add that the box from Gateway was crammed with software. The computer came with an operating system, without which it was useful only as a boat anchor. . . . Gateway also included many application programs. So the Hills' effort to limit *ProCD* to software would not avail them factually, even if it were sound legally — which it is not.

For their second sally, the Hills contend that *ProCD* should be limited to executory contracts (to licenses in particular), and therefore does not apply because both parties' performance of this contract was complete when the box arrived at their home. This is legally and factually wrong: legally because the question at hand concerns the *formation* of the contract rather than its *performance*, and factually because both contracts were incompletely performed. *ProCD* did not depend on the fact that the seller characterized the transaction as a license rather than as a contract; we treated it as a contract for the sale of goods and reserved the question whether for other purposes a "license" characterization might be preferable. 86 F.3d at 1450. All debates about characterization to one side, the transaction in *ProCD* was no more executory than the one here: Zeidenberg paid for the software and walked out of the store with a box under his arm, so if arrival of the box with the product ends the time for revelation of contractual terms, then the time ended in *ProCD* before Zeidenberg opened the box. But of course ProCD had not completed performance with delivery of the box, and neither had Gateway. One element of the transaction was the warranty, which obliges sellers to fix defects in their products. The Hills have invoked Gateway's warranty and are not satisfied with its response, so they are not well positioned to say that Gateway's obligations were fulfilled when the motor carrier unloaded the box. What is more, both ProCD and Gateway promised to help customers to use their products. Long-term service and information obligations are common in the computer business, on both hardware and software sides. Gateway offers "lifetime service" and has a round-the-clock telephone hotline to fulfil this promise. Some vendors spend more money helping customers use their products than on developing and manufacturing them. The document in Gateway's box includes promises of future performance that some consumers value highly; these promises bind Gateway just as the arbitration clause binds the Hills.

Next the Hills insist that *ProCD* is irrelevant because Zeidenberg was a "merchant" and they are not. Section 2-207(2) of the UCC, the infamous battle-of-the-forms section, states that "additional terms [following acceptance of an offer] are to be construed as proposals for addition to a contract. Between merchants such terms become part of the contract unless. . . ." Plaintiffs tell us that *ProCD* came out as it did only because Zeidenberg was a "merchant" and the terms inside ProCD's box were not excluded by the "unless" clause. This argument pays scant attention to the opinion in *ProCD*, which concluded that, when there is only one form, "sec. 2-207 is irrelevant." 86 F.3d at 1452. The question in *ProCD* was not whether terms were added to a contract after its formation, but how and when the contract was formed — in particular, whether a vendor may propose that a contract of sale be formed, not in the store (or over the phone) with the payment of money or a general "send me the product," but after the customer has had a chance to inspect both the item and the terms. *ProCD* answers "yes," for merchants and consumers alike. Yet again, for what little it is worth we observe that the Hills misunderstand the setting of *ProCD*. A "merchant" under the UCC "means a person who deals in goods of the kind or otherwise by his occupation holds himself out as having knowledge or skill peculiar to the practices or goods involved in the transaction," §2-104(1). Zeidenberg bought the product at a retail store, an uncommon place for merchants to acquire inventory. His corporation put ProCD's database on the Internet for anyone to browse, which led to the litigation but did not make Zeidenberg a software merchant.

At oral argument the Hills propounded still another distinction: the box containing ProCD's software displayed a notice that additional terms were within, while the box containing Gateway's computer did not. The difference is functional, not legal. Consumers browsing the aisles of a store can look at the box, and if they are unwilling to deal with the prospect of additional terms can leave the box alone, avoiding the transactions costs of returning the package after reviewing its contents. Gateway's box, by contrast, is just a shipping carton; it is not on display anywhere. Its function is to protect the product during transit, and the information on its sides is for the use of handlers ("Fragile!" "This Side Up!" "↑") rather than would-be purchasers.

Perhaps the Hills would have had a better argument if they were first alerted to the bundling of hardware and legal-ware after opening the box and wanted to return the computer in order to avoid disagreeable terms, but were dissuaded by the expense of shipping. What the remedy would be in such a case — could it exceed the shipping charges? — is an interesting question, but one that need not detain us because the Hills knew before they ordered the computer that the carton would include *some* important terms, and they did not seek to discover these in advance. Gateway's ads state that their products come with limited warranties and lifetime support. How limited was the warranty — 30 days, with service contingent on shipping the computer back, or five years, with free onsite service? What sort of support was offered? Shoppers have three principal ways to discover these things. First, they can ask the vendor to send a copy before deciding whether to buy. The Magnuson-Moss Warranty Act requires firms to distribute their warranty terms on request, 15 U.S.C. §2302(b)(1)(A); the Hills do not contend that Gateway would have refused to enclose the remaining terms too. Concealment would be bad for business, scaring some customers away and leading to excess returns from others. Second, shoppers can consult public sources (computer magazines, the Web sites of vendors) that may contain this information. Third, they may inspect the documents after the product's delivery. Like Zeidenberg, the Hills took the third option. By keeping the computer beyond 30 days, the Hills accepted Gateway's offer, including the arbitration clause.

The Hills' remaining arguments, including a contention that the arbitration clause is unenforceable as part of a scheme to defraud, do not require more than a citation to Prima Paint Corp. v. Flood & Conklin Mfg. Co., 388 U.S. 395 (1967). Whatever may be said pro and con about the cost and efficacy of arbitration (which the Hills disparage) is for Congress and the contracting parties to consider. Claims based on RICO are no less arbitrable than those founded on the contract or the law of torts. Shearson/American Express, Inc. v. McMahon, 482 U.S. 220, 238-242 (1987). The decision of the district court is vacated, and this case is remanded with instructions to compel the Hills to submit their dispute to arbitration.

STUDY GUIDE: What objection does Judge Vratil have to Judge Easterbrook's analysis of §2-207? Does Judge Vratil find that there was no mutual assent? If there was mutual assent, when did it occur and what were its terms? Do you see any difference between the problem of conflicting forms and the specific problem that arises in Hill *and this case?*

KLOCEK v. GATEWAY
United States District Court, District of Kansas,
104 F. Supp. 2d 1332 (2000)

VRATIL,* District Judge. William S. Klocek brings suit against Gateway, Inc. and Hewlett-Packard, Inc. on claims arising from purchases of a Gateway computer and a Hewlett-Packard scanner. . . . For reasons stated below, the Court overrules Gateway's motion to dismiss. . . .

Plaintiff brings individual and class action claims against Gateway, alleging that it induced him and other consumers to purchase computers and special support packages by making false promises of technical support. . . . Individually, plaintiff also claims breach of contract and breach

---

* Kathryn Hoefer Vratil (1949-†). Educated at the University of Kansas (B.A., 1971; J.D., 1975), Judge Vratil clerked for three years for the same U.S. District Court on which she now sits. She was named to the court in 1992 after practicing law in Kansas City, Kansas, and serving as a judge in the municipal court of the City of Prairie Village, Kansas. In 2008, she became the Chief Judge of the U.S. District Court for the District of Kansas. — R.B.

of warranty, in that Gateway breached certain warranties that its computer would be compatible with standard peripherals and standard internet services. . . .

Gateway asserts that plaintiff must arbitrate his claims under Gateway's Standard Terms and Conditions Agreement ("Standard Terms"). Whenever it sells a computer, Gateway includes a copy of the Standard Terms in the box which contains the computer battery power cables and instruction manuals. At the top of the first page, the Standard Terms include the following notice:

NOTE TO THE CUSTOMER

This document contains Gateway 2000's Standard Terms and Conditions. By keeping your Gateway 2000 computer system beyond five (5) days after the date of delivery, you accept these Terms and Conditions.

The notice is in emphasized type and is located inside a printed box which sets it apart from other provisions of the document. The Standard Terms are four pages long and contain 16 numbered paragraphs. Paragraph 10 provides the following arbitration clause:

DISPUTE RESOLUTION. Any dispute or controversy arising out of or relating to this Agreement or its interpretation shall be settled exclusively and finally by arbitration. The arbitration shall be conducted in accordance with the Rules of Conciliation and Arbitration of the International Chamber of Commerce. The arbitration shall be conducted in Chicago, Illinois, U.S.A. before a sole arbitrator. Any award rendered in any such arbitration proceeding shall be final and binding on each of the parties, and judgment may be entered thereon in a court of competent jurisdiction.

Gateway urges the Court to dismiss plaintiff's claims under the Federal Arbitration Act ("FAA"). The FAA ensures that written arbitration agreements in maritime transactions and transactions involving interstate commerce are "valid, irrevocable, and enforceable." Federal policy favors arbitration agreements and requires that we "rigorously enforce" them. . . .

Before granting a stay or dismissing a case pending arbitration, the Court must determine that the parties have a written agreement to arbitrate. . . . When deciding whether the parties have agreed to arbitrate, the Court applies ordinary state law principles that govern the formation of contracts. . . . If the parties dispute making an arbitration agreement, a jury trial on the existence of an agreement is warranted if the record reveals genuine issues of material fact regarding the parties' agreement.

Gateway urges the Court to follow the Seventh Circuit decision in *Hill*. That case involved the shipment of a Gateway computer with terms similar to the Standard Terms in this case, except that Gateway gave the customer 30 days — instead of 5 days — to return the computer. In enforcing the arbitration clause, the Seventh Circuit relied on its decision in *ProCD*, where it enforced a software license which was contained inside a product box. . . .

The Court is not persuaded that Kansas or Missouri courts would follow the Seventh Circuit reasoning in *Hill* and *ProCD*. In each case the

Seventh Circuit concluded without support that UCC §2-207 was irrelevant because the cases involved only one written form. This conclusion is not supported by the statute or by Kansas or Missouri law. Disputes under §2-207 often arise in the context of a "battle of forms," . . . but nothing in its language precludes application in a case which involves only one form. The statute provides:

Additional terms in acceptance or confirmation.

> (1) A definite and seasonable expression of acceptance or a written confirmation which is sent within a reasonable time operates as an acceptance even though it states terms additional to or different from those offered or agreed upon, unless acceptance is expressly made conditional on assent to the additional or different terms.
>
> (2) The additional terms are to be construed as proposals for addition to the contract [if the contract is not between merchants]. . . .

By its terms, §2-207 applies to an acceptance or written confirmation. It states nothing which requires another form before the provision becomes effective. In fact, the official comment to the section specifically provides that §§2-207(1) and (2) apply "where an agreement has been reached orally . . . and is followed by one or both of the parties sending formal memoranda embodying the terms so far agreed and adding terms not discussed." Official Comment 1 of UCC §2-207. Kansas and Missouri courts have followed this analysis. . . . Thus, the Court concludes that Kansas and Missouri courts would apply §2-207 to the facts in this case. . . .

In addition, the Seventh Circuit provided no explanation for its conclusion that "the vendor is the master of the offer." . . . In typical consumer transactions, the purchaser is the offeror, and the vendor is the offeree. . . . While it is possible for the vendor to be the offeror, . . . Gateway provides no factual evidence which would support such a finding in this case. The Court therefore assumes for purposes of the motion to dismiss that plaintiff offered to purchase the computer (either in person or through catalog order) and that Gateway accepted plaintiff's offer (either by completing the sales transaction in person or by agreeing to ship and/or shipping the computer to plaintiff).[55] . . .

Under §2-207, the Standard Terms constitute either an expression of acceptance or written confirmation. As an expression of acceptance, the Standard Terms would constitute a counter-offer only if Gateway expressly made its acceptance conditional on plaintiff's assent to the additional or different terms. . . ." [T]he conditional nature of the acceptance must be clearly expressed in a manner sufficient to notify the offeror that the offeree is unwilling to proceed with the transaction unless the additional or different terms are included in the contract." [Brown Machine v. Hercules, Inc.,

55. UCC §2-206(b) provides that "an order or other offer to buy goods for prompt or current shipment shall be constructed as inviting acceptance either by a prompt promise to ship or by the prompt or current shipment. . . ." The official comment states that "[e]ither shipment or a prompt promise to ship is made a proper means of acceptance of an offer looking to current shipment" UCC §2-206, Official Comment 2.

770 S.W.2d 416, 420 (Mo. App. 1989).[56]] Gateway provides no evidence that at the time of the sales transaction, it informed plaintiff that the transaction was conditioned on plaintiff's acceptance of the Standard Terms. Moreover, the mere fact that Gateway shipped the goods with the terms attached did not communicate to plaintiff any unwillingness to proceed without plaintiff's agreement to the Standard Terms. . . .

Because plaintiff is not a merchant, additional or different terms contained in the Standard Terms did not become part of the parties' agreement unless plaintiff expressly agreed to them. See K.S.A. §84-2-207, Kansas Comment 2 (if either party is not a merchant, additional terms are proposals for addition to the contract that do not become part of the contract unless the original offeror expressly agrees). Gateway argues that plaintiff demonstrated acceptance of the arbitration provision by keeping the computer more than five days after the date of delivery. Although the Standard Terms purport to work that result, Gateway has not presented evidence that plaintiff expressly agreed to those Standard Terms. Gateway states only that it enclosed the Standard Terms inside the computer box for plaintiff to read afterwards. It provides no evidence that it informed plaintiff of the five-day review-and-return period as a condition of the sales transaction, or that the parties contemplated additional terms to the agreement.[57] See *Step-Saver*, 939 F.2d at 99 (during negotiations leading to purchase, vendor never mentioned box-top license or obtained buyer's express assent thereto). The Court finds that the act of keeping the computer past five days was not sufficient to demonstrate that plaintiff expressly agreed to the Standard Terms. . . . Thus, because Gateway has not provided evidence sufficient to support a finding under Kansas or Missouri law that plaintiff agreed to the arbitration provision contained in Gateway's Standard Terms, the Court overrules Gateway's motion to dismiss. . . .

REFERENCE: Barnett, §§3.5.4-3.5.5

---

56. Courts are split on the standard for a conditional acceptance under §2-207. . . . On one extreme of the spectrum, courts hold that the offeree's response stating a materially different term solely to the disadvantage of the offeror constitutes a conditional acceptance. . . . At the other end of the spectrum, courts hold that the conditional nature of the acceptance should be so clearly expressed in a manner sufficient to notify the offeror that the offeree is unwilling to proceed without the additional or different terms. . . . The middle approach requires that the response predicate acceptance on clarification, addition or modification. . . .

57. The Court is mindful of the practical considerations which are involved in commercial transactions, but it is not unreasonable for a vendor to clearly communicate to a buyer — at the time of sale — either the complete terms of the sale or the fact that the vendor will propose additional terms as a condition of sale, if that be the case.

6

WRITTEN MANIFESTATIONS OF ASSENT

Contracts have long been associated with writings. The growth of the writ of assumpsit in the sixteenth century as the primary vehicle for the enforcement of private commitments (described in Chapter 9) was motivated by a desire to obviate the early common law's almost exclusive reliance on written contracts. We have already seen in Chapter 5 some of the problems that surround form contracts. In this chapter, we shall examine three other ways that writings can affect the enforcement of a contract. First (Section A), the existence of a writing may be considered privileged in some manner and given priority over *oral* communications when interpreting the meaning of assent. This circumstance is governed by the *parol evidence rule* although, as we shall discover, this rule also privileges some *written* manifestations of assent over others. Second (Section B), sometimes a writing fails to reflect the understanding of one or both parties. Under certain circumstances, these *mistakes in integration* may justify the reformation of a writing. Finally (Section C), the rise of the writ of assumpsit to protect against the *under*enforcement of informal commitments led in the seventeenth century to a legislative attempt by Parliament to combat the problem of *over*enforcement. This legislation was — and still is — known as the Statute of Frauds.

A. INTERPRETING A WRITING — THE PAROL EVIDENCE RULE

Raffles v. Wichelhaus concerned the problem of determining the meaning of an agreement. In *Raffles* there was a written contract. Attorney Mellish argued that parol evidence may be offered to resolve ambiguous terms in the writing. He was referring to evidence of meaning that is extrinsic to the writing itself. In this section, we continue our study of contractual interpretation begun in Chapter 5 in the special context of written agreements. How should a written manifestation of assent be interpreted in light of extrinsic oral *or written* evidence that may contradict it? The parol evidence rule was developed to answer this question. As we shall see, there is more than one approach to this rule.

THOMPSON v. LIBBEY
Supreme Court of Minnesota,
34 Minn. 374, 26 N.W. 1 (1885)

MITCHELL, J.* The plaintiff being the owner of a quantity of logs marked "H.C.A.," cut in the winters of 1882 and 1883, and lying in the Mississippi river, or on its banks, above Minneapolis, defendant and the plaintiff, through his agent, D. S. Mooers, having fully agreed on the terms of a sale and purchase of the logs referred to, executed the following written agreement:

Agreement.

Hastings, Minn., June 1, 1883.

I have this day sold to R. C. Libby, of Hastings, Minn., all my logs marked "H.C.A.," cut in the winters of 1882 and 1883, for ten dollars a thousand feet, boom scale at Minneapolis, Minnesota. Payments cash as fast as scale bills are produced.

J. H. Thompson,
per D. S. Mooers.
R. C. Libbey.

This action having been brought for the purchase money, defendant having pleaded a warranty of the quality of the logs, alleged to have been made at the time of the sale, and a breach of it, offered on the trial oral testimony to prove the warranty, which was admitted, over the objection of plaintiff that it was incompetent to prove a verbal warranty, the contract of sale being in writing. This raises the only point in the case.

No ground was laid for the reformation of the written contract, and any charge of fraud on part of plaintiff or his agent in making the sale was on the trial expressly disclaimed. No rule is more familiar than that "parol contemporaneous evidence is inadmissible to contradict or vary the terms of a valid written instrument," and yet none has given rise to more misapprehension as to its application. It is a rule founded on the obvious inconvenience and injustice that would result if matters in writing, made with consideration and deliberation, and intended to embody the entire agreement of the parties, were liable to be controlled by what Lord Coke expressively calls "the uncertain testimony of slippery memory." Hence, where the parties have deliberately put their engagements into writing in such terms as to import a legal obligation, without any uncertainty as to the object or extent of such engagement, it is conclusively presumed that the whole engagement of the parties, and the manner and extent of their undertaking, was reduced to writing. . . . Of course, the rule presupposed that the parties

---

* *William Mitchell* (1832-1900), a graduate of Jefferson College (Pennsylvania), was admitted to the Virginia bar in 1857. That same year he settled in Winona, Minnesota, where he practiced law (1857-1873) and was a member of the second state legislature of Minnesota (1859-1860). He served as judge of the Third Judicial District (1874-1881), then was appointed to a newly created position on the state's supreme bench, where he served until 1899. Upon retiring from the bench, he returned to private practice in the few months prior to his death. William Mitchell College of Law is named for him. — C.R.

intended to have the terms of their complete agreement embraced in the writing, and hence it does not apply where the writing is incomplete on its face and does not purport to contain the whole agreement, as in the case of mere bills of parcels, and the like.

But in what manner shall it be ascertained whether the parties intended to express the whole of their agreement in the writing? It is sometimes loosely stated that where the whole contract be not reduced to writing, parol evidence may be admitted to prove the part omitted. But to allow a party to lay the foundation for such parol evidence by oral testimony that only part of the agreement was reduced to writing, and then prove by parol the part omitted, would be to work in a circle, and to permit the very evil which the rule was designed to prevent. The only criterion of the completeness of the written contract as a full expression of the agreement of the parties is the writing itself. If it imports on its face to be a complete expression of the whole agreement, — that is, contain such language as imports a complete legal obligation, — [it is to be presumed that the parties introduced into it every material item and term;] and parol evidence cannot be admitted to add another term to the agreement, although the writing contains nothing on the particular one to which the parol evidence is directed. The rule forbids to add by parol when the writing is silent, as well as to vary where it speaks. . . .

. . . Our conclusion therefore is that the court erred in admitting parol evidence of a warranty, and therefore the order refusing a new trial must be reversed.

STUDY GUIDE: How does the method of applying the parol evidence rule exemplified by Masterson v. Sine differ from that used by the court in Thompson v. Libbey? Is there any way of drafting a contract ex ante so as to ensure that parol evidence will not be introduced at trial on the question of integration? What sources does Justice Traynor look to in announcing California's rule?

MASTERSON v. SINE
Supreme Court of California,
68 Cal. 2d 222, 436 P.2d 561 (1968)

TRAYNOR,* Chief Justice.

Dallas Masterson and his wife Rebecca owned a ranch as tenants in common. On February 25, 1958, they conveyed it to Medora and Lu Sine by a grant deed "Reserving unto the Grantors herein an option to purchase the above described property on or before February 25, 1968" for the "same

---

* Roger Traynor (1900-1983) studied at the University of California (A.B., J.D.). He was instructor of political science at the University of California at Berkeley from 1926 to 1929, and a professor of law at Berkeley from 1929 to 1940. In 1940, Traynor became an associate justice of the Supreme Court of California; he was named Chief Justice in 1964, a position which he held until retiring from the bench in 1970. After retirement, he taught law at the Universities of Virginia, Colorado, and Utah, and at the Hastings College of Law in San Francisco. — C.R.

consideration as being paid heretofore plus their depreciation value of any improvements Grantees may add to the property from and after two and a half years from this date." Medora is Dallas' sister and Lu's wife. Since the conveyance Dallas has been adjudged bankrupt. His trustee in bankruptcy and Rebecca brought this declaratory relief action to establish their right to enforce the option.

. . .

Trial Court reasoning →

The court also determined that the parol evidence rule precluded admission of extrinsic evidence offered by defendants to show that the parties wanted the property kept in the Masterson family and that the option was therefore personal to the grantors and could not be exercised by the trustee in bankruptcy.

Trial Court holding →

The court entered judgment for plaintiffs, declaring their right to exercise the option, specifying in some detail how it could be exercised, and reserving jurisdiction to supervise the manner of its exercise and to determine the amount that plaintiffs will be required to pay defendants for their capital expenditures if plaintiffs decide to exercise the option.

Defendant argument →

Defendants appeal. They contend that the option provision is too uncertain to be enforced and that extrinsic evidence as to its meaning should not have been admitted. The trial court properly refused to frustrate the obviously declared intention of the grantors to reserve an option to repurchase by an overly meticulous insistence on completeness and clarity of written expression. It properly admitted extrinsic evidence to explain the language of the deed (see Farnsworth, "Meaning" in the Law of Contracts (1967) 76 Yale L.J. 939, 959-965; Corbin, The Interpretation of Words and the Parol Evidence Rule (1965) 50 Cornell L.Q. 161) to the end that the consideration for the option would appear with sufficient certainty to permit specific enforcement. The trial court erred, however, in excluding the extrinsic evidence that the option was personal to the grantors and therefore nonassignable.

General Rule →

When the parties to a written contract have agreed to it as an "integration" — a complete and final embodiment of the terms of an agreement — parol evidence cannot be used to add to or vary its terms. When only part of the agreement is integrated, the same rule applies to that part, but parol evidence may be used to prove elements of the agreement not reduced to writing.

The crucial issue in determining whether there has been an integration is whether the parties intended their writing to serve as the exclusive embodiment of their agreement. The instrument itself may help to resolve that issue. It may state, for example, that "there are no previous understandings or agreements not contained in the writing," and thus express the parties' "intention to nullify antecedent understandings or agreements." (See 3 Corbin, Contracts (1960) §578, p. 411.) Any such collateral agreement itself must be examined, however, to determine whether the parties intended the subjects of negotiation it deals with to be included in, excluded from, or otherwise affected by the writing. Circumstances at the time of the writing may also aid in the determination of such integration.

California cases have stated that whether there was an integration is to be determined solely from the face of the instrument, and that the question for the court is whether it "appears to be a complete agreement." Neither of these strict formulations of the rule, however, has been consistently applied. The requirement that the writing must appear incomplete on its face has been repudiated in many cases where parol evidence was admitted "to prove the existence of a separate oral agreement as to any matter on which the document is silent and which is not inconsistent with its terms" — even though the instrument appeared to state a complete agreement. Even under the rule that the writing alone is to be consulted, it was found necessary to examine the alleged collateral agreement before concluding that proof of it was precluded by the writing alone. (See 3 Corbin, Contracts (1960) §582, pp. 444-446.) It is therefore evident that "The conception of a writing as wholly and intrinsically self-determinative of the parties' intent to make it a sole memorial of one or seven or twenty-seven subjects of negotiation is an impossible one." (9 Wigmore, Evidence (3d ed. 1940) §2431, p. 103.) For example, a promissory note given by a debtor to his creditor may integrate all their present contractual rights and obligations, or it may be only a minor part of an underlying executory contract that would never be discovered by examining the face of the note.

In formulating the rule governing parol evidence, several policies must be accommodated. One policy is based on the assumption that written evidence is more accurate than human memory. This policy, however, can be adequately served by excluding parol evidence of agreements that directly contradict the writing. Another policy is based on the fear that fraud or unintentional invention by witnesses interested in the outcome of the litigation will mislead the finder of facts. (Murray, The Parol Evidence Rule: A Clarification (1966) 4 Duquesne L. Rev. 337, 338-339.) McCormick has suggested that the party urging the spoken as against the written word is most often the economic underdog, threatened by severe hardship if the writing is enforced. In his view the parol evidence rule arose to allow the court to control the tendency of the jury to find through sympathy and without a dispassionate assessment of the probability of fraud or faulty memory that the parties made an oral agreement collateral to the written contract, or that preliminary tentative agreements were not abandoned when omitted from the writing. (See McCormick, Evidence (1954) §210.) He recognizes, however, that if this theory were adopted in disregard of all other considerations, it would lead to the exclusion of testimony concerning oral agreements whenever there is a writing and thereby often defeat the true intent of the parties. See McCormick, op. cit. supra, §216, p. 441.)

Evidence of oral collateral agreements should be excluded only when the fact finder is likely to be misled. The rule must therefore be based on the credibility of the evidence. [One such standard, adopted by section 240(1)(b) of the Restatement of Contracts, permits proof of a collateral agreement if it "is such an agreement as might *naturally* be made as a separate agreement by parties situated as were the parties to the written contract."] (Italics added; see McCormick, Evidence (1954) §216, p. 441; see also 3 Corbin, Contracts (1960) §583, p. 475, §594, pp. 568-569; 4 Williston, Contracts (3d ed. 1961) §638, pp. 1039-1045.) The draftsmen of the Uniform Commercial Code would exclude the evidence in still fewer instances: "If the additional terms are such that, if agreed upon, they would *certainly* have been included in the document in the view of the court, then evidence of their alleged making must be kept from the trier of fact." (Com. 3, §2-202, italics added.)

The option clause in the deed in the present case does not explicitly provide that it contains the complete agreement, and the deed is silent on the question of assignability. Moreover, the difficulty of accommodating the formalized structure of a deed to the insertion of collateral agreements makes it less likely that all the terms of such an agreement were included.[1] (See 3 Corbin, Contracts (1960) §587; 4 Williston, Contracts (3d ed. 1961) §645; 70 A.L.R. 752, 759 (1931); 68 A.L.R. 245 (1930).) The statement of the reservation of the option might well have been placed in the recorded deed solely to preserve the grantors' rights against any possible future purchasers and this function could well be served without any mention of the parties' agreement that the option was personal. There is nothing in the record to indicate that the parties to this family transaction, through experience in land transactions or otherwise, had any warning of the disadvantages of failing to put the whole agreement in the deed. This case is one, therefore, in which it can be said that a collateral agreement such as that alleged "might naturally be made as a separate agreement." A fortiori, the case is not one in which the parties "would certainly" have included the collateral agreement in the deed.

It is contended, however, that an option agreement is ordinarily presumed to be assignable if it contains no provisions forbidding its transfer or indicating that its performance involves elements personal to the parties. The fact that there is a written memorandum, however, does not necessarily preclude parol evidence rebutting a term that the law would otherwise presume. In American Industrial Sales Corp. v. Airscope, Inc., 44 Cal. 2d 393, 397-398, we held it proper to admit parol evidence of a contemporaneous collateral agreement as to the place of payment of a note, even though it contradicted the presumption that a note, silent as to the place of payment, is payable where the creditor resides. (For other examples of this approach, see Richter v. Union Land etc. Co. (1900) 129 Cal. 367, 375, 62 P. 39 (presumption of time of delivery rebutted by parol evidence); Wolters v. King (1897) 119 Cal. 172, 175-176, 51 P. 35 (presumption of time of payment rebutted by parol evidence); Mangini v. Wolfschmidt, Ltd., supra, 165 Cal. App. 2d 192, 198-201, 331 P.2d 728 (presumption of duration of an agency contract rebutted by parol evidence); Zinn v. Ex-Cell-O Corp. (1957) 148 Cal. App. 2d 56, 73-74, 306 P.2d 1017; see also Rest., Contracts, §240, com. c.) Of course a statute may preclude parol evidence to rebut a statutory presumption. Here, however, there is no such statute. In the absence of a controlling statute the parties may provide that a contract right or duty is nontransferable. Moreover, even when there is no explicit agreement — written or oral — that contractual duties shall be personal, courts will effectuate presumed intent to that effect if the circumstances indicate that performance by substituted person would be different from that contracted for.

---

1. The option was in the form of a reservation in a deed; however, in legal effect it is the same as if it had been contained in a separate document.

In the present case defendants offered evidence that the parties agreed that the option was not assignable in order to keep the property in the Masterson family. The trial court erred in excluding that evidence.

The judgment is reversed. ——> Holding

PETERS, TORBRINER, MOSK, and SULLIVAN, JJ., concur.

BURKE, J., dissenting. . . .

RESTATEMENT (SECOND) OF CONTRACTS

§209.   INTEGRATED AGREEMENTS

(1) An integrated agreement is a writing or writings constituting a final expression of one or more terms of an agreement.

(2) Whether there is an integrated agreement is to be determined by the court as a question preliminary to determination of a question of interpretation or to application of the parol evidence rule.

(3) Where the parties reduce an agreement to a writing which in view of its completeness and specificity reasonably appears to be a complete agreement, it is taken to be an integrated agreement unless it is established by other evidence that the writing did not constitute a final expression.

factors?

§210.   COMPLETELY AND PARTIALLY INTEGRATED AGREEMENTS

(1) A completely integrated agreement is an integrated agreement adopted by the parties as a complete and exclusive statement of the terms of the agreement.

(2) A partially integrated agreement is an integrated agreement other than a completely integrated agreement.

(3) Whether an agreement is completely or partially integrated is to be determined by the court as a question preliminary to determination of a question of interpretation or to application of the parol evidence rule.

§213.   EFFECT OF INTEGRATED AGREEMENT ON PRIOR AGREEMENTS (PAROL EVIDENCE RULE)

(1) A binding integrated agreement discharges prior agreements to the extent that it is inconsistent with them. ——> Written agreement trumps earlier words

(2) A binding completely integrated agreement discharges prior agreements to the extent that they are within its scope.

(3) An integrated agreement that is not binding or that is voidable and avoided does not discharge a prior agreement. But an integrated agreement, even though not binding, may be effective to render inoperative a term which would have been part of the agreement if it had not been integrated.

§214.   EVIDENCE OF PRIOR OR CONTEMPORANEOUS AGREEMENTS AND NEGOTIATIONS

Agreements and negotiations prior to or contemporaneous with the adoption of a writing are admissible in evidence to establish

(a) that the writing is or is not an integrated agreement;

(b) that the integrated agreement, if any, is completely or partially integrated;

(c) the meaning of the writing, whether or not integrated;

(d) illegality, fraud, duress, mistake, lack of consideration, or other invalidating cause;

(e) ground for granting or denying rescission, reformation, specific performance, or other remedy.

§216.   CONSISTENT ADDITIONAL TERMS

(1) Evidence of a consistent additional term is admissible to supplement an integrated agreement unless the court finds that the agreement was completely integrated.

(2) An agreement is not completely integrated if the writing omits a consistent additional agreed term which is

(a) agreed to for separate consideration, or

(b) such a term as in the circumstances might naturally be omitted from the writing.

STUDY GUIDE: Which view of the parol evidence rule is adopted by the Uniform Commercial Code? As a lawyer, how might you protect your clients from having their written contracts challenged by extrinsic evidence?

SALES CONTRACTS: THE UNIFORM COMMERCIAL CODE

§2-202.   FINAL WRITTEN EXPRESSION: PAROL OR EXTRINSIC EVIDENCE

Terms with respect to which the confirmatory memoranda of the parties agree or which are otherwise set forth in a writing intended by the parties as a final expression of their agreement with respect to such terms as are included therein may not be contradicted by evidence of any prior agreement or of a contemporaneous oral agreement but may be explained or supplemented

(a) by course of dealing or usage of trade (§1-205) or by course of performance (§2-208); and

(b) by evidence of consistent additional terms unless the court finds the writing to have been intended also as a complete and exclusive statement of the terms of the agreement.

REFERENCE: Farnsworth, §§7.2-7.4, 7.12-7.13
                  Calamari & Perillo, §§3.2-3.8, 3.16
                  Murray, §§83-86

STUDY GUIDE: *In the next two cases, consider what divides Justice Traynor and Judge Kozinski. Is one taking a more "objective" or less "contextual" approach than the other? Or do they differ about the trade-off between doing justice in a particular case and establishing a rule of law upon which contracting parties may rely? Who do you think is right?*

PACIFIC GAS AND ELECTRIC CO. v.
G. W. THOMAS DRAYAGE & RIGGING CO.
Supreme Court of California,
69 Cat, 2d 33, 69 Cat Rptr. 561, 442 P.2d 641 (1968)

TRAYNOR, C.J. Defendant appeals from a judgment for plaintiff in an action for damages for injury to property under an indemnity clause of a contract.

In 1960 defendant entered into a contract with plaintiff to furnish the labor and equipment necessary to remove and replace the upper metal cover of plaintiff's steam turbine. Defendant agreed to perform the work "at (its) own risk and expense" and to "indemnify" plaintiff "against all loss, damage, expense and liability resulting from . . . injury to property, arising out of or in any way connected with the performance of this contract." Defendant also agreed to procure not less than $50,000 insurance to cover liability for injury to property. Plaintiff was to be an additional named insured, but the policy was to contain a cross-liability clause extending the coverage to plaintiff's property.

During the work the cover fell and injured the exposed rotor of the turbine. Plaintiff brought this action to recover $25,144.51, the amount it subsequently spent on repairs. During the trial it dismissed a count based on negligence and thereafter secured judgment on the theory that the indemnity provision covered injury to all property regardless of ownership.

Defendant offered to prove by admissions of plaintiff's agents, by defendant's conduct under similar contracts entered into with plaintiff, and by other proof that in the indemnity clause the parties meant to cover injury to property of third parties only and not to plaintiff's property. Although the trial court observed that the language used was "the classic language for a third party indemnity provision" and that "one could very easily conclude that . . . its whole intendment is to indemnify third parties," it nevertheless held that the "plain language" of the agreement also required defendant to indemnify plaintiff for injuries to plaintiff's property. Having determined that the contract had a plain meaning, the court refused to admit any extrinsic evidence that would contradict its interpretation.

When a court interprets a contract on this basis, it determines the meaning of the instrument in accordance with the ". . . extrinsic evidence of the judge's own linguistic education and experience." (3 Corbin on

Contracts (1960 ed.) (1964 Supp. §579, p. 225, fn.56).) The exclusion of testimony that might contradict the linguistic background of the judge reflects a judicial belief in the possibility of perfect verbal expression. (9 Wigmore on Evidence (3d ed. 1940) §2461, p. 187.) This belief is a remnant of a primitive faith in the inherent potency[2] and inherent meaning of words.[3]

The test of admissibility of extrinsic evidence to explain the meaning of a written instrument is not whether it appears to the court to be plain and unambiguous on its face, but whether the offered evidence is relevant to prove a meaning to which the language of the instrument is reasonably susceptible. . . .

A rule that would limit the determination of the meaning of a written instrument to its four-corners merely because it seems to the court to be clear and unambiguous, would either deny the relevance of the intention of the parties or presuppose a degree of verbal precision and stability our language has not attained.

Some courts have expressed the opinion that contractual obligations are created by the mere use of certain words, whether or not there was any intention to incur such obligations.[4] Under this view, contractual obligations flow, not from the intention of the parties but from the fact that they used certain magic words. Evidence of the parties' intention therefore becomes irrelevant.

In this state, however, the intention of the parties as expressed in the contract is the source of contractual rights and duties.[5] A court must ascertain and give effect to this intention by determining what the parties meant by the words they used. Accordingly, the exclusion of relevant, extrinsic evidence to explain the meaning of a written instrument could be justified only if it were feasible to determine the meaning the parties gave to the words from the instrument alone.

If words had absolute and constant referents, it might be possible to discover contractual intention in the words themselves and in the manner in which they were arranged. Words, however, do not have absolute and constant referents. "A word is a symbol of thought but has no arbitrary and

2. E.g., "The elaborate system of taboo and verbal prohibitions in primitive groups; the ancient Egyptian myth of Khern, the apotheosis of the word, and of Thoth, the Scribe of Truth, the Giver of words and Script, the Master of Incantations; the avoidance of the name of God in Brahmanism, Judaism and Islam; totemistic and protective names in mediaeval Turkish and Finno-Ugrian languages; the misplaced verbal scruples of the 'Précieuses'; the Swedish peasant custom of curing sick cattle smitten by witchcraft, by making them swallow a page torn out of the psalter and put in dough. . . ." From Ullman, The Principles of Semantics (1963 ed.) 43. (See also Ogden and Richards, The Meaning of Meaning (rev. ed. 1956) pp. 24-47.)

3. " 'Rerum enim vocabula immutabilia sunt, homines mutabilia,' " (words are unchangeable, men changeable) from Dig. XXXIII, 10, 7, §2, de sup. leg. as quoted in 9 Wigmore on Evidence, op. cit. supra, §2461, p. 187.

4. "A contract has, strictly speaking, nothing to do with the personal, or individual, intent of the parties. A contract is an obligation attached by the mere force of law to certain acts of the parties, usually words, which ordinarily accompany and represent a known intent." (Hotchkiss v. National City Bank of New York (S.D.N.Y. 1911) 200 F. 287, 293. . . .)

5. "A contract must be so interpreted as to give effect to the mutual intention of the parties as it existed at the time of contracting, so far as the same is ascertainable and lawful." (Civ. Code, §1636. . . .)

fixed meaning like a symbol of algebra or chemistry, . . ." (Pearson v. State Social Welfare Board (1960) 54 Cal. 2d 184, 195 [5 Cal. Rptr. 553, 559, 353 P.2d 33, 391].) The meaning of particular words or groups of words varies with the ". . . verbal context and surrounding circumstances and purposes in view of the linguistic education and experience of their users and their hearers or readers (not excluding judges). . . . A word has no meaning apart from these factors; much less does it have an objective meaning, one true meaning." (Corbin, The Interpretation of Words and the Parol Evidence Rule (1965) 50 Cornell L.Q. 161, 187.) Accordingly, the meaning of a writing ". . . can only be found by interpretation in the light of all the circumstances that reveal the sense in which the writer used the words. The exclusion of parol evidence regarding such circumstances merely because the words do not appear ambiguous to the reader can easily lead to the attribution to a written instrument of a meaning that was never intended. (Citations omitted.)" (Universal Sales Corp. v. California Press Mfg. Co., supra, 20 Cal. 2d 751, 776 [128 P.2d 665, 679] (concurring opinion). . . .)

Although extrinsic evidence is not admissible to add to, detract from, or vary the terms of a written contract, these terms must first be determined before it can be decided whether or not extrinsic evidence is being offered for a prohibited purpose. The fact that the terms of an instrument appear clear to a judge does not preclude the possibility that the parties chose the language of the instrument to express different terms. That possibility is not limited to contracts whose terms have acquired a particular meaning by trade usage,[6] but exists whenever the parties' understanding of the words used may have differed from the judge's understanding.

Accordingly, rational interpretation requires at least a preliminary consideration of all credible evidence offered to prove the intention of the parties.[7] (Civ. Code, §1647; Code Civ. Proc. §1860. . . .) Such evidence includes testimony as to the "circumstances surrounding the making of the agreement . . . including the object, nature and subject matter of the writing . . ." so that the court can "place itself in the same situation in which the parties found themselves at the time of contracting." (Universal Sales Corp. v. California Press Mfg. Co., supra, 20 Cal. 2d 751, 761 [128 P.2d 665, 671]. . . .) If the court decides, after considering this evidence, that the language of a contract, in the light of all the circumstances, is "fairly

---

6. Extrinsic evidence of trade usage or custom has been admitted to show that the term "United Kingdom" in a motion picture distribution contract included Ireland . . . ; that the word "ton" in a lease meant a long ton or 2,240 pounds and not the statutory ton of 2,000 pounds . . . ; that the word "stubble" in a lease included not only stumps left in the ground but everything "left on the ground after the harvest time" . . . ; that the term "north" in a contract dividing mining claims indicated a boundary line running along the "magnetic and not the true meridian" . . . and that a form contract for purchase and sale was actually an agency contract. . . .

7. When objection is made to any particular item of evidence offered to prove the intention of the parties, the trial court may not yet be in a position to determine whether in the light of all of the offered evidence, the item objected to will turn out to be admissible as tending to prove a meaning of which the language of the instrument is reasonably susceptible or inadmissible as tending to prove a meaning of which the language is not reasonably susceptible. In such case the court may admit the evidence conditionally by either reserving its ruling on the objection or by admitting the evidence subject to a motion to strike. (See Evid. Code, §403.)

susceptible of either one of the two interpretations contended for. ...."
(Balfour v. Fresno C. & I. Co. (1895) 109 Cal. 221, 225 [44 P. 876,
877]. ...), extrinsic evidence relevant to prove either of such meanings is
admissible.[8]

In the present case the court erroneously refused to consider extrinsic
evidence offered to show that the indemnity clause in the contract was not
intended to cover injuries to plaintiff's property. Although that evidence
was not necessary to show that the indemnity clause was reasonably susceptible of the meaning contended for by defendant, it was nevertheless
relevant and admissible on that issue. Moreover, since that clause was reasonably susceptible of that meaning, the offered evidence was also admissible to prove that the clause had that meaning and did not cover injuries to
plaintiff's property. Accordingly, the judgment must be reversed. *—> Holding!*

PETERS, J., MOSK, J., BURKE, J., SULLIVAN, J., and PEEK, J., concurred.

MCCOMB, J., dissented.

*STUDY GUIDE: In the next case, do you agree with Judge Kozinski that the
doctrine embodied in* Pacific Gas *required reversal of the district court's
dismissal of Trident's complaint?*

TRIDENT CENTER v. CONNECTICUT
GENERAL LIFE INSURANCE CO.
United States Court of Appeals, Ninth Circuit,
847 F.2d 564 (1988)

KOZINSKI, C.J.:*

The parties to this transaction are, by any standard, highly sophisticated business people: Plaintiff is a partnership consisting of an insurance
company and two of Los Angeles' largest and most prestigious law firms;
defendant is another insurance company. Dealing at arm's length and from
positions of roughly equal bargaining strength, they negotiated a commercial loan amounting to more than $56 million. The contract documents are
lengthy and detailed; they squarely address the precise issue that is the

----

8. Extrinsic evidence has often been admitted in such cases on the stated ground that
the contract was ambiguous (e.g., Universal Sales Corp. v. California Press Mfg. Co., supra, 20
Cal. 2d 751, 761 [128 P.2d 665]). This statement of the rule is harmless if it is kept in mind
that the ambiguity may be exposed by extrinsic evidence that reveals more than one possible
meaning.

Alex Kozinski (1950-†) was born in Bucharest, Romania, and came to the United
States in 1962. He was educated at the University of California at Los Angeles (A.B., J.D.).
Upon graduation, Kozinski was a law clerk for the Honorable Anthony M. Kennedy on the
U.S. Court of Appeals for the Third Circuit (1975-1976) and for Chief Justice Warren E.
Burger (1976-1977). Thereafter, he practiced privately in Los Angeles and Washington,
D.C. (1977-1981), and concurrently in the Office of Counsel to President Reagan (1980-
1981). In 1982, he was appointed Chief Judge of the U.S. Claims Court, where he sat
until his current appointment to the U.S. Court of Appeals for the Ninth Circuit in 1985.
Kozinski was the youngest person ever appointed to the Court of Appeals to that date.
In 2007, he became Chief Judge. — K.T.

subject of this dispute; to all who read English, they appear to resolve the issue fully and conclusively.

Plaintiff nevertheless argues here, as it did below, that it is entitled to introduce extrinsic evidence that the contract means something other than what it says. This case therefore presents the question whether parties in California can ever draft a contract that is proof to parol evidence. Somewhat surprisingly, the answer is no.

Issue

FACTS

The facts are rather simple. Sometime in 1983 Security First Life Insurance Company and the law firms of Mitchell, Silberberg & Knupp and Manatt, Phelps, Rothenberg & Tunney formed a limited partnership for the purpose of constructing an office building complex on Olympic Boulevard in West Los Angeles. The partnership, Trident Center, the plaintiff herein, sought and obtained financing for the project from defendant, Connecticut General Life Insurance Company. The loan documents provide for a loan of $56,500,000 at 12 1/4 percent interest for a term of 15 years, secured by a deed of trust on the project. The promissory note provides that "[m]aker shall not have the right to prepay the principal amount hereof in whole or in part" for the first 12 years. Note at 6. In years 13-15, the loan may be prepaid, subject to a sliding prepayment fee. The note also provides that in case of a default during years 1-12, Connecticut General has the option of accelerating the note and adding a 10 percent prepayment fee.

Contract Terms

Everything was copacetic for a few years until interest rates began to drop. The 12 1/4 percent rate that had seemed reasonable in 1983 compared unfavorably with 1987 market rates and Trident started looking for ways of refinancing the loan to take advantage of the lower rates. Connecticut General was unwilling to oblige, insisting that the loan could not be prepaid for the first 12 years of its life, that is, until January 1996.

Trident then brought suit in state court seeking a declaration that it was entitled to prepay the loan now, subject only to a 10 percent prepayment fee. Connecticut General promptly removed to federal court and brought a motion to dismiss, claiming that the loan documents clearly and unambiguously precluded prepayment during the first 12 years. The district court agreed and dismissed Trident's complaint. The court also "*sua sponte,* sanction[ed] the plaintiff for the filing of a frivolous lawsuit." . . . Trident appeals both aspects of the district court's ruling.

Procedural Posture

DISCUSSION

I

Trident makes two arguments as to why the district court's ruling is wrong. First, it contends that the language of the contract is ambiguous and proffers a construction that it believes supports its position. Second, Trident argues that, under California law, even seemingly unambiguous contracts are subject to modification by parol or extrinsic evidence. Trident faults the district court for denying it the opportunity to present evidence that the contract language did not accurately reflect the parties' intentions.

A. *The Contract*

As noted earlier, the promissory note provides that Trident "shall not have the right to prepay the principal amount hereof in whole or in part before January 1996." Note at 6. It is difficult to imagine language that more clearly or unambiguously expresses the idea that Trident may not unilaterally prepay the loan during its first 12 years. Trident, however, argues that there is an ambiguity because another clause of the note provides that "[i]n the event of a prepayment resulting from a default hereunder or the Deed of Trust prior to January 10, 1996 the prepayment fee will be ten percent (10%)." Note at 6-7. Trident interprets this clause as giving it the option of prepaying the loan if only it is willing to incur the prepayment fee.

We reject Trident's argument out of hand. In the first place, its proffered interpretation would result in a contradiction between two clauses of the contract; the default clause would swallow up the clause prohibiting Trident from prepaying during the first 12 years of the contract. The normal rule of construction, of course, is that courts must interpret contracts, if possible, so as to avoid internal conflict. . . .

In any event, the clause on which Trident relies is not on its face reasonably susceptible to Trident's proffered interpretation. Whether to accelerate repayment of the loan in the event of default is entirely Connecticut General's decision. The contract makes this clear at several points. See Note at 4 ("in each such event [of default], the entire principal indebtedness, or so much thereof as may remain unpaid at the time, shall, *at the option of Holder*, become due and payable immediately" (emphasis added [by the court])); id. at 7 ("[i]n the event Holder exercises its *option to accelerate* the maturity hereof. . . ." (emphasis added [by the court])); Deed of Trust ¶2.01, at 25 ("in each such event [of default], Beneficiary *may* declare all sums secured hereby immediately due and payable. . . ." (emphasis added [by the court])). Even if Connecticut General decides to declare a default and accelerate, it "may rescind any notice of breach or default." Id. ¶2.02, at 26. Finally, Connecticut General has the option of doing nothing at all: "Beneficiary reserves the right at its sole option to waive noncompliance by Trustor with any of the conditions or covenants to be performed by Trustor hereunder." Id. ¶3.02, at 29.

Once again, it is difficult to imagine language that could more clearly assign to Connecticut General the exclusive right to decide whether to declare a default, whether and when to accelerate, and whether, having chosen to take advantage of any of its remedies, to rescind the process before its completion. Trident nevertheless argues that it is entitled to precipitate a default and insist on acceleration by tendering the balance due on the note plus the 10 percent prepayment fee. The contract language, cited above, leaves no room for this construction. It is true, of course, that Trident is free to stop making payments, which may then cause Connecticut General to declare a default and accelerate. But that is not to say that Connecticut General would be required to so respond. The contract quite clearly gives Connecticut General other options: It may choose to waive the default, or to take advantage of some other remedy such as the right to collect "all the income, rents, royalties, revenue, issues, profits, and proceeds of the Property." Deed of Trust ¶1.18, at 22. By interpreting the contract as Trident suggests, we would ignore those provisions giving Connecticut General, not Trident, the exclusive right to decide how, when and whether the contract will be terminated upon default during the first 12 years.

In effect, Trident is attempting to obtain judicial sterilization of its intended default. But defaults are messy things; they are supposed to be. Once the maker of a note secured by a deed of trust defaults, its credit rating may deteriorate; attempts at favorable refinancing may be thwarted by the need to meet the trustee's sale schedule; its cash flow may be impaired if the beneficiary takes advantage of the assignment of rents remedy; default provisions in its loan agreements with other lenders may be triggered. Fear of these repercussions is strong medicine that keeps debtors from shirking their obligations when interest rates go down and they become disenchanted with their loans.[9] That Trident is willing to suffer the cost and delay of a lawsuit, rather than simply defaulting, shows far better than anything we might say that these provisions are having their intended effect. We decline Trident's invitation to truncate the lender's remedies and deprive Connecticut General of its bargained-for protection.

B.   Extrinsic Evidence

Trident argues in the alternative that, even if the language of the contract appears to be unambiguous, the deal the parties actually struck is in fact quite different. It wishes to offer extrinsic evidence that the parties had agreed Trident could prepay at any time within the first 12 years by tendering the full amount plus a 10 percent prepayment fee. As discussed above, this is an interpretation to which the contract, as written, is not reasonably susceptible. Under traditional contract principles, extrinsic evidence is inadmissible to interpret, vary or add to the terms of an unambiguous integrated written instrument. . . .

Trident points out, however, that California does not follow the traditional rule. Two decades ago the California Supreme Court in Pacific Gas & Electric Co. v. G.W. Thomas Drayage & Rigging Co., 69 Cal. 2d 33, 442 P.2d 641, 69 Cal. Rptr. 561 (1968), turned its back on the notion that a contract can ever have a plain meaning discernible by a court without resort to extrinsic evidence. The court reasoned that contractual obligations flow not from the words of the contract, but from the intention of the parties. "Accordingly," the court stated, "the exclusion of relevant, extrinsic, evidence to explain the meaning of a written instrument could be justified only

---

9. This provides a symmetry with the situation where interest rates go up and it is the lender who is stuck with a loan it would prefer to turn over at market rates. In an economy where interest rates fluctuate, it is all but certain that one side or the other will be dissatisfied with a long-term loan at some time. Mutuality calls for enforcing the contract as written no matter whose ox is being gored.

if it were feasible to determine the meaning the parties gave to the words from the instrument alone." 69 Cal. 2d at 38, 442 P.2d 641, 69 Cal. Rptr. 561. This, the California Supreme Court concluded, is impossible: "If words had absolute and constant referents, it might be possible to discover contractual intention in the words themselves and in the manner in which they were arranged. Words, however, do not have absolute and constant referents." Id. In the same vein, the court noted that "[t]he exclusion of testimony that might contradict the linguistic background of the judge reflects a judicial belief in the possibility of perfect verbal expression. This belief is a remnant of a primitive faith in the inherent potency and inherent meaning of words." Id. at 37, 442 P.2d 641, 69 Cal. Rptr. 561 (citation and footnotes omitted).[10]

Under *Pacific Gas*, it matters not how clearly a contract is written, nor how completely it is integrated, nor how carefully it is negotiated, nor how squarely it addresses the issue before the court: the contract cannot be rendered impervious to attack by parol evidence. If one side is willing to claim that the parties intended one thing but the agreement provides for another, the court must consider extrinsic evidence of possible ambiguity. If that evidence raises the specter of ambiguity where there was none before, the contract language is displaced and the intention of the parties must be divined from self-serving testimony offered by partisan witnesses whose recollection is hazy from passage of time and colored by their conflicting interests. . . . We question whether this approach is more likely to divulge the original intention of the parties than reliance on the seemingly clear words they agreed upon at the time. . . .

Pacific Gas casts a long shadow of uncertainty over all transactions negotiated and executed under the law of California. As this case illustrates, even when the transaction is very sizeable, even if it involves only sophisticated parties, even if it was negotiated with the aid of counsel, even if it results in contract language that is devoid of ambiguity, costly and protracted litigation cannot be avoided if one party has a strong enough motive for challenging the contract. While this rule creates much business for lawyers and an occasional windfall to some clients, it leads only to frustration and delay for most litigants and clogs already overburdened courts.

It also chips away at the foundation of our legal system. By giving credence to the idea that words are inadequate to express concepts, *Pacific Gas* undermines the basic principle that language provides a meaningful constraint on public and private conduct. If we are unwilling to say that parties, dealing face to face, can come up with language that binds them, how can we send anyone to jail for violating statutes consisting of mere words lacking "absolute and constant referents"? How can courts ever enforce decrees, not written in language understandable to all, but encoded in a dialect reflecting, only the "linguistic background of the judge"? Can lower courts ever be faulted for failing to carry out the mandate of higher courts when "perfect verbal expression" is impossible? Are all attempts to

10. In an unusual footnote, the court compared the belief in the immutable meaning of words with " '[t]he elaborate system of taboo and verbal prohibitions in primitive groups . . . [such as] the Swedish peasant custom of curing sick cattle smitten by witchcraft, by making them swallow a page torn out of the psalter and put in dough. . . .' " Id. n.2 (quoting Ullman, The Principles of Semantics 43 (1963)).

develop the law in a reasoned and principled fashion doomed to failure as "remnant[s] of a primitive faith in the inherent potency and inherent meaning of words"?

Be that as it may. While we have our doubts about the wisdom of *Pacific Gas*, we have no difficulty understanding its meaning, even without extrinsic evidence to guide us. As we read the rule in California, we must reverse and remand to the district court in order to give plaintiff an opportunity to present extrinsic evidence as to the intention of the parties in drafting the contract.[11] It may not be a wise rule we are applying, but it is a rule that binds us. Erie R.R. Co. v. Tompkins, 304 U.S. 64, 78, 58 S. Ct. 817, 822, 82 L. Ed. 1188 (1938).

→ Erie Doctrine

II

In imposing sanctions on plaintiff, the district court stated:

> Pursuant to Fed. R. Civ. P. 11, the court, *sua sponte*, sanctions the plaintiff for the filing of a frivolous lawsuit. The court concludes that the language in the note and deed of trust is plain and clear. No reasonable person, much less firms of able attorneys, could possibly misunderstand this crystal-clear language. Therefore, this action was brought in bad faith.

Order of Dismissal at 3. Having reversed the district court on its substantive ruling, we must, of course, also reverse it as to the award of sanctions. While we share the district judge's impatience with this litigation, we would suggest that his irritation may have been misdirected. It is difficult to blame plaintiff and its lawyers for bringing this lawsuit. With this much money at stake, they would have been foolish not to pursue all remedies available to them under the applicable law. At fault, it seems to us, are not the parties and their lawyers but the legal system that encourages this kind of lawsuit. By holding that language has no objective meaning, and that contracts mean only what courts ultimately say they do, *Pacific Gas* invites precisely this type of lawsuit.[12] With the benefit of 20 years of hindsight, the California Supreme Court may wish to revisit the issue. If it does so, we commend to it the facts of this case as a paradigmatic example of why the traditional rule, based on centuries of experience, reflects the far wiser approach.

11. Nothing we say should be construed as foreclosing Connecticut General from moving for summary judgment after completion of discovery; given the unambiguous language of the contract itself, such a motion would succeed unless Trident were to come forward with extrinsic evidence sufficient to render the contract reasonably susceptible to Trident's alternate interpretation, thereby creating a genuine issue of fact resolvable only at trial.

12. This is not to say, of course, that all lawsuits seeking to challenge the interpretation of facially unambiguous contracts are necessarily immune from imposition of sanctions. Even under *Pacific Gas*, a party urging an interpretation lacking any objectively reasonable basis in fact might well be subject to sanctions for bringing a frivolous lawsuit.

CONCLUSION

Holding! { The judgment of the district court is reversed. The case is remanded for reinstatement of the complaint and further proceedings in accordance with this opinion. The parties shall bear their own costs on appeal.

Reread: Restatement §216 (p. 458)

Comparative Law Background: The Parol Evidence Rule Under the United Nations Convention on Contracts for the International Sale of Goods

DANIEL D. BARNHIZER, CISG AS AN ALTERNATIVE SYSTEM OF DEFAULT RULES GOVERNING THE SALE OF GOODS.[13] Just as Article 2 of the UCC establishes default rules governing contracts for the sale of goods within the U.S., so too does the United Nations Convention on Contracts for the International Sale of Goods ("CISG") for sales across international borders. The United Nations Conference on Contracts for the International Sales of Goods unanimously adopted the CISG in 1980, culminating decades of effort by the international community to establish a uniform law governing transnational sales contracts. The CISG was drafted by the United Nations Commission on International Trade Law ("UNCITRAL"), comprised of representatives from 36 nations, including the United States. The United States ratified the Convention in 1986, and the CISG became effective on January 1, 1988.

Like the UCC, the CISG establishes default rules applicable to contracts for the sale of goods. But unlike the UCC, the CISG governs contracts between parties with places of business in different countries unless those parties specify a different choice of law in their contract.[14] The purpose of the CISG is to reduce the often-greater legal uncertainty that accompanies international legal transactions, as compared with domestic contracting. In the international context, both parties are likely to lack full information regarding each other's legal regimes. Social, cultural and linguistic differences also increase the likelihood of misunderstandings and delays in communication or delivery. The resulting transactional inefficiencies range from difficulties in agreeing on the appropriate choice of law, to uncertainty as to contract terms negotiated according to unfamiliar legal rules and languages, to increased litigation costs arising from litigating disputes in foreign forums. By laying out a system of clear default rules around which the parties can reliably contract, the CISG arguably reduces potential transaction costs that would otherwise be required to resolve these uncertainties.

Many provisions of the CISG mirror rules contained in the UCC. Other provisions embody legal concepts derived from non-Anglo-American legal

---

13. [This selection was graciously written by Professor Barnhizer of the Michigan State University-Detroit College of Law for inclusion in this casebook. — EDS.]

14. The United States' ratification of the CISG requires that the parties must *both* have their places of business in countries that are signatories of the CISG.

systems that law students — indeed, many practicing attorneys who are untrained in foreign non-common-law legal systems — find unfathomable. For both litigators and transactional attorneys, knowledge of international agreements such as the CISG can be essential. As a multilateral treaty to which the United States is a party, the CISG is incorporated into state contract law through the Supremacy Clause of Art. VI, §2 of the United States Constitution.[15] Consequently, attorneys cannot safely assume their clients and practices are immune from international law merely because they practice solely within the United States.

COMPARING THE CISG AND THE UCC

The CISG is similar to the UCC in many ways, and U.S. courts have expressly held that "[c]aselaw interpreting analogous provisions of Article 2 of the [UCC], may also inform a court where the language of the relevant CISG provisions tracks that of the UCC."[16] But despite such similarities and interpretative overlaps, critical differences between the two contracting regimes present substantial pitfalls for the unwary. Two of the most significant differences involve the admissibility of parol evidence and ability of the winning party to recover attorneys' fees.[17]

1.   THE PAROL EVIDENCE RULE

Article 8 of the CISG eliminates the parol evidence rule and requires courts to consider all relevant evidence of the parties' intent to determine the contract terms:

Article 8(1).   For the purposes of this Convention statements made by and other conduct of a party are to be interpreted according to his intent where the other party knew or could not have been unaware what that intent was.

Article 8(3).   In determining the intent of a party or the understanding a reasonable person would have had, due consideration is to be given to all relevant circumstances of the case including the negotiations, any practices which the parties have established between themselves, usages and any subsequent conduct of the parties.

---

15. See, e.g., Asante Technologies, Inc. v. PMC-Sierra, Inc., 164 F. Supp. 2d 1142, 1150 (N.D. Cal. 2001) (party's choice of law provision designating California law to apply to any dispute held insufficient to opt out of CISG because "California is bound by the Supremacy Clause to the treaties of the United States" and therefore CISG — as a treaty of the United States — is California law).

16. Delchi Carrier SpA v. Rotorex Corp., 71 F.3d 1024, 1028 (2d Cir. 1995).

17. The CISG differs substantially from the UCC in numerous other respects, including the mailbox rule on the timing of acceptances by mail, the UCC's perfect tender rule, applicability of the CISG only to transactions between merchants, rules governing rejection of nonconforming goods, and rules governing delivery of goods.

U.S. courts have recognized that CISG Article 8 may produce dramatically different outcomes compared to purely domestic transactional disputes. For example, in MCC-Marble Ceramic Center, Inc. v. Ceramica Nuova D'Agostino, S.p.A.,[18] the court expressly held that applying the parol evidence rule to transnational sale of goods contracts would defeat the CISG's goals of good faith and uniformity of interpretation:

> [A]lthough jurisdictions in the United States have found the parol evidence rule helpful to promote good faith and uniformity in contract, as well as an appropriate answer to the question of how much consideration to give parol evidence, a wide number of other States Party to the CISG have rejected the rule in their domestic jurisdictions. One of the primary factors motivating the negotiation and adoption of the CISG was to provide parties to international contracts for the sale of goods with some degree of certainty as to the principles of law that would govern potential disputes and remove the previous doubt regarding which party's legal system might otherwise apply. Courts applying the CISG cannot, therefore, upset the parties' reliance on the Convention by substituting familiar principles of domestic law when the Convention requires a different result.[19]

The reasoning of *MCC-Marble* suggests that the benefits of promoting uniform rules in international sale of goods transactions outweigh the benefits of the parol evidence rule. But why is this so? First, in the international context, the parol evidence rule could cause greater uncertainty than it would prevent. Transnational sales of goods under the CISG not only are conducted across legal and linguistic barriers, but also can be conducted under informal contracting mechanisms. The CISG specifically rejects any formal requirements for sales contracts and provides for the enforcement of purely oral agreements.[20] In the face of such informal contracting mechanisms and heightened likelihood of miscommunication, even an apparently unambiguous written contract will often fail to reflect the terms of the parties' actual agreement.

Second, few legal regimes have adopted the parol evidence rule. Consequently, non-American contracting parties would be more likely to suffer undue surprise if they were forced to comply with the parol evidence rule after contracting in a foreign legal regime that allows parol evidence to vary or contradict the terms of a written agreement. The CISG default rule thus reflects the common sense understandings of most parties engaged in transnational sales of goods.

Third, the CISG's rule permitting parol evidence of the parties' intent illustrates how default rules can be set to remedy information asymmetries. The CISG's default rule permitting parol evidence requires parties who wish to take advantage of the parol evidence rule to notify the other party to the transaction of the existence of the rule by bargaining to opt out of the CISG default rule. In other words, if a party wishes to merge all prior negotiations into a final writing that prohibits the use of parol evidence to vary the terms

---

18. MCC-Marble Ceramic Center, Inc. v. Ceramica Nuova D'Agostino, S.p.A., 144 F.3d 1384 (11th Cir. 1998).

19. Id. at 1391 (internal citation omitted).

20. See CISG art. 11.

of the contract, the CISG requires that party to negotiate a merger clause into the agreement.

2.   ATTORNEYS' FEES UNDER THE CISG

The remedies provisions of the CISG demonstrate yet another pitfall for unwary attorneys who assume that familiar language in the international context requires the same outcome as in the attorney's home forum. For example, CISG Article 74 appears to embody the familiar common law standard that damages for breach of contract must be foreseeable:

> Damages for breach of contract by one party consist of a sum equal to the loss, including loss of profit, suffered by the other party as a consequence of the breach. Such damages may not exceed the loss which the party in breach foresaw or ought to have foreseen at the time of the conclusion of the contract, in light of the facts and matters of which he then knew or ought to have known, as a possible consequence of the breach of contract.

Indeed, the Second Circuit has specifically held that "[t]he CISG requires that damages be limited by the familiar principle of foreseeability established in Hadley v. Baxendale. . . ."[21]

Most American students and attorneys would not include attorneys' fees as foreseeable damages available to a successful litigant. Under the so-called American Rule governing awards of attorneys' fees, litigants must bear their own costs in any legal action, and attorneys' fees are generally not recoverable by the winning party. But at least one American court has held that the American Rule does not apply in disputes under the CISG:

> Although the norm in our own judicial system is for each litigant in a purely United-States-based dispute to bear the burden of its own legal expense, that does not at all equate to the notion that public policy (or anything else) forbids a federal court's judicial enforcement of a different rule that is appropriately brought into play — indeed, [one exception to the American Rule] expressly contemplates such enforcement where there is a statute (and a treaty calls for an a fortiori application of that notion) that instead establishes a "loser pays" regime.[22]

This distinction between contract litigation under the CISG and such litigation under the common law or the UCC makes sense in terms of the difficulties of transnational contracting. Like the parol evidence rule, the American Rule on attorneys' fees is a relative rarity — "loser pays" regimes are more common in the international context. Consequently, parties unfamiliar with the American Rule would more likely suffer undue surprise from its application to disputes over transnational sales of goods. Additionally, parties forced to litigate in a foreign forum will often suffer increased litigation expenses as a result of duplication of counsel, travel expenses, and

21. *Delchi Carrier*, 71 F.3d at 1029.
22. Zapata Hermanos Sucesores, S.A. v. Hearthside Baking Co., 2001 WL 1000927, at *3 (N.D. Ill. Aug. 29, 2001) (interpreting CISG art. 74 to require payment by losing party of prevailing party's attorney fees).

other litigation-related costs over and above the costs of purely domestic litigation. By providing for awards of attorneys' fees to the winning party, the CISG minimizes the effects of distance and disparate legal regimes that would otherwise tend to protect home-turf litigants from uncertain but meritorious claims by foreign claimants.

B. REFORMING A WRITING — MISTAKES IN INTEGRATION

Having considered the use of extrinsic evidence to supplement or contradict a writing, we now take up the closely related problem of inaccurate writings or mistakes in integration. We shall be concerned with the relationship between this issue and the parol evidence rule. We shall also see what, if anything, this doctrine may add to our understanding of the objective or subjective approach to interpreting assent that was discussed in Chapter 5.

STUDY GUIDE: How can the following case be reconciled with the materials we just studied concerning the parol evidence rule? Is not the court permitting extrinsic evidence to contradict a completely integrated agreement? What is the difference between the mistake made in the following case and a misunderstanding of the sort we studied in Chapter 5? Can this doctrine be reconciled with the objective approach to interpreting assent or does it undermine it? Notice too the court's rejection of the terminology of mutual mistake. We shall return to that issue in Chapter 17 when considering excuses that justify the avoidance of a contractual duty.

THE TRAVELERS INSURANCE CO. v. BAILEY
Supreme Court of Vermont, Windsor County,
124 Vt. 114, 197 A.2d 813 (1964)

BARNEY, J.* The plaintiff insurance company has come into equity asking for reformation of the annuity provisions of a life insurance policy on the basis of mistake. Thirty years after issuance of the original policy it tendered the defendant insured an amended policy which he refused. On trial, the chancellor found that the amended policy represented the true insuring agreement originally entered into by the parties and allowed reformation. The defendant appealed.

At the instance of his mother, the defendant, when nineteen, submitted an application to an agent of the plaintiff for a life insurance policy. The plan requested in the application was one insuring the defendant's life for five thousand dollars, with an annuity at age sixty-five for five hundred

---

Albert Wilkins Barney, Jr. (1920-2010) was educated at Yale University (A.B.) and Harvard University (LL.B.). After admission to the Vermont bar in 1949, he practiced law briefly before becoming a Municipal Court Judge (1951-1952) and a member of the Vermont Superior Court (1952-1959). Judge Barney joined the Supreme Court of Vermont in 1959. He served as Chief Justice of that body from 1974-1982, when he retired. — K.T.

dollars a year for the balance of his life, ten years certain. When the application was accepted and the policy prepared in the home office of the plaintiff, the correct descriptive information was inserted on the wrong policy form. The printed portion of the form used yielded the correct life insurance contract, but produced an annuity obligation to pay five hundred dollars a month for life, one hundred months certain. The application was made a part of the policy, by its terms. In accordance with its usual practice, the plaintiff did not retain a copy of the policy itself but kept a record of the information permitting reproduction of the policy if the occasion demanded.

> → Mistake

The premiums were regularly paid on the policy issued in 1931, and about the middle of 1961 the actual policy came into the possession of the defendant for the first time. The semi-annual premiums charged and paid were identical with the prescribed premium for five thousand dollars of life insurance with annuity at age sixty-five of five hundred dollars annually, with payment for ten years certain. This $40.90 semi-annual premium was applicable only to that policy plan, issued at the defendant's then age of nineteen, and no other. The plaintiff had no rate for and did not sell a policy for five thousand dollars life insurance with an annuity at age sixty-five of five hundred dollars monthly, payment for one hundred months certain.

> strong Evidence
>
> Travelers is asking the court to reform (re-write) contract

After being told by a third party that his policy could not have the provisions he claimed for it, the defendant took the policy to the office of the defendant's agent that sold the policy and made inquiry. Shortly thereafter, in late 1961, the amended policy was tendered. There is no evidence that the defendant then knew that his original policy provided for an annuity payment larger than he was entitled to in view of the premium paid and the life insurance coverage purchased.

[Vermont law, like that of many jurisdiction[s], imposes upon the party seeking reformation the duty of establishing, beyond a reasonable doubt, the true agreement to which the contract in question is to be reformed.] deNeergaard v. Dillingham, 123 Vt. 327, 331, 187 A.2d 494. That this was accomplished, in the judgment of the chancellor, is demonstrated by this finding in particular·

> The only agreement that the plaintiff and defendant made was for $5,000 insurance with annuity of $500 per year at attained age 65, ten years certain.

Adequate evidentiary support for all findings of fact, including this one, made in this case by the chancellor, appears from the transcript of the evidence.

Indeed, in his appeal the defendant does not question any of the findings relating to the facts already recited. His principal attack on the decision relates to the chancellor's finding that the mistake in issuing the policy furnished the defendant came about through no fault of the defendant, but solely through the negligence and inattention of the plaintiff. This, says the defendant, is a finding of unilateral mistake, and therefore, under the authority of New York Life Insurance Co. v. Kimball, 93 Vt. 147, 153, 106 A. 676, is not grounds for reformation. . . .

[Where, as here, an antecedent contract has been established by the requisite measure of proof, equity will act to bring the erroneous writing into conformity with the true agreement.] Burlington Building & Loan Assn. v. Cummings, 111 Vt. 447, 453, 17 A.2d 319. On the basis of the maxim, "Equity regards that as done which ought to be done," equity will deal generously with the correction of mistakes. Stone v. Blake, 118 Vt. 424, 427, 110 A.2d 702 [704]. This power has been regularly and frequently invoked in connection with real estate transactions, but there is nothing that requires that equity limit its application to that kind of case. . . .

Accordingly, we hold that where there has been established beyond a reasonable doubt a specific contractual agreement between parties, and a subsequent erroneous rendition of the terms of the agreement in a material particular, the party penalized by the error is entitled to reformation, if there has been no prejudicial change of position by the other party while ignorant of the mistake. [If such change of position can equitably be taken into account and adjusted for in the decree, reformation may be possible even then.] . . . Mistakes generally occur through some carelessness, and failure to discover a mistake may be in some degree negligent, but unless some prejudice to the other party's rights under the true contract results, so as to make its enforcement inequitable, reformation will not be refused because of the presence of some negligence. . . .

Change of position is raised as an issue by the defendant. It cannot be said that the defendant acted in reliance on the terms of the policy which, he testified, were not exactly known by him until he received the policy in 1961. But he argues that the mere passage of time, in this case thirty years, should overcome the chancellor's finding to the contrary and establish a change of position. But clearly this aging process was inevitable, and not a prejudicial act induced by the mistaken term in the policy. The defendant has not demonstrated that he was prejudiced by the existence of the error. . . .

Reformation was properly granted.
Decree affirmed.

RESTATEMENT (SECOND) OF CONTRACTS

§155.   WHEN MISTAKE OF BOTH PARTIES AS TO WRITTEN EXPRESSION JUSTIFIES REFORMATION

Where a writing that evidences or embodies an agreement in whole or in part fails to express the agreement because of a mistake of both parties as to the contents or effect of the writing, the court may at the request of a party reform the writing to express the agreement, except to the extent that rights of third parties such as good faith purchasers for value will be unfairly affected.

REFERENCE: Farnsworth, §7.5
Calamari & Perillo, §§9.31-9.36
Murray, §86(B)

C. REQUIRING A WRITING — THE STATUTE OF FRAUDS

When determining the existence of assent we are faced with the twin problems of underenforcement and overenforcement. In this context, *underenforcement* is the failure of the legal system to enforce a legitimate exercise of assent. *Overenforcement* is the erroneous enforcement of an alleged exercise of assent that in fact never occurred. There is no perfect solution to these problems because almost any effort to avoid one kind of error will lead to errors in the other direction. In the law of contracts this has led to a kind of doctrinal ping-pong match.

The tort writ of Assumpsit was adapted to the enforcement of private commitments, in part, because the actions of debt, detinue, and covenant provided inadequate protection of informal agreements, leading to systematic *under*enforcement of legitimate exercises of assent. The expanded enforcement of informal commitments, however, permitted more fraudulent contract claims to succeed creating a new problem of *over*enforcement. This, in turn, led to the judicial development of the doctrine of consideration and the passage by Parliament of the original Statute of Frauds in 1677 requiring that some contracts be formalized. Inevitably, the restoration of requirements of formality gave rise to instances of *under*enforcement. This, in turn, has led to the development of judicially created exceptions to such statutes — exceptions that unavoidably permit some degree of *over*enforcement.

The cases in this section do not purport to treat the problems raised by the Statute of Frauds comprehensively. They are intended instead to (a) raise the problem of requiring increased formality as a means of combatting fraudulent contractual claims, (b) introduce some of the many exceptions to the requirements of the statute that have arisen, and (c) consider how the elements of contract formation may perform a different function than that performed by the statute.

RESTATEMENT (SECOND) OF CONTRACTS

§110. CLASSES OF CONTRACTS COVERED

(1) The following classes of contracts are subject to a statute, commonly called the Statute of Frauds, forbidding enforcement unless there is a written memorandum or an applicable exception:

(a) a contract of an executor or administrator to answer for a duty of his decedent (the executor-administrator provision);

(b) a contract to answer for the duty of another (the suretyship provision);

(c) a contract made upon consideration of marriage (the marriage provision);

(d) a contract for the sale of an interest in land (the land contract provision);

(e) a contract that is not to be performed within one year from the making thereof (the one-year provision).

---

(2) The following classes of contracts, which were traditionally subject to the Statute of Frauds, are now governed by Statute of Frauds provisions of the Uniform Commercial Code:

✗ (a) a contract for the sale of goods for the price of $500 or more (Uniform Commercial Code §2-201);

(b) a contract for the sale of securities (Uniform Commercial Code §8-319);

(c) a contract for the sale of personal property not otherwise covered, to the extent of enforcement by way of action or defense beyond $5,000 in amount or value of remedy (Uniform Commercial Code §1-206).

(3) In addition the Uniform Commercial Code requires a writing signed by the debtor for an agreement which creates or provides for a security interest in personal property or fixtures not in the possession of the secured party.

(4) Statutes in most states provide that no acknowledgment or promise is sufficient evidence of a new or continuing contract to take a case out of the operation of a statute of limitations unless made in some writing signed by the party to be charged, but that the statute does not alter the effect of any payment of principal or interest.

(5) In many states other classes of contracts are subject to a requirement of a writing.

1. The Statute and Its Exceptions

STUDY GUIDE: *What is the theoretical justification for the exceptions discussed in the next two cases? In what manner will lawsuits contesting the application of the Statute of Frauds inevitably skew our perceptions of the merits of such statutes?*

BOONE v. COE
Court of Appeals of Kentucky,
153 Ky. 233, 154 S.W. 900 (1913)

Appeal from Monroe Circuit Court.

Action by W. H. Boone and another against J. F. Coe. From a judgment sustaining a demurrer to the petition and dismissing the petition, plaintiffs appeal. . . .

Opinion of the court by WILLIAM ROGERS CLAY,* Commissioner — Affirming.

Procedural Posture

---

*William Rogers Clay (1864-1938) received degrees from Transylvania University (A.B.) and Georgetown University (LL.B., LL.M.). Admitted to the Missouri bar in 1887, he practiced privately (1887-1907) and concurrently was private secretary to U.S. Senator James B. Beck (1887-1890), superintendent of schools, Lexington (1892-1903), and city solicitor (1904-1907). He was then appointed commissioner of the Court of Appeals of Kentucky (1907-1921) and became judge of the same court (1921-1938), where he served until his death. He served as Chief Justice of that body two terms (1927-1928, 1935-1936). Clay also played a vital role in the railway wage arbitration in the 1920s. — K.T.

Plaintiffs, W. H. Boone and J. T. Coe, brought this action against defendant, [sic] J. F. Coe, to recover certain damages, alleged to have resulted from defendant's breach of a parol contract of lease for one year to commence at a future date. It appears from the petition that the defendant was the owner of a large and valuable farm in Ford County, Texas. Plaintiffs were farmers, and were living with their families in Monroe County, Kentucky. [In the fall of 1909, defendant made a verbal contract with plaintiffs whereby he rented to them his farm in Texas for a period of twelve months, to commence from the date of plaintiffs' arrival at defendant's farm.] Defendant agreed that if plaintiffs would leave their said homes and businesses in Kentucky, and with their families, horses and wagons, move to defendant's farm in Texas, and take charge of, manage and cultivate same in wheat, corn and cotton for the twelve months next following plaintiffs' arrival at said farm, the defendant would have a dwelling completed on said farm and ready for occupancy upon their arrival, which dwelling plaintiffs would occupy as a residence during the period of said tenancy. Defendant also agreed that he would furnish necessary material at a convenient place on said farm out of which to erect a good and commodious stock and grain barn, to be used by plaintiffs. The petition further alleges that plaintiffs were to cultivate certain portions of the farm and were to receive certain portions of the crops raised, and that plaintiffs, in conformity with their said agreement, did move from Kentucky to the farm in Texas, and carried with them their families, wagons, horses, and camping outfit, and in going to Texas they traveled for a period of 55 days. [It is also charged that defendant broke his contract, in that he failed to have ready and completed on the farm a dwelling house in which plaintiffs and their families could move, and also failed to furnish the necessary material for the erection of a suitable barn; that on December 6th defendant refused to permit plaintiffs to occupy the house and premises, and failed and refused to permit them to cultivate the land or any part thereof; that on the _____ day of December, 1909, they started for their home in Kentucky, and arrived there after traveling for a period of four days.] It is charged that plaintiffs spent in going to Texas, in cash, the sum of $150; that the loss of time to plaintiffs and their teams in making the trip to Texas was reasonably worth $8 a day for a period of 55 days, or the sum of $440; that the loss of time to them and their teams during the period they remained in Texas was $8 a day for 22 days, or $176; that they paid out in actual cash for transportation for themselves, families and teams from Texas to Kentucky the sum of $211.80; that the loss of time to them and their teams in making the last named trip was reasonably worth the sum of $100; that in abandoning and giving up their homes and businesses in Kentucky they had been damaged in the sum of $150, making a total damage of $1,387.80, for which judgment was asked. Defendant's demurrer to the petition was sustained and the petition dismissed. Plaintiffs appeal.

Under the rule in force in this State the statute of frauds relates to the remedy or mode of procedure, and not to the validity of the contract. Though the land is located in Texas, the parol contract of lease was made here, and here it is sought to enforce it. If unenforceable under our statute, it cannot be enforced here. . . .

The statute of frauds . . . provides as follows:

No action shall be brought to charge any person:

   6. Upon any contract for the sale of real estate, or any lease thereof, for longer term than one year; nor

   7. Upon any agreement which is not to be performed within one year from the making thereof, unless the promise, contract, agreement, representation, assurance, or ratification, or some memorandum or note thereof, be in writing, and signed by the party to be charged therewith, or by his authorized agent; but the consideration need not be expressed in writing, it may be proved when necessary, or disproved by parol or other evidence.

[margin note: Not enforceable under statute of frauds / Issue]

A parol lease of land for one year, to commence at a future date, is within the statute. . . . – End of the lease would alter one year deadline

The question sharply presented is: May plaintiffs recover for expenses incurred and time lost on the faith of a contract that is unenforceable under the statute of frauds? . . .

[I]t is the general rule that damages cannot be recovered for violation of a contract within the statute of frauds. . . .

[margin note: General Rule]

To this general rule there are certain well recognized exceptions. . . . [I]t has been held that, where services have been rendered during the life of another, on the promise that the person rendering the service should receive at the death of the person served a legacy, and the contract so made is within the statute of frauds, a reasonable compensation may be recovered for the services actually rendered. It has also been held that the vendee of land under a parol contract is entitled to recover any portion of the purchase money he may have paid, and is also entitled to compensation for improvements. . . .

[margin note: Exception – i.e. benefit entered to other party and improvements to land]

And under a contract for personal services within the statute, an action may be maintained on a *quantum meruit* . . . [The doctrine of these cases proceeds upon the theory that the defendant has actually received some benefits from the acts of part performance, and the law, therefore, implies a promise to pay.] . . .

In the case under consideration, the plaintiffs merely sustained a loss. Defendant received no benefit. Had he received a benefit, the law would imply an obligation to pay therefor. Having received no benefit, no obligation to pay is implied. The statute says that the contract of defendant made with plaintiffs is unenforceable. Defendant, therefore, had the legal right to decline to carry it out. [To require him to pay plaintiffs for losses and expenses incurred on the faith of the contract without any benefit accruing to him would, in effect, uphold a contract upon which the statute expressly declares no action shall be brought] The statute was enacted for the purpose of preventing frauds and perjuries. That it is a valuable statute is shown by the fact that similar statutes are in force in practically all, if not all, of the states of the union. Being a valuable statute, the purpose of the law-makers in its enactment should not be defeated by permitting recoveries in cases to which its provisions were intended to apply.

[margin note: Can't reward damages b/c would doing so make it as they the Court would be enforcing the contract yet it is unenforceable under SoF]

The contrary rule was announced by this court in the case of McDaniel v. Hutcherson, 136 Ky. 412 [124 S.W. 384]. There the plaintiff lived in the State of Illinois. The defendant owned a farm in Mercer County, Kentucky.

The defendant agreed with plaintiff that if the plaintiff and his family would come to Kentucky and live with defendant, the defendant would furnish the plaintiff a home during defendant's life, and upon his death, would give plaintiff his farm. It was held that although the contract was within the statute of frauds, plaintiff could recover his reasonable expenses in moving to Kentucky, and reasonable compensation for loss sustained in giving up his business elsewhere. Upon reconsideration of the question involved, we conclude that the doctrine announced in that case is not in accord with the weight of authority, and should be no longer adhered to. It is therefore overruled.

Judgment affirmed. → Holding

RESTATEMENT (SECOND) OF CONTRACTS

§125. CONTRACT TO TRANSFER, BUY, OR PAY FOR AN INTEREST IN LAND

(1) A promise to transfer to any person any interest in land is within the Statute of Frauds.

(2) A promise to buy any interest in land is within the Statute of Frauds, irrespective of the person to whom the transfer is to be made.

(3) When a transfer of an interest in land has been made, a promise to pay the price, if originally within the Statute of Frauds, ceases to be within it unless the promised price is itself in whole or in part an interest in land.

(4) Statutes in most states except from the land contract and one-year provisions of the Statute of Frauds short-term leases and contracts to lease, usually for a term not longer than one year.

§129. ACTION IN RELIANCE; SPECIFIC PERFORMANCE

A contract for the transfer of an interest in land may be specifically enforced notwithstanding failure to comply with the Statute of Frauds if it is established that the party seeking enforcement, in reasonable reliance on the contract and on the continuing assent of the party against whom enforcement is sought, has so changed his position that injustice can be avoided only by specific enforcement.

§130. CONTRACT NOT TO BE PERFORMED WITHIN A YEAR

(1) Where any promise in a contract cannot be fully performed within a year from the time the contract is made, all promises in the contract are within the Statute of Frauds until one party to the contract completes his performance.

(2) When one party to a contract has completed his performance, the one-year provision of the Statute does not prevent enforcement of the promises of other parties.

STUDY GUIDE: In the next case, the court claims to be upholding the requirements of the statute, yet it gives the plaintiff a recovery. On what grounds? Was the defendant actually put in a worse position than had the contract been enforced?

RILEY v. CAPITAL AIRLINES, INC.
United States District Court, Southern District of Alabama, 185 F. Supp. 165 (1960)

DANIEL HOLCOMBE THOMAS, D.J.*

This is an action for breach of an oral contract allegedly entered into between L. G. Riley, a proprietorship and d/b/a Riley Enterprises, plaintiff herein, and Capital Airlines, Inc., defendant herein. The plaintiff seeks to recover by this action for merchandise, goods and chattels delivered to the defendant pursuant to the alleged contract, and in addition, seeks the recovery of damages for breach of the contract.

The contract which is the basis of this action is alleged to have been entered into the latter part of August 1956, by and between L. G. Riley and Victor H. Luecke, an employee of Capital Airlines, Inc. The plaintiff contends that he was given a five-year contract, with an option to renew, to supply water methanol to the defendant at its Mobile, Alabama, terminal for use in its turbo-prop jet aircraft.

The defendant denies that it entered into a five-year contract with the plaintiff at any time, and avers that all purchases made by it from the plaintiff were made pursuant to its Blanket Purchase Orders. The defendant further contends that if there was a contract between the parties, this action is barred by the Alabama Statute of Frauds.

Having considered the evidence, the major portion of which consisted of the testimony of witnesses, and the arguments of counsel, the Court, now, after due deliberation, makes the following findings of fact and conclusions of law:

FINDINGS OF FACT . . .

The Court is of the opinion that the facts when considered as a whole sustain the plaintiff's allegation that a five-year contract was made between the parties. Therefore, I find as a matter of fact that Capital Airlines, Inc., entered into a five-year contract with L. G. Riley whereby the latter was to supply the former with water methanol according to its demands and specifications.

---

* Daniel Holcombe Thomas (1906-2000) received his law training at the University of Alabama (LL.B.). He engaged in private practice with several Mobile County law firms and was briefly the assistant solicitor of Mobile County, except while serving with the United States Naval Reserve (1943-1945). In 1951, he was appointed judge of the U.S. District Court for the Southern District of Alabama. At the time of his death, he was one of the longest-serving federal judges in history. — K.T.

Having reached the conclusion that there was in fact a contract between the parties, there remains for the Court to determine whether or not this action is barred by the Statute of Frauds of the State of Alabama.

CONCLUSIONS OF LAW

. . . The Statute of Frauds of Alabama states in part:

> In the following cases, every agreement is void, unless such agreement, or some note or memorandum thereof, expressing the consideration, is in writing, and subscribed by the party to be charged therewith, or some other person by him thereunto lawfully authorized in writing:
>
> (1) Every agreement which by its terms, is not to be performed within one year from the making thereof.

Title 20, Code of Alabama, 1940, §3.

At first impression it would appear that the contract here in question falls within the statute and should therefore be unenforceable because it is obvious that it was not to be performed within the period of one year. . . . However, the plaintiff contends that the agreement does not fall within the purview of the statute inasmuch as the agreement is a contract for the sale of goods and should not be barred under Title 57, Code of Alabama of 1940, §10. That section states:

> Statute of frauds. (1) A contract to sell or a sale of any goods or choses in action of the value of five hundred dollars or upward shall not be enforceable by action unless the buyer shall accept part of the goods or choses in action so contracted to be sold or sold, and actually received the same, or give something in earnest to bind the contract, or in part payment, or unless some note or memorandum in writing of the contract or sale be signed by the party to be charged or his agent in his behalf. (2) . . . ; *but if the goods are to be manufactured by the seller especially for the buyer and are not suitable for sale to others in the ordinary course of the seller's business, the provisions of this section shall not apply* . . .

(Emphasis supplied.)

It is the plaintiff's theory that since the water methanol was manufactured specially for the defendant and was not suitable for sale to others in the ordinary course of plaintiff's business, the five-year contract comes within the statutory exemption and is enforceable. While this theory is plausible, I do not believe it applicable to the facts of the present case for the reason that here each specially mixed delivery of water methanol was paid for separately by the defendant upon receipt of the plaintiff's invoice. This was not a case of goods being specially manufactured followed by a subsequent breach by the buyer, as was the case in the landmark decision of Goddard v. Binney, 115 Mass. 450, 15 Am. Rep. 112, wherein a contract to build a carriage to the buyer's specifications was held to fall outside the statute of frauds of the Sales Act. Although it is true that in the instant case the plaintiff manufactured the product exclusively for the defendant and according to its specifications, there was no product or item manufactured in its entirety for delivery five years from the date of making the contract. The plaintiff mixed the product when the defendant requested it; each order was delivered, invoiced, and paid for separately. I think that as to each delivery there was a contract which fell outside the statute of frauds and was thus enforceable to the extent that it was executed. . . .

The unexecuted or executory portion of the five-year contract falls within the purview of the Alabama statute of frauds and is unenforceable. . . . To hold otherwise would be to defeat the very purpose for which the statute was devised, that is, the prevention of frauds which may be accomplished by setting up contracts of the interdicted class by parole testimony. . . .

The plaintiff contends that the doctrine of part performance removes the contract from the effects of the statute of frauds. I cannot concur in this view. In Franklin v. Matoa Gold Min. Co., 8 Cir., 1907, 158 F. 941 (8th Cir., 1907), Judge Philips, in an excellent discussion on the statute of frauds, states on page 947:

> There is much of illogical assertion by courts touching this question of part performance. In many cases there is utter confusion of part performance and entire performance. Of course, when a contract is performed on both sides there is no longer a contract to be executed and enforced. In such case the statute of frauds has no application. Without pursuing this question, it is sufficient to say that both the weight of reason and authority is that the doctrine of part performance by the buyer, such as paying the purchase price, and the like, obtains only in equity and has no place in an action at law founded on the contract for damages.

In Farrow v. Burns, 1922, 18 Ala. App. 350, 92 So. 236, 237, it is stated that:

> Whatever may be the law in other states, in this jurisdiction the partial performance of a contract, void under the statute of frauds, does not take it from under the influence of the statute . . . , so as to permit a recovery under the contract for any part of the contract remaining executory.

Consequently, part performance does not take the executory portion of the contract herein from the purview of the statute of frauds.

By its petition the plaintiff seeks recovery for "merchandise, goods and chattels sold by the Plaintiff to the Defendant on the 1st day of September, 1956, said merchandise, goods and chattels to be delivered over a period of five (5) years up to and including the 1st day of September, 1961, for which the Defendant now refuses to pay. . . ." The evidence is uncontradicted that the plaintiff received payment for each delivery of the product; therefore, there is nothing due the plaintiff on the executed portion of the contract, and inasmuch as the executory portion of the contract is void under the statute of frauds, the plaintiff is entitled to recover nothing for the breach of the parole [sic] agreement by the defendant. . . .

The Court finds as a matter of law that the plaintiff is not entitled to damages for breach of the contract because the statute of frauds of the State of Alabama bars enforcement of the executory portion thereof.

[The plaintiff has purchased expensive equipment in order to fulfill adequately the provisions of the contract. While under the above-expressed views I do not think the plaintiff entitled to recover damages for breach of the executory portion of the contract, I am of the opinion that he should be compensated for the loss in equipment which was purchased in good faith pursuant to the defendant's specifications.]In the landmark case of United States v. Behan, 1883, 110 U.S. 338, 344, 4 S. Ct. 81, 83, 28 L. Ed. 168, Mr. Justice Bradley, speaking for the Court, said:

[Plaintiff can collect reliance damages]

> Unless there is some artificial rule of law which has taken the place of natural justice in relation to the measure of damages, it would seem quite clear that the claimant ought at least to be made whole for his losses and expenditures. So far as appears, they were incurred in the fair endeavor to perform the contract which he assumed. If they were foolishly or unreasonably incurred, the government (defendant) should have proven this fact. It will not be presumed. The court finds that his expenditures were reasonable.

Justice Bradley states further on page 345 of 110 U.S., on page 84 of 4 S. Ct.:

> As before stated, the primary measure of damage is the amount of the party's loss; and this loss, as we have seen, may consist of two heads or classes of damage — actual outlay and anticipated profits.

The expenses for equipment incurred by the plaintiff were incurred in the fair endeavor to perform the contract which he assumed; consequently, he is entitled to recover the loss of these expenditures which the Court finds were reasonable. The defendant has failed to prove that the expenses were foolishly or unreasonably incurred.

Reasonable expenditures incurred by the plaintiff in anticipation of a valid contract were the purchases of the three tanks, the storage drums, the demineralizing equipment, a pump, and an air compressor. These items were obtained at a cost of $3,418.15. Inasmuch as the tanks in question have been sold for $700, I find the plaintiff is entitled to recover the amount of $2,718.15, as the loss in expenditures which were incurred in a fair endeavor to perform the contract.

In accordance with the foregoing, judgment shall be entered for the plaintiff and costs of these proceedings taxed against the defendant. *[→ Holding]*

SALES CONTRACTS: THE UNIFORM COMMERCIAL CODE

§2-201. FORMAL REQUIREMENTS; STATUTE OF FRAUDS

(1) Except as otherwise provided in this Section a contract for the sale of goods for the price of $500 or more is not enforceable by way of action or defense unless there is some writing sufficient to indicate that a contract for sale has been made between the parties and signed by the party against

whom enforcement is sought or by his authorized agent or broker. A writing is not insufficient because it omits or incorrectly states a term agreed upon but the contract is not enforceable under this paragraph beyond the quantity of goods shown in such writing.

(2) Between merchants if within a reasonable time a writing in confirmation of the contract and sufficient against the sender is received and the party receiving it has reason to know its contents, it satisfies the requirements of subsection (1) against such party unless written notice of objection to its contents is given within 10 days after it is received.

(3) A contract which does not satisfy the requirements of subsection (1) but which is valid in other respects is enforceable

(a) if the goods are to be specially manufactured for the buyer and are not suitable for sale to others in the ordinary course of the seller's business and the seller, before notice of repudiation is received and under circumstances which reasonably indicate that the goods are for the buyer, has made either a substantial beginning of their manufacture or commitments for their procurement; or

(b) if the party against whom enforcement is sought admits in his pleading, testimony or otherwise in court that a contract for sale was made, but the contract is not enforceable under this provision beyond the quantity of goods admitted; or

(c) with respect to goods for which payment has been made and accepted or which have been received and accepted (§2-606).

RESTATEMENT (SECOND) OF CONTRACTS

§139. ENFORCEMENT BY VIRTUE OF ACTION IN RELIANCE

(1) A promise which the promisor should reasonably expect to induce action or forbearance on the part of the promisee or a third person and which does induce the action or forbearance is enforceable notwithstanding the Statute of Frauds if injustice can be avoided only by enforcement of the promise. The remedy granted for breach is to be limited as justice requires.

(2) In determining whether injustice can be avoided only by enforcement of the promise, the following circumstances are significant:

(a) the availability and adequacy of other remedies, particularly cancellation and restitution;

(b) the definite and substantial character of the action or forbearance in relation to the remedy sought;

(c) the extent to which the action or forbearance corroborates evidence of the making and terms of the promise, or the making and terms are otherwise established by clear and convincing evidence;

(d) the reasonableness of the action or forbearance;

(e) the extent to which the action or forbearance was foreseeable by the promisor.

§143. UNENFORCEABLE CONTRACT AS EVIDENCE

The Statute of Frauds does not make an unenforceable contract inadmissible in evidence for any purpose other than its enforcement in violation of the Statute.

REFERENCE: Farnsworth, §§6.1-6.2, 6.4-6.12
               Calamari & Perillo, §§19.1-19.48
               Murray, §§69, 72-81

2. Satisfying the Requirement of a Writing

STUDY GUIDE: Why did the court think that the letter in the next case failed to satisfy the Statute of Frauds? Was its analysis correct? Is there a difference between establishing the elements of contract formation and satisfying the requirements of the statute? Is the function of the statute the same as the function of the elements of formation? In answering these questions, consider the Restatement sections that follow the case. Also pay attention to the role that the defendants' lawyer played in this story. Although the court's discussion of promissory estoppel has been retained, we shall discuss this theory of relief in Chapter 11.

SCHWEDES v. ROMAIN
Supreme Court of Montana,
179 Mont. 466, 587 P.2d 388 (1978)

MR. JUSTICE SHEEHY* delivered the opinion of the court.

Lawrence and Billy Ann Schwedes (Schwedes) brought suit in the District Court, Eleventh Judicial District, Flathead County against Dorlaine A. Romain and LeRoy Mudgett (respondents) to obtain either specific performance of an alleged contract with respondents for the sale of land, or damages for breach of such contract. Respondents, after discovery, moved for summary judgment in their favor, which was granted. Schwedes appeal from the summary judgment against them, and from the refusal of the District Court to alter, amend, or vacate the summary judgment.

We conclude the District Court should be affirmed in this case.

In 1976, respondents, as part of a business partnership, owned twenty acres of land on or near the Swan River in Flathead County. Schwedes,

---

*John C. Sheehy (1918-†) received his LL.B. at the University of Montana School of Law in 1943. He practiced privately more than 30 years in Billings, Montana, interrupted intermittently by service as a legislator (Representative and Senator) in four sessions of the Montana Legislature. He was appointed to the Montana Supreme Court in 1978, where he served until his retirement in 1991. — K.T.

residents of Santa Monica, California, searching for a place to retire in the Flathead Valley, received the following letter from Dorlaine A. Romain:

> Romain & Mudgett
> Aug. 9, 1976
> Bigfork, Mont. 59911

Mr. & Mrs. Laurence Schwedes
353 24th St.
Santa Monica, Calif. 90402

Dear Mr. Schwedes,

Concerning the Swan River property you were interested in. We have contacted Mr. Charles Hash, attorney of Kalispell and he informs us that the Title Ins. Co. says the acreage and survey is correct at 19.53 acres and should be sold as is. If there is any confusion at the courthouse it can be cleared with a simple Quit Claim from us to Kirbys without contacting the Albrechts.

We have agreed to sell to you for $60,000 cash if you are interested. There is $19,170.00 contract that could be assumed. This contract has 3 years left at 7 1/2% interest.

We have listed the property with the local realties at $65,000 with a 6% commission charge and have shown it several times but so far we have not heard anything interesting. We are interested in selling this year if possible and hope you will consider this price.

> Sincerely yours,
>
> Dorlaine Romain [sic]

Lawrence Schwedes on August 16, 1976 communicated acceptance of the respondents' offer by telephone call to Dorlaine A. Romain in Flathead County. Thereupon respondents employed an attorney, Tom Hoover, to attend to details relating to the closing of the real estate transaction. Mr. Hoover ordered a title insurance commitment with an effective date of September 9, 1976 and prepared appropriate deeds to be executed by respondents in favor of the Schwedes. A closing date was set for September 20, 1976, a date agreed upon by all the parties. However, before that date, Mr. Hoover, in a telephone conversation with Schwedes, indicated it would not be necessary for them to come to Flathead County to close the transaction until they were further notified by telephone by Mr. Hoover. Nevertheless, on the previously agreed upon closing date, September 20, 1976, Mr. Hoover called Schwedes to indicate that the title reports had been received and would be sent by mail to the Schwedes. At that time, Lawrence Schwedes offered in the telephone call to send the whole purchase price as agreed, but was told by Mr. Hoover that it would be unnecessary and that the Schwedes could take care of it when they came to close the transaction, which was then set for October 3, 1976.

On September 30, 1976, respondents sold the real property in question to a third party, identified in the record as the "Vornbrocks" from Alberta, Canada, for a consideration stated to be $64,000. The action in the District Court ensued.

It is clear from the record that no document in writing was signed by either of the Schwedes respecting the transaction; that Attorney Hoover had no authority in writing to bind respondents to the transaction; that respondents would have executed the necessary documents for the property transaction and authorized their delivery to the Schwedes if the purchase price had been delivered to them prior to the date of sale to the Vornbrocks; that the Schwedes did not take possession of the property, erected no improvements thereon, paid no taxes or other assessments on the property, nor any sums of money to respondents.

[margin: ? Evidence of no performance on the part of the appellant]

From our examination of the record, and our consideration of the briefs and oral argument herein, we must conclude (1) no enforceable contract between the parties existed; (2) there was no basis upon which the District Court could have granted specific performance to the Schwedes; and (3) even if a contract existed, there was no part performance thereof, nor estoppel against respondents, so as to take the contract out of the statute of frauds. Therefore, the summary judgment granted by the District Court against Schwedes was correct.

The four essential elements of a contract are (1) legally capable parties, (2) their consent, (3) a lawful object, and (4) consideration. Section 13-102, R.C.M. 1947. Here there is no evidence that any consideration moved from Schwedes to respondents. A mere oral promise to pay, as in this case, is not sufficient consideration to support a contractual obligation on the part of Schwedes. Such a promise must be binding and impose some legal obligation on the one making it. 17 Am. Jur. 2d 450, 451 Contracts §105. A contract is not made so long as, in the contemplation of both parties thereto, something remains to be done in order to establish contract relations. See Mahoney v. Lester (1946), 118 Mont. 551, 557, 168 P.2d 339.

[margin: ? Reasoning real estate contract under SoG under SoF / Is this true? Can exchange promises]

Respondents argue that the acceptance of the offer by Schwedes was not unqualified as required by §13-321, R.C.M. 1947, and therefore, this essential element of consent is also missing from the purported contract. Since this is an appeal from a summary judgment, we will not consider that point where the evidence may be conflicting, and the issue does not enter into our decision.

It is further true, however, that a contract for the sale of real estate is invalid unless it, or some note or memorandum thereof is in writing subscribed by the parties to be charged. Section 13-606(4), R.C.M. 1947. Here there is no writing, memorandum or note binding Schwedes to buy this property. Hence, the oral promise of Schwedes was not legally binding, and imposed no legal duty upon them.) → *[margin: Doesn't matter b/c Schwedes are trying to enforce the contract]*

Likewise, Schwedes may not rely, to establish a contract between them and respondents, on the fact that Attorney Hoover prepared and mailed a form of deed and a title report, or that he extended the time for payment. The attorney, as any other agent, has no power to bind respondents in this case unless his authority to act on behalf of respondents is in writing, subscribed by respondents. Section 13-606(4); Hartt v. Jahn (1921), 59 Mont. 173, 196 F. 153.

We now consider whether the Schwedes are entitled to specific performance.

To begin with, the Schwedes have no evidence upon which they can establish a valid enforceable contract. In that situation, they may not obtain specific performance of the purported contract:

> While it is universally recognized that equitable relief by way of specific performance does not follow as a matter of course by establishing the existence and validity of the contract, the performance of which is sought, the existence of a valid contract is essential to the remedy of specific performance. In order for equity to decree specific performance, it is necessary that there be in existence and in effect a contract valid at law and binding upon the parties against whom performance is sought, for specific performance is never applicable where there is no obligation to perform. . . .

71 Am. Jur. 2d 27, Specific Performance §13. . . .

As a third point, the Schwedes say the contract is not invalid under the statute of frauds because of partial performance, both by the Schwedes and the respondents. The acts of partial performance by Schwedes, relied upon by them, are that they secured financing and offered (but did not pay) the full purchase price to respondents' attorney. They further claim respondents partially performed by withholding their property from the market while the parties were negotiating, obtaining a title report and hiring an attorney to close the deal.

It appears to us that appellants have failed to distinguish between acts undertaken in *contemplation of eventual performance*, and acts which truly constitute part performance of a contract. Acts undertaken by a party under the first category are not such part performance of the contract as to take it out of the operation of the statute of frauds. Here, the actions of Schwedes in obtaining financing and offering to pay the full amount, with nothing further, did not constitute part performance of the contract.

Claimed acts of partial performance sufficient to take [] an otherwise unenforceable contract out of the statute of frauds must be unequivocally referable to that contract. . . . The sufficiency of acts to constitute such part performance can be decided as a matter of law. . . . Such acts as obtaining financing and making studies of the real property have been held insufficient part performance to preclude the defense of the statute of frauds. Gene Hancock Construction Co. v. Kempton & Snedigar Dairy (Ariz. 1973), 20 Ariz. App. 122, 510 P.2d 752, 755.

The actions of *respondents* relied on by Schwedes are acts undertaken in *contemplation of eventual performance* of the contract. Again, these do not constitute part performance to remove the operation of the statute of frauds. Further, the acts of the respondents may not be relied upon by Schwedes because in order to remove the contract from the operation of the statute of frauds, a party may rely only on his part performance and not on the purported partial performance of others.

> . . . So, it is often laid down as a general rule that the acts relied upon as part performance to remove a parol agreement for the sale of lands from the operation of the Statute of Frauds must have been performed by the parties seeking to enforce the agreement. Part performance by the parties sought to be charged does not take an agreement out of the Statute of Frauds. Since the

basis of the doctrine of part performance is to prevent a fraud upon the plaintiffs, it is true as a general proposition, that if a party who resists the enforcement of a contract chooses not to stand on what he has done under and in pursuance of it, the other party cannot be aided by it.

73 Am. Jur. 2d 38, Statute of Frauds §411.

The final issue of Schwedes is that respondents are estopped to deny the validity of the contract between them. Again Schwedes rely on the actions they claim constitute part performance as above set forth, and further upon the fact that it was respondents' attorney who told the Schwedes not to pay the purchase price on September 20, 1976, but to do it at a later closing date.

This contention is inapplicable and can be answered simply by quoting the comment in 56 A.L.R.3d at 1054, regarding Sinclair v. Sullivan Chevrolet Co. (Ill. 1964), 45 Ill. App. 2d 10, 195 N.E.2d 250, *affirmed* 31 Ill. 2d 507, 202 N.E.2d 516, as follows:

> . . . [T]he court explicitly stated that where a case is clearly within the statute of frauds, promissory estoppel is inapplicable, for the net effect would be to repeal the statute completely. The court cited [a] general rule that the moral wrong of refusing to be bound by an agreement because it does not comply with the statute of frauds, does not of itself authorize the application of the doctrine of estoppel, because the breach of a promise which the law does not regard as binding is not a fraud. The court also stated that acts performed in contemplation of the contract are not considered as sufficient part performance to bring the case within any exception to the statute of frauds, or to permit the application of doctrine of estoppel. . . .

Usually the courts will apply the doctrine of promissory estoppel to suspend the statute of frauds only in those situations when the statute would otherwise operate to perpetrate a fraud. 56 A.L.R.3d 1037, 1056. Such is not the case here.

For the foregoing reasons, the summary judgment granted by the District Court is affirmed.

RESTATEMENT (SECOND) OF CONTRACTS

§131. GENERAL REQUISITES OF A MEMORANDUM

Unless additional requirements are prescribed by the particular statute, a contract within the Statute of Frauds is enforceable if it is evidenced by any writing, signed by or on behalf of the party to be charged, which

(a) reasonably identifies the subject matter of the contract,

(b) is sufficient to indicate that a contract with respect thereto has been made between the parties or offered by the signer to the other party, and

(c) states with reasonable certainty the essential terms of the unperformed promises in the contract.

§133. MEMORANDUM NOT MADE AS SUCH

Except in the case of a writing evidencing a contract upon consideration of marriage, the Statute may be satisfied by a signed writing not made as a memorandum of a contract.

COMMENT

a. Rationale.   The rule of this section reflects the general assumption that the primary purpose of the Statute is evidentiary, that it was not intended to facilitate repudiation of oral contracts. The marriage provision, however, performs a cautionary function as well, and a subsequent writing does not satisfy the statute unless made as a memorandum of the agreement. See §124 Comment d. More than a merely evidentiary writing is also required to satisfy a statutory provision that "the contract" be in writing.

b. Communication; Delivery.   There is no requirement that a memorandum be communicated or delivered to the other party to the contract, or even that it be known to him or to anyone but the signer. A memorandum may consist of an entry in a diary or in the minutes of a meeting, of a communication to or from an agent of the party, of a public record, or of an informal letter to a third person. Where a written offer serves as a memorandum to charge the offeror, however, communication of the offer is essential; written instructions to an agent to make an offer do not suffice. And where the statute requires only the vendor's signature the memorandum is not effective to charge the vendee until he manifests assent to it.

Ethical Background: The Role of the Lawyer in Schwedes

In Schwedes v. Romain, the Romains' lawyer told the Schwedes that the closing had been postponed from September 20th to October 3rd. He also told them that their offer to forward the full purchase price was unnecessary. The delay in the closing date enabled the Romains to sell the property to another party on September 30th. And had the Schwedes made the payment (and the Romains accepted it) on September 20th, the court would most likely have found that the Statute of Frauds had been satisfied.

STUDY GUIDE: Did the lawyer do anything improper during this conversation? Consider the following provisions of the American Bar Association's Model Rules of Professional Conduct. What additional facts would you need to know to determine whether some of these provisions apply? Although the lawyer here did not formally represent the Schwedes, did he give them legal advice? Could he ethically have represented both parties to the transaction? What dangers arise from such joint representation? We shall return to these provisions — especially Rules 1.6, 1.16, and 4.1 — in Chapter 7 when discussing the case of International Telemeter Corp. v. Teleprompter Corp., a case that concerns the ethical constraints on lawyers when they negotiate contracts as agents for their clients.

AMERICAN BAR ASSOCIATION MODEL RULES
OF PROFESSIONAL CONDUCT (2002)

CLIENT-LAWYER RELATIONSHIP

RULE 1.2   SCOPE OF REPRESENTATION

(a) A lawyer shall abide by a client's decisions concerning the objectives of representation, subject to paragraphs (c), (d) and (e), and shall consult with the client as to the means by which they are to be pursued. . . .

(d) A lawyer shall not counsel a client to engage, or assist a client, in conduct that the lawyer knows is criminal or fraudulent, but a lawyer may discuss the legal consequences of any proposed course of conduct with a client and may counsel or assist a client to make a good faith effort to determine the validity, scope, meaning or application of the law.

(e) When a lawyer knows that a client expects assistance not permitted by the rules of professional conduct or other law, the lawyer shall consult with the client regarding the relevant limitations on the lawyer's conduct.

Comment

Criminal, Fraudulent and Prohibited Transactions

A lawyer is required to give an honest opinion about the actual consequences that appear likely to result from a client's conduct. The fact that a client uses advice in a course of action that is criminal or fraudulent does not, of itself, make a lawyer a party to the course of action. However, a lawyer may not knowingly assist a client in criminal or fraudulent conduct. There is a critical distinction between presenting an analysis of legal aspects of questionable conduct and recommending the means by which a crime or fraud might be committed with impunity.

When the client's course of action has already begun and is continuing, the lawyer's responsibility is especially delicate. The lawyer is not permitted to reveal the client's wrongdoing, except where permitted by Rule 1.6. However, the lawyer is required to avoid furthering the purpose, for example, by suggesting how it might be concealed. A lawyer may not continue assisting a client in conduct that the lawyer originally supposes is legally proper but then discovers is criminal or fraudulent. Withdrawal from the representation, therefore, may be required. . . .

RULE 1.6   CONFIDENTIALITY OF INFORMATION

(a) A lawyer shall not reveal information relating to representation of a client unless the client consents after consultation, except for disclosures that are impliedly authorized in order to carry out the representation, and except as stated in paragraph (b).

(b) A lawyer may reveal such information to the extent the lawyer reasonably believes necessary:

(1) to prevent the client from committing a criminal act that the lawyer believes is likely to result in imminent death or substantial bodily harm; or

(2) to establish a claim or defense on behalf of the lawyer in a controversy between the lawyer and the client, to establish a defense to a criminal charge or civil claim against the lawyer based upon conduct in which the client was involved, or to respond to allegations in any proceeding concerning the lawyer's representation of the client.

Comment

Withdrawal

If the lawyer's services will be used by the client in materially furthering a course of criminal or fraudulent conduct, the lawyer must withdraw, as stated in Rule 1.16(a)(1).

After withdrawal the lawyer is required to refrain from making disclosure of the client's confidences, except as otherwise provided in Rule 1.6. Neither this rule nor Rule 1.8(b) nor Rule 1.16(d) prevents the lawyer from giving notice of the fact of withdrawal, and the lawyer may also withdraw or disaffirm any opinion, document, affirmation, or the like. . . .

RULE 1.16 DECLINING OR TERMINATING REPRESENTATION

(a) Except as stated in paragraph ₁(c), a lawyer shall not represent a client or, where representation has commenced, shall withdraw from the representation of a client if:

(1) the representation will result in violation of the rules of professional conduct or other law;

(2) the lawyer's physical or mental condition materially impairs the lawyer's ability to represent the client; or

(3) the lawyer is discharged.

(b) except as stated in paragraph (c), a lawyer may withdraw from representing a client if

(1) withdrawal can be accomplished without material adverse effect on the interests of the client;

(2) the client persists in a course of action involving the lawyer's services that the lawyer reasonably believes is criminal or fraudulent;

(3) the client has used the lawyer's services to perpetrate a crime or fraud;

(4) a client insists upon taking action that the lawyer considers repugnant or with which the lawyer has a fundamental disagreement;

(5) the client fails substantially to fulfill an obligation to the lawyer regarding the lawyer's services and has been given reasonable warning that the lawyer will withdraw unless the obligation is fulfilled;

(6) the representation will result in an unreasonable financial burden on the lawyer or has been rendered unreasonably difficult by the client; or

(7) other good cause for withdrawal exists. . . .

(c) When ordered to do so by a tribunal, a lawyer shall continue representation notwithstanding good cause for terminating the representation.

(d) Upon termination of representation, a lawyer shall take steps to the extent reasonably practicable to protect a client's interests, such as giving reasonable notice to the client, allowing time for employment of other counsel, surrendering papers and property to which the client is entitled and refunding any advance payment of fee that has not been earned. The lawyer may retain papers relating to the client to the extent permitted by other law.

Comment

A lawyer should not accept representation in a matter unless it can be performed competently, promptly, without improper conflict of interest and to completion.

Mandatory Withdrawal

A lawyer ordinarily must decline or withdraw from representation if the client demands that the lawyer engage in conduct that is illegal or violates the Rules of Professional Conduct or other law. The lawyer is not obliged to decline or withdraw simply because the client suggests such a course of conduct; a client may make such a suggestion in the hope that a lawyer will not be constrained by a professional obligation. . . .

Optional Withdrawal

A lawyer may withdraw from representation in some circumstances. The lawyer has the option to withdraw if it can be accomplished without material adverse effect on the client's interests. Withdrawal is also justified if the client persists in a course of action that the lawyer reasonably believes is criminal or fraudulent, for a lawyer is not required to be associated with such conduct even if the lawyer does not further it. Withdrawal is also permitted if the lawyer's services were issued in the past even if that would materially prejudice the client. The lawyer also may withdraw where the client insists on a repugnant or imprudent objective.

A lawyer may withdraw if the client refuses to abide by the terms of an agreement relating to the representation, such as an agreement concerning fees or court costs or an agreement limiting the objectives of the representation. . . .

TRANSACTIONS WITH PERSONS OTHER THAN CLIENTS

RULE 4.1 TRUTHFULNESS IN STATEMENTS TO OTHERS

In the course of representing a client a lawyer shall not knowingly:
   (a) make a false statement of material fact or law to a third person; or
   (b) fail to disclose a material fact to a third person when disclosure is necessary to avoid assisting a criminal or fraudulent act by a client, unless disclosure is prohibited by Rule 1.6.

Comment

Misrepresentation

A lawyer is required to be truthful when dealing with others on a client's behalf, but generally has no affirmative duty to inform an opposing party of relevant facts. A misrepresentation can occur if the lawyer incorporates or affirms a statement of another person that the lawyer knows is false. Misrepresentations can also occur by failure to act.

Statements of Fact

This Rule refers to statements of fact. Whether a particular statement should be regarded as one of fact can depend on the circumstances. Under generally accepted conventions in negotiation, certain types of statements ordinarily are not taken as statements of material fact. Estimates of price or value placed on the subject of a transaction and a party's intentions as to an acceptable settlement of a claim are in this category, and so is the existence of an undisclosed principal except where nondisclosure of the principal would constitute fraud.

Fraud by Client

Paragraph (b) recognizes that substantive law may require a lawyer to disclose certain information to avoid being deemed to have assisted the client's crime or fraud. The requirement of disclosure created by this paragraph is, however, subject to the obligations created by Rule 1.6. . . .

RULE 4.3 DEALING WITH UNREPRESENTED PERSON

In dealing on behalf of a client with a person who is not represented by counsel, a lawyer shall not state or imply that the lawyer is disinterested. When the lawyer knows or reasonably should know that the unrepresented person misunderstands the lawyer's role in the matter, the lawyer shall make reasonable efforts to correct the misunderstanding.

3. Satisfying the Requirement of a Signature

STUDY GUIDE: U.C.C. §2-201 requires a writing that is "signed by the party against whom enforcement is sought or by his authorized agent or broker." Yet today many transactions are negotiated and consummated by e-mail or other forms of electronic transmissions. With such communications, what constitutes a signature? Does Judge Posner find the existence of a "signature" or the absence of any need for one? What is the difference? Notice also his acknowledgment that the parties can provide for greater protections than are afforded by the U.C.C.'s Statute of Frauds.

CLOUD CORP. v. HASBRO, INC.
United States Court of Appeals, Seventh Circuit,
314 F.3d 289 (2002)

POSNER, Circuit Judge.

"Wonder World Aquarium" is a toy that Hasbro, Inc., the well-known designer and marketer of toys, sold for a brief period in the mid-1990s. The toy comes as a package that contains (we simplify slightly) the aquarium itself, some plastic fish, and, depending on the size of the aquarium (for this varies), large or small packets of a powder that when dissolved in distilled water forms a transparent gelatinous filling for the aquarium. The gel simulates water, and the plastic fish can be inserted into it with tweezers to create the illusion of a real fish tank with living, though curiously inert, fish. "Pretend blood," included in some of the packages, can be added for even greater verisimilitude. The consumer can choose among versions of Wonder World Aquarium that range from "My Pretty Mermaid" to "Piranha Attack" — the latter a scenario in which the pretend blood is doubtless a mandatory rather than optional ingredient.

Hasbro contracted out the manufacture of this remarkable product. Southern Clay Products Company was to sell and ship Laponite HB, a patented synthetic clay, to Cloud Corporation, which was to mix the Laponite with a preservative according to a formula supplied by Hasbro, pack the mixture in the packets that we mentioned, and ship them to affiliates of Hasbro in East Asia. The affiliates would prepare and package the final product — that is the aquarium, the packet of gel, and the plastic fish (and "pretend blood") — and ship it back to Hasbro in the United States for distribution to retailers. . . .

Early in 1997 Hasbro discovered that its East Asian affiliates, the assemblers of the final package, had more than enough powder on hand to supply Hasbro's needs, which were diminishing, no doubt because Wonder World Aquarium was losing market appeal. Mistakenly believing that Hasbro's market was expanding rather than contracting, Cloud had manufactured a great many packets of powder in advance of receiving formal purchase orders for them from Hasbro. Hasbro refused to accept delivery of these packets or to pay for them. Contending that this refusal was a breach of contract, Cloud sued Hasbro in federal district court in Chicago. . . . After a bench trial, the district judge ruled in favor of Hasbro.

Cloud does not quarrel with the district judge's findings of fact, but only with her legal conclusions. The governing law is the Uniform Commercial Code as interpreted in Illinois.

The original understanding between Hasbro and Cloud regarding Cloud's role in the Wonder World Aquarium project . . . were set forth in the purchase orders that Hasbro sent Cloud, confirming discussions between employees of Cloud and Kathy Esposito, Hasbro's employee in charge of purchasing inputs for the company's foreign affiliates. Upon receipt of a purchase order, Cloud would send Hasbro an order acknowledgment and would order from Southern Clay Products the quantity of Laponite required to fill the purchase order.

In October 1995, which is to say a few months after the launch of Wonder World Aquarium, Hasbro sent a letter to all its suppliers, including

Cloud, that contained a "terms and conditions" form to govern future purchase orders. One of the terms was that a supplier could not deviate from a purchase order without Hasbro's written consent. . . . Hasbro placed its last purchase orders with Cloud in February and April 1996. The orders for February specified 2.3 million small packets and 3.2 million large ones. For April the numbers were 1.5 and 1.4 million. Hasbro notified Cloud of the formula that it was to use in making the packets and Cloud ordered Laponite from Southern Clay Products accordingly. . . .

Hasbro notified Cloud that it was to use a new formula in manufacturing the powder, a formula that required so much less Laponite that the same quantity would enable Cloud to produce a third again as many packets. Cloud determined that by using the new formula it could produce from the quantity of Laponite that it had on hand 4.5 million small and 5 million large packets, compared to the 3.8 and 3.9 million called for by the February and April orders but not yet delivered. . . . Athough it had received no additional purchase orders, Cloud sent Hasbro an order acknowledgment for 4.5 million small and 5 million large packets with a delivery date similar to that for the April order, but at a lower price per packet, reflecting the smaller quantity of Laponite, the expensive ingredient in the powder, in each packet.

Cloud's acknowledgment was sent in June. Hasbro did not respond to it — at least not explicitly. It did receive it, however. And Kathy Esposito continued having e-mail exchanges and phone conversations with Cloud. These focused on delivery dates and, importantly, on the quantities to be delivered on those dates. Importantly because some very large numbers — much larger than the February and April numbers, numbers consistent however with Cloud's order acknowledgment sent to Hasbro in June — appear in these and other e-mails written by her. In two of the e-mails the quantity Cloud is to ship is described as "more or less depending on the formula," consistent with Cloud's understanding that if the formula reduced the amount of Laponite per packet Cloud should increase the number of packets it made rather than return unused Laponite to Southern Clay Products. A notation made in August by another member of Hasbro's purchasing department, Maryann Ricci — "Cloud O/S; 4,000,000 sm; 3.5 million lg." — indicates her belief that Cloud had outstanding ("O/S") purchase orders for 4 million small and 3.5 million large packets. These numbers were far in excess of the undelivered portions of the February and April orders; and since all the earlier orders had, so far as we can determine, already been filled and so were no longer outstanding, she must have been referring to the numbers in Cloud's June order acknowledgment. . . .

For unexpressed reasons the district judge did not focus on the contractual provisions requiring that any modification of a purchase order be in writing. She considered only whether the UCC's statute of frauds required this, and ruled that it did. The quantity term in a contract for the sale of goods for more than $500 must be memorialized in a writing signed by the party sought to be held to that term, UCC §2-201(1), and so, therefore, must a modification of that term. UCC §2-209(3). However — and here we part company with the district judge — Kathy Esposito's e-mails, plus the notation that we quoted earlier signed by Maryann Ricci, another member of Hasbro's purchasing department, satisfy the statutory requirement. The UCC does not require that the contract itself be in writing, only that there be adequate documentary evidence of its existence and essential terms, which there was here.

But what shall we make of the fact that Kathy Esposito's e-mails contained no signature? The Electronic Signatures in Global and National Commerce Act provides that in all transactions in or affecting interstate or foreign commerce (the transactions between Cloud and Hasbro were in interstate commerce and affected both interstate and foreign commerce), a contract or other record relating to the transaction shall not be denied legal effect merely because it is in electronic form. That would be conclusive in this case — had the e-mails been sent after the Act took effect in 2000. But they were sent in 1996. The Act does not purport to be applicable to transactions that occurred before its effective date, and, not being procedural, it is presumed not to apply retroactively. But . . . we conclude without having to rely on the federal Act that the sender's name on an e-mail satisfies the signature requirement of the statute of frauds. . . .

Neither the common law nor the UCC requires a handwritten signature, even though such a signature is better evidence of identity than a typed one. It is not customary, though it is possible, to include an electronic copy of a handwritten signature in an e-mail, and therefore its absence does not create a suspicion of forgery or other fraud — and anyway an electronic copy of a signature could be a forgery.

The purpose of the statute of frauds is to prevent a contracting party from creating a triable issue concerning the terms of the contract — or for that matter concerning whether a contract even exists — on the basis of his say-so alone. That purpose does not require a handwritten signature, especially in a case such as this in which there is other evidence, and not merely say-so evidence, of the existence of the contract (more precisely, the contract modification) besides the writings. The fact that Cloud produced the additional quantity is pretty powerful evidence of a contract, as it would have been taking a terrible risk in doing so had it thought it would have no right to be paid if Hasbro refused to accept delivery but would instead be stuck with a huge quantity of a product that had no salvage value. Actually, in the case of a contract for goods specially manufactured by the buyer, partial performance by the seller takes the contract outside the statute of frauds, without more. UCC §2-201(3)(a). This may well be such a case; but we need not decide.

The background to the modification — the fact that the parties had dealt informally with each other . . . , and above all that Hasbro plainly wanted more product and wanted it fast — is further evidence that had Cloud asked for a written purchase order in June 1996 for the additional quantity, Hasbro would have given it, especially since Cloud was offering a lower price.

There is more: "between merchants [a term that embraces 'any transaction with respect to which both parties are chargeable with the knowledge or skill of merchants,' UCC §2-104(3)] if within a reasonable time a writing in confirmation of the contract and sufficient against the sender is received and the party receiving it has reason to know its contents, it satisfies the requirements of subsection 1 [the statute of frauds] . . . unless written notice of objection to its contents is given within 10 days after it is received." UCC §2-201(2). Cloud sent an order acknowledgment, reciting the increased quantity, shortly after the oral modification, and Hasbro did not object within ten days. . . .

But what of the contractual requirement of the buyer's consent in writing to any modification? Could that stiffen the requirements of the UCC's statute of frauds? Parties are free to incorporate stronger conditions for contractual modification than the UCC provides: "A signed agreement which excludes modification or rescission except by a signed writing cannot be otherwise modified or rescinded, but except as between merchants such a requirement on a form supplied by the merchant must be separately signed by the other party." UCC §2-209(2). The UCC's statute of frauds requires only quantity terms to be in writing. The contractual requirement that the buyer's consent be in writing was not limited to quantity terms, but this makes no difference, since those are the terms in dispute.

Could the contractual statute of frauds (to speak oxymoronically) be broader in a different sense? Specifically, could "consent in writing" require an explicit written statement of consent, missing here, rather than merely an inference of consent from a writing or series of writings? Maybe, but Hasbro does not argue that the contractual statute of frauds in this case has any different scope from the statutory, though it seems highly unlikely that a no-oral-modification clause would be subject to the exception in section 2-201(2) (quoted earlier) to the statute of frauds. Such a clause is added to a contract when the parties want to draft their own statute of frauds, as they are permitted to do; and there is no reason to suppose that they would want to adopt wholesale the limitations that the UCC imposes on its own statute of frauds. If they wanted those limitations they wouldn't need their own, customized clause.

So we may set section 2-201(2) to one side. That leaves intact, however, Cloud's argument, which we have accepted, that there was adequate evidence of written consent to the modification. . . . Cloud could have been more careful. But a failure to insist that every i be dotted and t crossed is not the same thing as being unreasonable. In any event, to repeat an earlier point, Hasbro did give its written consent to the modification.

We conclude that the June modification was enforceable and we therefore reverse the judgment and remand the case for a determination of Cloud's damages.

Statutory Background: Writings and the "E-SIGN" Act

On June 30, 2000, Congress enacted the Electronic Signatures in Global and National Commerce Act (E-SIGN) to facilitate the use of electronic records and signatures in interstate and foreign commerce by ensuring the validity and legal effect of contracts entered into electronically. The Act went into effect in October 2000.

§101.   GENERAL RULE OF VALIDITY

(a) IN GENERAL. — Notwithstanding any statute, regulation, or other rule of law (other than this title and title II), with respect to any transaction in or affecting interstate or foreign commerce

(1) a signature, contract, or other record relating to such transaction may not be denied legal effect, validity, or enforceability solely because it is in electronic form; and

(2) a contract relating to such transaction may not be denied legal effect, validity, or enforceability solely because an electronic signature or electronic record was used in its formation.

Statutory Background: Provisions for E-Signatures

UNIFORM ELECTRONIC TRANSACTIONS ACT (1999)

§9. ATTRIBUTION AND EFFECT OF ELECTRONIC RECORD AND ELECTRONIC SIGNATURE

(a) An electronic record or electronic signature is attributable to a person if it was the act of the person. The act of the person may be shown in any manner, including a showing of the efficacy of any security procedure applied to determine the person to which the electronic record or electronic signature was attributable.

(b) The effect of an electronic record or electronic signature attributed to a person under subsection (a) is determined from the context and surrounding circumstances at the time of its creation, execution, or adoption, including the parties' agreement, if any, and otherwise as provided by law.

UNIFORM COMPUTER INFORMATION TRANSACTIONS ACT (2001)

§213. DETERMINING ATTRIBUTION

(a) An electronic authentication, display, message, record, or performance is attributed to a person if it was the act of the person or its electronic agent, or if the person is bound by it under agency or other law. The party relying on attribution of an electronic authentication, display, message, record, or performance to another person has the burden of establishing attribution.

(b) The act of a person may be shown in any manner, including a showing of the efficacy of an attribution procedure that was agreed to or adopted by the parties or established by law.

(c) The effect of an electronic act attributed to a person under subsection (a) is determined from the context at the time of its creation, execution, or adoption, including the parties' agreement, if any, or otherwise as provided by law.

(d) If an attribution procedure exists to detect errors or changes in an electronic authentication, display, message, record, or performance, and was agreed to or adopted by the parties or established by law, and one party conformed to the procedure but the other party did not, and the nonconforming party would have detected the change or error had that party also conformed, the effect of noncompliance is determined by the agreement but, in the absence of agreement, the conforming party may avoid the effect of the error or change.

7

MULTIPARTY TRANSACTIONS

In the cases examined to this point, we have limited our focus solely to transactions between two parties. Contracts frequently involve additional parties, and several bodies of specialized doctrine have evolved to handle these sometimes complex multiparty transactions. In this chapter, we shall consider two: (a) transactions in which a party transfers either contractual rights or duties to a third party; and (b) situations in which persons who are not parties to a contract, but who may nonetheless stand to benefit from its performance, seek to enforce it.

A. TRANSFERRING RIGHTS OR DUTIES TO THIRD PARTIES

Legal Background: Introduction to Assignment and Delegation

E. ALLAN FARNSWORTH, CONTRACTS 680-682 (4TH ED. 2004): At the outset, it is vital to distinguish the *assignment of rights* from the *delegation of performance of duties*.[1] An obligee's transfer of a contract right is known as an *assignment* of the right. By an assignment, the obligee as *assignor* (B) transfers to an *assignee* (C) a right that the assignor has against an *obligor* (A). An obligor's empowering of another to perform the obligor's duty is known as a *delegation* of the performance of that duty. By a delegation, the obligor as *delegating party* (B) empowers a delegate (C) to perform a duty that the delegating party owes to an *obligee*.[2] A party to a contract that both assigns rights and delegates performance to another person will be referred to as a *transferor* (B); the other person will be referred to as a *transferee* (C); and the transaction will be called a *transfer*

---

1. The term *assignment of a contract* is sometimes used to refer to a transaction in which both rights are assigned and duties are delegated. . . . It is also used to refer to a transaction in which only rights are assigned. To avoid confusion, this term is not used in this treatise. For an early and forceful statement of the distinction between assignment and delegation, see Corbin, Assignment of Contract Rights, 74 U. Pa. L. Rev. 207, 216-218 (1926).

2. The terms *delegating party* and *delegate* are not as well established as *assignor* and *assignee*. See, e.g., U.C.C. §2-210 (using *party delegating* and *delegate*); Restatement Second §318(3) (using *delegating obligor* and *person delegated*). . . .

of the contract. It will be useful to apply this terminology to five common situations.[3]

The first situation is that of a prospective donor that wants to make a gift. If the prospective donor (B) wants to give $1,000 to a favorite grandchild (C), the prospective donor might, of course, simply give the child cash. However, if the prospective donor is short of cash but is owed $1,000 by a debtor (A), the prospective donor may instead assign the right to payment to the grandchild as a gift. As assignee, the grandchild will then own the right that the donor previously had against the debtor and will collect the $1,000 from the debtor.

The second situation is that of a retailer that sells to consumers on credit. If the retailer has sold a $1,000 stereo on credit to a consumer (A), the retailer may need cash to finance the business until the $1,000 has been paid. The retailer (B) may therefore assign the right to payment to a financial institution (C) in return for the immediate payment by it of $1,000, less a discount to compensate the financial institution for the loss of the use of the $1,000 until it can collect the money from the consumer.[4] The financial institution will then own the right that the retailer previously had against the consumer and will collect the $1,000 from the consumer.

The third situation is that of a wholesaler that sells to retailers on credit. If the wholesaler (B) has sold $10,000 worth of carpets on credit to a retailer (A), the wholesaler may need cash to finance the business until the $10,000 has been paid. The wholesaler may therefore assign the right to payment, which is known as an "account receivable," to a financial institution (C). However, in contrast to the situation just described, in which a retailer assigns a consumer debt, the wholesaler engages in what is known as "accounts receivable financing" and assigns accounts in bulk, rather than individually, so that the total of all accounts assigned might be, say, $1,000,000. Furthermore, the wholesaler does not assign them outright but only as security for a loan for, say, $800,000 (somewhat less than the value of the collateral). In what is called "non-notification financing," it is understood that the wholesaler, not the financial institution, will collect from the retailer and that the wholesaler will repay the loan out of the proceeds when the retailer has paid for the goods.[5] The financial institution's compensation is the interest on the secured loan.

The fourth situation is that of the builder that makes construction contracts. If the builder (B) has contracted with an owner (A) to build a building for $10,000,000, payable as the work progresses, the builder may need funds immediately to begin work. The builder may therefore assign

3. [T]o facilitate comparison, the obligor of the right that is assigned or the obligee of the duty the performance of which is delegated is often designated parenthetically as A, the assignor or delegating party as B, and the assignee or delegate as C. An analogous designation is used for the parties to similar transactions, even though they do not actually involve the assignment of a right or the delegation of performance of a duty.

4. The financial institution in this situation is usually a bank or finance company. The amount of the discount will also include its transaction costs. Since the financial institution has recourse against the retailer, should the consumer default, its risk of not being paid is slight.

5. The financial institution in this situation is usually a bank or finance company. In contrast to the situation described in the text, the financial institution often does not require the wholesaler to repay the loan as the proceeds are collected, but relies on the assignment of future accounts to secure the loan in the original amount. . . . There is an alternative to the transaction described in the text in which the financial institution (sometimes called a "factor") purchases the account outright, notifies the obligor, and collects the debt.

the right to payment from the owner to a financial institution (C) in return for a loan to help finance the construction. Here, in contrast to the wholesaler's account receivable in the situation just described, the builder's right to payment has not yet been earned, since it is constructively conditioned on performance of the contract. As the builder performs and the progress payments become due, they are collected and used to repay the loan.

The fifth and most complex situation is that of an owner of a business that furnishes goods or services to other businesses. If the owner (B) wants to sell the business to a buyer (C) as a going concern, the parties may also plan to transfer long-term contracts with, say, a supplier (A) and a customer (A'). With respect to both the supplier and the customer, such a transfer involves not only assignment but delegation. The seller wants both to assign to the buyer the seller's rights against the supplier and the customer, and also to delegate to the buyer the performances that the seller owes them. There are, therefore, two significant problems not present in the four earlier situations. The first is that, with respect to the supplier, the right that the seller wishes to assign is a right to a performance other than the payment of money. The second is that with respect to both the supplier and the customer, the seller wishes not only to assign rights but also to delegate performance of duties, the duty of paying the supplier for what is supplied and the duty of furnishing the customer with goods or services. If the seller can overcome these problems and transfer these contracts, the buyer will have both a right to be supplied by the supplier in return for payment and a right to be paid by the customer in return for furnishing goods or services.

1. Assignment of Contractual Rights

STUDY GUIDE: In the next case, notice the distinction made between an assignment and an agency relationship and between an assignment and a relationship of third-party beneficiary. We shall consider third-party beneficiary relationships in Section B. What is the "legal nicety" that the dissenting judge thinks is preventing the majority from doing "full justice" by finding an assignment here? In answering this question, you should consult Restatement (Second) §317, which was cited by the court and which appears after the case.

KELLY HEALTH CARE v. THE PRUDENTIAL INSURANCE CO. OF AMERICA
Supreme Court of Virginia,
226 Va. 376, 309 S.E.2d 305 (1983)

POFF, J.* delivered the opinion of the court.

The principal issue raised by this appeal is whether a health care provider was an assignee of benefits payable to an insured under a health insurance policy and, as such, entitled to recover against the insurer.

---

* *Richard Harding Poff* (1923-2011) was educated at Roanoke College and the University of Virginia (LL.B.). During World War II, he earned the Distinguished Flying Cross for flying 35 missions as a bomber pilot in Europe. He practiced privately for 20 years and served as a member of the 83d-92d Congresses representing the Sixth District of Virginia, during which time he was vice-chairman of the National Commission on Reform of Federal Crime Laws. Poff became a member of the Supreme Court of Virginia in 1972, serving until his retirement in 1988. — K.T.

William Green was insured under a group health insurance policy issued by the Prudential Insurance Company of America. Green's wife, covered as a dependent under the policy, incurred certain expenses as a patient in a facility operated by Kelly Health Care, Inc. Kelly submitted bills to Prudential which Prudential refused to pay. Kelly sued both Prudential and Green. The trial court entered a default judgment for Kelly against Green, but Kelly pursued its claim against Prudential on the theory that Kelly was Green's assignee.

As proof of an assignment, Kelly relied upon two documents drafted by Kelly and signed by Green. The first provided:

PAYMENT AGREEMENT FOR CONTRACTED SERVICES
I understand that nursing services provided to Joan Green by Kelly Health Care, Inc. may be paid directly to Kelly Health Care, Inc., by Prudential Insurance Co. under policy or contract number _____ . I accept full responsibility and will pay for all or any part of the services to the above patient not paid to Kelly Health Care, Inc., by the above insurance company within 15 days of the billing date.

The second document provided:

AUTHORIZATION OF BENEFITS TO KELLY HEALTH CARE
I hereby authorize payment directly to Kelly Health Care . . . of the nursing service benefits, if any, otherwise payable to me for their services as described below.

In a bench trial, Prudential moved for summary judgment on the pleadings, admissions, stipulation of facts, and legal memoranda. The parties stipulated that there was "no evidence showing delivery of [the first] document to the defendant Prudential," and it appears that the second document was not delivered to Prudential until several months following commencement of the services for which Kelly claimed payment. The trial court ruled that the documents constituted an authorization rather than an assignment, granted Prudential's motion for summary judgment, and dismissed Kelly's action against Prudential with prejudice.

As framed in Kelly's assignment of error, the principal issue on appeal is whether "[t]he Court erred in . . . ruling that the plaintiff did not have a valid assignment of benefits to the insurance policy of William J. Green." . . .

. . . The trial court ruled, and we agree, that there was no assignment, legal or equitable, in this case. An assignment is a transfer, but a transfer is not necessarily an assignment. If the transfer is less than absolute, it is not an assignment; the obligee must have intended, at the time of the transfer, to dispossess himself of an identified interest, or some part thereof, and to vest indefeasible title in the transferee. See Restatement (Second) of Contracts §317(1) (1981).

> The intention of the assignor is the controlling consideration. The intent to transfer a present ownership of the subject matter of the assignment to the assignee must be manifested by some word, written or oral, or by some act inconsistent with the assignor's remaining as owner. This has sometimes been called a "present appropriation." *The assignor must not retain any control over the fund or property assigned, any authority to collect, or any form of revocation.*

Nusbahm and Co. v. Atlantic Realty, 206 Va. 673, 681, 146 S.E.2d 205, 210 (1966) (emphasis added) (citations omitted).

Under this definition, the appointment of an agent or the grant of a power of attorney cannot qualify as an assignment. Both are revocable, and the latter expires at the grantor's death. One of the documents upon which Kelly relies does no more than appoint Kelly as Green's special agent with authority to collect payments from Prudential as Green's entitlement falls due. The other document granted Prudential authority in the nature of a power of attorney to make such payments.

> [A] mere communication to the holder of the fund (the obligor), containing no words of present assignment and merely authorizing and directing him to pay to a third party, may properly bear the interpretation that it is a mere power of attorney to the obligor himself, empowering him to effectuate a transfer by his own subsequent act. With this interpretation, the communication to the obligor is not an assignment; and, like most other powers of attorney, it is revocable by its creator and it is terminated by its creator's death.

4 Corbin on Contracts §862 (1951) (citations omitted).

As an alternative theory, Kelly argues that it is entitled to recover against Prudential as "a third party beneficiary under Prudential's insurance policy with Mr. Green." We disagree. The third party beneficiary doctrine is subject to the limitation that the third party must show that the parties to the contract clearly and definitely intended it to confer a benefit upon him. . . .

Kelly did not allege and does not argue that Prudential and Green "clearly and definitely" intended to confer the benefits of Green's policy upon it. Indeed, it could not. Kelly was only one member of a large class of health care providers. At best, Kelly was a potential and incidental, and never the intended, beneficiary of the contract.

Finding no error below, we will affirm the judgment.

Affirmed.

GORDON, R.J.,* dissenting.

Kelly appeals a summary judgment. We must therefore assume, as alleged by Kelly, that Prudential owes money to its insured, Green, and Green owes money to Kelly.

Under an instrument signed by Green and delivered to Prudential, Green authorized Kelly to receive and pocket the money Prudential owes. Green by his pleading admits he signed "a claim form and assignment" to Kelly. A letter from Prudential calls the instrument an "assignment of benefits."

Upon a remand, this suit offers the facility to do full justice. That facility should in my opinion be accommodated.

Green intended the instrument to be an assignment, and Prudential so regarded it. I would carry out the intent, rather than stick to a legal nicety. . . .

---

* *Thomas Christian Gordon, Jr.* (1915-2003) attended the University of Virginia (A.B., LL.B.) and was admitted to the Virginia bar in 1937. He practiced law at Richmond for nearly 30 years until he was appointed justice on the Supreme Court of Virginia in 1965. He resigned from the bench in 1972 and resumed private practice until retiring in 1983. Gordon was also a lecturer on law at the University of Virginia Law School (1970-1972) and the Marshall-Wythe Law School (1979-1981). — K.T.

RESTATEMENT (SECOND) OF CONTRACTS

§317. ASSIGNMENT OF A RIGHT

(1) An assignment of a right is a manifestation of the assignor's intention to transfer it by virtue of which the assignor's right to performance by the obligor is extinguished in whole or in part and the assignee acquires a right to such performance.

(2) A contractual right can be assigned unless

(a) the substitution of a right of the assignee for the right of the assignor would materially change the duty of the obligor, or materially increase the burden or risk imposed on him by his contract, or materially impair his chance of obtaining return performance, or materially reduce its value to him, or

(b) the assignment is forbidden by statute or is otherwise inoperative on grounds of public policy, or

(c) assignment is validly precluded by contract.

REFERENCE: Farnsworth, §§11.2-11.3
               Calamari & Perillo, §§18.1-18.3
               Murray, §§136, 137

STUDY GUIDE: Can you see a relationship between the challenge to the enforceability of an assignment in the next case and the challenges to the contracts in Shaheen v. Knight in Chapter 1? Is there a relationship between this case and the issues surrounding the remedy of specific performance we considered in Chapter 3? What is your opinion of the Massachusetts statute that the court seeks to interpret?

In re NANCE
United States Court of Appeals, First Circuit,
556 F.2d 602 (1977)

LEVIN H. CAMPBELL, C.J.*

Coolidge Bank and Trust Co. (the bank) petitioned the bankruptcy judge to have a debt of the bankrupt, James S. Nance, declared non-dischargeable. After an evidentiary hearing, the bankruptcy judge determined that the bankrupt had willfully and maliciously converted $24,000.09 which was the property of the bank, and that the bankrupt's liability to the bank for

---

* *Levin Hicks Campbell* (1927-†) was educated at Harvard University (A.B., LL.B.). He practiced privately in Boston and served as a member of the Massachusetts House of Representatives (1963-1964), before working in the office of the Massachusetts Attorney General (1965-1968). His judicial career began with an appointment to the Superior Court of Massachusetts in 1969. He briefly served on the U.S. District Court of Massachusetts (1972) before becoming a judge on the U.S. Court of Appeals for the First Circuit. He served as Chief Judge of that court from 1983 to 1990, and now holds senior status. He has been a member of the National Commission on Judicial Discipline and Removal since 1991. — K.T.

this amount was a non-dischargeable debt under section 17(a)(2) of the Bankruptcy Act, 11 U.S.C. §35(a)(2).[6] Nance appealed this ruling to the district court, which reversed on the ground that the Massachusetts "Assignment of Wages" statute, Mass. Gen. Laws Ann. ch. 154, had invalidated Nance's attempted assignment of deferred salary to the bank. The bank appeals.

I

Nance was a professional football player for the New England Patriots. He became a customer of the bank in 1968 or 1969 and soon acquired a checking account, a Master Charge account, an Executive Credit Agreement, and a commercial loan. By September 1970, the bank advised Nance that he was in arrears on many of his obligations and his loans should be brought up-to-date. Nance and his agent, Mr. Myers, met with the bank's officers on September 7, 1970 and gave assurances that the bank would be paid. At the meeting Nance executed a document entitled "Assignment of Contract." The subject of the purported assignment was "Standard Player contract Boston Patriots Football Club, Inc., and player James S. Nance, Jr., dated 9/7/70" covering the 1970, 1971, and 1972 playing seasons. The assignment recited Nance's "current" and "deferred" compensation for the three seasons.[7] At the bottom, just above Nance's signature, came the statement: "As to this contract and the above mentioned compensation, I do assign that portion of said contract over to the Coolidge Bank and Trust Company as collateral for any monies loaned to me" by the bank. Nance testified that the bank officers told him that the instrument was merely "something to pacify the board of directors" and was not true collateral. He said that he intended at the time to pay off his obligations to the bank from investment income and from his salary from the Patriots. The president of the bank testified to the contrary that both Nance and the bank understood that this assignment of Nance's current and deferred compensation was backup collateral.

Nance was traded to another club sometime after the 1971 season, and while he was there, Myers enjoyed "full power of attorney on all monies due (Nance) by the New England Patriots." An exhibit in the record reveals that in May, 1972, the Patriots' president wrote to Myers indicating his willingness to release Nance from the third year of his contract but showing strong opposition to a request from Myers that the Patriots accelerate payment of

---

6. Section 17(a)(2) provides, in pertinent part, "A discharge in bankruptcy shall release a bankrupt from all of his provable debts, whether allowable in full or in part, except such as . . . are liabilities for . . . willful and malicious injuries to the person or property of another. . . ."

7. The stated amounts were:

Season 1970, Current Compensation — $30,000, Deferred Compensation — $55,000;
Season 1971, Current Compensation — $30,000, Deferred Compensation — $70,000;
Season 1972, Current Compensation — $30,000, Deferred Compensation — $125,000.

Payment of the deferred compensation for 1970 was to begin in 1975 and run through 1980; payment of the deferred compensation for 1971 was to begin in 1981 and run through 1988.

Nance's deferred income. In September, 1972, bank auditors were questioning the adequacy of the bank's security for outstanding loans to Nance, and Nance executed a "Declaration of Revocable Trust" naming himself as sole beneficiary and designating the bank and Myers as trustees with "full and absolute power over all monies owed to (Nance) by the New England Patriots" and a right "to a sixty-day notification by the New England Patriots in the event that any monies owed the Settlor by (the Patriots) are to be paid directly to him or on his behalf." A copy of the 1970 Player Contract was attached to the trust instrument. The trust could not be altered, amended, revoked or terminated by Nance for one year after its execution without the agreement of the trustees.

The following month, the bank called Nance in and asked him to consolidate in one instrument all loans previously made to him by the bank. This he did by executing a demand note, dated October 6, 1972, in the amount of $55,809.32. . . . No new consideration was given. The note recited that Nance had deposited as collateral security the following property: "Assignment of Revocable Trust on monies owed to James Nance by the New England Patriots." The bank considered this assignment "backup collateral" on Nance's personal obligation on the note. Nance testified that he never told the bank that it would be paid out of his deferred compensation, but toward the end of his cross-examination, the following exchange took place:

Q: (D)o you deny that you intended to assign to the Coolidge Bank & Trust Company the deferred compensation that you were to receive from the Boston Patriots? . . .
A: At some point, yes if it came down to no other way of paying the Coolidge Bank, yes. . . .

By January, 1973, Nance was not current on interest obligations on the demand note. Contemplating legal action, the bank sought advice regarding the "Assignment of Contract" and "Declaration of Revocable Trust" executed by Nance. Counsel advised that both were questionable as legal documents to be enforced by the bank. The bank then called all parties together for a meeting on February 16, 1973. Nance testified that he felt the purpose of the meeting was to produce something "to appease the Board of Directors." The bank's president testified that the meeting was called to determine when the bank was "going to get paid based on the assignment of the collateral" and that Nance and Myers assured the bank "that they would pay out of this particular assignment this collateral and that Mr. Myers was about to enter into negotiations with the Patriots to produce this money." He testified further that the parties agreed to meet with the bank's counsel the following day "where, in the spirit of cooperation, an instrument could be perfected that would make (counsel) happy as far as collecting money from the Patriots." Another bank officer present at the meeting testified that it was his understanding that a meeting would take place the following day "to draft a new form and . . . to contact the Patriots regarding it." A meeting was held the following day between counsel, Nance and Myers. Myers testified that the bank's counsel had suggested that Nance execute a new agreement to collateralize the monies owed to

Nance by the Patriots but that Nance declined to sign any new document because he was engaged in delicate negotiations with the Patriots for accelerated payment of the deferred compensation. No new document was executed at this meeting.

On April 2, 1973 Nance wrote the bank indicating that he had requested of the Patriots "a fifteen thousand ($15,000.00) dollar advance against deferred income" and that the Patriots "acknowledg(e) that I have already earned the monies described in a previous assignment to the Coolidge Bank and Trust Co.," and stating his "intention to deliver up to the bank, fifteen thousand ($15,000.00) dollars sometime within the next two weeks; twenty-five thousand ($25,000.00) dollars within the first week of January, 1974 and the balance of all monies due within the first week of January, 1975." Nance did not pay the bank according to the schedule indicated, but the bank took no action. One bank officer testified that the bank did not proceed to collect on the collateral because of assurances by Myers and Nance on several occasions that Nance would make good on his debt.

In early December, 1973, Nance and the Patriots settled Nance's claim to deferred income for $64,056.59, of which $35,056.50 was credited to discharge a promissory note previously executed by Nance in favor of the Patriots. The balance of $29,000.09 was paid to Nance in two installments: $14,000.00 in December, 1973 and $15,000.09 in January, 1974. Nance turned over to the bank $5,000.00 out of the first installment, but failed to pay anything more on the note. In March, 1974, the bank brought an action in state court on its promissory note for the unpaid balance of $53,025.92. In July, 1974, Nance filed his petition for bankruptcy, which stayed the action in state court.

The bank then filed its petition with the bankruptcy judge seeking to establish the debt of the bankrupt to the bank as $24,000.09 and to have it declared a non-dischargeable debt. The bank had the burden of proving that the money Nance received from the Patriots was "property" of the bank and that it was willfully and maliciously converted. . . . The bankruptcy judge found that Nance "knew he was assigning his deferred income as security and intended to do so" and ruled that the bank held an effective assignment. . . .

On appeal from the bankruptcy judge, the district court recited the latter's finding that Nance "intended to assign to the Bank the deferred compensation payable to the Bankrupt by the (Patriots) to secure his existing indebtedness to the Bank in the amount of $55,709.32, and that the Bank agreed to the assignment" and ruled that this finding was supported by the evidence and "is not susceptible to attack as clearly erroneous." However, the district court reversed the order below on the ground that the assignment was ineffective because not in compliance with Mass. Gen. Laws Ann. ch. 154. Reciting the policy of the statute "to protect the wage earner," the district court rejected the bankruptcy judge's conclusion that the statute would not apply to an equitable assignment as between the parties. The court then looked to the language of the statute and construed the term "future wages" as used in section 3 of chapter 154 to "include all wages to be paid out, by an employer in the future, making the provisions of section 3 applicable to the assignment of deferred compensation here irrespective of whether the assignment is said to have ripened after the wages had been earned." Since the assignment was not made in accordance with the requirements of section 3, see note [8], infra, judgment was entered for Nance.

On appeal to this court, the bank argues that the district court erred in ruling that Nance's assignment of his claim to deferred income was invalid for failing to comply with the conditions set forth in section 3 of chapter 154. Nance, of course, urges support of the ruling. As additional grounds for reversing the bankruptcy judge's finding of non-dischargeability, Nance also argues that the bank never received an assignment from him, and that, even if it had, his actions did not amount to a willful and malicious conversion. We agree with the district court insofar as it ruled that the "Assignment of Contract" executed by Nance in 1970 was an assignment of "future wages" subject to state law and was invalid for failing to comply with the conditions set forth in section 3. However, we read the bankruptcy judge's findings as indicating a fresh assignment in October of 1972, by which time Nance had left the Patriots and had fully earned the deferred compensation in question. We think an assignment covering income fully earned would not be subject to the requirements of section 3 and effected a valid transfer to the bank. We affirm the bankruptcy judge's ruling that Nance's retention of funds received in settlement of his claim amounted to a willful and malicious conversion of the bank's property.

II

The "Assignment of Contract" executed by Nance on September 7, 1970 was plainly invalid. Made in advance of the 1970 playing season, and covering income to be earned then and in seasons to come, the assignment fell within the class of assignments subject to section 3; it was an "assignment of or order for future wages."[8] The section sets forth numerous conditions for the validity of an assignment none of which were met. To hold, as did the bankruptcy judge, that an assignment which does not conform to these statutory requirements is valid as between the parties because otherwise effective would be to defeat the language and clear intent of the statute, the object of which is to protect wage earners and their families. See 4 Corbin on Contracts §879, at 534 (1951).

---

8. Mass. Gen. Laws Ann. ch. 154, §3, provides:

No assignment of or order for future wages other than one subject to the preceding section shall be valid for a period exceeding two years from the making thereof, nor unless made to secure a debt contracted prior to or simultaneously with the execution of said assignment or order, nor unless executed in writing in the standard form set forth in section five and signed by the assignor in person and not by attorney, nor unless such assignment or order states the date of its execution, the money or the money value of goods actually furnished by the assignee and the rate of interest, if any, to be paid thereon. Three fourths of the weekly earnings or wages of the assignor shall at all times be exempt from such assignment or order, and no assignment or order shall be valid which does not so state on its face. No such assignment or order shall be valid unless the written acceptance of the employer of the assignor, and, if the assignor is a married man, the written consent of his wife to the making thereof, are endorsed thereon or attached thereto.

But the bankruptcy judge did not base his finding that Nance "knew he was assigning his deferred income as security and intended to do so" solely on the "Assignment of Contract" executed in 1970. He pointed also to the "Declaration of Revocable Trust" executed in September of 1972, to which a copy of the contract had been attached, and the demand note for $55,809.32 signed by Nance in October, 1972, which mentioned as collateral the Trust and the monies owed him by the Patriots. . . .

We come, then, to whether the district court was correct in holding Nance's assignment at this later time invalid for failing to comply with the requirements of section 3 of the Massachusetts "Assignment of Wages" statute. The district court was persuaded by the difference in language used in sections 2 and 3 of chapter 154 to define the class of assignments subject to the requirements of each section. Section 2 begins: "No assignment of or order for wages or salary to be earned in the future to secure a loan of less than three thousand dollars shall be valid. . . ."[9] Section 3 begins: "No assignment of or order for future wages other than one subject to the preceding section shall be valid. . . ."[10] The court thought that the use of different language "was meant to be expressive of the distinction between all wages to be paid out by an employer in the future and those wage payouts reflecting only work done by the assignor after the wage assignment is executed." While this is a possible reading, no reason for the legislature to have made such a marked distinction in the coverage of the two provisions has been called to our attention, and we think it more reasonable to construe the term "future wages" in section 3 as no more than a variation of the more specific terminology used in the preceding section 2, viz. "wages or salary to be earned in the future."[11] Thus where section 2 refers to any assignment of "wages or salary to be earned in the future" to

9. Mass. Gen. Laws Ann. ch. 154, §2, provides in full:

No assignment of or order for wages or salary to be earned in the future to secure a loan of less than three thousand dollars shall be valid against an employer of the person making such assignment or order until the assignment or order is accepted in writing by the employer, nor until the assignment or order and the acceptance of the same have been filed and recorded with the clerk of the city or town where the person making the assignment or order resides if he is a resident of the commonwealth, or in which he is employed if he is not a resident thereof; nor shall it be valid unless said assignment is substantially in the form prescribed in section five. No such assignment or order shall be recorded by the clerk of a city or town unless it states on its face that the sum of ten dollars per week, as earned, of the wages or salary so assigned is exempt from such assignment or order. No such assignment or order shall be valid when made by a married man unless the written consent of his wife to the making thereof is attached thereto. No such assignment or order shall be valid for a period exceeding one year from the making thereof. The fee for the filing and recording of such assignment shall be as provided by clause (2) of section thirty-four of chapter two hundred and sixty-two.

10. Section 3 is reproduced in full in note [8], supra.

11. Section 2 derives from "An Act to Regulate Further the Business of Making Small Loans," 1908 Mass. Acts ch. 605, while section 3 derives from a series of acts "Relative to the Assignment of Wages," e.g., 1905 Mass. Acts ch. 308. The two pieces of legislation containing the same language disparity as at present were soon combined into one chapter, 1910 Mass. Acts ch. 563, and later the interrelationship between the two was clarified by making section 3 applicable only to an assignment "other than one subject to the preceding section," 1929 Mass. Acts ch. 159. While the separate genesis of the two provisions makes it possible that

secure a loan of under three thousand dollars, section 3 applies to all *other* assignments of "wages or salary to be earned in the future." Under this interpretation, Nance's 1972 assignment of income already earned would not be subject to the requirements of section 3.

Our reading finds strong support in the remaining language of section 3. Three of the stated conditions for validity of an assignment would make little sense if read to apply to the assignment of deferred income occurring after the assignor had a vested right to it.

One such condition is that "Three fourths of the weekly earnings or wages of the assignor shall at all times be exempt from such assignment or order, and no such assignment or order shall be valid which does not so state on its face." As applied to an assignment of wages to be earned in the future, the exemption serves the clear purpose of protecting the assignor and his family from deprivation, suffering or a "hopeless condition of quasi-slavery" caused by one unwise assignment. R. Smith, The History and Purpose of the Wage Assignment Statutes with a Suggestion for an Amendment, 5 Mass. L.Q. 479, 485 (1920). No similar purpose would be served by applying the exemption to an assignment of income which the assignor has already earned but the receipt of which has been postponed past the usual payment cycle. After assigning a claim to deferred income, the assignor remains employable and his weekly wage or salary would not be affected; there is no risk that the assignment will plunge him or his family into deprivation, suffering or a "hopeless condition of quasi-slavery."

Section 3 provides further that "No such assignment or order shall be valid unless the written acceptance of the employer of the assignor" is endorsed on or attached to the assignment. Giving the employer a veto over an employee's assignment of his wages to be earned in the future can be justified on two grounds: the employer's paternalism might protect the employee from entering into an unwise assignment, and the employer has an interest himself in avoiding the impact on an employee's morale caused by an assignment. While the first ground might arguably be relevant in some cases where the income has already been earned, the employer's interest in not having his employees assign their income is relevant only if the assignment is of wages to be earned in the future. An employer might not want his employee to feel that he is working for the benefit of the assignee department store or credit house rather than for his own benefit. But if the employee's weekly check is not affected by an assignment, as in the case of deferred income, there is little likelihood of employee discontent. The statute, moreover, does not deal with the question of which employer to notify — present or former — if the assignor, as here, has moved on to another job. The present employer would have little reason to interfere, and the previous employer, while having an obvious interest in the subject of the assignment, has no strong interest in accepting or not accepting his former employee's decision to assign the claim.

---

each was intended to have different scope, the absence of any indication that such was the case, and the fact that they have now co-existed in the same statute for almost seventy years, makes it reasonable to construe the two sections *in pari materia*. Had the legislature intended the language in section 3 to be read as anything but a shorthand version of that in section 2, we might have expected any distinction to have been spelled out when the relationship between the provisions was clarified by amendment in 1929.

Finally, reading section 3 as applying to Nance's assignment of his claim to deferred income would make it difficult to adhere to the requirement that an assignment covered by the section must be executed "in the standard form set forth in section five."[12] The standard form permits assignment of "all claims and demands . . . against my present employer, and against any person whose employ I shall hereafter enter." Since Nance was no longer in the employ of the New England Patriots when he assigned his claim to deferred income, the standard form could not be used to effect an assignment of his claim. If section 3 were read to apply, Nance would therefore be unable to assign his claim; in order to be valid, the assignment would have to be executed "in the standard form," but the standard form would be incapable of effecting the assignment.[13]

It thus appears that to read section 3 as applying to an assignment of deferred income that has been fully earned would raise perplexing problems in trying to construe and apply the conditions for validity set forth in the section. The whole thrust of section 3, as evidenced by those conditions, is to protect a wage earner from assigning away in advance his entire means of supporting himself and his family. Its application is essentially prospective, binding, as section 7 of chapter 154 specifies, "all wages earned by the assignor within the period named in such assignment." We accordingly do not read the statutory language as applying to Nance's assignment of his 1970 and 1971 income which had been fully earned in the past. . . .

Reversed.

RESTATEMENT (SECOND) OF CONTRACTS

§321. ASSIGNMENT OF FUTURE RIGHTS

(1) Except as otherwise provided by statute, an assignment of a right to payment expected to arise out of an existing employment or other

---

12. Mass. Gen. Laws Ann. ch. 154, §5, provides in relevant part:

I . . . do hereby assign and transfer . . . all claims and demands, not exempt by law (which I now have, and all) which within a period of . . . from the date hereof I may and shall have against my present employer, and against any person whose employ I shall hereafter enter. . . .

13. Ironically some support for the argument that the term "future wages" contained in section 3 covers an assignment of deferred income can be found in language contained in the standard form of assignment which covers "all claims and demands . . . which I now have . . . against my present employer." This clause suggests that claims for income which has already been earned may be included in any assignment executed according to the standard form. We agree with that construction, at least insofar as it applies to claims for income already earned but not yet paid out according to the usual payment cycle. But the fact that such a claim must be included as part of a larger assignment of wages to be earned in the future from the same employer does not mean that an assignment of a claim to deferred income to be paid out over a ten-year period commencing five years after the income has been earned is covered by section 3. Where, as here, the assignment of deferred income is made at some date after the assignor has left the employ of the one liable for paying the deferred income, the standard form's reference to "all claims and demands . . . which I now have . . . against my present employer" would be inappropriate for the assignment in question.

continuing business relationship is effective in the same way as an assignment of an existing right.

(2) Except as otherwise provided by statute and as stated in Subsection (1), a purported assignment of a right expected to arise under a contract not in existence operates only as a promise to assign the right when it arises and as a power to enforce it.

REFERENCE: Farnsworth, §§11.4-11.5
                Calamari & Perillo, §18.9
                Murray, §§139, 140

2.   Delegation of Contractual Duties

We now move from the *assignment of rights* to the performance of another to the *delegation of duties* of performance under the contract. Delegation is treated differently than assignment. As Restatement (Second) §318(3) states: "Unless the obligee agrees otherwise, neither delegation of performance nor a contract to assume the duty made with the obligor by the person delegated discharges any duty or liability of the delegating obligor." One colorful way to remember this difference is offered by Professors Charles Knapp and Nathan Crystal:

> The essential difference between assignment and delegation lies here, in its effect on the original party. If assigning a right is like passing a football, then delegating a duty resembles more the dissemination of a catchy tune or a contagious disease: Passing it on is not the same thing as getting rid of it.[14]

In sum, even after a delegation has been made, the person originally bound will remain subject to that duty (a) unless that person is released by the other party or (b) until the duty is discharged by the rendering of performance. The next case concerns a different problem: which duties may be delegated.

STUDY GUIDE: The district court thought that the next case involved the impermissible delegation of duties of a personal nature. Why would such duties be nondelegable? Why did the court of appeals reject this characterization of the duties in question? On what grounds did dissenting Judge Posner criticize this aspect of the majority's decision? In addition to the issues of assignment and delegation raised by the next case, notice the court's discussion of whether or not the U.C.C. applies to a particular transaction.

14. Charles L. Knapp & Nathan M. Crystal, Problems in Contract Law: Cases and Materials 1233-1234 (3d ed. 1993).

SALLY BEAUTY CO. v. NEXXUS PRODUCTS CO.
United States Court of Appeals, Seventh Circuit,
801 F.2d 1001 (1986)

CUDAHY, C.J.*

Nexxus Products Company ("Nexxus") entered into a contract with Best Barber Beauty Supply Company, Inc. ("Best"), under which Best would be the exclusive distributor of Nevus hair care products to barbers and hair stylists throughout most of Texas. When Best was acquired by and merged into Sally Beauty Company, Inc. ("Sally Beauty"), Nexxus cancelled the agreement. Sally Beauty is a wholly-owned subsidiary of Alberto-Culver Company ("Alberto-Culver"), a major manufacturer of hair care products and a competitor of Nexxus'. Sally Beauty claims that Nexxus breached the contract by cancelling. Nexxus asserts by way of defense that the contract was not assignable or, in the alternative, not assignable to Sally Beauty. The district court granted Nexxus' motion for summary judgment, ruling that the contract was one for personal services and therefore not assignable. We affirm on a different theory — that this contract could not be assigned to the wholly-owned subsidiary of a direct competitor under §2-210 of the Uniform Commercial Code. . . .

The fact that this contract is considered a contract for the sale of goods and not for the provision of a service does not, as Sally Beauty suggests, mean that it is freely assignable in all circumstances. The delegation of performance under a sales contract (whether in conjunction with an assignment of rights, as here, or not) is governed by U.C.C. §2-210(1), Tex. Bus. & Com. Code §2-210(a) (Vernon 1968). The U.C.C. recognizes that in many cases an obligor will find it convenient or even necessary to relieve himself of the duty of performance under a contract, see Official Comment 1, U.C.C. §2-210 ("[T]his section recognizes both delegation of performance and assignability as normal and permissible incidents of a contract for the sale of goods."). The Code therefore sanctions delegation except where the delegated performance would be unsatisfactory to the obligee: "A party may perform his duty through a delegate unless otherwise agreed to or unless the other party has a substantial interest in having his original promisor perform or control the acts required by the contract": U.C.C. §2-210(1), Tex. Bus. & Com. Code Ann. §2-210(a) (Vernon 1968). Consideration is given to balancing the policies of free alienability of commercial

---

Richard D. Cudahy (1926-†) received degrees from the U.S. Military Academy (B.S.) and Yale University (J.D.), between which he served in the U.S. Army (1948-1950). He served as law clerk to the Presiding Judge of the U.S. Court of Appeals for the Second Circuit (1955-1956), then worked in the Department of State (1956-1957) before entering private practice in 1957. In 1968, Cudahy ran an unsuccessful campaign for Wisconsin attorney general. He served as commissioner and chairman of the Wisconsin Public Service Commission (1972-1975) prior to serving as judge on the U.S. Court of Appeals for the Seventh Circuit (1979-1994). In 1994, he assumed senior status. Cudahy has taught at Marquette Law School, the University of Wisconsin, the George Washington University School of Law, and the De Paul College of Law, as well as authoring a variety of articles on regulatory policy, environmental law, and international law. He has also served as a trustee of the Environmental Defense Fund and as Chairman of the Board of the International Human Rights Institute at De Paul University's College of Law. He continues to practice law as well as sit as a hearing officer for an arbitration and mediation firm. — K.T.

contracts and protecting the obligee from having to accept a bargain he did not contract for.

We are concerned here with the delegation of Best's duty of performance under the distribution agreement, as Nexxus terminated the agreement because it did not wish to accept Sally Beauty's substituted performance.[15] Only one Texas case has construed §2-210 in the context of a party's delegation of performance under an executory contract. In McKinnie v. Milford, 597 S.W.2d 953 (Tex. Civ. App. 1980, writ ref'd, n.r.e.), the court held that nothing in the Texas Business and Commercial Code prevented the seller of a horse from delegating to the buyer a preexisting contractual duty to make the horse available to a third party for breeding. "[I]t is clear that Milford [the third party] had no particular interest in not allowing Stewart [the seller] to delegate the duties required by the contract. Milford was only interested in getting his two breedings per year, and such performance could only be obtained from McKinnie [the buyer] after he bought the horse from Stewart'" Id. at 957. In *McKinnie*, the Texas court recognized and applied the U.C.C. rule that bars delegation of duties if there is some reason why the non-assigning party would find performance by a delegate a substantially different thing than what he had bargained for.

In the exclusive distribution agreement before us, Nexxus had contracted for Best's "best efforts" in promoting the sale of Nexxus products in Texas. U.C.C. §2-306(2), Tex. Bus. & Com. Code Ann. §2-306(b) (Vernon 1968), states that "[a] lawful agreement by either buyer or seller for exclusive dealing in the kind of goods concerned imposes unless otherwise agreed an obligation by the seller to use best efforts to supply the goods and by the buyer to use best efforts to promote their sale." This implied promise on Best's part was the consideration for Nexxus' promise to refrain from supplying any other distributors within Best's exclusive area. See Official Comment 5, U.C.C. §2-306. It was this contractual undertaking which Nexxus refused to see performed by Sally.

In ruling on Nexxus' motion for summary judgment, the district court noted: "Unlike Best, Sally Beauty is a subsidiary of one of Nexxus' direct competitors. This is a significant distinction and in the court's view, it raises serious questions regarding Sally Beauty's ability to perform the distribution agreement in the same manner as Best." Memorandum Opinion and Order at 7. In Berliner Foods Corp. v. Pillsbury Co., 633 F. Supp. 557 (D. Md. 1986), the court stated the same reservation more strongly on similar facts. Berliner was an exclusive distributor of Haagen-Dazs ice cream when it was sold to Breyer's, manufacturer of a competing ice cream line. Pillsbury Co., manufacturer of Haagen-Dazs, terminated the distributorship and Berliner sued. The court noted, while weighing the factors for and against a preliminary injunction, that "it defies common sense to require a manufacturer

15. If this contract is assignable, Sally Beauty would also, of course, succeed to Best's rights under the distribution agreement. But the fact situation before us must be distinguished from the assignment of contract rights that are no longer executory (e.g., the right to damages for breach or the right to payment of an account), which is considered in U.C.C. §2-210(2), Tex. Bus. & Com. Code Ann. §2-210(b) (Vernon 1968), and in several of the authorities relied on by appellants. The policies underlying these two situations are different and, generally, the U.C.C. favors assignment more strongly in the latter. See U.C.C. §2-210(2) (non-executory rights assignable even if agreement states otherwise).

to leave the distribution of its products to a distributor under the control of a competitor or potential competitor." Id. at 559-60.[16] We agree with these assessments and hold that Sally Beauty's position as a wholly-owned subsidiary of Alberto-Culver is sufficient to bar the delegation of Best's duties under the agreement. . . .

At oral argument, Sally Beauty argued that the case should go to trial to allow it to demonstrate that it could and would perform the contract as impartially as Best. It stressed that Sally Beauty is a "multi-line" distributor, which means that it distributes many brands and is not just a conduit for Alberto-Culver products. But we do not think that this creates a material question of fact in this case.[17] When performance of personal services is delegated, the trier merely determines that it is a personal services contract. If so, the duty is *per se* nondelegable. There is no inquiry into whether the delegate is as skilled or worthy of trust and confidence as the original obligor: [T]he delegate was not bargained for and the obligee need not consent to the substitution.[18] . . .

The judgment of the district court is Affirmed.

POSNER, Circuit Judge, dissenting.

My brethren have decided, with no better foundation than judicial intuition about what businessmen consider reasonable, that the Uniform Commercial Code gives a supplier an absolute right to cancel an exclusive-dealing contract if the dealer is acquired, directly or indirectly, by a competitor of the supplier. . . .

No case adopts the per se rule that my brethren announce. The cases ask whether, as a matter of fact, a change in business form is likely to impair performance of the contract. . . .

My brethren find this a simple case — as simple (it seems) as if a lawyer had undertaken to represent the party opposing his client. But notions of conflict of interest are not the same in law and in business, and judges can go astray by assuming that the legal-services industry is the pattern for the entire economy. The lawyerization of America has not reached that point. Sally Beauty, though a wholly owned subsidiary of Alberto-Culver,

---

16. The effort by the dissent to distinguish *Berliner* merely because the court there apparently assumed in passing that distributorship agreements were a species of personal service contracts must fail. The *Berliner* court emphasizes that the sale of a distributorship to a competitor of the supplier is by itself a wholly sufficient reason to terminate the distributorship.

17. We do not address here the situation in which the assignee is not completely under the control of a competitor. If the assignee were only a partially-owned subsidiary, there presumably would have to be fact-finding about the degree of control the competitor-parent had over the subsidiary's business decisions.

18. Of course, the obligee makes such an assessment of the prospective delegate. If it thinks the delegated performance will be as satisfactory, it is of course free to consent to the delegation. Thus, the dissent is mistaken in its suggestion that we find it improper — a "conflict of interest" — for one competitor to distribute another competitor's products. Rather, we believe only that it is commercially reasonable that the supplier in those circumstances have consented to such a state of affairs. To borrow the dissent's example, Isuzu allows General Motors to distribute its cars because it considers this arrangement attractive. Nor is distrust of one's competitors a trait unique to lawyers (as opposed to ordinary businessmen), as the dissent may be understood to suggest.

distributes "hair care" supplies made by many different companies, which so far as appears compete with Alberto-Culver as vigorously as Nexxus does. Steel companies both make fabricated steel and sell raw steel to competing fabricators. General Motors sells cars manufactured by a competitor, Isuzu. What in law would be considered a fatal conflict of interest is in business a commonplace and legitimate practice. The lawyer is a fiduciary of his client; Best was not a fiduciary of Nexxus.

Selling your competitor's products, or supplying inputs to your competitor, sometimes creates problems under antitrust or regulatory law — but only when the supplier or distributor has monopoly or market power and uses it to restrict a competitor's access to an essential input or to the market for the competitor's output. . . . There is no suggestion that Alberto-Culver has a monopoly of "hair care" products or Sally Beauty a monopoly of distributing such products, or that Alberto-Culver would ever have ordered Sally Beauty to stop carrying Nexxus products. Far from complaining about being squeezed out of the market by the acquisition, Nexxus is complaining in effect about Sally Beauty's refusal to boycott it!

How likely is it that the acquisition of Best could hurt Nexxus? Not very. Suppose Alberto-Culver had ordered Sally Beauty to go slow in pushing Nexxus products, in the hope that sales of Alberto-Culver "hair care" products would rise. Even if they did, since the market is competitive Alberto-Culver would not reap monopoly profits. Moreover, what guarantee has Alberto-Culver that consumers would be diverted from Nexxus to it, rather than to products closer in price and quality to Nexxus products? In any event, any trivial gain in profits to Alberto-Culver would be offset by the loss of goodwill to Sally Beauty; and a cost to Sally Beauty is a cost to Alberto-Culver, its parent. Remember that Sally Beauty carries beauty supplies made by other competitors of Alberto-Culver; Best alone carries "hair care" products manufactured by Revlon, Clairol, Bristol-Myers, and L'Oreal, as well as Alberto-Culver. Will these powerful competitors continue to distribute their products through Sally Beauty if Sally Beauty displays favoritism for Alberto-Culver products? Would not such a display be a commercial disaster for Sally Beauty, and hence for its parent, Alberto-Culver? Is it really credible that Alberto-Culver would sacrifice Sally Beauty in a vain effort to monopolize the "hair care" market, in violation of section 2 of the Sherman Act? Is not the ratio of the profits that Alberto-Culver obtains from Sally Beauty to the profits it obtains from the manufacture of "hair care" products at least a relevant consideration?

Another relevant consideration is that the contract between Nexxus and Best was for a short term. Could Alberto-Culver destroy Nexxus by failing to push its products with maximum vigor in Texas for a year? In the unlikely event that it could and did, it would be liable in damages to Nexxus for breach of the implied best-efforts term of the distribution contract. Finally, it is obvious that Sally Beauty does not have a bottleneck position in the distribution of "hair care" products, such that by refusing to promote Nexxus products vigorously it could stifle the distribution of those products in Texas; for Nexxus has found alternative distribution that it prefers — otherwise it wouldn't have repudiated the contract with Best when Best was acquired by Sally Beauty.

Not all businessmen are consistent and successful profit maximizers, so the probability that Alberto-Culver would instruct Sally Beauty to cease to push Nexxus products vigorously in Texas cannot be reckoned at zero. On this record, however, it is slight. And there is no principle of law that if something happens that trivially reduces the probability that a dealer will use his best efforts, the supplier can cancel the contract. Suppose there had been no merger, but the only child of Best's president had gone to work for Alberto-Culver as a chemist. Could Nexxus have canceled the contract, fearing that Best (perhaps unconsciously) would favor Alberto-Culver products over Nexxus products? That would be an absurd ground for cancellation, and so is Nexxus's actual ground. At most, so far as the record shows, Nexxus may have had grounds for "insecurity" regarding the performance by Sally Beauty of its obligation to use its best efforts to promote Nexxus products, but if so its remedy was not to cancel the contract but to demand assurances of due performance. See U.C.C. §2-609; Official Comment 5 to §2-306. The judgment should be reversed and the case remanded for a trial on whether the merger so altered the conditions of performance that Nexxus is entitled to declare the contract broken.

SALES CONTRACTS: THE UNIFORM COMMERCIAL CODE

STUDY GUIDE: In addition to those provisions that are pertinent to the previous case, notice that the Code atypically adopts an immutable or mandatory rule that a "right to damages for breach of the whole contract or a right arising out of the assignor's due performance of his entire obligation can be assigned despite agreement otherwise."

§2-210. DELEGATION OF PERFORMANCE; ASSIGNMENT OF RIGHTS

(1) A party may perform his duty through a delegate unless otherwise agreed or unless the other party has a substantial interest in having his original promisor perform or control the acts required by the contract. No delegation of performance relieves the party delegating of any duty to perform or any liability for breach.

(2) Unless otherwise agreed all rights of either seller or buyer can be assigned except where the assignment would materially change the duty of the other party, or increase materially the burden or risk imposed on him by his contract, or impair materially his chance of obtaining return performance. A right to damages for breach of the whole contract or a right arising out of the assignor's due performance of his entire obligation can be assigned despite agreement otherwise.

(3) Unless the circumstances indicate the contrary a prohibition of assignment of "the contract" is to be construed as barring only the delegation to the assignee of the assignor's performance.

(4) An assignment of "the contract" or of "all my rights under the contract" or an assignment in similar general terms is an assignment of rights and unless the language or the circumstances (as in an assignment for security) indicate to the contrary, it is a delegation of performance of the duties of the assignor and its acceptance by the assignee constitutes a promise by him to perform those duties. This promise is enforceable by either the assignor or the other party to the original contract.

(5) The other party may treat any assignment which delegates performance as creating reasonable grounds for insecurity and may without prejudice to his rights against the assignor demand assurances from the assignee (Section 2-609).

REFERENCE: Farnsworth, §§11.10-11.11
                Calamari & Perillo, §§18.25-18.32
                Murray, §141

B.   THIRD-PARTY BENEFICIARIES OF A CONTRACT

In the previous section we saw how the rights of one party can be transferred to another. In this section, we examine how parties to a contract can create rights in a third party. Persons who are benefited by a contract to which they are not a party are known as *third-party beneficiaries*. Traditionally, two types of third-party beneficiaries — so-called *creditor beneficiaries* and *donee beneficiaries* — have been allowed to enforce a contract to which they are not party. *Incidental beneficiaries* are third parties who cannot enforce the contract. Although modern commentators have questioned the usefulness of the distinction between creditor and donee beneficiaries, and the Restatement (Second) has abandoned these terms — referring instead to *intended beneficiaries* — creditor and donee beneficiaries still constitute the paradigm examples of third parties who may enforce the terms of a contract to which they are not a party.

Modern Term

REFERENCE: Farnsworth, §10.1
                Calamari & Perillo, §17.1
                Murray, §130

1.   The Birth of the Third-Party Beneficiary Rule

STUDY GUIDE: The next case is regarded as the origin of the American rule that third-party beneficiaries may sue on a contract. What doctrinal problems stood in the way of enforcing the promise against the defendant in this case? How did the court overcome these problems? Why was Lawrence suing Fox, rather than suing Holly, the man who purportedly owed him money?

LAWRENCE v. FOX
Court of Appeals of New York,
20 N.Y. 268 (1859)

An action lies on a promise made by the defendant upon valid consideration to a third person for the benefit of the plaintiff, although the plaintiff was not privy to the consideration.

Such promise is to be deemed made to the plaintiff, if adopted by him, though he was not a party nor cognizant of it when made. Per JOHNSON, Ch. J., and DENIO, J.

So *held*, where A loaned money to the defendant upon his promise to pay it to the plaintiff, to whom A stated that he owed and had promised to pay the like sum; there being no other evidence of the fact than such declaration.

APPEAL from the Superior Court of the city of Buffalo. On the trial before Mr. Justice Masten, it appeared by the evidence of a bystander, that one Holly, in November, 1857, at the request of the defendant, loaned and advanced to him $300, stating at the time that he owed that sum to the plaintiff for money borrowed of him, and had agreed to pay it to him the then next day; that the defendant in consideration thereof, at the time of receiving the money, promised to pay it to the plaintiff the then next day.

Upon this state of facts the defendant moved for a nonsuit, upon three several grounds, viz.: That there was no proof tending to show that Holly was indebted to the plaintiff; that the agreement by the defendant with Holly to pay the plaintiff was void for want of consideration, and that there was no privity between the plaintiff and defendant. The court overruled the motion, and the counsel for the defendant excepted. The cause was then submitted to the jury, and they found a verdict for the plaintiff for the amount of the loan and interest, $344.66, upon which judgment was entered; from which the defendant appealed to the Superior Court, at general term, where the judgment was affirmed, and the defendant appealed to this court. The cause was submitted on printed arguments.

H. GRAY,* J.

The first objection raised on the trial amounts to this: That the evidence of the person present, who heard the declarations of Holly giving directions as to the payment of the money he was then advancing to the defendant, was mere hearsay and therefore not competent. Had the plaintiff sued Holly for this sum of money no objection to the competency of this evidence would have been thought of; and if the defendant had performed his promise by paying the sum loaned to him to the plaintiff, and Holly had afterwards sued him for its recovery, and this evidence had been offered by the defendant, it would doubtless have been received without an objection from any source.

---

*Hiram Gray (1801-1890) was born in Salem, New York, and was admitted to the New York bar in 1823. He served in the House of Representatives from 1837-1839 and served on the New York Court of Appeals from 1847-1860. He was known for being stern with young attorneys, and some stated that he reminded them of Stonewall Jackson. — S.Q.

All the defendant had the right to demand in this case was evidence which, as between Holly and the plaintiff, was competent to establish the relation between them of debtor and creditor. For that purpose the evidence was clearly competent; it covered the whole ground and warranted the verdict of the jury. But it is claimed that notwithstanding this promise was established by competent evidence, it was void for the want of consideration. It is now more than a quarter of a century since it was settled by the Supreme Court of this State — in an able and pains-taking opinion by the late Chief Justice Savage, in which the authorities were fully examined and carefully analysed — that a promise in all material respects like the one under consideration was valid; and the judgment of that court was unanimously affirmed by the Court for the Correction of Errors. (Farley v. Cleaveland, 4 Cow., 432; *same case in error,* 9 *id.*, 639.) In that case one Moon owed Farley and sold to Cleaveland a quantity of hay, in consideration of which Cleaveland promised to pay Moon's debt to Farley; and the decision in favor of Farley's right to recover was placed upon the ground that the hay received by Cleaveland from Moon was a valid consideration for Cleaveland's promise to pay Farley, and that the subsisting liability of Moon to pay Farley was no objection to the recovery.

The fact that the money advanced by Holly to the defendant was a loan to him for a day, and that it thereby became the property of the defendant, seemed to impress the defendant's counsel with the idea that because the defendant's promise was not a trust fund placed by the plaintiff in the defendant's hands, out of which he was to realize money as from the sale of a chattel or the collection of a debt, the promise although made for the benefit of the plaintiff could not enure to his benefit. The hay which Cleaveland delivered to Moon was not to be paid to Farley, but the debt incurred by Cleaveland for the purchase of the hay, like the debt incurred by the defendant for money borrowed, was what was to be paid. That case has been often referred to by the courts of this State, and has never been doubted as sound authority for the principle upheld by it. (Barker v. Buklin, 2 Denio, 45; Hudson Canal Company v. The Westchester Bank, 4 *id.*, 97.) It puts to rest the objection that the defendant's promise was void for want of consideration. The report of that case shows that the promise was not only made to Moon but to the plaintiff Farley. In this case the promise was made to Holly and not expressly to the plaintiff; and this difference between the two cases presents the question, raised by the defendant's objection, as to the want of privity between the plaintiff and defendant.

As early as 1806 it was announced by the Supreme Court of this State, upon what was then regarded as the settled law of England, "That where one person makes a promise to another for the benefit of a third person, that third person may maintain an action upon it." Schermerhorn v. Vanderheyden (1 John. R., 140), has often been re-asserted by our courts and never departed from. The case of Seaman v. White has occasionally been referred to (but not by the courts) not only as having some bearing upon the question now under consideration, but as involving in doubt the soundness of the proposition stated in Schermerhorn v. Vanderheyden. In that case one Hill, on the 17th of August, 1835, made his note and procured it to be indorsed by Seaman and discounted by the Phœnix Bank. Before the note matured and while it was owned by the Phœnix Bank, Hill placed in the hands of the defendant,

Whitney, his draft accepted by a third party, which the defendant indorsed, and on the 7th of October, 1835, got discounted and placed the avails in the hands of an agent with which to take up Hill's note; the note became due, Whitney withdrew the avails of the draft from the hands of his agent and appropriated it to a debt due him from Hill, and Seaman paid the note indorsed by him and brought his suit against Whitney. Upon this state of facts appearing, it was held that Seaman could not recover: first, for the reason that no promise had been made by Whitney to pay, and second, if a promise could be implied from the facts that Hill's accepted draft, with which to raise the means to pay; the note, had been placed by Hill in the hands of Whitney, the promise would not be to Seaman, but to the Phœnix Bank who then owned the note; although, in the course of the opinion of the court, it was stated that, in all cases the principle of which was sought to be applied to that case, the fund had been appropriated by an express undertaking of the defendant with the creditor. But before concluding the opinion of the court in this case, the learned judge who delivered it conceded that an undertaking to pay the creditor may be implied from an arrangement to that effect between the defendant and the debtor. This question was subsequently, and in a case quite recent, again the subject of consideration by the Supreme Court, when it was held, that in declaring upon a promise, made to the debtor by a third party to pay the creditor of the debtor, founded upon a consideration advanced by the debtor, it was unnecessary to aver a promise to the creditor; for the reason that upon proof of a promise made to the debtor to pay the creditor, a promise to the creditor would be implied. And in support of this proposition, in no respect distinguishable from the one now under consideration, the case of Schermerhorn v. Vanderheyden, with many intermediate cases in our courts, were cited, in which the doctrine of that case was not only approved but affirmed. (The Delaware and Hudson Canal Company v. The Westchester County Bank, 4 Denio, 97.)

The same principle is adjudged in several cases in Massachusetts. I will refer to but few of them. (Arnold v. Lyman, 17 Mass., 400; Hall v. Marston, *Id.*, 575; Brewer v. Dyer, 7 Cush., 337, 340.) In Hall v. Marston the court say: "It seems to have been well settled that if A promises B for a valuable consideration to pay C, the latter may maintain assumpsit for the money"; and in Brewer v. Dyer, the recovery was upheld, as the court said, "upon the principle of law *long recognized and clearly established*, that when one person, for a valuable consideration, engages with another, by a simple contract, to do some act for the benefit of a third, the latter, who would enjoy the benefit of the act, may maintain an action for the breach of such engagement; that it does not rest upon the ground of any actual or supposed relationship between the parties as some of the earlier cases would seem to indicate, but upon the broader and more satisfactory basis, that the law operating on the act of the parties creates the duty, establishes a privity, and implies the promise and obligation on which the action is founded." There is a more recent case decided by the same court, to which the defendant has referred and claims that it at least impairs the force of the former cases as authority. It is the case of Mellen v. Whipple (1 Gray, 317). In that case one Rollins made his note for $500, payable to Ellis and Mayo, or order, and to secure its payment mortgaged to the payees a certain lot of ground, and then sold and conveyed the mortgaged premises to the defendant, by deed in which it was stated that the "granted premises were subject to a mortgage for $500, which mortgage, with the note for which it was given, the said Whipple is to assume and cancel." The deed thus made was accepted by Whipple, the mortgage was afterwards duly assigned, and the note indorsed by Ellis and Mayo to the plaintiff's intestate. After Whipple received the deed he paid to the mortgagees and their assigns the interest upon the mortgage and note for a time, and upon refusing to continue his payments was sued by the plaintiff as administratrix of the assignee of the mortgage and note. The court held that the stipulation in the deed that Whipple should pay the mortgage and note was a matter exclusively between the two parties to the deed; that the sale by Rollins of the equity of redemption did not lessen the plaintiff's security, and that as nothing had been put into the defendant's hands for the purpose of meeting the plaintiff's claim on Rollins, there was no consideration to support an express promise, much less an implied one, that Whipple should pay Mellen the amount of the note. This is all that was decided in that case, and the substance of the reasons assigned for the decision; and whether the case was rightly disposed of or not, it has not in its facts any analogy to the case before us, nor do the reasons assigned for the decision bear in any degree upon the question we are now considering.

But it is urged that because the defendant was not in any sense a trustee of the property of Holly for the benefit of the plaintiff, the law will not imply a promise. I agree that many of the cases where a promise was implied were cases of trusts, created for the benefit of the promiser. The case of Felton v. Dickinson (10 *Mass.*, 189, 190), and others that might be cited, are of that class; but concede them all to have been cases of trusts, and it proves nothing against the application of the rule to this case. The duty of the trustee to pay the *cestuis que trust*, according to the terms of the trust, implies his promise to the latter to do so. In this case the defendant, upon ample consideration received from Holly, promised Holly to pay his debt to the plaintiff; the consideration received and the promise to Holly made it as plainly his duty to pay the plaintiff as if the money had been remitted to him for that purpose, and as well implied a promise to do so as if he had been made a trustee of property to be converted into cash with which to pay. The fact that a breach of the duty imposed in the one case may be visited, and justly, with more serious consequences than in the other, by no means disproves the payment to be a duty in both. The principle illustrated by the example so frequently quoted (which concisely states the case in hand) "that a promise made to one for the benefit of another, he for whose benefit it is made may bring an action for its breach," has been applied to trust cases, not because it was exclusively applicable to those cases, but because it was a principle of law, and as such applicable to those cases. It was also insisted that Holly could have discharged the defendant from his promise, though it was intended by both parties for the benefit of the plaintiff, and therefore the plaintiff was not entitled to maintain this suit for the recovery of a demand over which he had no control. It is enough that the plaintiff did not release the defendant from his promise, and whether he could or not is a question not now necessarily involved; but if it was, I think it would be found difficult to maintain the right of Holly to discharge a judgment recovered by the plaintiff upon confession or otherwise, for the breach of the defendant's promise; and if he could not, how could he discharge the suit before judgment, or the promise before suit, made as it was for the plaintiff's benefit and in accordance with legal presumption accepted by him (Berley v. Taylor, 5 Hill, 577-584, *et seq.*), until his dissent was shown. The cases cited, and especially that of Farley v. Cleaveland, establish the validity of a parol promise; it stands then upon the footing of a written one. Suppose the defendant had given his note in which, for value received of Holly, he had promised to pay the plaintiff and the plaintiff had accepted the promise, retaining Holly's liability. Very clearly Holly could not have discharged that promise, be the right to release the defendant as it may. No one can doubt that he owes the sum of money demanded of him, or that in accordance with his promise it was his duty to have paid it to the plaintiff; nor can it be doubted that whatever may be the diversity of opinion elsewhere, the adjudications in this State, from a very early period, approved by experience, have established the defendant's liability; if, therefore, it could be shown that a more strict and technically accurate application of the rules applied, would lead to a different result (which I by no means concede), the effort should not be made in the face of manifest justice.

The judgment should be affirmed. ——> Holding

JOHNSON, Ch. J., DENIO, SELDED, ALLEN and STRONG, Js., concurred. JOHNSON, Ch. J., and DENIO, J., were of opinion that the promise was to be regarded as made to the plaintiff through the medium of his agent, whose action he could ratify when it came to his knowledge, though taken without his being privy thereto.

COMSTOCK, J. (Dissenting.)

The plaintiff had nothing to do with the promise on which he brought this action. It was not made to him, nor did the consideration proceed from him. If he can maintain the suit, it is because an anomaly has found its way into the law on this subject. In general, there must be privity of contract. The party who sues upon a promise must be the promisee, or he must have some legal interest in the undertaking. In this case, it is plain that Holly, who loaned the money to the defendant, and to whom the promise in question was made, could at any time have claimed that it should be performed to himself personally. He had lent the money to the defendant, and at the same time directed the latter to pay the sum to the plaintiff. This direction he could countermand, and if he had done so, manifestly the defendant's promise to pay according to the direction would have ceased to exist. The plaintiff would receive a benefit by a complete execution of the arrangement, but the arrangement itself was between other parties, and was under their exclusive control. If the defendant had paid the money to Holly, his debt would have been discharged thereby. So Holly might have released the demand or assigned it to another person, or the parties might have annulled the promise now in question, and designated some other creditor of Holly as the party to whom the money should be paid. It has never been claimed, that in a case thus situated, the right of a third person to sue upon the promise rested on any sound principle of law. . . .

GROVER, J., also dissented.

Judgment affirmed.

Relational Background

STUDY GUIDE: The following reading reveals that the facts in Lawrence v. Fox *were far more complicated and interesting than the court's opinion suggests. How does a knowledge of the relationship between Lawrence, Fox, and Hawley change your view of the case and the court's reasoning? Does this knowledge make the outcome in the case more or less defensible?*

ANTHONY JON WATERS, THE PROPERTY IN THE PROMISE: A STUDY OF THE THIRD PARTY BENEFICIARY RULE, 98 HARV. L. REV. 1109 (1985):   As one might have guessed about an idea so plainly at odds with the received wisdom of its time, the rule of Lawrence v. Fox is the product of a freakish combination of events. The facts of the case, the rules of pleading, and the substantive law were each in doubt or in flux, and each was resolved in such a way as to make possible the birth of the third party beneficiary rule. In order to appreciate how and why these elements combined as they did, it is necessary to delve in some depth into the history of the action "for money had and received for and to the use of the plaintiff," for it was in that form that Lawrence's action against Fox was brought.

. . .

By the middle of the nineteenth century — the time of Lawrence v. Fox — the action for money had and received had become a residual category in New York law, providing a theory of recovery in situations that the more tightly defined forms of action could not be made to fit. The New York courts regarded the action as essentially equitable in nature (even though it was demonstrably legal in lineage) and described it in very broad terms: "The action for money had and received, applies to almost every case where a person has received money, which in equity and good conscience he should refund to the true owner."

Consistent with this otherwise broad formulation of the action, New York courts strictly observed its proprietary limitations, as expressed by the words "the true owner." This demarcation was to become a central factor in Lawrence's case. In had-and-received cases, the courts had come to describe the defendant's relationship to the money as that of a trustee, who had no proper business with it but to deliver it to the rightful owner. If the defendant could show that he received the money under any circumstances that permitted him to use it for his own purposes (such as a loan), the action for money had and received would not lie.

Thus, in a case in which the plaintiff could establish ownership of money being held by the defendant, a promise "implied by law" — a pure fiction — was employed to permit recovery of plaintiff's property. But where the plaintiff's claim was instead founded on a promise by the defendant, then the action, being an action "on the promise," could be maintained only if the plaintiff had complied with the requisites of contractual liability; if the plaintiff was not a party to the promise (no privity), his action would fail.

. . .

The facts of Lawrence v. Fox, as recounted by the New York Court of Appeals, are these: One Holly, declaring that he owed Lawrence three hundred dollars, lent that amount to Fox, who promised Holly that he would repay it to Lawrence the next day. Fox did not pay, and Lawrence sued him. Lawrence prevailed at trial, on appeal, and, finally, in the New York Court of Appeals. What the Court of Appeals called the "principle of law" of the case is "that [when] a promise [is] made to one for the benefit of another, he for whose benefit it is made may bring an action for its breach." The mystery of Lawrence v. Fox is why Lawrence chose the tortuous route of suing Fox, with whom he had not dealt, rather than sue Holly, who was, it appears, his debtor.

Figure 1. Schematic Diagram of Lawrence v. Fox.

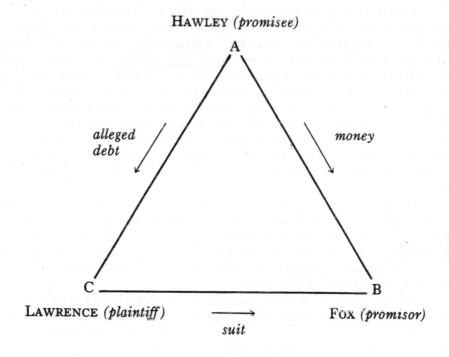

HAWLEY (*promisee*)

A

alleged debt   *money*

C ————————————————————— B

LAWRENCE (*plaintiff*)   ⟶   FOX (*promisor*)

suit

. . .

From the records of the case, we learn that "Holly" was in fact one Hawley, referred to in the complaint as Samuel Hawley. The Buffalo census of 1855 lists no Samuel Hawley, but of the eighteen Hawleys who are listed, only one appears to have had sufficient means to have been involved in a three hundred dollar cash transaction. He was Merwin Spencer Hawley, a prominent merchant. In 1856, Hawley was President of the Buffalo Board of Trade, an organization with which Fox, at some point, was also connected. It is admittedly possible that the Hawley who dealt with Fox, and who was allegedly indebted to Lawrence, was another

Hawley from out of town, or out of state. That would explain his absence from the census and from the courtroom. But there are indications of other reasons why Lawrence may have avoided suing Hawley, even if he was affluent and available. Those reasons — which I shall deal with shortly — taken together with the fact that Merwin Hawley was a wealthy Buffalonian who moved in the same social circles as Arthur Fox, make it more likely that he is the Hawley of Lawrence v. Fox. The assumption that Hawley was affluent and available in Buffalo when Lawrence sued Fox does nothing, however, to solve the mystery of why Lawrence chose not to sue him. The solution to that mystery lies in the nature of Lawrence's transaction with Hawley, of which Hawley's dealings with Fox on the next day are highly suggestive.

In 1854, when the transaction took place, three hundred dollars was a very large amount of money. Even among successful entrepreneurs, a loan the size of Hawley's to Fox, to be repaid a day later, must have been out of the ordinary. At trial in the Superior Court in Buffalo, Fox's attorney, Jared Torrance, shed some light on the nature of that transaction. The only witness in the case was William Riley, by whom Lawrence's attorney, Edward Chapin, had proved that Hawley paid three hundred dollars to Fox; that Hawley told Fox that he, Hawley, owed that amount to Lawrence; and that Fox promised Hawley that he would repay that amount to Lawrence. On cross-examination, Torrance elicited four facts: that Lawrence was not present when Hawley made the loan to Fox; that the deal took place at Mr. Purdy Merritt's on Washington Street; that there were "two or three persons present . . . doing nothing but standing near them"; and that Hawley counted out the money as he handed it to Fox.

The first fact, that Lawrence was not present, formed the basis of Fox's privity defense. This defense makes sense only in an action based on contract, a point to which we shall return. For now, it is the other three facts — the location, the bystanders, and the cash being counted out — that are noteworthy, for they suggest the milieu in which the transaction took place, and help to explain its character.

William Riley, the witness, was a horse dealer. He did his business near the canal, the life line of Buffalo's then-thriving commerce. Not many steps away was Mr. Purdy Merritt's establishment, where the transaction took place; Merritt was also a horse dealer. Torrance's cross-examination presented a more complete picture: two well-to-do merchants in a horse dealer's establishment down by the canal; a large amount of cash changing hands; and several other people present, loitering. Of these facts, not the least significant was the location:

> Canal Street was more than a street. It was the name of a district, a small and sinful neighborhood. . . . As late as the 1800's, there were ninety-three saloons there, among which were sprinkled fifteen other dives known as concert halls plus sundry establishments designed to separate the sucker from his money as swiftly as possible, painlessly by preference, but painfully if necessary. . . . It must have been an eternal mystery to the clergy and the good people of the town why the Lord never wiped out this nineteenth

century example of Sodom and Gamorrah with a storm or a great wave from Lake Erie.[19]

In his cross-examination of Riley, Attorney Torrance had gone as far as he could go to set the scene for what he then sought to prove directly, also by William Riley: that Hawley lent the money to Fox for Fox to gamble with it, and that this unlawful purpose was known to Hawley.

Trial Judge Joseph Masten did not, however, permit Riley to testify to the alleged link with gambling. Attorney Chapin, for Lawrence, successfully objected on two grounds, neither of which bears upon the probable truth or untruth of the evidence that Riley was prepared to give. As to that question, the facts that Torrance had already elicited do suggest a setting in which gambling could have been taking place. But there is one more fact, this one uncontroverted, that is entirely consistent with the allegation of a connection with gambling and is difficult to explain otherwise. That fact — the central mystery of this case — is that Lawrence chose to sue not his debtor, Hawley, but his debtor's debtor, Fox. If, as seems to be the fact, Hawley was a person of considerable wealth in Buffalo, and if, as alleged, he owed three hundred dollars to Lawrence, then Lawrence must have had compelling reason to neglect the obvious action — suing Hawley — in favor of the much more difficult task of seeking recovery from Fox. A gambling debt would have presented just such a reason. If Hawley's debt to Lawrence from the day before, in the round sum of three hundred dollars, was itself the outcome of gambling and thus unenforceable at law, Lawrence was well advised to look for someone other than Hawley to sue. Furthermore, if we look to the law of gamblers rather than the law of commerce, it is clear that Fox, and not Hawley, was both the villain and the obvious person to pursue.

Commercial transactions were not then and are not now structured in such a way as to leave a creditor with no better means of recovery than to sue his debtor's debtor. The series of events described in Lawrence v. Fox makes no commercial sense. Had Hawley's dealings with Fox conformed to the norms of commercial behavior, Hawley would have requested a negotiable instrument either made out to Lawrence, or to be endorsed in his favor, in return for his loan to Fox. And had Lawrence's dealings with Hawley been of a kind condoned and upheld by the law of the land, then Lawrence would surely have sued Hawley, and not Fox. It is not surprising, therefore, that there was no theory of recovery in the law of contract by which Lawrence could collect from Fox.

Had William Riley's further evidence been admitted, and not controverted, Torrance, for Fox, would presumably have argued that the indirect link with gambling tainted Hawley's loan to Fox so as to make it

---

19. L. Graham, Niagara Country 205-06 (1949). Graham describes the Canal Street district as "an irregular area, bounded on the west by the harbor, on the south by Main Street, on the east by The Terrace and on the north by Erie Street, roughly speaking." *Id.* at 205. According to the 1848 street map of Buffalo, Washington Street, where the transaction between Hawley and Fox took place, was one small block to the south of Main Street and parallel with it. For further descriptions of the Canal Street district, see Two Blocks of Riotous Sin Which Became Dante Pl. Catered Mostly to Sailors, Buffalo Com. Express, Oct. 26, 1952, at 1, col. 1. The Buffalo and Erie County Historical Society has a life-sized, "walk-through" re-creation of the Canal Street area on exhibit until the end of 1985.

unrecoverable, there being New York case law to support that position.[20] Chapin, for Lawrence, would have argued the opposite — that the loan itself was distinct from, and not tainted by, the borrower's purpose in borrowing, even if known to the lender.

. . .

Chapin needed a cause of action that avoided adverting to the nature of Lawrence's dealings with Hawley, and Hawley's with Fox, as far as possible, while still making out a claim to the money that Fox had promised Hawley he would pay to Lawrence. The cause of action had to focus as little as possible on the two transactions involved, and as much as possible on Lawrence's simple grievance: that Arthur Wellesley Fox had three hundred dollars that really belonged to Lawrence. The action for money had and received had obvious appeal: Chapin could make his client's claim fall within the broad definition adhered to by the New York courts if he limited his pleadings to certain facts and characterized the claim appropriately. Chapin followed the old standard form of pleading for money had and received but made more than a bald assertion that the defendant held money that properly belonged to the plaintiff. Such an assertion would once have sufficed for a common count, but the Field Code now called for the plaintiff to plead all that he intended to prove. And so he did.

The complaint told a simple story very similar to that recounted by the Court of Appeals. It alleged that on or about November 15, 1854, in Buffalso, Lawrence "loaned unto Samuel Hawley the sum of three hundred dollars in money," to be repaid the next day, and that on that next day "said Hawley delivered the said sum . . . to . . . Arthur W. Fox, to be by him delivered to this plaintiff . . . ." Lawrence, having "often requested" Fox "to deliver the same to him" — which Fox "wholly neglected and refused . . . to do" — "further said that the defendant was indebted to him in the sum of three hundred dollars for money had and received to and for the use of the plaintiff herein."

Chapin needed to prove the transaction between Hawley and Fox as he set it out in the complaint; specifically, he needed to prove that Hawley "delivered" the money to Fox — no more, no less. Had Torrance succeeded in proving that Fox had borrowed the money from Hawley, Chapin might well have lost the case because, as we have seen, in a common count action for money had and received, the difference between "delivered" and "lent" was the difference between winning and losing.

The grounds of Chapin's objection to Torrance's offer to prove, by William Riley, that the transaction was in fact a loan of money for Fox to gamble with, show clearly that Chapin understood the threat. Chapin's first objection, that "the loan was not set up in the answer," was procedural. It

---

20. See Ruckman v. Bryan, 3 Denio 340, 341 (N.Y. Sup. Ct. 1846) ("[M]oney knowingly lent for the purpose of betting or gaming [could not] be recovered from the borrower" (quoting Peck v. Briggs, 3 Denio 107, 108 (N.Y. Sup. Ct. 1846))). Existing New York law made gambling unlawful and provided that "[a]ll contracts for or on account of any money or property, or thing in action so wagered, bet or staked, shall be void." *See Ruckman,* 3 Denio at 342 (quoting 1 N.Y. Rev. Stat. pt. 1, ch. 20, tit. 8, §8, at 666 (1836)). *Peck* and *Ruckman* stated that the statutory language comprehended a loan knowingly made to further gambling. See *id.* at 342-43; *Peck,* 3 Denio at 108.

asserted that a general denial in the answer was not sufficient to allow the defendant to raise a loan defense at trial. The second objection — that even if the loan were proved, the evidence would afford no defense — perhaps reflects an understanding on Chapin's part that in an appropriate case, a post-Field Code court would not be constrained by the pre-Code limitations of one of the old common counts. Because this second objection referred to the whole of the offer of proof, including that Fox's purpose, known to Hawley, was to gamble, it may also mean that Chapin was ready to contest the legal relevance of such knowledge. On that very question, the case law was so uncertain that it raised problems for both sides and it may have been bargained out of the case later on.

Such speculation is perhaps less important than the simple fact that the court did sustain the objections. Whether Riley's account was true or not, by sustaining Chapin's objections, Judge Masten effectively removed this more complete story from the case, and "the counsel for the plaintiff did then and there rest." Chapin rested, as he had hoped to, on an incomplete story. And he won.

. . . In the foregoing discussion of Riley's evidence in chief and of Chapin's objections, we have relied upon the original, unaltered bill of exceptions, prepared after trial and before the appeal. On what appears to be the copy of the bill that made its way to the Court of Appeals, there are two inked-in alterations of substance. Each addresses the same point: the distinction between (1) a "delivery" of money, which could sustain an action for money had and received, and (2) a loan of money, which could sustain an action of debt, or of contract, by the lender but not an action by a third party, and not an action for money had and received. This distinction rendered the nature of Hawley's payment to Fox the most critical fact of the case and, as we shall see, the changes that were made to the bill of exceptions were to shape the rule of Lawrence v. Fox and, in time, the broader rule to which it gave rise.

The first handwritten change, an addition to the account of Riley's testimony, is straightforward. The unaltered version reads: "Hawley . . . at the special request of the defendant, advanced to him . . . the sum of three hundred dollars. . . ." In the altered version, the words "lent and" have been inserted before "advanced," the ambiguity resolved. Thus, Hawley, at Fox's request, "lent and advanced" to him three hundred dollars.

The second handwritten change, this one to the account of Chapin's objections to the admission of Riley's testimony, is consistent with the first and addresses the same distinction. The printed version reads:

First. — That the loan was not set up in the answer.

Second. — That if proved, it would constitute no defence to the action.

The altered version has the word "loan" deleted and "same" written above it. A specific objection to the evidence of loan has been changed to a general objection to the whole of Riley's story. In combination with the insertion of "lent and" before "advanced" in the account of Riley's testimony, this change shows an unambiguous acquiescence by Chapin in the very loan characterization he had so stealthily avoided in his pleadings, and so plainly objected to in court.

4

SUPERIOR COURT OF BUFFALO.

DON. R. LAWRENCE,

ags't

ARTHUR W. FOX.

And afterwards to wit: at a term of this court, held at the Court House in the city of Buffalo, on the 17th day of January, 1857, by, and before the Hon. Jos. G. Masten, one of the justices of said court, and a jury, the issues joined between said justices, came on to be tried; at which day came, the parties with their attorneys aforesaid, and the jurors of the jury aforesaid, being called, also came and were duly sworn to try the issues so joined.

9   And upon the trial of said case, the plaintiff to maintain the issues upon his part, called one, William Riley, and proved by him that one Holley, in the latter part of November, 1854, at the special request of the defendant, advanced to him the said defendant, the sum of three hundred dollars, and the defendant then and there in consideration thereof, undertook and agreed with said Holley that he would pay the said sum of three hundred dollars to the plaintiff herein, the next day.

10   It was further proved by said witness William Riley, that the said Holley, at the time of the delivery of the said money to the said defendant, and at the time of the agreement as aforesaid, stated to said defendant, that he was owing the said plaintiff, the said sum of three hundred dollars for money borrowed of him, the said plaintiff; and which said sum he had agreed to repay to said plaintiff herein the next day.

11   The counsel for the said defendant, did then and there move the court to strike out the testimony of what the said Holley said to the defendant, of his indebtedness to the plaintiff, upon the ground, that such testimony was improper, as it called for heresay evidence, being the declarations of third person. His Honor the Justice, did then and there deny said motion, to which decision the counsel for the defendant did then and there except.

On the *cross-examination* of said witness, it was also proved that at the time of the advance or delivery of said money by said Holley, to said defendant, and at the time of the agreement aforesaid, that said

Figure 2. The Bill of Exceptions, Lawrence v. Fox, 20 N.Y. 268 (1859).

5

plaintiff was not present; that said conversation occurred at the city of Buffalo, on Washington Street, at Mr. Purdy Merrit's; that there were two or three persons present; that they were doing nothing but standing near them; that the witness saw Holley count out the money to the defendant, and hand it to him.   12

The counsel for the defendant, then and there offered to prove by said witness, that the defendant borrowed the said money from the said Holley, with the purpose and intent to gamble with it illegally, and that Holley knew to what use he intended to apply it; to which offer the counsel for the said plaintiff, did then and there object, on the ground,

First.—That the *same* was not set up in the answer.

Second.—That if proved, it would constitute no defence to the action.

Whereupon, his Honor, the said Justice, did then and there sustain   13 the said objections, and the counsel for the defendant did then and there duly except; whereupon the counsel for the plaintiff did then and there rest.

And thereupon the counsel for said defendant, did then and there move and insist, that his Honor the said Justice, should non-suit the said plaintiff, on the ground.

First—that the plaintiff had not made out a cause of action for the reason, that it appeared from the proof, that there was no privity of the agreement or contract, proved between the parties, or between the plaintiff and said Holley.   14

Second.—There was no proof in the cause tending to show that the said Holley was indebted to, or owing the said plaintiff any sum whaever.

Third.—That the agreement was void, for want of consideration passing between the parties.

But his Honor, the said Justice, then and there refused to non-suit the said plaintiff, to which refusal of his Honor, the counsel for said defendant, did then and there except.

Whereupon the parties rested and the cause was submitted to the   15 jury, whereupon they rendered a verdict in favor of said plaintiff and against said defendant for the sum of three hundred and forty-four dollars and sixty-three cents.

And in as much as the ruling and decisions the of said Justice, and the defendant's exceptions thereto, do not appear upon the record of said trial therefore, the defendant by his said counsel, has made this bill of exceptions according to the statute in such case made and provided, this 11th day of March, 1857.

JOS. G. MASTEN, (L. S.) .

The legal explanation of Fox's liability to Lawrence changed between trial and final appeal. It changed as the bill of exceptions was changed and it changed because, for whatever reason, Chapin, Torrance, and Judge Masten agreed that the bill of exceptions should reflect that Hawley's "delivery" of money to Fox was in fact a loan. With the stroke of a pen, Lawrence's successful action for money being held was well on its way to being converted into an action on the promise by a creditor of the promisee.

We should attempt to understand how and why the bill of exceptions was altered. The bill was to serve the purpose of a record on appeal to the General Term. Had Fox not appealed, there would have been no bill of exceptions. It was the job of appellant's counsel, Jared Torrance, to draft the bill, to present it to Chapin and to Judge Masten, and to seek to have it sealed in a form as favorable to his client's interests as circumstances would allow. Thus, it is a fair inference that the handwritten alterations to the bill of exceptions in this case were the product of negotiation between counsel, perhaps involving the trial judge.

Whether Masten was "correct" in upholding Chapin's procedural objection that the loan had not been specifically pleaded depends in part on the nature of the action that was still being described as an action for money had and received seven years after the Field Code had abolished the common counts. The question of what constitutes new matter can be intimately related to the question of what constitutes the elements of a cause. Just as it may have been uncertain, after the Code, whether Chapin needed to plead Hawley's indebtedness to Lawrence, so it may have been uncertain whether the evidence offered by the defendant — to show that the money "delivered" was in fact a loan — constituted "new matter." It could not have been very clear to anyone that Chapin's argument was correct. Judge Masten may have reconsidered his position that a general denial of the allegation "that money was 'delivered' to the defendant 'to be by him delivered unto' the plaintiff" barred the introduction of evidence that the money was not "delivered" but "loaned." If Masten did have second thoughts about the admissibility of that evidence and communicated his concern to both attorneys before the bill was sealed — as one would expect him to have done — then counsel would presumably have tried to find the most effective way to deal with this change of events, and changing the bill of exceptions would have made good sense.

Although we do not know the precise reasons behind the inked-in changes, we should not lose sight of the important thing: the changes were made, and they transformed the most critical fact of the case. The "delivery" in Lawrence's complaint became the "loan" in the story that emerged from the Court of Appeals. This transformation was to force the highest court to design a new rule to explain the outcome precisely because when Hawley handed three hundred dollars to Fox, he was lending it to him. From the time that the bill of exceptions was altered, two appellate courts in Lawrence v. Fox and, eventually, countless courts throughout the land, would explain the third party's right as an action on the promise, because Hawley's payment of money to Fox was a loan. . . .

. . .

The hybrid origins of the action that emerged from Lawrence v. Fox have long been masked by its formulation as an action on the promise. Yet in its modern application, the third party beneficiary rule bears as much resemblance to a proprietary claim as to a conventional contract action.

In both respects — its formulation and its application — the present-day doctrine is faithful to the case from which it is derived, and it is as imprecisely classified as was Lawrence's claim against Fox.

So long as the object of the suit remained a bag of coins or a bundle of bills, it did not much matter whether the plaintiff's right was thought about as a right to the property, being money, or as a right to enforce the defendant's promise to pay. But when the object of such suits is broadened to include the benefit of all promises of which the plaintiff is "an intended beneficiary," the transformation from an essentially proprietary claim (had and received), to an action on the promise, matters very much. If the courts had persisted in looking for trust property, had-and-received style, before upholding the third party's claim, the third party beneficiary rule would never have attained its present importance, specifically in relation to the benefits of public programs.

It is one of the ironies of this story that the broadly equitable third party beneficiary rule, which today enables the beneficiaries of government programs, among others, to secure their intended benefits, grew out of what were apparently gambling-related transactions that took place in Purdy Merritt's establishment down by the canal, in Buffalo, in 1854. Twenty years later a eulogist wrote of Arthur W. Fox:

> There are not many men in Buffalo whose death would be more deeply regretted. . . . Possessing remarkable business enterprise and ability, he was also a man of strict and rigid integrity, always fulfilling in letter and spirit any engagement or undertaking into which he entered. Of him it might with literal truth be said, "his word is as good as his bond."

. . .

2. Intended Beneficiaries

STUDY GUIDE: In the next case involving a donee beneficiary, note the judge's statement that "the testatrix had in substance bequeathed the promise to plaintiff. . . ." Can you see why Professor Anthony Waters entitled his famous article on third-party beneficiaries, "The Property in the Promise" (p. 526)? In what sense can a promise be property?

SEAVER v. RANSOM
Court of Appeals of New York,
224 N.Y. 233, 120 N.E. 639 (1918)

POUND, J.* Judge Beman and his wife were advanced in years. Mrs. Beman was about to die. She had a small estate consisting of a

---

Cuthbert Winfred Pound (1864-1935) was educated at Cornell University and read law in a law office in Lockport, New York. He was admitted to the New York bar in 1886 and entered a private practice which lasted until 1905. During that time he also served as Lockport city attorney (1889-1891) and as a member of the state Senate (1894-1895). Pound taught law at Cornell from 1895 until 1904; concurrently he was a member and president

house and lot in Malone and little else. Judge Beman drew his wife's will according to her instructions. It gave $1,000 to plaintiff, $500 to one sister, plaintiff's mother, and $100 each to another sister and her son, the use of the house to her husband for life, and remainder to the American Society for the Prevention of Cruelty to Animals. She named her husband as residuary legatee and executor. Plaintiff was her niece, thirty-four years old, in ill health, sometimes a member of the Beman household. When the will was read to Mrs. Beman, she said that it was not as she wanted it; she wanted to leave the house to plaintiff. She had no other objection to the will, but her strength was waning and although the judge offered to write another will for her, she said she was afraid she would not hold out long enough to enable her to sign it. So the judge said, if she would sign the will, he would leave plaintiff enough in his will to make up the difference. He avouched the promise by his uplifted hand with all solemnity and his wife then executed the will. When he came to die it was found that his will made no provision for the plaintiff.

This action was brought and plaintiff recovered judgment in the trial court, on the theory that Beman had obtained property from his wife and induced her to execute the will in the form prepared by him by his promise, to give plaintiff $6,000, the value of the house, and that thereby equity impressed his property with a trust in favor of plaintiff. Where a legatee promises the testator that he will use property given him by the will for a particular purpose, a trust arises. . . . Beman received nothing under his wife's will but the use of the house in Malone for life. Equity compels the application of property thus obtained to the purpose of the testator, but equity cannot so impress a trust except on property obtained by the promise. Beman was bound by his promise, but no property was bound by it; no trust in plaintiff's favor can be spelled out.

An action on the contract for damages or to make the executors trustees for performance stands on different ground. . . . The Appellate Division properly passed to the consideration of the question whether the judgment could stand upon the promise made to the wife, upon a valid consideration, for the sole benefit of plaintiff. The judgment of the trial court was affirmed by a return to the general doctrine laid down in the great case of Lawrence v. Fox (20 N.Y. 268) which has since been limited as herein indicated.

Contracts for the benefit of third persons have been the prolific source of judicial and academic discussion. (Williston, Contracts for the Benefit of a Third Person, 15 Harvard Law Review, 767; Corbin, Contracts for the Benefit of Third Persons, 27 Yale Law Review, 1008.) The general rule, both in law and equity . . . was the privity between a plaintiff and a defendant is necessary to the maintenance of an action on the contract. The consideration must be furnished by the party to whom the promise was made. The contract cannot be enforced against the third party, and, therefore, it cannot be enforced by him. On the other hand, the right of the beneficiary to sue on a contract made expressly for his benefit has been fully

of the N.Y. Civil Service Commission (1900-1905). From 1905 to 1906, he was counsel to the Governor. His judicial career began with nine years on the Supreme Court. In 1915, he moved to the Court of Appeals of New York. He served as Chief Judge from 1932 to 1934, and retired at the end of that period. — C.R.

recognized in many American jurisdictions, either by judicial decision or by legislation, and is said to be "the prevailing rule in this country." (Hendrick v. Linsday, 93 U.S. 143 [23 L. Ed. 855]; Lehow v Simonton, 3 Col. 346.) It has been said that "the establishment of this doctrine has been gradual, and is a victory of practical utility over theory, of equity over technical subtlety. (Brantly on Contracts (2d ed.), p. 253.) The reasons for this view are that it is just and practical to permit the person for whose benefit the contract is made to enforce it against one whose duty it is to pay. Other jurisdictions still adhere to the present English rule (7 Halsbury's Laws of England, 342, 343; Jenks' Digest of English Civil Law, §229) that a contract cannot be enforced by or against a person who is not a party. (Exchange Bank v. Rice, 107 Mass. 37 [9 Am. Rep. 1]. . . .) In New York the right of the beneficiary to sue on contracts made for his benefit is not clearly or simply defined. It is at present confined, *first*, to cases where there is a pecuniary obligation running from the promisee to the beneficiary; "a legal right founded upon some obligation of the promisee in the third party to adopt and claim the promise as made for his benefit." (Farley v. Cleveland, 4 Cow. 432 [15 Am. Dec. 387]); Lawrence v. Fox, supra;] . . . *Secondly*, to cases where the contract is made for the benefit of the wife . . . , affianced wife . . . , or child . . . of a party to the contract. The close relationship cases go back to the early King's Bench case (1677), long since repudiated in England, of Dutton v. Poole (2 Lev. 211; *s.c.*, 1 Ventris, 318, 332). (Schermerhorn v. Vanderheyden, 1 Johns. 139 [3 Am. Dec. 304].) The natural and moral duty of the husband or parent to provide for the future of wife or child sustains the action on the contract made for their benefit. "This is the farthest the case[s] in this state have gone" says Cullen, J., in the marriage settlement case of Borland v. Welch (162 N.Y. 104, 110 [56 N.E. 556]).]

The right of the third party is also upheld in, *thirdly*, the public contract cases . . . where the municipality seeks to protect its inhabitants by covenants for their benefit,] and, *fourthly*, the cases where, at the request of a party to the contract, the promise runs directly to the beneficiary although he does not furnish the consideration.] . . . It may be safely said that a general rule sustaining recovery at the suit of the third party would include but few classes of cases not included in these groups, either categorically or in principle.

The desire of the childless aunt to make provision for a beloved and favorite niece differs imperceptibly in law or in equity from the moral duty of the parent to make testamentary provision for a child. The contract was made for the plaintiff's benefit. She alone is substantially damaged by its breach. The representatives of the wife's estate have no interest in enforcing it specifically. It is said in Buchanan v. Tilden that the common law imposes moral and legal obligations upon the husband and the parent not measured by the necessaries of life. It was, however, the love and affection or the moral sense of the husband and the parent that imposed such obligations in the cases cited, rather than any common-law duty of husband and parent to wife and child. If plaintiff had been a child of Mrs. Beman, legal obligation would have required no testamentary provision for her, yet the child could have enforced a covenant in her favor identical with the covenant of Judge Beman in this case. (De Cicco v. Schweizer [221 N.Y. 431, 117 N.E. 807].)

The constraining power of conscience is not regulated by the degree of relationship alone. The dependent or faithful niece may have a stronger claim than the affluent or unworthy son. No sensible theory of moral obligation denies arbitrarily to the former what would be conceded to the latter. We might consistently either refuse or allow the claim of both, but I cannot reconcile a decision in favor of the wife in Buchanan v. Tilden based on the moral obligations arising out of near relationship with a decision against the niece here on the ground that the relationship is too remote for equity's ken. No controlling authority depends upon so absolute a rule. . . .

Kellogg, P.J., writing for the court below well said:

> The doctrine of Lawrence v. Fox is progressive, not retrograde. The court of the late decisions is to enlarge, not to limit the effect of that case.

The court in that leading case attempted to adopt the general doctrine that any third person, for whose direct benefit a contract was intended, could sue on it. The headnote thus states the rule. Finch, J., in Gifford v. Corrigan (17 N.Y. 257, 262 [22 N.E. 756, 6 L.R.A. 610, 15 Am. St. Rep. 508]) says that the case rests upon that broad proposition; Edward T. Bartlett, J., in Pond v. New Rochelle Water Co. (183 N.Y. 330, 337 [76 N.E. 211, 213, 1 L.R.A. (N.S.) 958, 5 Ann. Cas. 504]) calls it "the general principle"; but Vrooman v. Turner [69 N.Y. 280] confined its application to the facts on which it was decided. "In every case which an action has been sustained," says Allen, J., "there has been a debt or duty owing by the promisee to the party claiming to sue upon the promise." (69 N.Y. 285 [25 Am. Rep. 195].) As late as Towsend v. Rackham (143 N.Y. 516, 523 [38 N.E. 731, 733]) we find Peckham, J., saying that "to maintain the action by the third person there must be this liability to him on the part of the promisee." Buchanan v. Tilden went further than any case since Lawrence v. Fox in a desire to do justice rather than to apply with technical accuracy strict rules calling for a legal or equitable obligation. . . .

But, on principle, a sound conclusion may be reached. If Mrs. Beman had left her husband the house on condition that he pay the plaintiff $6,000, and he accepted the devise, he would have become personally liable to pay the legacy, and plaintiff could have recovered in an action at law against him, whatever the value of the house. . . . That would be because the testatrix had in substance bequeathed the promise to plaintiff, and not because close relationship or moral obligation sustained the contract. The distinction between an implied promise to a testator for the benefit of a third party to pay a legacy and an unqualified promise on a valuable consideration to make provision for the third party by will is discernible but not obvious. The tendency of American authority is to sustain the gift in all such cases and to permit the donee-beneficiary to recover on the contract. . . . The equities are with the plaintiff and they may be enforced in this action, whether it be regarded as an action for damages or an action for specific performance to convert the defendants into trustees for plaintiff's benefit under the agreement.

The judgment should be affirmed, with costs.

RESTATEMENT (SECOND) OF CONTRACTS

STUDY GUIDE: In what manner does the Restatement adopt the distinction between creditor and donee beneficiaries? What is the relationship between the intention of the parties and these two types of beneficiaries?

§302. INTENDED AND INCIDENTAL BENEFICIARIES

(1) Unless otherwise agreed between promisor and promisee, a beneficiary of a promise is an intended beneficiary if recognition of a right to performance in the beneficiary is appropriate to effectuate the intention of the parties and either

(a) the performance of the promise will satisfy an obligation of the promisee to pay money to the beneficiary; or *(Creditor) (Lawrence v. Fox)*

(b) the circumstances indicate that the promisee intends to give the beneficiary the benefit of the promised performance. *(Donee) (Seaver v. Ransom)*

"*Facts*" (2) An incidental beneficiary is a beneficiary who is not an intended beneficiary.

3. Distinguishing Intended from Incidental Beneficiaries

STUDY GUIDE: You will recall that in Kelly Health Care, *the hospital sought to recover from an insurance company as an assignee. In the next case, a hospital asserts rights against an insurance company as a third-party beneficiary of a settlement agreement between the insurance company and the patient. In addition, the court considers briefly one circumstance in which a promisor may assert a defense against a beneficiary.*

SISTERS OF ST. JOSEPH OF PEACE, HEALTH, AND HOSPITAL SERVICES v. RUSSELL
Supreme Court of Oregon,
318 Or. 370, 867 P.2d 1377 (1994)

GRABER, J.*

This case involves principles relating to third-party beneficiary contracts.

---

* *Susan P. Graber* (1949-†) was educated at Wellesley College (B.A.) and Yale University (J.D.). She served as Assistant Attorney General of the Bureau of Revenue at Santa Fe, New Mexico (1972-1974), then engaged in private practice at Santa Fe (1974-1975), Cincinnati (1975-1978), and Portland, Oregon (1978-1988). In 1988, Graber was appointed to the Court of Appeals of Oregon; she was promoted to the Supreme Court of Oregon in 1990. She now sits on the U.S. Court of Appeals for the Ninth Circuit. — K.T.

FACTS AND PROCEDURAL BACKGROUND

On September 13, 1984, Russell was injured when the log scaler that he was operating rolled down a hill. As a result of that accident, Russell's back and arm were broken. Sacred Heart General Hospital (hospital) provided medical treatment for his injuries from September 13, 1984, through August 30, 1985.

Russell was uncertain who his employer was at the time of the injury. For that reason, he filed four separate workers' compensation claims against four purported employers. After a hearing concerning all four claims, a referee held that an employer insured by The Aetna Casualty & Surety Company (Aetna) was Russell's employer for workers' compensation purposes. The Workers' Compensation Board (Board) affirmed. Aetna and Russell sought judicial review in the Court of Appeals.

While those petitions for judicial review were pending, the four purported employers and their insurers, including Aetna, entered into a Disputed Claim Settlement (DCS) agreement with Russell. The Board approved the DCS agreement pursuant to ORS 656.289(4),[21] and Aetna and Russell dismissed their petitions for judicial review of the Board's order.

Plaintiff hospital then brought this action against Russell and Aetna to recover for the medical care that plaintiff had provided to Russell. Plaintiff pleaded two theories of recovery against Russell: contract implied in fact (Claim 1) and account stated (Claim 2). Plaintiff also pleaded a claim against Aetna (Claim 3). That claim was based on the theory that plaintiff was a third-party beneficiary of the DCS agreement, to which Russell and Aetna were parties. The case was tried to a jury.

> *[handwritten margin note: Provision of implied services not essential]*

At trial, plaintiff called Russell as a witness. Russell testified that he never agreed to "personally pay" plaintiff's bills, although he did not refuse the hospital's treatment and agreed that the treatment saved his life. plaintiff's only other witness was its director of patient accounts, who testified as to the charges billed and gave the opinion that the charges were reasonable. Plaintiff also introduced the DCS agreement and the hospital bills into evidence.

At the close of all the evidence, Aetna moved for a directed verdict . . . on Claim 3. Aetna argued two separate points: (a) that "there is no evidence of a third-party beneficiary contract," and (b) that "Plaintiff has . . . not presented any expert testimony sufficient to show that the [hospital] services that were allegedly provided to Defendant Russell were services which were reasonable . . . and necessary" to treat Russell's injuries. The trial court denied Aetna's motion. Thereafter, the jury returned a verdict for Russell on Claims 1 and 2 and for plaintiff against Aetna on Claim 3, the claim based on the DCS agreement.[22]

---

21. ORS 656.289(4) provides in part that, "in any case where there is a bona fide dispute over compensability of a claim, the parties may, with the approval of . . . the board . . . , by agreement make such disposition of the claim as is considered reasonable."

22. With respect to Claim 3, the jury verdict stated:

I. What is the amount that plaintiff is entitled to recover from defendant Aetna, if any, on plaintiff's third claim for relief? "$96,888.74."

The trial court entered judgment on the verdict. Aetna appealed, assigning as error the denial of its motion for a directed verdict on Claim 3.[23]

The Court of Appeals reversed. . . . That court rejected plaintiff's characterization of Claim 3 as one based entirely on its rights as a third-party beneficiary of an express contract, the DCS agreement. . . . The court concluded that, instead, plaintiff's express contract claim against Aetna "incorporates an implied agreement between plaintiff and Russell," so that plaintiff's right to recover depended on Russell's actual liability to plaintiff; plaintiff, therefore, could not recover unless it proved all the elements of Claim 1, its implied contract claim against Russell. . . . The court then held that, because "there was no admissible evidence that what was supplied was necessary for the care of Russell," the trial court erred in not granting Aetna's motion for directed verdict. . . . One judge concurred, stating that "[p]laintiff was, at best, an incidental beneficiary of the [DCS] agreement and not entitled to bring an action as a third-party beneficiary of Russell's contract." . . . (Warren, P.J., concurring.) One judge dissented, on the ground that the DCS agreement was ambiguous, that the jury was entitled to decide whether plaintiff was an intended third-party beneficiary of the DCS agreement, and that, "because the jury decided this case on the basis of an express contract, testimony concerning the reasonableness or necessity of the [medical] services [provided to Russell by plaintiff] is irrelevant." . . . (Landau, J., dissenting.) We allowed plaintiff's petition for review and now reverse the decision of the Court of Appeals.

PLAINTIFF AS THIRD-PARTY BENEFICIARY

Plaintiff's claim against Aetna was based on a single theory: "[t]hat Sacred Heart General Hospital became a third party beneficiary of" the DCS agreement between Aetna and Russell, "pursuant to said agreement." We begin by examining that assertion. . . .

As a general proposition, a third party's right to enforce a contractual promise in its favor depends on the intention of the parties to the contract. [Oregon case law recognizes three categories of third-party beneficiaries: donee beneficiaries, creditor beneficiaries, and incidental beneficiaries]. . . . For a plaintiff to be a donee beneficiary,

> it must appear that the [promisee's] intent in obtaining [the promisor's] promise to [perform] was to make a gift to [the] plaintiff or to confer a right to [performance] upon [the] plaintiff, which [performance] was not due *or claimed to be due* by the [promisee] to [the] plaintiff.

Northwest Airlines v. Crosetti Bros., 258 Or. 340, 346, 483 P.2d 70 (1971) (emphasis added). For a plaintiff to be a creditor beneficiary,

> the performance . . . by [the promisor] must be to "satisfy an actual *or supposed or asserted duty* of the promisee . . . to the [plaintiff]."

---

23. Plaintiff did not appeal concerning Claims 1 and 2, which were its claims against Russell. As a result, Claims 1 and 2 were not at issue on appeal and are not at issue on review.

Ibid. (emphasis added; citation omitted). Finally, if the third party has paid no value *and* there is no intention to confer a contract right on that party, then the party is an incidental beneficiary who is not entitled to an action on the contract. In those circumstances, "the contract will not be interpreted to promise performance to the third-party stranger to the contract even though the stranger may incidentally benefit from the contract." Aetna Casualty & Surety Co. v. OHSU, 310 Or. 61, 65, 793 P.2d 320 (1990). In short, the first two categories of beneficiaries are entitled to enforce directly contractual promises intended to be for their benefit, even though they are strangers to the contract. Incidental beneficiaries are not so entitled.

In this case, plaintiff gave medical care to Russell. Plaintiff billed Russell for that medical care. In other words, at the time the DCS agreement was signed, plaintiff had given something of value to Russell and was asserting that Russell had a duty to pay for it. In those circumstances, plaintiff was a creditor beneficiary of the DCS agreement *if* the parties intended that contract to benefit plaintiff. To determine whether Aetna and Russell intended to benefit the hospital, we must examine the DCS agreement.

In numbered paragraph 1 of the DCS agreement, Russell "allege[d] that he ha[d] incurred" certain "medical expenses" as a result of the injury that gave rise to the settlement, including "Sacred Heart Hospital, Eugene, OR [$]98,872.50." Paragraph 2 provided:

> That Aetna Casualty & Surety Co. will hold . . . Russell harmless in regard to the above alleged medical expenses, including, but not limited to all principal, interest, penalties, attorneys' fees or any other charges or claims or demands or causes of action or suit against him by reason of the above alleged medical bills and/or obligations. [Russell] agrees that as between Aetna and the medical providers, Aetna is free to make whatever arrangements they wish with regard to settlement of the alleged bills.

Paragraph 3 of the DCS agreement specified that Russell could keep the time loss payments that he had received from Aetna. Paragraph 4 awarded a lump sum settlement to Russell and his lawyers. Paragraph 5 absolved the four purported employers and their insurers of any further responsibility for Russell's

> disputed and denied conditions excepting, however, the terms [that] this agreement provide[,] and the parties agree that the sums heretofore set forth to be the sole responsibility of the carrier Aetna Casualty & Surety Company.

Paragraph 6 of the DCS agreement included various general provisions relating to the settlement and stated that, after the date of the DCS agreement, Russell would be responsible

> for his own temporary and permanent disability due to this injury and/or medical care and . . . for future medical expenses incurred due to these conditions and also including [Russell's] sole responsibility for any aggravation or permanent disability attendant thereto.

Paragraph 6 also provided:

> [Russell] and his attorney agree and warrant that the aboved named health care providers are the only health care providers which have provided services to [Russell] in relation to this claim and Aetna Casualty & Surety Company shall be solely responsible for resolving the claims of said creditors and as hereinabove set forth shall indemnify and hold [Russell] harmless therefrom including any and all claims, demands, causes of action or suit, attorney fees, penalties, interest or otherwise arising out of the aforesaid bills by medical providers but that [Russell] shall be solely responsible for any future obligations or bills incurred for treatment of his condition.

The trial court held that the DCS agreement was ambiguous and, accordingly, that the issue should be decided by the jury. This court has explained:

> Unambiguous contracts must be enforced according to their terms. Whether the terms of a contract are ambiguous in the first instance is a question of law. If a contract is ambiguous, the trier of fact will ascertain the intent of the parties and construe the contract consistent with the intent of the parties.

OSEA v. Rainier School Dist. No. 13, 311 Or. 188, 194, 808 P.2d 83 (1991) (citations omitted).

We conclude that the trial court did not err in denying Aetna's motion for a directed verdict on the asserted ground that "there is no evidence of a third-party beneficiary contract." In so concluding, we note that plaintiff did not move for a directed verdict in its favor on that question and that neither party asserts in this court that the jury received erroneous instructions or an erroneous verdict form with respect to that question. Our holding, therefore, is limited in scope.

The most natural reading of paragraph 2 is that Aetna *must pay the listed medical providers*, although it remains free to negotiate concerning the amount to be paid to a given provider and the payment arrangements, such as timing.

Aetna argues, however, that the DCS agreement also could be read to suggest that the parties intended to settle Russell's workers' compensation claim without concern for the ability of plaintiff or other third-party health care providers to receive payment.

Other provisions demonstrate an intention to require Aetna to pay the third parties listed in paragraph 1 of the DCS agreement. For example, in paragraph 5 ("the parties agree that *the sums heretofore set forth to be the sole responsibility of the carrier Aetna Casualty & Surety Company*.") (Emphasis added.) The phrase "the sums heretofore set forth" may be read to include the medical expenses listed in paragraph 1. Further, in paragraph 6, Russell

> warrant[s] that the above named health care providers are the only health care providers which have provided services to [Russell] in relation to this claim and Aetna Casualty & Surety Company shall be solely responsible for resolving the claims of said creditors.

Also in paragraph 6, Russell agrees to "be fully responsible for future medical expenses incurred." As a whole, paragraph 6 may be read to demonstrate that the parties *intended for all health care providers to be paid*, but simply divided the responsibility for payment between past and future expenses.

In deciding whether the parties to the DCS agreement intended to benefit plaintiff, the jury could consider, not only the terms of the contract, but also the circumstances under which the contract was made. See ORS 42.220 ("In construing an instrument, the circumstances under which it was made, including the situation of the subject and of the parties, may be shown so that the judge is placed in the position of those whose language the judge is interpreting."). . . . One of the circumstances was the potential liability facing Aetna and Russell at the time that they signed the DCS agreement.

Had Russell prevailed in his workers' compensation claim against Aetna's insured, Aetna would have been legally responsible for paying all of Russell's past and future medical bills attributable to his compensable injury, including the hospital bills at issue here. See ORS 656.245 (requiring insurer to provide medical services, including surgical, hospital, and nursing services, and medications and similar supplies, for every compensable injury). Had Russell's accident been held noncompensable, as Aetna was contending in the petition for judicial review that was pending at the time the DCS agreement was signed, Russell could have been legally responsible for paying all of his own medical expenses, including those owed to plaintiff. In the light of those circumstances, a possible interpretation of the DCS agreement was that all of the health care providers *must and would be paid* by someone and that the only question was who would be responsible to pay which bills — a question settled by Aetna's promise to pay past bills and Russell's promise to be responsible for future bills.

The jury also could infer from the extent of Russell's injuries, the extent of medical treatments provided, and the substantial size of the hospital bills that the parties to the DCS agreement intended to ensure that someone would pay plaintiff. Finally, from Russell's testimony that plaintiff's services saved his life, the jury could infer that Russell, at least, intended that plaintiff be paid by Aetna.

In summary, the trial court did not err in denying Aetna's motion for a directed verdict on the asserted ground that, as a matter of law, plaintiff was not an intended third-party beneficiary of the DCS agreement.

PROOF OF ENTITLEMENT TO RECOVERY

We turn to the question whether, in order to enforce the DCS agreement in its favor, plaintiff was required to prove that the medical services that it provided to Russell were necessary. Because of the procedural posture of the case, the same standard of review applies to this question as applied to the question whether plaintiff was an intended third-party beneficiary of the contract. Again, plaintiff did not seek a directed verdict in its favor and, again, there is no challenge to the adequacy of the jury instructions or the verdict form as to this question.

In general, a third-party creditor beneficiary's right to recover against the promisor is subject to any claim or defense arising from the beneficiary's own conduct or agreement. See Restatement (Second) of Contracts, §309(4) and comment c (1981) (so stating; "The conduct of the beneficiary . . . may give rise to claims and defenses which may be asserted against him by the obligor, and his right may be affected by the terms of an agreement made by him."). In this case, Aetna asserts that plaintiff provided medical services to Russell that were not proved to be necessary.

Assuming that Aetna's factual assertion is accurate,[24] plaintiff's claim is not barred by that defense. That is because the contract that a third-party beneficiary seeks to enforce may provide that some or all otherwise-available defenses do not apply.

Aetna argues that paragraph 2 of the DCS agreement can be read to suggest that the parties intended to condition the intention to benefit plaintiff on plaintiff's negotiations with Aetna regarding the hospital bills; the absence of proof that the hospital services were "necessary for the care of Russell" could be a basis for such negotiations.

Paragraph 5 of the DCS agreement, however, makes *"the sums heretofore set forth . . . the sole responsibility of the carrier Aetna."* (Emphasis added.) One of those *sums* is stated to be *the full and exact dollar amount of plaintiff's bills* for Russell's care. In addition, as discussed above, paragraph 6 may be read to suggest that the DCS agreement simply divided responsibility for payment of medical expenses, as between Russell and Aetna, based *only* on whether the expenses were for past or future care. Paragraph 6 refers to the medical providers, including plaintiff, as Russell's "creditors." As a whole, the paragraph suggests that the parties to the DCS agreement recognized that Russell's medical expenses, as listed in paragraph 1, were, in fact, owed.

The trial court did not err in denying Aetna's motion for a directed verdict on the asserted ground that plaintiff failed to prove a required element of its claim.

CONCLUSION

In summary, the trial court did not err in denying Aetna's motion for a directed verdict on either of the grounds asserted by Aetna. There are no other issues before us concerning the propriety of the jury's verdict, and that verdict must be sustained.

The decision of the Court of Appeals is reversed. The judgment of the circuit court is affirmed.

24. The parties agree that the following statement by the Court of Appeals, concerning the record in this case, is correct:

Plaintiff presented evidence that it provided to Russell the medical services for which it sought payment. Moreover, it presented evidence that the charges for the medical services were reasonable. However, there was no admissible evidence that what was supplied was necessary for the care of Russell.

Sisters of St. Joseph v. Russell, 122 Or. App. 188, 192, 857 P.2d 192 (1993).

RESTATEMENT (SECOND) OF CONTRACTS

§315. EFFECT OF A PROMISE OF INCIDENTAL BENEFIT

An incidental beneficiary acquires by virtue of the promise no right against the promisor or the promisee.

REFERENCE: Farnsworth, §§10.2-10.6
              Calamari & Perillo, §§17.2-17.4
              Murray, §§131, 133

III

ENFORCEABILITY

8

PRINCIPLES OF ENFORCEABILITY

The materials on assent dealt with the problems of determining the existence and meaning of a private commitment. We have yet to consider whether, when, and why the existence of a private commitment justifies legal enforcement. As Professor Arthur Corbin once wrote:

> The mere fact that one man promises something to another creates no legal duty and makes no legal remedy available in case of non-performance. To be enforceable, the promise must be accompanied by some other factor. . . . The question now to be discussed is what is this other factor. What fact or facts must accompany a promise to make it enforceable at law?[1]

Why should *any* private agreement be coercively enforced? Do *all* private commitments merit enforcement? If not, how do we distinguish those that do from those that do not?

Early English law answered these questions by the use of *formalities.* Only commitments under seal were readily enforceable.[2] After the rise of the writ of assumpsit, the answer to these questions was provided by the doctrine of *consideration.* In the late nineteenth and early twentieth centuries, this doctrine was supplemented by the doctrine of *promissory estoppel.* Historically, then, the common law of contract has provided at least three doctrinal criteria of enforceability. We shall devote a chapter to each. Chapter 9 concerns the doctrine of consideration. Chapter 10 discusses the function of formalities in determining enforceability. Chapter 11 covers the doctrine of promissory estoppel.

Our two goals throughout this part of the materials will be to understand the doctrines and to discern the theory or theories that underlie them. To these ends, we begin our study of these questions with a section in which existing theories of enforcement are categorized and summarized. Note that this organizational scheme is not the only way to divide up the

---

1. Arthur L. Corbin, Corbin on Contracts §110, at 490 (1963); see also Melvin A. Eisenberg, The Principles of Consideration, 67 Cornell L. Rev. 640, 640 (1982) ("A promise, as such, is not legally enforceable. The first great question of contract law, therefore, is what kinds of promises should be enforced.").

2. As will be discussed below, informal promises could be enforced in principle, but were subject to legal defenses inapplicable to contracts under seal.

world. Other have been presented by Morris Cohen[3] and by John Calamari and Joseph Perillo.[4]

A.   SIX CORE PRINCIPLES
OF ENFORCEABILITY[5]

Why should the law enforce the mutual assent of contracting parties? At least six reasons for enforcement have been offered. These reasons can be considered core principles of contractual enforcement. They are the principles of will, reliance, restitution, efficiency, fairness, and bargain. To some extent, contract law represents an amalgam of these principles. Contract scholars differ over the proper mix of these principles as well as the weight each is to be accorded. Most (but not all) think that no single theory can explain or adequately justify all contractual enforcement.

These six principles can be placed in three general categories. Will, reliance, and restitution principles are *party-based.* Efficiency and fairness principles are *standards-based.* The bargain principle is *process-based.* At least some of each principle's inability to explain and justify contractual enforcement is characteristic of its type. For this reason, each type shall be separately considered here. In the discussion that follows, the basic insight underlying each of the principles will be described and then its limitations will be explained. The object is not to refute any of these principles. To the contrary, each captures something important that is at stake when people make commitments to each other. Instead, the reason for discussing the limitations of these principles is to show how each, despite its attractiveness, is inadequate standing alone to provide a comprehensive theory of contractual obligation.

1.   Party-Based Principles

Principles described here as party-based are those that focus on one particular party to a transaction. The will principle is primarily concerned with protecting the promisor. The reliance principle is primarily concerned with protecting the promisee. The restitution principle is concerned with the unjust enrichment of the promisor.

a. The Will Principle.   According to the will principle, commitments are enforceable because the promisor has *willed* or freely chosen to be bound by his commitment. "According to the classical view, the law of contract gives expression to and protects the will of the parties, for the will is something inherently worthy of respect."[6] In this approach, the use of force

---

3. See Morris Cohen, The Basis of Contract, 46 Harv. L. Rev. 553 (1933).

4. See John Calamari and Joseph Perillo, The Philosophical Foundations of Contract Law, in The Law of Contracts 7-11 (3d ed. 1987).

5. This section is based on Randy E. Barnett, A Consent Theory of Contract, 86 Colum. L. Rev. 269, 271-291 (1986) (hereinafter cited as "A Consent Theory").

6. Cohen, supra note 3, at 575.

against a reneging promisor is morally justified because the promisor herself has undertaken the obligation in question. A promisor cannot complain about force being used against her, since she created the obligation being enforced.[7]

In this way, the will principle is able to distinguish contract from tort. In tort, the source of the obligation, or duty, is the law. In contract, the source of the obligation or duty being enforced is the promisor herself. The spirit of the will principle may best be exemplified by the traditional sentiment, often expressed by nineteenth- and early twentieth-century courts, that contracts require a "meeting of the minds." According to the materials we studied in Part II, mutual assent is thought necessary to create a contractual obligation. This aspect of contract doctrine is quite harmonious with the will principle.

Limitations of the Will Principle. The will principle depends for its moral force upon the notion that contractual duties are binding because they are freely assumed by those who are required to discharge them. This position leads quite naturally to an inquiry as to the promisor's actual state of mind at the time of agreement — the so-called *subjective* viewpoint — and indeed most important contractual duties probably are subjectively assented to by the promisor. However, what of those manifested commitments that lack subjective assent? Without a genuine commitment by the person who is to be subjected to a legal sanction, enforcement would seem to be unjustified by the will principle. After all, enforcement can hardly be based on will if the obligation was *not* chosen by the individual but instead was imposed by law the way that tort duties are.

Yet, it has long been recognized that a system of contractual enforcement would be unworkable if it required a subjective inquiry into the putative promisor's intent. Where we cannot discern the actual subjective intent or will of the parties, there is no practical problem since we may assume it corresponds to objectively manifested intentions. But where subjective intent can somehow be proved and it is contrary to objectively manifested behavior, the subjective intent should prevail if the moral integrity of the will principle is to be preserved.

Of course, any legal preference for the promisor's hidden subjective intent would disappoint a promisee who has acted in reliance on the appearance of a commitment. Moreover, permitting a subjective inquiry into the promisor's intent could also enable a promisor to fraudulently undermine otherwise perfectly clear agreements by generating and preserving extrinsic evidence of ambiguous or conflicting intentions. Such a strategy might create a de facto option in the promisor. The promisor could insist on enforcement if the contract continued to be in her interest, but if it were no longer advantageous, she could avoid the contract, by producing evidence of a differing subjective intent.[8] In sum, because the subjective

7. See Charles Fried, Contract as Promise 16 (1981) ("An individual is morally bound to keep his promises because he has *intentionally* invoked a convention whose function it is to give grounds — moral grounds — for another to expect the promised performance.") (emphasis added).

8. For a case in which a court suspected a party of using the mail-box rule in such a fashion, see Cohen v. Clayton Coal Company, 86 Colo. 270, 281 (1929).

approach relies on evidence inaccessible to the promisee, much less to third parties, an inquiry into subjective intent would undermine the security of transactions by greatly reducing the reliability of contractual commitments. As philosopher David Hume observed over 200 years ago:

> If the secret direction of the intention, said every man of sense, could invalidate a contract, where is our security? And yet a metaphysical schoolman might think, that where an intention was supposed to be requisite, if that intention really had no place, no consequence ought to follow, and no obligation be imposed.[9]

Not surprisingly, as we studied in Chapters 4 and 5, despite the oft-expressed traditional sentiment that contracts require a meeting of the minds, the objective approach has largely prevailed. A rigorous commitment to a will theory conflicts unavoidably with the practical need for a system of rules based to a large extent on objectively manifested states of mind.

Because a person's objective manifestations generally *do* reflect her subjective intentions, the doctrinal requirement of mutual assent tends in the vast majority of cases to honor the will principle. And, consistent with the will principle, we have seen that (a) the reasonable or objective meaning of assent may be overridden by proof of a contrary subjective agreement between *both* parties and (b) when a promisee has access to the subjective or actual understanding of the promisor, he may not rely on the objective, or reasonable, meaning of the promisor's conduct. In such circumstances, the courts will enforce the subjective over the objective meaning of assent. Nonetheless, the will principle has difficulty explaining the enforcement of the objective agreement where it can be shown that the subjective understanding of a promisor differs from her objectively manifested behavior. This accounts in part for the continued interest in reliance-based theories of contractual obligation.

b. The Reliance Principle. Some contract theorists are attracted to the idea that contractual enforcement is an effort to protect a promisee's reliance on the promises of others.[10] The reliance principle has the apparent virtue of explaining why persons may be bound by the common or objective meaning of their words regardless of their intentions. The reliance principle is based upon the intuition that we ought to be liable in contract law for harm caused by our *verbal* behavior (whether oral or written), in much the same way and for the same reasons that we are held liable in tort law for harmful consequences of other types of acts. In contrast with the will

9. David Hume, An Inquiry Concerning the Principles of Morals 30 n.5 (C. Hendel ed. 1957) (1st ed. 1751).

10. See, e.g., Grant Gilmore, The Death of Contract 71-72, 88 (1974). Patrick Atiyah appears to call for a reliance theory, although he also acknowledges that "the voluntary creation and extinction of rights and liabilities" should remain one of the "basic pillars of the law of obligations." P. S. Atiyah, The Rise and Fall of Freedom of Contract 779 (1979); see also Jay M. Feinman, Promissory Estoppel and Judicial Method, 97 Harv. L. Rev. 678, 716-717 (1984) ("reliance principle" undermines "classical" contract law doctrines); Stanley D. Henderson, Promissory Estoppel and Traditional Contract Doctrine, 78 Yale L.J. 343, 344 (1969) (rules of promissory estoppel create a contract grounded on effects of reliance).

principle, adherence to this principle makes contractual obligations appear to resemble closely the duties imposed by tort law if it does not entirely collapse the contract-tort distinction. As Grant Gilmore stated:

> We may take the fact that damages in contract have become indistinguishable from damages in tort as obscurely reflecting an instinctive, almost unconscious realization that the two fields, which had been artificially set apart, are gradually merging and becoming one.[11]

The reliance principle is also commonly thought to be reflected in the doctrine of promissory estoppel, which we will study in Chapter 11.

Limitations of the Reliance Principle. Contract theorists who seek to place exclusive reliance on the reliance principle have nonetheless faced a seemingly insuperable difficulty. As Morris Cohen wrote as early as 1933: "Clearly, not all cases of injury resulting from reliance on the word or act of another are actionable, and the theory before us offers no clue as to what distinguishes those which are."[12] This deficiency has led necessarily to the employment of such phrases as "justifiable" reliance or "reasonable" reliance. These adjectives, however, depend on usually vague or entirely unstated standards of evaluation that are unrelated to reliance because — whether justified or unjustified, reasonable or unreasonable — reliance is present in any event. Perhaps for this reason, while the literature is replete with discussion of the reliance principle, a comprehensive reliance theory of contract has never been systematically presented.

Furthermore, whether a person has "reasonably" relied on a promise depends to some degree on what most people would (or ought to) do. We cannot make this assessment entirely independently of the legal rule in effect in the relevant community, because what many people would do in reliance on a promise — especially repeat players with access to lawyers who are familiar with the legal rules in effect — is crucially affected by their perception of whether or not the promise is enforceable. Even though some people will rely upon the commitments of others for reasons having nothing to do with enforcement, a prediction that a promise can reasonably be expected to induce reliance by a promisee or third party in many cases will depend upon whether the promisee (or third party) believes that reliance will be legally protected. Therefore, a legal rule cannot be based solely on such a prediction without introducing a practical circularity into the analysis.

What if we limit enforceability to promises upon which reliance is reasonably foreseeable?[13] If a promise is defined, however, as in the Restatement (Second) of Contracts §2, as "a manifestation of intention to act or refrain from acting in a specified way, so made as to justify a promisee in understanding that a *commitment* has been made," then it would seem that *every* promisor should reasonably expect to induce reliance because every

11. G. Gilmore, supra note 10, at 88.
12. Cohen, supra note 3, at 579.
13. See, e.g., Restatement (Second) of Contracts §90(1) (1979) ("A promise which the promisor should reasonably expect to induce action or forbearance on the part of the promisee or a third person and which does induce such action is binding if injustice can be avoided only by the enforcement of the promise.").

promisor has by definition made a commitment. If this is correct, then "[t]he real issue is not whether the promisor should have expected the promisee to rely, but whether the extent of the promisee's reliance was reasonable."[14] But this returns us once again to the difficulties of discerning reasonable reliance.

In sum, any theory that purports to base contractual obligation solely on the reliance principle fails to resolve the basic question concerning enforceability: Which *potentially* reliance-inducing actions entail legal consequences and which do not? A person's actions in reliance on a commitment are not justified — and therefore legally protected — simply *because* he has relied. Rather, an important part of any account of why reliance on the words of others is legally protected will turn on some as yet undefined criteria or criterion that distinguishes reasonable, or justified, reliance from unreasonable and unjustified reliance. And this criterion will not, by assumption, be the presence of reliance itself.

Finally, the reliance principle does not explain cases in which the expectations of the promisees are legally protected despite the fact that they did *not* rely on the promise.[15] Such cases could be viewed as vindicating the promisee's *right* to rely on a promise, but enforcement cannot then be justified on the grounds that, as in tort law, the verbal conduct of the promisor has worked an injury to the promisee.

c. The Restitution Principle.

Another reason for enforcing a commitment is to prevent the unjust enrichment of a promisor who seeks to go back on her word. Contractual enforcement can be viewed as forcing such persons to disgorge the benefits that were obtained from the promisee. Such enrichment is considered to be unjust because it resulted from the breach of the commitment made by the promisor. As was early noted by Lon Fuller, in most instances, "the restitution interest is merely a special case of the reliance interest,"[16] insofar as the promisor's gain has resulted from the reliance of the promisee.

Limitations of the Restitution Principle. Although the restitution principle provides a reason for recovery in some cases, situations in which promisors have been enriched by the actions of the promisee or a third person are more rare either than cases in which promisors have subjectively willed to be bound or in which promisees have relied to their detriment on a promise. Therefore, even more than the reliance and will principles, the restitution principle cannot alone provide a comprehensive account of contractual obligation unless a great many cases in which contracts are currently enforced are wrongly decided. The unjust enrichment of the promisor is by no means a prerequisite of contractual obligation.

---

14. Eisenberg, supra note 1, at 659 (1982).

15. See, e.g., Allegheny College v. National Chautauqua County Bank of Jamestown, 246 N.Y. 369, 159 N.E. 173 (1927) (this case appears in Chapter 11). The outcome of this case has been incorporated into Restatement §90(2), which recommends enforcing "charitable subscriptions" without any showing of reliance.

16. Lon L. Fuller & William Perdue, The Reliance Interest in Contract Damages: 1, 46 Yale L.J. 52, 56 (1936).

Moreover, enrichment alone is insufficient to establish a legal obligation to disgorge benefits. *Unjust* enrichment is required. As John Wade observed, "the enrichment-principle provides for restitution only when enrichment is unjust. . . ."[17] When a person who breaks her promise is enriched at the promisee's expense, it surely seems unjust, but only because under certain circumstances there is thought to be something wrong with dishonoring one's commitment. To explain why this is so, a restitution principle is dependent on some other principle or principles — perhaps the will or reliance principles. In sum, the fact that a promisor is enriched at the promisee's expense does not tell us why the promise should be enforced until we know why it is unjust to break one's promise.

d. The Problem with Party-Based Theories. These difficulties reveal that the principles of will, reliance, and restitution have much in common with each other. Each principle must implicitly rest on unarticulated considerations apart from will, reliance, or restitution to distinguish enforceable from unenforceable commitments. Consequently, theories of contractual obligation based *solely* on any one of these principles will fail in their basic mission to distinguish adequately between those commitments that are worthy of legal protection and those that are not.

Each principle primarily focuses on one side of a contractual transaction: The will principle focuses on respecting the intentions of the promisor; the reliance principle focuses on correcting the injury to the promisee; the restitution principle focuses on the benefits gained by promisors. As a result, these principles standing alone cannot properly assess the inter*relational* quality of the process of contracting. The law of contract exists to facilitate transactions between persons. In such an enterprise, there is no obvious reason why either party should be the exclusive focus of attention. Because contractual enforcement must strike some balance between the will of the promisor and the reliance of the promisee, contractual enforcement cannot be premised solely on one or the other of these concerns. Consequently, while the phenomena of subjective intentions, reliance costs, and unjust enrichment are vital to a proper understanding of contractual obligation, something is missing in theories of contractual obligation focusing on only one of these core concerns.

2. Standards-Based Principles

Standards-based principles shift our focus away from the parties to a transaction and toward the substance of a contract to see if the commitments made by the parties conform to a standard of evaluation that the principle specifies as primary. Economic efficiency and substantive fairness are two such standards that have received wide attention.

17. John W. Wade, Restitution for Benefits Conferred Without Request, 19 Vand. L. Rev. 1183, 1185 (1966). In this article, Professor Wade attempts to summarize and systematize the circumstances accompanying enrichment that courts have accepted as constituting an injustice.

a. The Efficiency Principle.   One of the most familiar standards-based legal principles is the efficiency approach associated with the law and economics school. Economic efficiency is viewed by some in this school as the maximization of a concept of social wealth or welfare: "[T]he term efficiency will refer to the relationship between the aggregate benefits of a situation and the aggregate costs of the situation. . . . In other words, efficiency corresponds to 'the size of the pie.' "[18] According to this view, legal rules and practices are assessed to see whether they will expand or contract the size of this pie.[19]

Since the enforcement of contracts uses scarce resources, this practice can be justified on efficiency grounds only if the benefits to be gained from enforcement exceed the costs. Efforts to apply the efficiency principle tend to fall somewhere on the following continuum: At one end are analyses of the efficiency of enforcing promissory commitments *in general* or in the abstract. Why is it that enforcing promises in general tends on balance to be beneficial to the parties themselves and to society at large? At the other end are attempts to evaluate the efficiency of *particular* transactions or types of transactions. Why is it that any particular exchange or type of exchange is beneficial?

Limitations of the Efficiency Principle. The less abstract efficiency analysis becomes, the more difficulties are encountered. If we are to enforce only those real-world agreements that increase the overall wealth of society,[20] then it must be either claimed or assumed that a neutral observer (for example, an economist-judge) has access to this information — that is, knows which agreements increase wealth and which do not.[21] Two problems arise from this assumption or claim. The first concerns its truth. Can observers ever have information about value-enhancing exchanges independent of the demonstrated preferences of the market participants? More importantly, can a legal system practically base its decisions on such information? It has been persuasively argued that such knowledge is simply not available independently of the production of information by real

18. A. Mitchell Polinsky, An Introduction to Law and Economics 7 (1983); cf. Robert Cooter & Melvin A. Eisenberg, Damages for Breach of Contract, 73 Calif. L. Rev. 1432, 1460 (1985) ("Economists say that a contract is efficient if its terms maximize the value that can be created by the contemplated exchange.").

19. But cf. Jules L. Coleman, Efficiency, Utility and Wealth Maximization, 8 Hofstra L. Rev. 509, 512 (1980) ("Economists as well as proponents of the economic analysis of law employ at least four efficiency-related notions, including: (1) Productive efficiency, (2) Pareto optimality, (3) Pareto superiority, and (4) Kaldor-Hicks efficiency.").

20. Cf. Richard A. Posner, Gratuitous Promises in Economics and Law, 6 J. Leg. Stud. 411, 415 (1977) ("The question whether it is economical for society to recognize a promise as legally enforceable thus requires a comparison of utility of the promise to the promisor with the social cost of enforcing the promise." (citation omitted)).

21. See, e.g., Richard A. Posner, The Economics of Justice 62 (1981) ("The purist would insist that the relevant values are unknowable since they have not been revealed in an actual market transaction, but I believe that in many cases a court can make a reasonably accurate guess as to the allocation of resources that would maximize wealth."); id. at 79 ("The 'interpersonal comparison of utilities' is anathema to the modern economist, and rightly so, because there is no metric for making such a comparison. But the interpersonal comparison of values, in the economic sense, is feasible, although difficult, even when the values are not being compared in an explicit market.").

markets.[22] If it is not available, then it cannot provide workable criteria to distinguish enforceable from unenforceable promises.

Of course, after the commission of a tort or a breach of contract has occurred, the legal system may have no choice but to objectively assess subjective values as best it can. Perhaps for this reason, law and economics contracts scholars have focused most of their attention on remedies and contract defenses rather than issues of enforceability.[23] At issue here, however, is not how best to rectify breaches of contract, but rather why and which voluntary commitments are legally enforceable in the first place. It is appropriate to ask the transaction-specific efficiency advocate whether a court system empowered to use an efficiency analysis can outperform the market in recognizing value-enhancing exchanges. There is no evidence that this is possible, and good reason to think that it is not.[24]

The second problem is that, assuming such foreknowledge of value-enhancing exchanges is available, if we have direct access to information sufficient to know whether or not particular exchanges are value enhancing, why bother with contract law at all? Why not simply have a central authority use this knowledge to transfer entitlements independently of the parties' agreement, particularly given the fact that the need to reach agreements creates transaction costs? Or, why not let judges use this knowledge to ratify *efficient thefts* — that is, give thieves the option of obtaining title to property that they have taken from others without their consent, provided only that the thief pays court-assessed damages equal to the value to the victim of her property? Those who seek to apply the efficiency principle in a highly particularistic way are barred by their assumption about available information from responding that we need the market to provide such information.

In contrast with the examination of particular agreements, observations provided by economic theory at a more abstract level about the effects of certain contract rules or principles on the efficient allocation of resources may rightly influence our normative assessment of those rules or principles. This is particularly so when these effects are considered along with the effects such rules and principles would have on private autonomy, or *will*, and on reliance. Most notably, the efficient allocation of resources may require a market composed of consensual exchanges that reveal and

22. See, e.g., Harold Demsetz, Some Aspects of Property Rights, 9 J.L. Econ. 61, 67-68 (1966); Mario Rizzo, The Mirage of Efficiency, 8 Hofstra L. Rev. 641, 648-651 (1980); Jules L. Coleman, The Normative Basis of Economic Analysis: A Critical Review of Richard Posner's The Economics of Justice (book review), 34 Stan. L. Rev. 1105, 1109, n.6 (1982).

23. See, e.g., Timothy Muris, Cost of Completion or Diminution in Market Value: The Relevance of Subjective Value, 12 J. Legal Stud. 379 (1983) (discussing compensation for subjectively measured damages that result from breaches of contract).

24. The seminal work in this area was done by Ludwig von Mises and F. A. Hayek. See, e.g., Ludwig von Mises, Socialism 137-142 (rev. ed. 1951) (discussing why "artificial markets" are not possible); F. A. Hayek, The Use of Knowledge in Society, in Individualism and Economic Order 77, 77-78 (1948) ("The economic problem of society is thus not merely a problem of how to allocate 'given' resources. . . . It is rather a problem of how to secure the best use of resources known to any of the members of society, for ends whose relative importance only these individuals know.").

convey otherwise unobtainable information about personal preferences and economic opportunities.[25]

For example, economic analysis may suggest that demonstrated or manifested consent plays an important role in the law of contract. From this perspective, the transaction costs created by a requirement of consent are no worse from an efficiency standpoint than any other cost of production. The costs of negotiating to obtain the consent of another may be resources well spent because such negotiations serve to reveal valuable information that would otherwise be unknown to the parties themselves and unknowable to others.

In this way and in the abstract, demonstrated consent can be seen as playing an important role in any effort to achieve economic or allocative efficiency. Efficiency notions alone, however, cannot completely explain why certain commitments should be enforced unless it is also shown that economic efficiency — as opposed to the pursuit of other social goals — is or should be the exclusive goal of a legal order. No such comprehensive normative efficiency theory has yet been successfully presented.

> **_b. The Principle of Substantive Fairness._** Another standards-based school of thought attempts to evaluate the _substance_ of a transaction to see if it is _fair_[26] — an approach that must be distinguished from one that focuses on whether the contracting process is fair or unfair.[27] The substantive fairness principle has a long tradition dating back at least to the Christian "just price" theorists of the Middle Ages[28] and perhaps even to Aristotle.[29] Its modern incarnation in contract law can be found

---

25. Cf. Steven N. S. Cheung, The Theory of Share Tenancy 64 (1969) ("[C]ompetition conglomerates knowledge from all potential owners — the knowledge of alternative contractual arrangements and uses of the resource; and transferability of property rights ensures that the most valuable knowledge will be utilized."); Demsetz, supra note 22, at 65 ("[I]nsisting on voluntary consent tends to produce information accuracy when many costs and benefits are known only by the individuals affected.").

26. See, e.g., Melvin A. Eisenberg, The Bargain Principle and Its Limits, 95 Harv. L. Rev. 741, 754 (1982) ("[T]he new paradigm [of unconscionability] creates a theoretical framework that explains most of the limits that have been or should be placed upon . . . [the bargain] principle, based on the quality of the bargain.").

27. See, e.g., Arthur A. Leff, Unconscionability and the Code — The Emperor's New Clause, 115 U. Pa. L. Rev. 485 (1967) (distinguishing procedural from substantive unconscionability).

28. See Richard T. Ely, Outlines of Economics 827 (5th ed. 1930). But medieval just price theory actually may have been more market oriented and subjective than most modern commentators assume. See Raymond De Roover, The Concept of the Just Price: Theory and Economic Policy, 18 J. Econ. Hist. 418, 420, 421-434 (1958) (the just price was more market oriented); Bernard W. Dempsey, Just Price in a Functional Economy, 25 Am. Econ. Rev. 471, 474-476, 480-486 (1935) (the just price was more subjective). See also James Gordley, The Philosophical Origins of Modern Contract Doctrine 99 (1991) ("[T]he competitive market price was just in the sense that it preserved equality to the extent possible if need and scarcity were to be taken into account.").

29. See, e.g., Aristotle, Nichomachean Ethics 125 (M. Ostwald trans. 1962):

> Thus, if (1) proportional equality is established between the goods, and (2) reciprocity effected, the fair exchange we spoke of will be realized. But if there is no proportionality, the exchange is not equal and fair, and (the association of the two will) not hold together.

in nineteenth-century discussions of the adequacy of consideration (which we shall briefly encounter in Chapter 9) and more recently in some treatments of unconscionability[30] — a doctrine that we shall study in Chapter 16.

Limitations of the Principle of Substantive Fairness. The principle of substantive fairness presupposes a standard of value by which the substance of any agreement can be directly objectively evaluated.[31] Such a criterion has yet to be articulated and defended. Without such a criterion, theories of contractual enforcement based on the substantive fairness principle fall back on one or both of two incomplete approaches. Some such theories tend to focus all their attention on a small fraction of commitments — those that are thought to be so extreme as to "shock the conscience" of the courts. Consequently, most real world agreements are considered to be presumptively enforceable. Other theories appealing to substantive fairness tend to become process based — looking for either information asymmetries or what is called *unequal bargaining power.* The first of these responses attempts to find extreme instances of violations of a standard that cannot be articulated — or at least cannot be articulated for most transactions. The latter represents a movement away from the substantive fairness principle and toward a procedural fairness approach.[32]

Most importantly for this discussion, however, the principle of substantive fairness fails to address squarely the most central and common problem of contract theory: Which *conscionable* or unquestionably fair agreements should be enforced and which should not? After all, distinguishing between enforceable and unenforceable commitments was the original problem for which theories of contractual obligation have been devised. A useful theory of contractual obligation, therefore, ought to help us to discern those commitments that merit legal enforcement and the substantive fairness principle is inadequate to this task.

This may not have committed Aristotle to a "just price" position. Instead, he may only be attempting here to "explain" exchange transactions as a modern-day economist would, rather than normatively assess the "justice" of the exchange.

30. See, e.g., Restatement (Second) of Contracts §208 comment c (1979) ("Theoretically it is possible for a contract to be oppressive taken as a whole, even though there is no weakness in the bargaining process. . . .").

31. Cohen noted this problem with what he called the *equivalent* theory of contract. See Cohen, supra note 3, at 581 (Due to problems of measurement, modern law "professes to abandon the effort of more primitive systems to enforce material fairness within the contract. The parties to the contract must themselves determine what is fair."). As a purely descriptive matter, the idea that exchange occurs because goods are of equivalent or equal value captivated economists for centuries until it was shown to be quite false. In fact, exchange occurs because both parties ex ante perceive the value of the goods to be exchanged as unequal. Each subjectively perceives the good or service offered by the other to be of greater value (to an unknowable extent) than what they are willing to trade for it. See Carl Menger, Principles of Economics 180 (J. Dingwall & B. Hoselitz trans. 1981).

32. Professor Eisenberg, for example, confines his analysis to the identification of circumstances, or *norms,* that, if present, would call the fairness of the resulting agreement into question. For example, he discusses exploitation of distress, transactional incapacity, susceptibility to unfair persuasion, and price-ignorance. See Eisenberg, supra note 26, at 754-785. Eisenberg's resort to suspect circumstances, however, finesses the issue of discerning the quality of unfairness of the substantive bargain that he is seeking to police.

c. The Problem with Standards-Based Theories.   All standards-based principles face two problems, one that is obvious and another that is more subtle. The obvious problem, which has already been discussed, is identifying and defending the appropriate standard by which enforceable commitments can be distinguished from those that should be unenforceable. The more subtle problem arises from the fact that standards-based contract theories are types of what philosopher Robert Nozick has called "patterned" principles of distributive justice:

> [A] principle of distribution [is] patterned if it specifies that a distribution is to vary along with some natural dimension, weighted sum of natural dimensions, or lexicographic ordering of natural dimensions. . . .
>
>   Almost every suggested principle of distributive justice is patterned: to each according to his moral merit, or needs, or marginal product, or how hard he tries, or the weighted sum of the foregoing, and so on.[33]

The problem created by such patterned theories of justice — including theories based on some notion of efficiency — is that they require constant interferences with individual preferences. "Render possessions ever so equal, man's different degrees of art, care, and industry will immediately break that equality."[34] The maintenance of a pattern, therefore, requires either that persons be stopped from entering the contracts they desire, or that those in power "continually (or periodically) interfere to take from some persons resources that others for some reason chose to transfer to them."[35] Such interferences are at least presumptively suspect. They may sometimes even be objectionable according to the particular standard that is being used to justify the intervention. For example, inefficiency might be shown to be the ultimate result of interventions to achieve efficiency that thwart individual preferences in this way. And a system in which judges may — in the absence of fraud, duress, or some other demonstrable defect in the formation process — second-guess the wisdom of the parties may create more substantive unfairness than it cures. Somewhat paradoxically, we may achieve a more efficient and fairer resolution of contract disputes if contract law does not itself directly pursue either efficiency or fairness.[36]

3. Process Principles

A process principle shifts the focus of the inquiry away from the contract parties and the substance of their agreement to the manner in which

33. Robert Nozick, Anarchy, State and Utopia 156-157 (1974).

34. D. Hume, supra note 9, at 25.

35. R. Nozick, supra note 33, at 163. See generally his discussion of "how liberty upsets patterns." Id. at 160-164.

36. See John Gray, Indirect Utility and Fundamental Rights, Soc. Phil. Poly., Spring 1984, at 73, 85 ("If direct utilitarian policy is counterproductive, we must accept practical constraints on it, and there is nothing to say that these will not include the distributive constraints imposed by principles conferring weighty moral rights on individuals.") Larry Alexander, Pursuing the Good — Indirectly, 95 Ethics 315 (1985) (further elaborating this position).

their agreement was reached. We just discussed how theories based on substantive fairness tend in this direction. This approach seeks appropriate procedures for establishing enforceable obligations and then assesses any given transaction to see if these procedures were followed. The best-known principle of this sort is the bargain principle, which is now the reigning theory of the traditional doctrine of consideration that we shall study in Chapter 9.

a. The Bargain Principle.

The origin of the modern doctrine of consideration can be traced to the rise of the writ of assumpsit, one of the forms of action that once defined all common law causes of action. As was discussed in Chapter 1, until the late sixteenth and early seventeenth centuries, enforcement of private commitments was largely governed by such writs as debt, detinue, and covenant. These and other actions were not promise based. Debt and detinue, for example, were claims based not on a promise having been made, but on the existence of some underlying property right. Debt was an action for money owed, while detinue was an action for goods detained. The existence of an explicit promise was considered evidence that an underlying obligation existed.

The writ of covenant was based on the making of a promise, but unless the promise was made in the form of a sealed writing (in which case the writing itself was treated as a form of property), it was subject to the defense of *wager of law* or *compurgation.* To successfully wager law, a defendant who denied having made a promise needed to produce a number of oath-helpers (usually 12) who would swear that they believed the defendant's denial. The defense was based on the idea that, by taking such an oath, these compurgators were putting their eternal souls at risk. In a world in which this belief was widespread and before modern fact-finding procedures had been developed, this defense made some sense. Nonetheless, it made the enforcement of informal promises considerably uncertain. And this gave rise to a thriving legal practice in ecclesiastical courts enforcing informal promises based on actions for breach of faith (*fidei laesio*).[37]

To enlarge the protection of the informal promises (and thereby reclaim legal business being lost to ecclesiastical courts), common law lawyers and judges needed to base relief on a writ that was not subject to the wager of law defense. They found this in the writ of assumpsit, a writ that originally applied to a situation that we would now think of as based on the tort concept of malpractice. Essentially, early actions in assumpsit were based on the idea that (a) one voluntarily assumed an obligation to perform a certain action; (b) the action was performed improperly (malfeasance); and (c) as a result the obligee was injured. So, for example, if one promised to build a house, but as a result of having done so improperly, the house collapsed, injuring the plaintiff, the action would lie in assumpsit.

The writ of assumpsit was unavailable to enforce a simple contract due to two restrictions. First, it applied only to *mal*feasance, and not to *non*-feasance. That is, it applied only to improper performance and not to non-performance. Second, there was a rule stipulating that assumpsit was not appropriate if the action could be fit within the writs of debt or detinue. By

37. See R. H. Helmholz, Assumpsit and *Fidei Laesio,* 91 L.Q. Rev. 406 (1975).

the early seventeenth century both of these restrictions had been abolished and assumpsit was then available to those seeking to enforce informal promises.

The rise of assumpsit as a means of handling the problem of *under*-enforcing informal promises gave rise to the risk of *over*enforcement. Wager of law was traditionally not available as a defense to assumpsit because the very act of malperformance itself was inherently good evidence that a serious commitment had been made. Now, however, assumpsit was being used to enforce promises that had yet to be performed at all. As we saw in Chapter 6, the evidentiary problem created by the shift to the writ of assumpsit was ameliorated to some extent by the passage in 1677 of the first Statute of Frauds — originally entitled "An Act for Prevention of Frauds and Perjuries."

Moreover, when the voluntary assumption of obligation came to be viewed as the basis of contractual enforcement, no one seriously suggested that *every* demonstrable agreement merited legal enforcement. The number of agreements made every day are so numerous that for reasons of both practice and principle some distinction, apart from that made by purely evidentiary requirements, must be made between enforceable and unenforceable agreements. As we shall see in Chapter 9, the doctrine of consideration was devised to provide this distinction.[38] Where consideration is present, an agreement ordinarily will be enforced. And, most significantly, where there is no consideration, even if the commitment is clear and unambiguous, enforcement is supposed to be unavailable.

In the nineteenth century, the *bargain* theory of consideration was promoted by some — most notably Harvard law professors Oliver Wendell Holmes, Jr., and Christopher Langdell — as a doctrinal way of distinguishing enforceable from unenforceable commitments. Today it is the predominant theory of consideration and is embodied in §71 of the Restatement (Second) of Contracts:

(1) To constitute consideration, a performance or a return promise must be *bargained for*.
(2) A performance or return promise is *bargained for* if it is sought by the promisor in exchange for his promise and is given by the promisee in exchange for that promise.[39]

According to this approach, it is not *what* is bargained for that is important; all that matters is that each party's promise or performance is induced by the other's. It attempts to discern this mutuality of inducement from the motives and acts of both parties to the transaction.

The bargain principle had a number of decided advantages. First, the very existence of a bargain ("I'll do this for you, if you do that for me" — and *vice versa*) provides good evidence of the making of a serious promise — a promise that the parties intended should be enforced. Second, since most commercial commitments are part of explicit bargains, it captures a majority

---

38. See A. W. B. Simpson, A History of the Common Law of Contract 316-326 (1975) (discussing the origin and early meaning of the term "consideration") (excerpts from this book appear in Chapters 9 and 11).
39. Restatement (Second) of Contracts §71(1) & (2) (1979) (emphasis added).

of the sort of promises that are ordinarily intended to be legally binding. At the same time it tends to exclude most social promises — i.e., those between friends and family members — that are not intended to create or alter legal relations. Thus the bargain principle informing the doctrine of consideration addresses quite effectively the evidentiary problem raised by the writ of assumpsit, while striking a reasonable balance between over- and underenforcement of informal commitments.

Limitations of the Bargain Principle. The difficulties presented by the doctrine of consideration depend on which way the concept is viewed. If the doctrine is interpreted restrictively, then whole classes of serious agreements where legal enforcement is normally contemplated will be thought to be lacking consideration. In several kinds of cases promisees have traditionally had considerable difficulty obtaining legal relief for non-performance because bargained-for consideration is lacking, although it is generally conceded that the parties may have intended to be legally bound and that enforcement should therefore be available. These include promises to keep an offer open, promises to release a debt, promises to modify an obligation, promises to pay for past favors, promises to assume the obligations of another, promises to convey land, promises to give to charities, and those promises made by bailees to bailors or by family members to each other.

In each of these types of cases, a promise is made and then broken. The promisee then seeks to base his cause of action on the promise. In many of these cases, the promise is a serious and unambiguous one. In each situation, however, there is no bargain and therefore no consideration for the promise. Such cases as these invite attempts by judges and others to expand the concept of consideration beyond the bargain requirement. As we shall see in Chapter 11, cases in these categories produced the doctrine of promissory estoppel. Any attempt to capture these and other types of cases will, however, run afoul of an opposing difficulty.

If the web of consideration doctrine is woven too loosely, however, it will increasingly capture social agreements where legal enforcement is not contemplated — for example, promises of financial assistance between family members. Thus, any expanded concept of consideration threatens to undermine the doctrine's traditional function: distinguishing enforceable from unenforceable agreements in a predictable fashion to allow for private planning and to prevent the weight of legal coercion from falling upon those informal, or social, arrangements where the parties have not contemplated legal sanctions for breach.[40]

Each strategy to deal with the problems generated by a doctrine of consideration, therefore, wreaks havoc in its own way with a coherent theory of contractual obligation. With a restrictive definition like that of bargain, serious promises which merit enforcement are left unenforced. With a more expansive formulation, informal promises that are thought

---

40. See Cohen, supra note 3, at 573 ("Certainly, some freedom to change one's mind is necessary for free intercourse between those who lack omniscience."); Lon L. Fuller, Consideration and Form, 41 Colum. L. Rev. 799, 813 (1941) ("There is a real need for a field of human intercourse freed from legal restraints, for a field where men may without liability withdraw assurances they have once given." (citation omitted)).

to be properly outside the province of legal coercion will be made the subject of legal sanctions. The most recognized problem with the bargain principle is that it appears to have erred too far in the direction of under-enforcement. However, the bargain principle suffers in a more fundamental way from its purely process-based character.

b. The Limitations of a Process Principle.

The problem with a purely process principle of enforceability is not simply that it must strike a balance between over- and underenforcement. Such trade-offs cannot be completely avoided in any system that bases decision making on rules and principles of general application. As Aristotle observed, "all law is universal, but there are some things about which it is not possible to speak correctly in universal terms."[41] The real problem with a process principle such as the bargain theory of consideration is that it places substantial obstacles in the way of reducing such difficulties of enforcement.

First, a process principle's *exclusive* focus on the process that justifies contractual enforcement conceals the substantive values that must support any choice among possible processes. By obscuring these values, a process-based principle comes to treat the favored procedural devices as ends, rather than as means. Then, when the adopted procedures inevitably give rise to problems of fit between means and ends, a process principle that is divorced from ends cannot say why this has occurred or what is to be done about it. This inherent weakness of a process principle has plagued the bargain theory of consideration.

The bargain principle, which was devised to limit the applicability of assumpsit, fails to ensure the enforcement of certain reasonably well-defined categories of unbargained-for but serious commitments. Then, when courts are moved to enforce such commitments, the principal theory of consideration to which they adhere cannot account for these exceptions to the normal requirement of a bargain without appealing to concepts more fundamental than bargaining. Ironically, the rise of assumpsit — the source of the need for the consideration doctrine — was itself due to the inability of the then-existing process-based writ system to accommodate enforcement of informal but serious promises.[42]

Second, a process principle cannot itself explain why certain kinds of commitments are not and should not be enforceable. For example, as we studied in Chapter 1, it is widely recognized that agreements that are against public policy — such as agreements to perform illegal acts — should not be enforced. Similarly, as we studied in Chapter 3, slavery contracts are also thought to be unenforceable per se. If, however, agreements of these types were reached in conformity with all the procedural rules of the game, a principle that looks only to the rules of the game to decide issues of enforceability cannot say why such an otherwise procedurally proper agreement should be unenforceable.

---

41. Aristotle, supra note 29, at 141. See also H. L. A. Hart, The Concept of Law 125 (1961) ("[U]ncertainty at the borderline is the price to be paid for the use of general classifying terms in any form of communication concerning matters of fact.").

42. See A. W. B. Simpson, supra note 38, at 136-196 (discussing difficulties in enforcing informal contracts prior to the development of assumpsit).

These two types of problems, however, are not confined to process principles. As was seen above, party-based theories based on will, reliance, and restitution are also plagued by an inability to account for and explain exceptional agreements that are enforceable without recourse to their animating principles. And the will, reliance, and efficiency principles have as hard a time as process-based theories explaining why certain agreements are unenforceable due to so-called public policy exceptions to their respective norms of contractual obligation.

Notwithstanding the weaknesses inherent in process principles, they offer significant advantages over both party-based and standards-based principles. By employing a neutral criterion[43] for determining contractual enforcement, a good process-based doctrine can better preserve the relational balance between the contractual intent of promisors and the reliance of promisees than one-sided party-based theories, provided it identifies features of the contractual process that normally correspond both to the presence of contractual intent and substantial reliance. Further, by identifying judicially workable criteria of enforcement, a process principle can avoid the difficulties of extreme indeterminacy that were seen to plague standards-based theories. Process-based doctrine can, in short, better provide the traditionally acknowledged advantages of a system of generally applicable laws, such as facilitating private planning and helping to ensure equal treatment of similarly situated persons. Perhaps it is these advantages that have permitted the bargain principle to survive its frequent detractors.

The significant administrative advantages of process principles suggest that the best approach to contractual obligation may be one that preserves a procedural aspect of contract law, while recognizing that such procedures are dependent for their ultimate justification on more substantive principles. These substantive principles occasionally affect procedural analysis in two ways. First, these principles might suggest specific improvements in procedures governing contract formation that are appropriate in the event that previously adopted procedures have created well-defined problems of underenforcement. Second, these principles might serve to deprive certain procedurally immaculate agreements of their normal moral significance, thereby ameliorating identifiable problems of overenforcement.

4. Integrating the Core Principles of Enforceability

Each of the six principles just discussed — will, reliance, restitution, efficiency, substantive fairness, and bargain — implicates a core concern of the practice of contracting. The problem facing contract theory then is twofold: On the one hand, no single principle provides the sole method of understanding contractual enforcement; on the other hand, attempting

---

43. The phrase *neutral principles* refers only to the fact that such principles may be applied to the facts of a particular case in an impartial manner. The choice of which principles ought to be followed by legal decision makers is by no means a "neutral" — in the sense of value-free, or nonnormative — decision.

to pursue the six principles willy-nilly would make a hash of contract law. Perhaps the great bulk of contracts could be enforced consistently with all six principles. Still, enough cases would remain in which one principle or concern comes into conflict with others that, without some criterion by which conflicts among these principles can be assessed, we will experience great uncertainties and injustices in the administration of contract law.

If possible, therefore, it would be highly desirable to identify some mediating criteria of enforceability by which these various principles can be ordered with respect to each other so that some reasonable balance among them can be achieved. As the dominance of the bargain theory of consideration has shown, such a criterion need not be perfect to be preferable either to ignoring one or more of these core concerns or to pursuing more than one principle simultaneously. In sum, what is needed is a *rule of recognition*,[44] by which enforceable commitments can be identified, that facilitates the pursuit of each of these concerns while mediating the potential conflicts among them. But is such a criterion possible?

a. Consent to Be Legally Bound.
A casebook is probably not the place to advocate a particular and controversial solution even to so vexatious a problem as that just discussed. I shall only briefly describe the criterion that I have proposed elsewhere.[45] As we shall see in Chapter 10, it is a criterion that is explicitly acknowledged in English law and which I think underlies much of the doctrine of contract law we have inherited: Courts should presumptively enforce private commitments when there exists a *manifested intention to create a legal relation*. Another formulation of this criterion is that to determine the prima facie case of contract, we should determine whether there was a manifested intention to be legally bound.

I refer to this criterion as *consent*. This special sense of consent is to be distinguished from promise. To promise is to commit to do or refrain from doing something. To consent is to commit to being *legally* responsible for nonperformance of a promise. So consent is a commitment in addition to

44. This term is borrowed from H. L. A. Hart. See H. L. A Hart, supra note 41, at 92. According to Hart, "primary" rules are those which guide individual and associational conduct. "Secondary" rules are those which guide persons charged with administering the primary rules. A rule of recognition is a particular kind of secondary rule (or set of rules) adopted by a legal system to "recognize" or distinguish which of the potential "primary" rules that guide our conduct is valid.

45. See Randy E. Barnett, . . . and Contractual Consent, 3 S. Cal. Interdisc. L.J. 421 (1993); id., Sound of Silence: Default Rules and Contractual Consent, 78 Va. L. Rev. 821 (1992) [hereinafter cited as "Sound of Silence"]; id., Rational Bargaining Theory and Contract: Default Rules, Hypothetical Consent, the Duty to Disclose, and Fraud, 15 Harv. J. L. Pub. Poly. 783 (1992); id., Conflicting Visions: A Critique of Ian Macneil's Relational Theory of Contract, 78 Va. L. Rev. 1175 (1992); id., The Function of Several Property and Freedom of Contract, 9 Soc. Phil. Poly. 62 (1992) [hereinafter cited as "Freedom of Contract"]; id., Some Problems with Contract as Promise, 77 Cornell L. Rev. 1022 (1992); id., The Internal and External Analysis of Concepts, 11 Cardozo L. Rev. 525 (1990); id., Squaring Undisclosed Agency Law with Contract Theory, 75 Cal. L. Rev. 1969 (1987); id., Contract Remedies and Inalienable Rights, 4 Soc. Phil. Poly. 179 (1986) [hereinafter cited as "Inalienable Rights"]; id., A Consent Theory, supra note 5; id., Contract Scholarship and the Reemergence of Legal Philosophy (book review), 97 Harv. L. Rev. 1223 (1984); and Randy E. Barnett & Mary Becker, Beyond Reliance: Promissory Estoppel, Contract Formalities and Misrepresentation, 15 Hofstra L. Rev. 445 (1987).

the commitment inherent in a promise. Moreover, consent is to be distinguished from subjective assent. Consent is the voluntary communication by one person to another person of a particular message: that one intends to alter an already existing legal relation between the parties or to create a new one.[46] Some such criterion seems to have been incorporated into U.C.C. §2-204(3), which, as we saw in Chapters 4 and 5, permits the enforcement of a contract with one or more open terms "if the parties *intended to make a contract* and there is a reasonably certain basis of giving an appropriate remedy."[47]

A consent theory of enforceability does not purport to provide an independent principle or core concern of contract. Rather it seeks to provide a general criterion of contractual enforceability that strikes a reasonable and workable balance among the party-based, substance-based, and process principles already discussed. Requiring a manifested intention to be legally bound facilitates the *will* or private autonomy of the parties since one's manifested intention is highly likely to reflect an underlying subjective assent. The existence of a manifested intention to be legally bound would also help to distinguish those commitments upon which *reliance* is justified and merits legal protection from those that do not. Although *restitution*-based liability is not limited to contract — it can provide an independent basis for legal enforcement apart from consent, as we saw in Chapter 3 — the existence of a party's consent to be legally bound justifies forcing that party to disgorge her enrichment.

Adherence to a criterion of consent would tend to limit enforceability to value-enhancing or *efficient* commitments (whether gratuitous or as part of an exchange) in which ex ante the parties view enforceability to be worth more to them than its costs. To the extent that parties themselves are the best judge of their own interests, the substance of agreements that result from the parties' consent are also likely to be *fair*. But to the extent that these conditions do not obtain, the parties' consent provides only a prima facie basis for enforceability. Contract defenses that will be discussed in Part V allow consent to be set aside under circumstances such as misrepresentation, duress, various forms of incompetence, undue influence, etc., in which the consent of the parties may not produce substantively fair or efficient agreements.

Finally, the criterion of consent helps place the *bargain* principle in proper perspective. The existence of a bargain in a commercial context is very likely to indicate the existence of an intention to be legally bound. The absence of bargains in noncommercial settings is apt to reflect the absence of such consent. Nonetheless, the existence of a bargain is not dispositive of the issue of consent. For example, the *presence* of a bargain in the *commercial* context could be negated by evidence that the parties did not intend to be legally bound. By the same token, the *absence* of a bargain

46. Because every person stands in some legal relation to every other person, analytically there is no real difference between altering a preexisting legal relationship and creating a new one. Still, it is useful to distinguish between creating a *contractual* relationship between parties who previously had no such relationship and altering a contractual relationship that already exists.

47. U.C.C. §2-204(3).

in the *non*commercial context could be compensated by the existence of some other indicia of intention to be legally bound — perhaps a formality such as so-called nominal consideration.

Many of these situations will be considered in Chapter 10 and in the promissory estoppel cases we shall study in Chapter 11. In many of the promissory estoppel cases, some indicia of consent other than bargain appears to be present. So we may be wrong to conceive of the doctrine of promissory estoppel solely in terms of reliance. And under some circumstances, consent of a promisor to be legally bound may be manifested by her silence in the face of substantial reliance by the promisee of the sort that would not be incurred without a commitment to be legally bound. A possible doctrinal substitute for promissory estoppel based on the consent criteria is provided at the end of Chapter 11.

b. Limitations of the Consent Criterion.

b. Limitations of the Consent Criterion. Like any rule of law, limiting even prima facie contractual enforcement to those commitments that are accompanied by some formal or informal manifestation of intention to be legally bound will lead to some cases of over- and underenforcement from the standpoint of the underlying principles of enforceability. Particularly if limited to highly formalized manifestations of consent, it will fail to capture all promises that intuitions deem to be enforceable; but if expanded to include highly contextual indicia of consent such as those just discussed, it may lead to the enforcement of some commitments that should be left unenforced. Moreover, standing alone, consent to be legally bound does not immediately explain the limitations on its application, for example, in cases involving promises to perform illegal acts or consent to servitude.[48] And although the consent criterion accounts for much of existing contract doctrine, this "fit" alone does not entirely justify a conclusion that it should be the sole criterion of contractual obligation.[49]

REFERENCE: Barnett, §4.1
                         Calamari & Perillo, §1.4

B.   APPLYING THE PRINCIPLES OF ENFORCEABILITY TO A CASE

To understand and appreciate the core principles of enforceability, some will find it useful to discuss them in the context of real-world cases. In the next three chapters we shall be reading a wide variety of commercial and noncommercial cases in which enforceability is the principal concern. Each of these cases is best examined, however, in the context of some particular

---

48. My treatment of this subject involves the concept of underlying entitlements that parties bring to transactions and which are transferred by their consent. Some of these entitlements, however, are *inalienable* and cannot be transferred even *with* the consent of the parties. See Barnett, Inalienable Rights, supra note 45.

49. For additional normative support of the consent criterion, see Barnett, Sound of Silence, supra note 45; and Barnett, Freedom of Contract, supra note 45.

doctrine that governs enforceability, such as the doctrines of consideration or promissory estoppel. When considering the application of these doctrines to those cases, we may well ask whether and how they serve or disserve the core principles of enforceability. All of the most commonly occurring contractual disputes will implicate existing doctrines of enforceability. By virtue of its novelty, therefore, the famous "palimony" case of Marvin v. Marvin provides those who are interested with a rare opportunity to apply these core principles of enforceability directly to a particular case unmediated by a concern for prevailing contract doctrine.

Study Guide: Should promises between unmarried persons living together in an intimate relationship be enforced? Should promises between married persons? Promises between parents and children? None? All? If some, which? What, if anything, do the principles just discussed suggest for how this case ought to have been decided? Does the effort to apply them to the case reveal anything about their limitations? Is there a theoretical conflict between the majority and dissenting opinions? What is the practical and theoretical significance of whether the Family Law Act governs here? [Lee Marvin starred in such films as The Man Who Shot Liberty Valance *(one of my personal favorites),* Cat Ballou *(for which he won an Academy Award for best actor), and* The Dirty Dozen. *He remarried in 1984 and remained married until his death in 1987 at the age of 63. Having received the Purple Heart for wounds received while in the Marines during World War II, he was buried in Arlington National Cemetery. Since about 1980, Michelle Triola Marvin has been the live-in companion of actor Dick Van Dyke.]*

MICHELLE MARVIN v. LEE MARVIN

Supreme Court of California,
18 Cal. 3d 660, 557 P.2d 106 (1976)

TOBRINER, J.* During the past 15 years, there has been a substantial increase in the number of couples living together without marrying. Such nonmarital relationships lead to legal controversy when one partner dies or the couple separates. Courts of Appeal, faced with the task of determining property rights in such cases, have arrived at conflicting positions: two cases (In re Marriage of Cary (1973) 34 Cal. App. 3d 345 [109 Cal. Rptr. 862]; Estate of Atherley (1975) 44 Cal. App. 3d 758 [119 Cal. Rptr. 41]) have held that the Family Law Act (Civ. Code, §4000 et seq.) requires division of the property according to community property principles, and

* *Mathew Oscar Tobriner* (1904-1982) was educated at Stanford University (A.B., M.A.) and Harvard University (LL.B.) and was admitted to the California bar in 1928. He practiced law in San Francisco and Los Angeles for over 30 years, except while with the chief attorney solicitor's office of the Department of Agriculture (1932-1936), before being appointed justice of the District Court of Appeal for the First District of California (1956-1962). He left that post to accept an appointment to the Supreme Court of California in 1962, where he served until his death. — K.T.

one decision (Beckman v. Mayhew (1975) 49 Cal. App. 3d 529 [122 Cal. Rptr. 604]) has rejected that holding. We take this opportunity to resolve that controversy and to declare the principles which should govern distribution of property acquired in a nonmarital relationship.

We conclude: (1) The provisions of the Family Law Act do not govern the distribution of property acquired during a nonmarital relationship; such a relationship remains subject solely to judicial decision. (2) The courts should enforce express contracts between nonmarital partners except to the extent that the contract is explicitly founded on the consideration of meretricious sexual services. (3) In the absence of an express contract, the courts should inquire into the conduct of the parties to determine whether that conduct demonstrates an implied contract, agreement of partnership or joint venture, or some other tacit understanding between the parties. The courts may also employ the doctrine of quantum meruit, or equitable remedies such as constructive or resulting trusts, when warranted by the facts of the case.

In the instant case plaintiff and defendant lived together for seven years without marrying; all property acquired during this period was taken in defendant's name. When plaintiff sued to enforce a contract under which she was entitled to half the property and to support payments, the trial court granted judgment on the pleadings for defendant, thus leaving him with all property accumulated by the couple during their relationship. Since the trial court denied plaintiff a trial on the merits of her claim, its decision conflicts with the principles stated above, and must be reversed.

1. THE FACTUAL SETTING OF THIS APPEAL

Since the trial court rendered judgment for defendant on the pleadings, we must accept the allegations of plaintiff's complaint as true, determining whether such allegations state, or can be amended to state, a cause of action. . . . We turn therefore to the specific allegations of the complaint.

Plaintiff avers that in October of 1964 she and defendant "entered into an oral agreement" that while "the parties lived together they would combine their efforts and earnings and would share equally any and all property accumulated as a result of their efforts whether individual or combined." Furthermore, they agreed to "hold themselves out to the general public as husband and wife" and that "plaintiff would further render her services as a companion, homemaker, housekeeper and cook to . . . defendant."

Shortly thereafter plaintiff agreed to "give up her lucrative career as an entertainer [and] singer" in order to "devote her full time to defendant . . . as a companion, homemaker, housekeeper and cook;" in return defendant agreed to "provide for all of plaintiff's financial support and needs for the rest of her life."

Plaintiff alleges that she lived with defendant from October of 1964 through May of 1970 and fulfilled her obligations under the agreement. During this period the parties as a result of their efforts and earnings acquired in defendant's name substantial real and personal property, including motion picture rights worth over $1 million. In May of 1970, however, defendant compelled plaintiff to leave his household. He continued to support plaintiff until November of 1971, but thereafter refused to provide further support.

On the basis of these allegations plaintiff asserts two causes of action. The first, for declaratory relief, asks the court to determine her contract and property rights; the second seeks to impose a constructive trust upon one half of the property acquired during the course of the relationship.

Defendant demurred unsuccessfully, and then answered the complaint.... Following extensive discovery and pretrial proceedings, the case came to trial.... Defendant renewed his attack on the complaint by a motion to dismiss. [T]he parties had stipulated that defendant's marriage to Betty Marvin did not terminate until the filing of a final decree of divorce in January 1967....

After hearing argument the court granted defendant's motion and entered judgment for defendant. Plaintiff moved to set aside the judgment and asked leave to amend her complaint to allege that she and defendant reaffirmed their agreement after defendant's divorce was final. The trial court denied plaintiff's motion, and she appealed from the judgment.

2. PLAINTIFF'S COMPLAINT STATES A CAUSE OF ACTION FOR BREACH OF AN EXPRESS CONTRACT

In Trutalli v. Meraviglia (1932) 215 Cal. 698 [12 P.2d 430] we established the principle that nonmarital partners may lawfully contract concerning the ownership of property acquired during the relationship. We reaffirmed this principle in Vallera v. Vallera (1943) 21 Cal. 2d 681, 685 [134 P.2d 761], stating that "If a man and woman [who are not married] live together as husband and wife under an agreement to pool their earnings and share equally in their joint accumulations, equity will protect the interests of each in such property."

In the case before us plaintiff, basing her cause of action in contract upon these precedents, maintains that the trial court erred in denying her a trial on the merits of her contention. Although that court did not specify the ground for its conclusion that plaintiff's contractual allegations stated no cause of action, defendant offers some four theories to sustain the ruling; we proceed to examine them.

Defendant first and principally relies on the contention that the alleged contract is so closely related to the supposed "immoral" character of the relationship between plaintiff and himself that the enforcement of the contract would violate public policy. He points to cases asserting that a contract between nonmarital partners is unenforceable if it is "involved in" an illicit relationship ..., or made in "contemplation" of such a relationship.... A review of the numerous California decisions concerning contracts between nonmarital partners, however, reveals that the courts have not employed such broad and uncertain standards to strike down contracts. The decisions instead disclose a narrower and more precise standard: a contract between nonmarital partners is unenforceable only *to the extent* that it *explicitly* rests upon the immoral and illicit consideration of meretricious sexual services....

Although the past decisions hover over the issue in the somewhat wispy form of the figures of a Chagall painting, we can abstract from those decisions a clear and simple rule. The fact that a man and woman live together without marriage, and engage in a sexual relationship, does not in itself invalidate agreements between them relating to their earnings, property, or expenses. Neither is such an agreement invalid merely because the parties may have contemplated the creation or continuation of a nonmarital relationship when they entered into it. Agreements between nonmarital partners fail only to the extent that they rest upon a consideration of meretricious sexual services. Thus the rule asserted by defendant, that a contract fails if it is "involved in" or made "in contemplation" of a nonmarital relationship, cannot be reconciled with the decisions. . . .

Defendant secondly relies upon the ground suggested by the trial court: that the 1964 contract violated public policy because it impaired the community property rights of Betty Marvin, defendant's lawful wife. Defendant points out that his earnings while living apart from his wife before rendition of the interlocutory decree were community property under 1964 statutory law . . . and that defendant's agreement with plaintiff purported to transfer to her a half interest in that community property. But whether or not defendant's contract with plaintiff exceeded his authority as manager of the community property . . . , defendant's argument fails for the reason that an improper transfer of community property is not void *ab initio*, but merely voidable at the instance of the aggrieved spouse. . . .

In the present case Betty Marvin, the aggrieved spouse, had the opportunity to assert her community property rights in the divorce action. . . . The interlocutory and final decrees in that action fix and limit her interest. Enforcement of the contract between plaintiff and defendant against property awarded to defendant by the divorce decree will not impair any right of Betty's, and thus is not on that account violative of public policy.

Defendant's third contention is noteworthy for the lack of authority advanced in its support. He contends that enforcement of the oral agreement between plaintiff and himself is barred by Civil Code section 5134, which provides that "All contracts for marriage settlements must be in writing. . . ." A marriage settlement, however, is an agreement in contemplation of marriage in which each party agrees to release or modify the property rights which would otherwise arise from the marriage. . . . The contract at issue here does not conceivably fall within that definition, and thus is beyond the compass of section 5134.[50]

Defendant finally argues that enforcement of the contract is barred by Civil Code section 43.5, subdivision (d), which provides that "No cause of action arises for . . . breach of promise of marriage." This rather strained contention proceeds from the premise that a promise of marriage impliedly includes a promise to support and to pool property acquired after marriage . . . to the conclusion that pooling and support agreements not part of or accompanied by promise of marriage are barred by the section. We conclude that section 43.5 is not reasonably susceptible to the interpretation advanced by defendant, a conclusion demonstrated by the fact that since section 43.5 was enacted in 1939, numerous cases have enforced

50. Our review of the many cases enforcing agreements between nonmarital partners reveals that the majority of such agreements were oral. In two cases (Ferguson v. Schuenemann, supra, 167 Cal. App. 2d 413; Cline v. Festersen, supra, 128 Cal. App. 2d 380), the court expressly rejected defenses grounded upon the statute of frauds.

pooling agreements between nonmarital partners, and in none did court or counsel refer to section 43.5.

In summary, we base our opinion on the principle that adults who voluntarily live together and engage in sexual relations are nonetheless as competent as any other persons to contract respecting their earnings and property rights. Of course, they cannot lawfully contract to pay for the performance of sexual services, for such a contract is, in essence, an agreement for prostitution and unlawful for that reason. But they may agree to pool their earnings and to hold all property acquired during the relationship in accord with the law governing community property; conversely they may agree that each partner's earnings and the property acquired from those earnings remains the separate property of the earning partner.[51] So long as the agreement does not rest upon illicit meretricious consideration, the parties may order their economic affairs as they choose, and no policy precludes the courts from enforcing such agreements.

In the present instance, plaintiff alleges that the parties agreed to pool their earnings, that they contracted to share equally in all property acquired, and that defendant agreed to support plaintiff. The terms of the contract as alleged do not rest upon any unlawful consideration. We therefore conclude that the complaint furnishes a suitable basis upon which the trial court can render declaratory relief. . . . The trial court consequently erred in granting defendant's motion for judgment on the pleadings.

3.   PLAINTIFF'S COMPLAINT CAN BE AMENDED TO STATE A CAUSE OF ACTION FOUNDED UPON THEORIES OF IMPLIED CONTRACT OR EQUITABLE RELIEF

. . . We believe that the prevalence of nonmarital relationships in modern society and the social acceptance of them, marks this as a time when our courts should by no means apply the doctrine of the unlawfulness of the so-called meretricious relationship to the instant case. As we have explained, the nonenforceability of agreements expressly providing for meretricious conduct rested upon the fact that such conduct, as the word suggests, pertained to and encompassed prostitution. To equate the nonmarital relationship of today to such a subject matter is to do violence to an accepted and wholly different practice.

We are aware that many young couples live together without the solemnization of marriage, in order to make sure that they can successfully later undertake marriage. This trial period, preliminary to marriage, serves as some assurance that the marriage will not subsequently end in dissolution to the harm of both parties. We are aware, as we have stated, of the pervasiveness of nonmarital relationships in other situations.

---

51. A great variety of other arrangements are possible. The parties might keep their earnings and property separate, but agree to compensate one party for services which benefit the other. They may choose to pool only part of their earnings and property, to form a partnership or joint venture, or to hold property acquired as joint tenants or tenants in common, or agree to any other such arrangement. . . .

The mores of the society have indeed changed so radically in regard to cohabitation that we cannot impose a standard based on alleged moral considerations that have apparently been so widely abandoned by so many. Lest we be misunderstood, however, we take this occasion to point out that the structure of society itself largely depends upon the institution of marriage, and nothing we have said in this opinion should be taken to derogate from that institution. The joining of the man and woman in marriage is at once the most socially productive and individually fulfilling relationship that one can enjoy in the course of a lifetime.

We conclude that the judicial barriers that may stand in the way of a policy based upon the fulfillment of the reasonable expectations of the parties to a nonmarital relationship should be removed. As we have explained, the courts now hold that express agreements will be enforced unless they rest on an unlawful meretricious consideration. We add that in the absence of an express agreement, the courts may look to a variety of other remedies in order to protect the parties' lawful expectations.[52]

The courts may inquire into the conduct of the parties to determine whether that conduct demonstrates an implied contract or implied agreement of partnership or joint venture . . . , or some other tacit understanding between the parties. The courts may, when appropriate, employ principles of constructive trust . . . or resulting trust. . . . Finally, a nonmarital partner may recover in quantum meruit for the reasonable value of household services rendered less the reasonable value of support received if he can show that he rendered services with the expectation of monetary reward. . . .

Since we have determined that plaintiff's complaint states a cause of action for breach of an express contract, and, as we have explained, can be amended to state a cause of action independent of allegations of express contract,[53] we must conclude that the trial court erred in granting defendant a judgment on the pleadings.

The judgment is reversed and the cause remanded for further proceedings consistent with the views expressed herein.

WRIGHT, C.J., MCCOMB, J., MOSK, J., SULLIVAN, J., and RICHARDSON, J., concurred.

CLARK, J.* concurring and dissenting. The majority opinion properly permits recovery on the basis of either express or implied in fact agreement

52. We do not seek to resurrect the doctrine of common law marriage, which was abolished in California by statute in 1895. . . . Thus we do not hold that plaintiff and defendant were "married," nor do we extend to plaintiff the rights which the Family Law Act grants valid or putative spouses; we hold only that she has the same rights to enforce contracts and to assert her equitable interest in property acquired through her effort as does any other unmarried person.

53. We do not pass upon the question whether, in the absence of an express or implied contractual obligation, a party to a nonmarital relationship is entitled to support payments from the other party after the relationship terminates.

* *William Patrick Clark, Jr.* (1931-†) was educated at Stanford University (B.A.) and Loyola University Law School (J.D.) and began his political career as chief of staff to then-Governor Ronald Reagan (1966-1969). That year, he was appointed judge of the Superior Court of California, moving to the Court of Appeals of Los Angeles two years later. In 1973,

between the parties. These being the issues presented, their resolution requires reversal of the judgment. Here, the opinion should stop.

This court should not attempt to determine all anticipated rights, duties and remedies within every meretricious relationship — particularly in vague terms. Rather, these complex issues should be determined as each arises in a concrete case.

The majority broadly indicate that a party to a meretricious relationship may recover on the basis of equitable principles and in quantum meruit. However, the majority fail to advise us of the circumstances permitting recovery, limitations on recovery, or whether their numerous remedies are cumulative or exclusive. Conceivably, under the majority opinion a party may recover half of the property acquired during the relationship on the basis of general equitable principles, recover a bonus based on specific equitable considerations, and recover a second bonus in quantum meruit.

The general sweep of the majority opinion raises but fails to answer several questions. First, because the Legislature specifically excluded some parties to a meretricious relationship from the equal division rule of Civil Code section 4452, is this court now free to create an equal division rule? Second, upon termination of the relationship, is it equitable to impose the economic obligations of lawful spouses on meretricious parties when the latter may have rejected matrimony to avoid such obligations? Third, does not application of equitable principles — necessitating examination of the conduct of the parties — violate the spirit of the Family Law Act of 1969, designed to eliminate the bitterness and acrimony resulting from the former fault system in divorce? Fourth, will not application of equitable principles reimpose upon trial courts the unmanageable burden of arbitrating domestic disputes? Fifth, will not a quantum meruit system of compensation for services — discounted by benefits received — place meretricious spouses in a better position than lawful spouses? Sixth, if a quantum meruit system is to be allowed, does fairness not require inclusion of all services and all benefits regardless of how difficult the evaluation?

When the parties to a meretricious relationship show by express or implied in fact agreement they intend to create mutual obligations, the courts should enforce the agreement. However, in the absence of agreement, we should stop and consider the ramifications before creating economic obligations which may violate legislative intent, contravene the intention of the parties, and surely generate undue burdens on our trial courts.

By judicial overreach, the majority perform a nunc pro tunc marriage, dissolve it, and distribute its property on terms never contemplated by the parties, case law or the Legislature.

---

he was appointed justice on the Supreme Court of California (1973-1981), leaving the bench in 1981 to fill posts in the federal government, including Assistant Secretary of the Department of State (1981-1982), Assistant to President Ronald Reagan for National Security Affairs (1982-1983), and Secretary of the Interior (1983-1985). Since leaving the federal government, he has practiced privately and is currently director of a private international corporation. — K.T.

FRANCES MORONE v. FRANK MORONE, COURT OF APPEALS OF NEW YORK, 429 N.Y.S.2D 592 (1980): MEYER, J.* Historically, we have required the explicit and structured understanding of an express contract and have declined to recognize a contract which is implied from the rendition and acceptance of services. . . . The major difficulty with implying a contract from the rendition of services for one another by persons living together is that it is not reasonable to infer an agreement to pay for the services rendered when the relationship of the parties makes it natural that the services were rendered gratuitously. . . . As a matter of human experience personal services will frequently be rendered by two people living together because they value each other's company or because they find it a convenient or rewarding thing to do (see Marvin v. Marvin . . .). For courts to attempt through hindsight to sort out the intentions of the parties and affix jural significance to conduct carried out within an essentially private and generally noncontractual relationship runs too great a risk of error. Absent an express agreement, there is no frame of reference against which to compare the testimony presented and the character of the evidence that can be presented becomes more evanescent. There is, therefore, substantially greater risk of emotion-laden afterthought, not to mention fraud, in attempting to ascertain by implication what services, if any, were rendered gratuitously and what compensation, if any, the parties intended to be paid.

Similar considerations were involved in the Legislature's abolition by chapter 606 of the Laws of 1933 of common-law marriages in our State. Writing in support of that bill, Surrogate Foley informed Governor Lehman that it was the unanimous opinion of the members of the Commission to Investigate Defects in the Law of Estates that the concept of common-law marriage should be abolished because attempts to collect funds from decedents' estates were a fruitful source of litigation. Senate Minority Leader Fearon, who had introduced the bill, also informed the Governor that its purpose was to prevent fraudulent claims against estates and recommended its approval. The consensus was that while the doctrine of common-law marriage could work substantial justice in certain cases, there was no built-in method for distinguishing between valid and specious claims and, thus, that the doctrine served the State poorly.

The notion of an implied contract between an unmarried couple living together is, thus, contrary to both New York decisional law and the implication arising from our Legislature's abolition of common-law marriage.

REFERENCE: Farnsworth, §5.4
                 Murray, §99(J)

---

* *Bernard S. Meyer* (1916-2005) studied at Johns Hopkins University (B.S.), the University of Maryland at Baltimore (LL.B.), and Hofstra University (LL.D.). He was admitted to the Maryland bar in 1938 and later to the District of Columbia and New York bars. Judge Meyer served as Justice of the Supreme Court of New York State (1959-1972) before moving to the New York Court of Appeals (1979-1986). Judge Meyer continued in private practice as well as serving as a hearing officer for the National Arbitration and Mediation organization. — L.R.

STUDY GUIDE: *If an unmarried couple is permitted to make binding promises to each other in the context of* Marvin *and* Morone, *can a prospective spouse commit contractually to restrict the amount of alimony and child support he or she may collect upon divorce? The next case considers the enforceability of what are called pre- or antenuptial agreements.*

SARI POSNER v. VICTOR POSNER, SUPREME COURT OF FLORIDA, 257 SO. 2D 530 (1972):   BOYD, J.* . . . On the merits, the case involves the validity of an antenuptial agreement executed fourteen days before the marriage of the parties on December 30, 1960. After six years of marriage and two children, the parties were divorced by decree dated December 7, 1966. Under the terms of the antenuptial agreement, Posner, a very wealthy man, pays $600 per month in alimony and $600 per month per child for support. . . .

This Court, in its first opinion, held:[54]

> We have given careful consideration to the question of whether the change in public policy towards divorce requires a change in the rule respecting antenuptial agreements settling alimony and property rights of the parties upon divorce and have concluded that such agreements should no longer be held to be void ab initio as "contrary to public policy." *If such an agreement is valid when tested by the stringent rules prescribed in Del Vecchio v. Del Vecchio, supra, 143 So. 2d 17, for ante- and postnuptial agreements settling the property rights of the spouses in the estate of the other upon death, and if, in addition, it is made to appear that the divorce was prosecuted in good faith, on proper grounds, so that, under the rules applicable to postnuptial alimony and property settlement agreements referred to above, it could not be said to facilitate or promote the procurement of a divorce, then it should be held valid as to conditions existing at the time the agreement was made.* (e.s.) . . .

We reiterate that inadequate and disproportionate provision for the wife, even to the extent evidenced in the instant case, will not vitiate an antenuptial agreement. If the prospective wife has full knowledge of her rights, and in the absence of willful or unintentional fraud, or the withholding of material facts, she will . . . [not] be entitled to a greater share of her husband's wealth.

Freedom to contract includes freedom to make a bad bargain. But freedom to contract is not always absolute. The public interest requires that antenuptial agreements be executed under conditions of candor and fairness. As stated in Del Vecchio:[55]

> The relationship between the parties to an antenuptial agreement is one of mutual trust and confidence. Since they do not deal at arm's length they must

---

* *Joseph Arthur Boyd, Jr.* (1916-2007) studied at Piedmont College and the University of Miami Law School (J.D.). Prior to serving as justice on the Supreme Court of Florida (1969-1987), he held several government positions, including City Attorney for Hialeah, Florida (1951-1958), and County Commissioner for Dade County (1958-1968). Boyd also served in the Pacific and American theaters during World War II. — K.T.

54. Posner v. Posner, 233 So. 2d 381, 385 (Fla. 1970).
55. 143 So. 2d 17, 21 (Fla. 1962).

exercise a high degree of good faith and candor in all matters bearing upon the contract.

[After evaluating the evidence, the court concluded that: "The failure to disclose or show knowledge on the part of petitioner-wife of respondent's wealth plus the inadequate provision made for petitioner renders the antenuptial agreement void."]

9

THE DOCTRINE OF CONSIDERATION

A. THE HISTORICAL ORIGINS OF THE DOCTRINE

The traditional approach to identifying an enforceable commitment is known as the doctrine of consideration. As discussed in Chapter 8, this doctrine has come to be identified with the bargain theory of consideration. The bargain theory was adopted by both the first and second Restatements of Contracts. In this chapter we will read cases in which the existence of "bargained-for" consideration is the principal issue. Before examining these cases, however, it is useful to consider briefly the history of the doctrine. The doctrine of consideration is among the more baffling for first-year law students in part because the word "consideration" itself conveys little, if any, hint as to the content or purpose of the doctrine. It is helpful to consider how this term came to be associated with a legal doctrine and that the bargain theory was not the original conception of consideration. Accordingly, we now turn to the past.

Historical Background: The Origins of the Doctrine of Consideration

STUDY GUIDE: *When reading the following excerpt, notice how the term "consideration" referred to the motive for making a promise and how the recognized motives that justified enforcement originally included moral considerations and considerations of preexisting duties. The modern bargain theory of consideration that we shall study in the balance of this chapter excludes such motivations in its conception of consideration.*

A. W. B. SIMPSON, THE DOCTRINE OF CONSIDERATION — INTRODUCTION, in A HISTORY OF THE COMMON LAW OF CONTRACT: THE RISE OF THE ACTION OF ASSUMPSIT 316-317, 321-323, 325-326 (1975):   [W]here no debt was involved, since the promisor was not a debtor, the rise of assumpsit . . . involve[d] the recognition by the common law courts of a new liability. Promises to marry, for example, to build houses or to return lost dogs do not involve any obligation to pay a fixed sum of money, and promises to guarantee debts or pay marriage dowries did not give rise to debts according to the principles of the medieval law, although definite sums of money were involved. The extension of promissory liability into areas previously outside the scope of the common law generated a need for a new set of boundary markers. It was natural that in a doctrinal system of law there should be a place for a new body of doctrine, whose function was to define which promises should be actionable, and which should not give rise to legal liability. Such a corpus of doctrine was evolved in the sixteenth century, and one part of it is the doctrine of consideration, which delimits the actionability of informal promises *by reference to the circumstances in which the promise in question is made.*

It is important to notice in passing that other limiting doctrines are both conceivable and have in some cases been adopted by the common law. Thus one possibility is to insist upon some measure of formality such as writing, or the formal words once insisted upon in the stipulation of Roman Law. But until the passing of the Statute of Frauds in 1677 formality was in general treated as irrelevant in assumpsit. Other restrictions were imposed. Some promises, because of their content or subject-matter, fell outside the jurisdiction of the common law courts; this was so in the case of promises to marry, which until the mid-seventeenth century were regarded as wholly spiritual in nature. Other promises might be illegal, or contrary to public policy, or impossible to perform, or induced by fraud or duress; consideration is and always has been only one of the prerequisites of promissory liability. In modern law consideration is also intimately linked to the doctrine of offer and acceptance, and paralleled by the requirement of an intention to create legal relations; consequently the requirements for what we call "formation of contract" are complex. Neither doctrine is to be found in the period with which we are concerned, so that consideration was the characteristic doctrine of the action for breach of promise to a more striking degree than today. . . .

The Meaning of "Consideration."   Pleadings in assumpsit had always included matters of inducement. For example, in the pleadings against a negligent surgeon in 1369 the pleader explained the circumstances in which the surgeon undertook to look after an injured finger — the declaration stated that the middle finger of the plaintiff's right hand had been accidentally injured, and that the surgeon had been paid a proper fee of 6s. 8d. The development in the 1560s of the settled practice of setting out not *any* circumstances, but circumstances known as "the considerations," or "the causes and considerations," entails the acceptance of some general contractual theory, and the first step towards understanding this theory is to identify what was then meant by "considerations." The consideration, or considerations, for a promise meant the factors which the promisor considered when he promised, and which moved or motivated his promising. Although not a precise equivalent, "motive" is perhaps about as near as one can get by way of synonym. The essence of the doctrine of consideration, then, is the adoption by the common law of the idea that the legal effect of a promise should depend upon the factor or factors which motivated the promise. To decide whether a promise to do X is binding, you need to know why the promise was made. This basic idea can be elaborated in various ways — for example, one might or might not accept love of charity, or a future marriage, or a past payment, as sufficient in law to impose promissory liability. Whatever decisions are made about such matters as these can be fitted into the basic analysis.

Consideration and the Will.   The recognition by the common law that a promise, to give rise to legal liability in assumpsit, must be "supported" by good, sufficient, or adequate consideration, entails the idea that a promise on its own, an unsupported promise, is not sufficient to impose liability. Now in contemporary thought a promise was conceived of as an expression of will, and the effect of the doctrine was therefore that of depriving a bare or naked expression of will, the *nuda voluntas*, of legal significance; looked at from the point of view of a promisee, it deprived a mere volunteer (i.e., one whose claim depended solely upon the will of another) of an actionable claim. . . . In modern terms one can see the plausibility of the theory — a promise which lacks any adequate motive cannot have been serious, and therefore ought not to be taken seriously.

Promises Reinforcing Existing Obligations.   Granted this analysis it is plain that a promise to do something which one is already under an obligation to do, the promise being made in consideration of the circumstance giving rise to the obligation, is the paradigm or central case of a binding promise. For example, suppose *A* owes *B* a debt of £10, and because of this (in consideration . . .) promises to pay *B* £10. According to the theory the mere promise to pay £10 is not enough — it must be supported or bolstered up by an adequate motivating circumstance. What better circumstance than a pre-existing obligation to pay £10? Or again take an illustration used by St. Germain. My father is cold and needs a gown to keep him warm — I ought, of course, as his son to give him a gown, I have a natural duty to do so. If I now *promise* to give him a gown then the promise is binding. Hence in the early history of consideration it must be appreciated that what has come to be called pre-existing "moral" obligation — today associated with Lord Mansfield's activities in the eighteenth century — was not some curious aberration; it logically lay at the heart of the doctrine. . . . It is perhaps worth noticing in this connection that in everyday life promises are frequently used not so much to impose but to reinforce, or render more precise previously existing duties and obligations, the archetype here being the child's promise to be good, with such variants as the promise to tell the truth. . . .

Theories of Consideration.   With the exception of Sir John Salmond (with whose approach I am broadly in agreement), historians who have sought to produce explanations of the origin of the doctrine of consideration seem to me to have generally missed the point of what has to [be] explained. What is curious about the common law is not that it enforces business agreements (a somewhat ill-defined category), or that it holds binding promises which have been paid for — it would be extraordinary if it did not. The curiosity is that the actionability of informal promises is made to turn upon an analysis of the motivating reasons which induced the promisor to make the promise — the consideration or considerations for the promise.

REFERENCE: Barnett, §§4.2, 4.2.1
              Farnsworth, §§1.5-1.6
              Calamari & Perillo, §4.1
              Murray, §§2-3, 55

B.   The Bargain Theory of Consideration

Although *consideration* could refer to whatever circumstances render a commitment legally binding, in the twentieth century it came to be identified with the existence of a *bargain*. This is reflected in §17 of the Restatement (Second), which states that: "Except as stated in Subsection (2), the formation of a contract requires a bargain in which there is a manifestation of mutual assent to the exchange and a consideration."[1] Restatement (Second) §71(1), in turn, defines consideration in terms of a bargain: "To constitute consideration, a performance or a return promise must be bargained for." Section 71(2) defines *bargained for* as follows: "A performance or return promise is bargained for if it is sought by the promisor in exchange for his promise and is given by the promisee in exchange for that promise."

We may summarize the second Restatement's primary approach to enforceability as follows:

1.   A contract is an enforceable promise (§§1 and 2);
2.   With some exceptions (§17(2)), to be enforceable a promise must be supported by a consideration (§17(1));
3.   A promise is supported by a consideration if it is bargained for (§71(1));
4.   A promise is bargained for "if it is sought by the promisor in exchange for his promise and is given by the promisee in exchange for that promise" (§71(2)).

In sum, according to this theory of enforceability, to find that a commitment is legally enforceable on the grounds that it is supported by consideration, one must determine that it has been bargained for.

In this section, we consider a number of cases in which the bargained-for nature of a commitment is the primary issue. Most of these cases are clustered under traditional categories such as past consideration, moral consideration, preexisting duties, etc. Each of these doctrines can be viewed as involving different circumstances in which a bargain is, for one reason or another, absent. Before proceeding, let us consider one famous account of the crucial social function of bargaining.

Economics Background: Bargains and the Division of Labor

ADAM SMITH, LECTURES ON JURISPRUDENCE 347-348 (OXFORD: CLARENDON PRESS, 1978) [from GLASGOW UNIVERSITY LECTURE OF TUESDAY, MARCH 29, 1763]:   This division of work is not however the effect of any human policy, but is the necessary consequence of a naturall disposition altogether peculiar to men, viz the

---

1. Subsection (2) reads: "Whether or not there is a bargain a contract may be formed under special rules applicable to formal contracts or under the rules stated in §§82-94." We shall study the types of circumstances included in these sections in Chapters 10 and 11.

disposition to truck, barter, and exchange; and as this disposition is peculiar to man, so is the consequence of it, the division of work betwixt different persons acting in concert. It is observed that the hounds in a chance turn the hare towards one another, and in this manner are helpfull to each other and divide the labour, but this does not arise from any contract, as is evident since they generally quarrell about her after she is killed; no one ever saw them make any agreement giving one bone for another, nor make any signs by which they declared, This is mine and that is thine. — Dogs draw all the attention of others by their fawning and flattering. Man too some times uses this art, when no others will do, of gaining what he wants by fawning and adulation. But this is but seldom the case; he commonly falls upon other expedients. The other animals live entirely independent of others. And some times indeed when in danger its cries may draw the attention of man or other animalls; but this rarely is the case, and there seems to be no more provision made by nature in such cases than there is for one who is shipwrecked in the midst of the sea. The propagation of the kind and the preservation of the species goes on not-withstanding. Man continually standing in need of the assistance of others, must fall upon some means to procure their help. This he does not merely by coaxing and courting; he does not expect it unless he can turn it to your advantage or make it appear to be so. Mere love is not sufficient for it, till he applies in some way to your self love. A bargain does this in the easiest manner.

ADAM SMITH, THE WEALTH OF NATIONS 22 (5TH ED. LONDON, 1789):   Whoever offers to another a bargain of any kind, proposes to do this: Give me that which I want, and you shall have this which you want, is the meaning of every such offer; and it is in this manner that we obtain from one another the far greater part of those good offices which we stand in need of. It is not from the benevolence of the butcher, the brewer, or the baker, that we expect our dinner, but from their regard to their own interest. We address ourselves, not to their humanity but to their self-love, and never talk to them of our own necessities but of their advantages.

STUDY GUIDE: When reading each of the cases in Section B, consider whether or not the promise in question was bargained for according to the Restatement (Second).

1.   Distinguishing Bargains from Gratuitous Promises

The first item of business is learning to distinguish a bargain from alternative sorts of agreements. As should be apparent by now, legal reasoning often proceeds by positing two opposing theories or characterizations of a case and trying to decide which one most accurately describes the facts in question. The alternative to a bargained-for exchange is a gratuitous promise. Unlike bargained-for promises, gratuitous or "gift" promises are only effective upon actual delivery of the thing that was promised. Our purpose for reading about gratuitous promises in this chapter is to enable you to distinguish them from bargains. The next two cases present the very tricky problem of distinguishing between a bargained-for commitment and a conditioned, or contingent, gift.

STUDY GUIDE: How do you suppose one can tell the difference between a promise that is bargained for and one that is made on condition that certain actions or events occur? In the next case, should the promise be enforceable? We will return to the issue of enforcing donative promises to charity in Chapter 11 when discussing Judge Cardozo's opinion in Allegheny College v. National Chautauqua County Bank of Jamestown and Restatement (Second) of Contracts §90(2).

JOHNSON v. OTTERBEIN UNIVERSITY
Supreme Court of Ohio,
41 Ohio 527 (1885)

Error to the District Court of Wood County.

Otterbein University is an educational institution at Westerville, Ohio, incorporated under a special act passed February 13, 1849, and supported by donations, bequests, &c. In February, 1869, Johnson signed and delivered to Spangler, an agent of the institution, an instrument of which the following is a copy:

$100   WESTERVILLE, OHIO, May 6, 1869.

Three years after date, I promise to pay to the trustees of Otterbein University of Ohio, or their agents, one hundred dollars, with interest, at the rate of no per cent., to be used exclusively to liquidate the present, that is, February (1869) indebtedness of said University. Should this donation ever be used for any other purpose than herein specified, the trustees of said University shall be held bound to refund said sum of money to the donor.

JOHN JOHNSON.

This and similar notes given by other parties in 1868 and 1869, were turned over to the institution by Spangler and accepted as a fund with which to liquidate the indebtedness.

In December, 1876, the trustees brought suit in the common pleas of Wood county. The petition set forth a copy of the note and averred its delivery, maturity and nonpayment, and that the indebtedness of 1869, named in the note, was unpaid. The answer alleged that the note was without consideration, and this allegation was denied in the reply. This issue was tried in the common pleas, and judgment was entered against Johnson for the amount claimed. A motion for a new trial was overruled, and a bill of exceptions embodying all the testimony was taken. On error to the district court the judgment was affirmed. To reverse the judgment of affirmance is the object of the present proceeding.

The only testimony introduced at the trial consisted of the depositions of Spangler and Bender, agents of the university, taken in August, 1878. It appears that the note was given for no other consideration than as expressed on its face; that the indebtedness of the university in February,

1869, was $33,250; that about $16,000 was paid thereon out of the proceeds of notes taken in 1868 and 1869; that $15,150 was paid thereon with money borrowed for the purpose, and for which the institution was still indebted, but when this loan was made, whether before or after the commencement of the suit, is not stated; and that $6,500 is still due on the original indebtedness of 1869. . . .

MARTIN, J.* The writing sued on contains a distinct promise to pay one hundred dollars at a fixed time, a direction as to the application of the fund, and a provision that it shall be refunded in case of misapplication. The parties supposed that the writing provided for a donation to be made to the institution. It is an elementary principle that an executory contract to give is without consideration, and that a promise to pay money as a gift may be revoked at any time before payment. "The gift of the maker's own note is the delivery of a promise only, and not of the thing promised, and the gift therefore fails." Kent's Com. 438; Hamor v. Moore, 8 Ohio St., 243; Ohio Wesleyan Female College v. Love's Exr., 16 Id., 20. This doctrine is not disputed. But several claims are variously stated on behalf of the university which may be reduced to two heads. 1st. That there is a valid consideration: In this, that by acceptance the institution agreed to pay over the money, and thus there arose a case of mutual promises; and in this, that the promise and the liabilities incurred on the faith of it serve as considerations each for the other. 2d. That by force of the charter provisions, the promise is binding though it be without a consideration in law. [Discussion of the second theory is omitted.]

But grant, that by acceptance of the note, the university impliedly agreed to comply with the direction, that is to apply the proceeds to the payment of its indebtedness. Is that a promise to do an act of advantage to Johnson, or of detriment to the institution in the sense requisite to constitute it a legal consideration? We think it is not. If the writing had been in form a promissory note, or a mere promise to make a donation without any qualification, a necessary implication of a duty to apply its proceeds to proper corporate objects would arise upon acceptance. In the absence of special circumstances we fail to see how a duty to apply the fund to a particular corporate purpose can better serve as a consideration than a duty to apply it to corporate purposes not specified. The duty in either case is implied. The claim made involves the proposition that a promise in writing to make a gift to an educational institution is valid on acceptance. This is denied in Ohio Wesleyan Female College v. Love's Exr., supra. It, however, finds some support in the authorities.

The liabilities incurred by the institution on the faith, as it is said, of the promise, are not alluded to in the pleadings. The only reference to them in the record is found in the deposition of Mr. Bender, which was taken in August, 1878, some 19 months after Johnson's answer was filed. He testifies that $15,150 "has been paid by borrowing money from other parties, which money is still owing by the institution." He does not state when it was borrowed. Non constat, but that it was borrowed after the answer was

* *Charles D. Martin* (1829-1911) was educated at Kenyon College and was admitted to the Ohio bar in 1850. He practiced law privately at Lancaster, Ohio, and served as a member of the thirty-sixth Congress (1859-1861). Martin was appointed to the Supreme Court of Ohio in 1883, and after completing one term, he resumed his law practice until his death. — K.T.

filed when, if not before, the promise was revoked. In this state of the testimony we need not comment on the claims made by counsel as to the effect of these loans. . . .

It follows, from what has been said, that the judgments below are erroneous. We place the reversal on these legal propositions; that the creation of a fund with which to pay the previously incurred indebtedness of the institution was not a consideration in law for the promise; and that the acceptance of the writing containing the direction to apply the fund, does not, in a legal sense, give rise to a case of mutual promises.

Judgment reversed.

STUDY GUIDE: Was the court in the next case correct in finding a bargain rather than a conditioned gift? The parties are arguing about whether the nephew suffered a detriment, yet the court seemed more interested in the existence of a bargain. Why look for a bargained-for exchange instead of asking whether there was a benefit to the promisor or a detriment to the promisee? Also, this case is the first of several we shall read in Part III involving an executor of an estate refusing to honor a commitment alleged to have been made by the testator. Why do you suppose that executors would contest the validity of these sorts of claims? Might it be significant that such cases are so prevalent in the historical development of the doctrines of consideration and of promissory estoppel?

HAMER v. SIDWAY
Court of Appeals of New York,
124 N.Y. 538, 27 N.E. 256 (1891)

Appeal from order of the General Term of the Supreme Court in the fourth judicial department, made July 1, 1890, which reversed a judgment in favor of plaintiff entered upon a decision of the court on trial at Special Term and granted a new trial.

This action was brought upon an alleged contract.

The plaintiff presented a claim to the executor of William E. Story, Sr., for $5,000 and interest from the 6th day of February, 1875. She acquired it through several mesne assignments from William E. Story, 2d. The claim being rejected by the executor, this action was brought. It appears that William E. Story, Sr., was the uncle of William E. Story, 2d; that at the celebration of the golden wedding of Samuel Story and wife, father and mother of William E. Story, Sr., on the 20th day of March, 1869, in the presence of the family and invited guests he promised his nephew that if he would refrain from drinking, using tobacco, swearing and playing cards or billiards for money until he became twenty-one years of age he would pay him a sum of $5,000.[2] The nephew assented thereto and fully performed the

2. [In the defendant's brief to the appellate court (p. 4-5), the exchange is related as follows:

It is claimed by the plaintiff that William E. Story observed the little boy, fifteen years, one month and twenty days old, was drinking, smoking and playing cards and billiards

conditions inducing the promise. When the nephew arrived at the age of twenty-one years and on the 31st day of January, 1875, he wrote to his uncle informing him that he had performed his part of the agreement and had thereby become entitled to the sum of $5,000.[3] The uncle received the letter and a few days later and on the sixth of February, he wrote and mailed to his nephew the following letter:

BUFFALO, *Feb.* 6, 1875.

W. E. STORY, Jr.

DEAR NEPHEW — Your letter of the 31st ult. came to hand all right, saying that you had lived up to the promise made to me several years ago. I have no doubt but you have, for which you shall have five thousand dollars as I promised you. I had the money in the bank the day you was 21 years old that I intend for you, and you shall have the money certain. Now, Willie I do not intend to interfere with this money in any way till I think you are capable of taking care of it and the sooner that time comes the better it will please me. I would hate very much to have you start out in some adventure that you thought all right and lose this money in one year. The first five thousand dollars that I got together cost me a heap of hard work. You would hardly believe me when I tell you that to obtain this I shoved a jackplane many a day, butchered three or four years, then came to this city, and after three months' perseverance I obtained a situation in a grocery store. I opened this store early, closed late, slept in the fourth story of the building in a room 30 by 40 feet and not a human being in the building but myself. All this I done to live as cheap as I could to save something. I don't want you to take up with this kind of fare. I was here in the cholera season '49 and '52 and the deaths averaged 80 to 125 daily and plenty of smallpox. I wanted to go home, but Mr. Fisk, the gentleman I was working for, told me if I left then, after it got healthy he probably would not want me. I stayed. All the money I have saved I know just how I got it. It did not come to me in any mysterious way, and the reason I speak of this is that money got in this way stops longer with a fellow that gets it with hard knocks than it does when he finds it. Willie, you are 21 and you have many a thing to learn yet. This money you have earned much easier than I did besides acquiring good habits at the same time and you are quite welcome to the money; hope you will make good use of it. I was ten long years getting this together after I was your age. Now, hoping this will be satisfactory, I stop. One thing more. Twenty-one years ago I bought you 15 sheep. These sheep were put out to double every four years. I kept track of them the first

---

to such an extent as led the uncle, after a conference with the boy's father, James A. Story, in which the father consented thereto, to make a proposition to the boy before all assembled, in words as follows: "If you will not drink any liquor, will not smoke, will not play cards or billiards, until you are 21, I will give you $5,000 that day." And he further said: "Of course, if you want to play cards for fun, I do not consider that playing cards. I mean playing cards for money."

James Story testified that, at the wedding, his brother had also said to him: "You know when a boy of his age gets to going bad it always gains on him, and I want to hold out some inducement to stop it right here and now." Trial court record, p. 94. — EDS.]

3. [At trial, James Story recalled that the letter read: "Dear Uncle: — I am twenty-one years old to-day, and I am now my own boss, and I believe according to agreement [sic] there is due me $5,000. I have lived up to the contract to the letter in every sense of the word." Id. at 35. William Story, 2d, testified: "I do drink, smoke, play cards and billiards now to a moderate degree, and I have for a few years. I cannot tell you when I first commenced either one." Id. at 51. — EDS.]

eight years; I have not heard much about them since. Your father and grand-father promised me that they would look after them till you were of age. Have they done so? I hope they have. By this time you have between five and six hundred sheep, worth a nice little income this spring. Willie, I have said much more than I expected to; hope you can make out what I have written. Today is the seventeenth day that I have not been out of my room, and have had the doctor as many days. Am a little better today; think I will get out next week. You need not mention to father, as he always worries about small matters.

Truly Yours,

W. E. STORY

P.S. You can consider this money on interest.

The nephew received the letter and thereafter consented that the money should remain with his uncle in accordance with the terms and conditions of the letters. The uncle died on the 29th day of January, 1887, without having paid over to his nephew any portion of the said $5,000 and interest. . . .

PARKER, J.* The question which provoked the most discussion by counsel on this appeal, and which lies at the foundation of plaintiff's asserted right of recovery, is whether by virtue of a contract defendant's testator William E. Story became indebted to his nephew William E. Story, 2d, on his twenty-first birthday in the sum of five thousand dollars. The trial court found as a fact that

> on the 20th day of March, 1869, . . . William E. Story agreed to and with William E. Story, 2d, that if he would refrain from drinking liquor, using tobacco, swearing, and playing cards or billiards for money until he should become 21 years of age then he, the said William E. Story, would at that time pay him, the said William E. Story, 2d, the sum of $5,000 for such refraining, to which the said William E. Story, 2d, agreed,

and that he "in all things fully performed his part of said agreement."[4]

The defendant contends that the contract was without consideration to support it, and, therefore, invalid. He asserts that the promisee by refraining from the use of liquor and tobacco was not harmed but benefited; that which he did was best for him to do independently of his uncle's promise, and insists that it follows that unless the promisor was benefited, the

---

Alton Brooks Parker (1852-1926) received his legal training at Albany Law School (LL.B.). He practiced law in Kingston, New York, and held the positions of surrogate of Ulster County (1877-1885) and first assistant postmaster-general (1885). Parker was appointed justice of the Supreme Court of New York in 1885, and was elected to that post in 1886. His tenure on the bench included member of the Court of Appeals, Second Division (1889-1892), member of the general term (1893-1896), and of the Appellate Division (1898-1904). He resigned to accept the Democratic nomination for the Presidency in 1904. After an unsuccessful bid for the Presidency, Parker returned to private practice and was chief counsel for the impeachment trial of Governor Sulzer in 1913. — K.T.

4. [The trial court further found that plaintiff had "deprived himself of the right to continue to drink liquor and use tobacco, and on one occasion during the time when he had so agreed not to use liquor, refused to use the same when suffering from fever and ague in the West." Id. at 10. — EDS.]

contract was without consideration. A contention, which if well founded, would seem to leave open for controversy in many cases whether that which the promisee did or omitted to do was, in fact, of such benefit to him as to leave no consideration to support the enforcement of the promisor's agreement. Such a rule could not be tolerated, and is without foundation in the law. The Exchequer Chamber, in 1875, defined consideration as follows:

> A valuable consideration in the sense of the law may consist either in some right, interest, profit or benefit accruing to the one party, or some forbearance, detriment, loss or responsibility given, suffered or undertaken by the other.

Courts

> will not ask whether the thing which forms the consideration does in fact benefit the promisee or a third party, or is of any substantial value to anyone. It is enough that something is promised, done, forborne or suffered by the party to whom the promise is made as consideration for the promise made to him.

(Anson's Prin. of Con. 63.)

> In general a waiver of any legal right at the request of another party is a sufficient consideration for a promise.

(Parsons on Contracts, 444.)

> Any damage, or suspension, or forbearance of a right will be sufficient to sustain a promise.

(Kent, [Commentaries,] vol. 2, 465, 12th ed.)[5]
Pollock, in his work on contracts, page 166, after citing the definition given by the Exchequer Chamber already quoted, says:

> The second branch of this judicial description is really the most important one. Consideration means not so much that one party is profiting as that the other abandons some legal right in the present or limits his legal freedom of action in the future as an inducement for the promise of the first.

---

5. [Professors Farnsworth and Young note the following: "James Kent (1763-1847) began practice after three years as an apprentice and was active in Federalist politics. Hamilton introduced him to the writings of European authors on the civil law, which were to influence his later work. In 1793, largely through his Federalist connections, he was made Professor of Law at Columbia College. He attracted few students, and soon resigned to become a judge on the New York Supreme Court, then the highest court in the state. In 1814 he became Chancellor. Upon his retirement in 1823, he lectured again at Columbia for three years. Out of these lectures grew the "Commentaries on American Law," in four volumes, which became the most important American law book of the century. (It is the source of the quotation above.) Kent lived to prepare six editions; subsequent ones were revised by others. For his work on the Court of Chancery, he has been called the creator of equity in the United States." E. Allan Farnsworth & William F. Young, Cases and Materials on Contracts 43 (4th ed. 1988). Chicago-Kent College of Law is named for him. — EDS.]

Now, applying this rule to the facts before us, the promisee used tobacco, occasionally drank liquor, and he had a legal right to do so. That right he abandoned for a period of years upon the strength of the promise of the testator that for such forbearance he would give him $5,000. We need not speculate on the effort which may have been required to give up the use of those stimulants. It is sufficient that he restricted his lawful freedom of action within certain prescribed limits upon the faith of his uncle's agreement, and now having fully performed the conditions imposed, it is of no moment whether such performance actually proved a benefit to the promisor, and the court will not inquire into it, but were it a proper subject of inquiry, we see nothing in this record that would permit a determination that the uncle was not benefited in a legal sense. Few cases have been found which may be said to be precisely in point, but such as have been support the position we have taken.

In Shadwell v. Shadwell, 9 C.B.N.S. 159, an uncle wrote to his nephew as follows:

> MY DEAR LANCEY — I am so glad to hear of your intended marriage with Ellen Nicholl, and as I promised to assist you at starting, I am happy to tell you that I will pay you 150 pounds yearly during my life and until your annual income derived from your profession of a chancery barrister shall amount to 600 guineas, of which your own admission will be the only evidence that I shall require.
>
> Your Affectionate uncle,
>
> Charles Shadwell

It was held that the promise was binding and made upon good consideration. . . .

It will be observed that the agreement which we have been considering was within the condemnation of the Statute of Frauds, because not to be performed within a year, and not in writing. But this defense the promisor could waive, and his letter and oral statements subsequent to the date of final performance on the part of the promisee must be held to amount to a waiver. Were it otherwise, the statute could not now be invoked in aid of the defendant. It does not appear on the face of the complaint that the agreement is one prohibited by the Statute of Frauds, and, therefore, such defense could not be made available unless set up in the answer. . . . This was not done. . . .

The order appealed from should be reversed and the judgment of the Special Term affirmed, with costs payable out of the estate.

All concur. ——> *Holding*
Judgment for Sidway
reversed

Relational Background: Other Dealings Between Willie and His Uncle

STUDY GUIDE: After reading the previous case, one is likely to be sympathetic to Willie. One's sympathies might, however, be influenced by the additional facts that are included in the intermediate appellate court's opinion but which were omitted from the opinion of the Court of Appeals.

Note the issue of the alleged assignment or assignments. Also included is a brief portion of the appellate court's reasoning for rejecting the enforceability of the promise.

HAMER v. SIDWAY, SUPREME COURT, GENERAL TERM, FOURTH DEPARTMENT, 11 N.Y. SUPP. 182 (1890): MARTIN, J.* . . . The promise of the testator, as testified to by the plaintiff's witnesses, was that if his nephew would refrain from smoking, drinking and gambling, during his minority, he would give him $5,000 on the day he became of age. It will be observed that this promise was not that he would pay him that amount for any service to be performed for the testator, but that he would give him that amount as a gratuity, as an incentive to his nephew to become a sober and worthy man, free from evil and useless habits. In its ordinary and familiar signification, the word "give" means to transfer gratuitously, without any equivalent. Presumably the word was used in that sense by the testator. Unless the evidence shows that it was used in some other sense, its ordinary signification should be given it. We find no sufficient evidence in this case to hold that the word "give" was used other than in its ordinary sense. The evidence of the witness Judson shows that when Willie was a child only eight or ten years of age the testator contemplated making him a gift of that sum when he became of age, and that he frequently mentioned his purpose in the family of his brother, and that he also contemplated starting him in business at that time, if everything was favorable. Thus the purpose of the testator would seem not to have been a new one arising at that time, but one which had existed for years, and which was known to the family. This witness also testified that this contemplated gift was not only a subject of frequent conversation between the testator and his brother's family, but that he conversed with her in relation to it upon at least two occasions, and still she never heard anything about any contract between the testator and William. This testimony tends to sustain the appellant's claim that the arrangement between the parties was in the nature of a promised gift by the testator.

But it may be said that the correspondence between the parties when William became of age tends to show that the arrangement was as claimed by the respondent. It is true that William, in his letter to the testator, refers to the arrangement between them as an agreement or contract, and states that he believes there is his due $5,000, but in the testator's reply to that letter he mentions the $5,000 only as a sum which he had promised to his nephew. . . . On the contrary, the testator's letter is inconsistent with that idea, for, after stating that he had the money in the bank that he *intended* for him (William), and after he again promised that he should have it, the testator states unqualifiedly that he does not intend to interfere with this money in any way until he thinks William capable of taking care of it. Thus the testator, instead of recognizing any legal liability to pay the money when William became twenty-one years of age, treated the matter just as he

---

* *Celora E. Martin* (1834-1909) studied law privately at Newport, New York, and was admitted to the bar of that state in 1856. He practiced law at Whitney's Point until he was appointed justice of the Supreme Court in 1877; he was elected to the post later that same year. In 1887, Martin was designated Chief Justice of the general term, which position he held until his retirement in 1895. — K.T.

doubtless understood it, as a promise to make a gift at that time, and he then, in effect, refused to perfect the gift by delivery, but insisted upon attaining it under his own dominion and control until he should think William capable of taking care of it. When this letter was received by William the evidence fails to show that he objected to it, or claimed that he had any right to the money until such time as the testator should see fit to give it to him. This evidence is inconsistent with the existence of a valid contract, and consistent only with the appellant's theory that this transaction was a mere promise to make a gift, and that both parties so regarded it. We think the transaction between the testator and William E. Story amounted to no more than a promise on the part of the testator that he would give William $5,000 when he became twenty-one years of age, if he should prove himself worthy of it by abstaining from certain useless, evil, and expensive habits. . . .

Moreover, the evidence in this case is far from satisfactory. It tends to show quite clearly that the testator, during his lifetime, had fulfilled his promise to his nephew. Soon after the letter of the testator was written we find William engaged in business with his father. He had borrowed $2,500 of the testator, for which he gave his promissory note. Subsequently he and his father failed in business and were declared bankrupts. In the schedules filed in that proceeding he makes no mention of any claim or debt against the testator, and when required to state any and all money or debts that were due or owing to him, he declared there were none except those which were mentioned, which did not include this claim. He also declared upon his oath that there was no money held in trust for him by any one. After this the testator transferred to William and his father $11,000 worth of goods, for which he received two one-thousand dollar notes and a general release under seal executed by both, which was broad enough to cover this claim.[6]

The plaintiff seeks to avoid the effect of this evidence by proving that the plaintiff's claim had been previously assigned by William to his wife, and that the testator knew of such assignment when the release was given. The credibility of that testimony is materially shaken by the fact that when this action was brought no such assignment was alleged, but the plaintiff alleged in her complaint that she acquired title to this claim directly from William by an assignment made February 3, 1887. The plaintiff's attorney, who drew that complaint, also swears that such an assignment was before him when he drew it. It may be that the assignment was made by William to his wife, as alleged and proved, but it is certainly very remarkable that that fact should have been forgotten by them until the defendant pleaded a release as a defense to this action. It would seem that either William, his wife or the plaintiff, must have remembered the fact, if it

---

6. [Upon submission by the defendant's lawyers of proposed findings of fact to this effect, the trial judge specifically refused to find any of these facts to be true. And in his opinion, he stated: "There is nothing in the evidence which satisfies the Court that this money was ever paid to Wm. E. Story, 2d, during the lifetime, or that the obligation was in any manner released." Trial court record, p. 101. (My thanks to Professor Alexander Meiklejohn for bringing this to my attention as well as for supplying me with the trial and appellate court records.) Why the appellate judges of the Supreme Court rejected the trial judge's factual finding and why the Court of Appeals ignored this factual dispute between the lower courts remains unclear. — EDS.]

existed, either when the claim against the testator's estate was made, verified and presented, or when the original complaint in this action was prepared. Without stating the evidence in further detail, it certainly is not satisfactory to us. In a case like this, where the estate of a dead man is assaulted by dissatisfied relatives,[7] it is the duty of a court to scrutinize the evidence given to sustain such an assault quite carefully, and such a claim should be allowed only upon fair, reliable and consistent evidence, which shows that it is a just one. If there were no other questions in the case except the question whether the plaintiff's claim had been paid and released, we should be inclined to regard it as our duty to grant a new trial upon the ground that the decision was against the weight of evidence. We are, however, of the opinion that there was no legal contract between the parties sufficient to uphold the recovery in this case, and that the judgment should be reversed.

Judgment reversed and a new trial ordered, with costs to abide the event.

STUDY GUIDE: In the next case, was there consideration for the promise made as Justice Ormond thought, or was the promise a conditioned gift as the majority of justices thought? How do you tell the difference between a bargained-for exchange and a conditioned gift? If you apply the modern bargain theory of consideration that developed after this case was decided, what additional facts might change your conclusion about the presence or absence of a bargain? Can the result in this case be reconciled with Hamer v. Sidway? Note that the brief opinion (which appears in its entirety after the court's summary of the facts) was written by the dissenting justice, an archaic practice that probably resulted from the assignment of responsibility for writing the opinion before oral argument and decision.

KIRKSEY v. KIRKSEY
Supreme Court of Alabama,
8 Ala. 131 (1845)

Error to the Circuit Court of Talladega.

Assumpsit by the defendant, against the plaintiff in error. The question is presented in this Court, upon a case agreed, which shows the following facts:

The plaintiff was the wife of defendant's brother, but had for some time been a widow, and had several children. In 1840, the plaintiff resided on public land, under a contract of lease, she had held over, and was comfortably settled, and would have attempted to secure the land she lived on. The defendant resided in Talladega county, some sixty, or seventy miles off. On the 10th October, 1840, he wrote to her the following letter:

Dear Sister Antillico — Much to my mortification, I heard, that brother Henry was dead, and one of his children. I know that your situation is one of grief,

---

7. [The trial court record indicates that William Story 2d received nothing from his uncle's estate. He was, he told a witness, "left out in the cold and he explained to me what others had received from his uncle's estate." Id. at p. 60. — EDS.]

and difficulty. You had a bad chance before, but a great deal worse now. I should like to come and see you, but cannot with convenience at present. . . .

I do not know whether you have a preference on the place you live on, or not. If you had, I would advise you to obtain your preference, and sell the land and quit the country, as I understand it is very unhealthy, and I know society is very bad. If you will come down and see me, I will let you have a place to raise your family, and I have more open land than I can tend; and on the account of your situation, and that of your family, I feel like I want you and the children to do well.[8]

[margin handwritten: Offer (Promise)]

Within a month or two after the receipt of this letter, the plaintiff abandoned her possession, without disposing of it, and removed with her family, to the residence of the defendant, who put her in comfortable houses, and gave her land to cultivate for two years, at the end of which time he notified her to remove, and put her in a house, not comfortable, in the woods, which he afterwards required her to leave.

A verdict being found for the plaintiff, for two hundred dollars, the above facts were agreed, and if they will sustain the action, the judgment is to be affirmed, otherwise it is to be reversed. . . .

ORMOND, J.* The inclination of my mind, is, that the loss and inconvenience, which the plaintiff sustained in breaking up, and moving to the defendant's, a distance of sixty miles, is a sufficient consideration to support the promise, to furnish her with a house, and land to cultivate, until she could raise her family. My brothers, however think, that the promise on the part of the defendant, was a mere gratuity, and that an action will not lie for its breach. The judgment of the Court below must therefore be reversed, pursuant to the agreement of the parties.

[margin handwritten: Judge disagrees with majority opinion even though he is writing it]

Relational Background: "Dear Sister Antillico"

STUDY GUIDE: *Do the following additional facts affect your analysis of the presence or absence of consideration in* Kirksey?

WILLIAM R. CASTO & VAL D. RICKS, "DEAR SISTER ANTILLICO . . .": THE STORY OF KIRKSEY v. KIRKSEY, 94 GEO. L.J. 321, 324, 340-353, 371-372 (2006): Notwithstanding the surprising

---

8. [In their article excerpted after the case, Professors Castro and Ricks note that the omitted portion of this letter read: "I am not well at present, my family has been generally well, all but myself and my youngest son. We have not been very sick. The health of the County is tolerably good at present. I should like to know your situation." — EDS.]

*John J. Ormond (1795-1866) was a native of England and came with his parents to the vicinity of Charlottesville, Virginia, in his infancy. He was left an orphan at a tender age. As he lacked funds, prominent friends of the family contributed liberal aid to his elementary education and training. He evinced a strong taste for books. In 1827, he moved to Alabama and began practice in Lawrence County, which he represented as a Whig in the legislature in 1832 and 1833. In 1837, a Democratic legislature elected him to the Alabama Supreme Court, where he remained on the bench for 12 years until he declined further service because of feeble health. — R.B.

paucity of judicial citations, *Kirksey* truly is a famous case. Most first-year students and all contracts professors know the case's story of personal tragedy, good intentions gone awry, intrafamilial squabbling, and a broken promise. *Kirksey* is famous because it is a great teaching case — especially for first-semester students. Although the case seems straightforward and even simple, many ambiguities and puzzles lie beneath its still surface. Countless professors in countless classes have queried: Why did Isaac Kirksey invite his sister-in-law "Antillico" (an aberrant spelling of Angelico, we discovered) down to Talladega? Was he bargaining for something when he did? How many children did Angelico bring? Did Isaac mean for the children to work on his plantation (did he bargain for their labor)? Did Isaac and Angelico have an affair (was the consideration meretricious)? Why did Isaac move to evict his sister-in-law? Was she unbearable as a neighbor? Why did she sue? What result was she seeking? What evidence was presented at trial? Did she have evidence of consideration other than her trip to Talladega? Was her lawyer incompetent? Did the law of the time support Angelico's legal position, or is Ormond's conclusion based on something other than legal authority? Did the appellate court usurp the jury's factfinding role? Why did the dissenting judge write the majority opinion? Whatever happened to Angelico and her small children? The ensuing classroom discussion intrigues both professor and student. The case has even inspired poetry (of a sort).

Asking these questions serves pedagogy, though the questions are consistent with as many pedagogical objectives as there are questions. Indeed, our informal poll of contract law teachers revealed a long list of objectives for which professors use *Kirksey*. Because *Kirksey* is not a leading case, its very obscurity leaves the professor free to take the case wherever she will. That is one reason professors and students enjoy the case: it is delightfully ambiguous.

We intend to spoil that ambiguity and answer all of these questions. Henry Kirksey, Angelico's late husband, was the poorer brother of the entrepreneurial and litigious Isaac Kirksey, the writer of the letter. Though Isaac's invitation suggests to us today that Isaac was kind and generous, Isaac had an ulterior motive. He meant to place Angelico on public land to hold his place — his preference — so that he could buy the land later from the U.S. government at a lucrative discount. He was bargaining for her to act as a placeholder, and she knew it, though using that evidence later in court was problematic. . . .

Merely selling federal lands was insufficient as a land distribution policy in early America. Americans pushed the frontier forward by settling on federal lands before the lands were put up for sale. As early as 1783, a concerned Congress issued a proclamation forbidding settlement in Ohio and sent federal troops to remove settlers there. The troops drove off the squatters, burned their cabins, rooted up their potatoes and other crops, and destroyed their fences. When the troops left, the settlers returned.

Later, congressional acts forbade any settlement in the territories, but enforcement was politically unpopular and futile. From 1800 to 1841, Congress bowed to political pressure and curried settlers' voting favor by passing a series of acts designed to legalize the possession of squatters and protect the value of improvements these squatters had placed illegally on federal land. Most of these acts took the form of grants to squatters of a "preference" or "preemption" right, which was a "a right to become the purchaser at the minimum price . . . , in preference to all others" of the land each had settled and cultivated. . . . [I]n September 1841 Congress passed a standing preemption law. Under this law, any head of a family, widow, or single man over the age of twenty-one years who settled on surveyed public lands, improving and building or using a house on them, was given a preemption right to 160 acres including the dwelling. Anyone already owning 320 acres within the United States was ineligible. Anyone abandoning a residence on his or her own land to reside on public land was ineligible. The statute only granted one preemption right per person. If two persons settled on the same surveyed 160 acres, the first settler would win the preemption right. . . .

Isaac and Angelico's awareness of these laws becomes obvious if the facts we know about them are read against this background. In October 1840, Angelico was living on public land under a "contract of lease," not with the United States, but "with another." This last phrase in fact denotes that she was leasing from the holder of a preference. But Angelico had "held over," meaning that her term as a tenant had ended. If she was possessing adversely to her lessor, she may well have been the legal equivalent of a squatter against the United States. The *Kirksey* Court stated that had Isaac not offered her a place, Angelico "would have attempted to secure [the title to] the land she lived on." What was obvious to the Court — too obvious to mention, but not at all obvious to readers now — was that Angelico as a squatter may have already earned a preference in the property . . . in which case the land might have been hers for the minimum price of $1.25 per acre. Alternately, her continued possession may have given her a preference under a later act had she remained. Isaac's letter stressed the importance of preference rights: "I do not know whether you have a preference on the place you live on, or not. If you had, I would advise you to obtain your preference, and sell the land and quit the country." The preference was not to pass up, he implies. Isaac's advice assumed Angelico was relatively sophisticated about preference rights. The immediate exercise of a preference right that Isaac suggested makes sense economically only if the going price for land was greater than the federal minimum price of $1.25 per acre. If it was, then Angelico could make a quick profit by purchasing for $1.25 and immediately reselling. Isaac's recommendation assumed that Angelico knew what a preference right was and also that the going price for land exceeded the federal minimum. Their conversation thus revealed that both Isaac and Angelico were familiar with land acquisition laws of the time, and that Isaac was thinking about preferences when he wrote the letter.

Given that background, Isaac actually suggests his motive for inviting Angelico down to Talladega in the next sentence of the letter: "If you will come down and see me, I will let you have a place to raise your family, and I have more open land than I can tend. . . ." The last phrase is puzzling without the legal background. "Open land" can mean a number of things. . . . But Isaac's most probable meaning becomes clear once we understand that the phrase "open land" also meant land open to the public for settlement. "Open land" commonly meant just that in the 1830s and 1840s. In the context of Isaac's discussion of preferences, his reference to "open land" probably suggested that meaning to Angelico. "There you are on open land," Isaac seems to say, "but society is bad there. Come here instead. I will put you on open land as well, that I possess, and you will be no worse off economically and bettered health-wise and socially. You settle for me on open land that I possess, wherever that is, until the government grants me a preference, and you will always have a place to live." . . .

Under this interpretation, Isaac's motives become clear. He wished Angelico to settle on and cultivate public land for him until Congress granted another preference. Notwithstanding Isaac's large holdings, prior preference statutes would have given him a right to prefer more. Another general preemption act was expected in 1842. Moreover, leasing public land to another who functioned as placeholder had become common. Angelico leased under such an arrangement in Marshall County, before she moved to Talladega. Congress's Act of June 1, 1840, specifically approved such placeholding by a lessee, preserving the preference right to the lessor under certain conditions. If a preference-holder could lease land and keep the preference, surely Isaac could grant Angelico a license to preferred land and retain his rights, or so he thought. This interpretation of Isaac's letter also assists in understanding Angelico's motives. If she was leasing from a preference holder in Marshall County before she moved, she was no worse off holding likewise for Isaac in Talladega.

This interpretation of Isaac's letter further explains why Isaac placed his son in possession jointly with Angelico and later removed her. In September 1841, after Angelico had possessed under Isaac for roughly one year, Congress passed the standing preemption law. Whereas earlier statutes allowed any head of household a preference on cultivated federal land, the 1841 Act restricted preemption to those not already owning 320 acres. Isaac instantly became ineligible. That presented a problem for Isaac's scheme. Though Isaac was ineligible, Angelico was not. In the words of the statute, she was "[a] widow . . . over the age of twenty-one years, . . . a citizen of the United States, . . . who since the first day of June [1840], has made . . . a settlement in person on the public lands . . . and who has or shall erect a dwelling thereon. . . ." The Act therefore gave Angelico the ability to gain a preference for 160 acres. Whether her possession until September 1841 counted in her favor is debatable, but her possession after that date arguably began to give her rights. Had Isaac not taken some action, Angelico would have taken the land instead of him. She had to leave the property.

There was a delay in time. The Act was passed in September 1841, yet Angelico stayed in the house for at least another year. Why the delay? Various explanations are possible. . . . The most compelling reason for delay, though, is the puzzling fact that Isaac put his son in joint possession with Angelico. Isaac was waiting for his eldest son to be old enough to take Angelico's place. At some point in 1842, late or early — and the record does not say when — Isaac placed his son on the property, in "joint possession" of the house. But Isaac's oldest son, Albert Oscar Kirksey, turned 21 and became eligible for preemption rights only on February 22, 1843, a little over two years after Angelico moved into the house. Albert's possession in late 1841 would have counted toward his preemption right under the 1841 Act, but Isaac did not remove Angelico from the property until Albert turned twenty-one and could gain a preemption himself, two years after she took possession. . . . [O]nly interruption of Angelico's possession after Albert turned twenty-one would give Albert a clear claim. So Angelico had to go, and that is why Isaac in the end had to evict her. Eviction was delayed for several months in part because only then was a better placeholder eligible. . . .

That Isaac involved Angelico in his preference-grabbing scheme also explains the amount of the jury verdict. Isaac's breach of promise deprived Angelico of land to which she could have obtained a preference. Under the 1841 Act, a preference could be obtained on a maximum of 160 acres. When the preference holder finally purchased the land, she had to pay the "minimum price." Since 1820, the minimum price for all U.S. land sales had been $1.25 per acre. The jury's verdict of $200 (160 acres × $1.25 per acre) thus reflects a way to measure Angelico's expectations. The $200 would in fact have allowed her to buy the exact land at issue. She had, after all, settled on it. No one else could claim it before her. If Isaac paid the judgment, Angelico could march from the courthouse down to the land office and buy the property. Perhaps hope that she could obtain the property itself is what led her to remain in Talladega until 1845, after the Supreme Court's decision. Alternatively, the $200 is exactly the amount Angelico needed to settle somewhere else on 160 acres of federal land. . . .

A question remains: Why did Angelico's counsel not present this theory to the court? If she came as a placeholder, couldn't she argue that her doing so was detriment suffered in exchange for Isaac's promise? Perhaps, but arguing that to the court may not have served her ultimate goal if she wanted the land itself. If she did want to claim a preference on the property, claiming that she had come to Talladega as a placeholder for Isaac would have been a fatal move. . . . She may have been estopped to claim otherwise. Only if she left the placeholding out of her lawsuit could she later swear to the land office register without contest that she held independently of Isaac.

Both Angelico and Isaac may also have thought that presenting the placeholder plan before the jury would look as if both were trying to manipulate the preemption laws. Because the arrangement was clearly not a lease, which would have been legitimate, the scheme is only a hair's breadth removed from Angelico agreeing to take title herself and transfer it to Isaac. Perhaps neither wished the jury to think of them as manipulative, as trying to take unfair advantage of the law. So the complaint is crafted so as to omit any reference as to who owned the land. Rather than say that Isaac placed Angelico on federal land, the agreed statement of facts says that he placed her "on a part of the land then unoccupied." No lease is alleged, nor any license to use the land. Only breach of promise was put at issue. Rather than allege as a consideration that Isaac wanted Angelico to preserve a possible preemption right in the land he allowed her to possess — a consideration a judge might in fact find meretricious, given the settler's oath — Angelico's lawyer alleged only the consideration of her inconvenience in moving her family. That became the ultimate issue in the case. . . .

Harry Jones once asked, "Did you wonder what in God's name ever happened to the widow, Sister Antillico, and her small children . . . ?" Apparently she returned to Madison County, where she appears on the 1850 Census as the head of a household and the owner of land worth

$300. Six of her children, aged twelve to twenty-six, were living with her, and she owned three young girls as slaves. By 1860, Angelico had moved to St. Francis County, Arkansas, where at the age of sixty-eight she was living with her son Edwin. She does not appear in the 1870 census and presumably died in the 1860s. That is all we know.

As for Isaac, he continued to prosper. By 1850 he was a large slaveholder with fifty slaves, and in the late 1840s and 1850s, he gave land and slaves to his children as they married. In addition, in 1855 he sent his son, James Isaac ("Jim") Kirksey, Jr., and twenty slaves to Texas to work on his western holdings. Jim established a successful cotton plantation in Anderson County, Texas. On the eve of the Civil War, Isaac's slave holdings in Alabama had diminished to about forty slaves. He died in May 1865, at the end of the Civil War, without even an obituary in the local newspapers. His landholdings are now divided. Aside from the Kirksey opinion, little in Talladega County now reminds us of either Angelico or Isaac. Both, however, have descendants who gained fame. Angelico's great-grandson Morris Kirksey ran the 100 meters in 10.8 seconds to win a silver medal in the 1920 Olympics. And Isaac's daughter Eliza married Daniel Rather in March 1840; their great-great-grandson is Dan Rather, formerly of CBS News.

STUDY GUIDE: Both Hamer v. Sidway and Kirksey v. Kirksey involved unilateral contracts — i.e., a promise in return for a performance rather than a counterpromise. Here is another, more modern example of an overlooked bargain in the context of a unilateral contract. Can you articulate the "mutual inducement" here?

DAHL v. HEM PHARMACEUTICALS CORP., UNITED STATES COURT OF APPEALS, NINTH CIRCUIT, 7 F.3D 1399 (1993): KLEINFELD, Circuit Judge.* Dahl and seventeen others, afflicted with chronic fatigue syndrome, enrolled in an experimental program to test a new medication. . . . The patients received the medicine as part of the testing procedure used by the Food and Drug Administration to determine whether a medicine is safe and effective. When the test was over, HEM ceased providing the medication to the patients. They sued for injunctive and other relief, claiming that HEM promised to continue providing Ampligen to them after the study ended if statistical analysis showed efficacy compared to placebo. . . .

The patients submitted themselves to months of periodic injections with an experimental drug, or unbeknownst to them, mere saline solution, combined with intrusive and necessarily uncomfortable testing to

* *Andrew Jay Kleinfeld* (1945-†) was educated at Wesleyan University (B.A., 1966) and Harvard Law School (J.D., 1969) before serving as a law clerk to Judge J. A. Rabinowitz of the Alaska Supreme Court (1969-1971). Raised an easterner, he began his legal career as a solo practitioner in Fairbanks and recalls that, when he began in practice, each of the other local lawyers sent him one of their clients to help him get established. While in private practice, he also served as Magistrate, United States District Court for the District of Alaska in Fairbanks. In 1986, Judge Kleinfeld was appointed to the United States District Court for the District of Alaska, where he served until his appointment to the United States Court of Appeals for the Ninth Circuit, on which he now sits. In 2010, he assumed senior status. His wife, Judith Kleinfeld, is a professor of psychiatry at the University of Alaska and noted author. His son, Joshua Kleinfeld, is a law professor at Northwestern University School of Law. — R.B.

determine their condition as the tests proceeded. HEM sought to have them participate in its study so that it could obtain FDA approval for its new drug. HEM argues that because petitioners participated voluntarily and were free to withdraw, they had no binding obligation and so gave no consideration. Somehow the category of unilateral contracts appears to have escaped HEM's notice. The deal was, "if you submit to our experiment, we will give you a year's supply of Ampligen at no charge." . . . [9] In this case, the petitioners performed by submitting to the double-blind tests. They incurred the detriment of being tested upon for HEM's studies in exchange for the promise of a year's treatment of Ampligen. Upon completion of the double-blind tests, there was a binding contract.

Reread: Restatement, §3 (p. 15), §17 (p. 262), §18 (p. 263)

Study Guide: *Can you apply the following material from the Restatement (Second) to determine whether the uncle's promise in Hamer v. Sidway was a conditioned gift or bargained for?*

RESTATEMENT (SECOND) OF CONTRACTS

§24.   OFFER DEFINED

COMMENT

b. Proposal of Contingent Gift.   A proposal of a gift is not an offer within the present definition; there must be an element of exchange. Whether or not a proposal is a promise, it is not an offer unless it specifies a promise or performance by the offeree as the price or consideration to be given by him. It is not enough that there is a promise performable on a certain contingency.

[handwritten margin note: There must be an element of exchange in an offer]

ILLUSTRATION

2. *A* promises *B* $100 if *B* goes to college. If the circumstances give *B* reason to know that *A* is not undertaking to pay *B* to go to college but is promising a gratuity, there is no offer.

9. The form is . . . similar to the standard Brooklyn Bridge hypothetical case: Suppose A says to B, "I will give you $100 if you walk across the Brooklyn Bridge," and B walks — is there a contract? It is clear that A is not asking B for B's promise to walk across the Brooklyn Bridge. What A wants from B is the act of walking across the bridge. When B has walked across the bridge, there is a contract, and A is then bound to pay B $100. At that moment there arises a unilateral contract. A has bartered away his volition for B's act of walking across the Brooklyn Bridge. I. Maurice Wormser, The True Conception of Unilateral Contracts, 26 Yale L.J. 136, 136 (1916). HEM did not bargain for or seek a promise by the patients to submit to the double-blind testing. It sought and obtained their actual performance. Mutuality of promises was unnecessary.

§71.   REQUIREMENT OF EXCHANGE; TYPES OF EXCHANGE

(1) To constitute consideration, a performance or a return promise must be bargained for.

(2) A performance or return promise is bargained for if it is sought by the promisor in exchange for his promise and is given by the promisee in exchange for that promise. *(Interlocking inducements)* *(Key thing to understand is the nature of the exchange)*

(3) The performance may consist of

(a) an act other than a promise, or

(b) a forbearance, or

(c) the creation, modification, or destruction of a legal relation.

(4) The performance or return promise may be given to the promisor or to some other person. It may be given by the promisee or by some other person. *(Hamer v. Sidway)*

COMMENT

a. Other Meanings of "Consideration."   The word "consideration" has often been used with meanings different from that given here. It is often used merely to express the legal conclusion that a promise is enforceable. Historically, its primary meaning may have been that the conditions were met under which an action of assumpsit would lie. It was also used as the equivalent of the *quid pro quo* required in an action of debt. A seal, it has been said, "imports a consideration," although the law was clear that no element of bargain was necessary to enforcement of a promise under seal. On the other hand, consideration has sometimes been used to refer to almost any reason asserted for enforcing a promise, even though the reason was insufficient. In this sense we find references to promises "in consideration of love and affection," to "illegal consideration," to "past consideration," and to consideration furnished by reliance on a gratuitous promise.

Consideration has also been used to refer to the element of exchange without regard to legal consequences. Consistent with that usage has been the use of the phrase "sufficient consideration" to express the legal conclusion that one requirement for an enforceable bargain is met. Here §17 states the element of exchange required for a contract enforceable as a bargain as "a consideration." Thus "consideration" refers to an element of exchange which is sufficient to satisfy the legal requirement; the word "sufficient" would be redundant and is not used.

b. "Bargained for."   In the typical bargain, the consideration and the promise bear a reciprocal relation of motive or inducement: the consideration induces the making of the promise and the promise induces the furnishing of consideration. Here, as in the matter of mutual assent, the law is concerned with the external manifestation rather than the undisclosed mental state: it is enough that one party manifests an intention to induce the other's response and to be induced by it and that the other responds in accordance with the inducement. See §81; compare §§19, 20. But it is not enough that the promise induces the conduct of the promisee or that the conduct of the promisee induces the making of the promise; both elements must be present, or there is no bargain. Moreover a mere pretence of bargain does not suffice, as where there is a false recital of consideration or where the purported consideration is merely nominal. In such cases there is no consideration and the promise is enforced, if at all, as a promise binding without consideration under §§82-94. . . .

§81. CONSIDERATION AS MOTIVE OR INDUCING CAUSE

(1) The fact that what is bargained for does not of itself induce the making of a promise does not prevent it from being consideration for the promise.

(2) The fact that a promise does not of itself induce a performance or return promise does not prevent the performance or return promise from being consideration for the promise.

COMMENT

a. "Bargained for."   Consideration requires that a performance or return promise be "bargained for" in exchange for a promise; this means that the promisor must manifest an intention to induce the performance or return promise and to be induced by it, and that the promisee must manifest an intention to induce the making of the promise and to be induced by it. See §71 and Comment *b*. In most commercial bargains the consideration is the object of the promisor's desire and that desire is a material motive or cause inducing the making of the promise, and the reciprocal desire of the promisee for the making of the promise similarly induces the furnishing of the consideration.

b. Immateriality of Motive or Cause.   This section makes explicit a limitation on the requirement that consideration be bargained for. Even in the typical commercial bargain, the promisor may have more than one motive, and the person furnishing the consideration need not inquire into the promisor's motives. Unless both parties know that the purported consideration is mere pretense, it is immaterial that the promisor's desire for the consideration is incidental to other objectives and even that the other party knows this to be so. Compare §79 and Illustrations. Subsection (2) states a similar rule with respect to the motives of the promisee.

REFERENCE: Barnett, §§4.2.2, 4.4.3
                Farnsworth, §§2.2-2.5
                Calamari & Perillo, §§4.2(a), 4.5, 4.7
                Murray, §61

2. Past Consideration

We now turn our attention to the first of two doctrines associated with the requirement of consideration: the doctrines of past consideration and moral consideration. We shall consider how each doctrine is a logical implication of the bargain theory of consideration. So studying these doctrines is another way to test your comprehension of the bargain requirement as well as to assess its desirability.

STUDY GUIDE: The defendant in the next case is "Nelson L. Elmer and others, as administrators, etc.," which is the only indication in the opinion that Elmer died, as predicted by Josephine L. Moore, aka "Madame Sesemore," on September 15, 1899.

MOORE v. ELMER
Supreme Judicial Court of Massachusetts,
180 Mass. 15, 61 N.E. 259 (1901)

(Past Consideration)

The following is a copy of the contract sued on [spelling as in original]:

Performance has already occurred

Springfield, Mass., Jan 11th, 1898.

In Consideration of Business and Test Sittings Reseived from Mm. Sesemore, the Clairvoyant, otherwise known as Mrs. Josephene L. Moore on Numerous occasions I the undersighned do hear by agree to give the above named Josephene or her heirs, if she is not alive, the Balance of her Mortgage note whitch is the Herman E. Bogardus Mortgage note of Jan. 5, 1893, and the Interest on sane [sic] on or after the last day of Jan. 1900, if my Death occurs before then whitch she has this day Predicted and Claims to be the truth, and whitch I the undersighned Strongly doubt. Wherein if she is right I am willing to make a Recompense to her as above stated, but not payable unless death Occurs before 1900.

Issue is Promise - deciding whether this promise was made with consideration

Willard Elmer.

HOLMES, C.J. It is hard to take any view of the supposed contract in which, if it were made upon consideration, it would not be a wager. But there was no consideration. The bill alleges no debt of Elmer to the plaintiff prior to the making of the writing. It alleges only that the plaintiff gave him sittings at his request. This may or may not have been upon an understanding or implication that he was to pay for them. If there was such an understanding it should have been alleged or the liability of Elmer in some way shown. If, as we must assume and as the writing seems to imply, there was no such understanding, the consideration was executed and would not support a promise made at a later time. The modern authorities which speak of services rendered upon request as supporting a promise must be confined to cases where the request implies an undertaking to pay, and do not mean that what was done as a mere favor can be turned into a consideration at a later time by the fact that it was asked for. See Langdell, Contracts §92 et seq. . . .

It may be added that even if Elmer was under a previous liability to the plaintiff it is not alleged that the agreement sued upon was received in satisfaction of it, either absolutely or conditionally, and this again cannot

Holmes's deal test: she was paid. The contract was already happened so to speak so she can't collect now.

Must be a "live bargain"

Past uncompleted performance is not enough to induce promise. Performance w/ bargain no consideration

be implied in favor of the plaintiff's bill. It is not necessary to consider what further difficulties there might be in the way of granting relief.

Bill dismissed. ——→ *Holding*

Rule: Past consideration is not sufficient for enforcement of a contract unless the parties agreed prior to performing that compensation would be provided at a later time

REFERENCE: Barnett, §4.2.3
                  Farnsworth, §2.7
                  Calamari & Perillo, §4.3
                  Murray, §68(A)

3.   Moral Consideration

In the excerpt we read by Professor Simpson at the beginning of this chapter, he explained that the doctrine of consideration attempted to distinguish enforceable from unenforceable promises on the basis of the circumstances surrounding their making — in particular the motivation of the promisor for making the promise. A preexisting moral obligation to perform a particular act was considered to be a good reason for enforcing an express commitment to do so. As was just seen, the bargain theory stipulates that so-called past consideration will not constitute legal consideration and thereby justify legal enforcement. We now turn to another possible source of pre-existing obligation to do what one also promised to do: moral consideration.

STUDY GUIDE: Does the reasoning in this case depart from what Professor Simpson describes as the historical origins of the consideration doctrine? In what respect is it consistent with a bargain theory of consideration? How does the court distinguish those preexisting obligations that will support enforcement from those that will not? Classical natural rights theorists distinguished between two kinds of moral rights: perfect rights were those moral rights that were also legally enforceable; imperfect rights were those moral rights that depended upon suasion alone. How is this distinction reflected in the following opinion? Finally, notice the court's rejection of plaintiff's argument that "it is sufficient that [defendant's] ... promise was in writing, and was made deliberately, with a knowledge of all the circumstances." We shall return to this basis of enforceability in Chapter 10.

MILLS v. WYMAN
(Moral Consideration)

Supreme Judicial Court of Massachusetts,
20 Mass. (3 Pick.) 207 (1825)

This was an action of assumpsit brought to recover a compensation for the board, nursing, c., of Levi Wyman, son of the defendant, from the 5th to the 20th of February, 1821. The plaintiff then lived at Hartford, in Connecticut the defendant, at Shrewsbury, in this county. Levi Wyman, at the time when the services were rendered, was about 25 years of age, and had long ceased to be a member of his father's family. He was on his return from a voyage at sea, and being suddenly taken sick at Hartford, and being poor and in distress, was relieved by the plaintiff in the manner and to the extent above stated. On the 24th of February, after all the expenses had been incurred, the defendant wrote a letter to the plaintiff, promising to pay him such expenses. There was no consideration for this promise, except what grew out of the relation which subsisted between Levi Wyman and the defendant, and Howe J., before whom the cause was tried in the Court of Common Pleas, thinking this not sufficient to support the action, directed to nonsuit. To this direction the plaintiff filed exceptions.

J. Davis and Allen in support of the exceptions. The moral obligation of a parent to support his child is a sufficient consideration for an express promise.... The arbitrary rule of law, fixing the age of twenty-one years for the period of emancipation, does not interfere with this moral obligation, in case a child of full age shall be unable to support himself. Our statute of 1793, c.59, requiring the kindred of a poor person to support him, proceeds upon the ground of a moral obligation.

But if there was no moral obligation on the part of the defendant, it is sufficient that his promise was in writing, and was made deliberately, with a knowledge of all the circumstances. A man has a right to give away his property. [Parker C.J. There is a distinction between giving and promising.] The case of Bowers v. Hurd, 10 Mass. R. 427, does not take that distinction. [Parker C.J. That case has been doubted.][10] Neither does the case of Packard v. Richardson, 17 Mass. R. 122; and in this last case (p. 130) the want of consideration is treated as a technical objection....

The opinion of the Court was read, as drawn up by

PARKER, C.J.* General rules of law established for the protection and security of honest and fair-minded men, who may inconsiderately make promises without any equivalent, will sometimes screen men of a different character from engagements which they are bound in *foro conscientiœ* to perform. This is a defect inherent in all human systems of legislation. The rule that a mere verbal promise, without any consideration, cannot be enforced by action, is universal in its application, and cannot be departed from to suit particular cases in which a refusal to perform such a promise may be disgraceful.

The promise declared on in this case appears to have been made without any legal consideration. The kindness and services towards the sick son of the defendant were not bestowed at his request. The son was in no

---

10. [Though the practice of "doubting" a report was a technique common law judges sometimes used to avoid precedent with which they disagreed, in this case Chief Justice Parker was explicitly rejecting "his own opinion in Bowers v. Hurd, in which the supreme judicial court enforced a promise based solely on past good deeds." Geoffrey R. Watson, In the Tribunal of Conscience: Mills v. Wyman Reconsidered, 71 Tulane L. Rev. 1749, 1784 (1997). — EDS.]

Isaac Parker (1768-1830) graduated Harvard University in 1786. He began his public service career as a member of the U.S. House of Representatives from Massachusetts, Fifth Congress (1797-1799). In 1799, President John Adams appointed Parker U.S. Marshal for the Maine District (1799-1803). He later became a judge on the Massachusetts Supreme Court (1806-1830) and had served as Chief Justice of that court for 16 years at the time of his death. Parker was also one of the first professors of law at Harvard (1815-1827) and submitted a plan for a law school at Harvard in 1817, which was later adopted by the school. He also served as president of the Massachusetts Constitutional Convention in 1820. — K.T.

respect under the care of the defendant. He was twenty-five years old, and had long left his father's family. On his return from a foreign country, he fell sick among strangers, and the plaintiff acted the part of the good Samaritan, giving him shelter and comfort until he died. The defendant, his father, on being informed of this event, influenced by a transient feeling of gratitude, promises in writing to pay the plaintiff for the expenses he had incurred. But he has determined to break this promise, and is willing to have his case appear on record as a strong example of particular injustice sometimes necessarily resulting from the operation of general rules.

It is said a moral obligation is a sufficient consideration to support an express promise; and some authorities lay down the rule thus broadly; but upon examination of the cases we are satisfied that the universality of the rule cannot be supported, and that there must have been some preëxisting obligation, which has become inoperative by positive law, to form a basis for an effective promise. The cases of debts barred by the statute of limitations, of debts incurred by infants, of debts of bankrupts, are generally put for illustration of the rule. Express promises founded on such preexisting equitable obligations may be enforced; there is a good consideration for them; they merely remove an impediment created by law to the recovery of debts honestly due, but which public policy protects the debtors from being compelled to pay. In all these cases there was originally a quid pro quo; and according to the principles of natural justice the party receiving ought to pay; but the legislature has said he shall not be coerced; then comes the promise to pay the debt that is barred, the promise of the man to pay the debt of the infant, of the discharged bankrupt to restore to his creditor what by the law he had lost. In all these cases there is a moral obligation founded upon an antecedent valuable consideration. These promises therefore have a sound legal basis. They are not promises to pay something for nothing; not naked pacts; but the voluntary revival or creation of obligation which before existed in natural law, but which had been dispensed with, not for the benefit of the party obliged solely, but principally for the public convenience. If moral obligation, in its fullest sense, is a good substratum for an express promise, it is not easy to perceive why it is not equally good to support an implied promise. What a man ought to do, generally he ought to be made to do, whether he promise or refuse. But the law of society has left most of such obligations to the *interior* forum, as the tribunal of conscience has been aptly called. Is there not a moral obligation upon every son who has become affluent by means of the education and advantages bestowed upon him by his father, to relieve that father from pecuniary embarrassment, to promote his comfort and happiness, and even to share with him his riches, if thereby he will be made happy? And yet such a son may, with impunity, leave such a father in any degree of penury above that which will expose the community in which he dwells, to the danger of being obliged to preserve him from absolute want. Is not a wealthy father under strong moral obligation to advance the interest of an obedient, well disposed son, to furnish him with the means of acquiring and maintaining a becoming rank in life, to rescue him from the horrors of debt incurred by misfortune? Yet the law will uphold him in any degree of parsimony, short of that which would reduce his son to the necessity of seeking public charity.

Without doubt there are great interests of society which justify withholding the coercive arm of the law from these duties of imperfect obligation, as they are called; imperfect, not because they are less binding upon the conscience than those which are called perfect, but because the wisdom of the social law does not impose sanctions upon them.

A deliberate promise, in writing, made freely and without any mistake, one which may lead the party to whom it is made into contracts and expenses, cannot be broken without a violation of moral duty. But if there was nothing paid or promised for it, the law, perhaps wisely, leaves the execution of it to the conscience of him who makes it. It is only when the party making the promise gains something, or he to whom it is made loses something, that the law gives the promise validity. And in the case of the promise of the adult to pay the debt of the infant, of the debtor discharged by the statute of limitations or bankruptcy, the principle is preserved by looking back to the origin of the transaction, where an equivalent is to be found. An exact equivalent is not required by the law; for there being a consideration, the parties are left to estimate its value: though here the courts of equity will step in to relieve from gross inadequacy between the consideration and the promise.

These principles are deduced from the general current of decided cases upon the subject, as well as from the known maxims of the common law. The general position, that moral obligation is a sufficient consideration for an express promise, is to be limited in its application, to cases where at some time or other a good or valuable consideration has existed. . . .

[A legal obligation is always a sufficient consideration to support either an express or an implied promise; such as an infant's debt for necessaries, or a father's promise to pay for the support and education of his minor children.] But when the child shall have attained to manhood, and shall have become his own agent in the world's business, the debts he incurs, whatever may be their nature, create no obligation upon the father; and it seems to follow, that his promise founded upon such a debt has no legally binding force.

The cases of instruments under seal and certain mercantile contracts, in which considerations need not be proved, do not contradict the principles above suggested. The first import a consideration in themselves, and the second belong to a branch of the mercantile law, which has found it necessary to disregard the point of consideration in respect to instruments negotiable in their nature and essential to the interests of commerce.

Instead of citing a multiplicity of cases to support the positions I have taken, I will only refer to a very able review of all the cases in the note in 3 Bos. & Pul. 249. The opinions of the judges had been variant for a long course of years upon this subject, but there seems to be no case in which it was nakedly decided, that a promise to pay the debt of a son of full age, not living with his father, though the debt were incurred by sickness which ended in the death of the son, without a previous request by the father proved or presumed, could be enforced by action. . . .

For the foregoing reasons we are all of opinion that the non-suit directed by the Court of Common Pleas was right, and that judgment be entered thereon for costs for the defendant.

Relational Background: Levi Lives!

STUDY GUIDE: *In addition to fleshing out the events in question, Professor Watson reproduced the letter in which Seth Wyman Sr. allegedly made his promise to Daniel Mills and notes a problem with the court's interpretation of this commitment.*

GEOFFREY R. WATSON, IN THE TRIBUNAL OF CONSCIENCE: MILLS v. WYMAN RECONSIDERED, 71 TUL. L. REV. 1749, 1752-1758, 1760-1762, 1765-1768, 1806 (1997):   Levi Wyman was born on November 25, 1795, in Shrewsbury, Massachusetts, a suburb of Worcester. He was the seventh and last child of Seth and Mary Wyman. . . . Not much is known of Levi's childhood. He grew up in a relatively prosperous household, on a homestead of more than a hundred acres. It is not known what, if any, schooling he received. . . .

Sometime between 1815 and 1821, Levi left home. By 1821, according to the trial court in Mills v. Wyman, Levi "had long ceased to be a member of his father's family." Where he went, and why, is a mystery. The next we hear of him, Levi was in Hartford, Connecticut in February 1821, "on his return from a voyage at sea" — indeed, on his return from a "foreign country" — when he became very ill. . . .

The nature of Levi's illness is also a mystery. Court papers provide some tantalizing details. The illness was a protracted one: by all accounts it lasted at least two weeks. Daniel Mills, the Good Samaritan who housed and cared for Levi Wyman, arranged for two men to guard Levi for four days and nights while Levi "was in this derang'd state." Levi was so sick that "he leaped out of a chamber window to the imminent hazard of his life, and to the very great alarm of the family and the boarders." Mills provided Wyman with "1 gallon Spirits" and with "pills" provided by a Doctor Linde. Mills also hired John Lee Comstock, a prominent Hartford physician, to care for Wyman. Comstock found Levi "in a state of indisposition" and, for some time, "in a state of delirium" that required two or three persons "to prevent him from injuring himself." Although Dr. Comstock published dozens of books on subjects ranging from mineralogy to Greek history to philosophy, he left little further record of his diagnosis and treatment of Levi Wyman.

Perhaps the most interesting aspect of Levi's illness was the end of it. The Supreme Judicial Court pronounced Levi dead. It said that Mills "acted the part of the Good Samaritan, giving [Levi] shelter and comfort until he died." This finding might influence one's view of the case, since Mills is a less sympathetic plaintiff if his ministrations were ineffective.[11] But the court's report of Levi's death was somewhat exaggerated. All available evidence suggests that Levi in fact recovered and eventually settled in Springfield, Massachusetts. On March 3, 1821, Mills wrote to Levi's father, Seth Wyman, stating that "[i]t is with satisfaction that I can announce to you — that he has recovered his health in a measure so far that he has left this place a day or two since." In a postscript, Mills added: "Levi Started from here and contemplated on going home by the way of Springfield should his health

---

11. But cf. Cotnam v. Wisdom, 104 S.W. 164, 167 (Ark. 1907) (permitting restitutionary recovery by doctor even when patient died).

admit — was tolerable smart when he left here." Two of Mills's acquaintances, Nathaniel Wales and Norman Pease, also spoke of Levi's "recovery."

Moreover, there is evidence that Levi survived for years or even decades after the illness. In 1829 one Levi Wyman executed a quitclaim deed in favor of Seth Wyman, Jr., administrator of the estate of Colonel Seth Wyman. In exchange for five hundred dollars, this Levi Wyman quitclaimed all his rights in the "Real Estate whereof *my Hon. Father Seth Wyman* . . . died seized." Colonel Seth Wyman had only one son named Levi, the Levi Wyman of Mills v. Wyman. . . .

Other evidence also suggests that, while Levi outlived the Supreme Judicial Court's pronouncement of his death, he did not outgrow his habit of getting into trouble. Worcester County probate records from the 1820s and 1830s indicate that a Levi Wyman, a spendthrift and drunkard, had been assigned a legal guardian. In 1829, the Worcester County Probate Court appointed Henry Snow of Shrewsbury as guardian of "Levi Wyman of said Shrewsbury, who spends and wastes his estate by excessive drinking and idleness." The guardian's accounting of Levi's assets suggests that this is indeed our Levi Wyman, for the accounting mentions "One Bond for one hundred and fifty Dollars, signed by Seth Wyman" — presumably Seth Wyman, Jr. — and dated January 8, 1829. This was the day before Levi executed the quitclaim deed releasing his claims to any of the estate of his father. The only other property in Levi's name was "an old riding Saddle worth about one Dollar." . . .

It is not clear why the Supreme Judicial Court thought Levi was dead. No surviving court records suggest that he had died. Perhaps a stray suggestion of counsel at oral argument influenced the court; only the plaintiff's attorneys appeared in person. But it would hardly have been in Mills's interest to suggest that Levi had died while under his care.

Whatever his physical health in 1821 — sick or well, dead or alive — Levi's financial health was indisputably wretched. He was a "stranger" in Hartford, "totally unable to pay" for his room, board, and medical expenses. Those expenses amounted to about twenty-two dollars — a considerable sum in those days — and included six dollars for fourteen days' board and lodging, three dollars for "Room pine & Candles," one dollar for a gallon of "Spirits," six dollars in expenses for the two men hired to restrain Levi, and six dollars for Dr. Comstock's fee. Levi apparently did, however, volunteer that his father Seth Wyman would reimburse Mills. He was "confident that his father, Col. Seth Wyman, would readily pay" the bill. This confidence was either misplaced or feigned.

Levi Wyman left Hartford without paying Daniel Mills a penny. As Mills's acquaintances put it: "We never have known of any property of Levi Wyman since his sickness nor have we ever seen him since." The date of Levi's departure is uncertain. That date is of interest because it roughly corresponds with the date on which Seth Wyman supposedly promised to pay for Levi's expenses. Mills billed Seth for fourteen days lodging, but Mills didn't clearly indicate which fourteen days were involved. One bill carries the date February 20; another carries the date February 27. But on March 3, Mills reported to Seth Wyman that Levi Wyman had "left this place a day or two since," suggesting that Levi had left Mills's house at the very end of February or even early March. . . .

Anxious to be paid, Mills did not wait to contact Levi's father until Levi had departed. In early or middle February, Mills contacted Seth Wyman and advised him of Levi's condition. We don't have the text of Mills's first communication to Wyman, but Mills apparently suggested that Seth Wyman come see his son. On February 24, while Levi was probably still at Mills's house, Seth Wyman responded. This was the ostensible promise to pay Mills for services already rendered and the writing on which the litigation in Mills v. Wyman turned. It is worth quoting in full:

> Dear Sir
>
> I received a line from you relating to my Son Levi's sickness and requesting me to come up and see him, but as the going is very bad I cannot come up at the present, but I wish you to take all possible care of him and if you cannot have him at your house I wish you to remove him to some convenient place and if he cannot satisfy you for it I will.
> I want that you should write me again immediately how he does and greatly oblige your most obedient servant
>
> > Seth Wyman
>
> Shrewsbury Feb 24th 1821
> Mr. Daniel Mills

By this letter, Seth Wyman supposedly promised to pay Mills for services already rendered, for so-called "past consideration." But the letter does not clearly promise to pay for the services already rendered. It seems more directed at procuring future services from Daniel Mills — i.e., that he either "have him at your house" or "remove him to some convenient place." Wyman can be more fairly said to have been bargaining for future conduct and for real consideration than to have been making a sterile promise to pay for past services. The letter is understandably preoccupied with ensuring his son's safety hereafter, not in settling his debts heretofore. Not surprisingly, when the case came to trial, Wyman's first defense was that he never promised to pay Mills for past expenses.

Mills, however, interpreted Wyman's letter as a promise to pay Levi's existing debt, not just an offer to pay for future services. Mills was not concerned with arranging future accommodations for Levi. Mills wanted Levi's bill paid. By the time Mills received Seth Wyman's letter, i.e., in late February or even early March, Levi Wyman was leaving or perhaps already gone. Anxious to collect on his debt, Mills interpreted Wyman's letter as a guarantee of Levi's existing obligations. After advising Seth of Levi's departure, Mills wrote:

> [Levi] did not nor was not in any situation for to compensate me or the Phisitian in the Senst [?] For my trouble and expense I shall therefore agreeable to your Letter of guarantee make out any bill against you which you will find annexed to this — amounting to — $16.00 — Which I can assure you is more reasonable than it otherwise would have been — had it not been so unfortunate on your part — you will have the goodness to enclose said amount and forward it to me by mail as soon as convenient and oblige yours etc.
>
> > Daniel Mills
>
> City of Hartford 3d March 1821

The letter included Mills's itemized expenses and Dr. Comstock's bill for six dollars. There is no record of any response from Seth Wyman. Mills repeated his demand, to no avail, one month later. . . .

[W]hy did Seth refuse to pay the man who nursed Levi back to health? When Seth spoke of the "going being bad," did he mean his financial rather than physical health? Poverty seems an unlikely explanation for Seth's refusal to pay Mills. Seth Wyman was a man of means who became a moderately prominent citizen of his small home town. One source offers this laconic description of his life: "He had a farm and built the grist mill and saw mill. He was colonel of the militia, and selectman of the town. He was a large lumber dealer." Wyman's political career was short-lived; he served as a selectman for only one term, from 1814 to 1815. But he owned a considerable amount of property right up to the end of his life. Property records from Worcester County, for example, indicate that he bought and sold substantial amounts of real estate throughout his life. After his death in 1827, his real estate holdings were appraised at $7,924 and his personal property was valued at $2,033.76, for a grand total of almost $10,000. That was a large sum of money in those days, far more than most people earned in a year or even a decade. The probate court's inventory of the couple's possessions suggests they led a very comfortable life in the country.

Still, Seth's financial situation was not perfect. He had sizable debts. The administrator of his estate was ordered to sell $3,400 worth of property to satisfy Seth's creditors. In fact, the administrator ended up selling almost $5,000 worth of real and personal property to meet Seth's debts. Nor was Mary Wyman wealthy. She died with assets appraised at $246.78. Moreover, although Seth bought and sold property actively up until 1817, from 1817 until his death in 1827 he continued to sell real estate, but stopped buying it. Perhaps he sold land to keep cash flowing in as he grew too old to manage the family farm and the mills he had erected on it. What's more, he died intestate, even though he was survived by his wife, several children, and a number of other living relatives. The absence of a will again suggests uncertainty about his financial situation. While Seth could doubtless afford to pay Mills his $25, perhaps Seth's financial circumstances had deteriorated sufficiently that he was willing to fight a debt he did not think he owed. He took that determination with him to his grave: Seth's estate did not pay Daniel Mills anything.

One question of motive remains. Why did these two men take a twenty-five dollar dispute all the way to the Supreme Judicial Court of Massachusetts? Granted, twenty-five dollars was a significant sum of money, the equivalent of a month's pay or more, but it was not that large a sum when compared to court costs and attorney's fees. Moreover, not only did the Massachusetts court award costs to the victor, as is the practice today; it. also still followed the English rule on attorney's fees, thereby magnifying the risks of litigation for both parties. At the trial level, for example, Daniel Mills was ordered to pay Wyman's costs and fees, which totaled $10.74, $1.50 of which represented the attorney's fee. When Mills lost again on appeal, he was saddled with Wyman's costs in the Supreme Judicial Court as well; these totaled an additional $9.94, $2.50 of which represented defense counsel's fee on appeal, for a total of $20.68. In addition to all this, Mills presumably had to pay his own attorneys; he was represented by respected counsel at trial and by fairly prominent attorneys on appeal, and they presumably charged similarly for fees and costs. Thus he paid out more than he expected to win. In retrospect, it seems remarkable that either Mills or Wyman took the risk of being saddled with costs and fees that exceeded the actual amount in controversy. But they did. . . .

[M]any lawyers remember great common-law cases more for their facts than their reasoning. Ask a lawyer about the holding of Mills v. Wyman and you probably get a blank look. Ask if the lawyer remembers the case about father promising to pay the Good Samaritan for caring for the sick son, and you may get a smile of recognition. A former public defender once told me that her clients sometimes asserted they were lawyers, and she would test them by asking if they recognized the facts — not the holdings — of great cases. Mills v. Wyman is such a case. Everyone remembers the facts; no one remembers the holding.

For Mills, perhaps that is the way it should be. The rule in the case is eminently forgettable: it is as incoherent as it is inefficient. It will be a dead letter in another hundred years. But the facts of the case are memorable. Indeed, the story told by Justice Parker — Seth's hasty promise in a fleeting moment of gratitude, the death of Levi Wyman, Seth's willingness to stand up in court and be counted as a scoundrel — is more compelling than the story told by the surviving documents, in which Seth makes no promise, Levi does not die, and Seth deserves to win. For the law teacher, the reported facts are more convenient than the historical truth because they more poignantly illustrate the tension between law and morality. For the law student, the reported facts stand as a morality play for lawyers and as a reminder of the limits of the profession. The mythical facts of Mills are an important part of our legal culture. They lurk somewhere in our collective interior forum, in the tribunal of conscience.

STUDY GUIDE: In the case below, the court considers and rejects the defendant's theory about past consideration. Can that theory be reconciled with the holding in Mills? *What theory does the court adopt? Can the holding and theory in this case be reconciled with* Mills? *Should a promise to pay for the expenses of caring for livestock be treated differently than a promise to pay for the expenses of caring for children?*

BOOTHE v. FITZPATRICK
Supreme Court of Vermont,
36 Vt. 681 (1864)

BOOK ACCOUNT. The auditor reported that some time prior to the last of August, 1860, the defendant's bull was impounded by one Matthew Fox in Chittenden; that said bull by some means escaped from the pound and got into the plaintiff's pasture in Pittsford, about the 1st of September, 1860, and was kept by the plaintiff from that time until about the 20th of May following, when the defendant took him away. The plaintiff did not know who was owner of the animal, when it came into his pasture as above stated, but he made frequent inquiries in order to ascertain its owner. In the latter part of November, 1860, the plaintiff having ascertained that the defendant was the owner of said bull, sent word to the defendant that he, the plaintiff, had the defendant's bull; but it did not appear that the defendant got the word at that time. Some time after this, but at what time did not definitely appear, the plaintiff met the defendant in Pittsford, and described the bull in his possession to the defendant, who thereupon said it was his, and that he would pay him, (the plaintiff) for keeping; but also said to the plaintiff that Fox, who had impounded the bull, should pay it. Some time after the interview last referred to, the defendant went to the plaintiff in Pittsford and saw the bull, told the plaintiff that it was his, and that he would pay the plaintiff for keeping, but did not drive him away at that time. The plaintiff kept the bull through the winter, and at a reasonable time in the spring turned him out to pasture, when becoming troublesome, the plaintiff went to see the defendant in regard to taking him away. The defendant on this occasion informed the plaintiff that he would come and take him away the next day, and did, and at the same time offered the plaintiff his note for the amount charged for keeping. The plaintiff did not accept the note, but told the defendant that he might leave the amount with one Duncklee for the plaintiff, to which the defendant assented; but the defendant did not leave the amount with Duncklee, and the plaintiff's claim for keeping the bull remains unpaid. The amount charged was reasonable, and no more than a fair compensation for the keeping.

The plaintiff ascertained who the owner of the animal was, but at what time did not certainly appear, the plaintiff advertised said bull as an estray by posting up three notices in the town of Pittsford, where the bull was taken up; but no notice was published in a newspaper, although three were published in the county, nor was any copy left at the town clerk's office. Said bull was worth, when taken up and advertised as above stated, the sum of twelve dollars. The plaintiff made no entry of his claim on his book of accounts, nor did it appear that the plaintiff kept such book.

On the auditor's report, — the court, March Term, 1863, KELLOG, J., presiding, rendered a judgment in favor of the plaintiff. Exceptions by the defendant.

OPINION

PECK, J.

The defendant's counsel, without distinction between the part of the account that accrued before the defendant's promise to pay, and that which accrued after, insists that the promise was made upon a past consideration and not binding, in as much as there was never any previously existing legal obligation. As to all that part of the account that accrued after the defendant made his first promise to pay for the keeping, the plaintiff's right to recover is clear, as the subsequent keeping must be taken to have been upon the faith of that promise. When the defendant promised to take the bull away and pay for the keeping, the parties must have understood that the defendant was to pay for the keeping till he should take the bull away. As to the prior portion of the keeping, the promise was upon a past consideration, and the question is whether this is a legal objection to a recovery. It is urged that without an express promise there was at most but a moral obligation, and that a moral obligation is not sufficient to give a legally binding force to an express promise, except in cases where there had once existed a legal obligation, as in case of a debt barred by the statute of limitations or by a discharge in bankruptcy. This is so said in some reported cases, but no case is cited in which the question involved and decided establishes this as a general proposition. That it is not so, is evident from the cases in which it is decided that a minor making a contract may bind himself by a promise made after arriving at the age of majority without a new consideration. In such case there is no legal obligation previously existing, and yet the promise is binding. The same may be said of another class of cases where the consideration has enured to the benefit of the defendant, but without any request on his part, in which it is held that a subsequent promise is equivalent to a previous request, and creates a legal liability, where none existed before for want of a request. If the consideration, even without request, moves directly from the plaintiff to the defendant and enures directly to the defendant's benefit, the promise is binding, though made upon a past consideration. In this case there was such consideration. The plaintiff parted with what was of value to him, and it enured directly to the benefit of the defendant. A promise upon such past consideration is binding. This principle is fundamental and elementary, and is sustained by abundant authority. But for the defendant's promise the plaintiff could not recover for want of a request on the part of the defendant, as one can not thus be made debtor without his assent. The promise of the defendant obviates this objection, it being equivalent to a previous request. The cases cited by the defendant's counsel to show that a moral obligation is not a good consideration for an express promise, except where there had been a previous legal obligation, are not in conflict with these principles. It is true there are some expressions used by judges that taken literally without reference to the case then under consideration, would seem to be irreconcilable with this view. The language in these cases must be understood in reference to the cases in which the language is used. They were cases where the defendant had received no consideration beneficial to himself; not like this, where the defendant has received a valuable pecuniary benefit at the expense of the plaintiff.

There would be another objection to a recovery in this case in the absence of a promise by the defendant, arising from the provision of the statute prohibiting a party who takes up an estray, from recovering for keeping in case he neglects to advertise as the statute requires. But it was competent for the defendant to waive this objection, as he has done by an express promise to pay. There is no reason why he may not as well waive this defence by a promise to pay, as the defence of the statute of limitations or the defence of infancy. The plaintiff is entitled to recover his whole account.

Judgment affirmed.

STUDY GUIDE: When evaluating the court's reasoning in the next case, recall the case of Cotnam v. Wisdom in Chapter 3. Does that case (and the section in which it appears) help to provide a theory by which Webb *can be reconciled with Mills v. Wyman? Is the court correct when it says that "the services rendered by appellant were not gratuitous"? What might the court have meant by this statement?*

WEBB v. McGOWIN
Court of Appeals of Alabama,
27 Ala. App. 82, 168 So. 196 (1935)

BRICKEN, Presiding Judge.*

This action is in assumpsit. The complaint as originally filed was amended. The demurrers to the complaint as amended were sustained, and because of this adverse ruling by the court the plaintiff took a nonsuit, and the assignment of errors on this appeal are predicated upon said action or ruling of the court.

A fair statement of the case presenting the questions for decision is set out in appellant's brief, which we adopt.

[margin note: Plaintiff lost at trial, appealed to C.O.A]

On the 3d day of August, 1925, appellant while in the employ of the W. T. Smith Lumber Company, a corporation, and acting within the scope of his employment, was engaged in clearing the upper floor of mill No. 2 of the company. While so engaged he was in the act of dropping a pine block from the upper floor of the mill to the ground below; this being the usual and ordinary way of clearing the floor, and it being the duty of the plaintiff in the course of his employment to so drop it. The block weighed about 75 pounds.

As appellant was in the act of dropping the block to the ground below, he was on the edge of the upper floor of the mill. As he started to turn the block loose so that it would drop to the ground, he saw J. Greeley McGowin, testator of the defendants, on the ground below and directly under where the block would have fallen had appellant turned it loose. Had he turned it loose it would have struck McGowin with such force as to have caused him serious bodily harm or death. Appellant could have remained safely on the upper floor of the mill by turning the block loose and allowing it to drop, but had he done this the block would have fallen on McGowin and caused him serious injuries or death. The only safe and reasonable way to prevent this was for appellant to hold to the block and divert its direction in falling from the place where McGowin was standing and the only safe way to divert it so as to prevent its coming into contact with McGowin was for appellant to fall with it to the ground below. Appellant did this, and by holding to the block and falling with it to the ground below, he diverted the course of its fall in such way that McGowin was not injured. In thus preventing the injuries to McGowin appellant himself received serious bodily injuries, resulting in his right leg being broken, the heel of his right foot torn off and his right arm broken. He was badly crippled for life and rendered unable to do physical or mental labor.

On September 1, 1925, in consideration of appellant having prevented him from sustaining death or serious bodily harm and in consideration of the injuries appellant had received, McGowin agreed with him to care for and maintain him for the remainder of appellant's life at the rate of $15 every two weeks from the time he sustained his injuries to and during the remainder of appellant's life; it being agreed that McGowin would pay this sum to appellant

[margin note: Promise made after performance]

---

*Frank B. Bricken (1875-1951) graduated from the University of Alabama Law School with honors (1894). After his admission to the Alabama bar in the same year, Bricken established a private practice. He served as the city attorney of Luverne (1890-1893), the mayor of Luverne (1893-1896), and solicitor of the second judicial circuit (1899-1916). In 1916, Bricken was elected to the Court of Appeals of Alabama, where he continued to serve through reelection until his death. — J.B.

for his maintenance. Under the agreement McGowin paid or caused to be paid to appellant the sum so agreed on up until McGowin's death on January 1, 1934. After his death the payments were continued to and including January 27, 1934, at which time they were discontinued. Thereupon plaintiff brought suit to recover the unpaid installments accruing up to the time of the bringing of the suit.

The material averments of the different counts of the original complaint and the amended complaint are predicated upon the foregoing statement of facts.

In other words, the complaint as amended averred in substance: (1) That on August 3, 1925, appellant saved J. Greeley McGowin, appellee's testator, from death or grievous bodily harm; (2) that in doing so appellant sustained bodily injury crippling him for life; (3) that in consideration of the services rendered and the injuries received by appellant, McGowin agreed to care for him the remainder of appellant's life, the amount to be paid being $15 every two weeks; (4) that McGowin complied with this agreement until he died on January 1, 1934, and the payments were kept up to January 27, 1934, after which they were discontinued.

The action was for the unpaid installments accruing after January 27, 1934, to the time of the suit.

The principal grounds of demurrer to the original and amended complaint are: (1) It states no cause of action; (2) its averments show the contract was without consideration; (3) it fails to allege that McGowin had, at or before the services were rendered, agreed to pay appellant for them; (4) the contract declared on is void under the statute of frauds.

1. The averments of the complaint show that appellant saved McGowin from death or grievous bodily harm. This was a material benefit to him of infinitely more value than any financial aid he could have received. Receiving this benefit, McGowin became morally bound to compensate appellant for the services rendered. Recognizing his moral obligation, he expressly agreed to pay appellant as alleged in the complaint and complied with this agreement up to the time of his death; a period of more than 8 years.

[Had McGowin been accidentally poisoned and a physician, without his knowledge or request, had administered an antidote, thus saving his life, a subsequent promise by McGowin to pay the physician would have been valid. Likewise, McGowin's agreement as disclosed by the complaint to compensate appellant for saving him from death or grievous bodily injury is valid and enforceable.] → Analogy

Where the promisee cares for, improves, and preserves the property of the promisor, though done without his request, it is sufficient consideration for the promisor's subsequent agreement to pay for the service, because of the material benefit received. . . .

In Boothe v. Fitzpatrick, 36 Vt. 681, the court held that a promise by defendant to pay for the past keeping of a bull which had escaped from defendant's premises and been cared for by plaintiff was valid, although there was no previous request, because the subsequent premise obviated that objection; it being equivalent to a previous request. On the same principle, had the promisee saved the promisor's life or his body from grievous harm, his subsequent promise to pay for the services rendered would have been valid. Such service would have been far more material than caring for his bull. Any holding that saving a man from death or grievous bodily harm is not a material benefit sufficient to uphold a subsequent promise to pay for the service, necessarily rests on the assumption that saving life and preservation of the body from harm have only a sentimental value. The converse of this is true. Life and preservation of the body have material, pecuniary values, measurable in dollars and cents. Because of this, physicians practice their profession charging for services rendered in saving life and curing the body of its ills, and surgeons perform operations. The same is true as to the law of negligence, authorizing the assessment of damages in personal injury cases based upon the extent of the injuries, earnings, and life expectancies of those injured.

In the business of life insurance, the value of a man's life is measured in dollars and cents according to his expectancy, the soundness of his body, and his ability to pay premiums. The same is true as to health and accident insurance.

It follows that if, as alleged in the complaint, appellant saved J. Greeley McGowin from death or grievous bodily harm, and McGowin subsequently agreed to pay him for the service rendered, it became a valid and enforceable contract.

2. It is well settled that a moral obligation is a sufficient consideration to support a subsequent promise to pay where the promisor has received a material benefit, although there was no original duty or liability resting on the promisor. . . . In the case of State ex rel Bayer v. Funk, [105 Or. 134, 199 P. 592, 209 P. 113,] the court held that a moral obligation is a sufficient consideration to support an executory promise where the promisor has received an actual pecuniary or material benefit for which he subsequently expressly promised to pay.

The case at bar is clearly distinguishable from that class of cases where the consideration is a mere moral obligation or conscientious duty unconnected with receipt by promisor of benefits of a material or pecuniary nature. Park Falls State Bank v. Fordyce, [206 Wis. 628, 238 N.W. 516]. Here the promisor received a material benefit constituting a valid consideration for his promise.

3. Some authorities hold that, for a moral obligation to support a subsequent promise to pay, there must have existed a prior legal or equitable obligation, which for some reason had become unenforceable, but for which the promisor was still morally bound. This rule, however, is subject to qualification in those cases where the promisor, having received a material benefit from the promisee, is morally bound to compensate him for the services rendered and in consideration of this obligation promises to pay. In such cases the subsequent promise to pay is an affirmance or ratification of the services rendered carrying with it the presumption that a previous request for the service was made. . . .

Under the decisions above cited, McGowin's express promise to pay appellant for the services rendered was an affirmance or ratification of what appellant had done raising the presumption that the services had been rendered at McGowin's request.

4. The averments of the complaint show that in saving McGowin from death or grievous bodily harm, appellant was crippled for life. This was part

of the consideration of the contract declared on. McGowin was benefited. Appellant was injured. Benefit to the promisor or injury to the promisee is a sufficient legal consideration for the promisor's agreement to pay. . . .

5. Under the averments of the complaint the services rendered by appellant were not gratuitous. The agreement of McGowin to pay and the acceptance of payment by appellant conclusively shows the contrary. . . .

From what has been said, we are of the opinion that the court below erred in the ruling complained of; that is to say, in sustaining the demurrer, and for this error the case is reversed and remanded.

Reversed and remanded.

SAMFORD, J.* (concurring).

The questions involved in this case are not free from doubt, and perhaps the strict letter of the rule, as stated by judges, though not always in accord, would bar a recovery by plaintiff, but following the principle announced by Chief Justice Marshall in Hoffman v. Porter, Fed. Cas. No. 6,577, 2 Brock. 156, 159, where he says "I do not think that law ought to be separated from justice, where it is at most doubtful," I concur in the conclusions reached by the court.

WEBB v. McGOWIN
Supreme Court of Alabama,
232 Ala. 374, 168 So. 199 (1936)

FOSTER, J.**

We do not in all cases in which we deny a petition for certiorari to the Court of Appeals approve the reasoning and principles declared in the opinion, even though no opinion is rendered by us. It does not always seem to be important that they be discussed, and we exercise a discretion in that respect. But when the opinion of the Court of Appeals asserts important principles or their application to new situations, and it may be uncertain whether this court agrees with it in all respects, we think it advisable to be specific in that respect when the certiorari is denied. We think such a situation here exists.

Neither this court nor the Court of Appeals has had before it questions similar to those here presented, though we have held that the state may

* *William Hodges Samford* (1866-1940) was a student at the Alabama Agricultural and Mechanical College (now Alabama Polytechnical Institute) and was admitted to the Alabama bar in 1894. He practiced law in Troy (1894-1909) and Montgomery (1909-1917) and concurrently served as prosecuting attorney for the Law Court of Pike County (1895-1902), city attorney of Troy (1901-1907), and as a member of the Alabama Constitutional Convention (1901). He moved to the bench of the Alabama Court of Appeals in 1917 and remained there until his death. — K.T.

** *Arthur Borders Foster* (1872-1958) was educated at the University of Alabama (A.B., LL.B.). He practiced law at Troy, Alabama (1891-1915), served as register in chancery (1892-1898), and was a member of the Alabama House of Representatives (1903). In 1915, Foster was appointed judge of the 12th Judicial Circuit, from which position he resigned in 1923; thereafter, he practiced in Birmingham, Alabama, until his appointment to the Supreme Court of Alabama in 1928. He became Supernumerary Justice of the court in 1953, which position he held until his death. — K.T.

recognize a moral obligation, and pay it or cause it to be paid by a county, or city. . . .

Those cases do not mean to affirm that the state may recompense for nice ethical obligations, or do the courteous or generous act, without a material and substantial claim to payment, though it is not enforceable by law; nor that an executory obligation may be so incurred.

The opinion of the Court of Appeals here under consideration recognizes and applies the distinction between a supposed moral obligation of the promisor, based upon some refined sense of ethical duty, without material benefit to him, and one in which such a benefit did in fact occur. We agree with that court that if the benefit be material and substantial, and was to the person of the promisor rather than to his estate, it is within the class of material benefits which he has the privilege of recognizing and compensating either by an executed payment or an executory promise to pay. The cases are cited in that opinion. The reason is emphasized when the compensation is not only for the benefits which the promisor received, but also for the injuries either to the property or person of the promisee by reason of the service rendered.

Writ denied. ──> They declined to take the case

Relational Background: Was a Promise Made?

RICHARD DANZIG & GEOFFREY R. WATSON, THE CAPABILITY PROBLEM IN CONTRACTS (2D ED. 2004): There are a variety of accounts of the accident in the lumber mill at the W. T. Smith Lumber Company on the morning of August 3, 1925. Charles Howard Webb, Webb's grandson, visited the mill and has this understanding of the facts:

> [T]hey would take big logs and turn it into lumber. Now, part of a log, when they turn it into lumber, turns into waste. You have slabs that are cut off, which is the bark and stuff, and all that becomes . . . some of it is salvageable. . . . All of that waste was put on a conveyor that went several hundred feet away from the plant, and several feet high, to a burn pile. They had a chain, and pieces of metal attached to that chain, pick up scrap, take all way to end, drop into burn pile. To support the structure that the chain was on, you had a post . . . and sometimes lumber not properly placed on that chain would turn sideways, get caught on the post [and] actually stop the chain from moving. It would be a logjam.
>
> My grandfather had to go up and free up a logjam. Well, the piece of lumber that was causing it was big enough that he could just barely pick it up. He got it to the point where he could throw it off the chain and dispose of it. As he was getting ready to throw it, Mr. McGowin was on the spot where it would have landed. So he diverted it to go away from McGowin, and in the process he fell. . . . He followed the piece of lumber down. It resulted in a serious injury to [his] hip and leg. It was probably something [that would be] correctable today. [But it] was not [then].

[T]he McGowin estate seemed to acknowledge at least that Webb acted to protect McGowin from "danger." In its answer, the estate generally denied the allegations of the complaint but also alleged that J. Freeley McGowin was inspecting the works and machinery of the plant of . . . W. T. Smith Lumber Company; that the plaintiff was working on the upper floor of one of the mills of said lumber company removing some pieces of sawed-off timbers throwing the same to the ground floor; that as said J. Greeley McGowin approached the point where plaintiff was working, the plaintiff was about to throw down a piece of timber; that plaintiff seeing the danger of [sic] said J. Greeley McGowin, undertook to catch or intercept the falling timber and lost his balance and fell, thereby sustaining the injuries complained of.

. . .

The parties, however, had sharply different positions on whether any promise was made at all, what its content was, and whether it was made by Mr. Greeley or one of his employees. In an answer to interrogatories, the plaintiff asserted that "the wife and daughter of the plaintiff . . . witnessed a statement made by Mr. McGowin to the plaintiff" to pay Webb, in accordance with the court's reported version of the facts. But the estate's position was that McGowin made no such promise at all; that at most he merely instructed his bookkeeper to pay Webb; and that the term of such payments was to be limited by the statutory period for Workmen's Compensation. . . .

Accordingly, the McGowin estate . . . took the position that McGowin never made the promise alleged — or at least not the precise promise alleged. According to Calvin Poole III, grandson of the Calvin Poole who handled the case for the McGowin estate, McGowin never made a promise directly to Webb. Instead, Poole says, McGowin instructed the company bookkeeper to send Webb $15 every two weeks in accordance with the Workmen's Compensation statute. . . .

The estate also took the position, in the alternative, that even if McGowin did make some sort of oral promise to Webb, it was nothing more than a promise to make Workmen's Compensation payments — which, under Alabama law, would indeed have amounted to $15 every two weeks, but only for 300 weeks, not for life. "When the statutory requirements for the payment of workmen's compensation benefits ran out," the estate's attorneys argued, "Mr. McGowin, purely out of the kindness of his heart and prompted by appreciation for what Mr. Webb had done for him, caused W. T. Smith Lumber Company to continue the payments paid to Mr. Webb." . . .

After the Alabama Supreme Court decision came down, . . . the estate agreed to pay Webb a lump sum of $900 in exchange for dismissal of the suit. This sum represented less than three years' worth of payments, much less than Webb would have received had he collected $15 every two weeks until he died in 1943 or 1944. (If a court had awarded Webb the $15 payments retroactive to January 1934, Webb would have received a total of at least $3,500, although most of it would have come in $15 installments.) And Webb doubtless had to use some of the $900 settlement to pay his attorney, who did not normally work for free.

At least two of Joe Webb's grandchildren think that the McGowin family — most likely Mr. Greeley himself — also gave Webb use of a home and several acres of land outside Georgiana. These grandchildren have detailed memories of visiting that property while one or both grandparents lived there. This arrangement does not seem to have been part of the formal settlement in the case. Charles Howard Webb speculates that before Mr. Greeley died, he made an "oral agreement" with Joe Webb in which he gave Webb and his wife use of the house and land until they both passed away. When asked about such an arrangement, both Calvin Poole III and Pete Hamilton — grandsons of lawyers on each side — say they know nothing about it.

Calvin Poole came to regret the decision to settle, and some of the McGowins may have as well. Long afer Poole settled the case, he remembered it this way:

> There was no basis for a claim against the McGowin estate, and such a claim could not have been proven. The case was settled on the basis of expediency alone. It was desired to settle the administration of the estate, and the executors decided to settle the lawsuit for a more or less nominal sum rather than incur the expense and inconvenience of delaying the settlement of the estate.
>
> In the light of afterthought and for the vindication of the McGowin family in the court records, it would probably have been better to have had the record clarified by following up the case after reversal and requiring the plaintiff to prove the averments of his complaints.

Or, as Poole's grandson puts it today:

> Papa (my grandfather) always said that if he had known of the widespread publicity which the case would receive, he would have taken the case to trial so as to clear the McGowin family name. I always wondered if he weren't just as concerned about the Poole family name, since our name goes down in the law books as having lost the case in the Alabama Supreme Court.

Powell & Hamilton [Webb's law firm], for its part, doesn't seem to have regarded Webb v. McGowin as its most important case. C. E. Hamilton's grandson recalls that when Dempsey Powell was called on to eulogize Hamilton, Powell didn't list Webb v. McGowin among Hamilton's great successes. To be sure, Powell himself, rather than Hamilton, did most of the work on *Webb*. But there's no evidence that Powell thought of the case as his most important victory. The lawyer who now runs the office, Pete Hamilton, says he doesn't keep any mementos to the case on his office walls. To an experienced litigator like Dempsey Powell, a case that settled for $900 probably didn't rank among his most storied successes.

RESTATEMENT (SECOND) OF CONTRACTS

§86. PROMISE FOR BENEFIT RECEIVED   *(Webb v. McGowin)*

(1) A promise made in recognition of a benefit previously received by the promisor from the promisee is binding to the extent necessary to prevent injustice.

(2) A promise is not binding under Subsection (1)

(a) if the promisee conferred the benefit as a gift or for other reasons the promisor has not been unjustly enriched; or

(b) to the extent that its value is disproportionate to the benefit.

REFERENCE: Barnett, §4.2.2
                  Farnsworth, §2.8
                  Calamari & Perillo, §5.2
                  Murray, §68(B)

C.   CONTRACT MODIFICATION AND THE PREEXISTING DUTY RULE

We now shift our focus from initial contract formation to the attempts by parties to adjust their contractual obligations during the performance stage of the contract. The issue arises as to whether a promise to modify a pre-existing contractual relationship is enforceable. In this section, we read cases concerning whether the enforcement of such promises requires additional bargained-for consideration. We shall return to the topic of contract modification in Chapter 16 when we will take up the problem of one party using improper means to coerce the other to modify the contract.

STUDY GUIDE: Although the preexisting duty rule is a logical extension of the bargain theory of consideration, it has been heavily criticized. When reading the next few cases, consider the relationship between the rule governing enforceability provided by the consideration doctrine and the principles and policies that the rule is intended to serve. Are the problems inherent in enforcing promises made within an already existing contract the same as those which arise when first forming a contract? How might any differences justify a different doctrinal approach to the problem?

HARRIS v. WATSON
King's Bench,
Peake Rep. 102, 170 Eng. Rep. 94 [1791]

In this case the declaration stated, that the plaintiff being a seaman on board the ship "Alexander," of which the defendant was master and commander, and which was bound on a voyage to Lisbon: whilst the ship was on her voyage, the defendant, in consideration that the plaintiff would perform some extra work, in navigating the ship, promised to pay him five guineas over and above his common wages. There were other counts for work and labour, &c. The plaintiff proved that the ship being in danger, the defendant, to induce the seamen to exert themselves, made the promise stated in the first count.

LORD KENYON. — If this action was to be supported, it would materially affect the navigation of this kingdom. It has been long since determined, that when the freight is lost, the wages are also lost. This rule was founded on a principle of policy, for if sailors were in all events to have their wages, and in times of danger entitled to insist on an extra charge on such a promise as this, they would in many cases suffer a ship to sink, unless the captain would pay any extravagant demand they might think proper to make.

The plaintiff was nonsuited. → *Holding* *Dismissing case as a matter of law for the defendant*

[margin handwritten: In case involving seaman sailor clause to contractual obligation can't be made due to policy reason of perverse incentives]

STUDY GUIDE: In the next case, Lord Ellenborough faces a case very similar to that faced by Lord Kenyon in Harris v. Watson. How does his approach and reasoning to the problem differ from Lord Kenyon's approach? Why might a judge favor one approach over the other?

STILK v. MYRICK
Court of Common Pleas,
2 Camp. 317, 170 Eng. Rep. 1168 [1809]

This was an action for seaman's wages, on a voyage from London to the Baltic and back.

By the ship's articles, executed before the commencement of the voyage, the plaintiff was to be paid at the rate of £5 a month, and the principal question in the cause was, whether he was entitled to a higher rate of wages? — In the course of the voyage two of the seamen deserted; and the captain having in vain attempted to supply their places at Cronstadt, there entered into an agreement with the rest of the crew, that they should have the wages of the two who had deserted equally divided among them, if he could not procure two other hands at Gottenburgh. This was found impossible; and the ship was worked back to London by the plaintiff and eight more of the original crew, with whom the agreement had been made at Cronstadt.

[margin handwritten: Contractual obligation]

[margin handwritten: Modification of contractual terms]

Garrow for the defendant insisted, that this agreement was contrary to public policy, and utterly void. In West India voyages, crews are often thinned greatly by death and desertion; and if a promise of advanced wages were valid, exorbitant claims would be set up on all such occasions. This ground was strongly taken by Lord Kenyon in Harris v. Watson, Peak. Cas. 72, where that learned Judge held, that no action would lie at the suit of a sailor on a promise of a captain to pay him extra wages, in consideration of his doing more than the ordinary share of duty in navigating the ship; and his Lordship said, that if such a promise could be enforced, sailors would in many cases suffer a ship to sink unless the captain would accede to any extravagant demand they might think proper to make.

[margin handwritten: Policy reasons of sailors thwarting their ships for higher pay?]

The Attorney-General, contra, distinguished the case from Harris v. Watson, as the agreement here was made on shore, when there was no danger or pressing emergency, and when the captain could not be supposed to be under any constraint or apprehension. The mariners were not to be permitted on any sudden danger to force concessions from the captain; — but why should they be deprived of the compensation he voluntarily offers them in perfect security for their extra labour during the remainder of the voyage?

[margin handwritten: Plaintiff's argument that this case is different b/c the ship wasn't in danger at the time of modification]

LORD ELLENBOROUGH.* — I think Harris v. Watson was rightly decided; but I doubt whether the ground of public policy, upon which Lord Kenyon is stated to have proceeded, be the true principle on which the decision is to be supported. Here, I say, the agreement is void for want of consideration. There was no consideration for the ulterior pay promised to the mariners who remained with the ship. Before they sailed from London they had undertaken to do all that they could under all the emergencies of the voyage. They had sold all their services till the voyage should be completed. If they had been at liberty to quit the vessel at Cronstadt, the case would have been quite different; or if the captain had capriciously discharged the two men who were wanting, the others might not have been compellable to take the whole duty upon themselves, and their agreeing to do so might have been a sufficient consideration for the promise of an advance of wages. But the desertion of a part of the crew is to be considered an emergency of the voyage as much as their death; and those who remain are bound by the terms of their original contract to exert themselves to the utmost to bring the ship in safely to her destined port. Therefore, without looking to the policy of this agreement, I think it is void for want of consideration, and that the plaintiff can only recover at the rate of £5 a month.

Verdict accordingly.

STUDY GUIDE: Are the circumstances in the next case identical to those in the preceding case? Can one outcome be justified more easily than the other?

ALASKA PACKERS' ASS'N v. DOMENICO
United States Circuit Court of Appeals, Ninth Circuit,
117 F. 99 (1902)

Appeal from the District Court of the United States for the Northern District of California. . . .

ROSS, Circuit Judge.** The libel in this case was based upon a contract alleged to have been entered into between the libelants and the appellant corporation on the 22d day of May, 1900, at Pyramid Harbor, Alaska, by which it is claimed the appellant promised to pay each of the libelants,

* *Edward Law*, Lord Ellenborough (1750-1818) was admitted as a student at Lincoln's Inn in 1769. In 1771, Law became a pupil in a private London office. He worked as a pleader for five years before he was called to the bar in 1780. He was made a king's counsel in 1787, and later that year was elected a bencher of the Inner Temple, where he served until appointed in 1793 to the post of attorney-general and Serjeant of the County Palantine of Lancaster. He was knighted in 1802 by George III and served briefly in the House of Commons until he was appointed Lord Chief Justice of England later that year, which he remained at his death. — K.T.

** *Erskine Mayo Ross* (1845-1925) graduated Virginia Military Institute and was admitted to the California bar in 1869. He soon began his judicial career, being appointed justice of the Supreme Court of California in 1879. He resigned that post to serve on the U.S. District Court for the Southern District of California (1886-1895). He served as U.S. Circuit Judge for the Ninth Circuit (1895-1911) and was judge on the U.S. Circuit Court of Appeals from 1912 until his death. — K.T.

among other things, the sum of $100 for services rendered and to be rendered. In its answer the respondent denied the execution, on its part, of the contract sued upon, averred that it was without consideration, and for a third defense alleged that the work performed by the libelants for it was performed under other and different contracts than that sued on, and that, prior to the filing of the libel, each of the libelants was paid by the respondent the full amount due him thereunder, in consideration of which each of them executed a full release of all his claims and demands against the respondent.

The evidence shows without conflict that on March 26, 1900, at the city and county of San Francisco, the libelants entered into a written contract with the appellants, whereby they agreed to go from San Francisco to Pyramid Harbor, Alaska, and return, on board such vessel as might be designated by the appellant, and to work for the appellant during the fishing season of 1900, at Pyramid Harbor, as sailors and fishermen, agreeing to do "regular ship's duty, both up and down, discharging and loading; and to do any other work whatsoever when requested to do so by the captain or agent of the Alaska Packers' Association." By the terms of this agreement, the appellant was to pay each of the libelants $50 for the season, and two cents for each red salmon in the catching of which he took part.

On the 15th day of April, 1900, 21 of the libelants signed shipping articles by which they shipped as seamen on the Two Brothers, a vessel chartered by the appellant for the voyage between San Francisco and Pyramid Harbor, and also bound themselves to perform the same work for the appellant provided for by the previous contract of March 26th; the appellant agreeing to pay them therefor the sum of $60 for the season, and two cents each for each red salmon in the catching of which they should respectively take part. Under these contracts, the libelants sailed on board the Two Brothers for Pyramid Harbor, where the appellants had about $150,000 invested in a salmon cannery. The libelants arrived there early in April of the year mentioned, and began to unload the vessel and fit up the cannery. A few days thereafter, to wit, May 19th, they stopped work in a body, and demanded of the company's superintendent there in charge $100 for services in operating the vessel to and from Pyramid Harbor, instead of the sums stipulated for in and by the contracts; stating that unless they were paid this additional wage they would stop work entirely, and return to San Francisco. The evidence showed, and the court below found, that it was impossible for the appellant to get other men to take the places of the libelants, the place being remote, the season short and just opening; so that, after endeavoring for several days without success to induce the libelants to proceed with their work in accordance with their contracts, the company's superintendent, on the 22d day of May, so far yielded to their demands as to instruct his clerk to copy the contracts executed in San Francisco, including the words "Alaska Packers' Association" at the end, substituting, for the $50 and $60 payments, respectively, of those contracts, the sum of $100, which document, so prepared, was signed by the libelants before a shipping commissioner whom they had requested to be brought from Northeast Point; the superintendent, however, testifying that he at the time told the libelants that he was without authority to enter into any such contract, or to in any way alter the contracts made between them and the company in San Francisco. [Upon the return of the libelants to San Francisco at the close of the fishing season, they demanded pay in accordance with the terms of the alleged contract of May 22d, when the company denied its validity, and refused to pay other than as provided for by the contracts of March 26th and April 5th, respectively.] Some of the libelants, at least, consulted counsel, and, after receiving his advice, those of them who had signed the shipping articles before the shipping commissioner at San Francisco went before that officer, and received the amount due them thereunder, executing in consideration thereof a release in full, and the others paid at the office of the company, also receipting in full for their demands.

On the trial in the court below, the libelants undertook to show that the fishing nets provided by the respondent were defective, and that it was on that account that they demanded increased wages. On that point, the evidence was substantially conflicting, and the finding of the court was against the libelants, the court saying:

> The contention of libelants that the nets provided them were rotten and unserviceable is not sustained by the evidence. The defendants' interest required that libelants should be provided with every facility necessary to their success as fishermen, for on such success depended the profits defendant would be able to realize that season from its packing plant, and the large capital invested therein. In view of this self-evident fact, it is highly improbable that the defendant gave libelants rotten and unserviceable nets with which to fish. It follows from this finding that libelants were not justified in refusing performance of their original contract.

112 Fed. 554.

The evidence being sharply conflicting in respect to these facts, the conclusions of the court, who heard and saw the witnesses, will not be disturbed. . . .

The real questions in the case as brought here are questions of law, and, in the view that we take of the case, it will be necessary to consider but one of those. Assuming that the appellant's superintendent at Pyramid Harbor was authorized to make the alleged contract of May 22d, and that he executed it on behalf of the appellant, was it supported by a sufficient consideration? From the foregoing statement of the case, it will have been seen that the libelants agreed in writing, for certain stated compensation, to render their services to the appellant in remote waters where the season for conducting fishing operations is extremely short, and in which enterprise the appellant had a large amount of money invested; and, after having entered upon the discharge of their contract, and at a time when it was impossible for the appellant to secure other men in their places, the libelants, without any valid cause, absolutely refused to continue the services they were under contract to perform unless the appellant would consent to pay them more money. Consent to such a demand, under such circumstances, if given, was, in our opinion, without consideration, for the reason that it was based solely upon the libelants' agreement to render the exact services, and none other, that they were already under contract to render. The case shows that they willfully and arbitrarily broke that obligation. As a matter of course, they were liable to the appellant in damages, and it is quite probable, as suggested by the court below in its opinion, that they may have been unable to respond in damages. But we are unable to agree with the conclusions there drawn, from these facts, in these words:

> Under such circumstances, it would be strange, indeed, if the law would not permit the defendant to waive the damages caused by the libelants' breach, and enter into the contract sued upon, — a contract mutually beneficial to all the parties thereto, in that it gave to the libelants reasonable compensation for their labor, and enabled the defendant to employ to advantage the large capital it had invested in its canning and fishing plant.

Certainly, it cannot be justly held, upon the record in this case, that there was any voluntary waiver on the part of the appellant of the breach of the original contract. The company itself knew nothing of such breach until the expedition returned to San Francisco, and the testimony is uncontradicted that its superintendent at Pyramid Harbor, who, it is claimed, made on its behalf the contract sued on, distinctly informed the libelants that he had no power to alter the original or to make a new contract; and it would, of course, follow that, if he had no power to change the original, he would have no authority to waive any rights thereunder. The circumstances of the present case bring it, we think, directly within the sound and just observations of the supreme court of Minnesota in the case of King v. Railway Co., 61 Minn. 482, 63 N.W. 1105:

> No astute reasoning can change the plain fact that the party who refuses to perform, and thereby coerces a promise from the other party to the contract to pay him an increased compensation for doing that which he is legally bound to do, takes an unjustifiable advantage of the necessities of the other party. Surely it would be a travesty on justice to hold that the party so making the promise for extra pay was estopped from asserting that the promise was without consideration. A party cannot lay the foundation of an estoppel by his own wrong, where the promise is simply a repetition of a subsisting legal promise. There can be no consideration for the promise of the other party, and there is no warrant for inferring that the parties have voluntarily rescinded or modified their contract. The promise cannot be legally enforced, although the other party has completed his contract in reliance upon it. . . .

It results from the views above expressed that the judgment must be reversed, and the cause remanded, with directions to the court below to enter judgment for the respondent, with costs. It is so ordered.

Relational Background: Were the Fishing Nets Really Rotten?

STUDY GUIDE: *Though she provides a good deal more background information on this case than there is space for here — particularly information on "the Fish Trust" and the financial wherewithal of the Alaska Packers' Association — in the following excerpt, Professor Deborah Threedy questions the "self-evident fact" that Alaska Packers shared the same interest as the fishermen in maximizing the catch of salmon and therefore had no motive to supply deficient nets. When reading her "alternative narratives," ask yourself what difference, if any, they should make to the outcome of this case had they been proved at trial.*

DEBORA L. THREEDY, A FISH STORY: ALASKA PACKERS' ASSOCIATION v. DOMENICO, 2000 UTAH L. REV. 185, 201, 208-212, 219-220:   The cannery at Pyramid Harbor was the site of the confrontation between the fishermen and the company which led to the law suit. The Pyramid Harbor cannery was one of eighteen canneries Alaska Packers was operating in 1900. Pyramid Harbor is located on Chilkat Inlet, about eighty miles north of Juneau, Alaska. It is on the western side of the Inlet, a mile and a half south of Pyramid Island. The harbor "consists of a small cove in which two or three vessels may find anchorage." . . .

A.   THE QUESTION OF THE NETS

At trial the fishermen justified their refusal to work by arguing that Alaska Packers had provided them with substandard nets. The trial court, however, rejected this argument. Although all three of the libelants' witnesses testified that the nets were in poor condition, the court found that this contention was "not sustained by the evidence."

One possible reading of the trial transcript in the *Alaska Packers'* case is that the nets provided by the Alaska Packers were indeed serviceable, but that the fishermen did not realize this, due in large part to differences in language and experience. A review of the individual libelants quickly reveals that most were Italians. Testimony at the trial indicated that most were immigrants and that the majority did not speak English. An interpreter was present and, on at least one occasion, used at trial. The transcript itself indicates some language problems.

In addition, it appears that for most of the fishermen this was their first year fishing at Pyramid Harbor, although they testified they had experience in other places. The trial testimony strongly suggests that the type of nets used at Pyramid Harbor was different than the type used at other places, such as on the Columbia River.

The Pyramid Harbor fishermen used gill nets exclusively, which were supplied by the company. The nets from top to bottom are sixteen to eighteen feet deep (also described as thirty-two meshes deep). At Pyramid Harbor, each year the top sixteen meshes of the net were new; however, the bottom meshes were not. The bottom meshes were recycled from the top of the preceding year's net.

Apparently, reusing the nets in this way was unique to Pyramid Harbor. There was testimony at trial that on the Columbia River in Oregon and at Orca in Alaska the nets were new each year. The fishermen's complaints about the nets at trial appear to have focused on the old, reused portion of the nets. They testified that the nets were hanging in the cannery and that they could tear the meshes by pulling on them with two fingers. One testified that the fish broke right through the bottom of the nets where the mesh was old.

Murray, the superintendent of the cannery, testified that the reason for reusing the nets in this way was because fish are only caught in the upper portion of the net, the top seven or eight meshes. The lower part of the net is there merely to keep the net hanging properly. The reason that fish are only caught in the upper portion of the net at Pyramid Harbor had to do with the conditions of the water where they were fishing. At the point in the channel where they were fishing, the fresh river water floats on top of the denser salt water to a depth of six or seven feet. Because the salmon were found only in the muddy, nutrient-rich, fresh water, there was new netting for the top six or seven feet of the net, where the fish would be. The fish did not strike in the clear salt water that lay below the fresh river water.

Murray testified that when the men first complained to him about the nets, on May 19th, "I explained the way we fished, and the way we got our fish." He also was of the opinion that the few fishermen who had been at Pyramid Harbor before understood about the nets and "could fully explain the kinds of nets we used," although he did not know whether they had. Given the fishermen's language difficulties, and assuming that Murray did not speak Italian, the possibility exists that the men's understanding of what Murray was saying was incomplete.

Assuming for the moment that the fishermen did not understand that the nets were perfectly adequate for fishing at Pyramid Harbor, the case takes on a different complexion. Their misunderstanding might not have affected the ultimate outcome of the case because, after all, there still would not have been justification in fact for their strike. However, any suggestion of duress would have disappeared, as the fishermen would have had a good faith, albeit mistaken, reason for refusing to work.

B. DIVERGENT INTERESTS: AN ASSUMPTION CALLED INTO QUESTION

Another distinct possibility is that the nets were indeed substandard. The court disbelieved the fishermen because the court assumed that Alaska Packers' self-interest would lead it to furnish the fishermen with good nets. The court took it as a "self-evident fact" that Alaska Packers would provide adequate gear "for on (the fishermen's) success depended the profits defendant would be able to realize that season from its packing plant, and the large capital invested therein." The court thus assumed that the fishermen and Alaska Packers both wished to maximize the number of fish caught. This line of reasoning, however, over-simplifies the economics of the salmon canning industry at the turn of the century. While the fishermen certainly wanted to maximize the number of fish they caught, it should not be assumed that the cannery wanted to as well.

Certainly, the fishermen's self-interest would lead them to want to catch as many fish as possible. At the turn of the century, Alaskan fishermen's wages were made up of two components: "run money" and the price paid per fish.

From the earliest days of the industry fishermen sent to Alaska from the United States proper customarily have manned the company vessels on the voyage to and from the salmon fields. For this service they are paid what is known as "run money" — a flat sum for the season negotiated in advance. . . . [12]

The run money included payment for anything that was not fishing. As the testimony at trial showed, the fishermen were expected not only to sail the vessel from San Francisco to Pyramid Harbor, but also to unload supplies for the cannery, clean and mend the fishing nets and other equipment, close up the cannery at the end of the season, and load the packed cases of canned salmon onto the ship.

The greatest part of the fishermen's earnings, however, came from the price paid per fish. The original contract gave the men $50 in "run money" and four cents per red salmon per boat. As two men manned each boat, this worked out to two cents per man per fish.

Conversely, the canneries needed the fishermen to catch sufficient fish, but not too many. There were no facilities in 1900 for preserving the fish until they could be canned. Moreover, canning the fish was a very labor intensive operation. If the salmon harvest was too bountiful, the cannery workers would not be able to keep up and fish would rot before they could be canned.

Exactly this situation occurred in British Columbia in 1897: "[s]almon ran in vast numbers that year. . . . The vast numbers of fish delivered each day exceeded the cannery capacity. Until strict limits per boat were imposed on the fishermen, large amounts of salmon lay rotting in trenches dug to receive the overflow."[13] . . . In 1900, the government inspector for the Alaskan canneries commented that the waste in the Bristol Bay district was "strikingly large."

As it turned out, the salmon run during the 1900 season was exceptionally large. "From all parts of Alaska come reports of a large and steady run of salmon: The number of cases packed this year in Alaskan waters will be the greatest on record."[14] At least for Alaska Packers, this prediction proved true: in 1900 for the first time the total pack exceeded one million cases. Of course, in May when the fishermen made their demands, no one could know what the run would be like for that season, but they knew the possibility existed that the run could be very large.

There is very little in the trial testimony that sheds any light on the relation between the catch and the Pyramid Harbor cannery's ability to can that catch. Murray, the superintendent, testified that the pack in 1900 was 1,500 to 2,000 cases better than in 1899. He indicated that 2,000 cases represented about 20,000 fish. Murray also testified that the run in 1900 was about the same as the run in 1899. However, Mr. Banning, the attorney for the fishermen, failed to pin Murray down on the comparison between 1900's catch and that from 1899.

If the catches in the two years were comparable while the pack for 1900 increased by 2,000 cases, that would suggest that in 1899 the cannery was

---

12. [L. W. Casaday, Labor Unrest and the Labor Movement in the Salmon Industry of the Pacific Coast 267 (1938).]

13. Joseph E. Forester & Anne D. Forester, Fishing: British Columbia's Commercial Fishing History 21 (1975).

14. Coast Seamens Journal, Aug. 1, 1900.

unable to process at least 20,000 salmon.[15] It also would suggest that the company had a motive for making sure the fishermen's catch did not exceed the cannery's capacity.

This motive is reinforced by Alaska Packers' documents indicating the number of cases for which Pyramid Harbor was outfitted. Due to the distance between Alaska and the mainland, cannery superintendents had to plan for the season months before it began and without knowing what the run would be like. In 1900, Pyramid Harbor was outfitted (with materials such as tin, solder, labels, cases, etc.) to can 55,000 cases. In fact, that year it canned 55,601. This suggests that in 1900, Pyramid Harbor was operating pretty much at capacity for the season.

Moreover, in both 1898 and 1899 the pack at Pyramid Harbor had either met or exceeded the number of cases for which the cannery had been outfitted. This suggests that the cannery would not have had many extra supplies on hand from previous seasons. None of these facts, however, came out in the trial.

There is another possible reason for why the cannery might have provided substandard nets. As was pointed out above, Pyramid Harbor's cost per case of salmon was higher than most of the other Alaska Packers' canneries, and it spent more on fishing gear than other canneries of a comparable size. The reason for the disproportionate gear expenditure may have been the need to fish with gillnets, which are an inefficient means of fishing for salmon. Thus, if Murray, the superintendent, felt the need to reduce the cost per case, he may have chosen to economize on the nets by recycling portions of last year's nets.

Murray may have been willing to economize on the nets, even though this reduced, to some extent, the fishermen's catch, because he knew he could purchase fish from the local tribes. Each year, the cannery obtained a significant percentage of its fish from the Chilkat and Chilkoot fishermen. The records show that Pyramid Harbor regularly obtained 25% to 40% of its fish from the tribes. In 1900, it purchased over 200,000 fish from them.

Perhaps what Alaska Packers really needed the fishermen for was not fishing, but for sailing the vessel to and from San Francisco, unloading supplies upon arrival in Alaska, and loading the pack at the end of the season. In fact, Murray testified that it was "just as necessary" to have the men discharge the ship as it was to have them fish. The possibility that Alaska Packers was not concerned with maximizing the fishermen's catch due to the availability of fish from the local tribes was not raised at trial. . . .

The following demonstrates a likely scenario: In San Francisco, the men were not organized. They were of different nationalities, although predominantly Italian. They probably did not belong to a union. They scarcely knew their fellow fishermen. They were new to Alaska. After they arrived in Alaska, for the first time they had the opportunity to talk with the few fishermen who fished at Pyramid Harbor in the past and they discovered that the average catches were not what they thought they would be.

---

15. . . . A possible explanation for the increased pack is the fact that in 1900 the cannery bought 47,178 more fish from the local tribes than it had in 1899: 217,074 in 1900 versus 169,896 in 1899. . . . Given that 2,000 cases require about 20,000 fish, this would still leave the canner unable to process some 20,000 salmon.

The nets were different, not like they were used to using. Accordingly, their concerns about their ability to earn a living wage increased. In addition, they discovered that other nearby canneries were paying their fishermen more than Pyramid Harbor. Together in a foreign place, isolated from outside influences, they coalesced into a group and went on strike.

Interestingly, there appears to have been a repeat of the Pyramid Harbor strike two years later at Bristol Bay, in western Alaska. On June 24, 1902, seven hundred fishermen went on strike demanding an increase in pay per fish, from two to three cents per red salmon. The strike lasted four days, at which time the cannery gave in to the men's demands. Apparently, however, just as with this case, the company at the end of the season refused to pay the increased amount and the courts upheld the company. According to the *Coast Seaman's Journal*, there was a lesson to be learned here: "[t]heir present experience should teach the Alaskan fishermen that the proper place to raise wages is in San Francisco, and the proper time when they are signing articles. To wait until they are on the grounds and the fish begin to run is to take bigger risks than fish, to say the least."

STUDY GUIDE: *On what basis does the court in the following case find the contract modification enforceable? Can this case be distinguished from the situations in Stilk v. Myrick and Alaska Packers?*

BRIAN CONSTRUCTION AND DEVELOPMENT CO. v. BRIGHENTI

Supreme Court of Connecticut,
176 Conn. 162, 405 A.2d 72 (1978)

LOISELLE, Associate Justice.*

The plaintiff, a contractor, brought this action for damages against the defendant, a subcontractor, alleging that the defendant had breached a contract under which he had promised to perform certain excavation work for the plaintiff. The defendant counterclaimed. The court rendered judgment for the defendant on the plaintiff's claim and for the plaintiff on the defendant's counterclaim. From the judgment for the defendant, the plaintiff has appealed.

The relevant facts as found by the court are as follows: In early 1968, Joseph E. Bennett, doing business as Joseph E. Bennett Company, entered into a contract with Seymour B. Levine (hereinafter the owner) for the construction of a post office building in Bristol. Shortly thereafter, Bennett assigned the contract to the plaintiff, who, on October 10, 1968, entered into a written subcontract with the defendant. Pursuant to that contract,

Alva P. Loiselle (1910-†) was educated at the University of Connecticut (B.S., LL.D.) and admitted to practice in Connecticut in 1943. Prior to his judicial career, he was corporate counsel to Willimantic City (1945-1947) and an instructor at the University of Connecticut. He has served as judge of the Connecticut Court of Common Pleas (1952-1957); judge of the Connecticut Superior Court (1957-1971); and justice of the Connecticut Supreme Court, appointed to a term beginning in 1971. Loiselle is currently retired and serves as State Trial Referee. — K.T.

consisting of a standard subcontract agreement plus specifications, the
defendant agreed to perform "all Excavation, Grading, Site Work, Asphalt
Pavement, Landscaping, and Concrete Work" and "everything requisite and
necessary to finish the entire work properly." In return, the defendant was
to receive $104,326.

The defendant commenced excavation of the premises on October 15,
1968, at which time he discovered considerable debris below the surface,
consisting in part of concrete foundation walls, slab floors, underground
tanks, twisted metals and various combustible materials. Apparently, the
discovered walls and floor had been part of the basement of an old factory
which had previously been located on the site. The plaintiff had previously
taken test borings of the excavation site, the results of which had been given
to the defendant prior to the execution of the subcontract. The defendant
had relied upon those results, although they proved to be grossly inaccurate. Neither party had been aware of the rubble and, consequently, its
removal was not specifically called for by the plans and specifications
included in the subcontract, nor was the cost of its removal included in
the contract price. Nonetheless, the existence of the rubble necessitated
excavation beyond the depth anticipated in the plans and specifications
and the post office building could not be constructed without its removal.

A provision of the general contract between the owner and Bennett
provided that "no extra work or change shall be made unless in pursuance
of a written order from the Owner signed or countersigned by the Architect,
or a written order from the Architect stating that the Owner has authorized
the extra work or change." A separate provision of the contract specified
that each subcontractor was to make all claims for extras "to the Contractor
in the manner provided in the General Conditions of the Contract . . . for
like claims by the Contractor upon the Owner." A provision of the subcontract reiterated this requirement, adding that "no extra work or other
change will be commenced by the Sub-Contractor without the Contractor's
prior approval in writing." Similarly, both contracts included provisions
under which the subcontractor agreed to be bound to the contractor by
the terms of the general contract and to assume toward the contractor all
those obligations which he, under the contract, assumed towards the
owner.

Upon discovery of the unanticipated debris, the plaintiff notified the
architect, the attorney for the owner, representatives of the Bristol redeve-
lopment agency, which owned the building site, and representatives of the
postal service of the existence of the rubble.[16] All agreed that removal of the
rubble was requisite for completion of the building, yet none would issue
written authorization for its removal.

On October 21, 1968, the defendant ceased working on the excavation
site and notified the plaintiff of his refusal to continue. Subsequently, the
defendant offered to complete the subcontract if the plaintiff would have
the unsuitable material removed. The plaintiff refused this offer. He then
ordered the defendant to remove the rubble as part of "everything requisite
and necessary" under the subcontract. The defendant refused. When the

---

16. The plaintiff sought to notify the owner, but because the owner was ill, the plaintiff
was unable to reach him.

plaintiff was confronted with this situation, and no one would take the responsibility to authorize the removal of the rubble, although its removal was necessary for the contractor to complete his contract, he chose to enter into a further agreement with the defendant for work not included in the subcontract. The plaintiff and the defendant orally agreed that the defendant would be paid his costs for removing the unanticipated rubble, plus 10 percent. By letter dated November 7, 1968, the plaintiff confirmed this oral agreement. Although requested in the letter to do so, the defendant failed to sign and return a copy of the letter to the plaintiff. Nonetheless, the defendant returned to work, continuing until about November 13, 1968, at which point he left the job, refusing to return despite the plaintiff's request that he complete the work. The plaintiff completed his own contract with the owner, suffering, as a result of the defendant's abandonment, considerable damages.

On appeal to this court, . . . [the plaintiff] raises the issue of whether the oral agreement between it and the defendant constituted a valid agreement obligating the defendant to remove the unexpected rubble. Because we find this issue to be dispositive of the appeal, the other claims need not be specifically addressed.

It is an accepted principle of law in this state that when a party agrees to perform an obligation for another to whom that obligation is already owed, although for lesser remuneration, the second agreement does not constitute a valid, binding contract. . . .

> The basis of the rule is generally made to rest upon the proposition that in such a situation he who promises the additional compensation receives nothing more than that to which he is already entitled and he to whom the promise is made gives nothing that he was not already under legal obligation to give. 1 Williston on Contracts, §130. . . .

Where, however, the subsequent agreement imposes upon the one seeking greater compensation an additional obligation or burden not previously assumed, the agreement, supported by consideration, is valid and binding upon the parties. . . .

In Blakeslee v. Board of Water Commissioners, 106 Conn. 642, 656, 139 A. 106, 111, this court, in analyzing these traditional principles, articulated the evolving rule that

> where a contract must be performed under burdensome conditions not anticipated, and not within the contemplation of the parties at the time when the contract was made, and the promisee measures up to the right standard of honesty and fair dealing, and agrees, in view of the changed conditions, to pay what is then reasonable, just, and fair, such new contract is not without consideration within the meaning of that term, either in law or in equity. . . .

This principle has received recognition by courts of other jurisdictions confronted with situations comparable to that now before this court. In Evergreen Amusement Corporation v. Milstead, 206 Md. 610, 112 A.2d 901, the Maryland Court of Appeals found a subsequent oral agreement of the parties to a written construction contract valid, relying, in part, upon the theory of unforeseen circumstances. In that case, the plaintiff, operator of a drive-in movie theater, had entered into a written contract with the defendant, a contractor, pursuant to which the latter agreed to supply all the necessary materials and to perform the work needed to clear the theater site of timber, stumps, and waste material, and to grade the site as indicated on the accompanying plans. Once the work was underway, it became apparent that substantial, additional fill would be needed to complete the project, although neither party had anticipated this, both relying upon a topographical map which proved to be of doubtful accuracy. The court found that the parties, upon this discovery, entered into an oral agreement whereby the defendant would bring in the fill for additional compensation. On appeal, the plaintiff claimed that this agreement lacked consideration since the defendant promised only to do that which he had already agreed to do, i.e., to furnish all materials needed to grade the theater site. Relying upon the theory of unforeseen circumstances, the court held the agreement to be binding.

In another case involving facts similar to those now before us, a California Court of Appeal in Bailey v. Breetwor, 206 Cal. App. 2d 287, 23 Cal. Rptr. 740, without reference to the theory of unforeseen circumstances, determined that a subsequent oral agreement of parties to a written contract was valid where unanticipated, burdensome conditions, not contemplated by the parties at the time the written contract was executed, were encountered. In that case, the defendant owner had entered into a written contract with a construction company to grade and compact a building site for $2600. The work was subcontracted to the plaintiff, who agreed to perform the work in accordance with the general contract. Upon commencing his work, the plaintiff discovered, below the surface, an extensive amount of wet clay. The owner was notified of this and was advised that, although removal of this clay was not included in the subcontract, its removal was necessary for compliance with the city building code. In return for costs plus 10 percent, the plaintiff orally agreed to remove the clay. Determining that the oral agreement constituted a separate, binding contract, the court noted that "[t]his performance was clearly beyond the scope of the original contract. Bailey [the plaintiff] thus incurred a new detriment and Breetwor [the owner] received a new benefit constituting sufficient consideration for Breetwor's promise." Id., 292 [23 Cal. Rptr. 743].

Although the technical terminology apparent in these two cases differs, the underlying reasoning is similar. In each case, an unforeseen, burdensome condition was discovered during the performance of the original contract. The promise of additional compensation in return for the promise that the additional work required would be undertaken was held to constitute a separate, valid agreement. Such reasoning is applicable to the facts of this case. The unchallenged findings of the court reveal that the substantial rubble found beneath the surface of the site was not anticipated by either party, that its presence necessitated excavation beyond the depths required in the plans and specifications, that the cost of removing this rubble was not included in the contract price and that the parties entered into a separate oral agreement for the removal of the rubble. Under these circumstances, the subsequent oral agreement, that the defendant would remove this rubble in return for additional compensation, was binding as a new, distinct contract, supported by valid consideration. See Restatement (Second) Contracts §89D (Tentative Draft No. 2, 1965). The defendant's failure to comply with this agreement constitutes a breach of contract. . . .

There is error, the judgment for the defendant on the complaint is set aside and the case is remanded with direction to render judgment for the plaintiff to recover such damages as he may prove on a new trial limited to the issue of damages.

In this opinion the other judges concurred.

STUDY GUIDE: Notice how the Restatement (Second) has altered the pre-existing duty rule, while the Uniform Commercial Code has abolished it for contracts involving the sale of goods.

RESTATEMENT (SECOND) OF CONTRACTS

§89.   MODIFICATION OF EXECUTORY CONTRACT

A promise modifying a duty under a contract not fully performed on either side is binding

(a) if the modification is fair and equitable in view of circumstances not anticipated by the parties when the contract was made; or

(b) to the extent provided by statute; or

(c) to the extent that justice requires enforcement in view of material change of position in reliance on the promise.

SALES CONTRACTS: THE UNIFORM COMMERCIAL CODE

§2-209.   MODIFICATION, RESCISSION, AND WAIVER

(1) An agreement modifying a contract within this Article needs no consideration to be binding. . . .

OFFICIAL COMMENT

Purposes of Changes and New Matter

1. This section seeks to protect and make effective all necessary and desirable modifications of sales contracts without regard to the technicalities which at present hamper such adjustments.

2. Subsection (1) provides that an agreement modifying a sales contract needs no consideration to be binding. However, modifications made thereunder must meet the test of good faith imposed by this Act. The effective use of bad faith to escape performance on the original contract is barred, and the extortion of a "modification" without legitimate commercial reason is ineffective as a violation of

the duty of good faith. Nor can a mere technical consideration support a modification in bad faith.

The test of "good faith" between merchants or as against merchants includes "observance of reasonable standards of fair dealing in the trade" (Section 2-103), and may in some situations require an objectively demonstrable reason for seeking such modifications. But such matters as a market shift which makes performance come to involve a loss may provide such a reason even though there is no such unforeseen difficulty as would make out a legal excuse from performance under Sections 2-615 and 2-616. . . .

Study Guide: The requirement of consideration has been thought by some to be useful because it may prevent the enforcement of a modification obtained "coercively" sometime after the original bargain. The comments to U.C.C. §2-209 reject the preexisting duty rule as a way of policing the problem of the "extortion of a modification" in favor of a more direct approach. Consider the argument for this doctrinal change as summarized by Judge Richard Posner in the following opinion. To the extent that the problem of extorted contract modifications is no longer conceived in terms of consideration, we shall need to continue our discussion of it in Chapter 16 when discussing the concept of economic duress.

UNITED STATES v. STUMP HOME SPECIALTIES MANUFACTURING, UNITED STATES COURT OF APPEALS, SEVENTH CIRCUIT, 905 F.2D 1117 (1990): . . . Posner, Circuit Judge. The guarantors' second major argument is that the modification in the loan agreement is unenforceable because not supported by consideration. The black-letter rule is indeed that a contract may not be modified without consideration. A & S Corp. v. Midwest Commerce Banking Co., 525 N.E.2d 1290, 1292 (Ind. App. 1988), Wisconsin Knife Works v. National Metal Crafters, 781 F.2d 1280, 1285 (7th Cir. 1986); Farnsworth, Contracts 271-73 (1982). (The U.C.C. abrogates the rule for sales of goods, U.C.C. §2-209(1), but we do not have a sale of goods in this case.) And yet the cautionary, evidential, and other policies behind the requirement of consideration do not apply, or apply only with much attenuated strength, in the context of written modification. By hypothesis the parties already have a contract, so that the danger of mistaking casual promissory language for an intention to be legally bound is slight; moreover, we deal here with a written, not an oral, modification, so fabrication of a promise is harder.

The requirement of consideration has, however, a distinct function in the modification setting — although one it does not perform well — and that is to prevent coercive modifications. Since one of the main purposes of contracts and of contract law is to facilitate long-term commitments, there is often an interval in the life of a contract during which one party is at the mercy of the other. A may have ordered a machine from B that A wants to place in operation on a given date, specified in their contract; and in expectation of B's complying with the contract, A may have made commitments to his customers that it would be costly to renege on. As the date of scheduled delivery approaches, B may be tempted to demand that A agree to renegotiate the contract price, knowing that A will incur heavy expenses if B fails to deliver on time. A can always refuse to renegotiate, relying instead on his right to sue *B* for breach of contract if *B* fails to make delivery by the agreed date. But legal remedies are costly and uncertain, thereby opening the way to duress. Considerations of commercial reputation will deter taking advantage of an opportunity to exert duress on a contract partner in many cases, but not in all: For examples of duress in the contract-modification setting, see Austin Instrument, Inc. v. Loral Corp., 29 N.Y.2d 124, 324 N.Y.S.2d 22, 272 N.E.2d 533 (1971), and Alaska Packers' Assn. v. Domenico, 117 F. 99 (9th Cir. 1902). . . .

The rule that modifications are unenforceable unless supported by consideration strengthens *A*'s position by reducing *B*'s incentive to seek a modification. But it strengthens it feebly, as we pointed out in Wisconsin Knife Works v. National Metal Crafters, supra, 781 F.2d at 1285. The law does not require that consideration be adequate — that it be commensurate with what the party accepting it is giving up. Slight consideration, therefore, will suffice to make a contract or a contract modification enforceable. . . . And slight consideration is consistent with coercion. To surrender one's contractual rights in exchange for a peppercorn is not functionally different from surrendering them for nothing.

The sensible course would be to enforce contract modifications (at least if written) regardless of consideration and rely on the defense of duress to prevent abuse. Wisconsin Knife Works v. National Metal Crafters, supra, 781 F.2d at 1286; U.C.C. §2-209, official comment 2; Hillman, Contract Modification Under the Restatement (Second) of Contracts, 67 Cornell L. Rev. 680 (1982). All coercive modifications would then be unenforceable, and there would be no need to worry about consideration, an inadequate safeguard against duress. . . .

REFERENCE: Barnett, §4.2.4
               Farnsworth, §§4.21-4.23
               Calamari & Perillo, §§4.9-4.10
               Murray, §65

D.   ADEQUACY OF CONSIDERATION

As Judge Posner stated in the previous opinion: "The law does not require that consideration be adequate — that it be commensurate with what the party accepting it is giving up." The traditional position is stated by the court in Hardesty v. Smith, 3 Ind. 39 (1851):

> [T]he simple parting with a right which is one's own, and which he has the right to fix a price upon, must be a good consideration for a promise to pay that price. In such cases, the purchaser *gets a something*, and he is estopped by the exercise of his own judgment, uninfluenced by fraud, or warranty, or mistake of facts, at the time, to afterwards say it was not worth to him what he agreed to give.
>
> If there is not title in the seller, then, indeed, the purchaser does not get what he supposes he is buying, and may well say there is no consideration, unless where he purchases under such circumstances as show that he takes the risk of the title. But the doctrine of failure of consideration rests, as a

general rule, on the two doctrines of fraud and warranty. Where either of these exists, the party does not purchase upon his own unbiased judgment of the thing, and hence is not estopped as to the price; and hence, again, may show in evidence what, by the judgment of others, the thing purchased is really worth, where it is retained, rather than returned upon a rescission of the contract entirely.

Where, however, there is no fraud, or warranty, express or implied, or mistake as to facts, the parties are bound by the contracts they make. . . . When a party gets all the consideration he honestly contracted for, he cannot say he gets no consideration, or that it has failed. If this doctrine be not correct, then it is not true that parties are at liberty to make their own contracts. And if, where an article is fairly sold and purchased, for a stipulated consideration, a Court or jury may annul the bargain if they come to the conclusion the article sold was of no value, then they should be permitted, in every case, where they may conclude the article is worth something, to determine whether it is worth as much as has been promised for it, and, if it is not, to reduce the amount to be paid to that point; thus doing away with all special contracts, and putting all dealing upon the *quantum valebat* and the *quantum meruit* — a doctrine that would, indeed, produce litigation enough.

When considering the merits of the traditional doctrine governing inadequacy of consideration, keep in mind that we are here concerned with the prima facie case of contract. The possibility of considering the "fairness" of the exchange reemerges as part of several contract defenses, such as misrepresentation, economic duress, undue influence, and unconscionability. We shall study these defenses to the prima facie case in Chapters 15 and 16. When we do, consider why (or whether) this issue is better treated in defenses and what difference it makes to do so.

One basis for the traditional approach concerns the subjectivity of value, which we studied in Chapter 2. One economist who placed great stress on this issue was Ludwig von Mises.

Economics Background: Subjectivity and the Inequality of Exchange

LUDWIG VON MISES, HUMAN ACTION 203-204 (REV. ED. 1963): An inveterate fallacy asserted that things and services exchanged are of equal value. Value was considered as objective, as an intrinsic quality inherent in things and not merely as the expression of various people's eagerness to acquire them. People, it was assumed, first established the magnitude of value proper to goods and services by an act of measurement and then proceeded to barter them against quantities of goods and services of the same amount of value. This fallacy frustrated Aristotle's approach to economic problems and, for almost two thousand years, the reasoning of all those for whom Aristotle's opinions were authoritative. It seriously vitiated the marvelous achievements of classical economists and rendered the writings of their epigones, especially those of Marx and the Marxian school, entirely futile. The basis of modern economics is the cognition that it is precisely the disparity in the value attached to the objects exchanged that results in their being exchanged. People buy and sell only because they appraise the things given up less than those received. Thus the notion of a measurement of value is vain. An act of exchange is neither preceded nor accompanied by any process which could be called a measuring of value. An individual may attach the same value to two things; but then no exchange can result. But if there is a diversity in valuation, all that can be asserted with regard to it is that one *a* is valued higher, that it is preferred to one *b*. Values and valuations are intensive quantities and not extensive quantities. They are not susceptible to mental grasp by application of cardinal numbers.

STUDY GUIDE: Can the following "classic" case be reconciled with the traditional approach to adequacy of consideration or the subjectivity of value described by von Mises? Can it be reconciled with the bargain theory of consideration?

NEWMAN & SNELL's STATE BANK v. HUNTER
Supreme Court of Michigan,
243 Mich. 331, 220 N.W. 665 (1928)

FELLOWS, J.* Defendant is the widow of Lee C. Hunter, who died intestate January 25, 1926. His estate was insufficient to pay his funeral expenses and the widow's allowance. At the time of his death plaintiff bank held his note for $3,700, with 50 shares of the capital stock of the Hunter Company as collateral. This company was insolvent but was still doing business when the note was given; afterwards it was placed in the hands of a receiver and its assets were insufficient to pay its debts. The facts were agreed upon on the trial in the court below. We quote from the agreed statement of facts:

On March 1, 1926, the defendant gave the plaintiff the note described in the plaintiff's declaration in this cause, and the plaintiff surrendered to her therefor, and in consideration thereof, the note of said Lee C. Hunter. The defendant also paid the plaintiff the earned interest due on the deceased's note.

Defendant pleaded want of consideration. . . .

. . . Here we have the widow's note given to take up the note of her insolvent husband, a worthless piece of paper. When plaintiff surrendered this worthless piece of paper to the defendant, it parted with nothing of value and defendant received nothing of value, the plaintiff suffered no loss or inconvenience and defendant received no benefit. The weight of authority sustains defendant's contention, but, going back to fundamentals it seems clear to me that the transaction was without consideration. It is

---

* *Grant Fellows* (1865-1929) was admitted to the Michigan bar (1886). He practiced law in Hudson, Michigan (1890-1913), and served as Attorney General of Michigan (1913-1917). He left that post in 1917, when he was elected justice of the Supreme Court of Michigan. He served as Chief Justice of that court in 1922 and was reelected to the bench in 1924, serving an eight-year term at his death. — K.T.

urged that plaintiff's right as a creditor to administer the estate was valuable and was waived. Had there been assets or prospective undisclosed assets there might be some force to this contention. But the agreed statements of facts negative any such situation. Under the agreement of facts there was not enough in the estate to pay the funeral expenses or the widow's support.

We have now reached the question of whether the manner of handling the stock of the Hunter Company furnished a consideration. So far as the record discloses, this stock was retained by the bank and was treated as collateral to defendant's note, and it was so stated in that instrument. The bank, so far as the record discloses, never surrendered it to the defendant but kept it and has it today. But plaintiff's counsel insists that as matter of law it was transferred to defendant. They insist that whatever interest the bank had in the stock passed to defendant when her husband's note was surrendered to her, even though it was not as matter of fact given to her. But if we accept this theory and thus create a legal fiction, we must have in mind that she at once and in the same transaction re-hypothecated the stock to the bank. Stripped of all legal fiction, the cold facts are that, when the negotiations opened plaintiff had this stock and the worthless note of defendant's husband. When they ended, the bank still had the stock and defendant's note. Defendant had her husband's worthless note and she had nothing more. But this discussion is largely academic. The agreed statement of facts shows that the company was insolvent. The stock then had no book value. There is no statement that it had a market value, and in the absence of anything showing or tending to show a market value, we cannot assume it had such value or what it was. It was suggested on the argument that even though the company was insolvent, it might have been revived by the infusion of new money in the enterprise. But no one has come along with any infusion of such new blood, and value based on such a possibility is altogether too problematical to form a fixed basis of property rights. The record shows the affairs of the company have been wound up, and that creditors were not paid in full. Upon this record the stock was worthless. . . .

The judgment will be reversed, without a new trial.

STUDY GUIDE: Why are "pretended exchanges" insufficient to establish enforceability? We shall return to this issue in Chapter 10.

RESTATEMENT (SECOND) OF CONTRACTS

§79. ADEQUACY OF CONSIDERATION; MUTUALITY OF OBLIGATION

If the requirement of consideration is met, there is no additional requirement of   └→ when we have an exchange
  (a) a gain, advantage, or benefit to the promisor or a loss, disadvantage, or detriment to the promisee; or
  (b) equivalence in the values exchanged; or
  (c) "mutuality of obligation."

COMMENT...

d. Pretended Exchange.   Disparity in value, with or without other circumstances, sometimes indicates that the purported consideration was not in fact bargained for but was a mere formality or pretense. Such a sham or "nominal" consideration does not satisfy the requirement of §71. Promises are enforced in such cases, if at all, either as promises binding without consideration under §§82-94 or as promises binding by virtue of their formal characteristics under §6. See, for example, §§95-109 on contracts under seal.

§364.   EFFECT OF UNFAIRNESS

(1) Specific performance or an injunction will be refused if such relief would be unfair because . . .

(c) the exchange is grossly inadequate or the terms of the contract are otherwise unfair.

STUDY GUIDE: How does the claim in the next case differ from that in Newman? Is it not a "pretended exchange"? Does this situation remind you of Webb v. McGowin? Does this case suggest that the requirement of truly bargained-for consideration performs an "evidentiary function" (a concept we shall take up in the next chapter) by providing some proof that a commitment was really made by the promisor?

DYER v. NATIONAL BY-PRODUCTS, INC.

Supreme Court of Iowa,
380 N.W.2d 732 (1986)

SCHULTZ, J.* The determinative issue in this appeal is whether good faith forbearance to litigate a claim, which proves to be invalid and unfounded, is sufficient consideration to uphold a contract of settlement. The district court determined, as a matter of law, that consideration for the alleged settlement was lacking because the forborne claim was not a viable cause of action. We reverse and remand. → Holding

On October 29, 1981, Dale Dyer, an employee of National By-Products, lost his right foot in a job-related accident. Thereafter, the employer placed Dyer on a leave of absence at full pay from the date of his injury until August 16, 1982. At that time he returned to work as a foreman, the job he held prior to his injury. On March 11, 1983, the employer indefinitely laid off Dyer.

Dyer then filed the present lawsuit against his employer claiming that his discharge was a breach of an oral contract. He alleged that he in good

---

*Louis W. Schultz (1927-1993) was educated at Drake University Law School (LL.B.). After serving in the navy during World War II, Judge Schultz was in private practice from 1945 to 1960 and held the office of Iowa County Attorney from 1960 to 1968. After being a judge for the Sixth Judicial District (1971-1980), he was appointed to the Iowa Supreme Court where he served until his death. — J.B.

faith believed that he had a valid claim against his employer for his personal injury. Further, Dyer claimed that his forbearance from litigating his claim was made in exchange for a promise from his employer that he would have lifetime employment. The employer specifically denied that it had offered a lifetime job to Dyer after his injury.

Following extensive discovery procedures, the employer filed a motion for summary judgment claiming there was no genuine factual issue and that it was entitled to judgment as a matter of law. The motion was resisted by Dyer. The district court sustained the employer's motion on the basis that: (1) no reciprocal promise to work for the employer for life was present, and (2) there was no forbearance of any viable cause of action, apparently on the ground that workers' compensation provided Dyer's sole remedy.

On appeal, Dyer claims that consideration for the alleged contract of lifetime employment was his forbearance from pursuing an action against his employer. Accordingly, he restricts his claim of error to the second reasons advanced by the district court for granting summary judgment. . . . Dyer generally contends that an unresolved issue of material fact remains as to whether he reasonably and in good faith forbore from asserting a claim against his employer and his coemployees in exchange for the employer's alleged promise to employ him for life. Specifically, he asserts that the trial court erred because: (1) the court did not consider the reasonableness and good faith of his belief in the validity of the claim he forbore from asserting, and (2) the court considered the legal merits of the claim itself which Dyer forbore from asserting.

The employer, on the other hand, maintains that workers' compensation[17] benefits are Dyer's sole remedy for his injury and that his claim for damages is unfounded. It then urges that forbearance from asserting an unfounded claim cannot serve as consideration for a contract. For the purpose of this discussion, we shall assume that Dyer's tort action is clearly invalid and he had no basis for a tort suit against either his employer or his fellow employees. We recognize that the fact issue, as to whether Dyer in good faith believed that he had a cause of action based in tort against the employer, remains unresolved. The determinative issue before the district court and now on appeal is whether the lack of consideration for the alleged promise of lifetime employment has been established as a matter of law.

Preliminarily, we observe that the law favors the adjustment and settlement of controversies without resorting to court action. . . . Compromise is favored by law. . . . Compromise of a doubtful right asserted in good faith is sufficient consideration for a promise.

The more difficult problem is whether the settlement of an unfounded claim asserted in good faith is consideration for a contract of settlement.

17. It is undisputed that the employee was covered under workers' compensation. The Iowa workers' compensation act states in pertinent part that:

The rights and remedies provided in this chapter . . . for an employee on account of injury . . . for which benefits under this chapter . . . are recoverable, *shall be the exclusive and only rights and remedies of such employee* . . . at common law or otherwise, on account of such injury . . . against: (1) his or her employer. . . .

Iowa Code §85.20 (1983) (emphasis added).

Professor Corbin presents a view favorable to Dyer's argument when he states:

> [F]orbearance to press a claim, or a promise of such forbearance, may be a sufficient consideration even though the claim is wholly ill-founded. It may be ill-founded because the facts are not what he supposes them to be, or because the existing facts do not have the legal operation that he supposes them to have. In either case, his forbearance may be a sufficient consideration, although under certain circumstances it is not. The fact that the claim is ill-founded is not in itself enough to prevent forbearance from being a sufficient consideration for a promise.

1 Corbin on Contracts §140, at 595 (1963). Further, in the same section, it is noted that:

> The most generally prevailing, and probably the most satisfactory view is that *forbearance is sufficient if there is any reasonable ground for the claimant's belief that it is just to try to enforce his claim. He must be asserting his claim "in good faith";* but this does not mean he must believe that his suit can be won. It means that he must not be making his claim or threatening suit for purposes of vexation, or in order to realize on its "nuisance value."

. . . the Restatement (Second) of Contracts section 74 (1979), supports the Corbin view and states:

> Settlement of Claims
>   (1) Forbearance to assert or the surrender of a claim or defense which proves to be invalid is not consideration unless
>   (a) the claim or defense is in fact doubtful because of uncertainty as to the facts or the law, or
>   (b) the forbearing or surrendering party believes that the claim or defense may be fairly determined to be valid. . . .
>   Comment: . . .
>
>   b. *Requirement of good faith.* The policy favoring compromise of disputed claims is clearest, perhaps, where a claim is surrendered at a time when it is uncertain whether it is valid or not. Even though the invalidity later becomes clear, *the bargain is to be judged as it appeared to the parties at the time*; if the claim was then doubtful, no inquiry is necessary as to their good faith. Even though the invalidity should have been clear at the time, the settlement of an honest dispute is upheld. But a mere assertion or denial of liability does not make a claim doubtful, and *the fact that invalidity is obvious may indicate that it was known.* In such cases Subsection (1)(b) requires a showing of *good faith.*

(emphasis added). . . .

However, not all jurisdictions adhere to this view. Some courts require that the claim forborne must have some merit in fact or at law before it can provide consideration and these jurisdictions reject those claims that are obviously invalid. See Bullard v. Curry-Cloonan, 367 A.2d 127, 131 (D.C. App. 1976) ("[A]s a general principle, the forbearance of a cause of action advanced in good faith, which is neither absurd in fact nor obviously unfounded in law, constitutes good and valuable consideration."); . . . Charles

v. Hill, 260 N.W.2d 571, 575 (Minn. 1977) ("[A] wholly baseless or utterly unfounded claim is not consideration for a contract."). . . .

In fact, we find language in our own case law that supports the view which is favorable to the employer in this case. See Vande Stouwe v. Bankers' Life Co., 218 Iowa 1182, 1190, 254 N.W. 790, 794 (1934) ("A claim that is entirely baseless and without foundation in law or equity will not support a compromise."). . . . Additionally, Professor Williston notes that:

> While there is a great divergence of opinion respecting the kind of forbearance which will constitute consideration, the *weight of authority holds that although forbearance from suit on a clearly invalid claim is insufficient consideration for a promise*, forbearance from suit on a claim of doubtful validity is sufficient consideration for a promise if there is a sincere belief in the validity of the claim.

1 Williston on Contracts §135, at 581 (3d ed. 1957) (emphasis added).

We believe, however, that the better reasoned approach is that expressed in the Restatement (Second) of Contracts section 74. . . . As noted before, as a matter of policy the law favors compromise and such policy would be defeated if a party could second guess his settlement and litigate the validity of the compromise. The requirement that the forbearing party assert the claim in good faith sufficiently protects the policy of law that favors the settlement of controversies. Our holdings which are to the contrary to this view are overruled.

In the present case, the invalidity of Dyer's claim against the employer does not foreclose him, as a matter of law, from asserting that his forbearance was consideration for the alleged contract of settlement. However, the issue of Dyer's good faith must still be examined. In so doing, the issue of the validity of Dyer's claim should not be entirely overlooked.

> Although the courts will not inquire into the validity of a claim which was compromised in good faith, there must generally be reasonable grounds for a belief in order for the court to be convinced that the belief was honestly entertained by the person who asserted it. Sufficient consideration requires more than the bald assertion by a claimant who has a claim, and to the extent that the validity or invalidity of a claim has a bearing upon whether there were reasonable grounds for believing in its possible validity, evidence of the validity or invalidity of a claim may be relevant to the issue of good faith.

15A Am. Jur. 2d Compromise and Settlement §17, at 790. We conclude that the evidence of the invalidity of the claim is relevant to show a lack of honest belief in the validity of the claim asserted or forborne.

Under the present state of the record, there remains a material fact as to whether Dyer's forbearance to assert his claim was in good faith. Summary judgment should not have been rendered against him. Accordingly, the case is reversed and remanded for further proceedings consistent with this opinion.

REFERENCE: Farnsworth, §2.11
               Calamari & Perillo, §4.4
               Murray, §§60, 62(A)

10

THE INTENTION TO BE
LEGALLY BOUND

At least since the first restatement was published in 1932, there has existed a consensus that the bargain theory of consideration requires supplementation by other principles or theories of enforceability. Cases in which the enforcement of nonbargained-for commitments has been allowed are normally clustered under the doctrinal heading of *promissory estoppel*, and we shall study them in Chapter 11. Before doing so, however, it is useful to identify another reason why private commitments have been thought to be enforceable, which has tended to be neglected by contemporary scholars: persons' commitments should be enforced when they have manifested their intention to be legally bound. This criterion of enforceability preceded the rise of assumpsit and the doctrine of consideration and was never abandoned by English law. It is also manifested in U.C.C. §2-204(3), which, as we studied in Chapters 4 and 5, permits the enforcement of a contract in which one or more terms are left open if there is a reasonably certain basis for giving a remedy and "if the parties have *intended to make a contract.* . . ."[1]

The concept of intention to create legal relations can potentially be applied in two ways: First, the *presence* of a manifested intention to be legally bound can *justify* the enforcement of commitments that lack either bargained-for consideration or detrimental reliance. Second, the *absence* of such a manifestation or a manifested intention *not* to be legally bound might *prevent* the enforcement of even bargained-for commitments or those that have induced reliance. In Section A, we take up the first of these possibilities by examining a number of situations in which commitments either used to be or still are enforceable solely because of the existence of some type of *formality* that indicates an intention to be legally bound. In Section B, we consider cases in which the absence of such a manifested intention has undermined the enforcement of some commitments.

It should be stressed, however, that the cases in which the enforcement of nonbargained-for commitments is most intuitively appealing appear not in this chapter but in Chapter 11. In the nonbargain cases discussed there, the courts have applied the doctrine of promissory estoppel. Although this doctrine traditionally has been thought to be based on the principle of detrimental reliance, the material in this chapter will enable us to evaluate the extent to which the existence of detrimental reliance or the

1. U.C.C. §2-204(3).

presence of a manifested intention to be legally bound best explains the results in promissory estoppel cases.

Before reading the materials in this chapter, it is important for students to realize that the first Restatement of Contracts explicitly rejected the idea that contracts *require* an intention by the parties to create or alter their legal relations. Section 20 states:

> A manifestation of mutual assent by the parties to an informal contract is essential to its formation and the acts by which such assent is manifested must be done with the intent to do those acts; but, except as qualified by §§55, 71 & 72, neither mental assent to the promises in the contract, nor *real or apparent intent that the promises shall be legally binding* is essential.

(Emphasis added.) At first blush, the Restatement (Second) of Contracts appears to embrace the same approach:

§21. INTENTION TO BE LEGALLY BOUND

> Neither real nor apparent intention that a promise be legally binding is essential to the formation of a contract, but a manifestation of intention that a promise shall not affect legal relations may prevent the formation of a contract.

Does it?

Comparative Law Background: The English Law of Contract

STUDY GUIDE: *Professor Samuel Williston — who is cited below as denying that an intention to be legally bound was needed to create a contract — was the reporter for the first Restatement of Contracts. Does §21 of the second Restatement represent an embrace of the first Restatement's view of the intention to be legally bound? In what respect does it represent a movement in the direction of English law as described in the following excerpt? When reading the following, consider the role that presumptions play in legal theory. We shall return to this issue in Part V when we study circumstances in which the normal enforceability of mutual assent is undermined by the existence of other circumstances that constitute defenses to enforcement.*

INTENTION TO CREATE LEGAL RELATIONS, from CHESHIRE, FIBFOOT AND FURMSTON'S LAW OF CONTRACT 111-112 (12TH ED. 1991) (M. P. FURMSTON, ED.): The question now to be discussed is whether a contract necessarily results once the court has ruled that the parties must be taken to have made an agreement and that it is supported by consideration.[2] This conclusion is commonly denied. The law, it is said, does not proclaim the existence of a contract merely because of the presence of mutual promises. Agreements are made every day in domestic and

---

2. It is assumed here that the contract cannot be challenged on the ground that it violates public policy or is avoided by statute. . . .

in social life, where the parties do not intend to invoke the assistance of the courts should the engagement not be honoured. To offer a friend a meal is not to invite litigation. Contracts, in the words of Lord Stowell,

> must not be the sports of an idle hour, mere matters of pleasantry and badinage, never intended by the parties to have any serious effect whatever.[3]

It is therefore contended that, in addition to the phenomena of agreement and the presence of consideration, a third contractual element is required — the intention of the parties to create legal relations.

This view, commonly held in England,[4] has not passed unchallenged; and the criticism of it made by Professor Williston demands attention, not only as emanating from a distinguished American jurist, but as illuminating the whole subject now under discussion. In his opinion, the separate element of intention is foreign to the common law, imported from the Continent by academic influences in the nineteenth century[5] and useful only in systems which lack the test of consideration to enable them to determine the boundaries of contract.

> The common law does not require any positive intention to create a legal obligation as an element of contract. . . . A deliberate promise seriously made is enforced irrespective of the promisor's views regarding his legal liability.[6]

His own views may be reduced to three propositions:

(1) If reasonable people would assume that there was no intention in the parties to be bound, there is no contract.

(2) If the parties expressly declare or clearly indicate their rejection of contractual obligations, the law accepts and implements their intention.

(3) Mere social engagements, if accompanied by the requisite technicalities, such as consideration, may be enforced as contracts.

English lawyers may well be prepared to accept the first two of these propositions: decided cases refute the third.[7] But their acceptance does not necessarily justify the complete rejection of intention to create legal relations as an independent element in the formation of contract. It is certainly true, and of great significance, that the very presence of consideration normally implies the existence of such an intention. To make a bargain is to assume liability and to invite the sanction of the courts. Professor

3. Dalrymple v. Dalrymple (1811) 2 Hag. Con. 54, at 105.
4. E.g., Pollock on Contract (13th ed.) p. 3; Law Revision Committee, Sixth Interim Report, p. 15.
5. Historically this would appear correct. Simpson, 91 L.Q.R. 263-265.
6. Williston on Contracts (3d ed.) s.21. Williston has not lacked support: see Tuck, 21 Can. Bar. Rev. 123; Hamson, 54 L.Q.R. 233; Shatwell, 1 Sydney L. Rev. 289; Unger, 19 M.L.R. 96; Hepple, [1970] C.L.J. 122. . . . Cf. Chloros, 33 Tulane L. Rev. 607.
7. E.g., Balfour v. Balfour [1919] 2 K.B. 571. . . . See also Lens v. Devonshire Club [1914] Times, 4 December, discussed by Scrutton, L.J. in Rose and Frank Co. v. J R Crompton & Bros. Ltd. [1923] 2 K.B. 261.

Williston performed a valuable service by insisting that the emphasis laid by foreign systems on this element of intention is out of place in the common law, where it follows naturally from the very nature of contract. Consideration, bargain, legal consequences — these are interrelated concepts. But it is possible for this presumption to be rebutted. If *A* and *B* agree to lunch together and *A* promises to pay for the food if *B* will pay for the drink, it is difficult to deny the presence of consideration and yet equally clear that no legal ties are contemplated or created.[8] It seems necessary, therefore, to regard the intention to create legal relations as a separate element in the English law of contract, though, by the preoccupation of that law with the idea of bargain, one which does not normally obtrude upon the courts.

The cases in which a contract is denied on the ground that there is no intention to involve legal liability may be divided into two classes. On the one hand there are social, family or other domestic agreements, where the presence or absence of an intention to create legal relations depends upon the inference to be drawn by the court from the language used by the parties and the circumstances in which they use it.[9] On the other hand there are commercial agreements where this intention is presumed and must be rebutted by the party seeking to deny it. In either case, of course, intention is to be objectively ascertained.

A.   USING FORMALITIES TO MANIFEST AN INTENTION TO BE LEGALLY BOUND

You will recall that the shift to the writ of assumpsit was a means of addressing the underenforcement of *informal* commitments — that is, written and oral promises not under seal. In Chapter 9, we learned that the doctrine of consideration (together with the Statute of Frauds that we studied in Chapter 6) was devised as a means of limiting the potentially open-ended nature of assumpsit. Eventually, however, consideration was thought to be a general requirement of *all* contracts. This left the enforcement of formal contracts, such as those under seal, that lacked bargained-for consideration in an awkward position. Instead of assumpsit and its restrictive doctrine of consideration being the exception to a normal regime of formal commitments, it came to be said (as Judge Parker did in Mills v. Wyman) that such formal devices as the seal imported, or were a substitute for, a consideration.

In time, the legitimacy of enforcing formal commitments lacking consideration has been seriously undermined. Nonetheless, a few commitments are enforceable today entirely on the basis of formalities. Such promises need

8. It may be objected that there is only consideration if the promises are given in exchange for each other but some test of intention is needed to discover whether this is so.
9. It is not irrelevant to notice that by §1 (1) of the Law Reform (Miscellaneous Provisions) Act 1970, "an agreement between two persons to marry one another shall not under the law of England and Wales have effect as a contract giving rise to legal rights, and no action shall lie in England or Wales for breach of such an agreement, whatever the law applicable to the agreement."

not be bargained for; nor is there any required showing of detrimental reliance. Consider U.C.C. §2-205:

§2-205. FIRM OFFERS

An offer by a merchant to buy or sell goods in signed writing which by its terms gives assurances that it will be held open is not revokable, for lack of consideration, during the time stated or if no time is stated for a reasonable time, but in no event may such a period of irrevocability exceed three months; but any such term of assurance on a form supplied by the offeree must be separately signed by the offeror.

The Restatement (Second) also acknowledges the enforceability of certain commitments accompanied by formalities without any need to show either consideration or detrimental reliance. Restatement (Second) §87 states that an offer is binding as an option, when it "is in writing and signed by the offeror, recites a purported consideration for the making of the offer, and proposes an exchange on fair terms within a reasonable time. . . ." Restatement (Second) §88 states that a promise to be a surety is binding if "the promise is in writing and signed by the promisor and recites a purported consideration." In this section, we examine why such commitments may be enforceable despite the absence of consideration or detrimental reliance, and whether this basis of enforceability should be expanded.

In one of the most famous articles on contract ever written, "Consideration and Form,"[10] Lon Fuller identifies the distinct functions performed by the use of formalities. Although the entire article is well worth studying, consider the following summary and expansion of Fuller's analysis by Professors Calamari and Perillo:

Formalities serve important functions in many legal systems, particularly in relatively primitive societies. Important among these is the *evidentiary function.* Compliance with formalities provides reliable evidence that a given transaction took place. A *cautionary function* is also served. The ceremony of melting sealing wax onto parchment followed by impressing the melted wax with a signet ring was imposing. Before performing the required ritual the promisor had ample opportunity to reflect and deliberate on the wisdom of his act. Therefore the document can be accepted by the legal system as a serious act of volition. A third function is an earmarking or *channeling function.* The populace is made aware that the use of a given device will attain a desired result. When the device is used, the judicial task of determining the parties' intentions is facilitated. A fourth function is *clarification.* When the parties reduce their transaction to writing (and a contract under seal must be in writing) they are more likely to work out details not contained in their oral agreement. In addition, form requirements can work to serve regulatory and fiscal ends, to educate the parties as to the full extent of their obligations, to provide public notice of the transaction, and also to help management efficiency in an organizational setting.[11] (Emphasis added.)

In this section, we shall consider the continued role that formality plays in the law of contract.

---

10. Lon L. Fuller, Consideration and Form, 41 Colum. L. Rev. 799 (1941).
11. John D. Calamari and Joseph M. Perillo, Contracts §7.1 (5th ed. 2003).

STUDY GUIDE: When reading the cases in the next few sections, consider the advantages of enforcing formal (but not bargained-for) commitments. What theoretical or philosophical reasons can you offer for the decline of formal contracts? Consider as well how your views of the outcomes of the following cases are influenced by your sympathies (or the lack thereof) for the parties. Are these appropriate concerns for a court? Do they enhance or distort the ideal of equality before the law — or of law itself? Is there a reason why these cases might be peculiarly prone to such emotional influences?

1.   The Seal

Prior to the rise of assumpsit, the seal dominated the English common law of contract. One might say that the seal was to medieval English contract law what consideration became to modern contract law. The traditional view of the seal was summarized by the court in In re Conrad's Estate:

> It is well settled that a seal imports consideration. This is more than a mere presumption; the seal takes the place of proof of consideration and in the absence of fraud makes the promise enforceable without it. The defense of want of consideration is not available in an action on a sealed instrument. . . . Where, however, there is evidence of fraud upon the maker, the seal will be disregarded and proof of consideration will be required.
>
> Failure of consideration, on the other hand, is a valid defense to a sealed instrument. The distinction between want and failure of consideration has been pointed out in a number of cases.[12]

The court then quotes In re Killeen's Estate:

> There is, however, a distinction between want and failure of consideration; want of consideration embraces transactions or instances where none was intended to pass, while failure of consideration implies that a valuable consideration, moving from obligee to obligor, was contemplated. . . . Want of consideration is no defense, as this would contradict the terms of the instrument, while failure of consideration does not contradict the terms of the instrument, but shows that the consideration contemplated was never received.[13]

Notice that, by the time In re Conrad's Estate was decided, the theory of consideration so dominated thinking about contract enforceability that the seal was seen as "importing" a consideration rather than as an alternative to this requirement.

When reading the following cases, it is important for students to bear in mind that the rise of the bargain theory of consideration during the past century has been accompanied by a marked decline in the significance of the seal.

12. In re Conrad's Estate, 33 Pa. 561, 563, 3 A2d 697, 699 (1938).
13. In re Killeen's Estate, 310 Pa. 182, 187, 165 A. 34, 35 (1932).

[I]ts effect on the enforceability of promises was abolished in roughly half of the states of the United States and seriously curtailed in the rest. The most recent of these assaults on the seal came in the Uniform Commercial Code which, as its commentary explains, "makes it clear that every effect of the seal which relates to 'sealed instruments' as such is wiped out insofar as contracts for sale [of goods] are concerned." In jurisdictions where the seal has not been entirely abolished, its effect may be limited to raising a rebuttable presumption of consideration or to making applicable a longer period of limitations. It is essential in such jurisdictions to consult the particular state statutes relating to the seal and the decisions applying those statutes.[14]

Can you think of possible reasons why this decline has occurred — reasons that do not undermine the legitimacy of enforcing all formal commitments? When pondering this, consider the following description of the seal by Chancellor James Kent in the 1810 case of Warren v. Lynch (1810):

A scrawl with a pen is not a seal, and deserves no notice. . . . The calling a paper a deed will not make it one, if it want the requisite formalities. . . . The policy of the rule consists in giving ceremony and solemnity to the execution of important instruments, by means of which the attention of the parties is more certainly and effectually fixed, and frauds less likely to be practised upon the unwary.[15]

Now compare Chancellor Kent's description with the following definition of a seal contained in an 1892 New York statute:

The private seal of a person, other than a corporation, to any instrument or writing shall consist of a wafer, wax or other similar adhesive substance affixed thereto, paper or other similar substance affixed thereto, by mucilage or other adhesive substance, or of the word "seal," or the letters "L.S.," opposite the signature.[16]

We shall study cases about the seal in part because of the historical significance of this doctrine, but most importantly because of what these discussions of the seal reveal about the enforceability of both formal and informal agreements. These insights will be of particular importance when we study the promissory estoppel cases in Chapter 11.

STUDY GUIDE: In the next case, which of Lon Fuller's three functions of formality — evidentiary, cautionary, and channeling — are used by the court in its discussion of the seal? Notice that Peter Aller's written promise was neither bargained for, nor did it induce any detrimental reliance. Does the absence of these two rationales for enforcement mean that it should be unenforceable? If not, what is the rationale for its enforcement?

---

14. E. Allan Farnsworth, Contracts §2.16 (4th ed. 2004) (citations omitted).
15. Warren v. Lynch, 5 Johns. 239, 245-46 (N.Y. 1810).
16. 1892 N.Y. Laws, ch. 677, §13.

ALLER v. ALLER
Supreme Court of New Jersey,
40 N.J.L. 446 (1878)

The action was brought on the following instrument, viz.:

One day after date, I promise to pay my daughter, Angeline H. Aller, the sum of three hundred and twelve dollars and sixty-one cents, for value received, with lawful interest from date, without defalcation or discount, as witness my hand and seal this fourth day of September, one thousand eight hundred and seventy-three. $312.61. This note is given in lieu of one-half of the balance due the estate of Mary A. Aller, deceased, for a note given for one thousand dollars to said deceased by me. Peter H. Aller. [L. S.] Witnesses present, John J. Smith, John F. Grandin.

Both subscribing witnesses were examined at the trial, and it appeared that there was a note for $1000, dated May 1st, 1858, given by said Peter H. Aller to Mary Aller, upon which there were endorsements of payments — April 1st, 1863, $50; April 1st, 1866, $46; April 1st, $278.78.

Mary Ann Aller, the wife, died, and on the day after her burial, Peter H. Aller told his daughter, the plaintiff, to get the note, which he said was among her mother's papers. She brought it, read the note; he said there was more money endorsed on it than he thought; requested the witness John F. Grandin to add up the endorsements and subtract them from the principal, to divide the balance by two, and draw a note to each of her daughters, Leonora and Angelina, for one-half. After they were drawn by the witness, Peter H. Aller said: "Now here, girls, is a nice present for you," and gave them the notes. Angelina was directed to put the old note back among her mother's papers. Grandin was afterwards appointed administrator of Mary A. Aller, and as such, he says, he destroyed the old note. . . .

The action was brought by Angelina H. Aller, now Angelina H. McPherson, against Peter H. Aller in his lifetime and, after his death, continued against his executor, Michael Shurts.

The defendant, Peter H. Aller, was aged and feeble, and the plea was, therefore, filed in his lifetime, by consent, without affidavit. . . .

The verdict was for the plaintiff, and a rule to show cause was allowed at the Circuit.

The opinion of the court was delivered by SCUDDER, J.* Whether the note for $1000 could have been enforced in equity as evidence of an indebtedness by the husband to the wife during her life, is immaterial, for after her death he was entitled, as husband of his deceased wife, to administer on her estate, and receive any balance due on the note, after deducting legal charges, under the statute of distribution. The daughters could have no legal or equitable claim on this note against their father after their mother's decease. The giving of these two sealed promises in writing to them by their father was therefore a voluntary act on his part. That it was just and meritorious to divide the

---

* *Edward Wallace Scudder* (1822-1893) was educated at Princeton College and studied law privately. He served in the New Jersey Senate from 1863 to 1865 and was president of that body in 1865. Appointed to the Supreme Court of New Jersey in 1869, he served on the bench until his death. — K.T.

amount represented by the original note between these only two surviving children of the wife, if it was her separate property, and keep it from going into the general distribution of the husband's estate among his other children, is evident, and such appears to have been his purpose.

The question now is, whether that intention was legally and conclusively manifested, so that it cannot now be resisted. . . .

Our statute concerning evidence . . . which enacts that in any action upon an instrument in writing, under seal, the defendant in such action may plead and set up as a defence therein fraud in the consideration, is not applicable for here there is no fraud shown.

But it is said that the act of April 6th, 1875, . . . opens it to the defence of want of sufficient consideration, as if it were a simple contract, and, that being shown, the contract becomes inoperative.

The statute reads —

> that in every action upon a sealed instrument, or where a set-off is founded on a sealed instrument, the seal thereof shall be only presumptive evidence of a sufficient consideration, which may be rebutted, as if such instrument was not sealed, &c.

Suppose the presumption that the seal carries with it, that there is sufficient consideration, is rebutted, and overcome by evidence showing there was no such consideration, the question still remains, whether an instrument under seal, without sufficient consideration, is not a good promise, and enforceable at law. It is manifest here the parties intended and understood that there should be no consideration. The old man said: "Now here, girls, is a nice present for each of you," and so it was received by them. The mischief which the above quoted law was designed to remedy, was that where the parties intended there should be a consideration, they were prevented by the common law from showing none, if the contract was under seal. But it would be going too far to say that the statute was intended to abrogate all voluntary contracts, and to abolish all distinction between specialties and simple contracts.

It will not do to hold that every conveyance of land, or of chattels, is void by showing that no sufficient consideration passed when creditors are not affected. Nor can it be shown by authority that an executory contract, entered into intentionally and deliberately, and attested in solemn form by a seal, cannot be enforced. Both by the civil and the common law, persons were guarded against haste and imprudence in entering into voluntary agreements. The distinction between *"nudum pactum"* and *"pactum vestitum,"* by civil law, was in the formality of execution and not in the fact that in one case there was a consideration, and in the other none, though the former term, as adopted in the common law, has the signification of a contract without consideration. The latter was enforced without reference to the consideration, because of the formality of its ratification. 1 Parsons on Cont. (6th ed.). . . .

The early case of Sharington v. Strotton, Plow. 308, gives the same cause for the adoption of the sealing and delivery of a deed. It says, among other things,

> because words are oftentimes spoken by men unadvisedly and without deliberation, the law has provided that a contract by words shall not bind without

consideration. And the reason is, because it is by words which pass from men lightly and inconsiderately, but where the agreement is by deed there is more time for deliberation, &c. So that there is great deliberation used in the making of deeds, for which reason they are received as a *lien* final to the party, and are adjudged to bind the party without examining upon what cause or consideration they were made. . . .

In Smith on Contracts, the learned author, after stating the strictness of the rules of law, that there must be a consideration to support a simple contract to guard persons against the consequences of their own imprudence, says: "The law does not absolutely prohibit them from contracting a gratuitous obligation, for they may, if they will, do so by deed."

This subject of the derivation of terms and formalities from the civil law, and of the rule adopted in the common law, is fully described in Fonb. Eq. 335, note a. The author concludes by saying:

> If, however, an agreement be evidenced, by bond or other instrument, under seal, it would certainly be seriously mischievous to allow its consideration to be disputed, the common law not having pointed out any other means by which an agreement can be more solemnly authenticated. Every deed, therefore, in itself imports a consideration, though it be only the will of the maker, and therefore shall never be said to be *nudum pactum*. . . .

These statements of the law have been thus particularly given in the words of others, because the significance of writings under seal, and their importance in our common law system, seem in danger of being overlooked in some of our later legislation. If a party has fully and absolutely expressed his intention in a writing sealed and delivered, with the most solemn sanction known to our law, what should prevent its execution where there is no fraud or illegality? But because deeds have been used to cover fraud and illegality in the consideration, and just defences have been often shut out by the conclusive character of the formality of sealing, we have enacted in our state the two recent statutes above quoted. The one allows fraud in the consideration of instruments under seal to be set up as a defence, the other takes away the conclusive evidence of a sufficient consideration heretofore accorded to a sealed writing, and makes it only presumptive evidence. This does not reach the case of a voluntary agreement, where there was no consideration, and none intended by the parties. The statute establishes a new rule of evidence, by which the consideration of sealed instruments may be shown, but does not take from them the effect of establishing a contract expressing the intention of the parties, made with the most solemn authentication, which is not shown to be fraudulent or illegal. It could not have been in the mind of the legislature to make it impossible for parties to enter in to such promises; and without a clear expression of the legislative will, not only as to the admissibility, but the effect of such evidence, such construction should not be given to this law. Even if it should be held that consideration is required to uphold a deed, yet it might still be implied where its purpose is not within the mischief which the statute was intended to remedy. It was certainly not the intention of the legislature to abolish all distinction between simple contracts and specialties, for in the last clause of the section they say that all instruments executed with a scroll, or other device by way of scroll, shall be deemed sealed instruments. It is evident that they were to be continued with their former legal effect, except so far as they might be controlled by evidence affecting their intended consideration. . . .

The rule for a new trial should be discharged.

Statutory Background: New Jersey Changes Its Mind

STUDY GUIDE: *Would the following amendment of the New Jersey statute have affected the enforceability of Peter Aller's note to his daughter? If so, is this a development to be desired?*

After Aller v. Aller, the New Jersey state legislature amended the statute to read as follows:

> In any claim upon a sealed instrument, a party may plead and set up, in defense thereto, fraud in the consideration of the contract upon which recovery is sought, or want or failure of consideration, as if the instrument was not sealed. In such cases the seal shall be only presumptive evidence of sufficient consideration, which presumption may be rebutted as if the instrument were not sealed.

N.J. Stat. Ann. §2A:82-3 (1951).

STUDY GUIDE: *The seal is still alive in some places and Massachusetts is one of them. The following brief case shows how a seal can cut short the issue of enforceability. It also shows the court's reluctance to entertain arguments based on inadequacy of consideration.*

WAGNER v. LECTROX CORP.
Appeals Court of Massachusetts,
4 Mass. App. Ct. 815, 348 N.E.2d 451 (1976)

Before KEVILLE, GOODMAN and ARMSTRONG, JJ.*

RESCRIPT. The plaintiff's contention that the defendants' motion for summary judgment was improperly allowed because he had established

---

* *Edward Keville* (1912-2005) served as the chief secretary to Governor Herter, who subsequently appointed him to the Probate Court (1954-1979). In 1972, Keville was appointed as one of the six original Associate Justices of the Appeals Court, where he served until 1979.

Reuben Goodman (1913-1983) was the son of Russian immigrants. Raised speaking Yiddish, Goodman began learning English at the age of five. Educated at Harvard (A.B., LL.B.), Goodman had a long record of private and public service with the Massachusetts Defenders Committee and the Civil Liberties Union of Massachusetts and as a defense counsel in many celebrated trials. He was Chief Counsel for the Office of Price Administration (1943-1946) and, in 1946, served in the Department of Justice as an advisor to the South Korean Ministry of Justice in reorganizing the administrative branch of its interim government. From 1947 to 1950, he was in Tokyo with Allied forces to re-establish a civilian government and set up a new constitution.

Christopher J. Armstrong was educated at Yale College (A.B., LL.B.) before being admitted to the Massachusetts bar in 1961. Justice Armstrong was appointed as one of the six original Associate Justices of the Appeals Court in 1972. In 2000, he became Chief Justice of the Appeals Court. In 2009, he left the bench to enter private practice where he specializes in appellate advocacy. — J.B.

the existence of one or more genuine issues of material fact bearing on the enforceability of the license agreement against him is without merit. His deposition and counteraffidavit . . . did no more than disclose that he sought relief from the terms of the agreement which he came to regard "as a bad or uneven bargain." Hancock Bank & Trust Co. v. Shell Oil Co., . . . 309 N.E.2d 482 (1974). The plaintiff unsuccessfully asserts the existence of an issue whether there had been failure of consideration for the license granted the corporate defendant by him under the agreement. In making this claim he relies upon averments in his deposition and counteraffidavit that the written agreement did not express the entire understanding of the parties, that he executed the agreement in consideration of oral "assurances" by the individual defendants that certain proposals beneficial to him "would be acted upon later," but that no action was taken or agreement reached with respect to those proposals. Even if such "assurances" could prevail against the strictures imposed by the parol evidence rule and by the plain language of the written agreement . . . , the plaintiff's counteraffidavit failed to establish anything more than expectations on his part which fell short of a binding agreement. . . . It is not apparent how any insufficiency of the consideration recited in the written agreement could have affected the outcome of the case, since the agreement, being under seal, would not thereby have been rendered unenforceable. Schuster v. Baskin, 354 Mass. 137, 141, 236 N.E.2d 205 (1968). Marine Contractors Co. Inc. v. Hurley, . . . 310 N.E.2d 915 (1974). . . .

Judgment affirmed.

RESTATEMENT (SECOND) OF CONTRACTS

§95.   REQUIREMENTS FOR SEALED CONTRACT OR WRITTEN CONTRACT OR INSTRUMENT

(1) In the absence of statute a promise is binding without consideration if

(a) it is in writing and sealed; and

(b) the document containing the promise is delivered; and

(c) the promisor and promisee are named in the document or so described as to be capable of identification when it is delivered. . . .

SALES CONTRACTS: THE UNIFORM COMMERCIAL CODE

§2-203.   SEALS INOPERATIVE

The affixing of a seal to a writing evidencing a contract for sale or an offer to buy or sell goods does not constitute the writing a sealed instrument and the law with respect to sealed instruments does not apply to such a contract or offer.

REFERENCE: Barnett, §4.3
                    Farnsworth, §§2.16-2.19
                    Calamari & Perillo, §§7.1-7.9
                    Murray, §54

2. Nominal Consideration

We now turn our attention from the formality of the seal to that provided by so-called nominal consideration. As was seen in Chapter 9, the second Restatement declares such pretended exchanges to be ineffective. Comment *d* to Restatement (Second) §79 states:

> Disparity in value, with or without other circumstances, sometimes indicates that the purported consideration was not in fact bargained for but was a mere formality or pretense. Such a sham or "nominal" consideration does not satisfy the requirement of §71.

Although this implication of the bargain theory has become the rule in most situations, our purpose is, once again, to evaluate the merits of this basis of enforceability. One advocate of such enforcement was Lon L. Fuller, who contended that with nominal consideration:

> the desiderata underlying the use of formalities are . . . satisfied by the fact that the parties have taken the trouble to cast their transaction in the form of an exchange. The promise supported by nominal consideration then becomes enforceable for reasons similar to those which justify the enforcement of the promise under seal.[17]

Was Fuller right? If so, why did the Restatement (Second) reject this position?

STUDY GUIDE: Can you see the role that the concept of subjective value is playing in the following group of decisions? How has the doctrine of consideration appeared to swallow the whole of contract law? Is this justified in light of the origins of the doctrine? Why should not Mr. Schnell be able to legally bind himself in this manner?

SCHNELL v. NELL
Supreme Court of Indiana,
17 Ind. 29 (1861)

PERKINS, J.* — Action by J. B. Nell against Zacharias Schnell, upon the following instrument:

> This agreement, entered into this 13th day of February, 1856, between Zach. Schnell, of Indianapolis, Marion county, State of Indiana, as party of the

---

17. Lon L. Fuller, Consideration and Form, 41 Colum. L. Rev. 799, 820 (1941).

Samuel E. Perkins (1811-1879) served as a judge on the Indiana Supreme Court (1846-1864). Considered one of the "ablest lawyers" in the state, he returned to private practice in 1865, but in 1872, he was appointed to fill a vacancy on the Marion County Superior Court (1872-1877), where he sat until his election to the Indiana Supreme Court (1877-1879). In addition, he was a professor of law at Northwestern Christian University (1857-1870) and Indiana University (1870-1872), and prepared both the Indiana Digest (1858) and the Indiana Practice book (1859). — R.B.

first part, and J. B. Nell, of the same place, Wendelin Lorenz, of Stilesville, Hendricks, county, State of Indiana, and Donata Lorenz, of Frickinger, Grand Duchy of Baden, Germany, as parties of the second part, witnesseth: The said Zacharias Schnell agrees as follows: whereas his wife, Theresa Schnell, now deceased, has made a last will and testament, in which, among other provisions, it was ordained that every one of the above named second parties, should receive the sum of $200; and whereas the said provisions of the will must remain a nullity, for the reason that no property, real or personal, was in the possession of the said Theresa Schnell, deceased, in her own name, at the time of her death, and all property held by Zacharias and Theresa Schnell jointly, therefore reverts to her husband; and whereas the said Theresa Schnell has also been a dutiful and loving wife to the said Zach. Schnell, and has materially aided him in the acquisition of all property, real and personal, now possessed by him; for, and in consideration of all this, and the love and respect he bears to his wife; and, furthermore, in consideration of one cent, received by him of the second parties, he, the said Zach Schnell, agrees to pay the above named sums of money to the parties of the second part, to wit: $200 to the said J. B. Nell; $200 to the said Wendelin Lorenz; and $200 to the said Donata Lorenz, in the following installments viz., $200 in one year from the date of these presents; $200 in two years, and $200 in three years; to be divided between the parties in equal portions of $66 2/3 each year, or as they may agree, till each one has received his full sum of $200.

And the said parties of the second part, for, and in consideration of this, agree to pay the above named sum of money [one cent], and to deliver up to said Schnell, and abstain from collecting any real or supposed claims upon him or his estate, arising from the said last will and testament of the said Theresa Schnell, deceased.

In witness whereof, the said parties have, on this 13th day of February, 1856, set hereunto their hands and seals.

ZACHARIAS SCHNELL   [SEAL]
J. B. NELL   [SEAL]
WEN. LORENZ   [SEAL]

The complaint contained no averment of a consideration for the instrument, outside of those expressed in it; and did not aver that the one cent agreed to be paid, had been paid or tendered.

A demurrer to the complaint was overruled.

The defendant answered, that the instrument sued on was given for no consideration whatever.

He further answered, that it was given for no consideration, because his said wife, Theresa, at the time she made the will mentioned, and at the time of her death, owned neither separately, nor jointly with her husband, or any one else (except so far as the law gave her an interest in her husband's property,) any property, real or personal, &c.

The will is copied into the record, but need not be into this opinion.

The Court sustained a demurrer to these answers, evidently on the ground that they were regarded as contradicting the instrument sued on, which particularly set out the considerations upon which it was executed. But the instrument is latently ambiguous on this point. . . .

The case turned below, and must turn here, upon the question whether the instrument sued on does express a consideration sufficient to give it legal obligation, as against Zacharias Schnell. It specifies three distinct considerations for his promise to pay $600:

1.   A promise, on the part of the plaintiffs, to pay him one cent.
2.   The love and affection he bore his deceased wife, and the fact that she had done her part, as his wife, in the acquisition of property.
3.   The fact that she had expressed her desire, in the form of an inoperative will, that the persons named therein should have the sums of money specified.

The consideration of one cent will not support the promise of Schnell. It is true, that as a general proposition, inadequacy of consideration will not vitiate an agreement. . . . But this doctrine does not apply to a mere exchange of sums of money, of coin, whose value is exactly fixed, but to the exchange of something of, in itself, indeterminate value, for money, or, perhaps, for some other thing of indeterminate value. In this case, had the one cent mentioned been some particular one cent, a family piece, or ancient, remarkable coin, possessing an indeterminate value, extrinsic from its simple money value, a different view might be taken. As it is, the mere promise to pay six hundred dollars for one cent, even had the portion of that cent due from the plaintiffs been tendered, is an unconscionable contract, void, at first blush, upon its face, if it be regarded as a earnest one. Hardesty v. Smith, 3 Ind. 39. The consideration of one cent is, plainly, in this case, merely nominal, and intended to be so. As the will and testament of Schnell's wife imposed no legal obligation upon him to discharge her bequests out of his property, and as she had none of her own, his promise to discharge them was not legally binding upon him, on that ground. A moral consideration, only, will not support a promise. . . . And for the same reason, a valid consideration for his promise can not be found in the fact of a compromise of a disputed claim; for where such claim is legally groundless, a promise upon a compromise of it, or of a suit upon it, is not legally binding. . . . There was no mistake of law or fact in this case, as the agreement admits the will inoperative and void. The promise was simply one to make a gift. The past services of his wife, and the love and affection he had borne her, are objectionable as legal considerations for Schnell's promise, on two grounds: 1. They are past considerations. . . . 2. The fact that Schnell loved his wife, and that she had been industrious, constituted no consideration for his promise to pay J. B. Nell, and the Lorenzes, a sum of money. Whether, if his wife, in her lifetime, had made a bargain with Schnell, that, in consideration of his promising to pay, after her death, to the persons named, a sum of money, she would be industrious, and worthy of his affection, such a promise would have been valid and consistent with public policy, we need not decide. Nor is the fact that Schnell now venerates the memory of his deceased wife, a legal consideration for a promise to pay any third person money.

The instrument sued on, interpreted in the light of the facts alleged in the second paragraph of the answer, will not support an action. The demurrer to the answer should have been overruled. . . .

PER CURIAM — The judgment is reversed, with cost. Cause remanded &c.

Statutory Background: Documents Under Seal in Indiana

STUDY GUIDE: You may have noticed that Mr. Schnell's promise was made under seal. Here is a likely explanation for why the court did not consider this to be a basis of enforcement. This statute exemplifies the longstanding general trend toward diminishing the effectiveness of the seal.

LON L. FULLER, BASIC CONTRACT LAW 346 (1947):   Statutory provisions in Indiana, already in effect when Schnell v. Nell was decided, read as follows:

> A failure or want of consideration, in whole or in part, may be pleaded in any action, set-off or counter-claim upon or arising out of any specialty, bond or deed, except instruments negotiable by the law merchant and negotiated before falling due.

Burns' Ann. St. (1926) §390.

> There shall be no difference in evidence between sealed and unsealed writings; and every writing not sealed, shall have the same force and effect that it would have if sealed. A writing under seal, except conveyances of real estate, or any interest therein, may therefore be changed, or altogether discharged, by a writing not under seal. An agreement in writing, without a seal, for the compromise of a debt, is as obligatory as if a seal were affixed.

Id., §492.

STUDY GUIDE: Why does the Restatement (Second) allow nominal consideration to be effective under §87(1)(a), despite the fact that it is a "mere pretense"?

RESTATEMENT (SECOND) OF CONTRACTS

§71.   REQUIREMENT OF EXCHANGE; TYPES OF EXCHANGE

COMMENT

b. "Bargained for."   . . . Moreover, a mere pretense of bargain does not suffice, as where there is a false recital of consideration or where the purported consideration is merely nominal. In such cases there is no consideration and the promise is enforceable, if at all, as a promise binding without consideration under §§82-94. See Comments b and c to §87.

ILLUSTRATION

5.   A desires to make a binding promise to give $1000 to his son B. Being advised that a gratuitous promise is not binding, A offers to buy from B for $1000 a book worth less than $1. B accepts the offer knowing that the purchase of the book is a mere pretense. There is no consideration for A's promise to pay $1000.

§87.   OPTION CONTRACT

(1) An offer is binding as an option contract if it
    (a) is in writing and signed by the offeror, recites a purported consideration for the making of the offer, and proposes an exchange on fair terms within a reasonable time. . . .
[Paragraph (2) appears in Chapter 11.]

COMMENT

a. Consideration and Form.   The traditional common-law devices for making a firm offer or option contract are the giving of consideration and the affixing of a seal. See §§25, 95. But the firm offer serves a useful purpose even though no preliminary bargain is made: it is often a necessary step in the making of the main bargain proposed, and it partakes of the natural formalities inherent in business transactions. The erosion of the formality of the seal has made it less and less satisfactory as a universal formality. As literacy has spread, the personal signature has become the natural formality and the seal has become more and more anachronistic. The rules stated in this section reflect the judicial and legislative response to this situation. . . .

b. Nominal Consideration.   Offers made in consideration of one dollar paid or promised are often irrevocable under Subsection (1)(a). The irrevocability of an offer may be worth much or little to the offeree, and the courts do not ordinarily inquire into the adequacy of the consideration bargained for. See §79. Hence a comparatively small payment may furnish consideration for the irrevocability of an offer proposing a transaction involving much larger sums. But gross disproportion between the payment and the value of the option commonly indicates that the payment was not in fact bargained for but was a mere formality or pretense. In such a case there is no consideration as that term is defined in §71.

Nevertheless, such a nominal consideration is regularly held sufficient to support a short-time option proposing an exchange on fair terms. The fact that the option is an appropriate preliminary step in the conclusion of a socially useful transaction provides a sufficient substantive basis for enforcement, and a signed writing taking a form appropriate to a bargain satisfies the desiderata of form. In the absence of statute, however, the bargaining form is essential: a payment of one dollar by each party to the other is so obviously not a bargaining transaction that it does not provide the form of an exchange.

REFERENCE: Barnett, §4.3
             Farnsworth, §2.11
             Calamari & Perillo, §4.6
             Murray, §62(A) & (B)

3.   Recitals

With nominal consideration, a token actually changes hands. We now consider contracts in which a recital of good consideration is made. The overwhelming norm, as we shall see, is that such recitals give rise to, at most, a rebuttable presumption of consideration. Nonetheless, some commitments supported only by a recital of consideration are enforced despite the lack of consideration or detrimental reliance. Why? In light of the quotation from Lon Fuller on page 667, do you suppose he would have supported or opposed enforcing commitments on the basis of false recitals of consideration?

STUDY GUIDE: In what respect do such recitals resemble nominal consideration or pretended exchanges? In what respect are they different?

SMITH v. WHEELER

Supreme Court of Georgia,
233 Ga. 166, 210 S.E.2d 702 (1974)

JORDAN, J.*

Ira Wheeler and Charles Smith entered into an option agreement on March 17, 1973, whereby Wheeler gave Smith a one-year option to buy certain property located in Rockdale County. The option agreement, signed by both parties, states that it is "In consideration of the sum of one ($1.00) dollar to me in hand paid, receipt whereof is hereby acknowledged. . . ." It is undisputed that the one dollar consideration cited in the agreement was not paid at the time of execution.

On May 22, 1973, Wheeler, through his attorney, informed Smith in a letter that due to the fact that Smith had never paid the one dollar cited as consideration in the agreement he would take the position "that the purported option agreement is a legal nullity and not enforceable against him." Wheeler went on to state in the letter that he intended to sell the property shortly thereafter to another individual and that as far as he was concerned Smith had "no legal rights in the property." On March 11, 1974, Smith sent Wheeler notice by registered mail that he was prepared to exercise his option to buy the property and enclosed the one dollar consideration. In his letter, Smith stated that he was ready to pay $30,000 in cash and that the closing was scheduled for 11:00 A.M., March 15, 1974, at a local Savings and Loan Institution. Wheeler refused to receive delivery on the letter, and on April 23, 1974, filed a complaint in the Superior Court of Rockdale County asking that the option agreement between himself and the optionee be declared a nullity and stricken from the records in that it constituted an improper cloud upon his title to the subject property. He alleged in his complaint that the purported option agreement was of no legal force and effect due to the "failure of the Defendant-Optionee to deliver the One Dollar recited as the sole consideration of the option agreement." . . .

---

* *Robert Henry Jordan* (1916-1992) was educated at the University of Georgia (J.D.) and was admitted to practice in Georgia in 1941. He practiced law in Talbotton (1946-1960) and served in the Georgia State Senate (1953-1954, 1959-1960), where he was President pro tem in 1959. He moved to the bench in 1960 with his appointment to the Supreme Court of Georgia, where he served as Chief Justice (1980-1982). Jordan retired from that body in 1982. — K.T.

The plaintiff-appellee contended in the trial court and now contends on appeal that the option contract was unilateral in nature and since the optionor withdrew his offer prior to the tender and payment of the one dollar recited as consideration for the option agreement, the option is a nullity and has no legal force and effect. We do not agree with this contention and reverse the decision of the trial court.

The majority of cases from other jurisdictions hold that the offeror may prove that the consideration had not been paid and that no other consideration had taken its place. Bard v. Kent, 19 Cal. 2d 449 (122 P.2d 8, 139 A.L.R. 1032); Calamari & Perillo, Law of Contracts, §58 (1970). However, the minority rule, and what we consider to be the best view, is that even if it is shown that the dollar was not paid it does not void the contract. We have held many times that the recital of the one dollar consideration gives rise to an implied promise to pay which can be enforced by the other party. . . .

It was therefore error for the trial court to grant appellee's motion for judgment on the pleadings on the theory that there was a failure of consideration. There are material issues of fact concerning appellant's compliance with other terms of the option agreement, and the rights and obligations evolving therefrom.

Judgment reversed.

All the Justices concur, except INGRAM, J., who concurs specially.

JOLLES v. WITTENBERG, COURT OF APPEALS OF GEORGIA, 148 GA. APP 805, 253 S.E.2D 203 (1979): QUILLIAN, J.* . . . A contract under seal raises a prima facie presumption of consideration, which is rebuttable. . . . Thus, although a contract under seal imports consideration . . . , the defense of failure of consideration can be asserted. . . . However, any nominal consideration recited in sealed instruments is sufficient as a matter of law. . . .

Here the monetary consideration recited is $1, which was noted as received and admitted by the defendant as to its "adequacy." The parties stipulated that the $1 was not paid. But this evidence is not controlling. "Where a contract contains a recital of the payment of one dollar as its consideration, the contract is valid though the sum named was not actually paid. It creates an obligation to pay that sum, which can be enforced by the other party." Southern Bell & Co. v. Harris, 117 Ga. 1001(2), (44 S.E. 885); . . . Smith v. Wheeler, 233 Ga. 166, 168, (210 S.E.2d 702). Accordingly, we find the contract was supported by monetary consideration which was agreed to, in writing, by the appellant to be adequate. . . .

---

* *John Kelley Quillian* (1930-1988) studied at Piedmont College (A.B.) and the University of Georgia (LL.B.) and was admitted to the Georgia bar in 1954. He practiced law at Winder, Georgia, until his appointment in 1966 to the Court of Appeals of Georgia; he was elected to the post in 1971 and served there until 1984. — K.T.

RESTATEMENT (SECOND) OF CONTRACTS

§87.   OPTION CONTRACT

COMMENT

c. False Recital of Nominal Consideration.   A recital in a written agreement that a stated consideration has been given is evidence of the fact as against a party to the agreement, but such a recital may ordinarily be contradicted by evidence that no consideration was given or expected. See §218. In cases within Subsection (1)(a), however, the giving and recital of nominal consideration performs a formal function only. The signed writing has vital significance as a formality, while the ceremonial manual delivery of a dollar or a peppercorn is an inconsequential formality. In view of the dangers of permitting a solemn written agreement to be invalidated by oral testimony which is easily fabricated, therefore, the option agreement is not invalidated by proof that the recited consideration was not in fact given. A fictitious rationalization has sometimes been used for this rule: acceptance of delivery of the written instrument conclusively imports a promise to make good the recital, it is said, and that promise furnishes consideration. Compare §218. But the sound basis for the rule is that stated above.

§88.   GUARANTY

A promise to be surety for the performance of a contractual obligation, made to the obligee, is binding if

(a) the promise is in writing and signed by the promisor and recites a purported consideration. . . .

COMMENT

b. Nominal Consideration and Recital Thereof.   . . . The amount paid for a guaranty is often only a small fraction of the amount of the principal obligation; indeed, consideration may be furnished by the mere extension of credit to the principal obligor. Hence it would often be difficult to say whether a consideration of one dollar is adequate in amount, and courts do not ordinarily inquire into that question. See §79. Like §87 on option contracts, this Section goes further and precludes inquiry into the question whether the consideration recited in a written contract of guaranty was mere formality or pretense, or whether it was in fact given.

REFERENCE: Farnsworth, §2.17
Murray, §62(C)

4.   Written Expression of Intention to Be Legally Bound

Suppose that a person makes a written promise and also explicitly states in writing that she intends to be legally bound. Should such a promise be enforceable in the absence of bargained-for consideration or a formality like a seal, nominal consideration, or a recital of consideration? The traditional answer to this question, and the answer in most jurisdictions today, is that such commitments are not enforceable. Yet in 1925 the National Conference of Commissioners on Uniform State Law (the same institution that drafted the U.C.C.) proposed that states enact a statute that would have made such commitments enforceable in the absence of consideration. Section 1 of the Uniform Written Obligations Act, reads as follows:

> A written release or promise hereafter made and signed by the person releasing or promising shall not be invalid or unenforceable for lack of consideration, if the writing also contains an additional express statement, in any form of language, that the signer intends to be legally bound.

This statute was adopted by Pennsylvania in 1927, where it remains in effect.[18] Restatement (Second) of Contracts §95(2) states that:

> When a statute provides in effect that a written contract or instrument is binding without consideration . . . , in order to be subject to the statute a promise must either (a) be expressed in a document signed or otherwise assented to by the promisor and delivered; or (b) be expressed in a writing or writings to which both promisor and promisee manifest assent.

Before we examine cases in which the statute has been used, it will be illuminating to read an excerpt from proceedings of the 1925 meeting of the National Conference of Commissioners in which this proposal was debated. Perhaps most interesting of all in light of his identification with §20 of the first Restatement, the person who authored this proposal and defended it before the Commissioners was none other than Professor Samuel Williston.

Legislative Background: The Rationale for the Uniform Written Obligations Act

STUDY GUIDE: Why did Professor Williston think that this statute was desirable? Did he intend to abolish the requirement of consideration? Notice what is said about the seal, promises of gifts, nominal consideration, and charitable subscriptions. Why do you suppose that so few states enacted the act? What criticisms were offered by some commissioners? What does Commissioner Beers mean by exalting "form over substance"? Would such a proposal adequately perform the evidentiary, cautionary, and channelling functions of formality?

___

18. The official position of the National Conference of Commissioners with respect to this and other proposed uniform and model acts that have not received wide adoption is that "they are still recommended for consideration in states having need for legislation in the several fields involved." Handbook of the National Conference of Commissioners on Uniform State Laws 457 (1993).

HANDBOOK OF THE NATIONAL CONFERENCE OF
COMMISSIONERS ON UNIFORM STATE LAWS & PROCEEDINGS OF
THE THIRTY-FIFTH ANNUAL MEETING, DETROIT, MICHIGAN,
SEVENTH SESSION, FRIDAY, AUG. 28, 1925, PP. 193-202, 204, 211-
212, 215: . . . The Conference then went into a Committee of the Whole
to consider the Uniform Written Obligations Act . . . , Mr. Dinkelspiel of
California in the chair.

Mr. Williston read Section 1 of the Uniform Written Obligations Act. . . .

Mr. Beers: May I ask if it is the intention of the Committee to make enforcible [sic] a mere promise to make a gift? For instance, in a moment
of generosity my friend, Mr. Williston, says, "I promise to pay, or I will
pay $10,000," and he signs it.

Mr. Williston: That alone does not comply with Section 1. The writing
does not contain an express statement that the signer intends to be
legally bound.

Mr. Beers: Does it mean, for instance, suppose I feel good-natured and
I feel rich today and I promise to pay John Doe next week $10,000, and
I expressly state that I intend to be bound — (interrupted).

Mr. Williston: Yes, that is just what it is intended to mean.

Mr. Beers: It junks most of our prevailing notions of law, doesn't it? It is
pretty sweeping.

Mr. Williston: It substitutes for the common law use of a seal, this express
intention to be legally bound. If you write such a paper as that which
you have just alluded to and lick a wafer and put it on, at common law
you are bound. You had better not do it in Massachusetts and many
other states unless you want to pay $10,000, and it seems a better way to
effectuate that sort of purpose, to make an express statement that you
intend to do what you are doing and intend to create a legal obligation,
than to lick a wafer. It is something, it seems to me, that a person ought
to be able to do, if he wishes to do it, — to create a legal obligation to
make a gift. Why not? The result of having no such provision in many
states is the creation of a sort of fictitious consideration in regard to
subscription papers, by means of which courts for one reason or
another, as most of them do, enforce a promise to make a charitable
gift. They base their action on all sorts of reasons, and occasionally some
of them don't do it, but it creates a lot of litigation. I don't see why a man
should not be able to make himself liable if he wishes to do so.

Mr. Beers: Forgetting the question of the seal for the moment, I think it is
pretty well ground into most of us that if there is a consideration you
can make a binding promise, but that a gift must be a present thing.
Now, it may be that this will cure some defects in subscription papers
and things of that kind, but it would seem that it is so sweeping, so
broad, it makes such radical changes, that any little incidental good it
may do is very much overbalanced by the dangers which it opens up.
I, personally, am very much opposed to it.

Mr. Child: Do I understand, Professor Williston, that an express statement
to be bound must have an additional express statement of an intention
to be bound?

Mr. Williston: An express promise must have, in addition, an express statement that you intend legally to be bound, and not merely morally bound, as every promisor is by his promise.

Mr. Child: Do I understand that an express promise, as suggested by Mr. Beers, would need another express promise added to that?

Mr. Williston: Another express statement that you intend to be legally bound. That is not another express *promise*, but it is a statement that you intend your promise not simply to create the moral obligation which attaches to every promise, but you intend that it shall create a legal obligation. . . .

Mr. Freund: I would like to ask, suppose I sign a writing, "In consideration of love and affection I promise to pay my niece on her marriage day $10,000." Suppose she is already engaged to be married so that there would be no question of a new consideration, is that or is it not binding?

Mr. Williston: It is not binding under this.

Mr. Dutcher: But if you add "I expect to be legally bound by it," then it would be.

Mr. Williston: Then it would be.

Mr. Dutcher: As I understand it, this is an attempt to revive practically the old common law doctrine that a written contract under seal without consideration is legally enforceable. It substitutes for the seal the declaration of intention to be legally bound.

Mr. Williston: That is the purpose of it, to make uniform the law in regard to that sort of voluntary promise, and to make as a substitute for the very technical and easily substituted wafer an expression which nobody can misunderstand, which clearly indicates that it is intended to create a legal obligation.

Mr. Dutcher: I think in my state the courts never concern themselves with enforcement of any purely executory contract that hasn't a consideration.

Mr. Williston: I understand this would change the law of your state.

Mr. Dutcher: I was wondering what proportion of the states of the union practically abolish the common law doctrine and are similar to the laws of my own state, and what proportion of the states will have the affixation of a seal.

Mr. Williston: I think I can tell you roughly. I suppose that a minority of the states have abolished seals altogether, a somewhat large number but still a minority. A more common provision is that in a writing with a seal the consideration shall be presumed.

Mr. Dutcher: That's true in my state.

Mr. Williston: Now, that was a frequent way of explaining the common law doctrine that a seal rendered a promise binding. It was often said that the consideration was presumed, and it is very likely that many, if not most, of the states which made that statutory enactment merely were taking over a common law expression that consideration was presumed and then changed the meaning which was attached to those words in the English books, namely, that consideration was conclusively presumed, and made it mean consideration was presumed until the contrary was proved. Under precisely that form of statute in

New Jersey consideration is conclusively presumed.[19] You go across the river into New York, where they have the same statute substantially, the presumption is disputable. So it is in most states. In a certain number of states, perhaps ten or a dozen, I should think, the seal would still have its old common law effect, so far as consideration is concerned, without any statutory interference. Now, the purpose of this act is to make the law uniform on this subject, and instead of attempting to reinstate seals in their old effect, so far as consideration is concerned, this is suggested as a better way. Seals seem to be objectionable for several reasons. In the first place, people aren't generally likely to know what is the effect of licking a seal and putting it after a signature. In the second place, when a man has signed a document, a gratuitous promise, and given it to another, it is pretty easy for that other to lick a wafer and put it after the signature. That's a fraud that might be difficult to prove. In the third place, there has been a great deal of litigation in regard to what is a seal, and it raises a very difficult question. In one case a dash an eighth of an inch long was held to be a seal. When you cut as fine as that, you are getting into troublesome technicalities. Nevertheless it seems to me it is desirable that if a man really wants to make a gratuitous promise that he ought to be allowed to do so, that the law ought to give effect to his intent. Of course, if you disagree with that fundamental proposition, you disagree with the proposed act.

Mr. Dutcher: I think it is very desirable that the law should be uniform on the subject. The only question in my mind is whether the law should not be uniform that the courts should not concern themselves with the promise made without a consideration.

Mr. Williston: The result in states where that has been the attitude of the courts has generally been an upsetting of the law of consideration, for when they get to gratuitous promises, really gratuitous promises, which they wish to enforce, they hunt around and find something which they treat as consideration *pro hac vice*, though it is really not an agreed exchange. The subscription paper cases are the most striking example of what I am saying. Those are really, as the name implies, charitable subscriptions, which means they are gifts, promises to give simply because you are charitable.

Mr. Dixon: The effect of this would be to reenact the common law effect of a seal under the name and take away the plea of no consideration where the promise is in writing, is that true?

Mr. Williston: No. The promise must not only be in writing but there must be an additional express statement that the promisor intends to be legally bound.

Mr. Dixon: If there was no such statement made, but the promise was an unconditional agreement.

Mr. Williston: That would not be binding under this act. There must be, in addition, an express statement that the promisor intends to be legally bound. That is a requirement put in to make it clear that he knows what

19. [As was noted previously in this chapter, the New Jersey legislature eventually enacted a statute in which the presumption of consideration could be rebutted. — EDS.]

he is doing, that he intends it to be a legal obligation. I should not be in favor — some people are — but I am not in favor of any proposition that any promise in writing is binding simply because it is in writing. I think that's going too far, but when a man, in addition, in the same writing says that he intends to be legally bound, intends to subject himself to a legal obligation, I don't see why he shouldn't be allowed to do it. . . .

Mr. Beers: Mr. Chairman, doesn't the argument of Professor Williston really exalt the form above the substance? Isn't it a real fundamental rule that where a man makes a promise there must be something in the nature of a *quid pro quo* if he is to be held for it? Of course, we know that the doctrine of consideration can be whittled away until you don't know where you are, but after all isn't the principle fundamental that if a man is going to make a gift he must do it; he must put his hand in his pocket and hand over what he intends to give? Now, by a sort of hocus-pocus, there may be cases where that principle has been gotten away from by giving this peculiar effect to a seal, that in some way or other sticking something on imports a consideration, but isn't the safe rule for society the fact that if you are going to give a gift, you must do it? Now I think all of us have been at meetings where feelings were up and people were enthusiastic, and the example of the widow's mite came to us, and people made all kinds of promises, and some of them, alas, didn't fulfill them, but doesn't this open the door for all kinds of over-reaching. It simply says that you could give away your property, you can make all kinds of promises, but you must have one form of hocus-pocus instead of another; instead of licking a seal and putting it on, you must make a sort of argumentative statement, "I not only promise but I want to be bound by my promise." Isn't it a safe thing to leave the law exactly where it is, or, if we do anything, simply say that the seal in the case of a gratuitous promise shan't have any effect? The act, however, may have a useful scope, in that it may remove unnecessary formalities to releases, and if I owe you a doubtful obligation or if I owe you an obligation I can't satisfy, perhaps, and you want to cancel it, you are allowed to give me a release without any form of hocus-pocus, either licking something and putting it on, or making some sort of an indirect statement. I, therefore, move that these words be stricken out so that it may be restricted to releases and not be an invitation for all kinds of frauds and impositions, by getting people to make promises and then giving a form of language that will be binding on them forever after.

Mr. Child: May I ask the Commissioner what will he do; will he furnish no method of giving an option, for instance, to sell real estate without passing over a dollar? We now have gotten rid of the seal, for instance, in our state. We had the method of sticking on the seal, and then the consideration was imported and the option is good. Now we have done away with the seal but we have got no substitute. Will you give us no substitute for the seal? Will you give us no means of doing away with that fiction of passing over the dollar in an option?

Mr. Beers: If you want a provision against options, for heaven's sake have it, and say so, but don't open the door to let in the cat and at the same time let in the wolf.

President MacChesney: In our state we formerly had a good deal of difficulty with charitable subscriptions, and we have met it, I believe, as they have in many other states by a form of subscription card by which one agrees to subscribe in consideration of similar subscriptions by others. It seems to me that that is really a subterfuge. What is intended to be done, of course, is for a man really to subscribe for the charitable purposes, as has been said by Professor Williston, and this provision by which he says he promises to give and intends thereby to be legally bound, would seem to accomplish that in a direct method, which can be understood by the person signing it. There is a difference between a statement in a letter or an informal statement of intention to give, and a legal document which shall clearly express the intention to do so. So far as we are concerned, I think this is a distinct advance over our present method of evidencing the validity of such a transaction.

Mr. Rose: It seems to me that this is the most important act ever introduced into this body. In the simple law of contracts there comes the question of determining whether there is sufficient moral obligation to justify it being carried out. We avoided that in the common law by the use of the seal, but that has been abolished in my state and in a great many other states, and it brings us down simply and absolutely to the sordid question of a monetary consideration. If you give a dollar you may support the most enormous obligation, but no matter how great may be the moral duty to do a thing, no matter how solemnly you promise, unless a paltry dollar is paid, all these moral obligations are of no account. That, Mr. Chairman, seems a disgrace to our law as it is in the State of Arkansas and as it is in almost a majority of the states of the union. We have no method by which the contract may be made binding, or an obligation can be made binding unless you pass over a pitiable little sum of money. Now, a great many of these obligations are just as meritorious — take the obligation of which my brother Beers speaks. If I promise a man solemnly that I will give him $10,000, and write it out and say that that is my solemn obligation, upon the face of that he makes all sorts of investments; he changes his condition, and when I do not carry out my obligation I have done to him a very severe wrong; it may be an irreparable wrong, and it seems to me that the quicker we get back to the proposition that there can be some basis of obligation except the sordid monetary one, the better.

Mr. Piatt: I would like to ask the Chairman if this doesn't wipe out the defense of lack of consideration or failure of consideration to a contract?

Mr. Williston: By no means is it so wide as that. It wipes out the defense of lack of consideration in case you have a written promise with this additional statement, that the signer intends to be legally bound. Failure of consideration is another matter. Failure of consideration is properly used in a case where there was an agreement for consideration but the consideration has not been given or has for some reason, perhaps, impossibility, destruction or one thing and another, failed. . . .

Mr. Piatt: Let me give you another illustration as we have it in our state of a case of this sort. *A* gave his note for $5,000 to the Kansas City School

Board as a gift. The School Board proceeded as a result of that promise to incur some liability. *A* died before the note matured, and under the law of our state, as it stood, the note would have been void as against the estate if contested by the heirs for lack of consideration or no consideration, but our Supreme Court held that the note, while in effect a gift and without consideration, was enforceable because the incurring of an obligation by the School Board on the faith of the note created a consideration. Now this statute will wipe out that doctrine, won't it?

Mr. Williston: It is hoped that this statute will make it unnecessary for the court to say such things which are not true.

Mr. Piatt: Then we have this situation, Professor, if I understand it. It is not an uncommon thing for men to make promissory notes or promises of gifts to employees, or to other people, in very substantial sums, that don't take place and are not actually given but are not consummated until after death, and the heirs attack that kind of conveyance. This wipes that out, doesn't it?

Mr. Williston: If the man intended to be legally bound and the document so stating was signed and delivered, the estate is liable.

Mr. Piatt: And his estate and the heirs suffer by it?

Mr. Williston: When a man gives away money or incurs liability, his estate takes the consequence.

Mr. Evans: I think it has been the experience pretty generally of practitioners that whenever the issue of consideration is involved, it is an invitation to perjury. It is the most difficult issue that we have to meet. It is difficult to prove a consideration and it is difficult to prove that there was no consideration, and all things considered, it is one of the most difficult, if not the most difficult to meet. This act, if adopted, puts that question forever to sleep. Where a man promises to pay and then, after having promised to pay, solemnly says that it is his intention to be legally bound, I fail to see any reason under the shining sun why he should not be bound, and I fail to see wherein after doing that, promising that and expressing his intention to be bound, it can be said that there is any sort of hocus-pocus about it. . . .

Mr. Graham: Before the question is put, I would like to ask Professor Williston a question. In case this law is generally adopted, the form of petition for subscriptions, of course, would change. The form referred to by General MacChesney, binding each promisor because somebody else was bound, would be abandoned, it wouldn't be necessary, and we would have written or printed statements at the head of the subscription paper with this language either prominently written in or hidden in it somewhere. Suppose the person who circulates the petition misrepresents the contents of the statement to a would-be subscriber, and on the strength of that misrepresentation the party signs the petition. Would he be bound anyhow?

Mr. Williston: No, this says shall not be invalid for lack of consideration, but it does not say shall be valid in spite of fraud and misrepresentation.

Mr. Graham: There would be a great deal of that sort of thing. . . .

Mr. Crook: Section 2 of our By-Laws states that the object of this organization is to promote uniformity in state laws on all subjects where uniformity is deemed desirable and practical. I am opposed to the adoption of this whole act in any form. I don't believe it is within our province technically. I think we have gone to the extreme limit. We are not dealing with a subject that is now in confusion among the laws of the states. On the contrary, we are going to a question of the substitution of law, as has been well stated by the genetleman [sic] from Connecticut. It is very radical. We are getting into deep water; we are inviting confusion; we are going into the states of our country and asking them to adopt a law which I think will weaken the Conference and its influence in those states by reason of its very radical nature and the fact that it is not calculated to relieve confusion. It is going further, I believe, than we have gone at any time before. . . .

Mr. Williston: I should like to say one word with regard to the propriety of the act being within our province. It is to my mind something to render uniform a matter about which the law is distinctly in conflict. As a matter of fact, the law of Wyoming says that any written promise is binding without consideration. There are several states that say that written promises are presumed to have consideration whether they are sealed or not. Then there are, of course, the states which still retain the seal as a method of making a written promise binding. Some considerable number of states still have that rule, so that the law as to when a written promise is binding without consideration is a matter on which the present confusion of law and conflict is very great, and it is a matter, it seems to me, on which it is important to have the law of the several states uniform, for contracts made in one state are, of course, frequently of vital importance in another.

Mr. Ryall: Mr. Chairman, I would like to ask the Chairman of the Committee and the Committee of the Whole that has this matter in charge, because I feel they perhaps are better fitted than anybody here to answer this question specifically, would the Committee, if they deemed it possible, advise the abolition of the entire common law doctrine of consideration, or not?

Mr. Williston: Not for a minute.

Mr. Ryall: I asked that question, and I wanted to get a specific answer, for this reason: It seems to me that as this matter now stands we have practically done that, if we say that this contract is going to be binding, notwithstanding there is no consideration. In other words, the doctrine of necessity of consideration has gone and it is simply now a matter of whether the promisor says that he understands that there is no consideration in the sense of the common law definition and that he is going to be bound anyway. In other words, it has resolved itself now into a matter of — instead of a matter of what the law has looked upon and called consideration, it seems to me as the thing now stands it practically abolishes the doctrine of consideration.

Mr. Williston: I think that is not true at all. In Massachusetts we have the law of seals in force. You lick a wafer and put it on a promise and that promise is binding. I suppose it is no exaggeration to say that in Massachusetts, of a thousand contracts 999 of them rest for their validity on the doctrine of consideration, and perhaps one in 1,000 rests for its validity on the question of a seal, and if this statute is adopted, I have no doubt that the proportion will be about the same in any state which enacts it. The ordinary bargains of human life are made for a consideration and they will continue to be so if this statute is passed or not. The only effect of this statute will be that if there is no consideration for a promise and the parties, nevertheless, intend to be legally bound, they can be; but that case is, of course, always the exception. This enables a man to bind himself by promising to pay $10,000 gratuitously, if he wants to, but that is not the way parties ordinarily make contracts. . . .

President MacChesney: The act is declared adopted [by a vote of 23 in favor, 12 opposed and 1 divided] and will be recommended in accordance with the vote, it having received the requisite number of votes under the constitution. . . .

REFERENCE: Barnett, §§4.1, 4.3

STUDY GUIDE: When reading the next few cases, consider the purposes to which this statute has been put. Has it borne out the hopes of Williston or the fears of the Commissioners who opposed it?

THOMAS v. FIRST NATIONAL BANK OF SCRANTON
Superior Court of Pennsylvania,
173 Pa. Super. 205, 96 A.2d 196 (1953)

HIRT, J.*

This action in assumpsit was tried on stipulated facts. The defendant, a National Bank in the City of Scranton, had accepted the plaintiff as a depositor prior to October 12, 1950 and he then had funds with the bank, in a checking account. On the above date he delivered his check, drawn on the bank, to Sabor Dental Supply House as payee, in the sum of $1,225. On the following day plaintiff went to the bank for the purpose of stopping payment on the check and there signed a "Request to Stop Payment" on a printed form submitted to him by one of defendant's clerks. The request addressed to the bank, which he signed, contained the following:

> Should the check be paid through inadvertence, accident or oversight, it is expressly agreed that the Bank will in no way be held responsible. The Bank receives this request upon the express condition that it shall not be in any way liable for its act should the check be paid by it in the course of its business. The undersigned agrees to be legally bound hereby.

---

* *William Elmer Hirt* (1881-1963) graduated Princeton University (B.A.). He then read law in a private office in Erie, Pennsylvania, and was admitted to the Pennsylvania bar in 1908. He was engaged in law practice for the next 12 years. In 1920, he was appointed to the Court of Common Pleas of Erie County, and he was elected to that bench in 1921 and reelected in 1931. Hirt resigned in 1939 to accept appointment to the Superior Court of Pennsylvania, to which he was elected later that year; he retired from the bench in 1959 at the conclusion of his second term. He again engaged in the practice of law in Erie until the time of his death. — K.T.

On October 16, three days after the plaintiff signed the stop-payment order, the check was paid by the defendant bank on presentation, "through inadvertence, accident, or oversight" and was charged against the funds on deposit in plaintiff's account. This suit was brought to recover $1,225, when the defendant on demand refused to credit plaintiff's account with the amount of the check on which plaintiff had stopped payment. The case was tried without a jury resulting in a judgment in plaintiff's favor against the defendant for the amount of the check with interest. . . .

The majority of the cases and certainly the weight of authority support the view that a stipulation releasing a bank from liability on paying a check in disregard of a stop-payment request constitutes a valid enforceable contract. . . .

The decisions in some of the cases holding that such releases are unenforceable rest upon lack of consideration for the relinquishment of the depositor's absolute common law right to look to the bank for reimbursement. . . . The assertion of lack of consideration however is not available to the present plaintiff in seeking to avoid the limiting terms of his stop-payment request. The release which he signed specifically provides: "The undersigned agrees to be legally bound hereby." Plaintiff's agreement to that effect removes lack of consideration from the case as a ground for avoiding the effect of the release, under the Uniform Written Obligations Act of May 13, 1927, P.L. 985, 33 P.S. §6.

Judgment reversed and here entered for the defendant.

KAY v. KAY

Supreme Court of Pennsylvania,
460 Pa. 680, 334 A.2d 585 (1975)

JONES, C.J.*

On September 11, 1967, shortly before the divorce proceedings were commenced, the appellant and appellee entered into a separation agreement. By that agreement the appellant undertook, *inter alia*, to pay $20.00 per week to the appellee. Payments were to cease only in the event of appellee's remarriage.[20] The agreement was signed and sealed in the presence of the parties and the scrivener.

On February 1, 1973, appellee filed a complaint in equity seeking specific performance of the agreement as to the future payments and

---

* *Benjamin Rowlands Jones* (1906-1980) was a student at the Wyoming Seminary in Kingston, Pennsylvania, Princeton University (A.B.), and the University of Pennsylvania (LL.B.). Admitted to the Pennsylvania bar in 1930, he had practiced law for over 20 years when he was appointed Presiding Judge of the Orphans' Court of Luzerne County in 1952. Jones was promoted to the Pennsylvania Supreme Court in 1957 and served as Chief Justice of that body from 1972 until his retirement in 1977. Thereafter, he practiced law in Philadelphia until his death. — K.T.

20. The clause concerning support payments stated:

HUSBAND agrees to be legally bound to support his WIFE in the amount of $20.00 per week. HUSBAND further agrees and legally binds himself to continue said support of $20.00 per week subsequent to the Divorce. Said support shall continue until such time when WIFE should remarry and at which time said support shall cease.

recovery of past payments allegedly due and owing. The chancellor enforced the agreement and concluded that the appellant had made payments totalling $1,080 and that he owed the appellee at the time of final adjudication the sum of $5,660. The appellant took various exceptions to the chancellor's findings of fact and conclusions of law, those exceptions were denied, and this appeal followed. . . . We affirm. . . .

Appellant next argues that equity cannot enforce the agreement because . . . it is not supported by consideration. . . . Assuming arguendo that no consideration passed to the appellant in return for his undertaking, the support clause nevertheless states that the appellant intends to be legally bound by the agreement. Under the Uniform Written Obligations Act, the absence of consideration does not render the agreement unenforceable where such statements are made part of the contract. . . .

STUDY GUIDE: *Why did the courts in the next two cases refuse to apply the Uniform Written Obligations Act to the formal promise in question? Can you relate this outcome to the discussion between Professor Williston and the Commissioners on Uniform State Laws?*

FEDERAL DEPOSIT INSURANCE CORP. v. BARNESS
United States District Court, Eastern District of Pennsylvania,
484 F. Supp. 1134 (1980)

EDWARD R. BECKER, District Judge.*
[Defendant sought to avoid the enforcement by the FDIC of a promissory note which the defendant executed in the amount of $64,835 to the Centennial Bank of which he was a major shareholder. This note came into the possession of the FDIC when Centennial was closed by the Commonwealth of Pennsylvania. Defendant claimed that he signed the note entirely to aid Centennial by enabling it to satisfy HUD's loan guaranty requirements for a construction project that the bank was financing and that he received no benefit in return. Consequently, the defendant alleged that there was no consideration for the note.]

Plaintiff contends that the defense of no consideration is precluded by the Uniform Written Obligations Act, 33 P.S. §6, which provides that a signed promise is not invalid for lack of consideration "if the writing also contains an additional express statement, in any form of language, that the signer intends to be legally bound." Id. He contends that the words "the Undersigned . . . promises to pay to the order of Centennial Bank . . ." are an "additional express statement" within the meaning of the statute.

---

* *Edward Roy Becker* (1933-2006) received degrees from the University of Pennsylvania (A.B.) and Yale University (LL.B.). Admitted to the Pennsylvania bar in 1957, he practiced law in Philadelphia until 1970, when he was appointed U.S. District Judge. He served on that bench until appointment in 1982 to the U.S. Court of Appeals for the Third Circuit. Becker was also a lecturer at the University of Pennsylvania Law School (1978-1983) and served on numerous commissions. — K.T.

In Gershman v. Metropolitan Life Insurance Co., 405 Pa. 585, 176 A.2d 435 (1962), the Pennsylvania Supreme Court considered whether an agreement without legal consideration was nonetheless effective because it included the words "Approved by" followed by the obligor's signature. The Court gave short shrift to that argument:

> We merely say, in response to this argument, that we fail to see how the simple approval of the letter constituting the agreement can be considered as "an additional express statement . . . to be legally bound."

176 A.2d at 436-37. In Fedun v. Mike's Cafe, Inc., 204 Pa. Super. 356, 364-65, 204 A.2d 776, 780-81 (1964), *aff'd*, 419 Pa. 607, 213 A.2d 638 (1965), the court ruled that the words "(w)e . . . release you . . . and will not hold you. . . ." did not constitute the additional express statement required by the Uniform Written Obligations Act. . . .

The note sued on, like the agreements before the court in *Gershman* and *Fedun*, contains no "additional express statement." It contains only the bare promise to pay money. That promise alone is not sufficient to bring it within the terms of the Uniform Written Obligations Act:

> The purpose of this act, as declared by Professor Williston, who drafted it, was to make the law "substantially the same as it was when seals were in force, so far as the doctrine of consideration is concerned, except that in lieu of the formality of a seal, the formality of this statement is substituted." . . . The statement that the signer intends to be legally bound, in order to take the place of a seal, in a release or contract, as respects consideration, must be an additional express statement, to the effect that the signer intends to be legally bound. It is never to be inferred from circumstances.

Taylor v. Philadelphia, 126 Pa. Super. 196, 211-12, 190 A. 663, 669-70 (1937), *aff'd on opinion below*, 328 Pa. 383, 196 A. 64 (1938) (emphasis and citations omitted). Since the note contains no "additional express statement," the Uniform Written Obligations Act does not preclude the defense of no consideration. . . .

FIRST FEDERAL SAVINGS AND LOAN ASS'N OF PITTSTON v. REGGIE, SUPERIOR COURT OF PENNSYLVANIA, 376 PA. SUPER. 346, 546 A.2D 62 (1988):   The bank, for the first time on appeal, attempts to salvage the enforceability of the mortgage from this alleged lack of consideration by invoking the application of the Uniform Written Obligations Act. . . . However, the bank has altogether failed to specify the language in the mortgage which allegedly qualifies as a substitute for consideration under the Uniform Written Obligations Act. The trial court made no finding as to . . . whether the mortgage in fact contained the appropriate language to render it enforceable under the Act. Thus, since the bank has failed to support its allegations, we cannot hold this mortgage enforceable under the Act.

However, even if the mortgage were found enforceable notwithstanding the lack of consideration, the bank would not be entitled to summary judgment. The Reggies alleged that they were induced into signing the mortgage because of fraud and misrepresentations on the part of the bank. They allege that the bank misrepresented to them that they owed the pre-existing debt to the bank and that the bank could have foreclosed on their home. The Uniform Written Obligations Act would merely save the mortgage from unenforceability due to lack of consideration; it does not prevent an attack on the mortgage on the basis of fraud or material misrepresentation.

REFERENCE: Murray, §32(A)

B.   LACK OF INTENTION TO BE LEGALLY BOUND

In Section A, we considered enforcing nonbargained-for commitments by using various types of formalities to manifest an intention to be legally bound. In this section, we examine the possibility of avoiding enforcement, even of bargained-for commitments, by disclaiming the intention to be legally bound. This principle is contained in Restatement (Second) of Contracts §21, which states, "[A] manifestation of intention that a promise shall not affect legal relations may prevent the formation of a contract."

STUDY GUIDE: Cases in which employees seek to enforce employee handbooks as contracts have increased in frequency in recent years. Courts have gradually become more receptive to such claims. What follows is one approach. Notice the court's concern with the conspicuousness of disclaimers.

FERRERA v. A. C. NIELSEN
Court of Appeals of Colorado,
799 P.2d 458 (Colo. 1990)

Opinion by COYTE, J.*
Plaintiff, Beverly K. Ferrera, appeals the summary judgment entered in favor of defendant, A.H. [sic] Nielsen Co., d/b/a Neodata Services, on her claim that she was wrongfully discharged from employment. We affirm. . . .

Neodata had suspended Ferrera in 1985 after concluding that she had falsified her time card in violation of a company rule. In January 1987, Neodata concluded that Ferrera had again falsified her time card, and fired her.

Ferrera brought this action alleging wrongful discharge from employment under implied contract and promissory estoppel theories based on the employee handbook. Neodata moved for summary judgment. After Ferrera responded, the trial court entered summary judgment on an issue not raised by the parties: that the 1986 handbook could not constitute a contract because it contained a disclaimer, and denied Ferrera's subsequent motion for relief from judgment. . . .

---

* *Ralph H. Coyte* (1914-1998) was educated at the University of Colorado (B.A., LL.B.) and was admitted to practice in Colorado in 1940. He practiced law in Fort Collins until being appointed to the Colorado Court of Appeals in 1970. Coyte was also reporter for the 1970 volume of the Colorado Court of Appeals Reports. In 1983, he retired to private practice and sat on this case by assignment of the Chief Justice. — K.T.

Ferrera contends that the trial court erred in entering summary judgment on her breach of contract and promissory estoppel claims, arguing that the 1986 handbook constituted a contract limiting Neodata's right to discharge employees. We disagree.

Statements made in an employee handbook limiting an employer's right to discharge employees may be the basis for breach of implied contract and promissory estoppel claims by discharged employees. Continental Air Lines, Inc. v. Keenan, 731 P.2d 708 (Colo. 1987).

Under an implied contract theory, such statements must be a manifestation of the employer's willingness to enter into a bargain that would justify the employee in understanding that his or her assent was invited. Under a promissory estoppel theory, the promise must be one which the employer should reasonably have expected the employee to consider as a commitment from the employer. Continental Air Lines, Inc. v. Keenan, supra.

The 1986 handbook at issue here did not expressly require either just cause for discharge of employees or that the employer apply "progressive discipline" in all cases. Cf. Dickey v. Adams County School District No. 50, 773 P.2d 585 (Colo. App. 1988), aff'd, 791 P.2d 688 (Colo. 1990) (handbook expressly required "just and good causes" for dismissal); Cronk v. Intermountain Rural Electric Assn., 765 P.2d 619 (Colo. App. 1988) (handbook required just cause for dismissal). Instead, it expressly reserved the right to discharge an employee whose conduct "in the opinion of the Company" warrants it.

Moreover, the handbook contains the following disclaimer on page one:

IMPORTANT

This Handbook is not a contract but merely a condensation of various Company policies, procedures, and employee benefits to assist you in the conduct of Company business. . . .

Management has the right to change the policies and benefits of the Company in accordance with the needs of the business without notice.

The information contained in this Handbook is the most current at this time and supersedes all previous Handbooks by Neodata Services.

Summary judgment denying claims based on a handbook is appropriate if the employer has clearly and conspicuously disclaimed intent to enter a contract limiting the right to discharge employees. See Therrien v. United Air Lines, Inc., 670 F. Supp. 1517 (D. Colo. 1987).

Here, the disclaimer was sufficiently clear to inform employees that Neodata did not intend to be bound by the provisions of the handbook. . . .

The disclaimer was also sufficiently conspicuous. It was labeled "IMPORTANT" and was placed on the first page of the handbook. Ferrera signed an acknowledgement that she received a copy of the handbook, and alleged that she had read it.

Under these circumstances, we agree with the trial court that, as a matter of law, the 1986 handbook did not constitute a contract limiting Neodata's right to terminate employees.

Cronk v. Intermountain Rural Electric Assn., supra, does not require a different result. There, summary judgment was improper despite the presence of a disclaimer because the handbook included language requiring just cause for discharge. Here, by contrast, there was no such language. Moreover, excerpts from the record in *Cronk* submitted to the trial court in this case show that there the disclaimer was inconspicuously placed in an appendix to the handbook.

We conclude that the record establishes as a matter of law that Neodata made no promise in the 1986 handbook on which plaintiff could base an implied contract or promissory estoppel claim.

The judgment is affirmed.

REFERENCE: Murray, §32(B)

STUDY GUIDE: Why did the disclaimers in the company handbook fail to insulate the employer from liability in the next case?

EVENSON v. COLORADO FARM BUREAU MUTUAL INSURANCE CO., COURT OF APPEALS OF COLORADO, DIVISION II, 879 P.2D 402 (1993):   To rebut the presumption of employment "at-will" and enforce termination procedures found in an employee manual or handbook, an employee must demonstrate either that the manual or handbook resulted in a contract between the employer and the employee or that it formed the basis for a promissory estoppel claim. Continental Airlines, Inc. v. Keenan, 731 P.2d 708 (Colo. 1987). To establish that the manual resulted in a contract, the employee must establish that the employer's actions manifested to a reasonable person an intent to be bound by the provisions of the manual or handbook.

Such a manifestation of willingness to be bound can be inferred if there is no disclaimer in the manual stating that it does not constitute a contract or if such disclaimer, though present, is not clear and conspicuous. See Ferrera v. Nielsen, 799 P.2d 458 (Colo. App. 1990).

Furthermore, even if there is a disclaimer in the manual, an employer may nevertheless be found to have manifested an intent to be bound by its terms if the manual contains mandatory termination procedures or requires "just cause" for termination. See Allabashi v. Lincoln National Sales Corp., [824 P.2d 1 (Colo. App. 1991)] (conflict between disclaimer and other documents permits finding of implied contract); Cronk v. Intermountain Rural Electric Assn., 765 P.2d 619 (Colo. App. 1988) (handbook required just cause for dismissal); cf. Ferrera v. Nielsen, supra (no implied contract where disclaimer appeared conspicuously at beginning of manual and in big letters under heading "Important" and no evidence was presented indicating employee's justifiable reliance on the terms of the handbook).

If evidence in the record creates an issue as to whether an employment contract existed, then a directed verdict or summary judgment is inappropriate. . . . Such was the case here.

The discharge provisions of the Farm Bureau employee manual state:

We reserve the right to terminate the employee at management discretion. Employees have been hired at the discretion of the company and their employment may be terminated at its will and at any time.

The last section of the manual also contains a disclaimer provision opposite the signature page which notifies employees that

> the language used in this handbook is not intended to create, nor is it to be construed as a contract between the company and any one or all of its employees.

Finally, the manual's discipline procedure stated that "the steps for disciplinary action *may* be. . . ." (Emphasis added.) Thus, these provisions, on their face, suggest that the manual was not intended to create a binding obligation.

However, several Farm Bureau managers, including the Chief Personnel Officer, testified on Evenson's behalf that they regarded the disciplinary procedures as mandatory and treated them as mandatory. The Chief Personnel Officer also testified that he met with the CEO and a supervisor regarding the need for compliance with these disciplinary procedures before terminating Evenson. This evidence supported Evenson's position that the manual's disciplinary procedures were, in fact, treated by Farm Bureau as mandatory and binding.

Thus, conflicting evidence was presented as to whether the discipline procedures had to be followed before terminating an employee.

Further, while the disclaimer provisions are clear, they were not emphasized. Indeed, they contain nothing to make them conspicuous.

In the absence of conspicuous disclaimer provisions but with evidence that the employer thus treated the provisions as binding, whether the provisions in the manual constituted a contract between the parties is a question for the jury. . . . Thus, on the facts presented, we conclude that a factual dispute was present as to whether the disciplinary procedures were contractually binding. Hence, a directed verdict on the issue of whether there was an implied employment contract was improper, and the issue must be resolved on remand.

Our decision is consistent with Ferrera v. Nielsen, supra. In that case, unlike the situation here, a division of this court found that the disclaimer in the employee manual was both sufficiently clear and sufficiently conspicuous to inform employees that the employer did not intend to be bound. Also, there the employee apparently presented no evidence to bring into question the applicability of the disclaimer. . . .

STUDY GUIDE: *On what basis did the court in the next case conclude that there was "no enforceable 'contract' "? Was there no bargained-for consideration? Was there no reliance? Can the court's description of "the basic requisite of a contract" be squared with Restatement (Second) §21?*

EILAND v. WOLF, COURT OF APPEALS OF TEXAS, HOUSTON (1ST DISTRICT), 764 S.W.2D 827 (1989):   DUNN, J.* . . . The appellee alleged

---

* *D. Camille Dunn* (1925-†) was educated at the University of South Carolina (A.B.) and the University of Michigan (J.D.). Admitted to the bars of South Carolina in 1946 and Texas in 1963, she has practiced law in Orangeburg, South Carolina (1946-1963), and Texas (1963-1985). In 1985, Dunn was elected to the Court of Appeals of Texas, and was reelected in 1990. — K.T.

that he was a medical student at the University of Texas Medical Branch at Galveston, and that he had successfully completed all the requirements for graduation with the exception of one four-week elective course that he had failed and had not been allowed to retake. He alleged that because of the appellants' arbitrary and capricious actions, violation of his equal protection and due process rights, and breach of contractual rights, he was prevented from completing his academic work and that the appellants threatened to deny him a Degree of Doctor of Medicine, even if he successfully completed the one remaining elective course. The appellee contended that the appellants' conduct was a result of institutional bias against him, stemming from his obtaining a court order to reinstate him in his third year after he was not allowed to attend classes pending an appeal of a prior nonacademic dismissal. That dismissal, which was based on the appellee's failure to include some significant information on his loan application, was eventually overturned by the school. . . .

In 1981, when the appellee first enrolled in school, he received the school catalog, which he testified that he later used as a reference as he proceeded through school. The catalog provides:

DEGREE OF DOCTOR OF MEDICINE

The degree of Doctor of Medicine is awarded upon satisfactory completion of the prescribed curriculum in the School of Medicine, recommendation of the Faculty of Medicine, and certification by the Board of Regents. Candidates must (1) be at least 18 years of age at the time the degree is awarded; (2) present evidence of good moral character; (3) offer satisfactory evidence of having properly fulfilled all academic curricula including acceptable performance on Parts I and II of National Board Examinations; and (4) comply with all necessary legal and financial requirements.

Prior to graduation and receipt of diploma, all students must have arranged to take care of all just indebtedness in accordance with the rules outlined under Student Debts. . . .

Contract Claim.   Appellants also contend that the trial court erred in granting relief on the appellee's contract claim, because . . . appellants did not breach any contractual obligations to the appellee. . . .

The Texas Legislature has delegated to the University of Texas Board of Regents the duty of implementing statutes pertaining to the University of Texas Medical Branch. . . . Pursuant to this delegation of authority, the University of Texas Medical Branch catalog was compiled. All parties agree that the catalog is applicable to this case.

This Court once held that "a school's catalog constitutes a written contract between the educational institution and the patron, where entrance is under its terms." University of Texas Health Science Center v. Babb, 646 S.W.2d 502 (Tex. App. — Houston [1st Dist.] 1982, no writ). . . . We have found no other Texas cases that address whether a public university's catalog constitutes a contract with the student.

We find that the circumstances in the *Babb* case are distinguishable from the present situation. In *Babb*, there was an express statement in the school catalog that allowed a student who began school under the terms of a certain catalog to continue through the program under the same catalog. Given this statement, the student was held to have a right to rely on the catalog's terms.

In the case at bar, the first page of the applicable catalog contains the express notice that

> [t]he provisions of this catalogue are subject to change without notice and do not constitute an irrevocable contract between any student . . . and The University of Texas Medical School at Galveston. . . .

The catalog further provides,

> Since matriculation in medical school is a privilege and not a right, the faculty retains the prerogative to request withdrawal of any student who does not attain adequate academic performance or who does not exhibit the personal qualifications prerequisite to the practice of medicine. These criteria shall apply at all times during the curriculum. Academic performance will not be the only factor in determining admission, promotion, graduation, or request for withdrawal.

Further, regarding dismissals, the catalog states,

> It must be clearly understood by all matriculants that the Faculty of the School of Medicine has the authority to drop any student from the rolls . . . if circumstances of a legal, moral, health, social, or academic nature justify such a request.

We need not decide whether, as a rule, the catalog of a state university constitutes a contract between the student and the school. Given the express disclaimers in the document alleged to be a contract here, it is clear that no enforceable "contract" existed in the present case. A basic requisite of a contract is an intent to be bound, and the catalog's express language negates, as a matter of law, an inference of such intent on the part of the university. Thus, the trial court erred in granting recovery for the breach of an alleged contract based upon the medical school catalog. The appellants' contract claims are sustained. . . .

REFERENCE: Barnett, §§4.1, 4.3

11

THE DOCTRINE OF PROMISSORY ESTOPPEL

The practice of enforcing formal contracts (discussed in Chapter 10) long predates the rise of assumpsit with its corresponding doctrine of consideration. Assumpsit was developed to better protect *informal* commitments. The doctrine of consideration was then adopted to distinguish enforceable from unenforceable informal commitments. According to the *bargain theory* of consideration, any informal commitment that is not bargained for is unenforceable. Is this strictly true? Are there any circumstances that justify enforcing such non-bargained-for, but informal, commitments?

The *doctrine of promissory estoppel* has evolved to answer this question. In this chapter, we shall consider the content and coherence of this doctrine, first, by studying its historical origins in Sections A and B. Then, in Section C, we study some modern applications. It is commonly assumed that the principle underlying promissory estoppel is compensation for *detrimental reliance.* This theory is incorporated in §90 of both the first and second Restatements. In this chapter we shall consider the extent to which this theoretical account of the doctrine is persuasive.

Historical Background: Early Alternatives to the Doctrine of Consideration

A. W. B. SIMPSON, THE DOCTRINE OF CONSIDERATION — INTRODUCTION, from A HISTORY OF THE COMMON LAW OF CONTRACT: THE RISE OF THE ACTION OF ASSUMPSIT 323-325 (1975): Plainly the idea of relating promissory liability to an analysis of the motives for the promise is only one of a number of possible theories which share a reluctance to base liability simply upon the making of the promise alone. Where, for example, the promisor has been paid or recompensed for his promise, one might justify holding him to performance in order to prevent his being unjustly enriched, a rationale which has nothing to do with the inspection of the promisor's motive. Or one might conceive of such a promise as being a trick or deceit, and hold the promisor to it in accordance with the idea that people ought not be allowed to profit from their wrongs. Such contractual theories as these will be found lurking in modern case law as they are to be found in old cases, there being in this field nothing new under the sun. Now one such rationale for the enforcement of promises is the notion (variously formulated) of induced reliance. Promises do not simply give rise to expectations, they also serve to induce promisees to act in reliance upon them, changing their situation or circumstances in ways which they otherwise would not have done. Where there has been such induced reliance it seems fair to hold the promisor to the promise (or at least require him to compensate). . . .

. . . This notion was to find a confused expression in detriment consideration, and the confusion arises in this way. The detriment suffered in reliance upon the promise . . . is induced by the promise; it is not the motive for the promise. Consequently it is only by a perversion of both the meaning and the basic idea involved in the doctrine of consideration that "detriment to the promisee" could be portrayed as a form of consideration. In a tidy and more intelligible scheme of thought, induced injurious reliance as a ground for actionability would have been presented not as an aspect of the doctrine of consideration but as an alternative to it. But there has always in the common law been a tendency towards a sort of doctrinal monism — there must be *one* test for the formation of contract (offer and acceptance), *one* principle governing possession, *one* test for the actionability of promises. Hence the adoption of good consideration as *the* requirement for *all* promises, which necessitated a mystifying twisting of the meaning of the term. And even to this day the principle of induced reliance leads an uneasy existence somewhere on the borderline of contract, property, tort, and evidence, notoriously in cases now barbarously referred to as cases of equitable estoppel. The same point can be made, though less importantly, in relation to benefit consideration — put at its simplest the idea that a promisor who has been paid for his promise should perform it can be regarded as independent and alternative to, or supplementary to any *recherché* analysis of promissory motives. But benefit to the promisor was to become another aspect of the sole doctrine — consideration. Since orthodoxy required that all contracts by parole should be supported by consideration, whilst underlying common sense recognized a variety of justifications for holding men to promises, it was bound to happen that the doctrine of consideration became something of dog's breakfast. The position in modern tort law is similar — since all questions about liability for negligence are supposed to turn on the doctrine of the duty of care, one must expect the duty of care to be something of a dog's breakfast too. It is.

STUDY GUIDE: *Can you think of any dangers in extending enforcement to informal non-bargained-for promises? How do the concepts of underenforcement and overenforcement apply?*

A.   THE DEVELOPMENT OF PROMISSORY ESTOPPEL AS A SUBSTITUTE FOR CONSIDERATION

As a distinct doctrine of contract law, promissory estoppel is of relatively recent vintage. One way to understand it is to study the classic cases that led to its formulation. These early cases tended to cluster around certain factual situations. Many of these situations are represented in this section.

STUDY GUIDE: To solidify your grasp of the consideration requirement discussed in Chapter 9, when reading each of the cases in this section, make sure you understand why there was no bargained-for consideration to justify enforcing the promise. Had there been a true bargain, why might it have been difficult to detect or prove? It is commonly thought that promissory estoppel developed as a means of protecting detrimental reliance. Is this an accurate description of all the cases in this section? Is there any other factor or factors that these cases share? Why do you think these particular kinds of cases led to the perception that the bargain theory of consideration was incomplete?

1.   Family Promises

RICKETTS v. SCOTHORN
Supreme Court of Nebraska,
57 Neb. 51, 77 N.W. 365 (1898)

HOLMES, J. Action by Katie Scothorn against Andrew D. Ricketts, executor of the will of J. C. Ricketts, deceased. There was a judgment for plaintiff, and defendant brings error. . . .   ———> Procedural Posture

SULLIVAN, J.*

In the district court of Lancaster county the plaintiff Katie Scothorn recovered judgment against the defendant Andrew D. Ricketts, as executor of the last will and testament of John C. Ricketts, deceased. The action was based upon a promissory note, of which the following is a copy:

> May the first, 1891. I promise to pay to Katie Scothorn on demand, $2,000, to be at 6 per cent per annum.
>
> J. C. Ricketts

In the petition the plaintiff alleges that the consideration for the execution of the note was that she should surrender her employment as bookkeeper for Mayer Bros. and cease to work for a living. She also alleges that the note was given to induce her to abandon her occupation, and that, relying on it, and on the annual interest, as a means of support, she gave up the employment in which she was then engaged. These allegations of the petition are denied by the executor. The material facts are undisputed. They

*John Joseph Sullivan (1855-1926) studied law in a private office and at the University of Iowa (LL.B.). In 1898, he began the practice of law at Harvard, Iowa, and, in 1879, moved to Columbus, Nebraska, serving there as city attorney for several years. Thereafter, he served as County Judge of Platte County (1883-1886), a member of the state legislature (1886-1891), and district judge of the sixth judicial district (1891-1897). In 1897, he was elected judge of the Supreme Court of Nebraska and became Chief Justice in 1902, holding that position until 1904. He was appointed to the Supreme Court in 1908, qualified, and resigned after serving one day. Thereafter, he practiced law in Omaha until his death. — K.T.

are as follows: John C. Ricketts, the maker of the note, was the grandfather of the plaintiff. Early in May — presumably on the day the note bears date — he called on her at the store where she was working. What transpired between them is thus described by Mr. Flodene, one of the plaintiff's witnesses:

A: Well, the old gentleman came in there one morning about 9 o'clock — probably a little before or a little after, but early in the morning — and he unbuttoned his vest and took out a piece of paper in the shape of a note; that is the way it looked to me; and he says to Miss Scothorn, "I have fixed out something that you have not got to work any more." He says, "None of my grandchildren work and you don't have to."

Q: Where was she?

A: She took the piece of paper and kissed him, and kissed the old gentleman and commenced to cry.

It seems Miss Scothorn immediately notified her employer of her intention to quit work and that she did soon after abandon her occupation. The mother of the plaintiff was a witness and testified that she had a conversation with her father, Mr. Ricketts, shortly after the note was executed in which he informed her that he had given the note to the plaintiff to enable her to quit work; that none of his grandchildren worked and he did not think she ought to. For something more than a year the plaintiff was without an occupation, but in September, 1892, with the consent of her grandfather, and by his assistance, she secured a position as bookkeeper with Messrs. Funke & Ogden. On June 8, 1894, Mr. Ricketts died. He had paid one year's interest on the note, and a short time before his death expressed regret that he had not been able to pay the balance. In the summer or fall of 1892 he stated to his daughter, Mrs. Scothorn, that if he could sell his farm in Ohio he would pay the note out of the proceeds. He at no time repudiated the obligation. We quite agree with counsel for the defendant that upon this evidence there was nothing to submit to the jury, and that a verdict should have been directed peremptorily for one of the parties. The testimony of Flodene and Mrs. Scothorn, taken together, conclusively establishes the fact that the note was not given in consideration of the plaintiff pursuing, or agreeing to pursue, any particular line of conduct. There was no promise on the part of the plaintiff to do or refrain from doing anything. Her right to the money promised in the note was not made to depend upon an abandonment of her employment with Mayer Bros. and future abstention from like service. Mr. Ricketts made no condition, requirement, or request. He exacted no *quid pro quo*. He gave the note as a gratuity and looked for nothing in return. So far as the evidence discloses, it was his purpose to place the plaintiff in a position of independence where she could work or remain idle as she might choose. The abandonment by Miss Scothorn of her position as bookkeeper was altogether voluntary. It was not an act done in fulfillment of any contract obligation assumed when she accepted the note. The instrument in suit being given without any valuable consideration, was nothing more than a promise to make a gift in the future of the sum of money therein named. Ordinarily, such promises are not enforceable even when put in the form of a promissory note. . . . But it has often been held that an action on a note given to a church, college, or other like institution, upon the faith of which money has been expended or obligations incurred, could not be successfully defended on the ground of a want of consideration. . . . In this class of cases the note in suit is nearly always spoken of as a gift or donation, but the decision is generally put on the ground that the expenditure of money or assumption of liability by the donee, on the faith of the promise, constitutes a valuable and sufficient consideration. It seems to us that the true reason is the preclusion of the defendant, under the doctrine of estoppel, to deny the consideration. Such seems to be the view of the matter taken by the supreme court of Iowa in the case of Simpson Centenary College v. Tuttle, 71 Ia. 596, [33 N.W. 74,] where Rothrock, J., speaking for the court, said:

> Where a note, however, is based on a promise to give for the support of the objects referred to, it may still be open to this defense [want of consideration], unless it shall appear that the donee has, prior to any revocation, entered into engagements or made expenditures based on such promise, so that he must suffer loss or injury if the note is not paid. This is based on the equitable principle that, after allowing the donee to incur obligations on the faith that the note would be paid, the donor would be estopped from pleading want of consideration.

And in the case of Reimensnyder v. Gans, 110 Pa. St. 17, 2 Atl. Rep. 425, which was an action on a note given as a donation to a charitable object, the court said:

> The fact is that, as we may see from the case of Ryerss v. Trustees, 33 Pa. St. 114, a contract of the kind here involved is enforceable rather by way of estoppel than on the ground of consideration in the original undertaking.

It has been held that a note given in expectation of the payee performing certain services, but without any contract binding him to serve, will not support an action. . . . But when the payee changes his position to his disadvantage, in reliance on the promise, a right of action does arise. . . .

Under the circumstances of this case is there an equitable estoppel which ought to preclude the defendant from alleging that the note in controversy is lacking in one of the essential elements of a valid contract? We think there is. An estoppel *in pais* is defined to be "a right arising from acts, admissions, or conduct which have induced a change of position in accordance with the real or apparent intention of the party against whom they are alleged." Mr. Pomeroy has formulated the following definition:

> Equitable estoppel is the effect of the voluntary conduct of a party whereby he is absolutely precluded, both at law and in equity, from asserting rights which might perhaps have otherwise existed, either of property, of contract, or of remedy, as against another person who in good faith relied upon such conduct, and has been led thereby to change his position for the worse, and who on his part acquires some corresponding right either of property, of contract, or of remedy.

(2 Pomeroy, Equity Jurisprudence [sec.] 804.)

According to the undisputed proof, as shown by the record before us, the plaintiff was a working girl, holding a position in which she earned a salary of $10 per week. Her grandfather, desiring to put her in a position of independence, gave her the note, accompanying it with the remark that his other grandchildren did not work, and that she would not be obliged to work any longer. In effect he suggested that she might abandon her employment, and rely in the future upon the bounty which he promised. He, doubtless, desired that she should give up her occupation, but whether he did or not, it is entirely certain that he contemplated such action on her part as a reasonable and probable consequence of his gift. Having intentionally influenced the plaintiff to alter her position for the worse on the faith of the note being paid when due, it would be grossly inequitable to permit the maker, or his executor, to resist payment on the ground that the promise was given without consideration. The petition charges the elements of an equitable estoppel, and the evidence conclusively establishes them. If errors intervened at the trial they could not have been prejudicial. A verdict for the defendant would be unwarranted. The judgment is right and is

Affirmed.

Historical Background: The Doctrine of Equitable Estoppel

The court in Ricketts v. Scothorn speaks of *equitable* estoppel, not *promissory* estoppel. The following passage from John Norton Pomeroy's famous Treatise on Equity Jurisprudence appears immediately after the excerpt quoted by the court.

STUDY GUIDE: *Given the elements of equitable estoppel listed by Pomeroy, was the court correct to apply the doctrine to this case? To understand the situation to which the doctrine of equitable estoppel applies, consider the following hypothetical: A person calls her bank to ask if it has received her paycheck. When told by a clerk that it has, she proceeds to write checks against that amount of money. Suppose now that the clerk erred (he mistakenly looked at the previous month's deposit), the checks bounced, and the bank seeks to charge her a $25.00 penalty for each overdraft. As described by Pomeroy, how would the doctrine of equitable estoppel shield her against this liability? Why would promissory estoppel be inapposite?*

JOHN NORTON POMEROY, ESSENTIAL ELEMENTS CONSTITUTING THE ESTOPPEL, from A TREATISE ON EQUITY JURISPRUDENCE §805 (2D ED. 1892): In conformity with the principle already stated which lies at the basis of the doctrine, and upon the authority of decisions which have recognized and adopted that principle, the following are the essential elements which must enter into and form a part of an equitable estoppel in all of its phases and applications. One caution, however, is necessary, and very important. It would be unsafe and misleading to rely on these general requisites as applicable to every case, without examining the instances in which they have been modified or limited.

1.   There must be conduct — acts, language, or silence — amounting to a representation or concealment of material facts.

2.   These facts must be known to the party estopped at the time of his said conduct, or at least the circumstances must be such that knowledge of them is necessarily imputed to him.

3.   The truth concerning these facts must be unknown to the other party claiming the benefit of the estoppel, at the time when such conduct was done, *and at the time when it was acted upon by him.*

4.   The conduct must be done with the intention, or at least with the *expectation*, that it will be acted upon by the other party, or under such circumstances that it is both natural and probable that it will be so acted upon. There are several familiar species in which it is simply *impossible* to ascribe any *intention* or even *expectation* to the party estopped that his conduct will be acted upon by the one who afterwards claims the benefit of the estoppel.

5.   The conduct must be relied upon by the other party, and, thus relying, he must be led to act upon it.

6.   He must in fact act upon it in such a manner as to change his position for the worse; in other words, he must so act that he would suffer a loss if he were compelled to surrender or forego or alter what he has done by reason of the first party being permitted to repudiate his conduct and to assert rights inconsistent with it. [Italics in original.]

STUDY GUIDE: *Consider also the following exchange between Samuel Williston and the American Law Institute concerning the appropriate name for the doctrine embodied in the first §90 (then-numbered §88).*

DISCUSSION OF THE TENTATIVE DRAFT OF CONTRACTS, RESTATEMENT NO. 2, 4 AMERICAN LAW INSTITUTE PROCEEDINGS APPENDIX 61, 89-90 (1926):[1]

Merritt Lane (New Jersey):   May I ask the Reporter whether it was not the intent to cover under Section 88 what is now usually treated under the head of equitable estoppel?

Mr. Williston: I should say that was a very bad name for it.

Mr. Lane: What would you call it?

Mr. Williston: I don't know; and nearly anything can be called estoppel. When a lawyer or a judge does not know what other name to give for his decision to decide a case a certain way, he says there is an estoppel; but I should like to confine the meaning of the word to a misrepresentation of some fact that was relied upon. There is no misrepresentation of fact here; there is simply a gratuitous promise which the promisor knows is gratuitous and which the promisee knows is gratuitous. I have in my treatise used the term "promissory estoppel" for this sort of case; but there is the danger that the inference will be drawn that wherever a promise is reasonably relied upon it becomes binding. That would go farther than Section 88.

1. [The entire exchange is reprinted in Peter Linzer, A Contracts Anthology 339-349 (2d ed. 1995), and is well worth reading. — EDS.]

2.   Promises to Convey Land

*Study Guide: In what ways does the next case present a stronger argu-
ment for relief than Ricketts v. Scothorn? In what ways is it weaker? How
does the existence of rules governing property conveyances create peculiarly vexatious problems with promises to convey land? Do you see any
similarity between promises to convey land and claims made against
estates that a deceased had made an inter vivos gift?*

GREINER v. GREINER
Supreme Court of Kansas,
131 Kan. 760, 293 P. 759 (1930)

Action by Maggie Greiner against Frank Greiner, in which defendant
claimed affirmative relief. Judgment for defendant, and plaintiff
appeals. . . .

The opinion of the court was delivered by BURCH, J.: Maggie Greiner
commenced an action of forcible detention against her son, Frank Greiner,
to recover possession of a quarter section of land, and an additional tract of
eighty acres. Frank answered that his mother had given him the eighty-acre
tract under such circumstances that she not only could not reclaim it, but
that she should execute a conveyance to him. The district court ordered
plaintiff to execute a deed conveying the eighty-acre tract to defendant, and
plaintiff appeals.

Peter Greiner died testate, leaving a widow — the plaintiff — and sons
and daughters. His sons Henry, Frank and Nicholas and his daughter Kate,
were disinherited — were given five dollars apiece. Henry died in June,
1925, unmarried and intestate, and his mother inherited considerable property from him. She then concluded to place the other two disinherited sons
on an equal footing with those who had been favored in the will, and she
took active measures to accomplish her purpose. At first she intended to
give Frank and Nicholas land, about ninety acres apiece. Later, she entered
into a written contract to pay Nicholas $2,000. Frank had gone to Logan
county, had homesteaded a quarter section of land, and had lived there
sixteen or seventeen years. Mrs. Greiner lived in Mitchell county, and the
land in controversy lies in Mitchell county, not far from her home. [The brief
for plaintiffs says she inherited from Henry only a three-sevenths interest in
the eighty-acre tract] [The brief for defendant says she inherited the entire
interest, and Mrs. Greiner so testified] In any event, some deeds were to be
executed, and in July, 1926, Mrs. Greiner had Nicholas write to Frank and
tell Frank to come down, she was going to make settlement with him and
Nicholas. Frank came to Mitchell county and had a conversation with his
mother. At that time there was a house on the quarter section. In the conversation Mrs. Greiner told Frank she was going to pay him and Nicholas.
Frank told her he did not want money, he wanted a home — a little land for
a home. She said all right, she had the land, and she wanted him to move
into the house, and they would divide up later. He said that would be all
right, and he would move back. . . .

Frank moved back on September 20, 1926. Mrs. Greiner then determined to move the house from the quarter section to the eighty-acre tract, and give that specific tract to Frank. . . .

The buildings were moved from the quarter section to the eighty-acre tract, and Frank commenced to occupy the eighty-acre tract in the spring of 1927. . . .

The manner of assuring title to Frank came up. At first a will was contemplated. Louis Greiner testified as follows:

Q: Now did she say anything about this place, any arrangement, after those deeds were made here, and so on?
A: Well, we had fixed a date she was going to make a will to that effect, come to Beloit.
Q: Yes?
A: And in the meantime, she had signed some papers with Diebolt to pay Nick $2,000, and she called me up, and wanted me to come up one morning, and she told me what she had done.
Q: Yes?
A: Said Gustie had been raising so much storm about it, she wanted me to come and see if I couldn't get that paper back, and she would go to Beloit and make a will in favor of Frank and Nick; and so I went to Tipton with her, and we got this paper, and fixed a date to go to Beloit the next week; and the next week came, and I came there, and she absolutely wouldn't go; wouldn't do a thing.
Q: Did she say why?
A: She said Gustie told her if she would make a will they would move her off the place, that if she would make a will, she would be moved off the place at once.
Q: Then what was done about this place?
A: Well, she said that she would let Frank have it the way it was, and she wouldn't make a will.

Later, Mrs. Greiner said she was going to give Frank a deed.

August Greiner, "Gustie," a son favored in the will, lives with his mother. He returned from California a few days after she had made the written contract to pay Nicholas $2,000. The money has not yet been paid. August had a fight with Frank and Albert, and brought an action against them on account of it. He testified he helped move the house from the quarter section to the eighty-acre tract, but he testified he never heard that his mother intended to give the eighty-acre tract to Frank. A crystal gazer could tell why no deed to Frank has been executed.

An omission is noted in the testimony of Louis Greiner quoted above. Louis testified it was a settled fact that Frank was to move on the eighty, and his mother gave him that place as his share. The matter omitted consisted of a single question and answer as follows:

Q: That she was going to give him that?
A: Yes, sir.

In that way the learned counsel for plaintiff adroitly turned a settled fact into a matter of future intention, and the appeal is based chiefly on that legal distinction. The contention is that Maggie Greiner was going to settle with the disinherited boys; she was going to give Frank land; she was going to give Frank the eighty-acre tract; she was going to move the buildings; she was going to make a will; she was going to give Frank a deed; and these expressions of future intention did not make a contract with Frank that she would give him the eighty-acre if he would move from Logan county to Mitchell county.

A promise for breach of which the law gives remedy, or recognizes as creating a legal duty, is a contract. The promise need not be in any crystallized form of words: "I promise," "I agree," etc. Ritual scrupulousness is not required and, generally, any manifestation, by words or conduct or both, which the promisee is justified in understanding as an expression of intention to make a promise, is sufficient. . . . In this instance there is no doubt whatever respecting the intention of Maggie Greiner, either before or after she first sent for Frank to come to Mitchell county. Indeed, she fulfilled her intention up to the point of the formal matter of executing and delivering a deed. The only question is whether the untutored woman — she could not write — sufficiently expressed a promise to Frank when he came down to see her in response to the letter from Nicholas. The court has no hesitation in saying that Mrs. Greiner did promise to give Frank land for a home if he would move back to Mitchell county. Just at that point the promise was unenforceable because of indefiniteness. No particular land was specified. But the offer was later made perfectly definite. The eighty-acre tract was segregated for Frank, Mrs. Greiner fitted it for his occupancy as a home, and she gave him possession of it. . . .

Plaintiff says that there was no consideration for Maggie Greiner's promise; she did everything for Frank, and he did nothing for her. Section 90 of the American Law Institute's Restatement of the Law of Contracts reads as follows:

SECTION 90. *Promise Reasonably Inducing Definite and Substantial Action is Binding.* A promise which the promisor should reasonably expect to induce action or forbearance of a definite and substantial character on the part of the promisee and which does induce such action or forbearance, is binding if injustice can be avoided only by enforcement of the promise.

In this instance Frank did give up his homestead in Logan county, did move to Mitchell county, did establish himself and his family on the eighty-acre tract, made some lasting and valuable improvements upon it, and made other expenditures, relying on his mother's promise; and he lived on the land for nearly a year before he was served with notice to quit.

It is not necessary to review the conflicting evidence in detail. The evidence satisfied the district court that Mrs. Greiner should execute a deed to Frank. On the evidence favorable to him, and the inferences derivable from the evidence favorable to him, this court cannot say it would not be unjust to deny him a deed and to put off, and cannot say a money judgment would afford him adequate relief.

The judgment of the district court is affirmed.

RESTATEMENT (SECOND) OF CONTRACTS

§90.   PROMISE REASONABLY INDUCING ACTION OR FORBEARANCE

. . . (2) A charitable subscription or a marriage subscription is binding under Subsection (1) without proof that the promise induce action or forbearance.

3.   Promises of a Pension

STUDY GUIDE: What problems would Mrs. Feinberg face in using a reliance theory of promissory estoppel if she had retired because of illness? Would such a situation reveal any problem with this theoretical account of promissory estoppel? Suppose the company withdrew its promise of a pension after Mrs. Feinberg retired but before she became unable to work for another employer? How would this affect the applicability of §90? Does this reveal any problem with the formulation of the doctrine embodied in §90? Why did Mrs. Feinberg rely on the promise? Did she have a right to so rely?

FEINBERG v. PFEIFFER CO.
St. Louis Court of Appeals, Missouri,
322 S.W.2d 163 (1959)

DOERNER, Commissioner.

This is a suit brought in the Circuit Court of the City of St. Louis by plaintiff, a former employee of the defendant corporation, on an alleged contract whereby defendant agreed to pay plaintiff the sum of $200 per month for life upon her retirement. A jury being waived, the case was tried by the court alone. Judgment below was for plaintiff for $5,100, the amount of the pension claimed to be due as of the date of the trial, together with interest thereon, and defendant duly appealed. [*Procedural Posture*]

The parties are in substantial agreement on the essential facts. Plaintiff began working for the defendant, a manufacturer of pharmaceuticals, in 1910, when she was but 17 years of age. By 1947 she had attained the position of bookkeeper, office manager, and assistant treasurer of the defendant, and owned 70 shares of its stock out of a total of 6,503 shares issued and outstanding. Twenty shares had been given to her by the defendant or its then president, she had purchased 20, and the remaining 30 she had acquired by a stock split or stock dividend. Over the years she received substantial dividends on the stock she owned, as did all of the other stockholders. Also, in addition to her salary, plaintiff from 1937 to 1949, inclusive, received each year a bonus varying in amount from $300 in the beginning to $2,000 in the later years.

On December 27, 1947, the annual meeting of the defendant's Board of Directors was held at the Company's offices in St. Louis, presided over by

Max Lippman, its then president and largest individual stockholder. The other directors present were George L. Marcus, Sidney Harris, Sol Flammer, and Walter Weinstock, who, with Max Lippman, owned 5,007 of the 6,503 shares then issued and outstanding. At that meeting the Board of Directors adopted the following resolution, which, because it is the crux of the case, we quote in full:

> The Chairman thereupon pointed out that the Assistant Treasurer, Mrs. Anna Sacks Feinberg, has given the corporation many years of long and faithful service. Not only has she served the corporation devotedly, but with exceptional ability and skill. The President pointed out that although all of the officers and directors sincerely hoped and desired that Mrs. Feinberg would continue in her present position for as long as she felt able, nevertheless, in view of the length of service which she has contributed provision should be made to afford her retirement privileges and benefits which should become a firm obligation of the corporation to be available to her whenever she should see fit to retire from active duty, however many years in the future such retirement may become effective. It was, accordingly, proposed that Mrs. Feinberg's salary which is presently $350.00 per month, be increased to $400.00 per month, and that Mrs. Feinberg would be given the privilege of retiring from active duty at any time she may elect to see fit so to do upon a retirement pay of $200.00 per month for life, with the distinct understanding that the retirement plan is merely being adopted at the present time in order to afford Mrs. Feinberg security for the future and in the hope that her active services will continue with the corporation for many years to come. After due discussion and consideration, and upon motion duly made and seconded, it was —
>
> RESOLVED, that the salary of Anna Sacks Feinberg be increased from $350.00 to $400.00 per month and that she be afforded the privilege of retiring from active duty in the corporation at any time she may elect to see fit so to do upon retirement pay of $200.00 per month, for the remainder of her life.

At the request of Mr. Lippman his sons-in-law, Messrs. Harris and Flammer, called upon the plaintiff at her apartment on the same day to advise her of the passage of the resolution. Plaintiff testified on cross-examination that she had no prior information that such a pension plan was contemplated, that it came as a surprise to her, and that she would have continued in her employment whether or not such a resolution had been adopted. It is clear from the evidence that there was no contract, oral or written, as to plaintiff's length of employment, and that she was free to quit, and the defendant to discharge her, at any time.

Plaintiff did continue to work for the defendant through June 30, 1949, on which date she retired. In accordance with the foregoing resolution, the defendant began paying her the sum of $200 on the first of each month. Mr. Lippman died on November 18, 1949, and was succeeded as president of the company by his widow. Because of an illness, she retired from that office and was succeeded in October, 1953, by her son-in-law, Sidney M. Harris. Mr. Harris testified that while Mrs. Lippman had been president she signed the monthly pension check paid plaintiff, but fussed about doing so, and considered the payments as gifts. After his election, he stated, a new accounting firm employed by the defendant questioned the validity of the payments to plaintiff on several occasions, and in the Spring of 1956, upon

Promise to pay pension not made directly to plaintiff. Does that matter?

its recommendation, he consulted the Company's then attorney, Mr. Ralph Kalish. Harris testified that both Ernst and Ernst, the accounting firm, and Kalish told him there was no need of giving plaintiff the money. He also stated that he had concurred in the view that the payments to plaintiff were mere gratuities rather than amounts due under a contractual obligation, and that following his discussion with the Company's attorney plaintiff was sent a check for $100 on April 1, 1956. Plaintiff declined to accept the reduced amount, and this action followed. Additional facts will be referred to later in this opinion.

Appellant's first assignment of error relates to the admission in evidence of plaintiff's testimony over its objection, that at the time of trial she was sixty-five and a half years old, and that she was no longer able to engage in gainful employment because of the removal of a cancer and the performance of a colocholecystostomy operation on November 25, 1957. Its complaint is not so much that such evidence was irrelevant and immaterial, as it is that the trial court erroneously made it one basis for its decision in favor of plaintiff. As defendant concedes, the error (if it was error) in the admission of such evidence would not be a ground for reversal, since, this being a jury-waived case, we are constrained by the statutes to review it upon both the law and the evidence . . . , and to render such judgment as the court below ought to have given. . . . We consider only such evidence as is admissible, and need not pass upon questions of error in the admission and exclusion of evidence. . . . However, in fairness to the trial court it should be stated that while he briefly referred to the state of plaintiff's health as of the time of the trial in his amended findings of fact, it is obvious from his amended grounds for decision and judgment that it was not, as will be seen, the basis for his decision.

Appellant's next complaint is that there was insufficient evidence to support the court's findings that plaintiff would not have quit defendant's employ had she not known and relied upon the promise of defendant to pay her $200 a month for life, and the finding that, from her voluntary retirement until April 1, 1956, plaintiff relied upon the continued receipt of the pension installments. The trial court so found, and, in our opinion, justifiably so. Plaintiff testified, and was corroborated by Harris, defendant's witness, that knowledge of the passage of the resolution was communicated to her on December 27, 1947, the very day it was adopted. She was told at that time by Harris and Flammer, she stated, that she could take the pension as of that day, if she wished. She testified further that she continued to work for another year and a half, through June 30, 1949; that at that time her health was good and she could have continued to work, but that after working for almost forty years she thought she would take a rest. Her testimony continued:

Q: Now, what was the reason — I'm sorry. Did you then quit the employment of the company after you — after this year and a half?
A: Yes.
Q: What was the reason that you left?
A: Well, I thought almost forty years, it was a long time and I thought I would take a little rest.
Q: Yes.

A: And with the pension and what earnings my husband had, we figured we could get along.

Q: Did you rely upon this pension?

A: We certainly did.

Q: Being paid?

A: Very much so. We relied upon it because I was positive that I was going to get it as long as I lived.

Q: Would you have left the employment of the company at that time had it not been for this pension?

A: No.

Mr. Allen: Just a minute, I object to that as calling for a conclusion and conjecture on the part of this witness.

The Court: It will be overruled.

Q: (Mr. Agatstein continuing): Go ahead, now. The question is whether you would have quit the employment of the company at that time had you not relied upon this pension plan?

A: No, I wouldn't.

Q: You would not have. Did you ever seek employment while this pension was being paid to you —

A: (interrupting): No.

Q: Wait a minute, at any time prior — at any other place?

A: No, sir.

Q: Were you able to hold any other employment during that time?

A: Yes, I think so.

Q: Was your health good?

A: My health was good.

It is obvious from the foregoing that there was ample evidence to support the findings of fact made by the court below.

We come, then, to the basic issue in the case. While otherwise defined in defendant's third and fourth assignments of error, it is thus succinctly stated in the argument in its brief:

> . . . whether plaintiff has proved that she has a right to recover from defendant based upon a legally binding contractual obligation to pay her $200 per month for life.

It is defendant's contention, in essence, that the resolution adopted by its Board of Directors was a mere promise to make a gift, and that no contract resulted either thereby, or when plaintiff retired, because there was no consideration given or paid by the plaintiff. It urges that a promise to make a gift is not binding unless supported by a legal consideration; that the only apparent consideration for the adoption of the foregoing resolution was the "many years of long and faithful service" expressed therein; and that past services are not a valid consideration for a promise. Defendant argues further that there is nothing in the resolution which made its effectiveness conditional upon plaintiff's continued employment, that she was not under contract to work for any length of time but was free to quit whenever she wished, and that she had no contractual right to her position and could have been discharged at any time.

Plaintiff concedes that a promise based upon past services would be without consideration, but contends that there were two other elements which supplied the required element: First, the continuation by plaintiff in the employ of the defendant for the period from December 27, 1947, the date when the resolution was adopted, until the date of her retirement on June 30, 1949. And, second, her change of position, i.e., her retirement, and the abandonment by her of her opportunity to continue in gainful employment, made in reliance on defendant's promise to pay her $200 per month for life.

[We must agree with the defendant that the evidence does not support the first of these contentions. There is no language in the resolution predicating plaintiff's right to a pension upon her continued employment. She was not required to work for the defendant for any period of time as a condition to gaining such retirement benefits.] She was told that she could quit the day upon which the resolution was adopted, as she herself testified, and it is clear from her own testimony that she made no promise or agreement to continue in the employ of the defendant in return for its promise to pay her a pension. Hence there was lacking that mutuality of obligation which is essential to the validity of a contract. . . .

But as to the second of these contentions we must agree with plaintiff. By the terms of the resolution defendant promised to pay plaintiff the sum of $200 a month upon her retirement. Consideration for a promise has been defined in the Restatement of the Law of Contracts, Section 75, as:

> (1) Consideration for a promise is
>   (a) an act other than a promise, or
>   (b) a forbearance, or
>   (c) the creation, modification or destruction of a legal relation, or
>   (d) a return promise,
> bargained for and given in exchange for the promise.

As the parties agree, the consideration sufficient to support a contract may be either a benefit to the promisor or a loss or detriment to the promisee. . . .

Section 90 of the Restatement of the Law of Contracts states that:

> A promise which the promisor should reasonably expect to induce action or forbearance of a definite and substantial character on the part of the promisee and which does induce such action or forbearance is binding if injustice can be avoided only by enforcement of the promise.

This doctrine has been described as that of "promissory estoppel," as distinguished from that of equitable estoppel or estoppel in pais, the reason for the differentiation being stated as follows:

> It is generally true that one who has led another to act in reasonable reliance on his representations of fact cannot afterwards in litigation between the two deny the truth of the representations, and some courts have sought to apply this principle to the formation of contracts, where, relying on a gratuitous promise, the promisee has suffered detriment. It is to be noticed, however, that such a case does not come within the ordinary definition of estoppel. If there is any representation of an existing fact, it is only that the promisor at the time of making the promise intends to fulfill it. As to such intention there is usually no misrepresentation and if there is, it is not that which has injured the promisee. In other words, he relies on a promise and

not on a misstatement of fact; and the term "promissory" estoppel or something equivalent should be used to make the distinction.

Williston on Contracts, rev. ed., Sec. 139, Vol. 1.

In speaking of this doctrine, Judge Learned Hand said in Porter v. Commissioner of Internal Revenue, 2 Cir., 60 F.2d 673, 675, that ". . . 'promissory estoppel' is now a recognized species of consideration." . . .

Was there such an act on the part of plaintiff, in reliance upon the promise contained in the resolution, as will estop the defendant, and therefore create an enforceable contract under the doctrine of promissory estoppel? We think there was. One of the illustrations cited under Section 90 of the Restatement is:

> 2. *A* promises *B* to pay him an annuity during *B's* life. *B* thereupon resigns a profitable employment, as *A* expected that he might. *B* receives the annuity for some years, in the meantime becoming disqualified from again obtaining good employment. *A*'s promise is binding.

This illustration is objected to by defendant as not being applicable to the case at hand. The reason advanced by it is that in the illustration *B* became "disqualified" from obtaining other employment *before A* discontinued the payments, whereas in this case the plaintiff did not discover that she had cancer and thereby became unemployable until *after* the defendant had discontinued the payments of $200 per month. We think the distinction is immaterial. The only reason for the reference in the illustration to the disqualification of *A* is in connection with that part of Section 90 regarding the prevention of injustice. The injustice would occur regardless of when the disability occurred. Would defendant contend that the contract would be enforceable if the plaintiff's illness had been discovered on March 31, 1956, the day before it discontinued the payment of the $200 a month, but not if it occurred on April 2nd, the day after? Furthermore, there are more ways to become disqualified for work, or unemployable, than as the result of illness. At the time she retired plaintiff was 57 years of age. At the time the payments were discontinued she was over 63 years of age. It is a matter of common knowledge that it is virtually impossible for a woman of that age to find satisfactory employment, much less a position comparable to that which plaintiff enjoyed at the time of her retirement.

The fact of the matter is that plaintiff's subsequent illness was not the "action or forbearance" which was induced by the promise contained in the resolution. As the trial court correctly decided, such action on plaintiff's part was her retirement from a lucrative position in reliance upon defendant's promise to pay her an annuity or pension. In a very similar case, Ricketts v. Scothorn, 57 Neb. 51, 77 N.W. 365, 367, . . . the Supreme Court of Nebraska said:

> . . . According to the undisputed proof, as shown by the record before us, the plaintiff was a working girl, holding a position in which she earned a salary of $10 per week. Her grandfather, desiring to put her in a position of independence, gave her the note, accompanying it with the remark that his other grandchildren did not work, and that she would not be obliged to work any longer. In effect, he suggested that she might abandon her employment,

and rely in the future upon the bounty which he promised. He doubtless desired that she should give up her occupation, but, whether he did or not, it is entirely certain that he contemplated such action on her part as a reasonable and probable consequence of his gift. Having intentionally influenced the plaintiff to alter her position for the worse on the faith of the note being paid when due, it would be grossly inequitable to permit the maker, or his executor, to resist payment on the ground that the promise was given without consideration.

The Commissioner therefore recommends, for the reasons stated, that the judgment be affirmed.

PER CURIAM.

The foregoing opinion by DOERNER, C., is adopted as the opinion of the court. The judgment is, accordingly, affirmed. ——> Holding! for the plaintiff

STUDY GUIDE: *The facts in this case seem in many ways to be identical to those in* Pfeiffer. *How are they different? Why did the plaintiff in that case win, while Mr. Pitts lost? Is the plaintiff in* Pfeiffer *more sympathetic than the plaintiff in this case? Do the facts warrant such different treatment?*

PITTS v. McGRAW-EDISON CO.
United States Court of Appeals, Sixth Circuit,
329 F.2d 412 (1964)

SHACKELFORD MILLER, JR.,* Circuit Judge.

Plaintiff, L. U. Pitts, brought this action in the District Court to recover damages in the amount of $15,000 for an alleged breach of a retirement contract by the defendant. He also sought a declaration of rights with respect to future payments under the contract. Jurisdiction is based upon diversity of citizenship and the amount involved. Section 1332, Title 28 United States Code. Plaintiff appeals from a judgment dismissing the action. ——> Procedural Posture

The facts, which are mostly undisputed, are as follows. Plaintiff was a manufacturer's representative in Memphis, Tennessee, for a period of many years prior to July 1, 1955. For approximately twenty-five years preceding that date, he sold the products of the defendant's predecessor and the defendant, McGraw-Edison Company, on a commission basis in an assigned territory comprising several southern states. In his capacity as a manufacturer's representative he was an independent business man, hiring and firing his own employees, paying his own expenses and overhead, and managing his business as he saw fit. He had no written contract with the defendant and the defendant had no obligation to him except to compensate him on a commission basis for sales made in the assigned territory. The relationship between the parties was independent and was not that of

Contractor to recover lost benefits

* Shackelford Miller Jr. (1892-1965) was born in Louisville, Kentucky. He received his undergraduate degree from Princeton, and then attended Harvard Law School. After serving for six years on the U.S. District Court for the Western District of Kentucky, he was appointed to the U.S. Court of Appeals for the Sixth Circuit in 1945. He served on that court until his death. — S.Q.

employer and employee. It was terminable at will, without notice by either party at any time. The plaintiff was free to handle any other products he desired, including those of competitors of the defendant, and he did so until early in 1954, when on his own volition and without any requirement by the defendant, he discontinued his representation of other manufacturers.

At no time during the relationship of the parties did the plaintiff make contributions to a pension fund or a retirement fund of any kind.

In April 1955 when the plaintiff was approximately 67 years of age, he accompanied O. Dee Harrison, the sales manager for the defendant, to Little Rock, Arkansas, for a meeting with one Paul Thurman, who had formerly worked for the plaintiff but at the time was working the State of Arkansas as a factory representative for the defendant and others. At that meeting Mr. Harrison told the plaintiff that the defendant was making arrangements for the plaintiff to retire at a time shortly thereafter and for Thurman to take over the plaintiff's territory, with the plaintiff receiving an overwrite commission of 1% from the defendant on all sales made in that territory. Thereafter the plaintiff received a letter dated July 1, 1955, from O. Dee Harrison reading in part as follows:

"Dear Lou:

"Whether you know it or not, you are on retirement effective July 1st. But to make the matter of retirement a little less distasteful, we are going ahead as you and I talked last time we were together by paying each month 1% of the sales from the Mississippi and Tennessee states. You will get your check each month just as you have been in the habit of getting our check on commissions. Let us hope that there is enough to help keep a few pork chops on the table and a few biscuits in the oven.

"We are going to keep you on the list for bulletins, Lou, so that you will know what is going on. I know that you will help Paul in every way that you can, and I know that your help will be greatly appreciated by Paul."

There was an error in this letter regarding the territory to which it referred and Mr. Harrison corrected this error in a letter to the plaintiff dated July 20, 1955. In addition, this letter contained the following:

"Now in regard to your 1% deal, Lou, I have talked with our office in Boonville on this matter. There is a problem of keeping things straight without undue complications, also. So what I am going to do is to give you 1% on Paul's territory, which will enable Dorothy to quickly figure the thing each month. I am sorry I cannot include the rest of the United States, Lou, but I don't think this will be too bad a proposition for you."

The letter also said in closing:

"We will keep you on the mailing list and any time you can throw a little weight our way we will appreciate any effort you make, Lou. And any time you have any questions, don't be afraid to ask us about them."

Although plaintiff testified that the arrangements were completed at the April meeting in Little Rock, he unequivocally conceded on his cross-examination that the foregoing two letters contained the entire understanding between him and the defendant, and that there was nothing else either orally or in writing.

The plaintiff received a check from the defendant each month regularly from July 1955 through June 1960 covering the 1% commission on sales in the specified territory. The amounts received were:

For the last six months of 1955,	$ 759.67
For 1956,	2,630.23
For 1957,	2,696.31
For 1958,	2,629.04
For 1959,	4,337.38
For first six months of 1960	3,233.46

Under date of July 23, 1960, the plaintiff was advised by letter from the Division Controller of the defendant, reading in part as follows:

"Dear Mr. Pitts:

"I am enclosing our check #50064752 for $238.51 which, according to our records, completes the five year series of payments to be paid after your retirement from the Company."

[handwritten margin note: Mistake in terms]

Plaintiff wrote the defendant protesting the discontinuance of the payments. Mr. Harrison responded at some length, pointing out that the plaintiff was at no time an employee of the defendant, that he was not eligible for any company pension had there been one available, which there was not, and that in order to make the retirement a little less painful, the Company had voluntarily paid the 1% commission for a period of five years but was not willing to continue it for an additional period. He pointed out that this was the same position taken by the Company with respect to three other employees who were all retired at the same general period, and that he did not know of any other company which gave any separation pay at all to manufacturer's representatives who represented them.

This action followed. Following a trial to the Court without a jury, the District Judge held that the plaintiff was not entitled to recover any amount whatever and dismissed his complaint.

Plaintiff contends that the negotiations between the Company and him leading to his retirement were in substance an offer on the part of the Company that if he would retire as a manufacturer's representative on July 1, 1955, and turn over to his successor representative all of his customer account records containing valuable information on active and inactive accounts, which had been built up over a period of twenty years or more, the Company would pay him monthly thereafter a 1% overwrite commission on sales by the defendant in the territory which was at that time allotted to him; that after considering the offer, he accepted it and thereafter carried it out by retiring as a manufacturer's representative and turning over to his successor the stipulated records; and that the defendant breached the contract by refusing to make the payments after July 1, 1960.

Defendant contends that the so-called "retirement" of the plaintiff was actually not a "retirement" in that the plaintiff was not an employee of the defendant, but was a termination of defendant's business relations with the plaintiff, made effective by a unilateral act on its part, which it was legally authorized to do; that it was not an offer to the plaintiff on its part and acceptance thereof by the plaintiff; that it imposed no contractual obligation on its part to make any payment to the plaintiff; and that even if construed as a retirement contract between it and the plaintiff, it was void and unenforceable for lack of consideration.

In considering these contentions, it must be kept in mind that the plaintiff was an independent business man, not an employee of the defendant. His relationship with the defendant could be terminated by either party at any time without notice and without liability therefor. The plaintiff in his testimony concedes this, and it was so found as a fact by the District Judge. Unless the plaintiff is able to establish a valid contract obligating the defendant to pay the "retirement" benefits claimed, he has no cause of action.

Assuming, without so holding, that there was a promise by the defendant to pay the plaintiff the retirement benefits claimed, we are faced with the question of what consideration passed from the plaintiff to the defendant to make this promise enforceable.

Plaintiff vigorously argues that although he did not promise to do anything or to refrain from doing anything, as plainly appears from the two letters, and so conceded by him, consideration nevertheless exists because of the action taken by him at the request of the defendant, namely, his retirement as a manufacturer's representative, including other manufacturers as well as the defendant, and his turning over to the defendant his personal records pertaining to customers and sales over a period of years in the past. There would be merit in this contention if it was supported by the facts. Farabee-Treadwell Co. v. Union & Planters' Bank & Trust Co., 135 Tenn. 208, 216, 186 S.W. 92, L.R.A.1916F, 501; Meurer Steel Barrel Co., Inc. v. Martin, 1 F.2d 687, C.A.3d; Messick v. Powell, 314 Ky. 805, 809, 236 S.W.2d 897.

However, these factual contentions of the plaintiff were disputed by the evidence of the defendant. The District Judge made findings of fact that the plaintiff was not required by the terms of the letters, or by any other statements on the part of the defendant, or its agents, to do anything whatsoever; that upon his retirement on July 1, 1955, the plaintiff was free to handle the products of any other manufacturer or competitor if he so desired, to seek other employment, or to do as he pleased; that nothing in the arrangement circumscribed the plaintiff's actions or rights in any manner; and that the plaintiff was not obligated to perform any duties on behalf of the defendant. These findings are fully supported by the evidence. In fact, they were substantially conceded by the plaintiff in the cross-examination of him as a witness, in which he apparently contended that he did certain things for the defendant after his retirement although he was not required to do so.

On the basis of these facts, the District Judge ruled that the payments to the plaintiff over the period of July 1, 1955, to July 1, 1960, were without consideration, were the result of voluntary action on the part of the defendant, and were mere gratuities terminable by the defendant at will.

We concur in the ruling. Combs v. Standard Oil Co., 166 Tenn. 88, 59 S.W.2d 525; Judd v. Wasie, 211 F.2d 826, 832, C.A.8th; Big Cola Corporation v. World Bottling Co., 134 F.2d 718, C.A.6th; Tennessee Enamel Mfg. Co. v. Stoves, Inc., 192 F.2d 863, C.A.6th, cert. denied, 342 U.S. 946, 72 S. Ct. 561, 96 L. Ed. 704.

Plaintiff further contends that although defendant's promise may not be supported by legal consideration, it is nevertheless enforceable under the doctrine of promissory estoppel, which, as explained by the authorities, is different from the well recognized principle of estoppel in pais, based on misrepresentation of fact. Plaintiff relies upon this principle as explained and applied in Ricketts v. Scothorn, 57 Neb. 51, 77 N.W. 365, 42 L.R.A. 794; Sessions v. Southern California Edison Co., 47 Cal. App. 2d 611, 118 P.2d 935; and Feinberg v. Pfeiffer Company, (Mo. App. 1959) 322 S.W.2d 163.

Promissory estoppel is defined in Restatement, Contracts, Section 90, as follows:

> "A promise which the promisor should reasonably expect to induce action or forbearance of a definite and substantial character on the part of the promisee and which does induce such action or forbearance is binding if injustice can be avoided only by enforcement of the promise."

This principle appears to be of somewhat limited application in the United States. Annotation, 48 A.L.R.2d 1069, 1081, 1085. We are not shown that it has ever been recognized or applied as the law of Tennessee. The indications are to the contrary. Barnes v. Boyd, 18 Tenn. App. 55, 72 S.W.2d 573; Comment, 23 Tenn. Law Review, 423. We construe the ruling in Marsh v. State Bank & Trust Co., 153 Tenn. 400 (see page 406), 284 S.W. 380, 48 A.L.R. 1365, relied upon by plaintiff, to be based upon estoppel in pais, rather than upon promissory estoppel.

Although there may be other facts in the present case which prevent it from coming within the scope of that definition, we believe that an important fact is that the plaintiff in no way altered his position for the worse by reason of defendant's letters of July 1 and July 20, 1955. The District Judge found as a fact that the plaintiff gave up nothing to which he was legally entitled and was restricted in no way in his activities thereafter. Plaintiff gave up nothing in accepting retirement that he would not have lost if he had refused to accept it. We do not find in the present case the injustice required in order to enforce the alleged promise.

In the Nebraska, California and Missouri cases, referred to above and relied on by the plaintiff, the plaintiff in each case relinquished some right to which he or she was entitled in reliance upon the promise of the defendant. They are not applicable here. See also: Insurance Co. v. Mowry, 96 U.S. 544, 547, 24 L. Ed. 674; Faxton v. Faxon, 28 Mich. 159, 161.

The judgment is affirmed.

4. Construction Bids

STUDY GUIDE: In what way is the doctrine of promissory estoppel being interpreted as a consideration substitute? This approach will be contrasted with a different conception of promissory estoppel in the case of Hoffman v. Red Owl Stores, Inc.

JAMES BAIRD CO. v. GIMBEL BROS., INC.
United States Court of Appeals, Second Circuit,
64 F.2d 344 (1933)

L. HAND, Circuit Judge.*

The plaintiff sued the defendant for breach of a contract to deliver linoleum under a contract of sale; the defendant denied the making of the contract; the parties tried the case to the judge under a written stipulation and he directed judgment for the defendant. The facts as found, bearing on the making of the contract, the only issue necessary to discuss, were as follows: The defendant, a New York merchant, knew that the Department of Highways in Pennsylvania had asked for bids for the construction of a public building. It sent an employee to the office of a contractor in Philadelphia, who had possession of the specifications, and the employee there computed the amount of the linoleum which would be required on the job, underestimating the total yardage by about one-half the proper amount. In ignorance of this mistake, on December twenty-fourth the defendant sent to some twenty or thirty contractors, likely to bid on the job, an offer to supply all the linoleum by the specifications at two different lump sums, depending upon the quality used. These offers concluded as follows:

> If successful in being awarded the contract, it will be absolutely guaranteed, . . . and . . . we are offering these prices for reasonable (sic), prompt acceptance after the general contract has been awarded.

The plaintiff, a contractor in Washington, got one of these on the twenty-eighth, and on the same day the defendant learned its mistake and telegraphed all the contractors to whom it had sent the offer, that it withdrew it and would substitute a new one at about double the amount of the old. This withdrawal reached the plaintiff at Washington on the afternoon of the same day, but not until after it had put in a bid at Harrisburg

---

* *Learned Hand* (1872-1961) born Billings Learned Hand, dropped the name Billings in favor of Learned, his mother's maiden name. He studied at Harvard College (A.B., A.B., LL.B.) and became a member of the New York bar in 1897. Maintaining a private law practice for over ten years in New York City, he was appointed by President Taft to the U.S. District Court for the Southern District of New York in 1909. He was elevated by President Coolidge to the U.S. Court of Appeals for the Second Circuit in 1924, where he served until retirement in 1951. During his long and celebrated judicial career, Judge Hand wrote nearly 4,000 opinions. — K.T.

at a lump sum, based as to linoleum upon the prices quoted by the defendant. The public authorities accepted the plaintiff's bid on December thirtieth, the defendant having meanwhile written a letter of confirmation of its withdrawal, received on the thirty-first. The plaintiff formally accepted the offer on January second, and, as the defendant persisted in declining to recognize the existence of a contract, sued it for damages on breach.

Unless there are circumstances to take it out of the ordinary doctrine, since the offer was withdrawn before it was accepted, the acceptance was too late. Restatement of Contracts, §35 [now §36]. To meet this the plaintiff argues as follows: It was a reasonable implication from the defendant's offer that it should be irrevocable in case the plaintiff acted upon it, that is to say, used the prices quoted in making its bid, thus putting itself in a position from which it could not withdraw without great loss. While it might have withdrawn its bid after receiving the revocation, the time had passed to submit another, and as the item of linoleum was a very trifling part of the cost of the whole building, it would have been an unreasonable hardship to expect it to lose the contract on that account, and probably forfeit its deposit. While it is true that the plaintiff might in advance have secured a contract conditional upon the success of its bid, this was not what the defendant suggested. It understood that the contractors would use its offer in their bids, and would thus in fact commit themselves to supplying the linoleum at the proposed prices. The inevitable implication from all this was that when the contractors acted upon it, they accepted the offer and promised to pay for the linoleum, in case their bid were accepted.

It was of course possible for the parties to make such a contract, and the question is merely as to what they meant; that is, what is to be imputed to the words they used. Whatever plausibility there is in the argument, is in the fact that the defendant must have known the predicament in which the contractors would be put if it withdrew its offer after the bids went in. However, it seems entirely clear that the contractors did not suppose that they accepted the offer merely by putting in their bids. If, for example, the successful one had repudiated the contract with the public authorities after it had been awarded to him, certainly the defendant could not have sued him for a breach. If he had become bankrupt, the defendant could not prove against his estate. It seems plain therefore that there was no contract between them. And if there be any doubt as to this, the language of the offer sets it at rest. The phrase, "if successful in being awarded this contract," is scarcely met by the mere use of the prices in the bids. Surely such a use was not an "award" of the contract to the defendant. Again, the phrase, "we are offering these prices for . . . prompt acceptance after the general contract has been awarded," looks to the usual communication of an acceptance, and precludes the idea that the use of the offer in the bidding shall be the equivalent. It may indeed be argued that this last language contemplated no more than an early notice that the offer had been accepted, the actual acceptance being the bid, but that would wrench its natural meaning too far, especially in the light of the preceding phrase. The contractors had a ready escape from their difficulty by insisting upon a contract before they used the figures; and in commercial transactions it does not in the end promote justice to seek strained interpretations in aid of those who do not protect themselves. . . .

But the plaintiff says that even though no bilateral contract was made, the defendant should be held under the doctrine of "promissory estoppel." This is to be chiefly found in those cases where persons subscribe to a venture, usually charitable, and are held to their promises after it has been completed. It has been applied much more broadly, however, and has now been generalized in section 90, of the Restatement of Contracts. We may arguendo accept it as it there reads, for it does not apply to the case at bar. Offers are ordinarily made in exchange for a consideration, either a counter-promise or some other act which the promisor wishes to secure. In such cases they propose bargains; they presuppose that each promise or performance is an inducement to the other. . . . But a man may make a promise without expecting an equivalent; a donative promise, conditional or absolute. The common law provided for such by sealed instruments, and it is unfortunate that these are no longer generally available. The doctrine of "promissory estoppel" is to avoid the harsh results of allowing the promisor in such a case to repudiate, when the promisee has acted in reliance upon the promise. . . . Cf. Allegheny College v. National Bank, 246 N.Y. 369, 159 N.E. 173. . . . But an offer for an exchange is not meant to become a promise until a consideration has been received, either a counter-promise or whatever else is stipulated. To extend it would be to hold the offeror regardless of the stipulated condition of his offer. In the case at bar the defendant offered to deliver the linoleum in exchange for the plaintiff's acceptance, not for its bid, which was a matter of indifference to it. That offer could become a promise to deliver only when the equivalent was received; that is, when the plaintiff promised to take and pay for it. There is no room in such a situation for the doctrine of "promissory estoppel."

Nor can the offer be regarded as of an option, giving the plaintiff the right seasonably to accept the linoleum at the quoted prices if its bid was accepted, but not binding it to take and pay, if it could get a better bargain elsewhere. There is not the least reason to suppose that the defendant meant to subject itself to such a one-sided obligation. True, if so construed, the doctrine of "promissory estoppel" might apply, the plaintiff having acted upon it, though, so far as we have found, the decisions are otherwise. . . . As to that, however, we need not declare ourselves.

Judgment affirmed.

Relational Background: More About the "Mistake"

STUDY GUIDE: In light of the doctrine of mistake in integration, which we studied in Chapter 6, consider the following facts. Why was that justification for reformation apparently unavailable here? Also, make a note to refer back to these facts when, in Chapter 17, we discuss the defense of mistake.

LON L. FULLER, BASIC CONTRACT LAW 376 (1947): Gimbel actually relied on two defenses: (1) its offer was withdrawn before it was accepted; (2) its offer was based on a mistaken computation of such proportions that Baird ought to have known of the mistake. . . . The evidence on the issue of mistake was in such a state that it was difficult for the court to deal with it. The bid on the total job was about $2,000,000; Baird had to submit a $50,000 check with its bid. Gimbel's bid on the linoleum was about $15,000; other bids for this part of the job ran from about $29,000 to $32,000. Of the twenty five odd general contractors to whom Gimbel sent bids on the linoleum, three or four called to say that there must have been some mistake in Gimbel's bid. It appeared that their concern was not so much for Gimbel as for themselves; they feared that other general contractors would not notice the discrepancy in the linoleum bids and might therefore make a lower bid for the whole job, based on Gimbel's low bid on the linoleum. An expert called by Gimbel admitted that variations of as much as fifty percent were not unusual in bids on subcontracts for linoleum, but also testified that mistakes were very common. Baird's estimator testified that he had little time in which to prepare the bid on the whole job, and that he did not calculate the footage of linoleum required. He testified that Gimbel was the most responsible of the subcontractors offering to do the linoleum work, and that he depended on Gimbel to determine the footage correctly. Gimbel's witnesses were unable to explain satisfactorily just what mistake had been made by them, but assumed it must have consisted in leaving out whole floors of the building.

STUDY GUIDE: Is there a difference between Judge Hand's and Justice Traynor's theories of promissory estoppel that accounts for the different outcomes of these two cases?

DRENNAN v. STAR PAVING CO.
Supreme Court of California, En Banc,
51 Cal. 2d 409, 333 P.2d 757 (1958)

TRAYNOR, J. — Defendant appeals from a judgment for plaintiff in an action to recover damages caused by defendant's refusal to perform certain paving work according to a bid it submitted to plaintiff.

On July 28, 1955, plaintiff, a licensed general contractor, was preparing a bid on the "Monte Vista School Job" in the Lancaster school district. Bids had to be submitted before 8 P.M. Plaintiff testified that it was customary in that area for general contractors to receive the bids of subcontractors by telephone on the day set for bidding and to rely on them in computing their own bids. Thus on that day plaintiff's secretary, Mrs. Johnson, received by telephone between 50 and 75 subcontractors' bids for various parts of the school job. As each bid came in, she wrote it on a special form, which she brought into plaintiff's office. He then posted it on a master cost sheet setting forth the names and bids of all subcontractors. His own bid had to include the names of subcontractors who were to perform one-half of one per cent or more of the construction work, and he had also to provide a bidder's bond of 10 per cent of his total bid of $317,385 as a guarantee that he would enter the contract if awarded the work.

Late in the afternoon, Mrs. Johnson had a telephone conversation with Kenneth R. Hoon, an estimator for defendant. He gave his name and telephone number and stated that he was bidding for defendant for the paving work at the Monte Vista School according to plans and specifications and that his bid was $7,131.60. At Mrs. Johnson's request he repeated his bid. Plaintiff listened to the bid over an extension telephone in his office and posted it on the master sheet after receiving the bid form from Mrs. Johnson. Defendant's was the lowest bid for the paving. Plaintiff computed his own bid accordingly and submitted it with the name of defendant as the subcontractor for the paving. When the bids were opened on July 28th, plaintiff's proved to be the lowest, and he was awarded the contract.

On his way to Los Angeles the next morning plaintiff stopped at defendant's office. The first person he met was defendant's construction engineer, Mr. Oppenheimer. Plaintiff testified:

> I introduced myself and he immediately told me that they had made a mistake in their bid to me the night before, they couldn't do it for the price they had bid, and I told him I would expect him to carry through with their original bid because I had used it in compiling my bid and the job was being awarded them. And I would have to go and do the job according to my bid and I would expect them to do the same.

Defendant refused to do the paving work for less than $15,000. Plaintiff testified that he "got figures from other people" and after trying for several months to get as low a bid as possible engaged L & H Paving Company, a firm in Lancaster, to do the work for $10,948.60.

The trial court found on substantial evidence that defendant made a definite offer to do the paving on the Monte Vista job according to the plans and specifications for $7,131.60, and that plaintiff relied on defendant's bid in computing his own bid for the school job and naming defendant therein as the subcontractor for the paving work. Accordingly, it entered judgment for plaintiff in the amount of $3,817 (the difference between defendant's bid and the cost of the paving to plaintiff) plus costs.

Defendant contends that there was no enforceable contract between the parties on the ground that it made a revocable offer and revoked it before plaintiff communicated his acceptance to defendant.

There is no evidence that defendant offered to make its bid irrevocable in exchange for plaintiff's use of its figures in computing his bid. Nor is there evidence that would warrant interpreting plaintiff's use of defendant's bid as the acceptance thereof, binding plaintiff, on condition he received the main contract, to award the subcontract to defendant. In sum, there was neither an option supported by consideration nor a bilateral contract binding on both parties.

Plaintiff contends, however, that he relied to his detriment on defendant's offer and that defendant must therefore answer in damages for its refusal to perform. Thus the question is squarely presented: Did plaintiff's reliance make defendant's offer irrevocable?

Section 90 of the Restatement of Contracts states:

> A promise which the promisor should reasonably expect to induce action or forbearance of a definite and substantial character on the part of the promisee and which does induce such action or forbearance is binding if injustice can be avoided only by enforcement of the promise.

This rule applies in this state. . . .

Defendant's offer constituted a promise to perform on such conditions as were stated expressly or by implication therein or annexed thereto by operation of law. . . . Defendant had reason to expect that if its bid proved the lowest it would be used by plaintiff. It induced "action . . . of a definite and substantial character on the part of the promisee."

Had defendant's bid expressly stated or clearly implied that it was revocable at any time before acceptance we would treat it accordingly. It was silent on revocation, however, and we must therefore determine whether there are conditions to the right of revocation imposed by law or reasonably inferable in fact. In the analogous problem of an offer for a unilateral contract, the theory is now obsolete that the offer is revocable at any time before complete performance. Thus section 45 of the Restatement of Contracts provides:

> If an offer for a unilateral contract is made, and part of the consideration requested in the offer is given or tendered by the offeree in response thereto, the offeror is bound by a contract, the duty of immediate performance of which is conditional on the full consideration being given or tendered within the time stated in the offer, or, if no time is stated therein, within a reasonable time.

In explanation, comment b states that the

> main offer includes as a subsidiary promise, necessarily implied, that if part of the requested performance is given, the offeror will not revoke his offer, and that if tender is made it will be accepted. Part performance or tender may thus furnish consideration for the subsidiary promise. Moreover, merely acting in justifiable reliance on an offer may in some cases serve as sufficient reason for making a promise binding (see §90).

Whether implied in fact or law, the subsidiary promise serves to preclude the injustice that would result if the offer could be revoked after the offeree had acted in detrimental reliance thereon. Reasonable reliance resulting in a foreseeable prejudicial change in position affords a compelling basis also for implying a subsidiary promise not to revoke an offer for a bilateral contract.

The absence of consideration is not fatal to the enforcement of such a promise. It is true that in the case of unilateral contracts the Restatement finds consideration for the implied subsidiary promise in the part performance of the bargained-for exchange, but its reference to section 90 makes clear that consideration for such a promise is not always necessary. The very purpose of section 90 is to make a promise binding even though there was no consideration "in the sense of something that is bargained for and given in exchange." (See 1 Corbin, Contracts 634 et seq.) Reasonable reliance serves to hold the offeror in lieu of the consideration ordinarily required to make the offer binding. In a case involving similar facts the Supreme Court of South Dakota stated that

> we believe that reason and justice demand that the doctrine [of section 90] be applied to the present facts. We cannot believe that by accepting this doctrine as controlling in the state of facts before us we will abolish the requirement of a consideration in contract cases, in any different sense than an ordinary estoppel abolishes some legal requirement in its application. We are of the opinion, therefore, that the defendants in executing the agreement [which was not supported by consideration] made a promise which they should have reasonably expected would induce the plaintiff to submit a bid based thereon to the Government, that such promise did induce this action, and that injustice can be avoided only by enforcement of the promise.

Northwestern Engineering Co. v. Ellerman, 69 S.D. 397, 408 [10 N.W.2d 879, 884]; . . . cf. James Baird Co. v. Gimbel Bros., [2d Cir.,] 64 F.2d 344.

When plaintiff used defendant's offer in computing his own bid, he bound himself to perform in reliance on defendant's terms. Though defendant did not bargain for this use of its bid neither did defendant make it idly, indifferent to whether it would be used or not. On the contrary it is reasonable to suppose that defendant submitted its bid to obtain the subcontract. It was bound to realize the substantial possibility that its bid would be the lowest, and that it would be included by plaintiff in his bid. It was to its own interest that the contractor be awarded the general contract; the lower the subcontract bid, the lower the general contractor's bid was likely to be and the greater its chance of acceptance and hence the greater defendant's chance of getting the paving subcontract. Defendant had reason not only to expect plaintiff to rely on its bid but to want him to. Clearly defendant had a stake in plaintiff's reliance on its bid. Given this interest and the fact that plaintiff is bound by his own bid, it is only fair that plaintiff should have at least an opportunity to accept defendant's bid after the general contract has been awarded to him.

It bears noting that a general contractor is not free to delay acceptance after he has been awarded the general contract in the hope of getting a better price. Nor can he reopen bargaining with the subcontractor and at the same time claim a continuing right to accept the original offer. . . . In the present case plaintiff promptly informed defendant that plaintiff was being awarded the job and that the subcontract was being awarded to defendant.

[Court's discussion of mistake defense appears in Chapter 16.]

There is no merit in defendant's contention that plaintiff failed to state a cause of action, on the ground that the complaint failed to allege that plaintiff attempted to mitigate the damages or that they could not have been mitigated. Plaintiff alleged that after defendant's default, "plaintiff had to procure the services of the L & H Co. to perform said asphaltic paving for the sum of $10,948.60." plaintiff's uncontradicted evidence showed that he spent several months trying to get bids from other subcontractors and that he took the lowest bid. Clearly he acted reasonably to mitigate damages. In any event any uncertainty in plaintiff's allegation as to damages could have been raised by special demurrer. . . . It was not so raised and was therefore waived. . . .

The judgment is affirmed.

RESTATEMENT (SECOND) OF CONTRACTS

§87. OPTION CONTRACT

[Paragraph (1) appears in Chapter 10.]

(2) An offer which the offeror should reasonably expect to induce action or forbearance of a substantial character on the part of the offeree before acceptance and which does induce such action or forbearance is binding as an option contract to the extent necessary to avoid injustice.

REFERENCE: Barnett, §4.4.3
Farnsworth, §§3.23-3.25
Calamari & Perillo, §§6.1-6.3
Murray, §67D

5. Charitable Subscriptions

The next famous case concerns a charitable subscription. You may recall from Chapter 10 the comment by Professor Williston in his presentation to the Commissioners of Uniform State Laws. Referring to states that profess to enforce only those promises supported by consideration:

> [T]he attitude of the courts has generally been an upsetting of the law of consideration, for when they get to gratuitous promises, really gratuitous promises, which they wish to enforce, they hunt around and find something which they treat as consideration *pro hac vice*, though it is really not an agreed exchange. The subscription paper cases are the most striking example of what I am saying. Those are really, as the name implies, charitable subscriptions, which means they are gifts, promises to give simply because you are charitable.[2]

Notwithstanding Judge Cardozo's eschewing reliance on promissory estoppel, law professors have long taught the next case as a precursor to the doctrine. We review this case for two reasons: first, as a review of bargained consideration by evaluating Judge Cardozo's consideration analysis. Second, to note that (at least according to the Restatement) charitable subscriptions are enforceable notwithstanding the absence of detrimental reliance by a charity.

STUDY GUIDE: *Imagine that this is an examination question and you are asked to apply the bargain theory to the facts of this case to determine the presence or absence of consideration. Do you reach the same conclusion as Judge Cardozo? Compare this case with Johnson v. Otterbein University which we read in Chapter 9. Does the fact that the Restatement (Second) recommends the enforcement of charitable subscriptions without any*

---

2. Handbook of the National Conference of Commissioners on Uniform State Laws & Proceedings of the Thirty-Fifth Annual Meeting 198 (1925).

reliance suggest that something different is going on here than in the previous promissory estoppel cases we have read?

ALLEGHENY COLLEGE v. NATIONAL
CHAUTAUQUA COUNTY BANK OF JAMESTOWN
Court of Appeals of New York,
246 N.Y. 369, 159 N.E. 173 (1927)

CARDOZO, C.J. The plaintiff, Allegheny College, is an institution of liberal learning at Meadville, Pennsylvania. In June 1921, a "drive" was in progress to secure for it an additional endowment of $1,250,000. An appeal to contribute to this fund was made to Mary Yates Johnston of Jamestown, New York. In response thereto, she signed and delivered on June 15, 1921, the following writing:

Estate Pledge,

Allegheny College Second Century Endowment

Jamestown, N.Y., June 15, 1921.

In consideration of my interest in Christian Education, and in consideration of others subscribing, I hereby subscribe and will pay to the order of the Treasurer of Allegheny College, Meadville, Pennsylvania, the sum of Five Thousand Dollars; $5,000.

This obligation shall become due thirty days after my death, and I hereby instruct my Executor, or Administrator, to pay the same out of my estate. This pledge shall bear interest at the rate of _____ per cent per annum, payable annually, from _____ till paid. The proceeds of this obligation shall be added to the Endowment of said Institution, or expended in accordance with instructions on reverse side of this pledge.

Name	Mary Yates Johnston,
Address	306 East 6th Street,
	Jamestown, N.Y.
Dayton E. McClain	Witness
T. R. Courtis	Witness to authentic signature.

On the reverse side of the writing is the following indorsement:

In loving memory this gift shall be known as the Mary Yates Johnston Memorial Fund, the proceeds from which shall be used to educate students preparing for the Ministry, either in the United States or in the Foreign Field.

This pledge shall be valid only on the condition that the provisions of my Will, now extant, shall be first met.

Mary Yates Johnston

The subscription was not payable by its terms until thirty days after the death of the promisor. The sum of $1,000 was paid, however, upon account in December, 1923, while the promisor was alive. The college set the money aside to be held as a scholarship fund for the benefit of students preparing for the ministry. Later, in July, 1924, the promisor gave notice to the college that she repudiated the promise. Upon the expiration of thirty days following her death, this action was brought against the executor of her will to recover the unpaid balance.

The law of charitable subscriptions has been a prolific source of controversy in this State and elsewhere. We have held that a promise of that order is unenforceable like any other if made without consideration. . . . On the other hand, though professing to apply to such subscriptions the general law of contract, we have found consideration present where the general law of contract, at least as then declared, would have said that it was absent. . . .

A classic form of statement identifies consideration with detriment to the promisee sustained by virtue of the promise (Hamer v. Sidway, 124 N.Y. 538; Anson, Contracts [Corbin's ed.], p. 116; 8 Holdsworth, History of English Law, 10). So compendious a formula is little more than a half truth. There is need of many a supplementary gloss before the outline can be so filled in as to depict the classic doctrine.

> The promise and the consideration must purport to be the motive each for the other, in whole or at least in part. It is not enough that the promise induces the detriment or that the detriment induces the promise if the other half is wanting.

(Wisc. & Mich. Ry. Co. v. Powers, 191 U.S. 379, 386. . . .) If A promises B to make him a gift, consideration may be lacking, though B has renounced other opportunities for betterment in the faith that the promise will be kept.

The half truths of one generation tend at times to perpetuate themselves in the law as the whole truths of another, when constant repetition brings it about that qualifications, taken once for granted, are disregarded or forgotten. The doctrine of consideration has not escaped the common lot. As far back as 1881, Judge Holmes in his lectures on the Common Law (p. 292), separated the detriment which is merely a consequence of the promise from the detriment which is in truth the motive or inducement, and yet added that the courts "have gone far in obliterating this distinction." The tendency toward effacement has not lessened with the years. On the contrary, there has grown up of recent days a doctrine that a substitute for consideration or an exception to its ordinary requirements can be found in what is styled "a promissory estoppel" (Williston, Contracts, §§139, 116). Whether the exception has made its way in this State to such an extent as to permit us to say that the general law of consideration has been modified accordingly, we do not now attempt to say. Cases such as Siegel v. Spear Co. (234 N.Y. 479) and DeCicco v. Schweizer (221 N.Y. 431) may be signposts on the road. Certain, at least, it is that we have adopted the doctrine of promissory estoppel as the equivalent of consideration in connection with our law of charitable subscriptions. So long as those decisions stand, the question is not merely whether the enforcement of a charitable subscription can be squared with the doctrine of consideration in all its ancient rigor. The question may also be whether it can be squared with the doctrine of consideration as qualified by the doctrine of promissory estoppel. . . .

It is in this background of precedent that we are to view the problem now before us. The background helps to an understanding of the implications inherent in subscription and acceptance. This is so though we may find in the end that without recourse to the innovation of promissory estoppel the transaction can be fitted within the mould of consideration as established by tradition.

The promisor wished to have a memorial to perpetuate her name. She imposed a condition that the "gift" should "be known as the Mary Yates Johnston Memorial Fund." The moment that the college accepted $1,000 as a payment on account, there was an assumption of a duty to do whatever acts were customary or reasonably necessary to maintain the memorial fairly and justly in the spirit of its creation. The college could not accept the money, and hold itself free thereafter from personal responsibility to give effect to the condition. . . . More is involved in the receipt of such a fund than a mere acceptance of money to be held to a corporate use. . . . The purpose of the founder would be unfairly thwarted or at least inadequately served if the college failed to communicate to the world, or in any event to applicants for the scholarship, the title of the memorial. By implication it undertook, when it accepted a portion of the "gift," that in its circulars of information and in other customary ways, when making announcement of this scholarship, it would couple with the announcement the name of the donor. The donor was not at liberty to gain the benefit of such an undertaking upon the payment of a part and disappoint the expectation that there would be payment of the residue. If the college had stated after receiving $1,000 upon account of the subscription that it would apply the money to the prescribed use, but that in its circulars of information and when responding to prospective applicants it would deal with the fund as an anonymous donation, there is little doubt that the subscriber would have been at liberty to treat this statement as the repudiation of a duty impliedly assumed, a repudiation justifying a refusal to make payments in the future. Obligation in such circumstances is correlative and mutual. . . .

The longing for posthumous remembrance is an emotion not so weak as to justify us in saying that its gratification is a negligible good.

We think the duty assumed by the plaintiff to perpetuate the name of the founder of the memorial is sufficient in itself to give validity to the subscription within the rules that define consideration for a promise of that order. When the promisee subjected itself to such a duty at the implied request of the promisor, the result was the creation of a bilateral agreement. . . . There was a promise on the one side and on the other a return promise, made, it is true, by implication, but expressing an obligation that had been exacted as a condition of the payment. A bilateral agreement may exist though one of the mutual promises be a promise "implied in fact," an inference from conduct as opposed to an inference from words. . . .

No doubt there are times and situations in which limitations laid upon a promisee in connection with the use of what is paid by a subscriber lack the quality of a consideration, and are to be classed merely as conditions. . . .

It is often difficult to determine whether words of condition in a promise indicate a request for consideration or state a mere condition in a gratuitous promise. An aid, though not a conclusive test in determining which construction of the promise is more reasonable is an inquiry whether the happening of the condition will be a benefit to the promisor. If so, it is a fair inference that the happening was requested as a consideration.

(Williston, supra, §112.)

Such must be the meaning of this transaction unless we are prepared to hold that the college may keep the payment on account, and thereafter nullify the scholarship which is to preserve the memory of the subscriber. The fair implication to be gathered from the whole transaction is assent to the condition and the assumption of a duty to go forward with performance. . . . The subscriber does not say: I hand you $1,000, and you may make up your mind later, after my death, whether you will undertake to commemorate my name. What she says in effect is this: I hand you $1,000, and if you are unwilling to commemorate me, the time to speak is now.

The conclusion thus reached makes it needless to consider whether, aside from the feature of a memorial, a promissory estoppel may result from the assumption of a duty to apply the fund, so far as already paid, to special purposes not mandatory under the provisions of the college charter (the support and education of students preparing for the ministry), an assumption induced by the belief that other payments sufficient in amount to make the scholarship effective would be added to the fund thereafter upon the death of the subscriber. . . .

The judgment of the Appellate Division and that of the Trial Term should be reversed, and judgment ordered for the plaintiff as prayed for in the complaint, with costs in all courts.

KELLOGG, J. (dissenting). The Chief Judge finds in the expression "In loving memory this gift shall be known as the Mary Yates Johnston Memorial Fund" an offer on the part of Mary Yates Johnston to contract with Allegheny College. The expression makes no such appeal to me. Allegheny College was not requested to perform any act through which the sum offered might bear the title by which the offeror states that it shall be known. The sum offered was termed a "gift" by the offeror. Consequently, I can see no reason why we should strain ourselves to make it, not a gift, but a trade. Moreover, since the donor specified that the gift was made "In consideration of my interest in Christian education, and in consideration of others subscribing," considerations not adequate in law, I can see no excuse for asserting that it was otherwise made in consideration of an act or promise on the part of the donee, constituting a sufficient *quid pro quo* to convert the gift into a contract obligation. To me the words used merely expressed an expectation or wish on the part of the donor and failed to exact the return of an adequate consideration. But if an offer indeed was present, then clearly it was an offer to enter into a unilateral contract. The offeror was to be bound provided the offeree performed such acts as might be necessary to make the gift offered become known under the proposed name. This is evidently the thought of the Chief Judge, for he says: "She imposed a condition that the 'gift' should be known as the Mary Yates

Johnston Memorial Fund." In other words, she proposed to exchange her offer of a donation in return for acts to be performed. Even so there was never any acceptance of the offer and, therefore, no contract, for the acts requested have never been performed. The gift has never been made known as demanded. Indeed, the requested acts, under the very terms of the assumed offer, could never have been performed at a time to convert the offer into a promise. This is so for the reason that the donation was not to take effect until after the death of the donor, and by her death her offer was withdrawn. . . . Clearly, although a promise of the college to make the gift known, as requested, may be implied, that promise was not the acceptance of an offer which gave rise to a contract. The donor stipulated for acts, not promises.

> In order to make a bargain it is necessary that the acceptor shall give in return for the offer or the promise exactly the consideration which the offeror requests. If an act is requested, that very act and no other must be given. If a promise is requested, that promise must be made absolutely and unqualifiedly.

(Williston on Contracts, §73.)

> It does not follow that an offer becomes a promise because it is accepted; it may be, and frequently is, conditional, and then it does not become a promise until the conditions are satisfied; and in case of offers for a consideration, the performance of the consideration is always deemed a condition.

(Langdell, Summary of the Law of Contracts, §4.)

It seems clear to me that there was here no offer, no acceptance of an offer, and no contract. . . .

POUND, CRANE, LEHMAN and O'BRIEN, JJ., concur with CARDOZO, C.J.; KELLOGG, J. dissents in opinion, in which ANDREWS, J., concurs.

Judgment accordingly.

B.   PROMISSORY ESTOPPEL AS AN ALTERNATIVE TO BREACH OF CONTRACT

In the cases we have read to this point, it might have seemed appropriate to view the doctrine of promissory estoppel as offering a *substitute for consideration* when considering whether to enforce a promise. This was how the doctrine was originally conceived by Professor Williston. During the American Law Institute debate over what came to be §90 of the first Restatement of Contracts, the following exchange occurred, stimulated by a hypothetical posed by Reporter Samuel Williston in which Johnny's uncle promises to pay $1,000 knowing that Johnny intends to use the money to buy a car and Johnny, relying upon the promise, purchases the car, incurring a debt of $1,000:

Frederic R. Coudert (New York):   May I ask the learned Reporter, as I am unfamiliar with the literature on that particular subject, whether it could not be properly and logically supported on the ground of a quasi-contractual relation, because it would be necessary for the judge to decide first, whether substantial justice required that it be enforced rather than merely whether it falls within the technical rules of contracts. Would not that partake somewhat of the language of a quasi-contractual obligation rather than of a true contractual obligation?

Mr. Williston: I should say not. I should say anything was truly contractual where a promisor makes a promise and that promise is enforced. A contract to my mind is a binding promise, and in the case we are referring to, under the stated circumstances, the promise itself is binding. In such a case as I suggested a few moments ago where the status quo can be restored,[3] the promise would not be binding; and what the plaintiff will obtain is not the enforcement of the promise but the recovery of what he has given, or payment for what he has done. Such an obligation is quasi-contractual; but if what the court is asked to do and what it does, is to enforce the actual promise that is made, whatever the reason the court has for doing it, you are enforcing a contract.

Mr. Coudert: But is it not true that it only enforces it because justice requires it and not because it is a rule of contract law? I do not quarrel at all with it; it may be the necessary statement; but I am a little confused by the predicate that substantial justice can be done only in that way. Is that the only way to get at the existence of a true contract?

Mr. Williston: I do not care in what way you may make your true contracts. The definition of contract in the first part of the section is a binding promise. If any law in any state says that a promise is binding under certain circumstances, then that promise is a contract.[4]

In this section we consider two cases in which this conception of promissory estoppel is hard to sustain. Our goal will be to discern how the use of this doctrine here differs from its use in the previous section and whether the extension of promissory estoppel to this type of situation is warranted. These cases raise a number of intriguing questions. Does the incompatibility of viewing promissory estoppel as an alternative to an action for breach of contract mean that the previous conception of promissory estoppel as a consideration substitute was misconceived? Or might it not mean, instead, that there are several distinct causes of action lurking under the rubric of *promissory estoppel* that are concealed by forcing them together under a common doctrinal heading?

3. [In the variation on the hypothetical to which Professor Williston refers, Johnny has not yet taken possession of the car and can change his mind without incurring full liability for the purchase price to the dealer, but perhaps having to forfeit a nonrefundable deposit. — Eds.]

4. [Discussion of the Tentative Draft of Contracts, Restatement No. 2, 4 American Law Institute Proceedings Appendix 61, 94-95 (1926). Professor Linzer has noted that this exchange

is often reproduced as evidence of Williston's narrow view of the section and of his extreme formalism. The full debate, however, shows Williston to have defended section 88 energetically, and with a sense of the importance of doing justice that belies the received wisdom of Williston the old fuddy-duddy. . . . [In the full debate] Williston comes through as a much more human figure, and as one who understood the importance of the new concept.

As noted earlier in this chapter, Professor Linzer has reprinted the entire debate in Peter Linzer, A Contracts Anthology 339-349 (2d ed. 1995). — Eds.]

STUDY GUIDE: Is there some important difference between the outcomes of the next two cases and those in Section A? Does this difference tell us anything helpful about the true nature of the promissory estoppel claims being made here? The next case is commonly cited as a promissory estoppel case. Is it? Does the court use the term "promissory estoppel"? Can you think of another theory that might apply? Hint: It, too, is called "estoppel."

GOODMAN v. DICKER
United States Court of Appeals for the District of Columbia,
169 F.2d 684 (1948)

PROCTOR, Associate Justice.*

This appeal is from a judgment of the District Court in a suit by appellees for breach of contract.

Appellants are local distributors for Emerson Radio and Phonograph Corporation in the District of Columbia. Appellees, with the knowledge and encouragement of appellants, applied for a "dealer franchise" to sell Emerson's products. The trial court found that appellants by their representations and conduct induced appellees to incur expenses in preparing to do business under the franchise, including employment of salesmen and solicitation of orders for radios. Among other things, appellants represented that the application had been accepted;[5] that the franchise would be granted, and that appellees would receive an initial delivery of thirty to forty radios. Yet, no radios were delivered, and notice was finally given that the franchise would not be granted.

The case was tried without a jury. The court held that a contract had not been proven but that appellants were estopped from denying the same by reason of their statements and conduct upon which appellees relied to their detriment. Judgment was entered for $1500, covering cash outlays of $1150 and loss of $350, anticipated profits on sale of thirty radios.

The main contention of appellants is that no liability would have arisen under the dealer franchise had it been granted because, as understood by appellees, it would have been terminable at will and would have imposed no duty upon the manufacturer to sell or appellees to buy any fixed number

James McPherson Proctor (1882-1953), educated at George Washington University (LL.B.), was admitted to the District of Columbia bar in 1903. He worked in the office of the U.S. Attorney for the District from 1905 to 1913, when he entered private practice in the area. In 1931, Proctor was appointed to the United States District Court for the District of Columbia, where he served until moving to the United States Court of Appeals for the D.C. Circuit in 1948. He remained on that court until his death. — C.R.

5. [The letter from the defendant informing the plaintiffs that the franchise had been denied included the following passage:

During the numerous times that we have spoken about your franchise, your application was being held up for approval at the factory. I led you to believe that it had been accepted although I was trying to convey to you the fact that the application had been sent in to the factory, and usually, they accept same without hesitation.

Joint Appendix at 17-18, *as it appears in* Randy E. Barnett & Mary C. Becker, Beyond Reliance: Promissory Estoppel, Contract Formalities, and Misrepresentation, 15 Hofstra L. Rev. 443, 489 n. 213 (1987). — EDS.]

of radios. From this it is argued that the franchise agreement would not have been enforceable (except as to acts performed thereunder) and cancellation by the manufacturer would have created no liability for expenses incurred by the dealer in preparing to do business. Further, it is argued that as the dealer franchise would have been unenforceable for failure of the manufacturer to supply radios appellants would not be liable to fulfill their assurance that radios would be supplied.

We think these contentions miss the real point of this case. We are not concerned directly with the terms of the franchise. We are dealing with a promise by appellants that a franchise would be granted and radios supplied, on the faith of which appellees with the knowledge and encouragement of appellants incurred expenses in making preparations to do business. Under these circumstances we think that appellants cannot now advance any defense inconsistent with their assurance that the franchise would be granted. Justice and fair dealing require that one who acts to his detriment on the faith of conduct of the kind revealed here should be protected by estopping the party who has brought about the situation from alleging anything in opposition to the natural consequences of his own course of conduct. . . . In Dickerson v. Colgrove, 100 U.S. 578, 580, 25 L. Ed. 618, the Supreme Court, in speaking of equitable estoppel, said:

> The law upon the subject is well settled. The vital principle is that he who by his language or conduct leads another to do what he would not otherwise have done, shall not subject such person to loss or injury by disappointing the expectations upon which he acted. Such a change of position is sternly forbidden. . . . This remedy is always so applied as to promote the ends of justice. . . .

In our opinion the trial court was correct in holding defendants liable for moneys which appellees expended in preparing to do business under the promised dealer franchise. These items aggregated $1150. We think, though, the court erred in adding the item of $350 for loss of profits on radios promised under an initial order. The true measure of damage is the loss sustained by expenditures made in reliance upon the assurance of a dealer franchise. As thus modified, the judgment is

Affirmed.

STUDY GUIDE: *Can you theoretically distinguish Goodman v. Dicker from the next case? In contrast with Professor Williston's and Judge Hand's (in Baird v. Gimbel) view of promissory estoppel as a consideration substitute, how does the court in the next case conceive of the doctrine? What are the practical implications of adopting one conception or the other? Why did the court think that an action for fraud or deceit would not apply here?*

HOFFMAN v. RED OWL STORES, INC.
Supreme Court of Wisconsin,
26 Wis. 2d 683, 133 N.W.2d 267 (1965)

Action by Joseph Hoffman (hereinafter "Hoffman") and wife, plaintiffs, against defendants Red Owl Stores, Inc. (hereinafter "Red Owl") and Edward Lukowitz.

Promissory model ← *representation wl plaintiffs who incurred detriment/ change to their position in reliance on defendant's promise*

[The complaint alleged that Lukowitz, as agent for Red Owl, represented to and agreed with plaintiffs that Red Owl would build a store building in Chilton and stock it with merchandise for Hoffman to operate in return for which plaintiffs were to put up and invest a total sum of $18,000; that in reliance upon the above-mentioned agreement and representations plaintiffs sold their bakery building and business and their grocery store and business; also in reliance on the agreement and representations Hoffman purchased the building site in Chilton and rented a residence for himself and his family in Chilton; plaintiffs' actions in reliance on the representations and agreement disrupted their personal and business life; plaintiffs lost substantial amounts of income and expended large sums of money as expenses. Plaintiffs demanded recovery of damages for the breach of defendants' representations and agreements.]

The action was tried to a court and jury. The facts hereinafter stated are taken from the evidence adduced at the trial. Where there was a conflict in the evidence the version favorable to plaintiffs has been accepted since the verdict rendered was in favor of plaintiffs.

Hoffman, assisted by his wife, operated a bakery at Wautoma from 1956 until sale of the building late in 1961. The building was owned in joint tenancy by him and his wife. Red Owl is a Minnesota corporation having its home office at Hopkins, Minnesota. It owns and operates a number of grocery supermarket stores and also extends franchises to agency stores which are owned by individuals, partnerships, and corporations. Lukowitz resides at Green Bay and since September, 1960, has been divisional manager for Red Owl in a territory comprising Upper Michigan and most of Wisconsin in charge of 84 stores. Prior to September, 1960, he was district manager having charge of approximately 20 stores.

In November, 1959, Hoffman was desirous of expanding his operations by establishing a grocery store and contacted a Red Owl representative by the name of Jansen, now deceased. Numerous conversations were had in 1960 with the idea of establishing a Red Owl franchise store in Wautoma. In September, 1960, Lukowitz succeeded Jansen as Red Owl's representative in the negotiations. [Hoffman mentioned that $18,000 was

Representation made to plaintiff ← all the capital he had available to invest and he was repeatedly assured that this would be sufficient to set him up in business as a Red Owl store.] About Christmastime, 1960, Hoffman thought it would be a good idea if he bought a small grocery store in Wautoma and operated it in order that he gain experience in the grocery business prior to operating a Red Owl store in some larger community.[On February 6, 1961, on the advice of Lukowitz and Sykes, who had succeeded Lukowitz as Red Owl's district manager, Hoffman bought the inventory and fixtures of a small grocery store in Wautoma and leased the building in which it was operated.]

After three months of operating this Wautoma store, the Red Owl representatives came in and took inventory and checked the operations and found the store was operating at a profit.[Lukowitz advised Hoffman to sell the store to his manager, and assured him that Red Owl would find a larger store for him elsewhere.] Acting on this advice and assurance, Hoffman sold the fixtures and inventory to his manager on June 6, 1961. Hoffman was reluctant to sell at that time because it meant losing the summer tourist business, but he sold on the assurance that he would be operating in a new location by fall and that he must sell this store if he wanted a bigger one. Before selling, Hoffman told the Red Owl representatives that he had $18,000 for "getting set up in business" and they assured him that there would be no problems in establishing him in a bigger operation. The makeup of the $18,000 was not discussed; it was understood plaintiff's father-in-law would furnish part of it. By June, 1961, the towns for the new grocery store had been narrowed down to two, Kewaunee and Chilton. In Kewaunee, Red Owl had an option on a building site. In Chilton, Red Owl had nothing under option, but it did select a site to which plaintiff obtained an option at Red Owl's suggestion. The option stipulated a purchase price of $6,000 with $1,000 to be paid on election to purchase and the balance to be paid within thirty days. On Lukowitz's assurance that everything was all set plaintiff paid $1,000 down on the lot on September 15th.

On September 27, 1961, plaintiff met at Chilton with Lukowitz and Mr. Reymund and Mr. Carlson from the home office who prepared a projected financial statement. Part of the funds plaintiffs were to supply as their investment in the venture were to be obtained by sale of their Wautoma bakery building.

On the basis of this meeting Lukowitz assured Hoffman: ". . . [E]verything is ready to go. Get your money together and we are set." Shortly after this meeting Lukowitz told plaintiffs that they would have to sell their bakery business and bakery building, and that their retaining this property was the only "hitch" in the entire plan. On November 6, 1961, plaintiffs sold their bakery building for $10,000. Hoffman was to retain the bakery equipment as he contemplated using it to operate a bakery in connection with his Red Owl store. After sale of the bakery Hoffman obtained employment on the night shift at an Appleton bakery.

The record contains different exhibits which were prepared in September and October, some of which were projections of the fiscal operation of the business and others were proposed building and floor plans. Red Owl was to procure some third party to buy the Chilton lot from Hoffman, construct the building, and then lease it to Hoffman. No final plans were ever made, nor were bids let or a construction contract entered. Some time prior to November 20, 1961, certain of the terms of the lease under which the building was to be rented by Hoffman were understood between him and Lukowitz. The lease was to be for ten years with a rental approximating $550 a month calculated on the basis of 1 percent per month on the building cost, plus 6 percent of the land cost divided on a monthly basis. At the end of the ten-year term he was to have an option to renew the lease for an additional ten-year period or to buy the property at cost on an installment basis. There was no discussion as to what the installments would be or with respect to repairs and maintenance.

On November 22d or 23d, Lukowitz and plaintiffs met in Minneapolis with Red Owl's credit manager to confer on Hoffman's financial standing and on financing the agency. Another projected financial statement was there drawn up entitled, "Proposed Financing For An Agency Store." This showed Hoffman contributing $24,100 of cash capital of which only $4,600 was to be cash possessed by plaintiffs. Eight thousand was to be procured as a loan from a Chilton bank secured by a mortgage on the bakery fixtures, $7,500 was to be obtained on a 5 percent loan from the father-in-law, and $4,000 was to be obtained by sale of the lot to the lessor at a profit.

A week or two after the Minneapolis meeting Lukowitz showed Hoffman a telegram from the home office to the effect that if plaintiff could get another $2,000 for promotional purposes the deal could go through for $26,000. Hoffman stated he would have to find out if he could get another $2,000. He met with his father-in-law, who agreed to put $13,000 into the business provided he could come into the business as a partner. Lukowitz told Hoffman the partnership arrangement "sounds fine" and that Hoffman should not go into the partnership arrangement with the "front office." On January 16, 1962, the Red Owl credit manager teletyped Lukowitz that the father-in-law would have to sign an agreement that the $13,000 was either a gift or a loan subordinate to all general creditors and that he would prepare the agreement. On January 31, 1962, Lukowitz teletyped the home office that the father-in-law would sign one or other of the agreements. However, Hoffman testified that it was not until the final meeting some time between January 26 and February 2, 1962, that he was told that his father-in-law was expected to sign an agreement that the $13,000 he was advancing was to be an outright gift. No mention was then made by the Red Owl representatives of the alternative of the father-in-law signing a subordination agreement. At this meeting the Red Owl agents presented Hoffman with [a] . . . projected financial statement. . . . Hoffman interpreted [this] . . . statement to require of plaintiffs a total of $34,000 cash made up of $13,000 gift from his father-in-law, $2,000 on mortgage, $8,000 on Chilton bank loan, $5,000 in cash from plaintiff, and $6,000 on the resale of the Chilton lot. Red Owl claims $18,000 is the total of the unborrowed or unencumbered cash, that is, $13,000 from the father-in-law and $5,000 cash from Hoffman himself. Hoffman informed Red Owl he could not go along with this proposal, and particularly objected to the requirement that his father-in-law sign an agreement that his $13,000 advancement was an absolute gift. This terminated the negotiations between the parties.

The case was submitted to the jury on a special verdict with the first two questions answered by the court. This verdict, as returned by the jury, was as follows:

Question No. 1:   Did the Red Owl Stores, Inc., and Joseph Hoffmann on or about mid-May of 1961 initiate negotiations looking to the establishment of Joseph Hoffmann as a franchise operator of a Red Owl Store in Chilton?

Answer: Yes. (Answered by the Court.)

Question No. 2:   Did the parties mutually agree on all of the details of the proposal so as to reach a final agreement thereon?

Answer: No. (Answered by the Court.)

Question No. 3:   Did the Red Owl Stores, Inc., in the course of said negotiations, make representations to Joseph Hoffmann that if he fulfilled certain conditions that they would establish him as a franchise operator of a Red Owl Store in Chilton?

Answer: Yes.

Question No. 4:   If you have answered Question No. 3 "Yes," then answer this question: Did Joseph Hoffmann rely on said representations and was he induced to act thereon?

Answer: Yes.

Question No. 5: If you have answered Question No. 4 "Yes," then answer this question: Ought Joseph Hoffmann, in the exercise of ordinary care, to have relied on said representations?

Answer: *Yes.*

Question No. 6: *If you have answered Question No. 3 "Yes" then answer this question: Did Joseph Hoffmann fulfill all the conditions he was required to fulfill by the terms of the negotiations between the parties up to January 26?*

Answer: *Yes.*

Question No. 7: *What sum of money will reasonably compensate the plaintiffs for such damages as they sustained by reason of:*

(a) The sale of the Wautoma store fixtures and inventory?
    Answer: $16,735.
(b) The sale of the bakery building?
    Answer: $2,000.
(c) Taking up the option on the Chilton lot?
    Answer: $1,000.
(d) Expenses of moving his family to Neenah?
    Answer: $140.
(e) House rental in Chilton?
    Answer: $125.

Plaintiffs moved for judgment on the verdict while defendants moved to change the answers to Questions 3, 4, 5, and 6 from "Yes" to "No," and in the alternative for relief from the answers to the subdivisions of Question 7 or a new trial. On March 31, 1964, the circuit court entered the following order:

it Is Ordered in accordance with said decision on motions after verdict hereby incorporated herein by reference:

1. That the answer of the jury to Question No. 7 (a) be and the same is hereby vacated and set aside and that a new trial be had on the sole issue of the damages for loss, if any, on the sale of the Wautoma store, fixtures and inventory.
2. That all other portions of the verdict of the jury be and hereby are approved and confirmed and all after-verdict motions of the parties inconsistent with this order are hereby denied.

Defendants have appealed from this order and plaintiffs have cross-appealed from paragraph 1, thereof.

Currie, C.J.* The instant appeal and cross appeal present these questions:

*George Robert Currie (1900-1983) studied at the Wisconsin State Teachers College and the University of Wisconsin (LL.B.). Admitted to the Wisconsin bar in 1925, he practiced law in Sheboygan for over 25 years before his appointment to the Supreme Court of Wisconsin in 1951. He served as Chief Justice of that body from 1964 to 1968, when he retired from the bench. Currie also served in World War I. — K.T.

(1) Whether this court should recognize causes of action grounded on promissory estoppel as exemplified by sec. 90 of Restatement, 1 Contracts?
(2) Do the facts in this case make out a cause of action for promissory estoppel?
(3) Are the jury's findings with respect to damages sustained by the evidence?

[handwritten margin note: Questions presented]

RECOGNITION OF A CAUSE OF ACTION GROUNDED ON PROMISSORY ESTOPPEL

Sec. 90 of Restatement, 1 Contracts, provides (at p. 110):

A promise which the promisor should reasonably expect to induce action or forbearance of a definite and substantial character on the part of the promisee and which does induce such action or forbearance is binding if injustice can be avoided only by enforcement of the promise.

The Wisconsin Annotations to Restatement, Contracts, prepared under the direction of the late Professor William H. Page and issued in 1933, stated (at p. 53, sec. 90):

The Wisconsin cases do not seem to be in accord with this section of the Restatement. It is certain that no such proposition has ever been announced by the Wisconsin court and it is at least doubtful if it would be approved by the court.

Since 1933, the closest approach this court has made to adopting the rule of the Restatement occurred in the recent case of Lazarus v. American Motors Corp. (1963), 21 Wis. (2d) 76, 85, 123 N.W. (2d) 548, wherein the court stated:

We recognize that upon different facts it would be possible for a seller of steel to have altered his position so as to effectuate the equitable considerations inherent in sec. 90 of the Restatement.

While it was not necessary to the disposition of the *Lazarus* case to adopt the promissory-estoppel rule of the Restatement, we are squarely faced in the instant case with that issue. [Not only did the trial court frame the special verdict on the theory of sec. 90 of Restatement, 1 Contracts, but no other possible theory has been presented to or discovered by this court which would permit plaintiffs to recover] Of other remedies considered that of an action for fraud and deceit seemed to be the most comparable. An action at law for fraud, however, cannot be predicated on unfulfilled promises unless the promisor possessed the present intent not to perform. . . . [Here, there is no evidence that would support a finding that Lukowitz made any of the promises, upon which plaintiffs' complaint is predicated, in bad faith with any present intent that they would not be fulfilled by Red Owl.]

[handwritten margin note: Court wants to find a theory of recovery that will allow Hoftmer to recover damages]

Many courts of other jurisdictions have seen fit over the years to adopt the principle of promissory estoppel, and the tendency in that direction continues.[6] As Mr. Justice McFaddin, speaking in behalf of the Arkansas court, well stated, that the development of the law of promissory estoppel "is an attempt by the courts to keep remedies abreast of increased moral consciousness of honesty and fair representations in all business dealings." Peoples National Bank of Little Rock v. Linebarger Construction Co. (1951), 219 Ark. 11, 17, 240 S.W. (2d) 126. . . .

The Restatement avoids use of the term "promissory estoppel," and there has been criticism of it as an inaccurate term. . . . On the other hand, Williston advocated the use of this term or something equivalent. 1 Williston, Contracts (1st ed.), p. 308, sec. 139. Use of the word "estoppel" to describe a doctrine upon which a party to a lawsuit may obtain affirmative relief offends the traditional concept that estoppel merely serves as a shield and cannot serve as a sword to create a cause of action. . . . "Attractive nuisance" is also a much-criticized term. . . . However, the latter term is still in almost universal use by the courts because of the lack of a better substitute. The same is also true of the wide use of the term "promissory estoppel." We have employed its use in this opinion not only because of its extensive use by other courts but also since a more-accurate equivalent has not been devised.

Because we deem the doctrine of promissory estoppel, as stated in sec. 90 of Restatement, 1 Contracts, is one which supplies a needed tool which courts may employ in a proper case to prevent injustice, we endorse and adopt it.

APPLICABILITY OF DOCTRINE TO FACTS OF THIS CASE

The record here discloses a number of promises and assurances given to Hoffman by Lukowitz in behalf of Red Owl upon which plaintiffs relied and acted upon to their detriment.

Foremost were the promises that for the sum of $18,000 Red Owl would establish Hoffman in a store. After Hoffman had sold his grocery store and paid the $1,000 on the Chilton lot, the $18,000 figure was changed to $24,100. Then in November, 1961, Hoffman was assured that if the $24,100 figure were increased by $2,000 the deal would go through. Hoffman was induced to sell his grocery store fixtures and inventory in June, 1961, on the promise that he would be in his new store by fall. In November, plaintiffs sold their bakery building on the urging of defendants and on the assurance that this was the last step necessary to have the deal with Red Owl go through.

We determine that there was ample evidence to sustain the answers of the jury to the questions of the verdict with respect to the promissory

---

6. Among the many cases which have granted relief grounded upon promissory estoppel are: Goodman v. Dicker (D.C. 1948), 169 Fed. (2d) 684; Drennan v. Star Paving Co. (1958), 51 Cal. (2d) 409, 333 Pac. (2d) 757; Van Hook v. Southern California Waiters Alliance (1958), 158 Cal. App. (2d) 556, 323 Pac. (2d) 212; Chrysler Corp. v. Quimby (1958), 51 Del. 264, 144 Atl. (2d) 123, 144 Atl. (2d) 885; Lusk-Harbison-Jones, Inc. v. Universal Credit Co. (1933), 164 Miss. 693, 145 So. 623; Feinberg v. Pfeiffer Co. (Mo. App. 1959), 322 S.W. (2d) 163; Schafer v. Fraser (1955), 206 Or. 446, 290 Pac. (2d) 190, 294 Pac. (2d) 609; Northwestern Engineering Co. v. Ellerman (1943), 69 S.D. 397, 10 N.W. (2d) 879.

representations made by Red Owl, Hoffman's reliance thereon in the exercise of ordinary care, and his fulfillment of the conditions required of him by the terms of the negotiations had with Red Owl.

There remains for consideration the question of law raised by defendants that agreement was never reached on essential factors necessary to establish a contract between Hoffman and Red Owl. Among these were the size, cost, design, and layout of the store building; and the terms of the lease with respect to rent, maintenance, renewal, and purchase options[This poses the question of whether the promise necessary to sustain a cause of action for promissory estoppel must embrace all essential details of a proposed transaction between promisor and promisee so as to be the equivalent of an offer that would result in a binding contract between the parties if the promisee were to accept the same.]

[margin note: An issue to be resolved]

Originally the doctrine of promissory estoppel was invoked as a substitute for consideration rendering a gratuitous promise enforceable as a contract. . . . In other words, the acts of reliance by the promisee to his detriment provided a substitute for consideration. If promissory estoppel were to be limited to only those situations where the promise giving rise to the cause of action must be so definite with respect to all details that a contract would result were the promise supported by consideration, then the defendants' instant promises to Hoffman would not meet this test. However, sec. 90 of Restatement, 1 Contracts, does not impose the requirement that the promise giving rise to the cause of action must be so comprehensive in scope as to meet the requirements of an offer that would ripen into a contract if accepted by the promisee. Rather the conditions imposed are:

(1) Was the promise one which the promisor should reasonably expect to induce action or forbearance of a definite and substantial character on the part of the promisee?

(2) Did the promise induce such action or forbearance?

(3) Can injustice be avoided only by enforcement of the promise?[7]

[We deem it would be a mistake to regard an action grounded on promissory estoppel as the equivalent of a breach-of-contract action.] As Dean Boyer points out, it is desirable that fluidity in the application of the concept be maintained. 98 University of Pennsylvania Law Review (1950), 459, at page 497. While the first two of the above-listed three requirements of promissory estoppel present issues of fact which ordinarily will be resolved by a jury, the third requirement, that the remedy can only be invoked where necessary to avoid injustice, is one that involves a policy decision by the court. Such a policy decision necessarily embraces an element of discretion.

[margin note: Red Owl told to incur these detriments to his position and not justified]

We conclude that injustice would result here if plaintiffs were not granted some relief because of the failure of defendants to keep their promises which induced plaintiffs to act to their detriment.

---

7. See Boyer, 98 University of Pennsylvania Law Review (1950), 459, 460. "Enforcement" of the promise embraces an award of damages for breach as well as decreeing specific performance.

DAMAGES

Defendants attack all the items of damages awarded by the jury.

The bakery building at Wautoma was sold at defendants' instigation in order that Hoffman might have the net proceeds available as part of the cash capital he was to invest in the Chilton store venture. The evidence clearly establishes that it was sold at a loss of $2,000. Defendants contend that half of this loss was sustained by Mrs. Hoffman because title stood in joint tenancy. They point out that no dealings took place between her and defendants as all negotiations were had with her husband. Ordinarily only the promisee and not third persons are entitled to enforce the remedy of promissory estoppel against the promisor. However, if the promisor actually foresees, or has reason to foresee, action by a third person in reliance on the promise, it may be quite unjust to refuse to perform the promise. 1A Corbin, Contracts, p. 220, sec. 200. Here not only did defendants foresee that it would be necessary for Mrs. Hoffman to sell her joint interest in the bakery building, but defendants actually requested that this be done. We approve the jury's award of $2,000 damages for the loss incurred by both plaintiffs in this sale. . . .

We also determine it was reasonable for Hoffman to have paid $125 for one month's rent of a home in Chilton after defendants assured him everything would be set when plaintiff sold the bakery building. This was a proper item of damage.

Plaintiffs never moved to Chilton because defendants suggested that Hoffman get some experience by working in a Red Owl store in the Fox River Valley. Plaintiffs, therefore, moved to Neenah instead of Chilton. After moving, Hoffman worked at night in an Appleton bakery but held himself available for work in a Red Owl store. The $140 moving expense would not have been incurred if plaintiffs had not sold their bakery building in Wautoma in reliance upon defendants' promises. We consider the $140 moving expense to be a proper item of damage.

We turn now to the damage item with respect to which the trial court granted a new trial, i.e., that arising from the sale of the Wautoma grocery-store fixtures and inventory for which the jury awarded $16,735. The trial court ruled that Hoffman could not recover for any loss of future profits for the summer months following the sale on June 6, 1961, but that damages would be limited to the difference between the sales price received and the fair market value of the assets sold, giving consideration to any goodwill attaching thereto by reason of the transfer of a going business. There was no direct evidence presented as to what this fair market value was on June 6, 1961. The evidence did disclose that Hoffman paid $9,000 for the inventory, added $1,500 to it and sold it for $10,000 or a loss of $500. His 1961 federal income-tax return showed that the grocery equipment had been purchased for $7,000 and sold for $7,955.96. Plaintiffs introduced evidence of the buyer that during the first eleven weeks of operation of the grocery store his gross sales were $44,000 and his profit was $6,000 or roughly 15 percent. On cross-examination he admitted that this was gross and not net profit. Plaintiffs contend that in a breach-of-contract action damages may include loss of profits. However, this is not a breach-of-contract action.

The only relevancy of evidence relating to profits would be with respect to proving the element of goodwill in establishing the fair market value of the grocery inventory and fixtures sold. Therefore, evidence of profits would be admissible to afford a foundation for expert opinion as to fair market value.

Where damages are awarded in promissory estoppel instead of specifically enforcing the promisor's promise, they should be only such as in the opinion of the court are necessary to prevent injustice. Mechanical or rule-of-thumb approaches to the damage problem should be avoided. In discussing remedies to be applied by courts in promissory estoppel we quote the following views of writers on the subject:

> Enforcement of a promise does not necessarily mean Specific Performance. It does not necessarily mean Damages for breach. Moreover the amount allowed as Damages may be determined by the plaintiff's expenditures or change of position in reliance as well as by the value to him of the promised performance. Restitution is also an "enforcing" remedy, although it is often said to be based upon some kind of a rescission. In determining what justice requires, the court must remember all of its powers, derived from equity, law merchant, and other sources, as well as the common law. Its decree should be molded accordingly. 1A Corbin, Contracts, p. 221, sec. 200.
>
> The wrong is not primarily in depriving the plaintiff of the promised reward but in causing the plaintiff to change position to his detriment. It would follow that the damages should not exceed the loss caused by the change of position, which would never be more in amount, but might be less, than the promised reward. Seavey, Reliance on Gratuitous Promises or Other Conduct, 64 Harvard Law Review (1951), 913, 926.
>
> There likewise seems to be no positive legal requirement, and certainly no legal policy, which dictates the allowance of contract damages in every case where the defendant's duty is consensual. Shattuck, Gratuitous Promises — A New Writ?, 35 Michigan Law Review (1936), 908, 912.[8]

At the time Hoffman bought the equipment and inventory of the small grocery store at Wautoma he did so in order to gain experience in the grocery-store business. At that time discussion had already been had with Red Owl representatives that Wautoma might be too small for a Red Owl operation and that a larger city might be more desirable. Thus Hoffman made this purchase more or less as a temporary experiment. Justice does not require that the damages awarded him, because of selling these assets at the behest of defendants, should exceed any actual loss sustained measured by the difference between the sales price and the fair market value.

Since the evidence does not sustain the large award of damages arising from the sale of the Wautoma grocery business, the trial court properly ordered a new trial on this issue.

By the Court. — Order affirmed. Because of the cross appeal, plaintiffs shall be limited to taxing but two thirds of their costs.

---

8. For expression of the opposite view, that courts in promissory-estoppel cases should treat them as ordinary breach of contract cases and allow the full amount of damages recoverable in the latter, see Note, 13 Vanderbilt Law Review (1960), 705.

Relational Background: What Was the Promise in Red Owl Stores?

STUDY GUIDE: One of the difficult questions raised by the Wisconsin Supreme Court's opinion in Red Owl *concerns the promise upon which the Hoffmanns relied that was then the basis of an action for promissory estoppel. The Court emphasizes Lukowitz's statement that $18,000 of equity would be enough to make the deal. But, given the negotiating context, can this statement reasonably be construed as a promise by Red Owl through its agent? The following article, based on extensive interviews with Joseph Hoffmann, highlights another moment in the negotiations in which something more like a promise was made. It also uncovers information that might explain the real reason that Red Owl kept moving the goal posts on the amount of equity the Hoffmanns needed to make the deal. It also reveals that the Supreme Court misspelled Mr. Hoffmann's name. How does the statement in June that $18,000 would be enough differ from the statement in October about "the only hitch"? With the additional information stressed here, does this case more closely resemble* Goodman v. Dicker, *or is it still distinguishable?*

WILLIAM C. WHITFORD & STEWART MACAULAY, HOFFMAN v. RED OWL STORES: THE REST OF THE STORY, 61 HASTINGS L.J. 801 (2009):   Hoffman v. Red Owl Stores, Inc., is the most famous of the cases that founded a new area of contract law by allowing recovery of reliance expenses incurred before a contract had been formed. *Hoffman* also has been the most influential case in framing the issue of the rights of a relying party. It was also an influential decision giving meaning to the then-relatively new doctrine of promissory estoppel. *Hoffman* has now become a staple of contracts casebooks, and it is routinely discussed in law review articles and textbook discussions about recovery for "precontractual reliance." Some courts in other states have adopted the *Hoffman* rule, while others have rejected it.

We have had the unexpected good fortune to locate and interview Joseph Hoffmann,[9] the plaintiff in this famous case. We have been delighted to discover that Mr. Hoffmann remains in good health. And despite the many years that have passed since the events involved in the case, he still has a sharp recollection of many of the events leading up to the trial and appeal. Mr. Hoffmann told us many things about the events that provoked the litigation as well as the litigation itself. He raised points not reflected in the decision or in the scholarly literature spawned by the case. We have verified much of what he has told us from the full trial record. . . .

SALE OF THE BAKERY

Sometime during the first week of October [1961], Lukowitz telephoned Hoffmann from his office in Green Bay. According to Hoffmann's

---

9. Mr. Hoffmann has always spelled his name with two n's, as is made clear in the trial record. For unknown reasons, the Wisconsin Supreme Court used only one n, and the case name has been spelled that way ever since.

trial testimony, Lukowitz told him "that Minneapolis had told [Lukowitz] that the only hitch in this thing at the present time was that I had to get rid of my bakery and my bakery building." As Lukowitz knew, this had not been Hoffmann's intention. Hoffmann expressed a willingness to sell the bakery, nonetheless, if he was assured that the deal was going through. He pointed out that the bakery provided his family's livelihood, and by this time Hoffmann had six children. Lukowitz provided verbal reassurance, insisting that sale of the bakery was the only "hitch." A few days earlier, Lukowitz had shown Hoffmann a proposed floor plan for the Chilton store, which reinforced the idea that Red Owl was proceeding with the deal.

Hoffmann and his wife decided to sell the bakery business immediately, including the bakery equipment not set aside for the Chilton store, to a twenty-one-year-old bakery employee, Mike Grimm. The sale was entirely on credit, with Grimm agreeing to make monthly payments from business income. The bakery building was sold for $10,000 in cash to a local investor, who then rented it to Grimm. Hoffmann had to guarantee payment of the rent in order to get the investor to buy the building. The building sold for $2000 less than Hoffmann had previously valued it, but Hoffmann accepted the deal anyway because of Red Owl's insistence on a quick sale and his expectation that he would soon be set up in the Chilton store.

NEW OWNER AT WAUTOMA BAKERY — Michael Grimm, left, became the new owner of Tastee Bakerie Monday when he bought the business and equipment from Joe Hoffman. Mike, 21, is the son of Mr. and Mrs. Elver Grimm. He has worked for Hoffman in the bakery all but six months out of five years Hoffman has owned the bakery. Grimm says he is planning no changes for the present, but he will operate under the name of "Mike's Tastee Bakerie", Hoffman announced that he "will devote more of his time to his other interests".

LUKOWITZ'S WARNING OF TROUBLE AHEAD

Joe Hoffmann told us that he still remembers clearly a surprise visit by Ed Lukowitz to Wautoma shortly before the closing of the sale of the bakery on November 6th. Hoffmann and Lukowitz sat in Lukowitz's car while Hoffmann read over a memorandum that Lukowitz had received from Red Owl headquarters. Hoffmann remembers the memorandum stating or implying that because of financial difficulties at Red Owl, it would be necessary to restrict the company's investment in new franchises. The memorandum said nothing specifically about the Chilton store, and Lukowitz told Hoffmann that he hoped that it did not mean trouble for Hoffmann. However, Lukowitz had taken the time to drive unexpectedly from Green Bay to Wautoma to show the telegram to Hoffmann. We can infer that Lukowitz feared that the policy change might derail Joe's proposed Chilton franchise.

Nothing was said at trial about this conversation. Hoffmann remembers that his lawyers, in pretrial discovery, tried to get a copy of the memorandum that Lukowitz showed Hoffmann, but Red Owl said that they could not find it. There is no mention in the transcript of this unsuccessful discovery request. Nonetheless, Hoffmann's current recollection of his conversation with Lukowitz is very clear, including a vision of where on Main Street in Wautoma that the car was parked. We have come away from our conversations with Hoffmann convinced that the meeting with Lukowitz actually happened. . . .

THE FINAL PROPOSAL

. . . There was conflict in the testimony about what reasons Hoffmann gave for rejecting the final plan when it was first presented to him at the Appleton meeting. According to Walker, Hoffmann objected to having to continue to borrow the $8000 from the Chilton bank. Walker testified that Hoffmann said: "My father-in-law won't let me be in debt." Hoffmann testified that he gave as his reason: "I will not go to my father-in-law and ask him for a $13,000 gift." And according to the uncontradicted testimony of Hoffmann, neither he nor anybody else ever discussed with his father-in-law the possibility of making the contribution a gift.

Hoffmann recalls today another reason why he called the deal off. He remembers that he did not believe that Red Owl would grant him a franchise even if he had agreed to the $34,000 plan. Ever since the meeting in Minneapolis, he had been skeptical that Red Owl wanted to grant him a franchise on any conditions. He had gone to the meeting in Minneapolis with the expectation that the deal would be concluded, only to be told that he would need more money. Then he had been told by Lukowitz, who showed Hoffmann a telegram from headquarters to that effect, that $26,000 would suffice and he went to the Appleton meeting with that expectation, only to be disappointed again. To this day Hoffmann suspects that if he had agreed to the $34,000 plan, there would have been a later demand for even more money. . . .

WHAT WAS MOTIVATING THE PARTIES?

In this Part we attempt to provide insight into what was motivating the parties over the course of their interactions.

A.   HOFFMANN

Hoffmann's motives are easy to understand. He was a young man who had had considerable success in building his Wautoma bakery business. There were, however, limits to how much a bakery could grow in such a small town. Hoffmann wanted more. Originally, he wanted to open a store in Wautoma where he was well known. However, Red Owl officials wanted a store in a bigger town, and he was willing to move. Hoffmann at all times exhibited a keen awareness of the limited resources available to him, and he was concerned about excessive debt. At the beginning of his dealings with Red Owl, he thought that he could invest $18,000. He could get this by investing his approximately $10,000 savings plus $7500 that he would borrow from his father-in-law. In addition, he expected to use bakery equipment not needed in Wautoma in the new enterprise.

Red Owl's demands for more money and more sacrifices kept increasing. When Red Owl suggested that Hoffmann sell the Wautoma grocery in 1961, Hoffmann sought reassurance that his $18,000 would be enough to get him set up. Upon receiving it, he went along with the suggestion because Red Owl wanted him free to work on the new franchise over the summer. The next big Red Owl demand was that the Hoffmanns sell the Wautoma bakery. The record is very clear that Hoffmann and his wife questioned Lukowitz carefully about whether a deal was in hand before they agreed to sell the bakery business and building, and they were told that their continued ownership of the bakery and building was "the only hitch." The decision to sell the business was a big one. The family was giving up what had been their livelihood, and they were committing to moving from Wautoma. And the reassurance from Lukowitz was credible. Hoffmann had already met with officials from headquarters at the proposed lot in Chilton. They had information about his financial condition, and they had drafted the first proposed financial plan. Lukowitz represented that he had communicated with those officials before reassuring Hoffmann. . . .

The Hoffmanns' decision to sue may have been partly motivated by vindication. Certainly, they felt wronged. Their unsuccessful effort to obtain a Red Owl franchise had fundamentally changed their life. They were able to hire a lawyer on a contingency basis, so they did not have to invest any funds on a lawsuit whose success must have seemed problematic. In the end, they got a small recovery, which helped them meet living expenses for a large family during the lean years, while Joe was establishing himself in his new profession in life insurance sales and Shirley was just getting started in real estate sales.

B. ED LUKOWITZ

We choose to offer an account of the motivations of Ed Lukowitz separate from the rest of the Red Owl management because Lukowitz's motives are easier to understand and were probably different from the motives of the other Red Owl officials. Lukowitz was a new divisional manager at the time he first began offering encouragement to Hoffmann in the fall of 1960. Previously, he had been a district manager for ten years. One major new responsibility of a divisional manager concerned the establishment of new stores, and it appears that Lukowitz took that responsibility very seriously. It is also clear that Lukowitz became a strong advocate for Hoffmann within the Red Owl hierarchy. Hoffmann today remembers Lukowitz as "a real decent guy [who] had my interest at heart." Lukowitz not only had gotten to know Hoffmann and observe how he managed the Wautoma bakery and grocery, but he had a sense of how well Hoffmann was regarded in the Wautoma community. And Lukowitz's judgment was probably correct. Hoffmann became a great success in the life insurance business. Hoffmann believes he would have been a successful operator of a Red Owl grocery in Chilton.

At the same time, the record suggests that at times Lukowitz may have gone further in reassuring Hoffmann than was justified by the communications Lukowitz had with his superiors at headquarters. This is particularly true of the time when Hoffmann exercised the option to buy the Chilton lot and when the Hoffmanns sold the bakery business. Perhaps Lukowitz was reluctant to warn Hoffmann of the risks he was taking, for fear that Hoffmann, ever cautious about financial matters, would simply withdraw. Perhaps Lukowitz, a relative newcomer as a divisional manager, was overly optimistic that everything would work out, and hence thought there would be no harm in getting the Hoffmanns to overcome their caution.

Lukowitz denied that he had reassured Hoffmann at the time of the exercise of the option on the Chilton lot. "I told him we weren't quite ready yet and had too many details to work out. . . . I had to find out from Hopkins. This had to come from above." Lukowitz was never directly asked at trial about conversations he had with Hoffmann at the time they were advised to sell the bakery building and business. Lukowitz's testimony about the strength of the reassurances that he gave Hoffmann appears to us as that of a Red Owl employee who wanted to keep his job. The entire story suggests that Joe Hoffmann was a cautious man, and strong reassurances were needed to persuade him to do what Ed Lukowitz thought that he should do.

C. RED OWL

On appeal, Red Owl maintained that their primary concern was the amount of "equity capital" that Hoffmann would invest. They argued that their demands in that respect had not measurably increased over the course of their interactions with Hoffmann, as the final financial plan required only $18,000 in unencumbered cash — $5000 from Hoffmann and $13,000 from his father-in-law. A franchisor can have a legitimate interest in requiring investment of equity. An overleveraged investor may feel free to walk away from the investment at little cost to itself, essentially stiffing any creditors. A franchisee/investor feeling this way may act in an insufficiently risk-averse (or overly speculative) manner. These incentives are not consonant with the interests of the franchisor, who is an important creditor of the franchisee and who has long-term interests in brand reputation to protect.

Red Owl may have had a corporate policy requiring a minimum investment of "equity," and corporate officers in Minneapolis may have had difficulty in justifying a franchise for Hoffmann under that policy. All the proposed financial plans identified certain parts of the proposed investment as "equity" and seemed concerned that the "equity capital" totaled approximately $18,000. This would suggest that there was some kind of corporate commitment or policy that needed to be satisfied. . . .

[But there] is another possible account of Red Owl's motives, one suggested by Hoffmann's recounting to us of the warning that he received from Lukowitz about Red Owl's emerging financial difficulties. Despite the passage of more than forty-five years, Hoffmann remembers this conversation with clarity. Much of Lukowitz's and Red Owl's behavior is consistent with an assumption that Red Owl's Franchise Department changed its policy in late October so that it was inclined to invest less in small-town franchises and take less risk. According to Hoffmann, the tone of his meeting with Red Owl officials in Chilton in late September was very supportive, whereas the tone at the meeting in Minneapolis in late November was very different and Red Owl officials began suggesting that Hoffmann would need to raise more money. Their concern was clearly that Hoffmann needed to obtain additional total funds, whether borrowed or unborrowed, without any focus at this time on equity capital as such. . . .

In the end, it is impossible to know for sure what motivated Red Owl. What may have happened is that there was some kind of policy change in the Franchise Department, and this may have prompted the increasing demands that Hoffmann invest more in the business. Headquarters officials may or may not have known what Lukowitz had told Hoffmann. Red Owl officials may have felt that they were within their rights when they increased their asking price for a franchise. Or they may have known about Lukowitz's assurances but assumed that they faced no real threat of a lawsuit by Hoffmann because of cost barriers to litigation.

In this context, it may be useful to speculate about Red Owl's litigation strategy. At some point early in the litigation, and certainly after they had deposed Hoffmann, it must have become clear to Red Owl that Hoffmann's case relied on statements made to him by Lukowitz. Yet at no time in the trial did Red Owl try to distance themselves from Lukowitz by suggesting that it was not reasonable for Hoffmann to rely on Lukowitz as their agent. Rather, Red Owl's trial strategy was to suggest that Lukowitz had not made any representations that were not fulfilled, going to some length to stress that nobody in Red Owl ever found fault with Lukowitz's interactions with Hoffmann. But the jury apparently did not believe Lukowitz's claims that he had only offered opinions and advice. Hoffmann wanted more than that before he would act, and Lukowitz created the impression that he had cleared everything with the home office.

We can also ask why Red Owl chose to litigate this case so vigorously. The damages claimed were not great, and the ultimate settlement was for a modest amount. Simply from the perspective of saving litigation costs, an earlier settlement offer would seem to have been in Red Owl's best interests. We have no doubt that Red Owl believed strongly that the law favored them, but does a corporation like Red Owl litigate just to vindicate a legal position? One possible explanation for Red Owl's aggressive litigation perspective comes from Hoffmann's current recollection that there were other prospective franchisees in the same area of Wisconsin who were caught up in the policy change that required greater franchisee investment and whose deals consequently did not go through. If this recollection is correct, perhaps Red Owl feared that if Hoffmann got a settlement, other lawsuits would surely be forthcoming. We do not know whether other lawsuits were ever filed.

WHAT WE HAVE LEARNED

. . . [O]ur story suggests that the key reliance by the Hoffmanns was the sale of the bakery building and business. This was their livelihood. The sale ultimately became a career — changing event. And it was precisely at this point that the Hoffmanns hesitated, insisted on extra assurances that the deal would go through, and received them from Lukowitz. After Hoffmann had met with officials from Red Owl headquarters in Chilton, had given them a fully accurate statement of his financial affairs, and received Red Owl's first financial plan, Lukowitz telephoned Hoffmann and told him "that Minneapolis had told him (Lukowitz) that the only hitch in this thing at the present time was that I had to get rid of my bakery and my bakery building." Hoffmann relied on this statement to his detriment. It is very unlikely he would have sold his bakery absent Lukowitz's reassurances.

The supreme court's opinion does not reveal that there was anything special about this moment. It considers the key Red Owl assurance to be Lukowitz's statement in June, at the time of the sale of the Wautoma grocery, that $18,000 would be enough to set up Hoffmann in a Red Owl store. Lukowitz made such a statement, and without it Hoffmann might not have sold the Wautoma grocery. But Hoffmann had much less reason to understand that this assurance effectively promised him a franchise, as compared with Lukowitz's later statement that the sale of the bakery was "the only hitch." In June, a site for Hoffmann's franchise had not yet been selected, Red Owl had made no inquiry into Hoffmann's finances, and Hoffmann had no idea what headquarters officials knew or had told Lukowitz at that time. Further, the Wautoma grocery was a business that Hoffmann had purchased in order to gain experience in managing a grocery store and to demonstrate to Red Owl his managerial abilities in that field. It was not his livelihood, and he did not expect to own it for more than a short period. Moreover, by the time of the sale of the bakery, whatever assurance had been made about $18,000 being the outside limit of Hoffmann's investment was clearly no longer operative. By this time, Red Owl had accepted Hoffmann's proposal to invest his bakery equipment in addition to the $18,000, something that later financial plans considered as part of his equity contribution. Further, it was clear to Hoffmann that Red Owl anticipated investment of the proceeds of the sale of the bakery building, which would push Hoffmann's cash investment to over $18,000. . . .

We believe that Hoffmann knew that Lukowitz was not the ultimate decisionmaker[, but] . . . we also think that Hoffmann very reasonably understood that Lukowitz was authorized by Red Owl to convey decisions made at headquarters. In fact, Red Owl never disputed Lukowitz's agency in this regard. If a jury believed Hoffmann's testimony that Lukowitz said that the people at the home office had told him that the "only hitch" to Joe being granted a franchise was the sale of the bakery, we think the jury could reasonably find the statement to be a promise. This understanding is entirely consistent with the encouraging attitude of the Red Owl officials at the Chilton meeting. It is possible that Lukowitz overstated what he had been told by the home office officials. There is some reason to believe that some officials at the home office had not yet considered the adequacy of Hoffmann's proposed investment in the new franchise. But Lukowitz failed to convey this information, if he knew it. Moreover, Lukowitz knew he was persuading Joe Hoffmann to do something that Hoffmann did not want to do. Had Lukowitz only made carefully limited statements about what might influence the home office decision, Red Owl would have been justified in deciding to deny Hoffmann a franchise for good, bad, or no reason. But Hoffmann testified, credibly, that Lukowitz did make highly encouraging statements about Red Owl's commitments, which prompted significant reliance. . . .

In our own casebook we . . . ask whether there was any promise made by Ed Lukowitz or only opinions and encouragement. After reading the complete transcript and talking to Joe Hoffmann, we now view the situation differently. We think that the jury could reasonably have viewed Lukowitz's statements preceding the sale of the bakery as a promise on which Hoffmann reasonably relied to his substantial detriment. There are two particular issues that we must address to defend our judgment.

The first issue is whether Lukowitz's statements to the Hoffmanns in October should have bound Red Owl. The Hoffmanns knew, probably from the very beginning of the relationship, that Lukowitz was not authorized to commit Red Owl to granting a franchise. Lukowitz's superiors at Red Owl headquarters had to approve. But the Hoffmanns were reasonable in viewing Lukowitz as an agent authorized to communicate messages from those headquarters officials. Red Owl never really challenged this position at trial, probably because there was no reasonable basis for doing so. Lukowitz was a divisional manager in charge of over eighty stores in Wisconsin and upper Michigan. He was responsible for developing proposals for new franchises. And except for direct meetings with Hoffmann, all communications from Red Owl headquarters officials had been conveyed to Hoffmann through Lukowitz.

The second and more difficult issue is what kind of a promise is needed before the promisor becomes liable for some or all of the precontractual reliance losses of the promisee. The Supreme Court of Wisconsin raised this issue in the *Hoffman* case. It held that there had been no promise sufficient to make a contract because too many important details were never agreed upon, but that the promissory estoppel principle did not require a promise "so comprehensive in scope." The court never specifically addressed, however, what precisely are the characteristics that distinguish a promise sufficient to invoke promissory estoppel from mere advice, prediction, or enthusiastic expression of an opinion.

The opinion does refer to Lukowitz's statements that $18,000 "would establish Hoffman in a store" as "promises," and most previous interpretations of the case have assumed that was the promise the court meant to enforce. We have indicated our doubts that Lukowitz's statements to Hoffmann in June, at the time of the sale of the Wautoma grocery, should be considered as anything other than advice or encouragement. We suspect that Hoffmann himself viewed those statements as such. To impose liability based on those statements does raise serious questions about whether the requirement of a promise imposes any limits on liability for precontractual reliance.

But the statements made to Hoffmann in October, when he agreed to sell the bakery and building, seem to us much different. By that time, Hoffmann had met with Red Owl headquarters officials who appeared to approve the proposed location in Chilton. Those officials had reviewed Hoffmann's personal financial statement and then drafted a proposed financial plan for the franchise. And Hoffmann was being asked to sell the bakery and building so that he could invest more in the franchise than he had originally planned. In those circumstances, Lukowitz's statement that the sale of the bakery was "the last hitch" could be understood by an ordinary person as a commitment. Hoffmann says today that he understood it as a commitment. . . .

It is common to interpret a precedent as though the facts of the case are those stated in the opinion. From that perspective, *Hoffman* stands for enforcement of the "promise" that Hoffmann would get a franchise for an investment of $18,000. . . . [However,] because the court does not explain why Lukowitz's statements about the $18,000 should be considered a promise rather than a mere opinion or enthusiastic encouragement, the opinion does not help explain the limits on precontractual reliance. . . . [W]ith our view of the full facts, in its ultimate outcome Hoffman v. Red Owl Stores provides a mainstream example of precontractual liability. . . . Hoffmann relied on Red Owl's assurances in order to benefit the franchise project. He sold the bakery business and the building in order to get his money together and position himself to work on establishing the Chilton store as soon as possible. He was reluctant to do this because he knew that Red Owl had not yet signed a formal franchise contract. Yet he trusted Lukowitz's statement about the position of the home office — sale of the bakery was "the only hitch." Hoffmann probably did not think about his legal rights at this point, but he thought that he had a firm commitment from Red Owl. When the deal fell apart, he told the Red Owl representatives that he was considering seeing a lawyer. Further, once the Hoffmanns sold their bakery business, their bargaining position was compromised because they had only less attractive alternatives if the deal collapsed. Red Owl responded by demanding ever-increasing investments from Hoffmann. . . .

Put another way, if we accept the facts as we have reported them, Hoffman v. Red Owl Stores, far from being an outlier, is a very mainstream precontractual reliance case. The Wisconsin courts, in perhaps an inelegant but historically significant way, got it right.

RESTATEMENT (SECOND) OF CONTRACTS

STUDY GUIDE: The courts in both Drennan *and* Red Owl *relied on the version of §90 that appeared in the first Restatement. Identify all the differences between the old and new versions of §90. What do you suppose motivated these changes? What are the likely effects?*

§90.   PROMISE REASONABLY INDUCING ACTION OR FORBEARANCE

(1) A promise which the promisor should reasonably expect to induce action or forbearance on the part of the promisee or a third person and which does induce such action or forbearance is binding if injustice can be avoided only by enforcement of the promise. The remedy granted for breach may be limited as justice requires.

(2) A charitable subscription or a marriage settlement is binding under Subsection (1) without proof that the promise induced action or forbearance.

REFERENCE: Barnett, §4.4.1
                    Farnsworth, §2.19
                    Calamari & Perillo, §§6.1-6.4
                    Murray, §67

STUDY GUIDE: How would Goodman *and* Red Owl *be decided under the following provisions? Do they require any revision to address either or both fact situations and, if so, would any such revision be wise?*

RESTATEMENT (SECOND) OF TORTS (1977)

§526.   CONDITIONS UNDER WHICH MISREPRESENTATION IS FRAUDULENT (SCIENTER)

A misrepresentation is fraudulent if the maker
    (a) knows or believes that the matter is not as he represents it to be,
    (b) does not have the confidence in the accuracy of his representation that he states or implies, or
    (c) knows that he does not have the basis for his representation that he states or implies.

§530.   MISREPRESENTATION OF INTENTION

(1) A representation of the maker's own intention to do or not to do a particular thing is fraudulent if he does not have that intention.

(2) A representation of the intention of a third person is fraudulent under the conditions stated in §526.

Doctrinal Background: The Tort of Promissory Misrepresentation

STUDY GUIDE: *In the excerpt that follows, it is suggested that the doctrine of promissory estoppel is sometimes used to compensate for harms caused by some tortious misrepresentations. Does it matter which doctrinal category (e.g., tort or contract) is used to reach the result in these cases? Is this account consistent with §90 of the Restatement? Does this account of promissory estoppel apply to all the cases we have studied in this chapter or just to some? If only to some, what explains the rest?*

RANDY E. BARNETT & MARY E. BECKER, BEYOND RELIANCE: PROMISSORY ESTOPPEL, CONTRACT FORMALITIES, AND MISREPRESENTATIONS, 15 HOFSTRA L. REV. 443, 445-446, 485-492, 495 (1987):   In this article, we suggest that promissory estoppel serves two of the functions served by traditional contract and tort remedies available to parties in consensual relationships: the enforcement of some promises intended as legally binding and the imposition of liability to compensate for harm caused by some misrepresentations. . . .

Tort law provides a remedy for some negligent or reckless misrepresentations of fact. In almost all jurisdictions, liability will lie in tort if the speaker made a misrepresentation of fact negligently or with reckless disregard for the truth in order to induce desired reliance provided that the plaintiff reasonably relied in the desired manner.

In almost all American jurisdictions, tort law also provides a remedy for some promissory misrepresentations made to induce reasonable reliance desired by the speaker.

For liability to lie in tort, however, a promissory misrepresentation must be a lie when made. If at the time the promise is made to induce desired reliance, the promisor has no intention of performing, liability will be established. Liability will not lie in tort, however, if the promisor made the promise to induce desired reliance and hoped that the promise would be fulfilled. Thus, tort affords no general remedy for breach of a promise made to induce desired reliance even when the promisor knows that the promisee will consider the promise more reliable than it actually is.

A few courts have used promissory estoppel to impose liability when traditional contract or tort doctrines would also afford a remedy for the misrepresentation. In Goodman v. Dicker,[10] estoppel[11] was used to impose liability though liability could probably have been imposed under the then-existing tort standard. . . . In *Goodman*, the local distributors of a franchisor were held liable for the plaintiffs' reliance loss on an assurance that the franchisor had decided to award plaintiffs a franchise.

The plaintiffs had written the franchisor in New York (Emerson Radio Phonograph Corporation) and asked about a franchise. The defendants (Emerson Radio of Washington) responded, explaining to the plaintiffs that the franchisor had written suggesting that the defendants contact the

---

10. 69 F.2d 684 (D.C. Cir. 1948) (applying D.C. law).
11. The court used "estoppel" rather than "promissory estoppel" to describe the basis of liability. Id. at 685.

plaintiffs. After some discussions, the defendants gave the plaintiffs a franchise application. The application required the defendants' (the local distributor's) approval. The plaintiffs submitted the application to the defendants. The defendants signed the application, noting their approval, and submitted it to the franchisor. The plaintiffs' reliance on the defendants' assurance (that the franchisor had decided to award the franchise) was therefore "reasonable" the defendants appeared to be in a position to know about the franchisor's decision. The defendants offered the assurance to induce the plaintiffs to hire salesmen and to begin selling Emerson radios prior to the receipt of a formal franchise certificate.

Contrary to the defendants' assurance, the franchisor had not decided to award the plaintiffs a franchise. When the decision was made, it was negative. The plaintiffs sued the defendants for losses sustained in reliance on their assurance.

Liability might have been imposed in contract if the defendants gave the plaintiffs the impression that they (the defendants) were speaking as authorized agents of the franchisor when they assured the plaintiffs that the franchisor had made an affirmative decision. If so, the defendants would be liable for breach of their implied warranty of agency. Neither the trial court nor the appellate court, however, explicitly made such findings of fact.

It seems more likely that the decision is based on tort notions;[12] the imposition of liability is consistent with the then-existing tort standard. This mistaken assurance can be regarded as a false statement of fact: that the franchisor had made an affirmative decision when it had not.[13] Tort would afford a remedy for this misstatement of fact since the defendants made the misrepresentation negligently or recklessly: the defendants had no basis for thinking that the franchisor had made any decision. In addition, the assurance was made to induce the plaintiffs to rely in a way desired by the defendants.

In a few cases, promissory estoppel has been used to afford a remedy for misrepresentation beyond those available under traditional contract and tort doctrines. In these cases, it seems likely that the defendant made a promise in order to induce the plaintiff to rely in a desirable way, knowing that the plaintiff would regard the promise as more reliable than it actually

---

12. Not only did both courts fail to make the findings of fact necessary for contract liability, it is likely that the appellate court intended to base its decision on tort doctrines. Although the case is widely cited as a promissory estoppel case, the court itself did not use the words "promissory estoppel." The court mentions "estoppel," but cites equitable estoppel cases. The factual misrepresentation strand of traditional equitable estoppel is closely related to the modern tort of reckless or negligent factual misrepresentation. . . . Thus, it is likely that the *Goodman* court based liability on tortious misrepresentation of fact, rather than on promissory estoppel. True, the court refers to defendants' "promise" and "assurances that a franchise would be granted," . . . but it also notes that the defendants "represented that the application had been accepted." Id. at 684.

13. In the letter informing the plaintiffs that a franchise would not be awarded, the defendants virtually admitted the misrepresentation:

During the numerous times that we have spoken about your franchise, your application was being held up for approval at the factory. I led you to believe that it had been accepted although I was trying to convey to you the fact that the application had been sent in to the factory, and usually, they accept same without hesitation. Joint Appendix at 17-18, *Goodman* (No. 9786).

was. The best known of these cases is Hoffman v. Red Owl Stores.[14] The Hoffmans owned and operated a bakery in Wautoma, Wisconsin, but were interested in a franchise for a Red Owl grocery store. The defendant's agents repeatedly assured Mr. Hoffman that Red Owl would give the plaintiffs a franchise in Chilton for a total cash outlay of $18,000. Although the terms of the franchise were never worked out, Red Owl agents encouraged Mr. Hoffman to rely on their assurances in many specific and potentially costly ways desired by Red Owl. Apparently, the agents had made the representation that $18,000 would be enough without consulting Red Owl's credit manager regarding Hoffman's financial standing and the financing of the store. When the credit manager was consulted, the cash needed by Hoffman increased dramatically, and the deal fell through.

Liability would lie in contract, even under an objective standard, only for Hoffman's reliance on what Hoffman reasonably thought was an enforceable contract. Much of Hoffman's reliance occurred, however, at a very early point in negotiations prior to the parties agreeing on such basic terms as the town the store would be in. When negotiations finally broke down, long after most of Hoffman's reliance, the parties had yet to agree on the specifications for the new store or many of the terms of the lease. It is unlikely, even at that late date, that Hoffman reasonably thought that he and Red Owl had a legally binding franchise agreement.

Similarly, liability cannot be explained by the then-existing tort standard for promissory misrepresentation. At the time the Red Owl agents assured Hoffman that $18,000 cash would be enough, the agents hoped that it would be enough. As the court noted, a tort action for misrepresentation "cannot be predicated on unfulfilled promises unless the promisor possessed the present intent not to perform." Although the court imposed liability on the basis of promissory estoppel, it did not explain why liability was appropriate in the absence of either a contract or a tort.

If, however, a court considers liability appropriate when a promisor makes a promise in order to induce desired and detrimental reliance with the knowledge (or under circumstances such that he should know) that the promisee will consider the promise more reliable than it actually is, liability is understandable. Red Owl's agents apparently assured Hoffman that $18,000 cash would be enough without talking to the Red Owl employee who would ultimately decide how much cash would be required. The agents were (or should have been) more familiar than Hoffman with the allocation of authority within the Red Owl organization. They knew (or should have known) that the assurance would appear to Hoffman to be more reliable than it actually was.

Hoffman is the first of a small but continuing line of cases in which courts have used promissory estoppel to afford a remedy for negligent promissory misrepresentation, i.e., to afford relief when a promise is made to induce a promisee to rely in a desired way in circumstances such that the promisor knows (or should know) that the promise will appear to be more reliable than it is. In each of these cases, the plaintiff relied detrimentally on the defendant's promises. Consistent with this explanation of liability — that it is based on misrepresentation of the reliability of the promise — courts

14. 26 Wis. 2d 683, 133 N.W.2d 267 (1965).

have generally denied relief for losses sustained during preliminary negotiations no matter how reasonable the reliance.

The courts using promissory estoppel to impose liability for negligent promissory misrepresentation could reach the same result under tort, by changing the standard for promissory misrepresentation from lie-when-made to negligent or reckless. For over a hundred years, however, common law courts have repeatedly held that tort liability for promissory misrepresentation requires that the promise be a lie when made. The tort standard has become fairly rigid, and promissory estoppel is a relatively new, and certainly more flexible basis for liability. . . .

The use of promissory estoppel to remedy misrepresentation may nevertheless be problematical in all jurisdictions. Courts taking this approach impose liability by ritualistically invoking the black letter of promissory estoppel without ever addressing the only issue in the case: Whether liability should lie for this form of misrepresentation. Had the court in Hoffman v. Red Owl, for example, addressed the question of whether liability should be imposed for negligent promissory misrepresentation, given the facts of the case, it might have come to a different conclusion and certainly a more understandable one.

REFERENCE: Barnett, §4.4.4

Theoretical Background: The Death of Contract?

Having considered the conception of promissory estoppel as an alternative to an action for breach of contract, we are now in a position to appreciate the provocative thesis offered by Professor Grant Gilmore. In his marvelously entertaining and refreshingly brief 1974 monograph, The Death of Contract, Gilmore predicted the future effect of promissory estoppel on contract law. He maintained that §90 of both Restatements portends that the "classical" theory of contract is collapsing into a more "tort-like" theory. We then contrast this famous prediction with the ensuing development of contract law as described by Professors E. Allan Farnsworth and Robert A. Hillman. In Section D, we shall contrast Gilmore's theory with a completely different reconstruction of contract enforceability to see which provides the best explanation of the cases we have studied throughout Part III.

STUDY GUIDE: Consider whether Gilmore's prediction has come to pass. Does his "tort" conception of contract accurately explain the cases in this chapter and the other cases you have read in Chapters 8, 9, and 10?

GRANT GILMORE, THE DEATH OF CONTRACT 60-61, 87-90 (1974):   I have referred to the Restatement's schizophrenia. It is time to give chapter and verse. The first lesson will be the Restatement's definition of consideration (§75) taken in connection with its most celebrated section — §90, captioned Promise Reasonably Inducing Definite and Substantial Action.

First §75:

> (1) Consideration for a promise is:
>   (a) an act other than a promise, or

(b) a forbearance, or

(c) the creation, modification or destruction of a legal relation, or

(d) a return promise, bargained for and given in exchange for the promise.

(2) Consideration may be given to the promisor or to some other person.

It may be given by the promisee or by some other person.

This is, of course, pure Holmes. The venerable Justice took no part in the Restatement project. It is unlikely that he ever looked at the Restatement of Contracts. If, however, §75 was ever drawn to his attention, it is not hard to imagine him chuckling at the thought of how his revolutionary teaching of the 1880s had become the orthodoxy of a half-century later.

Now, §90:

A promise which the promisor should reasonably expect to induce action or forbearance of a definite and substantial character on the part of the promisee and which does induce such action or forbearance is binding if injustice can be avoided only by enforcement of the promise.

And what is that all about? We have become accustomed to the idea, without in the least understanding it, that the universe includes both matter and anti-matter. Perhaps what we have here is Restatement and anti-Restatement or Contract and anti-Contract. We can be sure that Holmes, who relished a good paradox, would have laughed aloud at the sequence of §75 and §90. The one thing that is clear is that these two contradictory propositions cannot live comfortably together: in the end one must swallow the other up. . . .

Speaking descriptively, we might say that what is happening is that "contract" is being reabsorbed into the mainstream of "tort." Until the general theory of contract was hurriedly run up late in the nineteenth century, tort had always been our residual category of civil liability.[15] As the contract rules dissolve, it is becoming so again. It should be pointed out that the theory of tort into which contract is being reabsorbed is itself a much more expansive theory of liability than was the theory of tort from which contract was artificially separated a hundred years ago.

We have had more than one occasion to notice the insistence of the classical theorists on the sharp differentiation between contract and tort — the refusal to admit any liability in "contract" until the formal requisites of offer, acceptance and consideration had been satisfied, the dogma that only "bargained-for" detriment or benefit could count as consideration, and notably, the limitations on damage recovery. Classical contract theory might well be described as an attempt to stake out an enclave within the general domain of tort. The dykes which were set up to protect the enclave have, it is clear enough, been crumbling at a progressively rapid rate. With

15. It is an historical truism that assumpsit, from which our theories of contract eventually emerged, was itself a split-off from the tort action of trespass on the case. Until the late nineteenth century the dividing line between "contract" and "tort" had never been sharply drawn. . . . No doubt the obscure realization that contract (or assumpsit) had its origins in tort accounted, at least in part, for the failure to make a clear distinction between contract and tort until the nineteenth century theorists insisted on drawing the line.

the growth of the ideas of quasi-contract and unjust enrichment, classical consideration theory was breached on the benefit side. With the growth of the promissory estoppel idea, it was breached on the detriment side. We are fast approaching the point where, to prevent unjust enrichment, any benefit received by a defendant must be paid for unless it was clearly meant as a gift; where any detriment reasonably incurred by a plaintiff in reliance on a defendant's assurances must be recompensed. When that point is reached, there is really no longer any viable distinction between liability in contract and liability in tort. We may take the fact that damages in contract have become indistinguishable from damages in tort as obscurely reflecting an instinctive, almost unconscious realization that the two fields, which had been artificially set apart, are gradually merging and becoming one.

A number of the developments which we noted in the preceding Lecture in tracing the twentieth century decline and fall from nineteenth century theory illustrate this basic coming together of contract and tort, as well as the "instinctive, almost unconscious" level on which the process has been working itself out.

The idea which we have come to know as "quasi-contract" was not part of the nineteenth century theory. We think of quasi-contract as a sort of no-man's-land lying between contract and tort. In the early part of the century the concept served to blur the sharp edges both of contract theory and tort theory. It was, as the courts readily admitted, a legal fiction: the "quasi-contract" was no contract at all but the admitted legal fiction served, or so it was thought, the ends of justice.

The "promissory estoppel" cases, like the quasi-contract cases, began to appear in the reports shortly after the turn of the century. The two concepts were, indeed, twins. As a matter of usage it came to be felt that quasi-contract was a better way of talking about the situation where plaintiff was seeking reimbursement for some benefit he had conferred on the defendant, while promissory estoppel was better for the situation where plaintiff was seeking recovery for loss or damage suffered as the result of reliance on the defendant's promises or representations. It would seem, as a matter of jurisprudential economy, that both situations could have been dealt with under either slogan but the legal mind has always preferred multiplication to division. And it may be that we still feel that the "benefit conferred" idea is a little closer to contract than it is to tort, so that contract (or quasi-contract) language is appropriate, while the "detrimental reliance" idea is a littler closer to tort than it is to contract, so that tort (or quasi-tort) language is appropriate.

In this connection the introductory Comment to revised §90 in Restatement (Second) is instructive:

> Obligations and remedies based on reliance are not peculiar to the law of contracts. This Section is often referred to in terms of "promissory estoppel," a phrase suggesting an extension of the doctrine of estoppel. Estoppel prevents a person from showing the truth contrary to a representation of fact made by him after another has relied on the representation. . . . Reliance is also a significant feature of numerous rules in the law of negligence, deceit and restitution. . . . In some cases those rules and this Section overlap; in others they provide analogies useful in determining the extent to which enforcement is necessary to prevent injustice.

[We seem to be in the presence of the phenomenon which, in the history of comparative religion, is called syncretism — that is, according to Webster, "the reconciliation or union of conflicting beliefs." I have occasionally suggested to my students that a desirable reform in legal education would be to merge the first-year courses in Contracts and Torts into a single course which we could call Contorts. Perhaps the same suggestion would be a good one when the time comes for the third round of Restatements.

STUDY GUIDE: Assuming the conclusions reached by Professor Farnsworth in the following excerpt are correct, can you think of any reasons why movement in the direction of protecting non-bargained-for reliance might have been arrested in the 1980s? Can this "stopping point" be theoretically justified?

E. ALLAN FARNSWORTH, DEVELOPMENTS IN CONTRACT LAW DURING THE 1980S: THE TOP TEN, 41 CASE W. RES. L. REV. 203, 218-222 (1990):   The third example of theoretical turnabout [in the 1980s] occurred in the tug of war between formalities and reliance. In contract law, a perennial tension between these two legal concepts gives rise to interesting issues concerning the enforceability of promises. Should the mere utterance of a promise, supported by what Holmes suggested was the formality of consideration,[16] be sufficient to bind the promisor, or should some reliance by the promisee be required? If the law requires some formality, such as a writing, to render a promise enforceable, should that formality be dispensed with if the promisee detrimentally relies upon the promise?

The 1970s saw a significant judicial erosion of the requirement of a writing imposed by Uniform Commercial Code §2-201, the statute of frauds for the sale of goods. Courts were confronted with a rash of grain cases that grew out of sharp price increases in 1973 and 1974. Farmers who made oral contracts to sell to grain elevators reneged on their contracts using the statute of frauds as a defense. The grain elevators claimed that they had relied on the farmers' promises by making resale contracts and that the farmers were therefore precluded from relying on the statute of frauds to avoid enforcement of the contracts. Although some courts adhered to the traditional position that such reliance did not make the farmers' oral promises enforceable, other courts accepted the argument of the grain elevators and enforced the farmers' oral promises.

The expansion of the role of reliance, and the simultaneous erosion of the role of formalities, did not continue in the 1980s. Indeed, . . . the trend appears to be in the other direction. . . .

The 1980s were also remarkable for the developments which did not take place. For example, Grant Gilmore made one of the more celebrated predictions of the 1970s in The Death of Contract:

> [W]e might say that what is happening is that "contract" is being reabsorbed into the mainstream of "tort." Until the general theory of contract was hurriedly run up late in the nineteenth century, tort had always been our

---

16. See Krell v. Codman, 154 Mass. 454, 456, 28 N.E. 578, 578 (1891) ("consideration is as much a form as a seal.").

residual category of civil liability. As the contract rules dissolve, it is becoming so again.[17]

Gilmore maintained that the facade of classical contract theory crumbled with the emergence of ideas such as unjust enrichment and promissory estoppel to supplement, and eventually supplant, bargain theory.[18] He further stated that these developments, as well as the similarity between tort and contract damages, leave no "viable distinction between liability in contract and liability in tort."[19]

The 1980s, however, did not witness the death of contract. Academic attempts to merge contracts into torts in courses called "contorts" failed to flourish and it may be argued that contracts, through liberal application of third party beneficiary doctrine, invaded the domain of tort during the 1980s. . . .

Indeed, as early as the 1981 Association of American Law Schools conference, Justice Abramson of the Wisconsin Supreme Court reported that contracts was "viable as a litigation category" and that Gilmore's report of the death of contract was highly exaggerated.[20] At the same conference, Gilmore himself attempted to provide "an explanation of why this field of law, which somebody or other said was dead, some time ago, is not only alive and well but bursting at the seams."[21]

Empirical Background: Promissory Estoppel in the Nineties

STUDY GUIDE: *Professor Hillman's study is based on a survey of all the reported decisions in the United States in which a promissory estoppel claim succeeded or failed or in which promissory estoppel was discussed from July 1, 1994, through June 30, 1996. Another portion of his findings appears later in this chapter.*

ROBERT A. HILLMAN, QUESTIONING THE "NEW CONSENSUS" ON PROMISSORY ESTOPPEL: AN EMPIRICAL AND THEORETICAL STUDY, 98 COLUM. L. REV. 580, 588 (1998):   The purpose of this Article is to present evidence of a fundamental misunderstanding of how courts apply the theory of obligation called promissory estoppel. Contrary to the accepted wisdom, the data and analysis presented here . . . demonstrate that the theory seldom leads to victory in reported decisions. . . . The . . . lack of success of the theory in the courts, contradicts theorists who predicted that promissory estoppel would "swallow up" the bargain theory of contract and become the dominant promissory theory of obligation. Although some writers have questioned the prediction, this Article is the first comprehensive empirical study that demonstrates promissory estoppel's limited role. . . .

17. G. Gilmore, The Death of Contract 87 (1974).
18. Id.
19. Id. at 88.
20. Kelso, The 1981 Conference on Teaching Contracts: A Summary and Appraisal, 32 J. Legal Educ. 616, 616 (1982).
21. Id. at 640.

1. *General win rates.* — [The data] show the generally low rate of success of promissory estoppel claimants. . . . [This data include] the outcomes of all 362 cases, which include not only cases decided on the merits, but also cases in which the promissory estoppel claimant either successfully survived an opposing motion or failed on its own motion for summary judgment . . . [and] the outcomes of the 299 cases decided on the merits of the promissory estoppel claim.

[P]romissory estoppel claims succeeded on the merits in 8.01% of the reported cases and succeeded by surviving an opposing motion in 15.74% of the reported cases, for a total win rate of 23.75%. . . . [O]nly 9.70% of promissory estoppel claims that reached a decision on the merits of the claim were successful. . . . [The data comparing] win rates on the merits of promissory estoppel cases in federal district courts and state trial courts with win rates of contract claims in federal district courts . . . show[] that the contract claims were 10 times more successful. . . .

2. *Lack of success in all subject areas and contexts, and the special problem of employment contracts.* . . . [Professor Hillman's data illustrate the lack of success across all subject areas, the high frequency of employment cases in the sample (47%), and the extremely low success rate in employment cases (4.23%) vs. the win rate of all other subject areas combined (14.65%). — Eds.]

3. *Reversal rates on review.* — The final [data] on win rates display the striking results of what happens to promissory estoppel claims upon appellate review. [P]arties bringing a promissory estoppel claim who won in lower courts had their victories overturned in appellate courts on the merits 43.24% of the time, whereas parties defending against a promissory estoppel claim who won below were reversed in appellate courts on the merits less than 2% of the time.

4. *Conclusions.* — As a whole, the win-rate data strongly suggest that promissory estoppel has not subsumed or even overshadowed other theories of promise enforcement in the courts. The win-rate data establish that promissory estoppel was very unsuccessful in reported decisions during 1994-1996 across a variety of subject matters and contexts. Further, even if they manage to succeed below, promissory estoppel claimants run a real risk of reversal on appeal. And promissory estoppel claimants in the employment setting are even more likely to lose than claimants in other areas.

REFERENCE: Barnett, §4.4.2

C. ESTABLISHING THE "ELEMENTS" OF PROMISSORY ESTOPPEL

Having identified two distinct conceptions of promissory estoppel, we now turn our attention to modern cases that have attempted to apply the doctrine. These cases illustrate that *both* conceptions of the doctrine are alive and well. They also reveal the difficulties of applying the black-letter of §90, the limitations that have been placed on its use, as well as the creative potential of §90 to avoid doctrinal barriers to enforcement. For ease of study, these cases are loosely divided according to the elements of promissory estoppel suggested by the wording of Restatement (Second) §90. That the elements of promise and reliance are critical to establishing a claim of promissory estoppel is borne out by two important and comprehensive empirical studies of reported cases, which appear at the end of this section.

1.   Promise

STUDY GUIDE: How does the theory of promissory estoppel articulated by the court in the next case differ from the court's theory in the Red Owl *case? Could the* Blatt *case be decided the same way under the wording of §90 of the Restatement (Second)?*

BLATT v. UNIVERSITY OF SOUTHERN CALIFORNIA
Court of Appeal of California, Second District,
5 Cal. App. 3d 935, 85 Cal. Rptr. 601 (1970)

SCHWEITZER, J.* — Appeal from a judgment dismissing an action following an order sustaining a general demurrer without leave to amend to the second amended complaint. The complaint is for injunctive and declaratory relief and seeks to compel the admission of plaintiff to membership in the Order of the Coif, a national honorary legal society.

THE PLEADINGS

Plaintiff was a June 1967 graduate of the School of Law, University of Southern California, and is a member of the California bar. Defendants are the University of Southern California, the national society known as the Order of the Coif, the local chapter of the society, and members of the committee of the local chapter having the authority and responsibility to elect members from graduating students.

The complaint alleges that the Order of the Coif (hereinafter referred to as the Order) gives recognition to high scholastic grade levels attained by law students; that members are elected from law students in the top 10 percent in scholarship in those accredited law schools having a chapter; that defendant University of Southern California has a chapter; that

Harold Wilton Schweitzer (1911-1983) was educated at Pomona College (B.A.) and the University of Southern California (LL.B.); he was admitted to the California bar in 1935 and began practice at Los Angeles in 1935. He served as judge on the Municipal Court of Los Angeles (1947-1952) and the Superior Court of Los Angeles (1952-1960) before being elected to the Court of Appeals. — K.T.

[e]lection to the Order of the Coif elevates the esteem, standing and position of the law student elected in the eyes of the school faculty, fellow students, judges, the legal profession and the public at large; and greatly enhances his employment possibilities and economic position after graduation and admittance to the Bar;

that plaintiff was a night law student at University of Southern California from September 1961 until graduation in June 1967; that the individual defendants were members of the selection committee of the local chapter of the Order and were authorized to establish the policy and rules for election of members within the limits of its constitution . . . ; that after plaintiff became a student the individual defendants represented to him that if he were in the top 10 percent of his graduating class, he "would be eligible for election to membership in the Order"; that plaintiff relied on these representations in order to attain membership in the Order, ranked fourth scholastically in his graduating class of 135 students, and was thereby in the top 10 percent of his class in scholarship.

The complaint further alleges that in addition to his scholastic achievement plaintiff received awards for excelling in six classes and the highest grade in another class; that he was of good moral character, "worthy of the honor," and that his non-election "was not due to his lack of worthiness, lack of character or unfitness"; that after his non-election the dean of the law school, who was also president of the local chapter of the Order, stated to plaintiff in a letter that plaintiff was "obviously the sort of student who should qualify for election" and added: "Both as your dean and as one of your instructors I wish to go on record as testifying to my pleasure and satisfaction in your performance throughout your law school career."

Plaintiff alleges that in June 1967 the committee elected seven or eight members to the Order who ranked below him in scholastic achievement; that plaintiff was not elected because "membership was restricted to students who, being eligible for the school's Law Review, accepted the invitation to work on the Law Review and completed their assignments successfully"; that said reason "was unreasonable, arbitrary and contrary to the representations" mentioned above, and was not applicable to plaintiff because it was a policy adopted after said representations were made to plaintiff; that prior to the adoption of the policy plaintiff served on the Law Review and submitted articles for publication therein; that after the adoption of the policy, plaintiff was not advised that it applied to him but was advised that the policy was applicable only to day students who thereafter became eligible for Law Review work; that plaintiff relied upon this advice and information and did not thereafter apply for or accept a Law Review assignment, although he did thereafter submit articles for publication in the Law Review, none of which, however, were published; and that other students who did not complete Law Review work and were in a similar position to plaintiff were elected to the Order.

The complaint concludes by alleging that plaintiff is qualified and entitled to membership in the Order, that defendants breached their promises and representations, and that he was denied membership therein by arbitrary and discriminatory action based upon erroneous and invalid reasons. The complaint seeks a declaration of the rights and duties of the parties, a determination that plaintiff is entitled to election to membership in the Order, and an order directing defendants to admit plaintiff to membership.

CONTENTIONS

On appeal plaintiff contends that the complaint sets forth a justiciable issue and that it sufficiently alleges a breach of contract and promissory estoppel. We hold that each contention is without merit and that defendants' demurrer to the second amended complaint was properly sustained without leave to amend. . . .

BREACH OF CONTRACT AND PROMISSORY ESTOPPEL

Plaintiff contends that his complaint states a cause of action for breach of contract; that the necessary elements of a contract are present; that there was an offer, representations by defendant individuals that if he ranked in the top 10 percent of his class, he *would be eligible* for election to membership in the Order; and that there was his acceptance, he "worked very hard" to and did achieve grades which placed him in the top 10 percent of his class. Plaintiff recognizes that the offer spoke in terms of eligibility for election and not that he would be elected, but states that there were only two requisites for election as to persons in the top 10 percent: first, "activities that contribute directly to legal education such as legal research and writing," and second, whether he was of fit character. He argues that since the complaint alleged, and the demurrer admitted that he was rejected for neither of these grounds, the court, in determining the sufficiency of the complaint, must accept as true his allegations that he complied with all the subjective and objective requirements for admittance.

Plaintiff seeks to establish a unilateral contract, one in which a promise is given in exchange for an act, forbearance or a thing. . . . There was no benefit flowing to defendants as a result of plaintiff's hard work or his class ranking. Any benefit that accrued inured to plaintiff. Consequently there was no consideration for any alleged promise or representations of defendants. Therefore, if any contract existed, it was because of the doctrine of promissory estoppel, a substitute for consideration. . . . Promissory estoppel is defined in section 90 of the Restatement of Contracts as:

> A promise which the promisor should reasonably expect to induce action or forbearance of a *definite and substantial character* on the part of the promisee and which does induce such action or forbearance is binding if injustice can be avoided only by enforcement of the promise.

(Emphasis added.)

Plaintiff argues that the alleged promise in this case is similar to cases where a promisor was estopped from denying the promised payment of a bonus, pension or reward, citing Van Hook v. Southern Cal. Waiters Alliance. . . . The classic case of Hamer v. Sidway, 124 N.Y. 538 [27 N.E. 256, 12 L.R.A. 463] is illustrative of his point. In *Hamer* it was held that abstaining from smoking and drinking, though in fact a benefit to the promisee's health and finances and of no benefit to the promisor, was a legal detriment; that if requested by the promisor, it was a sufficient substitute for consideration and would support an action based upon the principle of promissory estoppel.

An impassioned argument of detriment and change of position by plaintiff has been submitted. He points out that he might well have decided to take an easier path through law school and graduate with an average scholastic record instead of attaining excellence; that he had this initial choice; that after the individual defendants "enticed" him by their promises, he took the tougher road; that his extra effort for scholastic achievement was in reliance upon and motivated by the representations of the promised award. He compares election to the Order to a prize offered for certain achievements, stating that election is not a mere gratuity granted without achievement, but is the promised award for inspired achievement.

The bonus, pension and reward cases relied on by plaintiff are not applicable here since in each case the promisee suffered actual detriment in foregoing an act, in refusing other employment or in expending definite and substantial effort or money in reliance on a promise. Although it has been stated that "[t]he validity of the consideration does not depend upon its value, the law does not ordinarily weigh its quantum" (Blonder v. Gentile, 149 Cal. App. 2d 869, 875 [309 P.2d 147, 151]), we conclude that in this case the alleged promises or representations were such that it cannot be said that they induced "action . . . of a *definite and substantial character* on the part of the promisee." (Rest. Contracts, §90.) (Italics added.)

Furthermore, even if it be assumed that the doctrine of promissory estoppel were applicable, we note that plaintiff has not pleaded a breach of contract. There is no allegation that it was promised that he would in fact be admitted to membership if he graduated in the top 10 percent of his class. The allegation is that he "would be eligible for election" if he attained such position. The complaint alleges that his name was on the eligible list and did receive consideration by the election committee under the general standards set forth in the Order's constitution. This is all that the individual defendants promised. The facts pleaded do not support the alleged conclusion that there was a breach of contract.

Judgment affirmed.

STUDY GUIDE: In what respect is the next case similar to the preceding one? Is it different in any significant respect? Does it remind you of any cases in Chapter 10?

SPOONER v. RESERVE LIFE INSURANCE CO.
Supreme Court of Washington,
287 P.2d 735 (1955)

Action to recover renewal bonuses allegedly due insurance agents. The Superior Court, King County, HUGH TODD, J., rendered judgment for plaintiffs, and defendant appealed. . . .

HILL, J.*

[This appeal is from a judgment in favor of the plaintiff-respondents for the amount of bonuses to which they claim they are entitled for the period from February 29, 1952, through February 28, 1953. The respondents were, during that time, agents of the appellant insurance company.]

The following bulletin was issued by the appellant on February 29, 1952, to the respondents and other agents. (The italicized portions herein appear as underscored words in the bulletin as issued.)

Bulletin #160

TO: All Staff Members in Oregon, Washington, Colorado, Nebraska, Florida & North Carolina:

EXTRA EARNINGS AGREEMENT

Your Company has grown in size — premium wise — in the industry *from 421st place to 4th of its kind in five short years.*

That all-time record, we believe, speaks for itself. But what does it mean to You?

It means that you offer a "preferred" product. Because of the values *your* product provides, *and because of the promotional effort behind it* people tend to select *your* Company.

Your Home Office folks are well aware, however, that you in the field must enjoy a sense of real security and see the road of the future stretching clearly ahead. Our association must be mutually profitable and pleasant. We hope to make your job more interesting and that you will earn more money than you could anywhere else.

Now, in addition to present substantial commissions, we are announcing your Renewal Bonus Plan *which provides extra earnings.* This has been a long time in the making. It is, we believe, superior to anything of its kind ever introduced.]

Reserve wants *career* men — men who are as much concerned about *next year* as *next month.* To attract such workers, and inspire their best efforts, your Company now puts into effect a schedule of *Bonus Payments.*

Your *Renewal Bonus* earnings will depend upon the Quality of your business as well as the amount. If you do a good job, you will earn a substantial income. If you do an *outstanding* job, you will be *very handsomely* rewarded.

You will receive at the end of each 12 month period, a bonus in accordance with the following schedule: . . .

This renewal bonus is a *voluntary* contribution on the part of the Company. It is agreed by you and by us that it may be withheld, increased, decreased or discontinued, individually or collectively, with or without notice. Further, this Renewal Bonus is contingent upon you actually writing business for this Company as a licensed agent at the time such Bonus is paid.

It will be paid once a year — on the mean amount of your business in force. This annual method of payment cuts down the cost of keeping records.

---

*Matthew William Hill (1894-1989) was educated at the University of Washington (LL.B.) and was admitted to the bar of that state in 1917. He held a private practice in Bellingham and Seattle from 1918 to 1945, serving concurrently as title examiner for the state (1919-1921) and Assistant U.S. District Attorney (1923-1924). Hill served two years on the Superior Court for King County before his appointment to the Supreme Court of Washington in 1947. He retired from the bench in 1969. — K.T.

Also — *and most important* — during the year the *boys are separated from the men.* The boys will get no bonus. That Leaves More For The Men.

In return, I ask only that you give me your best efforts. That means that you will sell your business cleanly and strictly on the merits of the policy itself and follow the letter and spirit of the Company's rules and practices.

Twelve months from now the Accounting Department will get busy and tote up the amount of business you have in force which is produced by you from the date of this agreement. They must get out the lapses and put the reinstatements back in. All that takes time. But your first Renewal Bonus check will be sent to you as quickly as humanly possible after the 12 months is up.

If you welcome these Extra Earnings, and I know you will, and to avoid any possible future misunderstanding, sign the enclosed copy of this agreement and hand it to your Manager who will send it to me.

Remember: Nothing succeeds like Success!

                                            C. C. Bradley [signed]

                                            C. C. Bradley
                                            Vice President

CCB:j1

_____
Signature of Staff Member

If this bulletin was a promise to pay a bonus under certain conditions, it must be found that the respondents met those conditions by remaining with the appellant and selling insurance, maintaining a lapse ratio of twenty to thirty per cent. The pivotal question here is whether this bulletin contains an enforceable promise of a bonus if its conditions are met or, by reason of the following paragraph, presents only an illusion of a promise:

> This renewal bonus is a *voluntary contribution* on the part of the Company. It is agreed by you and by us that *it may be withheld* increased, *decreased* or discontinued, individually or collectively, with or *without notice.* Further, this Renewal Bonus is contingent upon you actually writing business for this Company as a licensed agent at the time such Bonus is paid. (Italics ours.)

We are not here concerned with a conventional bonus case such as *Scott v. J. F. Duthie & Co.,* 1923, 125 Wash. 470, 216 P. 853, 28 A.L.R. 328. In that case it was held that the offer and the performance of the conditions of the offer constituted an enforceable contract, the employer having procured, in addition to the faithful and efficient service to which he was entitled under the employment of the employee for an indefinite term of service, continuity of service for the period designated in his offer. . . .

Nor are we here concerned with the rarer but still enforcible [sic] bonus cases in which there is a purely gratuitous promise by the employer which induces action of a definite and substantial character on the part of the employee. The applicable rule in such cases is well stated in 1 Restatement, Contracts 110, §90, which reads as follows:

> A promise which the promisor should reasonably expect to induce action or forbearance of a definite and substantial character on the part of the promisee and which does induce such action or forbearance is binding if injustice can be avoided only by enforcement of the promise. . . .

But before this rule can be applied, there must be a real promise to be enforced. Action in reliance upon a supposed promise creates no obligation on an individual or corporation whose only promise is wholly illusory. 1 Corbin on Contracts 658, §201. Appellant insists that no enforcible [sic] promise to pay a bonus is contained in the bulletin. Our problem, as we have heretofore indicated, is whether the paragraph referred to, and particularly the portion reserving a right to decrease or withhold the bonus, makes an illusory promise of what would otherwise be an enforcible [sic] one.

A supposed promise may be illusory because it is so indefinite that it cannot be enforced . . . , or by reason of provisions contained in the promise which in effect make its performance optional or entirely discretionary on the part of the promisor. . . .

Respondents here have received their regular commissions. Appellant by its bulletin announced a voluntary contribution over and above those commissions. There can be no question but that the appellant was entitled to impose such conditions and terms on the payment of this voluntary bonus as it desired. The bulletin told the respondents in plain English that the company could withhold or decrease the bonus, with or without notice. The usual and ordinary meaning of "withhold" is "to refrain from paying that which is due." Dupuy v. Board of Education, 1930, 106 Cal. App. 533, 537, 289 P. 689, 691. "Withhold" cannot be construed to apply only to future, unearned bonus payments.

We do not defend what the appellant has done here. We think the trial court correctly applied the formula set out in the bulletin, and that the respondents have reason to be dissatisfied with what appellant has paid them. Nevertheless, it cannot be said that there has been a breach of a binding contract to pay a bonus. Appellant, while perilously near the perpetration of a fraud in the position it takes here, is still acting within the terms of its bulletin, in which it incorporated language that permitted it to withhold the bonus which it seemed to promise. We cannot disregard or suppress any of those terms. . . . The agents of the appellant had no choice but to accept the offer of a bonus with all the terms and limitations placed upon it, and if they were in any instance induced to stay with the company until the termination of the bonus period, it was because they were relying on the corporate conscience of the appellant and not upon an enforcible [sic] contract. There is a natural aversion to such one-sided propositions, but we cannot delete terms or words from an offer, nor can we ignore them, to make a binding contract for the parties where none exists. . . .

The judgment is reversed and the trial court is instructed to enter a judgment of dismissal.

Reread   Restatement §21 (p. 648)

STUDY GUIDE: *In the next case, why exactly does the court resort to a promissory estoppel theory? Was the unavailability of a normal cause of action for breach of contract due to the absence of bargained-for consideration? Notice the trial judge's respective views of government and of industry.*

YPSILANTI v. GENERAL MOTORS
Circuit Court of Michigan, Washtenaw County,
61 U.S.L.W. 2563 (1993)

Donald E. Shelton, Circuit Judge.*

This case was begun by the Charter Township of Ypsilanti against General Motors Corporation as a result of a February 1992 announced decision to transfer automobile assembly operations at General Motors' Willow Run plant in the township to a plant in Arlington, Texas, and then to close the Willow Run facility completely. The decision followed a highly publicized earlier determination by General Motors to select either Willow Run or Arlington for the transfer. General Motors chose Arlington and announced that it would begin transfer of the Willow Run operations to Arlington and would cease Willow Run operations completely after the end of production of 1993 models there.

PROCEDURAL HISTORY AND STATUS

The township complaint alleged that General Motors had entered into agreements with the township to obtain twelve year tax abatements on property in the Willow Run plant in 1984 and 1988 and that the closing of the plant prior to the expiration of those abatement periods would violate the agreements and representations General Motors had made to obtain those abatements. The complaint alleges five separate theories for relief: (1) breach of a contract created by the tax abatement statute; (2) breach of a contract created by the parties' conduct during and before the tax abatement application and approval process; (3) promissory estoppel; (4) unjust enrichment; and (5) misrepresentation.[22] The complaint seeks to have the Court enjoin General Motors from closing the facility or, alternatively, for monetary damages. Washtenaw County joined the suit as a plaintiff and joined in the township contract theories as a third party beneficiary, as well as asserting a theory of injunctive relief based upon an alleged violation of the tax abatement statute. The State of Michigan was involuntarily added as a necessary party by the Court pursuant to MCR 2.205. . . . Trial was conducted from January 11-22, 1993.

Donald E. Shelton (1944-†) was educated at Western Michigan University (B.A.) and the University of Michigan (J.D.). Admitted to practice in Illinois in 1969 and in Michigan in 1974, he held a legal practice in Ann Arbor, Michigan, from 1974 to 1990, during which he also held the post of mediator for the Washtenaw County Circuit Court (1981-1990). He was appointed to the Michigan Circuit Court for Washtenaw County in 1990 and became Chief Judge of the civil/criminal division in 1996. Prior to his appointment, he served as lecturer at the University of Maryland (1971-1973). Shelton also served as a captain in the United States Army Judge Advocate General's Corps from 1969 to 1974 — earning the Meritorious Service Medal in 1974 — and as mayor pro tem (1977-1978) and mayor (1978-1986) of the city of Saline. — K.T.

22. Plaintiff's misrepresentation count is not separately discussed but is considered as part of the promissory estoppel theory. The complaint also originally contained a count alleging a potential environmental nuisance but that count was voluntarily dismissed without prejudice prior to trial.

THE STATUTORY FRAMEWORK

Michigan, like over thirty other states, permits municipalities to offer property tax abatements to industries as a supposed means of retaining and adding employment opportunities. The statutory framework for such abatements was established in Act 198 of 1974, M.C.L. §207.551, et seq. The intent of the statute, as codified in §9(2)(e), is to provide tax abatements for industrial facilities which "will . . . have the reasonable likelihood to create employment, retain employment, prevent a loss of employment, or produce energy in the community in which the facility is located." . . .

FACTUAL BACKGROUND . . .

The two specific abatements at issue in this case were granted in 1984 and 1988. The 1984 abatement followed the course of events which had been established by the parties' prior relationship, with a briefing, plant tour and lunch for township officials prior to the public hearing on approval of the application. The application was in connection with a $175 million project which was described in §5e of the application: . . . Specifically, General Motors was changing the plant to produce its "H" model cars instead of the "X" model cars which had been produced at Willow Run. Section 10 of the application stated that the company expected to create 200 more jobs with the project and that 4,300 existing jobs would be retained as a result of the project. The township board passed a resolution approving the application for a twelve year abatement on July 17, 1984. Upon receipt of the township resolution, the State Tax Commission asked Washtenaw County to indicate whether it concurred in the abatement. The Board of Commissioners concurred in the 1984 Willow Run abatement application, . . . but conditioned its concurrence on a letter which further explained its intent: . . .

> The Board's approval of this application was based on its concern for economic development in Washtenaw County which results in increased job opportunities for unemployed and underemployed residents of our County. . . .

By 1988, the demand for "H" cars had declined and General Motors decided to produce a new rear wheel "B" model of the "Caprice." The Caprice had been manufactured at plants in Arlington, Texas, and Lakewood, Georgia. General Motors decided to close the Georgia plant and modify Willow Run so it could produce rear wheel drive cars, including the Caprice. The Willow Run modification was also designed to allow the plant the flexibility to change over between rear and front wheel drive car assembly in the future. . . .

The application for an abatement of taxes on the $75 million project was filed on October 7, 1988. . . . Section 10 of the application stated that no new jobs were expected to be created by the project but that 4,900 jobs "will be retained as a result of the project." Prior to the public hearing, Mr. Hughes prepared charts and graphs to show to the Board and prepared statements which both he and the Willow Run plant manager, Mr. Williams, would make to the Board. . . . At the hearing, Mr. Williams first read his prepared statement in which he described the rear wheel drive capacity sought by the project and then read the final remark which Mr. Hughes had prepared: ...

> Upon completion of this project and favorable market demand, it will allow Willow Run to continue production and maintain continuous employment for our employees. . . .

On the township side, the Township Assessor made his recommendation in a very telling comment to the Board: ...

> Needless to say I recommend approval of the petition. Based on the past history in dealing with the people of General Motors they've always done what they said they would do and they've kept the jobs there and they've kept the plant operating as an operational facility. . . .

The Board of Trustees unanimously approved . . . the Willow Run tax abatement application[] for a twelve year period. . . .

What happened thereafter is viewed differently by the parties. The plaintiffs view it as a poet once put it:[23]

> The document we sign with zeal
> And every pledge requirable,
> Because the terms therein, we feel,
> For us are most desirable.
> And this agreement, come what may,
> To every clause obedient,
> We'll keep forever and a day
> As long as it's expedient.

The defendant views it more as a different author did:[24]

> Business today consists in persuading crowds.

and

> A man's success in business today turns upon
> his power of getting people to believe he has
> something that they want.

In any event, despite some early success, General Motors did not convince people that they wanted as many Caprice cars as General Motors wanted to build. Caprice sedans were being manufactured at both the Willow Run and Arlington, Texas plants. Willow Run was also producing Buick and Cadillac station wagons. By late 1991, the demand for the Caprice had lessened and General Motors decided that the work being done at one of the plants would be transferred to the other and one would be closed. Willow Run

---

23. Arthur Guiterman, A Scrap of Paper, from Brave Laughter, E.P. Dutton & Co., Inc. (1943).

24. Gerald Stanley Lee, Crowds — A Moving Picture of Democracy, Doubleday, Page & Co. (1913).

was operating one shift per day and Arlington was operating two shifts per day. General Motors Vice President Joseph Spielman made the decision following a short two week process which involved getting "proposals" from each of the plants and the affected communities. He recommended, and the corporation announced in February of 1992, that the work being done on the one shift at Willow Run would be transferred to the Arlington plant, which would go on three shifts per day. Importantly however, the parties to this suit have stipulated that the defendant does not rely upon "economic necessity" as a defense to this action. . . . General Motors then gave the notice required by the federal "WARN" Act[25] that it intends to close Willow Run entirely.

THE STATUTE AND APPLICATION AS A CONTRACT

The initial question before the Court is whether the Act 198 statutory process results in a contract between the governments involved and the industry receiving the subsidy. . . .

The Court has concluded that, however unwisely, the state legislature did not intend to create contractual rights for the State or its subdivisions when it enacted Act 198 and that the statute does not therefore create an enforceable contract between the government and the subsidized industry. . . .

This Court's conclusion that the legislature did not, when it enacted Act 198, intend to impose contractual obligations on subsidized industries is not something of which the State should be proud. The relationship of government and industry in this country is necessarily one of conflict, for it is the purpose of government to provide for the common welfare of all and it is the antithetical purpose of an industry to strive solely for the profit of its owners. For example, contrary to the approach of the defendant in this case that "what is good for General Motors is good for the country,"[26] the truth is, as this case demonstrates, that what is good for General Motors may only coincidentally help, and often hurts, many of our people. Industry is the source of many of the jobs in our nation and it may well be that our nation needs a new relationship of trust and cooperation between government and industry in order to compete with heavily subsidized industries from other, perhaps less democratically and socially sophisticated, countries. But such an effort must be national in scope and must be a *real* partnership with industry, not one in which industry simply views government as a part of its "business climate" and another opportunity to increase profits. The tax abatement statutes in this State and others are not the product of a well thought out effort to forge such a new partnership. This tax subsidy policy results in pitting state against state and municipality against municipality in an inter-governmental bidding war. The local governments of this State are

25. 29 U.S.C. §2101 (1992).

26. The original statement was ". . . for many years I thought that what was good for our country was good for General Motors and vice versa." It was made by Charles Erwin Wilson in testimony before the U.S. Senate Armed Services Committee in January, 1953 just after his nomination to be Secretary of Defense for President Eisenhower and while he was still a large stockholder in General Motors. See Bohle, American Quotations, Gramercy Publishing Company (1986).

placed in a position where they feel that they have no choice but to give taxpayers' resources away under a statute which does not mandate that they receive anything in return for those foregone taxes. Moreover, it has been recognized by reputable economics scholars for over ten years that the tax subsidy program, at least as adopted in Michigan, simply does not work and has little if any effect on industry investment or location decisions.[27]

Unfortunately, however, this Court cannot interpret a statute to have other than its intended meaning because the legislature chose to act unwisely or improvidently. It is for the State legislature to attempt to undo what it has done, or perhaps for the federal government to finally intervene in this area on the basis that a national industrial policy regarding tax subsidies is needed. In any event, this Court is forced to read the statute as it currently stands and to hold that Act 198 does not, by itself, nor in conjunction with the completed application forms in this case, create a contract.

PROMISSORY ESTOPPEL

The rigid and technical rules of conventional contract law are designed to provide the framework for a Court to adjudicate the rights of parties in a contractual dispute. As with other generalized legal principles, these rigid rules sometimes fail us in our attempt to wring justice from a specific dispute between people whose expectations of each other are not fulfilled. Fortunately, our common law has also evolved concepts of equity which are designed to allow a Court the flexibility, which is the true hallmark of fairness, to do justice in such situations.

One such equitable concept in the law of contracts is the notion of promissory, or equitable, estoppel. As the Court of Appeals aptly described it:[28]

Application of the doctrine of promissory estoppel is based on the particular factual circumstances; as an equitable remedy, it is employed to alleviate an unjust result of strict adherence to established legal principles.

This doctrine is a well recognized feature of the common law of this State. ... The elements of promissory estoppel have been clearly identified:[29]

In order for a promise to be enforceable under the concept of promissory estoppel, there must be a (1) promise that the promisor should reasonably

27. See M. Wolkoff, Tax Abatement as an Incentive to Industrial Location, Michigan's Economic and Fiscal Structure. ... As Dr. Wolkoff concludes at p. 301:

... the existing empirical evidence suggests that it is unlikely that even full property tax abatement has had a major impact upon the level of investment. The inframarginal investor whose investment decisions were unaffected by reduced property taxes receives a windfall from state taxpayers.

28. Association of Hebrew Teachers v. Jewish Welfare Federation, 62 Mich. App. 54 (1975) at p. 60.

29. In re Timko Estate [51 Mich. App. 662, 666 (1974)].

have expected to induce action of a definite and substantial character on the part of the promisee, (2) which in fact produced reliance or forbearance of that nature, (3) in circumstances such that the promise must be enforced if injustice is to be avoided.

The plaintiffs in this case contend that, regardless whether the statute and application form created a contract by their own terms, General Motors, by its statements and conduct in connection with those and other applications, represented that it would provide continuous employment at the Willow Run plant if the government continued to provide tax abatement subsidies. The issue, in promissory estoppel terms, is whether those representations indeed constitute a promise and whether it is the type of promise that should be enforced by this Court to prevent an injustice.

For almost fifteen years before the 1988 abatement hearing, General Motors had established a repeated pattern of inducing the township to recommend approval of its tax abatement applications on both the Willow Run and Hydra-Matic plants. Each time General Motors wanted to substantially change the product line at one of the plants, it would "sell" the idea of a tax subsidy to the township with a ritual of "education" sessions and lunches. Every time, the inducement to the township was the same — jobs will be created or preserved at the plant — and it should have been, for that was the ostensible purpose of the abatement. And, to the credit of General Motors, each time it delivered and jobs were created or preserved at the plant, at least for the duration of that product line.

When General Motors decided to produce the Caprice sedans, as well as the Buick and Cadillac station wagons, at Willow Run, it approached the township for a subsidy as usual. This time, however, some things had changed. The township had a new supervisor and several new trustees who needed to be "educated" about the General Motors-Township tax subsidy arrangement, especially since General Motors had already announced that it was going to make the investment and build these particular cars at Willow Run. General Motors did not make any off-hand or casual statements to the Board at the public hearing on the abatement application. In the context of this background, when the plant manager, in the prepared statement on behalf of General Motors, stated that, subject to "favorable market demand," General Motors would "continue production and maintain continuous employment" at the Willow Run plant, it was a promise. The promise was clearly that if the township granted the abatement, General Motors would make the Caprice at Willow Run and not just transfer that work somewhere else. Our courts have accepted the following definition of a legal promise:[30]

> The fundamental element of promise seems to be an expression of intention by the promisor that his future conduct shall be in accordance with his present expression, irrespective of what his will may be when the time for performance arrives.

---

30. Mastaw v. Naiukow, 105 Mich. App. 25 (1981) *citing* Corbin, Contracts sec. 16.

A statement that the granting of the abatement would enable General Motors to provide continuous employment at the plant was a *quid pro quo* type of statement that is associated in its common sense meaning with a promise.

In the context of the abatement application hearing the statement was also a promise that General Motors "should reasonably have expected to induce action of a definite and substantial character on the part of" the township. General Motors clearly made the statement to induce the township to cut its property taxes on the $75 million project in half. Most importantly, the promise was needed because the township otherwise had no incentive to approve the application. General Motors could not simply promise that it would make the investment in the plant *if* it was granted the abatement because it had already publicly committed to make the investment without any mention of an abatement. The only logical reason the township would have to give up half of the taxes on the project is that General Motors represented, as it had done in the past, that as long as it made those cars it was going to make them in Willow Run.

General Motors asserts that the promise was conditioned upon "favorable market demand" and therefore a totally illusory one that the township could not reasonably have relied upon. . . . The author of the prepared statement testified at trial that when he used the phrase "favorable market demand" he meant enough Caprice and station wagon sales orders to keep *both* the Willow Run and Arlington plants operating at a level of two shifts each per day, 235 days a year. Such testimony is not credible. In the context of the corporate decision to transfer the Willow Run work to Arlington and the resulting trial almost five years later, this revelation of alleged intent is suspect. As indicated earlier, the intent of the parties is to be judged objectively by looking to the expressed, not unexpressed, words of the parties. . . . There was no mention of Arlington anywhere in the public hearing and no testimony that work levels at the Arlington plant had ever been discussed with township officials, much less been stated to be a condition of Willow Run's work level.

General Motors claims that if its view of the "favorable market demand" statement is not accepted, then the statement would be a promise to keep the plant open forever and such a promise is illogical and could never be reasonably relied upon by anyone. Certainly no one took the promise as such at the hearing and no one has suggested such a construction. The statement was made in the context of the decision to build the Caprice and the station wagons at the plant and it is apparent that "favorable market demand" referred to favorable market demand for *those cars.* General Motors' statement clearly meant that if there was a sufficient market demand to make the Caprice and the station wagons they would be made at Willow Run.[31] The fact is that there still is market demand for those cars but

31. There was testimony from General Motors vice president Joseph Spielman that no one below the level of the chief executive officer of the corporation would have the authority to make such a commitment regarding plant operations or employment levels in the context of a tax abatement. The Court finds to the contrary. The 1988 prepared statement had been thoroughly reviewed at corporate headquarters before it was made and the evidence further, and somewhat embarrassingly, showed that precisely such commitments had been made in

General Motors has decided to transfer the assembly of a third of them from Willow Run to Arlington.

The second element of promissory estoppel is that the promise produced "reliance or forbearance" of a definite and substantial character. If nothing else, and there is considerable else, the evidence that the township has given up over $2 million in local government taxes from 1988-92 for the 1988 abatement alone is sufficient to satisfy this element.

The final element is that the circumstances be such that General Motors' promise must be enforced "if injustice is to be avoided." The Court is mindful of the fact that two federal courts have refused to apply the promissory estoppel doctrine to prevent plant closings.[32] Neither of those situations involved specific representations or representations which were made as an inducement for a local government to approve a tax abatement. More important, in each of those situations, the corporation was simply closing a plant because it was economically necessary to close it and the courts concluded that the company never promised to operate a plant when there was no demand for its product. Here, General Motors has stipulated, as it must, that economic necessity is *not* a defense. Again, General Motors is not closing this plant because there is no demand for the cars which are made there. It simply has chosen to transfer the one shift of production of those cars at Willow Run to add a new third shift at another plant in Arlington, Texas.

Aside from these distinctions in the facts of those cases, this Court, perhaps unlike the judges there, simply finds that the failure to act in this case would result in a terrible injustice and that the doctrine of promissory estoppel should be applied. Each judge who dons this robe assumes the awesome, and lonely, responsibility to make decisions about justice, and injustice, which will dramatically affect the way people are forced to live their lives. Every such decision must be the judge's own and it must be made honestly and in good conscience. There would be a gross inequity and patent unfairness if General Motors, having lulled the people of the Ypsilanti area into giving up millions of tax dollars which they so desperately need to educate their children and provide basic governmental services, is allowed to simply decide that it will desert 4,500 workers and their families because it thinks it can make these same cars a little cheaper somewhere else. Perhaps another judge in another court would not feel moved by that injustice and would labor to find a legal rationalization to allow such conduct. But in this Court it is my responsibility to make that decision. My conscience will not allow this injustice to happen.[33]

---

other states by lower level officials after approval by corporate headquarters. Defendant Exs. 40 through 49.

32. Local 1330, United Steel Workers of America v. United States Steel Corp., 631 F.2d 1264 (6th Cir. 1980); Abbington v. Dayton Malleable, Inc., 561 F. Supp. 1290 (S.D. Ohio 1983). . . .

33. In light of the Court's finding that the doctrine of promissory estoppel requires enforcement of defendant's promise not to transfer the manufacture of Caprice sedans and Buick and Cadillac station wagons out of Willow Run, it is not necessary to reach plaintiffs' contentions regarding unjust enrichment or to attempt to specify the monetary damages that would be appropriate under that theory. Nor is it necessary to address the County's separate theory for injunctive relief.

ORDER

General Motors is hereby enjoined from transferring the production of its Caprice sedan, and Buick and Cadillac station wagons, from the Willow Run plant to any other facility.

STUDY GUIDE: When the appellate court considered whether General Motors made a promise, did they mean a promise as conventionally understood or a commitment amounting to a manifested intention to be legally bound? Put another way, is there a difference between a promise and a promise?

YPSILANTI v. GENERAL MOTORS
Court of Appeals of Michigan,
201 Mich. App. 128, 506 N.W.2d 556 (1993)

PER CURIAM. Defendant appeals from a February 9, 1993, order of the Washtenaw Circuit Court that enjoins defendant "from transferring the production of its Caprice sedan, and Buick and Cadillac [sic, Chevrolet] station wagons, from the Willow Run plant to any other facility." We reverse.

[The court's summary of the facts, procedural history, and trial court opinion are omitted.]

The elements of promissory estoppel are:

> A promise which the promisor should reasonably expect to induce action or forbearance on the part of the promisee or a third person and which does induce such action or forbearance is binding if injustice can be avoided only by enforcement of the promise. The remedy granted for breach may be limited as justice requires.

[1 Restatement Contracts, 2d, §90, p. 811.] Promissory estoppel requires an actual, clear, and definite promise. State Bank of Standish v. Curry, 442 Mich. 76, 84-85, 500 N.W.2d 104 (1993). Further, "reliance is reasonable only if it is induced by an actual promise." Id. at 84 [500 N.W.2d 104]. A determination that there was a promise will be overturned if it is clearly erroneous. Id.[34]

The trial court's finding that defendant promised to keep Caprice and station wagon production at Willow Run is clearly erroneous. First, the mere fact that a corporation solicits a tax abatement and persuades a municipality with assurances of jobs cannot be evidence of a promise. The very purpose of tax abatement legislation is to induce companies to locate and to continue business enterprises in the municipality. Even the trial court recognized this when it stated, "Every time, the inducement to the township

---

34. Plaintiffs' reliance on *Curry* is misplaced. It merely dealt with a situation in which there was a clear promise upon which the plaintiff detrimentally relied. *Curry*, rather than compelling a conclusion in plaintiffs' favor, points to why the doctrine does not apply to this case: the promise necessary to invoke the doctrine is distinguished from a statement of opinion or mere prediction of future events. Id. [442 Mich.] at 86 [500 N.W.2d 104].

was the same — jobs will be created or preserved at that plant, and it should have been, for that was the ostensible purpose of the abatement."

Second, representations of job creation and retention are a statutory prerequisite. An applicant for an industrial facilities exemption certificate must, among other things, certify that "[c]ompletion of the facility is calculated to, and will *at the time of issuance of the certificate* have the reasonable likelihood to create employment, retain employment, prevent a loss of employment, or produce energy in the community in which the facility is situated." M.C.L. §207.559(2)(e); M.S.A. §7.800(9)(2)(e); emphasis added.

Third, the fact that a manufacturer uses hyperbole and puffery in seeking an advantage or concession does not necessarily create a promise. For example, statements such as "We're partners" and "We look forward to growing together" were found not to constitute a promise to keep a collective bargaining agreement in force for the foreseeable future so as to create by promissory estoppel a continuing duty of the employer to honor an expired agreement. Marine Transport Lines, Inc. v. Intl. Organization of Masters, Mates, & Pilots, 636 F. Supp. 384 (S.D.N.Y., 1986). Nor did exhortations for union concessions in order to keep a foundry open constitute promises under promissory estoppel to prevent a foundry from closing. Abbington v. Dayton Malleable, Inc., 561 F. Supp. 1290 (S.D. Ohio, 1983), *aff'd* 738 F.2d 438 (CA 6, 1984). Similarly, exhortations to its employees to increase productivity and assurances that a plant would not be closed, as long as it was profitable, did not establish by promissory estoppel an obligation on a steel company to keep open a plant. Local 1330, United Steel Workers v. United States Steel Corp., 631 F.2d 1264 (CA 6, 1980).

Turning to the case at bar, almost all the statements the trial court cited as foundations for a promise were, instead, expressions of defendant's hopes or expectations of continued employment at Willow Run. The court summarized the corporation's concerted efforts to obtain abatements for Hydra-Matic between 1974 and 1981 as follows:

> Over the years, General Motors followed the example set in its first application and a course of conduct developed between General Motors and the township for the granting of tax abatements. Each time General Motors wanted an abatement to make a physical change in the plants, it would invite township officials to the plant for a briefing, a tour of the plant, and lunch. Then the formal application would be submitted and General Motors officials would appear at a public hearing before the entire Board, which would then approve the application. Each time, the Board was advised, in some specifics, of the impact of the improvements, and presumably the abatement, on production and employment levels in the plant.

The acts cited by the trial court were acts one would naturally expect a company to do in order to introduce and promote an abatement proposal to a municipality. The acts did not amount to a promise and, as course-of-conduct evidence, showed only efforts to take advantage of a statutory opportunity. They did not constitute assurances of continued employment. In any event, we note that the activity referred to by the trial court related to Hydra-Matic, not Willow Run.

The court cited the State Tax Commission's resolution regarding the 1984 Willow Run abatement in which the commission's approval "was based on its concern for economic development in Washtenaw County which results in increased job opportunities for unemployed and under-employed residents of our county." However, that was the commission's expectation, not defendant's promise.

In defendant's 1988 presentation, Russell Hughes, the Willow Run comp-troller, recited background, including: "Since the '81, '82 time-frame you can see that we've been basically maintaining about five thousand employees each year in a very consistent pattern." However, Hughes made the statement by way of history, and not as an assurance of future employment.

The circuit court also cited plant manager Harvey Williams' prepared statement:

> General Motors selected Willow Run to build these new vehicles because of our reputation for high quality, our continued harmonious rela-tionship and our spirit of all employees working together.
> . . . We are asking the Board to accept our application and pass on it favorably. To join the corporation in the kind of relationship we have in the Township in assuring future investments in our plant.

However, that language is nearly identical to the puffery the federal court found not to constitute a promise in *Marine Transport Lines, Inc.*, supra.

The trial court referred to the township assessor's remarks:

> Needless to say I recommend approval of the petition. Based on the past history in dealing with the people at General Motors, they've always done what they said they would do and they've kept the jobs there and they kept the plant operating as an operational facility.

Again, however, that was the assessor's evaluation, not defendant's promise.

The court quoted the State Tax Commission's resolution, which stated in part, "Where the facts indicate that positive results in gains in employ-ment and taxes appear justified . . . we will support all the local unit deci-sions." Once again, that was the commission's assessment, not defendant's promise of continuing employment.

Defendant's statement that the lower court principally relied on to find a promise was not sufficient to constitute a promise. Plant manager Williams stated:

> Good evening, my name is Harvey Williams and I am the plant manager of the Buick Oldsmobile Cadillac groups [sic] Willow Run plant.

> We are pleased to have this opportunity to appear before the Ypsilanti Township Board of Trustees. This application for an industrial facilities exemption certif-icate is for an investment totalling $75,000,000.00 for machinery and equipment. This will enable our plant to assemble a new full size car in the 1991 model year.

> This new rear wheel drive car is substantially larger then [sic] our current model. And specifically it will generate major booth, oven and conveyor changes in the paint shop and assembly line process, changes in the body, trim and chassis department. This change will also provide additional flexi-bility at our assembly plant. Essentially we would now have the capability to

produce either front or rear wheel drive cars with minimum modifications to our facility. *Upon completion of this project and favorable market demand, it will allow Willow Run to continue production and maintain continuous employment for our employees.*

I would like to introduce Russell Hughes, our controller, who will review pertinent charts pertaining to our request. (Emphasis added.)

Although the parties greatly dispute what the speaker meant by "favorable market demand" and even whether defendant should have been allowed to narrow it to Willow Run production, the fact is that the statement qualified defendant's expectation that the new abatement would allow it to continue production at the plant and maintain continuous employment for the employees. Again, even that statement was nothing more than the kind of hyperbole a corporation would use to obtain the tax abatement benefits afforded by the statute and willingly offered by the township. The trial court clearly erred in concluding that Williams' statement, and particularly the portion emphasized in the foregoing quotation, constituted a promise of continued Caprice and station wagon production at Willow Run as long as the company produces those vehicles.

Even if the finding of a promise could be sustained, reliance on the promise would not have been reasonable. "[T]he reliance interest protected by [Restatement]§90 is reasonable reliance." *Curry*, supra, [442 Mich.] at 84 [500 N.W.2d 104].

It has never been held that an abatement carries a promise of continued employment. Indeed, the history of this case shows that persons involved in the 1988 Willow Run abatement understood that defendant was not promising continued employment.

At a township board meeting in November 1988, Dillard Craiger, chairman of the Washtenaw County Board of Commissioners, opposed a tax break for Willow Run "unless a commitment was made by General Motors to remain operating at the present facility in Ypsilanti Township for that period of time thereby securing employment for the community." Craiger also complained that defendant had not given any commitments whatsoever. Outgoing Township Supervisor Ron Allen nevertheless endorsed defendant's request for tax relief, noting that "General Motors has never been overbearing or threatening" and cautioning "the Board not to take any action that would unravel the success that the Township has had [in dealing with General Motors] over the last several years." At a subsequent work session held on December 5, 1988, at least five of the seven board members — including new Township Supervisor Wesley Prater and Township Treasurer Ruth Ann Jamnick — decided to support the application.

At the public hearing at which plant manager Harvey Williams supposedly promised "continuous employment for our employees," plant comptroller Russell Hughes almost immediately warned that "[o]ne percent [market share] penetration that we lose at General Motors means ten thousand jobs for this corporation of our employees. In the assembly plant operation one percent means about twenty five hundred jobs throughout the U.S. and all assembly plants."

Other speakers then took the floor, several of whom specifically pointed out that defendant had not committed itself to continue operating the Willow Run plant for any particular period of time. Washtenaw County Commission Chairman Craiger, after listening to plant manager Williams' presentation, restated in detail his admonition from the previous month:

> The plant has not given us any commitments in any way that they will not "outsource" production, they will not tell you how long they are going to stay, they will not tell you that we only want it as long as we stay. Who knows, they might move tomorrow or two years from now and they will have been given three tax breaks with a hidden plan. . . .
>
> If Georgia or Alabama gives them a hundred percent [tax abatement], don't we have a right to bid on it? Don't we have that right, or should they just say, we're closing the plant because we got a better deal. . . . I would like to be able for them to tell us how long are they going to stay.

Others echoed this concern. A Mr. Smith referred to increases in his own property taxes and added: "I have eighteen years in and I'd like to see them stay here twelve years so I can retire, but they are not promising anything." Township Supervisor Prater, who chaired the meeting, then interjected a "point of clarification," explaining to Smith that "the abatement they are asking for is not on real estate tax, it's personal property tax." But Prater did not take issue with Smith's statement that no "promise" had been made, and Smith replied that "there should be some kind of proof by them that they are not going to . . . move out." Prater made no response. Other witnesses agreed with Smith that defendant had made no commitment to continue operations at Willow Run. Mr. Debs, president of the local union at the Willow Run plant, pointed out that "nobody can tell us what the sales are going to be" and that "no plant can stay open" if sales drop. A Mr. Alford remarked that "there were some legal issues there that cannot bind [Willow Run] or Hydra-Matic to giving jobs to Ypsilanti Township."

Defendant's representatives were not asked to respond to these comments, and no member of the township board took issue with them. Instead, Supervisor Prater urged the board to approve defendant's application. The township board then voted unanimously to approve a twelve-year abatement at Willow Run; the resolution contained no suggestion that approval was conditioned on a commitment to operate the plant for any particular period.

In short, defendant made no promises.

Reversed. Defendant may tax costs.

Relational Background: Settlement of the Case

JAMES BENNET, G.M. SETTLES SUIT OVER PLANT CLOSING, NEW YORK TIMES, APR. 15, 1994, P. 3:   The General Motors Corporation has tentatively settled a lawsuit filed by a Michigan township and county over the closing of an autombile [sic] assembly plant last year. Ypsilanti Township and Washtenaw County sued the auto maker after it announced that it would close the plant, known as Willow Run, because of flagging sales of its Chevrolet Caprice and other large rear-wheel-drive cars. The suit contended that General Motors had promised to build cars at Willow Run through the late 1990's in return for tax abatements, and having reneged on that promise owed $13.5 million in back taxes.

Under the agreement, General Motors will invest more than $80 million in new equipment and machinery to increase capacity at a transmission plant in the area. The investment will not result in new jobs, said Margaret G. Holmes, a G.M. spokeswoman. The company has also promised to clean up the closed factory to comply with state and Federal environmental laws, and to explore selling the plant or putting it to a different use.

12-Year Tax Abatements. The town and county will provide 12-year tax abatements worth 50 percent of the property taxes on the new investment. Ms. Holmes said it was not clear what the abatement would amount to.

Of the 2,400 people once employed at Willow Run, about 200 are left in jobs maintaining the plant. Many others retired, or moved to other G.M. plants, including the factory in Arlington, Tex., where G.M. consolidated production of rear-wheel-drive cars. Twenty skilled workers employed at Willow Run have yet to be placed at other jobs, Ms. Holmes said. The transmission plant next door to Willow Run employs 5,500 people.

Town officials seemed relieved to have completed the negotiations. "I have a new respect for General Motors, and I hope they do for the township," said Wesley E. Prater, township supervisor for Ypsilanti. The town board approved the settlement at a public hearing on Wednesday. The county has scheduled a public hearing next Wednesday on it.

2.   Reasonable Reliance

STUDY GUIDE: In the next case, why exactly was reliance on the promise found to be unreasonable? Also notice the close connection between gift law and the doctrine of promissory estoppel. Compare this case with Ricketts v. Scothorn. [To some, Elvis was "the King." Vernon Presley was his father.]

ALDEN v. VERNON PRESLEY
Supreme Court of Tennessee, 637 S.W.2d 862 (1982)

FONES, J.*
This is an action against the estate of Elvis Presley to enforce a gratuitous promise to pay off the mortgage on plaintiff's home made by decedent but not consummated prior to his death.

William Hardin Davis Fones (1917-2010) studied at Memphis State University and the University of Tennessee (J.D.) and was admitted to the Tennessee bar in 1942. He practiced law in Memphis for over twenty-five years, when, in 1971, he was appointed judge of the 15th Judicial Circuit Court of Tennessee at Memphis. In 1973, he was appointed to the Supreme Court of Tennessee where he served as Chief Justice twice (1974-1976, 1982-1984). Fones retired from the bench in 1990. He was decorated for service with the U.S. Army Air Corps (1942-1945). — K.T.

[The trial court denied recovery but the Court of Appeals found that plaintiff had relied upon the promise to her detriment and awarded plaintiff judgment on the theory of promissory estoppel.] → *Procedural Posture*

I . . .

Plaintiff, Jo Laverne Alden, is the mother of Ginger Alden, the former girlfriend of the late Elvis Presley. Presley was a singer of great renown throughout the world and a man of substantial wealth. In January of 1977, Presley became engaged to Ginger Alden. He was quite generous to several members of the Alden family including Ginger and her mother, the plaintiff. Gifts to plaintiff included the funds for landscaping the lawn and installing a swimming pool for the Alden home. Due to his close relationship with plaintiff's daughter, Presley also became aware of plaintiff's desire to obtain a divorce from her husband. Presley offered to pay all expenses incurred in the divorce proceeding, including furnishing plaintiff an attorney; to advance plaintiff money to purchase her husband's equity in the Alden home; and to pay off the remaining mortgage indebtedness on the Alden home.

[As a result of these promises, plaintiff filed for divorce on the grounds of irreconcilable differences. On August 1, 1977, a property settlement agreement was executed in which plaintiff paid her husband $5,325.00 for his equity in return for a deed conveying all of his interest in the home to plaintiff plus a release of the husband from all further liability upon the mortgage indebtedness on the Alden home.] The mortgage indebtedness at the time of the execution of the settlement agreement was in the sum of $39,587.66, and it is this amount which is the subject of the present suit, all the other gifts and promises to plaintiff having been fulfilled.

On August 16, 1977, Presley died suddenly leaving unpaid the mortgage indebtedness on the Alden home. On August 25, 1977, Drayton Beecher Smith, II, an attorney for the Presley estate, informed plaintiff that the estate would not assume liability for the mortgage indebtedness.

Plaintiff filed the present suit on February 14, 1978, to enforce the promise made by decedent to pay the home mortgage. On March 3, 1978, Smith informed plaintiff he could no longer represent her in the divorce action since he was serving as an attorney for decedent's estate. Plaintiff failed to employ new counsel and the divorce action was dismissed for failure to prosecute.

[Plaintiff re-filed her divorce action in April 1978, upon the same grounds and sought approval of the property settlement agreement executed in August, 1977, in conjunction with the original divorce suit. The divorce was granted in April, 1980, on the grounds of irreconcilable differences, and the property settlement was approved by the court. Plaintiff did not disclose to the court in the divorce case that decedent's estate had informed her it was not their intention to pay the mortgage on the Alden home.]

In the instant case, the trial court held that decedent did make a promise unsupported by consideration to plaintiff, that no gift was consummated for failure of delivery, that plaintiff and her husband suffered no detriment as she "wound up much better off after their association with

Elvis A. Presley than either would have been if he had never made any promise to Jo Laverne Alden," and that plaintiff did not rely upon the promise since her divorce petition was filed subsequent to the present suit and subsequent to being told that decedent's estate would not accept legal responsibility for decedent's promise.

The Court of Appeals concurred in the trial court finding that there was no gift for failure of delivery, holding that delivery is not complete unless "complete dominion and control of the gift is surrendered by the donor and acquired by the donee," *citing* Pamplin v. Satterfield, 196 Tenn. 297, 265 S.W.2d 886 (1954). . . .

[However, the Court of Appeals reversed the remainder of the trial court's decision by adopting and applying the doctrine of promissory estoppel holding that plaintiff had foregone remedies available to her in the divorce petition in reliance upon the promise made to her by decedent. The Court of Appeals reasoned the estate should be estopped from dishonoring that promise.]

We concur in the reasoning of the trial court and Court of Appeals' findings that decedent did not make a gift of the money necessary to pay off the mortgage as there was no actual or constructive delivery. We find it unnecessary to address the question of whether or not Tennessee recognizes the doctrine of promissory estoppel because plaintiff has failed, as a matter of law, to prove essential elements of promissory estoppel, to-wit: detrimental reliance, and a loss suffered as a result of detrimental reliance.

II

The Court of Appeals relied upon definitions of promissory estoppel found in the Restatement of Contracts and L. Simpson's Law of Contracts. Since these works present representative definitions of promissory estoppel we quote with approval from the Court of Appeals' opinion as follows:

A concise statement concerning promissory estoppel is found in Restatement of Contracts, Section 90, as follows:

A promise which the promisor should reasonably expect to induce action or forbearance of a definite and substantial character on the part of the promisee and which does induce such action or forbearance is binding if injustice can be avoided only by enforcement of the promise.

A more thorough examination of the doctrine, its elements and limitations is set forth in L. Simpson, Law of Contracts §61 (2d ed. 1965); to-wit:

Detrimental action or forbearance by the promisee in reliance on a gratuitous promise, within limits constitutes a substitute for consideration, or a sufficient reason for enforcement of the promise without consideration. This doctrine is known as promissory estoppel. A promisor who induces substantial change of position by the promisee in reliance on the promise is estopped to deny its enforceability as lacking consideration. The reason for the doctrine is to avoid an unjust result, and its reason defines its limits. No injustice results in refusal to enforce a gratuitous promise where the loss suffered in reliance is negligible, nor where the promisee's action in reliance was unreasonable or unjustified by the promise. The limits of promissory estoppel are: (1) the detriment suffered in reliance must be substantial in an economic sense; (2) the substantial loss to the promisee in acting in reliance must have been foreseeable by the promisor; (3) the promisee must have acted reasonably in justifiable reliance on the promise as made.

III

It is well established in this State that settlement agreements between husband and wife that purport to settle the legal obligations of alimony and child support, over which the Court has initial and continuing statutory authority to determine, are not binding until approved by the Court. See, e.g., . . . Osborne v. Osborne, 29 Tenn. App. 463, 197 S.W.2d 234 (1946). The terms of such agreements, "are merely evidential in value and may be followed by the court in its award of alimony — they should be given great consideration but are subject to close scrutiny by the court." 29 Tenn. App. at 466-467, 197 S.W.2d at 236.

The property settlement agreement that the Aldens entered into expressly provided that it was "subject to Court approval."

IV

The residence of the Aldens and the mortgage indebtedness thereon was obviously subject to such disposition as alimony, as the circumstances of the parties justified at the time that the divorce was granted, April 1980.

Mrs. Alden did not inform the court that the estate had denied legal responsibility for the mortgage indebtedness, after she had entered into the property settlement agreement, but instead, affirmatively sought approval of the property settlement agreement. Beyond question, she was entitled to relief from that portion of the property settlement agreement wherein she assumed the mortgage indebtedness, upon revealing to the divorce court that she agreed to assume the mortgage only because decedent promised to pay it off gratuitously, but that the estate denied liability subsequent to the execution of the property settlement agreement. She was represented by counsel and must be charged with the knowledge that those facts constituted a change of circumstances that, as a matter of law, entitled her to relief from that portion of the agreement.

In this action plaintiff has shown that decedent's promise induced her to assume a $39,587 mortgage as part of a property settlement agreement dated August 1, 1977. However, the property settlement agreement was not binding upon plaintiff or her husband until approved by the court and the estate's denial of liability for decedent's gratuitous promise before submission of the agreement to the court removed the element of detrimental reliance from the factual scenario of this case. It follows, plaintiff's reliance on the promise after August 25, 1977, was not reasonably justified and she suffered no loss as a result of justifiable reliance.

The judgment of the Court of Appeals is reversed and this case is dismissed. Costs are assessed against plaintiff.

3. Injustice of Nonenforcement

STUDY GUIDE: In the next case, does the court treat promissory estoppel as a consideration substitute or as an alternative theory of liability? Would the case have been decided any differently had it conceived of promissory estoppel the other way? Why does the court reject the plaintiff's misrepresentation claim? How does this case compare with Goodman v. Dicker and Hoffman v. Red Owl Stores? Does the following case suggest that the flexibility inherent in the "standards" provided by §90 is a two-edged sword for promisees? In similar circumstances, is there any way for parties (or their lawyers) to determine in advance of a judicial decision whether there is an enforceable obligation? If so, how? If not, what implications does this raise for the "rule of law"?

COHEN v. COWLES MEDIA CO.
Supreme Court of Minnesota,
457 N.W.2d 199 (1990)

SIMONETT, J.*

This case asks whether a newspaper's breach of its reporter's promise of anonymity to a news source is legally enforceable. We conclude the promise is not enforceable, neither as a breach of contract claim nor, in this case, under promissory estoppel. We affirm the court of appeals' dismissal of plaintiff's claim based on fraudulent misrepresentation, and reverse the court of appeals' allowance of the breach of contract claim.

Claiming a reporter's promise to keep his name out of a news story was broken, plaintiff Dan Cohen sued defendants Northwest Publications, Inc., publisher of the St. Paul Pioneer Press Dispatch (Pioneer Press), and Cowles Media Company, publisher of the Minneapolis Star and Tribune (Star Tribune). The trial court ruled that the First Amendment did not bar Cohen's contract and misrepresentation claims. The jury then found liability on both claims and awarded plaintiff $200,000 compensatory damages jointly and severally against the defendants. In addition, the jury awarded punitive damages of $250,000 against each defendant.

The court of appeals (2-1 decision) agreed that plaintiff's claims did not involve state action and therefore did not implicate the First Amendment; further, that even if First Amendment rights were implicated, those rights were outweighed by compelling state interests and, in any event, such rights were waived by the newspapers. The appeals panel ruled, however, that misrepresentation had not been proven as a matter of law and, therefore, set aside the punitive damages award. The panel upheld the jury's finding of a breach of contract and affirmed the award of $200,000

---

*John E. Simonett (1924-2011) received degrees from St. John's University (B.A.) and the University of Minnesota (LL.B.). He practiced law in Little Falls, Minnesota, for nearly 30 years, when he accepted his current appointment as justice of the Supreme Court of Minnesota in 1980, where he served until retirement in 1994. — K.T.

compensatory damages. Cohen v. Cowles Media Co., 445 N.W.2d 248 (Minn. App. 1989). We granted petitions for further review from all parties.

On October 27, 1982, in the closing days of the state gubernatorial election campaign, Dan Cohen separately approached Lori Sturdevant, the Star Tribune reporter, and Bill Salisbury, the Pioneer Press reporter, and to each stated in so many words:

> I have some documents which may or may not relate to a candidate in the upcoming election, and if you will give me a promise of confidentiality, that is that I will be treated as an anonymous source, that my name will not appear in any material in connection with this, and you will also agree that you're not going to pursue with me a question of who my source is, then I'll furnish you with the documents.

Sturdevant and Salisbury were experienced reporters covering the gubernatorial election and knew Cohen as an active Republican associated with the Wheelock Whitney campaign. Cohen told Sturdevant that he would also be offering the documents to other news organizations. Neither reporter informed Cohen that their promises of confidentiality were subject to approval or revocation by their editors. Both reporters promised to keep Cohen's identity anonymous, and both intended to keep that promise. At trial Cohen testified he insisted on anonymity because he feared retaliation from the news media and politicians. Cohen turned over to each reporter copies of two public court records concerning Marlene Johnson, the DFL candidate for lieutenant governor. The first was a record of a 1969 case against Johnson for three counts of unlawful assembly, subsequently dismissed; the second document was a 1970 record of conviction for petit theft, which was vacated about a year later.[35]

Both newspapers, on the same day, then interviewed Marlene Johnson for her explanation and reaction. The Star Tribune also assigned a reporter to find the original court records in the dead-storage vaults. The reporter discovered that Gary Flakne, known to be a Wheelock Whitney supporter, had checked out the records a day earlier; no one, before Flakne, had looked at the records for years. The reporter called Flakne and asked why he had checked out the records. Flakne replied, "I did it for Dan Cohen." The Star Tribune editors thereafter conferred and decided to publish the story the next day including Dan Cohen's identity. Acting independently, the Pioneer Press Dispatch editors also decided to break their reporter's promise and to publish the story with Cohen named as the source.[36]

---

35. Cohen then met with reporters for the Associated Press and WCCO-TV. They, too, promised Cohen anonymity and received the court documents. The Associated Press published the story and honored its promise. WCCO-TV did not run the story.

36. The court records obtained by Cohen did not contain the underlying facts of the unlawful assembly and petit theft charges. Apparently only after the reporters had gone to Johnson for an explanation did the full story become known. Johnson explained (and the newspapers duly reported in their stories) that the arrest for unlawful assembly (later dismissed) was for protesting the city's alleged failure to hire minority workers on construction projects, while the petit theft incident (theft up to $150) was for leaving a store with $6 of sewing materials at a time when Johnson was upset because of her father's death. These

The decision to identify Cohen in the stories was the subject of vigorous debate within the editorial staffs of the two newspapers. Some staff members argued that the reporter's promise of confidentiality should be honored at all costs. Some contended that the Johnson incidents were not newsworthy and did not warrant publishing, and, in any case, if the story was published, it would be enough to identify the source as a source close to the Whitney campaign. Other editors argued that not only was the Johnson story newsworthy but so was identification of Cohen as the source; that to attribute the story to a veiled source would be misleading and cast suspicion on others; and that the Johnson story was already spreading throughout the news media community and was discoverable from other sources not bound by confidentiality. Then, too, the Star Tribune had editorially endorsed the Perpich-Johnson ticket; some of its editors feared if the newspaper did not print the Johnson story, other news media would, leaving the Star Tribune vulnerable to a charge it was protecting the ticket it favored. Salisbury and Sturdevant both objected strongly to the editorial decisions to identify Cohen as the source of the court records. Indeed, Sturdevant refused to attach her name to the story.

Promising to keep a news source anonymous is a common, well-established journalistic practice. So is the keeping of those promises. None of the editors or reporters who testified could recall any other instance when a reporter's promise of confidentiality to a source had been overruled by the editor. Cohen, who had many years' experience in politics and public relations, said this was the first time in his experience that an editor or a reporter did not honor a promise to a source.

The next day, October 28, 1982, both newspapers published stories about Johnson's arrests and conviction. Both articles published Cohen's name, along with denials by the regular Whitney campaign officials of any connection with the published stories. Under the headline, *Marlene Johnson arrests disclosed by Whitney ally*, the Star Tribune also gave Johnson's explanation of the arrests and identified Cohen as a "political associate of IR gubernatorial candidate Wheelock Whitney" and named the advertising firm where Cohen was employed. The Pioneer Press Dispatch quoted Johnson as saying the release of the information was "a last-minute smear campaign."

The same day as the two newspaper articles were published, Cohen was fired by his employer. The next day, October 29, a columnist for the Star Tribune attacked Cohen and his "sleazy" tactics, with, ironically, no reference to the newspaper's own ethics in dishonoring its promise. A day later the Star Tribune published a cartoon on its editorial page depicting Dan Cohen with a garbage can labeled "last minute campaign smears."

Cohen could not sue for defamation because the information disclosed was true. He couched his complaint, therefore, in terms of fraudulent misrepresentation and breach of contract. We now consider whether these two claims apply here.

---

circumstances, of which Cohen was apparently unaware and which cast a somewhat different light on the two incidents, were likely to set in motion a boomerang effect. This suggestion of a boomerang may have prompted some of the editors to believe that Cohen's identity was newsworthy.

I

First of all, we agree with the court of appeals that the trial court erred in not granting defendants' post-trial motions for judgment notwithstanding the verdict on the misrepresentation claim.

For fraud there must be a misrepresentation of a past or present fact. A representation as to future acts does not support an action for fraud merely because the represented act did not happen, unless the promisor did not intend to perform at the time the promise was made. . . . Cohen admits that the reporters intended to keep their promises, as, indeed, they testified and as their conduct confirmed. Moreover, the record shows that the editors had no intention to reveal Cohen's identity until later when more information was received and the matter was discussed with other editors. These facts do not support a fraud claim. For this reason and for the other reasons cited by the court of appeals, we affirm the court of appeals' ruling. Because the punitive damages award hinges on the tort claim of misrepresentation, it, too, must be set aside as the court of appeals ruled. . . .

II

[In an omitted portion of the opinion, the court found that a breach of contract action did not lie because, though there was a bargain here, the "law does not create a contract where the parties intended none. . . . Nor does the law consider binding every exchange of promises. . . . We are not persuaded that in the special milieu of media news-gathering a source and a reporter ordinarily believe they are engaged in making a legally binding commitment."]

III

But if a confidentiality promise is not a legally binding contract, might the promise otherwise be enforceable? In Christensen v. Minneapolis Mun. Employees Retirement Bd., 331 N.W.2d 740, 747 (Minn. 1983), we declined to apply a "conventional contract approach, with its strict rules of offer and acceptance" in the context of public pension entitlements, pointing out this approach "tends to deprive the analysis of the relationship between the state and its employees of a needed flexibility." We opted instead for a promissory estoppel analysis. The doctrine of promissory estoppel implies a contract in law where none exists in fact. According to the doctrine, well-established in this state, a promise expected or reasonably expected to induce definite action by the promisee that does induce action is binding if injustice can be avoided only by enforcing the promise.[37]

In our case we have, without dispute, the reporters' unambiguous promise to treat Cohen as an anonymous source. The reporters expected

37. . . . This theory was not briefed by the parties but it surfaced during oral argument.

that promise to induce Cohen to give them the documents, which he did to his detriment. The promise applied only to Cohen's identity, not to anything about the court records themselves.

We are troubled, however, by the third requirement for promissory estoppel, namely, the requirement that injustice can only be avoided by enforcing the promise. Here Cohen lost his job; but whether this is an injustice which should be remedied requires the court to examine a transaction fraught with moral ambiguity. Both sides proclaim their own purity of intentions while condemning the other side for "dirty tricks." Anonymity gives the source deniability, but deniability, depending on the circumstances, may or may not deserve legal protection. If the court applies promissory estoppel, its inquiry is not limited to whether a promise was given and broken, but rather the inquiry is into all the reasons why it was broken.

Lurking in the background of this case has been the newspapers' contention that any state-imposed sanction in this case violates their constitutional rights of a free press and free speech.[38] . . .

Of critical significance in this case, we think, is the fact that the promise of anonymity arises in the classic First Amendment context of the quintessential public debate in our democratic society, namely, a political source involved in a political campaign. The potentiality for civil damages for promises made in this context chills public debate, a debate which Cohen willingly entered albeit hoping to do so on his own terms. In this context, and considering the nature of the political story involved, it seems to us that the law best leaves the parties here to their trust in each other.

We conclude that in this case enforcement of the promise of confidentiality under a promissory estoppel theory would violate defendants' First Amendment rights. . . . plaintiff's claim cannot be maintained on a contract theory. Neither is it sustainable under promissory estoppel. The judgment for plaintiff is reversed. . . .

COHEN v. COWLES MEDIA CO., 501 U.S. 663, 111 S. CT. 2513 (1991): Justice WHITE* delivered the opinion of the Court: The question before us is whether the First Amendment prohibits a plaintiff from

38. New York Times v. Sullivan, 376 U.S. 254, 84 S. Ct. 710, 11 L. Ed. 2d 686 (1964), holds that a state may not apply a state rule of law to impose impermissible restrictions on the federal constitutional freedoms of speech and press. The test is not the form which the state action takes — such as in this case, breach of contract or promissory estoppel — but, "whatever the form, whether such power has in fact been exercised." Id. at 265, 84 S. Ct. at 718. . . .

*Byron R. White (1917-2002), an All American football player at the University of Colorado, earned the name "Whizzer" for his talent as a running back. Following graduation, White played one season for the Pittsburgh Steelers and led the league in rushing. A Rhodes Scholar at Oxford University in 1939, White returned to the United States after the outbreak of war in Europe. He studied law at Yale and then resumed his football career with the Detroit Lions for the 1940-1941 season. When the United States entered the war, White joined the navy, serving in the Pacific. After the war, he completed his law degree at Yale and practiced in Denver. There he participated heavily in John F. Kennedy's 1960 presidential campaign, having known Kennedy while in England, in the navy, and when White clerked for Chief Justice Fred Vinson during Kennedy's first term in Congress. Kennedy appointed him deputy U.S. Attorney General and, in 1962, nominated him to the Supreme Court. He retired in 1993. — K.T.

recovering damages, under state promissory estoppel law, for a newspaper's breach of a promise of confidentiality given to the plaintiff in exchange for information. We hold that it does not. . . .

This case . . . is . . . controlled . . . by the . . . well-established line of decisions holding that generally applicable laws do not offend the First Amendment simply because their enforcement against the press has incidental effects on its ability to gather and report the news. As the cases relied on by respondents recognize, the truthful information sought to be published must have been lawfully acquired. The press may not with impunity break and enter an office or dwelling to gather news. Neither does the First Amendment relieve a newspaper reporter of the obligation shared by all citizens to respond to a grand jury subpoena and answer questions relevant to a criminal investigation, even though the reporter might be required to reveal a confidential source. . . . The press, like others interested in publishing, may not publish copyrighted material without obeying the copyright laws. . . . Similarly, the media must obey the National Labor Relations Act . . . and the Fair Labor Standards Act . . . ; may not restrain trade in violation of the antitrust laws . . . ; and must pay non-discriminatory taxes. . . . It is therefore beyond dispute that "[t]he publisher of a newspaper has no special immunity from the application of general laws. He has no special privilege to invade the rights and liberties of others." Associated Press v. NLRB, [301 U.S. 103, 132-133 (1937)]. Accordingly, enforcement of such general laws against the press is not subject to stricter scrutiny than would be applied to enforcement against other persons or organizations.

There can be little doubt that the Minnesota doctrine of promissory estoppel is a law of general applicability. It does not target or single out the press. Rather, in so far as we are advised, the doctrine is generally applicable to the daily transactions of all the citizens of Minnesota. The First Amendment does not forbid its application to the press. . . .

Respondents and *amici* argue that permitting Cohen to maintain a cause of action for promissory estoppel will inhibit truthful reporting because news organizations will have legal incentives not to disclose a confidential source's identity even when that person's identity is itself newsworthy. . . . But if this is the case, it is no more than the incidental, and constitutionally insignificant, consequence of applying to the press a generally applicable law that requires those who make certain kinds of promises to keep them. Although we conclude that the First Amendment does not confer on the press a constitutional right to disregard promises that would otherwise be enforced under state law, we reject Cohen's request that in reversing the Minnesota Supreme Court's judgment we reinstate the jury verdict awarding him $200,000 in compensatory damages. . . . The Minnesota Supreme Court's incorrect conclusion that the First Amendment barred Cohen's claim may well have truncated its consideration of whether a promissory estoppel claim had otherwise been established under Minnesota law and whether Cohen's jury verdict could be upheld on a promissory estoppel basis. Or perhaps the State Constitution may be construed to shield the press from a promissory estoppel cause of action such as this one. These are matters for the Minnesota Supreme Court to address and resolve in the first instance on remand. Accordingly, the judgment of the Minnesota

Supreme Court is reversed, and the case is remanded for further proceedings not inconsistent with this opinion.

So ordered.

COHEN v. COWLES MEDIA CO.
Supreme Court of Minnesota,
479 N.W.2d 387 (Minn. 1992)

SIMONETT, J.

This case comes to us on remand from the United States Supreme Court. We previously held that plaintiff's verdict of $200,000 could not be sustained on a theory of breach of contract. On remand, we now conclude the verdict is sustainable on the theory of promissory estoppel and affirm the jury's award of damages. . . .

Under promissory estoppel, a promise which is expected to induce definite action by the promisee, and does induce the action, is binding if injustice can be avoided only by enforcing the promise. *Cohen I*, 457 N.W.2d at 204; Restatement (Second) of Contracts §90(1) (1981). First of all, the promise must be clear and definite. As a matter of law, such a promise was given here. *Cohen I*, 457 N.W.2d at 204 ("[W]e have, without dispute, the reporters' unambiguous promise to treat Cohen as an anonymous source."). Secondly, the promisor must have intended to induce reliance on the part of the promisee, and such reliance must have occurred to the promisee's detriment. Here again, these facts appear as a matter of law. In reliance on the promise of anonymity, Cohen turned over the court records and, when the promises to keep his name confidential were broken, he lost his job. Id.

This leads to the third step in a promissory estoppel analysis: Must the promise be enforced to prevent an injustice? As the Wisconsin Supreme Court has held, this is a legal question for the court, as it involves a policy decision. Hoffman v. Red Owl Stores, Inc., 26 Wis. 2d 683, 698, 133 N.W.2d 267, 275 (1965). . . .

It is perhaps worth noting that the test is not whether the promise should be enforced to do justice, but whether enforcement is required to prevent an injustice. As has been observed elsewhere, it is easier to recognize an unjust result than a just one, particularly in a morally ambiguous situation. Cf. Edmond Cahn, The Sense of Injustice (1964). The newspapers argue it is unjust to be penalized for publishing the whole truth, but it is not clear this would result in an injustice in this case. For example, it would seem veiling Cohen's identity by publishing the source as someone close to the opposing gubernatorial ticket would have sufficed as a sufficient reporting of the "whole truth."

Cohen, on the other hand, argues that it would be unjust for the law to countenance, at least in this instance, the breaking of a promise. We agree that denying Cohen any recourse would be unjust. What is significant in this case is that the record shows the defendant newspapers themselves believed that they generally must keep promises of confidentiality given a news source. The reporters who actually gave the promises adamantly testified that their promises should have been honored. The editors who countermanded the promises conceded that never before or since have they reneged on a promise of confidentiality. A former Minneapolis Star managing editor testified that the newspapers had "hung Mr. Cohen out to dry because they didn't regard him very highly as a source." The Pioneer Press Dispatch editor stated nothing like this had happened in her 27 years in journalism. The Star Tribune's editor testified that protection of sources was "extremely important." Other experts, too, stressed the ethical importance, except on rare occasions, of keeping promises of confidentiality. It was this long-standing journalistic tradition that Cohen, who has worked in journalism, relied upon in asking for and receiving a promise of anonymity.

Neither side in this case clearly holds the higher moral ground, but in view of the defendants' concurrence in the importance of honoring promises of confidentiality, and absent the showing of any compelling need in this case to break that promise, we conclude that the resultant harm to Cohen requires a remedy here to avoid an injustice. In short, defendants are liable in damages to plaintiff for their broken promise.

This leaves, then, the issue of damages. For promissory estoppel, "[t]he remedy granted for breach may be limited as justice requires." Restatement (Second) of Contracts §90(1) (1981). See generally Midamar Corp. v. National-Ben Franklin Ins. Co., 898 F.2d 1333, 1338-39 (8th Cir. 1990); Hoffman v. Red Owl Stores, Inc., 26 Wis. 2d at 701, 133 N.W.2d at 276. In this case the jury was instructed:

> A party is entitled to recover for a breach of contract only those damages which: (a) arise directly and naturally in the usual course of things from the breach itself; or (b) are the consequences of special circumstances known to or reasonably supposed to have been contemplated by the parties when the contract was made.

This instruction, we think, provided an appropriate damages remedy for the defendants' broken promise, whether considered under a breach of contract or a promissory estoppel theory. There was evidence to support the jury's award of $200,000, and we see no reason to remand this case for a new trial on damages alone.

Our prior reversal of the verdict having been vacated, we now affirm the court of appeals' decision, but on promissory estoppel grounds. We affirm, therefore, plaintiff's verdict and judgment for $200,000 compensatory damages.

Affirmed on remand on different grounds.

REFERENCE: Murray, §67(B)

Empirical Background: The Elements of Promissory Estoppel

STUDY GUIDE: Professor Hillman's study is based on a survey of all the reported decisions in the United States in which a promissory estoppel claim succeeded or failed or in which promissory estoppel was discussed from July 1, 1994, through June 30, 1996. His mission was to establish the crucial role played by reliance in maintaining promissory estoppel claims. But his data also reveal the importance of establishing the existence of a promise.

ROBERT A. HILLMAN, QUESTIONING THE "NEW CONSENSUS" ON PROMISSORY ESTOPPEL: AN EMPIRICAL AND THEORETICAL STUDY, 98 COLUM. L. REV. 580, 583, 597-601 (1998): The data strongly demonstrate the crucial role reliance plays in courts' decisions either to deny or affirm a promissory estoppel claim at a preliminary motion or final judgment stage of a litigation. Moreover, the importance of reliance is consistent across variations in subject matter, the size and nature of the litigants, and the court rendering the judgment. . . .

1. *Reliance as a reason for success.* — [The data, which include all the successful promissory estoppel cases, on the merits or otherwise, show] the high rate of courts discussing reliance as a reason for success on the merits (93.10%) and for surviving an opposing motion (56.14%). Moreover, a discussion of reliance as a reason means that the court did more than merely state in one sentence or so that reliance is an element of promissory estoppel. A discussion means that the court specifically looked for and found reliance in the facts of the case. . . .

TABLE 5.1:
**Reasons for Failure of Promissory Estoppel
Claims Cases Decided on the Merits**

There was no definite promise	129
The promise was ambiguous	28
It would be unjust to enforce the promise	8
Reliance was not reasonable	86
There was no detrimental reliance	76
Reliance was unforeseeable	15
Reliance was too speculative	6
Reliance was not induced by the other party	23
The statute of frauds barred recovery	32
The parol evidence rule made evidence of a promise inadmissible	8
Another reason discussed for the failure of the claim	73
Reason for failure of claim unclear	5

2. *Reasons for failure.* — Table 5.1, which includes all the unsuccessful promissory estoppel cases on the merits, shows the reasons courts gave for the failure of a promissory estoppel claim. Percentages are omitted because courts often gave multiple reasons. The Table demonstrates that courts reject promissory estoppel claims on a wide variety of grounds and do not focus exclusively, or even in a clear preponderance of cases, on questions involving the promise. Although courts most often discuss the lack of a definite promise as a reason for failure, this justification does not mean that it is the only important factor even in those cases. Because each element of promissory estoppel is a prerequisite for recovery, it would not be unusual or telling that some courts that reject promissory estoppel claims never get to the issue of reliance, or to the issue of promise for that matter.

Table 5.2 groups the reliance-related reasons for failure of a promissory estoppel claim (no detrimental reliance, reliance was not reasonable, reliance was unforeseeable, reliance was too speculative, or reliance was not induced by the other party) and labels them "defects in reliance." The Table shows that in cases where promissory estoppel failed on the merits, one or more reasons relating to a defect in reliance were discussed in more than half the cases (151 cases or 55.93%). In fact, in 68 of the 151 cases, the court failed to discuss any promise-related reason (no definite promise, promise was ambiguous, or unjust to enforce the promise). . . .[39] Overall, the picture that emerges is that neither promise nor reliance dominates as a judicial reason for the failure of promissory estoppel claims. Rather, both elements are crucial to recovery.

TABLE 5.2:
**A Defect in Reliance as a Reason for Failure
of Promissory Estoppel Claims — Cases Decided on the Merits**

	N	*(%)*	*Total*
Defect in reliance discussed	*151*	*(55.93)*	*270*
Defect in reliance discussed and defect in promise not discussed [40]	*68*	*(25.19)*	*270*

[R]elevant to the question of the role of reliance in promissory estoppel cases, is the relatively high number of claims that fail in the business context at least in part because of a defect in reliance, namely about 48% (54 out of 113 cases). The figures were roughly comparable, but not quite as high, for reasons constituting a defect in the promise. These figures cast doubt on Farber and Matheson's thesis that courts are inclined to enforce promises "made in furtherance of an economic activity."[41] If courts were generally enforcing such promises without more, one would expect to see cases failing in the business context (by definition "economic activity") predominantly because of a defect in the promise. The result here should not be surprising if both promise and reliance are prerequisites for recovery on promissory estoppel grounds. Courts simply focused on one or the other element, found it wanting, and terminated the case.

STUDY GUIDE: In his study, Professor DeLong surveyed the 800 cases involving claims of promissory estoppel that were reported in 1995 and 1996. (Though it appeared first, this study was published too late to be discussed in Professor Hillman's article.) Like Hillman, he found that it was rare for promissory estoppel to be successfully asserted in commercial cases and that "courts rigorously enforce Section 90's requirement that the

---

39. One or more reasons constituting a defect in the promise were discussed in half of the cases (135 cases). The court failed to discuss a defect in reliance in only 52 of these cases.

40. [Professor Hillman does not report the category of "defects in promise discussed and defect in reliance not discussed." — EDS.]

41. [Daniel A. Farber & John H. Matheson, Beyond Promissory Estoppel: Contract Law and the "Invisible Handshake," 52 U. Chi. L. Rev. 903, 905 (1985) — EDS.]

*promise induce actual reliance (p. 948)." These strongly confirmatory
data are omitted from this excerpt. DeLong goes a further step by distinguishing between two types of reliance — performance reliance and
enforcement reliance. In a majority of the cases, he concludes from his
data, only if enforcement reliance is found to exist will courts recognize a
claim of promissory estoppel — and the difference between the two is
linked to the nature of the promise made by the promisor. Notice also
how this thesis dovetails with Hillman's findings on employment cases.*

SIDNEY W. DELONG, THE NEW REQUIREMENT OF
ENFORCEMENT RELIANCE IN COMMERCIAL PROMISSORY
ESTOPPEL: SECTION 90 AS CATCH-22, 1997 WIS. L. REV. 943, 953,
1003-1008, 1009-1014, 1021:   Two types of reliance are possible within
a legal system that differentiates between enforceable and unenforceable
promises. When a promisor makes a promise that the promisee recognizes
to be unenforceable, the promise can induce only "performance reliance."
The promisee relies solely on her estimate of the likelihood that the promisor will perform, without any expectation of a legal remedy if the reliance is
disappointed. The promisee decides whether and how much to rely by
assessing the promisor's honesty and reliability, the circumstances bearing
on the probability of performance and breach, the benefits that reliance
followed by performance would confer, and the costs that disappointed
reliance would impose. These factors determine the expected value of reliance on the promise.

    If, however, the promisor makes a promise that the promisee recog-
nizes to be legally enforceable, then the promise will induce what I will refer
to as "enforcement reliance." The promisee relies both on the credibility of
the promise and on the belief that she will have a legal remedy for some or
all of the costs of disappointed reliance if the promise is not performed. . . .

    It now seems apparent that legal doctrine in the courts is evolving in
sympathetic response to the aversion of commercial actors toward the risk
of estoppel liability. Many of the opinions reported in 1995 and 1996 lend
support to the thesis that, in order to prevail on a promissory estoppel
claim, a commercial promisee must now demonstrate not only that her
reliance was reasonable in light of the likelihood that the promisor
would perform, but also that she had a reasonable belief that the promise
was legally enforceable when made. Excluding those promises that are
already enforceable under bargain contract theory, this requires that the
promisor manifest an affirmative intention that the promise be enforceable
at the time of the promise. . . . [T]he ensuing reliance is reasonable because
the promise is enforceable, not vice versa.

    Although the promisor's manifestation of intention to be bound is
critical to these cases, the court's focus is usually on the promisee's actual
or presumed understanding of that manifestation. Enforcement is denied if
the court finds that the promisee was or should have been aware that the
promise was not intended to create an enforceable obligation. In the
following three situation-types, the promisee's actual or presumed legal
awareness proves fatal to her ability to enforce a reliance-inducing
commercial promise.

A. ENFORCEMENT RELIANCE PREVENTED BY THE PRESUMPTION OF AT-WILL EMPLOYMENT IN EMPLOYEE CLAIMS OF WRONGFUL TERMINATION

One of the most well-established examples of the requirement of enforcement reliance is in the refusal to apply promissory estoppel to enforce equivocal promises of non-terminable employment made by employers to employees. Over half of all the cases in the sample involved claims of wrongful termination from employment. These employees contended that they were not at-will employees and that their termination violated either an oral promise of permanent employment or a promised discharge procedure. Almost all of these claims failed, usually on a motion for summary judgment. The primary reason for the lack of success is that courts require such employees to demonstrate not that they reasonably relied on the likelihood that the employer would perform its promise, but instead that they had reasonable grounds to believe that the promises constituted a legally enforceable modification of their at-will status. This requirement often took the form of a demand that the employee prove a sufficiently "clear and definite," or "unambiguous," promise of permanent employment to alter their presumptive at-will status.

It may be instructive to sample the sorts of statements that courts have found to be inadequate to this task. . . . Employees have been held to have had no right to rely on language such as the following as a promise of permanent employment: "Don't worry about being fired"; "You will be here until you retire"; "I have no intention of firing you"; "You will not have to be concerned about job security because you have a job here as long as you want or until you retire"; "You will have continued and secure employment"; "You will have a job until you retire; we'll have you for the next twelve years"; "Your position will never be taken away and you can have it as long as you want it"; "You have full-time, permanent employment"; "I don't see a problem with you working until you are sixty-five"; "You will retire from this company"; "You will be the first person to work here for fifty years"; "You will never have to worry about your job"; "Should I look for another job?" "No, your job is secure"; "The only person that can eliminate you is yourself, you have a permanent job."

Such assurances instill employee loyalty and commitment to the job. . . . And just as obviously, the courts refuse to enforce these promises, reiterating with monotonous regularity that reliance on such employer assurances is "unreasonable" and "unforeseeable" in view of the prevailing at-will employment assumptions. In other words, employers give oral assurances seeking to induce reliance, employees predictably rely, and courts dutifully hold the reliance to be unforeseeable.

If the courts in these decisions were referring to performance reliance — the employee's reliance on a belief that the employer would do what he said he would do — then their conclusions would seem insupportable. Even though a strong presumption favors employment at-will in most jurisdictions, it is difficult to maintain, as the opinions do, that these statements are not "clear and definite" or "unambiguous." Expressions that are far less explicit than these statements have been held sufficient to create bargain contracts under the objective theory of contract formation.

Nor is it plausible that all of these employers were merely making general policy noises or speculations about the employees' future rather than promises. In some cases, no doubt, the employers were simply giving reassurances designed to make the employees feel appreciated and secure. These statements may not have been intended to induce any specific reliance. In other cases, however, the employers both intended, and were accurately understood, to be making a commitment to their employees, who were expected to rely upon it. If this seems unpersuasive, return to that litany of assurances and try the effect of inserting such statements as "remember that your employment is at-will and I can fire you at any time" or "don't rely on anything I am telling you." The resulting dissonance shows that these qualifications are wholly inconsistent with the assurances given. Yet the opinions cited hold that employees should have heard these unspoken qualifications when the assurances were given.

Finally, it is particularly unpersuasive to hold that reliance in such cases is literally unforeseeable. And if the courts were speaking of pure performance reliance, then their opinions seem incorrect. But it is not the performance reliance that the courts are finding to be unforeseeable: it is the reliance on having a legal claim or remedy that is deemed unreasonable and unforeseeable in light of the circumstances of the statements. . . . [C]ourts are, in effect, permitting employers to say "I unenforceably-promise not to terminate you." The inference is that such non-binding commitments have some value in the workplace that would be lost if employers could make no commitment at all, which might result if all such promises were legally enforceable. The employment cases thus imply that Section 90 is being interpreted to protect only enforcement reliance, leaving non-legal sanctions to protect performance reliance.

B. ENFORCEMENT RELIANCE PREVENTED BY DISCLAIMERS OF PROMISSORY LIABILITY

While a strong judicial presumption of unenforceability can prevent enforcement reliance, a more direct way to affect the promisee's awareness of non-enforceability is for the promisor to make an explicit disclaimer of liability for any oral promises he may make, either at the time of the disclaimer or afterward. An explicit disclaimer of liability has become the conventional defense to Section 90 liability for institutional promisors, "repeat players" such as employers, franchisors, lending institutions, and buyers and sellers of businesses. Most courts have given full effect to such disclaimers, whether they precede or follow the promise. These holdings are premised on an assumption of full and continuous awareness by the promisee of the legal effect of the disclaimer. . . .

The decisions occasionally allude to the difference between enforcement reliance and performance reliance. In Rennick v. O.P.T.I.O.N. Care, Inc., the plaintiffs failed to establish a Section 90 claim of a promise to issue a franchise because the letter of intent on which the claim was based specifically stated that it did not create a binding obligation. The plaintiffs argued that they had relied on oral promises preceding the letter and on the defendant's handshake as assurance that the franchise would be issued. The Ninth Circuit held that the reliance was unreasonable in light of the express language of the letter of intent:

> In light of the unequivocal nonbinding language in the letter of intent, reliance on the existence of a contract was unreasonable as a matter of law. The July 3 meeting and the letter of intent might have made [the plaintiffs'] actions prudent as a matter of business judgment, in contemplation of a probable contract, but they could not control whether the reliance would be reasonable for purposes of binding O.P.T.I.O.N. to a contract to which it expressly had as yet refused to agree [sic].[42]

The performance reliance may have been "prudent as a matter of business judgment" even though the statements and the handshake did not create grounds for enforcement reliance. The court seems to acknowledge that there is a place for performance reliance upon the unenforceable commercial promise or assurance.

In employment law, the employee handbook has evolved from being a possible source of contractual rights to being a barrier to their assertion. Disclaimers in handbooks or separate documents signed by the employees are now widely used by employers to bar claims of non-terminable, or continued, employment. Though employees are rarely "experienced, successful businessmen represented by capable attorneys," these written at-will agreements and handbook disclaimers usually prevent employers' subsequent, oral promises of job security from giving rise to liability under Section 90. Once the disclaimer is made, the employer can make reliance-inducing, unenforceable promises.

C. ENFORCEMENT RELIANCE PREVENTED BY THE PROMISEE'S KNOWLEDGE OF LEGAL RULES CONCERNING ENFORCEABILITY

Even in cases in which the promisor does not expressly disclaim an intention to be legally bound, a promisee may be unreasonable in relying on its legal enforceability. Many courts will find enforcement reliance unforeseeable in the absence of an affirmative manifestation of intention to be legally bound, even when the promisor deliberately induces reliance. For example, in Rhode Island Hospital Trust National Bank v. Varadian,[43] the counterclaimants in an action on a promissory note claimed the plaintiff bank breached an oral contract to lend an additional $43.5 million for a construction project. In answer to special interrogatories, the jury found that (1) the counterclaimants knew the bank intended to be bound only by an agreement in writing for the construction loan, but also (2) the bank did make the oral loan promise intending to induce reliance by the counterclaimants, and (3) they reasonably relied on the promise by executing the

---

42. [77 F.3d 309, 317 (9th Cir.), *cert. denied* 117 S. Ct. 174 (1996).]
43. 647 N.E.2d 1174 (Mass. 1995)

note and guarantee on which the bank had sued. Following a jury verdict in the counterclaimants' favor, the trial court entered judgment against the counterclaimants on their contract claim but in their favor on their promissory estoppel claim.

The Supreme Judicial Court of Massachusetts reversed the promissory estoppel judgment on the grounds that, given the finding that the counterclaimants understood the bank's intention not to be legally bound, they could not have understood the bank's statement to have been a "promise," in the sense of a commitment.[44] It also concluded that any reliance by the counterclaimants, experienced businessmen, on such a non-contractual "promise" would be unreasonable and unforeseeable as a matter of law.

If one interprets Section 90 to protect what I have called performance reliance, then the court begged the essential question. Given findings 2 and 3 (intent to induce reliance and actual reliance), it follows that the jury was wrong as a matter of law in finding 1 (no intent to be legally bound). If all parties were aware of Section 90 at the time of the oral promise, then the promisor's intention to be legally bound under the doctrine of promissory estoppel was manifested by its intentional inducement of the promisees' reliance. *Varadian*, however, rests on the principle that Section 90 cannot establish contract liability unless the promisor manifests an intention to be legally bound by some means other than by intentionally making a reliance-inducing promise.

Varadian contradicts the traditional, performance reliance protection version of Section 90. The text of Section 90 does not require that the promisor manifest an intention to be legally bound; the only intention that Section 90 seems to require of the promisor is the intention that the promise induce the promisee to rely on the promise. Yet the jury in *Varadian* found that the promisor had this intention and that the promisee did so rely. The *Varadian* court, however, defined "promise" for Section 90 purposes as a statement that both parties reasonably understand as a commitment to be legally bound, a narrower definition than that contained in the Restatement. *Varadian* suggests that Section 90 enforcement will be limited to those cases in which the promisor expressly states an intention to be legally bound by the promise.

The promisees in *Varadian* had reason to believe that the bank did not intend to make a legally binding commitment based on their dealings with the bank. Some courts find the "fatal knowledge" that bars enforcement reliance in the commercial promisee's general familiarity with business practice of formalizing serious agreements. A commercial promisor's failure to formalize even a serious, reliance-inducing promise may defeat the promisee's effort to establish enforcement reliance. . . .

Enforcement reliance becomes especially difficult to demonstrate in cases involving promisees who are attorneys and others who are aware of the rules of formal contract formation. Several courts in the sample held that even expressly requested reliance was legally unforeseeable if the promisee's education or experience made her aware that the accompanying promise was otherwise unenforceable as a bargain contract. . . .

---

44. Id. at 1179. Relying on earlier precedent, the court explained, "[a] promise made with an understood intention that it is not to be legally binding, but only expressive of a present intention, is not a contract." Id. . . .

The trend toward enforcement reliance is not universal. Some courts have enforced promises under Section 90 that legally aware promisees would have known were unenforceable under contract law principles. For example, courts have enforced promises under Section 90 in situations in which the original contract was unenforceable because of failure to agree on essential terms. . . .

CONCLUSION: THE TINY FUTURE
OF PROMISSORY ESTOPPEL

Promissory estoppel has not even unsettled "classical" bargain contract theory, much less led to its death. Instead, in the more general struggle between contract and tort law, formal contract is proving to be the more robust competitor. Sophisticated commercial promisors — employers, banks, franchisors, insurers, and other businesspeople — have learned how to avoid the risk of Section 90 liability. Having invoked the disclaimer shield, they become free to induce performance reliance by making unenforceable promises. Essential to their success has been a growing judicial consensus that Section 90 liability, unlike tort liability, must be deliberately incurred; that the promisor must not only make a promise but must also manifest an intention to be legally bound by the promise; that the promisee must not only have a reasonable expectation of performance but must also have an expectation of legal enforceability arising from some source outside Section 90 before her reliance will be protected under Section 90; and that it is not unjust to deny enforcement to a commercial promisee who relied without a reasonable expectation of a legal remedy for breach.

D.   A HYPOTHETICAL ALTERNATIVE
TO RESTATEMENT §90

In the final paragraph of his article, Professor DeLong observes:

> In the "heaven of legal concepts," commercial actors would not simply "promise": they would "enforceably-promise" or "unenforceably-promise," . . . promisees would rely accordingly, and contract law could be taught in one semester. In the absence of new verb-forms, it would seem that the courts are imposing a default rule of interpretation favoring "unenforceably-promise" on claims arising under Section 90. That approach has the merit of according with what appears to be the most common intention of commercial promisors. If courts were to adopt expressly the rule that commercial promises must be accompanied by a statement of intention to be bound in order to be enforceable under Section 90, they could more candidly acknowledge the existence of performance reliance. They could stop referring to promisee performance reliance as unreasonable or unforeseeable — it is neither — and could say more accurately that it is no justification for legal enforcement.[45]

---

45. Sidney W. DeLong, The New Requirement of Enforcement Reliance in Commercial Promissory Estoppel: Section 90 as Catch-22, 1997 Wis. L. Rev. 943, 1022.

Given the empirical information he and Professor Hillman provide, perhaps it is time to improve on the alternative to bargained-for consideration provided by Restatement (Second) of Contracts §90. At the end of the excerpt from The Death of Contract that appears in Section B of this chapter, Professor Gilmore refers to reforming the contract law in a "third round of Restatements." In that spirit, consider the following *purely hypothetical* replacement for §90.

STUDY GUIDE: How would the cases in Chapters 10 and 11 be decided under this proposal? How does its explanatory power compare with Gilmore's "tort" conception of contract? Does this section offer any advantages over the present §90? If adopted, do you see it creating any disadvantage? Would §21 (p. 648) have to be changed as well? How would this proposal work with the existing provisions from the Restatement (Second) of Torts that appears on page 740? Do the torts sections need to be revised in any way to handle the cases not well handled by the proposal?

RESTATEMENT (THIRD) OF CONTRACTS

§90.   ENFORCEABILITY OF NONBARGAIN PROMISES

In the absence of consideration as defined in §71, a promise is binding if

(1) the promise is accompanied by a formality that manifests an intention to be legally bound, such as:

(a) a seal, or

(b) the recital of a nominal consideration, or

(c) an expression of intention to be legally bound, or

(d) copies of a writing bearing the signatures of both parties; or

(2) with the knowledge of the promisor, the promise induces reliance by the promisee

(a) that is so substantial that would be unlikely in the absence of a manifested intention by the promisor to be legally bound, and

(b) the promisee expects the promise to be enforceable and is aware that the promisor has knowledge of the promisee's reliance, and

(c) the promisor remains silent concerning the promisee's reliance.

PERFORMANCE AND BREACH

12

PERFORMANCE

We have now concluded our study of the elements of an enforceable commitment. In Part II, we studied the element of mutual assent; in Part III we examined the element of enforceability. We now turn our attention to the matter of performance and breach. In this chapter, we discuss the performance phase of the contract. In Section A, we begin by considering the implied duty to perform one's commitment in good faith. In Section B, we consider implied warranties of merchantability and fitness for a particular use, as well as ways of contracting around such warranties. Having examined the duty of performance, in Chapter 14, we shall discuss different types of breach.

A. THE IMPLIED DUTY OF GOOD FAITH PERFORMANCE

In prior chapters we have run across the concept of *good faith performance.* For example, when discussing the alleged illusory nature of requirements contracts, we discussed the court's view that the quantity demanded must have been incurred in good faith. This concept was also implicated by Judge Cardozo's implying a duty to use best efforts in the case of Wood v. Lucy, Lady Duff-Gordon. Our previous consideration was confined to whether such a duty could fairly be implied when the parties are silent. In this section we examine what the duty of good faith performance *means* and how it may be breached.

The notion that all contracts contain an implied covenant to perform in good faith is commonly traced to the New York Court of Appeals opinion in Kirke La Shelle Co. v. Paul Armstrong Co., 263 N.Y. 79, 188 N.E. 163 (1933), in which it was stated that "in every contract there is an implied covenant that neither party shall do anything which will have the effect of destroying or injuring the right of the other party to receive the fruits of the contract, which means that in every contract there exists an implied covenant of good faith and fair dealing." Id. at 167. This principle was applied to the sale of goods by the Uniform Commercial Code §1-203:

> Every contract or duty within this Act imposes an obligation of good faith in its performance or enforcement.

Subsequently, it achieved an even wider application through its incorporation in the Restatement (Second) §205 which reads: *"Every contract* imposes upon each party a duty of good faith and fair dealing in its performance and its enforcement." (Emphasis added.)

What does the obligation of good faith performance entail? The U.C.C. offers the following less than entirely helpful definition in §1-201(19): " 'Good faith' means honesty in fact in the conduct or transaction concerned." And §2-103(1)(b) reads: " 'Good faith' *in the case of a merchant* means honesty in fact *and* the observance of reasonable commercial standards of fair dealing in the trade." (Emphasis added.) Comment a to Restatement §205 reads, in part:

> The phrase "good faith" is used in a variety of contexts, and its meaning varies somewhat with the context. Good faith performance or enforcement of a contract emphasizes faithfulness to an agreed common purpose and consistency with the justified expectations of the other party; it excludes a variety of types of conduct characterized as involving "bad faith" because they violate community standards of decency, fairness or reasonableness. The appropriate remedy for a breach of the duty of good faith also varies with the circumstances.

To gain a better grasp of what the duty of good faith performance requires in context, we shall confine our attention to a particular situation: commercial leases with "percentage of gross sales" rent clauses. You will read several cases in which the courts determine the requirement of this duty in different factual circumstances. You might then also look back to the cases in Chapter 5 (§A2) to see what the duty means in the context of requirements contracts and contracts for exclusive dealings.

When reading these cases ask yourself whether the duty of good faith performance represents a *restriction upon* or an *extension of* contractual freedom. When thinking about this last issue consider the following passage from U.C.C. §1-102(3) (emphasis added):

> The effect of provisions of this Act may be varied by agreement, except as otherwise provided in this Act and except that the *obligations of good faith*, diligence, reasonableness and care prescribed by this Act *may not be disclaimed by agreement* but the parties may by agreement determine the standards by which the performance of such obligations is to be measured if such standards are not manifestly unreasonable.

Should the implied duty of good faith be an immutable or a mandatory rule that is nondisclaimable (though subject to standards provided by the parties) as opposed to a default rule that can be varied by agreement? If so, does this necessarily represent a restriction on freedom of contract?

STUDY GUIDE: Can the results in the next three cases, each involving tenants, be reconciled? In the next case, what exactly did the tenant do that it was not supposed to do? Or is this the wrong question to ask? What do these cases reveal about the implied covenant of good faith? Is this duty implied-in-fact or implied-in-law? If the latter, is this a term that is being imposed *on the parties without their consent, or is it supplied by the court as a gap-filler that* facilitates *the parties' consent? In each of these cases ask yourself why the parties structured their leases the way they did.*

GOLDBERG 168-05 CORP. v. LEVY
Supreme Court of New York, Queens County,
170 Misc. 292, 9 N.Y.S.2d 304 (1938)

STEINBRINK, J.* This is a motion to dismiss the complaint for failure to state facts sufficient to constitute a cause of action.

Plaintiff sues to recover for the alleged breach of a leasehold agreement assigned to the plaintiff by the original lessor. As a first cause of action the following in substance is alleged: By agreement dated September 17, 1929, the plaintiff's assignor agreed to rent certain premises to the defendant Levy for a term expiring September 30, 1938; that the tenant was to pay a minimum rental of $13,800 per year and in addition thereto was to pay the difference between the said sum and ten percent of the gross receipts of the business conducted by the tenant on the leased premises; that it was further provided "in the event that the total gross sales of the Tenant for any one calendar year does not equal $101,000 . . . then the Tenant shall have the right to cancel said lease"; that the defendant Levy took possession of the premises under the said lease on October 10, 1929, and thereafter, with the knowledge and consent of the plaintiff's assignor, permitted the defendant Crawford Clothes, Inc., to occupy the premises "as though the same were occupied by" the defendant Levy, and to conduct therein a retail men's clothing business; that the defendant Levy, as officer, director, and chief stockholder of the defendant Crawford Clothes, Inc., operated and controlled the corporate defendant for his own use. It is then alleged that defendants, although obligated to do so,

> failed and refused to act in a fair and proper manner with relation to their obligations under the terms of the lease . . . by negligently or willfully permitting the said business to become mismanaged and by negligently or willfully diverting the proper channels of trade from said business to another store operated by said defendants, in the vicinity of the premises demised by said defendants from the plaintiff herein, and in general conducting themselves and their agents, servants, and employees in such a manner as to cause a reduction of the gross income of the sales of the demised premises below the amount of $101,000 per year;

that the defendant Levy, on June 1, 1937, gave notice of his intention to terminate the lease as of October 30, 1937, and on and after that day the defendants removed from the premises and refused to pay any further rentals. By reason of the foregoing plaintiff claimed to be damaged in the sum of $25,000.

It is not alleged in the complaint that the agreement sued upon contained an express provision obligating the tenant to refrain from conduct calculated to depress the annual gross receipts of the business below

---

Meier Steinbrink (1880-1967) received his legal training at New York University (LL.B.). Admitted to the New York state bar in 1901, he practiced in New York City (1901-1931), except while serving as special assistant to the Attorney General of the United States (1918, 1922). Steinbrink moved to the bench in 1932 upon his appointment to the Supreme Court of New York, serving later as official referee for several terms (1951-1956) and as special referee from 1957 until his death. — K.T.

the specified sum of $101,000. "A promise may be lacking, and yet the whole writing may be 'instinct with an obligation' imperfectly expressed." (Wood v. Duff-Gordon, 222 N.Y. 88, 91 [118 N.E. 214]; Alexander v. Equitable Life Assurance Society of United States, 233 N.Y. 300, 306 [135 N.E. 509].) It should be noted that the tenant promised to pay rental in part at least measured by a percentage of gross receipts of the business. This was a promise to use reasonable efforts to bring profits into existence. (Wood v. Duff-Gordon, supra.) The tenant could not avoid liability under the lease by abandoning premises. . . . By the same token he could not avoid liability by a diversion of business to another store which he operated in the same vicinity when such diversion is effected for the sole purpose of bringing the gross receipts below the specified figure and thereby laying the basis for a cancellation of the lease. Such conduct would be in direct violation of the covenant of good faith and fair dealing which exists in every contract. (Kirke La Shelle Co. v. [Paul] Armstrong Co., 263 N.Y. 79 [188 N.E. 163].) . . .

STUDY GUIDE: Do you agree with the majority that the tenant in the next case acted in good faith? Why do you suppose the majority thought that the behavior of this tenant differed from, for example, the tenant in the previous case? Is it simply the defendant's conduct in opening the fur department that is alleged to have been a breach of its duty of good faith, or is something else also needed to show such a breach? Should not the defendant be able to move around its departments as it sees fit? [For those who know Fifth Avenue, this building is now occupied by the women's clothing departments of Bergdorf-Goodman, though the street address has been changed to 754.]

MUTUAL LIFE INSURANCE CO. OF NEW YORK v. TAILORED WOMAN
Court of Appeals of New York, 309 N.Y. 248, 128 N.E.2d 401 (1955)

[The following statement of facts is taken from the Supreme Court opinion (123 N.Y.S.2d 349)]:

On or about June 29, 1939, plaintiff leased to the defendant the basement, first, second and third floors in the building known as No. 742 Fifth Avenue, in the Borough of Manhattan, for a term of ten years commencing October 1, 1939. (This lease will be referred to as the "main lease" and the premises thereby demised as the "main premises.") Paragraph 2 of the lease provides that the premises were to be used by the defendant for the sale, display, and/or the lawful manufacture of wearing apparel, accessories, jewelry and other items used, worn or carried by women and misses, and paragraph 37 provides that ". . . in conjunction therewith there may be other uses herein set forth and which will" (the store) "at all times contain a stock of first class merchandise and the business will be conducted and maintained in a manner substantially similar to the tenant's present store at 729 Fifth Avenue, New York City. . . ."

The lease (paragraph 30) also sets forth an undertaking on the part of the defendant to pay a fixed minimum annual rental and "in addition to said fixed and minimum rental, as additional rental a sum equal to 4 percent of the gross receipts for cash or credit, derived by the tenant . . . in excess of $1,200,000 in each year. . . ." "The term 'gross receipts' of said business, as used herein shall include all sales . . . and shall include all receipts and charges for goods, wares and merchandise sold on, in or from the demised premises. . . ."

Prior to October 1, 1939, the effective commencement date of this lease, defendant maintained a department for the sale of furs and sold furs in the premises then occupied by it at No. 729 Fifth Avenue and continued after the last-mentioned date to maintain a department for the sale of furs and sold furs in the premises occupied by it at 742 Fifth Avenue down to August 1, 1945.

On or about June 1, 1945, plaintiff leased to the defendant additional space on the fifth floor of the building at No. 742 Fifth Avenue for a term of one year and four months. This lease provided for a fixed rental but did not require the defendant to pay a percentage on sales effected on the fifth floor. (This lease will be referred to as the "fifth floor lease" and the premises as the "fifth floor premises.")

This lease also, as the main lease, authorized the defendant to use the demised premises for "the sale, display of all types of wearing apparel, accessories, worn or carried by women or misses and as workrooms." Paragraph 36 of the fifth floor lease provided that:

It is hereby understood and agreed that this lease will not have any effect on the lease dated June 29, 1939 between The Mutual Life Insurance Company of New York and The Tailored Woman, Inc., on the store, basement, second and third floor, in the building known as 742 Fifth Avenue. . . .

On August 1, 1945, and without notice to plaintiff, the defendant discontinued its fur department in the main premises and transferred and removed that department in toto to the fifth floor premises and has ever since there carried on all fur sales as well as sales of the other incidental merchandise which may be included in the category of furs.

DESMOND, J.* The facts of this controversy, and the issues, are set forth and discussed in the Appellate Division opinion. We will limit ourselves to a statement of our views on the principal questions of law.

Since plaintiff is suing for additional percentage rental under the 1939 ten-year lease of the lower three floors of 742 Fifth Avenue, New York City, it must base its claim on the covenants of that lease. Two only of those covenants are pertinent. We take them up in turn. The 4 percent percentage rental was to be paid on all sales made "on, in, and from the demised premises." After, by separate leases made in 1945, defendant had taken over from plaintiff part of the fifth floor (and the eighth floor, not involved

---

* *Charles S. Desmond* (1896-1987) studied at Canisius College (A.B., A.M.) and the University of Buffalo (LL.B.) and was admitted to the bar of New York in 1920. He practiced privately for 20 years in Buffalo before being appointed judge on the New York State Supreme Court in 1940. Within a year, he moved to the New York State Court of Appeals, serving from 1941 to 1966, and spending his last six years on that bench as Chief Judge (1960-1966). Desmond also served as a member of the law faculty at Cornell University and the State University of New York, and as lecturer at various law schools. — K.T.

here), defendant made it a practice to pay commissions, on fur sales made on the fifth floor, to salespeople on the lower floor who sent customers to the fifth-floor fur department. We think it not unreasonable to hold, with the Appellate Division, that such sales were, within the lease's intent, made "from" the main store and so subject to percentage rent. Such sales may be considered "main store" sales, as if a clerk in response to a telephone call took merchandise to a customer's home, and there effected a sale. It would be going too far, though, to hold that all fur sales were made "from" the lower store simply because, as hereinafter more fully explained, the fur department was moved up to the fifth floor after that floor had been "integrated" with the main store.

By the other language (of the 1939 percentage lease) which we find pertinent, the tenant promised that the store it would conduct in the lower three floors would "at all times contain a stock of first class merchandise" and would "be conducted and maintained in a manner substantially similar to the Tenant's present store at #729 Fifth Avenue" (that is, the store across the street from which defendant was moving). That verbiage is to be read with the purpose clause (of that same 1939 lease) which prescribed the sale of all kinds of women's apparel and accessories. Here, again, we agree with the Appellate Division that no more was intended than an agreement that there should be conducted, on the three lower floors of 742 Fifth Avenue, under the percentage lease, a woman's clothing shop of the same general character as defendant's store across the street. If plaintiff had desired further restrictions as to kinds of merchandise, etc., it should have insisted on them. Absent fraud or trickery (and the findings properly say there was none), defendant could carry on its business in the way that suited it so long as it did not deviate from those very broad and general lease specifications.

In 1945, defendant, needing more space, bought out a custom-made dress business which had been conducted in part of the fifth floor by another concern and made with plaintiff a new lease of that space at a flat no-percentage rent. Again, the lease terms went no further as to purpose than to state that the added space was to be used for the sale of female wearing apparel and accessories and for workrooms. The fifth floor custom-made dress department was not successful and was soon discontinued. Defendant then made such physical changes in the building that two elevators, which had theretofore served the first three floors from inside the main store, now could be, and were, used to carry passengers inside the store not only to and from the first three floors but to and from the fifth floor, also (and the eighth floor, although that is not important here). The result was that the first, second, third and fifth floors were, as the phrase goes, "integrated" into one store fronting on Fifth Avenue and served by elevators reached through the main store from the Fifth Avenue entrances. Formerly, the fifth floor could be reached by the use of two other elevators only, to which elevators entrance was from the side street lobby on the 57th Street side of the building. Then defendant moved its fur department to the fifth floor, and thereafter paid no percentage rent on fur sales.

Trial Term held that plaintiff did not acquiesce in these changes. The Appellate Division held that it did. The question of fact is a close one but, acquiescence or not, we think the undisputed facts forbade a recovery here by plaintiff of more than the percentage on certain fur sales, hereinbefore described as made on the fifth floor, but "from" the lower floors. There is nothing in the main lease to forbid the moving of the fur department and when plaintiff made the second, or fifth floor, lease, it again failed to include any restrictions as to particular kinds of merchandise to be sold in one or the other part of the building. It is clear enough that plaintiff did not contemplate, when it leased the fifth and eighth floors for a flat rental, that the fifth floor would be "integrated" with the lower floors into one store but such lack of foresight does not create rights or obligations. True, the second lease said that it would "not have any effect" on the earlier lease but the effect of the two leases, read together and enforcing both, was that defendant had the right to sell all kinds of women's apparel, etc., in any part of the four floors, so long as no other use was made of the premises. As we see it, defendant merely exercised that right when it moved the fur department. As to changing the elevator doors, if that were a violation of any implied covenants (certainly not of an express covenant) redress could be had by injunction or, perhaps, by the landlord putting the elevator doors back as they had been and charging the expense to the tenant. But such violations (if they were violations) could not result in a liability for additional rent not promised in the lease. Except as to the fur sales to customers sent upstairs, there were no additional sales "on, in or from" the premises covered by the percentage lease, even though certain activities with respect to furs continued to be carried on in the lower store.

In the view we take of the case, it is unnecessary to engage in interesting but unproductive computations or speculations as to whether or not the new "integrated" store actually produced more percentage rent for plaintiff than if the fur department and the elevators had not been changed. It is the fact, though, that plaintiff proved no loss in that respect.

In deciding this case as we do, we are not moving away from the good old rule that there is in every contract an implied covenant of fair dealing (Kirke La Shelle Co. v. [Paul] Armstrong Co., 263 N.Y. 79 [188 N.E. 163]). Defendant, as we see it, was merely exercising its rights. Nor do we reject such authorities as Cissna Loan Co. v. Baron (149 Wash. 386 [270 P. 1022]), which penalize unconscionable diversion of business from percentage-lease premises to others. The present case does not fit into that pattern.

The judgment should be affirmed, without costs.

BURKE, J.* (dissenting). The defendant is liable for additional percentage rental under the 1939 ten-year lease of the premises 742 Fifth Avenue, New York City, for sales of furs made on the fifth floor, as they were sales made on, in and from the main premises. . . .

The plaintiff alleges two causes of action. The first cause of action is based upon the theory that the fur sales were made "on, in or from" the main premises. All of the activities of the defendant from the initiation of the alterations to the actual sales were designed to hold out to the public that

---

Adrian P. Burke (1904-2000) was educated at Holy Cross College (A.B.) and Fordham University (LL.B.) and practiced law in New York City. He worked in the district attorney's office (1941-1953) and as City Counsel for the City of New York in 1954, when he was elected judge on the Court of Appeals in New York. He retired from the bench in 1974. — K.T.

the fur department was part of the premises 742 Fifth Avenue. The physical layout, the advertising, the window displays, the storage of the furs, and the use of the main store personnel characterized the fur department as an integral part of the main store operations. The second cause of action seeks damages upon the theory that if fur sales were not made "on, in or from" the main premises, nevertheless, the defendant, in removing the fur department from the main premises, violated express and implied covenants of the main lease against diversion of sales. It is implicit in every percentage rental agreement that the tenant has an obligation to conduct its business with regard for the landlord's interest in the tenant's gross receipts. "A promise may be lacking, and yet the whole writing may be 'instinct with an obligation,' imperfectly expressed." (Wood v. Duff-Gordon, 222 N.Y. 88, 91 [118 N.E. 214]. . . .) Unless a percentage rental agreement is so interpreted, the percentage requirement would have no meaning.

The question to be resolved is whether under the terms of the leases and the proof adduced at the trial, the plaintiff is entitled to recover on one or both causes of action. Both causes of action are well founded.

There is no doubt that the sales were made "on, in or from" the main premises. The evidence shows that the furs were delivered to the basement of the main store, prepared for display there, stored in the basement of the main store, packed and shipped out from the main store premises. The entire fur business was administered and conducted in the Fifth Avenue premises, yet the defendant would have us construe the leases so as to permit it to operate a fur department as part of a main store in a space with an address different from the address set forth in the lease of that space, doing a business with average annual gross receipts of over $600,000, for a fixed rental of $3,800 a year free from the percentage provisions of the main store lease. The leases fail to disclose such an authorization. The 742 Fifth Avenue lease limited the exclusive use of the entrances and elevators to three floors and basement. The 1 West 57th Street lease prohibited alterations without consent, and also prohibited any interference with the premises 742 Fifth Avenue.

We can perceive no distinction between the customer who was sent to the fifth floor fur department by salespeople on the lower floors, and the customers who responded to the advertisements or displays that proclaimed that the defendant's fur department was located at 742 Fifth Avenue. All these customers were patrons of the Fifth Avenue Tailored Woman store, and were attracted to that store by the advertisements and window displays using the Fifth Avenue address. Therefore, it necessarily follows that the terms of the lease of 742 Fifth Avenue must apply to all transactions taking place at that address.

Moreover in every contract there is an implied covenant that neither party shall do anything which shall have the effect of injuring or destroying the right of the other party to receive the fruits of the contract. (Kirke La Shelle Co. v. [Paul] Armstrong Co., 263 N.Y. 79 [188 N.E. 163].) The defendant cannot make a virtue of a violation of the lease. It made alterations without the written consent of the landlord of 1 West 57th Street. It violated the prohibition in paragraph 36 of the 1945 lease that the said lease was not to have any effect on the lease dated June 29, 1939, between the Mutual Life Insurance Co. of New York and the Tailored Woman, Inc. (1) by moving its fur department to the fifth-floor space from a lower floor, and (2) by advertising that the fifth-floor space described in the lease as space in the building known as 1 West 57th Street was located at 742 Fifth Avenue. The consequence of these violations was to bring about the condition wherein the defendant was using a Fifth Avenue address and sales space for the sale of furs at a rental rate of a side-street office salesroom.

Furthermore, under the terms of the 742 Fifth Avenue lease, the defendant agreed to maintain a business substantially similar to that which it had maintained at 729 Fifth Avenue, where the defendant had a fur department. As a result of the removal of the fur department to the fifth floor, the plaintiff was deprived of a substantial portion of the fruits of the contract. By excluding the fur sales from the calculations required by the percentage terms of the lease, the defendant excluded almost 20 percent of the average gross receipts collected at the premises 742 Fifth Avenue. Such an act constitutes an unreasonable diversion of business from a percentage leased premises to a fixed rental premises.

The intent of the parties as expressed in the two leases was that the fifth-floor space at 1 West 57th Street would be operated independently of the main premises. For example, the landlord by lease restricted the use of the elevators in 1 West 57th Street by providing that they would operate only until 1:00 P.M. on Saturdays and 6:00 P.M. on business days, whereas the elevators in 742 Fifth Avenue were within the absolute control of the defendant and could operate until 6:00 P.M. or later on Saturdays, business days and legal holidays only to the third floor.

The rent fixed for the fifth-floor space reflects the restrictions imposed on doing business in an off-street office salesroom space which is not serviced on Saturday afternoons or on legal holidays. Such restrictions are not incompatible with the use permitted by the 1 West 57th Street lease, i.e., the sale and display of women's wearing apparel. Such uses are commonly so restricted. In this very case the former tenant on the fifth floor was engaged in the women's wearing apparel business. The limitation of the use of the elevators to five and one-half days as well as the necessity of sharing the use of the elevators with the other tenants in 1 West 57th Street make it clear that any permitted diversion of business from the main store was intended to be confined to a five and one-half day operation with all the inconvenience of sharing public elevators. Naturally these conditions in themselves forbid the transfer of a major department from the main store to the off-street office salesroom.

Since the defendant, in order to avoid the restrictions of the 1 West 57th Street lease, elected, in violation of the provisions of the leases, to operate part of the fifth floor as an integral part of the main premises and to make fur sales on, in and from the main premises, it has subjected the gross receipts collected from these operations to the percentage rental terms of the main store lease. Such a conclusion is supported by the evidence, by a commonsense interpretation of the leases, and by the prevailing law in other jurisdictions. . . .

The judgment of the Appellate Division should be reversed and the judgment of the Trial Term reinstated. . . .

Judgment affirmed.

STUDY GUIDE: In what sense did Stop & Shop act in good faith? Or is the point of this case that it did not act in bad faith? Once again, what does this mean? Is not the closing of a store entirely a more serious action than that of shifting departments from one floor to another? Why then does the court refuse to find a lack of good faith? What does the court mean by "business judgment"? How is it relevant to the duty of good faith performance? Why does it matter whether or not the fixed rent is significantly below the fair rental value of the property?

What is the scope of performance?

What constitutes good performance?

STOP & SHOP, INC. v. GANEM

Supreme Judicial Court of Massachusetts,
347 Mass. 697, 200 N.E.2d 248 (1964)

WHITTEMORE, J.* The defendants in this bill for declaratory relief are lessors under a percentage lease. They have appealed from the final decree in the Superior Court that ruled that the lease does not expressly or impliedly require the plaintiff, as lessee, to use the demised premises for any particular purpose or to keep the premises open and there engage in the supermarket business. Except for brief testimony which is reported, the facts were stipulated. . . .

The lease, dated August 24, 1953, demised a lot and building at 154 Merrimack Street, Haverhill, for thirteen years and six months from September 1, 1953, for "the minimum rental" of $22,000 a year and the further rent of 1 1/4 percent "of all gross sales" above $1,269,230.60 "made by the lessee on the leased premises during each twelve month period." But the percentage rent was to be paid only if sales at the demised premises and at premises in Lawrence exceeded $3,000,000 a year. The lease recites that the Lawrence premises were leased to the plaintiff by the lessors of the Haverhill premises and certain other owners under a percentage lease containing a like limitation on the payment of percentage rent. The record shows no other facts relative to the Lawrence premises or the business conducted therein. The other lessors of the Lawrence premises, by stipulation in, and order of, this court, have now become parties, and all parties have stipulated that the issues may be determined as though the owners of the Lawrence premises were not concerned. We may, therefore, order declaratory relief on the present record. . . .

The lease required that the lessee should pay the amount of the increases in the annual real estate taxes and should receive the amount of the decreases therein, measured on the 1946 figure.

The lease does not state the purposes for which the premises are to be used. Nothing therein in terms requires that the premises be used for any

---

Arthur Easterbrook Whittemore (1896-1969) was educated at Harvard University (A.B., LL.B.) and was admitted to the Massachusetts bar in 1922. He practiced law with a Boston law firm (1922-1955), during which time he also spent two years in the state attorney general's office (1942-1944), then joined the bench of the Supreme Judicial Court of Massachusetts in 1955, where he served until his death. Whittemore also served in the infantry of the U.S. Army (1917-1919). — K.T.

purpose or bars the opening by the lessee of places of business competitive to the lessee's business in the demised premises. The lease does, however, require the lessee to use suitable cash registers to record all sales, to keep accurate books, to furnish statements of gross sales on demand, and at the end of each yearly period to furnish such a statement certified by a certified public accountant. The testimony showed that when the lease was made the plaintiff was engaged in the supermarket business and that the lessors knew it. The premises prior to August 24, 1953, had been used for the conduct of a market.

The plaintiff had occupied the premises as a supermarket through 1962. It had paid percentage rent in 1956 ($2,288.15) and in 1957 ($377.21) but in no other year, and had paid excess taxes in each year. The plaintiff intended to cease operating a supermarket in the premises shortly after January 1, 1963, but to continue to pay the minimum rent and any excess real estate taxes and otherwise to conform to the lease. The defendant lessors had threatened suit to compel the continued operation of a supermarket or, alternatively, for damages.

The defendant lessors filed a counterclaim which alleged that the plaintiff beginning in 1956 had opened two competing stores in Haverhill, one within one-half mile and the other within about one mile of the demised premises. The prayers of the counterclaim were (1) that the lease be reformed to provide that the plaintiff continuously operate the premises as a supermarket, (2) that the plaintiff be ordered to pay to the defendants as part of the rent of the demised premises 1 1/4 percent of gross sales from all the plaintiff's stores in Haverhill in excess of $1,269,230.60, and (3) for general relief. An interlocutory decree sustained the plaintiff's demurrer to the counterclaim "with leave to amend denied." The lessors took no appeal from that decree.

Other facts are referred to later in the opinion.

1. The issue presented by the bill for declaratory relief is whether there is in the lease an implied covenant to continue operations. . . . The counterclaim presents the issue whether the lessee may open competing stores and then discontinue operations. We consider first the issue under the bill.

The controlling principles are well established. An omission to specify an agreement in a written lease is evidence that there was no such understanding. . . . Covenants will not be extended by implication unless the implication is clear and undoubted. . . . Justice, common sense and the probable intention of the parties are guides to construction of a written instrument. . . .

> Since the governing principle . . . is the justifiable assumption by one party of a certain intention on the part of the other, the undertaking of each promisor in a contract must include any promises which a reasonable person in the position of the promisee would be justified in understanding were included.

Williston, Contracts (rev. ed.) §1293, p. 3682. . . .

The plaintiff contends that notwithstanding the interest of the lessors in having the premises operated so as to give it the benefit of possible percentage rent, the absence of an express requirement to operate together with a more than nominal minimum rent exclude the implication of a covenant to continue operations.

This may state too broad a rule. For even if there is a more than nominal minimum rent, other circumstances such as that the fixed rent is significantly below the fair rental value of the property might justify the conclusion that the parties intended that the lessors have the benefit of the percentage rent throughout the term.

The record does not show the fair rental value of the demised premises. An apparently substantial minimum rent in an apparently complete written lease, in the absence of a showing of disparity between the fixed rent and the fair rental value, gives ground for the inference that fixed rent and the lessee's self-interest in producing sales were the only assurance of rent that the lessor required. . . . Other circumstances may give rise to the same inference. . . . In cases where the minimum rent was not substantial continued operation has been held contemplated. . . .

In Smiley v. McLauthlin, 138 Mass. 363, this court held that where rent under a lease of a brick yard was to be computed on the basis of bricks made with no provision for minimum rent, there was no implied covenant that the lessee would operate the yard. The opinion stressed the extrinsic circumstances attending the making of the lease. "The premises leased were not a brick yard in operation, equipped for work, but barren, unoccupied land. The parties did not know the amount of clay on the land, nor whether brick could be made on the land at a profit. . . . The lease, applied to the subject matter, furnishes indications that the parties regarded the enterprise as experimental, and that any stipulation binding the lessee to work the yard was purposely omitted." Id. [138 Mass.] at 365. The questions may be asked whether the parties did not intend a contract, and if so whether an implied covenant at least to try to operate the brick yard was the only consideration given by the lessee. Compare Wood v. Lucy, Lady Duff-Gordon, 222 N.Y. 88 [118 N.E. 214] . . .

The minimum rent in this lease appears to be substantial. The figure of $22,000 is obviously not nominal in a lease that fixes as a base real estate tax figure the 1946 tax of $3,744.90. The total of real estate taxes for 1954 was $5,127.71. This roughly indicates the valuation for tax purposes of the demised premises at about the time the lease was made.

The burden of showing a disparity between fixed rent and fair rental value such as to furnish ground for implying a covenant to operate would be on the lessors. . . .

There is in this record no basis for implying a covenant to continue to operate beyond that time when in the business judgment of the lessee operations at the demised location[1] should cease. The lessors have not shown that "a reasonable person in the position of the . . . [lessors] would be justified in understanding" (Williston, Contracts [rev. ed.] §1293) that such a covenant was intended and hence implied.

The percentage rent provision of course gave the lessors an interest in the lessee's operations of the demised premises as a retail store. We assume, without deciding, that such interest could be protected against certain acts

1. As to discontinuance in connection with opening another store adjacent, or nearly adjacent, to the demised premises, see point 2.

of the lessee, as for example, discontinuance of operations for spite or to inflict harm. Such issues are outside this record for there is no intimation that the plaintiff has acted or proposes to act in respect of the leased premises otherwise than as its sound business judgment dictates in fairly promoting its retail business in Haverhill. . . .

[2.] The lessee, being free to disregard the effect on the lessors of its business decisions in respect of stopping operations, was free also to open stores elsewhere. We assume, without deciding, that had the lessee opened a competing store in the same location as the demised premises, that is adjacent, or nearly so, there might have been a basis for requiring it to regard the lessors' interest under the percentage rent provision in its conduct of the two stores. In such a case the lessee's acts would affirm the business advantage of remaining at the very place at which it had committed itself as tenant of the lessors. . . . But, on the allegations, this is plainly not such a case. At most we may infer that there is some overlap of the potential customer area of the two new stores with the demised premises.

The lessors do not contend that the counterclaim is to be read to allege that the lessee acted for other than sound business reasons or for the purpose of depreciating the worth of the demised premises rather than for the affirmative advantage of doing business elsewhere. In the circumstances we do not construe the allegation of sales of merchandise at lower prices as averring such a purpose. The counterclaim does not recite a policy of the lessee of setting unfair prices designed to draw customers from the demised premises or of unfair competition with the business in the demised premises. We intend no suggestion of the rule to be applied in such a case.

The defendants have not suggested that they could show such unfair competition, or that, the implications they contend for not being found in the lease, there was error in ordering the demurrer sustained "with leave to amend denied."

3. The interlocutory decree sustaining the demurrer and the final decree (construed as including a dismissal of the counterclaim) are affirmed.

So ordered. ——> *Holding for plaintiffs*

In commercial leases where a portion of the rent comes from sales the lessor cannot force the lessee to operate the business during the lease term even prohibit the the lessee from operating other business unless expressly provided for in the lease

STUDY GUIDE: In the next excerpt, notice the court's sensitivity to the fact that an implied rather than an expressed covenant is at issue. Why does this make a difference?

FOOD FAIR STORES, INC. v. BLUMBERG, COURT OF APPEALS OF MARYLAND, 234 MD. 521, 200 A.2D 166 (1963): PRESCOTT, J.* . . . Although percentage leases are generally governed by the rules of law applicable to ordinary leases, the peculiar features of provisions making rental

* *Stedman Prescott* (1896-1968) received his legal training at Georgetown University (LL.B.). Admitted to the Maryland bar in 1924, he entered the practice of law in Rockville (1924-1938), serving briefly as state's attorney for Montgomery County (1930) and as a state senator (1934). In 1938, Prescott joined the Sixth Judicial Circuit of Maryland serving as associate judge from 1938-1955 and as Chief Judge from 1955 to 1956. He left the circuit court to accept appointment to the Court of Appeals of Maryland in 1956. He retired from the bench in 1966, after spending the last two years of his term as Chief Judge of that court. Prescott also served in the U.S. Army during World War I. — K.T.

dependent in some way upon the percentage of income from, or gross sales of, business on the leased premises frequently present difficult questions of construction, which render such leases in the nature of agreements sui generis. . . . Considerable case law involving the construction of such leases has developed in recent years.

It has been held that where the percentage lease provides no minimum guaranteed rental or a purely nominal guarantee, the tenant is under an implied obligation to conduct the business in good faith. . . . It has also been held that if the guaranteed rental provides the landlord an adequate return on his investment and the percentage rental feature is in the nature of a bonus, there is no obligation upon the tenant as to the manner of conducting the business not expressed in the lease. . . . And it has been further held that the tenants under percentage leases were, or were not, under an implied obligation as to the manner of conducting tenants' businesses, depending upon the intention of the parties, as expressed by the provisions of the particular leases, interpreted with a due consideration of the circumstances surrounding the execution of the lease contracts. . . .

However, the construction and application of the percentage features of the leases have depended largely upon the specific wording of the individual leases, and the character and nature of the questions involved have varied widely, due to the circumstances of each particular case. Hence, it would serve no useful purpose to attempt to formulate a comprehensive set of rules of construction applicable to all cases of percentage leases.

For the purposes of the decision herein, we need only state that in every contract there exists an implied covenant that each of the parties thereto will act in good faith and deal fairly with the others. . . . And we adopt the principle expressed by the Louisiana Court in Selber Bros. v. Newstadt's Shoe Stores [194 La. 654] 194 So. 579, and thereafter, in substantially the same wording, by the Court of Appeals of California in Professional Building of Eureka v. Anita Frocks, Inc.[, 178 Cal. App. 2d 276,] 2 Cal. Rptr. 2d 914:

> Whether that doctrine [whether the lessor under a percentage lease guaranteeing a minimum rental has cause to complain when the business is conducted in such a way that it will not produce additional rent consisting of percentages of gross sales] is applicable to a given case depends upon the intention with which the parties entered into the contract of lease, as expressed in the contract, construed in the light of the circumstances in which the contract was made.

Applying the above principles to the allegations contained in the lessors' bill of complaint, we reach the conclusion that lessors cannot prevail. There is no allegation of a wilful intent on the part of the lessees to divert sales from lessors' store, nor was there an abandonment of the business. There is nothing in the record that showed a lack of good faith or fair dealing by the lessees. They were engaged in a highly competitive business (this feature thereof being very generally known) in a quickly growing community. The bill alleges that lessees expanded their business by opening two additional stores in the area and anticipated a third. There is nothing unusual in the large chain stores which sell food products in supermarkets adding to the number of their stores, when circumstances permit.

. . . We are dealing here only with an alleged *implied* covenant. There was, of course, no legal obstacle to prevent an express covenant being placed in the lease, so as to provide for lessors' contentions here. After considering the nature of lessees' business and the terms of the leases and after construing them in the light of the circumstances surrounding the parties at the time the leases were made, we are unable to conclude the parties impliedly covenanted that the lessees would not expand their business in the area of lessors' store. What the Supreme Court of Pennsylvania said in Dickey v. Phila. Minit-Man Corp.[, 377 Pa. 549,] 105 A.2d 580, is, we think, apposite here:

> If an implied covenant, as claimed by [the lessors] should be held to arise in such cases what would be the extent of the restriction thereby imposed upon the lessee[s]? Would it extend to each and every act on [their] part that might serve to reduce the extent of [their] business and thereby the percentage rental based thereon? Would it forbid [them], for example, if operating a retail store, from keeping it open for a fewer number of hours each day than formerly? Would it forbid [them] from dismissing salesmen whereby [their] business might be reduced in volume? Would it forbid [them] from discontinuing any department of [their] business even though [they] found it to be operating at a loss? It would obviously be quite unreasonable and wholly undesirable to imply an obligation that would necessarily be vague, uncertain and generally impracticable.

STUDY GUIDE: Does the theory enunciated by Judge Posner in the following excerpt illuminate the doctrine of good faith performance being applied in the lease cases we have just read? This case concerned the termination of a franchise by the franchisor, another specific type of contract in which the use of the concept of good faith has grown in recent years.

THE ORIGINAL GREAT AMERICAN CHOCOLATE CHIP COOKIE CO. v. RIVER VALLEY COOKIES, LTD., UNITED STATES COURT OF APPEALS, SEVENTH CIRCUIT, 970 F.2d 273 (1992): POSNER, Circuit Judge: . . . Illinois, like other states, requires, as a matter of common law, that each party to a contract act with good faith, and some Illinois cases say that the test for good faith "seems to center on a determination of commercial reasonability." Dayan v. McDonald's Corp., 125 Ill. App. 3d 972, 993, 81 Ill. Dec. 156, 171, 466 N.E.2d 958, 973 (1984). . . . The equation, tentative though it is ("seems to center on"), makes it sound as if, contrary to our earlier suggestion, the judges have carte blanche to declare contractual provisions negotiated by competent adults unreasonable and to refuse to enforce them. We understand the duty of good faith in contract law differently. There is no blanket duty of good faith; nor is reasonableness the test of good faith.

Contract law does not require parties to behave altruistically toward each other; it does not proceed on the philosophy that I am my brother's keeper. That philosophy may animate the law of fiduciary obligations but parties to a contract are not each other's fiduciaries, . . . even if the contract is a franchise. . . . Contract law imposes a duty, not to "be reasonable," but to avoid taking advantage of gaps in a contract in order to exploit the vulnerabilities that arise when contractual performance is sequential rather than simultaneous. . . . Suppose *A* hires *B* to paint his portrait to his satisfaction, and *B* paints it and *A* in fact is satisfied but says he is not in the hope of chivvying down the agreed-upon price because the portrait may be unsaleable to anyone else. This, as we noted in Morin Building Products Co. v. Baystone Construction, Inc., 717 F.2d 413, 415 (7th Cir. 1983), would be bad faith, not because any provision of the contract was unreasonable and had to be reformed but because a provision had been invoked dishonestly to achieve a purpose contrary to that for which the contract had been made. . . .

RESTATEMENT (SECOND) OF CONTRACTS

§205.   DUTY OF GOOD FAITH AND FAIR DEALING

Every contract imposes upon each party a duty of good faith and fair dealing in its performance and enforcement.

honestly

SALES CONTRACTS: THE UNIFORM COMMERCIAL CODE

§1-203.   OBLIGATION OF GOOD FAITH

Every contract or duty within this Act imposes an obligation of good faith in its performance or enforcement.

OFFICIAL COMMENT

This section sets forth a basic principle running throughout this Act. The principle involved is that in commercial transactions good faith is required in the performance and enforcement of all agreements or duties. Particular applications of this general principle appear in specific provisions of the Act. . . . The concept, however, is broader than any of these illustrations and applies generally, as stated in this section, to the performance or enforcement of every contract or duty within this Act. . . .

§2-103.   DEFINITIONS AND INDEX OF DEFINITIONS

(1) In this article unless the context otherwise requires. . . .
   (b) "Good faith" in the case of a merchant means honesty in fact and the observance of reasonable standards of fair dealing in the trade.

REFERENCE: Barnett, §5.1
                  Farnsworth, §7.17
                  Calamari & Perillo, §11.38
                  Murray, §93

B.   Implied and Express Warranties

The scope of performance is often defined by a warranty. When parties are silent, contract law supplies some warranties by default. Two provided by the Uniform Commercial Code are the implied warranty of merchantability and the implied warranty of fitness for a particular purpose. After considering the difference between these two implied warranties, we shall examine how parties may contract around them, either by adding an express warranty in addition to or in place of an implied warranty or by expressly disclaiming the implied warranties.

1.   Implied Warranties of Merchantability and Fitness for a Particular Purpose

Study Guide: In the next case, pay close attention to the defendant's argument. According to its theory of the case, why isn't it liable? According to the plaintiff, what must he show to prove the defendant's liability? How does the defendant's duty arise?

VLASES v. MONTGOMERY WARD & CO.
United States Court of Appeals, Third Circuit,
377 F.2d 846 (1967)

Gerald McLaughlin,* Circuit Judge.
This case revolves around the charge that defendant-appellant, Montgomery Ward, was liable for the breach of implied warranties in the sale of one day old chickens to the plaintiff-appellee, Paul Vlases. The latter came to this country from Greece when he was sixteen and until 1954 his primary occupation was that of a coal miner. He had always raised chickens but because of his job as a miner his flocks were small, ranging from between twenty-five to one hundred chicks. In 1958 plaintiff began the construction of a two story chicken coop large enough to house 4,000 chickens and a smaller side building where he could wash, grade and sell the eggs. Vlases worked alone on the coop, twelve hours a day, fifty-two weeks a year, until its completion in 1961. In November of 1961 plaintiff placed an order at defendant's outlet store in Brownsville, Pennsylvania for the purchase of 2,000 one day old chicks. The chickens selected by the plaintiff from Ward's catalogue were hybrid Leghorns and were noted for their excellent egg production. On December 21, 1961 plaintiff received the 2,200[2] chickens and placed them on the first floor of the coop which had been equipped with new brooders, feeders and within a short time, waters. As a further hygienic precaution wire and sugar cane were placed on the

* Gerald McLaughlin (1893-1977) was born in Newark, New Jersey. After serving in the Army during World War I, he attended Fordham College and Fordham Law School. He was nominated to the U.S. Court of Appeals for the Third Circuit in 1943 and became the senior justice in 1968. He remained on that court until his death. — S.Q.
2. As a bonus plaintiff received ten extra chickens per each one hundred ordered.

ground so the chickens would not come in contact with the dirt floor. For the first six months Vlases slept in the coop in order to give the new chicks his undivided attention.

During the first few weeks after delivery the chickens appeared to be in good health but by the third week plaintiff noticed that their feathers were beginning to fall off. This condition was brought to the attention of Mr. Howard Hamilton who represented the Agway Corporation which was supplying the plaintiff with feed on credit. In February of 1962 Mr. Hamilton took five chickens to the Bureau of Animal Industry Diagnostic Laboratory where they were examined by Dr. Daniel P. Ehlers. The examination revealed signs of drug intoxication and hemorrhagic disease involving the weakening of blood vessels. Four chicks were brought to Dr. Ehlers in May of 1962 and were found to be suffering from fatigue. On the 14th of August 1962 Mr. Hamilton brought three chickens to the laboratory where Dr. Ehlers' report noted that two of the chicks were affected with visceral leukosis, one with ocular leukosis, one had bumble foot and one had been picked. Visceral and ocular leukosis are two types of avian leukosis complex or bird cancer which disease infected plaintiff's flock either killing the chicks or causing those remaining to be destroyed.

Plaintiff in this two count suit in assumpsit charged negligence and breach of warranty with jurisdiction resting on the diversity provisions of 28 U.S.C.A. §1332. After the second day of trial the negligence claim was dropped leaving the breach of warranty as the sole problem for the jury's consideration. A verdict was returned in favor of the plaintiff in the amount of $23,028.77. Montgomery Ward appeals from the resultant judgment.

I

Appellant takes the position that an action for breach of implied warranties will not lie for the sale of one day old chicks where there is no human skill, knowledge or foresight which would enable the producer or supplier to prevent the occurrence of this disease, to detect its presence or to care for the sickness if it was present. The jury was instructed by the court that recovery on behalf of the plaintiff required a finding that the chickens were afflicted with leukosis at the time defendant made delivery. The expert testimony for both sides indicated that there was no way of determining whether newly hatched chicks have leukosis and that there is no medication available to prevent the disease from occurring.[3] Assuming the chickens were diseased upon their arrival the thrust of appellant's argument questions the sufficiency of the law to support a finding that Ward is liable under Pennsylvania law for the breach of implied warranties.

3. In the brief of appellee it was pointed out that preventive measures can be taken to reduce the incidents of avian leukosis in the hatcheries, such as strict hygienic supervision and insuring that the history of the breeding flock is free of the disease. However, there was no evidence introduced showing that the hatchery which supplied the eggs to Montgomery Ward failed to comply with the accepted health standards and for the purpose of this appeal it will be assumed that all necessary preventive steps were followed.

The two implied warranties before us are the implied warranty of merchantability, 12A P.S. §2-314,[4] and the implied warranty of fitness for a particular purpose, 12A P.S. §2-315.[5] Both of these are designed to protect the buyer of goods from bearing the burden of loss where merchandise, though not violating a promise expressly guaranteed, does not conform to the normal commercial standards or meeting the buyer's particular purpose, a condition upon which he had the right to rely.

Were it to be assumed that the sale of 2,000 chickens infected with avian leukosis transgressed the norm of acceptable goods under both warranties, appellant's position is that the action will not lie in a situation where the seller is unable to discover the defect or cure the damage if it could be ascertained. That theory does not eliminate the consequences imposed by the Code upon the seller of commercially inferior goods. It is without merit.

The fact that avian leukosis is nondetectable could be an important issue but only as bearing on the charge of negligence, which is no longer in this suit. The Pennsylvania decision in Vandenberg & Sons, N.V. v. Siter, 204 Pa. Super. 392, 204 A.2d 494 (1964), buttresses our conclusion in upholding the implied warranties. There latent defects in certain tulip and hyacinth bulbs went undetected in the face of two inspections and the court, though aware that the imperfections could only be uncovered after growth, limited its concern to the question of whether the seller's express provision that notice of any breach be communicated within a certain time, was reasonable. The entire purpose behind the implied warranty sections of the Code is to hold the seller responsible when inferior goods are passed along to the unsuspecting buyer. What the Code requires is not evidence that the defects should or could have been uncovered by the seller but only that the goods

4. Section 2-314:

"(1) Unless excluded or modified (Section 2-316), a warranty that the goods shall be merchantable is implied in a contract for their sale if the seller is a merchant with respect to goods of that kind. Under this section the serving for value of food or drink to be consumed either on the premises or elsewhere is a sale.

(2) Goods to be merchantable must be at least such as

(a) pass without objection in the trade under the contract description; and

(b) in the case of fungible goods, are of fair average quality within the description; and

(c) are fit for the ordinary purposes for which such goods are used; and

(d) run, within the variations permitted by the agreement, of even kind, quality and quantity within each unit and among all units involved; and

(e) are adequately contained, packaged, and labeled as the agreement may require; and

(f) conform to the promises or affirmations of fact made on the container or label if any.

(3) Unless excluded or modified (Section 2-316) other implied warranties may arise from course of dealing or usage of trade. As amended 1959, Oct. 2, P.L. 1023, §2."

5. Section 2-315:

"Where the seller at the time of contracting has reason to know any particular purpose for which the goods are required and that the buyer is relying on the seller's skill or judgment to select or furnish suitable goods, there is unless excluded or modified under the next section an implied warranty that the goods shall be fit for such purpose. As amended 1959, Oct. 2, P.L. 1023, §2."

upon delivery were not of a merchantable quality or fit for their particular purpose. If those requisite proofs are established the only exculpatory relief afforded by the Code is a showing that the implied warranties were modified or excluded by specific language under Section 2-316.[6] Lack of skill or foresight on the part of the seller in discovering the product's flaw was never meant to bar liability. The gravamen here is not so much with what precautions were taken by the seller but rather with the quality of the goods contracted for by the buyer. Even a provision specifically disclaiming any warrant against avian leukosis would not necessarily call for the defendant's freedom from liability. Section 1-102(3)[7] of the Code's General Provisions states that standards which are manifestly unreasonable may not be disclaimed and prevents the enforcement of unconscionable sales where, as in this instance, the goods exchanged are found to be totally worthless.

. . .

The judgment of the District Court will be affirmed.

6. Section 2-316:

"(1) Words or conduct relevant to the creation of an express warranty and words or conduct tending to negate or limit warranty shall be construed wherever reasonable as consistent with each other; but subject to the provisions of this Article on parol or extrinsic evidence (Section 2-202) negation or limitation is inoperative to the extent that such construction is unreasonable.

(2) Subject to subsection (3), to exclude or modify the implied warranty of merchantability or any part of it the language must mention merchantability and in case of a writing must be conspicuous, and to exclude or modify any implied warranty of fitness the exclusion must be by a writing and conspicuous. Language to exclude all implied warranties of fitness is sufficient if it states, for example, that "There are no warranties which extend beyond the description on the face hereof."

(3) Notwithstanding subsection (2)

(a) unless the circumstances indicate otherwise, all implied warranties are excluded by expressions like "as is," "with all faults" or other language which in common understanding calls the buyer's attention to the exclusion of warranties and makes plain that there is no implied warranty; and

(b) when the buyer before entering into the contract has examined the goods or the sample or model as fully as he desired or has refused to examine the goods there is no implied warranty with regard to defects which an examination ought in the circumstances to have revealed to him; and

(c) an implied warranty can also be excluded or modified by course of dealing or course of performance or usage of trade.

(4) Remedies for breach of warranty can be limited in accordance with the provisions of this Article on liquidation or limitation of damages and on contractual modification of remedy (Sections 2-718 and 2-719). As amended 1959, Oct. 2, P.L. 1023, §2."

7. Section 1-102(3):

"(3) The effect of provisions of this Act may be varied by agreement, except as otherwise provided in this Act and except that the obligations of good faith, diligence, reasonableness and care prescribed by this Act may not be disclaimed by agreement but the parties may by agreement determine the standards by which the performance of such obligations is to be measured if such standards are not manifestly unreasonable[.]"

SALES CONTRACTS: THE UNIFORM COMMERCIAL CODE

§2-314.   IMPLIED WARRANTY: MERCHANTABILITY; USAGE OF TRADE

(1) Unless excluded or modified (Section 2-316), a warranty that the goods shall be merchantable is implied in a contract for their sale if the seller is a merchant with respect to goods of that kind. Under this Section the serving for value of food or drink to be consumed either on the premises or elsewhere is a sale.

(2) Goods to be merchantable must be at least such as

(a) pass without objection in the trade under the contract description; and

(b) in the case of fungible goods, are of fair average quality within the description; and

(c) are fit for the ordinary purposes for which such goods are used; and

(d) run, within the variations permitted by the agreement, of even kind, quality and quantity within each unit and among all units involved; and

(e) are adequately contained, packaged, and labeled as the agreement may require; and

(f) conform to the promises or affirmations of fact made on the container or label if any.

(3) Unless excluded or modified (Section 2-316) other implied warranties may arise from course of dealing or usage of trade.

§2-315.   IMPLIED WARRANTY: FITNESS FOR PARTICULAR PURPOSE

Where the seller at the time of contracting has reason to know any particular purpose for which the goods are required and that the buyer is relying on the seller's skill or judgment to select or furnish suitable goods, there is unless excluded or modified under the next section an implied warranty that the goods shall be fit for such purpose.

§2-714.   BUYER'S DAMAGES FOR BREACH IN REGARD TO ACCEPTED GOODS . . .

(2) The measure of damages for breach of warranty is the difference at the time and place of acceptance between the value of the goods accepted and the value they would have had if they had been as warranted, unless special circumstances show proximate damages of a different amount.

(3) In a proper case any incidental and consequential damages under the next section may also be recovered.

REFERENCE: Murray, §101(B), (C), and (D)

2. Express Warranties

You will recall from Chapter 1 that in Shaheen v. Knight, the court refused to *imply* a "warranty of cure," although it said that "[a] doctor and his patient . . . are at liberty to contract for a particular result." In Hawkins v. McGee, Dr. McGee was alleged to have *expressly* warrantied the results of the operation. For this reason, we were not concerned with whether the injuries sustained by George Hawkins were foreseeable. In this way Dr. McGee's liability had been expanded by his consent. Express warranties are extremely common. They entail a promise to make good for losses within their scope, whether or not such losses were foreseeable, uncertain, or avoidable.

STUDY GUIDE: Pay attention to why the court finds some of the seller's statements to constitute a warranty and not others. Why draw a distinction between statements of fact and statements of opinion or "puffing"? We shall return to this distinction in Chapter 16 when discussing the defense of misrepresentation.

ROYAL BUSINESS MACHINES, INC. v. LORRAINE CORP.

*United States Court of Appeals, Seventh Circuit,
633 F.2d 34 (1980)*

BAKER, District Judge.*

This is an appeal from a judgment of the district court entered after a bench trial awarding Michael L. Booher and Lorraine Corp. (Booher) $1,171,216.16 in compensatory and punitive damages against Litton Business Systems, Inc. and Royal Business Machines, Inc. (Royal). The judgment further awarded Booher attorneys' fees of $156,800.00. It denied, for want of consideration, the recovery by Royal of a $596,921.33 indebtedness assessed against Booher earlier in the proceedings in a summary judgment. The judgment also granted Royal a set-off of $12,020.00 for an unpaid balance due on computer typewriters.

The case arose from commercial transactions extending over a period of 18 months between Royal and Booher in which Royal sold and Booher purchased 114 RBC I and 14 RBC II plain paper copying machines. In mid-August 1976, Booher filed suit against Royal in the Indiana courts claiming breach of warranties and fraud. On September 1, 1976, Royal sued Booher on his financing agreements in the district court and also removed the state litigation to the district court where the cases were consolidated.

Harold Albert Baker (1929-†) was educated at the University of Illinois (A.B., J.D.). Admitted to the bar in 1956, he practiced in Champaign, Illinois (1956-1978), prior to being appointed to his current post as Chief Judge of the U.S. District Court for the Central District of Illinois in 1978. Baker has also served in the U.S. Navy, as a member of the faculty of the College of Law, University of Illinois (1972-1978), and as senior counsel to the Presidential Commission on CIA Activities within the United States (1975). — K.T.

The issues in the cases arise under Indiana common law and under the U.C.C. as adopted in Indiana, Ind. Code §26-1-2-102 et seq. (1976). The contentions urged by Royal on appeal are that:

(1)   substantial evidence does not support the findings that Royal made certain express warranties or that it breached any express warranty and, as a matter of law, no warranties were made; and

(2)   substantial evidence does not support the findings that Royal breached the implied warranties of merchantability and fitness for a particular purpose. . . .

We reverse and remand for a new trial on the grounds set forth in this opinion.

EXPRESS WARRANTIES

We first address the question whether substantial evidence on the record supports the district court's findings that Royal made and breached express warranties to Booher. The trial judge found that Royal Business Machines made and breached the following express warranties:

(1)   that the RBC Model I and II machines and their component parts were of high quality;

(2)   that experience and testing had shown that frequency of repairs was very low on such machines and would remain so;

(3)   that replacement parts were readily available;

(4)   that the cost of maintenance for each RBC machine and cost of supplies was and would remain low, no more than 1/2 cent per copy;

(5)   that the RBC machines had been extensively tested and were ready to be marketed;

(6)   that experience and reasonable projections had shown that the purchase of the RBC machines by Mr. Booher and Lorraine Corporation and the leasing of the same to customers would return substantial profits to Booher and Lorraine;

(7)   that the machines were safe and could not cause fires; and

(8)   that service calls were and would be required for the RBC Model II machine on the average of every 7,000 to 9,000 copies, including preventive maintenance calls.

Substantial evidence supports the court's findings as to Numbers 5, 7, 8, and the maintenance aspect of Number 4, but, as a matter of law, Numbers 1, 2, 3, 6, and the cost of supplies portion of Number 4 cannot be considered express warranties.

Paraphrasing U.C.C. §2-313 as adopted in Indiana, . . . an express warranty is made up of the following elements: (a) an affirmation of fact or promise, (b) that relates to the goods, and (c) becomes a part of the basis of the bargain between the parties. When each of these three elements is present, a warranty is created that the goods shall conform to the affirmation of fact or to the promise.

With regard to express warranties see UCC 2-313(1)(a)

We require facts b/c the court looks at whether Opinion or if they have been informed really.

Examples of opinion

The decisive test for whether a given representation is a warranty or merely an expression of the seller's opinion is whether the seller asserts a fact of which the buyer is ignorant or merely states an opinion or judgment on a matter of which the seller has no special knowledge and on which the buyer may be expected also to have an opinion and to exercise his judgment. . . . General statements to the effect that goods are "the best," . . . or are "of good quality," . . . or will "last a lifetime" and be "in perfect condition," . . . are generally regarded as expressions of the seller's opinion or "the puffing of his wares" and do not create an express warranty.

No express warranty was created by Royal's affirmation that both RBC machine models and their component parts were of high quality. This was a statement of the seller's opinion, the kind of "puffing" to be expected in any sales transaction, rather than a positive averment of fact describing a product's capabilities to which an express warranty could attach. . . .

Similarly, the representations by Royal that experience and testing had shown that the frequency of repair was "very low" and would remain so lack the specificity of an affirmation of fact upon which a warranty could be predicated. These representations were statements of the seller's opinion.

The statement that replacement parts were readily available is an assertion of fact, but it is not a fact that relates to the goods sold as required by Ind. Code §26-1-2-313(1)(a) and is not an express warranty to which the goods were to conform. Neither is the statement about the future costs of supplies being 1/2 cent per copy an assertion of fact that relates to the goods sold, so the statement cannot constitute the basis of an express warranty.

It was also erroneous to find that an express warranty was created by Royal's assurances to Booher that purchase of the RBC machines would bring him substantial profits. Such a representation does not describe the goods within the meaning of U.C.C. §2-313(1)(b), nor is the representation an affirmation of fact relating to the goods under U.C.C. §2-313(1)(a). It is merely sales talk and the expression of the seller's opinion. See **Regal Motor Products v. Bender**, 102 Ohio App. 447, 139 N.E.2d 463, 465 (1956) (representation that goods were "readily saleable" and that the demand for them would create a market was not a warranty). . . .

On the other hand, the assertion that the machines could not cause fires is an assertion of fact relating to the goods, and substantial evidence in the record supports the trial judge's findings that the assertion was made by Royal to Booher.[8] The same may be said for the assertion that the machines were tested and ready to be marketed. See **Bemidji Sales Barn v. Chatfield**, 312 Minn. 11, 250 N.W.2d 185 (1977) (seller's representation that cattle "had been vaccinated for shipping fever and were ready for the farm" constituted an express warranty). See generally R. Anderson, Uniform Commercial Code §2-313:36 (2d ed. 1970) (author asserts that seller who sells with seal of approval of a third person, e.g., a testing laboratory, makes

---

8. Michael Booher testified at trial that in February or March of 1975 he called the service department at Royal Typewriter Company and spoke with either Bruce Lewis, national service manager, or with Joe Miller. Booher testified that he told the Royal representative that he had received a report of a fire in an RBC I machine at a customer's office. Booher then testified, "They told me that that couldn't happen." (Tr. Vol. IV, pp. 457-59.) For a discussion of whether the assertions about fires, maintenance, and service calls became part of the basis of the bargain, see infra. . . .

an express warranty that the product has been tested and approved and is liable if the product was in fact not approved). The record supports the district court's finding that Royal represented that the machines had been tested. . . .

As for finding 8 and the maintenance portion of Number 4, Royal's argument that those statements relate to predictions for the future and cannot qualify as warranties is unpersuasive.[9] An expression of future capacity or performance can constitute an express warranty. In Teter v. Schultz, 110 Ind. App. 541, 39 N.E.2d 802, 804 (1942), the Indiana courts held that a seller's statement that dairy cows would give six gallons of milk per day was an affirmation of fact by the seller relating to the goods. It was not a statement of value nor was it merely a statement of the seller's opinion. . . .

Whether a seller affirmed a fact or made a promise amounting to a warranty is a question of fact reserved for the trier of fact. . . . Substantial evidence in the record supports the finding that Royal made the assertion to Booher that maintenance cost for the machine would run 1/2 cent per copy and that this assertion was not an estimate but an assertion of a fact of performance capability.[10]

Finding Number 8, that service calls on the RBC II would be required every 7,000 to 9,000 copies, relates to performance capability and could constitute the basis of an express warranty. There is substantial evidence in the record to support the finding that this assertion was also made.[11]

While substantial evidence supports the trial court's findings as to the making of those four affirmations of fact or promises, the district court failed to make the further finding that they became part of the basis of the bargain. Ind. Code §26-1-2-313(1) (1976). While Royal may have made such affirmations to Booher, the question of his knowledge or reliance is another matter.[12]

---

9. In Number 4, the trial court found that the appellant warranted that the cost of maintenance for each RBC machine and cost of supplies was and would remain low, no more than 1/2 cent per copy, and in Number 8 that service calls were and would be required for the RBC Model II machine approximately every 7,000 to 9,000 copies.

10. Michael Booher testified at trial that Mr. Gavel, a Royal representative, told Booher in April 1974, at a meeting in Booher's Indianapolis office, that cost for service on the RBC I machine would be a half cent. (Tr. Vol. III, pp. 294-98.) Booher further testified that in July 1974, at a meeting in Chicago sponsored by Royal, he was told by Jack Airey, a Royal representative, that maintenance costs for the RBC II machine would be the same as on the RBC I, except that service costs should actually be a little less due to the reliability of the machine. (Tr. Vol. III, pp. 320-21.) Gavel testified by deposition taken on May 27, 1977, which was admitted into evidence at trial, that he told Booher that service costs for the RBC I machine would be half a cent (Gavel Dep., p. 28). He further testified in reference to the costs quoted to dealers on the RBC II machines that "(n)obody ever implied they were estimates," (Gavel Dep., p. 110).

11. Michael Booher testified at trial that at the Chicago meeting Royal representatives, Jack Airey and Roland Schultz, told him that the RBC II machines would require "a service call, a customer-related call about every nine thousand copies, and that we would have preventative maintenance calls about every twenty to twenty-one thousand copies. . . ." (Tr. Vol. III, p. 325.)

12. The requirement that a statement be part of the basis of the bargain in order to constitute an express warranty "is essentially a reliance requirement" and is inextricably intertwined with the initial determination as to whether given language may constitute an

This case is complicated by the fact that it involved a series of sales transactions between the same parties over approximately an 18-month period and concerned two different machines. The situations of the parties, their knowledge and reliance, may be expected to change in light of their experience during that time. An affirmation of fact which the buyer from his experience knows to be untrue cannot form a part of the basis of the bargain. . . . Therefore, as to each purchase, Booher's expanding knowledge of the capacities of the copying machines would have to be considered in deciding whether Royal's representations were part of the basis of the bargain. The same representations that could have constituted an express warranty early in the series of transactions might not have qualified as an express warranty in a later transaction if the buyer had acquired independent knowledge as to the fact asserted.

The trial court did not indicate that it considered whether the warranties could exist and apply to each transaction in the series. Such an analysis is crucial to a just determination. Its absence renders the district court's findings insufficient on the issue of the breach of express warranties.

Since a retrial on the questions of the breach of express warranties and the extent of damages is necessary, we offer the following observations. The court must consider whether the machines were defective upon delivery. Breach occurs only if the goods are defective upon delivery and not if the goods later become defective through abuse or neglect. . . .

In considering the promise relating to the cost of maintenance, the district court should determine at what stage Booher's own knowledge and experience prevented him from blindly relying on the representations of Royal. A similar analysis is needed in examining the representation concerning fire hazard in the RBC I machines. The court also should determine when that representation was made. If not made until February 1975, the representation could not have been the basis for sales made prior to that date. . . .

For the foregoing reasons the judgment of the district court is reversed, and the cause is remanded for a new trial on the remaining issues outlined herein. Each party is to bear its own costs.

---

express warranty since affirmations, promises and descriptions tend to become a part of the basis of the bargain. It was the intention of the drafters of the U.C.C. not to require a strong showing of reliance. In fact, they envisioned that all statements of the seller become part of the basis of the bargain unless clear affirmative proof is shown to the contrary. See Official Comments 3 and 8 to U.C.C. §2-313." Sessa v. Riegle, 427 F. Supp. 760, 766 (E.D. Pa. 1977), *aff'd without op.*, 568 F.2d 770 (3d Cir. 1978). Cf. Woodruff v. Clark County Farm Bureau Coop. Assn., 153 Ind. App. 31, 286 N.E.2d 188 (1972) where the court stated: "Whether such assertions (statements by the seller) constituted express warranties and whether (the buyer) *relied* upon these assertions are material issues of fact to be determined by the trier of fact." 286 N.E.2d at 199 (emphasis added [by the court]); Stamm v. Wilder Travel Trailers, 44 Ill. App. 3d 530, 358 N.E.2d 382 (1976) (reliance necessary in order to give rise to an express warranty). "[F]or all practical purposes it is suggested that no great change was wrought by the Code. Whether one speaks of reliance or basis of the bargain, little difference exists between the two. In neither case should the statement be required to have been the sole factor leading the buyer to purchase. In either case, the statement should, at least, be one of such factors. What is really crucial is whether the statement was made as an affirmation of fact, the goods did not live up to the statement, and the defect was not so apparent that the buyer could not be held to have discovered it for himself." Bender's U.C.C. Service, Dusenberg & King, Sales and Bulk Transfers §6.01, n.2 (Matthew Bender & Co. 1980).

SALES CONTRACTS: THE UNIFORM COMMERCIAL CODE

§2-313. EXPRESS WARRANTIES BY AFFIRMATION, PROMISE, DESCRIPTION, SAMPLE

(1) Express warranties by the seller are created as follows:

(a) Any affirmation of fact or promise made by the seller to the buyer which relates to the goods and becomes part of the basis of the bargain creates an express warranty that the goods shall conform to the description.

(b) Any description of the goods which is made part of the basis of the bargain creates an express warranty that the goods shall conform to the description.

(c) Any sample or model which is made part of the basis of the bargain creates an express warranty that the whole of the goods shall conform to the sample or model.

(2) It is not necessary to the creation of an express warranty that the seller use formal words such as "warrant" or "guarantee" or that he have a specific intention to make a warranty, but an affirmation merely of the value of the goods or a statement purporting to be merely the seller's opinion or commendation of the goods does not create a warranty.

STUDY GUIDE: In the previous case, the court stated: "An affirmation of fact which the buyer from his experience knows to be untrue cannot form a part of the basis of the bargain." The next case critically examines the meaning of this principle. Does the court reject this proposition? The court distinguishes between tort and contract conceptions of warranties. What is the difference between these two conceptions and why would each lead to a different approach to reliance on a warranty? Is there a difference in this regard between an implied and an express warranty? Do you see any similarity between this debate and that surrounding promissory estoppel? Is there a difference between compensating for detrimental reliance and protecting a person's right to rely on the commitment of another?

CBS, INC. v. ZIFF-DAVIS PUBLISHING CO.

Court of Appeals of New York,
75 N.Y.2d 496, 554 N.Y.S.2d 449, 553 N.E.2d 997 (1990)

HANCOCK, JR., J.*

A corporate buyer made a bid to purchase certain businesses based on financial information as to their profitability supplied by the seller. The bid

---

* *Stewart F. Hancock, Jr.* (1923-†) was educated at the U.S. Naval Academy and Cornell University Law School. Admitted to practice in New York, he practiced privately and as counsel to the city of Syracuse (1961-1963) and was an unsuccessful candidate for Senate (1966) before beginning his judicial career with his appointment to the New York Supreme Court (1971-1977), serving on the Appellate Division from 1977 to 1986. He was appointed to the Court of Appeals of New York in 1986. Since retiring from the bench in 1993, Hancock has returned to private practice, specializing in arbitration, mediation, and international civil litigation. He has also been a distinguished visiting professor/jurist in residence at Syracuse Law School (1994-present) and a lecturer at Albany and Touro law schools. — K.T.

was accepted and the parties entered into a binding bilateral contract for the sale which included, specifically, the seller's express warranties as to the truthfulness of the previously supplied financial information. Thereafter, pursuant to the purchase agreement, the buyer conducted its own investigation which led it to believe that the warranted information was untrue. The seller dismissed as meritless the buyer's expressions of disbelief in the validity of the financial information and insisted that the sale go through as agreed. The closing took place with the mutual understanding that it would not in any way affect the previously asserted position of either party. Did the buyer's manifested lack of belief in and reliance on the truth of the warranted information prior to the closing relieve the seller of its obligations under the warranties? This is the central question presented in the breach of express warranty claim brought by CBS Inc. (CBS) against Ziff-Davis Publishing Co. (Ziff-Davis). The courts below concluded that CBS's lack of reliance on the warranted information was fatal to its breach of warranty claim and, accordingly, dismissed that cause of action on motion under CPLR 3211(a)(7). We granted leave to appeal and, for reasons stated hereinafter, disagree with this conclusion and hold that the warranty claim should be reinstated.

I

The essential facts pleaded — assumed to be true for the purpose of the dismissal motion — are these. In September 1984, Goldman Sachs & Co., acting as Ziff-Davis's investment banker and agent, solicited bids for the sale of the assets and businesses of 12 consumer magazines and 12 business publications. The offering circular, prepared by Goldman Sachs and Ziff-Davis, described Ziff-Davis's financial condition and included operating income statements for the fiscal year ending July 31, 1984 prepared by Ziff-Davis's accountant, Touche Ross & Co. Based on Ziff-Davis's representations in the offering circular, CBS, on November 9, 1984 submitted a bid limited to the purchase of the 12 consumer magazines in the amount of $362,500,000. This was the highest bid.

On November 19, 1984 CBS and Ziff-Davis entered into a binding bilateral purchase agreement for the sale of the consumer magazine businesses for the price of $362,500,000. Under section 3.5 of the purchase agreement, Ziff-Davis warranted that the audited income and expense report of the businesses for the 1984 fiscal year, which had been previously provided to CBS in the offering circular, had "been prepared in accordance with generally accepted accounting principles" (GAAP) and that the report "present[ed] fairly the items set forth." Ziff-Davis agreed to furnish an interim income and expense report (Stub Report) of the businesses covering the period after the end of the 1984 fiscal year, and it warranted under section 3.6 that from July 31, 1984 until the closing, there had "not been any material adverse change in Seller's business of publishing and distributing the Publications, taken as a whole." Section 6.1 (a) provided that "all representations and warranties of Seller to Buyer shall be true and correct as of the time of the closing," and in section 8.1, the parties agreed that all "representations and warranties . . . shall survive the closing,

notwithstanding any investigation made by or on behalf of the other party."
In section 5.1 Ziff-Davis gave CBS permission to "make such investigation"
of the magazine businesses being sold "as [it might] desire" and agreed to
give CBS and its accountants reasonable access to the books and records
pertaining thereto and to furnish such documents and information as might
reasonably be requested.

Thereafter, on January 30, 1985 Ziff-Davis delivered the required Stub
Report. In the interim, CBS, acting under section 5.1 of the purchase agreement, had performed its own "due diligence" examination of Ziff-Davis's
financial condition. Based on this examination and on reports by its
accountant, Coopers & Lybrand, CBS discovered information causing it
to believe that Ziff-Davis's certified financial statements and other financial
reports were not prepared according to GAAP and did not fairly depict Ziff-
Davis's financial condition.

In a January 31, 1985 letter, CBS wrote Ziff-Davis that,

"[b]ased on the information and analysis provided [to it, CBS was] of the view
that there [were] material misrepresentations in the financial statements
provided [to CBS] by Touche Ross & Co., Goldman, Sachs & Co. and Ziff-
Davis." In response to this letter, Ziff-Davis advised CBS by letter dated February 4, 1985 that it "believe[d] that all conditions to the closing . . . were
fulfilled," that "there [was] no merit to the position taken by CBS in its [Jan.
31, 1985] letter" and that the financial statements were properly prepared
and fairly presented Ziff-Davis's financial condition. It also warned CBS that,
since all conditions to closing were satisfied, closing was required to be held
that day, February 4, 1985, and that, if it "should fail to consummate the
transactions as provided . . . Ziff-Davis intend[ed] *to pursue all of its rights
and remedies as provided by law.* (Emphasis added.)

CBS responded to Ziff-Davis's February 4, 1985 letter with its own February 4 letter, which Ziff-Davis accepted and agreed to. In its February 4 letter,
CBS acknowledged that "a clear dispute" existed between the parties. It stated
that it had decided to proceed with the deal because it had "spent considerable
time, effort and money in complying with [its] obligations . . . and recog-
niz[ed] that [Ziff-Davis had] considerably more information available."
Accordingly, the parties agreed "to close [that day] on a mutual understanding
that the decision to close, and the closing, [would] not *constitute a waiver of
any rights or defenses either of us may have*" (emphasis added) under the
purchase agreement. The deal was consummated on February 4.

CBS then brought this action claiming in its third cause of
action . . . that Ziff-Davis had breached the warranties made as to the magazines' profitability. Based on that breach, CBS alleged that "the price bid and
the price paid by CBS were in excess of that which would have been bid and
paid by CBS had Ziff-Davis not breached its representation and warranties."
Supreme Court granted Ziff-Davis's motion to dismiss the breach of warranty cause of action because CBS alleged "it did not believe that the representations set forth in Paragraphs 3.5 and 3.6 of the contract of sale were
true" and thus CBS did not satisfy "the law in New York [which] clearly
requires that this reliance be alleged in a breach of warranty action."
Supreme Court also dismissed CBS's fourth cause of action relating to an
alleged breach of condition. The Appellate Division, First Department,

unanimously affirmed for reasons stated by Supreme Court. There should
be a modification so as to deny the dismissal motion with respect to the
third cause of action for breach of warranties.

II

In addressing the central question whether the failure to plead reliance
is fatal to CBS's claim for breach of express warranties, it is necessary to
examine the exact nature of the missing element of reliance which Ziff-Davis
contends is essential. This critical lack of reliance, according to Ziff-Davis,
relates to CBS's disbelief in the truth of the warranted financial information
which resulted from its investigation *after* the signing of the agreement and
prior to the date of closing. The reliance in question, it must be emphasized,
does not relate to whether CBS relied on the submitted financial information in making its bid or relied on Ziff-Davis's express warranties as to the
validity of this information when CBS committed itself to buy the businesses
by signing the purchase agreement containing the warranties.

Under Ziff-Davis's theory, the reliance which is a necessary element for
a claim of breach of express warranty is essentially that required for a tort
action based on fraud or misrepresentation — i.e., a belief in the truth of the
representations made in the express warranty and a change of position in
reliance on that belief. Thus, because, prior to the closing of the contract on
February 4, 1985, CBS demonstrated its lack of belief in the truth of the
warranted financial information, it cannot have closed in reliance on it and
its breach of warranty claim must fail. This is so, Ziff-Davis maintains, despite
its unequivocal rejection of CBS's expressions of its concern that the submitted financial reports contained errors, despite its insistence that the
information it had submitted complied with the warranties and that there
was "no merit" to CBS's position, and despite its warnings of legal action if
CBS did not go ahead with the closing. Ziff-Davis's primary source for the
proposition it urges — that a change of position in reliance on the truth of
the warranted information is essential for a cause of action for breach of
express warranty — is language found in older New York cases such as
Crocker-Wheeler Elec. Co. v. Johns-Pratt Co. (29 App. Div. 300 [51 N.Y.S.
793], *aff'd*, 164 N.Y. 593 [58 N.E. 1086].).

CBS, on the other hand, maintains that the decisive question is
whether it purchased the express warranties as bargained-for contractual
terms that were part of the purchase agreement (see, e.g., Ainger v. Michigan Gen. Corp., 476 F. Supp. 1209, 1225 [S.D.N.Y. 1979], *aff'd*, 632 F.2d
1025 [2d Cir. 1980]). It alleges that it did so and that, under these circumstances, the warranty provisions amounted to assurances of the existence of
facts upon which CBS relied in committing itself to buy the consumer
magazines. Ziff-Davis's assurances of these facts, CBS contends, were the
equivalent of promises by Ziff-Davis to indemnify CBS if the assurances
proved unfounded. Thus, as continuing promises to indemnify, the express
contractual warranties did not lose their operative force when, prior to the
closing, CBS formed a belief that the warranted financial information was in
error. Indeed, CBS claims that it is precisely because of these warranties that
it proceeded with the closing, despite its misgivings.

As authority for its position, CBS cites, inter alia, Ainger v. Michigan Gen. Corp. (supra) and Judge Learned Hand's definition of warranty as

> an assurance by one party to a contract of the existence of a fact upon which the other party may rely. It is intended precisely to relieve the promisee of any duty to ascertain the fact for himself; *it amounts to a promise to indemnify the promisee for any loss if the fact warranted proves untrue, for obviously the promisor cannot control what is already in the past.*

(Metropolitan Coal Co. v. Howard, 155 F.2d 780, 784 [2d Cir. 1946] (emphasis added) . . .).

We believe that the analysis of the reliance requirement in actions for breach of express warranties adopted in Ainger v. Michigan Gen. Corp. (supra) and urged by CBS here is correct. The critical question is not whether the buyer believed in the truth of the warranted information, as Ziff-Davis would have it, but "whether [it] believed [it] was purchasing the [seller's] promise [as to its truth]." (Ainger v. Michigan Gen. Corp., supra, at 1225; . . . CPC Intl. v. McKesson Corp., 134 Misc. 2d 834 [513 N.Y.S.2d 319] (Sup. Ct., N.Y. County).) This view of "reliance" — i.e., as requiring no more than reliance on the express warranty as being a part of the bargain between the parties — reflects the prevailing perception of an action for breach of express warranty as one that is no longer grounded in tort, but essentially in contract. . . . The express warranty is as much a part of the contract as any other term. Once the express warranty is shown to have been relied on as part of the contract, the right to be indemnified in damages for its breach does not depend on proof that the buyer thereafter believed that the assurances of fact made in the warranty would be fulfilled. The right to indemnification depends only on establishing that the warranty was breached. . . .

If, as is allegedly the case here, the buyer has purchased the seller's promise as to the existence of the warranted facts, the seller should not be relieved of responsibility because the buyer, after agreeing to make the purchase, forms doubts as to the existence of those facts. . . . Stated otherwise, the fact that the buyer has questioned the seller's ability to perform as promised should not relieve the seller of his obligations under the express warranties when he thereafter undertakes to render the promised performance. . . .

Ziff-Davis repeatedly cites and the dissent relies upon language contained in the Appellate Division's opinion in Crocker-Wheeler Elec. Co. v. Johns-Pratt Co. (supra) which dealt with a claimed breach of an express warranty pertaining to the fitness of insulating material for a certain use. The court held that there was no actionable express warranty claim because the seller *made no warranty with respect to use of the material.* The language which Ziff-Davis quotes as a categorical proposition that should control the case before us — i.e., "[i]t is elementary that, in order to entitle the plaintiff to maintain an action for breach of an express warranty, *it must be established that the warranty was relied on*" (emphasis added) — is contained in dictum (29 App. Div., at 302 [51 N.Y.S. 793]).[13]

---

13. We note that this dictum has been criticized (see, 8 Williston, Contracts §973, at 501 [3d ed.]) and to the extent *Crocker-Wheeler* can be broadly read to require the rule of "reliance" urged by Ziff-Davis in this case it is not to be followed.

Viewed as a contract action involving the claimed breach of certain bargained-for express warranties contained in the purchase agreement, the case may be summarized this way. CBS contracted to buy the consumer magazine businesses in consideration, among other things, of the reciprocal promises made by Ziff-Davis concerning the magazines' profitability. These reciprocal promises included the express warranties that the audited reports for the year ending July 31, 1984 made by Touche Ross had been prepared according to GAAP and that the items contained therein were fairly presented, that there had been no adverse material change in the business after July 31, 1984, and that all representations and warranties would "be true and correct as of the time of the closing" and would "survive the closing, notwithstanding any investigation" by CBS.

Unquestionably, the financial information pertaining to the income and expenses of the consumer magazines was relied on by CBS in forming its opinion as to the value of the businesses and in arriving at the amount of its bid; the warranties pertaining to the validity of this financial information were express terms of the bargain and part of what CBS contracted to purchase. CBS was not merely buying identified consumer magazine businesses. It was buying businesses which it believed to be of a certain value based on information furnished by the seller which the seller warranted to be true. The determinative question is this: should Ziff-Davis be relieved from any contractual obligation under these warranties, as it contends that it should, because, prior to the closing, CBS and its accountants questioned the accuracy of the financial information and because CBS, when it closed, did so without *believing in* or *relying on* the truth of the information?

We see no reason why Ziff-Davis should be absolved from its warranty obligations under these circumstances. A holding that it should because CBS questioned the truth of the facts warranted would have the effect of depriving the express warranties of their only value to CBS — i.e., as continuing promises by Ziff-Davis to indemnify CBS if the facts warranted proved to be untrue (see, Metropolitan Coal Co. v. Howard, supra, at 784).[14] Ironically, if Ziff-Davis's position were adopted, it would have succeeded in pressing CBS to close despite CBS's misgivings and, at the same time, would have succeeded in *defeating* CBS's breach of warranties action because CBS harbored these *identical misgivings.*[15]

We agree with the lower courts that CBS's fourth cause of action, for breach of section 6.1(f) of the purchase agreement, was properly dismissed

14. In this regard, analogy to the Uniform Commercial Code is "instructive." While acceptance of goods by the buyer precludes rejection of the goods accepted (see, U.C.C. 2-607 [2]), the acceptance of nonconforming goods does not itself impair any other remedy for nonconformity (see, U.C.C. 2-607 [2]), including damages for breach of an express warranty (see, U.C.C. 2-714; see generally, 1 White and Summers, Uniform Commercial Code §10-1, at 501-502 [Practitioner's 3d ed.] . . .).

15. We make but one comment on the dissent: in its statement that our "holding discards reliance as a necessary element to maintain an action for breach of an express warranty" (dissenting opn., at 506 [at 455 of 554 N.Y.S.2d, at 1003 of 553 N.E.2d]) the dissent obviously misses the point of our decision. We do not hold that no reliance is required, but that the required reliance is established if, as here, the express warranties are bargained-for terms of the seller.

inasmuch as section 6.1(f) was a condition to closing, not a representation or warranty, and was waived by CBS.

The order of the Appellate Division should be modified, with costs to the appellant, by denying the motion to dismiss the third cause of action for breach of warranty and the order should be otherwise affirmed.

BELLACOSA, J.* (dissenting). The issue is whether a buyer may sue a seller, after consummating a business transaction, for breach of an express warranty on which the buyer chose not to rely. The holding discards reliance as a necessary element to maintain an action for breach of an express warranty. Predictability and reliability with respect to commercial transactions, fostered by 90 years of precedent, are thus sacrificed. I respectfully dissent and would affirm the order of the Appellate Division unanimously affirming Supreme Court's application of the sound and well-settled rule.

Plaintiff CBS contracted to purchase defendant Ziff-Davis's consumer magazine group pursuant to an Asset Purchase Agreement (APA). CBS specifically negotiated *the right to rely* on its own accountant's representations in assessing the validity of the financial information which had been, and would be, provided to CBS by Ziff-Davis (§5.1 of the APA). Given the factual and fiscal complexity of this $362,500,000 acquisition, CBS chose to rely on its own investigation. What the CBS inspectors found in the Ziff-Davis books differed significantly from the financial picture the seller had painted. CBS notified Ziff-Davis of the discrepancies by letter on January 31, 1985, four days before the closing date. Despite its protest to the contrary, it had a contractual right under section 6.1 (a) of the APA to avert the closing if "all representations and warranties of Seller to Buyer" were not true on the closing date. Clearly then, CBS chose to rely on the results of its own investigation and made a business judgment to consummate the purchase rather than cancel the deal. It took the business risk of a big deal and tried by this subsequent litigation to mitigate whatever risk, if any, inured from that choice; in other words, CBS wanted to have its cake and eat it, too.

Supreme Court determined CBS did not rely on the Ziff-Davis warranties. The Appellate Division made the same determination and the nonreliance is acknowledged by the majority. . . . The reliance element is thus unnecessarily excised as a matter of law from the legal proposition governing and defining the cause of action. If I am "missing the point" . . . , I believe it is because that is where the appellant's argument and the state of the law have led me.

Part of CBS's argument is that it should prevail because the closing day letter purports to reserve its rights as to the Ziff-Davis warranties and section 8.1 of the APA purports to be a kind of nonmerger survival clause. On a *sui generis* contract basis therefore, without affecting the traditional reliance element of the cause of action, this argument is enticing. Nevertheless,

Joseph W. Bellacosa (1937-†) received his legal training at St. John's University (J.D.). Upon graduation, he served as law secretary to the New York Courts, Appellate Division (1963-1970); professor of law and assistant dean at St. John's University (1970-1975); chief clerk to the New York Court of Appeals (1975-1983); and chief administrator of the courts of the State of New York (1985). In 1985, Bellacosa was appointed judge on the New York Court of Claims, serving until his current appointment as judge on the Court of Appeals of New York in 1987. — K.T.

I conclude — and the majority apparently agrees in this respect — that the argument is not dispositive. The warranties given to CBS created a right to rely on the financial data as part of the sales agreement, not a right not to rely on them, then consummate the deal and then sue on them besides. These aspects of the agreement, therefore, merely manifested the parties' intent not to allow the closing to operate as a waiver of CBS's right to rely — a right which was surrendered *before* the closing. If this issue were dispositive, it would render the case and the contract entirely *sui generis* and there would be no need to address or alter the long-standing test with its reliance element. However, the court confronts and decides the broader issue, and on that we see and understand the case all too well in a fundamentally different way.

"It is elementary that, in order to entitle the plaintiff to maintain an action for breach of an express warranty, it must be established that the warranty was relied on." (Crocker-Wheeler Elec. Co. v. Johns-Pratt Co., 29 App. Div. 300, 302 [51 N.Y.S. 793], *aff'd*, 164 N.Y. 593 [58 N.E. 1086].) This plain language proposition has been recognized by this court and by the Appellate Division. . . . The majority declares the oft-quoted principle of *Crocker-Wheeler* "is not to be followed" . . . , based in part on a dormant tort/contract categorical bifurcation drawn largely from Ainger v. Michigan Gen. Corp., 476 F. Supp. 1209. Also, part of the justification for this departure from stare decisis in the field of common-law commercial transactions — where the burden for change is very high — is Professor Williston's "criticism" of *Crocker-Wheeler*. Examination of the complete section of the quoted text, however, discloses a significant qualification: "[I]t is generally and rightly held that inspection by the buyer does not excuse the seller from liability for . . . an express warranty, *if the difference between the goods and the description was not detected*" (8 Williston, Contracts §973, at 501 [3d ed.] (nn. omitted; emphasis added)). "The difference" was definitively detected here by CBS pursuant to its express contractual right to personally assess the financial data.

In exchange for the long-standing, well-regarded and well-founded rule, New York law is subordinated to a theory advanced in Ainger v. Michigan Gen. Corp., 476 F. Supp., supra, at 1226. Among the problems of this approach, however, is that in affirming *Ainger* the Court of Appeals for the Second Circuit emphasized the limited impact of the District Court's categorical discussion of the precise issue before us. After stating that the District Court Judge's "finding of reliance made a discussion of New York law unnecessary," the Second Circuit said "[b]ecause there was reliance in this case, we will not speculate how the New York courts would decide a case in which there was none." (Ainger v. Michigan Gen. Corp., 632 F.2d 1025, 1026, n.1.) The reliance on CPC Intl. v. McKesson Corp. (134 Misc. 2d 834 [513 N.Y.S.2d 319]) also seems misplaced. Again, the trial court in that case extensively discussed the reliance question. However, the appellate courts in an entirely different procedural review significantly minimized the discussion of the pertinent subject matter (see, CPC Intl. v. McKesson Corp., 70 N.Y.2d 268, 285 [519 N.Y.S.2d 804, 514 N.E.2d 116] ["plaintiff, in contracting to purchase (defendant's corporation), relied solely on the warranties"], 120 A.D.2d 221, 229, 507 N.Y.S.2d 984 ["plaintiff relied solely upon the express warranties"]). Lack of reliance, therefore, was not part of the holdings in *Ainger* or *CPC*, even at their trial level citations by the majority. Yet those cases are accorded significant deference on the critical issue and they override superior longer-standing sources.

Finally, while I agree that analogy to the Uniform Commercial Code is "instructive" . . . , I believe the directly on-point express warranty section, U.C.C. 2-313, emphasizes the need to stand by our precedents and thus affirm. Official comment 3 of that section indicates that were this a transaction governed by the Uniform Commercial Code, CBS's nonreliance would take the seller's warranties out of the agreement, especially after a buyer consummates the deal with full knowledge and with open disagreement concerning key financial data. . . .

Thus, we are presented with no binding or persuasive authorities sufficient to warrant overturning a venerable rule of the kind used especially in the commercial world to reliably order affairs in such a way as to reasonably avoid litigation (see, Cardozo, Selected Writings of Benjamin Nathan Cardozo, The Growth of the Law, at 236 ["In this department of activity (commercial law), the current axiology still places stability and certainty in the forefront of the virtues."]). Allowing CBS to consummate the deal, and then sue on warranted financial data it personally investigated and verified as wrong beforehand, unsettles the finality, "stability and certainty" of commercial transactions and business relationships.

CBS chose — for business reasons it knows best — to complete its significant acquisition at the impressively high agreed price with its cyclopean eye wide open. That tips the scales in favor of retaining and applying the traditional rule requiring a reliance element to sue for breach of warranty.

I would affirm the order in its entirety and leave the law where it was and the parties where they put themselves. . . .

Order modified, etc.

REFERENCE: Murray, §101(B)

3.   Express Disclaimers of Warranty

Although the law of contract supplies certain warranties when the parties are silent, the parties may still contract around these "default rules." In Chapter 2, we observed one such method. Recall the disclaimer of liability by Federal Express:

> In any event, we will not be liable for any damage, whether direct, incidental, special, or consequential, in excess of the declared value of a shipment, whether or not FedEx has knowledge that such damages might be incurred, including but not limited to loss of income and profits.

The next case illustrates another method for contracting around the implied warranties of merchantability and fitness for a particular use.

STUDY GUIDE: Note the formalities that existed in the next case. Are they necessary, and if so, why?

SCHNEIDER v. MILLER

Court of Appeals of Ohio, Hancock County,
73 Ohio App. 3d 335, 597 N.E.2d 175 (1991)

THOMAS F. BRYANT, Presiding Judge.*

This is an appeal from a judgment entered in the Findlay Municipal Court in favor of defendant-appellee, Harold Robert Miller, d.b.a. Miller Motors or Classic Motors, and against plaintiff-appellant, R. Larry Schneider, following a bench trial.

On August 20, 1988, appellant learned that appellee had a 1966 Chevrolet Impala SS at his used car lot in Findlay. Appellant was in the market for such a car and, along with his brother-in-law (who had told him about the car), went to appellee's place of business to look at the car. Appellant took a test drive in the car and decided to purchase it.

When appellant returned to the car lot, he asked appellee about a squeaking noise in the car and appellee told him it was the brakes and they needed to be replaced. Appellee also pointed out to appellant that the trunk was rusted and it would cost about $500 to repair, and that the engine might need to be rebuilt at some point. Negotiations for the purchase price then began and the parties settled on a price of $2,580. Appellant made a down payment of $100 toward the purchase price.

On August 21, 1988, appellant returned to the car lot with his wife and stepson (for whom he was purchasing the car). He paid the balance of the purchase price, signed a bill of sale acknowledging that the car was sold "as is," and signed a separate document indicating that the car was sold "as is" with no warranty. The car was then driven by appellant or his stepson to their home in Marysville with a detour to Lakeview to show the car to someone attending a classic car show.

Within a day or two after taking the car to Marysville, appellant drove it to a repair shop to have the brakes replaced and the trunk repaired. On September 8, 1988, appellant wrote a letter to appellee seeking to rescind the contract. He offered to return the car to appellee in exchange for a return of the purchase price. Appellant alleged that the entire underside of the car was hardly attached to the frame because the frame was rusted, that the car was not safe to drive, could not be repaired and was a "death trap." Appellee refused to agree to rescind the contract and appellant subsequently brought suit.

After a bench trial, the trial court entered judgment in favor of appellee. The court denied appellant's claim for breach of warranty because the car was sold "as is" without any warranty. As to appellant's claim for fraud and deceit, the court held that appellee had not engaged in conduct that could be construed as a false representation nor had he concealed any

---

* *Thomas F. Bryant* (1932-†) was educated at Bowling Green State College (B.A.) and Ohio Northern University (J.D.) before serving as clerk to District Judge Girard E. Kalbfleisch, U.S. District Court for the Northern District of Ohio (1966-1968). After clerking, Bryant became an assistant professor of law at Ohio Northern University College of Law (1968-1970) and later an adjunct professor of law (1970-1975). Before joining the Court of Appeals of Ohio, Hancock County (1989-present), Judge Bryant served as Judge in the Findlay Municipal Court, Findlay, Ohio. Now retired from the bench, Judge Bryant is a veteran of the Korean War. — L.R.

material fact concerning the vehicle. The court also denied appellant's claim for rescission of the contract, holding that appellee made no assurances or guarantees that the vehicle was in any certain condition. The court further denied appellant's claim that appellee had engaged in unfair and deceptive practices in violation of R.C. 1345.02.

Appellant's first assignment of error on appeal is as follows:

> I. The court errored (sic) in its decision both factually and under the law in finding that there was no ground for recision [sic] and revocation of acceptance under Ohio Revised Code Section 1302.66. . . .

Appellant argues that the defects in this vehicle substantially impair its value to him and that he could not have reasonably discovered the defects prior to the purchase. Appellant admitted at trial that he took a test drive in the vehicle and saw the areas of the trunk that were rusted out. At no time did appellant testify that he could not have had this vehicle inspected by a mechanic or other knowledgeable person for defects. Furthermore, appellant admitted that appellee acknowledged the rust problem in the trunk of the car.

It is interesting to note that appellant owned another 1966 Chevrolet Impala SS at the time he purchased the vehicle which is the subject matter of this lawsuit. He testified at trial that he had experienced problems with rust on the underside of that car, but claimed that such knowledge did not put him on notice that more than just the trunk of this car could be rusted.

[In support of his contention that he is entitled to rescission or revocation of acceptance, appellant cites McCullough v. Bill Swad Chrysler-Plymouth, Inc. (1983), 5 Ohio St. 3d 181, 5 O.B.R. 398, 449 N.E.2d 1289, and Goddard v. General Motors Corp. (1979), 60 Ohio St. 2d 41, 14 O.O.3d 203, 396 N.E.2d 761. Both cases deal with warranties on new cars limiting the buyer's remedy to repair and replacement of defective parts. Neither case addresses the sale of a twenty-two year old car sold "as is" with no warranty. Appellant's reliance on these cases is misplaced.]

Appellant claims that "there has been a failure of 'essential purpose' to the contract when the alleged motor vehicle turns out to be nothing but 'junk.'" This is not a valid argument. Appellant apparently borrows the "failure of essential purpose" language from the law applicable to limited warranties. In particular, when a new car warranty is limited to repair and replacement of defective parts, a court will afford the purchaser additional relief if that limited warranty fails of its essential purpose. McCullough v. Bill Swad Chrysler-Plymouth, Inc., supra, and Goddard v. General Motors Corp., supra. The present case involves a car sold "as is" and does not involve a limited warranty.

Appellant has not shown that he accepted this vehicle on the reasonable assumption that its alleged nonconformity would be cured, nor has he shown that such nonconformity was induced by the difficulty of discovery before acceptance or by appellee's assurances. Accordingly, he is not entitled to revoke acceptance of the vehicle pursuant to that statute.

Appellant's next argument in support of his right to rescind or revoke acceptance is based on R.C. 1302.28, which relates to warranties of fitness for particular purpose. Appellant claims that appellee knew he was purchasing the car for his sixteen-year-old stepson to use as a motor vehicle, not for parts. He concludes that such knowledge on the part of appellee makes R.C. 1302.28 applicable.

Appellant completely ignores the portion of R.C. 1302.28 which provides that "there is *unless excluded or modified under section 1302.29 of the Revised Code* an implied warranty that the goods shall be fit for such purpose." (Emphasis added.) R.C. 1302.29 relates to exclusion or modification of warranties and is particularly applicable to the facts of this case. That statute provides in part:

> (C) Notwithstanding division (B) of this section:
> (1) unless the circumstances indicate otherwise all implied warranties are excluded by expressions like "as is," "with all faults," or other language which in common understanding calls the buyer's attention to the exclusion of warranties and makes plain that there is no implied warranty; and
> (2) when the buyer before entering into the contract has examined the goods or the sample or model as fully as he desired or has refused to examine the goods there is no implied warranty with regard to defects which an examination ought in the circumstances to have revealed to him[.]

Official Comment No. 7 to U.C.C. 2-316 (R.C. 1302.29) provides that terms like "as is" "in ordinary commercial usage are understood to mean that the buyer takes the *entire risk* as to the quality of the goods involved." (Emphasis added.) . . .

The evidence in this case is undisputed that appellant test drove this car and apparently examined it as fully as he desired before the purchase. Furthermore, he initialed the bill of sale directly underneath the notation which indicated that the car was sold "as is" and had more than one hundred thousand miles on it. Appellant also signed the bill of sale directly under language which provides:

> Purchaser agrees that this Order includes all of the terms and conditions on both the face and reverse side hereof, that this Order cancels and supersedes any prior agreement and as of the date hereof comprises the complete and exclusive statement of the terms of the agreement relating to the subject matters covered hereby[.]

It has been held that an integration clause such as this which provides that the entire agreement between the parties is contained within the four corners of the contract is effective to waive any implied warranty. Nick Mikalacki Constr. Co. v. M.J.L. Truck Sales, Inc. (1986), 33 Ohio App. 3d 228, 515 N.E.2d 24.

In addition to signing the bill of sale in two places, appellant also signed a Buyers Guide which indicates the vehicle is sold "AS IS — NO WARRANTY." This document instructs the buyer to read the back of the form which provides that one of the major defects that may occur in a used motor vehicle is "cracks, corrective welds, or [a] rusted through" frame.

Appellant is a practicing attorney who claims that he should not be held to the provisions of the documents which he signed. Such a claim is untenable.

Appellant claims that the trial court abused its discretion in basing its decision on inaccurate facts because the decision states that appellant used the car several weeks before taking it to the repair shop when the evidence shows that he had the car only two or three days. The trial court's decision states that appellant took the car to the repair shop "[a]fter several weeks of usage," but this is merely an observation by the trial court and clearly not the basis for its decision.

Appellant's first assignment of error is overruled.

Appellant's second assignment of error is:

> II. The court errored (sic) in its decision both factually and under Ohio law in finding that there was no ground for violation of the Consumer Practices Act under Ohio Revised Code Section 1345.03.

R.C. 1345.03 provides that no supplier shall commit an unconscionable act or practice in connection with a consumer transaction. Pursuant to the definitions contained in R.C. 1345.01(A) and 1345.01(C), appellee is subject to the provisions contained in R.C. Chapter 1345. Appellant produced no evidence at trial that appellee had knowledge of the alleged defect in this car at the time of the sale, nor did he produce any evidence that appellee attempted to conceal such defect even if he did have knowledge of it.

Appellant having produced no evidence of any conduct on the part of appellee which would have been a violation of the Consumer Sales Practices Act, appellant's second assignment of error is overruled. . . .

Accordingly, the judgment of the Findlay Municipal Court is affirmed.

Judgment affirmed. ——> *Holding for defendant-appellee*

PELC v. SIMMONS, APPELLATE COURT OF ILLINOIS, FIFTH DISTRICT, 249 ILL. APP. 3D 852, 620 N.E.2D 12 (1993): Justice WELCH.* Words do have meaning. "Sold as is" when posted on a used car means just that; to rule otherwise would make it meaningless and create a new body of law as to what words need be published and what words need to be said or not said in order to sell something without a warranty.

SALES CONTRACTS: THE UNIFORM COMMERCIAL CODE

§2-316.   EXCLUSION OR MODIFICATION OF WARRANTIES

(1) Words or conduct relevant to the creation of an express warranty and words or conduct tending to negate or limit warranty shall be construed wherever reasonable as consistent with each other; but subject to the provisions of this Article on parol or extrinsic evidence (Section 2-202) negation or limitation is inoperative to the extent that such construction is unreasonable.

(2) Subject to subsection (3), to exclude or modify the implied warranty of merchantability or any part of it the language must mention

---

* Thomas M. Welch (1939-†) studied at the University of Illinois (B.S.) and the University of Missouri (J.D.). After being admitted to the bar of Illinois in 1965, he began a career in public service as a magistrate of the Illinois Circuit Court (1965-1971), Assistant State's Attorney for Madison County (1971-1972), and City Attorney of Collinsville (1975-1980). Welch was elected to the Appellate Court of Illinois in 1980 and was again retained in his current position by election in 2010. — K.T.

merchantability and in case of a writing must be conspicuous, and to exclude or modify any implied warranty of fitness the exclusion must be by a writing and conspicuous. Language to exclude all implied warranties of fitness is sufficient if it states, for example, that "There are no warranties which extend beyond the description on the face hereof."

(3) Notwithstanding subsection (2)

(a) unless the circumstances indicate otherwise, all implied warranties are excluded by expressions like "as is," "with all faults" or other language which in common understanding calls the buyer's attention to the exclusion of warranties and makes plain that there is no implied warranty; and

(b) when the buyer before entering into the contract has examined the goods or the sample or model as fully as he desired or has refused to examine the goods there is no implied warranty with regard to defects which an examination ought in the circumstances to have revealed to him; and

(c) an implied warranty can also be excluded or modified by course of dealing or course of performance or usage of trade.

(4) Remedies for breach of warranty can be limited in accordance with the provisions of this Article on liquidation or limitation of damages and on contractual modification of remedy (Sections 2-718 and 2-719).

REFERENCE: Farnsworth, §§4.26, 4.28
                        Murray, §101(E)

STUDY GUIDE: *It is important to note that the Uniform Commercial Code applies to contracts with consumers, not just between merchants. Although the warranties provided by the U.C.C. are default rules, consumer protection statutes may supplement the U.C.C. by making some duties owed by merchants to consumers immutable.*

MORRIS v. MACK'S USED CARS
Supreme Court of Tennessee,
824 S.W.2d 538 (1992)

REID, C.J.* . . .

Disclaimers permitted by §47-2-316 of the Uniform Commercial Code (U.C.C.) may limit or modify liability otherwise imposed by the code, but

---

Lyle Reid (1930-†) was educated at the University of Tennessee (B.S., B.A., J.D.), worked in the state attorney general's office of Tennessee (1961-1963) and as county attorney for Haywood County (1964-1986), practiced privately for three years (1963-1966), and was a member of the General Assembly (1967-1968). In 1987, Reid took a seat on the Tennessee Court of Criminal Appeals, which he left to accept appointment as Chief Justice of the Supreme Court of Tennessee in 1990. From 1990 to 1994, he served as Chief Justice of the Tennessee Supreme Court, and he continued to serve on the Supreme Court as justice until 1998. Reid also served with the U.S. Air Force during the Korean War. He retired to private practice in 1994. In 1998, Judge Reid became vice president of litigation for Columbia/HCA Healthcare Corporation. He was associated with Wyatt, Tarrant & Combs from 2000 until he joined the Law Office of J. Houston Gordon in February 2002. — K.T.

such disclaimers do not defeat separate causes of action for unfair or deceptive acts or practices under the Consumer Protection Act, T.C.A. §§47-18-101 to -5002.

The U.C.C. contemplates the applicability of supplemental bodies of law to commercial transactions. Section 47-1-103, T.C.A., provides the following:

> Unless displaced by the particular provisions of chapters 1 through 9 of this title, the principles of law and equity, including the law merchant and the law relative to capacity to contract, principal and agent, estoppel, fraud, misrepresentation, duress, coercion, mistake, bankruptcy, or other validating or invalidating cause shall supplement its provisions.

Also, the supplementary nature of the Consumer Protection Act is made clear by T.C.A. §47-18-112, which states,

> The powers and remedies provided in this part shall be cumulative and supplementary to all other powers and remedies otherwise provided by law. The invocation of one power or remedy herein shall not be construed as excluding or prohibiting the use of any other available remedy.

A seller may disclaim all implied warranties pursuant to T.C.A. §47-2-316, which provides in pertinent part,

> *Exclusion or modification of warranties* . . . (3)(a) unless the circumstances indicate otherwise, all implied warranties are excluded by expressions like "as is," "with all faults" or other language which in common understanding calls the buyer's attention to the exclusion of warranties and makes plain that there is no implied warranty.

The Consumer Protection Act recognizes this right of exclusion or modification of warranties under the U.C.C. Section 47-18-113, T.C.A., provides,

> *Waiver of Rights.* (a) No provision of this part may be limited or waived by contract, agreement, or otherwise, notwithstanding any other provision of law to the contrary; provided, however, the provisions of this part shall not alter, amend, or repeal the provisions of the Uniform Commercial Code relative to express or implied warranties or the exclusion or modification of such warranties.

The above provision, however, also specifically precludes disclaimer of liability under the Consumer Protection Act. . . .

Claims under the U.C.C. and the Consumer Protection Act are distinct causes of action, with different components and defenses. The Consumer Protection Act is applicable to commercial transactions, also regulated by the U.C.C. . . .

The Tennessee Consumer Protection Act is to be liberally construed to protect consumers and others from those who engage in deceptive acts or practices. . . . In a case similar to the one before the Court, the seller's failure to disclose to the buyer that the vehicle had been in an accident and had been repaired constituted a violation of the Consumer Protection Act. See Paty v. Herb Adcox Chevrolet Co., 756 S.W.2d 697 (Tenn. Ct. App. 1988). To allow the seller here to avoid liability for unfair or deceptive acts or practices by disclaiming contractual warranties under the U.C.C. would contravene the broad remedial intent of the Consumer Protection Act.

13

CONDITIONS*

Sometimes a performance is due only if something happens or does not happen. This type of occurrence is called a "condition." Unless the condition is satisfied, nonperformance is not a breach. In his influential article on conditions, Arthur Corbin offered the following definition:

> The word "condition" is used in the law of property as well as in the law of contract and it is used with some variation in meaning. In the law of contract it is sometimes used in a very loose sense as synonymous with "term," "provision," or "clause." In such a sense it performs no useful service; instead, it affords one more opportunity for slovenly thinking. In its proper sense the word *"condition" means some operative fact subsequent to acceptance and prior to discharge*, a fact upon which the rights and duties of the parties depend. Such a fact may be an act of one of the two contracting parties, an act of a third party, or any other fact of our physical world. It may be a performance that has been promised or a fact as to which there is no promise. . . .
>
> *Express, implied and constructive conditions.* A certain fact may operate as a condition, because the parties intended that it should and said so in words. It is then an express condition. It may operate as a condition because the parties intended that it should, such intention being reasonably inferable from conduct other than words. It is then a condition implied in fact. Lastly, it may operate as a condition because the court believes that the parties would have intended it to operate as such if they had thought about it at all, or because the court believes that by reason of the *mores* of the time justice requires that it should so operate. It may then be described as a condition implied by law, or better as a *constructive condition*.[1]

[A condition is not the same thing as a promise.] To take a common example, imagine that you have bought a fire insurance policy. You pay the premiums. The insurance company is not required to perform, however, unless your house burns. The burning of the house is the *condition precedent* to the insurance company's duty to pay. The happening of the condition *precedes* the company's duty to pay, but you hardly promise the insurance company that your house is going to burn down. As should become apparent below, however, the distinction between conditions and promises often blurs.

---

*Note: The materials on conditions in this chapter (and portions of the next) were compiled by and edited with Professor David V. Snyder of the American University Washington College of Law.

1. Arthur L. Corbin, Conditions in the Law of Contract, 28 Yale L.J. 739, 743-744 (1919).

Your insurance policy might also provide that you cannot recover if you do not bring suit within a year after the fire. The failure to bring suit may be seen as a *condition subsequent.* As soon as the house burns, though, the company has a duty to pay. If you fail to bring suit within a year, the company's duty will be discharged. The condition subsequent — the failure to bring suit — occurs subsequent to the company's duty to pay and discharges that duty. (This "after the fact" effect is similar to the rule we studied in Chapter 4 whereby, while an acceptance of an offer by performance creates a contract, under certain circumstances the failure to timely notify the other party of this acceptance can cause, in the words of Restatement (Second) §54(3), "the contractual duty [to be] discharged").

This theoretically clear distinction between a condition precedent and a condition subsequent can be hard to put into practice, but much hinges on the distinction. Procedural law often gives the plaintiff the burden of pleading and proving conditions precedent but gives the defendant the burden for conditions subsequent. Several of the following cases therefore refer to this traditional distinction.

In this chapter, we seek to understand better the effects of a condition, the ways that courts interpret agreements to discern exactly what is a condition, and the tools courts use to avoid enforcing conditions in appropriate cases. In Chapter 14, we shall consider how courts use "constructive conditions" (and other doctrines) to decide whether nonperformance is justified in the absence of an express condition.

A. THE EFFECT OF A CONDITION

STUDY GUIDE: What effect does the failure of the condition have on the duty of the employer? Do you find the result of this case harsh? Should a court intervene if the contract made by the parties leads to a harsh result? Why would the company label the condition "precedent" rather than "subsequent"? Although the court's discussion of anticipatory repudiation is preserved, we shall not discuss that doctrine until Chapter 14.

INMAN v. CLYDE HALL DRILLING CO.
Supreme Court of Alaska
369 P.2d 498 (1962)

DIMOND, J.* This case involves a claim for damages arising out of an employment contract. The main issue is whether a provision in the contract,

---

* *John H. Dimond* (1918-†) was born in Valdez, Alaska, and completed his undergraduate education at Catholic University of America. Once in Valdez, in the 1930s, William Egan, later to become Alaska's first governor after statehood, was giving boxing lessons to Dimond and a group of other young men. When it came Dimond's turn to spar with Egan, his first punch knocked Egan through a window and onto the ground outside. After several minutes, Egan finally came through the door and said, "OK boys, the lesson is over for today." When serving as a platoon leader in the U.S. Army during World War II, Dimond saw action in three campaigns in the South Pacific, for which he received the Silver Star, the Bronze Star, the Purple Heart, the Asiatic Pacific Medal with two Bronze Stars, and the Philippine Liberation Service Medal with a Bronze Star. He ended his military service in 1945 as a Captain. Having

making written notice of a claim a condition precedent to recovery, is contrary to public policy.

Inman worked for the Clyde Hall Drilling Company as a derrickman under a written contract of employment signed by both parties on November 16, 1959. His employment terminated on March 24, 1960. On April 5, 1960, he commenced this action against the company claiming that the latter fired him without justification, that this amounted to a breach of contract, and that he was entitled to certain damages for the breach. In its answer the Company denied that it had breached the contract, and asserted that Inman had been paid in full the wages that were owing him and was entitled to no damages. Later the Company moved for summary judgment on the ground that Inman's failure to give written notice of his claim,[2] as required by the contract, was a bar to his action based on the contract.[3] The motion was granted, and judgment was entered in favor of the Company. This appeal followed.

A fulfillment of the thirty-day notice requirement is expressly made a "condition precedent to any recovery." Inman argues that this provision is void as against public policy. In considering this first question we start with the basic tenet that competent parties are free to make contracts and that they should be bound by their agreements. [In the absence of a constitutional provision or statute which makes certain contracts illegal or unenforceable, we believe it is the function of the judiciary to allow men to manage their own affairs in their own way.] As a matter of judicial policy the court should maintain and enforce contracts, rather than enable parties to escape from the obligations they have chosen to incur.

We recognize that "freedom of contract" is a qualified and not an absolute right, and cannot be applied on a strict, doctrinal basis. An established principle is that a court will not permit itself to be used as an instrument of inequity and injustice. As Justice Frankfurter stated in his dissenting opinion in United States v. Bethlehem Steel Corp., "The fundamental principle of law that the courts will not enforce a bargain where one party has unconscionably taken advantage of the necessities and distress of the other has found expression in an almost infinite variety of cases." In determining whether certain contractual provisions should be enforced,

---

received his bachelor's degree from the Catholic University of America before the war, he returned to Catholic for his J.D. Upon graduating, he began practicing law in Juneau in 1948. In 1959, Governor Egan named him a justice on the first Alaska Supreme Court following statehood, where he sat until his retirement in 1971. — R.B.

2. The fact that Inman did not give written notice was not disputed.

3. The portion of the contract with which we are concerned reads:

[You agree that you will, within thirty (30) days after any claim (other than a claim for compensation insurance) that arises out of or in connection with the employment provided for herein, give written notice to the Company for such claim, setting forth in detail the facts relating thereto and the basis for such claim; and that you will not institute any suit or action against the Company in any court or tribunal in any jurisdiction based on any such claim prior to six (6) months after the filing of the written notice of claim hereinabove provided for, or later than one (1) year after such filing. [Any action or suit on any such claim shall not include any item or matter not specifically mentioned in the proof of claim above provided. It is agreed that in any such action or suit, proof by you of your compliance with the provisions of this paragraph shall be a condition precedent to any recovery.]

the court must look realistically at the relative bargaining positions of the parties in the framework of contemporary business practices and commercial life. If we find those positions are such that one party has unscrupulously taken advantage of the economic necessities of the other, then in the interest of justice — as a matter of public policy — we would refuse to enforce the transaction. But the grounds for judicial interference must be clear. Whether the court should refuse to recognize and uphold that which the parties have agreed upon is a question of fact upon which evidence is required.

The facts in this case do not persuade us that the contractual provision in question is unfair or unreasonable. Its purpose is not disclosed. The requirement that written notice be given within thirty days after a claim arises may have been designed to preclude stale claims; and the further requirement that no action be commenced within six months thereafter may have been intended to afford the Company timely opportunity to rectify the basis for a just claim. But whatever the objective was, we cannot find in the contract anything to suggest it was designed from an unfair motive to bilk employees out of wages or other compensation justly due them.

There was nothing to suggest that Inman did not have the knowledge, capacity or opportunity to read the agreement and understand it; and the terms of the contract were imposed upon him without any real freedom of choice on his part; that there was any substantial inequality in bargaining positions between Inman and the Company. Not only did he attach a copy of the contract to his complaint, which negatives any thought that he really wasn't aware of its provisions, but he also admitted in a deposition that at the time he signed the contract he had read it, had discussed it with a Company representative, and was familiar with its terms. And he showed specific knowledge of the thirty-day notice requirement when, in response to a question as to whether written notice had been given prior to filing suit, he testified:

A. Well, now, I filed — I started my claim within 30 days, didn't I, from the time I hit here. I thought that would be a notice that I started suing them when I first came to town.
Q. You thought that the filing of the suit would be the notice?
A. That is right.

Under these circumstances we do not find that such a limitation on Inman's right of action is offensive to justice. We would not be justified in refusing to enforce the contract and thus permit one of the parties to escape his obligations. It is conceivable, of course, that a thirty-day notice of claim requirement could be used to the disadvantage of a workman by an unscrupulous employer. If this danger is great, the legislature may act to make such a provision unenforceable.[4] But we may not speculate on what in the future may be a matter of public policy in this state. It is our function to act only

4. In Oklahoma the constitution (art. XXIII, §9) provides: "Any provision of any contract or agreement, express or implied, stipulating for notice or demand other than such as may be provided by law, as a condition precedent to establish any claim, demand, or liability, shall be null and void." . . .

where an existent public policy is clearly revealed from the facts and we find that it has been violated. That is not the case here.

Inman's claim arose on March 24, 1960. His complaint was served on the Company on April 14. He argues that since the complaint set forth in detail the basis of his claim and was served within thirty days, he had substantially complied with the contractual requirement.

Service of the complaint probably gave the Company actual knowledge of the claim. But that does not serve as an excuse for not giving the kind of written notice called for by the contract. Inman agreed that no suit would be instituted "prior to six (6) months *after the filing of the written notice of claim.*" (emphasis ours). If this means what it says (and we have no reason to believe it does not), it is clear that the commencement of an action and service of the complaint was not an effective substitute for the kind of notice called for by the agreement. To hold otherwise would be to simply ignore an explicit provision of the contract and say that it had no meaning. We are not justified in doing that.

The contract provides that compliance with its requirement as to giving written notice of a claim prior to bringing suit "shall be a condition precedent to any recovery." Inman argues that this is not a true condition precedent — merely being labeled as such by the Company — and that noncompliance with the requirement was an affirmative defense which the Company was required to set forth in its answer under Civ. R. 8(c). He contends that because the answer was silent on this point, the defense was waived under Civ. R. 12(h).[5]

The failure to give advance notice of a claim where notice is required would ordinarily be a defense to set forth in the answer. But here the parties agreed that such notice should be a condition precedent to any recovery. This meant that the Company was not required to plead lack of notice as an affirmative defense, but instead, that Inman was required to plead performance of the condition or that performance had been waived or excused. The Company may not be charged under Civ. R. 12(h) with having waived a defense which it was not obliged to present in its answer.

Relying upon the doctrine of anticipatory breach of contract, Inman argues that when the Company discharged him it repudiated the employment agreement, and he was then excused from any further performance, including performance of the condition precedent of giving written notice of his claim.

What the Company allegedly did was not an anticipatory breach of contract in the strict sense of the term. Such a breach would have been committed only if the Company had repudiated its contractual duty before the time fixed for its performance had arrived. That was not the case here. Both parties had commenced performance on November 16, 1959, and they continued to perform until March 24, 1960. We believe Inman's real claim is that there was a breach of an existing duty accompanied by words or acts disclosing the Company's intention to refuse performance in the future,

---

5. This rule provides in part that "[a] party waives all defenses and objections which he does not present either by motion as hereinbefore provided or, if he has made no motion, in his answer or reply * * *."

and that this conferred upon him the privilege to deal with the contract as if broken altogether.

But even assuming that there had been a breach which excused Inman from further performance of his contractual obligation to work for the Company for the full term of the contract,[6] it does not follow that he was also excused from performing the condition precedent to commencement of this action for damages. He did not allege, nor does the record indicate, that his failure to give notice was caused by the Company's fault. There is no showing nor any inference that the Company, by words or conduct, induced Inman not to give the required notice, or led him to believe that giving notice would be a futile gesture. In fact, he admitted in his deposition that his reason for not complying with the condition was because he thought the filing of the suit would constitute the required notice.

Inman's last point is that the trial court erred in entering a final judgment. He argues that the failure to give written notice was merely a matter in abatement of his action until the condition could be performed, and that the most the court ought to have done was to dismiss the action without prejudice.

This argument is unsound. At the time judgment was entered Inman could no longer perform the condition precedent to recovery by giving written notice of his claim within thirty days after the claim arose, because this time limitation had expired. In these circumstances his right to seek redress from the court was barred and not merely abated. Final judgment in the Company's favor was proper.

The judgment is affirmed.

UNDERSTANDING THE EFFECTS OF CONDITIONS: A PROBLEM

Recall the facts of Carlill v. Carbolic Smoke Ball Co., which begins on page 310. The Smoke Ball Company offered a £100 reward for anyone who bought the smoke ball, used it according to the directions, and caught the flu. If you were the judge, when would you hold that a contract had been formed: when Mrs. Carlill bought the smoke ball, when she used it, or when she caught the flu? In your view, once the contract had been formed, did the Smoke Ball Company have a duty of immediate performance?

B.   WHAT EVENTS ARE CONDITIONS?

An event that is uncertain to occur — that is, an event other than the passage of time — may be a condition, a promise, or a "promissory condition" (which is both a promise and a condition). The event may also be none of these things; it might merely indicate at what point in time the parties

6. The contract provided that "The term of your employment will be on a twelve (12) month's basis terminable at the end of twelve (12) months by either the Company or yourself, or by the Company at any time on five (5) days previous written notice to you." Inman had worked approximately four months when his employment was terminated.

have contemplated a performance. Courts have long struggled to distinguish these different contractual devices.

1.   Is the Event a Condition, a Promise, or Both?

STUDY GUIDE: What tools do courts use to tell the difference between a promise and a condition? What are the different effects of a promise, a condition, and a promissory condition? Which interpretation do courts prefer? Why?

HOWARD v. FEDERAL CROP INSURANCE CORP.
United States Court of Appeals for the Fourth Circuit,
540 F.2d 695 (1976)

WIDENER, Circuit Judge.* Plaintiff-appellants sued to recover for losses to their 1973 tobacco crop due to alleged rain damage. The crops were insured by defendant-appellee, Federal Crop Insurance Corporation (FCIC). . . . The district court granted summary judgment for the defendant and dismissed all three actions. We remand for further proceedings.

Federal Crop Insurance Corporation, an agency of the United States, in 1973, issued three policies to the Howards, insuring their tobacco crops, to be grown on six farms, against weather damage and other hazards.

The Howards (plaintiffs) established production of tobacco on their acreage, and have alleged that their 1973 crop was extensively damaged by heavy rains, resulting in a gross loss to the three plaintiffs in excess of $35,000. The plaintiffs harvested and sold the depleted crop and timely filed notice and proof of loss with FCIC, but, prior to inspection by the adjuster for FCIC, the Howards had either plowed or disked under the tobacco fields in question to prepare the same for sowing a cover crop of rye to preserve the soil. When the FCIC adjuster later inspected the fields, he found the stalks had been largely obscured or obliterated by plowing or disking and denied the claims, apparently on the ground that the plaintiffs had violated a portion of the policy which provides that the stalks on any acreage with respect to which a loss is claimed shall not be destroyed until the corporation makes an inspection.

---

* H. Emory Widener, Jr. (1923-2007), was educated at Virginia Polytechnic Institute and State University (1940-1941), the U.S. Naval Academy (B.S.), and Washington and Lee University (LL.B.). After serving in the U.S. Navy from 1944 to 1949, he was called to the Virginia bar in 1951 and began his legal practice in Bristol, Virginia. While in practice, he served as an instructor at the Southern Seminary & Junior College (1950-1951), as a Lieutenant in the naval reserves (1951-1952), and as the U.S. Commissioner for the Western District of Virginia (1963-1966). He left private practice to become Judge (1969-1972) and Chief Judge (1971-1972) of the U.S. District Court Western District of Pennsylvania. Judge Widener served as Judge for the United States Court of Appeals for the Fourth Circuit, a position to which he was appointed in 1972. Widener taught at the University of Texas (1974), Washington and Lee University (1998), and the College of William and Mary (1999-2000). — L.R.

[The holding of the district court is best capsuled in its own words: "The inquiry here is whether compliance by the insureds with this provision of the policy was a condition precedent to the recovery. The court concludes that it was and that the failure of the insureds to comply worked a forfeiture of benefits for the alleged loss."]

There is no question but that apparently after notice of loss was given to defendant, but before inspection by the adjuster, plaintiffs plowed under the tobacco stalks and sowed some of the land with a cover crop, rye. The question is whether, under paragraph 5(f) of the tobacco endorsement to the policy of insurance, the act of plowing under the tobacco stalks forfeits the coverage of the policy. Paragraph 5 of the tobacco endorsement is entitled *Claims*. Pertinent to this case are subparagraphs 5(b) and 5(f), which are as follows:

> 5(b) *It shall be a condition precedent* to the payment of any loss that the insured establish the production of the insured crop on a unit and that such loss has been directly caused by one or more of the hazards insured against during the insurance period for the crop year for which the loss is claimed, and furnish any other information regarding the manner and extent of loss as may be required by the Corporation. (Emphasis added.)
>
> 5(f) The tobacco stalks on any acreage of tobacco of types 11a, 11b, 12, 13, or 14 with respect to which a loss is claimed *shall not be destroyed until the Corporation makes an inspection.* (Emphasis added.)

The arguments of both parties are predicated upon the same two assumptions. First, if subparagraph 5(f) creates a condition precedent, its violation caused a forfeiture of plaintiffs' coverage. Second, if subparagraph 5(f) creates an obligation (variously called a promise or covenant) upon plaintiffs not to plow under the tobacco stalks, defendant may recover from plaintiffs (either in an original action, or, in this case, by a counterclaim, or as a matter of defense) for whatever damage it sustained because of the elimination of the stalks. However, a violation of subparagraph 5(f) would not, under the second premise, standing alone, cause a forfeiture of the policy.]

Generally accepted law provides us with guidelines here. There is a general legal policy opposed to forfeitures. . . . Insurance policies are generally construed most strongly against the insurer. . . . When it is doubtful whether words create a promise or a condition precedent, they will be construed as creating a promise. . . . The provisions of a contract will not be construed as conditions precedent in the absence of language plainly requiring such construction. . . . Restatement of the Law, Contracts, §261.

Plaintiffs rely most strongly upon the fact that the term "condition precedent" is included in subparagraph 5(b) but not in subparagraph 5(f). It is true that whether a contract provision is construed as a condition or an obligation does not depend entirely upon whether the word "condition" is expressly used. . . . However, the persuasive force of plaintiffs' argument in this case is found in the use of the term "condition precedent" in subparagraph 5(b) but not in subparagraph 5(f). Thus, it is argued that the ancient maxim to be applied <u>is that the expression of one</u> <u>thing is the exclusion of another.</u>

Persuasive Legal Analysis

The defendant places principal reliance upon the decision of this court in Fidelity-Phenix Fire Insurance Company v. Pilot Freight Carriers, 193 F.2d 812, 31 A.L.R.2d 839 (4th Cir. 1952). Suit there was predicated upon a loss resulting from theft out of a truck covered by defendant's policy protecting plaintiff from such a loss. The insurance company defended upon the grounds that the plaintiff had left the truck unattended without the alarm system being on. The policy contained six paragraphs limiting coverage. Two of those imposed what was called a "condition precedent." They largely related to the installation of specified safety equipment. Several others, including paragraph 5, pertinent in that case, started with the phrase, "It is further warranted." In paragraph 5, the insured warranted that the alarm system would be on whenever the vehicle was left unattended. Paragraph 6 starts with the language: "The assured agrees, by acceptance of this policy, that the foregoing conditions precedent relate to matters material to the acceptance of the risk by the insurer." Plaintiff recovered in the district court, but judgment on its behalf was reversed because of a breach of warranty of paragraph 5, the truck had been left unattended with the alarm off. In that case, plaintiff relied upon the fact that the words "condition precedent" were used in some of the paragraphs but the word "warranted" was used in the paragraph in issue. <u>In rejecting that</u> <u>contention, this court said that "warranty" and "condition precedent" are</u> <u>often used interchangeably to create a condition of the insured's promise,</u> <u>and "[m]anifestly the terms 'condition precedent' and 'warranty' were</u> <u>intended to have the same meaning and effect."</u> 193 F.2d at 816.

Fidelity-Phenix thus does not support defendant's contention here. Although there is some resemblance between the two cases, analysis shows that the issues are actually entirely different. Unlike the case at bar, each paragraph in *Fidelity-Phenix* contained either the term "condition precedent" or the term "warranted." We held that, in that situation, the two terms had the same effect in that they both involved forfeiture. That is well established law.... <u>In the case at bar, the term "warranty" or "warranted" is in no</u> <u>way involved, either in terms or by way of like language, as it was in</u> *Fidelity-Phenix*. The issue upon which this case turns, then, was not involved in *Fidelity-Phenix.*

The Restatement of the Law of Contracts states:

§261. INTERPRETATION OF DOUBTFUL WORDS AS PROMISE OR CONDITION.

Where it is doubtful whether words create a promise or an express condition, they are interpreted as creating a promise; but the same words may sometimes mean that one party promises a performance and that the other party's promise is conditional on that performance.

Two illustrations (one involving a promise, the other a condition) are used in the Restatement:

2. *A*, an insurance company, issues to *B* a policy of insurance containing promises by *A* that are in terms conditional on the happening of certain events. The policy contains this clause: "provided, in case differences shall

arise touching any loss, *the matter shall be submitted to impartial arbitrators*, whose award shall be binding on the parties." This is a promise to arbitrate and does not make an award a condition precedent of the insurer's duty to pay.

3. *A*, an insurance company, issues to *B* an insurance policy in usual form containing this clause: "In the event of disagreement as to the amount of loss it shall be ascertained by two appraisers and an umpire. The loss shall *not be payable until 60 days after the award of the appraisers when such an appraisal is required.*" This provision is not merely a promise to arbitrate differences but makes an award a condition of the insurer's duty to pay in case of disagreement." (Emphasis added)

We believe that subparagraph 5(f) in the policy here under consideration fits illustration 2 rather than illustration 3. Illustration 2 specifies something to be done, whereas subparagraph 5(f) specifies something not to be done. Unlike illustration 3, subparagraph 5(f) does not state any conditions under which the insurance shall "not be payable," or use any words of like import. We hold that the district court erroneously held, on the motion for summary judgment, that subparagraph 5(f) established a condition precedent to plaintiffs' recovery which forfeited the coverage.[7] . . .

The explanation defendant makes for including subparagraph 5(f) in the tobacco endorsement is that it is necessary that the stalks remain standing in order for the Corporation to evaluate the extent of loss and to determine whether loss resulted from some cause not covered by the policy. However, was subparagraph 5(f) inserted because without it the Corporation's opportunities for proof would be more difficult, or because they would be impossible? Plaintiffs point out that the Tobacco Endorsement, with subparagraph 5(f), was adopted in 1970, and crop insurance goes back long before that date. Nothing is shown as to the Corporation's prior 1970 practice of evaluating losses. Such a showing might have a bearing upon establishing defendant's intention in including 5(f). Plaintiffs state, and defendant does not deny, that another division of the Department of Agriculture, or the North Carolina Department, urged that tobacco stalks be cut as soon as possible after harvesting as a means of pest control. Such an explanation might refute the idea that plaintiffs plowed under the stalks for any fraudulent purpose. Could these conflicting directives affect the reasonableness of plaintiffs' interpretation of defendant's prohibition upon plowing under the stalks prior to adjustment?

We express no opinion on these questions because they were not before the district court and are mentioned to us largely by way of argument rather than from the record. . . . Nothing we say here should preclude FCIC from asserting as a defense that the plowing or disking under of the stalks caused damage to FCIC if, for example, the amount of the loss was thereby made more difficult or impossible to ascertain whether the plowing or

---

7. The district court also referred to subparagraph 5(f) as a condition subsequent. The difference in terminology is of no consequence here.

disking under was done with bad purpose or innocently. To repeat, our narrow holding is that merely plowing or disking under the stalk does not of itself operate to forfeit coverage under the policy.

The case is remanded for further proceedings not inconsistent with this opinion. <u>Vacated and Remanded</u>.

[handwritten: The clause has created an obligation, not necessarily a condition precedent]

RESTATEMENT (SECOND) OF CONTRACTS

§227.   STANDARDS OF PREFERENCE WITH REGARD TO CONDITIONS

[handwritten margin: Promissory Condition]

[handwritten margin: · Must be spelled out completely]

(1) In resolving doubts as to whether an event is made a condition of an obligor's duty, and as to the nature of such an event, an interpretation is preferred that will reduce the obligee's risk of forfeiture, unless the event is within the obligee's control or the circumstances indicate that he has assumed the risk.

[handwritten margin: · Agreement between A and B]

(2) Unless the contract is of a type under which only one party generally undertakes duties, when it is doubtful whether

    (a) a duty is imposed on an obligee that an event occur, or

    (b) the event is made a condition of the obligor's duty, or

    (c) the event is made a condition of the obligor's duty and a duty is imposed on the obligee that the event occur,

the first interpretation is preferred if the event is within the obligee's control.

[handwritten margin: · A promises under agreement that B states that performance is a condition of B's performance · if A does not perform ↓ B has options can claim lack of condition but lose contractual benefits. Can also construe it as a promise and sue for breach]

2.   Is the Event a Condition, a Promise, or Neither?

CHIRICHELLA v. ERWIN
Court of Appeals of Maryland,
270 Md. 178, 310 A.2d 555 (1973)

LEVINE, J.* This appeal is from a decree for specific performance of a contract for the sale of real estate. Appellants (the Chirichellas) had contracted in June 1971 to sell their home in Silver Spring to appellees (the Erwins) for the sum of $39,000. Due to the refusal of the Chirichellas to settle, the Erwins finally sued them on August 31, 1972 for specific

---

Irving A. Levine (1924-†) completed his legal education at George Washington University (LL.B.) after serving in the U.S. Army Corps (1943-1945). He was admitted to practice in the District of Columbia in 1950 and Maryland in 1955. Judge Levine's judicial career began as Judge for the Maryland Tax Court (1965-1967) and continued with his service as Judge in the Maryland Circuit Court Sixth Judicial Circuit (1967-1972). Governor Marvin Mandel appointed Levine to the Maryland Court of Appeals in 1972, where he sat until 1978. — L.R.

performance.] At the conclusion of the trial, the circuit court for Montgomery County (Miller, J.) entered the decree from which this appeal is taken.

The contract entered into by the parties was the "standard" form used by the Montgomery County Board of Realtors. Paragraph Six of the form contract, entitled "Settlement," reads as follows:

> Within _____ days from date of acceptance hereof by the Seller, or as soon thereafter as a report of the title can be secured if promptly ordered, and/or survey, if required, and/or Government-insured loan, if used, can be processed, if promptly applied for, the Seller and Purchaser are required and agree to make full settlement in accordance with the terms hereof. . . .

Apparently when the real estate salesman initially submitted the contract to the Chirichellas, the words, "by Oct. 1, 1971 or sooner," had been inserted in the blank space. By mutual agreement, this language was amended to read, "Coincide with settlement of New Home in Kettering Approx. Oct. '71." No other reference to the "New Home in Kettering" appears in the contract.

The Chirichellas had contracted to purchase the "New Home" in April 1971. Their agreement provided that they were to settle "within fifteen (15) days from the date of completion." Although construction of the new house had not yet commenced when the Erwin contract was executed in April, the Chirichellas were confident that it would be completed by October unless unforeseen developments intervened. Their confidence proved to be unwarranted as the first settlement of the "New Home" was scheduled for June 15, 1972. The record does not indicate when construction actually commenced.

The June settlement on the "New Home" never materialized because the Chirichellas claimed it was not completed "in a workmanlike manner." . . . Settlement has never occurred on the "New Home" and it appears that it has been resold to another purchaser.

The first settlement of the contract on the house sold by the Chirichellas to the Erwins was also scheduled for June 15, 1972. Sometime prior to that date, but after October 1971, Mr. Erwin asked Mr. Chirichella to settle, but the latter refused because the "New Home" was not ready. The Chirichellas did not appear at the June 15 settlement, and it was rescheduled for August 9. When that proved to be futile, the Erwins filed their suit on August 31, 1972.

Although he was of the view that the Chirichellas' complaints concerning the "New Home" were justified, the chancellor concluded that the provision for settlement inserted in the Erwin contract was not a condition precedent to performance, but merely a requirement that settlement take place during the month of October 1971, or within a reasonable time thereafter. And, since more than a reasonable time had elapsed, the Erwins were entitled to a decree for specific performance. We agree, and therefore affirm.] —> Holding

Before this Court, the Chirichellas attack the chancellor's ruling on the same grounds raised below: That the contested provision was a condition precedent to performance on their part, and since that condition failed, the contract failed with it. . . .

A condition precedent has been defined as "a fact, other than mere lapse of time, which, unless excused, must exist or occur before a duty of immediate performance of a promise arises," 17 Am. Jur. 2d, Contracts, §320. . . . The question whether a stipulation in a contract constitutes a condition precedent is one of construction dependent on the intent of the parties to be gathered from the words they have employed and, in case of ambiguity, after resort to the other permissible aids to interpretation. . . . Although no particular form of words is necessary in order to create an express condition, such words and phrases as "if" and "provided that," are commonly used to indicate that performance has expressly been made conditional . . . as have the words "when," "after," "as soon as," or "subject to." . . .

We turn then to the question of whether the language in controversy here meets the definition of a condition precedent, i.e., whether it may be read to mean that settlement of the "New Home in Kettering" must have occurred before the Chirichellas' duty to settle with the Erwins arose. We think the provision in issue no more accomplishes that purpose than the words which it replaced. As we read the clause, "Coincide with settlement of New Home in Kettering Approx. Oct. '71," it merely fixes a convenient and appropriate time for settlement.

Although the amendment attempted to link one settlement with the other, its only effect was to insure that the October 1971 time designation not be regarded as of the essence. . . .

Here, whatever might have been the consequence had the phrase, "Approx. Oct. '71," not been added to the insertion, its inclusion effectively defeats the Chirichellas' argument. The result, as the chancellor ruled, was not to allow them to "avoid the contract," but to "delay settlement for a reasonable period of time while the [new] house was completed."

In sum, the Chirichellas' duty to perform by settling under their contract with the Erwins was not subject to the condition precedent that they first settle on the new house. Hence, they were required to do so within a reasonable time after October 1971. As suggested by the chancellor, that time had long since expired by January 29, 1973, the day of trial.

Decree affirmed; appellants to pay costs.

REFERENCE: Farnsworth, §§8.1-8.4
Calamari & Perillo, §§11.1-11.15
Murray, §§100, 102-104

C. AVOIDING CONDITIONS

As some of the previous cases show, the operation of a condition is sometimes harsh. Courts have developed various doctrines to avoid the effect of a condition. We shall consider three: waiver, estoppel, and excuse (although the term "excuse" is sometimes used more broadly to describe any doctrine that avoids the effect of a condition).

1. Waiver and Estoppel

Study Guide: What is the difference between waiver, modification, and estoppel? What policies underlie the doctrine of waiver? How does the estoppel discussed here differ from promissory estoppel?

CLARK v. WEST
Court of Appeals of New York,
193 N.Y. 349, 86 N.E. 1 (1908)

Appeal from Supreme Court, Appellate Division, Second Department.
Action by William L. Clark against John B. West. From a judgment of the Appellate Division of the Supreme Court reversing an interlocutory judgment overruling a demurrer to the complaint and sustaining the demurrer (125 App. Div. 64, 110 N.Y. Supp. 110), plaintiff, by permission, appeals, and the Appellate Division certifies questions. Reversed, and interlocutory judgment affirmed. . . .

WERNER, J.* . . . The contract before us, stripped of all superfluous verbiage, binds the plaintiff to total abstention from the use of intoxicating liquors during the continuance of the work which he was employed to do. The stipulations relating to the plaintiff's compensation provide that if he does not observe this condition he is to be paid at the rate of $2 per page, and if he does comply therewith he is to receive $6 per page. The plaintiff has written one book under the contract, known as "Clark & Marshall on Corporations," which has been accepted, published, and copies sold in large numbers by the defendant. The plaintiff admits that while he was at work on this book he did not entirely abstain from the use of intoxicating liquors. He has been paid only $2 per page for the work he has done. He claims that, despite his breach of this condition, he is entitled to the full compensation of $6 per page, because the defendant, with full knowledge of plaintiff's nonobservance of this stipulation as to total abstinence, has waived the breach thereof and cannot now insist upon strict performance in this regard. This plea of waiver presents the underlying question which determines the answers to the questions certified.

Briefly stated, the defendant's position is that the stipulation as to plaintiff's total abstinence is the consideration for the payment of the difference between $2 and $6 per page, and therefore could not be waived except by a new agreement to that effect based upon a good consideration; that the so-called waiver alleged by the plaintiff is not a waiver, but a modification of the contract in respect of its consideration. The plaintiff on the other hand, argues that the stipulation for his total abstinence was merely a condition precedent, intended to work a forfeiture of the additional

* *William E. Werner* (1855-1916) was born in Buffalo, New York. He read for the bar and was admitted in 1880, and he practiced in Rochester until becoming Clerk of the Municipal Court of Rochester in 1879. He was a special judge of Monroe County from 1884 to 1889 before being elected county judge in 1889. In 1894, he was elected a justice of the Supreme Court from the Seventh Judicial District, where he sat until his elevation by Governor Theodore Roosevelt to be an associate justice of the Court of Appeals, a position to which he was elected in 1904. In 1913, he was nominated for Chief Justice by the Republican Party but was defeated by Judge Willard Bartlett. He continued on the court until his death. — R.B.

compensation in case of a breach, and that it could be waived without any formal agreement to that effect based upon a new consideration.

The subject-matter of the contract was the writing of books by the plaintiff for the defendant. The duration of the contract was the time necessary to complete them all. The work was to be done to the satisfaction of the defendant, and the plaintiff was not to write any other books except those covered by the contract, unless requested so to do by the defendant, in which latter event he was to be paid for that particular work by the year. The compensation for the work specified in the contract was to be $6 per page, unless the plaintiff failed to totally abstain from the use of intoxicating liquors during the continuance of the contract, in which event he was to receive only $2 per page. That is the obvious import of the contract construed in the light of the purpose for which it was made, and in accordance with the ordinary meaning of plain language. It is not a contract to write books in order that the plaintiff shall keep sober, but a contract containing a stipulation that he shall keep sober so that he may write satisfactory books. When we view the contract from this standpoint, it will readily be perceived that the particular stipulation is not the consideration for the contract, but simply one of its conditions which fits in with those relating to time and method of delivery of manuscript, revision of proof, citation of cases, assignment of copyrights, keeping track of new cases and citations for new editions, and other details which might be waived by the defendant, if he saw fit to do so. . . . If that conclusion is well founded, there can be no escape from the corollary that this condition could be waived; and, if it was waived, the defendant is clearly not in a position to insist upon the forfeiture which his waiver was intended to annihilate. The forfeiture must stand or fall with the condition. If the latter was waived, the former is no longer a part of the contract. Defendant still has the right to counterclaim for any damages which he may have sustained in consequence of the plaintiff's breach, but he cannot insist upon strict performance. . . .

This whole discussion is predicated, of course, upon the theory of an express waiver. We assume that no waiver could be implied from the defendant's mere acceptance of the books and his payment of the sum of $2 per page without objection. It was the defendant's duty to pay that amount in any event after acceptance of the work. The plaintiff must stand upon his allegation of an express waiver, and if he fails to establish that he cannot maintain his action. . . .

The cases which present the most familiar phases of the doctrine of waiver are those which have arisen out of litigation over insurance policies where the defendants have claimed a forfeiture because of the breach of some condition in the contract . . . , but it is a doctrine of general application which is confined to no particular class of cases. A "waiver" has been defined to be the intentional relinquishment of a known right. It is voluntary and implies an election to dispense with something of value, or forego some advantage which the party waiving it might at its option have demanded or insisted upon . . . , and this definition is supported by many cases in this and other states. In the recent case of Draper v. Oswego Co. Fire R. Ass'n, 190 N.Y. 12, 16, 82 N.E. 755, Chief Judge Cullen, in speaking for the court upon this subject, said: "While that doctrine and the doctrine of equitable estoppel are often confused in insurance litigation, there is a clear distinction between the two. A 'waiver' is the voluntary abandonment or relinquishment by a party of some right or advantage. As said by my Brother Vann in the Kiernan Case, 150 N.Y. 190, 44 N.E. 698: 'The law of waiver seems to be a technical doctrine, introduced and applied by the court for the purpose of defeating forfeitures. . . . While the principle may not be easily classified, it is well established that, if the words and acts of the insurer reasonably justify the conclusion that with full knowledge of all the facts it intended to abandon or not to insist upon the particular defense afterwards relied upon, a verdict or finding to that effect establishes a waiver, which, if it once exists, can never be revoked.' The doctrine of equitable estoppel, or estoppel in pais, is that a party may be precluded by his acts and conduct from asserting a right to the detriment of another party who, entitled to rely on such conduct, has acted upon it. . . . As already said, the doctrine of waiver is to relieve against forfeiture. It requires no consideration for a waiver, nor any prejudice or injury to the other party." . . .

It remains to be determined whether the plaintiff has alleged facts which, if proven, will be sufficient to establish his claim of an express waiver by the defendant of the plaintiff's breach of the condition to observe total abstinence. In the 12th paragraph of the complaint, the plaintiff alleges facts and circumstances which we think, if established, would prove defendant's waiver of plaintiff's performance of that contract stipulation. These facts and circumstances are that, long before the plaintiff had completed the manuscript of the first book undertaken under the contract, the defendant had full knowledge of the plaintiff's nonobservance of that stipulation, and that with such knowledge he not only accepted the completed manuscript with out objection, but "repeatedly avowed and represented to the plaintiff that he was entitled to and would receive said royalty payments (i.e., the additional $4 per page), and plaintiff believed and relied upon such representations, . . . and at all times during the writing of said treatise on Corporations, and after as well as before publication thereof as aforesaid, it was mutually understood, agreed, and intended by the parties hereto, that, notwithstanding plaintiff's said use of intoxicating liquors, he was nevertheless entitled to receive and would receive said royalty as the same accrued under said contract." The demurrer not only admits the truth of these allegations, but also all that can by reasonable and fair intendment be implied therefrom. . . . Tested by these rules, we think it cannot be doubted that the allegations contained in the twelfth paragraph of the complaint, if proved upon the trial, would be sufficient to establish an express waiver by the defendant of the stipulation in regard to plaintiff's total abstinence. . . .

Order reversed, etc.

RESTATEMENT (SECOND) OF CONTRACTS

§84.   PROMISE TO PERFORM A DUTY IN SPITE OF NON-OCCURRENCE OF A CONDITION

(1) Except as stated in Subsection (2), a promise to perform all or part of a conditional duty under an antecedent contract in spite of the

non-occurrence of the condition is binding, whether the promise is made before or after the time for the condition to occur, unless

(a) occurrence of the condition was a material part of the agreed exchange for the performance of the duty and the promisee was under no duty that it occur; or

(b) uncertainty of the occurrence of the condition was an element of the risk assumed by the promisor.

(2) If such a promise is made before the time for the occurrence of the condition has expired and the condition is within the control of the promisee or a beneficiary, the promisor can make his duty again subject to the condition by notifying the promisee or beneficiary of his intention to do so if

(a) the notification is received while there is still a reasonable time to cause the condition to occur under the antecedent terms or an extension given by the promisor; and

(b) reinstatement of the requirement of the condition is not unjust because of a material change of position by the promisee or beneficiary; and

(c) the promise is not binding apart from the rule stated in Subsection (1).

COMMENT

b. "Waiver and "Estoppel"; Mistake. "Waiver" is often inexactly defined as "the voluntary relinquishment of a known right." When the waiver is reinforced by reliance, enforcement is often said to rest on "estoppel." . . .

STUDY GUIDE: Does the U.C.C. recognize waiver? Estoppel? What is the difference between the two? How are they related?

SALES CONTRACTS: THE UNIFORM COMMERCIAL CODE

Reread: U.C.C. §2-208 (p. 374).

§2-209. MODIFICATION, RESCISSION AND WAIVER

(1) An agreement modifying a contract within this Article needs no consideration to be binding.

(2) A signed agreement which excludes modification or rescission except by a signed writing cannot be otherwise modified or rescinded, but except as between merchants such a requirement on a form supplied by the merchant must be separately signed by the other party.

(3) The requirements of the statute of frauds section of this Article (Section 2-201) must be satisfied if the contract as modified is within its provisions.

(4) Although an attempt at modification or rescission does not satisfy the requirements of subsection (2) or (3) it can operate as a waiver.

(5) A party who has made a waiver affecting an executory portion of the contract may retract the waiver by reasonable notification received by the other party that strict performance will be required of any term waived, unless the retraction would be unjust in view of a material change of position in reliance on the waiver.

2. Excuse to Prevent Forfeiture

Study Guide: Does the distinction drawn by the majority remind you of the difference between conditions precedent and conditions subsequent? Does the holding of the majority have substantial economic consequences for lessors in general? What is the value of the approach advanced by the dissent?

J.N.A. REALTY CORP. v. CROSS BAY CHELSEA, INC.
Court of Appeals of New York,
42 N.Y.2d 392, 366 N.E.2d 1313, 397 N.Y.S.2d 958 (1977)

Wachtler, J.* J.N.A. Realty Corp., the owner of a building in Howard Beach, commenced this proceeding to recover possession of the premises claiming that the lease has expired. The lease grants the tenant, Cross Bay Chelsea, Inc., an option to renew and although the notice was sent, through negligence or inadvertence, it was not sent within the time prescribed in the lease. The landlord seeks to enforce the letter of the agreement. The tenant asks for equity to relieve it from a forfeiture.

The Civil Court, after a trial, held that the tenant was entitled to equitable relief. The Appellate Term affirmed, without opinion, but the Appellate Division, after granting leave, reversed and granted the petition. The tenant has appealed to this court.

Two primary questions are raised on the appeal. First, will the tenant suffer a forfeiture if the landlord is permitted to enforce the letter of the agreement. Secondly, if there will be a forfeiture, may a court of equity grant

---

* *Solomon Wachtler* (1930-†) was educated at Milford Academy and Washington and Lee University (B.A., LL.B.). After being admitted to practice in New York in 1956, he authored numerous articles while in private practice. In 1973, he was elected as Associate Judge of the New York Court of Appeals and was appointed Chief Judge by Governor Hugh Carey in 1986. Judge Wachtler was arrested in November 1992 following a bizarre 13-month harassment campaign against his former lover, the socialite and Republican Party fund-raiser, Joy Silverman. He pleaded guilty in April 1993 to a single federal felony count of threatening to kidnap Ms. Silverman's 14-year-old daughter. His actions, he told the court, were meant to force Ms. Silverman to "seek my help and protection." After submitting his resignation from the bar in 1993 following his guilty plea, he was disbarred. In October 1994, Wachtler was released from prison after serving 12 months of his 15-month sentence and then performed 500 hours of court-ordered community service. In 1995, Wachtler formed an alternative dispute resolution company in Long Island. More than fifty retired judges, corporate executives, public officials, and labor lawyers have agreed to mediate or arbitrate cases for Wachtler's firm. In 1997, his book *After the Madness: A Judge's Own Prison Memoir* was published by Random House. His license to practice law in New York was reinstated October 1, 2007. — R.B.

the tenant relief when the forfeiture would result from the tenant's own neglect or inadvertence. At the trial it was shown that J.N.A. Realty Corp. (hereafter JNA) originally leased the premises to Victor Palermo and Sylvester Vascellaro for a 10-year term commencing on January 1, 1964. Paragraph 58 of the lease, which was attached as part of a 12-page rider, granted the tenants an option to renew for a 10-year term provided "that Tenant shall notify the landlord in writing by registered or certified mail six (6) months prior to the last day of the term of the lease that tenant desires such renewal." The tenants opened a restaurant on the premises. In February, 1964 they formed the Foro Romano Corp. (Foro) and assigned the lease to the corporation. By December of 1967 the restaurant was operating at a loss and Foro decided to close it down and offer it for sale or lease. In March, 1968 Foro entered into a contract with Cross Bay Chelsea, Inc. (hereafter Chelsea), to sell the restaurant and assign the lease. As a condition of the sale Foro was required to obtain a modification of the option to renew so that Chelsea would have the right to renew the lease for an additional term of 24 years.

The closing took place in June of 1968. First JNA modified the option and consented to the assignment. The modification, which consists of a separate document to be attached to the lease, states: "the Tenant shall have a right to renew this lease for a further period of Twenty-Four (24) years, instead of Ten (10) years, from the expiration of the original term of said lease. . . . All other provisions of Paragraph #58 in said lease, . . . shall remain in full force and effect, except as hereinabove modified." Foro then assigned the lease and sold its interest in the restaurant to Chelsea for $155,000. The bill of sale states that "the value of the fixtures and chattels included in this sale is the sum of $40,000 and that the remainder of the purchase price is the value of the leasehold and possession of the restaurant premises." At that point five and one-half years remained on the original term of the lease.

In the summer of 1968 Chelsea reopened the restaurant. JNA's president, Nicholas Arena, admitted on the stand that throughout the tenancy it regularly informed Chelsea in writing of its obligations under the lease, such as the need to pay taxes and insurance by certain dates. For instance on June 13, 1973 JNA sent a letter to Chelsea informing them that certain taxes were due to be paid. When that letter was sent the option to renew was due to expire in approximately two weeks but JNA made no mention of this. A similar letter was sent to Chelsea in September, 1973. Arena also admitted that throughout the term of the tenancy he was "most assuredly" aware of the time limitation on the option. In fact there is some indication in the record that JNA had previously used this device in an attempt to evict another tenant. Nevertheless it was not until November 12, 1973 that JNA took any action to inform the tenant that the option had lapsed. Then it sent a letter noting that the date had passed and, the letter states, "not having heard from you as prescribed by paragraph #58 in our lease we must assume you will vacate the premises" at the expiration of the original term, January 1, 1974. By letter dated November 16, 1973 Chelsea, through its attorney, sent written notice of intention to renew the option which, of course, JNA refused to honor.

At the trial Chelsea's principals claimed that they were not aware of the time limitation because they had never received a copy of paragraph 58 of the rider. They had received a copy of the modification but they had assumed that it gave them an absolute right to retain the tenancy for 24 years after the expiration of the original term. However, at the trial and later at the Appellate Division, it was found that Chelsea had knowledge of, or at least was "chargeable with notice" of, the time limitation in the rider and thus was negligent in failing to renew within the time prescribed.

Chelsea's principals also testified that they had spent an additional $15,000 on improvements, at least part of which had been expended after the option had expired. Toward the end of the trial JNA's attorney asked the court whether it would "take evidence from" Arena that he had negotiated with another tenant after the option to renew had lapsed. However, the court held that this testimony would be immaterial.

It is a settled principle of law that a notice exercising an option is ineffective if it is not given within the time specified. . . . "At law, of course, time is always of the essence of the contract.". . . Thus the tenant had no legal right to exercise the option when it did, but to say that is simply to pose the issue; it does not resolve it. Of course the tenant would not be asking for equitable relief if it could establish its rights at law.

The major obstacle to obtaining equitable relief in these cases is that default on an option usually does not result in a forfeiture. The reason is that the option itself does not create any interest in the property, and no rights accrue until the condition precedent has been met by giving notice within the time specified. . . .

But when a tenant in possession under an existing lease has neglected to exercise an option to renew, he might suffer a forfeiture if he has made valuable improvements on the property. This of course generally distinguishes the lease option, to renew or purchase, from the stock option or the option to buy goods. This was a distinction which some of the older cases failed to recognize. . . .

Here, as noted, the tenant has made a considerable investment in improvements on the premises — $40,000 at the time of purchase, and an additional $15,000 during the tenancy. In addition, if the location is lost, the restaurant would undoubtedly lose a considerable amount of its customer good will. The tenant was at fault, but not in a culpable sense. It was, as Cardozo says, "mere venial inattention." There would be a forfeiture and the gravity of the loss is certainly out of all proportion to the gravity of the fault. Thus, under the circumstances of this case, the tenant would be entitled to equitable relief if there is no prejudice to the landlord.

However, it is not clear from the record whether JNA would be prejudiced if the tenant is relieved of its default. Because of the trial court's ruling, JNA was unable to submit proof that it might be prejudiced if the terms of the agreement were not enforced literally. Its proof of other negotiations was considered immaterial. It may be that after the tenant's default the landlord, relying on the agreement, in good faith, made other commitments for the premises. But if JNA did not rely on the letter of the agreement then, it should not be permitted to rely on it now to exact a substantial forfeiture for the tenant's unwitting default. This, however, must be resolved at a new trial.

Finally we would note, as the dissenters do, that it is possible to imagine a situation in which a tenant holding an option to renew might intentionally delay beyond the time prescribed in order to exploit a fluctuating market. However, as the dissenters also note, there is no evidence to suggest that that is what occurred here. On the contrary there has been an affirmed finding of fact that the tenant's late notice was due to negligence. Of course a tenant who has intentionally delayed should not be relieved of a forfeiture simply because this tenant, who was merely inadvertent, may be granted equitable relief. But, on the other hand, we do not believe that this tenant, or any tenant, guilty only of negligence should be denied equitable relief because some other tenant, in some other case, may be found to have acted in bad faith. By its nature equitable relief must always depend on the facts of the particular case and not on hypotheticals.

Accordingly, the order of the Appellate Division should be reversed and a new trial granted.

BREITEL, C.J. (dissenting). . . . Had an honest mistake or similar "excusable fault," as opposed to what is undoubtedly mere carelessness, occasioned the tenant's tardiness, absent prejudice to the landlord, equitable relief would be available. . . . At issue, instead, is the availability of equitable relief where the only excuse for the commercial tenant's dilatory failure to exercise its option to renew is sheer carelessness.

Enough has been said to uncover a common situation. Experienced and even hardened businessmen at cross-purposes over the renewal of a valuable lease term seek on the one hand to stand by the written agreement, and on the other, to loosen the applicable rules to receive *ad hoc* adjustment of equities and relief from economic detriment. The landlord wants a higher return. The tenant wants to keep the old bargain. Which of the profit-seeking parties in this particular case should prevail as a matter of morals is not within the province of the courts. The well-settled doctrine is that with respect to options, whether they be lease renewal options, options to purchase real or personal property, or stock options, time is of the essence. The exceptions, namely, estoppel, fraud, mistake, accident, or overreaching, are few. Commercial stability and certainty are paramount, and always the dangers of unsolvable issues of fact and speculative manipulation (as with stock options) are to be avoided.

The landlord should be awarded possession of the premises in accordance with the undisputed language and manifested intention of the written lease, its 12-page rider, and modification. It does not suffice that the tenant may suffer an economic detriment in losing the renewal period. Nor does it suffice that the delay in giving notice may have caused the landlord no "prejudice," other than loss of the opportunity to relet the property or renegotiate the terms of a lease on a fresh basis. Once an option to renew a lease has been conditioned upon the tenant's giving timely notice, the commercial lessee should not be heard to complain that through carelessness a valued asset has been lost, anymore than one would allow the landlord to complain of the economic detriment to him in agreeing to an improvident option to renew.

The court unanimously accepts the general rule at law: an option to renew a commercial lease must be exercised within the appointed time period. . . . Underlying the bar to equitable relief is the theory that until the condition precedent is fulfilled, that is, until the required timely notice is given, there is no "forfeiture" for which equity will extend protection. . . . While the rule has been bolstered by traditional concepts of estates in land, its basis has current commercial and economic validity.

In this State, as in others, relief has been afforded tenants threatened with loss of an expected renewal period. . . . But in New York, as elsewhere, the circumstances conditioning such relief have been carefully limited. It is only where the tenant can show, not mere negligence, but an excuse such as fraud, mistake, or accident, that is, one or more of the categories common and integral to invocation of equity, that courts have, despite the literal agreement and intention of the parties, stepped in to prevent a loss. . . .

Even in the case of excusable default by the tenant the court looks to the investment the tenant has made to bolster his right to equitable relief. But the fact of tenant investment alone is not enough to justify intervention. . . . In no case of accepted or acceptable authority . . . were improvements alone enough to help the negligent tenant. . . .

[U]nder the guise of sheer inadvertence, a tenant could gamble with a fluctuating market, at the expense of his landlord, by delaying his decision beyond the time fixed in the agreement. The market having resolved in favor of exercising the option, the landlord, even though the day appointed in the agreement has passed, could be held to the return set out in the option, although if the market had resolved otherwise, the tenant could not be held to the renewal period.

Considering investments in the premises or the renewal term a "forfeiture" as alone warranting equitable relief would undermine if not dissolve the general rule upon which there is agreement. For, it is difficult to imagine a dilatory commercial tenant, particularly one in litigation over a renewal, who would not or could not point, scrupulously or unscrupulously, to some threatened investment in the premises, be it a physical improvement or the fact of good will. As a practical matter, it is not unreasonable to expect the commercial tenant, as compared with his residential counterpart, to protect his business interests with meticulousness, a meticulousness to which he would hold his landlord. All he, or his lawyer, need do is red-flag the date on which he has to act.

Having established no excuse, other than its own carelessness, Chelsea's claim is unfounded. Even if Chelsea honestly thought it enjoyed a 30-year lease, it does not change the result. Nor is it helpful to argue that Chelsea, always represented by a lawyer, was unable to procure a copy of the entire lease agreement. Indeed, it borders on the utterly incredible that experienced, sophisticated businessmen and their lawyers would not have assembled and scrutinized every relevant document affecting a long-term lease covering, with a renewal, a 30-year period.

That adherence to well-settled principles, like a Statute of Limitations or a Statute of Frauds, works a hardship on some does not, alone, permit a court to depart from sound doctrine and principles. Even if precedent did not control the same doctrines and principles discussed should be applied.

Accordingly, I dissent and vote that the order of the Appellate Division should be affirmed, and the landlord awarded possession of the premises.

Order reversed, with costs, and a new trial granted.

RESTATEMENT (SECOND) OF CONTRACTS

§229. EXCUSE OF A CONDITION TO AVOID FORFEITURE

To the extent that the non-occurrence of a condition would cause disproportionate forfeiture, a court may excuse the non-occurrence of that condition unless its occurrence was a material part of the agreed exchange.

REFERENCE: Farnsworth, §§8.5-8.7
                      Calamari & Perillo, §§11.27-11.37
                      Murray, §§111, 112

14

BREACH

In Chapter 13, we saw that the duty of performance can be conditioned on the occurrence or nonoccurrence of an event. One of the events on which a duty of performance may be expressly conditioned is the promised performance of the other party. In the absence of an express condition, are there any circumstances that justify one party unilaterally putting an end to the contract? Courts have developed a number of doctrines to answer this question. We shall consider three: "constructive conditions" (that is, conditions that are implied), anticipatory repudiation, and material breach. We then conclude this chapter by examining two different ways to measure damages when the party in breach has substantially performed.

A. CONSTRUCTIVE CONDITIONS*

In the previous chapter, we examined how courts interpret express clauses in agreements to determine whether or not they are conditions. In other cases, courts "fill gaps" in agreements that lack an express condition by supplying what is called a "constructive condition." By definition, then, a constructive condition is one that is not expressed, but it nonetheless has the same effect: The breach of a constructive condition by one party can relieve the other party of its duty of performance. In Section B, we shall consider the doctrine of material breach. Because a material breach by one party can also relieve the other party of its duty of performance, these doctrines are very closely related. At the risk of oversimplification, we can distinguish them as follows: Finding a constructive condition depends on a backward-looking inquiry into the presumed intentions of the parties at the time of formation, whereas finding a material breach depends on a forward-looking inquiry into the likelihood of performance occurring in the future. (But this distinction, like most, gets muddy pretty quickly in the context of particular cases.) We shall see how the former inquiry sometimes resembles the duty of good-faith performance (which we studied in Chapter 12), while the latter resembles the doctrine of anticipatory repudiation, so we will postpone our study of material breach until after we read about anticipatory repudiation.

*Once again, we thank David V. Snyder of the American University Washington College of Law, for compiling and coediting the materials in this section.

STUDY GUIDE: *Given that performances in the next case were not expressly conditioned on each other, why did the court "construe" the agreement to include a condition? The rules in the following cases are still with us, for example in Restatement (Second) §237 and §§2-507 and 2-511 of the U.C.C.*

KINGSTON v. PRESTON
Court of King's Bench,
Lofft 194, 198, 98 Eng. Rep. 606, 608 (1773)

It was an action of debt, for nonperformance of convenants contained in certain articles of agreement between the plaintiff and the defendant. The declaration stated; — That, by articles made the 24th of March 1770, the plaintiff, for the considerations therein-after mentioned, covenanted, with the defendant, to serve him for one year and a quarter next ensuing, as a covenant-servant, in his trade of a silk-mercer at £200 a year, and in consideration of the premises, the defendant covenanted, that at the end of the year and a quarter, he would give up his business of a mercer to the plaintiff, and a nephew of the defendant, or some other person to be nominated by the defendant, and give up to them his stock in trade, at a fair valuation; and that, between the young traders, deeds of partnership should be executed for 14 years, and, from and immediately after the execution of the said deeds, the defendant would permit the said young traders to carry on the said business in the defendant's house.— Then the declaration stated a covenant by the plaintiff, that he would accept the business and stock in trade, at a fair valuation, with the defendant's nephew, or such other person, c. and execute such deeds of partnership, and, further, that the plaintiff should, and would, at, and before the sealing and delivery of the deeds, cause and procure good and sufficient security to be given to the defendant, to be approved of by the defendant, for the payment of £250 monthly, to the defendant, in lieu of a moiety of the monthly produce of the stock in trade, until the value of the stock should be reduced to £4000. — Then the plaintiff averred, that he had performed, and been ready to perform, his covenants, and assigned for breach, on the part of the defendant, that he had refused to surrender and give up his business, at the end of the said year and a quarter. —The defendant pleaded, 1. That the plaintiff did not offer sufficient security and, 2. That he did not give sufficient security for the payment of the £250 c. — And the plaintiff demurred generally to both pleas.— On the part of the plaintiff, the case was argued by Mr. Buller, who contended, that the covenants were mutual and independent, and, therefore, a plea of the breach of one of the covenants to be performed by the plaintiff was no bar to an action for a breach by the defendant of one of which he had bound himself to perform, but that the defendant might have his remedy for the breach by the plaintiff, in a separate action. On the other side, Mr. Grose insisted, that the covenants were dependent in their nature, and, therefore, performance must be alleged: the security to be given for the money, was manifestly the chief object of the transaction, and it would be highly unreasonable to construe the agreement, so as to oblige the defendant to give up a beneficial business, and valuable stock in trade, and trust to the plaintiff's personal security, (who might, and indeed was

admitted to be worth nothing,) for the performance of his part. —
In delivering the judgment of the court, LORD MANSFIELD* expressed himself
to the following effect: — There are three kinds of covenants: 1. Such as are
called mutual and independent, where either party may recover damages
from the other, for the injury he may have received by a breach of the
covenants in his favour, and where it is no excuse for the defendant, to
allege a breach of the covenants on the part of the plaintiff. 2. There are
covenants which are conditions and dependent, in which the performance
of one depends on the prior performance of another, and, therefore, till this
prior condition is performed, the other party is not liable to an action on his
covenant. 3. There is also a third sort of covenants, which are mutual conditions to be performed at the same time and, in these, if one party was
ready, and offered, to perform his part, and the other neglected, or refused
to perform his, he who was ready, and offered, has fulfilled his engagement,
and may maintain an action for the default of the other; though it is not
certain that either is obliged to do the first act. — His Lordship then proceeded to say, that the dependence or independence, of covenants was to
be collected from the evident sense and meaning of the parties, and, that,
however transposed they might be in the deed, their precedency must
depend on the order of time in which the intent of the transaction requires
their performance. That, in the case before the court, it would be the greatest injustice if the plaintiff should prevail: The essence of the agreement
was, that the defendant should not trust to the personal security of the
plaintiff, but, before he delivered up his stock and business, should have
good security for the payment of the money. The giving such security, therefore, must necessarily be a condition precedent. — Judgment was accordingly given for the defendant, because the part to be performed by the
plaintiff was clearly a condition precedent.[1]

*William Murray, Earl of Mansfield (1704-1793) was born in Scone (near Perth),
Scotland. In 1727, he received his B.A. from Oxford, his M.A. in 1730, and was then called
to the bar at Lincoln's Inn. In 1742, after a career as a barrister in the Court of Chancery,
Murray was made solicitor general and entered parliament. He continued as solicitor general
until his promotion to the position of attorney-general. Murray received his appointment as
Lord Chief Justice of the King's Bench, and his creation as Lord Mansfield in the county of
Nottingham on November 8, 1756. Known as "the founder of the commercial law of the
country," during the 32 years of his tenure, there were only two cases in which the whole
bench was not unanimous, and only two of his judgments were reversed on appeal. He
officially retired in 1788. — L.R.

1. This account of Kingston v. Preston is taken from the argument of one of the advocates in Jones v. Barkley, 2 Dougl. 685, 689, 99 Eng. Rep. 434, 437 (K.B. 1781). Blindly
trusting an advocate's characterization of a case can be dangerous, so the reporter's version
of the lead opinion is reproduced in this note. The reporter's version (Lofft 194, 198, 98 Eng.
Rep. 606, 608) is less straightforward but is perhaps more reliable — and more vivid.

The rule of law, to be sure is, that covenants independent cannot be set off one
against the other. There is another sort of covenants, which are, in their nature, conditions; and he who is to perform the first condition, cannot have his action till he has
performed.

There are also covenants reciprocal: such are all purchases; in which, if the seller
is ready, tendering the conveyance, and the buyer is not ready to pay the money, then
the seller shall not pass his estate without.

It would be the most monstrous case in the world, if the argument on the side of Mr. Buller's
client was to prevail. It's of the very essence of the agreement, that the defendant will not
trust the personal security of the plaintiff. A Court of Justice is to say, that by operation of law

MORTON v. LAMB
Court of King's Bench,
7 T.R. 125, 101 Eng. Rep. 890 (1797)

LORD KENYON, C.J.* If this question depended on the technical niceties of pleading, I should not feel so much confidence as I do: but it depends altogether on the true construction of this agreement. The defendant agreed with the plaintiff for a certain quantity of corn, to be delivered at Shardlow within a certain time, and there can be no doubt but that the parties intended that the payment should be made at the time of the delivery. It is not imputed to the defendant that he did not carry the corn to Shardlow, but that he did not deliver it to the plaintiff: to this declaration the defendant objects, and says "I did not deliver the corn to you (the plaintiff), because you do not say that you were ready to pay for it; and if you were not ready, I am not bound to deliver the corn", and the question is, whether that should or should not have been alleged. The case decided by Lord Holt in Salk. 112, if indeed so plain a case wanted that authority to support it, shews that where two concurrent acts are to be done, the party who sues the other for non-performance must aver that he had performed, or was ready to perform, his part of the contract. Then the plaintiff in this case cannot impute to the defendant the non-delivery of the corn, without alleging that he was ready to pay the price of it. A plaintiff, who comes into a Court of Justice, must shew that he is in a condition to maintain his action. But it has been argued that the delivery of the corn was a condition precedent, and some cases have been cited to prove it: but they do not appear to me to be applicable. In the one in *Saunders*, the party was to pull down a wall, and was then to be paid for it; there is no doubt but that the pulling down of the wall was a condition precedent to the payment; the act was to be done, and then the price was to be paid for it. So in the case in Salk. 171, where work was to be done, and then the workman was to be paid. And in ordinary cases of this kind the work is to be done before the wages are earned: but those cases do not apply to the present, where both the acts are to be done at the same time. Speaking of conditions precedent and subsequent in other cases only lead to confusion. In the case of Campbell

---

he shall, against his teeth. He is to let him into his house to squander every thing there, without any thing to rely on but what he has absolutely refused to trust. This payment, therefore, was a precedent condition before the covenant of putting into possession was to be performed on the part of the defendant.

*Lloyd Kenyon (Lord Kenyon) (1732-1802) was entered at the Middle Temple and called to the bar on February 7, 1756. Kenyon became known for attending courts in the Welsh and Oxford circuits and interposing, sometimes as *amicus curiae*, with some abtruse law or forgotten clause in an old act of parliament. His eccentric manner attracted the attention of Lord Thurlow, who, upon becoming Lord Chancellor, conferred upon Kenyon the chief justiceship of Chester. He was advanced to the attorney-generalship in 1782 and served until 1783, when both he and Lord Thurlow were turned out by the Coalition. Although he was subsequently reappointed under Mr. Pitt, Kenyon chose to receive the office of Master of the Rolls, and the honor of a baronetcy in 1784. After presiding at the Rolls for four years, he was raised, on the resignation of Lord Mansfield, to the head of the Court of the King's Bench on June 9, 1788, and was created a peer by the title of Lord Kenyon of Gredington on the same day. His presidency lasted 14 years until his death, which occurred in 1802. — L.R.

v. Jones, I thought, and still continue of that opinion, that whether covenants be or be not independent of each other, must depend on the good
sense of the case, and on the order in which the several things are to be
done: but here both things, the delivery of the corn by one, and the payment
by the other, were to be done at the same time; and as the plaintiff has not
averred that he was ready to pay for the corn, he cannot maintain this action
against the defendant for not delivering it.

[handwritten margin note: Money & Corn ? is the essence of the contract]

GROSE, J.* It is difficult to reconcile all the cases in the books on the
subject of conditions precedent; but the good sense to be extracted from
them all is, that if one party convenant to do one thing in consideration of
the other party's doing another, each must be ready to perform his part
of the contract at the time he charges the other with non-performance. Here
the question is, what was the intention of the parties; they clearly intended
that something should be done by each at the same time. The corn was to be
delivered at Shardlow to the plaintiff for a certain price to be therefore paid
by him, that is, at the time of the delivery; then the readiness to pay should
have been averred by the plaintiff. . . .

*STUDY GUIDE: The next case raises two distinct issues. First, was the
promise to pay the balance due on the house "conditioned" on the perfect
completion of all work or was it "independent"? Second, if independent,
what is the appropriate way to measure the expectation interest given the
nature of the breach: "cost of replacement" or "diminution in market
value"? We shall take up the first of these questions here and postpone
the second until the end of this chapter in Section C. For now, consider
why, given the various stipulations in the contract, Cardozo decided that
the promise to pay the balance due was not conditioned on perfectly
complete performance. Is Jacob & Youngs consistent with Morton v.
Lamb and Kingston v. Preston? Can its holding be seen as a response to
those cases that was intended "to mitigate the[ir] rigor"?*

JACOB & YOUNGS v. KENT
Court of Appeals of New York,
230 N.Y. 239, 129 N.E. 889 (1921)

CARDOZO, J. The plaintiff built a country residence for the defendant at a
cost of upwards of $77,000, and now sues to recover a balance of $3,483.46,
remaining unpaid. The work of construction ceased in June, 1914, and the
defendant then began to occupy the dwelling. There was no complaint of

---

* *Nash Grose* (approx. 1740-1814) was called to the bar at Lincoln's Inn in November
1766. After a short career as a barrister, he took the degree of serjeant in 1774 and soon
commanded the leading business in the Common Pleas until he was raised to the bench to
succeed Justice Edward Wiles in 1787 and received the usual honor of knighthood. After
occupying the same seat for 26 years, his failing health forced him to resign in 1813. He died
the following year, and his remains were interred in the Isle of Wight. His name should look
familiar from Kingston v. Preston. — L.R.

defective performance until March, 1915. One of the specifications for the plumbing work provides that

> all wrought iron pipe must be well galvanized, lap welded pipe of the grade known as "standard pipe" of Reading manufacture.

The defendant learned in March, 1915, that some of the pipe, instead of being made in Reading, was the product of other factories. The plaintiff was accordingly directed by the architect to do the work anew. The plumbing was then encased within the walls except in a few places where it had to be exposed. Obedience to the order meant more than the substitution of other pipe. It meant the demolition at great expense of substantial parts of the completed structure. The plaintiff left the work untouched, and asked for a certificate that the final payment was due. Refusal of the certificate was followed by this suit.

The evidence sustains a finding that the omission of the prescribed brand of pipe was neither fraudulent nor willful. It was the result of the oversight and inattention of the plaintiff's subcontractor. Reading pipe is distinguished from Cohoes pipe and other brands only by the name of the manufacturer stamped upon it at intervals of between six and seven feet. Even the defendant's architect, though he inspected the pipe upon arrival, failed to notice the discrepancy. The plaintiff tried to show that the brands installed, though made by other manufacturers, were the same in quality, in appearance, in market value and in cost as the brand stated in the contract — that they were, indeed, the same thing, though manufactured in another place. The evidence was excluded, and a verdict directed for the defendant. The Appellate Division reversed, and granted a new trial.

We think the evidence, if admitted, would have supplied some basis for the inference that the defect was insignificant in its relation to the project. The courts never say that one who makes a contract fills the measure of his duty by less than full performance. They do say, however, that an omission, both trivial and innocent, will sometimes be atoned for by allowance of the resulting damage, and will not always be the breach of a condition to be followed by a forfeiture. The distinction is akin to that between dependent and independent promises, or between promises and conditions. Anson on Contracts (Corbin's Ed.) §367; 2 Williston on Contracts, §842. Some promises are so plainly independent that they can never by fair construction be conditions of one another. . . . Others are so plainly dependent that they must always be conditions. Others, though dependent and thus conditions when there is departure in point of substance, will be viewed as independent and collateral when the departure is insignificant. . . . Considerations partly of justice and partly of presumable intention are to tell us whether this or that promise shall be placed in one class or in another. The simple and the uniform will call for different remedies from the multifarious and the intricate. The margin of departure within the range of normal expectation upon a sale of common chattels will vary from the margin to be expected upon a contract for the construction of a mansion or a "skyscraper." There will be harshness sometimes and oppression in the implication of a condition when the thing upon which labor has been expended is incapable of surrender because united to the land, and equity and reason in the implication of a like condition when the subject-matter, if defective, is in shape to be returned. From the conclusion that promises may not be treated as dependent to the extent of their uttermost minutiae without a sacrifice of justice, the progress is a short one to the conclusion that they may not be so treated without a perversion of intention. Intention not otherwise revealed may be presumed to hold in contemplation the reasonable and probable. If something else is in view, it must not be left to implication. There will be no assumption of a purpose to visit venial faults with oppressive retribution.

Those who think more of symmetry and logic in the development of legal rules than of practical adaptation to the attainment of a just result will be troubled by a classification where the lines of division are so wavering and blurred. Something, doubtless, may be said on the score of consistency and certainty in favor of a stricter standard. The courts have balanced such considerations against those of equity and fairness, and found the latter to be the weightier. The decisions in this state commit us to the liberal view, which is making its way, nowadays, in jurisdictions slow to welcome it. . . . Where the line is to be drawn between the important and the trivial cannot be settled by a formula. "In the nature of the case precise boundaries are impossible" (2 Williston on Contracts, §841). The same omission may take on one aspect or another according to its setting. Substitution of equivalents may not have the same significance in fields of art on the one side and in those of mere utility on the other. Nowhere will change be tolerated, however, if it is so dominant or pervasive as in any real or substantial measure to frustrate the purpose of the contract. . . . There is no general license to install whatever, in the builder's judgment, may be regarded as "just as good." . . . The question is one of degree, to be answered, if there is doubt, by the triers of the facts . . . , and, if the inferences are certain, by the judges of the law. . . . We must weigh the purpose to be served, the desire to be gratified, the excuse for deviation from the letter, the cruelty of enforced adherence. Then only can we tell whether literal fulfillment is to be implied by law as a condition. This is not to say that the parties are not free by apt and certain words to effectuate a purpose that performance of every term shall be a condition of recovery. That question is not here. This is merely to say that the law will be slow to impute the purpose, in the silence of the parties, where the significance of the default is grievously out of proportion to the oppression of the forfeiture. The willful transgressor must accept the penalty of his transgression. . . . For him there is no occasion to mitigate the rigor of implied conditions. The transgressor whose default is unintentional and trivial may hope for mercy if he will offer atonement for his wrong. . . .

In the circumstances of this case, we think the measure of the allowance is not the cost of replacement, which would be great, but the difference in value, which would be either nominal or nothing. Some of the exposed sections might perhaps have been replaced at moderate expense. The defendant did not limit his demand to them, but treated the plumbing as a unit to be corrected from cellar to roof. In point of fact, the plaintiff never reached the stage at which evidence of the extent of the allowance became necessary. The trial court had excluded evidence that the defect was unsubstantial, and in view of that ruling there was no occasion for the plaintiff to go farther with an offer of proof. We think, however, that the offer, if it had been made, would not of necessity have been defective because directed to difference in value. It is true that in most cases the cost of replacement is the measure. . . . The owner is entitled to the money which will permit him to complete, unless the cost of completion is grossly and unfairly out of proportion to the good to be attained. When that is true, the measure is the difference in value. Specifications call, let us say, for a foundation built of granite quarried in Vermont. On the completion of the building, the owner learns that through the blunder of a subcontractor part of the foundation has been built of granite of the same quality quarried in New Hampshire. The measure of allowance is not the cost of reconstruction. "There may be omissions of that which could not afterwards be supplied exactly as called for by the contract without taking down the building to its foundations, and at the same time the omission may not affect the value of the building for use or otherwise, except so slightly as to be hardly appreciable" (Handy v. Bliss, 204 Mass. 513, 519 . . .). The rule that gives a remedy in cases of substantial performance with compensation for defects of trivial or inappreciable importance, has been developed by the courts as an instrument of justice. The measure of the allowance must be shaped to the same end.

The order should be affirmed, and judgment absolute directed in favor of the plaintiff upon the stipulation, with costs in all courts.

McLAUGHLIN, J.* I dissent. The plaintiff did not perform its contract. Its failure to do so was either intentional or due to gross neglect which, under the uncontradicted facts, amounted to the same thing, nor did it make any proof of the cost of compliance, where compliance was possible.

Under its contract it obligated itself to use in the plumbing only pipe (between 2,000 and 2,500 feet) made by the Reading Manufacturing Company. The first pipe delivered was about 1,000 feet and the plaintiff's superintendent then called the attention of the foreman of the subcontractor, who was doing the plumbing, to the fact that the specifications annexed to the contract required all pipe used in the plumbing to be of the Reading Manufacturing Company. They then examined it for the purpose of ascertaining whether this delivery was of that manufacture and found it was. Thereafter, as pipe was required in the progress of the work, the foreman of the subcontractor would leave word at its shop that he wanted a specified number of feet of pipe, without in any way indicating of what manufacture. Pipe would thereafter be delivered and installed in the building, without any examination whatever. Indeed, no examination, so far as appears, was made by the plaintiff, the subcontractor, defendant's architect, or any one else, of any of the pipe except the first delivery, until after the building had

*Chester Bentine McLaughlin (1856-1929) graduated University of Vermont (A.B.) and studied law privately (1879-1881). He practiced law at Port Henry (1881-1896), serving as county judge and surrogate of Essex County, New York (1891-1895), and delegate to the New York Constitutional Convention (1894). He served two terms as justice on the Supreme Court of New York before being designated justice of the Appellate Division in 1898. He resigned from the Supreme bench in 1917 to accept appointment to the Court of Appeals of New York, to which he was elected in 1918. He retired from the bench in 1927, and became an official referee for the State of New York. — K.T.

been completed, plaintiff's [sic] architect then refused to give the certificate of completion, upon which the final payment depended, because all of the pipe used in the plumbing was not of the kind called for by the contract. After such refusal, the subcontractor removed the covering or insulation from about 900 feet of pipe which was exposed in the basement, cellar and attic, and all but 70 feet was found to have been manufactured, not by the Reading Company, but by other manufacturers, some by the Cohoes Rolling Mill Company, some by the National Steel Works, some by the South Chester Tubing Company, and some which bore no manufacturer's mark at all. The balance of the pipe had been so installed in the building that an inspection of it could not be had without demolishing, in part at least, the building itself.

I am of the opinion the trial court was right in directing a verdict for the defendant. The plaintiff agreed that all the pipe used should be of the Reading Manufacturing Company. Only about two-fifths of it, so far as appears, was of that kind. If more were used, then the burden of proving that fact was upon the plaintiff, which it could easily have done, since it knew where the pipe was obtained. The question of substantial performance of a contract of the character of the one under consideration depends in no small degree upon the good faith of the contractor. If the plaintiff had intended to, and had complied with the terms of the contract except as to minor omissions, due to inadvertence, then he might be allowed to recover the contract price, less the amount necessary to fully compensate the defendant for damages caused by such omissions. . . . But that is not this case. It installed between 2,000 and 2,500 feet of pipe, of which only 1,000 feet at most complied with the contract. No explanation was given why pipe called for by the contract was not used, nor was any effort made to show what it would cost to remove the pipe of other manufacturers and install that of the Reading Manufacturing Company. The defendant had a right to contract for what he wanted. He had a right before making payment to get what the contract called for. It is no answer to this suggestion to say that the pipe put in was just as good as that made by the Reading Manufacturing Company, or that the difference in value between such pipe and the pipe made by the Reading Manufacturing Company would be either "nominal or nothing." Defendant contracted for pipe made by the Reading Manufacturing Company. What his reason was for requiring this kind of pipe is of no importance. He wanted that and was entitled to it. It may have been a mere whim on his part, but even so, he had a right to this kind of pipe, regardless of whether some other kind, according to the opinion of the contractor or experts, would have been "just as good, better, or done just as well." He agreed to pay only upon condition that the pipe installed were made by that company and he ought not to be compelled to pay unless that condition be performed. . . . The rule, therefore, of substantial performance, with damages for unsubstantial omissions, has no application. . . .

What was said by this court in Smith v. Brady (supra) is quite applicable here:

> I suppose it will be conceded that everyone has a right to build his house, his cottage or his store after such a model and in such style as shall best accord

with his notions of utility or be most agreeable to his fancy. The specifications of the contract become the law between the parties until voluntarily changed. If the owner prefers a plain and simple Doric column, and has so provided in the agreement, the contractor has no right to put in its place the more costly and elegant Corinthian. If the owner, having regard to strength and durability, has contracted for walls of specified materials to be laid in a particular manner, or for a given number of joists and beams, the builder has no right to substitute his own judgment or that of others. Having departed from the agreement, if performance has not been waived by the other party, the law will not allow him to allege that he has made as good a building as the one he engaged to erect. He can demand payment only upon and according to the terms of his contract, and if the conditions on which payment is due have not been performed, then the right to demand it does not exist. To hold a different doctrine would be simply to make another contract, and would be giving to parties an encouragement to violate their engagements, which the just policy of the law does not permit. (p. 186.)

I am of the opinion the trial court did not err in ruling on the admission of evidence or in directing a verdict for the defendant.

For the foregoing reasons I think the judgment of the Appellate Division should be reversed and the judgment of the Trial Term affirmed.

HISCOCK, C.J., and HOGAN and CRANE, JJ., concur with CARDOZO, J. POUND and ANDREWS, JJ. concur with MCLAUGHLIN, J. Order affirmed, etc.

STUDY GUIDE: To understand the following per curiam opinion on the motion for reargument, you must know that the actual contract between Kent and Jacob & Youngs also contained the following provision: "Any work furnished by the Contractor, the material or workmanship of which is defective or which is not fully in accordance with the drawings and specifications, in every respect, will be rejected and is to be immediately torn down, removed, and remade or replaced in accordance with the drawings and specifications, whenever discovered." In light of this clause, was the stipulation in the contract that Reading pipe be used a condition, a promise, or a promissory condition? How did Cardozo distinguish them?

JACOB & YOUNGS v. KENT
Court of Appeals of New York,
230 N.Y. 656, 130 N.E. 933 (1921)

ON MOTION FOR REARGUMENT:

PER CURIAM. The court did not overlook the specification which provides that defective work shall be replaced. The promise to replace, like the promise to install, is to be viewed, not as a condition, but as independent and collateral, when the defect is trivial and innocent. [The law does not nullify the covenant, but restricts the remedy to damages.]

The motion for a reargument should be denied.

HISCOCK, C.J., and CARDOZO, POUND, MCLAUGHLIN, CRANE, and ANDREWS, JJ., concur.

Motion denied.

Relational Background: Why All the Fuss
About Reading Pipe?

STUDY GUIDE: How does the following discussion from Danzig cast light on the issue of subjectivity of value? In light of specification 22 of the contract quoted in this passage, could you argue that there was complete rather than substantial performance of the clause specifying the pipe? Finally, does this excerpt suggest that the concept of good faith may be helpful in determining whether the failure to install Reading pipe was an "independent promise" (or a material breach)?

RICHARD DANZIG, THE CAPABILITY PROBLEM IN CONTRACT LAW 120-125 (1978): . . .   George Edward Kent, the defendant in this case, was a successful New York lawyer who maintained two offices and two apartments in Manhattan as well as the mansion in Jericho (Long Island) whose construction provoked this litigation. In addition, George Kent acquired substantial wealth and political connections by his marriage (at age 38) to a daughter of W. R. Grace, then the owner of a large shipping line, and later Mayor of New York.

In 1913 when the Kents decided to build on land Mrs. Kent had acquired in Jericho during an earlier period, they hired an architect, William Wells Bosworth of New York City, who drew plans and specifications for a mansion on the property. In response to these plans Jacob and Youngs, a substantial, though not eminent, New York construction firm, tendered a "proposal" (an estimate of cost) for construction which was accepted. The contract and specifications for construction . . . were drawn and dated May 5 and May 7, 1913.

Why was pipe manufactured by the Philadelphia and Reading Iron and Coal Company specified? If Mr. Kent had a professional or financial connection with the Reading Company it remains buried. His surviving daughters, one born in 1898, another in 1911, are unaware of any such connection, as is his personal secretary of 20 years. While the latter entered Kent's employ in 1927, he saw most of Kent's papers and was consequently aware of his stockholdings and major clients for some years before that. In addition veteran employees at the remnants of what were the Reading Companies have never heard of a Kent or Grace connection and no member of either family shows up in the companies' annual reports as a director or officer from 1915-1945.

The contract specified a standard of pipe which cost 30% more than steel pipe — then the most widely used (and now the almost universally used) pipe. The makers of wrought iron pipe, however, claimed that the savings due to durability and low maintenance more than made up for the added expense.[2] The years from 1905-1920 saw a peak in the popularity of wrought iron pipe. For example Byers Co. reported a rise in the use of wrought iron pipe from 40-50% of the total market in New York City in the "few years" previous to 1916. This rise occurred, according to Byers, not in "cheap buildings sold to the public at large," but rather "in

---

2. A. M. Beyers Co., The Selection of Pipe for Modern Buildings 7 (1916).

skyscraper construction as well as in other large buildings planned and constructed with expertness and care." As an example of such a building a Byers publication printed a picture of a house built in Southampton, Long Island, another area like Jericho into which wealthy New Yorkers were moving after 1910. The house is very like that constructed for the Kents.

The Reading Company was by its account the largest manufacturer of wrought iron pipe in the country, having provided it for such famous New York buildings as the Metropolitan Life Insurance Building and the Chrysler Building. Indeed, its 1911 brochure asserted that "the majority of the modern and most prominent buildings in New York City are equipped with READING wrought iron pipe" and that "many leading architects and engineers have drawn their specifications in favor of wrought iron pipe, in instances prohibiting steel pipe entirely."

Interestingly, as this last comment suggests, these trade publications made their comparative claims not so much with reference to their competitors who made wrought iron pipe, as to those who made steel pipe. According to a pipe wholesaler interviewed in New York City in 1975, genuine wrought iron pipe was manufactured in the pre-war period by four largely non-competing companies: Reading, Cohoes, Byers and Southchester. According to this informant, all of these brands "were of the same quality and price. The manufacturer's name would make absolutely no difference in pipe or in price."

The testimony prepared for the Kent trial was to the same effect. If one reads between and around objections and exclusions of evidence it is apparent that Jacob and Youngs were prepared to show equality of price, weight, size, appearance, composition, and durability for all four major brands of wrought iron pipe. Indeed, in addition to other witnesses, an employee of the Reading Company was prepared to testify to this effect. Probably because of this evidence, Kent's briefs on appeal conceded that "experts could have testified that the substitute pipe was the same in quality in all respects. . . ." It appears that this concession crystallized into a "stipulation" before argument in the Court of Appeals, and that Cardozo's reference was to this when he directed a judgment for Jacob and Youngs.

Why then was Reading Pipe specified? Apparently because it was the normal trade practice to assure wrought iron pipe quality by naming a manufacturer. In contemporary trade bulletins put out by Byers and Reading, prospective buyers were cautioned that some steel pipe manufacturers used iron pipe and often sold under misleading names like "wrought pipe." To avoid such inferior products, Byers warned: "When wrought iron pipe is desired, the specifications often read 'genuine wrought iron pipe' but as this does not always exclude wrought iron containing steel scrap, it is safer to mention the name of a manufacturer known not to use scrap." Reading's brochure said: "If you want the best pipe, specify 'Genuine wrought iron pipe made from Puddled Pig Iron' and have the Pipe-Fitter furnish you with the name of the manufacturer."

The contract makes it especially clear that the use of Reading was primarily as a standard. Specification twenty-two says: "Where any particular brand of manufactured article is specified, it is to be considered as a standard. Contractors desiring to use another shall first make application in writing to the Architect stating the difference in cost and obtain their written approval of change." (Jacob and Youngs stressed the implications of this first sentence in their court of appeals brief.)

Why, given a realistic indifference to the maker of the pipe, did Kent refuse to pay for anything but Reading Pipe through three levels of litigation? Mr. Kent, according to some who knew him, carried cost consciousness "to an extreme point." As one put it: "The old man would go all over town to save a buck." Perhaps having paid the extra cost of wrought iron pipe, he felt cheated when not indisputably assured of the highest quality and purity with which Reading's name was associated. However, a Reading representative's willingness to testify for the plaintiff, and the apparent ability of Jacob and Youngs to show the equality of Byers, Cohoes, Southchester and Reading pipes (an equality probably realized by Kent's architect) suggest that Kent may have seized upon the pipe substitution as an expression of other dissatisfactions in his relationship with Jacob and Youngs. A summary of the construction process as revealed during the suit suggests anything but a harmonious relationship between builder and owner. . . .

While work was originally to be completed on the fifteenth of December, 1913, a modification was written and signed on the twenty-third of that month, extending the contract for an unspecified time and adding $580.00 to Kent's bill. (Complaint, paragraphs 6, 12, 13.) The reason given for the delay is that "the defendant failed to perform what he was to do under the said contract in time so the plaintiff's work could be completed by the said time," and because of "the defaults and delays of defendant." This language parallels one excuse for delay allowed in Art. III of the contract. The only duty which Kent seems to have owed Jacob and Youngs was to make payment, although the missing specifications may have detailed some preparatory work which Kent or his agents were to have done. Thus the delay and need for modification may have hinged on other troubles causing Kent to withhold payment at certain points. Paragraph 8 of the complaint notes "certain alterations and omissions entitled the defendant to a deduction of $4,031.41." Here again, there is evidence of unhappiness on Kent's part with work done by Jacob and Youngs. The whole price paid under the subcontract for the plumbing was only $6,000, so the earlier disputes were over equally large aspects of the contract.

The Kents moved into the house in June 1914, after twice as much time had passed for completion as the contract specified. Yet even Jacob and Youngs averred no more in their complaint than that "substantial completion" occurred by November 13, 1914. At that time a new modification entitled Jacob and Youngs to $240, and specified several "minor details of work" yet to be completed. The $3,483.46 outstanding on the contract would not be paid until these defaults were cured. (Complaint, paragraphs 14, 15.)

Moreover, though Kent occupied the house in June 1914 and work stopped except for "minor details" by November, Jacob and Youngs had not received the final payment or certificate by March 1915, 2 years after the contract was signed, and 1 1/2 years after it was to have been completed. (World War I began in Europe in the summer of 1914, probably complicating supply conditions.) Yet until then, Reading pipe was never mentioned as a subject of dispute. . . .

REFERENCE: Farnsworth, §§8.1, 8.10, 8.19
                 Calamari & Perillo, §§11.8, 11.12-11.26
                 Murray, §§102(C), 105, 112

B. PROSPECTIVE NONPERFORMANCE

1. Anticipatory Repudiation

One reason why a party will be able to cancel a contract is if, before the time for performance arrives, the other party indicates that she does not intend to perform and thereby "repudiates" the contract. Because this repudiation happens before performance is due, it is called "anticipatory repudiation." (You will recall that the court in Inman v. Clyde Hall Drilling Co. discussed this doctrine.)

STUDY GUIDE: When reading the cases in this section, note the connection between anticipatory repudiation and the doctrine of avoidability of damages that we studied in Chapter 2.

ALBERT HOCHSTER v. EDGAR DE LA TOUR
In the Queen's Bench,
2 E. & B. 678, 118 Eng. Rep. 922 [1853]

On the trial, before Erle, J., at the London sittings in last Easter Term, it appeared that plaintiff was a courier, who, in April, 1852, was engaged by defendant to accompany him on a tour, to commence on 1st June 1852, on the terms mentioned in the declaration. On the 11th May 1852, defendant wrote to plaintiff that he had changed his mind, and declined his services. He refused to make him any compensation. The action was commenced on 22d May. The plaintiff, between the commencement of the action and the 1st June, obtained an engagement with Lord Ashburton, on equally good terms, but not commencing till 4th July. The defendant's counsel objected that there could be no breach of the contract before the 1st of June. The learned Judge was of a contrary opinion, but reserved leave to enter a nonsuit on this objection. The other questions were left to the jury, who found for plaintiff.

Hugh Hill, in the same Term, obtained a rule Nisi to enter a nonsuit, or arrest the judgment. . . .

LORD CAMPBELL, C.J.,* now delivered the judgment of the Court.

On this motion in arrest of judgment, the question arises, Whether, if there be an agreement between *A.* and *B.*, whereby *B.* engages to employ *A.* on and from a future day for a given period of time, to travel with him into a

---

*Professors Farnsworth and Young report that *John Campbell* (1779-1861) was "a Scotsman of ancient lineage, matriculated at St. Andrews University at the age of eleven. Upon entering the English bar he predicted that he would become Lord Chancellor. His name is associated with a number of law reform statutes which he pressed as a member of Parliament, as Attorney General, and in the House of Lords. As a reward for his services to the government, he was made the first Baron Campbell. He won literary fame with his 'Lives of the Lord Chancellors,' followed by the 'Lives of the Chief Justices.' These works are full of good stories, inaccuracies, and harsh judgments; it was said that they had added a new sting to death. He held judicial office briefly as Lord Chancellor of Ireland, where he was not popular, and as Chief Justice of England from 1850 to 1859. Then he became Lord Chancellor of England, at the age of eighty." E. Allan Farnsworth & William F. Young, Cases and Materials on Contracts 737 (4th ed. 1988).

foreign country as a courier, and to start with him in that capacity on that day, A. being to receive a monthly salary during the continuance of such service, B. may, before the day, refuse to perform the agreement and break and renounce it, so as to entitle A. before the day to commence an action against B. to recover damages for breach of the agreement; A. having been ready and willing to perform it, till it was broken and renounced by B. The defendant's counsel very powerfully contended that, if the plaintiff was not contented to dissolve the contract, and to abandon all remedy upon it, he was bound to remain ready and willing to perform it till the day when the actual employment as courier in the service of the defendant was to begin; and that there could be no breach of the agreement, before that day, to give a right of action. But it cannot be laid down as a universal rule that, where by agreement an act is to be done on a future day, no action can be brought for a breach of the agreement till the day for doing the act has arrived. If a man promises to marry a woman on a future day, and before that day marries another woman, he is instantly liable to an action for breach of promise of marriage, Short v. Stone, (8 Q.B. 358). If a man contracts to execute a lease on and from a future day for a certain term, and, before that day, executes a lease to another for the same term, he may be immediately sued for breaking the contract, Ford v. Tiley, (6 B. C. 325). So, if a man contracts to sell and deliver specific goods on a future day, and before the day he sells and delivers them to another, he is immediately liable to an action at the suit of the person with whom he first contracted to sell and deliver them Bowdell v. Parsons, (10 East, 359). One reason alleged in support of such an action is, that the defendant has, before the day, rendered it impossible for him to perform the contract at the day; but this does not necessarily follow; for, prior to the day fixed for doing the act, the first wife may have died, a surrender of the lease executed might be obtained, and the defendant might have repurchased the goods so as to be in a situation to sell and deliver them to the plaintiff. Another reason may be, that, where there is a contract to do an act on a future day, there is a relation constituted between the parties in the meantime by the contract, and that they impliedly promise that in the meantime neither will do anything to the prejudice of the other inconsistent with that relation. As an example, a man and woman engaged to marry are affianced to one another during the period between the time of the engagement and the celebration of the marriage. In this very case, of traveller and courier, from the day of the hiring till the day when the employment was to begin, they were engaged to each other; and it seems to be a breach of an implied contract if either of them renounces the engagement. This reasoning seems in accordance with the unanimous decision of the Exchequer Chamber in Edlerton v. Emmens, [6 Com. B. 160,] which we have followed in subsequent cases in this Court. The declaration in the present case, in alleging a breach, states a great deal more than a passing intention on the part of the defendant which he may repent of, and could only be proved by evidence that he had utterly renounced the contract, or done some act which rendered it impossible for him to perform it. If the plaintiff has no remedy for breach of the contract unless he treats the contract as in force, and acts upon it down to the 1st June 1852, it follows that, till then, he must enter into no employment which will interfere with his promise "to start with the defendant on such travels on the day and year," and that he must then be properly equipped in all aspects as a courier for a three months' tour on the continent of Europe. But it is surely much more rational, and more for the benefit of both parties, that, after the renunciation of the agreement by the defendant, the plaintiff should be at liberty to consider himself absolved from any future performance of it, retaining his right to sue for any damage he has suffered from the breach of it. Thus, instead of remaining idle and laying out money in preparations which must be useless, he is at liberty to seek service under another employer, which would go in mitigation of the damages to which he would otherwise be for a breach of the contract. It seems strange that the defendant, after renouncing the contract, and absolutely declaring that he will never act under it, should be permitted to object that faith is given to his assertion, and that an opportunity is not left to him of changing his mind. If the plaintiff is barred of any remedy by entering into an engagement inconsistent with starting as a courier with the defendant on the 1st June, he is prejudiced by putting faith in the defendant's assertion: and it would be more consonant with principle, if the defendant were precluded from saying that he had not broken the contract when he declared that he entirely renounced it. Suppose that the defendant, at the time of his renunciation, had embarked on a voyage for Australia, so as to render it physically impossible for him to employ the plaintiff as a courier on the continent of Europe in the months of June, July, and August 1852: according to decided cases, the action might have been brought before the 1st June; but the renunciation may have been founded on other facts, to be given in evidence, which would equally have rendered the defendant's performance of the contract impossible. The man who wrongfully renounces a contract into which he has deliberately entered cannot justly complain if he is immediately sued for a compensation in damages by the man whom he has injured: and it seems reasonable to allow an option to the injured party, either to sue immediately, or to wait till the time when the act was to be done, still holding it as prospectively binding for the exercise of this option, which may be advantageous to the innocent party, and cannot be prejudicial to the wrongdoer. An argument against the action before the 1st of June, is urged from the difficulty of calculating the damages: but this argument is equally strong against an action before the 1st of September, when the three months would expire. In either case, the jury in assessing the damages would be justified in looking to all that had happened, or was likely to happen, to increase or mitigate the loss of the plaintiff down to the day of trial. We do not find any decision contrary to the view we are taking of this case. . . .

If it should be held that, upon a contract to do an act on a future day, a renunciation of the contract by one party dispenses with a condition to be performed in the meantime by the other, there seems no reason for requiring that other to wait till the day arrives before seeking his remedy by action: and the only ground on which the condition can be dispensed with seems to be, that the renunciation may be treated as a breach of the contract.

Upon the whole, we think that the declaration in this case is sufficient. It gives us great satisfaction to reflect that, the question being on the record, our opinion may be reviewed in a Court of Error. In the meantime we must give judgment for the plaintiff.

Judgment for Plaintiff.

STUDY GUIDE: *The doctrine of anticipatory repudiation gives rise to two dangers. One concerns the vulnerability of the party who accuses the other of repudiation; the other concerns the potential misuse of the doctrine by a party seeking to justify its breach. Can you identify these pitfalls in the next case? How do you think the case would have been decided had the market price fallen instead of having risen?*

HARRELL v. SEA COLONY, INC.
Court of Special Appeals of Maryland,
35 Md. App. 300, 370 A.2d 119 (1977)

MELVIN, J.*

By written contract, dated 14 November 1972, the appellant (plaintiff below), Sam L. Harrell, agreed to buy, and the appellee (one of the defendants below), Sea Colony, Inc., a Delaware corporation, agreed to sell for $74,900.00 a condominium unit to be constructed by Sea Colony, Inc. in Bethany Beach, Delaware. The contract called for a deposit of $11,235.00 and the balance of the purchase price to be paid "at settlement." The $11,235.00 deposit consisted of $5,000.00 cash paid by Harrell and the execution by him, pursuant to the contract, of a promissory note for $6,235.00, payable "at settlement." Other pertinent parts of the contract were the following provisions:

> . . . In the event of a default by the Purchaser hereunder, Seller shall have the right to retain the cash deposit and enforce the Note. . . .
> Settlement shall take place within thirty (30) days of the posting of written notice to the Purchaser of substantial completion of the above unit, and at the offices of an attorney selected by the Seller. . . .
> In the event the above unit is not delivered to the Purchaser on or before January 1, 1974, the Purchaser shall have the right to terminate the Agreement and secure refund of deposit.

On 12 January 1974, the parties agreed in writing to extend the limiting date for delivery to 31 December 1974.

On 12 November 1974, Harrell filed a declaration in the Circuit Court for Montgomery County against Sea Colony, Inc. (Sea Colony) and its agent, Carl M. Freeman Associates, Inc. (Freeman), seeking damages for an alleged anticipatory breach of the contract. Harrell claimed that the defendants had "repudiated" the contract and sold the condominium unit to another buyer

---

Ridgely P. Melvin, Jr. (1917-1999) was educated at Princeton University (A.B.) and the University of Maryland (LL.B.). Admitted to practice in Maryland in 1947, he was a member of the Maryland House of Delegates from 1954 to 1962 and a circuit judge from 1966 until his appointment to the Maryland Court of Special Appeals in 1974. He was elected to that post in 1976 and retired from the bench in 1981. Known affectionately as "Ridge," his obituary described him as "Maryland special appeals judge and ocean mariner extraordinaire." During World War II, Judge Melvin served as an officer aboard the battleship *Washington* in the Pacific naval campaign. As a devoted yachtsman from childhood, he won the Triton Class National Championship in the early 1970s. In 1985, he and his wife Lucy sailed their sloop *Song* across the Atlantic. For the next eight years, they lived aboard while sailing through European and Mediterranean waters. — K.T. & J.B.

for more than the contract price. He claimed as damages the $5,000.00 cash deposit as well as the difference between the contract price and the amount for which the unit was sold to the other buyer. Harrell also claimed, in his second amended declaration, punitive damages. After considerable pre-trial maneuverings, the case finally came on for trial before the court sitting without a jury on 6 May 1976.

The evidence before the trial judge consisted of various documentary exhibits and the live testimony of the appellant Harrell and that of Mr. Norman Dreyfuss who was an employee of Freeman. The judge concluded that the appellant had without justification unilaterally cancelled the contract and judgment was entered in favor of both appellees, Sea Colony and Freeman. Because we find the evidence legally insufficient to support the trial court's conclusion that Harrell unilaterally cancelled the contract, we shall vacate the judgment as to Sea Colony. As to Freeman, however, we shall affirm the judgment in its favor.

Regarding Freeman, the most the record shows is that after the contract of sale was executed by Harrell and Sea Colony, Freeman acted only as agent for Sea Colony, its disclosed principal. Freeman was not a party to the contract and its name nowhere appears therein. The general rule regarding an agent's contractual liability to a third party is set forth in A. S. Abell Co. v. Skeen, 265 Md. 53, 288 A.2d 596 (1972):

> . . . If an agent, acting for his principal, enters into an agreement with a third party, he is personally responsible under that contract *if the identity of his principal is not fully disclosed and is in fact unknown to the third party.* This concept encompasses two basic factual situations: where the third party knows there is an agency relationship but is unaware of the principal's identity; and where the third party is not even cognizant that an agency relationship exists. (Citations omitted.) *Generally, if an agent fully discloses the identity of his principal to the third party, then, absent an agreement to the contrary, he is insulated from liability.* (Citations omitted.) However, this is subject to exception when the purported principal that is disclosed is nonexistent or fictitious; or when the principal is legally incompetent. (Citations omitted.) Id. at 56 [288 A.2d at 597].

(Emphasis added.) Here, there is no indication that in his dealings with Freeman, Harrell was not fully aware that Freeman was no more than an agent for Sea Colony. Nor is there any evidence or claim that Sea Colony, as a corporate entity, is "nonexistent or fictitious" or "legally incompetent." Under these circumstances, we hold that the judgment in favor of Freeman was properly entered, albeit not for the reason given by the trial court.

We turn now to the principal issue raised in this appeal, and that is the correctness of the trial court's ruling that Harrell had breached the contract. There is no evidence that Sea Colony or its agent Freeman ever gave notice, written or otherwise, to Harrell "of substantial completion" of the condominium unit he had agreed to purchase. On 28 May 1974, Harrell requested of Dreyfuss that he be allowed to assign the contract. He was told that he could not do so.[3] Harrell testified that he then told Dreyfuss

---

3. The contract provided that it "shall not be assigned or transferred without written consent of the Seller."

that I would be interested in getting out of the contract, that the units were selling for substantially more than my contract price, we all knew this, and I asked them if they would be interested in taking my contract back and reselling the unit, they could make any additional profit on it, if they could, and he said that he would look into the matter and he would be in touch with me.

Mr. Dreyfuss, testifying for the defendants, corroborated much of Harrell's testimony concerning this conversation and did not contradict any of it. He said:

Mr. Harrell stated he wanted to cancel the contract, did not want to proceed with settlement, and indicated that he wanted another disposition of his deposit. He did discuss the matter of the assignability, and I informed him again it was not assignable, and that was pretty much the gist of the conversation.

He told me that the reason was his personal financial situation, which was such that he felt he could not proceed with the purchase of this unit.

It was this 28 May conversation that the trial court seems principally to have relied upon to conclude that Harrell had anticipatorily breached the contract. We think the conclusion was clearly erroneous, particularly in view of subsequent events.

Following the 28 May conversation between Harrell and Dreyfuss, Dreyfuss sent Harrell a letter in mid-July enclosing a "cancellation *request* which must be signed by you in order for us to process *your release.*" (Emphasis added.) The letter continued:

Please detail the reasons *for your request*, and the factors effecting your decision not to proceed with the settlement of Unit 901-S, Phase II.

Once we receive this information we will be able to proceed with the determination on the disposition of your deposit. (Emphasis added.)

Harrell responded with a letter dated 17 July 1974 as follows:

Dear Mr. Dreyfuss:

Enclosed herewith is the Release relative to the above. You will note that I have predicated this upon the refund of my deposit and execution of the Release by Sea Colony by July 25th. This is necessary due to the proximity of the completion of the building so that unless Sea Colony is going to release me from the Contract and refund my deposit I will need as much time as possible to take the necessary action to protect my interest in this matter.

Thank you for your consideration in this matter.

The "Release" enclosed with Harrell's letter was the "Cancellation Request" form sent to him in mid-July. He stated therein that he *"wishe[d] to rescind* his Agreement for the following reasons: Personal financial considerations and the refusal of Sea Colony to allow the assignment of this contract. *This Release is contingent upon refund of deposit by July 25, 1974."* (Emphasis added.)

On 18 August 1974, Sea Colony entered into a contract with a third party to sell the condominium unit for $82,000.00, i.e., $7,100.00 more than the original contract price that Harrell had agreed to pay. In the meantime, so far as the record discloses, there had been no communication between Harrell and Sea Colony or its agent. Thereafter, Harrell received the following letter from Freeman, dated 23 August 1974 — five days after Sea Colony had resold the unit to a third party:

> Dear Mr. Harrell:
>
> *We are accepting your request to cancel* your unit number 901-South of Sea Colony Phase II. However, due to your being unwilling to comply with the terms of the contract, we are keeping your deposit as liquidated damages. (Emphasis added.)

This letter was followed by another from Freeman, dated 28 August, 1974:

> Dear Mr. Harrell:
>
> Enclosed is an executed release which relieves you of any further obligation towards the purchase of a home in Sea Colony. Enclosed you will find your cancelled Promissory Note in the amount of $6,235.00.
>
> We are sorry that you are unable to proceed with the purchase of one of our homes. If in the future we can be of service, we would be pleased to have the opportunity to serve you.

The "executed release" enclosed with this letter consisted of the same "Cancellation Request" form that Harrell had forwarded to Freeman with his letter of 17 July 1974. The form contained a space for "Agency Approval" and was executed by an "authorized officer of seller." The executing officer, however, had crossed out Harrell's statement on the form that "This Release is contingent upon refund of deposit by July 25, 1974."

In our view, Sea Colony unilaterally attempted to convert Harrell's *request* for a mutual rescission of the contract to an anticipatory breach or repudiation on his part.

In 6 Corbin, Contracts, §973, the standard for determining an anticipatory breach of contract is set forth:

> In order to constitute an anticipatory breach of contract, *there must be a definite and unequivocal manifestation of intention on the part of the repudiator that he will not render the promised performance when the time fixed for it in the contract arrives.* Doubtful and indefinite statements that the performance may or may not take place and statements that, under certain circumstances that in fact do not yet exist, the performance will not take place, will not be held to create an immediate right of action. *A mere request for a change in the terms or a request for cancellation of the contract is not in itself enough to constitute a repudiation.* (Emphasis added.)

Measured against that standard, we think the evidence in this case falls short of warranting a finding that Harrell breached his contract. Sea Colony argues that Harrell's statements to Dreyfuss in their 28 May conversation that he (Harrell) "wanted to cancel the contract" and "did not want to proceed with settlement" because his "personal financial situation . . . was such that he felt he could not proceed with the purchase of this unit" amounted to an impermissible unilateral cancellation of the contract and that Sea Colony was therefore justified in retaining Harrell's $5,000 cash deposit and in re-selling the property to a third party. Sea Colony concedes that Harrell's "Cancellation Request" in July "was simply an offer of the appellant to rescind." It contends, however, that the "contract at that time was already breached" by Harrell and therefore Sea Colony "was under no obligation to even consider" the rescission offer.

As evidence of Harrell's alleged anticipatory breach of contract, in addition to Harrell's 28 May conversation with Dreyfuss, Sea Colony points to the fact that Harrell failed to answer requests from Sea Colony to choose which of two attorneys' offices he preferred as the location for settlement. As we have already noted, the contract provided that "Settlement shall take place within thirty (30) days of the posting of written notice to the Purchaser of substantial completion of the . . . unit, and *at the offices of an attorney selected by the Seller.*" (Emphasis added.) In early April 1974, Harrell received a letter from Freeman indicating that the "Seller" had "selected" two alternative law firms at which settlement would take place — one located in Delaware and one located in Bethesda, Maryland. The letter asked Harrell to "indicate which location would be more desirable for you." The letter concluded with this statement: "Once we have received your preferences, the attorney's office will be contacting you with regard to more specific information." Harrell did not reply to this letter, nor to an identical one he received in early May. His failure to reply cannot be regarded as even a partial breach of contract, for there is nothing in the contract imposing upon him a duty to do so — and, as we have already indicated, there is no evidence that at the time he received these letters the triggering event for scheduling a settlement (that event being written notice of substantial completion of the condominium unit) had occurred, or that he ever refused to attend a settlement, or otherwise refused or failed to fulfill any obligation imposed upon him by the contract.

In summary, we hold that the evidence as a whole is legally insufficient to permit a finding that there was "a definite and unequivocal manifestation of intention" on Harrell's part that "he . . . [would] not render the promised performance when the time fixed for it in the contract arrive[d]." 6 Corbin, Contracts, supra. See also, Friedman v. Katzner, 139 Md. 195, 114 A. 884 (1921), where the Court of Appeals, in discussing the doctrine of anticipatory breach, made it clear that the alleged repudiator's "refusal to perform must be positive and unconditional" in order that it may be treated as an anticipatory breach.

Because the trial court found that Harrell had breached the contract, it did not reach the precise issue of whether or not Sea Colony was guilty of an anticipatory breach as alleged by Harrell when it (Sea Colony) resold the property to a third party. Although it may be said that the trial court did, at least by implication, determine that issue, it did not do so in the context of a non-breach by Harrell. We think the issue should now be decided in that context by the court below upon remand rather than by us in the first instance. Md. Rule 1085. We think the issue can be determined by the trial court on the present record and see no necessity for further evidence to be taken. We point out, however, that on the evidence before it a finding by the trial court that Sea Colony breached the contract of sale may not be required. On the evidence, another possible finding would be that there was a mutual rescission of the contract effected by the words and conduct of the parties. Under the particular circumstances of this case, these two possible alternative findings (a breach by Sea Colony or mutual rescission) are mutually exclusive. If the latter finding be made, it would seem that Harrell is entitled to the return of his $5,000.00 deposit. If the former finding be made, he may, in addition to the deposit, be entitled to further damages for Sea Colony's breach.

Judgment for appellee Carl M. Freeman Associates, Inc. affirmed. Judgment for appellee Sea Colony, Inc. vacated. Case remanded for further proceedings not inconsistent with this opinion. Costs to be paid by Appellee Sea Colony, Inc.

SALES CONTRACTS: THE UNIFORM COMMERCIAL CODE

§2-610. ANTICIPATORY REPUDIATION

When either party repudiates the contract with respect to a performance not yet due the loss of which will substantially impair the value of the contract to the other, the aggrieved party may

(a) for a commercially reasonable time await performance by the repudiating party; or

(b) resort to any remedy for breach (Section 2-703 or Section 2-711), even though he has notified the repudiating party that he would await the latter's performance and has urged retraction; and

(c) in either case suspend his own performance or proceed in accordance with the provisions of this Article on the seller's right to identify goods to the contract notwithstanding breach or to salvage unfinished goods (Section 2-704).

§2-611. RETRACTION OF ANTICIPATORY REPUDIATION

(1) Until the repudiating party's next performance is due he can retract his repudiation unless the aggrieved party has since the repudiation cancelled or materially changed his position or otherwise indicated that he considers the repudiation final.

(2) Retraction may be by any method which clearly indicates to the aggrieved party that the repudiating party intends to perform but must include any assurance justifiably demanded under the provisions of this Article (Section 2-609).

(3) Retraction reinstates the repudiating party's rights under the contract with due excuse and allowance to the aggrieved party for any delay occasioned by the repudiation.

2. Adequate Assurances of Performance

The converse of the situation involving anticipatory repudiation arises when one party wishes to withhold performance because he suspects, for some reason, that the other party may not perform. May he suspend his performance pending the receipt from the other party of adequate assurances of due performance?

STUDY GUIDE: When reading the next case notice how the issue of adequate assurances of performance mirrors the issue of anticipatory repudiation. Once again, notice the danger for the party seeking assurances: That party is accused by the other party of repudiating — and thereby breaching — the contract.

SCOTT v. CROWN
Court of Appeals of Colorado,
765 P.2d 1043 (1988)

PLANK, J.*

In this breach of contract action, defendant, Dennis Crown d/b/a Crown Company (Buyer), appeals from a judgment entered in favor of plaintiffs, Larry and Vera Scott, and from the dismissal of Buyer's counterclaim against them. We reverse.

During February 1983, Larry Scott (Seller) and Buyer entered into contract No. 76 for the sale of 16,000 bushels of U.S. No. 1 wheat. Pursuant to the contract, Buyer paid Seller $2,000 as an advanced payment. With respect to payment of the contract balance, the agreement reads in part:

> Payment by Buyer is conditioned upon Sellers [sic] completion of Delivery of total quantity as set forth in this contract. Any payment made prior to completion of delivery is merely an accommodation. In making such accommodation, Buyer does not waive any condition of this contract to be performed by Seller.

Elsewhere, the contract provided that the full balance would be paid 30 days after shipment of the total contract quantity of grain.

By March 13, 1983, Seller had delivered all the wheat called for in the contract. Payment of the full contract balance of approximately $49,000 was due on April 13, 1983.

On March 1, 1983 Seller and Buyer executed contract 78-2 for the sale of 13,500 bushels of U.S. No. 1 wheat and contract No. 81-3 for the sale of approximately 30 truck loads of U.S. No. 1 wheat. These contracts are the subject of this action. With the exception of quantity, the contracts had

---

Leonard P. Plank (1932-†) was educated at Regis College (B.S.) and the University of Denver (LL.B.) and was admitted to practice in Colorado in 1961. That year, he began legal practice in Denver; he served as judge on the Denver County Court (1970-1974) and the Colorado District Court (1974-1988). He was appointed to the Colorado Court of Appeals in 1988, where he currently serves. — K.T.

identical terms and conditions as those in contract No. 76, including the above-quoted provision and the provision for full payment by Buyer 30 days after complete performance by Seller.

In early March 1983, Seller commenced performance of contract No. 78-2. By March 15, 1983, he had delivered to Buyer approximately 9,086 bushels of wheat. However, he ceased performance because of his belief that Buyer could not pay for the wheat.

Seller was contracting with other grain dealers while working with Buyer. Seller suffered a loss on an unrelated contract. When reviewing this loss with his banker, Seller was told that Buyer was not the "best grain trader" and was advised to contact an agent from the Department of Agriculture for additional information about Buyer. The agent, Mr. Witt, indicated there was an active complaint against Buyer concerning payments to other farmers.

The next day, one of Buyer's trucks appeared at Seller's farm to take another load of grain. Seller refused to deliver the grain. Instead, he testified that he told the driver:

> that we had the grain, but were trying to get in touch with Mr. Crown, and my attorney advised me not to load until we had made contact with Mr. Crown to settle some questions that we had.

Seller and Witt testified that during the period of March 21 through April 6, 1983, they and Seller's attorney had attempted to contact Buyer several times by telephone, but were not successful.

By a letter dated March 23, 1983, Buyer responded to Seller's refusal to load the wheat. Buyer stated that he had not breached the contracts; however, Seller had breached the agreements. Buyer pointed out the payment terms requiring shipment of the full quantity before payment was due and requested that Seller resume performance. Otherwise, Buyer would be forced to "resort to cover." —? 2-712?

Buyer followed up the letter with an April 4, 1983, correspondence in which he notified Seller that he was cancelling the contracts. However, he assured Seller that, if the contracts were performed, his company would pay according to the contract terms.

Through counsel, Seller replied by an April 6, 1983, letter. Counsel informed Buyer that his client had not been paid on the contracts and that Seller had received information that Buyer had been paid by his buyers. Counsel demanded assurances of performance that Buyer would pay for the grain shipped on the fully performed contract 76 and the partially performed contract 78-2. However, under the contract terms, payment was not due on contract 76 until April 13, 1983, and was not due on contract 78-2 until 30 days after full performance.

Buyer cancelled contracts 78-2 and 81-3 on April 7, 1983. He had previously contacted grain sellers in Denver and Salt Lake City to effect cover, but by this date the grain was no longer available.

Seller instituted suit on April 25, 1983, alleging breach of contract by Buyer in not paying in full for the grain prior to delivery pursuant to his demand for adequate assurance of performance.

The circumstances at issue bring this action within the scope of §4-2-609(1), C.R.S., of the Uniform Commercial Code. That section provides: "A contract for sale imposes an obligation on each party that the other's expectation of receiving due performance will not be impaired. When reasonable grounds for insecurity arise with respect to the performance of either party, the other may in writing demand adequate assurance of due performance and, until he receives such assurance, may if commercially reasonable suspend any performance for which he has not already received the agreed return."

By the express language of this provision, reasonable grounds for insecurity about the performance of either party must exist in order for the other party to exercise further rights.

Buyer alleges that Seller did not have reasonable grounds for insecurity and, further, that the demand for assurance of due performance was defective. We disagree that there were no reasonable grounds for insecurity, but agree that the demand for assurance of due performance was defective.

Whether Seller had reasonable grounds for insecurity is a question of fact. See AMF, Inc. v. McDonald's Corp., 536 F.2d 1167 (7th Cir. 1976). Since trial was to the court, we will not disturb the court's findings that Seller had reasonable grounds for insecurity unless it was clearly erroneous and not supported by the record. . . .

The trial court found that reasonable grounds for insecurity existed because: 1) Seller recently had had an unfortunate experience similar to the incident at issue with another grain dealer (i.e., a pattern of unreturned phone calls culminating in nonpayment for a grain delivery); 2) Investigator Witt had informed Seller that his office had active complaints by other farmers against Buyer; and 3) Buyer failed to make personal contact after Seller refused to load the wheat. This evidence supports the trial court's conclusion of reasonable grounds for insecurity.

There are, however, serious problems with the timing, form, and content of Seller's demand for assurances of performance. The court found that Seller had made an oral demand for assurances by his refusal [to] load the grain and his conversation with the driver on March 22, 1983. However, Seller did not make the written demand until his counsel's letter of April 6, 1983, some two weeks after he had suspended performance.

Generally, the express language of the statute is followed such that a demand for assurances of performance must be in writing in order to be effective. . . . However, in some cases an oral demand for assurances has sufficed. . . . In such cases, there appears a pattern of interaction which demonstrated a clear understanding between the parties that suspension of the demanding party's performance was the alternative, if its concerns were not adequately addressed by the other party.

In AMF, Inc. v. McDonald's Corp., supra, for example, McDonald's had ordered 23 computerized cash registers from AMF. However, a prototype machine installed at a McDonald's franchise performed poorly. McDonald's personnel then met with AMF and demanded that the order for their 23 units be held up pending resolution of the problems experienced in the prototype. AMF failed to resolve the problem, and McDonald's cancelled the order. The court expressly rejected AMF's argument that McDonald's had not made a written demand, and held that McDonald's had properly invoked the pertinent Uniform Commercial Code provision.

Here, Seller made only the oral statement to Buyer's driver before he suspended performance. In our view, that was insufficient to make that suspension justified under §4-2-609.

Also, there was not a subsequent pattern of interaction between the parties that would clearly demonstrate that Buyer understood that Seller had requested assurances of performance. Indeed, Buyer's letter of March 23, and April 4, 1983, demonstrated that he thought that Seller had inexcusably refused to perform the contracts. Hence, we conclude that the conditions necessary to validate an oral demand were not met here.

Moreover, even if we were to conclude that an oral demand would have been permissible here, the content of the alleged demand is deficient. In contrast to AMF, Seller did not communicate clearly to Buyer that he was demanding assurances of performance. He simply told Buyer's driver that he wanted to "settle" some questions with Buyer. A mere demand for meeting to discuss the contracts, even if it had been in writing, would not be sufficient to constitute a proper demand for assurances. . . .

Finally, a demand for performance assurances cannot be used as a means of forcing a modification of the contract. . . . When Seller's counsel made the demand for assurances of performance, he demanded performance beyond that required by the contracts. In the April 6, 1983, letter, counsel requested payment in full of contract 76 and payment for the grain delivered on contract 78-2. At that time, Buyer was not obligated under the terms of the contracts to make such payments.

Under these facts, we conclude that Seller did not have the right to suspend performance because he failed to act in a manner that would bring him within the scope of §4-2-609. Instead, Seller's action constituted an anticipatory repudiation which gave Buyer the right to cancel the contracts and resort to the buyer's remedies as provided in §4-2-713, C.R.S.

This matter is remanded to the trial court to determine the following factual issues relating to Buyer's damages: (1) whether the grain being delivered was U.S. No. 1 wheat or a lesser quality; (2) the date Buyer first learned of the breach; and (3) the fair market value of the wheat on the date Buyer learned of the breach. Seller is entitled to all credit for grain sold and delivered and for which payment was not received.

Accordingly, the judgment is reversed and the cause is remanded with directions that the court enter judgment for Buyer after making findings on these issues.

SALES CONTRACTS: THE UNIFORM COMMERCIAL CODE

§2-609.   RIGHT TO ADEQUATE ASSURANCE OF PERFORMANCE

(1) A contract for sale imposes an obligation on each party that the other's expectation of receiving due performance will not be impaired. When reasonable grounds for insecurity arise with respect to the

performance of either party the other may in writing demand adequate assurance of due performance and until he receives such assurance may if commercially reasonable suspend any performance for which he has not already received the agreed return.

(2) Between merchants the reasonableness of grounds for insecurity and the adequacy of any assurance offered shall be determined according to commercial standards.

(3) Acceptance of any improper delivery or payment does not prejudice the aggrieved party's right to demand adequate assurance of future performance.

(4) After receipt of a justified demand failure to provide within a reasonable time not exceeding thirty days such assurance of due performance as is adequate under the circumstances of the particular case is a repudiation of the contract.

REFERENCE: Barnett, §5.2
                Farnsworth, §§8.20-8.23
                Calamari & Perillo, §§12.1-12.10
                Murray, §110

3. Material Breach

In deciding whether the promisee can unilaterally put an end to the contract, instead of seeking to find a "constructive condition," courts sometimes try to determine whether a particular breach by the promisor was "material." One way to understand this is to say that parties are free to expressly empower the victim of *any* breach — however small — to cancel the contract. But, in the absence of such an express condition, courts will not *construe* or imply a condition empowering the victim of a breach to cancel the contract when there has been *substantial* performance. And a party has substantially performed unless his nonperformance constitutes a material breach. In other words, in the absence of an expressed or constructive condition to the contrary, *only if a breach is material does it relieve the nonbreaching party of its duty of performance under the contract*. Another way to understand this shift in terminology is to consider that, in determining whether a breach is material, a court is no longer interested solely in the parties' presumed intentions at the time of formation. It is now also concerned with whether the nature of the breach jeopardized the promisee's confidence in receiving additional performances in the future.

An analogy by which we may better understand the concept of material breach has been offered by Eric Andersen:

> In countries such as the United Kingdom that have parliamentary systems of government, the current administration (or "government") remains in office until the next election or until it falls under a vote of no-confidence. Contract formation may be likened to the installation of a new government. One who enters a contract presumably has sufficient confidence in its future performance to make the promises or to give the other consideration required to bind the contracting partner to the deal, just as a majority in

parliament has sufficient confidence in party leaders to entrust it with political power. This is not to say that the person has full or even great confidence about the outcome, but only sufficient confidence to enter a relationship in which new legal ŏbligations are created. With the creation of those obligations arises the interest in future performance. . . . [T]hat interest exists in the frame of reference created by the contract. Thus, even one who lacks great confidence that the agreement will be properly performed is legally entitled to look to the other party for full, proper performance, just as members of parliament are entitled to hold the government accountable to provide effective leadership even if its ability to govern well is in doubt.

A change of government under a regularly scheduled election may be compared to the full performance of a contract. A majority may be content to have the government retain power, despite flaws in its performance. Similarly, although one party may breach a contract, the other party, as a reasonable person, may be willing to seek only compensatory damages rather than end the contract.

A change of government under a vote of no-confidence is comparable to cancellation following material breach. Just as a majority in parliament may develop sufficient doubts about the government's ability to govern that they are prepared to undergo the uncertainties, confusion, and inefficiencies that accompany an unplanned election, a party to a contract may reasonably conclude that a breach has so impaired the interest in future performance that terminating the contract relationship is prudent, despite the disruptions and difficulties it may entail. When that point is reached, the materiality threshold has been crossed.[4]

According to this analogy, the doctrine of material breach has evolved to handle much the same problem as that of anticipatory repudiation: the promisee (like the Parliament) is no longer confident that she will receive the "future performance" she is due under the contract. For this reason the promisee wishes to cancel the contract and pursue other measures to secure performance (just as a Parliament may vote to hold an election for a new government). In the case of anticipatory repudiation, the promisee's lack of confidence in future performance stems from the promisor's having communicated a lack of willingness to perform. With material breach, the lack of confidence stems from the nature of a breach that has occurred. By this way of thinking, when a material breach has occurred, the injury to a promisee's "interest in future performance" is different from and in addition to any injury sustained as result of having received less than what was bargained for.

After reading two cases that address this issue, we turn our attention to the law governing the sale of goods. There, a more exacting standard known as the perfect tender doctrine had been adopted in the common law. We shall see how it has been modified by the Uniform Commercial Code. In Section C, we conclude our study of breach by examining two ways to measure expectation damages after there has been a *non*material breach — that is, after there has been substantial performance.

4. Eric G. Andersen, A New Look at Material Breach in the Law of Contracts, 21 U.C. Davis L. Rev. 1073, 1108-1109 (1988). Although the theory that material breach can best be understood as a way of protecting a party's interest in future performance is Professor Andersen's, he credits the analogy to a parliamentary vote of no-confidence to Richard A. Matasar.

STUDY GUIDE: *Does Andersen's theory that the concept of material breach is used to protect a party's "interest in future performance" help explain the decisions in the next two cases?*

B & B EQUIPMENT CO. v. BOWEN
Missouri Court of Appeals, Western District,
581 S.W.2d 80 (1979)

WASSERSTROM, J.* B & B Equipment Company, Inc. filed this suit to obtain a judgment declaring its right to terminate a contract under which defendant John A. Bowen was entitled to purchase 100 shares of the corporate stock. Bowen counterclaimed for a declaration that the contract is valid and subsisting and that he has a continuing right to purchase the 100 shares. The trial court rendered declaratory judgment as prayed by B & B, and Bowen appeals. *Procedural Posture*

B & B is the successor to Braymen Tractor Company which was originally owned by Mr. and Mrs. L. D. Braymen. The Braymens took Robert J. Jaecques and William L. Hughes into the business in 1964, first as employees and then later as partners and finally as equal stockholders in a corporate form of doing business.

In 1968, L. D. Braymen wanted to retire and Jaecques and Hughes desired to find someone to take Braymen's place. At that particular time, Bowen who had had prior experience in the same line of business, was unemployed and available. Accordingly, on December 28, 1968, the parties entered into an oral agreement with Bowen under which Bowen would become an equal participant in the business in place of Braymen. Bowen, however, did not have sufficient funds to pay the value of Braymens' 100 shares of stock, which was agreed to be $15,000. The corporation therefore agreed to buy the stock from the Braymens for $15,000 and in turn to sell that stock to Bowen for the same sum. Bowen was to and did pay $2,500 direct to the Braymens. B & B gave the Braymens its note for $12,500, payable with interest of 6% per annum. Bowen was to be entitled to all dividends on the 100 shares, and he agreed to pay back the dividends to B & B for application on the purchase price of the stock. When those payments for the stock totaled $12,500, plus whatever interest B & B had by then incurred to the Braymens, B & B was to deliver the 100 shares to Bowen. Under the agreement, Bowen was to assume as his primary responsibility all the corporate record keeping and bookkeeping, and he was in addition to devote his full time and attention to the corporate business in whatever capacity became necessary, including selling. The salaries of all three men were to be equal.

Promptly after the making of that agreement, Bowen did assume his new duties and at the beginning performed in a manner satisfactory to Jaecques and Hughes. Dividends were declared from 1969 to 1976 of

* *Solbert M. Wasserstrom* (1913-1995) received his education at the University of Missouri (B.A., J.D.) before being admitted to practice in Missouri in 1935. He practiced in Kansas City until being appointed to the Missouri Court of Appeals Kansas City District by Governor Warren E. Hearnes in 1972. Judge Wasserstrom was re-elected in 1974 and completed his term in 1986. — R.B.

which Bowen's share came to $7,156 and which were paid to him. He, in turn, repaid an equivalent amount on each occasion to be applied toward the stock purchase. However, starting in about 1972, Bowen began engaging in outside business activities and spent less time on his duties for B & B, with the result that Jaecques and Hughes became more and more dissatisfied with Bowen's performance. This dissatisfaction developed to the point that on April 27, 1976, a meeting was held between the three men in which Jaecques and Hughes informed Bowen that he was discharged. Approximately two or three weeks before that, B & B had paid a dividend for the year 1975, of which Bowen's share was $800, and at the time of the April 27 meeting Bowen had not yet repaid that sum to be credited on the stock purchase.

Following his discharge, Bowen retained counsel and on May 4 his lawyer wrote to the B & B attorney stating that Bowen would release any and all interest in the corporation for the sum of $82,350. On May 24, 1976, the corporation's attorney responded that B & B had elected to rescind the 1968 agreement and tendered to Bowen the sum of $9,656, representing the $2,500 paid by Bowen to the Braymens, together with the $7,156 dividends which Bowen had received from B & B and contributed toward payment of the stock. On June 2, 1976, Bowen's lawyer wrote rejecting the Corporation's tender and countered with a tender by Bowen of $5,344, plus whatever the amount of interest was that B & B had paid the Braymens, in exchange for which Bowen demanded the issuance to him of 100 shares of B & B stock.

The impasse thus created led to the present lawsuit. After hearing evidence without a jury, the trial court made findings of fact which included the following:

6. That on or about April 27, 1976 Jaecques and Hughes fired defendant as an employee and officer in the business. This action resulted from dissatisfaction with defendant in not devoting his full time and best efforts to the interest of the business. That defendant over a period of time did not properly keep the books of the plaintiff's business and did not devote his full time to his responsibility in the business. That defendant, as of April 27, 1976, had not paid to plaintiff the $800.00 dividend to be applied on defendant's obligation to purchase stock. That such actions and omissions and failure to act and perform on part of the defendant constituted a breach of the terms and conditions of the contract between plaintiff and defendant.

9. The court finds defendant did breach the conditions of the contract of December 28, 1968 as set out in paragraph 6 herein and that plaintiff was entitled to rescind the contract upon payment to defendant of the sum of $9,656.00 representing the total of the benefits received by plaintiff from defendant under said contract. . . .

Bowen's [argument] on appeal is that his "breach did not go to the very substance of the contract and further, any breach was waived and the trial court should have estopped assertions otherwise." The legal doctrine upon which Bowen rests this argument is that a rescission of a contract for breach by the other party must relate to a vital provision going to the very substance or root of the agreement, and cannot relate simply to a subordinate or incidental matter. . . . Bowen attempts to bring himself within that principle by arguing: "The contract respondent corporation and appellant entered into on December 28, 1968, was for the purchase of L. D. Braymen's One

Hundred (100) shares of stock. . . . The further agreement of employment with the respondent corporation was incidental to the major purpose of the contract, that of purchasing the stock of L. D. Braymen."

The argument just quoted turns the real situation up side down. Rather than the principal purpose of the agreement being the sale and purchase of stock, clearly the major purpose of the transaction between B & B and Bowen was the performance of services by Bowen. The stock itself was to go to Bowen on terms which can be explained only on the basis that Jaecques and Hughes were willing to let him become a one-third owner in expectation of valuable services to be contributed by Bowen. Indeed by far the major part of the purchase price was to come from the corporation itself in the nature of a bonus which could only be for services rendered.

B & B did not make this deal with Bowen in order to obtain needed capital. Instead the real purpose which stands out on this record as a whole is that Jaecques and Hughes wanted a "third partner" to take the place of the retiring partner Braymen. What they wanted were Bowen's services, not his money and in fact the only money which Bowen was ever to put up out of his own pocket was the initial $2,500. The only realistic appraisal of this situation is that the services to be performed by Bowen were the "very substance and root of the contract" so that his failure to adequately perform those duties did constitute a material breach warranting recission.

Bowen suggests that the definition of materiality should be amplified by utilization of the guidelines set forth in Restatement of Contracts, Section 275. Comment a to that section states that in determining whether a breach of contract is a material one, it is impossible to lay down a rule that can be applied with mathematical exactness and that such a determination depends upon considerations of inherent justice. Nevertheless, this section of the Restatement suggests certain guidelines, each of which will now be considered in connection with the facts of the present case:

A. *The extent to which the injured party will obtain the substantial benefit which he could have reasonably anticipated.* Here, B & B (the injured party) received some performance from Bowen for a period slightly in excess of five years, but those services were defective. . . . Jaecques and Hughes had agreed that Bowen could acquire a one-third ownership in their corporation on extremely favorable terms, in the expectation that they were obtaining an experienced partner who would devote his full time and attention to the company business. That expectation failed of fulfillment. It cannot reasonably be said that Jaecques and Hughes received the substantial benefit which they had a right to expect.

B. *The extent to which the injured party may be adequately compensated in damages for lack of complete performance.* Bowen suggests no way in which his breaches of contract may be measured in monetary terms. This situation does not lend itself to compensation in damages.

C. *The extent to which the party failing to perform has already partly performed or made preparations for performance.* Bowen here had partly performed, but defectively. Despite protests, he failed and neglected to make good the deficiencies. This guideline operates somewhat in Bowen's favor, but not decisively so.

D. *The greater or less hardship on the party failing to perform in terminating the contract.* The value of the 100 shares of B & B stock appreciated between December 1968 and April 1976. Bowen will receive the benefit of at least a substantial part of that increase by reason of the payment to him of the $7,156 in dividends declared by B & B during that period. To the extent that Bowen does not receive the full benefit of the increase in value of the 100 shares, his wound is self-inflicted by his defaults in performance. In addition, whatever loss is suffered by Bowen is more than counterbalanced by the hardship and unfairness which would be caused to Jaecques and Hughes by an opposite ruling.

E. *The willful, negligent or innocent behavior of the party failing to perform.* . . . Jaecques made protest and gave fair warning to Bowen concerning the unacceptability of Bowen's performance. Bowen's continuance in his unacceptable performance was at the very least negligent.

F. *The greater or less uncertainty that the party failing to perform will perform the remainder of the contract.* This particular criterion is of doubtful application in this present situation. If it be applicable, Bowen has had over five years in which to demonstrate his good faith and willingness to carry his share of the burden. Jaecques and Hughes cannot with fairness be required to experiment even longer in some vague hope of improvement.

Bowen also argues that B & B should not be permitted to rescind because that would be a violation of good faith and fair dealing on its part, because it had waived any claim of defect in Bowen's performance, and because it should be estopped to assert any such defect. All this multi-faceted argument rests on the assertion that B & B never protested to Bowen concerning the unacceptability of his performance of duty and that the corporation therefore caused him to rely upon a belief that his performance was satisfactory. That argument in all of its aspects fails because of the false factual premise. . . . Jaecques did protest to Bowen and gave him warnings. It cannot be fairly said that B & B failed in any duty of fair dealing or that it was waived or is estopped to assert its right of rescission. . . .

[The judgment is affirmed except as to the amount which is to be paid by B & B to Bowen. This case is remanded to the trial court for the purpose of determining the amount of income tax paid by Bowen attributable to the corporate earnings by B & B which were not distributed. That amount is to be added to the $9,656 paid by Bowen toward the 100 shares of capital stock, and the aggregate total of those two sums is to be paid to Bowen by B & B.

All concur.

LANE ENTERPRISES, INC. v. L. B. FOSTER CO.
Superior Court of Pennsylvania,
700 A.2d 465 (1997), rev'd on other grounds,
710 A.2d 54 (1998)

Cirillo, President Judge Emeritus.* L. B. Foster Company (Foster) appeals from the order entered in the Court of Common Pleas of Bedford County. We reverse.

Vincent A. Cirillo (1927-2000), a Korean War veteran, received his degrees from Villanova University (A.B.) and Temple University (LL.B.) before being admitted to the Pennsylvania bar and clerking for President Judge Harold G. Knight in Montgomery County (1955-

This appeal arises out of litigation concerning an agreement between Foster, a manufacturer of steel bridge components and Lane Enterprises, Inc. (Lane), a company specializing in the coating of steel materials. In the spring of 1992, Foster agreed to sell Hammond Construction, Inc. (Hammond) various bridge components for use in the construction of a bridge in Summit County, Ohio. This agreement (the Hammond Agreement) specified that Foster was to supply the bridge components in two separate stages. The Hammond Agreement also stated that the bridge components were to be coated in accordance with the Ohio Department of Transportation (ODOT) specifications.[5] Because Foster was not equipped to coat the bridge components that it manufactured, it sought an outside contractor, Lane, to perform the coating process. On September 23, 1992, Foster and Lane orally agreed that Lane would clean and coat the bridge components. The agreement was confirmed by Foster's purchase order which specified that all cleaning and coating performed by Lane was to be in compliance with ODOT standard specifications for construction and materials and that Lane was not to ship any coated components without prior approval from an ODOT inspector (The Lane Agreement). In addition, reflecting Foster's delivery obligations pursuant to the Hammond Agreement, the Lane Agreement provided that Lane clean and coat the bridge components in two separate stages, the first stage to be delivered in October of 1992 (Stage I) and the second stage in June of 1993 (Stage II). Pursuant to the Lane Agreement, Foster shipped Stage I of the uncoated bridge components to Lane's facility in Carlisle, Pennsylvania for processing. Lane then commenced the cleaning and coating process for the Stage I components. During cleaning, however, some steel residue (shot) as well as other surface contaminants remained on the steel and became trapped under the coating.[6] ODOT Inspectors visited Lane and examined the coated components. Although the ODOT inspectors were not fully satisfied with the amount of contamination trapped under the epoxy coating, they permitted shipment pending removal and re-application of the coating.

On January 5, 1993, Lane's quality assurance manager, Gary Hinkelman, wrote a letter to Foster detailing the problems that Lane faced while coating the Stage I components. Hinkelman explained Lane's inability to remove all of the contaminants and inquired as to whether Foster desired Lane to coat the Stage II components or retain Midwest Coating to complete Stage II. On January 27, 1993, a meeting was held at the bridge construction site. ODOT engineer David Nist conducted an inspection of the delivered stage I components. Nist performed a contamination test by chipping a piece of the epoxy coating which revealed backside contamination. Additionally, Nist's inspection revealed that the epoxy coating on the trimbars, components attached to the sides of the bridge floor, was readily removable. Nist then informed Lane that the coating procedure did not adhere to

---

1958). After serving as Assistant District Attorney (1958-1962), Assistant County Solicitor (1964-1971), and Commissioner of Lower Merion Township (1971), Judge Cirillo began his judicial career in 1982 as Judge for the Pennsylvania Court of Common Pleas Thirty-eighth Judicial District. In 1982, he was elected to the Superior Court of Pennsylvania. — R.B.

5. Coating the metallic bridge components is necessary to prevent corrosion.

6. Impurities trapped between the epoxy coating and the steel surface in construction parlance is called "backside contamination."

the Steel Structure Painting Council's surface preparation standard ten (SSPC SP-10) which was required for ODOT's approval. Nist, therefore, rejected the coated components.

A second on-site meeting was convened on February 5, 1993 to discuss how to rectify the situation. Representatives from Lane, Foster, and Hammond were all present. Lane representatives noted that pursuant to SSPC SP-10, ten to twenty percent backside contamination of an epoxy chip was acceptable. Via tele-conference, ODOT vehemently disagreed, stressing that SSPC SP-10 allowed zero percent backside contamination. Lane representatives then informed those present that if SSPC-10 required zero percent contamination, Lane would be unable to meet those requirements.

On February 8, 1993, ODOT sent a letter to Hammond formally rejecting the Stage I coated bridge components in their present condition. ODOT proposed, however, that if the unacceptable portions of the components underwent certain field repairs, ODOT would accept the components. Foster sent a letter to Lane advising that Foster would withhold payment until corrections were made. At this time, Foster still owed Lane $18,018.06 for Stage I. Lane agreed to assume the cost of the field repairs, which would be deducted from the $18,018.06 still owed to Lane. Hammond then subcontracted with Thomarios Painting to complete the field repairs at a cost of $10,935.84. After the repairs were completed, Lane requested the amount still owing on Stage I, $7,082.22.

ODOT eventually permitted Hammond to proceed with erection of the bridge, thus, presumably approving the repaired bridge components. On June 15, 1993, Foster sent Lane a letter inquiring as to whether Lane intended to perform Stage II of the Lane Agreement. The letter also stated that outstanding monies due Lane for Stage I, $7,082.22, would not be released until Lane gave assurances concerning its commitment to Stage II of the Lane Agreement. Lane responded that it would not discuss Stage II until Foster remitted the monies owed under Stage I. Foster sent a second letter on July 2, 1993, repeating its request for assurance of performance by Lane. Lane again responded that it would not proceed in any way until Foster satisfied the full payment for Stage I of the Lane Agreement. On August 17, 1993, Foster, faced with the prospect of delay damages under the Hammond Agreement, hired Encor Coating Incorporated (Encor) to complete Stage II at a cost of $99,329.15, $42,055.00 more than it would have paid Lane to complete Stage II under the agreement.

Foster then initiated suit against Lane by filing a writ of summons in Bedford County. Lane also initiated suit, filing a complaint in Cumberland County. The cases were subsequently consolidated in Bedford County and a bench trial ensued.

. . . The trial court found that Foster's failure to remit the final $7,082.22 on Stage I to Lane amounted to a breach of the Lane Agreement, thereby permitting Lane to suspend performance under the Lane Agreement. The trial court reasoned, therefore, that because Lane was legally entitled to suspend performance, Lane was not liable for any damages Foster incurred as a result of said suspension. Additionally, the trial court found that Lane was entitled to the $7,082.22 due and owing under the Lane Agreement.

Foster vehemently disagrees with the trial court's findings and conclusions. Foster argues that the withholding of Lane's $7,082.22 was not a material breach under established Pennsylvania contract law and thus Lane was not entitled to suspend its performance under the Lane Agreement. Additionally, Foster contends that it had the right to request adequate assurances of performance due to Lane's January 5, 1993 letter to Foster and that Lane's failure to provide such assurance amounted to a repudiation of the Lane Agreement. Foster concludes, therefore, that it is entitled to the amount over and above the full price of the Lane Agreement that it had to pay another contractor to coat the Stage II components less the $7,082.22 owed to Lane prior to Lane's breach.

Our initial inquiry must be whether the trial court erred in finding that Foster's withholding of $7,082.22 under the Lane Agreement constituted a material breach of that agreement. If the trial court did not err in so finding, then our inquiry ends because a material breach entitles the non-breaching party to suspend performance under the contract.

"When performance of a duty under a contract is due, any nonperformance is a breach." Restatement (Second) of Contracts §235(2) (1981). . . . If a breach constitutes a material failure of performance, then the non-breaching party is discharged from all liability under the contract. If, however, the breach is an immaterial failure of performance, and the contract was substantially performed, the contract remains effective. . . . John D. Calamari & Joseph M. Perillo, The Law of Contracts §11-22 (2d ed. 1977). In other words, the non-breaching party does not have a right to suspend performance.

Because Foster was in breach when it refused to remit the $7,082.22 still owing under Stage I of the Lane Agreement, it is necessary to ascertain whether such breach was material. . . . In determining materiality for purposes of breaching a contract, we consider the following factors:

> a) the extent to which the injured party will be deprived of the benefit which he reasonably expected;
> b) the extent to which the injured party can be adequately compensated for that part of the benefit of which he will be deprived;
> c) the extent to which the party failing to perform or to offer to perform will suffer forfeiture;
> d) the likelihood that the party failing to perform or offer to perform will cure his failure, taking account of all the circumstances including any reasonable assurances;
> e) the extent to which the behavior of the party failing to perform or offer to perform comports with standards of good faith and fair dealing.

Restatement (Second) of Contracts §241 (1981). . . .

In the present case, the trial court ruled that Foster's actions constituted a breach of its agreement with Lane. The trial court explained that because Foster gave Lane the opportunity to cure defects present in the coating and because Lane did in fact cure the defects, as evidenced by ODOT's permission to Hammond to commence construction with the coated components, Foster had no right to retain the $7,082.22 that it owed Lane for Stage I. The trial court, therefore, deduced that because Foster had no legitimate reason for failing to perform, Foster breached the Lane agreement.

The crux of Foster's contention is that although it may have breached the Lane agreement by withholding a small percentage of the sums due, this act was not a material breach. It is axiomatic, Foster asserts, that Lane was required to perform on Stage II of the Agreement. We agree. There has been no explicit finding that Foster's actions constituted a *material breach* of the agreement. . . . Moreover, applying the materiality test as set forth in the Restatement §241 . . . , we note that Foster failed to pay only $7,082.22 out of a $133,922.40 purchase order. . . . This amounts to a withholding of approximately 5% of the total contract price. *See* Calamari & Perillo, supra ("It is apparent that the ratio of the part performed to the part to be performed is an important question in determining . . . material breach.") Additionally, it is uncontradicted that Foster planned to remit the monies due once it received assurance from Lane that Lane could perform Stage II of the agreement. See 3A Corbin on Contracts §719 (time is generally not of the essence unless the parties have expressly manifested such an intent). Under these circumstances we conclude that the trial court erred in finding that Foster materially breached the Lane Agreement. Lane, therefore, was not entitled to suspend its responsibilities under the Lane Agreement. . . .

In light of our conclusion that Foster's breach did not materially impair the Lane Agreement, we must now determine whether Lane's failure to give Foster assurance of performance of Stage II of the Agreement amounted to an anticipatory breach. "Anticipatory breach of a contract occurs whenever there has been a definite and unconditional repudiation of a contract by one party communicated to another. A statement by a party that he will not or cannot perform in accordance with the agreement creates such a breach." Oak Ridge Const. Co., 351 Pa. Super. at 38, 504 A.2d at 1346. (1985). . . . Comment b to section 250 of the Restatement (Second) explains the nature of a repudiatory declaration:

> In order to reconstitute a repudiation, a party's language must be sufficiently positive to be reasonably interpreted to mean that the party will not or cannot perform. Mere expression of doubt as to willingness or ability to perform is not enough to constitute a repudiation. . . . However, language that under a fair reading amounts to a statement of intention not to perform except on conditions which go beyond the contract constitutes a repudiation.

Restatement (Second) of Contracts §250, cmt. b (1981). Accord Shafer v. A.I.T.S., Inc., 285 Pa. Super. 490, 428 A.2d 152 (1981) ("to be effective, a renunciation must be absolute and unequivocal.").

Although a statement by a party concerning its ability to perform may not be sufficiently absolute to constitute a repudiation of the contract, such a statement may warrant the other party to demand adequate assurance of performance, the failure of which may be treated as repudiation. . . . The Restatement explains:

> (1) where reasonable grounds arise to believe that the obligor will commit a breach by non-performance that would of itself give the obligee a claim for damages for total breach, the obligee may demand adequate assurance of due performance and may, if reasonable, suspend any performance for which he has not already received the agreed exchange until he receives such assurance

(2) The obligee may treat as a repudiation the obligor's failure to provide within a reasonable time such assurances of due performance as is adequate in the circumstances of the particular case.

Restatement (Second) of Contracts §251 (1981). If a party is warranted in demanding adequate assurances of performance, therefore, and none is forthcoming, the requesting party may treat the failure to respond as a repudiation of the contract. Id. . . .

The rationale for demanding adequate assurance of performance is explained as follows: Although a party does not ordinarily have the right to demand reassurance that the other contracting party will perform, a reasonable belief that the other contracting party will not or cannot perform permits the contracting party to demand adequate assurance. Restatement (Second) of Contracts §251 cmt. a (1981). The rule is closely related to the duty of good faith and fair dealing present in every contract. Id. Whether a party has a reasonable belief that the other party cannot perform is determined by the totality of the circumstances surrounding the agreement. Restatement (Second) of Contracts §251 cmt. c (1981). It should be noted, however, that "minor breaches may give reasonable grounds for a belief that there will be more serious breaches, and the mere failure of the obligee to press a claim for damages for those minor breaches will not preclude him from basing a demand for assurances on them." Id. Moreover, "conduct by a party that indicates doubt as to his willingness to perform but that is not sufficiently positive to amount to a repudiation may give reasonable grounds for such a belief." Id.

In the present case, we must first illustrate the circumstances out of which the Lane Agreement was created. The ultimate goal was to construct a bridge in Ohio. To that end, Hammond contracted with Foster for the manufacture of components and Foster contracted with Lane to clean and coat the components. In order to shield itself from liability under the Hammond Agreement, therefore, Foster required that the coating be approved by an ODOT engineer as a condition of the Lane Agreement. The contract did not, however, specify the level of contamination permitted between the coating and the steel components.

The evidence at trial showed that Lane had experienced difficulties in the cleaning and coating of the Stage I bridge components. In fact, after the coated components were shipped to the bridge construction site, ODOT engineers refused to approve the components until certain modifications were made. Due to the problems that Lane experienced, Lane's quality assurance manager wrote a letter to Foster explaining that it could not meet ODOT's claimed requirement of zero percent contamination because that level was unattainable. After receiving this letter Foster did not request assurance of performance nor did Foster claim that Lane had breached the contract. Rather, Foster made an agreement with Lane that the Stage I components would be modified by another firm and it would deduct the cost from the amount it owed Lane. The modifications were made by another company. Subsequent to the modifications, ODOT permitted Hammond to commence construction, thus presumably approving the coated components for use. Only after the repairs were made on the Stage I components did Foster demand assurance of performance by Lane on Stage II of the agreement.

Without citing any authority, the trial court found that because Foster had agreed that Lane would be responsible for the cost of the repairs, Foster lost its opportunity to demand assurance of performance on Stage II. We fail to see how Foster's agreement to permit Lane to pay to cure the defects resulted in a loss of Foster's right to demand assurance of performance with regard to Stage II. As comment c to the Restatement (Second) §251 explains: mere failure of the obligee to press a claim for damages for minor breaches will not preclude him from basing a demand for assurances. A material condition of the Lane Agreement was ODOT's approval of the coated components. Due to the difficulties that Lane experienced performing Stage I of the Agreement, coupled with Lane's lukewarm expression of its ability to perform, we find that Foster had reasonable grounds to demand assurance of performance.[7] Jonnet, supra. Foster requested that Lane provide some assurance that it would complete Stage II. Lane refused to give such assurances and thus we find that Lane, not Foster, materially breached the agreement.

Having concluded that Lane materially breached the Lane Agreement, our final task is to instruct the trial court on the proper allocation of damages. Here, as a direct result of Lane's breach, Foster was required to pay another contractor $42,055.00 more than it would have paid Lane to complete Stage II of the Lane Agreement. Because this amount flowed directly from the breach, Lane is required to pay Foster this amount in damages. *See . . .* Keystone Floor Products Co. v. Beattie Mfg. Co., 432 F. Supp. 869 (E.D. Pa. 1977) (breaching party must pay for any damages that naturally and ordinarily result from the breach as well as any other reasonably foreseeable damages so long as they were within the contemplation of the parties at the time of the contract). Foster, however, failed to remit $7,082.22 owed to Lane from Stage I of the Lane Agreement, which also was a breach. Accordingly, Foster is entitled to recover from Lane the cost of finding another contractor to complete stage II ($42,055.00) which is to be offset by the amount that Foster withheld from Lane for completing Stage I ($7,082.22). Foster is entitled, therefore, to a net award of $34,972.78. On remand, the trial court shall enter an order consistent with this opinion.

Order reversed. Case remanded. Jurisdiction relinquished.

DID SHAWN KEMP MATERIALLY BREACH? A PROBLEM

Shawn Kemp was an NBA basketball player for the Portland Trailblazers who was nearing the end of a professional career that began in 1989. In 1992, he signed an agreement with Reebok to endorse a line of basketball shoes that included the following provisions:

5.1 *Exclusivity:* Player warrants and represents that he has not authorized and, during the Term of Agreement, will not authorize or permit the use of his

7. The trial court also indicated that ODOT's failure to provide approval to the coated components for Stage I was a reasonable ground upon which to demand assurance of performance. Specifically, the trial court found persuasive the testimony of defense expert Paul Krauss that ODOT's understanding of the contamination was faulty. Even assuming that ODOT's engineers were mistaken regarding the proper contamination specifications, only a Monday Morning Quarterback could conclude that Foster's concerns were unreasonable.

performance, the Player Endorsement, or any part thereof, nor will he render services in connection with any radio or television commercial or participate in any other activity for the purpose of advertising or promoting any service or product which, in the Company's reasonable opinion, is competitive with or antithetical to Company's products and/or the Endorsed Goods, including, but not limited to footwear or athletic apparel and accessories of any nature or kind.

5.2 *Use:* . . . It is agreed and understood that Player shall use exclusively the type of Company basketball shoes and other Endorsed Goods as Company shall request while participating in any and all games, practices, workouts and other athletic activities as a professional basketball player. Player further agrees not to appear in public in any product that is competitive with Company's products and/or Endorsed Goods and to wear Endorsed Goods where appropriate.

5.3 *No Disparagement:* Player agrees that at no time during and after the Term of the Agreement will he disparage his association with the Company, the products of Company, its advertising agencies or others connected with Company. . . .

The contract commenced in October 1992 and was extended in 1997 to run until the end of September 2002. Under the extension, he was to receive approximately $11.2 million over the last five years of the agreement.

In April 2000, when Kemp was playing for the Cleveland Cavaliers, the *Akron Beacon Journal* published an article entitled "Footnoting Prose of Pros' Footwear: Kemp and His Teammates Stroll Down Memory Lane, Recalling Their Favorite Kinds of Shoes Growing Up." Near the beginning of the story is the following: "'My all time favorite pair I would probably have to say was Air Force II by Nike,' said Kemp, not caring the least that he has an endorsement deal with Reebok. 'They were worn by Durell Griffith and Moses Malone. Oh, yeah, you had to have them. When I got a pair of Air Force IIs, I was the coolest kid in school. I'd wear them around just to let everybody know I'm a basketball player.' " The story then includes quotes from other players and concludes with this: "Kemp says today's shoes aren't as good as the old ones, because they're made to be lighter. Kemp calls them 'throw-aways,' because they rip so easily. 'I might go back next year to (Reebok) Kamakazes,' Kemp said. 'They've got a real crazy design. That's the shoe I started out wearing my third year and wore when I made my first All-Star Game (in his fourth season of 1992-93).' Kemp has plenty of Kamakazes in his basement. Alas, he has no Air Force IIs."

Later that same month Reebok terminated his endorsement agreement, claiming that by making these statements Kemp has breached the contract provisions quoted above. In its termination letter, Reebok's attorney states, "Given that you have been contractually obligated since 1992 to wear Reebok footwear exclusively during all athletic workouts, practices, tournaments, games, exhibitions and to otherwise fulfill your obligations under the Agreement, it is patently clear your comments could only have been directed at Reebok footwear." Under the terms of the agreement, this meant Reebok refused to pay approximately $4.1 million still due for the final 2½ years of the contract.

Did Kemp materially breach his agreement with Reebok? Was Reebok justified in terminating its agreement with Kemp, or by attempting to do so has Reebok breached the agreement itself? Does Eric Andersen's approach help you answer this? Does Restatement §241 (quoted in *Lane Enterprises*)? Would it affect your answer — and if so, why — to know that Kemp's career was in significant decline by 2000? Would it affect your answer — and if so, why — to know that Reebok was doing very poorly in the sales of basketball shoes and cut its endorsement contracts from around 50 to just a few (including Allen Iverson and Steve Francis)? Would proof of these facts be admissible in a suit by Kemp against Reebok for breach of contract?

REFERENCE: Barnett, §5.2
                 Farnsworth, §§8.15-8.16
                 Calamari & Perillo, §11.18
                 Murray, §§108-109

4.   The Perfect Tender Rule: Cure and Rescission

When determining a buyer's right to reject nonconforming goods, the common law applied what came to be known as "the perfect tender doctrine." If taken literally, this would appear to be a more exacting standard than that of material breach. In this section, we consider how the Uniform Commercial Code treats this issue.

STUDY GUIDE: In what respect has the U.C.C. adopted the so-called perfect tender rule? How does the U.C.C. treatment differ, if at all, from the common law concept of material breach?

RAMIREZ v. AUTOSPORT
Supreme Court of New Jersey,
88 N.J. 277, 440 A.2d 1345 (1982)

The opinion of the Court was delivered by POLLOCK, J.*
This case raises several issues under the Uniform Commercial Code ("the Code" and "U.C.C.") concerning whether a buyer may reject a tender of goods with minor defects and whether a seller may cure the defects. We consider also the remedies available to the buyer, including cancellation of the contract. The main issue is whether plaintiffs, Mr. and Mrs. Ramirez, could reject the tender by defendant, Autosport, of a camper van with minor defects and cancel the contract for the purchase of the van.

---

* Stewart Glasson Pollock (1932-†) studied at Hamilton College (B.A.) and New York University (LL.B.). After he was admitted to the New Jersey bar in 1958, he worked in the U.S. attorney's office in Newark (1958-1960) and practiced privately in Morristown (1960-1974, 1976-1978). He served as counsel to the governor of New Jersey (1978-1979) and was appointed to the bench of the Supreme Court of New Jersey in 1979. He retired in 1999. — K.T.

Procedural Posture

[The trial court ruled that Mr. and Mrs. Ramirez rightfully rejected the van and awarded them the fair market value of their trade-in van. The Appellate Division affirmed in a brief per curiam decision which, like the trial court opinion, was unreported. We affirm the judgment of the Appellate Division.] — > *Holding*

I

Following a mobile home show at the Meadowlands Sports Complex, Mr. and Mrs. Ramirez visited Autosport's showroom in Somerville. On July 20, 1978 the Ramirezes and Donald Graff, a salesman for Autosport, agreed on the sale of a new camper and the trade-in of the van owned by Mr. and Mrs. Ramirez. Autosport and the Ramirezes signed a simple contract reflecting a $14,100 purchase price for the new van with a $4,700 trade-in allowance for the Ramirez van, which Mr. and Mrs. Ramirez left with Autosport. After further allowance for taxes, title and documentary fees, the net price was $9,902. [Because Autosport needed two weeks to prepare the new van, the contract provided for delivery on or about August 3, 1978.]

On that date, Mr. and Mrs. Ramirez returned with their checks to Autosport to pick up the new van. Graff was not there so Mr. White, another salesman, met them. Inspection disclosed several defects in the van. The paint was scratched, both the electric and sewer hookups were missing, and the hubcaps were not installed. White advised the Ramirezes not to accept the camper because it was not ready.

Mr. and Mrs. Ramirez wanted the van for a summer vacation and called Graff several times. Each time Graff told them it was not ready for delivery. Finally, Graff called to notify them that the camper was ready. On August 14 Mr. and Mrs. Ramirez went to Autosport to accept delivery, but workers were still touching up the outside paint. Also, the camper windows were open, and the dining area cushions were soaking wet. Mr. and Mrs. Ramirez could not use the camper in that condition, but Mr. Leis, Autosport's manager, suggested that they take the van and that Autosport would replace the cushions later. Mrs. Ramirez counteroffered to accept the van if they could withhold $2,000, but Leis agreed to no more than $250, which she refused. Leis then agreed to replace the cushions and to call them when the van was ready.

On August 15, 1978 Autosport transferred title to the van to Mr. and Mrs. Ramirez, a fact unknown to them until the summer of 1979. Between August 15 and September 1, 1978 Mrs. Ramirez called Graff several times urging him to complete the preparation of the van, but Graff constantly advised her that the van was not ready. He finally informed her that they could pick it up on September 1.

When Mr. and Mrs. Ramirez went to the showroom on September 1, Graff asked them to wait. And wait they did — for one and a half hours. No one from Autosport came forward to talk with them, and the Ramirezes left in disgust.

On October 5, 1978 Mr. and Mrs. Ramirez went to Autosport with an attorney friend. Although the parties disagreed on what occurred, the general topic was whether they should proceed with the deal or Autosport should return to the Ramirezes their trade-in van. Mrs. Ramirez claimed they rejected the new van and requested the return of their trade-in. Mr. Lustig, the owner of Autosport, thought, however, that the deal could be salvaged if the parties could agree on the dollar amount of a credit for the Ramirezes. Mr. and Mrs. Ramirez never took possession of the new van and repeated their request for the return of their trade-in. Later in October, however, Autosport sold the trade-in to an innocent third party for $4,995. Autosport claimed that the Ramirez' van had a book value of $3,200 and claimed further that it spent $1,159.62 to repair their van. By subtracting the total of those two figures, $4,359.62, from the $4,995.00 sale price, Autosport claimed a $600-700 profit on the sale.

On November 20, 1978 the Ramirezes sued Autosport seeking, among other things, rescission of the contract. Autosport counterclaimed for breach of contract.

II

Our initial inquiry is whether a consumer may reject defective goods that do not conform to the contract of sale. The basic issue is whether under the U.C.C., adopted in New Jersey as N.J.S.A. 12A:1-101 et seq., a seller has the duty to deliver goods that conform precisely to the contract. We conclude that the seller is under such a duty to make a "perfect tender" and that a buyer has the right to reject goods that do not conform to the contract. That conclusion, however, does not resolve the entire dispute between buyer and seller. A more complete answer requires a brief statement of the history of the mutual obligations of buyers and sellers of commercial goods.

In the nineteenth century, sellers were required to deliver goods that complied exactly with the sales agreement. See Filley v. Pope, 115 U.S. 213, 220, 6 S. Ct. 19, 21, 29 L. Ed. 372, 373 (1885) (buyer not obliged to accept otherwise conforming scrap iron shipped to New Orleans from Leith, rather than Glasgow, Scotland, as required by contract); Columbian Iron Works & Dry-Dock Co. v. Douglas, 84 Md. 44, 47, 34 A. 1118, 1120-1121 (1896) (buyer who agreed to purchase steel scrap from United States cruisers not obliged to take any other kind of scrap). That rule, known as the "perfect tender" rule, remained part of the law of sales well into the twentieth century. By the 1920s the doctrine was so entrenched in the law that Judge Learned Hand declared "[t]here is no room in commercial contracts for the doctrine of substantial performance." Mitsubishi Goshi Kaisha v. J. Aron & Co., Inc., 16 F.2d 185, 186 (2 Cir. 1926).

The harshness of the rule led courts to seek to ameliorate its effect and to bring the law of sales in closer harmony with the law of contracts, which allows rescission only for material breaches. . . . Nevertheless, a variation of the perfect tender rule appeared in the Uniform Sales Act. N.J.S.A. 46:30-75 (purchasers permitted to reject goods or rescind contracts for any breach of warranty); N.J.S.A. 46:30-18 to -21 (warranties extended to include all the seller's obligations to the goods). . . . The chief objection to the continuation of the perfect tender rule was that buyers in a declining market would reject goods for minor nonconformities and force the loss on surprised sellers. See Hawkland, Sales and Bulk Sales Under the Uniform Commercial

Code, 120-122 (1958), cited in N.J.S.A. 12A:2-508, New Jersey Study Comment 3.

To the extent that a buyer can reject goods for any nonconformity, the U.C.C. retains the perfect tender rule. <u>Section 2-106 states that goods conform to a contract "when they are in accordance with the obligations under the contract."</u> N.J.S.A. 12A:2-106. Section 2-601 authorizes a buyer to reject goods if they "or the tender of delivery fail in any respect to conform to the contract." N.J.S.A. 12A:2-601. The Code, however, mitigates the harshness of the perfect tender rule and balances the interests of buyer and seller. See Restatement (Second), Contracts, §241 comment (b) (1981). The Code achieves that result through its provisions for revocation of acceptance and cure. N.J.S.A. 12A:2-608, 2-508.

Initially, the rights of the parties vary depending on whether the rejection occurs before or after acceptance of the goods. Before acceptance, the buyer may reject goods for any nonconformity. N.J.S.A. 12A:2-601. Because of the seller's right to cure, however, the buyer's rejection does not necessarily discharge the contract. N.J.S.A. 12A:2-508. Within the time set for performance in the contract, the seller's right to cure is unconditional. Id., subsec. (1); see id., Official Comment 1. Some authorities recommend granting a breaching party a right to cure in all contracts, not merely those for the sale of goods. Restatement (Second), Contracts, ch. 10, especially §§237 and 241. <u>Underlying the right to cure in both kinds of contracts is the recognition that parties should be encouraged to communicate with each other and to resolve their own problems.</u> Id., Introduction p. 193.

The rights of the parties also vary if rejection occurs after the time set for performance. After expiration of that time, the seller has a further reasonable time to cure if he believed reasonably that the goods would be acceptable with or without a money allowance. N.J.S.A. 12A:2-508(2). The determination of what constitutes a further reasonable time depends on the surrounding circumstances, which include the change of position by and the amount of inconvenience to the buyer. N.J.S.A. 12A:2-508, Official Comment 3. Those circumstances also include the length of time needed by the seller to correct the nonconformity and his ability to salvage the goods by resale to others. See Restatement (Second), Contracts, §241 comment (d). Thus, the Code balances the buyer's right to reject nonconforming goods with a "second chance" for the seller to conform the goods to the contract under certain limited circumstances. N.J.S.A. 12A:2-508, New Jersey Study Comment 1.

After acceptance, the Code strikes a different balance: <u>the buyer may revoke acceptance only if the nonconformity substantially impairs the value of the goods to him.</u> N.J.S.A. 12A:2-608. . . . See generally, Priest, Breach and Remedy for the Tender of Non-Conforming Goods under the Uniform Commercial Code: An Economic Approach, 91 Harv. L. Rev. 960, 971-973 (1978). This provision protects the seller from revocation for trivial defects. . . . It also prevents the buyer from taking undue advantage of the seller by allowing goods to depreciate and then returning them because of asserted minor defects. . . . <u>Because this case involves rejection of goods, we need not decide whether a seller has a right to cure substantial defects that justify revocation of acceptance.</u> See Pavesi v. Ford Motor Co., 155 N.J. Super. 373, 378, [382 A.2d 954] (App. Div. 1978) (right to cure after acceptance limited to trivial defects). . . .

Other courts agree that the buyer has a right of rejection for any non-conformity, but that the seller has a countervailing right to cure within a reasonable time. . . .

One New Jersey case, Gindy Mfg. Corp. v. Cardinale Trucking Corp., suggests that, because some defects can be cured, they do not justify rejection. 111 N.J. Super. 383, 387 n.1, 268 A.2d 345 (Law Div. 1970). . . . Nonetheless, we conclude that the perfect tender rule is preserved to the extent of permitting a buyer to reject goods for any defects. Because of the seller's right to cure, rejection does not terminate the contract. Accordingly, we disapprove the suggestion in *Gindy* that curable defects do not justify rejection.

A further problem, however, is identifying the remedy available to a buyer who rejects goods with insubstantial defects that the seller fails to cure within a reasonable time. The Code provides expressly that when "the buyer rightfully rejects, then with respect to the goods involved, the buyer may cancel." N.J.S.A. 12A:2-711. "Cancellation" occurs when either party puts an end to the contract for breach by the other. N.J.S.A. 12A:2-106(4). Nonetheless, some confusion exists whether the equitable remedy of rescission survives under the Code. . . .

The Code eschews the word "rescission" and substitutes the terms "cancellation," "revocation of acceptance," and "rightful rejection." N.J.S.A. 12A:2-106(4); 2-608; and 2-711 and Official Comment 1. Although neither "rejection" nor "revocation of acceptance" is defined in the Code, rejection includes both the buyer's refusal to accept or keep delivered goods and his notification to the seller that he will not keep them. . . . Revocation of acceptance is like rejection, but occurs after the buyer has accepted the goods. Nonetheless, revocation of acceptance is intended to provide the same relief as rescission of a contract of sale of goods. N.J.S.A. 12A:2-608 Official Comment 1; N.J. Study Comment 2. In brief, revocation is tantamount to rescission. . . . Similarly, subject to the seller's right to cure, a buyer who rightfully rejects goods, like one who revokes his acceptance, may cancel the contract. N.J.S.A. 12A:2-711 and Official Comment 1. We need not resolve the extent to which rescission for reasons other than rejection or revocation of acceptance, e.g., fraud and mistake, survives as a remedy outside the Code. . . .

Although the complaint requested rescission of the contract, plaintiffs actually sought not only the end of their contractual obligations, but also restoration to their pre-contractual position. That request incorporated the equitable doctrine of restitution, the purpose of which is to restore plaintiff to as good a position as he occupied before the contract. . . . In U.C.C. parlance, plaintiffs' request was for the cancellation of the contract and recovery of the price paid. N.J.S.A. 12A:2-106(4), 2-711.

General contract law permits rescission only for material breaches, and the Code restates "materiality" in terms of "substantial impairment." . . . The Code permits a buyer who rightfully rejects goods to cancel a contract of sale. N.J.S.A. 12A:2-711. Because a buyer may reject goods with insubstantial defects, he also may cancel the contract if those defects remain uncured. Otherwise, a seller's failure to cure minor defects would compel a buyer to accept imperfect goods and collect for any loss caused by the nonconformity. N.J.S.A. 12A:2-714.

Although the Code permits cancellation by rejection for minor defects, it permits revocation of acceptance only for substantial impairments. That distinction is consistent with other Code provisions that depend on whether the buyer has accepted the goods. Acceptance creates liability in the buyer for the price, N.J.S.A. 12A:2-709(1), and precludes rejection. N.J.S.A. 12A:2-607(2); N.J.S.A. 12A:2-606, New Jersey Study Comment 1. Also, once a buyer accepts goods, he has the burden to prove any defect. N.J.S.A. 12A:2-607(4). . . . By contrast, where goods are rejected for not conforming to the contract, the burden is on the seller to prove that the nonconformity was corrected. . . .

Underlying the Code provisions is the recognition of the revolutionary change in business practices in this century. The purchase of goods is no longer a simple transaction in which a buyer purchases individually-made goods from a seller in a face-to-face transaction. Our economy depends on a complex system for the manufacture, distribution, and sale of goods, a system in which manufacturers and consumers rarely meet. Faceless manufacturers mass-produce goods for unknown consumers who purchase those goods from merchants exercising little or no control over the quality of their production. In an age of assembly lines, we are accustomed to cars with scratches, television sets without knobs and other products with all kinds of defects. Buyers no longer expect a "perfect tender." If a merchant sells defective goods, the reasonable expectation of the parties is that the buyer will return those goods and that the seller will repair or replace them.

Recognizing this commercial reality, the Code permits a seller to cure imperfect tenders. Should the seller fail to cure the defects, whether substantial or not, the balance shifts again in favor of the buyer, who has the right to cancel or seek damages. N.J.S.A. 12A:2-711. In general, economic considerations would induce sellers to cure minor defects. See generally Priest, supra, 91 Harv. L. Rev. 973-974. Assuming the seller does not cure, however, the buyer should be permitted to exercise his remedies under N.J.S.A. 12A:2-711. The Code remedies for consumers are to be liberally construed, and the buyer should have the option of cancelling if the seller does not provide conforming goods. See N.J.S.A. 12A:1-106.

To summarize, the U.C.C. preserves the perfect tender rule to the extent of permitting a buyer to reject goods for any nonconformity. Nonetheless, that rejection does not automatically terminate the contract. A seller may still effect a cure and preclude unfair rejection and cancellation by the buyer. N.J.S.A. 12A:2-508, Official Comment 2; N.J.S.A. 12A:2-711, Official Comment 1.

III

The trial court found that Mr. and Mrs. Ramirez had rejected the van within a reasonable time under N.J.S.A. 12A:2-602. The court found that on August 3, 1978 Autosport's salesman advised the Ramirezes not to accept the van and that on August 14, they rejected delivery and Autosport agreed to replace the cushions. Those findings are supported by substantial credible evidence, and we sustain them. . . . Although the trial court did not find whether Autosport cured the defects within a reasonable time, we find that Autosport did not effect a cure. Clearly the van was not ready for delivery during August, 1978 when Mr. and Mrs. Ramirez rejected it, and Autosport had the burden of proving that it had corrected the defects. Although the Ramirezes gave Autosport ample time to correct the defects, Autosport did not demonstrate that the van conformed to the contract on September 1. In fact, on that date, when Mr. and Mrs. Ramirez returned at Autosport's invitation, all they received was discourtesy.

On the assumption that substantial impairment is necessary only when a purchaser seeks to revoke acceptance under N.J.S.A. 12A:2-608, the trial court correctly refrained from deciding whether the defects substantially impaired the van. The court properly concluded that plaintiffs were entitled to "rescind" — i.e., to "cancel" — the contract. . . .

For the preceding reasons, we affirm the judgment of the Appellate Division.

SALES CONTRACTS: THE UNIFORM COMMERCIAL CODE

§2-106. DEFINITIONS: "CONTRACT"; "AGREEMENT"; "CONTRACT FOR SALE"; "SALE"; "PRESENT SALE"; "CONFORMING" TO CONTRACT; "TERMINATION"; "CANCELLATION"

(4) "Cancellation" occurs when either party puts an end to the contract for breach by the other and its effect is the same as that of "termination" except that the cancelling party also retains any remedy for breach of the whole contract or any unperformed balance.

§2-508. CURE BY SELLER OF IMPROPER TENDER OR DELIVERY; REPLACEMENT

(1) Where any tender or delivery by the seller is rejected because nonconforming and the time for performance has not yet expired, the seller may seasonably notify the buyer of his intention to cure and may then within the contract time make a conforming delivery.

(2) Where the buyer rejects a non-conforming tender which the seller had reasonable grounds to believe would be acceptable with or without money allowance the seller may if he seasonably notifies the buyer have a further reasonable time to substitute a conforming tender.

§2-601. BUYER'S RIGHTS ON IMPROPER DELIVERY

Subject to the provisions of this Article on breach in installment contracts (Section 2-612) and unless otherwise agreed under the sections on contractual limitations of remedy (Sections 2-718 and 2-719), if the goods or the tender of delivery fail in any respect to conform to the contract, the buyer may

(a) reject the whole; or
(b) accept the whole; or
(c) accept any commercial unit or units and reject the rest.

§2-602. MANNER AND EFFECT OF RIGHTFUL REJECTION

(1) Rejection of goods must be within a reasonable time after their delivery or tender. It is ineffective unless the buyer seasonably notifies the seller.

(2) Subject to the provisions of the two following sections on rejected goods (Sections 2-603 and 2-604),

(a) after rejection any exercise of ownership by the buyer with respect to any commercial unit is wrongful as against the seller; and

(b) if the buyer has before rejection taken physical possession of goods in which he does not have a security interest under the provisions of this Article (subsection (3) of Section 2-711), he is under a duty after rejection to hold them with reasonable care at the seller's disposition for a time sufficient to permit the seller to remove them; but

(c) the buyer has no further obligations with regard to goods rightfully rejected.

(3) The seller's rights with respect to goods wrongfully rejected are governed by the provisions of this Article on Seller's remedies in general (Section 2-703).

§2-606. WHAT CONSTITUTES ACCEPTANCE OF GOODS

(1) Acceptance of goods occurs when the buyer

(a) after a reasonable opportunity to inspect the goods signifies to the seller that the goods are conforming or that he will take or retain them in spite of their non-conformity; or

(b) fails to make an effective rejection (subsection (1) of Section 2-602), but such acceptance does not occur until the buyer has had a reasonable opportunity to inspect them; or

(c) does any act inconsistent with the seller's ownership; but if such act is wrongful as against the seller it is an acceptance only if ratified by him.

(2) Acceptance of a part of any commercial unit is acceptance of that entire unit.

§2-607. EFFECT OF ACCEPTANCE; NOTICE OF BREACH; BURDEN OF ESTABLISHING BREACH AFTER ACCEPTANCE; NOTICE OF CLAIM OR LITIGATION TO PERSON ANSWERABLE OVER

(1) The buyer must pay at the contract rate for any goods accepted.

(2) Acceptance of goods by the buyer precludes rejection of the goods accepted and if made with knowledge of a non-conformity cannot be revoked because of it unless the acceptance was on the reasonable assumption that the non-conformity would be seasonably cured but acceptance does not of itself impair any other remedy provided by this Article for non-conformity.

(3) Where a tender has been accepted

(a) the buyer must within a reasonable time after he discovers or should have discovered any breach notify the seller of breach or be barred from any remedy; and

(b) if the claim is one for infringement or the like (subsection (3) of Section 2-312) and the buyer is sued as a result of such a breach he must so notify the seller within a reasonable time after he receives notice of the litigation or be barred from any remedy over for liability established by the litigation.

(4) The burden is on the buyer to establish any breach with respect to the goods accepted.

(5) Where the buyer is sued for breach of a warranty or other obligation for which his seller is answerable over

(a) he may give his seller written notice of the litigation. If the notice states that the seller may come in and defend and that if the seller does not do so he will be bound in any action against him by his buyer by any determination of fact common to the two litigations, then unless the seller after seasonable receipt of the notice does come in and defend he is so bound.

(b) if the claim is one for infringement or the like (subsection (3) of Section 2-312) the original seller may demand in writing that his buyer turn over to him control of the litigation including settlement or else be barred from any remedy over and if he also agrees to bear all expense and to satisfy any adverse judgment, then unless the buyer after seasonable receipt of the demand does turn over control the buyer is so barred.

(6) The provisions of subsections (3), (4) and (5) apply to any obligation of a buyer to hold the seller harmless against infringement or the like (subsection (3) of Section 2-312).

§2-608. REVOCATION OF ACCEPTANCE IN WHOLE OR IN PART

(1) The buyer may revoke his acceptance of a lot or commercial unit whose non-conformity substantially impairs its value to him if he has accepted it

(a) on the reasonable assumption that its non-conformity would be cured and it has not been seasonably cured; or

(b) without discovery of such non-conformity if his acceptance was reasonably induced either by the difficulty of discovery before acceptance or by the seller's assurances.

(2) Revocation of acceptance must occur within a reasonable time after the buyer discovers or should have discovered the ground for it and before any substantial change in condition of the goods which is not caused by their own defects. It is not effective until the buyer notifies the seller of it.

(3) A buyer who so revokes has the same rights and duties with regard to the goods as if he had rejected them.

§2-709. ACTION FOR THE PRICE

(1) When the buyer fails to pay the price as it becomes due the seller may recover, together with any incidental damages under the next section, the price

(a) of goods accepted or of conforming goods lost or damaged within a commercially reasonable time after risk of their loss has passed to the buyer; and

(b) of goods identified to the contract if the seller is unable after reasonable effort to resell them at a reasonable price or the circumstances reasonably indicate that such effort will be unavailing.

(2) Where the seller sues for the price he must hold for the buyer any goods which have been identified to the contract and are still in his control except that if resale becomes possible he may resell them at any time prior to the collection of the judgment. The net proceeds of any such resale must be credited to the buyer and payment of the judgment entitles him to any goods not resold.

(3) After the buyer has wrongfully rejected or revoked acceptance of the goods or has failed to make a payment due or has repudiated (Section 2-610), a seller who is held not entitled to the price under this section shall nevertheless be awarded damages for non-acceptance under the preceding section.

§2-711. BUYER'S REMEDIES IN GENERAL; BUYER'S SECURITY INTEREST IN REJECTED GOODS

(1) Where the seller fails to make delivery or repudiates or the buyer rightfully rejects or justifiably revokes acceptance then with respect to any goods involved, and with respect to the whole if the breach goes to the whole contract (Section 2-612), the buyer may cancel and whether or not he has done so may in addition to recovering so much of the price as has been paid

(a) "cover" and have damages under the next section as to all the goods affected whether or not they have been identified to the contract; or

(b) recover damages for non-delivery as provided in this Article (Section 2-713).

(2) Where the seller fails to deliver or repudiates the buyer may also

(a) if the goods have been identified recover them as provided in this Article (Section 2-502); or

(b) in a proper case obtain specific performance or replevy the goods as provided in this Article (Section 2-716).

(3) On rightful rejection or justifiable revocation of acceptance a buyer has a security interest in goods in his possession or control for any payments made on their price and any expenses reasonably incurred in their inspection, receipt, transportation, care and custody and may hold such goods and resell them in like manner as an aggrieved seller (Section 2-706).

REFERENCE: Farnsworth, §8.12
                  Calamari & Perillo, §11.20
                  Murray, §109D

C.   COST OF COMPLETION VS. DIMINUTION IN VALUE: THE EXPECTATION INTEREST REVISITED

In Jacob & Youngs v. Kent, Judge Cardozo found that, while the builder may have breached the contract, because it had nonetheless *substantially performed*, the owner must pay the balance due on the house, less any damages he might have sustained as a result of the breach. Judge Cardozo then considered the issue of the appropriate measure of damages when there has been substantial, but not complete, performance. The owner asked for "cost of replacement, which would be great" (p. 976), whereas Cardozo found he was only entitled to the "difference in value, which would be either nominal or nothing" (id.). He then offered the following rule:

> It is true that in most cases the cost of replacement is the measure. . . . The owner is entitled to the money which will permit him to complete, unless the cost of completion is grossly and unfairly out of proportion to the good to be attained. When that is true, the measure is the difference in value [(p. 977)].

The next two cases examine these two different ways to measure expectation damages and the merits of using one calculation or the other. Since this concerns the proper measure of damages, we might well have studied it when we initially considered the expectation interest and its limits in Chapter 2. Nevertheless, it is useful to evaluate this rule after learning about the doctrines of good faith and material breach because that is the context in which it arises in contracts disputes.

STUDY GUIDE: In the following case, both the majority and the dissent cite Judge Cardozo's opinion in Jacob & Youngs *in support of their position. Which one is correct? Is the court's use of the concept of "willful" breach helpful here? When is a breach of contract not willful?*

GROVES v. JOHN WUNDER CO.
Supreme Court of Minnesota,
205 Minn. 163, 286 N.W. 235 (1939)

STONE, J.*

Action for breach of contract. Plaintiff got judgment for a little over $15,000. Sorely disappointed by that sum, he appeals.

---

* *Royal A. Stone* (1875-1942) graduated from Washington University College of Law at St. Louis and was admitted to legal practice in 1897. He served as Assistant Attorney General (1905-1907) and with the infantry in the Spanish-American War and World War I. Stone was appointed Associate Justice of the Minnesota Supreme Court in 1923 and elected to the same the following year. Stone was re-elected to consecutive terms, serving until his death. — K.T.

In August, 1927, S. J. Groves & Sons Company, a corporation (hereinafter mentioned simply as Groves), owned a tract of 24 acres of Minneapolis suburban real estate. It was served or easily could be reached by railroad trackage. It is zoned as heavy industrial property. But for lack of development of the neighborhood its principal value thus far may have been in the deposit of sand and gravel which it carried. The Groves company had a plant on the premises for excavating and screening the gravel. Nearby defendant owned and was operating a similar plant.

In August, 1927, Groves and defendant made the involved contract. For the most part it was a lease from Groves, as lessor, to defendant, as lessee; its term seven years. Defendant agreed to remove the sand and gravel and to leave the property "at a uniform grade, substantially the same as the grade now existing at the roadway . . . on said premises, and that in stripping the overburden . . . it will use said overburden for the purpose of maintaining and establishing said grade."

Under the contract defendant got the Groves screening plant. The transfer thereof and the right to remove the sand and gravel made the consideration moving from Groves to defendant, except that defendant incidentally got rid of Groves as a competitor. On defendant's part it paid Groves $105,000. So that from the outset, on Groves' part the contract was executed except for defendant's right to continue using the property for the stated term. (Defendant had a right to renewal which it did not exercise.)

Defendant breached the contract deliberately. It removed from the premises only "the richest and best of the gravel" and wholly failed, according to the findings, "to perform and comply with the terms, conditions, and provisions of said lease . . . with respect to the condition in which the surface of the demised premises was required to be left." Defendant surrendered the premises, not substantially at the grade required by the contract "nor at any uniform grade." Instead, the ground was "broken, rugged, and uneven." Plaintiff sues as assignee and successor in right of Groves.

As the contract was construed below, the finding is that to complete its performance 288,495 cubic yards of overburden would need to be excavated, taken from the premises, and deposited elsewhere. The reasonable cost of doing that was found to be upwards of $60,000. But, if defendant had left the premises at the uniform grade required by the lease, the reasonable value of the property on the determinative date would have been only $12,160. The judgment was for that sum, including interest, thereby nullifying plaintiff's claim that cost of completing the contract rather than difference in value of the land was the measure of damages. The gauge of damage adopted by the decision was the difference between the market value of plaintiff's land in the condition it was when the contract was made and what it would have been if defendant had performed. The one question for us arises upon plaintiff's assertion that he was entitled, not to that difference in value, but to the reasonable cost to him of doing the work called for by the contract which defendant left undone.

1. Defendant's breach of contract was wilful. There was nothing of good faith about it. Hence, that the decision below handsomely rewards bad faith and deliberate breach of contract is obvious. That is not allowable. Here the rule is well settled, and has been since Elliott v. Caldwell, 43 Minn. 357, 45 N.W. 845, 9 L.R.A. 52, that, where the contractor wilfully and

fraudulently varies from the terms of a construction contract, he cannot sue thereon and have the benefit of the equitable doctrine of substantial performance. That is the rule generally. . . .

Jacob & Youngs, Inc. v. Kent, 230 N.Y. 239, 243, 244, 129 N.E. 889, 891, 23 A.L.R. 1429, is typical. It was a case of substantial performance of a building contract. (This case is distinctly the opposite.) Mr. Justice Cardozo, in the course of his opinion, stressed the distinguishing features. "Nowhere," he said, "will change be tolerated, however, if it is so dominant or pervasive as in any real or substantial measure to frustrate the purpose of the contract." Again, "the willful transgressor must accept the penalty of his transgression."

2. In reckoning damages for breach of a building or construction contract, the law aims to give the disappointed promisee, so far as money will do it, what he was promised. . . .

Never before, so far as our decisions show, has it even been suggested that lack of value in the land furnished to the contractor who had bound himself to improve it any escape from the ordinary consequences of a breach of the contract. . . .

Even in case of substantial performance in good faith, the resulting defects being remediable, it is error to instruct that the measure of damage is "the difference in value between the house as it was and as it would have been if constructed according to contract." The "correct doctrine" is that the cost of remedying the defect is the "proper" measure of damages. Snider v. Peters Home Building Co., 139 Minn. 413, 414, 416, 167 N.W. 108.

Value of the land (as distinguished from the value of the intended product of the contract, which ordinarily will be equivalent to its reasonable cost) is no proper part of any measure of damages for wilful breach of a building contract. The reason is plain.

The summit from which to reckon damages from trespass to real estate is its actual value at the moment. The owner's only right is to be compensated for the deterioration in value caused by the tort. That is all he has lost.[8] [But not so if a contract to improve the same land has been breached by the contractor who refuses to do the work, especially where, as here, he has been paid in advance. The summit from which to reckon damages for that wrong is the hypothetical peak of accomplishment (not value) which would have been reached had the work been done as demanded by the contract.

The owner's right to improve his property is not trammeled by its small value. It is his right to erect thereon structures which will reduce its value. If that be the result, it can be of no aid to any contractor who declines performance. As said long ago in Chamberlain v. Parker, 45 N.Y. 569, 572: "A man may do what he will with his own, . . . and if he chooses to erect a monument to his caprice or folly on his premises, and employs and pays another to do it, it does not lie with a defendant who has been so employed and paid for building it, to say that his own performance would not be beneficial to the plaintiff." . . .

Suppose a contractor were suing the owner for breach of a grading contract such as this. Would any element of value, or lack of it, in the land have any relevance in reckoning damages? Of course not. The contractor

8. So also in condemnation cases, where the owner loses nothing of promised contractual performance.

would be compensated for what he had lost, i.e., his profit. Conversely, in such a case as this, the owner is entitled to compensation for what he has lost, that is, the work or structure which he has been promised, for which he has paid, and of which he has been deprived by the contractor's breach.

To diminish damages recoverable against him in proportion as there is presently small value in the land would favor the faithless contractor. It would also ignore and so defeat plaintiff's right to contract and build for the future. To justify such a course would require more of the prophetic vision than judges possess. This factor is important when the subject matter is trackage property in the margin of such an area of population and industry as that of the Twin Cities. . . .

It is suggested that because of little or no value in his land the owner may be unconscionably enriched by such a reckoning. The answer is that there can be no unconscionable enrichment, no advantage upon which the law will frown, when the result is but to give one party to a contract only what the other has promised; particularly where, as here, the delinquent has had full payment for the promised performance.

3. It is said by the Restatement, Contracts, §346, Comment b: "Sometimes defects in a completed structure cannot be physically remedied without tearing down and rebuilding, at a cost that would be imprudent and unreasonable. The law does not require damages to be measured by a method requiring such economic waste. If no such waste is involved, the cost of remedying the defect is the amount awarded as compensation for failure to render the promised performance."

The "economic waste" declaimed against by the decisions applying that rule has nothing to do with the value in money of the real estate, or even with the product of the contract. The waste avoided is only that which would come from wrecking a physical structure, completed, or nearly so, under the contract. The cases applying that rule go no further. . . . Absent such waste, as it is in this case, the rule of the Restatement, Contracts, §346, is that "the cost of remedying the defect is the amount awarded as compensation for failure to render the promised performance." That means that defendants here are liable to plaintiff for the reasonable cost of doing what defendants promised to do and have wilfully declined to do.

It follows that there must be a new trial. . . .

The judgment must be reversed with a new trial to follow.

So ordered.

JULIUS J. OLSON, J.* (dissenting). . . .

Since there is no issue of fact we should limit our inquiry to the single legal problem presented: What amount in money will adequately compensate plaintiff for his loss caused by defendant's failure to render performance? . . .

*Julius Johann Olson (1875-1955) received legal training at the University of Minnesota (LL.B.). Born in Norway, he was brought to America in 1883. He was admitted to the Minnesota bar in 1900 and practiced at Warren until 1930, when he was appointed district judge. In 1932, he was elected for a term of six years, leaving that court in 1934 to accept appointment to the Supreme Court of Minnesota. Elected to that post in 1934, he served on that bench until his retirement in 1948. — K.T.

As the rule of damages to be applied in any given case has for its purpose compensation, not punishment, we must be ever mindful that, "If the application of a particular rule for measuring damages to given facts results in more than compensation, it is at once apparent that the wrong rule has been adopted." Crowley v. Burns Boiler & Mfg. Co., 100 Minn. 178, 187, 110 N.W. 969, 973.

We have here then a situation where, concededly, if the contract had been performed, plaintiff would have had property worth, in round numbers, no more than $12,000. If he is to be awarded damages in an amount exceeding $60,000 he will be receiving at least 500 per cent more than his property, properly leveled to grade by actual performance, was intrinsically worth when the breach occurred. To so conclude is to give him something far beyond what the parties had in mind or contracted for. There is no showing made, nor any finding suggested, that this property was unique, specially desirable for a particular or personal use, or of special value as to location or future use different from that of other property surrounding it. Under the circumstances here appearing, it seems clear that what the parties contracted for was to put the property in shape for general sale. And the lease contemplates just that, for by the terms thereof defendant agreed "from time to time, as the sand and gravel are removed from the various lots . . . leased, it will surrender said lots to the lessor" if of no further use to defendant "in connection with the purposes for which this lease is made."

The theory upon which plaintiff relies for application of the cost of performance rule must have for its basis cases where the property or the improvement to be made is unique or personal instead of being of the kind ordinarily governed by market values. His action is one at law for damages, not for specific performance. As there was no affirmative showing of any peculiar fitness of this property to a unique or personal use, the rule to be applied is, I think, the one applied by the court. The cases bearing directly upon this phase so hold. Briefly, the rule here applicable is this: Damages recoverable for breach of a contract to construct is the difference between the market value of the property in the condition it was when delivered to and received by plaintiff and what its market value would have been if defendant had fully complied with its terms. . . .

The principle for which I contend is not novel in construction contract cases. It is well stated in McCormick, Damages, §168, pp. 648, 649, as follows:

> In whatever way the issue arises, the generally approved standards for measuring the owner's loss from defects in the work are two: First, in cases where the defect is one that can be repaired or cured without undue expense, so as to make the building conform to the agreed plan, then the owner recovers such amount as he has reasonably expended, or will reasonably have to spend, to remedy the defect. Second, if, on the other hand, the defect in material or construction is one that cannot be remedied without an expenditure for reconstruction disproportionate to the end to be attained, or without endangering unduly other parts of the building, then the damages will be measured not by the cost of remedying the defect, but by the difference between the value of the building as it is and what it would have been worth if it had been built in conformity with the contract.

And the same thought was expressed by Mr. Justice Cardozo in Jacob & Youngs, Inc. v. Kent, 230 N.Y. 239, 244, 129 N.E. 889, 891, 23 A.L.R. 1429,

1433, thus: "The owner is entitled to the money which will permit him to complete, unless the cost of completion is grossly and unfairly out of proportion to the good to be attained. When that is true, the measure is the difference in value." . . .

No one doubts that a party may contract for the doing of anything he may choose to have done (assuming what is to be done is not unlawful) "although the thing to be produced had no marketable value." (45 N.Y. page 572.) . . .

But that is not what plaintiff's predecessor in interest contracted for. Such a provision might well have been made, but the parties did not. They could undoubtedly have provided for liquidated damages for nonperformance . . . or they might have determined in money what the value of performance was considered to be and thereby have contractually provided a measure for failure of performance.

. . . In what manner has plaintiff been hurt beyond the damages awarded? As to him "economic waste" is not apparent. Assume that defendant abandoned the entire project without taking a single yard of gravel therefrom but left the premises as they were when the lease was made, could plaintiff recover damages upon the basis here established? The trouble with the prevailing opinion is that here plaintiff's loss is not made the basis for the amount of his recovery but rather what it would cost the defendant. No case has been decided upon that basis until now. . . .

. . . I think the judgment should be affirmed.

STUDY GUIDE: *Is there any relevant difference between* Groves v. John Wunder *and the next case? Does this factor support or undercut the outcome reached by the court? Are your sympathies for the party in breach different here than in* Jacob & Youngs? *If so, why? Consider what this says both for and against the role of sympathies in deciding cases.*

PEEVYHOUSE v. GARLAND COAL MINING CO.
Supreme Court of Oklahoma,
382 P.2d 109 (1962), cert. denied, 375 U.S. 906 (1963)

JACKSON, J.*

In the trial court, plaintiffs Willie and Lucille Peevyhouse sued the defendant, Garland Coal and Mining Company, for damages for breach of contract. Judgment was for plaintiffs in an amount considerably less than was sued for. Plaintiffs appeal and defendant cross-appeals.

In the briefs on appeal, the parties present their argument and contentions under several propositions; however, they all stem from the basic question of whether the trial court properly instructed the jury on the measure of damages.

* *Floyd Louis Jackson* (1902-†) was educated at the University of Oklahoma (LL.B.) and was admitted to the Oklahoma bar in 1927 and the Texas bar in 1928. He began his legal career at Burkburnett, Texas, in 1928, and removed to Walters, Oklahoma, where he served as County Attorney for Cotton County (1931-1936) and practiced privately (1936-1942). He joined the bench as judge of the Fifth Judicial District Court in 1946, moving to the Oklahoma Supreme Court in 1955. He retired from the court in 1973. — K.T.

Briefly stated, the facts are as follows: plaintiffs owned a farm containing coal deposits, and in November, 1954, leased the premises to defendant for a period of five years for coal mining purposes. A "stripmining" operation was contemplated in which the coal would be taken from pits on the surface of the ground, instead of from underground mine shafts. In addition to the usual covenants found in a coal mining lease, defendant specifically agreed to perform certain restorative and remedial work at the end of the lease period. It is unnecessary to set out the details of the work to be done, other than to say that it would involve the moving of many thousands of cubic yards of dirt, at a cost estimated by expert witnesses at about $29,000.00. However, plaintiffs sued for only $25,000.00.

During the trial, it was stipulated that all covenants and agreements in the lease contract had been fully carried out by both parties, except the remedial work mentioned above; defendant conceded that this work had not been done.

Plaintiffs introduced expert testimony as to the amount and nature of the work to be done, and its estimated cost. Over plaintiffs' objections, defendant thereafter introduced expert testimony as to the "diminution in value" of plaintiffs' farm resulting from the failure of defendant to render performance as agreed in the contract — that is, the difference between the present value of the farm, and what its value would have been if defendant had done what it agreed to do.

At the conclusion of the trial, the court instructed the jury that it must return a verdict for plaintiffs, and left the amount of damages for jury determination. On the measure of damages, the court instructed the jury that it might consider the cost of performance of the work defendant agreed to do, "together with all of the evidence offered on behalf of either party."

It thus appears that the jury was at liberty to consider the "diminution in value" of plaintiffs' farm as well as the cost of "repair work" in determining the amount of damages.

It returned a verdict for plaintiffs for $5000.00 — only a fraction of the "cost of performance," *but more than the total value of the farm even after the remedial work is done.*

On appeal, the issue is sharply drawn. Plaintiffs contend that the true measure of damages in this case is what it will cost plaintiffs to obtain performance of the work that was not done because of defendant's default. Defendant argues that the measure of damages is the cost of performance "limited, however, to the total difference in the market value before and after the work was performed."

It appears that this precise question has not heretofore been presented to this court. In Ardizonne v. Archer, 72 Okl. 70, 178 P. 263, this court held that the measure of damages for breach of a contract to drill an oil well was the reasonable cost of drilling the well, but here a slightly different factual situation exists. The drilling of an oil well will yield valuable geological information, even if no oil or gas is found, and of course if the well is a producer, the value of the premises increases. In the case before us, it is argued by defendant with some force that the performance of the remedial work defendant agreed to do will add at the most only a few hundred dollars to the value of plaintiffs' farm, and that the damages should be limited to that amount because that is all plaintiffs have lost.

Plaintiffs rely on Groves v. John Wunder Co., 205 Minn. 163, 286 N.W. 235, 123 A.L.R. 502. In that case, the Minnesota court, in a substantially similar situation, adopted the "cost of performance" rule as opposed to the "value" rule. The result was to authorize a jury to give plaintiff damages in the amount of $60,000, where the real estate concerned would have been worth only $12,160, even if the work contracted for had been done.

It may be observed that Groves v. John Wunder Co., supra, is the only case which has come to our attention in which the cost of performance rule has been followed under circumstances where the cost of performance greatly exceeded the diminution in value resulting from the breach of contract. Incidentally, it appears that this case was decided by a plurality rather than a majority of the members of the court.

Defendant relies principally upon Sandy Valley E. R. Co. v. Hughes, 175 Ky. 320, 194 S.W. 344; Bigham v. Wabash-Pittsburg Terminal Ry. Co., 223 Pa. 106, 72 A. 318; and Sweeney v. Lewis Const. Co., 66 Wash. 490, 119 P. 1108. These were all cases in which, under similar circumstances, the appellate courts followed the "value" rule instead of the "cost of performance" rule. Plaintiff points out that in the earliest of these cases (*Bigham*) the court cites as authority on the measure of damages an earlier Pennsylvania *tort* case, and that the other two cases follow the first, with no explanation as to why a measure of damages ordinarily followed in cases sounding in tort should be used in contract cases. Nevertheless, it is of some significance that three out of four appellate courts have followed the diminution in value rule under circumstances where, as here, the cost of performance greatly exceeds the diminution in value.

The explanation may be found in the fact that the situations presented are artificial ones. It is highly unlikely that the ordinary property owner would agree to pay $29,000 (or its equivalent) for the construction of "improvements" upon his property that would increase its value only about ($300) three hundred dollars. The result is that we are called upon to apply principles of law theoretically based upon reason and reality to a situation which is basically unreasonable and unrealistic.

In Groves v. John Wunder Co., supra, in arriving at its conclusions, the Minnesota court apparently considered the contract involved to be analogous to a building and construction contract, and cited authority for the proposition that the cost of performance or completion of the building as contracted is ordinarily the measure of damages in actions for damages for the breach of such a contract.

In an annotation following the Minnesota case beginning at 123 A.L.R. 515, the annotator places the three cases relied on by defendant (*Sandy Valley, Bigham* and *Sweeney*) under the classification of cases involving "grading and excavation contracts."

We do not think either analogy is strictly applicable to the case now before us. The primary purpose of the lease contract between plaintiffs and defendant was neither "building and construction" nor "grading and excavation." It was merely to accomplish the economical recovery and marketing of coal from the premises, to the profit of all parties. The special provisions of the lease contract pertaining to remedial work were incidental to the main object involved.

Even in the case of contracts that are unquestionably building and construction contracts, the authorities are not in agreement as to the factors to be considered in determining whether the cost of performance rule or the value rule should be applied. The American Law Institute's Restatement of the Law, Contracts, Volume 1, Sections 346(1)(a)(i) and (ii) submits the proposition that the cost of performance is the proper measure of damages "if this is possible and does not involve *unreasonable economic waste*"; and that the diminution in value caused by the breach is the proper measure "if construction and completion in accordance with the contract would involve *unreasonable economic waste."* (Emphasis supplied.) In an explanatory comment immediately following the text, the Restatement makes it clear that the "economic waste" referred to consists of the destruction of a substantially completed building or other structure. Of course no such destruction is involved in the case now before us.

On the other hand, in McCormick, Damages, Section 168, it is said with regard to building and construction contracts that ". . . in cases where the defect is one that can be repaired or cured without *undue expense*" the cost of performance is the proper measure of damages, but where ". . . the defect in material or construction is one that cannot be remedied without *an expenditure for reconstruction disproportionate to the end to be attained*" (emphasis supplied) the value rule should be followed. The same idea was expressed in Jacob & Youngs, Inc. v. Kent, 230 N.Y. 239, 129 N.E. 889, 23 A.L.R. 1429, as follows:

> The owner is entitled to the money which will permit him to complete, unless the cost of completion is grossly and unfairly out of proportion to the good to be attained. When that is true, the measure is the difference in value.

It thus appears that the prime consideration in the Restatement was "economic waste"; and that the prime consideration in McCormick, Damages, and in Jacob & Youngs, Inc. v. Kent, supra, was the relationship between the expense involved and the "end to be attained" — in other words, the "relative economic benefit."

In view of the unrealistic fact situation in the instant case, and certain Oklahoma statutes to be hereinafter noted, we are of the opinion that the "relative economic benefit" is a proper consideration here. This is in accord with the recent case of Mann v. Clowser, 190 Va. 887, 59 S.E.2d 78, where, in applying the cost rule, the Virginia court specifically noted that ". . . the defects are remediable from a practical standpoint and the costs *are not grossly disproportionate to the results to be obtained*" (emphasis supplied). . . .

We therefore hold that where, in a coal mining lease, lessee agrees to perform certain remedial work on the premises concerned at the end of the lease period, and thereafter the contract is fully performed by both parties except that the remedial work is not done, the measure of damages in an action by lessor against lessee for damages for breach of contract is ordinarily the reasonable cost of performance of the work; however, where the contract provision breached was merely incidental to the main purpose in view, and where the economic benefit which would result to lessor by full performance of the work is grossly disproportionate to the cost of performance, the damages which lessor may recover are limited to the diminution in value resulting to the premises because of the non-performance.

We believe the above holding is in conformity with the intention of the Legislature as expressed in the statutes mentioned, and in harmony with the better-reasoned cases from the other jurisdictions where analogous fact situations have been considered. It should be noted that the rule as stated does not interfere with the property owner's right to "do what he will with his own" (Chamberlain v. Parker, 45 N.Y. 569), or his right, if he chooses, to contract for "improvements" which will actually have the effect of reducing his property's value. Where such result is in fact contemplated by the parties, and is a main or principal purpose of those contracting, it would seem that the measure of damages for breach would ordinarily be the cost of performance. . . .

Under the most liberal view of the evidence herein, the diminution in value resulting to the premises because of non-performance of the remedial work was $300.00. After a careful search of the record, we have found no evidence of a higher figure, and plaintiffs do not argue in their briefs that a greater diminution in value was sustained. It thus appears that the judgment was clearly excessive, and that the amount for which judgment should have been rendered is definitely and satisfactorily shown by the record. . . .

We are of the opinion that the judgment of the trial court for plaintiffs should be, and it is hereby, modified and reduced to the sum of $300.00, and as so modified it is affirmed.

WELCH, DAVISON, HALLEY, and JOHNSON, JJ., concur.

WILLIAMS, C.J., BLACKBIRD, V.C.J., and IRWIN and BERRY, JJ., dissent.

IRWIN, J.* (dissenting).

By the specific provisions in the coal mining lease under consideration, the defendant agreed as follows:

> . . . 7b Lessee agrees to make fills in the pits dug on said premises on the property line in such manner that fences can be placed thereon and access had to opposite sides of the pits.
> [7]c Lessee agrees to smooth off the top of the spoil banks on the above premises.
> 7d Lessee agrees to leave the creek crossing the above premises in such a condition that it will not interfere with the crossings to be made in pits as set out in 7b. . . .
> 7f Lessee further agrees to leave no shale or dirt on the high wall of said pits. . . .

Following the expiration of the lease, plaintiffs made demand upon defendant that it carry out the provisions of the contract and to perform those covenants contained therein.

Defendant admits that it failed to perform its obligations that it agreed and contracted to perform under the lease contract and there is nothing in the record which indicates that defendant could not perform its obligations.

*Pat Irwin (1921-1999) studied at Southwestern State College and the University of Oklahoma (LL.B.). After serving as County Attorney for Dewey County (1949-1950) and secretary to the Oklahoma School Land Commission (1955-1958), he accepted appointment to the Supreme Court of Oklahoma in 1959, serving until 1983. He spent two terms as that court's Chief Justice (1969-1970, 1981-1982) and became U.S. Magistrate for the Western District of Oklahoma in 1983. — K.T.

Therefore, in my opinion defendant's breach of the contract was wilful and not in good faith. —> necessary antecedent?

Although the contract speaks for itself, there were several negotiations between the plaintiffs and defendant before the contract was executed. Defendant admitted in the trial of the action, that plaintiffs insisted that the above provisions be included in the contract and that they would not agree to the coal mining lease unless the above provisions were included.

In consideration for the lease contract, plaintiffs were to receive a certain amount as royalty for the coal produced and marketed and in addition thereto their land was to be restored as provided in the contract.

Defendant received as consideration for the contract, its proportionate share of the coal produced and marketed and in addition thereto, the *right to use* plaintiffs' land in the furtherance of its mining operations.

The cost for performing the contract in question could have been reasonably approximated when the contract was negotiated and executed and there are no conditions now existing which could not have been reasonably anticipated by the parties. Therefore, defendant had knowledge, when it prevailed upon the plaintiffs to execute the lease, that the cost of performance might be disproportionate to the value or benefits received by plaintiff for the performance.

Defendant has received its benefits under the contract and now urges, in substance, that plaintiffs' measure of damages for its failure to perform should be the economic value of performance to the plaintiffs and not the cost of performance.

If a peculiar set of facts should exist where the above rule should be applied as the proper measure of damages, (and in my judgment those facts do not exist in the instant case) before such rule should be applied, consideration should be given to the benefits received or contracted for by the party who asserts the application of the rule.

Defendant did not have the right to mine plaintiffs' coal or to use plaintiffs' property for its mining operations without the consent of plaintiffs. Defendant had knowledge of the benefits that it would receive under the contract and the approximate cost of performing the contract. With this knowledge, it must be presumed that defendant thought that it would be to its economic advantage to enter into the contract with plaintiffs and that it would reap benefits from the contract, or it would have not entered into the contract.

Therefore, if the value of the performance of a contract should be considered in determining the measure of damages for breach of a contract, the value of the benefits received under the contract by a party who breaches a contract should also be considered. However, in my judgment, to give consideration to either in the instant action, completely rescinds and holds for naught the solemnity of the contract before us and makes an entirely new contract for the parties. . . .

In my judgment, we should follow the case of Groves v. John Wunder Company, 205 Minn. 163, 286 N.W 235, 123 A.L.R. 502, which defendant agrees "that the fact situation is apparently similar to the one in the case at bar," and where the Supreme Court of Minnesota held:

> The owner's or employer's damages for such a breach (i.e. breach hypothesized in 2d syllabus) are to be measured, not in respect to the value of the land

to be improved, but by the reasonable cost of doing that which the contractor promised to do and which he left undone.

The hypothesized breach referred to states that where the contractor's breach of a contract is wilful, that is, in bad faith, he is not entitled to any benefit of the equitable doctrine of substantial performance.

In the instant action defendant has made no attempt to even substantially perform. The contract in question is not immoral, is not tainted with fraud, and was not entered into through mistake or accident and is not contrary to public policy. It is clear and unambiguous and the parties understood the terms thereof, and the approximate cost of fulfilling the obligations could have been approximately ascertained. There are no conditions existing now which could not have been reasonably anticipated when the contract was negotiated and executed. The defendant could have performed the contract if it desired. It has accepted and reaped the benefits of its contract and now urges that plaintiffs' benefits under the contract be denied. If plaintiffs' benefits are denied, such benefits would inure to the direct benefit of the defendant.

Therefore, in my opinion, the plaintiffs were entitled to specific performance of the contract and since defendant has failed to perform, the proper measure of damages should be the cost of performance. Any other measure of damage would be holding for naught the express provisions of the contract; would be taking from the plaintiffs the benefits of the contract and placing those benefits in defendant which has failed to perform its obligations; would be granting benefits to defendant without a resulting obligation; and would be completely rescinding the solemn obligation of the contract for the benefit of the defendant to the detriment of the plaintiffs by making an entirely new contract for the parties.

I therefore respectfully dissent to the opinion promulgated by a majority of my associates.

RESTATEMENT (SECOND) OF CONTRACTS

Study Guide: Does the following Restatement section adopt or modify the substantial performance doctrine as articulated by Judge Cardozo? Does it reconcile the three previous cases?

§348. ALTERNATIVES TO LOSS IN VALUE OF PERFORMANCE . . .

(2) If a breach results in defective or unfinished construction and the loss in value to the injured party is not proved with sufficient certainty, he may recover damages based on

(a) the diminution in the market price of the property caused by the breach, or

(b) the reasonable cost of completing performance or of remedying the defects if that cost is not clearly disproportionate to the probable loss of value to him. . . .

REFERENCE: Barnett, §2.3.7
                Farnsworth, §12.13
                Calamari & Perillo, §§14.28-14.29
                Murray, §119

Relational and Legal Background: Is Peevyhouse *a Lesson in Lawyering or Corruption?*

STUDY GUIDE: *In her massive study of the* Peevyhouse *case, Professor Judith Maute reveals previously unknown facts about the dispute. Her research teaches valuable lessons to future lawyers about the all-too-common tendency of lawyers to avoid adequate preparation in favor of "shooting-from-the-hip." It also examines the charge that the decision was a product of corruption among members of the Oklahoma Supreme Court. (In order to present here as much of her findings as possible, most footnotes, reflecting Professor Maute's copious research, have been omitted.)*

JUDITH L. MAUTE, PEEVYHOUSE v. GARLAND COAL CO. REVISITED: THE BALLAD OF WILLIE AND LUCILLE, 89 NW. U. L. REV. 1341, 1350, 1358-1363, 1366-1369, 1372-1373, 1399-1401, 1403, 1405-1406, 1446-1447, 1451-1452, 1454-1455, 1465-1470 (1995):

> We picked a fine time to strip mine, Lucille.
> It sure looks to me like we got a raw deal.
> We picked a fine time to strip mine, Lucille.
> It sure looks to me like we got a raw deal.
> That smooth city-slicker said we'd all get rich quicker.
> I should have known it warn't real.
> We picked a fine time to strip mine, Lucille. . . .
>
> We picked a fine time to strip mine, Lucille.
> Make no mistake, hon, we got a raw deal.
> I never went to law school,
> I didn't know the value rule,
> I thought sure we'd win our appeal,
> The Supreme Court done gyped us, Lucille.[9] . . .
>
> That smooth talkin' stranger, I knew he was danger,
> The minute he walked in our yard.
> But his smooth city ways put us in a daze,
> And that's when we let down our guard.
> He said that his goal was to mine all the coal,
> Lying beneath our farm.
> But, he said not to worry, because in a hurry,
> They'd put back our dirt with no harm. . . .

---

9. Copyright Todd Lowrey, class of 1991, and William Blodgett, class of 1988, University of Minnesota, J.D. Sung to the tune of "It's a fine time to leave me, Lucille." (Originally written by Roger Bowling and Hal Bynum.) . . .

The Peevyhouse land, while quite small in relation to the total acreage and quantity of coal Garland expected to be mined, was key to a profitable mining operation. The targeted vein cut through the Peevyhouses' back twenty-acre parcel and a small portion of their forty-acre parcel. By leasing the Peevyhouses' sixty acres, Garland could move its mining operation efficiently from northwest to southeast.

It appears Garland was strongly motivated to obtain the Peevyhouse lease in order to divert Cedar Creek from the mining site onto their land. Cedar Creek naturally ran north of the property, passing through the heavily mined land owned by neighbors Nolen and Fowler, and eventually flowed onto the northeast corner of Peevyhouses' forty-acre parcel. Its diversion from the mining site was essential to avoid interference with ongoing mining operations.[10] Even before execution of the Peevyhouse lease, Garland began pumping water from the creek onto the Peevyhouses' land. Garland began blasting for the diversion immediately after the lease was signed.

The Peevyhouses were opposed to permitting any mining on their land. An earlier mining operation stopped at their property line, leaving behind the disturbed land, including a dangerous pit, highwall and unsightly overburden. Their reluctance, combined with Garland's need to divert the creek, undoubtedly enhanced their bargaining power. Nevertheless, there is no indication they used this power to exact unreasonably favorable contract terms. The Peevyhouses waived the right to payment of $3,000 for surface damages in exchange for the promised remedial work. From Garland's perspective, the exchange appeared economically rational. It saved $3,000 immediate cash outlay, enabled prompt creek diversion and obtained rights to mine the Peevyhouse land. Alternatively, Garland might have purchased the land outright. It bought a 1.6 acre triangle of land from Thomas Laird, who owned the twenty-acre strip immediately south of the Peevyhouse twenty-acre parcel and refused to lease the property to Garland. Had the Peevyhouses refused to lease, Garland's mining operation could have skipped over their property and moved to the next leased property along the coal bed. It had done so previously when it could not reach agreement with another local property owner.

Lease negotiations between Cumpton and the Peevyhouses extended over several sessions. The two men dealt directly with each other while Lucille participated behind the scenes, assisting Willie in identifying issues and desired terms. The Peevyhouses were an astute and careful negotiating team. While they lacked advanced education and sophisticated business experience, the final agreement reflects sound judgment and survival skills acquired from living off the land.

The written contract clearly anticipated leaving an open pit on the Peevyhouses' land. This shows that Garland planned to make the last cut on their land, leaving behind a water-filled pit and the diverted creek.

10. Letter from R. W. Funston, P. E. to Charles Dietrich (March 22, 1990). . . . He explains:

> A creek is diverted by constructing a new channel around the mining operations and typically back into the original creek downstream so as to not affect downstream water rights. The original creek is then blocked off to divert water into the new channel.

To minimize the long-term consequences of the mining, Peevyhouses negotiated remedial provisions that would provide access to a small amount of land north of the pit, assure its future utility as pasture land, and enhance the safety of persons and livestock when near the pit.

The Peevyhouses rejected many of the standardized lease terms. The Peevyhouses insisted on striking several provisions they thought gave the lessee inordinate powers. Most important, they gave up the customary advance payment for surface damages. Because they wanted the land restored to usable condition after the mining, they agreed to forego payment of $3,000 ($50 per acre for 60 acres) in exchange for Garland's promise to do remedial work. Willie explained his view that it was not right to take money for land and allow work to be done on it that would make the land worthless in the future. . . .

In comparison to other land owners who leased their land without protective restrictions, Garland left the Peevyhouse personal acreage in relatively good condition. Because the Peevyhouses refused to lease the land on which they lived, gardened, or used for pasture, the stripmining activity was somewhat removed from their daily life.

This mining operation took place along a V-shaped stretch extending approximately fifteen miles. . . .

Although Garland continued mining in Haskell County until January 1958, it mined this particular segment during 1956 and 1957. It removed substantial quantities of coal from the other leased properties, but comparatively little coal from the Peevyhouse land. The Peevyhouses received merely $500 beyond the $2,000 advance royalty. Garland's profits earned from sale of coal removed from the Peevyhouse land ranged from $25,000 to $34,500. This figure does not include other economic benefits Garland derived from the lease, such as creek diversion.[11] . . .

When Garland prepared to stop mining, Burl Compton explained to Willie Peevyhouse that the coal depth fell from forty-five to seventy feet below the surface shortly after the mining operation moved onto their land. Compton claimed that despite a ready market for coal, the price was not high enough to justify the increased costs of extraction of the coal located at the lower depth.

To evaluate Garland's asserted reason for leaving, I examined its operations map, which depicts course of activity, coal depths, and test borings for the mined segment. Contrary to Garland's assertion, there was little if any difference in the coal depth on Peevyhouse land as compared to adjacent areas that Garland fully mined. The operations map indicates coal depths ranging from thirty to sixty feet from the surface, whereas the coal bed on Peevyhouse land was about twenty-five to forty-eight feet deep. . . .

If Garland stopped working this segment because the coal depth increased extraction costs, then this decision was based on generally applicable conditions and nothing unique about the Peevyhouse property. . . .

---

11. Garland extracted about 12,500 tons of coal from the Peevyhouse land at a cost of 20¢ a ton. Stigler coal sold for $6.70 a ton in the spring of 1957. Estimated production costs range from $3.94 to $4.70 a ton, giving the operator a net profit of somewhere between $2.00 and $2.76 per ton. . . .

Garland offered no excuse as to why it did not perform the promised remedial work. . . .

On February 29, 1960, [the Peevyhouses' attorney Woodrow] McConnell filed an action for money damages in Oklahoma County District Court, Oklahoma City. . . .

Quite possibly McConnell gave little thought to specific relief. Assuming he considered it, given equity's historical reluctance to become involved with construction disputes, McConnell could have reasonably predicted such relief was unlikely. His professional orientation also may have influenced the decision. As one who primarily practiced tort law, he was accustomed to seeking money damages. Moreover, because the case had been taken on a contingency basis, he had an interest in creating a fund from which he could recover a fee.

Regardless of the reason for not seeking specific performance, Garland's counsel perceived this election as evidence of opportunistic, strategic behavior. . . .

Word of the *Peevyhouse* decision spread quickly through the Oklahoma legal community. Many prominent lawyers thought it was wrongly decided and found ways to communicate their disagreement with members of the court. Distinguished University of Oklahoma law professor Eugene Kuntz debated the case over coffee with Justice Jackson. Oklahoma City University Professor (and now Oklahoma Supreme Court Justice) Marian Opala invited Justice Jackson to defend the decision before his contracts class. Seven weeks after the initial decision, ten highly regarded local attorneys and academics filed an amicus brief urging the court to reconsider and award plaintiffs the cost measure. They claimed to represent clients who enter contracts with comparable risks "projected into the future," and their concern with proper legal development. In three short pages, amicus forcefully argued for the sanctity of contracts.

> [A]t the very least, the express and unambiguous terms of contracts entered into by private individuals . . . cannot constitutionally be abrogated by it. Moreover, short of the wall of impossibility of performance, when contractual promises are broken, this Court should lend its aid to promisees relying on the promises of competent promisors and lend its most vigorous sanction, to insure to future promisees that the aid of this Court is certain and unwavering, particularly being mindful of the interests sought to be safeguarded by the promisee in stipulating for terms, and not alone the objective of the promisor.

Days later plaintiffs petitioned for rehearing and oral argument. McConnell's brief was verbose, burying otherwise viable arguments in excess prose or in abrasive attacks on the court. . . .

Justice Williams was known on the court for perpetual indecision. . . . Originally Justice Williams voted with Justice Jackson's five-to-three majority opinion. Conference minutes indicate that when the court discussed the request for rehearing on February 25, Justice Williams switched his vote to the dissent. The amicus brief may have persuaded him the case was wrongly decided. Justice Jackson may also have had second thoughts, for he passed on voting that day. Justice Welch, who did not vote on December 11, now voted to rule in favor of Garland. Because of the four-to-four stalemate, *Peevyhouse* was backlisted, to be reconsidered at a future conference.

When the court discussed *Peevyhouse* on March 15, Justice Jackson recommended and voted to deny rehearing. Neither Justice Williams nor Justice Welch voted. Once more, the case was backlisted. Finally, on March 25, with all nine justices voting, the court denied rehearing on a five-to-four vote. Justice Welch, who had not previously participated in a dispositive vote in this case, cast his vote for Garland Coal. Justice Williams remained with the dissent. . . .

Confidential court records demonstrate that this case, involving relatively low stakes, commanded unusual attention. *Peevyhouse* was discussed in conference eight times in as many months. This sharply contrasts with the typical case presented and finally decided in one court conference. Whatever the cause, it was a troublesome case for the court. . . .

Willie and Lucille Peevyhouse still live on the land located outside Stigler. The land they leased to Garland has changed little from when the mining stopped more than thirty-five years ago. The rough, rocky surface on the highwall and spoil banks is sparsely vegetated. About half of the leased acreage remains unusable.

The diversion of Cedar Creek caused long-term harm. It eroded the makeshift fills and now flows into the abandoned mining pit instead of the diversionary channel. It carved a new path flowing out of the southeast portion of the pit. The renegade creek washed out a bridge on the property southwest of Peevyhouses owned by Lucille's parents. The dry diversionary channel is overgrown with weeds. Because the unmined area south of the pit often floods after heavy rains, it lies fallow and overgrown with scrub. Their adult son has begun clearing the area so the fertile land can again be used. . . .

IV. Strains on the Quality of Justice. . . .   The unearthed facts in *Peevyhouse* raise disturbing questions about the quality of justice. The Peevyhouses bargained effectively to obtain contractual protection of their legitimate interests. When Garland breached, they sought legal redress but ultimately were denied meaningful contract enforcement. Meanwhile, the adversary system maintained the illusion that diminution damages protected their expectations of contract performance.

What went wrong? . . .

From the outset, it appeared that McConnell lacked sufficient grasp of the relevant facts and law, both essential to theory development. The problem is circular: lacking adequate knowledge of the underlying applicable law, the advocate is unaware of factual matters germane to theory development and rebuttal to the opposition.

In *Peevyhouse*, for example, . . . the complaint would have differentiated between the leased and unleased parcels, and specifically alleged the separate consideration the Peevyhouses gave to obtain the remedial promises. This trade-off in lieu of payment for surface damages strongly related to contract interpretation and substantial performance doctrine. The competent advocate would have anticipated parol evidence objections and acquired mastery over the legal issues key to admission: non-integration of the writing, the failure of consideration challenged the existence of a legally enforceable contract, and the general admissibility of evidence on surrounding circumstances to aid interpretation.

By contrast, [Garland's attorney Clyde] Watts understood Garland's viewpoint enough to suggest the impracticability excuse and property line dispute, both of which triggered waste considerations and risk allocation. McConnell never stood "toe to toe" with Watts on these issues, and failed to pierce the defense with demands for proof. If the plaintiffs' side adequately understood the law of impracticability and mistake, it could have before trial gathered information to defeat those claims. Instead, it fearfully avoided confronting those issues. As a consequence, the defense obscured the litigation with meager suggestions of excuse.

As superior litigators know well, fact-gathering and legal research in advance of litigation are crucial to theory development and trial preparation. These time-consuming tasks may seem endless, with much time spent pursuing avenues that ultimately bear no fruit. Despite the frustrations, this time is not wasted. It enables the skilled advocate to discard weaker claims while developing a theory and presentation effectively supported by the evidence, law and policy. Such efforts also prepare to rebut assertions taken by the opposition. . . .

There were significant disparities between the advocacy skills of the parties' respective counsel. Watts was well-prepared, having adeptly planned a trial strategy with supporting witnesses and documentation, knew the weaknesses in his case, and formulated a plan to limit unfavorable evidence. Watts litigated the case aggressively, demonstrating the killer instinct possessed by many successful litigators. He took control from the outset, battering McConnell's initial efforts with constant interruptions. In short time, Watts obtained dismissal of the tort claim and stipulations that limited evidence to proving damages to the leased acreage caused by the breach. He objected frequently, disrupting the flow of plaintiffs' case, avoiding attention to contract interpretation, and diverting attention from adverse testimony. He cross-examined effectively, anticipating points he wanted made, and stopping when that was done. When presenting the defense, Watts asked his witnesses crisp, direct questions that usually elicited articulate and concise responses. They clearly understood their roles and performed well, likely the product of adept witness preparation. Sometimes he warned defense witnesses about dangerous territory with speaking objections. . . .

V. The Supreme Court Bribery Scandal: Tantalizing Speculation Questioning the Quality of Justice.   . . . Some suspect *Peevyhouse* is a tainted decision.[12] In 1964, word broke of a bribery scandal involving several members of the Oklahoma Supreme Court, including two justices who voted with the *Peevyhouse* majority. Justice Corn, who was on senior status and did not participate in the case, pled guilty to tax evasion and gave

12. See, e.g., . . . John H. Jackson; Lee C. Bollinger, Contract Law in Modern Society, Cases and Materials 44 (2d ed. 1980) and Ian R. Macneil, Contracts: Exchange Transactions and Relations, Cases and Materials 132 (2d ed. 1978).

a statement implicating three others: Johnson, Welch and Bayless. Justice Johnson was impeached and convicted and Justice Welch resigned during impeachment proceedings. . . .

Was *Peevyhouse* tainted by the Supreme Court bribe scandal? Definitive proof is impossible. Suspicions persist based on the voting records of Justices Welch and Johnson, both listed in the *Pacific Reporter* as voting consistently with the majority. Supreme Court conference minutes show Welch did not participate in a dispositive vote on the case until March 1963, when the court denied plaintiffs' second rehearing petition. In September 1963, a court order retroactively added Welch to the original decision, which became necessary to preserve the original majority opinion after Williams switched to the dissent. . . .

There is no evidence that a bribe was paid in *Peevyhouse* or that Ned Looney sought favorable treatment from the court. However, overwhelming evidence shows that Justice Welch voted in favor of interests represented by the Looney, Watts law firm, especially in close cases where his vote could make a difference. *Peevyhouse* is such a case. Improper judicial bias may well have determined its outcome. Thus, if one defines taint as limited to bribery, then *Peevyhouse* is probably unblemished. If the definition includes all cases with outcomes affected by improper judicial bias, then *Peevyhouse* appears tainted.

The court's conference minutes catalogue Justice Welch's participation in the case. When considered against the backdrop of his vote in other close cases, his votes in *Peevyhouse* indicate that he voted when needed to secure a favorable outcome for the firm's client. . . .

Cases that reflect Judge Welch's vote demonstrate his tendency to favor the interests represented by the Looney, Watts firm. . . .

Overall, Welch voted with the majority or authored the majority opinions in 49% of the cases; he dissented in 7% of the cases. In examining Welch's overall voting pattern, there is a moderate statistically significant correlation reflecting a pro-Looney, Watts bias. In those cases where the interest represented by the Looney, Watts firm prevailed, Welch voted with the majority or authored majority opinions 67% of the time. He dissented, openly voicing opposition to the prevailing Looney, Watts interest only twice.[13] By contrast, he dissented in 13.8% of the cases where the firm lost.

Welch's bias is most striking in the seventeen close cases where his vote could affect the outcome. A close case is defined as one where the court was split on the final vote, with five or six justices in the majority. He voted in every close case. In all but one case Welch supported the interest represented by the Looney, Watts firm. In each case where the Looney, Watts interest lost, Welch dissented. In seven of the eight cases where the Looney interest prevailed, Welch voted with or authored the majority opinion. Only once did Welch dissent against the winning Looney interest. . . . Because of the small sample, normal statistical tests are considered less reliable.

Welch's likely favoritism is further evidenced by comparing how the other judges voted in the seventeen close cases. Welch voted for the interest represented by the Looney, Watts firm 94% of the time. No other judge came

---

13. That is, Welch dissented in 1.8% of the cases when the firm prevailed.

close. Johnson, who participated in fourteen of the cases, voted for the Looney, Watts interest nine times (64%). Corn supported the firm's interest in six of the eleven cases in which he participated (55%). The "loyalty rating" of other judges participating in most of the close cases ranged from a high of 47% to a low of 15%.

Welch appeared loyal to the Looney firm interest when it mattered. He never voted dispositively to defeat a Looney case, and cast the deciding vote in three cases, including *Peevyhouse*. Welch's conference votes in *Peevyhouse* suggest that he stayed his hand and did not participate in any dispositive vote until necessary for Garland to prevail.

V

DEFENSES TO CONTRACTUAL OBLIGATION

15

LACK OF CONTRACTUAL CAPACITY

A. INTRODUCTION — REBUTTING THE PRIMA FACIE CASE OF CONTRACT

We now have completed our study of the elements of an action in contract — mutual assent, enforceability, and breach. A determination that a contract exists and a breach of contract has occurred does not exhaust the inquiry that is required to determine the appropriateness of granting relief. There are long-accepted defenses based on factual circumstances that undermine the enforceability of an otherwise valid contract. The term *defense* can be used in a variety of ways. For example, in response to a claim of breach of contract a person could deny ever having signed the contract and claim the signature on the document was a forgery. This type of response is not what we shall be calling a defense. Rather, it is better termed a *denial.*

In addition to contesting the facts, however, the other party might allege additional facts and circumstances that deprive the prima facie case of contract (even if it is accepted as true) of its normal moral significance, thereby avoiding the obligation that is normally incurred when one breaches a contract. In other words, when a party alleges the prima facie case of breach of contract, he or she is entitled to prevail *if* the claims are believed and *if* the other party offers no response to these claims beyond a denial. What is meant by a *defense* here is what the common law referred to as a "plea in avoidance" — the setting out of additional facts and circumstances that rebut or avoid the normal significance of the prima facie case of contractual obligation, breach, and damages. Even though the facts that comprise the prima facie case of contract are established to be true, if the facts constituting a defense are also established, the person seeking contractual enforcement is not ordinarily entitled to a remedy. (The excerpt that follows explains this conception of prima facie cases, legal defenses, and possible responses to defenses.) Some defenses may also be asserted affirmatively by the promisor to avoid the enforcement of a contract *before* any breach occurs.

While the description of defenses to this point is generally accepted, a further, more contentious claim about legal defenses can also be made: A legal defense must describe comparatively *unusual* or *exceptional* circumstances if it is not to undermine the efficacy of the cause of action

931

against which it defends. If the facts needed to establish the prima facie contract defense were pervasive or common, then few if any causes of action for breach of contract would prevail and whatever purpose is served by such causes of action would be defeated. Put another way, if maintaining a legal cause of action for breach of contract is desirable, then defenses to that cause of action cannot be permitted to completely undermine it. This imperative sometimes leads to what appear to be arbitrary limits on the reach of a contract defense whose underlying logic can be extended considerably farther than the doctrine allows.

For purposes of study, we shall divide contract defenses or pleas in avoidance into three categories, although other organizations are surely possible and, as we shall see, some doctrines do not fit neatly into one category. First are defenses discussed in this chapter — incompetence and infancy — which describe circumstances in which the promisor's capacity to assent to a contract is somehow deficient. These defenses are often asserted by a promisor before a breach is alleged to avoid the enforcement of a contract that satisfies the normal requirements of mutual assent and enforceability. Second, we will study defenses alleging that one person obtained the contractual consent of the other by improper means. These defenses — misrepresentation, duress, undue influence, and unconscionability — will be discussed in Chapter 16. Third, we shall consider defenses in which it is alleged that there has been a failure of a basic assumption underlying the contract. That is, one or both parties assumed a certain state of affairs to be true and, for some reason, this belief later turned out to be incorrect. These defenses — mistake, impossibility, and frustration — will be discussed in Chapter 17. The overriding theoretical question of the next three chapters is this: Why exactly is it that establishing each of these defenses deprives the prima facie case of contract of its normal moral significance?

Theoretical Background: Legal Rules as Presumptions

STUDY GUIDE: When reading the following, note the three different ways that a person might respond to a legal claim: denial, demurrer, and plea in avoidance. Any defenses alleged in cases to this point in the course have been either denials or demurrers. In contrast, the defenses to contractual obligation covered in Part V refer only to pleas in avoidance. Professor Epstein's analysis of legal rules as presumptions is of great assistance in understanding the logical relationship between each of these defenses and the elements of contractual obligation — mutual assent and enforceability — that we studied in Parts II and III.

RICHARD A. EPSTEIN, PLEADINGS AND PRESUMPTIONS, 40 U. CHI. L. REV. 556, 557 (1973):   ... Legal systems use many of the terms that have a central place in both logic and the sciences, but often with subtle, though crucial, differences in meaning. One such term is of special importance here. The legal system uses the term "sufficient," as in the expression "facts sufficient to state a cause of action." But it would be a mistake to assume that this term carries over its logical connotation into the law.

In logic, we say that A is a sufficient condition for B, when, if A is true, then B of necessity follows. When the law tries to generate absolute or universal propositions that make certain conditions sufficient, in the logical sense, for the creation of responsibility, there is always room to doubt whether the conclusion follows from the premise. Consider, for example, the proposition that a man should be held responsible to someone whom he harms.[1] The proposition has its appeal, but its truth is not absolute. To treat it as such would be unjust in at least some cases, for at the very least cases of consent and self-defense are apparent exceptions to the general rule.[2] Since there are exceptions, it is tempting to argue that the general principle is worth nothing at all; in logic, one counter example would be sufficient to show that a supposedly general principle is false. If law were treated as a closed logical system, the sector of possible and plausible exceptions to every proposed rule would defeat all attempts to formulate general legal principles. But even if the law is not a closed system of logic, it does not follow that it is impossible to bring order to the legal system. The question is not whether there are exceptions to propositions that purport to be sufficient to create liability. Rather, the question is why it is necessary to think of exceptions to the general proposition at all.

Compare, for example, the proposition that a man should be held responsible because he has harmed another with the proposition that he should be held responsible because he has thought of another. Both statements purport to be universal, and both are in some sense false. There is, nonetheless, a crucial difference between them. The second proposition would not be entitled to a presumption of validity in any system of legal thought. One hardly feels compelled even to give a reason why a man who has thought of another should not be held liable to him. It is, however, arguable that the first proposition, though not conclusive, is entitled to a presumption of validity that retains its force in general even if subject to exceptions in particular cases. It may not by itself state all of the relevant considerations, but it says enough that the party charged should be made to explain or deny the allegation to avoid responsibility; the plaintiff has given a reason why the defendant should be held liable, and thereby invites the defendant to provide a reason why, in this case, the presumption should not be made absolute. The presumption lends structure to the argument, but it does not foreclose its further development. . . .

Division of Elements of a Case into Claim and Defense. The simple division of the elements of a lawsuit into claim and defense, generally accepted in the modern law, cannot be retained in a system of rules based on presumptions. To see the weakness of the division, we need only consider the options available to the defendant once the plaintiff has stated what he regards to be his prima facie case. First, in any system of pleading,

---

1. See Epstein, A Theory of Strict Liability, 2 J. Legal Studies 151 (1973), where I argued for this position on substantive grounds.

2. I do not discuss here the fact that many rules of law will take, for reasons of administrative convenience, an absolute form. It may well prove too costly to administer a set of "just" laws. But it is important to know what one thinks is right in the abstract, because only if that is known will it be possible to decide what substantive points must be sacrificed to administrative convenience.

the defendant can deny the truth of the plaintiff's allegations. A denial does not speak to the legal sufficiency of the plaintiff's allegations; it raises an issue of fact. The question could be simple: did the defendant have the green light when he entered the intersection? Or it could be quite complex: did the activities of the defendant amount to an unreasonable restraint of trade? Whatever the question, a denial will in the end require a judgment of true or false.

Second, if the defendant is unable or unwilling to dispute the truth of the plaintiff's allegations, he can argue that, as a matter of legal policy, the allegations made do not give any reason for the court to disturb the parity that existed between the parties at the outset of the lawsuit. The defendant's demurrer assumes the truth of the plaintiff's allegations but challenges their legal sufficiency. It does not tell us how to decide the legal issue it raises, for it only responds to the formal needs of the system. If the demurrer is sustained, then the defendant's conduct is, in effect, held not to require any explanation, and we reach a dead end in the development of substantive law that makes further pleas neither possible nor necessary. As it has so often been said, a bad plea is a sufficient answer to a bad cause of action.

Where it is not possible to question either the truth or the sufficiency of the plaintiff's prima facie case, the defendant's third course is to enter a plea in avoidance.[3] Since the allegations of a prima facie case can create only a presumption of liability, the defendant must be allowed to offer an explanation of the conduct alleged in the complaint. That explanation must admit the truth of all the plaintiff's allegations, and concede that the complaint states a prima facie case. It must also allege "new matter," consistent with all prior allegations, sufficient to defeat the inference from facts to liability that the plaintiff seeks to establish.

As we have seen, if the defendant chooses to deny or demur, the issue is joined and it remains only to decide a question of fact or a point of law. When, however, an affirmative plea in avoidance is entered, the issue cannot, as a matter of logic, be joined. The plaintiff must be allowed to respond to the defendant's affirmative plea in any of the three ways that were open to the defendant after the plaintiff stated his prima facie case. Denial of the defendant's allegations is as appropriate as a denial of the allegations in the prima facie case, for their truth could be disputed in either case.[4] Similarly, a demurrer is appropriate to determine the legal sufficiency of the defense. What is crucial, however, is that a further plea in avoidance is proper as well. Once the model of logically sufficient conditions is abandoned, the plaintiff must speak in terms of presumptions and not of absolute rules. The same requirement applies to the defendant: the modern division of a case into claim and defense should not obscure the fact that we work within a system

3. At common law, the plea was known as one of confession and avoidance. The term "confession" was added because the defendant could not plead in avoidance if he denied or demurred. As an administrative matter, there was no doubt much efficiency to this system of elections, but it was doubtless productive of much injustice as well. Today, the defendant is allowed, in most jurisdictions, a free choice amongst these alternatives. But these rules of election are of no concern here because we are only interested in seeing how these options fit into the formal structure of a legal argument.

4. The Federal Rules do not provide for joinder of issue where the plaintiff wishes to deny affirmative defenses raised in the answer. Fed. R. Civ. Pro. Rule 8(d).

of presumptions. The defendant's plea in avoidance only raises a presumption that the defendant can explain the conduct attributed to him. That explanation should in principle be subject to a further exception, again introducing new matter, consistent with all prior allegations, to override the defense established by the defendant's plea.

Indeed, three stages of pleading may not be enough, for there is no logical point at which the legal system, rather than the parties, can decide that all matter relevant to the lawsuit has been introduced. If the plaintiff replies with a further plea in avoidance at the third stage of the case, the defendant must be given a further opportunity to counter the plaintiff's affirmative plea — the explanation of the explanation — by a further plea in avoidance. The system presupposes the "essential incompleteness of legal rules," for the case remains subject to further elaboration until one of the parties decides to join an issue either of law or of fact. As the common law system of special pleadings, with its uncouth replications, rejoinders, surrejoinders and the like, recognized, some cases can only be adequately framed after many rounds of argument. The federal rules, with their reduced emphasis on the pleadings, do not allow the parties to develop the case in the manner required by a system of presumptions because the pleadings typically end at the second stage.

The strengths of a system of indefinite pleas can be illustrated by a simple three-stage argument. Let X represent the plaintiff's prima facie case, Y the defendant's plea in avoidance, and Z the plaintiff's response thereto.[5] Is it necessary to put the argument in this form, or could it be said that X and Z together make a prima facie case to which Y is an insufficient defense? If it could, then the two-staged argument of modern pleading systems sets out, and in a more efficient form, all of the information conveyed by the complicated structure of common law pleading. As reformulated into two stages, however, the argument does not indicate how the case should be decided if X is true, and both Y and Z are false. The two-stage argument indicates that X and Z together make a prima facie case, but it does not and cannot tell us that while X is always material, Z is relevant to the argument if and only if Y is true. If Z is intended to be an exception to an exception (here Y), it cannot be treated as a part of the prima facie case.

To give the argument concrete form, assume that X is "the defendant did not keep his part of the bargain," Y is "the defendant was an infant," and Z is "the plaintiff delivered necessaries to the infant in the performance of his part of the bargain." If these allegations are true, then it does not matter whether the parties are limited to pleading single statements of claim and

---

5. Note that these three allegations must be consistent with each other since the pattern of argument assumes that all of them can be true at one time. The requirement of consistency does not apply, however, whenever one of the inconsistent pleas will be immaterial after the introduction of the evidence. Thus there is no reason to say that the defendant cannot plead two inconsistent affirmative defenses in response to a prima facie case, so long as each of those answers is consistent with it. Here the inconsistency in the pleadings does not signal a permanent defect in the structure of the argument. The Federal Rules are clearly correct from a pleading standpoint when they allow inconsistent allegations to be made alternatively in a claim or defense, or indeed in any other plea as well. Fed. R. Civ. Pro. 8(e)(2).

defense or are allowed to continue indefinitely until one of them decides to join an issue. Both theories yield the same substantive result. Even if the plaintiff is required to prove as part of his prima facie case both that the defendant did not keep his part of the bargain (X) and that the plaintiff provided necessaries when he kept his (Z), he will be able to recover, as a matter of substantive law, regardless of whether the defendant can show that he is an infant (Y).

Suppose, however, that the plaintiff proves that the defendant did not keep his part of the bargain (X), and that the defendant is not an infant (not Y). Under these circumstances, it is not clear whether the plaintiff should be allowed to recover without also proving that he provided necessaries (Z). In the previous hypothetical, where X, Y, and Z were true, the plaintiff was required to show, as part of his prima facie case, both that he had provided necessaries and that the defendant did not keep his part of the bargain. If that requirement accurately reflected the requirements of the substantive law, then the plaintiff does not make out a prima facie case by showing only that the defendant did not keep his part of the bargain. Under the substantive law, however, this allegation does state a prima facie case. It is not clear, therefore, why the plaintiff should be required to include in his prima facie case an allegation that he provided the defendant with necessaries when the defendant's infancy might never be put in issue. If the delivery of necessaries (Z) is material only if it can be shown that the defendant is an infant, then it follows that the issues of necessaries should be raised only after the infancy question is pleaded as a defense.[6] That is the result under a system of indefinite pleas: the plaintiff's provision of necessaries is a sufficient reply to the defense of infancy, which raises only a presumption that the defendant is not liable. It is thus possible to treat the proposition "defendant did not keep his part of the bargain" (X) as the entire prima facie case even though it does not contain all the allegations that the plaintiff may need to prove in order to recover.

A system of staged pleadings can also help to clarify difficult issues of substantive law, a point illustrated by the case of the infant's contract. When the plaintiff states a prima facie case merely by alleging that the defendant did not keep his part of the bargain, the appropriate measure of damages is the value of the defendant's performance to the plaintiff, that is, the price of

6. The common law system of staged pleading is used to account for infant's liability in Guardians of Pontypridd Union v. Drew, [1927] 1 K.B. 214. "The old course of pleading was a count for goods sold and delivered, a plea of infancy, and a replication that the goods were necessaries; and then the plaintiff did not necessarily recover the price alleged, he recovered a reasonable price for the necessaries." Id. at 220.

Two points should be noted about the argument. First, it is not clear that the prima facie case need contain an allegation that the goods were delivered, since the nonperformance of a fully executory contract is in general actionable. The delivery of the goods should be raised in the replication. Second, it does not follow that this form of pleading "does not imply a consensual contract" for the supply of the goods alone is insufficient without the agreement. See generally Miles, The Infant's Liability for Necessaries, 43 L.Q. Rev. 389 (1927) (discussion of the basis of infant's liability).

the goods. The defendant then relies on the defense of infancy, which, in effect, reduces the measure of damages to zero. Since the plaintiff may plead further, however, the issues of liability and damages are not yet finally resolved. When the plaintiff shows that he provided the defendant with necessaries, he is again entitled to recover. But now the appropriate measure of damages is the value of the plaintiff's performance to the defendant, if it is less than the value of defendant's promise. The measure of recovery thus depends upon the last valid plea in the case shown to be true. A system of staged pleadings shows that it is futile to search for a single standard of recovery applicable to every contract case.

The three-stage argument also illustrates how difficult it is to classify actions by their theories of recovery. The prima facie case in the example above is appropriate to a contract action. To the extent that considerations of jurisdiction, venue, statutes of limitations, conflicts of law and so on turn on the characterization of the prima facie case, the action must be treated as one in contract. When attention is directed to the third stage of the argument, however, the action seems to be asked on quasi-contractual notions; the defendant has been unjustly enriched in that he received from the plaintiff a benefit for which he has not paid. Nonetheless, since the plaintiff must plead and prove the agreement between the parties in order to reach the third stage of the argument, the action should not be classified as quasi-contractual. It cannot be said simply that the defendant "is bound, not because he has agreed, but because he has been supplied." The case has two "becauses," the first of which is the agreement to purchase. Had there been no agreement between the parties, the plaintiff might still be able to recover, but not on the simple allegation that he provided the defendant with necessaries. The allegation presupposes the two prior stages of the argument, the first of which alleged the agreement. By itself it does not state a cause of action.

REFERENCE: Barnett, §6.1

B.   DEFICIENCIES IN CONTRACTUAL CAPACITY

The prima facie case of contract requires a manifestation of assent of a type that merits legal enforcement. When people manifest their assent we normally presume that this manifestation represents their actual subjective assent. We also ordinarily presume that persons are capable of making their own decisions about their lives. On rare occasions these presumptions can be shown to be incorrect. The defenses to be considered in this section — incompetence and infancy — describe circumstances that, if shown to exist, rebut the normal presumption that persons are capable of making decisions on their own behalf. In this way, they deprive a manifestation of assent of its normal ability to bind the promisor and justify legal enforcement.

One further clarifying note: Each of the pleas in avoidance described in this chapter may also be characterized as "bars to enforcement." They are available not only to persons who are alleged to have breached a contract in ways we discussed in Chapter 14 but also are typically used affirmatively by a party to avoid enforcement of a contract *before* any breach occurs.

1. Incompetence

STUDY GUIDE: *Is the issue in the next case that there was no manifestation of assent that would ordinarily be enforceable? Or is it that there is some articulable reason why this particular manifestation of assent does not provide the normal justification for enforcement? Can you articulate the reason? If it is so irrational for Mrs. Ortelere to make the choice she did, why is the option she chose made available to employees?*

ORTELERE v. TEACHERS' RETIREMENT
BOARD OF NEW YORK
Court of Appeals of New York,
25 N.Y.2d 196, 303 N.Y.S.2d 362, 250 N.E.2d 460 (1969)

BREITEL, J.

This appeal involves the revocability of an election of benefits under a public employees' retirement system and suggests the need for a renewed examination of the kinds of mental incompetency which may render voidable the exercise of contractual rights. The particular issue arises on the evidently unwise and foolhardy selection of benefits by a 60-year-old teacher, on leave for mental illness and suffering from cerebral arteriosclerosis, after service as a public schoolteacher and participation in a public retirement system for over 40 years. The teacher died a little less than two months after making her election of maximum benefits, payable to her during her life, thus causing the entire reserve to fall in. She left surviving her husband of 38 years of marriage and two grown children.

There is no doubt that any retirement system depends for its soundness on an actuarial experience based on the purely prospective selections of benefits and mortality rates among the covered group, and that retrospective or adverse selection after the fact would be destructive of a sound system. It is also true that members of retirement systems are free to make choices which to others may seem unwise or foolhardy. The issue here is narrower than any suggested by these basic principles. It is whether an otherwise irrevocable election may be avoided for incapacity because of known mental illness which resulted in the election when, except in the barest actuarial sense, the system would sustain no unfavorable consequences.

The husband and executor of Grace W. Ortelere, the deceased New York City schoolteacher, sues to set aside her application for retirement without option, in the event of her death. It is alleged that Mrs. Ortelere, on February 11, 1965, two months before her death from natural causes, was not mentally competent to execute a retirement application. By this application, effective the next day, she elected the maximum retirement allowance (Administrative Code of City of New York, §B20-46.0). She thus revoked her earlier election of benefits under which she named her husband a beneficiary of the unexhausted reserve upon her death. Selection of the maximum allowance extinguished all interests upon her death.

Following a nonjury trial in Supreme Court, it was held that Grace Ortelere had been mentally incompetent at the time of her February 11 application, thus rendering it "null and void and of no legal effect." The Appellate Division, by a divided court, reversed the judgment of the Supreme Court and held that, as a matter of law, there was insufficient proof of mental incompetency as to this transaction (31 A.D.2d 139).

Mrs. Ortelere's mental illness, indeed, psychosis, is undisputed. It is not seriously disputable, however, that she had complete cognitive judgment or awareness when she made her selection. A modern understanding of mental illness, however, suggests that incapacity to contract or exercise contractual rights may exist, because of volitional and affective impediments or disruptions in the personality, despite the intellectual or cognitive ability to understand. It will be recognized as the civil law parallel to the question of criminal responsibility which has been the recent concern of so many and has resulted in statutory and decisional changes in the criminal law (e.g., A.L.I. Model Penal Code, §4.01; Penal Law, §30.05; Durham v. United States, 214 F.2d 862).

Mrs. Ortelere, an elementary schoolteacher since 1924, suffered a "nervous breakdown" in March, 1964 and went on a leave of absence expiring February 5, 1965. She was then 60 years old and had been happily married for 38 years. On July 1, 1964 she came under the care of Dr. D'Angelo, a psychiatrist, who diagnosed her breakdown as involutional psychosis, melancholia type. Dr. D'Angelo prescribed, and for about six weeks decedent underwent, tranquilizer and shock therapy. Although moderately successful, the therapy was not continued since it was suspected that she also suffered from cerebral arteriosclerosis, an ailment later confirmed. However, the psychiatrist continued to see her at monthly intervals until March, 1965. On March 28, 1965 she was hospitalized after collapsing at home from an aneurysm. She died ten days later; the cause of death was "Cerebral thrombosis due to H[ypertensive] H[eart] D[isease]."

As a teacher she had been a member of the Teachers' Retirement System of the City of New York. . . . This entitled her to certain annuity and pension rights, preretirement death benefits, and empowered her to exercise various options concerning the payment of her retirement allowance.

Some years before, on June 28, 1958, she had executed a "Selection of Benefits under Option One" naming her husband as beneficiary of the unexhausted reserve. Under this option upon retirement her allowance would be less by way of periodic retirement allowances, but if she died before receipt of her full reserve the balance of the reserve would be payable to her husband. On June 16, 1960, two years later, she had designated her husband as beneficiary of her service death benefits in the event of her death prior to retirement.

Then on February 11, 1965, when her leave of absence had just expired and she was still under treatment, she executed a retirement application, the one here involved, selecting the maximum retirement allowance payable during her lifetime with nothing payable on or after death. She also, at this time, borrowed from the system the maximum cash withdrawal permitted, namely, $8,760. Three days earlier she had written the board, stating that she intended to retire on February 12 or 15 or as soon as she received "the information I need in order to decide whether to take an option or maximum allowance." She then listed eight specific questions, reflecting great understanding of the retirement system, concerning the various alternatives available. An extremely detailed reply was sent, by letter of February 15, 1965, although by that date it was technically impossible for her to change her selection. However, the board's chief clerk, before whom Mrs. Ortelere executed the application, testified that the questions were "answered verbally by me on February 11th." Her retirement reserve totalled $62,165 (after deducting the $8,760 withdrawal), and the difference between electing the maximum retirement allowance (no option) and the allowance under "option one" was $901 per year or $75 per month. That is, had the teacher selected "option one" she would have received an annual allowance of $4,494 or $375 per month, while if no option had been selected she would have received an annual allowance of $5,395 or $450 per month. Had she not withdrawn the cash the annual figures would be $5,247 and $6,148 respectively.

Following her taking a leave of absence for her condition, Mrs. Ortelere had become very depressed and was unable to care for herself. As a result, her husband gave up his electrician's job, in which he earned $222 per week, to stay home and take care of her on a full-time basis. She left their home only when he accompanied her. Although he took her to the Retirement Board on February 11, 1965, he did not know why she went, and did not question her for fear "she'd start crying hysterically that I was scolding her. That's the way she was. And I wouldn't upset her."

The Orteleres were in quite modest circumstances. They owned their own home, valued at $20,000, and had $8,000 in a savings account. They also owned some farm land worth about $5,000. Under these circumstances, as revealed in this record, retirement for both of the Orteleres or the survivor of them had to be provided, as a practical matter, largely out of Mrs. Ortelere's retirement benefits.

According to Dr. D'Angelo, the psychiatrist who treated her, Mrs. Ortelere never improved enough to "warrant my sending her back [to teaching]." A physician for the Board of Education examined her on February 2, 1965 to determine her fitness to return to teaching. Although not a psychiatrist but rather a specialist in internal medicine, this physician "judged that she had apparently recovered from the depression" and that she appeared rational. However, before allowing her to return to teaching, a report was requested from Dr. D'Angelo concerning her condition. It is notable that the Medical Division of the Board of Education on February 24, 1965 requested that Mrs. Ortelere report to the board's "panel psychiatrist" on March 11, 1965.

Dr. D'Angelo stated "[a]t no time since she was under my care was she ever mentally competent"; that "[m]entally she couldn't make a decision of any kind, actually, of any kind, small or large." He also described how involutional melancholia affects the judgment process:

> They can't think rationally, no matter what the situation is. They will even tell you, "I used to be able to think of anything and make any decision. Now," they say, "even getting up, I don't know whether I should get up or whether I should stay in bed." Or, "I don't even know how to make a slice of toast

any more." Everything is impossible to decide, and everything is too great an effort to even think of doing. They just don't have the effort, actually, because their nervous breakdown drains them of all their physical energies.

While the psychiatrist used terms referring to "rationality," it is quite evident that Mrs. Ortelere's psychopathology did not lend itself to a classification under the legal test of irrationality. It is undoubtedly, for this reason, that the Appellate Division was unable to accept his testimony and the trial court's finding of irrationality in the light of the prevailing rules as they have been formulated.

The well-established rule is that contracts of a mentally incompetent person who has not been adjudicated insane are voidable. Even where the contract has been partly or fully performed it will still be avoided upon restoration of the *status quo*. . . .

Traditionally, in this State and elsewhere, contractual mental capacity has been measured by what is largely a cognitive test (Aldrich v. Bailey, 132 N.Y. 85; 2 Williston, Contracts (3d ed.), §256; see 17 C.J.S. Contracts §133[1], subd. e, pp. 860-862). Under this standard the "inquiry" is whether the mind was "so affected as to render him wholly and absolutely incompetent to comprehend and understand the nature of the transaction" (Aldrich v. Bailey, supra, at p. 89). A requirement that the party also be able to make a rational judgment concerning the particular transaction qualified the cognitive test (Paine v. Aldrich, 133 N.Y. 544, 546, Note, "Civil Insanity": The New York Treatment of the Issue of Mental Incompetency in Non-Criminal Cases, 44 Cornell L.Q. 76). Conversely, it is also well recognized that contractual ability would be affected by insane delusions intimately related to the particular transaction (Moritz v. Moritz, 153 App. Div. 147, *aff'd*, 211 N.Y. 580, see Green, Judicial Tests of Mental Incompetency, 6 Mo. L. Rev. 141, 151).

These traditional standards governing competency to contract were formulated when psychiatric knowledge was quite primitive. They fail to account for one who by reason of mental illness is unable to control his conduct even though his cognitive ability seems unimpaired. When these standards were evolving it was thought that all the mental faculties were simultaneously affected by mental illness. (Green, Mental Incompetency, 38 Mich. L. Rev. 1189, 1197-1202.) This is no longer the prevailing view (Note, Mental Illness and the Law of Contracts, 57 Mich. L. Rev. 1020, 1033-1036).

Of course, the greatest movement in revamping legal notions of mental responsibility has occurred in the criminal law. The nineteenth century cognitive test embraced in the *M'Naghten* rules has long been criticized and changed by statute and decision in many jurisdictions (see *M'Naghten's Case*, 10 Clark Fin. 200 8 Eng. Rep. 718 [House of Lords, 1843];Weihofen, Mental Disorder as a Criminal Defense [1954], pp. 65-68; British Royal Comm. on Capital Punishment [1953], ch. 4; A.L.I. Model Penal Code, §4.01, supra; cf. Penal Law, §30.05).

While the policy considerations for the criminal law and the civil law are different, both share in common the premise that policy considerations must be based on a sound understanding of the human mind and, therefore, its illnesses. Hence, because the cognitive rules are, for the most part, too restrictive and rest on a false factual basis they must be re-examined.

Once it is understood that, accepting plaintiff's proof, Mrs. Ortelere was psychotic and because of that psychosis could have been incapable of making a voluntary selection of her retirement system benefits, there is an issue that a modern jurisprudence should not exclude, merely because her mind could pass a "cognition" test based on nineteenth century psychology.

There has also been some movement on the civil law side to achieve a modern posture. For the most part, the movement has been glacial and has been disguised under traditional formulations. Various devices have been used to avoid unacceptable results under the old rules by finding unfairness or overreaching in order to avoid transactions. . . .

In this State there has been at least one candid approach. In Faber v. Sweet Style Mfg. Corp., (40 Misc. 2d 212) Mr. Justice Meyer wrote: "[i]ncompetence to contract also exists when a contract is entered into under the compulsion of a mental disease or disorder but for which the contract would not have been made" (noted in 39 N.Y.U. L. Rev. 356). This is the first known time a court has recognized that the traditional standards of incompetency for contractual capacity are inadequate in light of contemporary psychiatric learning and applied modern standards. Prior to this, courts applied the cognitive standard giving great weight to objective evidence of rationality. . . .

It is quite significant that Restatement, 2d, Contracts, states the modern rule on competency to contract. This is in evident recognition, and the Reporter's Notes support this inference, that, regardless of how the cases formulated their reasoning, the old cognitive test no longer explains the results. Thus, the new Restatement section reads: "(1) A person incurs only voidable contractual duties by entering into a transaction if by reason of mental illness or defect . . . (b) he is unable to act in a reasonable manner in relation to the transaction and the other party has reason to know of his condition." (Restatement, 2d, Contracts [T.D. No. 1, April 13, 1964], §18C. . . .)

The avoidance of duties under an agreement entered into by those who have done so by reason of mental illness, but who have understanding, depends on balancing competing policy considerations. There must be stability in contractual relations and protection of the expectations of parties who bargain in good faith. On the other hand, it is also desirable to protect persons who may understand the nature of the transaction but who, due to mental illness, cannot control their conduct. Hence, there should be relief only if the other party knew or was put on notice as to the contractor's mental illness. Thus, the Restatement provision for avoidance contemplates that "the other party has reason to know" of the mental illness (id.).

When, however, the other party is without knowledge of the contractor's mental illness and the agreement is made on fair terms, the proposed Restatement rule is: "The power of avoidance under subsection (1) terminates to the extent that the contract has been so performed in whole or in part or the circumstances have so changed that avoidance would be inequitable. In such a case a court may grant relief on such equitable terms as the situation requires." (Restatement, 2d, Contracts, supra, §18C, subd. [2].)

The system was, or should have been, fully aware of Mrs. Ortelere's condition. They, or the Board of Education, knew of her leave of absence for medical reasons and the resort to staff psychiatrists by the Board of Education. Hence, the other of the conditions for avoidance is satisfied.

Lastly, there are no significant changes of position by the system other than those that flow from the barest actuarial consequences of benefit selection.

Nor should one ignore that in the relationship between retirement system and member, and especially in a public system, there is not involved a commercial, let alone an ordinary commercial, transaction. Instead the nature of the system and its announced goal is the protection of its members and those in whom its members have an interest. It is not a sound scheme which would permit 40 years of contribution and participation in the system to be nullified by a one-instant act committed by one known to be mentally ill. This is especially true if there would be no substantial harm to the system if the act were avoided. On the record none may gainsay that her selection of a "no option" retirement while under psychiatric care, ill with cerebral arteriosclerosis, aged 60, and with a family in which she had always manifested concern, was so unwise and foolhardy that a factfinder might conclude that it was explainable only as a product of psychosis.

On this analysis it is not difficult to see that plaintiff's evidence was sufficient to sustain a finding that, when she acted as she did on February 11, 1965, she did so solely as a result of serious mental illness, namely, psychosis. Of course, nothing less serious than medically classified psychosis should suffice or else few contracts would be invulnerable to some kind of psychological attack. Mrs. Ortelere's psychiatrist testified quite flatly that as an involutional melancholiac in depression she was incapable of making a voluntary "rational" decision. Of course, as noted earlier, the trial court's finding and perhaps some of the testimony attempted to fit into the rubrics of the traditional rules. For that reason rather than reinstatement of the judgment at Trial Term there should be a new trial under the proper standards frankly considered and applied.

Accordingly, the order of the Appellate Division should be reversed, without costs, and the action remanded to Special Term for a new trial.

JASEN, J.* (dissenting).

Where there has been no previous adjudication of incompetency, the burden of proving mental incompetence is upon the party alleging it. I agree with the majority at the Appellate Division that the plaintiff, the husband of the decedent, failed to sustain the burden incumbent upon him of proving deceased's incompetence.

The evidence conclusively establishes that the decedent, at the time she made her application to retire, understood not only that she was retiring, but also that she had selected the maximum payment during her lifetime.

* *Matthew Jasen* (1915-2006) was educated at Canisius College and the State University of New York (LL.B.). Admitted to the New York bar in 1940, he held a legal practice at Buffalo (1949-1957), except while serving as a judge on the U.S. Military Government Court in Heidelberg, Germany (1946-1949). He also served as a justice on the New York Supreme Court (1957-1967) before being elected to the Court of Appeals of New York in 1968. After his retirement from the bench in 1985, Judge Jasen dedicated his time to the Volunteer Lawyers Project, which provides legal services to the poor. — K.T.

Indeed, the letter written by the deceased to the Teachers' Retirement System prior to her retirement demonstrates her full mental capacity to understand and to decide whether to take on option or the maximum allowance. The full text of the letter reads as follows:

February 8, 1965

Gentlemen:

I would like to retire on Feb. 12 or Feb. 15. In other words, just as soon as possible after I receive the information I need in order to decide whether to take an option or maximum allowance. Following are the questions I would like to have answered:

1. What is my "average" five-year salary?
2. What is my maximum allowance?
3. I am 60 years old. If I select option four-a with a beneficiary (female) 27 years younger, what is my allowance?
4. If I select four-a on the pension part only, and take the maximum annuity, what is my allowance?
5. If I take a loan of 89% of my year's salary before retirement, what would my maximum allowance be?
6. If I take a loan of $5,000 before retiring, and select option four-a on both the pension and annuity, what would my allowance be?
7. What is my total service credit? I have been on a leave without pay since Oct. 26, 1964.
8. What is the "factor" used for calculating option four-a with the above beneficiary?

Thank you for your promptness in making the necessary calculations. I will come to your office on Thursday afternoon of this week.

It seems clear that this detailed, explicit and extremely pertinent list of queries reveals a mind fully in command of the salient features of the Teachers' Retirement System. Certainly, it cannot be said that the decedent could possess sufficient capacity to compose a letter indicating such a comprehensive understanding of the retirement system, and yet lack the capacity to understand the answers.

As I read the record, the evidence establishes that the decedent's election to receive maximum payments was predicated on the need for a higher income to support two retired persons — her husband and herself. Since the only source of income available to decedent and her husband was decedent's retirement pay, the additional payment of $75 per month which she would receive by electing the maximal payment was a necessity. Indeed, the additional payments represented an increase of 20% over the benefits payable under option 1. Under these circumstances, an election of maximal income during decedent's lifetime was not only a rational, but a necessary decision.

Further indication of decedent's knowledge of the financial needs of her family is evidenced by the fact that she took a loan for the maximum amount ($8,760) permitted by the retirement system, at the time she made application for retirement.

Moreover, there is nothing in the record to indicate that the decedent had any warning, premonition, knowledge or indication at the time of retirement that her life expectancy was, in any way, reduced by her condition.

Decedent's election of the maximum retirement benefits, therefore, was not so contrary to her best interests so as to create an inference of her mental incompetence.

Indeed, concerning election of options under a retirement system, it has been held:

> Even where no previous election has been made, the court must make the election for an incompetent which would be in accordance with what would have been his manifest and reasonable choice if he were sane, and, in the absence of convincing evidence that the incompetent would have made a different selection, it is *presumed that he would have chosen the option yielding the largest returns in his lifetime.*

(Schwartzberg v. Teachers' Retirement Bd., 273 App. Div. 240, 242-243, *aff'd*, 298 N.Y. 741; emphasis supplied.)

Nor can I agree with the majority's view that the traditional rules governing competency to contract "are, for the most part, too restrictive and rest on a false factual basis."

The issue confronting the courts concerning mental capacity to contract is under what circumstances and conditions should a party be relieved of contractual obligations freely entered. This is peculiarly a legal decision, although, of course, available medical knowledge forms a datum which influences the legal choice. It is common knowledge that the present state of psychiatric knowledge is inadequate to provide a fixed rule for each and every type of mental disorder. Thus, the generally accepted rules which have evolved to determine mental responsibility are general enough in application to encompass all types of mental disorders, and phrased in a manner which can be understood and practically applied by juries composed of laymen.

The generally accepted test of mental competency to contract which has thus evolved is whether the party attempting to avoid the contract was capable of understanding and appreciating the nature and consequences of the particular act or transaction which he challenges. . . . This rule represents a balance struck between policies to protect the security of transactions between individuals and freedom of contract on the one hand, and protection of those mentally handicapped on the other hand. In my opinion, this rule has proven workable in practice and fair in result. A broad range of evidence including psychiatric testimony is admissible under the existing rules to establish a party's mental condition. (See 2 Wigmore, Evidence [3d ed.], §§227-233.) In the final analysis, the lay jury will infer the state of the party's mind from his observed behavior as indicated by the evidence presented at trial. Each juror instinctively judges what is normal and what is abnormal conduct from his own experience, and the generally accepted test harmonizes the competing policy considerations with human experience to achieve the fairest result in the greatest number of cases.

As in every situation where the law must draw a line between liability and nonliability, between responsibility and nonresponsibility, there will be borderline cases, and injustices may occur by deciding erroneously that an individual belongs on one side of the line or the other. To minimize the chances of such injustices occurring, the line should be drawn as clearly as possible.

The Appellate Division correctly found that the deceased was capable of understanding the nature and effect of her retirement benefits, and exercised rational judgment in electing to receive the maximum allowance during her lifetime. I fear that the majority's refinement of the generally accepted rules will prove unworkable in practice, and make many contracts vulnerable to psychological attack. Any benefit to those who understand what they are doing, but are unable to exercise self-discipline, will be outweighed by frivolous claims which will burden our courts and undermine the security of contracts. The reasonable expectations of those who innocently deal with persons who appear rational and who understand what they are doing should be protected.

Accordingly, I would affirm the order appealed from. . . .

Order reversed, without costs, and a new trial granted.

RESTATEMENT (SECOND) OF CONTRACTS

§12.   CAPACITY TO CONTRACT

(1) No one can be bound by contract who has not legal capacity to incur at least voidable contractual duties. Capacity to contract may be partial and its existence in respect of a particular transaction may depend upon the nature of the transaction or upon other circumstances.

(2) A natural person who manifests assent to a transaction has full legal capacity to incur contractual duties thereby unless he is

    (a) under guardianship, or

    (b) an infant, or

    (c) mentally ill or defective, or

    (d) intoxicated.

§15.   MENTAL ILLNESS OR DEFECT

(1) A person incurs only voidable contractual duties by entering into a transaction if by reason of mental illness or defect

    (a) he is unable to understand in a reasonable manner the nature and consequences of the transaction, or

    (b) he is unable to act in a reasonable manner in relation to the transaction and the other party has reason to know of his condition.

(2) Where the contract is made on fair terms and the other party is without knowledge of the mental illness or defect, the power of avoidance under Subsection (1) terminates to the extent that the contract has been so performed in whole or in part or the circumstances have so changed that

avoidance would be unjust. In such a case a court may grant relief as justice requires.

REFERENCE: Barnett, §§6.2, 6.2.1
               Farnsworth, §§4.6-4.8
               Calamari & Perillo, §§8.11-8.14
               Murray, §§23, 27

2. Infancy

STUDY GUIDE: *In light of the theory of defenses articulated by Richard Epstein in the excerpt in Section A, is the court in the next case correct when it asserts that: "An infant's liability for necessaries is based not upon his actual contract to pay for them but upon a contract implied by law, or, in other words, a quasi-contract"? If not, then what is the basis for such liability? What is the purpose of the exception for necessaries?*

[handwritten margin note: Lack of capacity; misrepresentation; duress impede mutual assent]

WEBSTER STREET PARTNERSHIP, LTD. v. SHERIDAN
Supreme Court of Nebraska,
220 Neb. 9, 368 N.W.2d 439 (1985)

KRIVOSHA, C.J.*

Webster Street Partnership, Ltd. (Webster Street) appeals from an order of the district court for Douglas County, Nebraska, which modified an earlier judgment entered by the municipal court of the city of Omaha, Douglas County, Nebraska. The municipal court entered judgment in favor of Webster Street and against the appellees, Matthew Sheridan and Pat Wilwerding, in the amount of $630.94. On appeal the district court found that Webster Street was entitled to a judgment in the amount of $146.75 and that Sheridan and Wilwerding were entitled to a credit in the amount of $150. The district court therefore entered judgment in favor of Sheridan and Wilwerding and against Webster Street in the amount of $3.25. It is from this $3.25 judgment that appeal is taken to this court.

Webster Street is a partnership owning real estate in Omaha, Nebraska. On September 18, 1982, Webster Street, through one of its agents, Norman Sargent, entered into a written lease with Sheridan and Wilwerding for a second floor apartment at 3007 Webster Street. The lease provided that Sheridan and Wilwerding would pay to Webster Street by way of monthly rental the sum of $250 due on the first day of each month until August 15, 1983. The lease also required the payment of a security deposit in the

---

* *Norman Krivosha* (1934-†) was educated at the University of Nebraska (B.S., J.D.). He served as City Attorney at Lincoln, Nebraska (1969-1970), and was appointed Chief Justice on the Supreme Court of Nebraska in 1978. Krivosha served on that bench for nearly a decade before resigning in 1987. — K.T.

amount of $150 and a payment of $20 per month for utilities during the months of December, January, February, and March. Liquidated damages in the amount of $5 per day for each day the rent was late were also provided for by the lease.

The evidence conclusively establishes that at the time the lease was executed both tenants were minors and, further, that Webster Street knew that fact. At the time the lease was entered into, Sheridan was 18 and did not become 19 until November 5, 1982. Wilwerding was 17 at the time the lease was executed and never gained his majority during any time relevant to this case.

The tenants paid the $150 security deposit, $100 rent for the remaining portion of September 1982, and $250 rent for October 1982. They did not pay the rent for the month of November 1982, and on November 5 Sargent advised Wilwerding that unless the rent was paid immediately, both boys would be required to vacate the premises. The tenants both testified that, being unable to pay the rent, they moved from the premises on November 12. In fact, a dispute exists as to when the two tenants relinquished possession of the premises, but in view of our decision that dispute is not of any relevance.

In a letter dated January 7, 1983, Webster Street's attorney made written demand upon the tenants for damages in the amount of $630.94. On January 12, 1983, the tenants' attorney denied any liability, refused to pay any portion of the amount demanded, stated that neither tenant was of legal age at the time the lease was executed, and demanded return of $150 security deposit.

Webster Street thereafter commenced suit against the tenants and sought judgment in the amount of $630.94, which was calculated as follows:

Rent due Nov.	$250.00
Rent due Dec.	250.00
Dec. utility allowance	20.00
Garage rental	40.00
Clean up and repair	46.79
Broken window, degrease	
kitchen stove, shampoo	
carpet, etc.	
Advertising	24.15
Re-rental fee	150.00
	780.94
Less security deposit	150.00
	$630.94

To this petition the tenants filed an answer alleging that they were minors at the time they signed the lease, that the lease was therefore voidable, and that the rental property did not constitute a necessary for which they were otherwise liable. In addition, Sheridan cross-petitioned for the return of the security deposit, and Wilwerding filed a cross-petition seeking the return of all moneys paid to Webster Street. Following trial, the municipal court of the city of Omaha found in favor of Webster Street and against both tenants in the amount of $630.94.

The tenants appealed to the district court for Douglas County. The district court found that the tenants had vacated the premises on November 12, 1982, and therefore were only liable for the 12 days in which they actually occupied the apartment and did not pay rent. The district court also permitted Webster Street to recover $46.79 for cleanup and repairs. The tenants, however, were given credit for their $150 security deposit, resulting in an order that Webster Street was indebted to the tenants in the amount of $3.25.

Webster Street then perfected an appeal to this court assigning but one error in terms which provide little assistance to the court in considering the appeal. The assignment of error, in pertinent part, reads as follows: "The District Court . . . abused [its] discretion and committed errors of law in improperly modifying the judgment of the Municipal Court. . . ." It appears, in fact, to be Webster Street's position that the district court erred in failing to find that Sheridan had ratified the lease within a reasonable time after obtaining majority, and was therefore responsible for the lease, and that the minors had become emancipated and were therefore liable, even though Wilwerding had not reached majority. Webster Street is simply wrong in both matters.

As a general rule, an infant does not have the capacity to bind himself absolutely by contract. See Smith v. Wade, 169 Neb. 710, 100 N.W.2d 770 (1960); 43 C.J.S. Infants §166 (1978). The right of the infant to avoid his contract is one conferred by law for his protection against his own improvidence and the designs of others. See Burnand v. Irigoyen, 30 Cal. 2d 861, 186 P.2d 417 (1947). The policy of the law is to discourage adults from contracting with an infant; they cannot complain if, as a consequence of violating that rule, they are unable to enforce their contracts. As stated in Curtice Co. v. Kent, 89 Neb. 496, 500, 131 N.W. 944, 945 (1911): "The result seems hardly just to the [adult], but persons dealing with infants do so at their peril. The law is plain as to their disability to contract, and safety lies in refusing to transact business with them."

However, the privilege of infancy will not enable an infant to escape liability in all cases and under all circumstances. For example, it is well established that an infant is liable for the value of necessaries furnished him. 42 Am. Jur. 2d Infants §65 (1969). . . . An infant's liability for necessaries is based not upon his actual contract to pay for them but upon a contract implied by law, or, in other words, a quasi-contract. 42 Am. Jur. 2d, supra.

Just what are necessaries, however, has no exact definition. The term is flexible and varies according to the facts of each individual case. In Cobbey v. Buchanan, 48 Neb. 391, 397, 67 N.W. 176, 178 (1896), we said:

> The meaning of the term "necessaries" cannot be defined by a general rule applicable to all cases; the question is a mixed one of law and fact, to be determined in each case from the particular facts and circumstances in such case.

A number of factors must be considered before a court can conclude whether a particular product or service is a necessary. As stated in Schoenung v. Gallet, 206 Wis. 52, 54, 238 N.W. 852, 853 (1931):

> The term "necessaries," as used in the law relating to the liability of infants therefor, is a relative term, somewhat flexible, except when applied to such

things as are obviously requisite for the maintenance of existence, and depends on the social position and situation in life of the infant, as well as upon his own fortune and that of his parents. The particular infant must have an actual need for the articles furnished; not for mere ornament or pleasure. The articles must be useful and suitable, but they are not necessaries merely because useful or beneficial. Concerning the general character of the things furnished, to be necessaries the articles must supply the infant's personal needs, either those of his body or those of his mind. However, the term "necessaries" is not confined to merely such things as are required for a bare subsistence. There is no positive rule by means of which it may be determined what are or what are not necessaries, for what may be considered necessary for one infant may not be necessaries for another infant whose state is different as to rank, social position, fortune, health, or other circumstances, the question being one to be determined from the particular facts and circumstances of each case.

(Citation omitted.) This appears to be the law as it is generally followed throughout the country.

In Ballinger v. Craig, 95 Ohio App. 545, 121 N.E.2d 66, (1953), the defendants were husband and wife and were 19 years of age at the time they purchased a house trailer. Both were employed. However, prior to the purchase of the trailer, the defendants were living with the parents of the husband. The Court of Appeals for the State of Ohio held that under the facts presented the trailer was not a necessary. The court stated:

To enable an infant to contract for articles as necessaries, he must have been in actual need of them, and obliged to procure them for himself. They are not necessaries as to him, however necessary they may be in their nature, if he was already supplied with sufficient articles of the kind, or if he had a parent or guardian who was able and willing to supply them. The burden of proof is on the plaintiff to show that the infant was destitute of the articles, and had no way of procuring them except by his own contract.

(Citation omitted.) This appears to be the law as it is generally followed throughout the country. . . .

In 42 Am. Jur. 2d Infants §67 at 68-69 (1969), the author notes:

Thus, articles are not necessaries for an infant if he has a parent or guardian who is able and willing to supply them, and an infant residing with and being supported by his parent according to his station in life is not absolutely liable for things which under other circumstances would be considered necessaries.

The undisputed testimony is that both tenants were living away from home, apparently with the understanding that they could return home at any time. Sheridan testified:

Q: During the time that you were living at 3007 Webster, did you at any time, feel free to go home or anything like that?
A: Well, I had a feeling I could, but I just wanted to see if I could make it on my own.
Q: Had you been driven from your home?
A: No.

Q: You didn't have to go?
A: No.
Q: You went freely?
A: Yes.
Q: Then, after you moved out and went to 3417 for a week or so, you were again to return home, is that correct?
A: Yes, sir.

It would therefore appear that in the present case neither Sheridan nor Wilwerding was in need of shelter but, rather, had chosen to voluntarily leave home, with the understanding that they could return whenever they desired. One may at first blush believe that such a rule is unfair. Yet, on further consideration, the wisdom of the rule is apparent. If, indeed, landlords may not contract with minors, except at their peril, they may refuse to do so. In that event, minors who voluntarily leave home but who are free to return will be compelled to return to their parents' home — a result which is desirable. We therefore find that both the municipal court and the district court erred in finding that the apartment, under the facts in this case, was a necessary.

Having therefore concluded that the apartment was not a necessary, the question of whether Sheridan and Wilwerding were emancipated is of no significance. The effect of emancipation is only relevant with regard to necessaries. If the minors were not emancipated, then their parents would be liable for necessaries provided to the minors. As we recently noted in Accent Service Co., Inc. v. Ebsen, 209 Neb. 94, 96, 306 N.W.2d 575, 576 (1981):

> In general, even in the absence of statute, parents are under a legal as well as a moral obligation to support, maintain, and care for their children, the basis of such a duty resting not only upon the fact of the parent-child relationship, but also upon the interest of the state as parens patriae of children and of the community at large in preventing them from becoming a public burden. However, various voluntary acts of a child, such as marriage or enlistment in military service, have been held to terminate the parent's obligation of support, the issue generally being considered by the courts in terms of whether an emancipation of the child has been effectuated. In those cases involving the issue of whether a parent is obligated to support an unmarried minor child who has voluntarily left home without the consent of the parent, the courts, in actions to compel support from the parent, have uniformly held that such conduct on the part of the child terminated the support obligation. . . .

If, on the other hand, it was determined that the minors were emancipated and the apartment was a necessary, then the minors would be liable. But where, as here, we determine that the apartment was not a necessary, then neither the parents nor the infants are liable and the question of emancipation is of no moment.

Because the rental of the apartment was not a necessary, the minors had the right to avoid the contract, either during their minority or within a reasonable time after reaching their majority. See Smith v. Wade, 169 Neb. 710, 100 N.W.2d 770 (1960). Disaffirmance by an infant completely puts an end to the contract's existence, both as to him and as to the adult with whom he contracted. Curtice Co. v. Kent, 89 Neb. 496, 131 N.W. 944 (1911). Because the parties then stand as if no contract had ever existed, the infant can recover payments made to the adult, and the adult is entitled to the return of whatever was received by the infant. Id.

The record shows that Pat Wilwerding clearly disaffirmed the contract during his minority. Moreover, the record supports the view that when the agent for Webster Street ordered the minors out for failure to pay rent and they vacated the premises, Sheridan likewise disaffirmed the contract. The record indicates that Sheridan reached majority on November 5. To suggest that a lapse of 7 days was not disaffirmance within a reasonable time would be foolish. Once disaffirmed, the contract became void; therefore, no contract existed between the parties, and the minors were entitled to recover all of the moneys which they paid and to be relieved of any further obligation under the contract. The judgment of the district court for Douglas County, Nebraska, is therefore reversed and the cause remanded with directions to vacate the judgment in favor of Webster Street and to enter a judgment in favor of Matthew Sheridan and Pat Wilwerding in the amount of $500, representing September rent in the amount of $100, October rent in the amount of $250, and the security deposit in the amount of $150.

Reversed and remanded with directions.

HALBMAN v. LEMKE, SUPREME COURT OF WISCONSIN, 99 WIS. 2D 241, 251, 298 N.W.2D 562, 567 (1980): Callow, J.* . . . [M]odifications of the rules governing the capacity of infants to contract are best left to the legislature. Until such changes are forthcoming, however, we hold that, absent misrepresentation or tortious damage to the property, a minor who disaffirms a contract for the purchase of an item which is not a necessity may recover his purchase price without liability for use, depreciation, damage, or other diminution in value. . . .

We believe this result is consistent with the purpose of the infancy doctrine.

STUDY GUIDE: *Though an apartment is not a necessary, according to the previous case, a lawyer is, according to the next. Why would not the rationale of Statler v. Dodson apply as well to shelter?*

ZELNICK v. ADAMS, SUPREME COURT OF VIRGINIA, 561 S.E.2D 711, 716 (2002): Lemons, Justice.** Certainly, the provision of legal

---

* *William Grant Callow* (1921-†) received degrees from the University of Wisconsin (Ph.B., J.D.). He served in the Waukesha city attorney's office (1948-1960) and then as county judge in Waukesha (1961-1977). He was a member of the Supreme Court of Wisconsin from 1978 to 1992. Callow taught at the University of Minnesota (1951-1952) and the Wisconsin Judicial College (1968-1975). He served with the U.S. Marine Corps (1943-1945) and the U.S. Air Force (1951-1952). He now acts as a neutral specializing in the arbitration and mediation of all types of cases. — K.T.

** *Donald W. Lemons* (1949-†) received his B.A. (1970) from the University of Virginia. After graduation, he was an assistant dean for student affairs and an assistant professor at the University of Virginia School of Law before entering private practice in 1978. In 1995, he was appointed a judge of the Circuit Court of the City of Richmond, where he served until 1998,

services may fall within the class of necessaries for which a contract by or on behalf of an infant may not be avoided or disaffirmed on the grounds of infancy. Generally, contracts for legal services related to prosecuting personal injury actions, and protecting an infant's personal liberty, security, or reputation are considered contracts for necessaries. . . . "[W]hether attorney's services are to be considered necessaries or not depends on whether or not there is a necessity therefor. If such necessity exists, the infant may be bound. . . . If there is no necessity for services, there can be no recovery" for the services. Fenn v. Hart Dairy Co., 83 S.W.2d 120, 124 (1935). The Supreme Court of Appeals of West Virginia recently addressed this issue in a paternity action against the estate of an infant's father, brought by the infant's mother on the infant's behalf. Statler v. Dodson, 466 S.E.2d 497 (1995). The court held that contracts for legal services by infants should be regarded as contracts for necessaries in some instances because "[i]f minors are not required to pay for legal representation, they will not be able to protect their various interests." Id. at 503.

Historical Background: The Extension of Childhood

STUDY GUIDE: *The* Webster *case treated seventeen- and eighteen-year-olds as "infants," and therefore incapable of making responsible choices on their own behalf. Consider this legal categorization in light of the following excerpt concerning children's rights. Also keep this history in mind as you read the next case.*

HILLARY RODHAM, CHILDREN'S RIGHTS: A LEGAL PERSPECTIVE, in CHILDREN'S RIGHTS: CONTEMPORARY PERSPECTIVES 21, 24-25 (PATRICIA A. VARDIN & ILENE N. BRODY, EDS. 1979): Many of the modern conflicts between parents and children arise because of the "invention" of adolescence. Children in the Middle Ages became adults at the age of seven, at which time a boy was apprenticed to a tradesman, or otherwise sent out to find his fortune, and a girl was trained for future domestic responsibilities. The concept of childhood gradually was expanded until children became more and more dependent on their parents and parents became less and less dependent on their children for economic support and sustenance. During the nineteenth century in this country, the idea of compulsory education provided an opportunity for children to be trained, and took them out of an increasingly smaller work force, so that they would not compete with adults. Child labor laws continued this trend and so did the imposition of age requirements for school attendance. All of these developments ran parallel with the accelerated industrialization and shrinking frontiers of the twentieth century. A boy or girl of fifteen who wished to seek his or her fortune in the

---

when he was elected by the Virginia General Assembly to serve as a judge of the Court of Appeals of Virginia. In 2000, he was elected by the General Assembly to a twelve-year term on the Virginia Supreme Court. He also teaches at the University of Richmond School of Law. — R.B.

nineteenth century or even more recently might have run off to sea or otherwise absented himself or herself from home without becoming a status offender or causing family disagreements that could become legal problems.

⌊Because children now remain in the family for longer periods, during which they are still dependent but becoming more and more adult, the opportunities for intrafamily disputes have increased dramatically⌉

STUDY GUIDE: In the next case, the court notes that, at common law, an infant could disaffirm a contract executed by a parent on his or her behalf. Is that rule defensible? In Halbman, *the court said that any modification of the defense of infancy should be made by the legislature. The following is one court's interpretation of a statute that alters the common law rule governing contracts made by parents on behalf of infants that provoked a vigorous dissent. How does Judge Jasen distinguish the minor's power to avoid contracts asserted in this case from the situation in* Webster Street Partnership, Ltd. v. Sheridan? *Judge Jasen also dissented in the* Ortelere *case. Are his opinions in these two cases consistent? [Born in 1965, Brooke Shields went from child model to actress, starring in films such as* The Blue Lagoon *and the television series* Suddenly Susan. *During that time she also graduated from Princeton University.]*

BROOKE SHIELDS v. GROSS
Court of Appeals of New York,
58 N.Y.2d 338, 461 N.Y.S.2d 254, 448 N.E.2d 108 (1983)

SIMONS, J.*

The issue on this appeal is whether an infant model may disaffirm a prior unrestricted consent executed on her behalf by her parent and maintain an action pursuant to section 51 of the Civil Rights Law against her photographer for republication of photographs of her. We hold that she may not.

Plaintiff is now a well-known actress. For many years prior to these events she had been a child model and in 1975, when she was 10 years of age, she obtained several modeling jobs with defendant through her agent, the Ford Model Agency. One of the jobs, a series of photographs to be financed by Playboy Press, required plaintiff to pose nude in a bathtub. It was intended that these photos would be used in a publication entitled "Portfolio 8" (later renamed "Sugar and Spice"). Before the photographic sessions, plaintiff's mother and legal guardian, Teri Shields, executed two

---

* *Richard Duncan Simons* (1927-†) was educated at Colgate University (A.B.). He interrupted his legal studies to serve in the U.S. Navy during World War II, returning afterward to the University of Michigan (LL.B.); he was admitted to the New York bar in 1952. He held a private practice in Rome, New York, for over ten years; during that time, he was also counsel to the City of Rome (1955-1963). In 1964, he was appointed to the New York Supreme Court, serving in the Appellate Division from 1971 until he was appointed to the New York Court of Appeals in 1983, where he sat until 1996. — K.T.

consents in favor of defendant.[7] After the pictures were taken, they were used not only in "Sugar and Spice" but also, to the knowledge of plaintiff and her mother, in other publications and in a display of larger-than-life photo enlargements in the windows of a store on Fifth Avenue in New York City. Indeed, plaintiff subsequently used the photos in a book that she published about herself and to do so her mother obtained an authorization from defendant to use them. Over the years defendant has also photographed plaintiff for Penthouse Magazine, New York Magazine and for advertising by the Courtauldts and Avon companies.

In 1980 plaintiff learned that several of the 1975 photographs had appeared in a French magazine called Photo and, disturbed by that publication and by information that defendant intended others, she attempted to buy the negatives. In 1981, she commenced this action in tort and contract seeking compensatory and punitive damages and an injunction permanently enjoining defendant from any further use of the photographs. Special Term granted plaintiff a preliminary injunction. Although it determined that as a general proposition consents given by a parent pursuant to section 51 barred the infant's action, it found that plaintiff's claim that the consents were invalid or restricted the use of the photographs by Playboy Press presented questions of fact. After a nonjury trial the court ruled that the consents were unrestricted as to time and use and it therefore dismissed plaintiff's complaint. In doing so, however, it granted plaintiff limited relief. On defendant's stipulation it permanently enjoined defendant from using the photographs in "pornographic magazines or publications whose appeal is of a predominantly prurient nature" and it charged him with the duty of policing their use. The Appellate Division, [88 A.D.2d 846, 451 N.Y.S.2d 419] by a divided court, modified the judgment on the law and granted plaintiff a permanent injunction enjoining defendant from using the pictures for purposes of advertising or trade. . . .

The parties have filed cross appeals. Defendant requests reinstatement of the trial court's judgment. Plaintiff requests, in the alternative, that the order of the Appellate Division be modified by striking the limitation enjoining use only for purposes of advertising and trade, or that the order of the Appellate Division should be affirmed or, failing both of these, that a new trial be granted. Since the Appellate Division accepted the trial court's findings that the consents were valid and unrestricted as to time and use, we are presented with only a narrow issue of law concerning the legal effect to be given to the parent's consents.

---

7. The consents provided in pertinent part:

I hereby give the photographer, his legal representatives, and assigns, those for whom the photographer is acting, and those acting with his permission, or his employees, the right and permission to copyright and/or use, reuse and/or publish, and republish photographic pictures or portraits of me, or in which I may be distorted in character, or form, in conjunction with my own or a fictitious name, on reproductions thereof in color, or black and white made through any media by the photographer at his studio or elsewhere, for any purpose whatsoever; including the use of any printed matter in conjunction therewith.

I hereby waive any right to inspect or approve the finished photograph or advertising copy or printed matter that may be used in conjunction therewith or to the eventual use that it might be applied.

Historically, New York common law did not recognize a cause of action
for invasion of privacy (. . . Roberson v. Rochester Folding Box Co., 171 N.Y.
538). In 1909, however, responding to the *Roberson* decision, the Legislature enacted sections 50 and 51 of the Civil Rights Law. Section 50 is penal
and makes it a misdemeanor to use a living person's name, portrait or
picture for advertising purposes without prior "written consent." Section
51 is remedial and creates a related civil cause of action on behalf of the
injured party permitting relief by injunction or damages. . . . Section 51 of
the statute states that the prior "written consent" which will bar the civil
action is to be as "above provided," referring to section 50, and section 50,
in turn, provides that: "A person, firm or corporation that uses for advertising purposes, or for the purposes of trade, the name, portrait or picture
of any living person *without having first obtained the written consent of
such person, or if a minor of his or her parent or guardian, is guilty of a
misdemeanor*" (emphasis added).

Thus, whereas in *Roberson*, the infant plaintiff had no cause of action
against the advertiser under the common law for using her pictures, the
new statute gives a cause of action to those similarly situated unless they
have executed a consent or release in writing to the advertiser before use
of the photographs. The statute acts to restrict an advertiser's prior
unrestrained common-law right to use another's photograph until written
consent is obtained. Once written consent is obtained, however, the
photograph may be published as permitted by its terms. . . .

Concededly, at common law an infant could disaffirm his written
consent . . . or, for that matter, a consent executed by another on his or
her behalf. . . . Notwithstanding these rules, it is clear that the Legislature
may abrogate an infant's common-law right to disaffirm . . . or, conversely, it
may confer upon infants the right to make binding contracts. . . . Where a
statute expressly permits a certain class of agreements to be made by infants,
that settles the question and makes the agreement valid and enforceable.
That is precisely what happened here. The Legislature, by adopting section
51, created a new cause of action and it provided in the statute itself the
method for obtaining an infant's consent to avoid liability. Construing the
statute strictly, as we must since it is in derogation of the common law . . . ,
the parent's consent is binding on the infant and no words prohibiting
disaffirmance are necessary to effectuate the legislative intent. Inasmuch
as the consents in this case complied with the statutory requirements,
they were valid and may not be disaffirmed. . . .

It should be noted that plaintiff did not contend that the photographs
were obscene or pornographic. Her only complaint was that she was embarrassed because "they [the photographs] are not me now." The trial court
specifically found that the photographs were not pornographic and it
enjoined use of them in pornographic publications. Thus, there is no
need to discuss the unenforceability of certain contracts which violate
public policy (see, e.g., Penal Law, §235.00 et seq.) or to equate an infant's
common-law right to disaffirm with that principle, as the dissent apparently
does.

Finally, it is claimed that the application of the statute as we interpret it
may result in unanticipated and untoward consequences. If that be so, there
is an obvious remedy. A parent who wishes to limit the publicity and

exposure of her child need only limit the use authorized in the consent, for a defendant's immunity from a claim for invasion of privacy is no broader than the consent executed to him. . . .

The order of the Appellate Division should be modified by striking the further injunction against use of the photographs for uses of advertising and trade, and as so modified, the order should be affirmed.

JASEN, J. (dissenting).

Since I believe that the interests of society and this State in protecting its children must be placed above any concern for trade or commercialism, I am compelled to dissent. The State has the right and indeed the obligation to afford extraordinary protection to minors.

At the outset, it should be made clear that this case does not involve the undoing of a written consent given by a mother to invade her infant daughter's privacy so as to affect *prior* benefits derived by a person relying on the validity of the consent pursuant to sections 50 and 51 of the Civil Rights Law. Rather, what is involved is the right of an infant, now 17 years of age, to disaffirm her mother's consent with respect to *future use* of a nude photograph taken of her at age 10.

The majority holds, as a matter of law, not only in this case but as to all present and future consents executed by parents on behalf of children pursuant to sections 50 and 51 of the Civil Rights Law, that once a parent consents to the invasion of privacy of a child, the child is forever bound by that consent and may never disaffirm the continued invasion of his or her privacy, even where the continued invasion of the child's privacy may cause the child enormous embarrassment, distress and humiliation.

I find this difficult to accept as a rational rule of law, particularly so when one considers that it has long been the rule in this State that a minor enjoys an almost absolute right to disaffirm a contract entered into either by the minor or by the minor's parent on behalf of the minor . . . and the statute in question does not in any manner abrogate this salutary right.

This right has been upheld despite the fact that the minor held himself out to be an adult . . . or that a parent also attempted to contractually bind the minor. . . . Significantly, whether or not the minor can restore the other contracting party to the position he was in prior to entering the contract is pertinent only to the extent that the minor, by disaffirming the contract, cannot put himself into a better position than he was in before entering the contract. . . . In the past, this court has noted that those who contract with minors do so at their own peril. . . .

Understandably, such a broad right has evolved as a result of the State's policy to provide children with as much protection as possible against being taken advantage of or exploited by adults. "The right to rescind is a legal right established for the protection of the infant" (Green v. Green [69 N.Y. 553] at p. 556). This right is founded in the legal concept that an infant is incapable of contracting because he does not understand the scope of his rights and he cannot appreciate the consequences and ramifications of his decisions. Furthermore, it is feared that as an infant he may well be under the complete influence of an adult or may be unable to act in any manner which would allow him to defend his rights and interests. . . . Allowing a minor the right to disaffirm a contract is merely one way the common law developed to resolve those inequities and afford children the protection they require to compensate for their immaturity.

Can there be any question that the State has a compelling interest in protecting children? Indeed, the most priceless possessions we have in the Nation are our children. Recognizing this compelling interest in children, the State has assumed the role of *parens patriae*, undertaking with that role the responsibility of protecting children from their own inexperience. Acting in that capacity, the State has put the interests of minors above that of adults, organizations or businesses. . . . The broad right given a minor to disaffirm a contract is, of course, an obvious example of the State's attempt to afford an infant protection against exploitation by adults. . . . Thus, I am persuaded that, in this case, 17-year-old Brooke Shields should be afforded the right to disaffirm her mother's consent to use a photograph of her in the nude, taken when she was 10 years old, unless it can be said, as the majority holds, that the Legislature intended to abrogate that right when it enacted sections 50 and 51 of the Civil Rights Law.

The legislative history of this statute enacted in the early 1900s is understandably scarce. The case law prior to its passage, however, indicates that a minor's right to disaffirm a contract under the common law was well established at that time. Additionally, it is well accepted that this statute was enacted in response to this court's decision in Roberson v. Rochester Folding Box Co., (171 N.Y. 538, [64 N.E. 442] . . .), in which the court held that a minor had no recourse against an entrepreneur who made commercial use out of her picture without her consent. Apparently, in order to alleviate litigation over whether or not consent had been given, the Legislature required that such consent be in writing and, if the person was a minor, that the parent sign the consent form. There is no indication that by requiring consent from the minor's parents, the Legislature intended in any way to abrogate that minor's right to disaffirm a contract at some future date. Indeed, the requirement of parental consent, like the broad right to disaffirm a contract, was granted in order to afford the minor as much protection against exploitation as possible. The assumption, of course, was that a parent would protect the child's interests. But if that assumption proves invalid, as may well be the case if a minor upon reaching the age of maturity realizes that the parent, too, has been exploiting him or her or had failed to adequately guard his or her interest by giving consent for pictures which caused humiliation, embarrassment and distress, then the child should be able to cure the problem by disaffirming the parent's consent. To say, as does the majority, that the mother could have limited her consent avoids the issue. If the parent has failed to put any restrictions on the consent, as occurred in this case, and has thus failed to protect the child's future interests, I see no reason why the child must continue to bear the burden imposed by her mother's bad judgment. This means the child is forever bound by its parent's decisions, even if those decisions turn out to have been exploitative of the child and detrimental to the child's best interests. . . .

The fact that when an infant disaffirms a contract there may be harsh results to the person or commercial enterprise attempting to exploit the child has never caused the courts to alter the scope of the protection that right affords the child. The overriding interest of society in protecting its children has long been held to outweigh the interests of merchants who attempt to contract with children. . . .

. . . The failure of the Legislature to cover child models in this provision indicates to me that they intended child models to retain the protections afforded by the common-law right to disaffirm a contract. It is unfortunate that by virtue of the majority's interpretation of the Civil Rights Law those children may not in the future be afforded protection against exploitation by their own parents.

It is even more unfortunate that by its interpretation of sections 50 and 51 the majority takes away a large part of the protection those children had at common law . . .

Order modified, with costs to defendant, in accordance with the opinion herein and, as so modified, affirmed.

RESTATEMENT (SECOND) OF CONTRACTS

§14. INFANTS

Unless a statute provides otherwise, a natural person has the capacity to incur only voidable contractual duties until the beginning of the day before the person's eighteenth birthday.

REFERENCE: Barnett, §6.2.2
Farnsworth, §§4.3-4.5
Calamari & Perillo, §§8.3-8.9
Murray, §§25, 26

16

ASSENT IMPROPERLY OBTAINED AND ASSENT TO IMPROPER TERMS

In the previous chapter we studied defenses involving situations in which a person's normal capacity to make decisions on his or her own behalf is called into question. In this chapter we set these concerns aside and turn our attention to circumstances in which the assent of *competent* persons is obtained by means that are considered to be improper (although, as we shall see, with the defenses of undue influence and unconscionability, this distinction begins to erode). In other words, each of the promisors in the cases in this chapter manifested their assent to contract and were competent to do so. Nonetheless, their assent was alleged to have been induced by conduct on the part of the promisee that undermines the normal significance of a manifestation of assent. Our concern will be to understand what kind of conduct by promisees has this effect. Finally, we will turn to those very rare cases where courts refuse to enforce contracts based solely on their substance, even when there is no suggestion that assent was improperly attained.

A. MISREPRESENTATION

STUDY GUIDE: Notice the court's distinction between misrepresentation as a defense to contract and fraud as a cause of action in tort. What is the difference between these two legal theories? Also, you may wish to consider the difference, if any, between an innocent misrepresentation and a warranty, as well as to compare this misrepresentation and the statements made by Lukowitz in Red Owl Stores. *Although it seems obvious, ask yourself exactly why misrepresentation is a good reason to release someone from their contractual obligation. Would the case be decided the same way if the seller in the next case knew of the termites but said nothing about them? We shall return to the closely related issue of one's duty to disclose information in Chapter 17 in the section on unilateral mistake. Finally, notice the defendant's effort to rely on a merger clause in the contract.*

HALPERT v. ROSENTHAL
Supreme Court of Rhode Island,
107 R.I. 406, 267 A.2d 730 (1970)

KELLEHER, J.*

This is a civil action wherein the plaintiff vendor seeks damages for the breach by the defendant vendee of a contract for the sale of real estate. The defendant filed a counterclaim in which he sought the return of his deposit. A jury trial was held in the Superior Court. The jury found for the defendant and judgment followed. The case is before us on the plaintiff's appeal.

On February 21, 1967, the parties hereto entered into a real estate agreement whereby plaintiff agreed to convey a one-family house located in Providence on the southeasterly corner of Wayland and Upton Avenues to defendant for the sum of $54,000. The defendant paid a deposit of $2,000 to plaintiff. The agreement provided for the delivery of the deed and the payment of the balance of the purchase price by June 30, 1967.

On May 17, 1967, a termite inspection was made of the premises, and it was discovered that the house was inhabited by termites. The defendant then notified plaintiff that, because of the termite infestation, he was not going to purchase the property. The defendant did not appear for the title closing which plaintiff had scheduled for June 30, 1967.

The plaintiff immediately commenced this suit. Her complaint prayed for specific performance or monetary damages. When the case came on for trial, the property had been sold to another buyer for the sum of $35,000. The plaintiff then sought to recover from defendant the $19,000 difference between the selling price called for in the sales agreement and the actual selling price. The defendant in his answer alleged that plaintiff and her agent had, during the preagreement negotiation, intentionally misrepresented the house as being free of termites. The defendant's counterclaim sought the return of the $2,000 deposit.

At the conclusion of the presentation of all the evidence, plaintiff made a motion for a directed verdict on the issue of the alleged fraudulent misrepresentations. The trial justice reserved decision on the motion and submitted the case to the jury. After the jury's verdict, he denied the motion.

This case is unique in that plaintiff made no motion for a new trial. Her appeal is based for the most part on the trial court's refusal to direct a verdict in her favor on the counterclaim. She has also alleged that the trial justice erred in certain portions of his charge to the jury and in failing to adopt some 15 requests to charge submitted by plaintiff.

The absence of a motion for a new trial narrows the scope of an inquiry on appeal. Instead of being concerned with the credibility of witnesses or the weight of the evidence as we would be were we reviewing the usual motion for a new trial, we apply the standards applicable to a motion for a

---

* *Thomas F. Kelleher* (1923-1995) was educated at Providence College and Boston University (LL.B.). After graduation he practiced law in Smithfield, Rhode Island, where he also served later as probate judge and as city solicitor. From 1955 to 1966, Kelleher was a member of the Rhode Island House of Representatives. He became a justice on the Supreme Court of Rhode Island in 1966 where he remained until his death. — C.R.

directed verdict. In doing so, it is our duty to consider all of the evidence and reasonable inferences deducible therefrom in the light most favorable to defendant. . . .

Since we consider only the evidence favorable to defendant, we shall set forth defendant's version of three different occasions in 1967 when the alleged misrepresentations relative to absence of any termites were made.

1. In early February, defendant and his wife inspected the Halpert home. They asked the agent about termites and he told them that there was no termite problem and that he had never experienced any termite problem with any of the houses he sold in the East Side section of Providence.

2. Later on in February, defendant, his wife, his sister-in-law and his brother-in-law met plaintiff. The brother-in-law inquired about the presence of termites; plaintiff said that there were no termites in the house.

3. When defendant was about to sign the purchase and sales agreement, he asked plaintiff's real estate agent whether it might not be advisable if the home be inspected for termites before the agreement was signed. The agent told defendant that such a step was unnecessary because there were no termite problems in the house.

The plaintiff contends that any statements or representations attributed to her or her agent were qualified in that when asked about the termites, they replied that to the best of their knowledge or experience the Wayland Avenue property was termite free. What she overlooks is that in our consideration of the correctness of the denial of her motion for a direction, we can consider only that evidence and the reasonable inferences flowing therefrom which favor defendant. We do not weigh the evidence to determine whether her or her agent's representations were qualified or unqualified.

In contending that she was entitled to a directed verdict, plaintiff contends that to sustain the charge of fraudulent misrepresentation, some evidence had to be produced showing that either she or her agent knew at the time they said there were no termites in the house, that such a statement was untrue. Since the representations made to defendant were made in good faith, she argues that, as a matter of law, defendant could not prevail on his counterclaim.

The defendant concedes that there was no evidence which shows that plaintiff or her agent knowingly made false statements as to the existence of the termites but he maintains that an innocent misrepresentation of a material fact is grounds for rescission of a contract where, as here, a party relies to his detriment on the misrepresentation.

We affirm the denial of the motion for a directed verdict.

The plaintiff, when she made her motion for a directed verdict, stated that her motion was restricted to the issue of "fraud." The word "fraud" is a generic term which embraces a great variety of actionable wrongs. LaCourse v. Kiesel, 366 Pa. 385, 77 A.2d 877. It is a word of many meanings and defies any one all-inclusive definition. Fraud may become important either for the purpose of giving the defrauded person the right to sue for damages in an action for deceit or to enable him to rescind the contract. 12 Williston, Contracts §1487 at 322 (Jaeger 3d ed. 1970). In this jurisdiction a party who has been induced by fraud to enter into a contract may pursue either one of two remedies. He may elect to rescind the contract to recover what he has paid under it, or he may affirm the contract and sue for damages in an action for deceit. . . .

The distinction between a claim for damages for intentional deceit and a claim for rescission is well defined. Deceit is a tort action, and it requires some degree of culpability on the misrepresenter's part. Prosser, Law of Torts (3d ed.) §100. An individual who sues in an action of deceit based on fraud has the burden of proving that the defendant in making the statements knew they were false and intended to deceive him. . . . On the other hand, a suit to rescind an agreement induced by fraud sounds in contract. It is this latter aspect of fraud that we are concerned with in this case, and the pivotal issue before us is whether an innocent misrepresentation of a material fact warrants the granting of a claim for rescission. We believe that it does.

When he denied plaintiff's motion, the trial justice indicated that a false, though innocent, misrepresentation of a fact made as though of one's knowledge may be the basis for the rescission of a contract. While this issue is one of first impression in this state, it is clear that the trial judge's action finds support in the overwhelming weight of decision and textual authority which has established the rule that where one induces another to enter into a contract by means of a material misrepresentation, the latter may rescind the contract. It does not matter if the representation was "innocent" or fraudulent.

In 12 Williston, supra, §1500 at 400-01, Professor Jaeger states:

> It is not necessary, in order that a contract may be rescinded for fraud or misrepresentation, that the party making the misrepresentation should have known that it was false. Innocent misrepresentation is sufficient, for though the representation may have been made innocently, it would be unjust and inequitable to permit a person who has made false representations, even innocently, to retain the fruits of a bargain induced by such representations.

This statement of law is in accord with Restatement of Contracts, §476 at 908 which states:

> Where a party is induced to enter into a transaction with another party that he was under no duty to enter into by means of the latter's fraud or material misrepresentation, the transaction is voidable as against the latter. . . .

Misrepresentation is defined as

> . . . any manifestation by words or other conduct by one person to another that, under the circumstances, amounts to an assertion not in accordance with the facts. Restatement of Contracts, §470 at 890-91.

The comment following this section explains that a misrepresentation may be innocent, negligent or known to be false. A misrepresentation becomes material when it becomes likely to affect the conduct of a reasonable man with reference to a transaction with another person. Restatement of Contracts, §470(2) at 891. Section 28 of Restatement of Restitution is also in accord with this proposition of law that a transaction can be rescinded for innocent misrepresentation of a material fact. In addition, many courts have also adopted this rule. . . .

In Watkins v. Grady County Soil & Water Conservation District (Okl.) 438 P.2d 491, 495, the court ordered cancellation of an easement agreement that was procured by a material misrepresentation honestly made with no intent to deceive. The court reasoned that the question is "... not whether the representation is knowingly false, but whether the other party believed it to be true and thus was misled by such misrepresentations into making the contract."

In Williams v. Benson, 3 Mich. App. 9, 141 N.W.2d 650, the court indicated that relief would be available if there was in fact a misrepresentation, though made innocently, and if its deceptive influence was effective, the consequences to the plaintiff being as serious as though it proceeded from a vicious purpose. Citing Converse v. Blumrich, 14 Mich. 109, the court said that in determining whether relief is appropriate, courts must look to the effect of the untrue statement upon the person to whom it is made, rather than to the motive of the one making the representation.

In Ham v. Hart, 58 N.M. 550, 273 P.2d 748, the court in holding that the honesty and good faith of the person making misrepresentations is immaterial, quoted the following excerpt from 1 Story Equity Jurisprudence §272 (14 ed.):

> Whether the party thus misrepresenting a material fact knew it to be false, or made the assertion without knowing whether it were true or false, is wholly immaterial; for the affirmation of what one does not know or believe to be true is equally in morals and law as unjustifiable as the affirmation of what is known to be positively false. And even if the party innocently misrepresents a material fact by mistake, it is equally conclusive; for it operates as a surprise and imposition upon the other party. 58 N.M. at 552, 273 P.2d at 749.

It is true that some courts require proof of knowledge of the falsity of the misrepresentation before a contract may be invalidated. Wilkinson v. Appleton, 28 Ill. 2d 184, 190 N.E.2d 727; Classic Bowl, Inc. v. AMF Pinspotters, Inc., 403 F.2d 463; Southern Roofing & Petroleum Co. v. Aetna Ins. Co., 293 F. Supp. 725. However, the weight of authority follows the view that the misrepresenter's good faith is immaterial. We believe this view the better one.

A misrepresentation, even though innocently made, may be actionable, if made and relied on as a positive statement of fact. The question to be resolved in determining whether a wrong committed as the result of an innocent misrepresentation may be rectified is succinctly stated in 12 Williston, supra, §1510 at 462 as follows:

> When a defendant has induced another to act by representations false in fact although not dishonestly made, and damage has directly resulted from the action taken, who should bear the loss?

The question we submit is rhetorical. The answer is obvious. Simple justice demands that the speaker be held responsible. Accordingly, we hold that here defendant vendee could maintain his counterclaim.

The plaintiff's second contention is to the effect that even if an innocent misrepresentation without knowledge of its falsity may under certain circumstances entitle the misrepresentee to relief by way of rescission,

defendant cannot maintain his action because the sales agreement contains a merger clause. This provision immediately precedes the testimonium clause and provides that the contract ". . . contains the entire agreement between the parties, and that it is subject to no understandings, conditions or representations other than those expressly stated herein." The plaintiff argues that in order to enable a purchaser to rescind a contract containing a merger clause because of a misrepresentation, proof of a fraudulent misrepresentation must be shown. We find no merit in this argument.

If, as plaintiff concedes, a merger clause, such as is found within the sales contract now before us, will not prevent a rescission based on a fraudulent misrepresentation, . . . there is no valid reason to say that it will prevent a rescission of an agreement which is the result of a false though innocent misrepresentation where both innocent and fraudulent misrepresentations render a contract voidable. See Restatement of Contracts, §476. As we observed before, the availability of the remedy of rescission is motivated by the obvious inequity of allowing a person who has made the innocent misrepresentation to retain the fruits of the bargain induced thereby. If we are to permit a party to rescind a contract which is the result of an innocent misrepresentation, the "boiler plate" found in the merger clause shall not bar the use of this remedy. . . .

Before leaving this phase of plaintiff's appeal, we think it appropriate that we allude to the tendency of many courts to equate an innocent misrepresentation with some species of fraud. Usually the word "fraud" connotes a conscious dishonest conduct on the part of the misrepresenter. Fraud, however, is not present if the speaker actually believes that what he states as the truth is the truth. We believe that it would be better if an innocent misrepresentation was not described as some specie of fraud. Unqualified statements imply certainty. Reliance is more likely to be placed on a positive statement of fact than a mere expression of opinion or a qualified statement. The speaker who uses the unqualified statement does so at his peril. The risk of falsity is his. If he is to be liable for what he states, the liability is imposed because he is to be held strictly accountable for his words. Responsibility for an innocent misrepresentation should be recognized for what it is — an example of absolute liability rather than as many courts have said, an example of constructive fraud. See 12 Williston, supra, §1510; 1 Harper and James, The Law of Torts §7.7. . . .

The plaintiff complains that the trial justice erred when he told the jury that defendant could recover even though he might have been "negligent" in signing the sales agreement.[1] The thrust of this objection is plaintiff's contention that either defendant's neglect to include in the contract a clause which would have protected his interest in the event termites were found on the property or his failure to have the premises inspected for termites prevents his recovery of the deposit. Such an argument is really aimed at the question of whether or not defendant was justified in relying on the representations made by plaintiff and her agent. We can see nothing patently absurd or ridiculous in the statements attributed to them which

---

1. The plaintiff concedes that this court has permitted the victim of an intentional misrepresentation to recover even though he had failed to make any investigation into the truth or falsity of the statements made to him. . . .

would warrant us in saying that defendant should be denied relief because of his failure to do what plaintiff now says he should have done. On the record before us, defendant was amply justified in believing that the home he was purchasing was free of termites. . . .

The appeal of the plaintiff is denied and dismissed, and the case is remanded to the Superior Court for entry of judgment thereon.

RESTATEMENT (SECOND) OF CONTRACTS

§159.   MISREPRESENTATION DEFINED

A misrepresentation is an assertion that is not in accord with the facts.

Can be intentional or mistake?

§162.   WHEN A MISREPRESENTATION IS FRAUDULENT OR MATERIAL

(1) A misrepresentation is fraudulent if the maker intends his assertion to induce a party to manifest his assent and the maker

(a) knows or believes that the assertion is not in accord with the facts, or

(b) does not have the confidence that he states or implies in the truth of the assertion, or

(c) knows that he does not have the basis that he states or implies for the assertion.

(2) A misrepresentation is material if it would be likely to induce a reasonable person to manifest his assent, or if the maker knows that it would be likely to induce the recipient to do so.

§164.   WHEN A MISREPRESENTATION MAKES A CONTRACT VOIDABLE

(1) If a party's manifestation of assent is induced by either a fraudulent or a material misrepresentation by the other party upon which the recipient is justified in relying, the contract is voidable by the recipient.

(2) If a party's manifestation of assent is induced by either a fraudulent or a material misrepresentation by one who is not a party to the transaction upon which the recipient is justified in relying, the contract is voidable by the recipient, unless the other party to the transaction in good faith and without reason to know of the misrepresentation either gives value or relies materially on the transaction.

§167.   WHEN A MISREPRESENTATION IS AN INDUCING CAUSE

A misrepresentation induces a party's manifestation of assent if it substantially contributes to his decision to manifest his assent.

STUDY GUIDE: How would one distinguish the innocent *misstatements about termites as made in the previous case and the* honest *misstatements about land value made in the next? Does the concept of subjective value discussed in Chapter 2 help explain the distinction the court draws between* fact *and* opinion? *Can you imagine why the representation of* possession *was considered by the court to be material, whereas the representation of* ownership *was not?*

BYERS v. FEDERAL LAND CO.

United States Circuit Court of Appeals, Eighth Circuit,
3 F.2d 9 (1924)

MUNGER, District Judge.*

This suit was brought for the cancellation of a contract for the purchase of land. The parties will be designated as in the trial court. The defendant the Federal Land Company was a corporation organized under the laws of Wyoming and doing business at Cheyenne, Wyo. The other defendant, J. R. Carpenter, was its president. The plaintiff entered into a written contract on January 23, 1920, to purchase from the Federal Land Company 320 acres of land in Wyoming, for which he was to pay $2,800 in cash and a balance of $8,400, with interest, in 50 semiannual installments. In the contract the Federal Land Company agreed "to convey or cause to be conveyed" to the plaintiff the land mentioned when the plaintiff should have made these payments. The plaintiff was given the privilege, if he was not in default, of paying any amount on the contract at any interest-paying date.

This suit was begun September 15, 1922. The plaintiff's bill alleged the making of this contract, and prayed for its cancellation, and for recovery of the amounts he had paid under it. The grounds for his relief, shortly stated, were that the Federal Land Company had induced the plaintiff to sign this contract by fraudulently representing to him, contrary to the facts: (1) That the Federal Land Company was the actual owner of the land; (2) that it was in the actual possession thereof; and (3) that it was of the value of $35 per acre. The answers denied the making of these alleged representations. At the trial there was evidence that the real estate brokers acting as agents for the Federal Land Company had stated to the plaintiff, at the time of the preliminary negotiations leading up to the making of this contract, that the land was worth $35 an acre. The proofs were that the land was then worth about $15 per acre. The plaintiff lived at Hastings, Neb., several hundred miles from this land, which was situated about eight miles from Cheyenne, Wyo. The brokers, who made this statement as to value, also lived at Hastings and were engaged in the business of dealing in real estate. There was no relationship of special trust or confidence between them and the

---

* *Thomas Charles Munger* (1861-1941) was a student at Iowa (now Grinnell) College and the Union College of Law, Chicago, prior to admittance to the bar in 1885. A member of the Nebraska legislature (1895-1897) and county attorney for Lancaster County (1897-1901), he was appointed U.S. District Judge for the District of Nebraska in 1907, serving until his death. — K.T.

plaintiff, or between the vendor and the plaintiff. They also represented to the plaintiff that the Federal Land Company was the owner of this land. Before the contract was executed, the other defendant, Carpenter, who was the president of the Federal Land Company, came to Hastings, and he there executed the contract of sale on behalf of the Federal Land Company at the same time that the plaintiff signed it.

The written contract for the sale of the land contained no statement as to the possession of the land after its execution, except as implied in the covenant to convey the land when final payment had been made. There was no evidence of any direct statement to the plaintiff that the Federal Land Company was in possession of this land, but the plaintiff testified that the possession of the land was to be given at once upon the execution of the contract, and as a part of the same transaction there was a lease executed by the plaintiff to the defendant Carpenter of this land and of some adjoining land for a period of five years beginning on the March 1st following, at an annual cash rental of $1,000 per year, payable annually, with an agreement therein that Carpenter should cause to be broken 160 acres of the sod on the land agreed to be conveyed in 1920, and a like amount in 1921, for which he was to be paid from the rental.

The plaintiff had not seen this land prior to the contract and relied on the statements made by the agents and Carpenter. He saw the land in March, 1920. He paid the installment of the purchase price in September, 1920, when it was due, and paid the taxes due upon the land in the January following; but it was not shown that he knew the facts as to possession or value at these times. These facts and others were brought out in the testimony, and at the close of the plaintiff's evidence, the court sustained a motion by the defendants to dismiss the plaintiff's bill on the ground that no actionable misrepresentations had been proved, and the plaintiff has appealed.

It was undisputed in the evidence that the plaintiff had acted upon a representation on the part of the defendant Federal Land Company that this land was owned by it, but in fact the land was owned by another company. This company, however, had entered into a written contract with the Federal Land Company, prior to the date of the plaintiff's contract, to sell this land to the Federal Land Company, and it appeared that the land company which had agreed to sell the land to the Federal Land Company wrote several letters to the plaintiff, many months before this suit was brought, stating that a deed would be delivered to plaintiff at any time when he had complied with his contract. The plaintiff did not answer these letters. It was one of the essentials of the plaintiff's case to prove not only a misrepresentation, but a material misrepresentation. The plaintiff did not undertake to prove the inability of the Federal Land Company to comply with its contract to "convey or cause to be conveyed" this land. What evidence was given tended to indicate its ability and willingness to have the title conveyed to the plaintiff upon his compliance with his contract. The representation as to ownership was not a material misrepresentation to the plaintiff under these circumstances.

The representation as to the value of the land, as already stated, was made by the real estate brokers who lived in the same city as the plaintiff, in Hastings, Neb. He testifies that they told him the land was worth $35 an acre, was cheap at $35. He testified at one time that he relied on the representation as to ownership and possession and at another time that he relied on the representations [sic]. There was no evidence that suggested that these brokers had any special knowledge of or had ever seen this land, or that the plaintiff announced any special reliance on their statement of value.

An honest opinion as to the monetary value of property, stated as an opinion is not a fraudulent misrepresentation . . . , but a statement as an opinion, if it is not the real opinion may be a misrepresentation. . . . A statement of the monetary value or worth of an article, although not expressly phrased as an opinion or estimate, may nevertheless be a representation of an opinion and not of a fact. This is especially true as to property without a definite or known value, or as to property which has only a speculative value. A statement of the value of property for which there is a generally accepted market price, such as bonds of the government, grain or cattle, may be a misrepresentation of a fact. . . . A statement as to value of property may also be actionable as a fraudulent representation of fact under some circumstances, where there is a special reliance placed upon it and superior knowledge on the part of the maker. . . . In such a case it may also be said that the statement of value when the value is known to be different from that stated is a fraudulent misrepresentation of an opinion as existing that does not exist. A statement of the monetary value of property with no definite market value such as a mine, an invention, old and used goods or of lands, is generally made and understood as an expression of opinion only, and not as representation of a fact, and is not ordinarily an actionable misrepresentation. . . .

In this case there was no attempt to prove that the agents who stated the value of this land were acting in bad faith, or did not honestly believe that the land was worth what was represented as its value. It was a time of general speculation in lands and overestimates of value that subsequent events have proved extravagant were quite generally assigned to both urban and rural lands. For land of the nature of that involved here situated in a grazing region, somewhat unreliable for the raising of crops without irrigation, but located at a convenient distance from a city, the capital of the state, there was often a speculative, but real, sale value in excess of what is now regarded as the fair value at that time. But the purchaser of lands of this nature usually understands that no definite value can be assigned to such property, and that an expression of value is but an opinion, even though it is not stated as the thought, opinion, or estimate of the speaker. What was said by these brokers was evidently intended as but an opinion, and the plaintiff cannot be heard to say that he relied upon such an opinion.

The remaining claim of misrepresentation relates to the possession of the land. While there was no statement, in words, that the Federal Land Company held possession of the land, the statement that possession would be given to the plaintiff at once, coupled with the making of the lease, whereby Carpenter assumed to take the land as lessee after the 1st of March, and to plough it, and to pay rent therefor to plaintiff for five years, was intended to convey the impression that possession was held by the Federal Land Company, and was surrendered to the plaintiff, and accepted from him by Carpenter, because a lease of lands ordinarily imports the transfer of possession. . . . The evidence shows that the Federal Land Company never had possession of this land, that the plaintiff was never given possession, and Carpenter did not offer to perform his part of the lease. A misrepresentation may be made by words, but it may also consist of conduct. . . .

The misrepresentation as to the delivery of possession was material, because of the value of such possession during the long period that the contract might continue, and is evidenced by the substantial amount that Carpenter agreed to pay as yearly rent. In view of this false representation, and of the fact that plaintiff was not shown to have lost his right to ask for a rescission of his contract, the court should not have sustained the motion to dismiss the bill as to the Federal Land Company.

An order will be entered, remanding the case, with directions to enter a decree as prayed in plaintiff's bill against the Federal Land Company.

STUDY GUIDE: *In the next case, why did a statement of* opinion *provide the basis for a defense of misrepresentation? How did this expression of opinion differ from the opinion expressed in the previous case? Is every dance instructor really contractually obligated to tell the truth, the* whole *truth, and nothing but the truth to a pupil? Do you think that the remedy sought might have influenced the outcome in this case? If so, should it? This case comes very close to implicating the defense of undue influence that we shall discuss in Section C of this chapter. Keep this case in mind so that, when we get to that topic, you may consider how the theory of misrepresentation advanced here differs, if it does, from the defense of undue influence.*

VOKES v. ARTHUR MURRAY, INC.
District Court of Appeal of Florida,
212 So. 2d 906 (1968)

PIERCE, J.*

This is an appeal by Audrey E. Vokes, plaintiff below, from a final order dismissing with prejudice, for failure to state a cause of action, her fourth amended complaint, hereinafter referred to as plaintiff's complaint.

Defendant Arthur Murray, Inc., a corporation, authorizes the operation throughout the nation of dancing schools under the name of "Arthur Murray School of Dancing" through local franchised operators, one of whom was defendant J. P. Davenport whose dancing establishment was in Clearwater.

William C. Pierce (1903-†) was educated at Georgia Technical Preparatory School and Atlanta Law School (LL.B.). He left school at the age of 14 to work in a railroad yard. He later worked in the circulation department of a newspaper and with a publishing company before receiving his law degree. Pierce served as counsel for the Department of Agriculture for 30 years and was appointed to the District Court of Appeal of Florida in 1965. He served on that bench until retiring in 1972, having spent the last two years of his tenure as Chief Justice. — K.T.

Plaintiff Mrs. Audrey E. Vokes, a widow of 51 years and without family, had a yen to be "an accomplished dancer" with the hopes of finding "new interest in life." So, on February 10, 1961, a dubious fate, with the assist of a motivated acquaintance, procured her to attend a "dance party" at Davenport's "School of Dancing" where she whiled away the pleasant hours, sometimes in a private room, absorbing his accomplished sales technique, during which her grace and poise were elaborated upon and her rosy future as "an excellent dancer" was painted for her in vivid and glowing colors. As an incident to this interlude, he sold her eight 1/2-hour dance lessons to be utilized within one calendar month therefrom, for the sum of $14.50 cash in hand paid, obviously a baited "come-on."

Thus she embarked upon an almost endless pursuit of the terpsichorean art during which, over a period of less than sixteen months, she was sold fourteen "dance courses" totalling in the aggregate 2,302 hours of dancing lessons for a total cash outlay of $31,090.45, all at Davenport's dance emporium. All of these fourteen courses were evidenced by execution of a written "Enrollment Agreement — Arthur Murray's School of Dancing" with the addendum in heavy black print, "No one will be informed that you are taking dancing lessons. Your relations with us are held in strict confidence," setting forth the number of "dancing lessons" and the "lessons in rhythm sessions" currently sold to her from time to time, and always of course accompanied by payment of cash of the realm.

These dance lesson contracts and the monetary consideration therefor of over $31,000 were procured from her by means and methods of Davenport and his associates which went beyond the unsavory, yet legally permissible, perimeter of "sales puffing" and intruded well into the forbidden area of undue influence, the suggestion of falsehood, the suppression of truth, and the free exercise of rational judgment, if what plaintiff alleged in her complaint was true. From the time of her first contact with the dancing school in February, 1961, she was influenced unwittingly by a constant and continuous barrage of flattery, false praise, excessive compliments, and panegyric encomiums, to such extent that it would be not only inequitable, but unconscionable, for a Court exercising inherent chancery power to allow such contracts to stand.

She was incessantly subjected to overreaching blandishment and cajolery. She was assured she had "grace and poise"; that she was "rapidly improving and developing in her dancing skill"; that the additional lessons would "make her a beautiful dancer, capable of dancing with the most accomplished dancers"; that she was "rapidly progressing in the development of her dancing skill and gracefulness," etc., etc. She was given "dance aptitude tests" for the ostensible purpose of "determining" the number of remaining hours of instructions needed by her from time to time.

At one point she was sold 545 additional hours of dancing lessons to be entitled to award of the "Bronze Medal" signifying that she had reached "the Bronze Standard," a supposed designation of dance achievement by students of Arthur Murray, Inc.

Later she was sold an additional 926 hours in order to gain the "Silver Medal," indicating she had reached "the Silver Standard," at a cost of $12,501.35.

At one point, while she still had to her credit about 900 unused hours of instructions, she was induced to purchase an additional 24 hours of lessons to participate in a trip to Miami at her own expense, where she would be "given the opportunity to dance with members of the Miami Studio."

She was induced at another point to purchase an additional 126 hours of lessons in order to be not only eligible for the Miami trip but also to become "a life member of the Arthur Murray Studio," carrying with it certain dubious emoluments, at a further cost of $1,752.30.

At another point, while she still had over 1,000 unused hours of instruction she was induced to buy 151 additional hours at a cost of $2,049.00 to be eligible for a "Student Trip to Trinidad," at her own expense as she later learned.

Also, when she still had 1,100 unused hours to her credit, she was prevailed upon to purchase an additional 347 hours at a cost of $4,235.74, to qualify her to receive a "Gold Medal" for achievement, indicating she had advanced to "the Gold Standard."

On another occasion, while she still had over 1,200 unused hours, she was induced to buy an additional 175 hours of instruction at a cost of $2,472.75 to be eligible "to take a trip to Mexico."

Finally, sandwiched in between other lesser sales promotions, she was influenced to buy an additional 481 hours of instruction at a cost of $6,523.81 in order to "be classified as a Gold Bar Member, the ultimate achievement of the dancing studio."

All the foregoing sales promotions, illustrative of the entire fourteen separate contracts, were procured by defendant Davenport and Arthur Murray, Inc., by false representations to her that she was improving in her dancing ability, that she had excellent potential, that she was responding to instructions in dancing grace, and that they were developing her into a beautiful dancer, whereas in truth and in fact she did not develop in her dancing ability, she had no "dance aptitude," and in fact had difficulty in "hearing that musical beat." The complaint alleged that such representations to her "were in fact false and known by the defendant to be false and contrary to the plaintiff's true ability, the truth of plaintiff's ability being fully known to the defendants, but withheld from the plaintiff for the sole and specific intent to deceive and defraud the plaintiff and to induce her in the purchasing of additional hours of dance lessons." It was averred that the lessons were sold to her "in total disregard to the true physical, rhythm, and mental ability of the plaintiff." In other words, while she first exulted that she was entering the "spring of her life," she finally was awakened to the fact there was "spring" neither in her life nor in her feet.

The complaint prayed that the court decree the dance contracts to be null and void and to be cancelled, that an accounting be had, and judgment entered against, the defendants "for that portion of the $31,090.45 not charged against specific hours of instruction given to the plaintiff." The Court held the complaint not to state a cause of action and dismissed it with prejudice. We disagree and reverse. ─› Holding

The material allegations of the complaint must, of course, be accepted as true for the purpose of testing its legal sufficiency. Defendants contend that contracts can only be rescinded for fraud or misrepresentation when the alleged misrepresentation is as to a material fact, rather than an opinion, prediction or expectation, and that the statements and representations set forth at length in the complaint were in the category of "trade puffing," within its legal orbit.

It is true that "generally a misrepresentation, to be actionable, must be one of fact rather than of opinion." Tonkovich v. South Florida Citrus Industries, Inc., Fla. App. 1966, 185 So. 2d 710; Kutner v. Kalish, Fla. App. 1965, 173 So. 2d 763. But this rule has significant qualifications, applicable here. It does not apply where there is a fiduciary relationship between the parties, or where there has been some artifice or trick employed by the representor, or where the parties do not in general deal at "arm's length" as we understand the phrase, or where the representee does not have equal opportunity to become apprised of the truth or falsity of the fact represented. . . . As stated by Judge Allen of this Court in Ramel v. Chasebrook Construction Company, Fla. App. 1961, 135 So. 2d 876:

> . . . A statement of a party having . . . superior knowledge may be regarded as a statement of fact although it would be considered as opinion if the parties were dealing on equal terms.

It could be reasonably supposed here that defendants had "superior knowledge" as to whether plaintiff had "dance potential" and as to whether she was noticeably improving in the art of terpsichore. And it would be a reasonable inference from the undenied averments of the complaint that the flowery eulogiums heaped upon her by defendants as a prelude to her contracting for 1,944 additional hours of instruction in order to attain the rank of the Bronze Standard, thence to the bracket of the Silver Standard, thence to the class of the Gold Bar Standard, and finally to the crowning plateau of a Life Member of the Studio, proceeded as much or more from the urge to "ring the cash register" as from any honest or realistic appraisal of her dancing prowess or a factual representation of her progress.

Even in contractual situations where a party to a transaction owes no duty to disclose facts within his knowledge or to answer inquiries respecting such facts, the law is if he undertakes to do so he must disclose the *whole truth*. . . . From the face of the complaint, it should have been reasonably apparent to defendants that her vast outlay of cash for the many hundreds of additional hours of instruction was not justified by her slow and awkward progress, which she would have been made well aware of if they had spoken the "whole truth."

In Hirschman v. Hodges, etc., 1910, 59 Fla. 517, 51 So. 550, it was said that —

> . . . what is plainly injurious to good faith ought to be considered as a fraud sufficient to impeach a contract,

and that an improvident agreement may be avoided —

> . . . because of surprise, or mistake, *want of freedom, undue influence, the suggestion of falsehood, or the suppression of truth*. (Emphasis supplied.)

We repeat that where parties are dealing on a contractual basis at arm's length with no inequities or inherently unfair practices employed, the Courts will in general "leave the parties where they find themselves." But in the case sub judice, from the allegations of the unanswered complaint, we cannot say that enough of the accompanying ingredients, as mentioned in the foregoing authorities, were not present which otherwise would have barred the equitable arm of the Court to her. In our view, from the showing made in her complaint, plaintiff is entitled to her day in Court.

It accordingly follows that the order dismissing plaintiff's last amended complaint with prejudice should be and is reversed.

Reversed.

RESTATEMENT (SECOND) OF CONTRACTS

§168.   RELIANCE ON ASSERTIONS OF OPINION

(1) An assertion is one of opinion if it expresses only a belief, without certainty, as to the existence of a fact or expresses only a judgment as to quality, value, authenticity, or similar matters.

(2) If it is reasonable to do so, the recipient of an assertion of a person's opinion as to facts not disclosed and not otherwise known to the recipient may properly interpret it as an assertion

(a) that the facts known to that person are not incompatible with his opinion, or

(b) that he knows facts sufficient to justify him in forming it.

§169.   WHEN RELIANCE ON AN ASSERTION OF OPINION IS NOT JUSTIFIED

To the extent that an assertion is one of opinion only, the recipient is not justified in relying on it unless the recipient

(a) stands in such a relation of trust and confidence to the person whose opinion is asserted that the recipient is reasonable in relying on it, or

(b) reasonably believes that, as compared with himself, the person whose opinion is asserted has special skill, judgment or objectivity with respect to the subject matter or

(c) is for some other special reason particularly susceptible to a misrepresentation of the type involved.

REFERENCE: Farnsworth, §§4.10-4.15
               Calamari & Perillo, §§9.13-9.21, 9.23
               Murray, §96

B. DURESS

Perhaps the paradigm defense to contract is that of physical duress. It seems obvious that one's "consent" to contract is not binding if it was obtained by the use or threatened use of force. Lord Coke summarized the following circumstances that justified contract avoidance: "1. for fear of losse of life, 2. of losse of member, 3. of mayhem, and 4. of imprisonment. . . ."[2] This paradigm of duress is addressed by §174 of the Restatement (Second) of Contracts, which reads: "If conduct that appears to be a manifestation of assent by a party who does not intend to engage in that conduct is physically compelled by duress, the conduct is not effective as a manifestation of assent." The cases in this section concern one effort to extend the doctrine of duress beyond its epitome described by Lord Coke.

Economic duress is commonly thought to be a species of duress. Yet in situations involving economic duress, our attention is shifted from the impropriety of the means of obtaining assent to the economic straits confronted by the party who has consented. In this respect, economic duress seems to share some features in common with the defenses of mistake, impracticability, and frustration that we shall study in Chapter 17. Notwithstanding this focus on the circumstances of the party who has consented, however, there is something unseemly or improper about another person *exploiting* this situation. In this subsection, we shall read cases that exemplify the phenomenon of economic duress. Our goals will be to fathom the theory, if there be one, that lurks beneath this doctrine and to see how it may be defined so as not to undermine the prima facie case of contract.

STUDY GUIDE: Why do you think that the judge in the next case was unwilling to find duress on the facts of the case? Why might he have been reluctant to consider the economic circumstances of one party to a contract in determining whether that party's manifestation of assent was truly voluntary? Was the case correctly decided? Is it possible that the theory informing the doctrine of good faith performance that we studied in Chapter 12 might be of some assistance here?

---

2. E. Coke, Second Institute 482-483 (1642), as it appears in E. Allen Farnsworth, Contracts 257 (4th ed. 2004). The quotation continues by listing circumstances that do not justify recovery: "otherwise it is for fear of battery, which might be very light, or for burning of his houses, or taking away, or destroying of his goods or the like, for there he may have satisfaction in damages." Id. Compare this qualification with the following statement by William Blackstone:

> A fear of battery . . . is no duress; neither is the fear of having one's house burned, or one's goods taken away or destroyed; . . . because in these cases, should the threat be performed, a man may have satisfaction by recovering equivalent damages: but no suitable atonement can be made for the loss of life, or limb.

1 Blackstone's Commentaries 131 as it appears in John D. Calamari & Joseph M. Perillo, Contracts 336-337 (3d ed. 1987).

HACKLEY v. HEADLEY
Supreme Court of Michigan,
45 Mich. 569, 8 N.W. 511 (1881)

Cooley, J.* Headley sued Hackley & McGordon to recover compensation for cutting, hauling and delivering in the Muskegon river a quantity of
logs. The performance of the labor was not disputed. . . . The
defendants. . . . claimed to have had a full and complete settlement with
Headley, and produced his receipt in evidence thereof. Headley admitted
the receipt, but insisted that it was given by him under duress, and the verdict
which he obtained in the circuit court was in accordance with this claim. . . .
    . . . The paper reads as follows:

> Muskegon, Mich., August 3, 1875

> Received from Hackley & McGordon their note for four thousand dol-
> lars, payable in thirty days, at First National Bank, Grand Rapids, which is in
> full for all claims of every kind and nature which I have against Hackley &
> McGordon.
>   Witness: Thomas Hume   John Headley.

Headley's account of the circumstances under which this receipt was
given is in substance as follows: on August 3, 1875, he went to Muskegon,
the place of business of Hackley & McGordon, from his home in Kent
county, for the purpose of collecting the balance which he claimed was
due him under the contract. The amount he claimed was upwards of
$6,200, estimating the logs by the Scribner scale. He had an interview
with Hackley in the morning, who insisted that the estimate should be
according to the Doyle scale, and who also claimed that he had made payments to others amounting to some $1400 which Headley should allow.
Headley did not admit these payments, and denied his liability for them if
they had been made. Hackley told Headley to come in again in the
afternoon, and when he did so Hackley said to him:

> My figures show there is $4260 and odd dollars in round numbers your due,
> and I will just give you $4000. I will give you our note for $4000.

To this Headley replied:

> I cannot take that; it is not right, and you know it. There is over $2000 besides
> that belongs to me, and you know it.

* *Thomas MacIntyre Cooley* (1824-1898) was admitted to the Michigan bar in 1846 and
served as official reporter for the Supreme Court of Michigan in 1858. Thereafter, he served
as professor of law at the University of Michigan (1859-1884) and professor and dean of the
School of Political Science (1859-1898). In 1864, he was appointed Justice of the Supreme
Court of Michigan, serving as Chief Justice from 1868 to 1869. After his retirement from the
bench in 1878, he became a lecturer on constitutional law at Johns Hopkins University and
was chairman of the U.S. Interstate Commerce Commission (1887-1891). He was the author
of several highly influential works, especially his Treatise on the Constitutional Limitations
Which Rest upon the Legislative Power of the United States of the American Union, which
first appeared in 1868 and went through eight editions. Thomas M. Cooley Law School in
Lansing, Michigan, is named for him. — K.T.

Hackley replied:

That is the best I will do with you.

Headley said:

I cannot take that, Mr. Hackley,

and Hackley replied,

You do the next best thing you are a mind to. You can sue me if you please.

Headley then said,

I cannot afford to sue you, because I have got to have the money, and I cannot wait for it. If I fail to get the money today, I shall probably be ruined financially, because I have made no other arrangement to get the money only on this particular matter.

Finally he took the note and gave the receipt, because at the time he could do nothing better, and in the belief that he would be financially ruined unless he had immediately the money that was offered him, or paper by means of which the money might be obtained.

If this statement is correct, the defendants not only took a most unjust advantage of Headley, but they obtained a receipt which, to the extent that it assumed to discharge anything not honestly in dispute between the parties and known by them to be owing to Headley beyond the sum received, was without consideration and ineffectual. But was it a receipt obtained by duress? That is the question which the record presents. The circuit judge was of opinion that if the jury believed the statement of Headley they would be justified in finding that duress existed; basing his opinion largely upon the opinion of this court in Vyne v. Glenn, 41 Mich. 112.

Duress exists when one by the unlawful act of another is induced to make a contract or perform some act under circumstances which deprive him of the exercise of free will. It is commonly said to be of either the person or the goods of the party. Duress of the person is either by imprisonment, or by threats, or by an exhibition of force which apparently cannot be resisted. It is not pretended that duress of the person existed in this case; it is if anything duress of goods, or at least of that nature, and properly enough classed with duress of goods. Duress of goods may exist when one is compelled to submit to an illegal exaction in order to obtain them from one who has them in possession but refuses to surrender them unless the exaction is submitted to.

The leading case involving duress of goods is Astley v. Reynolds, 2 Strange, 915. The plaintiff had pledged goods for £20, and when he offered to redeem them, the pawnbroker refused to surrender them unless he was paid £10 for interest. The plaintiff submitted to the exaction, but was held entitled to recover back all that had been unlawfully demanded and taken. This, say the court, "is a payment by compulsion: the plaintiff might have such an immediate want of his goods that an action of trover would not do his business: where the rule *volenti non fit injuria* is applied, it must be when the party had his freedom of exercising his will, which this man had not: we must take it he paid the money relying on his legal remedy to get it back again." The principle of this case was approved in Smith v. Bromley, Doug. 695, and also in Ashmole v. Wainwright, 2 Q.B. 837. The latter was a suit to recover back excessive charges paid to common carriers who refused until payment was made to deliver the goods for the carriage of which the charges were made. There has never been any doubt but recovery could be had under such circumstances. . . . The case is like it of one [sic] having securities in his hands which he refuses to surrender until illegal commissions are paid. . . . So if illegal tolls are demanded, for passing a raft of lumber, and the owner pays them to liberate his raft, he may recover back what he pays. . . . So one may recover back money which he pays to release his goods from an attachment which is sued out with knowledge on the part of the plaintiff that he has no cause of action. . . . Nor is the principle confined to payments made to recover goods: it applies equally well when money is extorted as a condition to the exercise by the party of any other legal right; for example when a corporation refuses to suffer a lawful transfer of stock till the exaction is submitted to . . . or a creditor withholds his certificate from a bankrupt. . . . And the mere threat to employ colorable legal authority to compel payment of an unfounded claim is such duress as will support an action to recover back what is paid under it. . . .

But where the party threatens nothing which he has not a legal right to perform, there is no duress. Skeate v. Beale, 11 Ad. El. 983 Preston v. Boston, 12 Pick. 14. When therefore a judgment creditor threatens to levy his execution on the debtor's goods, and under fear of the levy the debtor executes and delivers a note for the amount, with sureties, the note cannot be avoided for duress. Wilcox v. Howland, 23 Pick. 167. Many other cases might be cited, but it is wholly unnecessary. We have examined all to which our attention has been directed, and none are more favorable to the plaintiff's case than those above referred to. Some of them are much less so; notably Atlee v. Bachhouse, 3 M. W. 633 Hall v. Schultz, 4 John. 240; Silliman v. United States, 101 United States 465.

In what did the alleged duress consist in the present case? Merely in this: that the debtors refused to pay on demand a debt already due, though the plaintiff was in great need of the money and might be financially ruined in case he failed to obtain it. It is not pretended that Hackley & McGordon had done anything to bring Headley to the condition which made this money so important to him at this very time, or that they were in any manner responsible for his pecuniary embarrassment except as they failed to pay this demand. The duress, then, is to be found exclusively in their failure to meet promptly their pecuniary obligation. But this, according to the plaintiff's claim, would have constituted no duress whatever if he had not happened to be in pecuniary straits and the validity of negotiations, according to this claim, must be determined, not by the defendants' conduct, but by the plaintiff's necessities. The same contract which would be valid if made with a man easy in his circumstances, becomes invalid when the contracting party is pressed with the necessity of immediately meeting his bank paper. But this would be a most dangerous, as well as a most unequal doctrine; and if accepted, no one could well know when he would be safe in dealing on the ordinary terms of negotiation with a party who professed to be in great need.

The case of Vyne v. Glenn, 41 Mich. 112, differs essentially from this. There was not a simple withholding of moneys in that case. The decision was made upon facts found by referees who reported that the settlement upon which the defendant relied was made at Chicago, which was a long distance from plaintiff's home and place of business; that the defendant forced the plaintiff into the settlement against his will, by taking advantage of his pecuniary necessities, by informing plaintiff that he had taken steps to stop the payment of money due to the plaintiff from other parties, and that he had stopped the payment of a part of such moneys; that defendant knew the necessities and financial embarrassments in which the plaintiff was involved, and knew that if he failed to get the money so due to him he would be ruined financially; that plaintiff consented to such settlement only in order to get the money due to him, as aforesaid, and the payment of which was stopped by defendant, and which he must have to save him from financial ruin. The report, therefore, showed the same financial embarrassment and the same great need of money which it is claimed existed in this case, and the same withholding of moneys lawfully due, but it showed over and above all that an unlawful interference by defendant between the plaintiff and other debtors, by means of which he had stopped the payment to plaintiff of sums due to him from such other debtors. It was this keeping of other moneys from the plaintiff's hands, and not the refusal by defendant to pay his own debt, which was the ruling fact in that case, and which was equivalent, in our opinion, to duress of goods.

These views render a reversal of the judgment necessary, and the case will be remanded for a new trial with costs to the plaintiffs in error.[3]

The other justices concurred.

STUDY GUIDE: In Chapter 9, when we studied the preexisting duty rule, it was argued by Judge Posner in United States v. Stump Home Specialties that opportunistic behavior to obtain contract modifications should be policed directly, rather than by using the doctrine of consideration to deny enforcement. We now consider one of the cases he cited in support of this approach. How do the circumstances alleged to constitute duress differ from those of the previous case? Which set of facts is more compelling? Is this case correctly decided? Once again, consider whether this case is reminiscent in any way of the good faith performance situations we studied in Chapter 12.

3. [At the new trial, plaintiff prevailed, this time arguing that the payment of a reduced sum was a "settlement" of a claim that lacked consideration. On appeal the Michigan Supreme Court this time affirmed the judgment, but for reasons that are hard to fathom. While apparently accepting the plaintiff's lack-of-consideration theory, it added that:

> All the authorities admit that when the other of the parties to a transaction sets it up against the other as an effective compromise, the latter may hinder it from operating in that sense and with that force by showing that his opponent acted unfairly or oppressively and asserted claims which he knew to be void of right with the design of getting the terms which he knew were nominally assented to.

Headley v. Hackley, 50 Mich. 43, 45 (1883). No mention is made of duress. Justice Cooley, who wrote the previous opinion in the case, concurred without opinion. Does this opinion reflect a reason — distinct from that of economic duress or consideration — why an agreement to modify a contract may be avoided? — EDS.]

AUSTIN INSTRUMENT v. LORAL CORP.
Court of Appeals of New York,
29 N.Y.2d 124, 324 N.Y.S.2d 22, 272 N.E.2d 533 (1971)

FULD, C.J.*

The defendant, Loral Corporation, seeks to recover payment for goods delivered under a contract which it had with the plaintiff Austin Instrument, Inc., on the ground that the evidence establishes, as a matter of law, that it was forced to agree to an increase in price on the items in question under circumstances amounting to economic duress.

In July of 1965, Loral was awarded a $6,000,000 contract by the Navy for the production of radar sets. The contract contained a schedule of deliveries, a liquidated damages clause applying to late deliveries and a cancellation clause in case of default by Loral. The latter thereupon solicited bids for some 40 precision gear components needed to produce the radar sets, and awarded Austin a subcontract to supply 23 such parts. That party commenced delivery in early 1966.

In May, 1966, Loral was awarded a second Navy contract for the production of more radar sets and again went about soliciting bids. Austin bid on all 40 gear components but, on July 15, a representative from Loral informed Austin's president, Mr. Krauss, that his company would be awarded the subcontract only for those items on which it was low bidder. The Austin officer refused to accept an order for less than all 40 of the gear parts and on the next day he told Loral that Austin would cease deliveries of the parts due under the existing subcontract unless Loral consented to substantial increases in the prices provided for by that agreement — both retroactively for parts already delivered and prospectively on those not yet shipped — and placed with Austin the order for all 40 parts needed under Loral's second Navy contract. Shortly thereafter, Austin did, indeed, stop delivery. After contacting 10 manufacturers of precision gears and finding none who could produce the parts in time to meet its commitments to the Navy,[4] Loral acceded to Austin's demands; in a letter dated July 22, Loral wrote to Austin that

> We have feverishly surveyed other sources of supply and find that because of the prevailing military exigencies, were they to start from scratch as would have to be the case, they could not even remotely begin to deliver on time to meet the delivery requirements established by the Government. . . . Accordingly, we are left with no choice or alternative but to meet your conditions.

Loral thereupon consented to the price increases insisted upon by Austin under the first subcontract and the latter was awarded a second

---

* *Stanley Howells Fuld* (1903-2003) studied at the College of the City of New York (A.B.) and Columbia University (LL.B.) and was admitted to the New York bar in 1926. He practiced privately in New York City (1926-1946), except while working in the National Recovery Administration (1935), and the offices of the District Attorney of New York City (1935-1944) and the Attorney General (1944-1945). He was appointed to the Court of Appeals of New York in 1946 and served as Chief Judge prior to his retirement in 1973. — K.T.

4. The best reply Loral received was from a vendor who stated he could commence deliveries sometime in October.

subcontract making it the supplier of all 40 gear parts for Loral's second contract with the Navy.[5] Although Austin was granted until September to resume deliveries, Loral did, in fact, receive parts in August and was able to produce the radar sets in time to meet its commitments to the Navy on both contracts. After Austin's last delivery under the second subcontract in July, 1967, Loral notified it of its intention to seek recovery of the price increases.

On September 15, 1967, Austin instituted this action against Loral to recover an amount in excess of $17,750 which was still due on the second subcontract. On the same day, Loral commenced an action against Austin claiming damages of some $22,250 — the aggregate of the price increases under the first subcontract — on the ground of economic duress. The two actions were consolidated and, following a trial, Austin was awarded the sum it requested and Loral's complaint against Austin was dismissed on the ground that it was not shown that "it could not have obtained the items in question from other sources in time to meet its commitment to the Navy under the first contract." A closely divided Appellate Division affirmed (35 A.D.2d 387 [316 N.Y.S.2d 528, 532]). There was no material disagreement concerning the facts; as Justice Steuer stated in the course of his dissent below, "[t]he facts are virtually undisputed, nor is there any serious question of law. The difficulty lies in the application of the law to these facts." (35 A.D.2d 392 [316 N.Y.S.2d 534].)

The applicable law is clear and, indeed, is not disputed by the parties. A contract is voidable on the ground of duress when it is established that the party making the claim was forced to agree to it by means of a wrongful threat precluding the exercise of his free will. . . . The existence of economic duress or business compulsion is demonstrated by proof that "immediate possession of needful goods is threatened" (Mercury Mach. Importing Corp. v. City of New York, 3 N.Y.2d 418, 425 [165 N.Y.S.2d 517, 520, 144 N.E.2d 400]) or, more particularly, in cases such as the one before us, by proof that one party to a contract has threatened to breach the agreement by withholding goods unless the other party agrees to some further demand. . . . However, a mere threat by one party to breach the contract by not delivering the required items, though wrongful, does not in itself constitute economic duress. It must also appear that the threatened party could not obtain the goods from another source of supply and that the ordinary remedy of an action for breach of contract would not be adequate.

We find without any support in the record the conclusion reached by the courts below that Loral failed to establish that it was the victim of economic duress. On the contrary, the evidence makes out a classic case, as a matter of law, of such duress.

It is manifest that Austin's threat — to stop deliveries unless the prices were increased — deprived Loral of its free will. As bearing on this, Loral's relationship with the Government is most significant. As mentioned above, its contract called for staggered monthly deliveries of the radar sets, with clauses calling for liquidated damages and possible cancellation on default. Because of its production schedule, Loral was, in July, 1966, concerned with meeting its delivery requirements in September, October and November, and it was for the sets to be delivered in those months that the withheld

5. Loral makes no claim in this action on the second subcontract.

gears were needed. Loral had to plan ahead, and the substantial liquidated damages for which it would be liable, plus the threat of default, were genuine possibilities. Moreover, Loral did a substantial portion of its business with the Government, and it feared that a failure to deliver as agreed upon would jeopardize its chances for future contracts. These genuine concerns do not merit the label "'self-imposed, undisclosed and subjective'" which the Appellate Division majority placed upon them. It was perfectly reasonable for Loral, or any other party similarly placed, to consider itself in an emergency, duress situation.

Austin, however, claims that the fact that Loral extended its time to resume deliveries until September negates its alleged dire need for the parts. A Loral official testified on this point that Austin's president told him he could deliver some parts in August and that the extension of deliveries was a formality. In any event, the parts necessary for production of the radar sets to be delivered in September were delivered to Loral on September 1, and the parts needed for the October schedule were delivered in late August and early September. Even so, Loral had to "work . . . around the clock" to meet its commitments. Considering that the best offer Loral received from the other vendors it contacted was commencement of delivery sometime in October, which, as the record shows, would have made it late in its deliveries to the Navy in both September and October, Loral's claim that it had no choice but to accede to Austin's demands is conclusively demonstrated.

We find unconvincing Austin's contention that Loral, in order to meet its burden, should have contacted the Government and asked for an extension of its delivery dates so as to enable it to purchase the parts from another vendor. Aside from the consideration that Loral was anxious to perform well in the Government's eyes, it could not be sure when it would obtain enough parts from a substitute vendor to meet its commitments. The only promise which it received from the companies it contacted was for *commencement* of deliveries, not full supply, and, with vendor delay common in this field, it would have been nearly impossible to know the length of the extension it should request. It must be remembered that Loral was producing a needed item of military hardware. Moreover, there is authority for Loral's position that nonperformance by a subcontractor is not an excuse for default in the main contract. (See, e.g., McBride & Wachtel, Government Contracts, §35.10, [11].) In light of all this, Loral's claim should not be held insufficiently supported because it did not request an extension from the Government.

Loral, as indicated above, also had the burden of demonstrating that it could not obtain the parts elsewhere within a reasonable time, and there can be no doubt that it met this burden. The 10 manufacturers whom Loral contacted comprised its entire list of "approved vendors" for precision gears, and none was able to commence delivery soon enough.[6] As Loral was producing a highly sophisticated item of military machinery requiring parts made to the strictest engineering standards, it would be unreasonable to hold that Loral should have gone to other vendors, with whom it was

6. Loral, as do many manufacturers, maintains a list of "approved vendors," that is, vendors whose products, facilities, techniques and performance have been inspected and found satisfactory.

either unfamiliar or dissatisfied, to procure the needed parts. As Justice Steuer noted in his dissent, Loral "contacted all the manufacturers whom it believed capable of making these parts" (35 A.D.2d at p. 393 [316 N.Y.S.2d at p. 534]), and this was all the law requires.

It is hardly necessary to add that Loral's normal legal remedy of accepting Austin's breach of the contract and then suing for damages would have been inadequate under the circumstances, as Loral would still have had to obtain the gears elsewhere with all the concomitant consequences mentioned above. In other words, Loral actually had no choice, when the prices were raised by Austin, except to take the gears at the "coerced" prices and then sue to get the excess back.

Austin's final argument is that Loral, even if it did enter into the contract under duress, lost any rights it had to a refund of money by waiting until July, 1967, long after the termination date of the contract, to disaffirm it. It is true that one who would recover moneys allegedly paid under duress must act promptly to make his claim known. . . . In this case, Loral delayed making its demand for a refund until three days after Austin's last delivery on the second subcontract. Loral's reason — for waiting until that time — is that it feared another stoppage of deliveries which would again put it in an untenable situation. Considering Austin's conduct in the past, this was perfectly reasonable, as the possibility of an application by Austin of further business compulsion still existed until all of the parts were delivered.

In sum, the record before us demonstrates that Loral agreed to the price increases in consequence of the economic duress employed by Austin. Accordingly, the matter should be remanded to the trial court for a computation of its damages.

The order appealed from should be modified, with costs, by reversing so much thereof as affirms the dismissal of defendant Loral Corporation's claim and, except as so modified, affirmed. —> the holding

BERGAN, J.* (dissenting).

Whether acts charged as constituting economic duress produce or do not produce the damaging effect attributed to them is normally a routine type of factual issue.

Here the fact question was resolved against Loral both by the Special Term and by the affirmance at the Appellate Division. It should not be open for different resolution here.

In summarizing the Special Term's decision and its own, the Appellate Division decided that "the conclusion that Loral acted deliberately and voluntarily, without being under immediate pressure of incurring severe business reverses, precludes a recovery on the theory of economic duress" (35 A.D.2d 387, 391 [316 N.Y.S.2d 528, 532]).

*Francis Bergan (1902-1998) was educated at the New York State College for Teachers, Siena College (A.B.), and Albany Law School (LL.B.) and was admitted to the New York bar in 1923. Bergan was a member of the New York Assembly (1926-1929) and the staff of the Attorney General of New York (1931) before beginning his judicial career in 1930. His posts before serving as justice on the Court of Appeals of New York (1963-1972) include judge on the City Court of Albany (1930-1933), judge on the Police Court of the City of Albany (1933-1935), and justice on the Supreme Court of New York (1935-1949) and the Appellate Division (1949-1963). — K.T.

When the testimony of the witnesses who actually took part in the negotiations for the two disputing parties is examined, sharp conflicts of fact emerge. Under Austin's version the request for a renegotiation of the existing contract was based on Austin's contention that Loral had failed to carry out an understanding as to the items to be furnished under that contract and this was the source of dissatisfaction which led both to a revision of the existing agreement and to entering into a new one.

This is not necessarily and as a matter of law to be held economic duress. On this appeal it is needful to look at the facts resolved in favor of Austin most favorably to that party. Austin's version of events was that a threat was not made but rather a request to accommodate the closing of its plant for a customary vacation period in accordance with the general understanding of the parties.

Moreover, critical to the issue of economic duress was the availability of alternative suppliers to the purchaser Loral. The demonstration is replete in the direct testimony of Austin's witnesses and on cross-examination of Loral's principal and purchasing agent that the availability of practical alternatives was a highly controverted issue of fact. On that issue of fact the explicit findings made by the Special Referee were affirmed by the Appellate Division. Nor is the issue of fact made the less so by assertion that the facts are undisputed and that only the application of equally undisputed rules of law is involved.

Austin asserted and Loral admitted on cross-examination that there were many suppliers listed in a trade registry but that Loral chose to rely only on those who had in the past come to them for orders and with whom they were familiar. It was, therefore, at least a fair issue of fact whether under the circumstances such conduct was reasonable and made what might otherwise have been a commercially understandable renegotiation an exercise of duress.

The order should be affirmed.

STUDY GUIDE: On what grounds did the court distinguish the following case from Austin? Why did it deny the claim that the contract modification was a product of economic duress? Was there no hardship? Can you use the underlying theory of this case to understand better the previous two cases?

UNITED STATES v. PROGRESSIVE ENTERPRISES
United States District Court, Eastern District of Virginia,
418 F. Supp. 662 (1976)

CLARKE, District Judge.*

This action was brought to recover the unpaid balance allegedly due for the purchase of a cast iron deaerator supplied by the plaintiff, Crane

*J. Calvitt Clarke, Jr. (1920-2004), studied at the University of Virginia (B.A., LL.B.) and was admitted to the Virginia bar in 1944. He had practiced law in Richmond, Virginia, for 30 years when he was appointed judge of the U.S. District Court for the Eastern District of Virginia in 1975. He assumed senior status in 1991. Clarke was also a candidate for Congress in 1954. — K.T.

Company (hereinafter referred to as "Crane"), to the defendant, Progressive Enterprises, Inc. (hereinafter referred to as "Progressive") to be installed as part of defendant's contract with the United States. Jurisdiction of the District Court is based upon the Miller Act, 40 U.S.C. §270b(a) and (b).

The material facts of the case are not in serious dispute. Plaintiff, on May 3, 1974, submitted a written proposal to furnish the machine to defendant for $5,238.00, the price quoted as firm for acceptance within fifteen days. After the expiration of the fifteen-day period, Progressive submitted its bid dated June 7, 1974, for the government contract without arranging for an extension of the fifteen-day period. Progressive was awarded the government contract on June 14, 1974. Shortly thereafter, on June 17, 1974, Progressive verified the continued effectiveness of the quoted price for a thirty-day period. On July 1, 1974, Progressive accepted the offer to sell by submission of a purchase order. (The price agreed to at that time was $5,217.00 because of the exclusion of a part included in the original price quotation.)

Crane, through its authorized selling agent, Hawkins-Hamilton Co., advised Progressive that "[b]ecause of rapidly escalating material costs, your purchase order can only be accepted subject to current price in effect at time of shipment." This communication went on to quote a current price of $7,350.00.

The parties agree that the July 1, 1974 purchase order was an effective acceptance of Crane's offer to sell. However, apparently without protest to or discussion with Crane or its agent, Progressive agreed to the higher price and, on August 7, 1974, submitted a second purchase order for the machine, this time at $7,350.00. Thereafter, the machine was delivered and Progressive paid $5,550.88 and asserted the balance not to be due because the increased price was not a valid modification of the contract. Crane then instituted this suit to recover $2,218.32 plus interest from March 2, 1975, representing the difference between the higher agreed price with interest and the amount paid by the defendant.

Crane contends that Progressive acquiesced in the increased price and that the August 7, 1974, purchase order effectively modified the existing contract. Section 2-209 of the Uniform Commercial Code (Virginia Code §8.2-209) provides:

> (1) An agreement modifying a contract within this Article needs no consideration to be binding.

This change from the common law of contracts supports the common business practice of adjusting the terms of agreements as conditions change.

The ability to modify a sales agreement is limited by the general U.C.C. requirement of good faith.[7] Official Comment 2 to §2-209 clearly expresses this requirement and elaborates on its meaning in the context of contract modifications:

> The effective use of bad faith to escape performance on the original contract terms is barred, and the extortion of a "modification" without legitimate

---

7. "Good faith" in the case of a merchant means honesty in fact and the observance of reasonable commercial standards of fair dealing in the trade. U.C.C. §2-103(b).

commercial reason is ineffective as a violation of the duty of good faith. Nor can a mere technical consideration support a modification made in bad faith.

. . . But such matters as a market shift which makes performance come to involve a loss may provide such a reason even though there is no such unforeseen difficulty as would make out a legal excuse from performance under Sections 2-615 and 2-616.

The letters of May 3 and July 11, 1974, from Crane's agent support a finding that the seller's costs had increased, justifying a request for modification of the price to Progressive. Although Progressive possessed the contractual right to refuse to modify and to demand performance on the original terms, it failed to do so and gave objective assent to the higher price.

Notwithstanding this objective assent and apparent modification, it is the contention of Progressive that the modification of the contract price was the result of economic duress and, hence, unenforceable. This claim is based upon its obligation under its contract with the United States Government to supply the ordered machine within a specific time and the fact that Crane was the only supplier of the exact machine required to fulfill the Government contract.

The evidence reveals, however, that in making its bid to the Government, Progressive was not relying on the lower price quoted because the time period for acceptance had expired. Thus, Progressive is not in the position of a contractor who justifiably relied on a price quotation only to find itself squeezed by repudiation of the quoted price.

The evidence shows further that Progressive at no time protested the increased price, or in any way attempted to enforce the terms of the earlier, lower price contract.

In Austin Instrument, Inc. v. Loral Corp., 29 N.Y.2d 124, 324 N.Y.S.2d 22, 272 N.E.2d 533 (1971), a closely divided New York Court of Appeals discussed the defense of economic duress and gave judgment to the buyer in a situation similar to the one at bar. In that case, however, the buyer communicated the facts of its predicament and warned that the modification was accepted only because there existed no alternative. Similarly, in Rose v. Vulcan Materials Co., 282 N.C. 643, 194 S.E.2d 521 (1973), cited by Progressive, the buyer expressly reserved the right to sue for the overcharges. Such situations, where the inability to obtain alternative sources of supply is communicated, are more analogous to the seeking of cover from the only available source, the original seller. Where no such protest or notice is given, the seller has no idea that anything other than a new contract has been made. If the buyer wishes not to accede to the increased demand, the seller must be dealt with honestly to be able to consider other possibilities.

In the context of a lengthy, on-going business relationship, seeking modification of a sales price is not uncommon and, given increased costs, is a fair method of doing business in order to preserve the desirability of the relationship for both parties. In such a situation, the parties must be able to rely on objective, unequivocal manifestations of assent. The secret intention of Progressive never to pay the higher price (as admitted by its president) is hardly in keeping with the good faith requirement of the U.C.C. of honesty in fact. If a seller in this situation cannot enforce such a modification, sought in good faith and objectively agreed to, the provisions of U.C.C. §2-209(1) would be hollow indeed. To avoid this predicament, the buyer must at least display some protest against the higher price in order to put the seller on notice that the modification is not freely entered into.

The availability of equitable relief belies Progressive's claim that it had no available remedies if it desired to enforce the original terms. Also, notification to Crane of the possible damages because of the threatened breach could have led to withdrawal of the requested increase. In any case, Progressive did nothing to alert Crane to the possibility that it did not mean what it said. Accordingly, it must be held to its agreement.

By reason of the foregoing, it is hereby ordered that judgment be entered for the plaintiff in the amount of $2,218.32 plus interest from March 2, 1975, against both defendants, the Fidelity and Deposit Company of Maryland being surety on Progressive's Miller Act bond.

RESTATEMENT (SECOND) OF CONTRACTS

§175. WHEN DURESS BY THREAT MAKES A CONTRACT VOIDABLE

(1) If a party's manifestation of assent is induced by an improper threat by the other party that leaves the victim no reasonable alternative, the contract is voidable by the victim.

(2) If a party's manifestation of assent is induced by one who is not a party to the transaction, the contract is voidable by the victim unless the other party to the transaction in good faith and without reason to know of the duress either gives value or relies materially on the transaction.

§176. WHEN A THREAT IS IMPROPER

(1) A threat is improper if
   (a) what is threatened is a crime or a tort, or the threat itself would be a crime or a tort if it resulted in obtaining property,
   (b) what is threatened is a criminal prosecution,
   (c) what is threatened is the use of civil process and the threat is made in bad faith, or
   (d) the threat is a breach of the duty of good faith and fair dealing under a contract with the recipient.

(2) A threat is improper if the resulting exchange is not on fair terms, and
   (a) the threatened act would harm the recipient and would not significantly benefit the party making the threat,
   (b) the effectiveness of the threat in inducing the manifestation of assent is significantly increased by prior unfair dealing by the party making the threat, or
   (c) what is threatened is otherwise a use of power for illegitimate ends.

REFERENCE: Barnett, §6.3.3
              Farnsworth, §§4.16-4.19
              Calamari & Perillo, §§9.1-9.8
              Murray, §94

C. UNDUE INFLUENCE

STUDY GUIDE: *How does the following case differ from the situation described in Vokes v. Arthur Murray, Inc.? How does undue influence differ from duress and why should it be a defense to a contract? Does the defense of undue influence have attributes both of obtaining consent by improper means and of incompetence to consent? Does it matter why the school administrators acted as they did? Do you think it is an accident that many of the undue influence cases cited by the court involve women (as did Vokes in this chapter and Ortelere in Chapter 15)?*

ODORIZZI v. BLOOMFIELD SCHOOL DISTRICT
District Court of Appeal of California, Second District,
246 Cal. App. 2d 123, 54 Cal. Rptr. 533 (1966)

FLEMING, J.*

Appeal from a judgment dismissing plaintiff's amended complaint on demurrer.

Plaintiff Donald Odorizzi was employed during 1964 as an elementary school teacher by defendant Bloomfield School District and was under contract with the district to continue to teach school the following year as a permanent employee. On June 10 he was arrested on criminal charges of homosexual activity, and on June 11 he signed and delivered to his superiors his written resignation as a teacher, a resignation which the district accepted on June 13. In July the criminal charges against Odorizzi were dismissed under Penal Code, section 995, and in September he sought to resume his employment with the district. On the district's refusal to reinstate him he filed suit for declaratory and other relief.

Odorizzi's amended complaint asserts his resignation was invalid because obtained through duress, fraud, mistake, and undue influence and given at a time when he lacked capacity to make a valid contract. Specifically, Odorizzi declares he was under such severe mental and emotional strain at the time he signed his resignation, having just completed the process of arrest, questioning by the police, booking, and release on bail, and having gone for 40 hours without sleep, that he was incapable of rational thought or action. While he was in this condition and unable to think clearly, the superintendent of the district and the principal of his school came to his apartment. They said they were trying to help him and had his best interests at heart, that he should take their advice and immediately resign his position with the district, that there was no time to consult an attorney, that if he did not resign immediately the district would suspend and dismiss him from his position and publicize the

* *Macklin Fleming* (1911-2010) studied at Yale University (A.B., LL.B.) and was admitted to practice law in New York in 1938 and California in 1946. He practiced briefly in New York and Washington, D.C., before removing to San Francisco in 1949, serving there with the U.S. Attorney's office (1949-1954). He then held a private practice in Los Angeles before appointment to the Superior Court of California in 1959. Fleming served on that bench until he was appointed Justice on the California Court of Appeal in 1964; he retired in 1981. — K.T.

proceedings, his "aforedescribed arrest" and cause him "to suffer extreme embarrassment and humiliation"; but that if he resigned at once the incident would not be publicized and would not jeopardize his chances of securing employment as a teacher elsewhere. Odorizzi pleads that because of his faith and confidence in their representations they were able to substitute their will and judgment in place of his own and thus obtain his signature to his purported resignation. A demurrer to his amended complaint was sustained without leave to amend.

By his complaint plaintiff in effect seeks to rescind his resignation pursuant to Civil Code, section 1689, on the ground that his consent had not been real or free within the meaning of Civil Code, section 1567, but had been obtained through duress, menace, fraud, undue influence, or mistake. A pleading under these sections is sufficient if, stripped of its conclusions, it sets forth sufficient facts to justify legal relief. . . . In our view the facts in the amended complaint are insufficient to state a cause of action for duress, menace, fraud, or mistake, but they do set out sufficient elements to justify rescission of a consent because of undue influence. We summarize our conclusions on each of these points.

1. No duress or menace has been pleaded. Duress consists in unlawful confinement of another's person, or relatives, or property, which causes him to consent to a transaction through fear. (Civ. Code, §1569.) Duress is often used interchangeably with menace . . . , but in California menace is technically a threat of duress or a threat of injury to the person, property, or character of another. (Civ. Code, §1570; Restatement, Contracts, §§492, 493.) We agree with respondent's contention that neither duress nor menace was involved in this case, because the action or threat in duress or menace must be unlawful, and a threat to take legal action is not unlawful unless the party making the threat knows the falsity of his claim. . . . The amended complaint shows in substance that the school representatives announced their intention to initiate suspension and dismissal proceedings under Education Code, section 13403, 13408 et seq. at a time when the filing of such proceedings was not only their legal right but their positive duty as school officials. . . . Although the filing of such proceedings might be extremely damaging to plaintiff's reputation, the injury would remain incidental so long as the school officials acted in good faith in the performance of their duties. . . . Neither duress nor menace was present as a ground for recission.

2. Nor do we find a cause of action for fraud, either actual or constructive. (Civ. Code, §§1571 to 1574.) Actual fraud involves conscious misrepresentation, or concealment, or non-disclosure of a material fact which induces the innocent party to enter the contract. (Civ. Code, §1572; Pearson v. Norton, 230 Cal. App. 2d 1, 7 [40 Cal. Rptr. 634]; Restatement, Contracts, §471.) A complaint for fraud must plead misrepresentation, knowledge of falsity, intent to induce reliance, justifiable reliance, and resulting damage. . . . While the amended complaint charged misrepresentation, it failed to assert the elements of knowledge of falsity, intent to induce reliance, and justifiable reliance. A cause of action for actual fraud was therefore not stated. . . .

Constructive fraud arises on a breach of duty by one in a confidential or fiduciary relationship to another which induces justifiable reliance by the latter to his prejudice. (Civ. Code, §1573.) Plaintiff has attempted to bring himself within this category, for the amended complaint asserts the existence of a confidential relationship between the school superintendent and principal as agents of the defendant, and the plaintiff. Such a confidential relationship may exist whenever a person with justification places trust and confidence in the integrity and fidelity of another. . . . Plaintiff, however, sets forth no facts to support his conclusion of a confidential relationship between the representatives of the school district and himself, other than that the parties bore the relationship of employer and employee to each other. Under prevailing judicial opinion no presumption of a confidential relationship arises from the bare fact that parties to a contract are employer and employee; rather, additional ties must be brought out in order to create the presumption of a confidential relationship between the two. . . . The absence of a confidential relationship between employer and employee is especially apparent where, as here, the parties were negotiating to bring about a termination of their relationship. In such a situation each party is expected to look after his own interests, and a lack of confidentiality is implicit in the subject matter of their dealings. We think the allegations of constructive fraud were inadequate.

3. As to mistake, the amended complaint fails to disclose any facts which would suggest that consent had been obtained through a mistake of fact or of law. The material facts of the transaction were known to both parties. Neither party was laboring under any misapprehension of law of which the other took advantage. The discussion between plaintiff and the school district representatives principally attempted to evaluate the probable consequences of plaintiff's predicament and to predict the future course of events. The fact that their speculations did not forecast the exact pattern which events subsequently took does not provide the basis for a claim that they were acting under some sort of mistake. The doctrine of mistake customarily involves such errors as the nature of the transaction, the identity of the parties, the identity of the things to which the contract relates, or the occurrence of collateral happenings. (Rest., Contracts, §502, com. e.) Errors of this nature were not present in the case at bench.

4. However, the pleading does set out a claim that plaintiff's consent to the transaction had been obtained through the use of undue influence.

Undue influence, in the sense we are concerned with here, is a shorthand legal phrase used to describe persuasion which tends to be coercive in nature, persuasion which overcomes the will without convincing the judgment. . . . The hallmark of such persuasion is high pressure, a pressure which works on mental, moral, or emotional weakness to such an extent that it approaches the boundaries of coercion. In this sense, undue influence has been called overpersuasion. (Kelly v. McCarthy, 6 Cal. 2d 347, 364 [57 P.2d 118].) Misrepresentations of law or fact are not essential to the charge, for a person's will may be overborne without misrepresentation. By statutory definition undue influence includes "taking an unfair advantage of another's weakness of mind, or . . . taking a grossly oppressive and unfair advantage of another's necessities or distress." (Civ. Code, §1575.) While most reported cases of undue influence involve persons who bear a confidential relationship to one another, a confidential or authoritative relationship between the parties need not be present when the undue influence involves unfair advantage taken of another's weakness or distress. . . .

We paraphrase the summary of undue influence given the jury by Sir James P. Wilde in Hall v. Hall, L.R. 1, P. & D. 481, 482 (1868):

> To make a good contract a man must be a free agent. Pressure of whatever sort which overpowers the will without convincing the judgment is a species of restraint under which no valid contract can be made. Importunity or threats, if carried to the degree in which the free play of a man's will is overborne, constitute undue influence, although no force is used or threatened. A party may be led but not driven, and his acts must be the offspring of his own volition and not the record of someone else's.

In essence undue influence involves the use of excessive pressure to persuade one vulnerable to such pressure, pressure applied by a dominant subject to a servient object. In combination, the elements of undue susceptibility in the servient person and excessive pressure by the dominating person make the latter's influence undue, for it results in the apparent will of the servient person being in fact the will of the dominant person.

Undue susceptibility may consist of total weakness of mind which leaves a person entirely without understanding (Civ. Code, §38); or, a lesser weakness which destroys the capacity of a person to make a contract even though he is not totally incapacitated (Civ. Code, §39 . . .); or, the first element in our equation, a still lesser weakness which provides sufficient grounds to rescind a contract for undue influence (Civ. Code, §1575 . . .). Such lesser weakness need not be longlasting nor wholly incapacitating, but may be merely a lack of full vigor due to age . . . , physical condition, . . . emotional anguish, . . . or a combination of such factors. The reported cases have usually involved elderly, sick, senile persons alleged to have executed wills or deeds under pressure. (Malone v. Malone, 155 Cal. App. 2d 161 [317 P.2d 65] (constant importuning of a senile husband); Stewart v. Marvin, 139 Cal. App. 2d 769 [294 P.2d 114] (persistent nagging of elderly spouse).) In some of its aspects this lesser weakness could perhaps be called weakness of spirit. But whatever name we give it, this first element of undue influence resolves itself into a lessened capacity of the object to make a free contract.

In the present case plaintiff has pleaded that such weakness at the time he signed his resignation prevented him from freely and competently applying his judgment to the problem before him. Plaintiff declares he was under severe mental and emotional strain at the time because he had just completed the process of arrest, questioning, booking, and release on bail and had been without sleep for 40 hours. It is possible that exhaustion and emotional turmoil may wholly incapacitate a person from exercising his judgment. As an abstract question of pleading, plaintiff has pleaded that possibility and sufficient allegations to state a case for rescission.

Undue influence in its second aspect involves an application of excessive strength by a dominant subject against a servient object. Judicial consideration of this second element in undue influence has been relatively rare, for there are few cases denying persons who persuade but do not misrepresent the benefit of their bargain. Yet logically, the same legal consequences should apply to the results of excessive strength as to the results of undue weakness. Whether from weakness on one side, or strength on the other, or a combination of the two, undue influence occurs whenever there results that kind of influence or supremacy of one mind over another by which that other is prevented from acting according to his own wish or judgment, and whereby the will of the person is over-borne and he is induced to do or forbear to do an act which he would not do, or would do, if left to act freely.

(Webb v. Saunders, 79 Cal. App. 2d 863, 871 [181 P.2d 43, 47].) Undue influence involves a type of mismatch which our statute calls unfair advantage. (Civ. Code, §1575.) Whether a person of subnormal capacities has been subjected to ordinary force or a person of normal capacities subjected to extraordinary force, the match is equally out of balance. If will has been overcome against judgment, consent may be rescinded.

The difficulty, of course, lies in determining when the forces of persuasion have overflowed their normal banks and become oppressive flood waters. There are second thoughts to every bargain, and hindsight is still better than foresight. Undue influence cannot be used as a pretext to avoid bad bargains or escape from bargains which refuse to come up to expectations. A woman who buys a dress on impulse, which on critical inspection by her best friend turns out to be less fashionable than she had thought, is not legally entitled to set aside the sale on the ground that the saleswoman used all her wiles to close the sale. A man who buys a tract of desert land in the expectation that it is in the immediate path of the city's growth and will become another Palm Springs, an expectation cultivated in glowing terms by the seller, cannot rescind his bargain when things turn out differently. If we are temporarily persuaded against our better judgment to do something about which we later have second thoughts, we must abide the consequences of the risks inherent in managing our own affairs. . . .

However, overpersuasion is generally accompanied by certain characteristics which tend to create a pattern. The pattern usually involves several of the following elements: (1) discussion of the transaction at an unusual or inappropriate time, (2) consummation of the transaction in an unusual place, (3) insistent demand that the business be finished at once, (4) extreme emphasis on untoward consequences of delay, (5) the use of multiple persuaders by the dominant side against a single servient party, (6) absence of third-party advisers to the servient party, (7) statements that there is no time to consult financial advisers or attorneys. If a number of these elements are simultaneously present, the persuasion may be characterized as excessive. The cases are illustrative:

Moore v. Moore, 56 Cal. 89, 93, and 81 Cal. 195 [22 P. 589, 874]. The pregnant wife of a man who had been shot to death on October 30 and buried on November 1 was approached by four members of her husband's family on November 2 or 3 and persuaded to deed her entire interest in her husband's estate to his children by a prior marriage. In finding the use of undue influence on Mrs. Moore, the court commented:

It was the second day after her late husband's funeral. It was at a time when she would naturally feel averse to transacting any business, and she might reasonably presume that her late husband's brothers would not apply to her at such a time to transact any important business, unless it was of a nature that would admit of no delay. And as it would admit of delay, the only reason which we can discover for their unseemly haste is, that they thought that she would be more likely to comply with their wishes then than at some future time, after she had recovered from the shock which she had then so recently experienced. If for that reason they selected that time for the accomplishment of their purpose, it seems to us that they not only took, but that they designed to take, an unfair advantage of her weakness of mind. If they did not, they probably can explain why they selected that inappropriate time for the transaction of business which might have been delayed for weeks without injury to any one. In the absence of any explanation, it appears to us that the time was selected with reference to just that condition of mind which she alleges that she was then in.

Taking an unfair advantage of another's weakness of mind is undue influence, and the law will not permit the retention of an advantage thus obtained. (Civ. Code, §1575.)

Weger v. Rocha, 138 Cal. App. 109 [32 P.2d 417]. Plaintiff, while confined in a cast in a hospital, gave a release of claims for personal injuries for a relatively small sum to an agent who spent two hours persuading her to sign. At the time of signing plaintiff was in a highly nervous and hysterical condition and suffering much pain, and she signed the release in order to terminate the interview. The court held that the release had been secured by the use of undue influence.

Fyan v. McNutt (1934) 266 Mich. 406 [254 N.W. 146] (1934). At issue was the validity of an agreement by Mrs. McNutt to pay Fyan, a real estate broker, a five-percent commission on all moneys received from the condemnation of Mrs. McNutt's land. Earlier, Fyan had secured an option from Mrs. McNutt to purchase her land for his own account and offer it for sale as part of a larger parcel to Wayne County for an airport site. On July 25 Fyan learned from the newspapers that the county would probably start condemnation proceedings rather than obtain an airport site by purchase. Fyan, with four others, arrived at Mrs. McNutt's house at 1 A.M. on July 26 with the commission agreement he wanted her to sign. Mrs. McNutt protested being awakened at that hour and was reluctant to sign, but Fyan told her he had to have the paper in Detroit by morning, that the whole airport proposition would fall through if she did not sign then and there, that there wasn't time to wait until morning to get outside advice. In holding the agreement invalid the Michigan Supreme Court said:

> The late hour of the night at which her signature was secured over her protest and plea that she be given until the next day to consider her action, the urge of the moment, the cooperation of the others present in their desire to obtain a good price for their farm lands, the plaintiff's anxiety over the seeming weakness of his original option, all combined to produce a situation in which, to say the least, it is doubtful that the defendant had an opportunity to exercise her own free will. . . . A valid contract can be entered into only when there is a meeting of the minds of the parties under circumstances conducive to a free and voluntary execution of the agreement contemplated. It must be conceived in good faith and come into existence under circumstances that do not deprive the parties of the exercise of their own free will.

The difference between legitimate persuasion and excessive pressure, like the difference between seduction and rape, rests to a considerable extent in the manner in which the parties go about their business. For example, if a day or two after Odorizzi's release on bail the superintendent of the school district had called him into his office during business hours and directed his attention to those provisions of the Education Code compelling his leave of absence and authorizing his suspension on the filing of written charges, had told him that the district contemplated filing written charges against him, had pointed out the alternative of resignation available to him, had informed him he was free to consult counsel or any adviser he wished and to consider the matter overnight and return with his decision the next day, it is extremely unlikely that any complaint about the use of excessive pressure could ever have been made against the school district.

But, according to the allegations of the complaint, this is not the way it happened, and if it had happened that way, plaintiff would never have resigned. Rather, the representatives of the school board undertook to achieve their objective by overpersuasion and imposition to secure plaintiff's signature but not his consent to his resignation through a high-pressure carrot-and-stick technique — under which they assured plaintiff they were trying to assist him, he should rely on their advice, there wasn't time to consult an attorney, if he didn't resign at once the school district would suspend and dismiss him from his position and publicize the proceedings, but if he did resign the incident wouldn't jeopardize his chances of securing a teaching post elsewhere.

Plaintiff has thus pleaded both subjective and objective elements entering the undue influence equation and stated sufficient facts to put in issue the question whether his free will had been overborne by defendant's agents at a time when he was unable to function in a normal manner. It was sufficient to pose ". . . the ultimate question . . . whether a free and competent judgment was merely influenced, or whether a mind was so dominated as to prevent the exercise of an independent judgment." (Williston on Contracts, §1625 (rev. ed.); Rest., Contracts, §497, com. c.) The question cannot be resolved by an analysis of pleading but requires a finding of fact.

We express no opinion on the merits of plaintiff's case, or the propriety of his continuing to teach school (Ed. Code, §13403), or the timeliness of his rescission (Civ. Code, §1691). We do hold that his pleading, liberally construed, states a cause of action for rescission of a transaction to which his apparent consent had been obtained through the use of undue influence.

The judgment is reversed.

Relational Background: Donald Odorizzi's Story

STUDY GUIDE: Until now, all that was known about this well-known contracts case were the facts presented in the previous judicial opinion. The following was prepared by Professor Kellye Y. Testy of the Seattle University School of Law, and is excerpted from a portion of her unpublished paper, "An Ode to Odorizzi: *Law's Undue Influence." I am grateful to Professor Testy for allowing me to reproduce a portion of her work-in-progress. All rights to this excerpt are reserved to Kellye Y. Testy.*

The *Odorizzi* case is commonly used by contracts teachers to teach the defense of undue influence. The case is appealing to both teachers and students for a number of reasons. Foremost is that contracts cases (as opposed to will contests) discussing undue influence at any length are rare. Furthermore, the opinion's discussion of undue influence is particularly well-developed, including an element-by-element discussion of the doctrine as well as a comparison of undue influence with other policing tools such as duress, fraud, and mistake. The procedural posture of the case — Odorizzi is appealing the defendant School District's successful motion to dismiss — paves the way for the court's doctrinal emphasis and results in perfect fodder for the steady first-year diet of acontextual legal doctrine. Teachers get a lot of mileage out of one case, so they are happy. Students get a rule — even one with clearly articulated elements — for their outlines, so they are happy.

And importantly, both teachers and students can breathe a sigh of relief: Odorizzi's appeal is successful; he's entitled to his day in court on his claim that he should be able to rescind his contract of resignation on the basis of undue influence. Even for someone whom we are obliquely told had been "arrested on criminal charges of homosexual activity," the law has done the right thing. It is tempting to see this case as much of law is presented during the first-year: one more piece of evidence that the law is making its sometimes slow, but ever-sure, march from dark evil to brilliant justice.

There is something more you need to know.

Undue influence is not a winning argument in contracts cases, and Odorizzi did not ultimately win this one. . . .

As the opinion indicates, Donald William Odorizzi was arrested on June 10, 1964 on criminal charges of homosexual activity. To be precise, Odorizzi was initially charged under California Penal Code §288a (oral copulation). The arresting officer swore that Don dialed a random phone number and asked the man who answered the call whether he wanted to have sex. The man said that he did and would meet Don in a designated parking lot after making an excuse to his wife and children. After meeting there, Don and the man went to Don's apartment. At the apartment, Don went into his bedroom and the man followed and stood in front of Don while Don sat down on the bed. When Don reached up to touch him, the man arrested Don, identifying himself as officer Ronald Arrington.[8]

This is the story that Arrington testified to. This is also the story that another officer in Arrington's department rushed, the day after Don's arrest, to tell the secretary of the School District where Don taught.[9] This is the story that then caused the superintendent and principal of Don's school to come to his home the evening of June 11 to obtain the resignation Don later sought to rescind. This is the story that provided the basis for the State's decision to revoke Don's teaching certificate.[10] And this is the story that followed Don throughout all of his legal proceedings and for the thirty-four years after his arrest.

8. Preliminary Examination Transcript, State v. Odorizzi, No. F-2556 (June 19, 1964) at 14 [hereinafter Transcript].

9. Interview with Donald Odorizzi (May 23, 1998) [hereinafter Odorizzi Interview]; Tangents Newsletter, Vol. I, No. 2 (Nov. 1965).

10. Decision of the California State Board of Education (September 13, 1966).

But this is not what Don says really happened the evening of June 10, 1964. According to Don,[11] he started that evening feeling depressed and alone. His live-in lover, Bud, had left him and had now been gone for over two weeks. Don went out, met someone he liked, and the two men went to Don's apartment and eventually ended up in bed together. Unfortunately, Bud decided to come back home that evening. When he came in and saw Don with another man he was upset and decided to call the police to report "homosexual activity." When officer Arrington arrived, Bud let him into the apartment and then left the officer to arrest Don. Arrington then proceeded with the arrest, constructing (possibly with Bud's help) the version of events that followed Don for the next thirty-four years. Once Don realized that Arrington's version of the circumstances of his arrest did not match his own, Don kept quiet about the fabricated story thinking he was somehow protecting Bud and having little idea of the repercussions that would flow from the officer's report.

Don was taken into custody where he was grilled and ridiculed about his sex life on tape for over three hours. Thinking he would lend credence to the fabricated story to which he was still committed, Don said that this was not the first time that he had called random numbers seeking sex with men. Under pressure, he also said that he had frequented a bathhouse on earlier occasions. After many hours of questioning and taunting by the police, he was jailed and not released until around 1:00 P.M. the following day. After his release he then spent several hours traveling to and from a bonding agent and visiting with an attorney.[12]

Shortly after arriving home, Don's friend Jim Schneider[13] arrived. Before the two men had time to talk, Robert Ferris and Donald Anderson, the superintendent and principal of Don's school, also arrived at Don's apartment around 8:00 P.M. The two school officials had earlier called Don expressing sympathy and wanting to come by and "talk" about what had happened. Without prior warning, however, they arrived with a resignation in hand, seeking to get Don's signature.[14] For over two hours, Ferris and Anderson sought to get Don to resign his teaching post while Schneider simultaneously sought to convince Don to resist resigning. Schneider wanted Don to use the situation to advance the rights of teachers who either were or were alleged to be homosexuals.[15] Schneider and Ferris spent

11. Odorizzi Interview (May 23, 1998).

12. Odorizzi Interview (May 23, 1998).

13. At the time, Schneider worked for an organization called "Tangents," which published a magazine and a newsletter under the same name. The organization was dedicated to advancing law reform on behalf of homosexuals.

14. The deposition of Donald R. Anderson, principal of Aloha school where Odorizzi was employed, indicates that Anderson and acting superintendent Robert E. Ferris had decided to call on Odorizzi that evening to obtain his resignation and that they did not tell him the purpose of their visit over the telephone. Deposition of Donald R. Anderson, Odorizzi v. Bloomfield School Dist., No. 848-053 (April 12, 1967) at 31-34 [hereinafter Anderson Deposition].

15. I use the term "homosexuals" rather than other terms such as "gay" because it is the term used during this pre-Stonewall time. For a history of the modern gay liberation movement, see John D'Emilio, A New Beginning: The Birth of Gay Liberation, in Sexual Politics, Sexual Communities: The Making of a Homosexual Minority in the United States, 1940-1970 at 231 (1983).

considerable time and effort bickering over the issue of homosexuality and its prevalence in society.[16]

At one point, Schneider telephoned Don Slater — founder of One, Incorporated, a nascent organization seeking to advocate civil rights for homosexuals — to get Slater's advice. According to Schneider, Slate agreed that Don should not sign the resignation and Schneider conveyed this to Don. Also present at some points during the discussion was the now-notorious roommate Bud. Bud's contribution to Don's decision-making process was to tell him to "just do what you want to do, Don, don't listen to any of these guys."[17] And of course, in the end we know that Don decided to sign. Around 10:00 P.M. he abruptly signed in pencil one of the two copies of a resignation that Ferris had prepared because he "had to get them out of the house."[18] Slater then put Don in touch with attorney Herbert Selwyn for representation in the criminal case. Selwyn argued that the crime charged had not been committed because no act sufficient to constitute the crime or its attempt had been performed by Don. The statute Odorizzi was alleged to have violated was §288a of the California Penal Code, which at the time provided: "Any person participating in an act of copulating the mouth of one person with the sexual organ of another is punishable by imprisonment in the state prison for not exceeding 15 years or by imprisonment in the county jail not to exceed one year. . . ."[19] Specifically, Selwyn argued that reaching to touch or even touching a fully clothed person does not consti-tute oral copulation or even a substantial step in oral copulation. This was a solid line of argument given that courts had been and were requiring "some penetration however slight" to satisfy the "copulation" requirement.[20]

That Don was arrested under §288a rather than §647 (disorderly con-duct) lends support to Don's assertion that the officer fabricated the cir-cumstances of Don's arrest. Officers were well aware that the oral copulation statute required some penetration and commonly wrote their arrest reports to satisfy this requirement.[21] Moreover, officers were also well aware that convictions were rarely obtained for conduct observed within a private residence because such observance often exceeded search and sei-zure requirements.[22] Accordingly, the most common provision for punish-ing homosexual conduct was §647, which provides punishment for acts of solicitation as well as for the actual commission of a lewd act.[23] Thus, had events transpired as the arresting officer testified, Odorizzi would routinely have been charged with violating §647, not §288a. Even the transcript of Don's preliminary hearing reveals some uncertainty as to whether the State was seeking to find Don guilty of oral copulation or attempted oral copulation.

16. Deposition of Robert E. Ferris, Odorizzi v. Bloomfield School Dist., No. 848-053 (April 12, 1967) [hereinafter Ferris Deposition]; Anderson Deposition.

17. Odorizzi and Schneider Interviews (May 23, 1998); Ferris Deposition at 57.

18. Odorizzi Interview (May 23, 1998).

19. Cal. Pen. Code §288a (pre-1971 amendments).

20. See Project, The Consenting Adult Homosexual and the Law: An Empirical Study of Enforcement and Administration in Los Angeles County, 13 UCLA Law Rev. 643, 680 (1966).

21. Id.

22. Id. at 689.

23. Id. at 684.

Although Don recalls that the judge did not seem to find Selwyn's defense convincing,[24] Selwyn was called into chambers for a conference. After he emerged, the judge granted his §995 motion,[25] the charges against Don were dismissed on July 9, 1964, and not refiled. Don never understood exactly why the charges were dropped, but turned his attention to getting his teaching job back. He loved teaching and had always been rated as a "good to excellent" teacher. His parents were working-class folks (his father was a coal miner) who Don thought had sacrificed much to help him obtain his teaching degree at Colorado State College in Greeley, Colorado. Don felt an enormous weight of responsibility to not waste his degree. Nonetheless, the School District refused to reinstate Don, and eventually he was connected with Burton Marks' law office for assistance. There, working with young lawyer Stuart Simke, he filed suit to rescind his resignation on the basis that it was obtained coercively. As we know from the reported appellate decision, Don's complaint was met with a successful motion to dismiss, which was then reversed on appeal.

Unfortunately for Don, however, this was not the only proceeding pending. The State Board of Education began decertification proceedings against him on the basis of his arrest and subsequent statements to police. Simke sought to hold that action at bay, arguing both that the civil appeal would adequately address the same issues and also that the statements on which the decertification action depended were inadmissible evidence because they had been obtained illegally. Simke's well-written brief to the State cited the recently decided and now-famous *Miranda*[26] decision to argue that Don's custodial interrogation was done without proper constitutional safeguards. Moreover, Simke himself was surprised by the State's vigorous pursuit of Don, writing: "Our problems have been complicated, however, by reason of the fact that the Committee of Credentials for the State Board has now taken action. This is somewhat surprising since they generally will leave the matter to the County or School District. . . . I am afraid that their philosophy is to starve you."[27] Their theory worked.

With both the civil and administrative cases pending, Don's legal needs and debt were mounting quickly. Slater attempted to raise money for Don's defense and to enlist the ACLU in assisting with his representation. Both efforts failed miserably. Meanwhile, the State was undeterred by Simke's arguments and continued proceedings to revoke Don's license. Don's letter to his lawyer in December, 1965 is revealing: "I feel that I am FIGHTING FOR MY LIFE and would never really be satisfied until the Supreme Court has ruled that I have no right to my job or to the practice of my profession as

24. The judge at Don's preliminary hearing certainly did not find Selwyn convincing, interrupting his argument to ask: "How much greater indignity must you expose the police officer to in his duty than this enormous indignity that was apparently committed? I will not buy it. I cannot see that an officer has to go beyond this state of humiliation."

25. Section 995 of the California Penal Code sets out grounds and procedures for setting aside either an indictment or an information when proper procedures have not been followed or where no reasonable or probable cause exists for arrest. Dismissals under this section are many and varied. See Cal. Pen: Code §995 (West 1985).

26. Miranda v. Arizona, 384 U.S. 436 (1966).

27. Letter from Stuart A. Simke to Donald W. Odorizzi (Oct. 22, 1965).

a teacher. Shall an agency of the State be empowered to eviscerate me for the rest of my life over the allegation of a crime that was not committed?"

The answer to Don's question was a resounding "yes." The State officially revoked Don's license on October 15, 1966. Thus, when Don finally learned on November 7, 1966 that he had "won" the civil appeal, it was cold comfort indeed. Ironically, Selwyn's earlier billing letter to Don had gloated: "I wish to inform you that for a total consideration of $1250.00 I successfully defended you against a criminal charge, which successful outcome was necessary to protect your certificate as a school teacher. Had you been convicted of this charge, the State would have taken your certificate from you, thus diminishing your ability to earn a living."

Faced with the reality that he would likely never teach again, mounting legal fees that would take years to pay off, and a job that did not permit him time to attend to his legal affairs, Don reluctantly agreed to dismiss his suit against both the School District and the State Board of Education. His letter to Slater, thanking him for the support and assistance, reveals his state of mind:

> Almost three years ago we started my legal actions with the courts to get my teaching credentials back. As up to date very little has been accomplished except legal bills.
>
> As of now it will take over three years to pay off the lawyers bills and money that I have borrowed from friends.
>
> I see no hope of ever teaching school again, which my lawyer agrees with. You have asked for contributions from members of the organization with no success. After a great deal of thought I am forced to drop the case.
>
> I want to thank you and the few people who helped and showed an interest in the case. I know that you spent a great deal of time on this matter and it was truly appreciated.[28]

To add insult to injury, even the IRS had to get in on this legal rampage against Don. In June 1965, his 1964 federal tax return was audited because his deduction for legal expenses related to his employment looked suspiciously large to the IRS. As it turned out, Don had paid *more* legal fees than he had claimed.

After giving Simke the go-ahead to dismiss his lawsuits, Don turned to trying to put the incident behind him and to paying off his huge legal expenses. The prominence of his case, however, has not escaped his notice. He first learned of its presence in law school classrooms through a friend whose daughter had attended law school. And although he has sought to live a very private life, he has been taunted about the case on numerous occasions over the years. Although he's a stocky, 5'9'' 60-year old man who looks like any guy you would expect to see drinking beer at a bowling alley, even now he has to get a "straight" friend to go to the rest room with him at work because of the harassment he receives there in his blue-collar job. All in a day's work — a daily reminder that this case was anything but a win. . . .

28. Letter from Don Odorizzi to Don Slater (May 9, 1967).

RESTATEMENT (SECOND) OF CONTRACTS

§177. WHEN UNDUE INFLUENCE MAKES
A CONTRACT VOIDABLE

(1) Undue influence is unfair persuasion of a party who is under the domination of the person exercising the persuasion or who by virtue of the relation between them is justified in assuming that that person will not act in a manner inconsistent with his welfare.

(2) If a party's manifestation of assent is induced by undue influence by the other party, the contract is voidable by the victim.

(3) If a party's manifestation of assent is induced by one who is not a party to the transaction, the contract is voidable by the victim unless the other party to the transaction in good faith and without reason to know of the undue influence either gives value or relies materially on the transaction.

REFERENCE: Barnett, §6.3.4
                Farnsworth, §4.20
                Calamari & Perillo, §§9.9-9.12
                Murray, §95

D. UNCONSCIONABILITY

In Chapter 9, we learned that courts will not normally inquire into the adequacy of consideration. In Chapter 10, however, we saw that courts will sometimes deny enforcement to "sham" exchanges involving nominal consideration. In Chapter 15, we examined cases in which the unfairness of the bargain coupled with the diminished capacity of the promisor was seen as justifying contract avoidance. We are now in a good position to evaluate the next group of cases, in which the courts have scrutinized an exchange under the doctrine of unconscionability.

When doing so, one should consider a widely discussed distinction between so-called *procedural* and *substantive* conceptions of unconscionability identified by Professor Arthur A. Leff in his classic and highly entertaining article, Unconscionability and the Code — The Emperor's New Clause, 115 U. Pa. L. Rev. 485, 486-487 (1967):

> Let us begin the story the way so many good stories begin, with ritual incantation: to make a contract one needs (i) parties with capacity, (ii) manifested assent, and (iii) consideration. This is all very simple.[29] If these criteria are met, a party to the resulting nexus who has made promises is obligated to carry them out, unless he can maintain successfully one of the standard contract-law defenses, such as fraud, duress, mistake, impossibility or illegality. These "defenses" might be classified in divers ways to serve various analytical purposes. For our particular needs, however, there is a simple way of grouping them which is signally illuminating: some of these defenses have to do with the *process of contracting* and others have to do with the resulting *contract*. When

---

29. This simplicity is, of course, of a rather special kind. Robert Frost once remarked (at a "saying" of his poetry): "e equals mc^2; what's so hard about that? Of course, what e, m and c are is harder."

fraud and duress are involved, for instance, the focus of attention is on what took place between the parties at the making of the contract. With illegality, on the other hand, the material question is instead the content of the contract once "made." The law may legitimately be interested both in the way agreements come about and in what they provide. A "contract" gotten at gunpoint may be avoided; a classic dicker over Dobbin may come to naught if horse owning is illegal. Hereafter, to distinguish the two interests, I shall often refer to bargaining naughtiness as "procedural unconscionability," and to the evils in the resulting contract as "substantive unconscionability."

Professor Leff then proceeds to analyze the legislative history of U.C.C. §2-302 (which appears in the text after the next case) to see whether one or both of these conceptions explains the intended scope of the Code's prohibition of an "Unconscionable Contract or Clause."

Ever since Leff wrote, many (but not all) contracts scholars and courts have found the distinction between substantive and procedural unconscionability useful to understand the concept of unconscionability. Can you see the source of its appeal? When reading the cases in this section, consider whether *you* find this distinction helpful. If you find yourself more attracted to one conception of unconscionability than the other, try to articulate why you feel as you do.

STUDY GUIDE: Can the next very famous and much-discussed case be squared with the traditional reluctance to examine the adequacy of consideration? Can the power claimed by the court be limited in a principled fashion or does it represent the undoing of freedom of contract? How does the defense of unconscionability relate, if at all, to the other defenses we have studied in this chapter? In Chapter 15? In particular, compare this contract provision with the contested portions of the contract in Vokes v. Arthur Murray. Is there anything problematic about extending lack of capacity or undue influence theories to the facts of this case? In what respect do these unconscionability cases represent "obtaining assent by improper means," or is this categorization of the doctrine too confining?

WILLIAMS v. WALKER-THOMAS FURNITURE CO.
United States Court of Appeals, District of Columbia Circuit,
350 F.2d 445 (1965)

J. SKELLY WRIGHT, Circuit Judge:*
Appellee, Walker-Thomas Furniture Company, operates a retail furniture store in the District of Columbia. During the period from 1957 to 1962

James Skelly Wright (1911-1988) was educated at Loyola University (Ph.D., LL.B.), serving as a high school teacher (1931-1935) while working toward his law degree. He embarked on his legal career with the U.S. attorney's office in New Orleans (1937-1942, 1945-1946), serving as U.S. attorney for the Eastern District of Louisiana (1948-1949). In 1949, he joined the federal courts as U.S. District Judge (1949-1962). In 1962, he was promoted to judge on the Court of Appeals for the District of Columbia, serving as Chief Judge of that court from 1978 to 1981. In 1981, Wright became judge on the Temporary Emergency Court of Appeals of the United States, and served there as Chief Judge from 1982 until his retirement in 1987. He served as a faculty member of Loyola University (1936-1937) and Loyola University School of Law (1950-1962), and as a lecturer on law at several law schools. He left the practice of law from 1942 to 1946 to serve as lieutenant commander with the U.S.C.G. — K.T.

each appellant in these cases purchased a number of household items from Walker-Thomas, for which payment was to be made in installments. The terms of each purchase were contained in a printed form contract which set forth the value of the purchased item and purported to lease the item to appellant for a stipulated monthly rent payment. The contract then provided, in substance, that title would remain in Walker-Thomas until the total of all the monthly payments made equaled the stated value of the item, at which time appellants could take title. In the event of a default in the payment of any monthly installment, Walker-Thomas could repossess the item.

The contract further provided that

> the amount of each periodical installment payment to be made by [purchaser] to the Company under this present lease shall be inclusive of and not in addition to the amount of each installment payment to be made by [purchaser] under such prior leases, bills or accounts; *and all payments now and hereafter made by [purchaser] shall be credited pro rata on all outstanding leases, bills and accounts* due the Company by [purchaser] at the time each such payment is made." (Emphasis added.)

The effect of this rather obscure provision was to keep a balance due on every item purchased until the balance due on all items, whenever purchased, was liquidated. As a result, the debt incurred at the time of purchase of each item was secured by the right to repossess all the items previously purchased by the same purchaser, and each new item purchased automatically became subject to a security interest arising out of the previous dealings.

On May 12, 1962, appellant Thorne purchased an item described as a Daveno, three tables, and two lamps, having total stated value of $391.10. Shortly thereafter, he defaulted on his monthly payments and appellee sought to replevy all the items purchased since the first transaction in 1958. Similarly, on April 17, 1962, appellant Williams bought a stereo set of stated value of $514.95.[30] She too defaulted shortly thereafter, and appellee sought to replevy all the items purchased since December, 1957. The Court of General Sessions granted judgment for appellee. The District of Columbia Court of Appeals affirmed, and we granted appellants' motion for leave to appeal to this court.

Appellants' principal contention, rejected by both the trial and the appellate courts below, is that these contracts, or at least some of them, are unconscionable and, hence, not enforceable. In its opinion in Williams v. Walker-Thomas Furniture Company, 198 A.2d 914, 916 (1964), the District of Columbia Court of Appeals explained its rejection of this contention as follows:

> Appellant's second argument presents a more serious question. The record reveals that prior to the last purchase appellant had reduced the balance in her account to $164. The last purchase, a stereo set, raised

---

30. At the time of this purchase her account showed a balance of $164 still owing from her prior purchases. The total of all the purchases made over the years in question came to $1,800. The total payments amounted to $1,400.

the balance due to $678. Significantly, at the time of this and the preceding purchases, appellee was aware of appellant's financial position. The reverse side of the stereo contract listed the name of appellant's social worker and her $218 monthly stipend from the government. Nevertheless, with full knowledge that appellant had to feed, clothe and support both herself and seven children on this amount, appellee sold her a $514 stereo set.

We cannot condemn too strongly appellee's conduct. It raises serious questions of sharp practice and irresponsible business dealings. A review of the legislation in the District of Columbia affecting retail sales and the pertinent decisions of the highest court in this jurisdiction disclose, however, no ground upon which this court can declare the contracts in question contrary to public policy. We note that were the Maryland Retail Installment Sales Act, Art. 83 secs. 128-153, or its equivalent, in force in the District of Columbia, we could grant appellant appropriate relief. We think Congress should consider corrective legislation to protect the public from such exploitive contracts as were utilized in the case at bar.

We do not agree that the court lacked the power to refuse enforcement to contracts found to be unconscionable. In other jurisdictions, it has been held as a matter of common law that unconscionable contracts are not enforceable.[31] While no decision of this court so holding has been found, the notion that an unconscionable bargain should not be given full enforcement is by no means novel. In Scott v. United States, 79 U.S. (12 Wall.) 443, 445, 20 L. Ed. 438 (1870), the Supreme Court stated:

... If a contract be unreasonable and unconscionable, but not void for fraud, a court of law will give to the party who sues for its breach damages, not according to its letter, but only such as he is equitably entitled to. ...

Since we have never adopted or rejected such a rule, the question here presented is actually one of first impression.

Congress has recently enacted the Uniform Commercial Code, which specifically provides that the court may refuse to enforce a contract which it finds to be unconscionable at the time it was made. 28 D.C. Code §2-302 (Supp. IV 1965). The enactment of this section, which occurred subsequent to the contracts here in suit, does not mean that the common law of the District of Columbia was otherwise at the time of enactment, nor does it preclude the court from adopting a similar rule in the exercise of its powers to develop the common law for the District of Columbia. In fact, in view of the absence of prior authority on the point, we consider the congressional adoption of §2-302 persuasive authority for following the rationale of the cases from which the section is explicitly derived.[32] Accordingly, we hold that where the element of unconscionability is present at the time a contract is made, the contract should not be enforced.

31. Campbell Soup Co. v. Wentz, 3 Cir., 172 F.2d 80 (1948); Indianapolis Morris Plan Corporation v. Sparks, 132 Ind. App. 145,172 N.E.2d 899 (1961); Henningsen v. Bloomfield Motors, Inc., 32 N.J. 358, 161 A.2d 69, 84-96, 75 A.L.R.2d 1 (1960). Cf. 1 Corbin, Contracts §128 (1963).

32. See Comment, §2-302, Uniform Commercial Code (1962). Compare Note, 45 Va. L. Rev. 583, 590 (1959), where it is predicted that the rule of §2-302 will be followed by analogy in cases which involve contracts not specifically covered by the section. ...

Unconscionability has generally been recognized to include an absence of meaningful choice on the part of one of the parties together with contract terms which are unreasonably favorable to the other party. Whether a meaningful choice is present in a particular case can only be determined by consideration of all the circumstances surrounding the transaction. In many cases the meaningfulness of the choice is negated by a gross inequality of bargaining power.[33] The manner in which the contract was entered is also relevant to this consideration. Did each party to the contract, considering his obvious education or lack of it, have a reasonable opportunity to understand the terms of the contract, or were the important terms hidden in a maze of fine print and minimized by deceptive sales practices? Ordinarily, one who signs an agreement without full knowledge of its terms might be held to assume the risk that he has entered a one-sided bargain.[34] But when a party of little bargaining power, and hence little real choice, signs a commercially unreasonable contract with little or no knowledge of its terms, it is hardly likely that his consent, or even an objective manifestation of his consent, was ever given to all the terms. In such a case the usual rule that the terms of the agreement are not to be questioned[35] should be abandoned and the court should consider whether the terms of the contract are so unfair that enforcement should be withheld.[36]

In determining reasonableness or fairness, the primary concern must be with the terms of the contract considered in light of the circumstances existing when the contract was made. The test is not simple, nor can it be mechanically applied. The terms are to be considered "in the light of the general commercial background and the commercial needs of the particular

33. . . . Inquiry into the relative bargaining power of the two parties is not an inquiry wholly divorced from the general question of unconscionability, since a one-sided bargain is itself evidence of the inequality of the bargaining parties. This fact was vaguely recognized in the common law doctrine of intrinsic fraud, that is, fraud which can be presumed from the grossly unfair nature of the terms of the contract. See the oft-quoted statement of Lord Hardwicke in Earl of Chesterfield v. Janssen, 28 Eng. Rep. 82, 100 (1751):

. . . [Fraud] may be apparent from the intrinsic nature and subject of the bargain itself; such as no man in his senses and not under delusion would make. . . .

34. See Restatement, Contracts §70 (1932); Note, 63 Harv. L. Rev. 494 (1950). See also Daley v. People's Building, Loan Savings Assn., 178 Mass. 13, 59 N.E. 452, 453 (1901), in which Mr. Justice Holmes, while sitting on the Supreme Judicial Court of Massachusetts, made this observation:

. . . Courts are less and less disposed to interfere with parties making such contracts as they choose, so long as they interfere with no one's welfare but their own. . . . It will be understood that we are speaking of parties standing in an equal position where neither has any oppressive advantage or power. . . .

35. This rule has never been without exception. In cases involving merely the transfer of unequal amounts of the same commodity, the courts have held the bargain unenforceable for the reason that "in such a case, it is clear, that the law cannot indulge in the presumption of equivalence between the consideration and the promise." 1 Williston, Contracts §115 (3d ed., 1957).

36. See the general discussion of "Boiler-Plate Agreements" in Llewellyn, The Common Law Tradition 362-371 (1960).

trade or case."[37] Corbin suggests the test as being whether the terms are "so extreme as to appear unconscionable according to the mores and business practices of the time and place." 1 Corbin, op. cit. supra Note 2. We think this formulation correctly states the test to be applied in those cases where no meaningful choice was exercised upon entering the contract.

Because the trial court and the appellate court did not feel that enforcement could be refused, no findings were made on the possible unconscionability of the contracts in these cases. Since the record is not sufficient for our deciding the issue as a matter of law, the cases must be remanded to the trial court for further proceedings.

So ordered.

DANAHER, Circuit Judge* (dissenting):

The District of Columbia Court of Appeals obviously was as unhappy about the situation here presented as any of us can possibly be. Its opinion in the *Williams* case, quoted in the majority text, concludes: "We think Congress should consider corrective legislation to protect the public from such exploitive contracts as were utilized in the case at bar."

My view is thus summed up by an able court which made no finding that there had actually been sharp practice. Rather the appellant seems to have known precisely where she stood.

There are many aspects of public policy here involved. What is a luxury to some may seem an outright necessity to others. Is public oversight to be required of the expenditures of relief funds? A washing machine, e.g., in the hands of a relief client might become a fruitful source of income. Many relief clients may well need credit, and certain business establishments will take long chances on the sale of items, expecting their pricing policies will afford a degree of protection commensurate with the risk. Perhaps a remedy when necessary will be found within the provisions of the "Loan Shark" law, D.C. Code §26-601 et seq. (1961).

I mention such matters only to emphasize the desirability of a cautious approach to any such problem, particularly since the law for so long has allowed parties such great latitude in making their own contracts. I dare say there must annually be thousands upon thousands of installment credit transactions in this jurisdiction, and one can only speculate as to the effect the decision in these cases will have.[38]

I join the District of Columbia Court of Appeals in its disposition of the issues.

---

37. Comment, Uniform Commercial Code sec. [2-302].

John Anthony Danaher (1899-1990) studied at Yale University (A.B.) and Yale Law School and was admitted to the bar of Connecticut in 1922. He practiced law in New York City (1921-1922) and in Hartford, Connecticut, and Washington, D.C. (1922-1953), except while serving as Assistant U.S. Attorney (1922-1934), Secretary of the State of Connecticut (1933-1935), and U.S. Senator (1939-1945). In 1953, Danaher joined the bench as a U.S. Circuit Judge on the U.S. Court of Appeals in Washington, D.C. (1953-1969), and then became Senior U.S. Circuit Judge in Hartford from 1969 until his retirement in 1980. — K.T.

38. However the provision ultimately may be applied or in what circumstances, D.C. Code §28-2-302 (Supp. IV, 1965) did not become effective until January 1, 1965.

Study Guide: Commenting on this U.C.C. section, Professor Leff observed: "If reading this section makes anything clear it is that reading this section alone makes nothing clear about the meaning of 'unconscionable' except perhaps that it is pejorative." Do you agree? If so, does it matter?

SALES CONTRACTS: THE UNIFORM COMMERCIAL CODE

§2-302.   UNCONSCIONABLE CONTRACT OR CLAUSE

(1) If the court as a matter of law finds the contract or any clause of the contract to have been unconscionable at the time it was made the court may refuse to enforce the contract, or it may enforce the remainder of the contract without the unconscionable clause, or it may so limit the application of any unconscionable clause as to avoid any unconscionable result.

(2) When it is claimed or appears to the court that the contract or any clause thereof may be unconscionable the parties shall be afforded a reasonable opportunity to present evidence as to its commercial setting, purpose and effect to aid the court in making the determination.

Study Guide: Do the following Restatement (Second) section and commentary make the concept of unconscionability any clearer? Can you see the influence of Professor Leff's distinction on these comments? Do they suggest a possible theoretical relationship between substantive and procedural unconscionability?

RESTATEMENT (SECOND) OF CONTRACTS

§208.   UNCONSCIONABLE CONTRACT OR TERM

If a contract or term thereof is unconscionable at the time the contract is made a court may refuse to enforce the contract, or may enforce the remainder of the contract without the unconscionable term, or may so limit the application of any unconscionable term as to avoid any unconscionable result.

COMMENT

a. Scope. Like the obligation of good faith and fair dealing (§205), the policy against unconscionable contracts or terms applies to a wide variety of types of conduct. The determination that a contract or term is or is not unconscionable is made in the light of its setting, purpose and effect. Relevant factors include weaknesses in the contracting process like those involved in more specific rules as to contractual capacity, fraud, and other invalidating causes; the policy also overlaps with rules which render particular bargains or terms unenforceable on grounds of public policy.

Policing against unconscionable contracts or terms has sometimes been accomplished "by adverse construction of language, by manipulation of the rules of offer and acceptance or by determinations that the clause is contrary to public policy or to the dominant purpose of the contract." Uniform Commercial Code §2-302 Comment 1. Particularly in the case of standardized agreements, the rule of this Section permits the court to pass directly on the unconscionability of the contract or clause rather than to avoid unconscionable results by interpretation. Compare §211.

b. Historic Standards. Traditionally, a bargain was said to be unconscionable in an action at law if it was "such as no man in his senses and not under delusion would make on the one hand, and as no honest and fair man would accept on the other"; damages were then limited to those to which the aggrieved party was "equitably" entitled. Hume v. United States, 132 U.S. 406 (1889), quoting Earl of Chesterfield v. Janssen, 2 Ves. Sen. 125, 155, 28 Eng. Rep. 82, 100 (Ch. 1750). Even though a contract was fully enforceable in an action for damages, equitable remedies such as specific performance were refused where "the sum total of its provisions drives too hard a bargain for a court of conscience to assist." Campbell Soup Co. v. Wentz, 172 F.2d 80, 84 (3d Cir. 1948). Modern procedural reforms have blurred the distinction between remedies at law and in equity. For contracts for the sale of goods, Uniform Commercial Code §2-302 states the rule of this Section without distinction between law and equity. Comment 1 to that section adds, "The principle is one of the prevention of oppression and unfair surprise (Cf. Campbell Soup Co. v. Wentz, . . .) and not of disturbance of allocation of risks because of superior bargaining power."

c. Overall Imbalance. Inadequacy of consideration does not of itself invalidate a bargain, but gross disparity in the values exchanged may be an important factor in a determination that a contract is unconscionable and may be sufficient ground, without more, for denying specific performance. See §§79, 364. Such a disparity may also corroborate indications of defects in the bargaining process, or may affect the remedy to be granted when there is a violation of a more specific rule. Theoretically it is possible for a contract to be oppressive taken as a whole, even though there is no weakness in the bargaining process and no single term which is in itself unconscionable. Ordinarily, however, an unconscionable contract involves other factors as well as overall imbalance. . . .

d. Weakness in the Bargaining Process. A bargain is not unconscionable merely because the parties to it are unequal in bargaining position, nor even because the inequality results in an allocation of risks to the weaker party. But gross inequality of bargaining power, together with terms unreasonably favorable to the stronger party, may confirm indications that the transaction involved elements of deception or compulsion, or may show that the weaker party had no meaningful choice, no real alternative, or did not in fact assent or appear to assent to the unfair terms. Factors which may contribute to a finding of unconscionability in the bargaining process include the following: belief by the stronger party that there is no reasonable probability that the weaker party will fully perform the contract; knowledge of the stronger party that the weaker party will be unable to receive substantial benefits from the contract; knowledge of the stronger party that the weaker party is unable reasonably to protect his interests by reason of physical or mental infirmities, ignorance, illiteracy or inability to understand the language of the agreement, or similar factors. . . .

e. Unconscionable Terms. Particular terms may be unconscionable whether or not the contract as a whole is unconscionable. Some types of terms are not enforced, regardless of context; examples are provisions for unreasonably large liquidated damages, or limitations on a debtor's right to redeem collateral. See Uniform Commercial Code §§2-718, 9-501(3). Other terms may be unconscionable in some contexts but not in others. Overall imbalance and weaknesses in the bargaining process are then important. . . .

f. Law and Fact. A determination that a contract or term is unconscionable is made by the court in the light of all the material facts. Under Uniform Commercial Code §2-302, the determination is made "as a matter of law," but the parties are to be afforded an opportunity to present evidence as to commercial setting, purpose and effect to aid the court in its determination. Incidental findings of fact are made by the court rather than by a jury, but are accorded the usual weight given to such findings of fact in appellate review. An appellate court will also consider whether proper standards were applied. . . .

g. Remedies. Perhaps the simplest application of the policy against unconscionable agreements is the denial of specific performance where the contract as a whole was unconscionable when made. If such a contract is entirely executory, denial of money damages may also be appropriate. But the policy is not penal: unless the parties can be restored to their pre-contract positions, the offending party will ordinarily be awarded at least the reasonable value of performance rendered by him. Where a term rather than the entire contract is unconscionable, the appropriate remedy is ordinarily to deny effect to the unconscionable term. In such cases as that of an exculpatory term, the effect may be to enlarge the liability of the offending party.

In Chapter 5, we considered whether all the terms in form contracts — sometimes pejoratively dubbed "contracts of adhesion" — are enforceable to the same extent as terms in negotiated contracts. We now turn to the closely related issue of whether some form contracts' terms are unenforceable because they are unconscionable.

STUDY GUIDE: When reading the next three cases, consider how the application of the defense of unconscionability to form contracts compares with the approach adopted by the Supreme Court in the Carnival Cruise case. In particular, how does the Supreme Court's inquiry into the "fundamental fairness" of the terms in a form contract compare with the defense of unconscionability? Are they the same?

In re REALNETWORKS

United States District Court, Northern District of Illinois,
Eastern Division,
2000 WL 631341 (2000)

KOCORAS, J. [RealNetworks' "clickwrap" agreement required arbitration in Washington state.] Intervenor argues that the License Agreement is procedurally unconscionable because it failed to provide fair notice of its contents and did not provide a reasonable opportunity to understand its terms before it was enforced. Both of these assertions are incorrect. Intervenor claims that the arbitration provision does not provide fair notice because it is "buried" in the License Agreement. Although burying important terms in a "maze of fine print" may contribute to a contract being found unconscionable, the arbitration provision in the License Agreement is not buried. . . . The License Agreement sets out the arbitration provision in the same size font as the rest of the agreement. . . . Moreover, it is not buried in the middle of the entire agreement or located in a footnote or appendix, but rather comprises the attention-getting final provision of the agreement. Although RealNetworks could have titled the heading containing the arbitration clause, the choice of law provision, and the forum selection clause in a more descriptive manner than "Miscellaneous," RealNetworks' titling it such does not necessarily bury the provision. While RealNetworks did not set off the arbitration provision and purposely draw attention to it, neither did RealNetworks bury the provision in a sea of words. Although burying an arbitration clause could contribute to a finding of unconscionability, the Court is unaware of, and Intervenor has not pointed to, any Washington state caselaw that provides that an arbitration clause is unconscionable if the contract does not draw attention to it.

Moreover, Intervenor claims that the user is not given a reasonable opportunity to understand the arbitration provision because the License Agreement comes in a small pop-up window, which is visually difficult to read, and because it cannot be printed. The Court has already discussed at length the capability of printing the License Agreement, and again rejects Intervenor's contention that the License Agreement cannot be printed. The Court also finds that the size of the pop-up window, although smaller than the desktop, does not make the License Agreement visually difficult to read. The Court finds disingenuous Intervenor's assertion that the License Agreement appears "in very fine print, requiring the user to position himself just inches from the monitor in order to read it." The font size of the License Agreement is no smaller, and possibly larger, than the font size of all the words appearing on the computer's own display. If Intervenor needs to plaster his face against the screen to read the License Agreement, he must then have to do the same to read anything on his computer, in which case, doing so does not seem like an inordinate hardship or an adjustment out of the ordinary for him. In addition, the user has all day to review the License Agreement on the screen. The pop-up window containing the License Agreement does not disappear after a certain time period; so, the user can scroll through it and examine it to his heart's content.

Because the arbitration agreement is not buried in fine print and because a user is given ample opportunity to understand the arbitration provision, the Court does not find that the arbitration agreement is procedurally unconscionable.

In addition, Intervenor asserts that the arbitration provision is substantively unconscionable because it chooses a geographically distant forum, it fails to provide for classwide arbitration, and the costs of arbitration are prohibitive.

The Court rejects Intervenor's claim that choosing Washington state as the arbitration forum renders the arbitration agreement substantively unconscionable. The designation of any state as a forum is bound to be distant to some potential litigants of a corporation that has a nationwide reach. Intervenor would have the Court essentially preclude arbitration agreements from having any forum selection clause in order to prevent the designation of a distant forum to any of these litigants. This Court is not willing to do so. Arbitration provisions containing forum selection clauses have previously been upheld. . . . Moreover, some courts have even found that the forum non conveniens doctrine is inapplicable in the context of arbitrations covered under the FAA. . . . Thus, that Washington is a distant arbitration forum for some does not render the arbitration clause substantively unconscionable.

Intervenor also claims that because litigants cannot pursue classwide arbitration without an arbitration provision providing for it, . . . RealNetworks is effectively preventing potential litigants from seeking classwide arbitration by not expressly providing for classwide arbitration. Further, Intervenor reasons that because consumers in cases such as this have relatively small claims, these consumers' rights to bring a case would essentially be vitiated because the costs of the litigation would be so prohibitive. This Court previously rejected this argument in its prior decision [in this case]. . . . The Seventh Circuit, along with other courts in this district, have considered this issue and upheld arbitration agreements that do not provide for class action and have even upheld arbitration agreements that expressly prohibit class actions. . . . Thus, the Court will not find the License Agreement substantively unconscionable because it does not provide for class arbitration.

Further, the Court rejects Intervenor's argument that allegedly prohibitive arbitration costs render the License Agreement unconscionable. The Seventh Circuit has found that the costs of arbitration do not prevent the enforcement of a valid arbitration agreement. . . . As such, the potential arbitration costs do not render the arbitration clause substantively unconscionable.

STUDY GUIDE: How does the California treatment of the unconscionability of an arbitration agreement in a form contract differ from that of the previous case? Does its characterization of form contracts as "contracts of adhesion" undermine its requirement that both procedural and substantive unconscionability be shown for the defense to succeed?

DISCOVER BANK v. SUPERIOR COURT
California Supreme Court,
36 Cal. 4th 148, 113 P.3d 1100 (2005)

MORENO, J.*

This case concerns the validity of a provision in an arbitration agreement between Discover Bank and a credit cardholder forbidding classwide arbitration. The credit cardholder, a California resident, alleges that Discover Bank had a practice of representing to cardholders that late payment fees would not be assessed if payment was received by a certain date, whereas in actuality they were assessed if payment was received after 1:00 p.m. on that date, thereby leading to damages that were small as to individual consumers but large in the aggregate. Plaintiff filed a complaint claiming damages for this alleged deceptive practice, and Discover Bank successfully moved to compel arbitration pursuant to its arbitration agreement with plaintiff.

Plaintiff now seeks to pursue a classwide arbitration, which is well accepted under California law. But plaintiff's arbitration agreement with Discover Bank has a clause forbidding classwide arbitration. . . . [W]e conclude that, at least under some circumstances, the law in California is that class action waivers in consumer contracts of adhesion are unenforceable, whether the consumer is being asked to waive the right to class action litigation or the right to classwide arbitration. . . .

I. FACTUAL AND PROCEDURAL BACKGROUND

Plaintiff Christopher Boehr obtained a credit card from defendant Discover Bank in April 1986. . . . When plaintiff's credit card was issued, the agreement did not contain an arbitration clause. Discover Bank subsequently added the arbitration clause in July 1999, pursuant to a change-of-terms provision in the agreement. Relying on the change-of-terms provision, Discover Bank added the arbitration clause by sending to its existing cardholders (including plaintiff) a notice that stated in relevant part: "NOTICE OF AMENDMENT. . . . WE ARE ADDING A NEW ARBITRATION SECTION WHICH PROVIDES THAT IN THE EVENT YOU OR WE ELECT TO RESOLVE ANY CLAIM OR DISPUTE BETWEEN US BY ARBITRATION, NEITHER YOU NOR WE SHALL HAVE THE RIGHT TO LITIGATE THAT CLAIM IN COURT OR TO HAVE A JURY TRIAL ON THAT CLAIM. THIS ARBITRATION SECTION WILL NOT APPLY TO LAWSUITS FILED BEFORE THE EFFECTIVE DATE."

---

* *Carlos R. Moreno* (1948-†) graduated with a degree in political science from Yale and earned his J.D. from Stanford in 1975. He began his legal career serving as a deputy city attorney with the Los Angeles City Attorney's office prosecuting criminal and civil consumer protection cases. In 1979, Moreno left for private practice and represented clients in commercial litigation. In 1986, Justice Moreno was appointed to the Municipal Court, Compton Judicial District, and in 1993, was subsequently elevated to the Los Angeles County Superior Court. Under President Clinton, he joined the United States District Court for the Central District of California in 1998. In 2001, Justice Moreno was confirmed to the Supreme Court of California. Moreno left the judiciary for private practice in 2011. — R.B.

In addition, the arbitration clause precluded both sides from participating in classwide arbitration, consolidating claims, or arbitrating claims as a representative or in a private attorney general capacity: ". . . NEITHER YOU NOR WE SHALL BE ENTITLED TO JOIN OR CONSOLIDATE CLAIMS IN ARBITRATION BY OR AGAINST OTHER CARDMEMBERS WITH RESPECT TO OTHER ACCOUNTS, OR ARBITRATE ANY CLAIM AS A REPRESENTATIVE OR MEMBER OF A CLASS OR IN A PRIVATE ATTORNEY GENERAL CAPACITY." . . .

Existing cardholders were notified that if they did not wish to accept the new arbitration clause, they must notify Discover Bank of their objections and cease using their accounts. Their continued use of an account would be deemed to constitute acceptance of the new terms. Plaintiff did not notify Discover Bank of any objection to the arbitration clause or cease using his account before the stated deadline.

On August 15, 2001, Boehr filed a putative class action complaint in superior court against Discover Bank. Plaintiff alleged . . . that Discover Bank breached its cardholder agreement by imposing a late fee of approximately $29 on payments that were received on the payment due date, but after Discover Bank's undisclosed 1:00 P.M. "cut-off time." Discover Bank also allegedly imposed a periodic finance charge (thereby disallowing a grace period) on new purchases when payments were received on the payment due date, but after 1:00 P.M. . . . Discover Bank moved to compel arbitration of plaintiff's claim on an individual basis and to dismiss the class action pursuant to the arbitration agreement's class action waiver.

Plaintiff opposed the motion, contending among other things that the class action waiver was unconscionable and unenforceable under California law.[39] Discover Bank, on the other hand, argued that the FAA requires the enforcement of the express provisions of an arbitration clause, including class action waivers. Discover Bank contended that under section 2 of the FAA, arbitration agreements should not be singled out for suspect status under state laws applicable only to arbitration provisions. . . .

II. DISCUSSION

A. Class Action Law Suits and Class Action Arbitration

Before addressing the questions at issue in this case, we first consider the justifications for class action lawsuits. These justifications were set forth in Justice Mosk's oft-quoted majority opinion in *Vasquez v. Superior Court* (1971) 4 Cal.3d 800, 808, 94 Cal. Rptr. 796, 484 P.2d 964 (*Vasquez*): "Frequently numerous consumers are exposed to the same dubious practice by the same seller so that proof of the prevalence of the practice as to one consumer would provide proof for all. Individual actions by each of the defrauded consumers is often impracticable because the amount of

---

39. Plaintiff also contended below that the unilateral addition of the arbitration clause was unconscionable under California law. That contention was rejected by the trial court and the Court of Appeal, and the issue was not raised in the petition for review. Accordingly, we do not address the issue. . . .

individual recovery would be insufficient to justify bringing a separate action; thus an unscrupulous seller retains the benefits of its wrongful conduct. A class action by consumers produces several salutary by-products, including a therapeutic effect upon those sellers who indulge in fraudulent practices, aid to legitimate business enterprises by curtailing illegitimate competition, and avoidance to the judicial process of the burden of multiple litigation involving identical claims. The benefit to the parties and the courts would, in many circumstances, be substantial." . . .

B.　The Enforceability of Class Action Waivers

. . . [P]laintiff contends that class action or arbitration waivers in consumer contracts, and in this particular contract, should be invalidated as unconscionable under California law.

> To briefly recapitulate the principles of unconscionability, the doctrine has both a "procedural" and a "substantive" element, the former focusing on "oppression" or "surprise" due to unequal bargaining power, the latter on "overly harsh" or "one-sided" results. The procedural element of an unconscionable contract generally takes the form of a contract of adhesion, "which, imposed and drafted by the party of superior bargaining strength, relegates to the subscribing party only the opportunity to adhere to the contract or reject it." Substantively unconscionable terms may take various forms, but may generally be described as unfairly one-sided. (Little v. Auto Stiegler, Inc. (2003) 29 Cal. 4th 1064, 1071, 130 Cal. Rptr. 2d 892, 63 P.3d 979.)

We agree that at least some class action waivers in consumer contracts are unconscionable under California law. First, when, a consumer is given an amendment to its cardholder agreement in the form of a "bill stuffer" that he would be deemed to accept if he did not close his account, an element of procedural unconscionability is present. Moreover, although adhesive contracts are generally enforced, class action waivers found in such contracts may also be substantively unconscionable inasmuch as they may operate effectively as exculpatory contract clauses that are contrary to public policy. As stated in Civil Code section 1668: "All contracts *which have for their object, directly or indirectly, to exempt anyone from responsibility for his own fraud, or willful injury* to the person or property of another, or violation of law, whether willful or negligent, are against the policy of the law." (Italics added.)

Class action and arbitration waivers are not, in the abstract, exculpatory clauses. But because, as discussed above, damages in consumer cases are often small and because "[a] company which wrongfully exacts a dollar from each of millions of customers will reap a handsome profit" ([Linder v. Thrifty Oil Co. (2000) 23 Cal. 4th 429, 446, 97 Cal. Rptr. 2d 179, 2 P.3d 27]), "the class action is often the only effective way to halt and redress such exploitation." Moreover, such class action or arbitration waivers are indisputably one-sided. "Although styled as a mutual prohibition on representative or class actions, it is difficult to envision the circumstances under which the provision might negatively impact Discover [Bank], because credit card companies typically do not sue their customers in class action lawsuits." ([Szetela v. Discover Bank (2002) 97 Cal. App. 4th 1094, 1101, 118 Cal. Rptr. 2d 862]) Such one-sided, exculpatory contracts in a contract of adhesion, at least to the extent they operate to insulate a party from liability that otherwise would be imposed under California law, are generally unconscionable. . . .

[We are not] persuaded by the rationale stated by some courts that the potential availability of attorney fees to the prevailing party in arbitration or litigation ameliorates the problem posed by such class action waivers. There is no indication other than these courts' unsupported assertions that, in the case of small individual recovery, attorney fees are an adequate substitute for the class action or arbitration mechanism. Nor do we agree with the concurring and dissenting opinion that small claims litigation, government prosecution, or informal resolution are adequate substitutes.

We do not hold that all class action waivers are necessarily unconscionable. But when the waiver is found in a consumer contract of adhesion in a setting in which disputes between the contracting parties predictably involve small amounts of damages, and when it is alleged that the party with the superior bargaining power has carried out a scheme to deliberately cheat large numbers of consumers out of individually small sums of money, then, at least to the extent the obligation at issue is governed by California law, the waiver becomes in practice the exemption of the party "from responsibility for [its] own fraud, or willful injury to the person or property of another." (Civ. Code, §1668.) Under these circumstances, such waivers are unconscionable under California law and should not be enforced. . . .

III. DISPOSITION

The judgment of the Court of Appeal is reversed, and the cause is remanded for proceedings consistent with this opinion.

Concurring and Dissenting Opinion by BAXTER, J.* . . .

The majority suggests that class waivers in standard consumer contracts may violate California's arguably "fundamental" statutory policy against direct or indirect "exculpatory" clauses. (See Civ. Code, §1668.) In the majority's view, such waivers may have an exculpatory effect because, given the usually modest amount of each cardholder's personal claim against Discover Bank, litigation or arbitration on an individual basis is impractical and uneconomic. The majority posits that because cardholders

---

Marvin R. Baxter (1940-†) attended California State University, where he graduated with a degree in economics, before attending the Hastings College of Law, where he completed his J.D. in 1966. Baxter served as Fresno County deputy district attorney for two years before moving into private civil practice for 13 years. Additionally, Baxter became the Appointments Secretary to Governor George Deukmejian and assisted in the appointment of more than 700 judges. In 1988, Baxter was appointed to the California Court of Appeal, Fifth Appellate District. In 1991, Baxter joined the Supreme Court of California as an associate justice. — R.B.

and their attorneys have no incentive to pursue such claims except by aggregating them with other similar complaints, Discover Bank will escape liability or punishment for its improper practices.

I find this analysis unpersuasive for several reasons. At the outset, I cannot accept the facile premise that lack of a class remedy is equivalent to exculpation of an alleged wrongdoer. Class treatment, in whatever forum, is a relatively recent invention, designed to encourage and facilitate the resolution of certain kinds of disputes. It may provide valuable procedural leverage to one side. But as we noted in Washington Mutual [v. Superior Court (2001) 24 Cal. 4th 906, 103 Cal. Rptr. 2d 320, 15 P.3d 1071], "[c]lass actions are provided *only as a means to enforce substantive law*." They must not be confused with the substantive law to be enforced. Even if the unavailability of class relief makes a plaintiff's pursuit of a particular claim "less convenient" (Moses H. Cone Hospital v. Mercury Constr. Corp. (1983) 460 U.S. 1, 19), such claims may nonetheless be pursued on an individual basis.

Moreover, the majority exaggerates the difficulty of pursuing modest claims where class treatment is unavailable and overlooks the many other means by which Discover Bank could be called to account for the mischarges plaintiff alleges. For example:

(1) The cardholder may contact the bank and attempt to resolve the matter informally. Discover Bank's cardholder agreement specifically provides a 60-day period in which to contact the company with billing questions and disputes. plaintiff's complaint does not state that he pursued this avenue. (Indeed, though the complaint asserts widespread improper billing practices by Discover Bank, it does not allege that the bank has ever mischarged plaintiff himself. Plaintiff admitted in his deposition that he does not know whether Discover Bank has ever done so.)

(2) ... The agreement includes several provisions designed to make the individual arbitration process fair and accessible. Under the agreement's terms, Discover Bank will arbitrate in the federal judicial district where the cardholder resides. Further, the cardholder may obtain an advance of all forum costs and will never pay forum costs exceeding those he or she would have had to pay in court litigation.

(3) For claims under $5,000, the cardholder may proceed in small claims court. (See Code Civ. Proc., §116.210 et seq.) In the cardholder agreement, Discover Bank promises that it "will not invoke [its] right to arbitrate an individual claim," involving less than $5,000, which is pending only in a small claims court. The only mandatory expense of a small claims action is a modest filing fee plus the actual cost of any mail service by the court clerk. The claim is pled by filling out a standard form. No formal discovery is permitted, and neither party may be represented by a lawyer, though free advisory assistance is available to the claimant.

(4) The cardholder may arbitrate, pursuant to the terms of the cardholder agreement, his rights under such federal statutes as [the

Truth-in-Lending Act].[40] This statute imposes mandatory disclosure requirements for consumer credit transactions, including
those arising on credit card accounts. As to the latter, the statute
provides for detailed disclosure of the terms on which credit is
being extended, including annual percentage rates, methods of
computing outstanding balances, finance charges, grace periods,
and late fees. The cardholder, if he or she prevails, may recover
actual damages, twice the finance charge imposed in connection
with each violative transaction, and attorney fees and costs.

(5) If Discover Bank's conduct violates California's unfair competition statutes, which broadly prohibit "any unlawful, unfair or
fraudulent business act or practice," the Attorney General and
designated local law enforcement officials (who are not bound
by the cardholder agreement) may sue on the People's behalf
for injunctive relief and for mandatory civil penalties of up to
$2,500 for each violation. The amount of a civil penalty shall be
calculated in accordance with "any one or more of the relevant
circumstances . . . including, but not limited to . . . the nature and
seriousness of the misconduct, the number of violations, the per-
sistence of the misconduct, the length of time over which the
misconduct occurred, the willfulness of the defendant's misconduct, and the defendant's assets, liabilities, and net worth."

(6) Finally, in the highly regulated banking and credit industry, other
means of sanctioning and remediating illegal conduct are
available. . . .

Under these circumstances, it cannot be said that, by upholding cardholders' contractual waiver of a class remedy . . . , we would effectively
absolve Discover Bank of its objectionable conduct. Thus, there is no
basis to conclude that enforcement of the class waiver . . . would contravene a fundamental California statutory policy against exculpatory
agreements.

*STUDY GUIDE: The next case expands upon the unconscionability doc-
trine of Discover Bank. Where does the issue of "bargaining power" fit
into the California court's analysis of unconscionability? Does the
majority equate the "adhesive" nature of a contract with procedural
unconscionability? If so, is this position reconcilable with the Supreme
Court's decision in Carnival Cruise (Chapter 5)? Does the majority disagree
with the dissent's insistence that, to be unenforceable, a contract must be
both procedurally and substantively unconscionable? If not, on what are
they disagreeing? Can you see any advantages to consumers of mandatory
arbitration clauses in form contracts? Do these advantages extend to a*

---

40. [F]ederal circuits addressing the issue have uniformly held that claimants must
arbitrate TILA claims pursuant to agreement, that arbitration precludes class relief under
TILA, that arbitration agreements containing express waivers of class treatment, even for
small individual amounts in dispute, are not unconscionable with respect to TILA claims, and
that, although TILA contemplates class actions, it includes no "unwaivable" right to class
relief.

waiver of the right to bring a class action lawsuit? Should any such analysis of advantage affect an analysis of unconscionability? If so, how? If not, why not? What is the relationship between the court's analysis of unconscionability and its view of public policy? [This may be the only case in the casebook in which both the majority and dissenting opinions were written by former schoolteachers; it is certainly the only case where both opinions were authored by women.]

GATTON v. T-MOBILE USA, INC.
Court of Appeal of California,
152 Cal. App. 4th 571 (2007)

GEMELLO, J.* . . .

-Mobile USA, Inc., appeals from an order denying its motion to compel arbitration of actions challenging the early termination fee charged to cellular telephone service subscribers and challenging the practice of selling locked handsets that a subscriber cannot use when switching carriers. T-Mobile contends the court erred in concluding that the arbitration clause in its service agreement is unconscionable. . . . [W]e hold that the adhesive nature of the service agreement established a minimal degree of procedural unconscionability notwithstanding the availability of market alternatives and that the high degree of substantive unconscionability arising from the class action waiver rendered the arbitration provision unenforceable. . . .

We affirm the trial court order.

FACTUAL AND PROCEDURAL BACKGROUND

THE PARTIES AND THE SERVICE AGREEMENTS

T-Mobile USA, Inc. (T-Mobile), is a cellular telephone provider in California. Plaintiffs are or were subscribers to T-Mobile. All plaintiffs executed service agreements drafted by T-Mobile. Each agreement incorporated terms and conditions drafted by T-Mobile. Directly above the signature line in the service agreement executed by plaintiffs is a short paragraph stating, "By signing below, you acknowledge you . . . have received a copy of this Agreement. . . . You also acknowledge you have received and reviewed the T-Mobile Terms and Conditions, and agree to be bound by them. . . . All disputes are subject to mandatory arbitration in accordance with paragraph 3 of the Terms and Conditions."

Linda M. Gemello (1945-†) was born in Montreal. Her first career was teaching English at Mountain View's Los Altos High School in the late 1960s and at Santa Clara University in the early 1970s. She received both her B.A. and J.D. degrees from Santa Clara. After graduating from law school in 1980, she worked as an associate for four years and a partner for 12 years at a Millbrae law firm before becoming a San Mateo County Superior Court judge in 1996. She was appointed to the Court of Appeals by Governor Gray Davis in 2002. The San Mateo County Trial Lawyers named Justice Gemello "Trial Judge of the Year" in 2000. — R.B.

The introductory paragraph to the terms and conditions incorporated into the agreement states: "Welcome to T-Mobile. BY ACTIVATING OR USING OUR SERVICE YOU AGREE TO BE BOUND BY THE AGREEMENT. Please carefully read these Terms and Conditions ("T & C's") as they describe your Service and affect your legal rights. IF YOU DON'T AGREE WITH THESE T & C'S, DO NOT USE THIS SERVICE OR YOUR UNIT." Similarly, the handset shipping box was sealed across the closing seam with a sticker that stated: "IMPORTANT [¶] Read the enclosed T-Mobile Terms & Conditions. By using T-Mobile service, you agree to be bound by the Terms & Conditions, including the mandatory arbitration and early termination fee provisions." The terms and conditions were also included in a "Welcome Guide" enclosed in the boxes containing the handsets.

Section 3 of the terms and conditions incorporated into the agreement is entitled "Mandatory Arbitration; Dispute Resolution." It includes language waiving any right to seek classwide relief.[41]

The terms and conditions incorporated into each of the plaintiff's agreements included a mandatory arbitration clause including a class action waiver. . . .

The action of plaintiffs Gatton, Hull, Nguyen, and Vaughan, brought on behalf of themselves individually and on behalf of all similarly situated California residents, challenges the [$200 per telephone] fee imposed by

---

41. Section 3 of the arbitration agreement provides:

YOU WILL FIRST NEGOTIATE WITH [T-MOBILE] IN GOOD FAITH TO SETTLE ANY CLAIM OR DISPUTE BETWEEN YOU AND US IN ANY WAY RELATED TO OR CONCERNING THE AGREEMENT, OR OUR PROVISION TO YOU OF GOODS, SERVICES OR UNITS ("CLAIM"). YOU MUST SEND A WRITTEN DESCRIPTION OF YOUR CLAIM TO OUR REGISTERED AGENT. [] IF YOU DO NOT REACH AGREEMENT WITH US WITHIN 30 DAYS, INSTEAD OF SUING IN COURT, YOU AGREE THAT ANY CLAIM MUST BE SUBMITTED TO FINAL, BINDING ARBITRATION WITH THE AMERICAN ARBITRATION ASSOCIATION ("AAA") UNDER ITS PUBLISHED WIRELESS INDUSTRY ARBITRATION RULES, WHICH ARE A PART OF THE AGREEMENT BY THIS REFERENCE AND ARE AVAILABLE BY CALLING THE AAA AT [listed telephone number] OR VISITING ITS WEB SITE AT [listed]. . . . You will pay your share of the arbitrator's fees except (a) for claims less than $25, we will pay all arbitrator's fees and (b) for claims between $25 and $1,000, you will pay $25 for the arbitrator's fee. You and we agree to pay our own other fees, costs and expenses including. . . .

Neither you nor we may be a representative of other potential claimants or a class of potential claimants in any dispute, nor may two or more individuals' disputes be consolidated or otherwise determined in one proceeding. While the prohibition on consolidated or classwide proceedings in this Sec. 3 will continue to apply: (a) you may take claims to small claims court, if they qualify for hearing by such court and (b) if you fail to timely pay amounts due, we may assign your account for collection and the collection agency may pursue such claims in court limited strictly to the collection of the past due debt and any interest or cost of collection permitted by law or the Agreement. YOU AND WE ACKNOWLEDGE AND AGREE THAT THIS SEC. 3 WAIVES ANY RIGHT TO A JURY TRIAL OR PARTICIPATION AS A PLAINTIFF OR AS A CLASS MEMBER IN A CLASS ACTION. IF A COURT OR ARBITRATOR DETERMINES THAT YOUR WAIVER OF YOUR ABILITY TO PURSUE CLASS OR REPRESENTATIVE CLAIMS IS UNENFORCEABLE, THE ARBITRATION AGREEMENT WILL NOT APPLY AND OUR DISPUTE WILL BE RESOLVED BY A COURT OF APPROPRIATE JURISDICTION, OTHER THAN A SMALL CLAIMS COURT. SHOULD ANY OTHER PROVISION OF THIS ARBITRATION AGREEMENT BE DEEMED UNENFORCEABLE, THAT PROVISION SHALL BE REMOVED, AND THE AGREEMENT SHALL OTHERWISE REMAIN BINDING.

T-Mobile for termination of the service agreement before its expiration date. . . . The action of plaintiffs Nguyen and Grant, brought on behalf of themselves individually and on behalf of all similarly situated California residents, challenges the practice of installing a locking device in T-Mobile handsets that prevents its subscribers from switching cell phone providers without purchasing a new handset. . . .

MOTION TO COMPEL ARBITRATION

T-Mobile moved to compel arbitration of the two actions in accord with the service agreement. Plaintiffs opposed the motion on the ground[] that . . . the arbitration clause was unconscionable.

The trial court denied the motion to compel. It concluded . . . that the arbitration provision was unconscionable and therefore unenforceable. The trial court held that although the indications of procedural unconscionability were "not particularly strong," under Discover Bank v. Superior Court (2005) 36 Cal. 4th 148, 30 Cal. Rptr. 3d 76, 113 P.3d 1100, the arbitration clause was substantively unconscionable because its prohibition on class arbitrations or participation in a class action was against public policy.

DISCUSSION

Appellant T-Mobile contends the trial court erred in denying its motion to compel because the class action waiver did not render the arbitration provision unconscionable. . . . An agreement to arbitrate is valid except when grounds exist for revocation of a contract. Unconscionability is one ground on which a court may refuse to enforce a contract. . . . Unconscionability has a procedural and a substantive element; the procedural element focuses on the existence of oppression or surprise and the substantive element focuses on overly harsh or one-sided results. To be unenforceable, a contract must be both procedurally and substantively unconscionable, but the elements need not be present in the same degree. The analysis employs a sliding scale: "the more substantively oppressive the contract term, the less evidence of procedural unconscionability is required to come to the conclusion that the term is unenforceable, and vice versa."

THE *DISCOVER BANK* DECISION

Our analysis of the challenged arbitration provision is governed by the California Supreme Court decision *Discover Bank*. There, the court considered an unconscionability challenge to an arbitration provision prohibiting classwide arbitration in an agreement between a credit card company and its cardholders. The provision was added to the agreement by a notice sent to cardholders.

The court emphasized the "important role of class action remedies in California law." . . . In analyzing the unconscionability issue, *Discover Bank* first concluded that "when a consumer is given an amendment to its cardholder agreement in the form of a 'bill stuffer' that he would be deemed to accept if he did not close his account, an element of procedural unconscionability is present." Turning to the substantive element, the court stated "although adhesive contracts are generally enforced [citation], class action waivers found in such contracts may also be substantively unconscionable inasmuch as they may operate effectively as exculpatory contract clauses that are contrary to public policy. As stated in Civil Code section 1668: '*All contracts which have for their object, directly or indirectly, to exempt anyone from responsibility for his own fraud, or willful injury* to the person or property of another, or violation of law, whether willful or negligent, are against the policy of the law.'" (Italics added.) The court acknowledged that class action and class arbitration waivers are not, in the abstract, exculpatory clauses, but because damages in consumer cases are often small and "because '[a] company which wrongfully exacts a dollar from each of millions of customers will reap a handsome profit,' 'the class action is often the only effective way to halt and redress such exploitation.'" Moreover, the court recognized that such class action and class arbitration waivers are "indisputably one-sided." "Although styled as a mutual prohibition on representative or class actions, it is difficult to envision the circumstances under which the provision might negatively impact Discover [Bank], because credit card companies typically do not sue their customers in class action lawsuits."

In light of those considerations, *Discover Bank* held that when a waiver of classwide relief "is found in a consumer contract of adhesion in a setting in which disputes between the contracting parties predictably involve small amounts of damages, and when it is alleged that the party with the superior bargaining power has carried out a scheme to deliberately cheat large numbers of consumers out of individually small sums of money, then, at least to the extent the obligation at issue is governed by California law, the waiver becomes in practice the exemption of the party 'from responsibility for [its] own fraud, or willful injury to the person or property of another.' (Civ. Code, §1668.) Under these circumstances, such waivers are unconscionable under California law and should not be enforced."

Against this legal backdrop, we consider the specific provision challenged here.

PROCEDURAL UNCONSCIONABILITY

The procedural element of the unconscionability analysis concerns the manner in which the contract was negotiated and the circumstances of the parties at that time. The element focuses on oppression or surprise. "Oppression arises from an inequality of bargaining power that results in no real negotiation and an absence of meaningful choice."[42] Surprise is defined as "the extent to which the supposedly agreed-upon terms of the

42. Oppression in the manner of formation of the contract is distinguished from substantive oppressiveness of the challenged provision. Even if the manner of formation of a contract involves oppression and thereby satisfies the procedural unconscionability element, the challenged provision is unenforceable only if it is unduly unfair or oppressive in substance.

bargain are hidden in the prolix printed form drafted by the party seeking to enforce the disputed terms."

In their reply brief, plaintiffs did not dispute T-Mobile's assertion that the surprise aspect of procedural unconscionability is absent because the arbitration provision was fully disclosed to T-Mobile's customers. In response to our request for supplemental briefing, plaintiffs first urged that surprise is not necessary to find procedural unconscionability. Plaintiffs then asserted that we could find surprise because T-Mobile did not specifically bring to the attention of its customers that the arbitration provision included a class action waiver and because the print used in the agreement was small. We conclude that plaintiffs have not shown surprise. The arbitration provision was not disguised or hidden, and T-Mobile made affirmative efforts to bring the provision to the attention of its customers, including by referencing the provision on a sticker placed across the closing seam of the handset shipping box. A finding of procedural unconscionability in this case cannot be based on the existence of surprise.

The California Supreme Court has consistently reiterated that "[t]he procedural element of an unconscionable contract generally takes the form of a contract of adhesion." *Discover Bank*. Appellate courts considering unconscionability challenges in consumer cases have routinely found the procedural element satisfied where the agreement containing the challenged provision was a contract of adhesion. . . .

Whether the challenged provision is within a contract of adhesion pertains to the oppression aspect of procedural unconscionability. A contract of adhesion is "imposed and drafted by the party of superior bargaining strength" and "relegates to the subscribing party only the opportunity to adhere to the contract or reject it." *Discover Bank*. This definition closely parallels the description of the oppression aspect of procedural unconscionability, which "arises from an inequality of bargaining power that results in no real negotiation and an absence of meaningful choice." It is clear that the T-Mobile service agreement was a contract of adhesion: T-Mobile drafted the form agreement, its bargaining strength was far greater than that of individual customers, and customers were required to accept all terms and conditions of the agreement as presented or forgo T-Mobile's telephone service.

Nevertheless, T-Mobile argues that there was no oppression in the formation of the agreements because plaintiffs had the option of obtaining mobile phone service from one of two other providers whose agreements did not contain class action waivers. Preliminarily, we note that the evidence of the availability of market alternatives is exceedingly slim. More fundamentally, we reject the contention that the existence of market choice altogether negates the oppression aspect of procedural unconscionability. "Procedural unconscionability focuses on the manner in which the disputed clause is presented to the party in the weaker bargaining position. When the weaker party is presented the clause and told to 'take it or leave it' without the opportunity for meaningful negotiation, oppression, and therefore procedural unconscionability, are present." The existence of consumer choice decreases the extent of procedural unconscionability but does not negate the oppression and obligate courts to enforce the challenged provision regardless of the extent of substantive unfairness. The existence of consumer choice is relevant, but it is not determinative of the entire issue.[43]

We considered market alternatives as a relevant factor in our decision in Marin Storage [v. Benco Contracting & Engineering, Inc. (2001) 89 Cal. App. 4th 1042, 107 Cal. Rptr. 2d 645]. There, a general contractor challenged the enforceability of an indemnification provision in a form subcontract created by a crane rental company. The procedural element was satisfied because the agreement at issue was "a contract of adhesion and, hence, procedurally unconscionable." But the degree of procedural unconscionability was limited because the contractor was sophisticated and had choice in selecting crane providers; in fact the plaintiff had done business with ten other firms. We also considered substantive unconscionability and concluded that, viewed in its commercial context, the indemnification provision was not overly one-sided or unreasonable. Balancing the procedural and substantive elements, we concluded that "[i]n light of the low level of procedural unfairness . . . a greater degree of substantive unfairness than has been shown here was required before the contract could be found substantively unconscionable."

The Marin Storage approach is consistent with the instruction in [Armendariz v. Foundation Health Psychcare Services, Inc. (2000) 24 Cal. 4th 83, 114, 99 Cal. Rptr. 2d 745, 6 P.3d 669], that the elements of procedural and substantive unconscionability "need not be present in the same degree." The court explained: "Essentially a sliding scale is invoked which disregards the regularity of the procedural process of the contract formation, that creates the terms, in proportion to the greater harshness or unreasonableness of the substantive terms themselves. In other words, the more substantively oppressive the contract term, the less evidence of procedural unconscionability is required to come to the conclusion that the term is unenforceable, and vice versa." . . .

The rule T-Mobile asks us to adopt disregards the sliding scale balancing required by Armendariz; in the absence of evidence of surprise, the proposed rule would allow any evidence of consumer choice to trump all other considerations, mandating courts to enforce the challenged provisions without considering the degree of substantive unfairness and the potential harm to important public policies. Although contracts of adhesion are well accepted in the law and routinely enforced, the inherent inequality of bargaining power supports an approach to unconscionability that preserves the role of the courts in reviewing the substantive fairness of challenged provisions. Otherwise, the imbalance of power creates an opportunity for overreaching in drafting form agreements. The possibility of overreaching is even greater in ordinary consumer transactions involving relatively inexpensive goods or services because consumers have little incentive to carefully scrutinize the contract terms or to research whether there are adequate alternatives with different terms, and companies have every business incentive to craft the terms carefully and to their advantage. The unconscionability doctrine ensures that companies are not permitted

43. Notably, we believe the issue before us is properly framed as whether the existence of market choice negates the existence of oppression, not whether choice renders a contract nonadhesive.

to exploit this dynamic by imposing overly one-sided and onerous terms. In sum, there are provisions so unfair or contrary to public policy that the law will not allow them to be imposed in a contract of adhesion, even if theoretically the consumer had an opportunity to discover and use an alternate provider for the good or service involved.

We reject the rule proposed by T-Mobile. Instead we hold that absent unusual circumstances,[44] use of a contract of adhesion establishes a minimal degree of procedural unconscionability notwithstanding the availability of market alternatives. If the challenged provision does not have a high degree of substantive unconscionability, it should be enforced. But, under *Armendariz*, we conclude that courts are not obligated to enforce highly unfair provisions that undermine important public policies simply because there is some degree of consumer choice in the market. . . .

We conclude that plaintiffs showed a minimal degree of procedural unconscionability arising from the adhesive nature of the agreement. But this is "the beginning and not the end of the analysis insofar as enforceability of its terms is concerned." Under the sliding scale approach, plaintiffs were obligated to make a strong showing of substantive unconscionability to render the arbitration provision unenforceable.

SUBSTANTIVE UNCONSCIONABILITY

The substantive element of the unconscionability analysis focuses on overly harsh or one-sided results. In light of *Discover Bank*, we conclude that the challenged provision has a high degree of substantive unconscionability.

In considering whether class action waivers may be unconscionable, *Discover Bank* emphasized that class actions are often the only effective way to halt corporate wrongdoing and that class action waivers are "indisputably one-sided" because companies typically do not sue their customers in class action lawsuits. The court did not conclude that all class action waivers are necessarily unconscionable, but the court did hold that "when the waiver is found in a consumer contract of adhesion in a setting in which disputes between the contracting parties predictably involve small amounts of damages, and when it is alleged that the party with the superior bargaining power has carried out a scheme to deliberately cheat large numbers of consumers out of individually small sums of money," then the waiver is exculpatory in effect and unconscionable under California law. . . .

In the consumer context, class actions and arbitrations are "often inextricably linked to the vindication of substantive rights." *Discover Bank*. There is nothing extraordinary about the circumstances of this case that distinguishes it from the typical consumer class actions described in *Discover Bank*. Because it is directly within the scope of the holding in that case, we conclude that the class action waiver has a high degree of

---

44. . . . Where the plaintiff is highly sophisticated and the challenged provision does not undermine important public policies, a court might be justified in denying an unconscionability claim for lack of procedural unconscionability even where the provision is within a contract of adhesion.

substantive unconscionability. Applying the sliding scale test for unconscionability, even though the evidence of procedural unconscionability is limited, the evidence of substantive unconscionability is strong enough to tip the scale and render the arbitration provision unconscionable. The trial court properly denied the motion to compel arbitration.

The order denying the motion to compel arbitration is affirmed. Costs are awarded to plaintiffs.

JONES, P.J.,* concurring and dissenting.

Under compulsion of *Discover Bank*, I concur in my colleagues' conclusion that the arbitration clauses before us are substantively unconscionable because of the prohibition in the mandatory arbitration provision against the pursuit of any remedy by a plaintiff as a representative of other potential claimants or class of claimants. But I cannot agree that the contracts are also procedurally unconscionable. In my view, plaintiffs do not show, on the record before us, either surprise or oppression to support their procedural unconscionability claim. In the absence of both procedural and substantive elements of unconscionability, this court should decline to exercise its discretion to refuse to enforce the disputed clause. The trial court erred when it denied the motion to compel arbitration, and its order so holding should be reversed. . . .

It is well settled that an agreement to arbitrate is valid, irrevocable, and enforceable except when grounds exist for the revocation of any contract (Code Civ. Proc., §§1281, 1281.2, subd. (b)), and it is equally settled that a court can refuse to enforce an unconscionable provision in a contract. (Civ. Code, §1670.5.) . . .

While the existence of a contract of adhesion is frequently the starting point for a procedural unconscionability analysis, adhesiveness and procedural unconscionability are discrete concepts. In my view, a contract of adhesion is not per se procedurally unconscionable. Even assuming the parties to the agreement do not have equal bargaining power, a realistic opportunity for the weaker party to avail him- or herself of meaningful market alternatives can obviate oppression for purposes of procedural unconscionability. I do not disagree . . . that the availability of alternate sources of a product or service without binding the consumer to the objectionable class action waiver is not the "determinative" factor. But it is a relevant factor. Indeed, the greater the number of alternatives available to the consumer, the more bargaining power is shifted to the consumer. I do not suggest that the existence of marketplace choice altogether negates the oppression aspect of procedural unconscionability. The extent and significance of meaningful alternatives must be assessed in the light of the

---

* *Barbara Jones* (1943-†) became the first female to serve as Presiding Justice of the Court of Appeal, First Appellate District, Division 5, in 1996 after sitting for four years as a Judge of the San Francisco Superior Court. A 1965 graduate of Duke University, she received her J.D. degree from the University of San Francisco School of Law in 1974, where she served on the Law Review. For over 16 years, Justice Jones practiced civil litigation, emphasizing general business and personal injury matters before being appointed to the bench by Governor Pete Wilson. She was born in Plainfield, New Jersey, and, prior to entering law school, was an elementary school teacher and editor of social studies textbooks as well as executive secretary to a U.S. congressman. Her interests include gardening and road cycling. — R.B.

particular circumstances of each transaction. Analyzed in this light, I conclude the service agreement herein has not been shown to be procedurally unconscionable.

As T-Mobile argues, and plaintiffs do not dispute, when plaintiffs entered into their service agreements with T-Mobile, two other nationwide wireless telephone companies, Nextel and Sprint, had service agreements that did not contain a class action waiver provision, and, in the case of Nextel, no arbitration agreement at all.

Furthermore, this agreement was presented to the customer at the time of the initial purchase, and, even after the purchase, the customer had a 14-day return period from date of activation, or a 30-day return period from date of purchase if not activated. These facts distinguish it from . . . *Discover Bank*, in which the bank sent their existing bankcard customers a mandatory arbitration/class action waiver provision as a "bill stuffer" addendum to their existing service agreements and forced the customers either to accept the new terms or to cancel their established accounts. While the T-Mobile customers may not have been able to negotiate the arbitration/class action waiver provision in the service agreement as part of their purchase negotiation, they were not confronted with a post-purchase choice of either accepting a more restrictive clause to an extant agreement, or forgoing entirely the service they had originally agreed to and enjoyed.

As *Armendariz* and other decisions make plain, adhesive contracts of employment present very different policy considerations from the adhesive consumer contract for a service such as a cell phone. Employment contracts that contain mandatory arbitration clauses are especially susceptible to being oppressive because "in the case of preemployment arbitration contracts, the economic pressure exerted by employers on all but the most sought-after employees may be particularly acute, for the arbitration agreement stands between the employee and necessary employment, and few employees are in a position to refuse a job because of an arbitration requirement."

Nothing like the economic pressure of obtaining or retaining employment is present in this case. However useful, convenient, or necessary cell phones may be, they are qualitatively different from the offer of a job, or the offer of continued employment, or the imposition of a more restrictive policy to an existing employment or after one has accepted employment, for which the job seeker or employee has no realistic alternative. An employee who has no opportunity to negotiate an employer's mandatory arbitration clause in the employment contract is limited to agreeing to the clause or forfeiting a paycheck and livelihood, and often crucial attendant benefits such as health care insurance or an employer-sponsored pension program. Here, the contract at issue concerned a non-unique consumer good — mobile phone service — available new and used from several sources. There was no evidence that plaintiffs were unaware of the existence of other cell phone providers or that the services of the other providers were not available to them.

Notwithstanding the imbalance in the bargaining power between T-Mobile and its cell phone subscribers, plaintiffs have not persuaded me there is procedural unconscionability in the making of the service agreement. Plaintiffs were fully apprised of the terms of the service agreement, and they did not present evidence of lack of meaningful alternative sources or other arrangements to meet their cellular telephone needs. In these circumstances, T-Mobile's conduct cannot be deemed oppressive.

As I stated at the outset, the *Armendariz* analytic framework requires *both* procedural and substantive elements before a court can exercise its discretion to refuse to enforce a contract under the unconscionability doctrine. Because there is an absence on this record of both the surprise and oppression factors of procedural unconscionability, the service agreement is not unconscionable, and T-Mobile's motion to compel arbitration should be granted.

REFERENCE: Barnett, §3.5
                 Farnsworth, §§4.27-4.28
                 Calamari & Perillo, §§9.37-9.40
                 Murray, §97

E.   ENFORCEABILITY OF ARBITRATION CLAUSES IN FORM CONTRACTS

As evidenced by the previous cases, clauses barring classwide arbitration claims in form contracts have come under special scrutiny in California and elsewhere. Part of this is due to the policy arguments favoring class action suits described in *Discover Bank*. But some of this scrutiny is motivated by a longstanding judicial hostility toward clauses mandating private arbitration. This hostility was such that in 1925, Congress enacted the Federal Arbitration Act (FAA) to protect mandatory arbitration clauses from being treated less favorably by states than other contracts clauses. In essence, the Act prohibits discrimination by state legislatures and courts against these particular clauses, giving rise to the need to detect whether a statute or court decision is discriminating or not. In the next case, the U.S. Supreme Court considers whether the rule in *Discover Bank* is discriminatory.

STUDY GUIDE: Under California unconscionability doctrine, does the adverse treatment of classwide arbitration clauses arise from a hostility to arbitration, or from a hostility to form contracts? Or does that not matter to the discriminatory effect on arbitration clauses that is barred by the FAA? Hint. In equal protection cases, the Court sometimes looks for a "disparate impact" of a state law or practice upon constitutionally protected groups. Perhaps that approach is influencing its protection of arbitration clauses from discrimination.

AT&T MOBILITY v. CONCEPCION
United States Supreme Court,
563 U.S. 333 (2011)

JUSTICE SCALIA* delivered the opinion of the Court.

---

*Antonin Scalia (1936-2016) received his A.B. from Georgetown University and the University of Fribourg, Switzerland, and his LL.B. from Harvard Law School, and was a Sheldon Fellow of Harvard University from 1960 to 1961. He was in private practice in Cleveland, Ohio, from 1961 to 1967, a Professor of Law at the University of Virginia from

Section 2 of the Federal Arbitration Act (FAA) makes agreements to arbitrate "valid, irrevocable, and enforceable, save upon such grounds as exist at law or in equity for the revocation of any contract." 9 U.S.C. §2. We consider whether the FAA prohibits States from conditioning the enforceability of certain arbitration agreements on the availability of classwide arbitration procedures.

In February 2002, Vincent and Liza Concepcion entered into an agreement for the sale and servicing of cellular telephones with AT&T Mobility LCC (AT&T). The contract provided for arbitration of all disputes between the parties, but required that claims be brought in the parties' "individual capacity, and not as a plaintiff or class member in any purported class or representative proceeding." . . .

The revised agreement provides that customers may initiate dispute proceedings by completing a one-page Notice of Dispute form available on AT&T's Web site. AT&T may then offer to settle the claim; if it does not, or if the dispute is not resolved within 30 days, the customer may invoke arbitration by filing a separate Demand for Arbitration, also available on AT&T's Web site. In the event the parties proceed to arbitration, the agreement specifies that AT&T must pay all costs for nonfrivolous claims; that arbitration must take place in the county in which the customer is billed; that, for claims of $10,000 or less, the customer may choose whether the arbitration proceeds in person, by telephone, or based only on submissions; that either party may bring a claim in small claims court in lieu of arbitration; and that the arbitrator may award any form of individual relief, including injunctions and presumably punitive damages. The agreement, moreover, denies AT&T any ability to seek reimbursement of its attorney's fees, and, in the event that a customer receives an arbitration award greater than AT&T's last written settlement offer, requires AT&T to pay a $7,500 minimum recovery and twice the amount of the claimant's attorney's fees.[45]

The Concepcions purchased AT&T service, which was advertised as including the provision of free phones; they were not charged for the phones, but they were charged $30.22 in sales tax based on the phones' retail value. In March 2006, the Concepcions filed a complaint against AT&T in the United States District Court for the Southern District of California. The complaint was later consolidated with a putative class action alleging, among other things, that AT&T had engaged in false advertising and fraud by charging sales tax on phones it advertised as free.

In March 2008, AT&T moved to compel arbitration under the terms of its contract with the Concepcions. The Concepcions opposed the motion, contending that the arbitration agreement was unconscionable and

---

1967 to 1971, and a Professor of Law at the University of Chicago from 1977 to 1982. He was also a visiting professor of law at the Georgetown Law Center University and Stanford University. He was chairman of the American Bar Association's Section of Administrative Law, 1981-1982, and its Conference of Section Chairmen, 1982-1983. He served the federal government as General Counsel of the Office of Telecommunications Policy from 1971 to 1972, Chairman of the Administrative Conference of the United States from 1972 to 1974, and Assistant Attorney General for the Office of Legal Counsel from 1974 to 1977. President Reagan appointed him to the United States Court of Appeals for the District of Columbia Circuit in 1982, and in 1986 nominated him to be an Associate Justice of the Supreme Court. — R.B.

45. The guaranteed minimum recovery was increased in 2009 to $10,000.

unlawfully exculpatory under California law because it disallowed class-wide procedures. The District Court denied AT&T's motion. It described AT&T's arbitration agreement favorably, noting, for example, that the informal dispute resolution process was "quick, easy to use" and likely to "promp[t] full or . . . even excess payment to the customer without the need to arbitrate or litigate"; that the $7,500 premium functioned as "a substantial inducement for the consumer to pursue the claim in arbitration" if a dispute was not resolved informally; and that consumers who were members of a class would likely be worse off. Laster v. T-Mobile USA, Inc., (SD Cal., Aug. 11, 2008). Nevertheless, relying on the California Supreme Court's decision in Discover Bank v. Superior Court, 36 Cal. 4th 148, 113 P.3d 1100 (2005), the court found that the arbitration provision was unconscionable because AT&T had not shown that bilateral arbitration adequately substituted for the deterrent effects of class actions.

The Ninth Circuit affirmed, also finding the provision unconscionable under California law as announced in *Discover Bank*. It also held that the *Discover Bank* rule was not preempted by the FAA because that rule was simply "a refinement of the unconscionability analysis applicable to contracts generally in California." . . .

We granted certiorari.

II

The FAA was enacted in 1925 in response to widespread judicial hostility to arbitration agreements. Section 2, the "primary substantive provision of the Act," Moses H. Cone Memorial Hospital v. Mercury Constr. Corp, 460 U.S. 1, 24 (1983), provides, in relevant part, as follows:

> A written provision in any maritime transaction or a contract evidencing a transaction involving commerce to settle by arbitration a controversy thereafter arising out of such contract or transaction . . . shall be valid, irrevocable, and enforceable, save upon such grounds as exist at law or in equity for the revocation of any contract.

We have described this provision as reflecting both a "liberal federal policy favoring arbitration," *Moses H. Cone*, and the "fundamental principle that arbitration is a matter of contract," Rent-A-Center, West, Inc. v. Jackson, 561 U.S. _____ (2010). In line with these principles, courts must place arbitration agreements on an equal footing with other contracts, and enforce them according to their terms.

The final phrase of §2, however, permits arbitration agreements to be declared unenforceable "upon such grounds as exist at law or in equity for the revocation of any contract." This saving clause permits agreements to arbitrate to be invalidated by "generally applicable contract defenses, such as fraud, duress, or unconscionability," but not by defenses that apply only to arbitration or that derive their meaning from the fact that an agreement to arbitrate is at issue. The question in this case is whether §2 preempts California's rule classifying most collective-arbitration waivers in consumer contracts as unconscionable. We refer to this rule as the *Discover Bank* rule.

Under California law, courts may refuse to enforce any contract found "to have been unconscionable at the time it was made," or may "limit the application of any unconscionable clause." Cal. Civ. Code Ann. §1670.5(a). A finding of unconscionability requires "a 'procedural' and a 'substantive' element, the former focusing on 'oppression' or 'surprise' due to unequal bargaining power, the latter on 'overly harsh' or 'one-sided' results." Armendariz v. Foundation Health Psychcare Servs., Inc., 24 Cal. 4th 83, 114 (2000).

In *Discover Bank*, the California Supreme Court applied this framework to class-action waivers in arbitration agreements and held as follows:

> [W]hen the waiver is found in a consumer contract of adhesion in a setting in which disputes between the contracting parties predictably involve small amounts of damages, and when it is alleged that the party with the superior bargaining power has carried out a scheme to deliberately cheat large numbers of consumers out of individually small sums of money, then . . . the waiver becomes in practice the exemption of the party "from responsibility for [its] own fraud, or willful injury to the person or property of another." Under these circumstances, such waivers are unconscionable under California law and should not be enforced. (quoting Cal. Civ. Code Ann. §1668).

California courts have frequently applied this rule to find arbitration agreements unconscionable.

III

A

The Concepcions argue that the *Discover Bank* rule, given its origins in California's unconscionability doctrine and California's policy against exculpation, is a ground that "exist[s] at law or in equity for the revocation of any contract" under FAA §2. . . . When state law prohibits outright the arbitration of a particular type of claim, the analysis is straightforward: The conflicting rule is displaced by the FAA. But the inquiry becomes more complex when a doctrine normally thought to be generally applicable, such as duress or, as relevant here, unconscionability, is alleged to have been applied in a fashion that disfavors arbitration. In Perry v. Thomas, 482 U.S. 483 (1987), for example, we noted that the FAA's preemptive effect might extend even to grounds traditionally thought to exist "at law or in equity for the revocation of any contract." We said that a court may not "rely on the uniqueness of an agreement to arbitrate as a basis for a state-law holding that enforcement would be unconscionable, for this would enable the court to effect what . . . the state legislature cannot."

An obvious illustration of this point would be a case finding unconscionable or unenforceable as against public policy consumer arbitration agreements that fail to provide for judicially monitored discovery. The rationalizations for such a holding are neither difficult to imagine nor different in kind from those articulated in *Discover Bank*. A court might reason that no consumer would knowingly waive his right to full discovery, as this would enable companies to hide their wrongdoing. Or the court might simply say that such agreements are exculpatory — restricting discovery would be of greater benefit to the company than the consumer, since the former is more likely to be sued than to sue. See *Discover Bank* (arguing that class waivers are similarly one-sided). And, the reasoning would continue, because such a rule applies the general principle of unconscionability or public-policy disapproval of exculpatory agreements, it is applicable to "any" contract and thus preserved by §2 of the FAA. In practice, of course, the rule would have a disproportionate impact on arbitration agreements; but it would presumably apply to contracts purporting to restrict discovery in litigation as well.

Other examples are easy to imagine. The same argument might apply to a rule classifying as unconscionable arbitration agreements that fail to abide by the Federal Rules of Evidence, or that disallow an ultimate disposition by a jury (perhaps termed "a panel of twelve lay arbitrators" to help avoid preemption). Such examples are not fanciful, since the judicial hostility towards arbitration that prompted the FAA had manifested itself in "a great variety" of "devices and formulas" declaring arbitration against public policy. Robert Lawrence Co. v. Devonshire Fabrics, Inc., 271 F.2d 402, 406 (CA2 1959). And although these statistics are not definitive, it is worth noting that California's courts have been more likely to hold contracts to arbitrate unconscionable than other contracts. Broome, An Unconscionable Application of the Unconscionability Doctrine: How the California Courts are Circumventing the Federal Arbitration Act, 3 Hastings Bus. L.J. 39, 54, 66 (2006); Randall, Judicial Attitudes Toward Arbitration and the Resurgence of Unconscionability, 52 Buffalo L. Rev. 185, 186-187 (2004). . . .

The overarching purpose of the FAA, evident in the text of §§2, 3, and 4, is to ensure the enforcement of arbitration agreements according to their terms so as to facilitate streamlined proceedings. Requiring the availability of classwide arbitration interferes with fundamental attributes of arbitration and thus creates a scheme inconsistent with the FAA.

B

. . . California's *Discover Bank* rule . . . interferes with arbitration. Although the rule does not require classwide arbitration, it allows any party to a consumer contract to demand it ex post. The rule is limited to adhesion contracts, but the times in which consumer contracts were anything other than adhesive are long past. . . . Hill v. Gateway 2000, Inc., 105 F. 3d 1147, 1149 (CA7 1997). The rule also requires that damages be predictably small, and that the consumer allege a scheme to cheat consumers. The former requirement, however, is toothless and malleable (the Ninth Circuit has held that damages of $4,000 are sufficiently small . . .), and the latter has no limiting effect, as all that is required is an allegation. Consumers remain free to bring and resolve their disputes on a bilateral basis under *Discover Bank*, and some may well do so; but there is little incentive for lawyers to arbitrate on behalf of individuals when they may do so for a class and reap far higher fees in the process. And faced with inevitable class arbitration, companies would have less incentive to continue resolving potentially duplicative claims on an individual basis. . . .

[C]lass arbitration, to the extent it is manufactured by *Discover Bank* rather than consensual, is inconsistent with the FAA. First, the switch from bilateral to class arbitration sacrifices the principal advantage of arbitration — its informality — and makes the process slower, more costly, and more likely to generate procedural morass than final judgment. . . . [B]efore an arbitrator may decide the merits of a claim in classwide procedures, he must first decide, for example, whether the class itself may be certified, whether the named parties are sufficiently representative and typical, and how discovery for the class should be conducted. . . .

Second, class arbitration requires procedural formality. The AAA's rules governing class arbitrations mimic the Federal Rules of Civil Procedure for class litigation. And while parties can alter those procedures by contract, an alternative is not obvious. If procedures are too informal, absent class members would not be bound by the arbitration. For a class-action money judgment to bind absentees in litigation, class representatives must at all times adequately represent absent class members, and absent members must be afforded notice, an opportunity to be heard, and a right to opt out of the class. At least this amount of process would presumably be required for absent parties to be bound by the results of arbitration.

We find it unlikely that in passing the FAA Congress meant to leave the disposition of these procedural requirements to an arbitrator. Indeed, class arbitration was not even envisioned by Congress when it passed the FAA in 1925; as the California Supreme Court admitted in *Discover Bank*, class arbitration is a "relatively recent development." And it is at the very least odd to think that an arbitrator would be entrusted with ensuring that third parties' due process rights are satisfied.

Third, class arbitration greatly increases risks to defendants. Informal procedures do of course have a cost: The absence of multilayered review makes it more likely that errors will go uncorrected. Defendants are willing to accept the costs of these errors in arbitration, since their impact is limited to the size of individual disputes, and presumably outweighed by savings from avoiding the courts. But when damages allegedly owed to tens of thousands of potential claimants are aggregated and decided at once, the risk of an error will often become unacceptable. Faced with even a small chance of a devastating loss, defendants will be pressured into settling questionable claims. . . .

The dissent claims that class proceedings are necessary to prosecute small-dollar claims that might otherwise slip through the legal system. But States cannot require a procedure that is inconsistent with the FAA, even if it is desirable for unrelated reasons. Moreover, the claim here was most unlikely to go unresolved. As noted earlier, the arbitration agreement provides that AT&T will pay claimants a minimum of $7,500 and twice their attorney's fees if they obtain an arbitration award greater than AT&T's last settlement offer. The District Court found this scheme sufficient to provide incentive for the individual prosecution of meritorious claims that are not immediately settled, and the Ninth Circuit admitted that aggrieved customers who filed claims would be "essentially guarantee[d]" to be made whole. Indeed, the District Court concluded that the Concepcions were better off under their arbitration agreement with AT&T than they would have been as participants in a class action, which "could take months, if not years, and which may merely yield an opportunity to submit a claim for recovery of a small percentage of a few dollars."

* * *

Because it "stands as an obstacle to the accomplishment and execution of the full purposes and objectives of Congress," Hines v. Davidowitz, 312 U.S. 52, 67 (1941), California's *Discover Bank* rule is preempted by the FAA. The judgment of the Ninth Circuit is reversed, and the case is remanded for further proceedings consistent with this opinion.

It is so ordered.

JUSTICE BREYER,* with whom JUSTICE GINSBURG, JUSTICE SOTOMAYOR, and JUSTICE KAGAN join, dissenting.

The Federal Arbitration Act says that an arbitration agreement "shall be valid, irrevocable, and enforceable, *save upon such grounds as exist at law or in equity for the revocation of any contract.*" 9 U.S.C. §2 (emphasis added). California law sets forth certain circumstances in which "class action waivers" in any contract are unenforceable. In my view, this rule of state law is consistent with the federal Act's language and primary objective. It does not "stan[d] as an obstacle" to the Act's "accomplishment and execution." Hines v. Davidowitz, 312 U.S. 52, 67 (1941). And the Court is wrong to hold that the federal Act pre-empts the rule of state law. . . .

The *Discover Bank* rule is consistent with the federal Act's language. It "applies equally to class action litigation waivers in contracts without arbitration agreements as it does to class arbitration waivers in contracts with such agreements." [*Discover Bank*.] Linguistically speaking, it falls directly within the scope of the Act's exception permitting courts to refuse to enforce arbitration agreements on grounds that exist "for the revocation of *any* contract." 9 U.S.C. §2 (emphasis added). . . .

Because California applies the same legal principles to address the unconscionability of class arbitration waivers as it does to address the unconscionability of any other contractual provision, the merits of class proceedings should not factor into our decision. If California had applied its law of duress to void an arbitration agreement, would it matter if the procedures in the coerced agreement were efficient?

**Stephen G. Breyer* (1938-†) received an A.B. from Stanford University, a B.A. from Magdalen College, Oxford, and an LL.B. from Harvard Law School. After clerking for Justice Arthur Goldberg during the 1964 term, he served as a Special Assistant to the Assistant U.S. Attorney General for Antitrust. From 1967 to 1990 he was a professor at the Harvard Law School, and from 1977 to 1980 he also held an appointment at Harvard's Kennedy School of Government. During his academic tenure, he took leaves to assume various government positions: Assistant Special Prosecutor of the Watergate Special Prosecution Force (1973), Special Counsel of the U.S. Senate Judiciary Committee (1974-1975), and Chief Counsel of the committee (1979-1980). In 1980, he was nominated by President Carter to the United States Court of Appeals for the First Circuit, serving as its Chief Judge from 1990 to 1994. He was a member of the Judicial Conference of the United States from 1990 to 1994, and the United States Sentencing Commission from 1985 to 1989. In 1994, President Clinton nominated him as an Associate Justice of the Supreme Court. — R.B.

Regardless, the majority highlights the disadvantages of class arbitrations, as it sees them. But class proceedings have countervailing advantages. In general agreements that forbid the consolidation of claims can lead small dollar claimants to abandon their claims rather than to litigate. I suspect that it is true even here, for as the Court of Appeals recognized, AT&T can avoid the $7,500 payout (the payout that supposedly makes the Concepcions' arbitration worthwhile) simply by paying the claim's face value, such that "the maximum gain to a customer for the hassle of arbitrating a $30.22 dispute is still just $30.22." Laster v. AT&T Mobility LLC, 584 F. 3d 849, 855, 856 (CA9 2009).

What rational lawyer would have signed on to represent the Concepcions in litigation for the possibility of fees stemming from a $30.22 claim? See, e.g., Carnegie v. Household Int'l, Inc., 376 F. 3d 656, 661 (CA7 2004) ("The realistic alternative to a class action is not 17 million individual suits, but zero individual suits, as only a lunatic or a fanatic sues for $30"). In California's perfectly rational view, nonclass arbitration over such sums will also sometimes have the effect of depriving claimants of their claims (say, for example, where claiming the $30.22 were to involve filling out many forms that require technical legal knowledge or waiting at great length while a call is placed on hold). *Discover Bank* sets forth circumstances in which the California courts believe that the terms of consumer contracts can be manipulated to insulate an agreement's author from liability for its own frauds by "deliberately cheat[ing] large numbers of consumers out of individually small sums of money." 36 Cal. 4th, at 162-163, 113 P.3d, at 1110. Why is this kind of decision — weighing the pros and cons of all class proceedings alike — not California's to make? . . .

By using the words "save upon such grounds as exist at law or in equity for the revocation of any contract," Congress retained for the States an important role incident to agreements to arbitrate. 9 U.S.C. §2. Through those words Congress reiterated a basic federal idea that has long informed the nature of this Nation's laws. We have often expressed this idea in opinions that set forth presumptions. See, e.g., Medtronic, Inc. v. Lohr, 518 U.S. 470, 485 (1996) ("[B]ecause the States are independent sovereigns in our federal system, we have long presumed that Congress does not cavalierly pre-empt state-law causes of action"). But federalism is as much a question of deeds as words. It often takes the form of a concrete decision by this Court that respects the legitimacy of a State's action in an individual case. Here, recognition of that federalist ideal, embodied in specific language in this particular statute, should lead us to uphold California's law, not to strike it down. We do not honor federalist principles in their breach.

With respect, I dissent.

Study Guide: *In the next case, the California Court of Appeal had to decide how much of California's law of unconscionability survived the U.S. Supreme Court's opinion in AT&T Mobility v. Concepcion. How does the court distinguish this case from* AT&T Mobility? *Do you find its argument persuasive? Would Justice Scalia? How could Empire Today LLC redraft its employment contracts to avoid the outcome in this case?*

SAMANIEGO v. EMPIRE TODAY, LLC
California Court of Appeal,
205 Cal. App. 4th 1138, 140 Cal. Rptr. 3d 492 (2012)

SIGGINS,* J.

Empire Today, LLC (Empire), a national carpet and flooring business, appeals from the superior court's refusal to compel contractual arbitration of claims by carpet installers that Empire violated multiple provisions of the California Labor Code. The court found the arbitration provision was unconscionable under California law. We affirm. We hold the provision is unconscionable and unenforceable under Armendariz v. Foundation Health Psychcare Services, Inc. (2000) 24 Cal. 4th 83, 99 Cal. Rptr. 2d 745, 6 P.3d 669 (*Armendariz*); that our consideration of the issues is governed by California law; and that the recent decision of the Supreme Court of the United States in AT & T Mobility LLC v. Concepcion (2011) _____ U.S. _____, 131 S. Ct. 1740, 179 L. Ed. 2d 742 (*Concepcion*) does not change our analysis.

BACKGROUND

Plaintiffs Salome Samaniego and Juventino Garcia work or worked as carpet installers for Flooring Install, Inc., an alleged subsidiary or affiliate of Empire. When they were initially hired, and again later during their employment, plaintiffs were given form contracts and told to sign them if they wanted to work for Empire. The second contract (the Agreement), which is at issue here, was captioned "Flooring Install, Inc. Subcontractor Installer Agreement." Both contracts were presented only in English, although Garcia cannot read English and Samaniego has difficulty reading more than simple written English. The contracts were offered on a non-negotiable, take-it or leave-it basis, with little or no time for review.

The Agreement is 11 single-spaced pages of small-font print riddled with complex legal terminology. The arbitration provision is set forth in the 36th of 37 sections. It provides: "Any dispute or claim arising from any provision of this Agreement or relating in any way to the business relationship between Flooring Install and the Subcontractor shall be submitted to arbitration before a single arbitrator pursuant to the Commercial Arbitration Rules of the American Arbitration Association. . . . [¶] **Both Flooring Install and the Subcontractor are hereby agreeing to choose arbitration, rather than litigation or some other means of dispute resolution, to address their grievances or alleged grievances with the expectation that this resolution process may be more cost-effective and expedient for the parties than litigation. By entering into this Agreement and the arbitration provisions of this section, both parties are giving up their constitutional right to have any dispute decided in a court of law before**

---

*Peter John Siggins (1955-†) is from San Francisco and attended Hastings College of Law. He began his legal career as a deputy attorney general. Arnold Schwarzenegger appointed him to the California Court of Appeal, First District in 2005. — S.Q.

a jury and, instead, are accepting the use of arbitration, other than as set forth immediately below. [¶] DUE TO THE POSSIBLE IMMEDIATE AND IRREPARABLE NATURE OF THE HARM, THE PARTIES AGREE THAT THIS SECTION SHALL NOT APPLY TO ANY CLAIMS BROUGHT BY ANY PARTY FOR DECLARATORY OR PRELIMINARY INJUNCTIVE RELIEF INVOLVING [specified sections] OF THIS AGREEMENT."

The Agreement also includes a shortened six-month statute of limitations for subcontractors to sue under the agreement and a unilateral fee-shifting provision that requires them to pay any attorneys' fees Empire might incur "to enforce any of its rights hereunder or to collect any amounts due." Although the Agreement directs that arbitration will be governed by the commercial rules of the American Arbitration Association, those rules were not attached to it or otherwise provided to plaintiffs.

Samaniego and Garcia filed this putative class action challenging Empire's allegedly unlawful misclassification of its carpet installers as independent contractors. The complaint alleges numerous Labor Code violations, including that Empire failed to pay minimum wage and overtime compensation; refused to indemnify employees for job-related expenses; wrongfully deducted from employee pay; coerced employees to make purchases from the company; failed to provide required meal periods; and failed to pay all wages due upon installers' termination.

Empire moved to stay the action and compel arbitration pursuant to the Agreement. The court found the Agreement was "highly unconscionable from a procedural standpoint" and demonstrated "strong indicia of substantive unconscionability," and therefore denied Empire's motion to compel. It also denied Empire's request for reconsideration in light of the United States Supreme Court's decision in *Concepcion, supra*, 131 S. Ct. 1740, which was issued several weeks after the denial of Empire's motion. Empire timely appealed.

DISCUSSION

I.   THE TRIAL COURT CORRECTLY REFUSED TO COMPEL ARBITRATION

The primary questions presented for our consideration are: (1) whether the agreement to arbitrate is unconscionable and, therefore, unenforceable under California law; (2) whether the court properly declined to enforce the entire arbitration clause rather than sever unconscionable provisions; and (3) whether the court correctly applied California law despite an Illinois choice-of-law provision in the Agreement. We answer each of these questions in the affirmative.

. . .

B.   *Unconscionability*

California law on unconscionability is well established. " ' "[U]nconscionability has generally been recognized to include an absence of meaningful choice on the part of one of the parties together with contract terms which are unreasonably favorable to the other party." [Citation.] Phrased another way, unconscionability has both a "procedural" and a "substantive" element.' [Citation.] ' "The procedural element requires oppression or surprise. [Citation.] Oppression occurs where a contract involves lack of negotiation and meaningful choice, surprise where the allegedly unconscionable provision is hidden within a prolix printed form. [Citation.] The substantive element concerns whether a contractual provision reallocates risks in an objectively unreasonable or unexpected manner." [Citation.] Under this approach, both the procedural and substantive elements must be met before a contract or term will be deemed unconscionable. Both, however, need not be present to the same degree. A sliding scale is applied so that "the more substantively oppressive the contract term, the less evidence of procedural unconscionability is required to come to the conclusion that the term is unenforceable, and vice versa." ' [Citations.]" (Lhotka v. Geographic Expeditions, Inc. (2010) 181 Cal. App. 4th 816, 821, 104 Cal. Rptr. 3d 844 (*Lhotka*); *Armendariz, supra*, 24 Cal. 4th at p. 114, 99 Cal. Rptr. 2d 745, 6 P.3d 669.)

1.   PROCEDURAL UNCONSCIONABILITY

Empire stakes its position that the Agreement was not procedurally unconscionable primarily on Roman v. Superior Court (2009) 172 Cal. App. 4th 1462, 92 Cal. Rptr. 3d 153 (*Roman*), which also addressed an employment contract. The plaintiff, a receptionist, argued the arbitration clause in her employment application was unconscionable solely because it was part of an adhesion contract. (*Id.* at pp. 1470-1471, 92 Cal. Rptr. 3d 153.) The trial court found the degree of procedural unfairness was minimal. (*Ibid.*) "The arbitration provision was not buried in a lengthy employment agreement. Rather, it was contained on the last page of a seven-page employment application, underneath the heading 'Please Read Carefully, Initial Each Paragraph and Sign Below.' It was set forth in a separate, succinct (four-sentence) paragraph that Roman initialed, affirming she had seen it." (*Id.* at p. 1471, 92 Cal. Rptr. 3d 153.) This minimal measure of procedural unconscionability, unaccompanied (the court went on to find) by *any* measure of substantive unconscionability, was not enough to render the arbitration agreement unconscionable. (*Id.* at pp. 1471-1476, 1466, 92 Cal. Rptr. 3d 153.)

Roman has little bearing on the issues in this case. Here, based on properly admitted, uncontroverted evidence, the superior court found as follows. "After being hired but before starting work, both Plaintiffs were required to take computer tests and complete certain paperwork, including a subcontractor agreement. They were told that they were 'required' to sign these documents, including the agreement, if they wanted to work for Empire. Both Plaintiffs are not able to read English (at all, or sufficiently well) and both Plaintiffs asked for a Spanish translation of the documents (including the agreement) in Spanish [*sic*] but were told none were available. Plaintiffs both signed all of the paperwork as instructed, but were not provided a copy." Plaintiffs were later presented with new agreements, also in English only, "and told that they were required to sign it if they wanted to keep working. Mr. Samaniego was directed to sign it immediately, and was told that he could not take it home for review. Mr. Garcia was permitted 24 hours to review and return his agreement, signed, which he did." In short, "[p]laintiffs perform manual labor, do not speak English as a first language, have limited or no literacy in English, and were told they could not continue employment if they did not sign the agreements."

Moreover, Empire failed to provide plaintiffs with a copy of the relevant arbitration rules. This is significant. In Harper v. Ultimo (2003) 113 Cal. App. 4th 1402, 1406, 7 Cal. Rptr. 3d 418, the court held it was oppressive to reference the Better Business Bureau arbitration rules, but not attach the rules to the agreement. "The customer is forced to go to another source to find out the full import of what he or she is about to sign — and must go to that effort *prior* to signing." (*Ibid.*) "Numerous cases have held that the failure to provide a copy of the arbitration rules to which the employee would be bound, supported a finding of procedural unconscionability. [Citations.]" (Trivedi v. Curexo Technology Corp. (2010) 189 Cal. App. 4th 387, 393-394, 116 Cal. Rptr. 3d 804.)

The Agreement was comprised of 11 pages of densely worded, single-spaced text printed in small typeface. The arbitration clause is the penultimate of 37 sections which, in contrast to *Roman*, were neither flagged by individual headings nor required to be initialed by the subcontractor. (See *Roman, supra*, 172 Cal. App. 4th at pp. 1470-1471, 92 Cal. Rptr. 3d 153; see also Gutierrez v. Autowest, Inc. (2003) 114 Cal. App. 4th 77, 89, 7 Cal. Rptr. 3d 267 [arbitration clause inconspicuous, printed in eight-point typeface on the opposite side of the signature page; buyer not told the lease contained an arbitration clause or required to initial it].) Taken together, these factors amply support the trial court's finding that the Agreement was procedurally unconscionable.

2.   Substantive Unconscionability

The Agreement also demonstrates "strong indicia of substantive unconscionability," as the trial court found. "Substantive unconscionability focuses on the one-sidedness or overly harsh effect of the contract term or clause." (*Lhotka, supra*, 181 Cal. App. 4th at pp. 824-825, 104 Cal. Rptr. 3d 844.) Empire asserts that none of the contractual terms amount to substantive unconscionability. But it supports its argument only with authority for the general proposition that a contractual provision that unilaterally shortens a limitations period to six months, taken alone, does not necessarily render an adhesion contract substantively unconscionable. (See Soltani v. Western & Southern Life Ins. Co. (9th Cir. 2001) 258 F.3d 1038, 1043 [citing California cases].) The import of such a clause is quite different in the context of the statutory wage and hour claims asserted here. The Labor Code provides the bases for the class claims, and it affords employees three or four years to assert them. Where, as in this case, arbitration provisions undermine statutory protections, courts have readily found unconscionability. (*Nyulassy, supra*, at p. 1283, 16 Cal. Rptr. 3d 296; *Martinez, supra*, at p. 117, 12 Cal. Rptr. 3d 663; Wherry v. Award, Inc. (2011) 192 Cal. App. 4th 1242, 1249, 123 Cal. Rptr. 3d 1 (*Wherry*).) As noted in *Armendariz, supra*, "an arbitration agreement cannot be made to serve as a vehicle for the waiver of statutory rights created by the FEHA." (24 Cal. 4th at p. 101, 99 Cal. Rptr. 2d 745, 6 P.3d 669.)

In any event, the limitations period is just one of several one-sided provisions. The Agreement also requires plaintiffs to pay any attorneys' fees incurred by Empire, but imposes no reciprocal obligation on Empire. Again, such a clause contributes to a finding of unconscionability. (See *Wherry, supra*, 192 Cal. App. 4th at pp. 1248-1249, 123 Cal. Rptr. 3d 1.) Empire argues this clause is of no moment because, after all, one-way fee shifting provisions that benefit only employers violate both the Labor Code and commercial arbitration rules, "which means that Empire cannot recover its attorney's fees from plaintiffs even if it prevails in arbitration." In other words, according to Empire, it isn't unconscionable because it's illegal and, hence, unenforceable. To state the premise is to refute Empire's logic. The argument is unpersuasive.

In addition, the Agreement exempts from the arbitration requirement claims typically brought by employers — namely, those seeking declaratory and preliminary injunctive relief to protect Empire's proprietary information and non-competition/non-solicitation provisions — while restricting to arbitration any and all claims plaintiffs might bring. Empire notes in this regard that "not all lack of mutuality in an adhesive arbitration agreement is invalid." True enough. (*Cf.* Flores v. Transamerica HomeFirst, Inc. (2001) 93 Cal. App. 4th 846, 855, 113 Cal. Rptr. 2d 376.) But at issue here is whether the multiple one-sided provisions in the Agreement, considered together, support the trial court's finding that it exhibits strong indicia of substantive unconscionability. They do, and we therefore have no difficulty affirming the denial of Empire's motion to compel arbitration.

. . .

IV.   CONCEPCION

Finally, Empire contends the United States Supreme Court's recent decision in *Concepcion, supra*, 131 S. Ct. 1740, extends the Federal Arbitration Act (FAA) so broadly as to preempt each "unconscionability-based rationale" that supported the trial court's refusal to compel arbitration here. Empire reads *Concepcion* too broadly.

In Discover Bank v. Superior Court (2005) 36 Cal. 4th 148, 30 Cal. Rptr. 3d 76, 113 P.3d 1100 (*Discover Bank*), the California Supreme Court held that arbitration agreements in adhesive consumer contracts that forbid classwide arbitration are, as a general matter, unconscionable. It stated: "We do not hold that all class action waivers are necessarily unconscionable. But when the waiver is found in a consumer contract of adhesion in a setting in which disputes between the contracting parties predictably involve small amounts of damages, and when it is alleged that the party with the superior bargaining power has carried out a scheme to deliberately cheat large numbers of consumers out of individually small sums of money, then, at least to the extent the obligation at issue is governed by California law, the waiver becomes in practice the exemption of the party 'from responsibility for [its] own fraud, or willful injury to the person or property of another.'" Under these circumstances, the Court held such waivers are unconscionable and, therefore, unenforceable. (*Id.* at pp. 162-163, 30 Cal. Rptr. 3d 76, 113 P.3d 1100.)

Concepcion addresses whether the FAA preempts the *Discover Bank* rule. (131 S. Ct. at p. 1746.) The United States Supreme Court held that it does, because "[r]equiring the availability of classwide arbitration interferes with fundamental attributes of arbitration and thus creates a scheme inconsistent with the FAA." (*Id.* at p. 1748.) But at the same time as the Court repudiated the categorical rule in *Discover Bank*, it explicitly reaffirmed that the FAA "permits agreements to arbitrate to be invalidated by 'generally applicable contract defenses, such as fraud, duress, or unconscionability,' [although] not by defenses that apply only to arbitration or that derive their meaning from the fact that an agreement to arbitrate is at issue." (*Id.* at p. 1746, 30 Cal. Rptr. 3d 76, 113 P.3d 1100; 9 U.S.C. §2; see Mission Viejo Emergency Medical Associates v. Beta Healthcare Group (2011) 197 Cal. App. 4th 1146, 1158, fn.4, 128 Cal. Rptr. 3d 330.) In short, arbitration agreements remain subject, post-*Concepcion*, to the unconscionability analysis employed by the trial court in this case.

DISPOSITION

The order denying Empire's motion for a stay and to compel arbitration is affirmed.

Commercial Background: Contracting Around Government Courts and State-Created Contract Law

STUDY GUIDE: Is the dispute resolution system described in the following excerpt extralegal or a rival legal system to that provided by government courts? Can you imagine why government judges might be hostile to such a system? Notice how this system reinforces moral norms of behavior. Would there be any drawbacks to governmental court systems attempting to accomplish the same thing? Think about Professor Bernstein's concluding observation that, as the shared religious norms have declined, the norms of the diamond business have been maintained for reasons of self-interest or profit. What does this imply for the stability of morality in other domains of modern society where no such incentives exist? Alternative dispute resolution also exists in realms less insular than that of the diamond industry. How might such a system work? As the use of various forms of ADR expands, what continued role, if any, do you see for government courts?

LISA BERNSTEIN, OPTING OUT OF THE LEGAL SYSTEM: EXTRALEGAL CONTRACTUAL RELATIONS IN THE DIAMOND INDUSTRY, 21 J. LEG. STUD. 115, 119-121, 124-130, 148-151, 157 (1992):   Business disputes arise in all industries, and the diamond industry is no exception. Unlike the situation in many other industries, however, diamond industry disputes are resolved not through the courts and not by the application of legal rules announced and enforced by the state. The diamond industry has systematically rejected state-created law. In its place, the sophisticated traders who dominate the industry have developed an elaborate, internal set of rules, complete with distinctive institutions and sanctions, to handle disputes among industry members. This article explores the reasons that this system of private governance has developed and endured within the diamond trade. . . .

The largest and most important trading club ("bourse") in the United States is the New York Diamond Dealers Club. Its membership is comprised of sight holders, manufacturers, wholesalers, and brokers. Club membership gives a dealer prestige and an important economic advantage. In the diamond industry, access to a steady supply of goods is essential to the operation of a profitable brokerage or manufacturing business. Although it is possible to buy stones on the "open market," a dealer who does not have access to the trading clubs — essential links in the worldwide diamond distribution network — will be at a competitive disadvantage. Approximately 80 percent of the rough diamonds coming into the United States pass through the hands of a DDC member, as do 15-20 percent of the polished stones. In addition, 20-50 percent of the transactions conducted by or on behalf of foreign or out of town dealers are concluded in the club.

The New York DDC currently has 2,000 members; in most years there is a waiting list for admission. Although requirements for membership are strict, the main constraint on membership is space, not the inability of dealers to meet the membership requirements. As a condition of membership, a dealer must sign an agreement to submit all disputes arising from the diamond business between himself and another member to the club's arbitration system. The agreement to arbitrate is binding. Unless the club opts not to hear the case, the member may not seek redress of his grievances in court. If he does so, he will be fined or expelled from the club. Furthermore, since the agreement to arbitrate is binding, the court will not hear the case. . . .

The New York DDC is a member of the World Federation of Diamond Bourses (WFDB), an umbrella organization composed of the world's twenty diamond bourses. A dealer who is a member of any one bourse in the world federation is automatically allowed to trade at all member bourses. Each bourse has similar trade rules, and, like the individual bourses, the WFDB has an arbitration system to resolve differences between its members. As a condition of membership in the federation, each bourse is required to enforce the arbitration judgments of other member bourses to the extent permitted by the law of the country in which it operates. . . .

Around 150 disputes per year are submitted to the DDC's arbitration system. Of these, an estimated 85 percent are settled during the mandatory prearbitration conciliation procedure. . . .

The DDC's procedural rules clearly reflect the industry's preference for the voluntary resolution of disputes. The bylaws are structured to give the parties control over the dispute resolution process and to create financial incentives to settle. For example, prior to an arbitration hearing, the parties are required to participate in a conciliation proceeding, and "whenever an adjustment by conciliation is consummated, the chairman of [the three-person conciliation] panel may refund the arbitration fee or any part of the same."[46]

An important feature of the arbitration system is the secrecy of the proceedings. The arbitrators are not required to make findings of fact and do not produce written decisions explaining their reasoning. As long as judgments are complied with, the fact of the arbitration as well as its outcome are officially kept secret.

Procedural Aspects of Arbitration.   There are two dispute resolution bodies in the DDC, the Floor Committee and the Board of Arbitrators; both are composed of club members elected for two-year terms. Before a dispute is referred to arbitration, the Floor Committee must find that a material issue of fact exists. The standard used is similar to the familiar standard for granting summary judgment.

The Floor Committee has the authority to exclude a member from the trading hall for up to twenty days and/or impose a fine of up to $1,000 when the member "fails to meet his commercial obligations to another member and no material issue of fact is involved or a member causes a disturbance or conducts himself in the clubrooms in a manner unbecoming a member of the club." A decision of the Floor Committee may be appealed by filing a written request and paying the $100 appeal fee. Unless the panel finds that a material issue of fact exists and recommends that the case be referred to arbitration, the decision of the appeal panel is final. Neither the Floor Committee nor the appeal panel are required to make any findings of fact.

Any member of the DDC who has a claim "arising out of or related to the diamond business" against another member has the right to file a written complaint against the member who must then submit to DDC adjudication. At the time he files the complaint, the plaintiff must pay a small arbitration fee, but at the conclusion of the case the panel "shall decide which of the litigants shall pay the arbitration fee and the expenses which were necessarily incurred, and . . . may refund the arbitration fee or any part of it." Arbitrators are required to render their decision within ten days of the hearing.

Arbitration awards can be appealed if notice of appeal is filed with the board of directors within ten days of the parties' receipt of the judgment. The appellant must pay a fee three times the original arbitration fee and "deposit cash or sufficient security to cover the amount of the judgment." The appeals board is composed of five arbitrators who did not hear the original case, and it too is "under no obligation to specify any findings of fact which are reversed or modified nor set forth any new findings of fact."

The decisions of the arbitration board can be appealed to New York State court under New York law, but arbitration awards can only be vacated for procedural irregularities, such as an arbitrator engaging in an ex parte communication or a failure to allow the parties to be represented by counsel.[47] The substantive rule of decision is not reviewed. . . .

46. DDC Arbitration Bylaws, Art. 12 §8.

47. . . . In addition, New York law requires that the arbitration process be free from the appearance of bias. See, for example, Rabinowitz v. Olewski, 100 A.D.2d 539; 473 N.Y.2d 232 (2d Dept. 1984) (where the court ordered a stay of DDC arbitration and directed that the case

Substantive Aspects of Arbitration. The DDC Board of Arbitrators does not apply the New York law of contract and damages, rather it resolves disputes on the basis of trade customs and usages. Many of these are set forth with particularity in the club's bylaws, and others simply are generally known and accepted. Although at first glance diamond transactions appear to be simple buy-sell agreements, complicated controversies often arise, particularly in the sale of polished stones. In general, disputes fall into three main classes: those that have explicit remedies prescribed in the trade rules; those that have no explicit remedies prescribed but are common enough that they are dealt with consistently according to widely known customs; and those complex disputes that the arbitrators either decline to hear or decide in accordance with rules of decision and damage measures that neither party can predict ex ante.

The dispute resolution system in the diamond industry shows some sensitivity to concerns of institutional competence. Under its bylaws, the club has the right to refuse to arbitrate a claim when it does not arise out of the diamond business, or "(1) involves complicated statutory rights; (2) is 'forum non conveniens' in that it is burdensome or inconvenient to handle the claim in the Club; (3) involves nonmembers; (4) has been conciliated, mediated, arbitrated or litigated outside the Club and/or the parties have sought remedies elsewhere; (5) is not in the ordinary course of commercial dealings."[48] When the club refuses to hear a case, the parties are permitted to seek remedies outside the club.

In complex cases that are neither explicitly covered by the trade rules nor dealt with according to established custom, it is difficult to determine what substantive rules of decision are applied. Arbitrators explain that they decide complex cases on the basis of trade custom and usage, a little common sense, some Jewish law, and, last, common-law legal principles. There are *no* general rules of damages. When calculating damages, the arbitrators look at the stone, consider the circumstances, and apply their business experience. Many dealers feel that the arbitrators have redistributive instincts; they cite the unpredictability of the decisions as well as the arbitrators' tendency to "split the difference" as an important motivation to settle their disputes on their own. This may be a reason why, while 150 arbitration complaints are filed each year, only thirty to forty go to judgment. The arbitrators announce their judgment, but they neither make findings of fact nor explain their reasoning. The absence of explicit findings of fact and written opinions is a precaution to prevent people from complaining, rightly or wrongly, that the arbitrators were biased, unfair, or relied on evidence that lacked probative value. The arbitration board is like a jury black box. Diamond dealers eschew arbitration for many of the

---

be heard by an independent arbitrator after a letter surfaced in the club accusing the plaintiff of being sympathetic to the Palestine Liberation Organization; since it was clear that a substantial injustice might result were the case heard by the predominantly Jewish DDC and there was the "appearance of impropriety and specter of bias among the DDC").

48. [DDC Arbitration Bylaws, Art.] 12 §1b. See, for example, Finker v. The Diamond Registry, 469 F. Supp. 674 (S.D.N.Y. 1979) (where the DDC agreed to decide issues concerning the ownership of goods held on memorandum (consignment) but "refused to involve itself in the dispute concerning the trademark registration and alleged infringement").

same reasons that businessmen in general are wary of jury trials, primarily the uncertainty of the outcome.

A person who is found to have breached an agreement or engaged in unethical conduct is sometimes ordered to pay punitive damages or a fine in the form of a donation to charity in addition to compensating the other party for his loss. Thus, unlike court awards that, while unpredictable, are at least bounded by expectation damages, arbitration awards have a completely uncertain component. In one case, a dealer falsely accused another dealer of stealing a stone. The accuser subsequently remembered where he had put the stone and apologized to the other dealer. As the incident had become widely known throughout the club, however, the wrongly accused dealer brought an arbitration action against the owner of the stone for impugning his good name. The board ordered the man to make a full public apology and a fifty thousand dollar donation to a Jewish charity.

Enforcing Arbitration Judgments.   The DDC bylaws provide that "[a]ll decisions of arbitration panels including floor committee arbitrations which are not complied with within 10 working days, together with the picture of the non-complying member, shall be posted in a conspicuous place in the Club rooms." This information is communicated to all bourses in the world federation. As a condition of membership in the federation, each bourse agrees to enforce the judgments of all member bourses. Since most diamond dealers frequently transact in foreign bourses, this reciprocity of enforcement greatly increases the penalty for failing to voluntarily comply with an arbitration judgment.

The arbitration board can also suspend or expel a member for failing to pay a judgment or failing to pay his diamond-related creditors without making special arrangements through the club's private bankruptcy system. . . .

In general, the Board of Arbitrators uses suspension more frequently than expulsion to secure compliance with its decisions. . . .

Under New York law, binding arbitration awards can be confirmed in civil court. If this is done, the judgment has the same force and effect as an initial court award. In practice, however, it is rarely necessary for a party to a DDC arbitration to seek confirmation of a judgment. While arbitration awards are officially kept secret, a confirmation proceeding in court would quickly become public knowledge. Thus, the dealer against whom the judgment was entered would suffer severe damage to his reputation. Furthermore, if a member refuses to pay a judgment and the party who prevailed finds it necessary to obtain a court enforcement order, the DDC bylaws require the losing party to pay an additional 15 percent of the award to cover his opponent's legal expenses. Another enforcement mechanism sometimes invoked by the arbitrators is a proceeding in Jewish rabbinical courts against the party who refuses to comply. Because these courts have the authority to ban an individual from participation in the Jewish community, this is a powerful threat against Orthodox members of the diamond industry. . . .

The Substantive and Procedural Advantages of Arbitration over Adjudication.   In the diamond industry, arbitration has important substantive and procedural advantages over adjudication. It enables parties to resolve disputes and enforce judgments quickly, inexpensively, and secretly, thereby containing damage to reputation and reducing the actual damage suffered by the promisee in event of breach.

Unlike courts, whose award of damages is limited by either expectation damages or a valid liquidated damages clause, the DDC bylaws allow arbitrators to award any measure of damages they think is appropriate, including punitive damages. They can also order one or both of the parties to pay a fine to a third-party beneficiary such as a charity. The authority to award punitive damages means that they can make the promisee whole, and the authority to order payment of a fine enables them to create a deterrent to breach contract. Since transactors know they may be forced to pay a penalty in the event of breach, their incentive to breach in the first place will be greatly reduced.

Although DDC arbitrators have industry expertise and sophisticated business judgment, they are not much better than courts at valuing lost profit or business opportunities forgone. Because arbitration hearings are held soon after the filing of the complaint, however, and because decisions are rendered and enforced shortly thereafter, the harm suffered by the promisee, while still difficult to quantify, is minimized. The inability of even expert dealers to accurately assess lost profit when a seller breaches a promise to deliver a stone may be the reason that possession is typically transferred at the time of contracting. Similarly, the difficulty of valuing lost business opportunities when a buyer fails to pay may account for the premium on speed: the sooner the promisee is paid, the fewer transactions he will be required to forgo. The bourse's ability to resolve disputes promptly is considered so important that even if a dealer fails to appear for an arbitration, the hearing is held and he is bound by the panel's decision. The Floor Committee is also available during trading hours to resolve minor disputes as soon as they arise.

In disputes other than breach of a promise to pay money or deliver a stone, which are dealt with in the bylaws or according to well-established custom, arbitrators' verdicts may be more accurate and predictable than those of a court since arbitrators possess industry expertise and are permitted to consider information that would be excluded in court under the rules of evidence. If a diamond dispute were decided by a court, the application of industry custom would be highly unpredictable: unlike a DDC arbitrator, who can apply his own knowledge of industry custom, a judge would have to determine the content of customary norms from the conflicting testimony of expert witnesses. The uncertainty introduced by a judge's need to resolve conflicting testimony would greatly reduce the expected benefit to the promisee of having a legally enforceable contract.

Under the club's bylaws, the existence of a dispute and its resolution are kept secret so long as the arbitrators' judgment is paid promptly. Consequently, unlike filing a claim in court, initiating an arbitration does not affect the parties' ability to borrow or enter into implicit capital market transactions during the pendency of the dispute, which, in turn, minimizes the financial harm suffered by the promisee. The reputation damage suffered by the promisee is reduced by the practice of keeping disputes secret after a judgment is rendered since other transactors may view mere participation in an arbitration as a signal that a dealer was unwilling to renegotiate deals when unforeseen circumstances arose; they might demand additional protections or charge a higher price when dealing with him in the future.

The rapid enforcement of judgments is another advantage of DDC arbitration. Unlike a court, the DDC has the ability to bring unique pressures on the losing party to pay: it can put him out of business almost instantaneously by hanging his picture in the clubroom of every bourse in the world with a notice that he failed to pay his debt. Thus, the threat of publicity and the practice of keeping disputes secret as long as judgments are paid gives the defendant an incentive to promptly comply with the arbitrators' judgment. In addition, trade rules try to minimize the likelihood of a judgment-proof debtor in two ways: by making individual members as well as the corporations they trade for liable for arbitration judgments; and by providing for the expulsion of any member who files, voluntarily or involuntarily, for personal or corporate bankruptcy in court instead of going through the club's own bankruptcy procedure, which requires the debtor to make 100 percent restitution to his diamond industry creditors. . . .

In complex cases not covered by the trade rules or industry custom, diamond industry arbitration suffers from the same weakness as most commercial arbitration: unpredictability. The lack of written decisions and a tradition of stare decisis makes it difficult for market participants to make rational breach decisions and to determine in advance the type of sanctioned behavior. In order to increase predictability, many bourses in the world federation have relaxed the norm of complete secrecy. Arbitrators publish written announcements of the principles used to decide novel cases while keeping the parties and other identifying facts secret. The WFDB recently proposed compiling a computer data base of these statements of principle to promote worldwide uniformity of arbitrated judgments and to prevent "forum shopping." They also proposed additional uniform training programs for all arbitrators. Younger WFDB officials fear that if such changes are not introduced the system will be perceived as arbitrary and unjust, and its legitimacy may decline. Recently, there has been increasing pressure on the New York bourse to relax the secrecy norm and to permit arbitrators to issue policy statements in novel or complex cases — a change that would enable the industry to capture the benefits of arbitration (secrecy, informality, and speed) and litigation (the creation of precedent and stare decisis). . . .

The customs and institutions in the diamond industry emerged for reasons wholly unrelated to shortcomings in the legal system; yet, even as the force of the old enforcement mechanisms of religion and secondary social bonds began to disintegrate, a network of trading clubs, designed to promote the dissemination of information about reputation and socialization among members, emerged to fill the gap. . . .

In the diamond industry, "trust" and "reputation" have an actual market value. As an elderly Israeli diamond dealer explained, "[W]hen I first entered the business, the conception was that truth and trust were simply *the* way to do business, and nobody decent would consider doing it differently. Although many transactions are still consummated on the basis of trust and truthfulness, this is done because these qualities are viewed as good for business, a way to make a profit."[49]

F. PUBLIC POLICY

Most limitations on the enforcement of contracts are based on some imperfection in how the contracts are formed, what one scholar has called "bargaining naughtiness."[50] Duress provides a very clear example of these concerns, but so do doctrines such as misrepresentation and unconscionability. Sometimes, however, courts will refuse to enforce a contract because of the substantive content of the contract itself. The doctrines of illegality and public policy thus present the starkest limitations in the law of contracts on the freedom of the parties to author their own obligations. The cases below provide examples of how the courts mark these outer limits of freedom of contract and the sources on which they drawn in discerning those limits.

STUDY GUIDE: In A.Z. v. B.Z., the court struggles with contracts surrounding new reproductive technologies. Notice that before reaching the issue of public policy, the court tries to dispose of the contract using other doctrines. Why might this be the case? Do you find the court's arguments persuasive?

A.Z. v. B.Z.
Supreme Judicial Court of Massachusetts,
431 Mass. 150, 725 N.E.2d 1051 (2000)

COWIN,* J.

We transferred this case to this court on our own motion to consider for the first time the effect of a consent form between a married couple and an in vitro fertilization (IVF) clinic (clinic) concerning disposition of frozen preembryos.[51] B.Z., the former wife (wife) of A.Z. (husband), appeals from a judgment of the Probate and Family Court that included, inter alia,[52] a

---

49. Interview with author, summer 1989.

50. Arthur Allen Leff, Unconscionability and the Code — The Emperor's New Clause, 115 U. Pa. L. Rev. 485, 487 (1967).

*Judith Cowin (1942-†) was educated at Wellesley College and Harvard Law School. After a long legal career in various public departments, including time as an assistant district attorney, she was appointed to the Massachusetts Superior Court in 1991 and then the Massachusetts Supreme Judicial Court in 1999. She retired from the Massachusetts Supreme Judicial Court in 2011. — S.Q.

51. We use the term "preembryo" to refer to the four-to-eight cell stage of a developing fertilized egg. See 62 Ethics Committee of the American Fertility Society, Ethical Considerations of Assisted Reproductive Technologies, Fertility and Sterility at 29S-30S (Supp. 1 Nov. 1994) (explaining terminology and transformation of single cell into multicellular newborn).

52. The issue arose in the context of a divorce proceeding.

permanent injunction in favor of the husband, prohibiting the wife "from utilizing" the frozen preembryos held in cryopreservation[53] at the clinic. The probate judge bifurcated the issue concerning the disposition of the frozen preembryos from the then-pending divorce action.[54] The wife appeals only from the issuance of the permanent injunction.[55] On February 8, 2000, we issued an order affirming the judgment of the Probate and Family Court. The order stated: "It is ordered that the permanent injunction entered on the docket on March 25, 1996 in Suffolk County Probate Court (Docket No. 95 D 1683 DV) be, and the same hereby is, affirmed. Opinion or opinions to follow." This opinion states the reasons for that order.

1. *Factual background.* We recite the relevant background facts as determined by the probate judge in his detailed findings of fact after a hearing concerning disposition of the preembryos at which both the husband and wife were separately represented by counsel. The probate judge's findings are supplemented by the record where necessary.

a. *History of the couple.* The husband and wife were married in 1977. . . . [T]he wife did become pregnant, but she suffered an ectopic pregnancy,[56] as a result of which she miscarried and her left fallopian tube was removed.

. . .

. . . IVF involves injecting the woman with fertility drugs in order to stimulate production of eggs which can be surgically retrieved or harvested. After the eggs are removed, they are combined in a petri dish with sperm produced by the man, on the same day as the egg removal, in an effort to fertilize the eggs. If fertilization between any of the eggs and sperm occurs, preembryos are formed that are held in a petri dish for one or two days until a decision can be made as to which preembryos will be used immediately and which will be frozen and stored by the clinic for later use. Preembryos that are to be utilized immediately are not frozen.

. . .

They underwent IVF treatment from 1988 through 1991. As a result of the 1991 treatment, the wife conceived and gave birth to twin daughters in 1992. During the 1991 IVF treatment, more preembryos were formed than were necessary for immediate implantation, and two vials of preembryos were frozen for possible future implantation.

---

53. Cryopreservation is the "[m]aintenance of the viability of excised tissues or organs at extremely low temperatures." Stedman's Medical Dictionary 375 (25th ed. 1990).

54. The husband and wife separated in August, 1995, and later that month the husband filed for divorce. In September, 1995, the husband filed a motion for an ex parte temporary restraining order regarding a vial of frozen preembryos stored at the IVF clinic. The judge did not act on the motion, but ordered a hearing at which counsel for both the husband and the wife stipulated to a "standstill order." The judge then bifurcated the issue presented here from the pending divorce action, but stated that the disposition of the issue concerning the frozen preembryos would be a final determination incorporated into the final divorce judgment. The probate judge's order granting the husband a permanent injunction in this case was subsequently incorporated in the final divorce decree.

55. Although he participated in the probate proceedings, the husband did not appear or file a brief in this court.

56. An ectopic pregnancy is one that occurs outside the uterus, the normal locus of pregnancy. Stedman's Medical Dictionary 488 (25th ed. 1990). In this case, the pregnancy occurred in and ruptured the fallopian tube, requiring surgery to remove it.

In the spring of 1995, before the couple separated, the wife desired more children and had one of the remaining vials of preembryos thawed and one preembryo was implanted. She did so without informing her husband.[57] The husband learned of this when he received a notice from his insurance company regarding the procedure. During this period relations between the husband and wife deteriorated. The wife sought and received a protective order against the husband under G.L. c. 209A. Ultimately, they separated and the husband filed for divorce.

At the time of the divorce, one vial containing four frozen preembryos remained in storage at the clinic. Using one or more of these preembryos, it is possible that the wife could conceive; the likelihood of conception depends, inter alia, on the condition of the preembryos which cannot be ascertained until the preembryos are thawed. The husband filed a motion to obtain a permanent injunction, prohibiting the wife from "using" the remaining vial of frozen preembryos.

b. *The IVF clinic and the consent forms.* In order to participate in fertility treatment, including GIFT and IVF, the clinic required egg and sperm donors (donors) to sign certain consent forms for the relevant procedures. Each time before removal of the eggs from the wife, the clinic required the husband and wife in this case to sign a preprinted consent form concerning ultimate disposition of the frozen preembryos. The wife signed a number of forms on which the husband's signature was not required. The only forms that both the husband and the wife were required to sign were those entitled "Consent Form for Freezing (Cryopreservation) of Embryos" (consent form), one of which is the form at issue here.[58]

Each consent form explains the general nature of the IVF procedure and outlines the freezing process, including the financial cost and the potential benefits and risks of that process. The consent form also requires the donors to decide the disposition of the frozen preembryos on certain listed contingencies: "wife or donor" reaching normal menopause or age forty-five years; preembryos no longer being healthy; "one of us dying"; "[s]hould we become separated"; "[s]hould we both die." Under each contingency the consent form provides the following as options for disposition of the preembryos: "donated or destroyed — choose one or both." A blank line beneath these choices permits the donors to write in additional alternatives not listed as options on the form, and the form notifies the donors that they may do so.[59] The consent form also informs the donors that they may change their minds as to any disposition, provided that both donors convey that fact in writing to the clinic.

. . .

---

57. No pregnancy resulted. One vial of frozen preembryos remains stored at the clinic. A whole vial must be thawed at one time; single preembryos cannot be removed from the vial and thawed individually.

58. The clinic required that a consent form be completed each time before the egg retrievals, regardless of whether any preembryos were ultimately produced and frozen. Once preembryos are produced and frozen, a new consent form does not need to be filled out by the husband and wife to authorize a thawing and transfer of frozen preembryos, unless they change their prior choices.

59. On one occasion, the wife called the clinic to inquire about the form and was advised that "she could cross out any of the language on the form and fill in her own [language] to fit her wishes."

c. *The execution of the forms.* Every time before eggs were retrieved from the wife and combined with sperm from the husband, they each signed a consent form.[60] The husband was present when the first form was completed by the wife in October, 1988. They both signed that consent form after it was finished. The form, as filled out by the wife, stated, inter alia, that if they "[s]hould become separated, [they] both agree[d] to have the embryo(s) . . . return[ed] to [the] wife for implant." The husband and wife thereafter underwent six additional egg retrievals for freezing and signed six additional consent forms, one each in June, 1989, and February, 1989, two forms in December, 1989, and one each in August, 1990, and August, 1991. The August, 1991, consent form governs the vial of frozen preembryos now stored at the clinic.

Each time after signing the first consent form in October, 1988, the husband always signed a blank consent form. Sometimes a consent form was signed by the husband while he and his wife were traveling to the IVF clinic; other forms were signed before the two went to the IVF clinic. Each time, after the husband signed the form, the wife filled in the disposition and other information, and then signed the form herself. All the words she wrote in the later forms were substantially similar to the words she inserted in the first October, 1988, form. In each instance the wife specified in the option for "[s]hould we become separated," that the preembryos were to be returned to the wife for implantation.

2. *The Probate Court's decision.* The probate judge concluded that, while donors are generally free to agree as to the ultimate disposition of frozen preembryos, the agreement at issue was unenforceable because of "change in circumstances" occurring during the four years after the husband and wife signed the last, and governing, consent form in 1991:[61] the birth of the twins as a result of the IVF procedure, the wife's obtaining a protective order against the husband, the husband's filing for a divorce, and the wife's then seeking "to thaw the preembryos for implantation in the hopes of having additional children." The probate judge concluded that "[n]o agreement should be enforced in equity when intervening events have changed the circumstances such that the agreement which was originally signed did not contemplate the actual situation now facing the parties." In the absence of a binding agreement, the judge determined that the "best solution" was to balance the wife's interest in procreation against the husband's interest in avoiding procreation. Based on his findings,[62] the judge determined that the husband's interest in avoiding procreation outweighed the wife's interest in having additional children and granted the permanent injunction in favor of the husband.

3. *Legal background.* While IVF has been available for over two decades and has been the focus of much academic commentary,[63] there is little

---

60. The husband and wife signed a total of seven consent forms. All the forms were preprinted and identical to the consent form described above.

61. There was considerable delay between the entry of judgment in the Probate Court on May 14, 1996, and the argument on the present appeal. The delay was due to the fact that portions of the record were missing and had to be reconstructed.

62. In view of our disposition, it is unnecessary to summarize these findings.

63. See, e.g., Coleman, Procreative Liberty and Contemporaneous Choice: An Inalienable Rights Approach to Frozen Embryo Disputes, 84 Minn. L. Rev. 55 (1999); Note, To Have

law on the enforceability of agreements concerning the disposition of frozen preembryos. Only three States have enacted legislation addressing the issue. See Fla. Stat. Ann. §742.17 (West 1997) (requiring couples to execute written agreement for disposition in event of death, divorce or other unforeseen circumstances); N.H. Rev. Stat. Ann. §§168-B:13 thru 168-B:15, 168-B:18 (1994 & Supp.1999) (requiring couples to undergo medical examinations and counseling and imposing a fourteen-day limit for maintenance of ex utero prezygotes[64]); La. Rev. Stat. Ann. §§9:121-9:133 (1991) (providing that "prezygote considered 'juridical person' that must be implanted[,]" Kass v. Kass, 91 N.Y.2d 554, 563, 673 N.Y.S.2d 350, 696 N.E.2d 174 [1998]).

Two State courts of last resort, the Supreme Court of Tennessee and the Court of Appeals of New York, have dealt with the enforceability of agreements between donors regarding the disposition of preembryos and have concluded that such agreements should ordinarily be enforced. The Supreme Court of Tennessee, in Davis v. Davis, 842 S.W.2d 588 (Tenn. 1992), cert. denied sub nom. Stowe v. Davis, 507 U.S. 911, 113 S. Ct. 1259, 122 L. Ed. 2d 657 (1993), considered the issue in a dispute between a husband and his former wife after the two were divorced. The wife sought to donate the preembryos at issue to another couple for implantation.[65] The court stated that agreements between donors regarding disposition of the preembryos "should be presumed valid and should be enforced."[66] Id. at 597. In that case, because there was no agreement between the donors regarding disposition of the preembryos, the court balanced the equitable interests of the two parties and concluded that the husband's interest in avoiding parenthood outweighed the wife's interest in donating the preembryos to another couple for implantation. Id. at 603.

The Court of Appeals of New York, in Kass v. Kass, *supra*, agreed with the Tennessee court's view that courts should enforce agreements where potential parents provide for the disposition of frozen preembryos.[67] Id. at

---

or Not to Have: Whose Procreative Rights Prevail in Disputes over Dispositions of Frozen Embryos?, 27 Conn. L. Rev. 1377 (1995); Forster, The Legal and Ethical Debate Surrounding the Storage and Destruction of Frozen Human Embryos: A Reaction to the Mass Disposal in Britain and the Lack of Law in the United States, 76 Wash. U. L.Q. 759 (1998); Robertson, Prior Agreements for Disposition of Frozen Embryos, 51 Ohio St. L.J. 407 (1990); Sheinbach, Examining Disputes over Ownership Rights to Frozen Embryos: Will Prior Consent Documents Survive if Challenged by State Law and/or Constitutional Principles?, 48 Cath. U. L. Rev. 989 (1999); Note, Divergent Conceptions: Procreational Rights and Disputes over the Fate of Frozen Embryos, 7 B.U. Pub. Int. L.J. 315 (1998); Walter, His, Hers, or Theirs — Custody, Control, and Contracts: Allocating Decisional Authority over Frozen Embryos, 29 Seton Hall L. Rev. 937 (1999).

64. Ex utero prezygotes are fertilized eggs being stored outside the body.

65. When the suit commenced, the wife had sought custody of the preembryos for herself for implantation. By the time the case reached the Supreme Court of Tennessee, the wife had changed her position. Davis v. Davis, 842 S.W.2d 588, 589 (Tenn. 1992), cert. denied sub nom. Stowe v. Davis, 507 U.S. 911, 113 S. Ct. 1259, 122 L. Ed. 2d 657 (1993).

66. The Supreme Court of Tennessee used the term "embryo" to describe the fertilized egg. Id. We use the term "preembryo" throughout for consistency.

67. The Court of Appeals of New York used the term "pre-zygotes" to refer to the fertilized egg. Kass v. Kass, 91 N.Y.2d 554, 557 n.1, 673 N.Y.S.2d 350, 696 N.E.2d 174 (1998). We continue to use the term "preembryo" for consistency.

565, 673 N.Y.S.2d 350, 696 N.E.2d 174. The issue arose in that case also in the context of a dispute between a husband and his former wife after divorce. The wife sought custody of the preembryos for implantation. According to the New York court, agreements "should generally be presumed valid and binding, and enforced in any dispute between [the donors]."[68] *Id.*, citing Davis v. Davis, *supra* at 597. While recognizing that it is difficult for donors to anticipate the future of their relationship, the court concluded that such agreements minimize misunderstanding, maximize procreative liberty, and provide needed certainty to IVF programs. Kass v. Kass, *supra*. The court determined that the consent form signed by the donors with the IVF clinic unequivocally manifested the donors' mutual intent, and that this intent was further highlighted by the divorce instrument, which was consistent with the consent form and had been signed only months before suit was begun. *Id.* at 567, 673 N.Y.S.2d 350, 696 N.E.2d 174. Therefore the court enforced the agreement that provided that the frozen preembryos be donated to the IVF clinic. *Id.* at 567-569, 673 N.Y.S.2d 350, 696 N.E.2d 174.

4. *Legal analysis.* This is the first reported case involving the disposition of frozen preembryos in which a consent form signed between the donors on the one hand and the clinic on the other provided that, on the donors' separation, the preembryos were to be given to one of the donors for implantation. In view of the purpose of the form (drafted by and to give assistance to the clinic) and the circumstances of execution, we are dubious at best that it represents the intent of the husband and the wife regarding disposition of the preembryos in the case of a dispute between them. In any event, for several independent reasons, we conclude that the form should not be enforced in the circumstances of this case.

First, the consent form's primary purpose is to explain to the donors the benefits and risks of freezing, and to record the donors' desires for disposition of the frozen preembryos at the time the form is executed in order to provide the clinic with guidance if the donors (as a unit) no longer wish to use the frozen preembryos. The form does not state, and the record does not indicate, that the husband and wife intended the consent form to act as a binding agreement between them should they later disagree as to the disposition. Rather, it appears that it was intended only to define the donors' relationship as a unit with the clinic.

Second, the consent form does not contain a duration provision.[69] The wife sought to enforce this particular form four years after it was signed by the husband in significantly changed circumstances and over the husband's objection. In the absence of any evidence that the donors agreed on the time period during which the consent form was to govern their conduct, we cannot assume that the donors intended the consent form to govern the

68. The consent form signed by the donors in the *Kass* case provided that the preembryos should be disposed of by donating them to scientific research. *Id.* at 560, 673 N.Y.S.2d 350, 696 N.E.2d 174. The court did not address a circumstance in which the form stated that the preembryos be given to one of the donors for implantation in the donor.

69. See supra at 154-155, 725 N.E.2d at 1053-1054.

disposition of the frozen preembryos four years after it was executed, especially in light of the fundamental change in their relationship (i.e., divorce).

Third, the form uses the term "[s]hould we become separated" in referring to the disposition of the frozen preembryos without defining "become separated." Because this dispute arose in the context of a divorce, we cannot conclude that the consent form was intended to govern in these circumstances. Separation and divorce have distinct legal meanings.[70] Legal changes occur by operation of law when a couple divorces that do not occur when a couple separates. Because divorce legally ends a couple's marriage, we shall not assume, in the absence of any evidence to the contrary, that an agreement on this issue providing for separation was meant to govern in the event of a divorce.

The donors' conduct in connection with the execution of the consent forms also creates doubt whether the consent form at issue here represents the clear intentions of both donors. The probate judge found that, prior to the signing of the first consent form, the wife called the IVF clinic to inquire about the section of the form regarding disposition "upon separation": that section of the preprinted form that asked the donors to specify either "donated" or "destroyed" or "both." A clinic representative told her that "she could cross out any of the language on the form and fill in her own [language] to fit her wishes." Further, although the wife used language in each subsequent form similar to the language used in the first form that she and her husband signed together, the consent form at issue here was signed in blank by the husband, before the wife filled in the language indicating that she would use the preembryos for implantation on separation. We therefore cannot conclude that the consent form represents the true intention of the husband for the disposition of the preembryos.

Finally, the consent form is not a separation agreement that is binding on the couple in a divorce proceeding pursuant to G.L. c. 208, §34. The consent form does not contain provisions for custody, support, and maintenance, in the event that the wife conceives and gives birth to a child. See G.L. c. 208, §1A; C.P. Kindregan, Jr. & M.L. Inker, Family Law and Practice §50.3 (2d ed. 1996). In summary, the consent form is legally insufficient in several important respects and does not approach the minimum level of completeness needed to denominate it as an enforceable contract in a dispute between the husband and the wife.

With this said, we conclude that, even had the husband and the wife entered into an unambiguous agreement between themselves regarding the disposition of the frozen preembryos, we would not enforce an agreement that would compel one donor to become a parent against his or her

---

70. See, e.g., G.L. c. 191, §9 (revocation of dispositions in will to former spouse upon divorce or annulment; decree of separation does not terminate status of husband and wife and is not divorce for purposes of statute); DuMont v. Godbey, 382 Mass. 234, 236, 415 N.E.2d 188 (1981) ("Divorce, but not separation, revokes will provisions for the former spouse . . ."); Campagna v. Campagna, 337 Mass. 599, 605, 150 N.E.2d 699 (1958) (decree of living apart for justifiable cause does not sever marital relationship and therefore does not change status of property held by tenancy by entirety); Bernatavicius v. Bernatavicius, 259 Mass. 486, 489, 156 N.E. 685 (1927) ("A tenancy by the entirety . . . cannot continue after the tenants have become divorced and thus have ended the legal relationship to each other, which constitutes the essence of that tenancy").

will.[71] As a matter of public policy, we conclude that forced procreation is not an area amenable to judicial enforcement. It is well-established that courts will not enforce contracts that violate public policy.[72] Beacon Hill Civic Ass'n v. Ristorante Toscano, Inc., 422 Mass. 318, 320-321, 662 N.E.2d 1015 (1996). Commonwealth v. Henry's Drywall Co., 366 Mass. 539, 543, 320 N.E.2d 911 (1974). Exxon Corp. v. Esso Workers' Union, Inc., 118 F.3d 841, 844-845 (1st Cir. 1997). While courts are hesitant to invalidate contracts on these public policy grounds, the public interest in freedom of contract is sometimes outweighed by other public policy considerations; in those cases the contract will not be enforced.[73] Beacon Hill Civic Ass'n v. Ristorante Toscano, Inc., *supra*. To determine public policy, we look to the expressions of the Legislature and to those of this court. Capazzoli v. Holzwasser, 397 Mass. 158, 160, 490 N.E.2d 420 (1986).

The Legislature has already determined by statute that individuals should not be bound by certain agreements binding them to enter or not enter into familial relationships. In G.L. c. 207, §47A, the Legislature abolished the cause of action for the breach of a promise to marry. In G.L. c. 210, §2, the Legislature provided that no mother may agree to surrender her child "sooner than the fourth calendar day after the date of birth of the child to be adopted" regardless of any prior agreement.

Similarly, this court has expressed its hesitancy to become involved in intimate questions inherent in the marriage relationship. Doe v. Doe, 365 Mass. 556, 563, 314 N.E.2d 128 (1974). "Except in cases involving divorce or separation, our law has not in general undertaken to resolve the many delicate questions inherent in the marriage relationship. We would not order either a husband or a wife to do what is necessary to conceive a

---

71. That is the relief sought by the wife in this case. We express no view regarding whether an unambiguous agreement between two donors concerning the disposition of frozen preembryos could be enforced over the contemporaneous objection of one of the donors, when such agreement contemplated destruction or donation of the preembryos either for research or implantation in a surrogate. We also recognize that agreements among donors and IVF clinics are essential to clinic operations. There is no impediment to the enforcement of such contracts by the clinics or by the donors against the clinics, consistent with the principles of this opinion.

72. The New York court noted that the wife had not argued that the consent form violated public policy, and suggested that in some circumstances agreements may be unenforceable for that reason. Kass v. Kass, 91 N.Y.2d 554, 565 n.4, 673 N.Y.S.2d 350, 696 N.E.2d 174 (1998).

73. We have refused to enforce contracts in a variety of contexts because of a conflict with public policy. See, e.g., Beacon Hill Civic Ass'n v. Ristorante Toscano, Inc., 422 Mass. 318, 322-325, 662 N.E.2d 1015 (1996) (contract in which neighborhood association promised not to oppose beer and wine license in exchange for promise of restaurant not to seek general alcohol license violates public policy); Loranger Constr. Co. v. C. Franklin Corp., 355 Mass. 727, 730, 247 N.E.2d 391 (1969) (covenant restraining trade violates public policy if not limited reasonably in time and space); DiLeo v. Daneault, 329 Mass. 590, 595-596, 109 N.E.2d 824 (1953) (contract requiring proprietor of union barber shop to join barbers' union violates public policy); Allen v. Lawrence, 318 Mass. 210, 213, 61 N.E.2d 133 (1945) (contract in which public official agrees to accept lower salary than established by law violates public policy); New Haven Road Constr. Co. v. Long, 269 Mass. 16, 18, 168 N.E. 161 (1929) (contract requiring payment to private contractor for use of public highway violates public policy); Parsons v. Trask, 73 Mass. 473, 7 Gray 473, 478 (1856) (contract establishing unlimited period of servitude violates public policy).

child or to prevent conception, any more than we would order either party to do what is necessary to make the other happy." *Id.*

In our decisions, we have also indicated a reluctance to enforce prior agreements that bind individuals to future family relationships.[74] In R.R. v. M.H., 426 Mass. 501, 689 N.E.2d 790 (1998), we held that a surrogacy agreement in which the surrogate mother agreed to give up the child on its birth is unenforceable unless the agreement contained, inter alia, a "reasonable" waiting period during which the mother could change her mind. *Id.* at 510, 689 N.E.2d 790. In Capazzoli v. Holzwasser, *supra*, we determined, as an expression of public policy, that a contract requiring an individual to abandon a marriage is unenforceable. And, in the same spirit, we stated in Gleason v. Mann, 312 Mass. 420, 425, 45 N.E.2d 280 (1942), that agreements providing for a general restraint against marriage are unenforceable.

We glean from these statutes and judicial decisions that prior agreements to enter into familial relationships (marriage or parenthood) should not be enforced against individuals who subsequently reconsider their decisions. This enhances the "freedom of personal choice in matters of marriage and family life." Moore v. East Cleveland, 431 U.S. 494, 499, 97 S. Ct. 1932, 52 L. Ed. 2d 531 (1977), quoting Cleveland Bd. of Educ. v. LaFleur, 414 U.S. 632, 639-640, 94 S. Ct. 791, 39 L. Ed. 2d 52 (1974).

We derive from existing State laws and judicial precedent a public policy in this Commonwealth that individuals shall not be compelled to enter into intimate family relationships, and that the law shall not be used as a mechanism for forcing such relationships when they are not desired. This policy is grounded in the notion that respect for liberty and privacy requires that individuals be accorded the freedom to decide whether to enter into a family relationship. See Commonwealth v. Stowell, 389 Mass. 171, 173, 449 N.E.2d 357 (1983). "There are 'personal rights of such delicate and intimate character that direct enforcement of them by any process of the court should never be attempted.'" Doe v. Doe, *supra* at 559, 314 N.E.2d 128, quoting Kenyon v. Chicopee, 320 Mass. 528, 534, 70 N.E.2d 241 (1946).

In this case, we are asked to decide whether the law of the Commonwealth may compel an individual to become a parent over his or her contemporaneous objection. The husband signed this consent form in 1991. Enforcing the form against him would require him to become a parent over his present objection to such an undertaking. We decline to do so.

---

74. We have enforced agreements regarding the family relationship once the parties have freely entered into that relationship, but these cases have not involved the issue of procreation. See G.L. c. 209, §2 (married woman may make contracts with husband); Ames v. Perry, 406 Mass. 236, 241, 547 N.E.2d 309 (1989), quoting White v. White, 141 Vt. 499, 503, 450 A.2d 1108 (1982) (providing that "divorcing parents may in some cases bind themselves in contract on matters involving their children"); Stansel v. Stansel, 385 Mass. 510, 432 N.E.2d 691 (1982) (enforcing separation agreement); Rosenberg v. Lipnick, 377 Mass. 666, 673, 389 N.E.2d 385 (1979) (enforcing antenuptial agreement). Cf. Wilcox v. Trautz, 427 Mass. 326, 327, 693 N.E.2d 141 (1998) (enforcing agreement between unmarried cohabitants).

STUDY GUIDE: *In A.Z. v. B.Z., the court had to decide whether to announce a new public policy limiting freedom of contract. In the next case, the court must consider whether to extend or limit a very old public policy. Pay close attention to the various theories considered by the court as to why this contract might not be enforceable. What is the difference between saying that the contract is "illegal" and saying that it "violates public policy"? How do the majority and the dissent read the same law and history so differently?*

MEYER v. HAWKINSON

Supreme Court of North Dakota,
2001 ND 78, 626 N.W.2d 262 (2001)

KAPSNER, Justice.

Clyde and Dorothy Meyer appeal from the district court's grant of summary judgment for Donald M. and Marilyn F. Hawkinson, dismissing Meyers' claim for enforcement of an alleged contract to share proceeds of the Western Canadian Lottery. The district court granted summary judgment because the alleged contract had an unlawful object and would be unenforceable as contrary to North Dakota's public policy against gambling. We hold the public policy of the state of North Dakota would not allow our courts to enforce an alleged contract to share proceeds of a winning lottery ticket. We affirm.

I

On August 16, 1997, Clyde Meyer drove his wife, Dorothy Meyer, and their friends, Donald and Marilyn Hawkinson, from Fargo, North Dakota to Winnipeg, Canada to attend the horse races. They planned to split the cost of gas for the trip, as was their custom. After checking into the hotel, Donald Hawkinson purchased a lottery ticket with three quick pick numbers at the hotel gift shop, and then he returned to the lounge to tell Marilyn Hawkinson and the Meyers about his purchase. Clyde Meyer claims Donald Hawkinson said to Clyde, "Go buy three lottery tickets and we'll split." Clyde Meyer testified he directly turned around, walked to the gift stand, and bought three lottery tickets.

The following day Donald Hawkinson discovered that one of his lottery ticket numbers was a winner of $1.6 million Canadian ($1.2 million U.S.). Clyde claims he went to meet his wife in the restaurant and thought he told her, "We won the lottery, Don's ticket."

The parties had been friends for over forty years, often gambling together. Donald frequently bought lottery tickets, but the parties never pooled their funds to purchase lottery tickets. On this occasion, after Donald won the lottery, he paid for all the Meyers' drinks and meals.

. . . Two to three weeks later, Donald told Clyde there would be no equal sharing of the winnings, and Clyde said he understood there would be no equal split, but he thought Donald would share the winnings. On about September 17, 1997, Donald sent each of the Meyers $2,500 as a gesture of friendship. Dorothy Meyer stated Clyde expected Donald to buy him a motor home, and so their friendship ended.

Clyde and Dorothy Meyer filed a civil action against Donald and Marilyn Hawkinson to enforce a contract to share equally in the lottery winnings. . . . [T]he district court granted summary judgment for the Hawkinsons, reasoning even if the alleged contract existed, such an agreement would be contrary to North Dakota's public policy against gambling. The district court concluded the alleged contract would be unenforceable because its object, although lawful in Canada, is unlawful in North Dakota as it violates state anti-gambling statutes. The Meyers appealed.

. . .

III

The Meyers argue the district court erred in granting Hawkinsons' motion for summary judgment by finding as a matter of law the alleged contract between the parties is unenforceable because it is contrary to the public policy of North Dakota. We disagree.

Gambling differs from other business transactions, and ordinary remedies usually are not available to enforce gambling debts. It is essential to the existence of a contract to have a lawful object. A contract is void if the consideration given for the contract is unlawful. A contract is unlawful if it is (1) contrary to an express provision of law; (2) contrary to the policy of express law, although not expressly prohibited; or (3) otherwise contrary to good morals.

A

The Meyers argue the alleged contract is not contrary to an express provision of law because it was entered into in Canada where the lottery is legal and because the alleged contract does not violate the laws of North Dakota. However, whether the alleged contract is contrary to express provision of law in North Dakota is essential to determining whether the contract is enforceable. The question is whether such a contract is enforceable in the courts of North Dakota or whether our courts will not be used to enforce such contracts because they are contrary to the public policy of this state.

The Constitution of North Dakota, Article XI, §25, provides:

> The legislative assembly shall not authorize any game of chance, lottery, or gift enterprises, under any pretense, or for any purpose whatever. However, the legislative assembly may authorize by law bona fide nonprofit veterans', charitable, educational, religious, or fraternal organizations, civic and service clubs, or such other public-spirited organizations as it may recognize, to conduct games of chance when the entire net proceeds of such games of chance are to be devoted to educational, charitable, patriotic, fraternal, religious, or other public-spirited uses.

In 1976, a constitutional amendment gave the legislature limited authority to authorize some forms of gambling. Under that limited constitutional authorization, the legislature enacted N.D.C.C. ch. 53-06.1 describing which games of chance are authorized in North Dakota, the persons and organizations authorized to hold such games of chance, and a regulatory licensing structure to ensure fairness and to ensure proceeds are devoted to purposes required by the constitution. Under N.D.C.C. §53-06.1-11.1(2), a licensed organization shall disburse gambling proceeds only for a specified list of educational, charitable, patriotic, fraternal, religious, or public-spirited uses.

Under North Dakota law, gambling is defined as risking any money or other thing of value for gain, contingent on a lot, chance, or the happening or outcome of an event over which the person taking the risk has no control. N.D.C.C. §12.1-28-01(1). In addition, N.D.C.C. §12.1-28-02(2) makes it a class A misdemeanor to: ". . . Sell, purchase, receive, or transfer a chance to participate in a lottery, whether the lottery is drawn in state or out of state, and whether the lottery is lawful in the other state or country. . . ."

Clearly, an alleged contract to share proceeds of a $1.2 million lottery would be illegal if entered into in North Dakota.

Our state constitution expressly forbids lotteries and games of chance unless the entire net proceeds are devoted to public-spirited uses statutorily specified as educational, charitable, patriotic, fraternal, and religious. In addition, N.D.C.C. §12.1-28-02(2), which criminalizes sales, purchases, receipt, or transfer of lottery chances, comprehensively forbids such activities whether the lottery is in state or out of state. By express terms, the statute prohibits these activities even if the lottery is legal in the other state or country. The statute also criminalizes dissemination of information about a lottery with intent to encourage participation in the lottery. Although §12.1-28-02(2) refers to lottery chances, not proceeds, a chance to share proceeds is really a chance to participate in a lottery.

The alleged contract between the Meyers and Hawkinsons to share lottery winnings is a wager, or "risking any money . . . or other thing of value for gain, contingent [on a] lot, chance, . . . or the happening or outcome of an event . . . over which the person taking the risk has no control," and constitutes gambling under the statutory definition of gambling. See N.D.C.C. §12.1-28-01(1). This Court will not enforce contracts which have an unlawful purpose or unlawful consideration. See N.D.C.C. §§9-01-02, 9-05-04; see also Erickson v. North Dakota State Fair Ass'n of Fargo, 211 N.W. 597, 599, 54 N.D. 830, 836 (N.D. 1926) (refusing to enforce an alleged contract to run an illegal horse race for prize money because courts will not aid parties engaged in illegal transactions, but rather will leave the parties where it finds them); Drinkall v. Movius State Bank, 88 N.W. 724, 727, 11 N.D. 10 (N.D. 1901) (holding neither party to an illegal contract may be aided by the courts, either to set it aside or enforce it).

We conclude the alleged contract if entered into in North Dakota would violate the express law against gambling. However, the contract was not created in North Dakota, so that does not end our inquiry. The contract may still be unlawful if contrary to the public policy underpinning express law, although not expressly prohibited.

B

The Meyers argue the alleged contract to share lottery proceeds is not void as against public policy. We are not persuaded.

Public policy is a principle of law whereby contracts will not be enforced if they have a tendency to be injurious to the public or against the public good. Johnson v. Peterbilt of Fargo, Inc., 438 N.W.2d 162, 163 (N.D. 1989). Whether the contract is against public policy is generally provided for by the state constitution or statute. Id.; see, e.g., N.D.C.C. §9-08-02 (providing that all contracts which have for their object exemption of persons from responsibility for their own fraud or willful injury to the person or property of another, or wilful or negligent violation of law, are against the policy of the law). However, when a contract is inconsistent with fair and honorable dealing, contrary to sound policy, and offensive to good morals, the courts have the authority to declare the contract void as against public policy. *Johnson*, at 164; see also N.D.C.C. §9-08-01 (deeming contracts unlawful if contrary to express law; contrary to policy of express law, although not expressly prohibited; or contrary to good morals).

Despite the constitutional amendment authorizing some limited forms of gambling, the legislature's anti-gambling message remains especially strong regarding lotteries. Section 12.1-28-02(2), N.D.C.C., prohibits the sale, purchase, receipt, or transfer of a chance to participate in a lottery, whether the lottery is drawn in state or out of state, and whether the lottery is lawful in the other state or country. (Emphasis added.) We regard the underlined language as clear indication of the public policy against lotteries. The use of our courts in the manner requested by the Meyers would frustrate that policy. In addition to the legislature, the voters have demonstrated opposition to lotteries. In 1986, a constitutional amendment proposed authorizing a state-operated lottery for the purpose of providing tax relief for the citizens of North Dakota. This proposed amendment met strong resistance. Ultimately, the proposed amendment to establish a North Dakota lottery was defeated in the November 1986 general election.

The Meyers argue that by refusing them an opportunity to enforce this contract, the courts would only reward those who convert the property of others. They cite cases from other jurisdictions which have enforced alleged contracts to split the proceeds of lotteries, although the lotteries were not legal in the state where the contract was formed. . . .

Other jurisdictions have refused to enforce contracts to split lottery proceeds because if the winning ticket is not jointly owned, then the parties are wagering against each other on the outcome of the lottery, which violates state statutes against wagering on the outcome of uncertain events over which no party has control. In Dickerson v. Deno, 770 So. 2d 63, 64 (Ala. 2000), the court voided an agreement to share winnings between Alabama holders of individually owned Florida lottery tickets. Because the tickets were owned by each individual party, they could only receive the proceeds from the winning lottery ticket as a result of their side agreement to share, not as a result of an ownership interest in the winning ticket. Id. at 66. Thus, the court reasoned the contract was founded on gambling consideration as it was a wager, hedging their bets in an attempt to increase each party's odds of winning the Florida lottery, an uncertain event none of the parties controlled. Id. at 66-67.

One jurisdiction even refused to enforce an agreement to split lottery proceeds between joint owners of the winning ticket, reasoning their joint venture was formed for the purpose of wagering on the outcome of a contingent event. See Cole v. Hughes, 114 N.C. App. 424, 442 S.E.2d 86, 88-89 (1994) (voiding a joint venture agreement entered into in North Carolina to purchase Virginia lottery tickets and equally share winnings because North Carolina statute prohibits wagers depending on any chance event and voids contracts for the purpose of such wagering). When the parties then tried to enforce their joint venture agreement in Virginia, where the winning lottery ticket was purchased legally, that jurisdiction also refused to enforce the contract because the agreement was based on gambling consideration. See Hughes v. Cole, 251 Va. 3, 465 S.E.2d 820, 827 (1996) (voiding the joint venture agreement entered into in North Carolina to purchase Virginia lottery tickets and share winnings, because a Virginia statute prohibited gaming contracts, even though the lottery was legal in Virginia).

In this case, the Meyers and Hawkinsons did not pool their money to jointly purchase the winning lottery ticket, and therefore Hawkinsons are not converting Meyers' property. Rather, Clyde Meyer and Donald Hawkinson were allegedly exchanging promises to share winnings from their individually owned lottery tickets on the happening of the uncertain event that the numbers drawn in the Canadian lottery matched one of their ticket numbers. Consequently, the alleged contract between Hawkinson and Meyer was a wager or side bet, that is, an attempt to hedge their bets and increase their odds of winning the Canadian lottery.

We have recognized that courts must be mindful of the right of individuals to enter contracts, when the court is faced with deciding whether a contract is against public policy. Martin v. Allianz Life Ins. Co. of North America, 1998 ND 8, ¶20, 573 N.W.2d 823. We have also acknowledged that the legislature is much better suited than the courts for setting the public policy of the state. Id. The statutory language, as well as the legislative and electoral history, comprehensively and clearly convey the policy underlying North Dakota's repeated rejection of a state-operated lottery and high-stakes gambling. See Trinity Med. Ctr., Inc. v. Holum, 544 N.W.2d 148, 152 (N.D. 1996) (providing the "cardinal rule" of statutory construction is that our interpretation must be consistent with legislative intent and done in a manner which will accomplish the policy goals and objectives of the statute). Therefore, we affirm the trial court's grant of summary judgment by finding as a matter of law the alleged contract between Clyde Meyer and Donald Hawkinson is contrary to public policy of the state of North Dakota and unenforceable in our courts.

V

The judgment of dismissal is affirmed.

SANDSTROM, Justice, dissenting.

Because the majority misapprehends the history of gambling in North Dakota and the working of our gambling laws, and misstates the public policy of our state, I respectfully dissent.

I

Although a quarter of a century ago, a credible argument might have been made that the public policy of North Dakota opposed the enforcement of a contract relating to gambling, no such argument can prevail today.

The early years of our statehood were shaped by the corruption of the Louisiana Lottery, the last of the so-called "great national lotteries." So corrupt that it was kicked out of Louisiana, the lottery company, seeking to establish the state as its new base of operations, came to "buy" the North Dakota legislature during its first session. The report of the Pinkerton detectives would establish there was good reason to believe the legislature was for sale. Governor John Miller, and others of great integrity, had secretly hired the Pinkerton Detectives to document the buying of votes at $500 per vote. Senate Bill 167 was introduced to permit lotteries. While the bill passed the Senate, when the investigation of the Pinkerton Detectives was revealed, the reaction was so strong that the bill was indefinitely postponed in the House. The people sent virtually a whole new legislature to Bismarck for the Second Legislative Assembly and proceeded as rapidly as the cumbersome procedures of the day would permit to adopt the First Amendment to the North Dakota Constitution, prohibiting all "lottery, or gift enterprises."

Over the next 85 years, North Dakota had a rather mixed history on gambling, ranging from Attorney General Nels Johnson, 1945-48, driving the slot machines out of the state, to Elmo Christiansen, in 1954, being convicted of conspiracy to bring illegal gambling into the state. In 1964 and 1968, constitutional amendments to permit parimutuel betting on horse and dog races were defeated. Id. at 6. In 1972, the text of the First Amendment to the North Dakota Constitution was submitted separately to the voters considering a new state constitution. The gambling provision failed to get the majority vote needed for inclusion in the new constitution and therefore would have been omitted had the new constitution been adopted.

The 1973 legislature, in adopting the New Criminal Code to be effective July 1, 1975, greatly increased the penalties for gambling — from misdemeanors to mostly felonies.

The 1975 legislature, at the urging of then-Attorney General Allen I. Olson, proposed a constitutional amendment to legalize gambling for charitable purposes. The aftermath of Watergate and the resignation of President Richard Nixon emphasized the importance of obeying the law and changing, rather than violating, laws with which the people did not agree. Olson cracked down on widespread illegal gambling and urged the people to speak with their ballots.

After the 1976 approval of the constitutional amendment, the 1977 legislature legalized charitable gambling, requiring the entire net proceeds go to "[n]onprofit veterans, charitable, educational, religious, and fraternal organizations, civic and service clubs, and public-spirited organizations."

The 1981 legislature made North Dakota only the third state in the nation — following Nevada and New Jersey — to legalize "Blackjack" or "Twenty-one." North Dakota became the third state with casinos — this before state lotteries became widespread, before modern riverboat gambling, and before the rise of Indian gambling.

In 1993, after the rise of modern state lotteries, the North Dakota legislature repealed the ban on lottery advertising — as long as the lottery was legal where it was conducted. North Dakota's legalization of advertising of out-of-state lotteries cannot be reconciled with the majority's claimed public policy against them.

. . .

The majority holds "the public policy of the state of North Dakota would not allow our courts to enforce an alleged contract to share proceeds of a winning lottery ticket." The majority misstates the public policy of this State. In the context of contract enforcement, the concept of public policy "is vague and variable." 17A Am. Jur. 2d Contracts §258 (1991). Public policy related to contract enforcement is fluid, flexible, and ever-changing:

> Public policy has been described as the will-o'-the-wisp of the law which varies and changes with the interests, habits, needs, sentiments, and fashions of the day; the public policy of one generation may not, under changed conditions, be the public policy of another. Thus, the very reverse of that which is public policy at one time may become public policy at another time.

Id. (footnotes omitted).

. . .

Courts, including this Court, increasingly decline to render contracts invalid on the basis of public policy. The court's power "to declare a contract void as against public policy must be exercised with caution and only in cases that are free from doubt." 17A Am. Jur. 2d Contracts §264 (1991) (footnote omitted). As stated in Johnson v. Peterbilt of Fargo, Inc., 438 N.W.2d 162, 164 (N.D. 1989):

> When a court is faced with deciding whether a contract is against public policy, it must also be mindful of an individual's right to enter into a contract. "It is not the court's function to curtail the liberty to contract by enabling parties to escape their valid contractual obligation on the ground of public policy unless the preservation of the general public welfare imperatively so demands." Tschirgi v. Merchants National Bank of Cedar Rapids, 253 Iowa 682, 690, 113 N.W.2d 226, 231 (1962).

. . .

Because the majority misperceives our history, misunderstands our law, and misstates our public policy, I cannot concur. Because the majority ignores its duty to enforce lawful contracts, I respectfully dissent.

Legal Background: Freedom of Contract

STUDY GUIDE: *The following case concerned a claim that "a contract by which an inventor agrees to sell what he may invent, or acquire a patent for before he has invented it, is against public policy . . . because it would discourage inventions; that if a man knows that he cannot obtain any pecuniary benefit from his invention, having already received the price for it, he will not invent, or if he does invent will keep it secret, and will not take out a patent." What does Jessel's reply to this argument imply for other arguments based on public policy such as those included in the preceding opinion?*

PRINTING AND NUMERICAL REGISTERING CO. v. SAMPSON, 19 EQ. 462 (ROLLS CT. 1875): JESSEL, M.R.*: . . . It must not be forgotten that you are not to extend arbitrarily those rules which say that a given contract is void as being against public policy, because if there is one thing which more than another public policy requires it is that men of full age and competent understanding shall have the utmost liberty of contracting, and that their contracts when entered into freely and voluntarily shall be held sacred and shall be enforced by Courts of justice. Therefore, you have this paramount public policy to consider — that you are not lightly to interfere with this freedom of contract. Now, there is no doubt public policy may say that a contract to commit a crime . . . is necessarily void. The decisions have gone further, and contracts to commit an immoral offence . . . or to induce another to do something against the general rules of morality, though far more indefinite than the previous class, have always been held to be void. I should be sorry to extend the doctrine much further. I do not say there are no other cases to which it does apply; but I should be sorry to extend it much further. . . .

REFERENCE: Farnsworth, §5.1
               Calamari & Perillo, §22.1
               Murray, §99

STUDY GUIDE: Would §178 apply to A.Z. v. B.Z. or Meyer v. Hawkinson? If so, which section?

RESTATEMENT (SECOND) OF CONTRACTS

§178.   WHEN A TERM IS UNENFORCEABLE ON GROUNDS OF PUBLIC POLICY

(1) A promise or other term of an agreement is unenforceable on grounds of public policy if legislation provides that it is unenforceable or the interest in its enforcement is clearly outweighed in the circumstances by a public policy against the enforcement of such terms.

(2) In weighing the interest in the enforcement of a term, account is taken of

(a) the parties' justified expectations

(b) any forfeiture that would result if enforcement were denied, and

---

* *Sir George Jessel* (1824-1883) studied at University College, London (B.A., M.A.) and was called to the bar in 1847. He served in Parliament and was Solicitor-General before his appointment as Master of the Rolls in 1873, at which time he resigned his seat in Parliament. Jessel ascended to the bench during the time in which the courts of chancery and law were being merged in England. He later served concurrently as president of the Chancery Division of the Court of Appeals; he was relieved of his duties on the Rolls Court in 1881, and sat on the appeals court until five days before his death. — K.T.

(c) any special public interest in the enforcement of the particular term.

(3) In weighing a public policy against enforcement of a term, account is taken of

(a) the strength of that policy as manifested by legislation or judicial decisions,

(b) the likelihood that a refusal to enforce the term will further that policy,

(c) the seriousness of any misconduct involved and the extent to which it was deliberate, and

(d) the directness of the connection between that misconduct and the term.

§179. BASES OF PUBLIC POLICIES AGAINST ENFORCEMENT

A public policy against the enforcement of promises or other terms may be derived by the court from

(a) legislation relevant to such a policy, or

(b) the need to protect some aspect of the public welfare, as is the case for the judicial policies against, for example,

(i) restraint of trade . . .

(ii) impairment of family relations . . . , and

(iii) interference with other protected interests . . . .

17

FAILURE OF A BASIC ASSUMPTION

The previous chapter concerned defenses based on improper ways of obtaining a person's assent to contract. The defenses clustered in this chapter are based on an entirely different phenomenon. As computer researchers struggling to develop "artificial intelligence" have painfully realized, beginning in infancy every person learns far more about the world than she could possibly articulate — even to herself. Any parent can testify to the untold number of questions that children ask eliciting information that adults unconsciously take for granted. Until subjected to the barrage, one cannot fully appreciate the immense store of knowledge one possesses. One is also struck by one's inability to articulate what one knows perfectly well.

Each of us brings this virtual infinity of knowledge and skill to every interpersonal interaction and much, perhaps most, of this knowledge we hold in common. For example, even persons who have never conceived of the concept of gravity know that to build a tower out of toy blocks we have to begin *at the bottom*, not at the top. (An elaborately programmed computer used for one artificial intelligence experiment did not "realize" this basic fact and responded to a command to stack blocks by starting at the top. It then had to be reprogrammed with this basic assumption.) This vast repository of shared knowledge about the world and how it works is often referred to as "common sense." Common sense makes communication by means of a common language possible.

Add to the infinity of knowledge about the present world the inherent uncertainty of future events and we immediately can see that the seductive idea that a contract can anticipate and articulate every contingency that might arise before, during, or after performance is sheer fantasy. For this reason, contracts must be silent on an untold number of items. And many of these silent assumptions that underlie *every* agreement are as basic as the assumption that the sun will rise tomorrow. They are simply *too* basic to merit mention. This phenomenon was described by Lon L. Fuller as follows:

> Words like "intention," "assumption," "expectation" and "understanding" all seem to imply a *conscious* state involving an awareness of alternatives and a deliberate choice among them. It is, however, plain that there is a psychological state which can be described as a "tacit assumption" that does not involve a consciousness of alternatives. The absent-minded professor stepping from his office into the hall as he reads a book "assumes" that the floor of

the hall will be there to receive him. His conduct is conditioned and directed by this assumption, even though the possibility that the floor has been removed does not "occur" to him, that is, is not present in his mental processes.

In experiments with animals the relative strength of such "assumptions" can be roughly measured. If a rat is trained for months to run through a particular maze, the sudden interposition of a barrier in one of the channels will have a very disruptive effect on its behavior. For some time after encountering the barrier, it will be likely to engage in random and apparently pointless behavior, running in circles, scratching itself, etc. The degree to which the barrier operates disruptively reflects the strength of the "assumption" made by the rat that it would not be there. If the maze has been frequently changed, and the rat has only recently become accustomed to its present form, the introduction of a barrier will act less disruptively. In such a case, after a relatively short period of random behavior, the rat will begin to act purposely, will retrace its steps, seek other outlets, etc. In this situation the "assumption" that the channel would not be obstructed has not been deeply etched into the rat's nervous system; it behaves as if it "half-expected" some such impediment.

In a similar way, where parties have entered a contract an unexpected obstacle to performance may operate disruptively in varying degrees. To one who has contracted to carry goods by truck over a route traversing a mountain pass, a landslide filling the pass may be a very disruptive and unexpected event. But one who originally contracted to build the roadway through the mountains might view the same event occurring during the course of construction as a temporary set-back and a challenge to his resourcefulness. One who contracts to deliver goods a year from now at a price now fixed certainly "takes into account" the possibility of some fluctuation in price levels, but may feel that a tenfold inflation was contrary to an "assumption" or "expectation" that price variations would occur within the "normal" range, and that this expectation was "the foundation of the agreement."[1]

Thankfully, our shared basic tacit assumptions about the world usually hold true and we need never address them. Yet occasionally the unexpected occurs and contracting parties (and their lawyers and courts) must decide who between them bears the risk of these developments. A series of doctrines has evolved to handle the problem of when the occurrence of different kinds of failures of basic assumptions made by contracting parties justifies excusing them from performance. We examine these doctrines in this chapter.

In Section A we consider defenses based on mistaken assumptions about basic facts that exist *at the time* of contract formation. In Section B we consider defenses based on unanticipated events that occur sometime *after* formation. Because the seeds of the future always lie somewhere in the present, at times it is hard to distinguish in practice between these two kinds of failures of basic assumptions. Although these categories survive, if any portion of contract law is in need of further theoretical and doctrinal development, it is this one. One of our concerns in this chapter will be to ask whether the traditional distinctions between mistake, impracticability, and frustration remain useful as devices for determining the proper allocation of risk and, if so, why. In these sections, we also examine one common response to an assertion of a failure of a basic assumption: that the party

1. Lon L. Fuller, Basic Contract Law 666-667 (1947).

seeking to avoid the contract *assumed the risk* of the unexpected event. Finally, in Section C, we conclude our discussion of contract defenses — and contract law — with a consideration of the special problems that arise when allocating risks within *long-term* contractual relationships. We shall use this as an opportunity both to review the concepts studied in Sections A and B, and to highlight a distinctive approach to contracts that some professors may well have stressed throughout the course: the *relational theory of contract.*

A. MISTAKES OF PRESENT EXISTING FACTS

Just as a mere promise does not give rise to a contract, the mere fact that it was a "mistake" to enter into a contract does not provide a valid defense to its enforcement. Because everyone who breaches a contract in some sense made a mistake by entering into it, to permit any mistake to justify avoidance would be effectively to eliminate contractual enforcement. Still, the existence of a mistake, coupled with other circumstances, can sometimes constitute a defense. In particular, Restatement (Second) §151 defines a mistake as "a belief that is not in accord with the facts." In this section we shall consider the circumstances that elevate this sort of mistake into a valid plea in avoidance.

1. Mutual Mistake

STUDY GUIDE: What is the theoretical difference between a "mistake" and a "misunderstanding" of the sort we analyzed in Chapter 4? How does the next case differ from Raffles v. Wichelhaus? Note that this is the same court that six years earlier decided Hackley v. Headley. Is there a way of explaining why the court in the next case rescinds the contract, while the court in Hackley *refused to do so?*

SHERWOOD v. WALKER
Supreme Court of Michigan,
66 Mich. 568, 33 N.W. 919 (1887)

MORSE, J.* Replevin for a cow. Suit commenced in justice's court. Judgement for plaintiff; appealed to circuit court of Wayne county, and

---

* *Allen Benton Morse* (1839-1921) was educated at the Agricultural College at Lansing, Michigan, and the University of Michigan. He interrupted his legal studies to enlist in the Union Army at the outbreak of the Civil War, and advanced in rank until becoming acting assistant adjutant general on the staff of Gen. F. T. Sherman. Morse took part in many famous battles of the War, including Bull Run, Antietam, and Chickamagua; he lost an arm in the storming of Missionary Ridge. After the War, he resumed his law work and was admitted to the Michigan bar in 1865. For the next 20 years, he was engaged in private practice, with periods of concurrent service as the Ionia prosecuting attorney (1867-1871), as a member of the state senate (1875-1876), and as the mayor of Ionia (1882). Morse became a member of the Supreme Court of Michigan in 1885, and remained on the bench until 1892; the last two

verdict and judgment for plaintiff in that court. The defendants bring error, and set out 25 assignments of the same.

The main controversy depends upon the construction of a contract for the sale of the cow.

The plaintiff claims that the title passed, and bases his action upon such claim.

The defendants contend that the contract was executory, and by its terms no title to the animal was acquired by the plaintiff.

The defendants reside at Detroit, but are in business at Walkerville, Ontario, and have a farm at Greenfield, in Wayne county, upon which were some blooded cattle supposed to be barren as breeders. The Walkers are importers and breeders of polled Angus cattle.

The plaintiff is a banker living at Plymouth, in Wayne county. He called upon the defendants at Walkerville for the purchase of some of their stock, but found none there that suited him. Meeting one of the defendants afterwards, he was informed that they had a few head upon this Greenfield farm. He was asked to go out and look at them, with the statement at the time that they were probably barren, and would not breed.

May 5, 1886, plaintiff went out to Greenfield, and saw the cattle. A few days thereafter, he called upon one of the defendants with the view of purchasing a cow, known as "Rose 2d of Aberlone." After considerable talk, it was agreed that defendants would telephone Sherwood at his home in Plymouth in reference to the price. The second morning after this talk he was called up by the telephone, and the terms of the sale were finally agreed upon. He was to pay five and one-half cents per pound, live weight, fifty pounds shrinkage. He was asked how he intended to take the cow home, and replied that he might ship her from King's cattle-yard. He requested defendants to confirm the sale in writing, which they did by sending him the following letter:

WALKERVILLE, May 15, 1886

T.C. Sherwood, President, etc.

DEAR SIR:

We confirm sale to you of the cow Rose 2d of Aberlone, lot 56 of our catalogue, at five and a half cents per pound, less fifty pounds shrink. We inclose herewith order on Mr. Graham for the cow. You might leave check with him, or mail to us here, as you prefer.

Yours truly,

HIRAM WALKER & SONS.

years were spent as Chief Justice of that court. He resigned from that court to wage an unsuccessful campaign for the governorship of Michigan. Soon after, Morse was named Ambassador to Scotland by President Grover Cleveland. He returned to practice law in Ionia after four years in Glasgow, and ended his career there. — C.R.

The order upon Graham enclosed in the letter read as follows:

WALKERVILLE, May 15, 1886.

George Graham:

You will please deliver at King's cattle-yard to Mr. T.C. Sherwood, Plymouth, the cow Rose 2d of Aberlone, lot 56 of our catalogue. Send halter with the cow, and have her weighed.

Yours truly,

HIRAM WALKER & SONS.

On the twenty-first of the same month the plaintiff went to the defendants' farm at Greenfield, and presented the order and letter to Graham, who informed him that the defendants had instructed him not to deliver the cow. Soon after, the plaintiff tendered to Hiram Walker, one of the defendants, $80, and demanded the cow. Walker refused to take the money or deliver the cow. The plaintiff then instituted this suit.

After he had secured possession of the cow under the writ of replevin, the plaintiff caused her to be weighed by the constable who served the writ, at a place other than King's cattle-yard. She weighed 1,420 pounds.

When the plaintiff, upon the trial in the circuit court, had submitted his proofs showing the above transaction, defendants moved to strike out and exclude the testimony from the case, for the reason that it was irrelevant, and did not tend to show that the title to the cow passed, and that it showed that the contract of sale was merely executory. The court refused the motion, and an exception was taken.

The defendants then introduced evidence tending to show that at the time of the alleged sale it was believed by both the plaintiff and themselves that the cow was barren and would not breed; that she cost $850, and if not barren would be worth from $750 to $1,000; that after the date of the letter, and the order to Graham, the defendants were informed by said Graham that in his judgment the cow was with calf, and therefore they instructed him not to deliver her to plaintiff, and on the twentieth of May, 1886, telegraphed plaintiff what Graham thought about the cow being with calf, and that consequently they could not sell her. The cow had a calf in the month of October following.

On the nineteenth of May, the plaintiff wrote Graham as follows:

PLYMOUTH, May 19, 1886.

Mr. George Graham
Greenfield

DEAR SIR:

I have bought Rose or Lucy from Mr. Walker, and will be there for her Friday morning, nine or ten o'clock. Do not water her in the morning.

Yours, etc.

T.C. SHERWOOD

Plaintiff explained the mention of the two cows in this letter by testifying that, when he wrote this letter, the order and letter of defendants were at his house, and, writing in a hurry, and being uncertain as to the name of the cow, and not wishing his cow watered, he thought it would do no harm to name them both, as his bill of sale would show which one he had purchased. Plaintiff also testified that he asked defendants to give him a price on the balance of their herd at Greenfield, as a friend thought of buying some, and received a letter dated May 17, 1886, in which they named the price of five cattle, including Lucy at $90, and Rose 2d at $80. When he received the letter he called defendants up by the telephone, and asked them why they put Rose 2d in the list, as he had already purchased her. They replied that they knew he had, but thought it would make no difference if plaintiff and his friend concluded to take the whole herd.

The foregoing is the substance of all the testimony in the case. . . .

It is evident to my mind [the defendants] had perfect confidence in the integrity and responsibility of the plaintiff, and that they considered the sale perfected and completed when they mailed the letter and order to the plaintiff. They did not intend to place any conditions precedent in the way, either of payment of the price, or the weighing of the cow, before the passing of the title. They cared not whether the money was paid to Graham, or sent to them afterwards, or whether the cow was weighed before or after she passed into the actual manual grasp of the plaintiff. The refusal to deliver the cow grew entirely out of the fact that, before the plaintiff called upon Graham for her, they discovered she was not barren, and therefore of greater value than they had sold her for. . . .

It appears from the record that both parties supposed this cow was barren and would not breed, and she was sold by the pound for an insignificant sum as compared with her real value if a breeder. She was evidently sold and purchased on the relation of her value for beef, unless the plaintiff had learned of her true condition, and concealed such knowledge from the defendants. Before the plaintiff secured the possession of the animal, the defendants learned that she was with calf, and therefore of great value, and undertook to rescind the sale by refusing to deliver her. The question arises whether they had a right to do so.

The circuit judge ruled that this fact did not avoid the sale and it made no difference whether she was barren or not. I am of the opinion that the court erred in this holding. I know that this is a close question, and the dividing line between the adjudicated cases is not easily discerned. But it must be considered as well settled that a party who has given an apparent consent to a contract of sale may refuse to execute it, or he may avoid it after it has been completed, if the assent was founded, or the contract made, upon the mistake of a material fact, — such as the subject-matter of the sale, the price, or some collateral fact materially inducing the agreement; and this can be done when the mistake is mutual. . . . Huthmacher v. Harris' Admr's, 38 Penn. St. 491; . . . Gibson v. Pelkie, 37 Mich. 380. . . .

If there is a difference or misapprehension as to the substance of the thing bargained for, if the thing actually delivered or received is different in substance from the thing bargained for and intended to be sold, — then there is no contract; but if it be only a difference in some quality or accident, even though the mistake may have been the actuating motive to the purchaser or seller, or both of them, yet the contract remains binding.

> The difficulty in every case is to determine whether the mistake or misapprehension is as to the substance of the whole contract, going, as it were, to the root of the matter, or only to some point, even though a material point, an error as to which does not affect the substance of the whole consideration.

Kennedy v. Panama, etc., Mail Co., L.R. 2 Q.B. 580, 587.

It has been held, in accordance with the principles above stated, that where a horse is bought under the belief that he is sound, and both vendor and vendee honestly believe him to be sound, the purchaser must stand by his bargain, and pay the full price, unless there was a warranty.

It seems to me, however, in the case made by this record, that the mistake or misapprehension of the parties went to the whole substance of the agreement. If the cow was a breeder, she was worth at least $750; if barren, she was worth not over $80. The parties would not have made the contract of sale except upon the understanding and belief that she was incapable of breeding, and of no use as a cow. It is true she is now the identical animal that they thought her to be when the contract was made; there is no mistake as to the identity of the creature. Yet the mistake was not of the mere quality of the animal, but went to the very nature of the thing. A barren cow is substantially a different creature than a breeding one. There is as much difference between them for all purposes of use as there is between an ox and a cow that is capable of breeding and giving milk. If the mutual mistake had simply related to the fact whether she was with calf or not for one season, then it might have been a good sale; but the mistake affected the character of the animal for all time, and for her present and ultimate use. She was not in fact the animal, or the kind of animal, the defendants intended to sell or the plaintiff to buy. She was not a barren cow, and, if this fact had been known, there would have been no contract. The mistake affected the substance of the whole consideration, and it must be considered that there was no contract to sell or sale of the cow as she actually was. The thing sold and bought had in fact no existence. She was sold as a beef creature would be sold; she is in fact a breeding cow, and a valuable one.

The court should have instructed the jury that if they found that the cow was sold, or contracted to be sold, upon the understanding of both parties that she was barren, and useless for the purpose of breeding, and that in fact she was not barren, but capable of breeding, then the defendants had a right to rescind, and to refuse to deliver, and the verdict should be in their favor.

The judgment of the court below must be reversed, and a new trial granted, with cost of this court to defendants.

CAMPBELL, C.J. and CHAMPLIN, J., concurred.

SHERWOOD, J.,* (dissenting). I do not concur in the opinion given by my brethren in this case. I think the judgments before the justice and at the circuit were right.

---

* *Thomas Russell Sherwood* (1827-1896) studied law with Gen. Ira Bellows of Pittsford, New York, and then in the office of Jared and George Wilson of Canandaigua. He was admitted to the New York bar in 1851, and practiced law in Port Jervis for one year. In 1852,

I agree with Brother Morse that the contract made was not within the statute of frauds, and that payment for the property was not a condition precedent to the passing of the title from the defendants to the plaintiff. And I further agree with him that the plaintiff was entitled to a delivery of the property to him when the suit was brought, unless there was a mistake made which would invalidate the contract; and I can find no such mistake.

There is no pretense there was any fraud or concealment in the case, and an intimation or insinuation that such a thing might have existed on the part of either of the parties would undoubtedly be a greater surprise to them than anything else that has occurred in their dealings or in the case.

As has already been stated by my brethren, the record shows that the plaintiff is a banker, and farmer as well, carrying on a farm, and raising the best breeds of stock, and lived in Plymouth, in the county of Wayne, 23 miles from Detroit; that the defendants lived in Detroit, and were also dealers in stock of the higher grades; that they had a farm at Walkerville, in Canada, and also one in Greenfield in said county of Wayne, and upon these farms the defendants kept their stock. The Greenfield farm was about 15 miles from the plaintiff's. In the spring of 1886 the plaintiff, learning that the defendants had some "polled Angus cattle" for sale, was desirous of purchasing some of that breed, and meeting the defendants, or some of them, at Walkerville, inquired about them, and was informed that they had none at Walkerville, "but had a few head left on their farm in Greenfield, and asked the plaintiff to go and see them, stating that in all probability they were sterile and would not breed." In accordance with said request, the plaintiff, on the fifth day of May, went out and looked at the defendants' cattle at Greenfield, and found one called "Rose 2d," which he wished to purchase, and the terms were finally agreed upon at five and one-half cents per pound, live weight, 50 pounds to be deducted for shrinkage. The sale was in writing, and the defendants gave an order to the plaintiff directing the man in charge of the Greenfield farm to deliver the cow to plaintiff. This was done on the fifteenth of May. On the twenty-first of May plaintiff went to get his cow, and the defendants refused to let him have her; claiming at the time that the man in charge at the farm thought the cow was with calf, and, if such was the case, they would not sell her for the price agreed upon.

The record further shows that the defendants, when they sold the cow, believed the cow was not with calf, and barren; that from what the plaintiff had been told by the defendants (for it does not appear he had any other knowledge or facts from which he could form an opinion) he believed the cow was farrow, but still thought she could be made to breed.

The foregoing shows the entire interview and treaty between the parties as to the sterility and qualities of the cow sold to the plaintiff. The cow had a calf in the month of October.

There is no question but that the defendants sold the cow representing her of the breed and quality they believed the cow to be, and that the purchaser so understood it. And the buyer purchased her believing her

---

Sherwood moved to Kalamazoo, Michigan, where he practiced until 1883. In 1878, he ran unsuccessfully for Congress on the Greenback ticket. Sherwood was elected on the Union ticket to the Supreme Court of Michigan in 1883. He left the court at the expiration of his term in 1889. — C.R.

to be of the breed represented by the sellers, and possessing all the qualities stated, and even more. He believed she would breed. There is no pretense that the plaintiff bought the cow for beef, and there is nothing in the record indicating that he would have bought her at all only that he thought she might be made to breed. Under the foregoing facts, — and these are all that are contained in the record material to the contract, — it is held that because it turned out that the plaintiff was more correct in his judgment as to one quality of the cow than the defendants, and a quality, too, which could not by any possibility be positively known at the time by either party to exist, the contract may be annulled by the defendants at their pleasure. I know of no law, and have not been referred to any, which will justify any such holding, and I think the circuit judge was right in his construction of the contract between the parties.

It is claimed that a mutual mistake of a material fact was made by the parties when the contract of sale was made. There was no warranty in the case of the quality of the animal. When a mistaken fact is relied upon as ground for rescinding, such fact must not only exist at the time the contract is made, but must have been known to one or both of the parties. Where there is no warranty, there can be no mistake of fact when no such fact exists, or, if in existence, neither party knew of it, or could know of it; and that is precisely this case. If the owner of Hambletonian horse had speeded him, and was only able to make him go a mile in three minutes, and should sell him to another, believing that was his greatest speed, for $300, when the purchaser believed he could go much faster, and made the purchase for that sum, and a few days thereafter, under more favorable circumstances, the horse was driven a mile in 2 minutes 16 sec., and was found to be worth $20,000, I hardly think it would be held, either at law or in equity, by any one, that the seller in such case could rescind the contract. The same legal principles apply in each case.

In this case neither party knew the actual quality and condition of this cow at the time of the sale. The defendants say, or rather said, to the plaintiff, "they had a few head left on their farm in Greenfield, and asked plaintiff to go and see them, stating to plaintiff that in all probability they were sterile and would not breed." Plaintiff did go as requested, and found there these cows, including the one purchased, with a bull. The cow had been exposed, but neither knew she was with calf or whether she would breed. The defendants thought she would not, but the plaintiff says that he thought she could be made to breed, but believed she was not with calf. The defendants sold the cow for what they believed her to be, and the plaintiff bought her as he believed she was, after the statements made by the defendants. No conditions whatever were attached to the terms of sale by either party. It was in fact as absolute as it could well be made, and I know of no precedent as authority by which this court can alter the contract thus made by these parties in writing, and interpolate in it a condition by which, if the *defendants should be mistaken in their belief that the cow was barren*, she could be returned to them and their contract should be annulled.

It is not the duty of courts to destroy contracts when called upon to enforce them, after they have been legally made. There was no mistake of any such material fact by either of the parties in the case as would license the vendors to rescind. There was no difference between the parties, nor misapprehension, as to the substance of the thing bargained for, which was a cow supposed to be barren by one party, and believed not to be by the other. As to the quality of the animal, subsequently developed, both parties were equally ignorant, and as to this each party took his chances. If this were not the law, there would be no safety in purchasing this kind of stock.

I entirely agree with my brethren that the right to rescind occurs whenever "the thing actually delivered or received is different in substance from the thing bargained for, and intended to be sold; but if it be only a difference in some quality or accident, even though the misapprehension may have been the actuating motive" of the parties in making the contract, yet it will remain binding. In this case the cow sold was the one delivered. What might or might not happen to her after the sale formed no element in the contract.

The case of Kennedy v. Panama Mail Co., L.R. 2 Q.B. 588, and the extract cited therefrom in the opinion of my brethren, clearly sustains the views I have taken. . . .

According to this record, whatever the mistake was, if any, in this case, it was upon the part of the defendants, and while acting upon their own judgment. It is, however, elementary law, and very elementary, too, "that the mistaken party, acting entirely upon his own judgment, without any common understanding with the other party in the premises as to the quality of an animal, is remediless if he is injured through his own mistake." Leake, Cont. 338. . . .

The case of Huthmacher v. Harris' Adm'rs, 38 Penn. St. 491, is this: A party purchased at an administrator's sale a drill-machine, which had hid away in it by the deceased a quantity of notes, to the amount of about $3,000, money to the amount of over $500, and two silver watches and a pocket compass of the value of $60.25. In an action of trover for the goods, it was held that nothing but the machine was sold or passed to the purchaser, neither party knowing that the machine contained any such articles. . . .

The foregoing are all the authorities relied on as supporting the positions taken by my brethren in this case. I fail to discover any similarity between them and the present case; and I must say, further, in such examination as I have been able to make, I have found no adjudicated case going to the extent, either in law or equity, that has been held in this case. In this case, if either party had superior knowledge as to the qualities of this animal to the other, certainly the defendants had such advantage.

I understand the law to be well settled that "there is no breach of any implied confidence that one party will not profit by his superior knowledge as to facts and circumstances" equally within the knowledge of both, because neither party reposes in any such confidence unless it be specially tendered or required, and that a general sale does not imply warranty of any quality, or the absence of any; and if the seller represents to the purchaser what he himself believes as to the qualities of an animal, and the purchaser buys relying upon his own judgment as to such qualities, there is no warranty in the case, and neither has a cause of action against the other if he finds himself to have been mistaken in judgment.

The only pretense for avoiding this contract by the defendants is that they erred in judgment as to the qualities and value of the animal. . . .

The judgment should be affirmed.

STUDY GUIDE: *Why does the mistake defense fail in the next case? Was there no mistake? Or was there a reason why the mistake that was made was not sufficient to establish a defense? Does the reasoning of this case undercut the opinion in Sherwood v. Walker? Notice that now-Chief Justice Sherwood, who dissented in* Sherwood, *wrote the opinion for the majority, while Justice Morse did not participate.*

NESTER v. MICHIGAN LAND & IRON CO.
Supreme Court of Michigan,
69 Mich. 290, 37 N.W. 278 (1888)

SHERWOOD, C.J. On the sixteenth of September, 1885, the defendant entered into a written contract with the complainant, whereby the defendant sold him all the merchantable pine fit for saw logs on certain lands owned by the defendant, . . . for the sum of $27,000, payable, one-quarter down, and the remainder in equal annual installments, with interest. By the terms of the contract, the timber was not to be cut faster than paid for.

The complainant, having made but one payment, without consent of defendant, cut and carried away to his mill all the pine upon the lands mentioned, and, in the month of March following, the defendant sued out of the circuit court of Baraga county a writ of replevin to seize the logs. The bill in this case is filed to enjoin the prosecution of this suit, and to compel the defendant to accept about one-half of the purchase price for the timber sold, on the ground that both parties in their estimate of the quality of the timber standing upon the land when sold were mistaken, that a large portion of it was unsound, and that the yield of the quality sold furnished only about half the quantity anticipated or estimated, in consequence of the amount decayed.

The complainant avers that he purchased the pine relying on the representation of the defendant's agents who made the sale as to the quantity of the qualities mentioned in the contract; but that it turned out that such representations were not correct, although believed to be correct when made by the agents.

The complainant offers to have a decree rendered against him for such a sum as the court finds may be equitably due to the defendant upon the contract for the timber.

The decree of the court below is in favor of the complainant, and finds that he shall pay the defendant $12,798.48, instead of $27,000, as agreed upon in the contract, and less than half the sum the complainant agreed to pay. From this decree the defendant appeals to this court.

The defendant, in its answer to the complainant's bill, says it is a large owner of pine lands which it holds for sale; that it has estimates of the timber on its lands, but it never represents or warrants these estimates to be correct; that the complainant has long been an extensive lumberman and purchaser of pine lands; that on August 14, 1883, the defendant gave complainant an option to purchase within 60 days a large amount of pine lands, including those described in the contract, for $172,146; and at the same time the complainant was given a letter containing the following, in regard to the pine of said lands:

> There is a large amount of pine on these lands. The lowest estimate on any one section is 90 M. feet; and the largest one, over four million feet. The others are between these figures; but for the most part are nearer the latter than the former. Sections 1, 11 and 14, in 48-52; sections 23, 33, 35, in 49-32; and section 19, town 50-33, — are among the best.

This is the only statement made as to said pine, and was based, as complainant well knew, on the estimates received by the defendant from its agents for its own use; that defendant's agents then believed, and still believe, that such estimate was a fair one; that it was not expected that complainant would buy relying on such estimate, and he did not thus buy; that such option expired without action by complainant.

Defendant further says, in its answer, that early in 1884, and in the month of February, another option was given complainant for the purchase of the lands afterwards bought, and other lands, for 60 days, for the sum of $87,486; and that, soon after, complainant caused said lands to be examined by his own agents, and they showed their estimates to the defendant's officers; that he claimed at that time that the pine was defective, and that the price should be reduced in consequence, and also proposed to have the lands examined by the agents of both parties, and that he be allowed to purchase by the thousand the merchantable pine found on the land; that this offer was refused by the defendant; that he had the option to purchase the last-named lands, within 60 days, for the sum of $80,981.25, but this offer was not accepted.

In December, 1884, complainant was given an option to buy the pine on the lands in question within 30 days for $35,000, and on January 12th thereafter he offered $22,000; that on February 7, 1885, the same pine was offered to complainant for $27,000; that complainant replied to this last proposition that the price was too high, or that in substance; that the defendant declined to take less; that complainant then made an offer of $24,000, which was refused; that finally, complainant, fearing the purchase by another, accepted the defendant's last offer, and on the sixteenth day of September thereafter the contract was completed, and put in writing, and $6,750 was paid thereon by the complainant.

And the answer, continuing, further says and avers that —

> complainant acted, and proposed to act, during the whole of said negotiations, on information derived from his own agents, and understood perfectly that in buying said pine he took the risk of quality and quantity;

that

> The steps provided in said contract for giving complainant the right to cut and take away a portion of said pine, corresponding to the amount paid, have not been taken, and, in consequence, all of the cutting and carrying away of such pine has been unlawful, and the title of the same remains in defendant. Defendant claims that it has a perfect right to prosecute said replevin suit. It asks that the injunction forbidding this be dissolved. It asks, also, that it recover its costs in this suit, and for such other relief as may be agreeable to equity. . . .

[N]o one pretends [that], if the timber had been sound, but that the amount would have filled the estimate of either party. That all the means of ascertaining its soundness were equally accessible to both parties, and that each did what they saw fit to test the quality before concluding the contract, and that it was equally impossible to ascertain the extent of the defective timber until it was actually cut, and that each had reason to believe, and did believe, that it was defective, and the defendant refused to sell to the complainant except as it stood.

[It appears] that the complainant was a lumberman with 25 years' experience in the various branches of business, and was not unfamiliar with the region and timber where the pine in question grew.

It further appears that, when the parties came to make their contract, it was drafted by no novice in the business. It is full in its provisions, but it contains nothing that can be construed into a promise or guaranty as to the quantity or quality of timber or logs the tract sold to complainant should contain. The significance of this fact is of first importance, and can neither be overlooked nor misunderstood. Especially is this so, when it is considered that the parties had the matter under consideration for three months before the purchase was made, and that the principal question of contention during all that time was the amount of timber, of the quality desired, which the tract offered would be likely to yield. It is this important portion of the agreement between the parties — one of more consequence than any other contained in the contract — which the complainant claims was allowed to rest in parol, and which he now asks this court, under the foregoing facts as we find them, to have interpolated into the contract.

We know of no rule in equity which will permit this to be done. I hardly think counsel for complainant would think it equitable or just, if, when the timber was cut, it had been found to contain twice the number of feet either party had estimated, that the complainant should be held to pay defendant $54,000, instead of $27,000 as promised. Yet, if the doctrine they base their present claim upon is correct, there is no reason, why, under such circumstances, the complainant should not be held to pay that amount. We know of no case which will sustain the complainant's case upon the facts before us. That of Sherwood v. Walker, 66 Mich. 568 (33 N.W. Rep. 919), will come the nearest to it of any referred to. That is, however, somewhat different upon its facts, and the rule applied in that case can never be resorted to except in a case where all the facts and circumstances are precisely the same as in that. . . . [W]e think the evidence clearly shows in this case that, while Seymour stated to the complainant what the estimates were which the company had made of the pine for his own private purposes, he told the complainant the company would not sell promising to the purchaser any such amount, and that the complainant must purchase, if at all, upon his own estimate; that he had such estimate made by his own men; that he knew the estimate could not be made with any degree of certainty by any one, — to use the language of his own estimate, that "it is all guesswork any way;" that the company made no representation to the complainant as to the amount of timber of the quality sold, which they intended Mr. Nester to rely upon, or which Mr. Nester did rely upon, in making his purchase, but that he made the purchase upon his own estimate, or that of his men, as to such quantity; and that to hold otherwise would be making a new contract for the parties, instead of enforcing the one made by themselves.

We therefore think the decree at the circuit should be reversed, and bill dismissed, with costs of both courts.

CHAMPLIN and LONG, JJ., concurred. MORSE, J. did not sit.

STUDY GUIDE: Does the following case square with the cases we have just discussed? Would the court have decided differently had the buyer known that the stone was a diamond? Reconsider this question after reading the cases in the next section.

WOOD v. BOYNTON
Supreme Court of Wisconsin,
64 Wis. 265, 25 N.W. 42 (1885)

Appeal from circuit court, Milwaukee county.

TAYLOR, J.* This action was brought in the circuit court for Milwaukee county to recover the possession of an uncut diamond of the alleged value of $1,000. The case was tried in the circuit court and, after hearing all the evidence in the case, the learned circuit judge directed the jury to find a verdict for the defendants. The plaintiff excepted to such instruction, and, after a verdict was rendered for the defendants, moved for a new trial upon the minutes of the judge. The motion was denied, and the plaintiff duly excepted, and, after judgment was entered in favor of the defendants, appealed to this court.

The defendants are partners in the jewelry business. On the trial it appeared that on and before the 28th of December, 1883, the plaintiff was the owner of and in the possession of a small stone of the nature and value of which she was ignorant; that on that day she sold it to one of the defendants for the sum of one dollar. Afterwards it was ascertained that the stone was a rough diamond, and of the value of about $700. After learning this fact the plaintiff tendered the defendants the one dollar, and ten cents as interest, and demanded a return of the stone to her. The defendants refused to deliver it, and therefore she commenced this action.

The plaintiff testified to the circumstances attending the sale of the stone to Mr. Samuel B. Boynton, as follows:

> The first time Boynton saw that stone he was talking about buying the topaz, or whatever it is, in September or October. I went into his store to get a little pin mended, and I had it in a small box, — the pin, — a small ear-ring; . . . this stone, and a broken sleeve-button were in the box. Mr. Boynton turned to give me a check for my pin. I thought I would ask him what the stone was, and

---

* *David Taylor* (1818-1891) was educated at Union College and was admitted to the bar of New York in 1844. He practiced there for two years before removing to Wisconsin and opening a law partnership there. Taylor was a member of the State Assembly in 1853 and of the State Senate from 1855 to 1856 and again from 1869 to 1870. He was appointed to the bench in 1857 and served on the Judicial Circuit Court until his retirement, upon which he returned to private practice until his death. Taylor also served as a member of two commissions to produce Revised Statutes (1858 and 1878), and produced an annotated compilation of Wisconsin's public laws, known as Taylor's Statutes. — K.T.

I took it out of the box and asked him to please tell me what that was. He took it in his hand and seemed some time looking at it. I told him I had been told it was a topaz, and he said it might be. He says, "I would buy this; would you sell it?" I told him I did not know but what I would. What would it be worth? And he said he did not know; he would give me a dollar and keep it as a specimen, and I told him I would not sell it; and it was certainly pretty to look at. He asked me where I found it, and I told him in Eagle. He asked about how far out, and I said right in the village, and I went out. Afterwards, and about the 28th of December, I needed money pretty badly, and thought every dollar would help, and I took it back to Mr. Boynton and told him I had brought back the topaz, and he says, "Well, yes; what did I offer you for it?" and I says, "One dollar;" and he stepped to the change drawer and gave me the dollar, and I went out.

In another part of her testimony she says:

Before I sold the stone I had no knowledge whatever that it was a diamond. I told him that I had been advised that it was probably a topaz, and he said probably it was. The stone was about the size of a canary bird's egg, nearly the shape of an egg, — worn pointed at one end; it was nearly straw color, — a little darker.

She also testified that before this action was commenced she tendered the defendants $1.10, and demanded the return of the stone, which they refused. This is substantially all the evidence of what took place at and before the sale to the defendants, as testified to by the plaintiff herself. She produced no other witness on that point.

The evidence on the part of the defendant is not very different from the version given by the plaintiff, and certainly is not more favorable to the plaintiff. Mr. Samuel B. Boynton, the defendant to whom the stone was sold, testified that at the time he bought this stone, he had never seen an uncut diamond; had seen cut diamonds, but they are quite different from the uncut ones; "he had no idea this was a diamond, and it never entered his brain at the time." Considerable evidence was given as to what took place after the sale and purchase, but that evidence has very little if any bearing upon the main point in the case.

This evidence clearly shows that the plaintiff sold the stone in question to the defendants, and delivered it to them in December, 1883, for a consideration of one dollar. The title to the stone passed by the sale and delivery to the defendants. How has that title been divested and again vested in the plaintiff? The contention of the learned counsel for the appellant is that the title became vested in the plaintiff by the tender to the Boyntons of the purchase money, with interest, and a demand of a return of the stone to her. Unless such tender and demand revested the title in the appellant, she cannot maintain her action.

The only question in the case is whether there was anything in the sale which entitled the vendor (the appellant) to rescind the sale and so revest the title in her. The only reasons we know of for rescinding a sale and revesting the title in the vendor so that he may maintain an action at law for the recovery of the possession against his vendee are (1) that the vendee was guilty of some fraud in procuring a sale to be made to him; (2) that there was a mistake made by the vendor in delivering an article which was not the article sold, — a mistake in fact as to the identity of the thing sold with thing delivered upon the sale. This last is not in reality a rescission of the sale made, as the thing delivered was not the thing sold, and no title ever passed to the vendee by such delivery.

In this case, upon the plaintiff's own evidence, there can be no just ground for alleging that she was induced to make the sale she did by any fraud or unfair dealings on the part of Mr. Boynton. Both were entirely ignorant at the time of the character of the stone and of its intrinsic value. Mr. Boynton was not an expert in uncut diamonds, and had made no examination of the stone, except to take it in his hand and look at it before he made the offer of one dollar, which was refused at the time, and afterwards accepted without any comment or further examination made by Mr. Boynton. The appellant had the stone in her possession for a long time, and it appears from her own statement that she had made some inquiry as to its nature and qualities. If she chose to sell it without further investigation as to its intrinsic value to a person who was guilty of no fraud or unfairness which induced her to sell it for a small sum, she cannot repudiate the sale because it is afterwards ascertained that she made a bad bargain. . . .

There is no pretense of any mistake as to the identity of the thing sold. It was produced by the plaintiff and exhibited to the vendee before the sale was made, and the thing sold was delivered to the vendee when the purchase price was paid. . . . Suppose the appellant had produced the stone, and said she had been told that it was a diamond, and she believed it was, but had no knowledge herself as to its character or value, and Mr. Boynton had given her $500 for it, could he have rescinded the sale if it had turned out to be a topaz or any other stone of very small value? Could Mr. Boynton have rescinded the sale on the ground of mistake? Clearly not, nor could he rescind it on the ground that there had been a breach of warranty, because there was no warranty, nor could he rescind it on the ground of fraud, unless he could show that she falsely declared that she had been told it was a diamond, or, if she had been so told, still she knew it was not a diamond. . . .

It is urged, with a good deal of earnestness, on the part of the counsel for the appellant that, because it has turned out that the stone was immensely more valuable than the parties at the time of the sale supposed it was, such fact alone is a ground for the rescission of the sale, and that fact was evidence of fraud on the part of the vendee. Whether inadequacy of price is to be received as evidence of fraud, even in a suit in equity to avoid a sale, depends upon the facts known to the parties at the time the sale is made.

When this sale was made the value of the thing sold was open to the investigation of both parties, neither knew its intrinsic value, and, so far as the evidence in this case shows, both supposed that the price paid was adequate. How can fraud be predicated upon such a sale, even though after-investigation showed that the intrinsic value of the thing sold was hundreds of times greater than the price paid? It certainly shows no such fraud as would authorize the vendor to rescind the contract and bring an action at law to recover the possession of the thing sold. Whether the fact would have any influence in an action in equity to avoid the sale we need not consider. . . .

We can find nothing in the evidence from which it could be justly inferred that Mr. Boynton, at the time he offered the plaintiff one dollar for the stone, had any knowledge of the real value of the stone, or that he entertained even a belief that the stone was a diamond. It cannot, therefore, be said that there was a suppression of knowledge on the part of the defendant as to the value of the stone which a court of equity might seize upon to avoid the sale. The following cases show that, in the absence of fraud or warranty, the value of the property sold, as compared with the price paid, is no ground for a rescission of a sale. Wheat v. Cross, 31 Md. 99; Lambert v. Heath, 15 Mees. W. 487 Bryant v. Pember, 45 Vt. 487; Kuelkamp v. Hidding, 31 Wis. 503-511.

However unfortunate the plaintiff may have been in selling this valuable stone for a mere nominal sum, she has failed entirely to make out a case either of fraud or mistake in the sale such as will entitle her to a rescission of such sale so as to recover the property sold in an action at law.

By the court. — The judgment of the circuit court is affirmed.

STUDY GUIDE: We conclude our consideration of mutual mistake with a modern Michigan Supreme Court opinion reconsidering the venerable case of Sherwood v. Walker *and applying the approach adopted by the Restatement (Second). Why did the court find that the existence of a mutual mistake of fact failed to justify a remedy of rescission? Why did the court reject the "substance-value" distinction employed by the court in* Sherwood? *Notice that the doctrine of mistake in basic assumptions appears so similar to that of failure of consideration that the appellees originally pleaded only the latter theory. Can you see how many problems formerly handled under the doctrine of consideration — like extorted modifications, which used to be handled by the doctrine of past consideration — are now being addressed by distinct defenses to contract rather than as denials that consideration was received? Perhaps this reveals that what formerly was conceived as a denial was, in actuality, additional factual circumstances that undermined the significance, as opposed to denying the existence, of elements of the prima facie case of contract.*

LENAWEE COUNTY BOARD OF HEALTH v. MESSERLY
Supreme Court of Michigan,
417 Mich. 17, 331 N.W.2d 203 (1982)

RYAN, J.*

In March of 1977, Carl and Nancy Pickles, appellees, purchased from appellants, William and Martha Messerly, a 600-square-foot tract of land upon which is located a three-unit apartment building. Shortly after the

---

* *James L. Ryan* (1932-†) was educated at Detroit Catholic Central High School, which led to his focus on Jesuit studies at the University of Detroit (1950-1956) before entering its law school (LL.B., 1956). He served first as a U.S. Navy JAG officer (1956-1960) and then became a certified military judge in the Navy Reserve (1960-1992), attaining the rank of captain prior to his retirement. Ryan entered private practice, while serving as an elected justice of the peace. He was elected to the Third Judicial Circuit of Michigan in 1966, prior to his appointment and subsequent election to the Michigan Supreme Court in 1975. In 1985, Ryan was appointed to the Sixth Circuit Court of Appeals, where he assumed senior status in 2000 and retired from the bench in 2010. Judge Ryan has taught evidence at the University of Detroit, the Thomas M. Cooley Law School, and the National Judicial College. — J.B.

transaction was closed, the Lenawee County Board of Health condemned the property and obtained a permanent injunction which prohibits human habitation on the premises until the defective sewage system is brought into conformance with the Lenawee County sanitation code.

We are required to determine whether appellees should prevail in their attempt to avoid this land contract on the basis of mutual mistake and failure of consideration. We conclude that the parties did entertain a mutual misapprehension of fact, but that the circumstances of this case do not warrant rescission.

I

The facts of the case are not seriously in dispute. In 1971, the Messerlys acquired approximately one acre plus 600 square feet of land. A three-unit apartment building was situated upon the 600-square-foot portion. The trial court found that, prior to this transfer, the Messerlys' predecessor in title, Mr. Bloom, had installed a septic tank on the property without a permit and in violation of the applicable health code. The Messerlys used the building as an income investment property until 1973 when they sold it, upon land contract, to James Barnes who likewise used it primarily as an income-producing investment.[2]

Mr. and Mrs. Barnes, with the permission of the Messerlys, sold approximately one acre of the property in 1976, and the remaining 600 square feet and building were offered for sale soon thereafter when Mr. and Mrs. Barnes defaulted on their land contract. Mr. and Mrs. Pickles evidenced an interest in the property, but were dissatisfied with the terms of the Barnes-Messerly land contract. Consequently, to accommodate the Pickleses' preference to enter into a land contract directly with the Messerlys, Mr. and Mrs. Barnes executed a quit claim deed which conveyed their interest in the property back to the Messerlys. After inspecting the property, Mr. and Mrs. Pickles executed a new land contract with the Messerlys on March 21, 1977. It provided for a purchase price of $25,500. A clause was added to the end of the land contract form which provides:

> 17. Purchaser has examined this property and agrees to accept same in its present condition. There are no other or additional written or oral understandings.

Five or six days later, when the Pickleses went to introduce themselves to the tenants, they discovered raw sewage seeping out of the ground. Tests conducted by a sanitation expert indicated the inadequacy of the sewage system. The Lenawee County Board of Health subsequently condemned the property and initiated this lawsuit in the Lenawee Circuit Court against the Messerlys as land contract vendors, and the Pickleses, as vendees, to obtain

---

2. James Barnes was married shortly after he purchased the property. Mr. and Mrs. Barnes lived in one of the apartments on the property for three months and, after they moved, Mrs. Barnes continued to aid in the management of the property.

a permanent injunction proscribing human habitation of the premises until the property was brought into conformance with the Lenawee County sanitation code. The injunction was granted, and the Lenawee County Board of Health was permitted to withdraw from the lawsuit by stipulation of the parties.

When no payments were made on the land contract, the Messerlys filed a cross-complaint against the Pickleses seeking foreclosure, sale of the property, and a deficiency judgment. Mr. and Mrs. Pickles then counterclaimed for rescission against the Messerlys, and filed a third-party complaint against the Barneses, which incorporated, by reference, the allegations of the counterclaim against the Messerlys. In count one, Mr. and Mrs. Pickles alleged failure of consideration. Count two charged Mr. and Mrs. Barnes with willful concealment and misrepresentation as a result of their failure to disclose the condition of the sanitation system. Additionally, Mr. and Mrs. Pickles sought to hold the Messerlys liable in equity for the Barneses' alleged misrepresentation. The Pickleses prayed that the land contract be rescinded.[3]

After a bench trial, the court concluded that the Pickleses had no cause of action against either the Messerlys or the Barneses as there was no fraud or misrepresentation. This ruling was predicated on the trial judge's conclusion that none of the parties knew of Mr. Bloom's earlier transgression or of the resultant problem with the septic system until it was discovered by the Pickleses, and that the sanitation problem was not caused by any of the parties. The trial court held that the property was purchased "as is," after inspection and, accordingly, its "negative . . . value cannot be blamed upon an innocent seller." Foreclosure was ordered against the Pickleses, together with a judgment against them in the amount of $25,943.09.[4]

Mr. and Mrs. Pickles appealed from the adverse judgment. The Court of Appeals unanimously affirmed the trial court's ruling with respect to Mr. and Mrs. Barnes but, in a two-to-one decision, reversed the finding of no cause of action on the Pickleses' claims against the Messerlys. Lenawee County Board of Health v. Messerly, 98 Mich. App. 478; 295 N.W.2d 903 (1980). It concluded that the mutual mistake between the Messerlys and the Pickleses went to a basic, as opposed to a collateral, element of the contract, and that the parties intended to transfer income-producing rental property but, in actuality, the vendees paid $25,500 for an asset without value.

We granted the Messerlys' application for leave to appeal. . . .

II

We must decide initially whether there was a mistaken belief entertained by one or both parties to the contract in dispute and, if so, the resultant legal significance.

---

3. Linehan Realty Company and Andrew E. Czmer, doing business as Andrew Realty Company, were also named as third-party defendants, but were later dismissed from the lawsuit by stipulation of the parties.

4. The parties stipulated that this amount was due on the land contract, assuming that the contract was valid and enforceable.

A contractual mistake "is a belief that is not in accord with the facts." 1 Restatement Contracts, 2d, §151, p. 383. The erroneous belief of one or both of the parties must relate to a fact in existence at the time the contract is executed. Richardson Lumber Co. v. Hoey, 219 Mich. 643, 189 N.W. 923 (1922); Sherwood v. Walker, 66 Mich. 568, 580, 33 N.W 919 (1887) (Sherwood, J., dissenting). That is to say, the belief which is found to be in error may not be, in substance, a prediction as to a future occurrence or non-occurrence. . . .

The Court of Appeals concluded, after a *de novo* review of the record, that the parties were mistaken as to the income-producing capacity of the property in question. . . . We agree. The vendors and the vendees each believed that the property transferred could be utilized as income-generating rental property. All of the parties subsequently learned that, in fact, the property was unsuitable for any residential use.

Appellants assert that there was no mistake in the contractual sense because the defect in the sewage system did not arise until after the contract was executed. The appellees respond that the Messerlys are confusing the date of the inception of the defect with the date upon which the defect was discovered.

This is essentially a factual dispute which the trial court failed to resolve directly. Nevertheless, we are empowered to draw factual inferences from the facts found by the trial court. . . .

An examination of the record reveals that the septic system was defective prior to the date on which the land contract was executed. The Messerlys' grantor installed a nonconforming septic system without a permit prior to the transfer of the property to the Messerlys in 1971. More-over, virtually undisputed testimony indicates that, assuming ideal soil con-ditions, 2,500 square feet of property is necessary to support a sewage system adequate to serve a three-family dwelling. Likewise, 750 square feet is mandated for a one-family home. Thus, the division of the parcel and sale of one acre of the property by Mr. and Mrs. Barnes in 1976 made it impossible to remedy the already illegal septic system within the confines of the 600-square-foot parcel.[5]

Appellants do not dispute these underlying facts which give rise to an inference contrary to their contentions.

Having determined that when these parties entered into the land con-tract they were laboring under a mutual mistake of fact, we now direct our attention to a determination of the legal significance of that finding.

A contract may be rescinded because of a mutual misapprehension of the parties, but this remedy is granted only in the sound discretion of the court. . . . Appellants argue that the parties' mistake relates only to the quality or value of the real estate transferred, and that such mistakes are

---

5. It is crucial to distinguish between the date on which a belief relating to a particular fact or set of facts becomes erroneous due to a change in the fact, and the date on which the mistaken nature of the belief is discovered. By definition, a mistake cannot be discovered until after the contract is executed. If the parties were aware, prior to the execution of a contract, that they were in error concerning a particular fact, there would be no misappre-hension in signing the contract. Thus stated, it becomes obvious that the date on which a mistaken fact manifests itself is irrelevant to the determination whether or not there was a mistake.

collateral to the agreement and do not justify rescission, citing A & M Land Development Co. v. Miller, 354 Mich. 681 94 N.W.2d 197 (1959).

In that case, the plaintiff was the purchaser of 91 lots of real property. It sought partial rescission of the land contract when it was frustrated in its attempts to develop 42 of the lots because it could not obtain permits from the county health department to install septic tanks on these lots. This Court refused to allow rescission because the mistake, whether mutual or unilateral, related only to the value of the property.

> There was here no mistake as to the form or substance of the contract between the parties, or the description of the property constituting the subject matter. The situation involved is not at all analogous to that presented in Scott v. Grow, 301 Mich. 226; 3 N.W.2d 254; 141 A.L.R. 819 (1942). There the plaintiff sought relief by way of reformation of a deed on the ground that the instrument of conveyance had not been drawn in accordance with the intention and agreement of the parties. It was held that the bill of complaint stated a case for the granting of equitable relief by way of reformation. In the case at bar plaintiff received the property for which it contracted. The fact that it may be of less value than the purchaser expected at the time of the transaction is not a sufficient basis for the granting of equitable relief, neither fraud nor reliance on misrepresentation of material facts having been established.

354 Mich. 693-694.

Appellees contend, on the other hand, that in this case the parties were mistaken as to the very nature of the character of the consideration and claim that the pervasive and essential quality of this mistake renders rescission appropriate. They cite in support of that view Sherwood v. Walker, 66 Mich. 568; 33 N.W. 919 (1887), the famous "barren cow" case. In that case, the parties agreed to the sale and purchase of a cow which was thought to be barren, but which was, in reality, with calf. When the seller discovered the fertile condition of his cow, he refused to deliver her. In permitting rescission, the Court stated:

"It seems to me, however, in the case made by this record, that the mistake or misapprehension of the parties went to the whole substance of the agreement. . . ."

As the parties suggest, the foregoing precedent arguably distinguishes mistakes affecting the essence of the consideration from those which go to its quality or value, affording relief on a per se basis for the former but not the latter. . . .

However, the distinctions which may be drawn from *Sherwood* and *A & M Land Development Co.* do not provide a satisfactory analysis of the nature of a mistake sufficient to invalidate a contract. Often, a mistake relates to an underlying factual assumption which, when discovered, directly affects value, but simultaneously and materially affects the essence of the contractual consideration. It is disingenuous to label such a mistake collateral. . . .

Appellant and appellee both mistakenly believed that the property which was the subject of their land contract would generate income as rental property. The fact that it could not be used for human habitation deprived the property of its income-earning potential and rendered it less valuable. However, this mistake, while directly and dramatically affecting the property's value, cannot accurately be characterized as collateral because it also affects the very essence of the consideration. "The thing sold and bought [income-generating rental property] had in fact no existence." Sherwood v. Walker, 66 Mich. 578.

We find that the inexact and confusing distinction between contractual mistakes running to value and those touching the substance of the consideration serves only as an impediment to a clear and helpful analysis for the equitable resolution of cases in which mistake is alleged and proven. Accordingly, the holdings of *A & M Land Development Co.* and *Sherwood* with respect to the material or collateral nature of a mistake are limited to the facts of those cases.

Instead, we think the better-reasoned approach is a case-by-case analysis whereby rescission is indicated when the mistaken belief relates to a basic assumption of the parties upon which the contract is made, and which materially affects the agreed performances of the parties. . . . Richardson Lumber Co. v. Hoey, 219 Mich. 643; 189 N.W 923 (1922). 1 Restatement Contracts, 2d, §152, pp. 385-386. Rescission is not available, however, to relieve a party who has assumed the risk of loss in connection with the mistake. . . . 1 Restatement Contracts, 2d, §§152, 154, pp. 385-386, 402-406.

All of the parties to this contract erroneously assumed that the property transferred by the vendors to the vendees was suitable for human habitation and could be utilized to generate rental income. The fundamental nature of these assumptions is indicated by the fact that their invalidity changed the character of the property transferred, thereby frustrating, indeed precluding, Mr. and Mrs. Pickles' intended use of the real estate. Although the Pickleses are disadvantaged by enforcement of the contract, performance is advantageous to the Messerlys, as the property at issue is less valuable absent its income-earning potential. Nothing short of rescission can remedy the mistake. Thus, the parties' mistake as to a basic assumption materially affects the agreed performances of the parties.

Despite the significance of the mistake made by the parties, we reverse the Court of Appeals because we conclude that equity does not justify the remedy sought by Mr. and Mrs. Pickles.

Rescission is an equitable remedy which is granted only in the sound discretion of the court. . . . A court need not grant rescission in every case in which the mutual mistake relates to a basic assumption and materially affects the agreed performance of the parties.

In cases of mistake by two equally innocent parties, we are required, in the exercise of our equitable powers, to determine which blameless party should assume the loss resulting from the misapprehension they shared.[6] Normally that can only be done by drawing upon our "own notions of what is reasonable and just under all the surrounding circumstances."[7]

---

6. This risk-of-loss analysis is absent in both *A & M Land Development Co.* and *Sherwood,* and this omission helps to explain, in part, the disparate treatment in the two cases. Had such an inquiry been undertaken in *Sherwood,* we believe that the result might have been different. Moreover, a determination as to which party assumed the risk in *A & M Land Development Co.* would have alleviated the need to characterize the mistake as collateral so as to justify the result denying rescission. Despite the absence of any inquiry as to the assumption of risk in those two leading cases, we find that there exists sufficient precedent to warrant such an analysis in future cases of mistake.

7. Hathaway v. Hudson, 256 Mich. 702, 239 N.W. 859, *quoting* 9 C.J., p. 1161.

Equity suggests that, in this case, the risk should be allocated to the purchasers. We are guided to that conclusion, in part, by the standards announced in §154 of the Restatement of Contracts 2d, for determining when a party bears the risk of mistake. . . . Section 154(a) suggests that the court should look first to whether the parties have agreed to the allocation of the risk between themselves. While there is no express assumption in the contract by either party of the risk of the property becoming uninhabitable, there was indeed some agreed allocation of the risk to the vendees by the incorporation of an "as is" clause into the contract which, we repeat, provided:

> Purchaser has examined this property and agrees to accept same in its present condition. There are no other or additional written or oral understandings.

That is a persuasive indication that the parties considered that, as between them, such risk as related to the "present condition" of the property should lie with the purchaser. If the "as is" clause is to have any meaning at all, it must be interpreted to refer to those defects which were unknown at the time that the contract was executed.[8] Thus, the parties themselves assigned the risk of loss to Mr. and Mrs. Pickles.[9]

We conclude that Mr. and Mrs. Pickles are not entitled to the equitable remedy of rescission and, accordingly, reverse the decision of the Court of Appeals.

RESTATEMENT (SECOND) OF CONTRACTS

§151. MISTAKE DEFINED

A mistake is a belief that is not in accord with the facts.

COMMENT

a. Belief as to Facts.   In this Restatement the word "mistake" is used to refer to an erroneous belief. A party's erroneous belief is therefore said to be a "mistake" of that party. The belief need not be an articulated one, and a party may have a belief as to a fact when he merely makes an assumption with respect to it, without being aware of alternatives. The word "mistake" is not used here, as it is sometimes used in common speech, to refer to an improvident act, including the making of a contract, that is the result of such an erroneous belief. This usage is avoided here for the sake of clarity and consistency. Furthermore, the erroneous belief must relate to the facts as they exist at the time of the making of the contract. A party's

---

8. An "as is" clause waives those implied warranties which accompany the sale of a new home. . . . Since implied warranties protect against latent defects, an "as is" clause will impose upon the purchaser the assumption of the risk of latent defects, such as an inadequate sanitation system, even when there are no implied warranties.

9. An "as is" clause does not preclude a purchaser from alleging fraud or misrepresentation as a basis for rescission. . . . However, Mr. and Mrs. Pickles did not appeal the trial court's finding that there was no fraud or misrepresentation, so we are bound thereby.

prediction or judgment as to events to occur in the future, even if errone-ous, is not a "mistake" as that word is defined here. An erroneous belief as to the contents or effect of a writing that expresses the agreement is, however, a mistake. Mistake alone, in the sense in which the word is used here, has no legal consequences. The legal consequences of mistake in connection with the creation of contractual liability are determined by the rules stated in the rest of this Chapter. . . .

§152. WHEN MISTAKE OF BOTH PARTIES MAKES A CONTRACT VOIDABLE

(1) Where a mistake of both parties at the time a contract was made as to a basic assumption on which the contract was made has a material effect on the agreed exchange of performances, the contract is voidable by the adversely affected party unless he bears the risk of the mistake under the rule stated in §154.

(2) In determining whether the mistake has a material effect on the agreed exchange of performances, account is taken of any relief by way of reformation, restitution, or otherwise.

§154. WHEN A PARTY BEARS THE RISK OF A MISTAKE

A party bears the risk of a mistake when
(a) the risk is allocated to him by agreement of the parties, or
(b) he is aware, at the time the contract is made, that he has only limited knowledge with respect to the facts to which the mistake relates but treats his limited knowledge as sufficient, or
(c) the risk is allocated to him by the court on the ground that it is reasonable in the circumstances to do so.

COMMENT

a. Rationale. Absent provision to the contrary, a contracting party takes the risk of most supervening changes in circumstances, even though they upset basic assumptions and unexpectedly affect the agreed exchange of performances, unless there is such extreme hardship as will justify relief on the ground of impracticability of performance or frustration of purpose. A party also bears the risk of many mistakes as to existing circumstances even though they upset basic assumptions and unexpectedly affect the agreed exchange of performances. For example, it is commonly understood that the seller of farm land generally cannot avoid the contract of sale upon later discovery by both parties that the land contains valuable mineral deposits, even though the price was negotiated on the basic assumption that the land was suitable only for farming and the effect on the agreed exchange of performances is material. In such a case a court will ordinarily allocate the risk of the mistake to the seller, so that he is under a duty to perform regardless of the mistake. The rule stated in this Section determines whether a party bears the risk of a mistake for the purposes of both §§152 and 153. Stating these rules in terms of the allocation of risk avoids such artificial and specious distinctions as are sometimes drawn between "intrinsic" and "extrinsic" mistakes or between mistakes that go to the "identity" or "existence" of the subject matter and those that go merely to its "attributes," "quality" or "value." Even though a mistaken party does not bear the risk of a mistake, he may be barred from avoidance if the mistake was the result of his failure to act in good faith and in accordance with reasonable standards of fair dealing. See §157.

b.   Allocation by Agreement.   The most obvious case of allocation of the risk of a mistake is one in which the parties themselves provide for it by their agreement. Just as a party may agree to perform in spite of impracticability or frustration that would otherwise justify his non-performance, he may also agree, by appropriate language or other manifestations, to perform in spite of mistake that would otherwise justify his avoidance. An insurer, for example, may expressly undertake the risk of loss of property covered as of a date already past. Whether the agreement places the risk on the mistaken party is a question to be answered under the rules generally applicable to the scope of contractual obligations, including those on interpretation, usage and unconscionability. . . .

c.   Conscious Ignorance.   Even though the mistaken party did not agree to bear the risk, he may have been aware when he made the contract that his knowledge with respect to the facts to which the mistake relates was limited. If he was not only so aware that his knowledge was limited but undertook to perform in the face of that awareness, he bears the risk of the mistake. It is sometimes said in such a situation that, in a sense, there was not mistake but "conscious ignorance." . . .

d.   Risk Allocated by the Court.   In some instances it is reasonably clear that a party should bear the risk of a mistake for reasons other than those stated in Subparagraphs (a) and (b). In such instances, under the rule stated in Subparagraph (c), the court will allocate the risk to that party on the ground that it is reasonable to do so. A court will generally do this, for example, where the seller of farm land seeks to avoid the contract of sale on the ground that valuable mineral rights have newly been found. See Comment a. In dealing with such issues, the court will consider the purposes of the parties and will have recourse to its own general knowledge of human behavior in bargain transactions, as it will in the analogous situation in which it is asked to supply a term under the rule stated in §204. The rule stated in Subsection (c) is subject to contrary agreement and to usage (§221).

§157.   EFFECT OF FAULT OF PARTY SEEKING RELIEF

A mistaken party's fault in failing to know or discover the facts before making the contract does not bar him from avoidance or reformation under the rules stated in this Chapter, unless his fault amounts to a failure to act in good faith and in accordance with reasonable standards of fair dealing.

§158.   RELIEF INCLUDING RESTITUTION

(1) In any case governed by the rules stated in this Chapter, either party may have a claim for relief including restitution under the rules stated in §§240 and 376.

(2) In any case governed by the rules stated in this Chapter, if those rules together with the rules stated in Chapter 16 will not avoid injustice, the court may grant relief on such terms as justice requires including protection of the parties' reliance interests.

REFERENCE: Barnett, §6.4.1
                Farnsworth, §§9.2, 9.3
                Calamari & Perillo, §§9.9-9.12, 9.25-9.26
                Murray, §92(A)-(D), (I)

2.   Unilateral Mistake and the Duty to Disclose

Normally to establish a defense of mistake the mistake must have been mutual — that is, shared by both parties. In the cases considered in this section, however, a mistake by *one* party is offered as a defense to performance. We shall consider here whether the distinction between mutual and unilateral mistake is defensible. We shall also discuss the close relationship between unilateral mistake and the defense of misrepresentation, which we studied in Chapter 16.

STUDY GUIDE: When reading the next case and the excerpt that follows, recall the case of Baird v. Gimbel discussed in Chapter 11 and the additional facts noted concerning Gimbel's defense of mistake. Can you see now why the mistake defense failed there? Could this contract have been reformed due to mistake in integration, of the type we studied in Chapter 6? What is required before reformation is allowed? Is the defense of unilateral mistake based on the same theory as that which undergirds the doctrine of mutual mistake?

TYRA v. CHENEY
Supreme Court of Minnesota,
129 Minn. 428, 152 N.W. 835 (1915)

[Action by Joseph Tyra, etc., against Robert J. Cheney, etc. Verdict for plaintiff, and, from denial of alternative motion for judgment or new trial, defendant appeals.] . . .

HOLT, J.* The defendant had the contract to add to and repair a school building in Minneapolis, Minnesota. Plaintiff did some work and furnished some material in the performance of the contract. This action was to recover the reasonable value thereof, less certain admitted payments. In defense an express contract was pleaded, and judgment tendered for $27, the unpaid balance. Verdict for plaintiff, and defendant appeals from the order denying his motion in the alternative for judgment or a new trial.

Plaintiff's contention, in brief, was: About the last of July, 1912, he offered to bid on the roofing and sheet metal work required in defendant's contract. Lacking time to put the bid, or estimate, in formal shape, he, on July 27, gave to defendant's estimator the figures for the various items, namely, $963 for the new part of the building; $2,410 for the old part; $400 for registers, and $251 for metal covered doors; the total bid being about $4,025. On August 1st he was told the bid came too late, but, nevertheless, he could send it in writing. Plaintiff undertook to do so on the third, but now claims the item of $963 for the new part of the building was left out through oversight. A few days thereafter, upon inquiring about his chance of securing the work, he was told that his bid was too high. However, he persisted in the attempt to induce defendant to use, instead of the specified metal doors, metal doors of plaintiff's make. He succeeded, and, late in August, was awarded a separate contract for the doors for $295. Nothing further was heard from defendant until in September, when plaintiff was told to go ahead with the work. Defendant denies ever receiving any estimate, bid or figures, except the written bid. The court, in submitting the case, charged that the burden was upon plaintiff to show, by a fair preponderance of testimony, that when, in September, 1912, defendant gave plaintiff the direction to proceed with the work, it was done with knowledge of plaintiff's mistake of $963 in the written bid, and of his resting under the belief that it conformed to the oral bid of $4,025, so that it might be truthfully found that defendant did not accept the written bid of $3,062 in good faith, then plaintiff could recover the reasonable value, otherwise the verdict must be limited to the amount tendered in the answer. We believe this theory sound. If cognizant of the mistake in plaintiff's bid, and that the latter was unaware of its occurrence, defendant had no right to claim that, when he told plaintiff to go ahead with the work, their minds met upon the price mistakenly stated in the bid. Nor should plaintiff be allowed to profit by his own mistake, so as to hold defendant to the oral bid. There was a failure to enter a binding contract. One cannot snap up an offer or bid knowing that it was made in mistake. . . . This also disposes of alleged errors in admitting evidence of reasonable value.

Andrew Holt (1855-1948) attended St. Ansgar's Academy (now Gustavus Adolphus College), St. Peter, Minnesota, and the University of Minnesota (LL.B.). Admitted to the Minnesota bar in 1881, he practiced privately until becoming judge on the Municipal Court of Minneapolis in 1894, serving for 10 years before his appointment to the Minnesota District Court. Holt served on the Supreme Court of Minnesota from 1912 to 1942. He was the first member of the Supreme Court of Minnesota to have been born in that State. — K.T.

The court, after charging that plaintiff must prove by a fair preponderance of the evidence that defendant in bad faith sought to take advantage of the mistake in the written bid, said:

> That means that the evidence in favor of that theory of the case must be to your minds, in some degree, more convincing than that to the contrary.

The expression "in some degree" is criticized. This was not an action to reform a contract, where clear and convincing proof of mistake is required, but a case where it is claimed the mistake of one party was knowingly and in bad faith sought to be taken advantage of by another in attempting to enter a contract. In such a case, virtually one of fraud, a fair preponderance of evidence determines the issue. If the phrase, "in some degree," was not an accurate enough statement, as applied to the quantum of proof required, the court's attention should have been called thereto at the time. It is also claimed the testimony upon the reasonable value widely diverged, hence prejudicial error for the court to say:

> I think there is not very much dispute in the evidence as to what the reasonable value was. You will perceive that the plaintiff's testimony as to what the reasonable value was, is just the amount of his bid, plus the $963.

Defendant offered no testimony upon reasonable value, except that of one person who bid on most of plaintiff's work. He testified only to the value of the work included in his bid. Adding thereto the value of what other work was furnished by plaintiff, the jury might reach the conclusion that the reasonable value of all was about $3,500. The verdict is practically on that basis, so that, even if the court was not warranted in the statement, the jury were not misled nor defendant prejudiced.

The verdict is assailed as not supported. We are not permitted to weigh the evidence. This is the province of the jury. There is positive and direct testimony to sustain the verdict under the pleadings and theory of the law correctly applied to the issues by the learned trial court. A further review of such testimony would serve no useful purpose.

The order is affirmed.

DRENNAN v. STAR PAVING CO., 51 CAL. 2D 409, 333 P.2D 757, 761 (CAL. 1958): . . . Defendant contends, however, that its bid was the result of mistake and that it was therefore entitled to revoke it. It relies on the rescission cases of M. F. Kemper Const. Co. v. City of Los Angeles, 37 Cal. 2d 696, [235 P.2d 7], and Brunzell Const. Co. v. G. J. Weisbrod, Inc., 134 Cal. App. 2d 278, [285 P.2d 989]. (See also, Lemoge Electric v. San Mateo County, 46 Cal. 2d 659, 662, [297 P.2d 638].) In those cases, however, the bidder's mistake was known or should have been to the offeree, and the offeree could be placed in status quo. Of course, if plaintiff had reason to believe that defendant's bid was in error, he could not justifiably rely on it, and section 90 would afford no basis for enforcing it. . . . Plaintiff, however, had no reason to know that defendant had made a mistake in submitting its bid, since there was usually a variance of 160 per cent between the highest and lowest bids for paving in the desert around Lancaster. He committed himself to performing the main contract in reliance on defendant's figures. Under these circumstances defendant's mistake, far from relieving it of its obligation, constitutes an additional reason for enforcing it, for it misled plaintiff as to the cost of doing the paving. Even had it been clearly understood that defendant's offer was revocable until accepted, it would not necessarily follow that defendant had no duty to exercise reasonable care in preparing its bid. It presented its bid with knowledge of the substantial possibility that it would be used by plaintiff; it could foresee the harm that would ensue from an erroneous underestimate of the cost. Moreover, it was motivated by its own business interest. Whether or not these considerations alone would justify recovery for negligence had the case been tried on that theory . . . , they are persuasive that defendant's mistake should not defeat recovery under the rule of section 90 of the Restatement of Contracts. As between the subcontractor who made the bid and the general contractor who reasonably relied on it, the loss resulting from the mistake should fall on the party who caused it. . . .

REFERENCE: Farnsworth, §9.4
               Calamari & Perillo, §9.27
               Murray, §92(e)

RESTATEMENT (SECOND) OF CONTRACTS

§153.   WHEN MISTAKE OF ONE PARTY MAKES A CONTRACT VOIDABLE

Where a mistake of one party at the time a contract was made as to a basic assumption on which he made the contract has a material effect on the agreed exchange of performances that is adverse to him, the contract is voidable by him if he does not bear the risk of the mistake under the rule stated in §154, and

(a) the effect of the mistake is such that enforcement of the contract would be unconscionable, or

(b) the other party had reason to know of the mistake or his fault caused the mistake.

STUDY GUIDE: In the next case, consider why Chief Justice Marshall might have limited his discussion to "intelligence of extrinsic circumstances, which might influence the price of the commodity" (our emphasis). Is there a principled distinction between this kind of information and the information concerning termites that was involved in Halpert v. Rosenthal, or the stone that was involved in Wood v. Boynton? Is this distinction subject to the same criticism as was leveled by the court in Lenawee against the substance/value distinction in mistake? Are there questions to which one is not entitled to a truthful reply? What is the relationship between the doctrine of misrepresentation discussed in Chapter 16, and the so-called duty to disclose information discussed in the next case? Notice the similarity between misrepresentation and unilateral mistake. How does the principle discussed here compare with the insider trading of stocks?

LAIDLAW v. ORGAN
United States Supreme Court,
15 U.S. (2 Wheat.) 178 (1817)

Error to the district court for the Louisiana district.

The defendant in error filed his petition, or libel, in the court below, stating, that on the 18th day of February, 1815, he purchased of the plaintiffs in error one hundred and eleven hogsheads of tobacco, as appeared by the copy of a bill of parcels annexed, and that the same were delivered to him by the said Laidlaw Co., and that he was in the lawful and quiet possession of the said tobacco, when, on the 20th day of the said month, the said Laidlaw & Co., by force, and of their own wrong, took possession of the same, and unlawfully withheld the same from the petitioner, notwithstanding he was at all times, and still was, ready to do and perform all things on his part stipulated to be done and performed in relation to said purchase, and had actually tendered to the said Laidlaw & Co. bills of exchange for the amount of the purchase money, agreeably to the said contract to his damage, &c. Wherefore the petition prayed that the said Laidlaw & Co. might be cited to appear and answer to his plaint, and that judgment might be rendered against them for his damages, &c. . . .

On the 20th of April, 1815, the cause was tried by a jury, who returned the following verdict, to wit: "The jury find for the plaintiff, for the tobacco named in the petition, without damages, payable as per contract." Whereupon the court rendered judgment

> that the plaintiff recover of the said defendants the said 111 hogsheads of tobacco, mentioned in the plaintiff's petition, and sequestered in this suit, with his costs of suit to be taxed; and ordered, that the marshal deliver the said tobacco to the said plaintiff, and that he have execution for his costs aforesaid, upon the said plaintiff's depositing in this court his bills of exchange for the amount of the purchase money endorsed, &c., for the use of the defendants, agreeably to the verdict of the jury.

On the 29th of April, 1815, the plaintiffs in error filed the following bill of exceptions, to wit:

> Be it remembered, that on the 20th day of April, in the year of our Lord, 1815, the above cause came on for trial before a jury duly sworn and empannelled, the said Peter Laidlaw Co. having filed a disclaimer, and Boorman and Johnston of the city of New-York, having filed their claim. . . . And it appearing in evidence in the said cause, that on the night of the 18th of February, 1815, Messrs. Livingston, White, and Shepherd brought from the British fleet the news that a treaty of peace had been signed at Ghent by the American and

British commissioners, contained in a letter from Lord Bathurst to the Lord
Mayor of London, published in the British newspapers, and that Mr. White
caused the same to be made public in a handbill on Sunday morning,
8 o'clock, the 19th of February, 1815, and that the brother of Mr. Shepherd,
one of these gentlemen, and who was interested in one-third of the profits of
the purchase set forth in said plaintiff's petition, had, on Sunday morning, the
19th of February, 1815, communicated said news to the plaintiff that the said
plaintiff, on receiving said news, called on Francis Girault, (with whom he had
been bargaining for the tobacco mentioned in the petition, the evening previous,) said Francis Girault being one of the said house of trade of Peter
Laidlaw Co., soon after sunrise on the morning of Sunday, the 19th of
February, 1815, before he had heard said news. Said Girault asked if there
was any news which was calculated to enhance the price or value of the article
about to be purchased and that the said purchase was then and there made,
and the bill of parcels annexed to the plaintiff's petition delivered to the
plaintiff between 8 and 9 o'clock in the morning of that day; and that in
consequence of said news the value of said article had risen from 30 to 50
per cent. There being no evidence that the plaintiff had asserted or suggested
any thing to the said Girault, calculated to impose upon him with respect to
said news, and to induce him to think or believe that it did not exist; and it
appearing that the said Girault, when applied to, on the next day, Monday, the
20th of February, 1815, on behalf of the plaintiff, for an invoice of said
tobacco, did not then object to the said sale, but promised to deliver the
invoice to the said plaintiff in the course of the forenoon of that day; the
court charged the jury to find for the plaintiff. Wherefore, that justice, by
due course of law, may be done in this case, the counsel of said defendants,
for them, and on their behalf, prays the court that this bill of exceptions be
filed, allowed, and certified as the law directs.

(Signed,) DOMINICK A. HALL,

District Judge.

New-Orleans, this 3d day of May, 1815.

On the 29th of April, 1815, a writ of error was allowed to this court, and on
the 3d of May, 1815, the defendant in error deposited in the court below,
for the use of the plaintiffs in error, the bills of exchange mentioned in the
pleadings, according to the verdict of the jury and the judgment of the court
thereon, which bills were thereupon taken out of court by the plaintiffs
in error. . . .

Mr. C. J. Ingersoll, for the plaintiffs in error. 1. The first question is,
whether the sale, under the circumstances of the case, was a valid sale;
whether fraud, which vitiates every contract, must be proved by the communication of positive misinformation, or by withholding information
when asked. Suppression of material circumstances within the knowledge
of the vendee, and not accessible to the vendor, is equivalent to fraud, and
vitiates the contract. . . . Pothier, in discussing this subject, adopts the distinction of the forum of conscience, and the forum of law; but he admits that
fides est servanda. . . . The parties treated on an unequal footing, as the one
party had received intelligence of the peace of Ghent, at the time of
the contract, and the other had not. This news was unexpected, even at
Washington, much more at New-Orleans, the recent scene of the most

sanguinary operations of the war. In answer to the question, whether there was any news calculated to enhance the price of the article, the vendee was silent. This reserve, when such a question was asked, was equivalent to a false answer, and as much calculated to deceive as the communication of the most fabulous intelligence. Though the plaintiffs in error, after they heard the news of peace, still went on, in ignorance of their legal rights, to complete the contract, equity will protect them. . . . 3. The court below had no right to charge the jury absolutely to find for the plaintiff. It was a mixed question of fact and law, which ought to have been left to the jury to decide. . . .

Mr. Key contra, . . . 2. The judge's charge was right, there being no evidence of fraud. The vendee's silence was not legal evidence of fraud, and, therefore, there was no conflict of testimony on this point: it was exclusively a question of law; the law was with the plaintiff; and, consequently, the court did right to instruct the jury to find for the plaintiff. . . . 4. The only real question in the cause is, whether the sale was invalid because the vendee did not communicate information which he received precisely as the vendor *might* have got it had he been equally diligent or equally fortunate? And, surely, on this question there can be no doubt. Even if the vendor had been entitled to the disclosure, he waived it by not insisting on an answer to his question; and the silence of the vendee might as well have been interpreted into an *affirmative* as a *negative* answer. But, on principle, he was not bound to disclose. Even admitting that his conduct was unlawful, *in foro conscientiae*, does that prove that it was so in the civil forum? Human laws are imperfect in this respect, and the sphere of morality is more extensive than the limits of civil jurisdiction. The maxim of *caveat emptor* could never have crept into the law, if the province of ethics had been co-extensive with it. There was, in the present case, no circumvention or manoeuvre practised by the vendee, unless rising earlier in the morning, and obtaining by superior diligence and alertness that intelligence by which the price of commodities was regulated, be such. It is a romantic equality that is contended for on the other side. Parties never can be precisely equal in knowledge, either of facts or of the inferences from such facts, and both must concur in order to satisfy the rule contended for. The absence of all authority in England and the United States, both great commercial countries, speaks volumes against the reasonableness and practicability of such a rule.

Mr. C. J. Ingersoll, in reply. Though the record may not show that any thing tending to mislead by positive assertion was said by the vendee, in answer to the question proposed by Mr. Girault, yet it is a case of manoeuvre; of mental reservation; of circumvention. The information was monopolized by the messengers from the British fleet, and not imparted to the public at large until it was too late for the vendor to save himself. The rule of law and of ethics is the same. It is not a romantic, but a practical and legal rule of equality and good faith that is proposed to be applied. . . . The judge undertook to decide from the testimony, that there was no fraud; in so doing he invaded the province of the jury; he should have left it to the jury, expressing his opinion merely.

Mr. Chief Justice MARSHALL* delivered the opinion of the court.

The question in this case is, whether the intelligence of extrinsic circumstances, which might influence the price of the commodity, and which was exclusively within the knowledge of the vendee, ought to have been communicated by him to the vendor? The court is of opinion that he was not bound to communicate it. It would be difficult to circumscribe the contrary doctrine within proper limits, where the means of intelligence are equally accessible to both parties. But at the same time, each party must take care not to say or do anything tending to impose upon the other. The court thinks that the absolute instruction of the judge was erroneous, and that the question, whether any imposition was practised by the vendee upon the vendor ought to have been submitted to the jury. For these reasons the judgment must be reversed, and the cause remanded to the district court of Louisiana, with directions to award a *venire facias de novo.*

Venire de novo awarded.

STUDY GUIDE: *How would the* Laidlaw *case have been decided under the following provisions?*

RESTATEMENT (SECOND) OF CONTRACTS

§160. WHEN ACTION IS EQUIVALENT TO AN ASSERTION (CONCEALMENT)

Action intended or known to be likely to prevent another from learning a fact is equivalent to an assertion that the fact does not exist.

§161. WHEN NON-DISCLOSURE IS EQUIVALENT TO AN ASSERTION

A person's non-disclosure of a fact known to him is equivalent to an assertion that the fact does not exist in the following cases only:

(a) where he knows that disclosure of the fact is necessary to prevent some previous assertion from being a misrepresentation or from being fraudulent or material.

---

* *John Marshall* (1755-1835) attended the College of William and Mary and served in the Revolutionary War (1775-1781), fighting in the battles of Brandywine, Germantown, and Monmouth, and at Valley Forge. Admitted to the Virginia bar in 1780, he held several public offices in that state and was a delegate to the Virginia Convention to ratify the U.S. Constitution in 1788. In the following years, he declined the posts of attorney general of the United States (1795) and minister to France (1796) and justice on the Supreme Court of the United States (1798), before serving as a member of the U.S. House of Representatives from Virginia, 6th Congress (1799-1800), where he successfully defended John Adams on charges of usurping judicial powers. He then declined the post of U.S. Secretary of War in 1800 and became U.S. Secretary of State later that year. Marshall served as Chief Justice of the Supreme Court from 1801 until his death. — K.T.

(b) where he knows that disclosure of the fact would correct a mistake of the other party as to a basic assumption on which that party is making the contract and if non-disclosure of the fact amounts to a failure to act in good faith and in accordance with reasonable standards of fair dealing.

(c) where he knows that disclosure of the fact would correct a mistake of the other party as to the contents or effect of a writing, evidencing or embodying an agreement in whole or in part.

(d) where the other person is entitled to know the fact because of a relation of trust and confidence between them.

THE BASEBALL CARD CASE: A PROBLEM

Twelve-year-old card collector Bryan Wrzesinski, owner of some 40,000 baseball cards, spotted a 1968 Nolan Ryan/Jerry Koosman rookie card at Ball-Mart, a newly opened baseball card store in Itasca, Illinois. The price of the card was marked "1200/." An inexperienced sales clerk interpreted this figure to mean $12.00 and accepted that amount in exchange for the card. The proprietor of the Ball-Mart, Joe Irmen, claimed that the card had been offered for sale at $1,200 (a price in line with its market value) and asked for it back. Wrzesinski refused to reverse the transaction. After two days of trial on Irmen's suit for replevin or money damages, and moments before the judge was to issue her decision, the parties announced a settlement: the card would be sold at auction and the proceeds given to charity.[10]

Consider how this case would have been resolved under Restatement §153 had it not been settled. What about §§160 and 161? What fact or facts would need to be established to determine the proper outcome? Suppose that the card had been clearly marked $12.00 and that the owner of the store who marked it was mistaken as to its value. Same result under *Laidlaw*? Under the Restatement (Second)? (As an aside, what does this case say about the defense of infancy?)

REFERENCE: Barnett, §6.4.2
               Farnsworth, §4.11
               Calamari & Perillo, §9.20
               Murray, §96(A)

B.   CHANGED CIRCUMSTANCES

The previous section described circumstances where a mistake about facts existing at the time of contract formation could provide a valid defense to enforcement. Can later developments or changed circumstances occurring *after* formation, which diminish the utility of the contract to one party, ever provide a valid defense? Since the seeds of the future lie always in the present, it is sometimes difficult to draw a line between a mistake of present existing

10. Andrew Kull, Unilateral Mistake: The Baseball Card Case, 70 Wash. U. L.Q. 57, 57 (1992).

fact and a mistake about a future contingency. Nevertheless, the law governing contract defenses has attempted to do so. In this section we shall strive to understand this distinction, as well as to consider if it makes any sense.

At least two types of changed circumstances have been considered by the courts. The first involves unforeseen *increases in the costs of performance* by one party. This type of unanticipated change animates what was traditionally called *impossibility* and is now usually referred to as *impracticability*. The second involves *reductions in the value* a party attaches to the performance to be received from the other party. This type of unanticipated change animates what is called *frustration of purposes*.

Study Guide: Why make a distinction between mistakes about present existing facts and those which concern future events? Consider once again the excerpt from Lon Fuller about tacit assumptions, which appears at the beginning of this chapter. Finally, Anglo-American writers and courts have sometimes assumed that the common law developed entirely apart from the civil law of Europe. When reading the cases in this section, notice the role that civil law principles and authorities played in these common law developments.

1. Impossibility and Impracticability

Study Guide: When reading the next case, consider whether the appropriateness of the default rule chosen by the court in light of conventional tacit assumptions might account for the counterintuitive nature of the result. In other words, what is the most likely meaning of silence about this contingency and which party should have the burden of contracting around the default rule?

PARADINE v. JANE
Aleyn 26, 82 Eng. Rep. 897 [1647]

In debt the plaintiff declares upon a lease for years rendering rent at the four usual feasts; and for rent behind for three years . . . brings his action; the defendant pleads that a certain German prince, by name Prince Rupert, an alien born, enemy to the King and kingdom, had invaded the realm with an hostile army of men; and with the same force did enter upon the defendant's possession, and him expelled, and held out of possession . . . whereby he could not take the profits; whereupon the plaintiff demurred, and the plea was resolved insufficient. . . .

2. He hath not averred that the army were all aliens, which shall not be intended, and then he hath his remedy against them; and Bacon cited 33 H. 6. 1. e. where the gaoler in bar of an escape pleaded, that alien enemies broke the prison, &c. and exception taken to it, for that he ought to shew of what countrey they were, viz. Scots, &c.

3. It was resolved, that the matter of the plea was insufficient; for though the whole army had been alien enemies, yet he ought to pay his

rent. And this difference was taken, that where the law creates a duty or charge, and the party is disabled to perform it without any default in him, and hath no remedy over, there the law will excuse him. As in the case of waste, if a house be destroyed by tempest, or by enemies, the lessee is excused. . . . [B]ut when the party by his own contract creates a duty or charge upon himself, he is bound to make it good, if he may, notwithstanding any accident by inevitable necessity, because he might have provided against it by his contract. And therefore if the lessee covenant to repair a house, though it be burnt by lightning, or thrown down by enemies, yet he ought to repair it. . . . Another reason was added, that as the lessee is to have the advantage of casual profits, so he must run the hazard of casual losses, and not lay the whole burthen of them upon his lessor; and . . . though the land be surrounded, or gained by the sea, or made barren by wildfire, yet the lessor shall have his whole rent: and judgment was given for the plaintiff.

Historical Background: The "Alien" Prince Rupert

In his discussion of Paradine v. Jane, John D. Wladis notes that "Prince Rupert was in fact the King's nephew and commanded Royalist troops during the [English] Civil War. In his plea, the defendant's attorney most likely portrayed him as an alien enemy in an attempt to rely on precedent excusing performance interfered with by alien enemies."[11] Wladis then goes on to speculate that "[t]he court's refusal to interpret the plea as alleging that not only Prince Rupert but also the members of his army were alien enemies may have been the court's way of taking judicial notice that the Royalist forces commanded by Rupert were subjects of the King and thus not alien enemies."[12]

Historical Background: One View of How and Why Paradine v. Jane Became a Leading Case

GRANT GILMORE, THE DEATH OF CONTRACT 44-46 (1974):   The effect of the application of the objective theory to such areas of the law as mistake was of course to narrow the range within which mistake could be successfully pleaded as a defense. That is, it is no longer enough that I was subjectively mistaken, even with respect to a fundamental term of the contract. To get out of my contract (or to be successful in arguing that no contract was ever formed) I must show that my mistake was justifiable or excusable in the light of the generally accepted standards of the community. Just as the Holmesian formulation of consideration had exploded the

11. John D. Wladis, Common Law and Uncommon Events: The Development of the Doctrine of Impossibility of Performance in English Contract Law, 75 Geo. L.J. 1575, 1579 n.21 (1987).
12. Id. at 1580 n.24.

"vulgar error that any benefit or detriment would do"[13] as a consideration to support a contract, so the "objectification" of the mistake cases exploded the equally vulgar error that any mistake (or failure of the "minds" to "meet") would do as an escape from contractual liability. Now there are "mistakes" and "mistakes" and only some of them will do. With the narrowing of the range of availability of such excuses as mistake,[14] we move toward the ideal of absolute liability which . . . was one of the basic ideas of the great theory.[15]

No legal system has ever carried into practice a theory of absolute contractual liability. Our own system, during the nineteenth century, may be the only one which has ever proclaimed such a theory. The proclamation was made in this country long before Holmes came on the scene and, at least in this country, was steadfastly adhered to, mostly as a matter of ritual incantation, throughout the century. The source of the absolute liability idea in English law was always confidently stated to be the seventeenth century case of Paradine v. Jane. In that case, a landlord's action to recover rent, the tenant had pleaded that he should be excused from payment because, during the term of the lease, he had been evicted from the land by a royalist army under the command of Prince Rupert. The plea was held bad: "Though the whole army had been alien enemies, yet he ought to pay his rent." Two hundred years later we find Morton, J., for the Massachusetts court, explaining the "general rule" on excuse by reason of impossibility in this fashion:

> [W]here the law imposes a duty upon anyone, inevitable accident may excuse the non-performance; for the law will not require of a party what, without any fault of his, he becomes unable to perform. But where the party by his agreement voluntarily assumes or creates a duty or charge upon himself, he shall be bound by his contract, and the nonperformance of it will not be excused by accident or inevitable necessity; for if he desired any such exception, he should have provided for it in his contract.[16]

---

13. [Gilmore is here quoting his own characterization of Holmes in an earlier lecture. — EDS.]

14. That Holmes was consciously engaged in such a "narrowing" process is entirely clear. The lecture on Void and Voidable Contracts in The Common Law is devoted to the argument that excuses from liability such as mistake, fraud, misrepresentation, and so on should be confined within the narrowest possible range. . . .

15. [In a previous lecture, Gilmore described "the great theory" promoted by Holmes and Langdell as

> dedicated to the proposition that, ideally, no one should be liable to anyone for anything. Since the ideal was not attainable, the compromise solution was to restrict liability within the narrowest possible limits. Within those limits, however, liability was to be absolute. . . . Liability, although absolute — at least in theory — was nevertheless to be severely limited. The equitable remedy of specific performance was to be avoided so far as possible. . . . Money damages for breach of contract were to be "compensatory," never punitive. . . . The "compensatory" damages, which were theoretically recoverable, turned out to be a good deal less than enough to compensate the victim for the losses which in fact he might have suffered. Damages in contract, it was pointed out were one thing and damages in tort another; the contract-breaker was not to be held responsible, as the tortfeasor was, for all the consequences of his actions.

Grant Gilmore, The Death of Contract 14-15 (1974) — EDS.]

16. Adams v. Nichols, 19 Pick. (Mass. 1837) 275, 276.

This language was copied, almost word for word, from one of the seventeenth century reports of Paradine v. Jane[17] — a case which, in all probability, Judge Morton had never read and which he did not cite.

The story of the transmission of the Paradine v. Jane language from mid-seventeenth century England to mid-nineteenth century America is one of the curiosities of the legal literature. In its own day *Paradine* does not seem to have been a particularly celebrated case, nor does its seventeenth century meaning, so far as we can determine it, necessarily have much or anything to do with what came to be its nineteenth century meaning. One possibility is that the seventeenth century court meant merely that the tenant could not interpose his plea in the landlord's action for the rent but could bring an independent action against the landlord to recover whatever damages he had suffered as the result of his eviction by Prince Rupert; indeed, *Paradine* is cited to that proposition in a case decided in 1723.[18] Another possibility is that the court looked on the leasehold as a fully executed transaction, with the tenant bearing the risk of eviction in the same way that a buyer of chattels would bear the risk of their loss or destruction after receiving delivery of them from the seller.[19] The modern vogue of *Paradine* dates from Serjeant Williams's edition, first published in 1802, of Saunders, which was a collection of late seventeenth century cases. One of the cases in Saunders, Walton v. Waterhouse,[20] involved a covenant by a tenant to rebuild after a fire. In a lengthy note to Walton v. Waterhouse, Williams paraphrased the language used in the Aleyn report of *Paradine* and it was Williams's note which Judge Morton, in the Massachusetts case just referred to, cited and copied out. Indeed, there are several early nineteenth century references to Paradine v. Jane which assume that the case, given the context in which Williams had put it, involved a tenant's covenant to rebuild.

However, all this is mere bibliographical amusement. The importance of the story lies in the facts that the Williams edition of Saunders was highly successful — having been many times reprinted both in England and in the United States — and that the Note to Walton v. Waterhouse became celebrated — the apparent meaning of the Note being that English law for two hundred years past had steadfastly

---

17. According to the report in Aleyn. . . . : "[W]here the law creates a duty or charge, and the party is disabled to perform it without any default in him, and hath no remedy over, there the law will excuse him. . . . [B]ut when the party by his own contract creates a duty, or charge upon himself, he is bound to make it good, if he may, notwithstanding any accident by inevitable necessity, because he might have provided against it in his contract."

The report of the case in Style has no analogue to the second sentence quoted above. According to Style, the decision went on this ground: "[I]f the tenant for years covenant to pay rent, though the lands let him be surrounded with water, yet he is chargeable with the rent, much more here." The analogy of the land surrounded by water also appears in the Aleyn report.

18. Monk v. Cooper, 2 Strange 763, 93 Eng. Rep. 833 (K.B. 1723). . . .

19. This is the explanation of the case which was put forward by Professor Corbin; see 6 Corbin, Contracts §1322 (1962).

20. 2 Wms Saunders 420, 85 Eng. Rep. 1233 (K.B. 1684).

adhered to a theory of absolute contractual liability.[21] Such a theory evidently made sense to the judges — particularly the American judges — of a hundred years and more ago.

STUDY GUIDE: Can you explain how the holding in the next case is consistent with that in Paradine v. Jane? Notice the use of pleading in the alternative.

TAYLOR v. CALDWELL
In the King's Bench,
3 B. & S. 825, 122 Eng. Rep. 309 (1863)

The declaration alleged that by an agreement, bearing date the 27th May, 1861, the defendants agreed to let, and the plaintiffs agreed to take, on the terms therein stated, The Surrey Gardens and Music Hall, Newington, Surrey, for the following days, that is to say, Monday the 17th June, 1861, Monday the 15th July, 1861, Monday the 5th August, 1861, and Monday the 19th August, 1861, for the purpose of giving a series for four grand concerts and day and night fêtes, at the Gardens and Hall on those days respectively, at the rent of sum of 100*l.* for each of those days. It then averred the fulfillment of conditions &c., on the part of the plaintiffs and breach by the defendants, that they did not nor would allow the plaintiffs to have the use of The Surrey Music Hall and Gardens according to the agreement, but wholly made default therein, c., whereby the plaintiffs lost divers moneys paid by them for printing advertisements of and in advertising the concerts, and also lost divers sums expended and expenses incurred by them in preparing for the concerts and otherwise in relation thereto, and on the faith of the performance by the defendants of the agreement on their part, and had been otherwise injured, &c.

Pleas. First. Traverse of the agreement.

Second. That the defendants did allow the plaintiffs to have the use of The Surrey Music Hall and Gardens according to the agreement, and did not make any default therein, &c.

Third. That the plaintiffs were not ready willing or able to take The Surrey Music Hall and Gardens.

Fourth. Exoneration before breach.

Fifth. That at the time of the agreement there was a general custom of the trade and business of the plaintiffs and the defendants, with respect to which the agreement was made, known to the plaintiffs and the defendants, and with reference to which they agreed, and which was part of the agreement, that in the event of the Gardens and Music Hall being destroyed or so far damaged by accidental fire as to prevent the entertainments being given according to the intent of the agreement, between the time of making the

---

21. *Paradine* is still cited to this proposition in our own day. See, e.g., Simpson, Handbook of the Law of Contracts 359 (2d ed. 1965); Berman, Excuse for Nonperformance in the Light of Contract Practices in International Trade, 63 Colum. L. Rev. 1413, 1417 (1963).

agreement and the time appointed for the performance of the same, the agreement should be rescinded and at an end. . . .

Issue on all the pleas. . . .

On the 11th June the Music Hall was destroyed by an accidental fire, so that it became impossible to give the concerts. Under these circumstances a verdict was returned for the plaintiff, with leave reserved to enter a verdict for the defendants on the second and third issues.

Petersdorff Serjt. in Hilary Term, 1862, obtained a rule to enter a verdict for the defendants generally.

The rule was argued in Hilary Term, 1863 (January 28th); before Cockburn C.J., Wightman, Crompton and Blackburn JJ.

H. Tindal Atkinson shewed cause. . . .

. . . The destruction of the premises by fire will not exonerate the defendants from performing their part of the agreement. In Paradine v. Jane (Al. 26) it is laid down that, where the law creates a duty or charge, and the party is disabled to perform it without any default in him, and hath no remedy over, there the law will excuse him; but when the party, by his own contract, creates a duty or charge upon himself, he is bound to make it good, if he may, notwithstanding any accident by inevitable necessity, because he might have provided against it by his contract. And there accordingly it was held no plea to an action for rent reserved by lease that the defendant was kept out of possession by an alien enemy whereby he could not take the profits.

Pearce, in support of the rule. . . .

. . . The words "God's will permitting" [in the contract] override the whole agreement. . . .

The judgment of the court was now delivered by BLACKBURN, J.* . . .

The parties inaccurately call this a "letting," and the money to be paid a "rent"; but the whole agreement is such as to shew that the defendants were to retain the possession of the Hall and Gardens so that there was to be no demise of them, and that the contract was merely to give the plaintiffs the use of them on those days. Nothing however, in our opinion, depends on this. The agreement then proceeds to set out various stipulations between the parties as to what each was to supply for these concerts and entertainments, and as to the manner in which they should be carried on. The effect of the whole is to shew that the existence of the Music Hall in the Surrey Gardens in a state fit for a concert was essential for the fulfillment of the contract — such entertainments as the parties contemplated in their agreement could not be given without it.

After the making of the agreement, and before the first day on which a concert was to be given, the Hall was destroyed by fire. This destruction, we must take it on the evidence, was without the fault of either party, and

* *Colin Blackburn,* Baron Blackburn (1813-1896), was educated at Eton and Trinity College, Cambridge (B.A., M.A.), and was called to the bench in 1838. Known more as a legal reporter than as a pleader, he was appointed to the Queen's Bench by Lord Campbell in 1859. In 1876, he was bestowed with the honor of one of two newly created posts of life Peer, or Lord of Appeal in Ordinary. He continued service until his retirement from the bench in 1886. Baron Blackburn was also the author of the eight-volume treatise on contracts for the sale of land, published in 1845. — K.T.

was so complete that in consequence the concerts could not be given as intended. And the question we have to decide is whether, under these circumstances, the loss which the plaintiffs have sustained is to fall upon the defendants. The parties when framing their agreement evidently had not present to their minds the possibility of such a disaster, and have made no express stipulation with reference to it, so that the answer to the question must depend upon the general rules of law applicable to such a contract.

There seems no doubt that where there is a positive contract to do a thing, not in itself unlawful, the contractor must perform it or pay damages for not doing it, although in consequence of unforeseen accidents, the performance of his contract has become unexpectedly burthensome or even impossible. . . . But this rule is only applicable when the contract is positive and absolute, and not subject to any condition either express or implied: and there are authorities which, as we think, establish the principle that where, from the nature of the contract, it appears that the parties must from the beginning have known that it could not be fulfilled unless when the time for the fulfillment of the contract arrived some particular specified thing continued to exist, so that, when entering into the contract, they must have contemplated such continuing existence as the foundation of what was to be done; there, in the absence of any express or implied warranty that the thing shall exist, the contract is not to be construed as a positive contract, but as subject to an implied condition that the parties shall be excused in case, before breach, performance becomes impossible from the perishing of the thing without default of the contractor.

There seems little doubt that this implication tends to further the great object of making the legal construction such as to fulfill the intention of those who entered into the contract. For in the course of affairs men in making such contracts in general would, if it were brought to their minds, say that there should be such a condition.

Accordingly, in the Civil law, such an exception is implied in every obligation of the class which they call obligatio de certo corpore. . . . The general subject is treated of by Pothier, who in his Traité des Obligations, partie 3, chap. 6, art. 3, §668 states the result to be that the debtor corporis certi is freed from his obligation when the thing has perished, neither by his act, nor his neglect, and before he is in default, unless by some stipulation he has taken on himself the risk of the particular misfortune which has occurred.

Although the Civil law is not of itself authority in an English Court, it affords great assistance in investigating the principles on which the law is grounded. And it seems to us that the common law authorities establish that in such a contract the same condition of continued existence of the thing is implied in English law.

There is a class of contracts in which a person binds himself to do something which requires to be performed by him in person; and such promises, e.g. promises to marry, or promises to serve for a certain time, are never in practice qualified by an express exception of the death of the party; and therefore in such cases the contract is in terms broken if the promisor dies before fulfillment. Yet it was very early determined that, if the performance is personal, the executors are not liable. . . . See 2 Wms.

Exors. 1560, 5th ed., where a very apt illustration is given. "Thus," says the learned author,

> if an author undertakes to compose a work, and dies before completing it, his executors are discharged from this contract: for the undertaking is merely personal in its nature, and, by the intervention of the contractor's death, has become impossible to be performed.

. . . In Hall v. Wright (E.B. & E. 746, 749), Crompton, J., in his judgment, puts another case.

> Where a contract depends upon personal skill, and the act of God renders it impossible, as, for instance, in the case of a painter employed to paint a picture who is struck blind, it may be that the performance might be excused.

It seems that in those cases the only ground on which the parties or their executors, can be excused from the consequences of the breach of the contract is, that from the nature of the contract there is an implied condition of the continued existence of the life of the contractor, and, perhaps in the case of the painter of his eyesight. In the instances just given, the person, the continued existence of whose life is necessary to the fulfillment of the contract, is himself the contractor, but that does not seem in itself to be necessary to the application of the principle; as is illustrated by the following example. In the ordinary form of an apprentice deed the apprentice binds himself in unqualified terms to "serve until the full end and term of seven years to be fully complete and ended," during which term it is covenanted that the apprentice his master "faithfully shall serve," and the father of the apprentice in equally unqualified terms binds himself for the performance by the apprentice of all and every covenant on his part. . . . It is undeniable that if the apprentice dies within the seven years, the covenant of the father that he shall perform his covenant to serve for seven years is not fulfilled, yet surely it cannot be that an action would lie against the father? Yet the only reason why it would not is that he is excused because of the apprentice's death.

These are instances where the implied condition is of the life of a human being, but there are others in which the same implication is made as to the continued existence of a thing. For example, where a contract of sale is made amounting to a bargain and sale, transferring presently the property in specific chattels, which are to be delivered by the vendor at a future day; there, if the chattels, without the fault of the vendor, perish in the interval, the purchaser must pay the price and the vendor is excused from performing his contract to deliver, which has thus become impossible.

That this is the rule of the English law is established by the case of Rugg v. Minett (11 East, 210), where the article that perished before delivery was turpentine, and it was decided that the vendor was bound to refund the price of all those lots in which the property had not passed; but was entitled to retain without deduction the price of those lots in which the property had passed, though they were not delivered, and though in the conditions of sale, which are set out in the report, there was no express qualification of the promise to deliver on payment. . . .

This also is the rule in the Civil law, and it is worth noticing that Pothier . . . treats this as merely an example of the more general rule that every obligation de certo corpore is extinguished when the thing ceases to exist. . . .

It may, we think, be safely asserted to be now English law, that in all contracts of loan of chattels or bailments if the performance of the promise of the borrower or bailee to return the things lent or bailed, becomes impossible because it has perished, this impossibility (if not arising from the fault of the borrower or bailee from some risk which he has taken upon himself) excuses the borrower or bailee from the performance of his promise to redeliver the chattel. . . .

. . . The principle seems to us to be that, in contracts in which the performance depends on the continued existence of a given person or thing, a condition is implied that the impossibility of performance arising from the perishing of the person or thing shall excuse the performance.

In none of these cases is the promise in words other than positive, nor is there any express stipulation that the destruction of the person or thing shall excuse the performance but that excuse is by law implied, because from the nature of the contract it is apparent that the parties contracted on the basis of the continued existence of the particular person or chattel. In the present case, looking at the whole contract, we find that the parties contracted on the basis of the continued existence of the Music Hall at the time when the concerts were to be given; that being essential to their performance.

We think, therefore, that the Music Hall having ceased to exist, without fault of either party, both parties are excused, the plaintiffs from taking the gardens and paying the money, the defendants from performing their promise to give the use of the Hall and Gardens and other things. Consequently the rule must be absolute to enter the verdict for the defendants.

Rule absolute.

RESTATEMENT (SECOND) OF CONTRACTS

§261.   DISCHARGE BY SUPERVENING IMPRACTICABILITY

Where, after a contract is made, a party's performance is made impracticable without his fault by the occurrence of an event the non-occurrence of which was a basic assumption on which the contract was made, his duty to render that performance is discharged, unless the language or the circumstances indicate the contrary.

§263.   DESTRUCTION, DETERIORATION OR FAILURE TO COME INTO EXISTENCE OF THING NECESSARY FOR PERFORMANCE

If the existence of a specific thing is necessary for the performance of a duty, its failure to come into existence, destruction, or such deterioration as makes performance impracticable is an event the non-occurrence of which was a basic assumption on which the contract was made.

SALES CONTRACTS: THE UNIFORM COMMERCIAL CODE

§2-613.   CASUALTY TO IDENTIFIED GOODS

Where the contract requires for its performance goods identified when the contract is made, and the goods suffer casualty without the fault of either party before the risk of loss passes to the buyer, or in a proper case under a "no arrival, no sale" term (Section 2-324) then

(a) if the loss is total the contract is avoided; and

(b) if the loss is partial or the goods have so deteriorated as no longer to conform to the contract the buyer may nevertheless demand inspection and at his option either treat the contract as avoided or accept the goods with due allowance from the contract price for the deterioration or the deficiency in quantity but without further right against the seller.

STUDY GUIDE: The next case involves a breach of contract action brought against the estate of River Phoenix, a young actor who has achieved cult status since his untimely death in 1993 of a drug overdose at the age of 23. He appeared in a string of hit movies, including Stand by Me, The Mosquito Coast, Little Nikita, Indiana Jones and the Last Crusade *(in which he played young Indiana Jones), and* My Own Private Idaho. *Did not River Phoenix breach his contract with the production companies insured by the plaintiffs and those whose rights they are asserting?*

CNA & AMERICAN CASUALTY v. ARLYN PHOENIX
District Court of Appeal of Florida, First District,
678 So. 2d 378 (1996)

JOANOS, Judge.* . . . The case arises from the unfortunate death of the young actor, River Phoenix, originally of Gainesville, Florida, apparently due to an overdose of illegal drugs, before completion of two films, "Dark Blood" and "Interview with the Vampire," in which he had contracted to appear. As a result of the death, the "Dark Blood" project was totally abandoned. "Interview with the Vampire" was completed with another actor replacing Phoenix. CNA and American Casualty, which are both

---

* *James E. Joanos* (1934-†) is a graduate of Florida State University (B.S., 1956), and after serving as an officer in the U.S. Air Force (1956-1959), he received his law degree from Yale Law School in 1962 and entered private practice. He served in the Florida House of Representatives from 1968 to 1971. In 1971, he became a judge in the Felony Court of Record for Leon County, Florida, and moved to the Second Judicial Circuit of Florida in 1973 and to the First District Court of Appeal in 1980, where he served as its Chief Judge from 1991 to 1993. He retired to private practice in 2001. He has taught as an adjunct professor at the Florida State University College of Law. — R.B.

members of the CNA group of insurance companies, had written entertainment package insurance policies covering various aspects of the two productions. After paying the policy holders, CNA and American Casualty became subrogated to the claims the insureds had against the estate.[22]

CNA attempted to state a cause of action for breach of contract against Phoenix's estate, based on an "actor loanout agreement," between Jude Nile, a corporation owned and run by Phoenix and his mother, Arlyn Phoenix, and Scala Productions. The agreement, signed by Phoenix, allegedly included a general obligation not to do anything which would deprive the parties to the agreement of its benefits. CNA further alleged that by deliberately taking illegal drugs in quantities in excess of those necessary to kill a human being, Phoenix deprived the parties of his services and breached his obligation. American Casualty also couched its complaint for declaratory judgment in terms of breach of contract based on an actor loanout agreement between Jude Nile and Geffen Pictures, which gave Geffen the right to loan Phoenix to Time Warner. . . .

The estate moved to dismiss . . . , contending there could be no cause of action for breach of contract because the personal services contracts were rendered impossible to perform due to the death. . . . After hearings, the trial court granted the motion[] to dismiss with prejudice.

On appeal, CNA and American Casualty contend that the defense of impossibility of performance does not apply in this case because that doctrine requires that the impossibility be fortuitous and unavoidable, and that it occur through no fault of either party. They contend that because the death occurred from an intentional, massive overdose of illegal drugs, that this is not a situation in which neither party was at fault. The trial court very clearly ruled that even if the death was a suicide (there is no indication in the record that it was) or the result of an intentional, self-inflicted act, the doctrine of impossibility of performance applied.

Appellants have candidly conceded that no case authorities exist in support of their position concerning fault in a case of impossibility due to death. Appellants ask this court to find support for their theory in the following language of the Restatement of Contracts 2d §§261 and 262:

§261 Where, after a contract is made, a party's performance is made impracticable without his fault by the occurrence of an event the nonoccurrence of which was a basic assumption on which the contract was made, his duty to render that performance is discharged, unless the language or the circumstances indicate the contrary.

§262 If the existence of a particular person is necessary for the performance of a duty, his death or such incapacity as makes performance impracticable is an event the nonoccurrence of which was a basic assumption on which the contract was made.

Appellants contend the Restatement dictates that impossibility of performance due to the destruction of one's own health is not the sort of conduct

---

22. CNA paid out over $5.7 million under its policy. American Casualty had not yet paid all claims, and sought a declaratory judgment on the coverage issue. It had paid out $15,000 of approximately $400,000 in claims.

that will excuse performance, citing Handicapped Children's Education Board v. Lukaszewski, 332 N.W.2d 774 (Wis. 1983), and that the same reasoning should apply in a case of self-induced death. Appellants also suggest a policy basis for the ruling they advocate, arguing that in a society dealing with increasing problems created by illegal drug abuse, such conduct should not excuse the performance of the contract.

At oral argument of this case, it became apparent that any attempt to discern fault in a death case such as this one, or in a similar case, perhaps involving the use of tobacco or alcohol would create another case by case and hard to interpret rule of law. Being mindful that there are already too many of these in existence, we are not persuaded by the facts or the arguments presented to depart from the clear and unambiguous rule that death renders a personal services contract impossible to perform. See 17A Am. Jur. 2d "Contracts" §688 (1991). In such contracts, "there is an implied condition that death shall dissolve the contract." Id. With this implied condition in mind, we believe the parties to the agreements could have provided specifically for the contingency of loss due to the use of illegal drugs, as they provided for other hazardous or life threatening contingencies.[23] We affirm the trial court's ruling that the doctrine of impossibility of performance applies in this case. . . .

REFERENCE: Farnsworth, §§9.5, 9.6, 9.9
              Calamari & Perillo, §§13.1-13.11, 13.13-13.15, 13.19, 13.23
              Murray, §§113, 114

STUDY GUIDE: Was performance in the next case impossible? If not, what is now viewed as the nature of this defense? Was there an expressed assumption of the risk of the Suez Canal closing? If not, how did the court decide how the risk was allocated under the contract? Was Transatlantic asserting a defense to its contract? If not, what was it claiming?

TRANSATLANTIC FINANCING CORP. v. UNITED STATES

United States Court of Appeals District of Columbia Circuit,
363 F.2d 312 (1966)

J. SKELLY WRIGHT, Circuit Judge:
This appeal involves a voyage charter between Transatlantic Financing Corporation, operator of the SS CHRISTOS, and the United States covering

---

23. "Interview With the Vampire" provided:

From the date two (2) weeks before the scheduled start date of principal photography until the completion of all services required of Employee hereunder, Employee will not ride in any aircraft other than as a passenger on a scheduled flight of a United States or other major international air carrier maintaining regularly published schedules, or engage in any ultrahazardous activity without Producer's written consent in each case.

The entertainment package policies contained exclusions based on similar activities.

carriage of a full cargo of wheat from a United States Gulf port to a safe port in Iran. The District Court dismissed a libel filed by Transatlantic against the United States for costs attributable to the ship's diversion from the normal sea route caused by the closing of the Suez Canal. We affirm.

On July 26, 1956, the Government of Egypt nationalized the Suez Canal Company and took over operation of the Canal. On October 2, 1956, during the international crisis which resulted from the seizure, the voyage charter in suit was executed between representatives of Transatlantic and the United States. The charter indicated the termini of the voyage but not the route. On October 27, 1956, the SS CHRISTOS sailed from Galveston for Bandar Shapur, Iran, on a course which would have taken her through Gibraltar and the Suez Canal. On October 29, 1956, Israel invaded Egypt. On October 31, 1956, Great Britain and France invaded the Suez Canal Zone. On November 2, 1956, the Egyptian Government obstructed the Suez Canal with sunken vessels and closed it to traffic.

On or about November 7, 1956, Beckmann, representing Transatlantic, contacted Potosky, an employee of the United States Department of Agriculture, who appellant concedes was unauthorized to bind the Government, requesting instructions concerning disposition of the cargo and seeking an agreement for payment of additional compensation for a voyage around the Cape of Good Hope. Potosky advised Beckmann that Transatlantic was expected to perform the charter according to its terms, that he did not believe Transatlantic was entitled to additional compensation for a voyage around the Cape, but that Transatlantic was free to file such a claim. Following this discussion, the CHRISTOS changed course for the Cape of Good Hope and eventually arrived in Bandar Shapur on December 30, 1956.

Transatlantic's claim is based on the following train of argument. The charter was a contract for a voyage from a Gulf port to Iran. Admiralty principles and practices, especially stemming from the doctrine of deviation, require us to imply into the contract the term that the voyage was to be performed by the "usual and customary" route. The usual and customary route from Texas to Iran was, at the time of contract, via Suez, so the contract was for a voyage from Texas to Iran via Suez. When Suez was closed this contract became impossible to perform. Consequently, appellant's argument continues, when Transatlantic delivered the cargo by going around the Cape of Good Hope, in compliance with the Government's demand under claim of right, it conferred a benefit upon the United States for which it should be paid in *quantum meruit*.

The doctrine of impossibility of performance has gradually been freed from the earlier fictional and unrealistic strictures of such tests as the "implied term" and the parties' "contemplation." Page, The Development of the Doctrine of Impossibility of Performance, 18 Mich. L. Rev. 589, 596 (1920). It is now recognized that "A thing is impossible in legal contemplation when it is not practicable; and a thing is impracticable when it can only be done at an excessive and unreasonable cost" Mineral Park Land Co. v. Howard, 172 Cal. 289, 293, 156 P. 458, 460, L.R.A. 1916F, 1 (1916). The doctrine ultimately represents the ever-shifting line, drawn by courts hopefully responsive to commercial practices and mores, at which the community's interest in having contracts enforced according to their terms is outweighed by the commercial senselessness of requiring performance. When the issue is raised, the court is asked to construct a condition of performance based on the changed circumstances, a process which involves at least three reasonably definable steps. First, a contingency — something unexpected — must have occurred. Second, the risk of the unexpected occurrence must not have been allocated either by agreement or by custom. Finally, occurrence of the contingency must have rendered performance commercially impracticable.[24] Unless the court finds these three requirements satisfied, the plea of impossibility must fail.

The first requirement was met here. It seems reasonable, where no route is mentioned in a contract, to assume the parties expected performance by the usual and customary route at the time of contract. Since the usual and customary route from Texas to Iran at the time of contract was through Suez, closure of the Canal made impossible the expected method of performance. But this unexpected development raises rather than resolves the impossibility issue, which turns additionally on whether the risk of the contingency's occurrence had been allocated and, if not, whether performance by alternative routes was rendered impracticable.

Proof that the risk of a contingency's occurrence has been allocated may be expressed in or implied from the agreement. Such proof may also be found in the surrounding circumstances, including custom and usages of the trade. The contract in this case does not expressly condition performance upon availability of the Suez route. Nor does it specify "via Suez" or, on the other hand, "via Suez or Cape of Good Hope." Nor are there provisions in the contract from which we may properly imply that the continued availability of Suez was a condition of performance. Nor is there anything in custom or trade usage, or in the surrounding circumstances generally, which would support our constructing a condition of performance. The numerous cases requiring performance around the Cape when Suez was closed, see e.g., Ocean Tramp Tankers Corp. v. V/O Sovfracht (The Eugenia), (1964) 2 Q.B. 226, and cases cited therein, indicate that the Cape route is generally regarded as an alternative means of performance. So the implied expectation that the route would be via Suez is hardly adequate proof of an allocation to the promisee of the risk of closure. In some cases, even an express expectation may not amount to a condition of performance.[25] The doctrine of deviation supports our assumption that

---

24. Compare UCC §2-615(a), which provides that, in the absence of an assumption of greater liability, delay or non-delivery by a seller is not a breach if performance as agreed is made "impracticable" by the occurrence of a "contingency" the non-occurrence of which was a "basic assumption on which the contract was made." To the extent this limits relief to "unforeseen" circumstances, comment 1, see the discussion below, and compare UCC §2-614(1). There may be a point beyond which agreement cannot go, UCC §2-615, comment 8, presumably the point at which the obligation would be "manifestly unreasonable," §1-102(3), in bad faith, §1-203, or unconscionable, §2-302. . . .

25. UCC 2-614(1) provides: "Where without fault of either party . . . the agreed manner of delivery . . . becomes commercially impracticable but a commercially reasonable substitute is available, such substitute performance must be tendered and accepted." Compare Mr. Justice Holmes' observation: "You can give any conclusion a logical form. You always can imply a condition in a contract. But why do you imply it? It is because of some belief as to the practice of the community or of a class, or because of some opinion as to policy. . . ." Holmes, The Path of the Law, 10 Harv. L. Rev. 457, 466 (1897).

parties normally expect performance by the usual and customary route, but it adds nothing beyond this that is probative of an allocation of the risk.[26]

There are two clauses which allegedly demonstrate that time is of importance in this contract. One clause computes the remuneration "in steaming time" for diversions to other countries ordered by the charterer in emergencies. This proves only that the United States wished to reserve power to send the goods to another country. It does not imply in any way that there was a rush about the matter. The other clause concerns demurrage and despatch. The charterer agreed to pay Transatlantic demurrage of $1,200 per day for all time in excess of the period agreed upon for loading and unloading, and Transatlantic was to pay despatch of $600 per day for any saving in time. Of course this provision shows the parties were concerned about time, but the fact that they arranged so minutely the consequences of any delay or speedup of loading and unloading operates against the argument that they were similarly allocating the risk of delay or speed-up of the voyage.

If anything, the circumstances surrounding this contract indicate that the risk of the Canal's closure may be deemed to have been allocated to Transatlantic. We know or may safely assume that the parties were aware, as were most commercial men with interests affected by the Suez situation, see *The Eugenia*, supra, that the Canal might become a dangerous area. No doubt the tension affected freight rates, and it is arguable that the risk of closure became part of the dickered terms. We do not deem the risk of closure so allocated, however. Foreseeability or even recognition of a risk does not necessarily prove its allocation. Parties to a contract are not always able to provide for all the possibilities of which they are aware, sometimes because they cannot agree, often simply because they are too busy. Moreover, that some abnormal risk was contemplated is probative but does not necessarily establish an allocation of the risk of the contingency which actually occurs. In this case, for example, nationalization by Egypt of the Canal Corporation and formation of the Suez Users Group did not necessarily indicate that the Canal would be blocked even if a confrontation resulted. The surrounding circumstances do indicate, however, a willingness by Transatlantic to assume abnormal risks, and this fact should legitimately cause us to judge the impracticability of performance by an alternative route in stricter terms than we would were the contingency unforeseen.

We turn then to the question whether occurrence of the contingency rendered performance commercially impracticable under the circumstances of this case. The goods shipped were not subject to harm from the longer, less temperate Southern route. The vessel and crew were fit to proceed

26. The deviation doctrine, drawn principally from admiralty insurance practice, implies into all relevant commercial instruments naming the termini of voyages the usual and customary route between those points. Insurance is cancelled when a ship unreasonably "deviates" from this course, for example by extending a voyage or by putting in at an irregular port, and the shipowner forfeits the protection of clauses of exception which might otherwise have protected him from his common law insurer's liability to cargo. . . . The doctrine's only relevance . . . is that it provides additional support for the assumption we willingly make that merchants agreeing to a voyage between two points expect that the usual and customary route between those points will be used. The doctrine provides no evidence of an allocation of the risk of the route's unavailability.

around the Cape. Transatlantic was no less able than the United States to purchase insurance to cover the contingency's occurrence. If anything, it is more reasonable to expect owner-operators of vessels to insure against the hazards of war. They are in the best position to calculate the cost of performance by alternative routes (and therefore to estimate the amount of insurance required), and are undoubtedly sensitive to international troubles which uniquely affect the demand for and cost of their services. The only factor operating here in appellant's favor is the added expense, allegedly $43,972.00 above and beyond the contract price of $305,842.92, of extending a 10,000 mile voyage by approximately 3,000 miles. While it may be an overstatement to say that increased cost and difficulty of performance never constitute impracticability, to justify relief there must be more of a variation between expected cost and the cost of performing by an available alternative than is present in this case, where the promisor can legitimately be presumed to have accepted some degree of abnormal risk, and where impracticability is urged on the basis of added expense alone.

We conclude, therefore, as have most other courts considering related issues arising out of the Suez closure, that performance of this contract was not rendered legally impossible. Even if we agreed with appellant, its theory of relief seems untenable. When performance of a contract is deemed impossible it is a nullity. In the case of a charter party involving carriage of goods, the carrier may return to an appropriate port and unload its cargo, subject of course to required steps to minimize damages. If the performance rendered has value, recovery in *quantum meruit* for the entire performance is proper. But here Transatlantic has collected its contract price, and now seeks *quantum meruit* relief for the additional expense of the trip around the Cape. If the contract is a nullity, Transatlantic's theory of relief should have been *quantum meruit* for the entire trip, rather than only for the extra expense. Transatlantic attempts to take its profit on the contract, and then force the Government to absorb the cost of the additional voyage. When impracticability without fault occurs, the law seeks an equitable solution, and *quantum meruit* is one of its potent devices to achieve this end. There is no interest in casting the entire burden of commercial disaster on one party in order to preserve the other's profit. Apparently the contract price in this case was advantageous enough to deter appellant from taking a stance on damages consistent with its theory of liability. In any event, there is no basis for relief.

Affirmed.

SALES CONTRACTS: THE UNIFORM COMMERCIAL CODE

§2-615.   EXCUSE BY FAILURE OF PRESUPPOSED CONDITIONS

Except so far as a seller may have assumed a greater obligation and subject to the preceding section on substituted performance:

(a) Delay in delivery or non-delivery in whole or in part by a seller who complies with paragraphs (b) and (c) is not a breach of his duty under a contract for sale if performance as agreed has been made impracticable by the occurrence of a contingency the non-occurrence of which was a basic assumption on which the contract was made or by compliance in good faith with any applicable foreign or domestic governmental regulation or order whether or not it later proves to be invalid.

(b) Where the causes mentioned in paragraph (a) affect only a part of the seller's capacity to perform, he must allocate production and deliveries among his customers but may at his option include regular customers not then under contract as well as his own requirements for further manufacture. He may so allocate in any manner which is fair and reasonable.

(c) The seller must notify the buyer seasonably that there will be delay or non-delivery and, when allocation is required under paragraph (b), of the estimated quota thus made available for the buyer.

2. Frustration of Purposes

STUDY GUIDE: As nothing in the agreement made the promise to pay conditional on the occurrence of the coronation procession, in the next case why should the person who let the room be able to get his or her money back? Are not hotels justified in retaining nonrefundable deposits on rooms they reserve, and doctors justified in charging for office appointments that patients miss? Can the agreements in the next case be distinguished somehow from these other examples? Is Taylor v. Caldwell good authority for the court's opinion?

KRELL v. HENRY
L.R. 2 K.B. 740 (Ct. App. 1903)

Appeal from a decision of DARLING, J.

The plaintiff, Paul Krell, sued the defendant, C. S. Henry, for £50., being the balance of the sum of £75., for which the defendant had agreed to hire a flat at 56A, Pall Mall on the days of June 26 and 27, for the purpose of viewing the processions to be held in connection with the coronation of His Majesty [Edward VII]. The defendant denied his liability, and counterclaimed for the return of the sum of £25., which had been paid as a deposit, on the ground that, the processions not having taken place owing to the serious illness of the King, there had been a total failure of consideration for the contract entered into by him.

. . . On June 17, 1902, the defendant noticed an announcement in the windows of the plaintiff's flat to the effect that windows to view the coronation processions were to be let. The defendant interviewed the housekeeper on the subject, when it was pointed out to him what a good view of the processions could be obtained from the premises, and he eventually agreed with the housekeeper to take the suite for the two days in question for a sum of £75.

On June 20 the defendant wrote the following letter to the plaintiff's solicitor: —

I am in receipt of yours of the 18th instant, inclosing form of agreement for the suite of chambers on the third floor at 56A, Pall Mall, for which I have agreed to take for the two days, the 26th and 27th instant, for the sum of £75. For reasons given you I cannot enter into the agreement, but as arranged over the telephone I inclose herewith cheque for £25. as deposit, and will thank you to confirm to me that I shall have the entire use of these rooms during the days (not the nights) of the 26th and 27th instant. You may rely that every care will be taken of the premises and their contents. On the 24th inst. I will pay the balance, viz., £50., to complete the £75. agreed upon.

On the same day the defendant received the following reply from the plaintiff's solicitor: —

> I am in receipt of your letter of today's date inclosing cheque for £25. deposit on your agreeing to take Mr. Krell's chambers on the third floor at 56A, Pall Mall for the two days, the 26th and 27th June, and I confirm the agreement that you are to have the entire use of these rooms during the days (but not the nights), the balance, of £50., to be paid to me on Tuesday next the 24th instant.

The processions not having taken place on the days originally appointed . . . the defendant declined to pay the balance of £50. alleged to be due from him under the contract in writing of June 20 constituted by the above two letters. Hence the present action.

Darling J., on August 11, 1902, held, upon the authority of Taylor v. Caldwell . . . that there was an implied condition in the contract that the procession should take place, and gave judgment for the defendant on the claim and counter-claim.

The plaintiff appealed. . . .

VAUGHAN WILLIAMS,* L.J. read the following written judgment: — The real question in this case is the extent of the application in English law of the principle of the Roman law which has been adopted and acted on in many English decisions, and notably in the case of Taylor v. Caldwell. That case at least makes it clear that

> where from the nature of the contract, it appears that the parties must from the beginning have known that it could not be fulfilled unless, when the time for the fulfillment of the contract arrived, some particular specified thing continued to exist, so that when entering into the contract they must have contemplated such continued existence as the foundation of what was to be done; there, in the absence of any express or implied warranty that the thing shall exist, the contract is not to be considered a positive contract, but as subject to an implied condition that the parties shall be excused in case, before breach, performance becomes impossible from the perishing of the thing without default of the contractor.

Thus far it is clear that the principle of the Roman law has been introduced into the English law. The doubt in the present case arises as to how far this

*Vaughan Williams (1838-1916) was born in Queen Square, Bloomsbury, the son of a justice in the court of common pleas. He studied jurisprudence at Christ Church, Oxford, and graduated in 1860. He read law in the chambers of Hassard Hume Dodgson and was called to the bar by Lincoln's Inn in 1864. He spent several years in private practice but also devoted himself to scholarship, publishing a well-regarded treatise, The Law and Practice of Bankruptcy, in 1870. In 1890, he was knighted and appointed to serve as a judge of the Queen's Bench Division. After seven years, Williams was promoted to be a lord justice of appeal and served in that capacity for seventeen years. He retired in 1914. — R.B.

principle extends. . . . It is said, on the one side, that the specified thing, state of things, or condition the continued existence of which is necessary for the fulfillment of the contract, so that the parties entering into the contract must have contemplated the continued existence of that thing, condition, or state of things as the foundation of what was to be done under the contract, is limited to things which are either the subject-matter of the contract or a condition or state of things, present or anticipated, which is expressly mentioned in the contract. But, on the other side, it is said that the condition or state of things need not be expressly specified, but that it is sufficient if that condition or state of things clearly appears by extrinsic evidence to have been assumed by the parties to be the foundation or basis of the contract, and the event which causes the impossibility is of such a character that it cannot reasonably be supposed to have been in the contemplation of the contracting parties when the contract was made. In such a case the contracting parties will not be held bound by the general words which, though large enough to include, were not used with reference to a possibility of a particular event rendering performance of the contract impossible. I do not think that the principle of the civil law as introduced into the English law is limited to cases in which the event causing the impossibility of performance is the destruction or non-existence of some thing which is the subject-matter of the contract or of some condition or state of things expressly specified as a condition of it. I think that you first have to ascertain, not necessarily from the terms of the contract, but, if required, from necessary inferences, drawn from surrounding circumstances recognised by both contracting parties, what is the substance of the contract, and then to ask the question whether that substantial contract needs for its foundation the assumption of the existence of a particular state of things. If it does, this will limit the operation of the general words, and in such case, if the contract becomes impossible of performance by reason of the non-existence of the state of things assumed by both contracting parties as the foundation of the contract, there will be no breach of the contract thus limited. Now what are the facts of the present case? The contract is contained in two letters of June 20 which passed between the defendant and the plaintiff's agent, Mr. Cecil Bisgood. These letters do not mention the coronation, but speak merely of the taking of Mr. Krell's chambers, or, rather, of the use of them, in the daytime of June 26 and 27, for the sum of £75, £25 then paid, balance £50. to be paid on the 24th. But the affidavits, which by agreement between the parties are to be taken as stating the facts of the case, shew that the plaintiff exhibited on his premises, third floor, 56A, Pall Mall, an announcement to the effect that windows to view the Royal coronation procession were to be let, and that the defendant was induced by that announcement to apply to the housekeeper on the premises, who said that the owner was willing to let the suite of rooms for the purpose of seeing the Royal procession for both days, but not nights, of June 26 and 27.

In my judgment the use of the rooms was let and taken for the purpose of seeing the Royal procession. It was not a demise of the rooms, or even an agreement to let and take the rooms. It is a license to use rooms for a particular purpose and none other. And in my judgment the taking place of those processions on the days proclaimed along the proclaimed route, which passed 56A, Pall Mall, was regarded by both contracting parties as the foundation of the contract; and I think that it cannot reasonably be supposed to have been in the contemplation of the contracting parties, when the contract was made, that the coronation would not be held on the proclaimed days, or the processions not take place on those days along the proclaimed route; and I think that the words imposing on the defendant the obligation to accept and pay for the use of the rooms for the named days, although general and unconditional, were not used with reference to the possibility of the particular contingency which afterwards occurred. It was suggested in the course of the argument that if the occurrence, on the proclaimed days, of the coronation and the procession in this case were the foundation of the contract, and if the general words are thereby limited or qualified, so that in the event of the non-occurrence of the coronation and procession along the proclaimed route they would discharge both parties from further performance of the contract, it would follow that if a cabman was engaged to take some one to Epsom on Derby Day at a suitable enhanced price for such a journey, say 10*l.*, both parties to the contract would be discharged in the contingency of the race at Epsom for some reason becoming impossible; but I do not think this follows, for I do not think that in the cab case the happening of the race would be the foundation of the contract. No doubt the purpose of the engager would be to go to see the Derby, and the price would be proportionately high; but the cab had no special qualifications for the purpose which led to the selection of the cab for this particular occasion. Any other cab would have done as well. Moreover, I think that, under the cab contract, the hirer, even if the race went off, could have said, "Drive me to Epsom; I will pay you the agreed sum; you have nothing to do with the purpose for which I hired the cab," and that if the cabman refused he would have been guilty of a breach of contract, there being nothing to qualify his promise to drive the hirer to Epsom on a particular day. Whereas in the case of the coronation, there is not merely the purpose of the hirer to see the coronation procession, but it is the coronation procession and the relative position of the rooms which is the basis of the contract as much for the lessor as the hirer; and I think that if the King, before the coronation day and after the contract, had died, the hirer could not have insisted on having the rooms on the days named. It could not in the cab case be reasonably said that seeing the Derby race was the foundation of the contract, as it was of the licence in this case. Whereas in the present case, where the rooms were offered and taken, by reason of their peculiar suitability from the position of the rooms for a view of the coronation procession, surely the view of the coronation procession was the foundation of the contract, which is a very different thing from the purpose of the man who engaged the cab — namely, to see the race — being held to be the foundation of the contract. Each case must be judged by its own circumstances. In each case one must ask oneself, first, what, having regard to all the circumstances, was the foundation of the contract? Secondly, was the performance of the contract prevented? Thirdly, was the event which prevented the performance of the contract of such a character that it cannot reasonably be said to have been in the contemplation of the parties at the date of the contract? If all these questions are answered in the affirmative (as I think they should be in this case), I think both parties are discharged from further performance of the contract. I think that the coronation procession was the foundation of this contract, and that the non-happening of it prevented the performance of the contract; and, secondly, I think that the non-happening of the procession . . . was an event "of such a character that it cannot reasonably be supposed to have been in the contemplation of the contracting parties when the contract was made. . . ." The test seems to be whether the event which causes impossibility was or might have been anticipated and guarded against. . . . I myself am clearly of opinion that in this case, where we have to ask ourselves whether the object of the contract was frustrated by the non-happening of the coronation and its procession on the days proclaimed, parol evidence is admissible to shew that the subject of the contract was rooms to view the coronation procession, and was so to the knowledge of both parties. . . . This disposes of the plaintiff's claim for £50 unpaid balance of the price agreed to be paid for the use of the rooms. The defendant at one time set up a crossclaim for the return of the £25 he paid at the date of the contract. As that claim is now withdrawn it is unnecessary to say anything about it. . . . I think this appeal ought to be dismissed.

[The concurring opinions of ROMER, L.J., and STIRLING, L.J. are omitted.]

Appeal dismissed.

Historical Background: The Ailing King

E. ALLAN FARNSWORTH & WILLIAM F. YOUNG, CONTRACTS 848 (4TH ED. 1988):   Two processions were planned in connection with the coronation: that on Coronation Day, and a "Pageant" of the following day. Experience of the Diamond Jubilee (1897) provided some guidance for the pricing of space to see the processions. At that time a club-house had been "let to a speculator for £200, who realized £500 by his bargain." C. Pascoe, The Pageant & Ceremony of The Coronation 213 (1902). But there were complications in the early summer of 1902, in that the routes of the processions had not been determined. Pall Mall — "club-land of the empire" — was thought to be a certainty for the Pageant procession but for Coronation Day two shorter routes, not including Pall Mall, were thought to be under consideration. One writer of the time estimated that prices for the Pageant ought not to exceed those paid for Victoria's Jubilee — "that is to say, if the Route be not [curtailed]. Of course, the lesser the opportunity of seeing the Pageant, the higher will be the prices asked for accommodation." Id. at 212.

On June 22 Commons was informed that the King had just undergone an operation for appendicitis, and that the coronation was indefinitely postponed. V. Cowles, Edward VII and His Circle 240 (1956). It was performed on August 9. Though some of the captains and the princes (kings were not invited) had departed London, the splendor of the ceremony was "scarcely dimmed." Pall Mall was on the coronation route. London Illustrated News, Aug. 14, 1902.

Legal Background: Should the Loss "Lie Where It Fell"?

STUDY GUIDE: Why was the Rule of Chandler v. Webster so widely criticized? Can you see any problem with the current approach requiring a judicial allocation of losses?

While Krell v. Henry is the coronation case best known for recognizing the defense of frustration of purposes, the case of Chandler v. Webster is best known for its approach to how a frustrated contract should be remedied. The following passage of the opinion became known as "the Rule of Chandler v. Webster":

> [W]here, from causes outside the volition of the parties, something which was the basis of, or essential to the fulfilment of, the contract, has become impossible, so that, from the time when the fact of that impossibility has been ascertained, the contract can no further be performed by either party, it remains a perfectly good contract up to that point, and everything previously done in pursuance of it must be treated as rightly done, but the parties are both discharged from further performance of it. . . . The rule adopted by the Courts in such cases is I think to some extent an arbitrary one, the reason for its adoption being that it is really impossible in such cases to work out with any certainty what the rights of the parties in the event which has happened should be. Time has elapsed, and the position of both parties may have been more or less altered, and it is impossible to adjust or ascertain the rights of the parties with exactitude. That being so, the law treats everything that has already been done in pursuance of the contract as validly done, but relieves the parties of further responsibility under it.[27]

In other words, the loss should "lie where it happened to fall" when the intervening event occurred.

This rule was widely condemned as unjust insofar as it resulted in a windfall gain for the parties who happened to collect a prepayment, and a windfall loss to the party who was responsible enough to leave a deposit. In 1942, the rule was reversed by the House of Lords in Fibrosa S.A. v. Fairbairn Lawson Combe Barbour, Ltd.[28] That case involved a contract in which a Polish textile manufacturer ordered some flax-hackling machines be constructed by an English manufacturer at a price of £4,800. After the Polish company had made an initial payment of £1,000, Germany invaded Poland. An agent of the Polish company requested its money back on the ground that performance was now impossible. Both the trial and appellate courts, following Chandler v. Webster, held that the English company was not obliged to return the deposit. The House of Lords reversed and held that the deposit was to be refunded, thus reversing *Chandler*. The Lords did not think they were authorized, however, to allow a set-off against the deposit to compensate the English company for the work they had done in preparation to perform the contract. Thus, in 1943, Parliament passed the Frustrated Contracts Act which provided that amounts previously paid and the value of other benefits by one party shall be recoverable, subject to possible set-off for expenses incurred and benefits conferred by the other party.

REFERENCE: Farnsworth, §§9.7-9.8
               Calamari & Perillo, §13.12
               Murray, §§115, 116

---

27. Chandler v. Webster, [1904] 1 K.B. at 499-500.
28. Fibrosa SA. v. Fairbairn Lawson Combe Barbour, Ltd., [1942] 1 K.B. 12, 28 (C.A. 1941).

STUDY GUIDE: Here is a modern application of the principle involved in the Coronation Cases. What does Justice Traynor think are the undesirable consequences of extending too far the doctrine of frustration of purposes? Is there a reason why a landlord, rather than a tenant, should assume the risk of the tenant's purposes being substantially frustrated? How does the doctrine of mitigation of damages figure in the application of this defense?

LLOYD v. MURPHY
Supreme Court of California,
25 Cal. 2d 48, 153 P.2d 47 (1944)

TRAYNOR, J.

On August 4, 1941, plaintiffs leased to defendant for a five-year term beginning September 15, 1941, certain premises located at the corner of Almont Drive and Wilshire Boulevard in the city of Beverly Hills, Los Angeles County, "for the sole purpose of conducting thereon the business of displaying and selling new automobiles (including the servicing and repairing thereof and of selling the petroleum products of a major oil company) and for no other purpose whatsoever without the written consent of the lessor" except "to make an occasional sale of a used automobile." Defendant agreed not to sublease or assign without plaintiffs' written consent. On January 1, 1942, the federal government ordered that the sale of new automobiles be discontinued. It modified this order on January 8, 1942, to permit sales to those engaged in military activities, and on January 20, 1942, it established a system of priorities restricting sales to persons having preferential ratings of A-1-j or higher. On March 10, 1942, defendant explained the effect of these restrictions on his business to one of the plaintiffs authorized to act for the others, who orally waived the restrictions in the lease as to use and subleasing and offered to reduce the rent if defendant should be unable to operate profitably. Nevertheless defendant vacated the premises on March 15, 1942, giving oral notice of repudiation of the lease to plaintiffs, which was followed by a written notice on March 24, 1942. Plaintiffs affirmed in writing on March 26th their oral waiver and, failing to persuade defendant to perform his obligations, they rented the property to other tenants pursuant to their powers under the lease in order to mitigate damages. On May 11, 1942, plaintiffs brought this action praying for declaratory relief to determine their rights under the lease, and for judgment for unpaid rent. Following a trial on the merits, the court found that the leased premises were located on one of the main traffic arteries of Los Angeles County; that they were equipped with gasoline pumps and in general adapted for the maintenance of an automobile service station; that they contained a one-story storeroom adapted to many commercial purposes; that plaintiffs had waived the restrictions in the lease and granted defendant the right to use the premises for any legitimate purpose and to sublease to any responsible party; that defendant continues to carry on the business of selling and servicing automobiles at two other places. Defendant testified that at one of these locations he sold new automobiles exclusively and when asked if he were aware that many new automobile dealers were continuing in business replied: "Sure. It is just the location that I couldn't make a go, though, of automobiles." Although there was no finding to that effect, defendant estimated in response to inquiry by his counsel, that 90 per cent of his gross volume of business was new car sales and 10 per cent gasoline sales. The trial court held that war conditions had not terminated defendant's obligations under the lease and gave judgment for plaintiffs, declaring the lease as modified by plaintiffs' waiver to be in full force and effect, and ordered defendant to pay the unpaid rent with interest, less amounts received by plaintiffs from re-renting. Defendant brought this appeal, contending that the purpose for which the premises were leased was frustrated by the restrictions placed on the sale of new automobiles by the federal government, thereby terminating his duties under the lease.

Although commercial frustration was first recognized as an excuse for nonperformance of a contractual duty by the courts of England (Krell v. Henry, [1903] 2 K.B. 740 [C.A.]; Blakely v. Muller, 19 T.L.R. 186 [K.B.]; see McElroy and Williams, *The Coronation Cases*, 4 Mod. L. Rev. 241) its soundness has been questioned by those courts (see Maritime National Fish, Ltd. v. Ocean Trawlers, Ltd., [1935] A.C. 524, 528-29; 56 L.Q. Rev. 324, arguing that Krell v. Henry, supra, was a misapplication of Taylor v. Caldwell, 3 B. & S. 826 [1863], the leading case on impossibility as an excuse for nonperformance), and they have refused to apply the doctrine to leases on the ground that an estate is conveyed to the lessee, which carries with it all risks. . . . Many courts, therefore, in the United States have held that the tenant bears all risks as owner of the estate . . . , but the modern cases have recognized that the defense may be available in a proper case, even in a lease. As the author declares in 6 Williston, Contracts (rev. ed. 1938), §1955, pp. 5485-5487,

> The fact that [a] lease is a conveyance and not simply a continuing contract and the numerous authorities enforcing liability to pay rent in spite of destruction of leased premises, however, have made it difficult to give relief. That the tenant has been relieved, nevertheless, in several cases indicates the gravitation of the law toward a recognition of the principle that fortuitous destruction of the value of performance wholly outside the contemplation of the parties may excuse a promisor even in a lease. . . .
>
> Even more clearly with respect to leases than in regard to ordinary contracts the applicability of the doctrine of frustration depends on the total or nearly total destruction of the purpose for which, in the contemplation of both parties, the transaction was entered into.

The principles of frustration have been repeatedly applied to leases by the courts of this state . . . and the question is whether the excuse for nonperformance is applicable under the facts of the present case.

Although the doctrine of frustration is akin to the doctrine of impossibility of performance (see Civ. Code, §1511; 6 Cal. Jur. 435-450; 4 Cal. Jur. Ten-year Supp. 187-192;Taylor v. Caldwell, supra) since both have developed from the commercial necessity of excusing performance in cases of extreme hardship, frustration is not a form of impossibility even under the modern definition of that term, which includes not only cases of physical impossibility but also cases of extreme impracticability of performance. . . . Performance remains possible but the expected value of performance to the party seeking to be excused has been destroyed by a fortuitous event, which supervenes to cause an actual but not literal failure of consideration. Krell v. Henry, supra; . . . 6 Williston, op. cit. supra, §§1935, 1954, pp. 5477, 5480; Restatement, Contracts, §288.

The question in cases involving frustration is whether the equities of the case, considered in the light of sound public policy, require placing the risk of a disruption or complete destruction of the contract equilibrium on defendant or plaintiff under the circumstances of a given case (Fibrosa Spolka Akcyjina v. Fairbairn Lawson Combe Barbour, Ltd., [1942] 167 L.T.R. [H.L.] 101, 112-113; see Smith, Some Practical Aspects of the Doctrine of Impossibility, 32 Ill. L. Rev. 672, 675; Patterson, Constructive Conditions in Contracts, 42 Colum. L. Rev. 903, 949; 27 Cal. L. Rev. 461), and the answer depends on whether an unanticipated circumstance, the risk of which should not be fairly thrown on the promisor, has made performance vitally different from what was reasonably to be expected (6 Williston, op. cit. supra, §1963, p. 5511; Restatement, Contracts, §454). The purpose of a contract is to place the risks of performance upon the promisor, and the relation of the parties, terms of the contract, and circumstances surrounding its formation must be examined to determine whether it can be fairly inferred that the risk of the event that has supervened to cause the alleged frustration was not reasonably foreseeable. If it was foreseeable there should have been provision for it in the contract, and the absence of such a provision gives rise to the inference that the risk was assumed.

The doctrine of frustration has been limited to cases of extreme hardship so that businessmen, who must make their arrangements in advance, can rely with certainty on their contracts. . . . The courts have required a promisor seeking to excuse himself from performance of his obligations to prove that the risk of the frustrating event was not reasonably foreseeable and that the value of counterperformance is totally or nearly totally destroyed, for frustration is no defense if it was foreseeable or controllable by the promisor, or if counterperformance remains valuable. . . .

Thus laws or other governmental acts that make performance unprofitable or more difficult or expensive do not excuse the duty to perform a contractual obligation. . . . It is settled that if parties have contracted with reference to a state of war or have contemplated the risks arising from it, they may not invoke the doctrine of frustration to escape their obligations. . . .

At the time the lease in the present case was executed the National Defense Act, Public Act No. 671 of the 76th Congress, [54 Stats. 601] §2A [50 U.S.C.A. Appendix §1152(a)], approved June 28, 1940, authorizing the President to allocate materials and mobilize industry for national defense, had been law for more than a year. The automotive industry was in the process of conversion to supply the needs of our growing mechanized army and to meet lend-lease commitments. Iceland and Greenland had been occupied by the army. Automobile sales were soaring because the public anticipated that production would soon be restricted. These facts were commonly known and it cannot be said that the risk of war and its consequences necessitating restriction of the production and sale of automobiles was so remote a contingency that its risk could not be foreseen by defendant, an experienced automobile dealer. Indeed, the conditions prevailing at the time the lease was executed, and the absence of any provision in the lease contracting against the effect of war, gives rise to the inference that the risk was assumed. Defendant has therefore failed to prove that the possibility of war and its consequences on the production and sale of new automobiles was an unanticipated circumstance wholly outside the contemplation of the parties.

Nor has defendant sustained the burden of proving that the value of the lease has been destroyed. The sale of automobiles was not made impossible or illegal but merely restricted and if governmental regulation does not entirely prohibit the business to be carried on in the leased premises but only limits or restricts it, thereby making it less profitable and more difficult to continue, the lease is not terminated or the lessee excused from further performance. . . . Defendant may use the premises for the purpose for which they were leased. New automobiles and gasoline continue to be sold. Indeed, defendant testified that he continued to sell new automobiles exclusively at another location in the same county.

Defendant contends that the lease is restrictive and that the government orders therefore destroyed its value and frustrated its purpose. Provisions that prohibit subleasing or other uses than those specified affect the value of a lease and are to be considered in determining whether its purpose has been frustrated or its value destroyed. See Owens, The Effect of the War Upon the Rights and Liabilities of Parties to a Contract, 19 California State Bar Journal 132, 143. It must not be forgotten, however, that "The landlord has not covenanted that the tenant shall have the right to carry on the contemplated business or that the business to which the premises are by their nature or by the terms of the lease restricted shall be profitable enough to enable the tenant to pay the rent but has imposed a condition for his own benefit; and, certainly, unless and until he chooses to take advantage of it, the tenant is not deprived of the use of the premises." (6 Williston, Contracts, op. cit. supra, §1955, p. 5485; see, also, People v. Klopstock, 24 Cal. 2d 897, 901, [151 P.2d 641].) In the present lease plaintiffs reserved the rights that defendant should not use the premises for other purposes than those specified in the lease or sublease without plaintiffs' written consent. Far from preventing other uses or subleasing they waived these rights, enabling defendant to use the premises for any legitimate purpose and to sublease them to any responsible tenant. This waiver is significant in view of the location of the premises on a main traffic artery in Los Angeles County and their adaptability for many commercial purposes. The value of these rights is attested by the fact that the premises were rented soon after defendants vacated them. It is therefore clear that the governmental restrictions on the sale of new cars has not destroyed the value of the lease. Furthermore, plaintiffs offered to lower the rent if defendant should be unable to operate profitably, and their conduct was at all times fair and cooperative.

The consequences of applying the doctrine of frustration to a leasehold involving less than a total or nearly total destruction of the value of the leased premises would be undesirable. Confusion would result from different decisions purporting to define "substantial" frustration. Litigation would be encouraged by the repudiation of leases when lessees found their businesses less profitable because of regulations attendant upon a national emergency.

Many lessees have been affected in varying degrees by the widespread governmental regulations necessitated by war conditions.

The cases that defendant relies upon are consistent with the conclusion reached herein. In Industrial Development Land Co. v. Goldschmidt, supra, the lease provided that the premises should not be used other than as a saloon. When national prohibition made the sale of alcoholic beverages illegal, the court excused the tenant from further performance on the theory of illegality or impossibility by a change in domestic law. The doctrine of frustration might have been applied, since the purpose for which the property was leased was totally destroyed and there was nothing to show that the value of the lease was not thereby totally destroyed. In the present case the purpose was not destroyed but only restricted, and plaintiffs proved that the lease was valuable to defendant. In Grace v. Croninger, supra [12 Cal. App. 2d 603, 55 P.2d 941], the lease was for the purpose of conducting a "saloon and cigar store, and for no other purpose" with provision for subleasing a portion of the premises for bootblack purposes. The monthly rental was $650. It was clear that prohibition destroyed the main purpose of the lease, but since the premises could be used for bootblack and cigar store purposes, the lessee was not excused from his duty to pay the rent. In the present case new automobiles and gasoline may be sold under the lease as executed and any legitimate business may be conducted or the premises may be subleased under the lease as modified by plaintiff's waiver. Colonial Operating Corp. v. Hannon Sales & Service, Inc., 34 N.Y.S.2d 116, was reversed in 265 App. Div. 411 [39 N.Y.S.2d 217], and Signal Land Corp. v. Loecher, 35 N.Y.S.2d 25 Schantz v. American Auto Supply Co., Inc., 178 Misc. 909 [36 N.Y.S.2d 747]; and Canrock Realty Corp. v. Vim Electric Co., Inc., 37 N.Y.S.2d 139, involved government orders that totally destroyed the possibility of selling the products for which the premises were leased. No case has been cited by defendant or disclosed by research in which an appellate court has excused a lessee from performance of his duty to pay rent when the purpose of the lease has not been totally destroyed or its accomplishment rendered extremely impracticable or where it has been shown that the lease remains valuable to the lessee.

The judgment is affirmed.

RESTATEMENT (SECOND) OF CONTRACTS

§265. DISCHARGE BY SUPERVENING FRUSTRATION

Where, after a contract is made, a party's principal purpose is substantially frustrated without his fault by the occurrence of an event the nonoccurrence of which was a basic assumption on which the contract was made, his remaining duties to render performance are discharged, unless the language or the circumstances indicate the contrary.

REFERENCE: Farnsworth, §9.6
               Calamari & Perillo, §§13.16, 13.18

C. ALLOCATION OF RISK
IN LONG-TERM CONTRACTS

For a variety of reasons, contracts — even those with clauses that expressly allocate some risks — do not cover every contingency. First, it is impossible to articulate all that we tacitly assume to be true about the world. Second, the future is inherently unpredictable at times. Third, it often is not worth investing the resources needed to anticipate, specify, and negotiate about very remote contingencies. Fourth, our interests change over time. Moreover, the longer a period of time a contract is intended to cover, the more these factors lead to the potential for developments that are not or cannot be specified in advance.

For these reasons, "relational contract" theorists have stressed that, beyond a certain point, contracts governing long-term relations come to appear less like individual bargains, in which all the terms can be discerned from the intentions of the parties at the time of formation, and more like *constitutions* governing polities — requiring similar modes of ongoing interpretation. Some build upon this insight to claim that *all* or almost all contracts, to some degree, resemble long-term agreements.

The undisputed originator of relational theory is Professor Ian Macneil.[29] At the core of his sweeping, complex, and controversial theory of social exchange is a descriptive insight that has been widely accepted by contracts scholars: all contracts can be viewed on a spectrum from highly *discrete* contracts, on the one end, to highly *intertwined* contracts, on the other.[30]

Discrete contracts:

> are characterized by short duration, limited personal interactions, and precise party measurements of easily measured objects of exchange. They require a minimum of future cooperation between the parties. No sharing of benefits or burdens occurs, nor is altruism expected. The parties are bound precisely

---

29. See, e.g., Ian R. Macneil, The New Social Contract: An Inquiry into Modern Contractual Relations (1980).

30. In most of his writings, Macneil labeled the poles of this continuum, *discrete* and *relational*, but this led to what he now views as an undesirable ambiguity and confusion:

> "[R]elational" has been used to mean two different things. It is used globally to describe all relations in which exchange occurs, and since all exchange, even the most discrete, occurs in relations, all exchange is thereby "relational." But it is also used to mean the opposite of discrete, that is, exchange occurring in relatively intertwined patterns, as for example, much of the exchange in nuclear families and within corporations.
>
> Thus the spectrum of exchange relations is ambiguously described when its poles are labeled discrete and relational. This ambiguity may have some bad effects, even apart from simple confusion. It may, for example, contribute to the erroneous, but extremely common, belief that discrete transactions can and do occur free of relations. For that reason, *I propose from hereon to describe the poles of this spectrum of exchange relations as discrete at one end and intertwined at the other*. Both, of course, are always relative terms; just as seemingly discrete transactions are in fact parts of relations, and hence intertwined, so too, elements of discreteness penetrate all human relations.

Ian R. Macneil, Relational Contract Theory as Sociology: A Reply to Professors Lindenberg and de Vos, 143 J. of Institutional and Theoretical Econ. 272, 276 (1987) (emphasis added) (citations omitted).

and tightly. The parties view themselves as free of entangling strings. Everything is clearly defined and presentiated. If trouble is anticipated at all, it is anticipated only if someone or something turns out unexpectedly badly. . . .

Discreteness and presentation are themselves not the same phenomenon, in spite of their merger in discrete contracts. Discreteness is the separating of a transaction from all else between the participant at the same time and before and after. Its ideal, never achieved in life, occurs when there *is* nothing else between the parties, never has been, and never will be. Presentation, on the other hand, is the bringing of the future into the present. Underlying both is the ideal of 100 percent planning of the future.[31]

In contrast, intertwined contracts:

are of significant duration (for example, franchising). Close whole person relations form an integral aspect of the relation (employment). The object of exchange typically includes both easily measured quantities (wages) and quantities not readily measured (the projection of personality by an airline stewardess). Many individuals with individual and collective poles of interest are involved in the relation (industrial relations). Future cooperative behavior is anticipated (the players and management of the Oakland Raiders). The benefits and burdens of the relation are to be shared rather than divided and allocated (a law partnership). The bindingness of the relation is limited (again a law partnership in which in theory each member is free to quit almost at will). The entangling strings of friendship, reputation, interdependence, morality, and altruistic desires are integral parts of the relation (a theatrical agent and his clients). Trouble is expected as a matter of course (a collective bargaining agreement). Finally the participants never intend or expect to see the whole future of the relation as presentiated at any single time, but view the relation as an ongoing integration of behavior which will grow and vary with events in a largely unforeseeable future (a marriage; a family business).[32]

In sum, according to Macneil, *discreteness* refers to the idea that each transaction can be viewed as an identifiable event at a particular moment in time that is entirely separate from any other transaction; whereas, in fact, such discrete transactions are, by far, the exception to the rule. Most commercial contracts establish an ongoing relation between the parties. Most discrete transactions take place within a matrix of more complex ongoing relations. *Presentiation* refers to the idea that every future contingency can be reduced to a present expectation during a magical moment of contract conception; whereas it is the nature of the future to be uncertain and only an infinitesimal fraction of all future contingencies can either be conceived or explicitly taken into account.

While this insight is now widely accepted, contracts scholars differ over its doctrinal and normative implications.[33] Macneil divides theories of

31. Id. at 275 (citations omitted) (Macneil is quoting here from his own earlier writing).

32. Ian R. Macneil, Restatement (Second) of Contracts and Presentiation, 60 Va. L. Rev. 589, 595 (1974).

33. See, e.g., Randy E. Barnett, Conflicting Visions: A Critique of Ian Macneil's Relational Theory of Contract, 78 Va. L. Rev. 1175 (1992).

contract into three categories. *Classical* contract theories, according to Macneil, looked largely to assent at the time of formation to determine the meaning of a contract that may extend long into the future — an approach akin to the view that one's personality can largely be traced to genetic factors that are determined at the moment of conception. *Relational* contract theory, on the other hand, views a contract as existing within a complex web of relations that color and influence its meaning, both initially and especially as time goes by — a view akin to the idea that one's personality is more influenced by the social environment than by heredity. Finally, Macneil identifies *neoclassical* contract theory (as exemplified by the second Restatement), as attempting to qualify classical contract with relational considerations — for example, by taking course of dealing and performance and usage of trade into account when interpreting assent, by creating "fictions" about what parties "implicitly" understood, and by formulating defenses to contract like undue influence that permit relational considerations to limit the scope of original assent. Although Macneil views the neoclassical approach as an improvement over classical theories, ultimately, he finds it to be inadequate and unsatisfactory as compared with a fully relational approach.

As Macneil himself would admit, all this is pretty difficult to grasp upon first exposure. So why bother? And why bother in this chapter? The answer is that relational considerations are at their most compelling in highly intertwined contracts that remain in effect over a long period of time. When conflicts arise between parties to such contracts we are sometimes faced with starkly different approaches. On the one hand, we can try to "interpret" such contracts by using doctrines such as impracticability and, especially, frustration of purposes to approximate what the parties intended. Or we can view such contracts essentially the way constitutions (or marriages) are viewed: as establishing a relationship that is ongoing, the maintenance of which may require periodic *intervention* (as opposed to interpretation) by judges (or arbitrators), given changing circumstances, expectations, and interests.

These two approaches to long-term contracts are exemplified by the last two cases we shall study in this course. The first case has been hailed as reflecting a more relational spirit of contract.[34] The last case, authored by Judge Posner, takes a more traditional approach. Our concern will be to discern whether the service of relations *ends* — such as the end of preserving ongoing relations that parties find to be in their mutual advantage — requires distinctly relational *means* — such as court adjustment of terms. To preserve advantageous long-term relationships, must we depart from "classical" contract principles as qualified by the "neoclassical" interpretive techniques and defenses to contract?

STUDY GUIDE: Do you think the outcome in the next case was influenced by the fact that Essex apparently was reselling some of the aluminum? Consider how the remedial approach taken by the judge might be viewed

---

34. See Richard E. Speidel, The New Spirit of Contract, 2 J. Law & Comm. 193 (1982).

as acting to preserve an ongoing relation. Would the relation necessarily have ended had the contract term been enforced, or had the contract been rescinded? How might it have continued? (Section numbers from the Restatement (Second) used by the court are from a tentative draft. They have been replaced by the final restatement numbers in brackets.)

ALUMINUM COMPANY OF AMERICA v. ESSEX GROUP, INC.

United States District Court, Western District of Pennsylvania, 499 F. Supp. 53 (1980)

TEITELBAUM, District J.*

Plaintiff, Aluminum Company of America (ALCOA), brought the instant action against defendant, Essex Group, Inc. (Essex). . . . The first count requests the Court to reform or equitably adjust an agreement entitled the Molten Metal Agreement entered into between ALCOA and Essex. . . .

In 1966 Essex made a policy decision to expand its participation in the manufacture of aluminum wire products. Thus, beginning in the spring of 1967, ALCOA and Essex negotiated with each other for the purpose of reaching an agreement whereby ALCOA would supply Essex with its long-term needs for aluminum that Essex could use in its manufacturing operations.

By December 26, 1967 the parties had entered into what they designated as a toll conversion service contract known as the Molten Metal Agreement under which Essex would supply ALCOA with alumina which ALCOA would convert by a smelting process into molten aluminum. Under the terms of the Molten Metal Agreement, Essex delivers alumina to ALCOA which ALCOA smelts (or toll converts) into molten aluminum at its Warrick, Indiana, smelting facility. Essex then picks up the molten aluminum for further processing.

The price provisions of the contract contained an escalation formula which indicates that $.03 per pound of the original price escalates in accordance with changes in the Wholesale Price Index-Industrial Commodities (WPI) and $.03 per pound escalates in accordance with an index based on the average hourly labor rates paid to ALCOA employees at the Warrick plant. The portion of the pricing formula which is in issue in this case . . . is the production charge which is escalated by the WPI. ALCOA contends that this charge was intended by the parties to reflect actual changes in the cost of the non-labor items utilized by ALCOA in the production of aluminum from alumina at its Warrick, Indiana smelting plant. In count one of this suit ALCOA asserts that the WPI used in the Molten Metal Agreement was in fact incapable of reasonably reflecting changes in the non-labor costs at ALCOA's

---

*Hubert I. Teitelbaum (1915-1995) studied at the University of Pittsburgh (A.B., J.D.) and was admitted to the Pennsylvania bar in 1940. He worked in the Federal Bureau of Investigation (1940-1943) and was assistant U.S. Attorney (1955-1958) and U.S. Attorney (1958-1961) prior to his appointment to United States District Court for the Western District of Pennsylvania in 1971. Teitelbaum retired from the bench in 1988. — K.T.

Warrick, Indiana smelting plant and has in fact failed to so reflect such changes.

    . . . ALCOA is seeking reformation or equitable adjustment of the Molten Metal Agreement so that pursuant to count one of its complaint, the pricing formula with respect to the non-labor portion of the production charge will be changed to eliminate the WPI and substitute the actual costs incurred by ALCOA for the non-labor items used at its Warrick, Indiana smelting plant. . . .

    The Court finds, based upon consideration of all the evidence, that ALCOA is entitled to reformation of the Molten Metal Agreement. . . .

    The facts pertinent to count one are few and simple. In 1967 ALCOA and Essex entered into a written contract in which ALCOA promised to convert specified amounts of alumina supplied by Essex into aluminum for Essex. The service is to be performed at the ALCOA works at Warrick, Indiana. The contract is to run until the end of 1983. Essex has the option to extend it until the end of 1988. The price for each pound of aluminum converted is calculated by a complex formula which includes three variable components based on specific indices. The initial contract price was set at fifteen cents per pound, computed as follows:

A.	Demand Charge	$0.05/lb.
B.	Production Charge	
	(i) Fixed component	.04/lb.
	(ii) Non-labor production	.03/lb.
	(iii) Labor production cost component	.03/lb.
Total initial charge		$0.15/lb.

The demand charge is to vary from its initial base in direct proportion to periodic changes in the Engineering News Record Construction Cost-20 Cities Average Index published in the Engineering News Record. The Non-labor Production Cost Component is to vary from its initial base in direct proportion to periodic changes in the Wholesale Price Index-Industrial Commodities (WPI-IC) published by the Bureau of Labor Statistics of the United States Department of Labor. The Labor Production Cost Component is to vary from its initial base in direct proportion to periodic changes in ALCOA's average hourly labor cost at the Warrick, Indiana works. The adjusted price is subject to an over-all "cap" price of 65 percent of the price of a specified type of aluminum sold on specified terms, as published in a trade journal, American Metal Market.

    The indexing system was evolved by ALCOA with the aid of the eminent economist Alan Greenspan. ALCOA examined the non-labor production cost component to assure that the WPI-IC had not tended to deviate markedly from their non-labor cost experience in the years before the contract was executed. Essex agreed to the contract including the index provisions after an examination of the past record of the indices revealed an acceptable pattern of stability.

    ALCOA sought, by the indexed price agreement, to achieve a stable net income of about 4¢ per pound of aluminum converted. This net income represented ALCOA's return (i) on its substantial capital investment devoted to the performance of the contracted services, (ii) on its management, and (iii) on the risks of short-falls or losses it undertook over an extended period. The fact that the non-labor production cost component of ALCOA's costs was priced according to a surrogate, objective index opened the door to a foreseeable fluctuation of ALCOA's return due to deviations between ALCOA's costs and the performance of the WPI-IC. The range of foreseeable deviation was roughly three cents per pound. That is to say that in some years ALCOA's return might foreseeably (and did, in fact) rise to seven cents per pound, while in other years it might foreseeably (and did, in fact) fall to about one cent per pound. . . .

Essex sought to assure itself of a long term supply of aluminum at a favorable price. Essex intended to and did manufacture a new line of aluminum wire products. The long term supply of aluminum was important to assure Essex of the steady use of its expensive machinery. A steady production stream was vital to preserve the market position it sought to establish. The favorable price was important to allow Essex to compete with firms like ALCOA which produced the aluminum and manufactured aluminum wire products in an efficient, integrated operation.

In the early years of the contract, the price formula yielded prices related, within the foreseeable range of deviation, to ALCOA's cost figures. Beginning in 1973, OPEC actions to increase oil prices and unanticipated pollution control costs greatly increased ALCOA's electricity costs. Electric power is the principal non-labor cost factor in aluminum conversion, and the electric power rates rose much more rapidly than did the WPI-IC. As a result, ALCOA's production costs rose greatly and unforeseeably beyond the indexed increase in the contract price. . . .

During the most recent years, the market price of aluminum has increased even faster than the production costs. At the trial ALCOA introduced the deposition of Mr. Wilfred Jones, an Essex employee whose duties included the sale of surplus metal. Mr. Jones stated that Essex had resold some millions of pounds of aluminum which ALCOA had refined. The cost of the aluminum to Essex (including the purchase price of the alumina and its transportation) was 36.35 cents per pound around June of 1979. Mr. Jones further stated that the resale price in June 1979 at one cent per pound under the market, was 73.313 cents per pound, yielding Essex a gross profit of 37.043 cents per pound. This margin of profit shows the tremendous advantage Essex enjoys under the contract as it is written and as both parties have performed it. A significant fraction of Essex's advantage is directly attributable to the corresponding out of pocket losses ALCOA suffers. ALCOA has sufficiently shown that without judicial relief or economic changes which are not presently foreseeable, it stands to lose in excess of $75,000,000 out of pocket, during the remaining term of the contract. . . .

ALCOA argues that it is entitled to relief on the grounds of impracticability and frustration of purpose. The Court agrees. . . .

The focus of the doctrines of impracticability and of frustration is distinctly on hardship. Section [261] declares a party is discharged from performing a contract where a supervening event renders his performance impracticable. Comment d discusses the meaning of "impracticability." The comment states the word is taken from Uniform Commercial Code

§2-615(a). It declares that the word denotes an impediment to performance lying between "impossibility" and "impracticality."

> Performance may be impracticable because *extreme and unreasonable difficulty, expense, injury, or loss to one of the parties will be involved.* . . .

A mere change in the degree of difficulty or expense due to such causes as increased wages, prices of raw materials, or costs of construction, unless well beyond the normal range, does not amount to impracticability since it is this sort of risk that a fixed-price contract is intended to cover. . . .

. . . This strict standard of severe disappointment is clearly met in the present case. ALCOA has sufficiently proved that it will lose well over $60 million dollars out of pocket over the life of the contract due to the extreme deviation of the WPI-IC from ALCOA's actual costs. . . .

. . . Essex argues that the causes of ALCOA's losses are due to market price increases to which the doctrine of impracticability does not apply. . . . The official comment to §2-615 lends strength to Essex's claim.

> 1. This section excuses a seller from timely delivery of goods contracted for, where his performance has become commercially impracticable because of unforeseen supervening circumstances not within the contemplation of the parties at the time of contracting.

However,

> 4. Increased cost alone does not excuse performance unless the rise in cost is due to some unforeseen contingency which alters the essential nature of the performance. Neither is a rise or a collapse in the market in itself a justification, for that is exactly the type of business risk which business contracts made at fixed prices are intended to cover. But a severe shortage of raw materials or of supplies due to a contingency such as war, embargo, local crop failure, unforeseen shutdown of major sources of supply or the like, which either causes a marked increase in cost or altogether prevents the seller from securing supplies necessary to his performance is within the contemplation of this section.

Several of the cases cited by Essex rely on comment 4 in denying claims for relief. Transatlantic Financing Corp. v. United States, 363 F.2d 312 (D.C. Cir. 1966); . . . Eastern Air Lines, Inc. v. Gulf Oil Corp., 415 F. Supp. 429 (S.D. Fla. 1975). . . . Each is distinguishable from the present case in the absolute extent of the loss and in the proportion of loss involved. . . .

Transatlantic Financing Corp. v. United States, supra, was one of the "Suez" cases. The carrier had contracted to transport a cargo from the United States to Iran for a specified price. The contract did not specify the route, but both parties knew the most direct route was by way of Suez. When the Canal was closed the carrier had to divert its ships around Cape Horn, adding three thousand miles to the expected ten thousand mile voyage, and adding an expense of about $44,000 to the contract price of about $306,000. Judge J. Skelly Wright, for a unanimous panel, found that "circumstances surrounding the contract indicate that the risk of the Canal's closure may be deemed to have been allocated to Transatlantic." But he found this conclusion doubtful enough to cause him to reject a direct application of the risk allocation rule. He went on:

> The surrounding circumstances do indicate, however, a willingness by Transatlantic to assume abnormal risks, and this fact should legitimately cause us to judge the impracticability of performance by an alternate route in stricter terms than we would were the contingency unforeseen.

Id. at 318-19. Judge Wright then held . . . that there must be more than a twelve percent cost increase to constitute impracticability.

Here ALCOA's loss is more than a thousand times greater than the carrier's loss. And the circumstances surrounding the contract show a deliberate avoidance of abnormal risks. . . .

Eastern Air Lines Inc. v. Gulf Oil Corp., supra, follows the pattern of these cases except in one detail. Gulf had contracted to furnish jet fuel to Eastern in designated cities from June 1972 until January 31, 1977. The price was tied to a specific trade journal report of posted prices for a specified type of domestic oil. During the contract the price of imported oil soared. Domestic oil was subjected to a complex and shifting body of regulations including a "two-tier" price control scheme regulating the price of "old oil" but not the price of "new oil." The specified trade journal reacted to the new system by publishing prices only for the regulated "old oil." Gulf sought to escape the burden of its contract and Eastern sued to compel Gulf to perform it.

The court required Gulf to perform the contract. It found that Gulf had failed to prove its defense. The "cost" figures in evidence included built in intra-company profits such that the court could not "determine how much it costs Gulf to produce a gallon of jet fuel for sale to Eastern, whether Gulf loses money or makes a profit on its sale of jet fuel to Eastern, either now or at the inception of the contract, or at any time in between." Id. at 440. Thus Gulf failed to prove it had suffered losses on the contract.

In the course of the decision the court declared that relief was available under §2-615 for an *unforeseeable* failure of a pre-supposed condition. It inferred this requirement from Comment 8 to §2-615[35] and from the Suez cases. If it were generally adopted, this requirement would reduce the occasions for excusing performance under §2-615. Judge Wright rejected such a requirement in *Transatlantic Financing*, declaring:

> Foreseeability or even recognition of a risk does not necessarily prove its allocation. . . . Parties to a contract are not always able to provide for all the possibilities of which they are aware, sometimes because they cannot agree, often simply because they are too busy. Moreover, that some abnormal risk was contemplated is probative but does not necessarily establish an allocation of the risk of the contingency which actually occurs. 363 F.2d at 318.

---

35. 8. The provisions of this section are made subject to assumption of greater liability by agreement and such agreement is to be found not only in the expressed terms of the contract but in the circumstances surrounding the contracting, in trade usage and the like. Thus the exemptions of this section do not apply when the contingency in question is sufficiently foreshadowed at the time of contracting to be included among the business risks which are fairly to be regarded as part of the dickered terms, either consciously or as a matter of reasonable, commercial interpretation from the circumstances. . . .

The question is important in the developing doctrine of impracticability. The Indiana cases are silent on it. The Court believes that Indiana courts would find Judge Wright's approach is more in keeping with the spirit and purpose of the Uniform Commercial Code than is the strict approach of Judge King in *Eastern Air Lines.* The Code, embodied in Title 26, Burns Ind. Stat. Ann. (1974) seeks to accommodate the law to sound commercial sense and practice. Courts must decide the point at which the community's interest in predictable contract enforcement shall yield to the fact that enforcement of a particular contract would be commercially senseless and unjust. The spirit of the Code is that such decisions cannot justly derive from legal abstractions. They must derive from courts sensitive to the mores, practices and habits of thought in the respectable commercial world. . . .

The Court holds that ALCOA is entitled to relief under the doctrine of impracticability. The cases Essex relies on and the other cases discovered by the Court are all distinguishable with respect to the gravity of harm which the aggrieved contracting party was liable to suffer. Except for *Transatlantic Financing*, they are also distinguishable with respect to the question of allocation of the risk, inferred from the circumstances known to the parties at the time of the contract and from the contract terms. . . .

This leaves the question of framing a remedy for ALCOA. Essex argues that reformation is not available. It cites many Indiana cases declaring that reformation is only available to correct writings which, through mistake, do not reflect the agreement of the parties. The declarations to that effect are clear. . . .

But the point is immaterial here. This case does not fall within reformation as a traditional head of equity jurisprudence. It does fall within the more general rules of equitable restitution. Courts have traditionally applied three remedial rules in cases of mistake, frustration and impracticability. In some cases courts declare that no contract ever arose because there was no true agreement between the parties, Raffles v. Wichelhaus . . . or because the parties were ignorant of existing facts which frustrated the purpose of one party or made performance impracticable. Restatement 2d of Contracts [§266]. In some other cases the courts hold that a contract is voidable on one of the three theories. In these cases the customary remedy is rescission. In both classes of cases where one or both parties have performed under the supposed contract, the courts award appropriate restitution in the light of the benefits the parties have conferred on each other. The aim is to prevent unjust enrichment. The courts in such cases often call this remedy "reformation" in the loose sense of "modification." See III Palmer, Law of Restitution §13.9 (1978). . . .

The same ends can be achieved under a long term executory contract by a similar remedy. To decree rescission in this case would be to grant ALCOA a windfall gain in the current aluminum market. It would at the same time deprive Essex of the assured long term aluminum supply which it obtained under the contract and of the gains it legitimately may enforce within the scope of the risk ALCOA bears under the contract. A remedy which merely shifts the windfall gains and losses is neither required nor permitted by Indiana law.

To frame an equitable remedy where frustration, impracticability or mistake prevent strict enforcement of a long term executory contract requires a careful examination of the circumstances of the contract, the purposes of the parties, and the circumstances which upset the contract. For some long term executory contracts rescission with or without restitution will be the only sensible remedy. Where developments make performance of the contract economically senseless or purposeless, to modify the contract and to enforce it as modified would be highly inappropriate. But in cases like the present one modification and enforcement may be the only proper remedy.[36] See Parev Products Co. v. I. Rokeach and Sons, Inc., 124 F.2d 147 (2d Cir. 1941). In this case Essex sought an assured long term supply of aluminum at a price which would let it earn a profit on its finished products. ALCOA, facing ordinary market risks in 1967, sought a long term, limited risk use for its Warrick Works. A remedy modifying the price term of the contract in light of the circumstances which upset the price formula will better preserve the purposes and expectations of the parties than any other remedy. Such a remedy is essential to avoid injustice in this case.

During the trial the parties agreed that a modification of the price term to require Essex to pay ALCOA the ceiling price specified in the contract would be an appropriate remedy if the Court held for ALCOA. The Court understands from the parties that ALCOA will continue to suffer a substantial but smaller out of pocket loss at this price level. But ALCOA has not argued that the ceiling price term is subject to the same basic assumptions about risk limitation as is the indexed price term. Accordingly the Court adopts the ceiling price term as part of the remedy it grants to ALCOA.

The Court must recognize, though, that before the contract expires economic changes may make this remedy excessively favorable to ALCOA. To deal with that possibility, the Court must frame a remedy which is suitable to the expectations and to the original agreement of the parties. A price fixed at the contract ceiling could redound to ALCOA's great profit and to Essex's great loss in changed circumstances. Therefore the Court adopts the following remedial scheme. For the duration of the contract the price for each pound of aluminum converted by ALCOA shall be the lesser of the current Price A or Price B indicated below.

Price A shall be the contract ceiling price computed periodically as specified in the contract.

Price B shall be the greater of the current Price B1 or Price B2. *Price B1* shall be the price specified in the contract, computed according to the terms of the contract. *Price B2* shall be that price which yields ALCOA a profit of one cent per pound of aluminum converted. This will generally yield Essex the benefit of its favorable bargain, and it will reduce ALCOA's disappointment to the limit of risk the parties expected in making the contract. The profit shall be computed using the same accounting methods used for the production of plaintiff's exhibit 431. The profit and the resulting price shall be computed once each calendar quarter, as soon after the close of the quarter as the necessary information may be assembled. When Price B2 applies, ALCOA shall bill Essex periodically, as specified in the contract at the price specified at the last quarterly price computation. Essex shall pay

---

36. The remedial provisions of the new Restatement agree. [§172(2)] declares that a court may frame a remedy by supplying a term which is reasonable in the circumstances to avoid injustice. The same provision appears in [§158(2)].

those bills according to the payment terms previously observed by the parties. When the next quarterly price computation is completed, that price shall be applied retroactively to the aluminum converted during the previous quarter. ALCOA shall refund any surplus payment by Essex upon the computation of the price or shall bill Essex for any additional money due.

ALCOA shall keep detailed records of the pertinent costs, indices and computations used to calculate Prices A, B1 and B2 and shall preserve them for two years beyond the termination of the contract. ALCOA shall send Essex, in the manner and at the times specified in the contract, the price information called for in the contract, as well as a quarterly statement of Price B2 whether or not that price then applies. The statement of Price B2 need not specify the elements from which it was calculated. . . .

CONCLUSION

This case is novel. The sums of money involved are huge. The Court has been considerably aided by the thorough and commendable work of all of the counsel who have participated in the case. There remains a need for a few concluding remarks concerning the theory of Count One of this case and its limitations.

One of the principal themes in the development of commercial contract doctrines since the 1920's has been the need for a body of law compatible with responsible commercial practices and understandings. The old spirit of the law manifest in Paradine v. Jane . . . is gone. The new spirit of commercial law in Indiana and elsewhere appears in the Uniform Commercial Code, in new developments of implied covenants, and in the new Restatement.

At stake in this suit is the future of a commercially important device — the long term contract. Such contracts are common in many fields of commerce. Mineral leases, building and ground leases, and long term coal sales agreements are just three examples of such contracts. If the law refused an appropriate remedy when a prudently drafted long term contract goes badly awry, the risks attending such contracts would increase. Prudent business people would avoid using this sensible business tool. Or they would needlessly suffer the delay and expense of ever more detailed and sophisticated drafting in an attempt to approximate by agreement what the law could readily furnish by general rule.

Another aspect of the new spirit of commercial law is important in this case. Much of the story of modern business law and of modern management concerns deals with the problem of risk limitation. The development of the concept of limited liability in the modern corporation illustrates this development. So do the proliferation of insurance, the development of no-fault auto insurance, and the recurring analysis of a party's capacity to anticipate losses and spread them or insure against them. *Force majeure* clauses, price indexing agreements and "double net" leases all aim to clarify and to limit the risk of long term contracts. Responsible business managers are attentive to risk control.

Corporate managers are fiduciaries. Law, founded on good sense, requires them to act with care in the management of businesses owned by other people. Attention to risk limitation is essential to the fiduciary duty of corporate managers. Courts must consider the fiduciary duty of management and the established practice of risk limitation in interpreting contracts and in the application of contract doctrines such as mistake, frustration and impracticability. Corporate managers should not gamble with corporate funds. Generally they do not. Courts should not presume that they do, nor should they frame rules founded on such a presumption. Instead, courts should be alert to indications that the parties to a commercial contract sought to limit their risks, and should interpret the contracts and frame remedies to protect that purpose. . . .

This attitude toward contract law and toward the work of the courts will disturb some people even at this late date. It strains against half-remembered truths and remembered half-truths from the venerated first year course in Contract Law. The core of the trouble lies in the hoary maxim that the courts will not make a contract for the parties. The maxim requires three replies. First, courts today can indeed make contracts for the parties. Given certain minimal indicators of an intent to contract, the courts are today directed to impose on the parties the necessary specific provisions to complete the process. See U.C.C. §§2-204, 2-207, 2-208; U.L.T.A. §§2-201-2-204. Second, a distinction has long been noted between judicial imposition of initial terms and judicial interpretations and implications of terms to resolve disputes concerning contracts the parties have made for themselves. The maxim bears less weight when it is applied to dispute resolution than it does when it is applied to questions of contract formation. This case is plainly one of dispute resolution. Third, the maxim rests on two sensible notions: (1) Liability under the law of contract rests on assent, not imposition. (2) Judges are seldom able business men; they seldom have the information, ability, or time to do a good job of contracting for the parties. Neither of these notions applies here. The parties have made their own contract. The Court's role here is limited to framing a remedy for a problem they did not foresee and provide for. And while the Court willingly concedes that the managements of ALCOA and Essex are better able to conduct their business than is the Court, in this dispute the Court has information from hindsight far superior to that which the parties had when they made their contract. The parties may both be better served by an informed judicial decision based on the known circumstances than by a decision wrenched from words of the contract which were not chosen with a prevision of today's circumstances. The Court gladly concedes that the parties might today evolve a better working arrangement by negotiation than the Court can impose. But they have not done so, and a rule that the Court may not act would have the perverse effect of discouraging the parties from resolving this dispute or future disputes on their own. Only a rule which permits judicial action of the kind the Court has taken in this case will provide a desirable practical incentive for businessmen to negotiate their own resolution to problems which arise in the life of long term contracts.[37] . . .

---

37. The Court is aware of the practical incentive to negotiation which lies in the delay, expense and uncertainty of litigation. This case shows that at times these burdens are insufficient to prompt settlements.

Procedural Background: The Aftermath
of the ALCOA Decision

Judge Teitelbaum's reformation of the contract was never put into effect.

> The parties settled the case after oral argument to the United States Court of Appeals for the Third Circuit. Judge Arlen M. Adams, a member of the Third Circuit Court of Appeals, requested the parties to attend a conciliation session between the time briefs were filed and oral argument was scheduled, a relatively unusual procedure.
>
> Following oral argument ALCOA indicated an interest in settling the case. The parties conferred at length, with ALCOA giving ground in its demands. It appears that the case was settled on the basis that the original contract would continue in effect until December 31, 1981; that during the balance of the original time of the contract, ALCOA would sell at a more favorable price; and that ALCOA would extend the time of the contract for a period of five years on a favorable price basis, albeit not as favorable as during the contract period.[38]

Professor John Wladis reports that, as a result of this settlement, the trial court decision lacks precedential value, based on a conversation he had with

> Professor Fairfax Leary, Jr., who had spoken with judges of the United States Court of Appeals for the Third Circuit. The Alcoa opinion was characterized as having the precedential value of a law review article. The procedural developments in the case after the District Court opinion were as follows: The case was appealed to the United States Court of Appeals for the Third Circuit. Before the appeal was decided, the parties reached settlement. Joint Motion Requesting Voluntary Dismissal of appeal at 2-3, Aluminum Co. of Am. v. Essex Group, Inc., No. 80-1604 (3d Cir. Feb. 5, 1981). They made a joint court's judgment, and remand of the case with directions to dismiss. Id. at 3-4. The Third Circuit granted this relief. By order dated March 4, 1981, District Court Judge Teitelbaum dismissed the action.[39]

REFERENCE: Farnsworth, §9.2

STUDY GUIDE: The doctrines of impracticability and frustration can be viewed as implicit default rules, both of which require a finding that the nonperforming party did not assume the risk of an unforeseen change in circumstances. Most long-term contracts contain what are commonly called force majeure *or* act of god *clauses that explicitly allocate some of the risks of unforeseen events. The next case concerns, in part, the interpretation of such a clause. How would you explain the difference between Judge Posner's approach to long-term contracts and that of Judge*

---

38. Stewart Macauley, John Kidwell, William Whitford, & Marc Galanter, Contracts: Law in Action 1180 (1995).

39. John D. Wladis, Impracticability as Risk Allocation: The Effect of Changed Circumstances upon Contract Obligations for the Sale of Goods, 22 Ga. L. Rev. 503, 586 n.333 (1988).

Teitelbaum in ALCOA? *Which approach is really more* relational? *Which approach represents the best way for courts to deal with changed circumstances in long-term contracts? Which approach best approximates the tacit assumptions of the parties?*

NORTHERN INDIANA PUBLIC SERVICE CO.
v. CARBON COUNTY COAL CO.
United States Court of Appeals, Seventh Circuit,
799 F.2d 265 (1986)

POSNER, Circuit Judge.

These appeals bring before us various facets of a dispute between Northern Indiana Public Service Company (NIPSCO), an electric utility in Indiana, and Carbon County Coal Company, a partnership that until recently owned and operated a coal mine in Wyoming. In 1978 NIPSCO and Carbon County signed a contract whereby Carbon County agreed to sell and NIPSCO to buy approximately 1.5 million tons of coal every year for 20 years, at a price of $24 a ton subject to various provisions for escalation which by 1985 had driven the price up to $44 a ton.

NIPSCO's rates are regulated by the Indiana Public Service Commission. In 1983 NIPSCO requested permission to raise its rates to reflect increased fuel charges. Some customers of NIPSCO opposed the increase on the ground that NIPSCO could reduce its overall costs by buying more electrical power from neighboring utilities for resale to its customers and producing less of its own power. Although the Commission granted the requested increase, it directed NIPSCO, in orders issued in December 1983 and February 1984 (the "economy purchase orders"), to make a good faith effort to find, and wherever possible buy from, utilities that would sell electricity to it at prices lower than its costs of internal generation. The Commission added ominously that "the adverse effects of entering into long-term coal supply contracts which do not allow for renegotiation and are not requirement contracts, is a burden which must rest squarely on the shoulders of NIPSCO management." Actually the contract with Carbon County did provide for renegotiation of the contract price — but one-way renegotiation in favor of Carbon County; the price fixed in the contract (as adjusted from time to time in accordance with the escalator provisions) was a floor. And the contract was indeed not a requirements contract: it specified the exact amount of coal that NIPSCO must take over the 20 years during which the contract was to remain in effect. NIPSCO was eager to have an assured supply of low-sulphur coal and was therefore willing to guarantee both price and quantity.

Unfortunately for NIPSCO, as things turned out it was indeed able to buy electricity at prices below the costs of generating electricity from coal bought under the contract with Carbon County; and because of the "economy purchase orders," of which it had not sought judicial review, NIPSCO could not expect to be allowed by the Public Service Commission to recover in its electrical rates the costs of buying coal from Carbon County. NIPSCO therefore decided to stop accepting coal deliveries from Carbon

County, at least for the time being; and on April 24, 1985, it brought this diversity suit against Carbon County in a federal district court in Indiana, seeking a declaration that it was excused from its obligations under the contract either permanently or at least until the economy purchase orders ceased preventing it from passing on the costs of the contract to its rate-payers. In support of this position it argued that . . . NIPSCO's performance was excused or suspended — either under the contract's *force majeure* clause or under the doctrines of frustration or impossibility — by reason of the economy purchase orders.

On May 17, 1985, Carbon County counterclaimed for breach of con-tract and moved for a preliminary injunction requiring NIPSCO to continue taking delivery under the contract. On June 19, 1985, the district judge granted the preliminary injunction, from which NIPSCO has appealed. Also on June 19, rejecting NIPSCO's argument that it needed more time for pretrial discovery and other trial preparations, the judge scheduled the trial to begin on August 26, 1985. Trial did begin then, lasted for six weeks, and resulted in a jury verdict for Carbon County of $181 million. The judge entered judgment in accordance with the verdict, rejecting Carbon County's argument that in lieu of damages it should get an order of specific performance requiring NIPSCO to comply with the contract. Upon entering the final judgment the district judge dissolved the preliminary injunction, and shortly afterward the mine — whose only customer was NIPSCO — shut down. NIPSCO has appealed from the damage judgment, and Carbon County from the denial of specific performance. . . .

. . . The contract permits NIPSCO to stop taking delivery of coal "for any cause beyond [its] reasonable control . . . including but not limited to . . . orders or acts of civil . . . authority . . . which wholly or partly pre-vent . . . the utilizing . . . of the coal." This is what is known as a *force majeure* clause. . . . NIPSCO argues that the Indiana Public Service Commis-sion's "economy purchase orders" prevented it, in whole or part, from using the coal that it had agreed to buy, and it complains that the district judge instructed the jury incorrectly on the meaning and application of the clause. The complaint about the instructions is immaterial. The judge should not have put the issue of *force majeure* to the jury. It is evident that the clause was not triggered by the orders.

All that those orders do is tell NIPSCO it will not be allowed to pass on fuel costs to its ratepayers in the form of higher rates if it can buy electricity cheaper than it can generate electricity internally using Carbon County's coal. Such an order does not "prevent," whether wholly or in part, NIPSCO from using the coal; it just prevents NIPSCO from shifting the burden of its improvidence or bad luck in having incorrectly forecasted its fuel needs to the backs of the hapless ratepayers. The purpose of public utility regulation is to provide a substitute for competition in markets (such as the market for electricity) that are naturally monopolistic. Suppose the market for electric-ity were fully competitive, and unregulated. Then if NIPSCO signed a long-term fixed-price fixed-quantity contract to buy coal, and during the life of the contract competing electrical companies were able to produce and sell electricity at prices below the cost to NIPSCO of producing electricity from that coal, NIPSCO would have to swallow the excess cost of the coal. It could not raise its electricity prices in order to pass on the excess cost to its consumers, because if it did they would buy electricity at lower prices from NIPSCO's competitors. By signing the kind of contract it did, NIPSCO gambled that fuel costs would rise rather than fall over the life of the contract; for if they rose, the contract price would give it an advantage over its (hypothetical) competitors who would have to buy fuel at the current market price. If such a gamble fails, the result is not *force majeure*.

This is all the clearer when we consider that the contract price was actually fixed just on the downside; it put a floor under the price NIPSCO had to pay, but the escalator provisions allowed the actual contract prices to rise above the floor, and they did. This underscores the gamble NIPSCO took in signing the contract. It committed itself to paying a price at or above a fixed minimum and to taking a fixed quantity at that price. It was willing to make this commitment to secure an assured supply of low sulphur coal, but the risk it took was that the market price of coal or substitute fuels would fall. A *force majeure* clause is not intended to buffer a party against the normal risks of a contract. The normal risk of a fixed-price contract is that the market price will change. If it rises, the buyer gains at the expense of the seller (except insofar as escalator provisions give the seller some protection); if it falls, as here, the seller gains at the expense of the buyer. The whole purpose of a fixed-price contract is to allocate risk in this way. A *force majeure* clause interpreted to excuse the buyer from the consequences of the risk he expressly assumed would nullify a central term of the contract.

The Indiana Public Service Commission is a surrogate for the forces of competition, and the economy fuel orders are a device for simulating the effects in a competitive market of a drop in input prices. The orders say to NIPSCO, in effect: "With fuel costs dropping, and thus reducing the costs of electricity to utilities not burdened by long-term fixed-price contracts, you had better substitute those utilities' electricity for your own when their prices are lower than your cost of internal generation. In a freely competitive market consumers would make that substitution; if you do not do so, don't expect to be allowed to pass on your inflated fuel costs to those consumers." Admittedly the comparison between competition and regulation is not exact. In an unregulated market, if fuel costs skyrocketed NIPSCO would have a capital gain from its contract (assuming the escalator provisions did not operate to raise the contract price by the full amount of the increase in fuel costs, a matter that would depend on the cause of the increase). This is because its competitors, facing higher fuel costs, would try to raise their prices for electricity, thus enabling NIPSCO to raise its price, or expand its output, or both, and thereby increase its profits. The chance of this "windfall" gain offsets, on an ex ante (before the fact) basis, the chance of a windfall loss if fuel costs drop, though NIPSCO it appears was seeking a secure source of low-sulphur coal rather than a chance for windfall gains. If as is likely the Public Service Commission would require NIPSCO to pass on any capital gain from an advantageous contract to the ratepayers (which is another reason for thinking NIPSCO wasn't after windfall gains — it would not, in all likelihood, have been allowed to keep them), then it ought to allow NIPSCO to pass on to them some of the capital loss from a disadvantageous contract — provided that the contract, when made, was prudent. Maybe it was not; maybe the risk that NIPSCO took was excessive. But all this was a matter between NIPSCO and the Public Service Commission, and NIPSCO did not seek judicial review of the economy purchase orders.

If the Commission had ordered NIPSCO to close a plant because of a safety or pollution hazard, we would have a true case of *force majeure*. As a regulated firm NIPSCO is subject to more extensive controls than unregulated firms and it therefore wanted and got a broadly worded *force majeure* clause that would protect it fully (hence the reference to partial effects) against government actions that impeded its using the coal. But as the only thing the Commission did was prevent NIPSCO from using its monopoly position to make consumers bear the risk that NIPSCO assumed when it signed a long-term fixed-price fuel contract, NIPSCO cannot complain of *force majeure*; the risk that has come to pass was one that NIPSCO voluntarily assumed when it signed the contract.

. . . The district judge refused to submit NIPSCO's defenses of impracticability and frustration to the jury, ruling that Indiana law does not allow a buyer to claim impracticability and does not recognize the defense of frustration. Some background (on which see Farnsworth, Contracts §§9.5-9.7 (1982)) may help make these rulings intelligible. In the early common law a contractual undertaking unconditional in terms was not excused merely because something had happened (such as an invasion, the passage of a law, or a natural disaster) that prevented the undertaking. See Paradine v. Jane, Aleyn 26, 82 Eng. Rep. 897 (K.B. 1647). Excuses had to be written into the contract; this is the origin of *force majeure* clauses. Later it came to be recognized that negotiating parties cannot anticipate all the contingencies that may arise in the performance of the contract; a legitimate judicial function in contract cases is to interpolate terms to govern remote contingencies — terms the parties would have agreed on explicitly if they had had the time and foresight to make advance provision for every possible contingency in performance. Later still, it was recognized that physical impossibility was irrelevant, or at least inconclusive; a promisor might want his promise to be unconditional, not because he thought he had superhuman powers but because he could insure against the risk of nonperformance better than the promisee, or obtain a substitute performance more easily than the promisee. . . . Thus the proper question in an "impossibility" case is not whether the promisor could not have performed his undertaking but whether his nonperformance should be excused because the parties, if they had thought about the matter, would have wanted to assign the risk of the contingency that made performance impossible or uneconomical to the promisor or to the promisee; if to the latter, the promisor is excused.

Section 2-615 of the Uniform Commercial Code takes this approach. It provides that "delay in delivery . . . by a seller . . . is not a breach of his duty under a contract for sale if performance as agreed has been made impracticable by the occurrence of a contingency the non-occurrence of which was a basic assumption on which the contract was made. . . ." Performance on schedule need not be impossible, only infeasible — provided that the event which made it infeasible was not a risk that the promisor had assumed. Notice, however, that the only type of promisor referred to is a seller; there is no suggestion that a buyer's performance might be excused by reason of impracticability. The reason is largely semantic. Ordinarily all the buyer has to do in order to perform his side of the bargain is pay, and while one can think of all sorts of reasons why, when the time came to pay, the buyer might not have the money, rarely would the seller have intended to assume the risk that the buyer might, whether through improvidence or bad luck, be unable to pay for the seller's goods or services. To deal with the rare case where the buyer or (more broadly) the paying party might have a good excuse based on some unforeseen change in circumstances, a new rubric was thought necessary, different from "impossibility" (the common law term) or "impracticability" (the Code term, picked up in Restatement (Second) of Contracts §261 (1979)), and it received the name "frustration." Rarely is it impracticable or impossible for the payor to pay; but if something has happened to make the performance for which he would be paying worthless to him, an excuse for not paying, analogous to impracticability or impossibility, may be proper. See Restatement, supra, §265, comment a.

The leading case on frustration remains Krell v. Henry, [1903] 2 K.B. 740 (C.A.). Krell rented Henry a suite of rooms for watching the coronation of Edward VII, but Edward came down with appendicitis and the coronation had to be postponed. Henry refused to pay the balance of the rent and the court held that he was excused from doing so because his purpose in renting had been frustrated by the postponement, a contingency outside the knowledge, or power to influence, of either party. The question was, to which party did the contract (implicitly) allocate the risk? Surely Henry had not intended to insure Krell against the possibility of the coronation's being postponed, since Krell could always relet the room, at the premium rental, for the coronation's new date. So Henry was excused.

NIPSCO is the buyer in the present case, and its defense is more properly frustration than impracticability; but the judge held that frustration is not a contract defense under the law of Indiana. . . . At all events, the facts of the present case do not bring it within the scope of the frustration doctrine, so we need not decide whether the Indiana Supreme Court would embrace the doctrine in a suitable case.

For the same reason we need not decide whether a *force majeure* clause should be deemed a relinquishment of a party's right to argue impracticability or frustration, on the theory that such a clause represents the integrated expression of the parties' desires with respect to excuses based on supervening events; or whether such a clause either in general or as specifically worded in this case covers any different ground from these defenses; or whether a buyer can urge impracticability under §2-615 of the Uniform Commercial Code, which applies to this suit. Regarding the last of these questions, although the text says "seller," Official Comment 9 to the section says that in some circumstances "the reason of the present section may well apply and entitle the buyer to the exemption," and many courts have done just that. . . . The rub is that Indiana has not adopted the "Official Comments" to the U.C.C. It has its own official comments, and they seem critical of Official Comment 9: "Comment 9 discusses 'exemption' for the buyer, but the text of the section is applicable only to sellers." Burns Ind. Stat. Ann. §26-1-2-615, Ind. Comment. It may be, therefore, that buyers cannot use §2-615 in Indiana. But it is not clear that this has substantive significance. Section 1-103 of the Uniform Commercial Code authorizes the courts to apply common law doctrines to the extent consistent with the

Code — this is the basis on which NIPSCO is able to plead frustration as an alternative defense to §2-615; and the essential elements of frustration and of impracticability are the same. With §2-615 compare Restatement, supra, §§261 (impossibility/impracticability) and 265 (frustration); and see id., §265, comment a. NIPSCO gains nothing by pleading §2-615 of the Uniform Commercial Code as well as common law frustration, and thus loses nothing by a ruling that buyers in Indiana cannot use §2-615.

Whether or not Indiana recognizes the doctrine of frustration, and whether or not a buyer can ever assert the defense of impracticability under §2-615 of the Uniform Commercial Code, these doctrines, so closely related to each other and to *force majeure* as well, . . . cannot help NIPSCO. All are doctrines for shifting risk to the party better able to bear it, either because he is in a better position to prevent the risk from materializing or because he can better reduce the disutility of the risk (as by insuring) if the risk does occur. Suppose a grower agrees before the growing season to sell his crop to a grain elevator, and the crop is destroyed by blight and the grain elevator sues. Discharge is ordinarily allowed in such cases. . . . The grower has every incentive to avoid the blight; so if it occurs, it probably could not have been prevented; and the grain elevator, which buys from a variety of growers not all of whom will be hit by blight in the same growing season, is in a better position to buffer the risk of blight than the grower is.

Since impossibility and related doctrines are devices for shifting risk in accordance with the parties' presumed intentions, which are to minimize the costs of contract performance, one of which is the disutility created by risk, they have no place when the contract explicitly assigns a particular risk to one party or the other. As we have already noted, a fixed-price contract is an explicit assignment of the risk of market price increases to the seller and the risk of market price decreases to the buyer, and the assignment of the latter risk to the buyer is even clearer where, as in this case, the contract places a floor under price but allows for escalation. If, as is also the case here, the buyer forecasts the market incorrectly and therefore finds himself locked into a disadvantageous contract, he has only himself to blame and so cannot shift the risk back to the seller by invoking impossibility or related doctrines. . . . It does not matter that it is an act of government that may have made the contract less advantageous to one party. . . . Government these days is a pervasive factor in the economy and among the risks that a fixed-price contract allocates between the parties is that of a price change induced by one of government's manifold interventions in the economy. Since "the very purpose of a fixed price agreement is to place the risk of increased costs on the promisor (and the risk of decreased costs on the promisee)," the fact that costs decrease steeply (which is in effect what happened here — the cost of generating electricity turned out to be lower than NIPSCO thought when it signed the fixed-price contract with Carbon County) cannot allow the buyer to walk away from the contract. . . .

. . . This completes our consideration of NIPSCO's attack on the damages judgment and we turn to Carbon County's cross-appeal, which seeks specific performance in lieu of the damages it got. Carbon County's counsel virtually abandoned the cross-appeal at oral argument, noting that the mine was closed and could not be reopened immediately — so that if specific performance (i.e., NIPSCO's resuming taking the coal) was ordered, Carbon County would not be able to resume its obligations under the contract without some grace period. In any event the request for specific performance has no merit. Like other equitable remedies, specific performance is available only if damages are not an adequate remedy, . . . and there is no reason to suppose them inadequate here. The loss to Carbon County from the breach of contract is simply the difference between (1) the contract price (as escalated over the life of the contract in accordance with the contract's escalator provisions) times quantity, and (2) the cost of mining the coal over the life of the contract. Carbon County does not even argue that $181 million is not a reasonable estimate of the present value of the difference. Its complaint is that although the money will make the owners of Carbon County whole it will do nothing for the miners who have lost their jobs because the mine is closed and the satellite businesses that have closed for the same reason. Only specific performance will help them.

But since they are not parties to the contract their losses are irrelevant. Indeed, specific performance would be improper as well as unnecessary here, because it would force the continuation of production that has become uneconomical. . . . No one wants coal from Carbon County's mine. With the collapse of oil prices, which has depressed the price of substitute fuels as well, this coal costs far more to get out of the ground than it is worth in the market. Continuing to produce it, under compulsion of an order for specific performance, would impose costs on society greater than the benefits. NIPSCO's breach, though it gave Carbon County a right to damages, was an efficient breach in the sense that it brought to a halt a production process that was no longer cost-justified. . . . The reason why NIPSCO must pay Carbon County's loss is not that it should have continued buying coal it didn't need but that the contract assigned to NIPSCO the risk of market changes that made continued deliveries uneconomical. The judgment for damages is the method by which that risk is being fixed on NIPSCO in accordance with its undertakings.

With continued production uneconomical, it is unlikely that an order of specific performance, if made, would ever actually be implemented. If, as a finding that the breach was efficient implies, the cost of a substitute supply (whether of coal, or of electricity) to NIPSCO is less than the cost of producing coal from Carbon County's mine, NIPSCO and Carbon County can both be made better off by negotiating a cancellation of the contract and with it a dissolution of the order of specific performance. Suppose, by way of example, that Carbon County's coal costs $20 a ton to produce, that the contract price is $40, and that NIPSCO can buy coal elsewhere for $10. Then Carbon County would be making a profit of only $20 on each ton it sold to NIPSCO ($40-$20), while NIPSCO would be losing $30 on each ton it bought from Carbon County ($40-$10). Hence by offering Carbon County more than contract damages (i.e., more than Carbon County's lost profits), NIPSCO could induce Carbon County to discharge the contract and release NIPSCO to buy cheaper coal. For example, at $25, both parties would be better off than under specific performance, where Carbon County gains only $20 but NIPSCO loses $30. Probably, therefore, Carbon County is seeking specific performance in order to have bargaining leverage with NIPSCO, and we can think of no reason why the law should give it such leverage. We add that if Carbon County obtained and enforced an order for specific performance this would mean that society was spending $20 (in our hypothetical example) to produce coal that could be gotten elsewhere for $10 — a waste of scarce resources. . . .

To summarize, the appeal from the grant of the preliminary injunction is dismissed as moot; the other orders appealed from are affirmed. No costs will be awarded in this court, since we have turned down Carbon County's appeals as well as NIPSCO's.

So ordered.

REFERENCE: Farnsworth, §9.1
               Calamari & Perillo, §13.19

STUDY GUIDE: The following survey examines the attitudes of corporate counsel toward long-term contracts and the problems that sometimes surround them. Do these results support or undercut the approach described in ALCOA? *Are they relevant to fashioning a legal rule?*

Empirical Background: Survey
of Corporate Counsel

RUSSELL J. WEINTRAUB, A SURVEY OF CONTRACT PRACTICE AND POLICY, 1992 WIS. L. REV. 1, 16-19, 22-24, 30, 41-42: In June 1988, I sent a questionnaire to the general counsels of 182 corporations of various sizes in all parts of the United States.[40] The questionnaire sought information on a broad range of contract practices and solicited opinion on how the law should deal with some classic contract problems. Questions three and four asked whether the respondent entered into long-term contracts to buy or sell products or services and, if so, what contract provisions were used to protect against substantial changes in market prices during the term of the contract:

> 3. Does your company enter into long-term contracts to sell your products or services or to buy another company's products or services? "Long-term" means for more than 1 year.

	F	%
yes → if your answer is "yes," go to question 4	74	89.2
no → if your answer is "no," go to question 5	9	10.8

---

40. . . . The corporations receiving questionnaires varied in size from those having annual sales in excess of a billion dollars to those with less than ten million. Eighty-four questionnaires were returned, of which one was discarded as unreliable. (Many answers on the discarded questionnaire had comments such as "probably" and "impossible to answer, this company too large.") Not counting the discarded questionnaire, the survey produced a response rate of 45.6%.

4. If your company enters into long-term contracts to sell or buy, mark the category or categories that describe how the contracts provide protection against substantial changes in market prices during the term of the contracts. (MORE THAN ONE BOX MAY BE MARKED.)

		F	%[41]
[A]	indexing	53	71.6
[B]	option to cancel at intervals	49	66.2
[C]	force majeure clause not addressed specifically to deviation between contract and market prices	30	40.5
[D]	clause providing for renegotiation if substantial deviation between contract and market prices	31	41.9
[E]	other[42]	13	17.6
[F]	no provision in contract for excuse if other party performs	12	16.2

The vast majority of respondents entered into long-term contracts to buy or sell products or services, including 100% of the manufacturers of consumer products other than food, manufacturers of hard goods and utilities supplying gas or electricity.

The most common method for protecting against a market shift during the contract term was "indexing" (71.6%), followed closely by an "option to cancel at intervals" (66.2%). Almost half of the respondents (41.9%) addressed the problem directly by including a "clause providing for renegotiation if [there is a] substantial deviation between contract and market prices." This kind of renegotiation clause was most commonly used by food producers (66%), producers of petroleum products (62.6%), conglomerates (50%), and manufacturers of hard goods (50%). Five respondents commented that the method used depended on the type of contract. Only three respondents marked "no provision" without also checking another box. One of these three respondents commented that it dealt only in contracts for services.

---

41. The percentage of responses (%) indicated in question four is the percentage of the 74 respondents who indicated that they did enter into long-term contracts.

42. "Other" methods that were stated for protecting against market shifts and the number of respondents who indicated each method are: foreign currency adjustment (one); escalation other than indexing (one); adjusting contract prices to meet best prices to other customers, referred to by respondents as "most favored nation" clause (two); "right to buy competitive products at lower price which are credited against contractual requirements" (one); periodic renegotiation whether or not there is a difference between contract and market prices (one); price changes based on regulatory commission orders (three, all utilities); "annual price review and negotiation" (one, who also marked option to cancel at intervals and force majeure); "very often government contracts allow for downward adjustments only unless there is a contract modification (one, from a company that has both government and other contracts); "price goes up if raw material goes up" (one, really a kind of indexing); "crude oil contracts float with 'posted price' — market price for that area of the country" (one); "subscription levels" (one, the "media company"); "advance payment so that money can be invested at U.S. rates which vary with inflation — we back with letter of credit" (one); "in the sale of a commodity, such as solder where tin makes up 70% of the cost, pricing is geared to the market price of tin at the time of sale" (one); "price term tracks actual costs" (one, who did not check "indexing"); "cost plus fixed fee" (one).

C. Request from the Other Party for Relief. Questions five and six asked whether the respondent would agree to a change in price, if requested by a supplier or customer after a market shift and, if so, why:

5. If, because of a shift in market prices, one of your suppliers or customers requested a modification of the contracted-for price, would your company always insist on compliance with the contract?

	F[43]	%
yes → go to question 7	4	4.9
not always → go to question 6	78	95.1

6. If your company would sometimes agree to a modification of the contracted-for price, which of the following factors would be relevant to the decision? (MORE THAN ONE BOX MAY BE MARKED.)

		F	%[44]
[A]	the request was reasonable under trade practice	59	75.6
[B]	if the request is made by a supplier, the additional cost can be passed on to customers	20	25.6
[C]	if the request is made by a buyer, our company will make a reasonable profit even if the request is granted	22	28.2
[D]	relations with the company making the request have been long and satisfactory	62	79.5
[E]	either the company making the request or our company is much larger	6	7.7
[F]	other	18	23.1

The overwhelming majority of respondents (95.1%) indicated that they would sometimes grant a supplier's or customer's request for price modification. The respondents least likely to grant such requests were manufacturers of hard goods, 16.7% of whom answered that they would always insist on compliance.

Custom clearly played a key role in identifying those situations in which relief was appropriate. Indeed, 75.6% of the respondents stated that they gave relief when "the request was reasonable under trade practice." The most common reason (79.5%) for granting modification was "relations with the company making the request have been long and satisfactory." . . .

D. Request to the Other Party for Relief. Questions seven and eight were the converse of five and six and asked how frequently the

---

43. One respondent did not answer question five, so the frequency total is 82.

44. This is the percentage of the 78 respondents who indicated that they would sometimes agree to a price adjustment.

respondent had requested relief from a contractual commitment and the experience when the request was made:

7. How frequently has your company asked relief from or modification of its contractual obligations?

		F	%
[A]	never → go to Question 9	13	17.1
[B]	an average of less than once per year	32	42.1
[C]	an average of 1 to 5 times per year	17	22.4
[D]	an average of over 5 times per year	14	18.4
	Comments[45]		

8. Describe your company's experience when it has asked relief from or modification of its contractual obligations. MORE THAN ONE BOX MAY BE MARKED. IF MORE THAN ONE BOX IS MARKED, INDICATE THE RELATIVE FREQUENCY OF EACH EXPERIENCE BY INSERTING A NUMBER IN EACH BOX SELECTED, WITH 1 INDICATING THE MOST FREQUENT EXPERIENCE, 2 THE NEXT, ETC.

		F[46]	%
[A]	amicable working out of the problem by modification of performance of the contract in question	58	87.9
[B]	amicable working out of the problem by adjustments in future contracts	44	66.7
[C]	request refused and we performed[47]	32	48.5
[D]	dispute resolved by arbitration	12	18.2
[E]	suit was filed and settled before judgment	22	33.3
[F]	suit was filed and litigated to judgment	17	25.8
[G]	other[48]	3	4.5

The great majority of respondents had requested relief from contractual obligations (82.9%), although for most this was a rare occurrence (42.1% indicating less than once per year). Companies most likely to request relief more than five times per year were conglomerates (38.1%), and a combined category of chemical and pharmaceutical companies (28.6%).

45. Comments to question seven on the frequency of requesting relief were: "50 times a year worldwide" (from a petroleum products producer with annual sales of over $1 billion); "don't know, probably *D*" (over five times per year); "rarely but dependent upon market conditions at the time"; "depends on economy"; "some operating units practically never, some more than five per year"; "very frequently." One respondent apparently did not understand that the question concerned unilateral relief, not modifications of performance on both sides, and wrote "poor question: modifications are constant, relief relatively rare."

46. The figures in the "F" column are the total number of respondents who indicated they had the relevant experience when they requested relief from a contractual obligation. It was not until the fourth level of frequency of experience that more than four respondents reported a resort to litigation.

47. One respondent marked C, struck out "and we performed" and wrote in "gas not sold." Apparently the respondent's request for relief was refused, respondent did not perform and no suit was brought.

48. One "other" response was "litigation in progress."

It was not until the fourth level of frequency of experience that more than four respondents reported a resort to litigation. On the rare occasions when litigation resulted from the denial of respondent's request for relief, different groups of companies reported the following experiences: diversified companies, 61.1% had experience with litigation that was settled before judgment, 38.9% had a case litigated to judgment; producers of petroleum products, 50% had a case that was settled; 37.5% had a case litigated to judgment. Gas and electric utilities were the only group in which more companies reported experience with litigation to judgment than with pre-judgment settlement (10% reported a settled case, 40% reported litigating to judgment). This further indicates that regulation has a significant effect on the reaction of the regulated industry to contract disputes.

E. The Need for Legal Sanctions. Question nine asked respondents' views on the need for legal sanctions:

9. If there were no legal sanctions for breach of contract and compliance depended on nonlegal sanctions (e.g., reputation in the business community, intra-corporate incentives for good performance), what is your estimate of how business operations would be affected?[49]

		F	%
[A]	not much if at all	14	17.7
[B]	substantially and detrimentally	52	65.8
[C]	substantially and beneficially	0	0.0
[D]	substantially with about an even amount of detriment and benefit	13	16.5

No respondent thought that business operations would improve substantially if there were no legal sanctions, and 65.8% thought that there would be a substantial detrimental effect. A respondent who checked *A* (not much effect) commented, "business objectives are more important than legal sanctions." A communications and information management company with annual sales of $1 billion or more did not mark a box but commented:

Our conduct would change very little because our reputation is critical on a long term basis. My concern would be that smaller companies and start up operations would be substantially disadvantaged. We would be less inclined to take service or products from them. They have no reputation and [there would be] no legal penalty for non-performance.

Respondents who thought business operations would deteriorate without legal sanctions made the following comments: "I suspect that business in general would tend to the lowest common denominator. Probably would be more uncertainty and sharp practices. Legal sanctions for breach of contract are absolutely essential to business. A contract sets the rules for virtually every transaction." A respondent with annual sales of $1 billion or more and a mix of government and commercial contracts commented,

49. Four respondents did not answer this question, so the figures in the "%" column are the percentages of 79 respondents who checked each box.

"[p]articularly when selling to a monopsony,[50] legal relief is critical." One comment perhaps illuminates a reason for our trade imbalance: "Japanese operations would be adversely affected to a much smaller extent if at all." Another respondent wrote, "the Anglo-Saxon legal system of contract law works very well."[51] A respondent who thought that without legal sanctions there would be a substantial change with equal amounts of benefit and detriment commented, "a contract is generally no better than the person with whom you contract."

The gas and electric utilities were almost unanimous in believing that legal sanctions were essential for desirable business operation. Twelve of the thirteen who answered this question (92.3%) marked B (substantial detrimental effect) suggesting, again, the effect of regulation. . . .

H. *Three Hypotheticals to Test Attitudes Toward Pure Expectancy.*   The final three questions were in the form of hypothetical situations. Respondents were instructed that "your answer should reflect your view of what the law should be, rather than your view of current law." . . .

The third and final hypothetical situation in the survey concerned frustration of contract that is so severe performance would result in the promisor's liquidation.

17. Company *A* has contracted to sell *B* a fixed quantity of fuel oil per month at a fixed price for 10 years. An unprecedented OPEC oil embargo causes the cost of the oil to *A* to far exceed the price that *B* has agreed to pay. *A*'s loss over the 10 years of the contract would be so large as to require liquidation of *A*. *B* can pass on the added cost of oil to its customers without suffering a competitive disadvantage. *A* refuses to deliver the oil at the contract price and *B* sues *A* for the difference between the contract price of the oil and the much higher price that *B* must pay to obtain oil from other sources. What result should the court reach?

		F	%[52]
[A]	*B* should receive a judgment for the difference between the contract price and the market price	28	35.0
[B]	*A* should be excused from performance	11	13.7
[C]	The contract price should be adjusted to avoid ruinous loss to *A*, but give *B* a significant savings over current market price	37	46.2
[D]	other:	4	5.0

50. A "monopsony" is a market in which the product or service of several sellers is sought by only one buyer. A classic example is the hiring of labor in a "company town" in which a worker either works for the dominant firm or is unemployed. See Paul A. Samuelson, Economics 548-49 (11th ed. 1980).

51. Yet this same respondent marked question 16 "no" (no expectancy damages when a unique product does not perform as warranted) and marked C as the answer to question 17 (the best response to frustration of contract is equitable adjustment of the price).

52. Three respondents did not answer question 17, so the figures in the "%" column are based on the 80 respondents who did answer. Two of the three respondents who did not mark an answer did comment in a manner that suggested they should be counted as *C*, thus further increasing the plurality in favor of price adjustment. One said that a poll of counsel representing different operating units resulted in four *C*'s, one *B*, and one *A*. The other wrote, "*A* is the correct legal result — *C* is the correct commercial compromise."

The most interesting responses were from the gas and electric utilities who would be in the position of *B*, the buyer. Of the twelve utilities who responded to this question, only four (33.3%) marked *A* (expectancy), two (16.7%) marked *B* (excuse), and six (50%) marked *C* (adjust price). One utility commented, "*C* is the best practical answer, but regulators may resist passing on the costs to customers and may require *B* to sue *A* for price difference."

Two respondents who marked *A* (expectancy) indicated in comments that this represented their position in either actual or possible litigation. A seller of petroleum products said, "because I am '*B*.' " A utility commented, "our conduct at that time (Westinghouse uranium case) is consistent with this response."

Of respondents who favored full recovery, nine indicated lack of sympathy with company *A* for failing to draft the contract to provide for this situation. Two of the respondents who would adjust the price, also thought that *A* should have drafted a better contract.

Two who marked response *A* (expectancy) commented that the legal rules were simply a background for what would be a probable accommodation between the parties. Two respondents, one who marked *A* and one who marked "other," commented that as a practical matter the seller would go into bankruptcy reorganization and an equitable solution would emerge from those proceedings.[53]

---

53. [And on this note, we end our study of contracts. — EDS.]

Table of Judges

1153

TABLE OF CASES

Principal cases are italicized.

TABLE OF STATUTES

Principal excerpts are italicized.

INDEX